UMBC LIBRARY

THE ROUTLEDGE COMPANION TO ENGLISH FOLK PERFORMANCE

This broad-based collection of essays is an introduction both to the concerns of contemporary folklore scholarship and to the variety of forms that folk performance has taken throughout English history.

Combining case studies of specific folk practices with discussion of the various different lenses through which they have been viewed since becoming the subject of concerted study in Victorian times, this book builds on the latest work in an ever-growing body of contemporary folklore scholarship. Many of the contributing scholars are also practicing performers and bring experience and understanding of performance to their analyses and critiques. Chapters range across the spectrum of folk song, music, drama and dance, but maintain a focus on the key defining characteristics of folk performance – custom and tradition – in a full range of performances, from carol singing and sword dancing to playground rhymes and mummers' plays.

As well as being an essential reference for folklorists and scholars of traditional performance and local history, this is a valuable resource for readers in all disciplines of dance, drama, song and music whose work coincides with English folk traditions.

Peter Harrop is Professor Emeritus of Drama at the University of Chester, formerly Senior Pro-Vice-Chancellor. His 2019 monograph *Mummers' Plays Revisited* is published by Routledge as part of their series Advances in Theatre and Performance. In 2013 he edited *Performance Ethnography: Dance, Drama, Music* (with Dunja Njaradi).

Steve Roud is a freelance writer, researcher and consultant, formerly Head of Local Studies Library and Archives, London Borough of Croydon and the Honorary Librarian of the Folklore Society. His most recent works include the widely reviewed and critically acclaimed *Folk Song in England* (2017) as well as *The New Penguin Book of English Folk Songs* (2012) (with Julia Bishop).

ROUTLEDGE THEATRE AND PERFORMANCE COMPANIONS

THE ROUTLEDGE COMPANION TO THEATRE OF THE OPPRESSED
Edited by Kelly Howe, Julian Boal, and José Soeiro

THE ROUTLEDGE COMPANION TO THEATRE AND POLITICS
Edited by Peter Eckersall and Helena Grehan

THE ROUTLEDGE COMPANION TO DANCE STUDIES
Edited by Helen Thomas and Stacey Prickett

THE ROUTLEDGE COMPANION TO PERFORMANCE PRACTITIONERS
Edited by Franc Chamberlain and Bernadette Sweeney

THE ROUTLEDGE COMPANION TO PERFORMANCE PHILOSOPHY
Edited by Laura Cull Ó Maoilearca and Alice Lagaay

THE ROUTLEDGE COMPANION TO THEATRE AND PERFORMANCE HISTORIOGRAPHY
Edited by Tracy Davis and Peter Marx

THE ROUTLEDGE COMPANION TO APPLIED PERFORMANCE
Edited by Tim Prentki and Ananda Breed

THE ROUTLEDGE COMPANION TO ENGLISH FOLK PERFORMANCE
Edited by Peter Harrop and Steve Roud

THE ROUTLEDGE PANTOMIME READER
Jennifer Schacker and Daniel O'Quinn

For more information about this series, please visit: https://www.routledge.com/handbooks/products/SCAR30

THE ROUTLEDGE COMPANION TO ENGLISH FOLK PERFORMANCE

Edited by Peter Harrop and Steve Roud

LONDON AND NEW YORK

First published 2021
by Routledge
2 Park Square, Milton Park, Abingdon, Oxon OX14 4RN

and by Routledge
605 Third Avenue, New York, NY 10158

Routledge is an imprint of the Taylor & Francis Group, an informa business

© 2021 selection and editorial matter, Peter Harrop and Steve Roud; individual chapters, the contributors

The right of Peter Harrop and Steve Roud to be identified as the authors of the editorial material, and of the authors for their individual chapters, has been asserted in accordance with sections 77 and 78 of the Copyright, Designs and Patents Act 1988.

All rights reserved. No part of this book may be reprinted or reproduced or utilised in any form or by any electronic, mechanical, or other means, now known or hereafter invented, including photocopying and recording, or in any information storage or retrieval system, without permission in writing from the publishers.

Trademark notice: Product or corporate names may be trademarks or registered trademarks, and are used only for identification and explanation without intent to infringe.

British Library Cataloguing-in-Publication Data
A catalogue record for this book is available from the British Library

Library of Congress Cataloging-in-Publication Data
A catalog record has been requested for this book

ISBN: 978-0-367-27992-9 (hbk)
ISBN: 978-1-032-02196-6 (pbk)
ISBN: 978-0-429-29906-3 (ebk)

Typeset in Bembo
by codeMantra

For the grandchildren: Henry, Maisie and Harvey.
For the second cousins: Jacqueline, Stephanie, Daisy, Clover, Charlie, Ted, and Bella.

CONTENTS

List of figures   *x*
List of contributors   *xii*

   Introduction   1
   Peter Harrop and Steve Roud

PART I
Folk drama, theatre and performance   9
Peter Harrop

1   Towards an anatomy of English customary drama: theatre, stage, play   16
   Thomas Pettitt

2   Performing calendrical pressures: Shrovetide processions and shroving perambulations in premodern England   44
   Taylor Aucoin

3   Robin Hood folk-performance in fifteenth- and sixteenth-century England   64
   John Marshall

4   Alongside the mummers' plays: customary elements in amateur and semi-professional theatre 1730–1850   77
   Peter Harrop

5   The Alderley Mummers' play: a story of longevity   101
   Duncan Broomhead

6	A performance bestiary Mike Pearson	120
7	Performing community: village life and the spectacle of worship in the work of Charles Marson Katie Palmer Heathman	145
8	Boxing Day fancy dress in Wigan Anna FC Smith	158

PART II
Folk dance
Peter Harrop — **177**

9	Merry neets and bridewains: contemporary commentaries on folk music, dance and song in the Lake Counties during the Romantic period Sue Allan	184
10	Sword dancing in England: texts and sources from the eighteenth and nineteenth centuries Stephen D. Corrsin	203
11	From country gardens to British festivals: the morris dance revival, 1886–1951 Matt Simons	225
12	The English country dance, Cecil Sharp and authenticity Derek Schofield	248
13	Douglas Kennedy and folk dance in English schools Chloe Middleton-Metcalfe	261
14	Fancy footwork: reviewing the English clog and step dance revival Alexandra Fisher	277
15	Expanding a repertoire: Leicester Morrismen and the Border morris John Swift	295
16	Dancing with tradition: clog, step and short sword rapper in the twenty first century Libby Worth	315

17	'Sequins, bows and pointed toes': girls' carnival morris—the 'other' morris dancing community *Lucy Wright*	336

PART III
Folk song and music   **355**
Steve Roud

18	Re-crafting love and murder: print and memory in the mediation of a murdered sweetheart ballad *Thomas Pettitt*	362
19	Burlesquing the ballad *Steve Gardham*	384
20	The rise and fall of the west gallery: popular religious music in the eighteenth and nineteenth centuries *Vic Gammon*	408
21	The drive for an English identity in music and the foundation of the Folk-Song Society *Arthur Knevett*	441
22	'No art more dangerous' – Eve Maxwell-Lyte and folk song *Martin Graebe*	464
23	Creativity versus authenticity in the English folk song revival *Brian Peters*	473
24	Folk choirs: their origins and contribution to the living tradition *Paul Wilson and Marilyn Tucker*	498
25	'Past Performances on Paper': a case study of the manuscript tunebook of Thomas Hampton *Rebecca Dellow*	528
26	The performers in the playground: children's musical practices in play *Julia Bishop*	550

Index   *585*

FIGURES

1.1	Distribution, communication, interaction	20
2.1	The band and other processors carrying the footballs aloft before the Shrove Tuesday match in Dorking (1885)	47
2.2	Scottish wedding procession with ball-money or ba' siller collection in the fore	48
2.3	Types of Shrovetide Perambulatory House-Visits in England and Wales. Mapped by Settlement and Historic County	51
3.1	St Brannock's Church, Braunton, Devon	69
3.2	St Brannock's Church House, Braunton, Devon	70
4.1	An imagining of *The Siege of Troy* at Jobson's Booth with live performers. 'Three Welch girls from Monmouth on the right, and two drunken colliers from Kingswood on the left […] Edwin carried some brandy in a pint bottle'	86
5.1	Alderley Mummers 1920. Left to Right: Enterer In – Clement Barber, Doctor – Thomas Barber, Prince Paradise- Alec Barber, St George – George Barber, Beelzebub – Ernest Barber, Colonel Slasher – Henry Barber, Young Ball (horse) – Obadiah Barber, Groom – Albert Barber	108
5.2	Alderley Mummers Play 2016. Left to Right. Enterer In – Dave Houghton, Doctor – Tom Kitchen. Prince Paradise- Tony Lepp, St. George – Roger Jackson, Beelzebub – Geoff Smith, Colonel Slasher – Simon Whomsley, Young Ball (horse) – Peter Jackson, Groom – Nicholas Houseman	116
6.1	West Halton Plough Jags, 1898	120
6.2	Map of North-west Lincolnshire	121
6.3	Burton Stather Plough Jags 1907	134
6.4	Burringham Plough Jags, pre-First World War	137
6.5	Plough Jags, probably West Halton	139
8.1	Getting ready at home, 'Labyrinth' theme group, Boxing Day 2017	159
8.2	Putin and friends, Boxing Day 2018	164
8.3	Fancy dress group 'scouser' theme, Boxing Day 2018	169
8.4	Perambulations, Boxing Day 2018	171
9.1	'Arnside Wedding'	196
15.1	Leicester Morrismen's first border morris performance, December 1981	302
15.2	Red Leicester at the evening ceilidh in Towersey, August 1997	307

15.3	Summary analysis of the number of teams dancing Border morris in 2019	309
16.1	Demon Barber Roadshow in *Time Gentlemen Please* at Carriageworks Theatre, Leeds, 2010	323
16.2	'Morris Locking' from *Step Hop House* by Folk Dance Remixed performed at Urban Village Fete, Greenwich 2015	326
16.3	Tower Ravens Rapper dancing their Piccadilly dance at Sidmouth Folk Festival, 2018	330
17.1	Members of Orcadia Morris Dancers, 2016	337
17.2	Map showing the geographic spread of all current morris troupes	342
17.3	Map showing the geographic spread of morris troupes, including teams no longer active	343
17.4	Platt Bridge Juniors lining up before a performance at Blackpool Winter Gardens, 2019	348
21.1	The circular letter that announced the Folk Song Society in 1898	449
22.1	Eve Maxwell-Lyte in her stage costume	465
24.1	'Whittingham Fair'	512
24.2	'The Lark in the Morning'	515
24.3	'The Sweet Nightingale'	519
25.1	Walter Soobroy's name written on printed music and matching handwriting in the manuscript	530
25.2	'Runns Hornpipe'	531
25.3	'O Come all ye faithful'	533
25.4	'Highland Schottische'	534
25.5	'Waltz' by S. Musgrave, showing octave doubling	538
25.6	Soobroy's string band	541
25.7	'Step Dancing in the Tap Room'	542
26.1	'One Two Three A-Leary'	553
26.2	'One Two Three A-Lairy'	554
26.3	'Plainsie Clapsie'	555
26.4	Rhythmic ostinato of 'The Cup Song' ('When I'm Gone'), (Roud 32904)	555
26.5	'My Man John'	556
26.6	Photograph of 'My Man John'	557
26.7	'[Rosy Apple]', Skipping	558
26.8	'[Queen Mary]', Liverpool girls (c.1915)	562
26.9	'Queen Mary', 'Bonnie Dundee' and 'Stella' compared	563
26.10	'The Big Ship Sails'	565
26.11	'The Big Ship Sails' and 'Poor Mary'	566
26.12	'My Mother Said' (n.d.)	570
26.13	'My Mummy Sent Me Shopping'	571
26.14	Letter from headteacher to Iona and Peter Opie, 23 May 1960	574
26.15	'Chinese Breakdown' (1934), 'Merry-go-round Broke Down' (1937) and 'Pretty Little Dutch Girl' (1977) compared	576
26.16	'Lemonade' and 'iPhone' compared	578

CONTRIBUTORS

Sue Allan was born and bred in Cumbria. She has been performing and researching the songs, dances and tunes of the county for over 40 years, in 2017 completing a PhD on its distinctive regional corpus of folk songs. As an independent scholar she has presented and published papers on fiddlers, folk song, ballad sellers and morris dancing in Cumbria and, in 2020, a book on dialect poet Robert Anderson. As a performer, originally a singer, she went on to co-found and perform with Carlisle Sword and Clog and Throstle's Nest Morris teams, and the Ellen Valley Band.

Taylor Aucoin is a Postdoctoral Research Fellow at the University of Exeter, specialising in the social and cultural history of medieval and early modern Britain. His research examines how practices and traditions of work and play influenced social relations, identities and politics in the past. Taylor is currently adapting his doctoral thesis on medieval and early modern Shrovetide into a monograph, while pursuing new research projects on premodern football, and labour and freedom in preindustrial England. He also runs 'Merry Shrovetide', an annual festival exploring the history of Pancake Day and Carnival in Britain via public events and performances.

Julia Bishop is a researcher specialising in children's folklore and traditional song. She studies continuity and change in contemporary children's play and does historical research into the collections of Iona and Peter Opie, James Ritchie and Norman Douglas. Her folk song research is historical in focus, exploring vernacular musicianship through musical analysis. She has published numerous articles and is co-editor of *The New Penguin Book of English Folk Songs* (2012) and *The Lifework and Legacy of Iona and Peter Opie* (2019), and co-author of *Changing Play: Play, Media and Commercial Culture From the 1950s to the Present Day* (2014).

Duncan Broomhead has been a researcher and performer of traditional Mummers' Plays for over forty years. During that period, he has interviewed ex-performers in Staffordshire, Lancashire, Yorkshire and Cumbria, but his special interest is in folk plays and related customs from his home county of Cheshire, particularly the Alderley Mummers Play. He is the secretary of the Traditional Drama Research Group and is also webmaster of their Folk Play website (https://folkplay.info/). He is the keeper of the Photographic Archive for the Morris Ring, the oldest of the three national organisations for morris dancers and mummers.

Contributors

Stephen D. Corrsin received his doctorate in Russian and East European history from the University of Michigan, Ann Arbor. He is the author of several books, including *Warsaw before the First World War: Poles and Jews in the Third City of the Russian Empire*; *Jews in America: From New Amsterdam to the Yiddish Stage*; and most importantly for this collection, *Sword Dancing in Europe: A History*, published by the Folklore Society in 1997. He has also published articles on the historiography of German and Austrian sword dances, and on the peculiar history of the notion of "ritual" dances in England. In addition, he has performed English sword dances in the United States and Canada, as well as dances derived from German, Austrian, and Czech examples, translated by him from published descriptions.

Rebecca Dellow is an experienced and versatile fiddle player who fuses traditions from around the British Isles. Fiddle playing in her family goes back at least five generations, to her great great grandfather Thomas Hampton, from Hereford. It was his hand-written tune book which inspired her PhD at the University of Sheffield. Since then, Rebecca has continued to carry out tune research, contributing to academic journals and conferences, and uses the research to develop her performance as a traditional musician. She has played in numerous duos and bands across many traditional genres and regularly collaborates with poet Adam Horovitz, exploring the connections between poetry and music.

Alexandra Fisher is a community clog dancer and researcher based in Lancashire. Alex is a member of The Instep Research Team and has been a clog dancer since 1984. She has studied clog dance traditions in Cumbria, Lancashire, Northumberland, and Durham and has an MA in Dance Studies (University of Surrey). Her dissertation (2000) focuses on the clog dancer Jackie Toaduff. Conference papers include 'In Search of Street Clog Dance: New Thoughts on Step-Dance Analysis' (Stepping On, Cecil Sharp House, November 2019) and for recent articles see *English Dance and Song* (Winter 2018 and Winter 2019).

Vic Gammon has been interested in traditional song and music since his teenage years and first researched popular church music in the 1970s. He retired from Newcastle University in 2010, where he was Senior Lecturer in Folk and Traditional Music. He remains actively engaged in research. He has published widely, including a book of essays, *Desire, Drink and Death in English Folk and Vernacular Song* (2008). Many of his writings can be accessed at https://newcastle.academia.edu/VicGammon. He is an active singer and instrumentalist, playing the tenor banjo, anglo-concertina and melodeon. He lives in Hexham, Northumberland.

Steve Gardham is an independent researcher who has spent the last 50 years studying the relationship between traditional songs and those that have been the product of some form of commercial activity. He has edited five anthologies of traditional folk songs and has written numerous articles on the subject mainly built around individual histories of particular songs. He has also spent almost all of his life performing folk music and organising folk events.

Martin Graebe is an independent researcher, writer and singer, who has studied and written about a number of the people who have figured in the history of traditional song. His book, *As I Walked Out; Sabine Baring-Gould and the Search for the Folk Songs of Devon and Cornwall* (Signal Books, 2017), has received both the Katharine Briggs Folklore Award and the W. G Hoskins Prize. He has been the Secretary of the Traditional Song Forum since its inception. He is also, with his wife Shan, a respected performer of traditional song.

Contributors

Peter Harrop is Professor Emeritus in Drama at the University of Chester, formerly Senior Pro-Vice-Chancellor. His 2019 monograph *Mummers' Plays Revisited* is published by Routledge as part of their series Advances in Theatre and Performance. In 2013 he co-edited *Performance Ethnography: Dance, Drama, Music* with dance ethnographer Dunja Njaradi. He gained his PhD (1980) from the Institute of Dialect and Folklife Studies at the University of Leeds, contributes to the website of the Traditional Drama Research Group at https://folkplay.info/ and has published in a range of folklore, theatre and performance studies journals.

Arthur Knevett has had a lifelong interest in traditional song. He has been an organiser and resident of a number of folk clubs since the 1960s and has specialised in singing English traditional songs and ballads. In 2009 he retired from his post as Head of the Teacher Education Department at Grimsby University Centre. In 2011, he completed a PhD at the University of Sheffield on the history of the Folk-Song Society, analysing its foundation and development in a social, cultural and political context.

John Marshall has spent all his academic career teaching in university departments of Drama. He taught at the Department of Drama: Theatre, Film and Television (now Department of Theatre), University of Bristol for 20 years. Following his retirement, he was appointed Senior Research Fellow in Theatre. He has published extensively in the areas of medieval English theatre and Robin Hood in performance. He has recently had published, by Routledge, a collection of his articles and chapters in *Early English Performance: Medieval Plays and Robin Hood Games*.

Chloe Middleton-Metcalfe is completing her PhD in the dance department at Roehampton university under Dr Sara Houston and Professor Theresa Buckland. Her thesis examines English social folk dance and focuses on events organised by and for non-specialists. She has authored two online resources: *An Introductory Bibliography of Traditional Social Folk Dance* (2019) published by the Vaughan Williams Memorial Library and *A Beginners Guide to English Folk Costumes* (2014) published by the English Folk Dance and Song Society. For more details visit: https://roehampton-online.academia.edu/ChloeMetcalfe

Katie Palmer Heathman is an independent scholar. She has been Research Associate (Modern British History) at Durham University, and was awarded her PhD from the University of Leicester in 2016. Her thesis reassessed the relationships of the early twentieth-century folk revival with contemporary social, political and religious thought. She has also worked on expressions of community, socialism and cultural nationalism in the use of folk tunes as hymn tunes by Percy Dearmer and Ralph Vaughan Williams ('"Lift Up a Living Nation": Community and Nation, Socialism and Religion in The English Hymnal, 1906', *Cultural and Social History*, 14:2).

Mike Pearson is Emeritus Professor of Performance Studies at Aberystwyth University and an honorary professor at Exeter University. Since 1970, he has devised and directed theatre professionally, in Wales and internationally. He currently creates performance as a solo artist with senior performer's group Good News From The Future and for National Theatre Wales, with whom his productions have included *The Persians* (2010), *Coriolan/us* (2012), *Iliad (2014)* and *The Storm Cycle* (2018–2020). He is co-author of *Theatre/Archaeology* (2001), and author of *In Comes I: Performance, Memory and Landscape* (2006), *Site-Specific Performance* (2010) and *Marking Time: Performance, Archaeology and the City* (2012).

Contributors

Brian Peters has been a professional performer, researcher and educator in the field of English traditional song for over thirty years, playing concerts and tutoring classes in the UK, North America and Australia. He has published research on song origins and Appalachian balladry and is a regular reviewer for the *Folk Music Journal*. As a singer he has a particular affinity for modal tunes, supernatural ballads and the industrial songs of North-West England, and he always admits to his reconstructions.

Thomas Pettitt is a cultural historian affiliated with the Institut for Kulturvidenskaber (Cultural Sciences Institute) of the University of Southern Denmark, his research field encompassing several aspects (news and rumour, narrative and song, custom and drama) of late-medieval and early-modern English Vernacular Culture. His approaches also encompass the exploration of European dimensions, and derivative or analogous folk traditions. Most of his scholarly production in this field is accessible at or via https://southerndenmark.academia.edu/ThomasPettitt, including elaborations of the theory that with the closing of the 'Gutenberg Parenthesis', digital technology and the internet represent, under several significant headings, a resumption of pre-modern conditions.

Steve Roud is a freelance writer, researcher and consultant, formerly Head of Local Studies Library and Archives, London Borough of Croydon and from 1983 until 1999 the Honorary Librarian of the Folklore Society, University College London. His most recent works include the widely reviewed and critically acclaimed *Folk Song in England* (Faber, 2017) as well as *The New Penguin Book of English Folk Songs* (Penguin, 2012) (with Julia Bishop), *Ballads in the Street: The Interface between Print and Oral Traditions* (Ashgate, 2014) (with David Atkinson) and *Street Literature of the Long Nineteenth Century* (Cambridge Scholars, 2017) (with David Atkinson). He has established several pioneering and major electronic resources including The Folk Song Index (available on the Vaughan Williams Memorial website).

Derek Schofield is a doctoral student at De Montfort University, Leicester, researching the history of the English folk dance revival. He has written books and articles on several aspects of the English folk music and dance revival, is a former editor of *English Dance and Song* magazine and is currently the reviews editor of the *Folk Music Journal*. He is a retired college lecturer and manager.

Matt Simons is a historian, with a particular interest in English cultural and intellectual history of the early twentieth century. In 2019, he received a doctorate from De Montfort University, Leicester, for his thesis entitled 'Morris Men: Dancing Englishness, c.1905–1951'. It provides a critical reappraisal of the early morris dance revival, articulated principally through a series of intellectual biographies. As of October 2020, Matt is Associate Lecturer in Modern British History at De Montfort University, Leicester.

Anna FC Smith is a multimedia artist from Greater Manchester. She studied Critical Fine Art Practice at The University of Brighton. Focusing on custom and communal histories, her practice combines research, sculpture and performance. Her writing has featured in publications including *Harry Hill's TV Burp as Carnival*, *Art 511 Mag* and *The Morris Dancer*. Her research into clog-fighting in Lancashire was featured on the BBC's Q.I. Smith worked with folklorist Doc Rowe on the project 'Lore and The Living Archive'. She is currently collaborating with Helen Mather on 'These Lancashire Women Are Witches In Politics' in association with The Turnpike.

Contributors

John Swift is an industrial chemist by training and retired in 2018 after spending nearly fifty years in industry, working principally in the fields of quality, technical and environmental management. John has had a strong interest in folk music and dance since his time at university in 1960s. He took up morris dancing in 1976, first with Kesteven Morris in Lincolnshire and then between 1984 and 2004 with Leicester Morrismen. A previous paper on 'The Role of Repertoire' was delivered at *The Evolving Morris* conference in 1990 and published in 1991 by The Morris Ring and the Morris Federation.

Marilyn Tucker and **Paul Wilson** are co-founders of Wren Music, which runs an extensive programme of participatory folk music projects in Devon for all ages, including folk choirs. They are recipients of the English Folk Dance and Song Society Gold Badge Award. As a contribution to the Full English Folk Song Archive, Wren co-ordinated the digitizing of the Baring-Gould collection. Marilyn and Paul perform as a duo and their repertoire includes many traditional songs from Devon, including songs from Marilyn's family. They are both published songwriters and folk song collectors. They have performed at a variety of venues, from London's South Bank to a fishing co-op in Newfoundland, and have been invited to folk festivals including VAKA (Iceland), St. Johns (Newfoundland) and Galtelli (Sardinia). Marilyn holds a BA in Social Sciences from Exeter University. Paul studied music at Dartington College of Arts and holds an honorary MA in Music Education from Plymouth University. They have been invited to give talks and practical workshops on inclusive folk music practice at conferences in the UK and Europe – for example Budapest, Riga and Florence.

Libby Worth is Reader in Contemporary Performance Practices, Royal Holloway, University of London. She is a movement practitioner with research interests in physical theatres, site-based performance, the Feldenkrais Method and in folk/traditional and amateur dance. She is co-editor of *Theatre, Dance and Performance Training* and has published on Anna Halprin (2004, 2018), Ninette de Valois (2012), and Jasmin Vardimon's Dance Theatre (2016). She has written chapters on clog and sword dancing for *Time and Performer Training* (2019, she co-edited), improvisation and everyday life for *Oxford Handbook of Dance Improvisation* (2019) and 'Dancing Swords and Somersaults: Precariousness in Amateur Traditional Dancing', *Performance Research* 'On Amateurs' (2020).

Lucy Wright is an artist and researcher, currently based at the University of Leeds, where she works as Research Fellow on the Arts and Humanities Research Council funded project, 'Cultural Participation: Stories of Success, Histories of Failure'. She has written extensively about British carnival performance, and in 2017 staged '"This Girl Can" Morris Dance', an exhibition of photographs documenting the girls' carnival morris dancing community at Cecil Sharp House in London. Her integrated practice of artistic research draws on her background in ethnomusicology and a strong interest in socially engaged art. In 2019 her monograph, *21st Century Folk Art*, was published by Social Art Publications. For more information, see www.artistic-researcher.co.uk.

INTRODUCTION

Peter Harrop and Steve Roud

As a starting point, so we can get rid of the inverted commas as soon as possible, 'folk' performance arises in an unofficial, homemade, amateur, occasionally semi-professional performance culture. Furthermore, folk performance culture has placed a particular value on a link to the past through the idea of the performed reiteration of songs, dances and plays, sometimes at the same times of year and sometimes in the same places. In this way, folk performance has a particular role in the formation of cultural memory. However, just because there is already something to perform, imaginative and talented people do not stop making new work.

Over a 600-year period (from which the evidence is drawn), the folk repertoire has been endlessly creative, generally conservative, frequently mischievous, occasionally resistant, critical and oppositional. It has never stayed the same. It has responded to the culture of which it is part, including the early cultures of performing arts emerging from medieval court pageantry and, from the fifteenth century, in the rise of professional theatre and entertainment. There has been a good deal of two-way traffic over an extended period.

Folklore is a broad description including at the very least superstitions and belief systems, oral literature and narrative, storytelling, children's games and customary activity. In determining the scope of this volume, 'folk performance' has been confined to folk song and music, folk dance and folk drama. There are obvious overlaps and many occasions when all of these forms are simultaneously present and in operation, usually in the context of special occasions such as important life moments or calendar customs, or their intersection at, for example, birthdays. Song, however, required no excuse whatsoever and appears to have been ubiquitous. Notwithstanding its everyday and individual qualities, it can be as participatory or theatrical as required.

Of our performance categories, folk 'drama' is most likely to be a misnomer. It can be theatrical – but so can everything discussed in this volume; it *can* be conventionally dramatic but neither plot nor character is prerequisite. It always harnesses performativity, that is to say an organised, heightened and contextualised expressivity. There are communal understandings (more or less) that during specified occasions, language, movement, apparel, spatial patterning and interactions may be temporarily extraordinary while adhering to a (more or less) prescribed structure. Over the last 50 years, the word performance has been used in preference to drama in order to encompass these cultural activities, and for the purposes of this volume drama, theatre and performance constitute Part I; dance Part II; and song and music Part III. Our scope is a broadly defined performing arts.

The founding folklorists had operated within an intellectual framework that considered folk performance as fundamental to other arts. The more knowledge we unearth about performance history, and the more we understand the interplay of folk arts with other amateur, semi-professional and professional arts, certainly from the fifteenth century onwards, the less extraordinary the folk arts seem. Indeed, it was the Victorian decision to view folklore as utterly separate from the wider culture that now seems extraordinary. Recent research recognises that folk drama, folk dance and folk song have quite separate histories and thereby require different questions of us. We will best understand the history of folk dance, for example, by understanding dance history, and by viewing dance history in the context of broader cultural history, yet never losing sight of the moment of dance, of bodies moving in space. This is exemplified in Sue Allan's chapter on dance in the Lake Counties. Historically, from the late nineteenth century and through much of the twentieth, the bundling together of *some* performance under the rubric folk has done much to obfuscate and blinker.

In broad terms, Part I (folk drama, theatre and performance) discusses and references as far back as the fourteenth century, Part II (folk dance) references as far back as the sixteenth century but discussion is for the most part focussed from the eighteenth, and Part III (folk song and music) both references and discusses from the eighteenth century onwards. All three parts do also acknowledge contemporary twenty-first-century folk performances. The volume commences with multi-modal, mobile and flexible forms of folk performance – wherein dance, drama and music often seem interwoven. It then foregrounds the more immediately dramatic (though often with song and dance attached) before shifting to dance, generally with a concomitant musicality, finally focussing directly on song and music.

These, then, are our folk performing arts. But what about our 'English'?

Given some earlier readings of folklore, it is important that the English of our title is understood as a self-imposed editorial 'constraining order' and not any search for the essence of Englishness within folk practice. Artistic practices from England have obviously exchanged and engaged with the cultural traditions of Scotland, Wales, Northern Ireland and the Republic of Ireland as well as further afield. However, even when folk practices appear closely related to those of other nations, there are matters of language, culture, nationalism and history that deserve far fuller treatment than this volume could have hoped to encompass.

We also acknowledge that some elements of the performances we think of as unequivocally English may well have arrived from other places. A musical tuning perhaps, or particular dance figures, or a personage such as a Quack Doctor. Whether brought home by travellers, or arriving as part of an immigrant's intangible heritage or as items of repertoire of the foreign entertainers visiting since at least the seventeenth century, these souvenirs of other performance do take root. Within our porous delineation of English, performers and audience members have also sailed away, or been press-ganged, or transported, only to perform again as part of a diaspora. Indeed, customary practices from the old and new worlds have interwoven in the naluyuk and jannying traditions of Labrador and Newfoundland, for example, or in the Jumbies' performances of Trinidad and Tobago, and of course this happens in England as well. Folk performances and their component parts are in flux; they pass through, change, move around, evolve and mutate, resettle as something different. In this regard, 'folk performance in England' might be a better term than 'English folk performance'.

But here in England, whatever their originations, past travels or intertextual adventures, some songs, airs, dances and performed events have come to constitute a 'performance of the local'. They have proved themselves to be much more than passing trade in the history of popular performance. They have been reiterated sufficiently often to assume a customary dimension, achieving a familiarity and embodiment that acquires the status of tradition or which has tradition conferred upon it. All of these combine together to form our subject of study and also raise two general questions.

First, what is happening on the ground as a newly created performance work (and they were all once newly created performance works) gradually becomes customary and acquires the status of tradition? Further, and rhetorically, how many reiterations are required in order to achieve a raison d'être that emphasises tradition? At what point does a participant rationalise a once newly minted performance as traditional? How many hands, voices, and bodies should a phrase or movement pass across; how many modifications and refinements are required; how much amendment and forgetting?

Self-evidently, all performance depends on traditions of one kind or another, be they professional, amateur, pedagogical or apprenticed, logocentric, aural, visual or otherwise contextual. So, second, what is it about a folk tradition that differentiates it from any other performance tradition?

The three introductions and 26 chapters that follow suggest different and contrasting answers for these two questions. Our contributors collectively unpick and rework the presumed usefulness of folk as a construct, but none of them abandon it.

Part I: folk drama, theatre and performance

The first four chapters of Part I provide some formulations for a customary theatre at stages of remove from its increasingly professional, commercial and institutional counterpart. First, Thomas Pettitt offers a survey and framework that facilitates appreciation of the attributes of a customary theatre. He incorporates both the auspices – the temporal and socio-cultural conditions under which such a theatre might operate (crudely, points of a year and points of a life) – and what he terms the 'stages' – the engineered and stage managed assemblies and encounters that underpin such performances and make them possible.

In Chapter 2, Taylor Aucoin develops a longitudinal study – readable within Pettitt's framework – focussed on Shrove Tuesday. He describes various performance forms and emphases arising from the intersection of religious, economic and social calendars. John Marshall contrasts this survey approach with a detailed study of a Robin Hood game held in Braunton, Devon, in 1562, which through its association with Whitsun Church Ales – Parish fund raising events – also falls under temporal auspices.

In Chapter 4, Peter Harrop considers points of contact along a blurred border between the customary and professional theatres from the eighteenth to the nineteenth centuries: a time of rapid expansion in professional theatre, most obviously in the numbers of new theatre buildings in regional centres and market towns, and in the numbers of touring and strolling players penetrating into rural areas on a new scale. This was the period when it became possible for the first folklorists to envisage a new folk drama, the mummers' play.

Chapters 5–7 share at least a partial focus on the period of the first folk revival. Duncan Broomhead examines a single mummers' play from the early nineteenth century through to the present day. Mike Pearson focusses on Lincolnshire to consider performances known locally as Plough Jagging. His archive-based investigation allows a performance maker's reimagining of a performance landscape and conditions pertaining, a perambulating cadge through the January cold as the nineteenth century turned to the twentieth. Katie Palmer Heathman's chapter is an important outlier, considering the dramatic experiments of John Marson, a Christian Socialist seeking an authentic voice for his parishioners. He took as source material the fifteenth-century pageant of The Second Shepherds Play of The Towneley Cycle and encouraged his parishioners to freely improvise the narrative content, mirroring the folk revival to seek a spiritual revival. All three examples attach themselves to the Christmas period as broadly conceived – and attend at big houses, public houses and the Church, respectively.

In the final chapter, Anna Smith discusses disguise and fancy dress in Wigan. This is a contemporary development that harnesses the perambulatory and guised trappings of early modern performance, yet with no obvious point of connection to earlier folk idioms, folk revivals or folk establishments. These days it is sections of the press that issue proclamations in the guise of disapproving editorial accompanied by photographs – the more Hogarthian the better.

Part II: folk dance

The contributors to this section are engaged with eighteenth- and post-eighteenth-century dance. Sue Allan starts in the late eighteenth century and moves into the nineteenth to examine contemporary accounts of country dance in that most favoured romantic setting of the Lake District. Stephen Corrsin takes a similar chronological start point but moves through to the early twentieth century with his survey of English hilt and point sword dancing. In demonstrating that the sword dance is a recent development in England, despite earlier best efforts to discern 'traces of ancient mystery', Corrsin, like Allan, reminds us that earlier readings do not simply disappear from popular perception and continue to shape our present understanding.

In Chapter 3, Matt Simons continues the lines of inquiry of morris dance scholars such as John Forrest, Keith Chandler and Michael Heaney into the period of the folk revival and beyond. He demonstrates that careful consideration of the morris dance revival reveals some important truths about early twentieth-century national identity. In Chapters 4 and 5, Derek Schofield and Chloe Middleton-Metcalfe, respectively, consider Cecil Sharp's ideas of art and authenticity with regard to country dance, and his successor Peter Kennedy's ambivalent attitude to country dance in education. These chapters all reflect on the power of personalities to shape not only the folk revival, but the very shape of what was being revived. The well-known disputes between Mary Neal and Cecil Sharp regarding the social efficacy of dance had a broader base than is usually discussed.

Fittingly, in the light of those discussions of authenticity, Alexandra Fisher considers the reasons behind the revival movement's late embrace of clog and step dance while also foregrounding both the stage background of the form and its competitive leanings. As she points out, these dance forms were too redolent of the popular, too urban and too modern, to catch the attention of the early collectors of folk dance. Her chapter reveals a long interplay between stage acts, street and pub dancing, and straightforward competition. Unusually in the context of this volume, this was a form that allowed space for the virtuosic individual.

John Swift considers the late development of Border Morris from a few scattered notes in the Sharp manuscripts through to a popular and widespread form. It is, in essence, a study of transmission as it appeared from the 'inside'. Swift also mentions his personal experience of the use of blackface (see below) within Border Morris, the now historical reasons why he and his peers rejected the practice and noting a series of related folk agency undertakings at the time of going to press.

Libby Worth considers contemporary step and rapper dancing, providing a degree of continuity from Corrsin and Fisher's earlier chapters, exploring current attitudes to tradition and change through conversation with practitioners. Lastly, Lucy Wright approaches girl's carnival morris, a folk form that predated and then existed in strict parallel with two folk revivals, remaining untouched and untroubled by either. No revival required. In bringing our considerations up to date, Worth and Wright raise different but important issues about the possibilities for folk performance futures, in Wright's phrase, 'outside of the ideological frameworks of the folk movement'. Chapters 8 and 24 by Anna Smith, Paul Wilson and Marilyn Tucker embrace the same conversation in Parts I and III, respectively.

Blackface

There has been much heated debate in recent years about the presence of blackened faces in many English calendar customs, a debate which has been exacerbated and obfuscated by different sides arguing from different bases, including dubious historical claims and confusing elements which can be categorised as origin, intent, development and perspective.

We can be reasonably clear about the early evidence for symbolic mask use in religious drama or the introduction of representational stage make-up. However, we do not normally know the origin of most traditional customs, or the original intent, and we rarely know when and why particular features were introduced. Occasionally we do – for example, the Father Christmas character in the mummers play cannot have dressed in the now familiar red robes and white beard before they became standardised in general society in the early twentieth century.

But as mentioned later in the context of song, it is an almost invariable feature of oral or semi-oral traditions that knowledge of origin is quickly lost, and the resultant vacuum is filled with explanations which fit the reasoning of the current time rather than the actual past.

When folklorists and other outsiders first encountered calendar customs, the communities almost invariably had a putative historical narrative (i.e. a legend) about their activity. Once those outsiders started declaring that customs were ancient ceremonies, luck-bringing rituals and the like, these explanations were often adopted by the performers themselves.

This is not to say that morris dancers or mummers 'do not know why they do it', but rather that their motives are unlikely to be those of the original performers.

In the case of a feature such as blackface, there are a number of possibilities of 'meaning', all of which can be evidenced in England over the last six centuries.

- symbolic – denoting good or evil or other
- representational – dressing in character
- camouflage – e.g. poachers operating at night
- disguise – to conceal the identity of the wearer

But there is one datable historical event which cuts sharply through this debate – the rise of blackface minstrelsy from the 1840s onwards. It is difficult to overstate how popular the blackface craze was for the rest of the nineteenth century, affecting equally the working and middle classes, and becoming a staple of popular culture which lasted well over 100 years. There is no doubt about the origin of this as a parody of black people (particularly slaves and recently freed slaves in the USA), or that it continued to be so. A widespread peripatetic custom was created – going 'niggering' – which involved blacking up and singing minstrel songs, and there is some evidence that this new custom replaced older ones, such as mumming.

Participants in modern customs which can only be dated back 200 years have no evidence of connection with older theatrical forms, nor can they claim that their customary activity was illegal or required them to disguise their identities. If seeking to be 'representational', the intent may not be racist, but the effect is. Taking all the evidence into consideration, it is almost certain that the blackfaces in these either originated or were introduced as a result of the minstrelsy craze, and cannot be claimed as 'English' tradition unconnected with some form of stereotypical racial intent.

Part III: folk song and music

As will be repeated in the later introduction to Part III, any attempt to understand folk song and music must be concerned with more than just the items themselves (the repertoire), but must also take into account the style, context and personnel of the genre, if such it is. Without these aspects, it is impossible to envision, let alone describe, a genre called 'folk' at all.

The first three chapters in this section, by Tom Pettitt, Steve Gardham and Vic Gammon, while highlighting particular categories of repertoire, all set them into wider, and deeper, contexts. Thomas Pettitt uses 'sweetheart murder' ballads to introduce notions of how our investigation must take into account not just the interplay between 'oral' and printed material, but also what goes on in the singer's head, in memory between learning and performance.

Many well-known songs engendered 'answer' or 'extension' songs, and many were also parodied – either with newly published songs or within traditional settings (in particular in bawdy versions).

And, as Steve Gardham demonstrates, an 'answer' could achieve a greater longevity than the original, until only the historian knows that the song was once a joke. As indicated above, this is a perennial feature of 'folklore'. Within the traditional process, knowledge of origins (and original meanings) is usually very quickly lost, and is often replaced by other explanations, which become folklore in themselves.

The subject of vernacular church music (now often called 'West Gallery' music) has only relatively recently caught the attention of the 'folk' world, and is a good example of the expansion of the field and the realisation that instead of policing our definitional borders, we need to understand how porous they really are. Vic Gammon's extended piece is both an examination of the evidence and a masterful summing up of where we are now in our understanding of an important phenomenon.

In Folk Song Studies, we also have to factor in two 'revivals' (a loaded word, but there is no real alternative), and it is as well to remind ourselves that it can signify 'revival of interest' and 'revival of performance', and the two are not necessarily the same. This is indeed one of the severe fault-lines in any longitudinal study of the subject, when, for want of better words, old-style (traditional) and current (revival) and future can be so different as to stretch the putative connections beyond breaking point.

Arthur Knevett's chapter on the formation of the Folk Song society in 1898 throws light on the thinking at the most important moment in the development of 'folk song studies', and identifies the mixed motives of the key players, combining aesthetics, antiquarianism and cultural nationalism. It is interesting to see that the struggle between the 'pedants' and the 'fakers' – a tension which echoes down the ages in folk – was already in play.

Martin Graebe's case study of Eve Maxwell-Lyte is a reminder that the first revival put 'folk song' on the national cultural map, albeit in a form barely recognisable to its original performers and achieved a niche market in the commercial entertainment industry.

Introduction

Chapters 23 and 24, by Brian Peters and Paul Wilson and Marilyn Tucker, all of whom are writing with long-standing 'insider' experience, highlight different manifestations of post-war revivals of performance, and the ways in which they have spawned a range of new (and not so new) enthusiasms and styles.

The editors decided early on not to include a great deal of musical analysis in this volume. Musical analysis rapidly moves into specialist areas which exclude many general readers at whom the book is aimed, although Chapters 24 and 26 have overt musical content and indicate areas worthy of further study.

In addition, most of this section is devoted to song (but song is half-music), although Rebecca Dellow's chapter focusses on instrumental music per se. She identifies a similar trajectory to song research in that an earlier concentration on 'folk tunes' has in recent years been replaced by an interest in 'what tunes the folk played'. This broadening of focus, and the new respect for historical sources, is very welcome indeed.

The final chapter, Julia Bishop's survey of an important, but neglected, aspect of children's folklore – the musical side – reminds us forcefully that the *people* need also to be centre stage in our investigations. Every individual is part of multiple communities – by residence, ethnicity, gender, occupation, interest and so on – but the one we all go through is childhood, and it is there we learn not only our first songs and tunes, but what we expect songs and tunes to be like.

But what about the social context? This is there throughout most of the chapters, including references to physical settings such as churches, concert halls, choirs, folk clubs and the more 'natural' habitats of homes, playgrounds and so on. But Chapter 9, Sue Allan's expert chapter, placed in the dance section for convenience, is particularly relevant here. By slicing the folklore cake in a different way, and concentrating on a particular region, the author demonstrates how song, music, dance and custom come together, and how local forces, such as dialect and local identity, come into play. And this microcosm can be set into the wider world of pan-European romanticism, high literature and even tourism.

This whole section can be summed up in the mundane observation that 'when people get together for a good time they dance and sing'. But what they dance and sing, and how they do it, is the fascinating stuff of the area of folklore studies investigated in this section.

Conclusion

The founding folklorists collected, catalogued and mapped the texts, times and sites of performance. They were collecting with a sense of urgency since they feared that these enactments might disappear completely. They were working to record an extinction. The participants in the folk revival seized on the outcome and process of that collecting, joining a widespread effort to breathe life back into the songs and dances. Both efforts continue to the present day.

Trying to communicate the experience of performance, now and in the past, and trying to understand reiteration, duration, time and place as components, in addition to matters of repertoire, style and personnel, also comprise valuable work. These seem unusually foregrounded in some genres of folk performance and may constitute special features.

Although folk is a helpful descriptor for a range of material, it is also an evasive term; the more one tries to pin it down, the more its definitional and distinctive qualities seem to slide away. It is often remarked in performance studies that 'the difference between performance and everyday life is straightforward until you stop to think about it'. The difference between folk performance and other performance has often been perceived as largely self-evident.

Given our recent appreciation of the porous borders mentioned above, perhaps it is once more time to stop to think about it.

Parts I, II and III carry separate introductions. Although each is clearly focussed on a particular genre, a number of more general points have been spread across them. With that in mind, it may be helpful to consider them in relation to one another as well as precursors to the chapters they specifically introduce.

Brought together in this way, reaching across drama, dance, song and music, English folk performance is an extraordinary body of material. Rich, varied, vibrant and possessed of multiple histories, it is testament to the creative and organisational agency of ordinary but talented people. Often working with the most limited resources, they have harnessed their performance-making abilities to the creation of art and cultural memory.

Steve Roud is a historian with an interest in folk culture. Peter Harrop has a background in performing arts and a wide-ranging interest in performance and community. We hope these respective approaches prove complementary for the reader.

PART I

Folk drama, theatre and performance

Peter Harrop

This is a broader field than the performance of plays by actors for an audience. In addition to performance *per se*, the folk art described and discussed in Part I accommodates the performative (heightened, expressive communication) and the presentational alongside the dramatic. Participation is central and there is often a fluidity in matters of display and spectatorship (sometimes doing, sometimes watching, always involved). Folk performance is a space where social role, persona, disguise, presentation, representation, personage and stage character often intermingle. Folk performances highlight the customary in their reiterated routes, visits, encounters and assemblies, games, pageants and parades, sometimes plays, and in the familiar personages that occasionally turn up – a St George here, a quack doctor there, Men-Women, a Jack in the Green, a Robin Hood or hobby-horse. Folk performances accompany the heightened expectations, behaviours and interactions of marked moments. They are a creative response to the 'extra' ordinary and shared reiterations that mark points of the year, points of our lives, and make special the places where we live.

The 'mists of time' that still cling to folk performance are for the most part the lingering effect of first-rate Victorian smoke machines. That smoke clears to reveal a history of widespread creativity, agency and organization, always interwoven with the broader culture of which it is part. Folk performance often engages with the parallel yet accessible track of popular professional and semi-professional theatre from the fifteenth century onwards and is sometimes barely separable from it. Indeed, folk performances so often achieve other lives across print media, art and theatre, that it can sometimes be difficult to disentangle a customary reiteration from an artistic appropriation, or even to establish a direction of travel. In the case of the mummers' play, surely the best-known example of an English folk drama, the earliest suggestion of a performance and the earliest example of a printed text fall very close together.

An example: rough music

Our cover illustration is the 1726 William Hogarth engraving 'Hudibras Encounters the Skimmington'. This is a depiction of *charivari* or 'rough music', a persistent and widespread European performance form intended to humiliate those responsible for transgressing normative marital relations. Hogarth's work was first printed in a new edition of Samuel Butler's

1664 satirical work *Hudibras* and shows the eponymous Presbyterian attempting to disrupt a community performance.[1]

The enactment – in general terms – mocks a local couple whose transgressions might have included domestic abuse or unfaithfulness, or simply being part of an unpopular marriage, or a second marriage, or marriage deemed inappropriate by discrepancy of age, wealth or background. In the picture itself, one performer represents the husband sitting backwards on a horse and carrying a distaff, while another, a man dressed as a woman, represents his wife beating him with a ladle – the 'skimmington' of the title. Just a few feet away, a cuckold's horns and petticoats are held aloft over other symbols of marital discord. The central personages are parading through a village accompanied by a crowd, some playing rough music; one contributor is throwing or swinging a cat to contribute to the cacophony. Production values are obviously in play; there are two main actors, seemingly two musicians, horses, instruments, costumes and properties. Some are more makeshift than others, some more impromptu – such as the poor, pressganged cat. Children have joined in – one child, though cropped out from our cover, is happily stealing sausages – then, in the background, there are the faces of the crowd. They look angry. This is a rumbustious public display, but also personal and up-close for the targeted couple, even where wrongdoing may have been popularly ascribed to a single partner. It is a crowded, layered, personalized discord of role reversal, cross-dressing, gendered properties and persistent noise. Seventeenth-century accounts describe the engagement of immediate and near neighbours, sometimes willing participants, sometimes coerced to take part in the enactment as retribution for their perceived tolerance of matters they must surely have known about. Outcomes for those targeted, though not violent, could be long lasting and occasionally tragic.

Descriptions of rough music (referenced regionally by words and phrases such as 'skimmington' or 'riding the stang') illustrate, in Thomas Pettit's telling phrase, a highly performative 'folk law'. Performances were both commonplace and noteworthy enough to allow the folklorist Violet Alford to make a comparison of some 250 examples from across Europe citing one French example dating back as far as 1377.[2] Unsurprisingly, given issues of distribution and longevity, this is a broad spectrum of customary activity, manifesting very differently at different times and places. Its legality in England, for example, was being questioned by 1500; yet, the most detailed accounts are found only from the 1560s onwards. At the other end of a significant duration – not all folk productions enjoy such long runs – there is a detailed newspaper account from Berkshire in 1930[3] and mention of other more recent contenders.

Three more examples: popular and courtly mumming, mummers' plays

Mummers' plays circumscribed a discussion of English folk drama for much of the twentieth century and not in a helpful way. The word 'mumming' first crops up in the fourteenth century to describe small groups of people playing a game of conceal and reveal. Wearing each other's clothes, sometimes cross-dressed, with masks or facial disguises, keeping silent to further disguise their identities, they would seek entry to private houses to play the hosts at dice and perhaps dance with them. This was risky as well as risqué and the first effort to put a stop to it was a London proclamation made in 1334. It was specifically forbidden by an Act of Parliament in 1511, but there were further proclamations in Newcastle upon Tyne and Chester as late as the 1550s. Indeed, the Reverend Henry Bourne of Newcastle was still complaining about it in arguably the first work of folklore, his *Popular Antiquities* of 1725. 'Mumming; which is a changing of Clothes between Men and Women; who when dress'd in each other's Habits, go from one Neighbour's house to another, and partake of their

Christmas-Cheer, and make Merry with them in Disguise…'.[4] Medieval mumming seems to have aspired to a sustained frisson, right on the edge of multiple gate-crashing, but with an expectation that the masked visitor/intruder would prove entertaining or rewarding in some way, the central game of dice neatly reflecting the uncertain outcome of the visitation.

Despite the earlier prohibition, a 1377 'mumming' was held as part of the celebration of Prince Richard's tenth birthday. One hundred and thirty costumed and masked men, bearing torches, cavalcaded from the City of London to Kennington: their dice precisely loaded to ensure the Prince won three games in succession, each time securing a different gold gift. No risk involved here – this was the structure of a popular custom, but event managed with theatrical precision. Without suggesting a direct line of descent, such elaborate and gilded theatricality never went away; its later manifestation as the Stuart masque disdained the complex dramatic narrative of popular public theatre while honing the symbolic, referential and allusive qualities of pictorial performance.

Popular mumming continued as a Christmastime custom, often under alternative regional names such as 'guising', and increasingly as an activity for children, certainly into the twentieth century – indeed, we hear its echo at Halloween. But by the 1770s, the word mummer started to be used in a quite different way. It achieved popularity as a generic term for a not very good actor, coincidentally at a time when strolling players were becoming a familiar sight across much of the country. The precise phrase 'mummers' play', however, was not coined until 1849, although hindsight enables us to discern a few early mummers' play performances from the second half of the eighteenth century followed by a burgeoning across much of the country throughout the nineteenth.

Mummers' plays are short, amateur performances, in verse, performed by men and boys, usually toured around private and public houses in return for gifts of food, drink and money. They are associated with different points of the year in different regions, from Halloween through Christmas and New Year to Easter, and there are endless creative variants and embellishments as one would expect from a widespread custom with long duration. Numerous detailed studies have shown regional variations with certain characters and narrative features proving more popular in particular places and at particular times. Similarly, their performers have capitalized on, or have already been involved with, other local customs that combine to elaborate the basic structure and provide local appeal. In Cheshire, the play attaches to soulcaking, a Halloween custom, and features a wild horse (usually a real horse's skull, treated and blackened, on a post, with a snapping jaw). In Yorkshire, the play has interwoven with the regional longsword dance (a late eighteenth-century European import) to provide a unique motif. In Lincolnshire during the 1880s and 1890s, a recruiting sergeant took a central role, and there are elements of comic courtship not found in other parts of the country. By far, the most common plot line, both over time and geographically, includes a fight between two heroes – usually St George and an exotic foreign adversary, closely followed by the ministrations of a quack doctor. Following recent work by Thomas Pettitt[5] and Peter Harrop,[6] we can see that the plays combine multiple arrangements of already familiar character types, of well-travelled pan-European moments of dramatic action captured in the phrase 'theatergrams', of established dramatic formulas and idiosyncratic extracts from specific early modern stage plays.

Theatrical backdrop

None of the dramatic activities and plays considered in Part I ever existed in a theatrical vacuum; in the present state of evidence, there is nothing to suggest a 'folk' theatre predating a 'non-folk' theatre. From the mid-fourteenth century, for example, trade guilds, civic and church authorities were dramatizing the Bible, working together to produce the mystery cycles, a 200-year span of performances that lasted until a gradual post-Reformation suppression in the mid-to-late 1500s. Morality plays (then referred to as interludes) developed throughout the same period, both as large-scale outdoor performances but more usually as private indoor productions, sometimes religious, sometimes secular. The range of court pageantry has already been alluded to; guildhalls and grand houses also provided multiple sites of theatrical experimentation, as did the commercial theatre buildings of the 1560s and 1570s. Court entertainment was increasingly harnessed to the pursuit of classical allusion, political symbolism and scenic sophistication leading towards the masque. In the public domain, theatre continued to expand and prosper until the closure of its buildings in 1642, followed by the interregnum of 1649–1660. But there was no real cessation and many sub-genres of the Elizabethan and Jacobean theatres – short pieces like jigs and drolls, for example – pursued a speakeasy existence at inns, seasonal fairs and other venues. The re-opening and scenic re-invention of the theatres from the point of Restoration in 1660 was followed by a national network of theatre buildings, touring and repertory companies, and significant increases in the movement of strolling players across most of the country. From the fourteenth to the eighteenth centuries, the period during which most of the activities discussed in Parts I and II first emerged (some were later, none were earlier), the interplay of these strands removes any possibility of an unsullied and perfectly quarantined folk drama.

Strange familiars

Several personages appear across various folk performances, cropping up with no explanation. They have been described as supernumerary, but they are overwhelmingly present. These include the animal disguises – most frequently horses of various shapes and sizes, occasionally bulls or rams, infrequently dragons. These beasts, and half-person half-beasts, are sometimes quiet bystanders, more often careering and boisterous, over-excited and occasionally threatening. Hobby-horses were particularly fashionable during the fifteenth century and up to the mid-sixteenth. They featured in court entertainments, watch parades, and attached to morris dancing for a brief period. From the nineteenth century to the present, a variety of beasts have re-invented across a greater geographical range, attending a wider range of events, appearing at May Day in Padstow, Cornwall, for example, or accompanying Cheshire soul-cakers at Halloween. Lincolnshire sieve horses are discussed in Chapter 6. Works by Violet Alford and Christopher Cawte have done much to provide an overview of these creatures, but no comparable study has yet addressed the Men-Women of English folk. These are usually men in non-specific historical drag, no actorly pretence of gendered representation, who attach versions of their multiple selves to plays, dances and parades. They are most likely an eighteenth century 'stepping out' from the ever popular cross gender dressing of early popular mumming and later guising. The late eighteenth-century Jack in the Green, popular through till the mid-nineteenth century, was a feature of May Day celebrations and has more recently conflated with a range of post-Frazerian incarnations. There are many others, often a summation of local imagination and creativity, attaching to one place only. They may not contribute to dramatic action, but they occasionally offer commentary, and they always add impact.

Popular antiquities to performance studies

A very gradual development from the establishment of antiquarianism (the Society of Antiquaries founded in London in 1707), through the pervading influence of romanticism and the eventual coining of 'folklore' in 1846, coalesced in the long half-century from c1865 to c1925. The establishment and vigour of the Folklore Society (1878), the Folk-Song Society (1898) and the English Folk Dance Society (1911) capture the disproportionate influence of that short period on conceptions of English folk. Between the earliest works of anthropology and a fully fledged folk revival, ideas about cultural evolutionism, survivalism, pagan origins, 'lost-in-the-mists-of-time-ness' and 'merrie-Englandism' entered and settled in the public consciousness, rather like folk dance in schools.

Because the histories of folk forms are now better-documented and understood, it has become more straightforward to separate them from the folkloric accretions that post-date their emergence (though not always by many years). The mummers' play, for example, had barely been going for a century before it was being understood as an ancient 'rite of spring' or some such vagary. This is an important clarification – in order to look properly at these performances, we need to extract them from the fascinating folklore that so often and so romantically obscures them. Otherwise, 'folk performance' comes to mean 'performance about which people have constructed folklore'. But it is also true that such separation is really only possible for the sake of argument; after all, how might one exclude the underlying mix of identity politics (quintessential Englishness) and magical realism (ancient pagan origins) of the Edwardian folk revival?

The twenty-first-century reality is that folk performances retain a direct engagement with performance skills, but alongside a complex social aesthetic premised on custom, particular understandings of history and changing perceptions of authenticity – a heady and fascinating mix. It is interesting to reflect that the older a (hypothetical) custom actually is, the shorter the proportion of its existence that might realistically be termed 'folk', since folk is unequivocally a nineteenth-century understanding. While history (the narrative sweep), historicity (provenance, dates, evidence) and historiography (the frame of reference of any act of history writing) should be intellectually separable, if only to understand the ways in which they inform one another, they remain resolutely and enjoyably intertwined in performance.

It is here, amidst what the Canadian anthropologist Mat Levitt has described as the intertextuality and metafolklore, that we find fresh insights.[7] His straightforward demonstration of the ease with which fellow mummers can hold widely differing views about the history and purpose of their collective activity, together in the here-and-now, provides a sharp ethnographic riposte to singular or static explanations of 'folk'. Diana Taylor's conceptual foregrounding of archive and repertoire is especially helpful in this regard; on the one hand, folk performances have been chloroformed and pinned like butterflies in collecting cases; on the other hand, they have persistently re-entered and re-invented the repertoire.[8] They are simultaneously part of the intellectual construct of folklore, yet still insist on making theatrical entrances. The antiquarian archive of 'collected' folk performances, of dusty classifications, taxonomies and mappings has never subjugated their romantic dynamism and liberating misbehaviours.

Given the centrality of iteration and reiteration to customary performance, Richard Schechner's conception of acting and theatre as 'restored behaviour' is applicable.[9] So is Joseph Roach's subsequent argument 'about the stimulus of restored behaviour to the production of cultural memory'.[10] Furthermore, because those validating reiterations of customary performance are never the same twice, I raise Jacques Derrida's famous différance. This conception, with its twin inference of endless difference alongside meaning deferred time and again, lends itself to folk performances.[11] Here, the gradual shifts in the nature of customary performances over time are accompanied by gradual shifts in the constitution of audience, and gradual shifts in the ways those performances are read and understood.

The nineteenth-century 'outsider' folklorist was capable of juxtaposing a romantic, creative impulse with an uncomfortable 'othering' and imposed atavism. The creative fictions of their readings required the performer/participant *not* to grasp the 'true' nature of their own performances. The made-up archival meanings (Thomas Hardy's 'fossilised survival' and Charlotte Burne's 'this world-old drama' to take two well-known examples)[12] became more fascinating than the actual customary repertoire. When these are superimposed on the variants of morris dances, sword dances and mummers' plays, we find acts of local creativity dismissed as degeneration from a fictitious original or ecotype, and a static interpretation foisted on endlessly different and deferred meanings, the consequence of multiple performances by different people at different times in different places.

But we should not forget that this critique has an unassailable corollary; however skewed the intellectual framework that influenced the pioneering collectors, and however biased their bases for collection may now appear, they bequeathed a far greater body of material for us to revisit than would otherwise have been the case.

Conclusion: indicators of a folk drama?

The volume is obviously a companion and not a solution; nonetheless, there are some features, variously reflected in this introduction and in the following chapters, that indicate sufficient commonality to support the idea of some broadly recognizable features of folk drama.

Spatial arrangements: In the late 1960s, the distinguished folklorist Herbert Halpert produced a typology of mumming which first focused attention on the spatial arrangements at play across that body of customary activity. For over a quarter of a century, Thomas Pettitt has also explored and developed those ideas with reference to both early modern pageantry and customary drama more broadly. The titles of three of his contributions indicate his scope and focus: *Social and Spatial Patterning in Customary Encounters*; *The Morphology of the Parade*; and lastly *Moving Encounters; Choreographing Stage and Spectators*.[13] His opening contribution to this volume draws on that body of work. The complex spatial patterns of customary drama are rarely mirrored in other forms of theatre; even the recent interest in site-specificity, mobilities and walking performances has not come close to the range of customary forms. The pageants, parades, promenades, perambulations, peregrinations and processions that move people together and apart, that facilitate different kinds of encounters and assemblies, that make possible arrivals and departures, entrances and exits, are a central feature of customary drama which seems to foreground movement, visiting and assemblage. This provides shape and emphasis for inculcating and sustaining an important social aesthetic.

Reiteration and duration, time and place: Taylor Aucoin, in Chapter 2, demonstrates continuity for Shrove Tuesday customs and performances, but these have changed utterly over the years, responding (and this is the basis of his argument) to different periods and circumstances. All folk performances come and go, are revived in different places and change with time. Notwithstanding, they somehow achieve a special relationship between people, time and place, and they appear to do so quite quickly. Whatever meaning is derived from events during an individual experience of them seems to depend on their perceived longevity rather than any necessity for the real thing. Two parallel processes are at work. First, the annual, seasonal or calendrical repetition of the same thing in the same place (which is rare in other theatres – to take even the most obvious example, it is not usually the same pantomime in the same theatre with the same actors *every* year) can soon impact on social arrangements and memories. Second, those performances attaching to the life cycle have built-in significance for the individuals concerned – these are, after all, moments from which subsequent life dates will be measured, visual and emotional memories formed, and they are also always indicative of other significant moments: one birthday, wedding or funeral summoning other such events, welcome or not. Both sets of performances assume significance as physical and temporal reference points, a shared understanding of the nature of the event further enhancing the social aesthetic.

Romanticism, context and technique: Knowing oneself to be part of a reiteration, whether as a performer, participant or spectator, however boisterous the event, has a quietly serious dimension. Marvin Carlson has spoken of things coming back in the theatre as a 'ghosting' and Derrida has arrived at the idea of 'hauntology' to consider questions of the presence of the past in the present.[14] Mummers' plays are not the only folk performances that have a remarkable capacity to remind us of their own past performances in the present moment of our watching. The term pentimento, usually used of paintings, describes how earlier iterations can show through the surface of a present 'finished' version. With these ideas in play, it seems reasonable to ask whether the following explorations highlight techniques that emphasize continuity, that demonstrate a readable distinction in performance between customary and non-customary theatres, that suggest in some way what a 'folk' performance might be.

Notes

1 Samuel Butler, *Hudibras* (London: W. Rogers, 1684).
2 Violet Alford, 'Rough Music or Charivari', *Folklore*, 70.4. 1959, pp. 505–518. See also Martin Ingram Ridings, 'Rough Music and the "Reform of Popular Culture"' in *Early Modern England, Past & Present*, 105 (November 1984), pp. 79–113 and Edward Palmer Thompson, *Customs in Common: Studies in Traditional Popular Culture* (London: The Merlin Press, 1991), the chapter entitled Rough Music.
3 Graham Seal, 'A Hussiting in Berkshire, 1930', *Folklore*, 98.1. 1987, pp. 91–94.
4 Henry Bourne, *Antiquitates Vulgares* (Newcastle: J. White, 1725), pp. 147–148.
5 Thomas Pettitt, 'Beyond the Bad Quarto: Exploring the Vernacular Afterlife of Early Modern Drama', *Journal of Early Modern Studies*, 8, 2019, 133–171, https://oajournals.fupress.net/index.php/bsfm-jems/article/view/7107/7105 [accessed 22 February 2020].
6 Peter Harrop, *Mummers' Plays Revisited* (London: Routledge, 2020).
7 Mathew James Levitt, 'The Laughing Storyteller: Metafolklore about the Origin of Mummers' Plays', unpublished MA Thesis, University of Alberta, 2011 and Ghosts Under the Marquee Lights: Mummers in Alberta, England, and Newfoundland, unpublished PhD thesis, University of Alberta, 2016.
8 Diana Taylor, *The Archive and the Repertoire: Performing Cultural Memory in the Americas* (Durham, NC: Duke University Press, 2007).
9 Richard Schechner, *Between Theatre and Anthropology* (Philadelphia: University of Pennsylvania Press, 1985), pp. 35–116.
10 Joseph Roach, *Cities of the Dead, Circum-Atlantic Performance* (New York: Colombia University Press, 1996), p. 73.
11 Jacques Derrida and Alan Bass, *Writing and Difference* (Chicago, IL: University of Chicago Press, 1978).
12 Thomas Hardy, *The Return of the Native* (London: MacMillan, 1912), p. 144. and Charlotte Burne, *Shropshire Folklore, Part lll* (London: Trubner and co., 1886), p. 492.
13 See the bibliography at https://southerndenmark.academia.edu/ThomasPettitt/Theatre-&-Custom [accessed 24 November 2020] for these and related papers.
14 Marvin Carlson, *The Haunted Stage, The Theatre as Memory Machine* (Michigan: Michigan University Press, 2003) and Jacques Derrida et al., *The Spectre of Marx* (London: Routledge, 2006).

1

TOWARDS AN ANATOMY OF ENGLISH CUSTOMARY DRAMA

Theatre, stage, play

Thomas Pettitt

Introductory remarks

A significant segment of the English Performance Culture covered by this collection comprises activities which are 'customary' in the sense of being observed as customs in their own right, or traditionally performed under arrangements which are themselves customary. Any customary activity qualifying as a performance of some kind has the potential for displaying dramatic features, and those that do can usefully be perceived, in a more than metaphorical sense, as a 'theatre', their auspices and material contexts, respectively, equivalent to playhouses and stages, in and on which customary 'plays' are performed.[1] What follows will accordingly offer an 'anatomy' of dramatic folk performance *as performance*, rather than as 'traces of ancient mystery' (Walter Scott, *Marmion*), or as essentially reflections of contemporary social relationships.

The history of this 'customary' theatre is distinct from, but has significantly interacted with, that of 'regular', or 'legitimate' theatre over the last several centuries, although the relationship was seriously distorted by the once fashionable theory, now discarded by folklorists if lingering among theatre historians, that the most elaborate and dramatic customs reported from the nineteenth century derived from ancient fertility rituals, and therefore must have existed in the Middle Ages.[2] It was indeed from those same rituals, according to some, that western theatre itself may have evolved.[3]

As the professionalized, institutional, cultural system we know today, English theatre emerged in the early modern period, and did so in close contact with customary dramatic performances – *such as they were at the time* – and whose influence is discernible in many features of dramatic context, form and content, for example, in the work of Shakespeare and his contemporaries.[4] In succeeding centuries, as institutional theatre was further consolidated, and as once vigorous customary performance traditions, under the successive blows of the Reformation, the Agrarian and the Industrial Revolutions, declined into mere 'folk' customs, the movement of dramatic material has rather been in the opposite direction.[5]

However, in the late medieval and Renaissance periods, the customary segment of performance culture examined here also included activities conventionally treated by theatre historians as 'pageantry'. Typically associated with royal, noble, civic or guild auspices, on closer inspection, it most often proves to comprise customs also observed by others, only now with the spectacular enhancement and artistic sophistication enabled by greater wealth and status. Conversely, most dramatic customs at humbler social levels also qualified as 'pageantry', only without the gold-plating. The identity of the two fields has been obscured by scholarly emphasis on the high-cultural superstructure of pageantry (pictorial and literary art) rather than its vernacular basis (crafting movement and action).[6]

While alert to historical change, the following matrix of categorical distinctions is designed to be valid for the study of customary drama over the period ca 1400–ca 1900,[7] but the closer it approaches the performances themselves, the more, necessarily, it will focus on the better-documented recent phases of tradition, recorded as 'Popular Antiquities' from the early eighteenth century and as 'Folklore' from the mid-nineteenth, down to the Great War, which took such a heavy toll on both English folk and folklorists.

Customary theatres (auspices)

Temporal auspices (incidence)

However else understood, definitive to custom is *iteration*: the same, deliberate, action is undertaken, over time, many times. A particularly relevant criterion for categorizing and analysing customs is accordingly their *incidence* (their temporal auspices).

Most familiar in more recent times are *annual* customs, but they qualify as such in various ways.[8] Some are strictly *calendrical*, observed on the same date each year, to which may be added those associated with a particular weekday in relation to a specific date – say the first Monday after Epiphany, 6 January ('Plough Monday'); the first Sunday after 1 October (village wakes – at least according to legislation of 1563); the Sunday closest to St Andrew's Day, 30 November (Advent Sunday). Others are geared to the ecclesiastical combination of solar and lunar calendars deployed to establish the date of Easter Sunday for each year, and with it a lengthy concatenation of 'movable' feasts stretching over some 15 weeks from Carnival/Shrovetide to Ascension, Whitsun and Corpus Christi, whose calendar dates can therefore shift within a 30-day range. There are also customs whose incidence is annual, but seasonal rather than strictly calendrical, typically when determined by the rhythm of agrarian production (arable; pastoral) which, in turn, could be affected by local climate and weather.[9]

From this temporal perspective, other customs have what might be termed a *biographical* incidence, marking transitions between the life cycle phases of an individual.[10] They accordingly qualify as 'rites of passage', although the term has a much wider range (and is provocative of unbridled theorizing).

In pre-modern times, the *birth* of a child might involve a 'gossips' feast' for the womenfolk attending on the mother's labour, as well as a more formal feast in connection with the church christening, and in the latter connection processions to and from the church.[11] Celebration of an annual 'birthday' thereafter would generally be under private auspices, but in the case of locally significant households, it could explode into quite significant customary activity (sometimes re-cycling material from calendar celebrations) in connection with the heir's *coming of age* at 21.[12]

The transition from single to married state provoked another, *nuptial*, cluster of customary observances, including not merely a wedding feast, but the bridal procession from home to church and that of the newlyweds from church to the venue for the feast.[13]

The *death* of an individual also gave rise to various customary observances, including the processional transfers of the coffin from the deceased's home to the church, and thence to the graveyard, accompanied by a deal (depending on status) of traditional pomp and circumstance. Interment was followed by a funeral feast, to which all those participating in the obsequies were invited, or (in the case of the local destitute) offered a dole at the gate.[14] Much of this persisted until relatively modern times, but England (in contrast to Ireland) lost at an early stage the customary activities of the night-time vigils over the laid out body, in the vernacular, 'lyke-wakes', intervening between the death and the funeral. To judge from the Irish analogues and sporadic documentary hints, these will once have involved a strange mixture of mourning, condolence, ceremony and pastimes, the latter sometimes with distinctly dramatic features.[15]

While 'biographical' in relation to the individual concerned, when they also provoked autonomous customary performances by others outside the family circle, the latter qualify as purely *occasional* customs with an incidence determined by the sporadic occurrence of performance-prompting events or situations, as and when they arose. This category would also encompass activities prompted by coronations, military victories, successful or thwarted revolutions, or local scandals and socio-economic disputes.

Socio-cultural auspices (function)

Inherent in the iterative nature of custom is the sustained engagement of its *participants*: from one performance to the next, many will be the same, while over time some will drop out, others join in, ensuring the persistence, as well as enabling the variation, of the tradition itself. Participants, accordingly, were less likely to be an ad hoc group brought together primarily for the continuance of the custom (as may be the case in recent revivals), and more likely to belong to an existing group, whose membership and cohesion were determined by other factors and functions, but for which the observance of the custom was a significant aspect of that collective identity. Classification of customary performances can therefore also be based on the categories to which groups belonged, of which, historically, there have been basically three: the household, the community and the association.

The most familiar *household* now is the *domestic* group with a 'nuclear' family at its core and (until recently) the male householder at its head, but the further we go back, and the higher up the social scale, the more it might also encompass resident-dependent relatives, live-in servants and apprentices. And there were also *institutional* households, typically ecclesiastical (monasteries, friaries, cathedral chapters), or educational (university colleges; inns of court; boarding schools), which paralleled the domestic with regard to living, sleeping and eating under the same roof under the control of a household head.[16]

A *community* is a collectivity of households based on spatial contiguity, upon which is superimposed some kind of organizational unity. They are sometimes configured as a wider community (say a city) and its sub-communities (parishes; wards; precincts), but the latter can overlap, and furthermore manors, significant land-holding units in pre-modern times, often had boundaries cutting across those of the other types.[17]

Falling somewhat between communities and households (in having aspects of each) were the *associations* in which individuals came together on the basis of other common factors. Most familiar among the formal associations was the guild, a characteristic late medieval formation, whose membership shared craft, trade or devotional interests, and for which customary performances were a significant, verging on definitive, activity.[18] Even smaller communities could have several of these, and there were other, equally or less formal, groupings under other designations, not least the various youth-groups (demarcated by age, gender and neighbourhood), active in many customary activities.[19] The in every way smallest but also the longest surviving associations were the playground and back-street 'gangs' of children who convened on a regular basis for traditional pastime and mischief.[20]

Inevitably, such neat categories are challenged by the realities on the ground (which the demarcations are designed to analyse), not least in the case of a major landed household and those in some way subservient to it: the lord of the manor and his villeins; the Squire and his tenants; the farmer and his labourers. From some perspectives, the subordinate group functions as an association whose members have common interests, not least in relation to the dominant household, where 'custom', often manifested as 'customs', was an important aspect. But the group may in other respects be perceived as an (extra-mural) extension of the 'great' household concerned, at whose customary observances they might have a right to attend.

While many customary activities were observed under the auspices of one such group, under the temporal circumstances surveyed above, there were others occurring under the quite different auspices of deliberate, organized *engagements* between two groups (or their representatives). Many permutations of community, household and association figured in such inter-group engagements, including the participation of two of the same kind (which could include a sub-community engaging with the wider community of which it was a part). Other than a general expectancy that certain things happen under certain circumstances, mutual pre-arrangement was rare, so normally the engagement was initiated by an *active group*, and a *reactive group* responded in accordance with the protocols of the custom concerned (unless say in periods where the custom concerned was under fire from some segments of society). Engagement customs can therefore most usefully be categorized in terms of the active group's motivation, and surveying the field as a whole, it seems to have been relatable to one or more of three primary factors:

1. the DISTRIBUTION of material resources

    – on an axis between achieving redistribution in favour of the reactive group (*donation*) and (more often) in favour of the active group (*exaction*); midway between them is the preservation of the ('customary') *status quo*;

2. the COMMUNICATION of the active group's attitude to the reactive

    – on an axis between a positive extreme (*benevolence*) and a negative (*malevolence*): midway between them the demonstration that the attitude was conditional on specified criteria;

3. an INTERACTION of some kind with the reactive group or their property

    – on an axis between positive intervention (*beneficence* – for example in benedictions conceived of as effective) and negative (*maleficence* – effective maledictions, i.e. curses, or outright physical violence). In between lay a spectrum from engagement in convivial pastimes and other social interaction to increasing degrees of mischief and vandalism.

In most engagement customs motivations were mixed, but these axes establish a three-dimensional zone within which a given custom can be located, reflecting both the admixture of motives, and the positive/negative degree of each. Furthermore, envisaging motivation

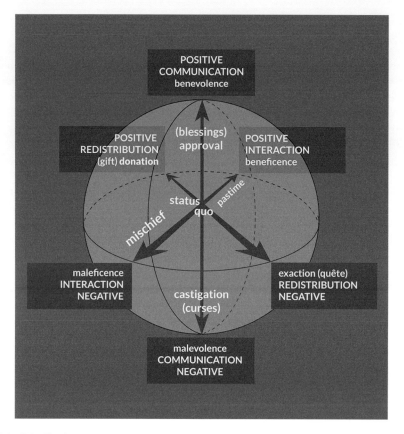

Figure 1.1 Distribution, communication, interaction
Source: Diagram copyright the author, version design Paul Loudon.

in this way enables detection and formulation of changes in a given custom over time. They may also prove useful in exploring the re-deployment of customs in general, and engagement customs in particular, in social unrest and rebellion (Figure 1.1).[21]

The customary stages (material contexts)

More directly related to the performances themselves are the material contexts in which they were carried out – whatever it is in customary drama that corresponds to the stages of conventional theatres – and while inevitably less elaborate, the spatial arrangements by which performance and spectators are brought together are decidedly more varied.

Assemblies

Closest to conventional theatre is the context in which participants, typically of a single group, often extended by guests and dependents, assemble under customary auspices for a range of traditional activities. The norm for a household, depending on period and status, would be an indoor location – hall, chamber, parlour, kitchen and perhaps by extension an enclosed garden or courtyard. More formal and wealthy associations might similarly assemble at a guildhall, others at a tavern or the residence of their current leader. Communities might also have access to an indoor venue in the form of a meeting house or a church nave, but would just as likely convene in an outdoor setting like a designated playfield, a churchyard, town square or market place.

The performance space in such venues, indoors and out, would normally be a flat area on the same level as spectators (to the extent they were distinguished from performers), who would stand or sit at its periphery in a complete or partial circle. For particularly elaborate outdoor performances, a temporary raised structure (as in the 'theatre' of public punishments, a 'scaffold') might have been erected to secure both a definitive performance space and better sightlines. In the case of fully dramatic performances, this would correspond to the booth stages in those early modern Flemish paintings depicting a community festival (*kermesse*) on which a performance is under way alongside other customary activities.[22] In England, a flat wagon might have been more common, but either way we are here approaching the uncertain boundary between customary drama and an autonomous dramatic work performed in a customary festive context, but which might equally be performed under quite other auspices. The indoor equivalent, including the development of a raised stage, is the (Tudor) 'interlude' which emerged within, but eventually broke free from, the winter (and wedding) revels in the great halls of late medieval and early modern noble and institutional households.[23]

Encounters

Customary performances could also take place in the material context of a spatial *encounter* between performers and spectators who were not already assembled for the purpose.[24] This generally meant that they belonged to (or represented) different social groups, so that a custom performed in the context of an encounter was also, under socio-cultural auspices, an inter-group engagement, with whatever that implied (as discussed above) for its purpose and function. Under these circumstances, a necessary prerequisite for an encounter between two groups would be their relative movement, but there seem to be no significant instances of both groups moving simultaneously and converging – which would require coordination. It was therefore necessary for one of the groups concerned, the performers or the spectators, to approach and penetrate the space occupied by the other. Classification is complicated by the circumstance that the *active* group in the (socio-cultural) *engagement* is not necessarily the *mobile* group in the (contextual) *encounter*.

By far the most frequent permutation, certainly in 'folk' tradition, is the *house-visit*, in which the performing group approach a residence (typically of a domestic or institutional household), establish contact either at the threshold or inside, go through their performance and depart. In material terms, while it is under way, the performance space will resemble that of a group assembly, in this case household revels, but no arrangements will have been made at the venue, where the residents are going about whatever is their normal business at the time of year and time of day concerned. So in addition to whatever fuss was needed to get into the building, a performance space would have to be cleared of people, pets and furniture, a process which is effectively part of the performance itself. Similar business (depending on purpose) will conclude the encounter and attend their exit.

The content of the house-visit performance (discussed further below) will vary, naturally enough, in relation to the purpose of the visitors, but so will the wider structure of the custom. Communicative engagements castigating the behaviour of a particular family will visit only that one house, while interactive mischief-visits will more likely go from house to house down the street in pursuit of opportunities. Redistributive customs in pursuit of largesse in return for a performance can choose between two basic strategies: offering a short, simple performance at a large number of houses, content with modest returns at each, selecting a few 'great houses' in the vicinity in anticipation of greater generosity and accordingly offering a more elaborate performance at each. The latter procedure can also encompass a particular house-visit which has been timed (by prior agreement or tradition) to coincide with an ongoing customary revel at the household concerned (typically at Christmas or harvest-time or in connection with a wedding). In such cases, the performance of the visitors will supplement whatever is ongoing by way of dramatic pastime and entertainment generated from within the group. Such encounters will probably have been conducive to the exchange of dramatic material between household and visit customs.

There is also an encounter type, the *reception*, which is the reverse of the house-visit, with the mobile but now reactive group (who will become the audience) approaching a residence with non-customary intent (like coming for a visit) and on arrival and entry being received with a customary performance by the active but stationary group within (typically members of the household resident there). Other than the perfunctory formalities welcoming dinner guests at the front door, this form is represented in England almost exclusively by the elaborate and sophisticated multimedia Welcomes staged by early modern nobility on the arrival of the Tudor or Stuart monarch who was to be their guest for a number of days in the course of a royal progress into the provinces. Considerable elaboration and sophistication were enabled not merely by the wealth of the hosts and their access to professional producers and performers, but by the fact that in this configuration the timing of the visit was known in advance to the stationary group and the performance space was under their control in the interim. The concentric landscape of the aristocratic residence, with greater and lesser parks, outer and inner courtyards, also made for greater complexity.[25]

The permutations of active and mobile groups represented by visits and receptions (Welcomes) are repeated in contexts where the encounter is staged in the open rather than as one group approaches and enters a building. In the case of an active stationary group, this involves what can be designated the *interception* of a mobile group as it progresses through the landscape, typically the streets of a town, with a view merely to getting from one place to another. Here too significance is largely historical. By the late nineteenth century, the interception was confined to very minor, marginally dramatic, forms in which a stationary group of children, at a location on a thoroughfare, displayed an exhibition of some kind – girls (in late summer) a 'grotto'; boys (up to 5 November) a 'guy' – in hopes of attracting largesse from passers-by.[26] England seems largely to have been spared the quite widespread European custom in which the progress of a wedding procession was blocked by a chain or rope (*Wegsperre*; *barrière*) which could be passed only on the payment of a toll (however, much of this was cloaked as remuneration for proffered refreshment).[27]

However, this form of customary encounter was massively significant in the late medieval and Renaissance civic pageantry which intercepted and engaged with an important figure processing through the community's streets: a monarch on their way from the Tower of London to their coronation at Westminster, or subsequently visiting a major city for the first time; a foreign potentate or royal spouse arriving from a channel port; a newly elected mayor making his way between important venues for his inauguration; assize judges arriving for sessions at a county town. Whatever spectacle was achieved by the train of the mobile group, even when classified as a 'Triumph', it was overshadowed by the stationary 'pageants' (with visual, verbal, musical, dramatic elements) by which they were intercepted along their path.[28]

But conversely, many groups undertook a deliberate passage through a landscape (urban or rural), with a view to an encounter (and generally engagement) with those it passed on the way.[29] The term *parade* may be deployed to reflect this aspect of deliberate, encounter-seeking movement, going beyond the more inward (or upward) focus of mere processions. It applies equally to the most demonstrative 'marching watch' of the greater cities and the most humble of 'hock cart' parades on their way through the village with the last load of corn. And in addition to any symbolism manifested on the way, the route of the parade itself could be a form of demonstration or communication, for example, in following or traversing a boundary, or stating a relationship between the points of departure and arrival.[30]

Uniquely among the 'stages' surveyed, that of the parade is mobile *during* the encounter, with all that implies for the manner of the performance it encompasses, which audiences could see and hear only as it approached and passed by. There were however customary variants, which we might distinguish as 'perambulations', in which the parade stopped at (precisely) 'stations', for performances whose dramaturgy could be closer to that of stationary arrangements. In medieval English drama (most of which was 'customary' in several respects), the pattern is seen in the performance of some local mystery cycles, which brought their stages with them as pageant wagons, but is also recognizable in other traditions. Other mobile groups might simply pause for a performance in encountering a suitably large group of people.

There were also conglomerate forms in which a group assembled for customary activities at separate venues (say one for sporting contests and one for subsequent feasting), and paraded from the one to the other in a spectacular manner that would have attracted the attention of the community at large whose territory they traversed. The parade of the harvest hock cart just mentioned similarly linked the ceremonies associated with the cutting of the last sheaf in the last field ('crying the neck') and the ensuing 'harvest home' at which customary performances (as we shall see) would also figure.[31]

Customary plays (performances)

Predictably, not every segment in this multidimensional matrix of incidence, socio-cultural auspices and material contexts will have hosted performances throughout the history of customary activities encompassed by this survey. Nonetheless, examining all those forms which do qualify for attention is out of the question under the present constraints. What follows will therefore comprise glances at three clusters of customary dramatic performance, representing various orientations in relation to the auspices and contexts (theatres and stages) surveyed above:

1. Castigation customs
    - occasional, malevolent encounters, staged in a variety of material contexts, with a limited variety of forms and materials;
2. Dramatic pastimes and entertainments
    - free-standing performances characteristic of both seasonal and biographical group assemblies, in a wide variety of forms and materials;
3. House-visit shows
    - semi-dramatic and dramatic materials embedded within a wider performance in the context of a specific form of inter-group encounter with a generally calendrical incidence.

Castigating malfeasance (folk law)

Castigation customs are a striking reminder that folk performance can be a serious, not to say nasty, business, rather than picturesque intangible heritage. The category has an unusually straightforward demarcation, although obscured by inconsistent terminology and criteria. Thus, the Italian *mattinata* specifies the time of day of performances (actually nocturnal); the French *charivari*, whatever it originally meant, refers to the castigation of a particular kind of malfeasance (second marriages); the common English terms invoke aspects of performance: 'riding' the material context, 'skimmington', one of the symbolic objects displayed in the demonstration, and 'rough music', an aural feature.

My 'castigation custom', translating the useful German *Rügebrauch*,[32] specifies a category of folk performance defined strictly in terms of its socio-cultural auspices: an engagement in which the active group communicates malevolence towards the reactive. Incidence is accordingly occasional, triggered by sporadic events or circumstances, but there is wide variation under other headings: material context (parade, interception, house-visit, assembly), form and content (including varying degrees of the dramatic).[33]

In a given society during a particular period, castigation customs amount to a *folk law*, reprehending behaviour unacceptable in terms of traditional mores and standards, but not subject to sanction by official judicial systems.[34] From one perspective, therefore, further categorization can meaningfully be based on the *offences* triggering the castigation, which in a pan-European perspective can be catalogued as follows:

— sexual irregularity

    between unmarried people ('fornication')
    between males (sodomy)

— nuptial irregularity

    discrepancy between bride and groom in:
        age; status; wealth;
        community (marrying an 'outsider')

    the bride's virginity disputed
    a second marriage for one of the parties

— conjugal irregularity

    wife dominant (shrew or scold)
    wife neglects husband ('gadding'; 'tippling')
    adultery
        by husband;
        by wife (making husband a cuckold)
    husband violent (wife-beater)
    cohabitation (couple are not legally married).

The range of offences triggering customary castigation will vary between regions, perhaps even communities. A striking example is the general absence of customary castigation of nuptial irregularity in a broad swathe of northern Europe encompassing England,

Scandinavia and northern Germany, in contrast to its prevalence elsewhere, notably France (*charivari*) and Italy (*mattinata*). And in any one area, what triggers customary castigation can vary over time. For example by the late nineteenth century, parts of England (notably Cornwall and East Anglia) had belatedly acquired nuptial castigations corresponding to the *charivari* (although more directed at discrepancies in age than at second marriages), while concurrently the focus on conjugal irregularity shifted from the domineering wife to the wife-beating husband.

Castigation customs were also directed at perceived malfeasance in the social and economic spheres, such as price-increases, strike-breaking and the abrogation of traditional rights.[35] It is an open question however whether they are autonomous customs, or opportunistic transfers to these spheres of forms of customary castigation already traditional in matters of interpersonal relationships.[36]

The reactive group (aka culprits, soon to become victims) is typically a household within a community, while the active group at least claims to be representing the community at large or perhaps one of its sub-communities (typically a youth-group). In communicating communal malevolence, castigation customs basically involved an engagement between the culpable individuals or household and the community, but under the circumstances, performance was also designed to advertise both the infringement and its castigation to the community at large. *Performances* tend accordingly to occur in outdoor, public spaces.

This is also true of the *house-visit* castigation, in that with a view to public visibility (not to mention the resistance of the reactive group), the 'visit' would likely penetrate no further than the threshold, subsequent performance being in the street or yard in front of the house. And while in other house-(to-house)-visit customs, the performers would likely walk purposefully to the venue, drawing attention to themselves (to alert those inside) only on their immediate approach, the movement of participants in a castigatory house-visit custom would as a matter of course attract attention by means of spectacle and noise (rough music), simultaneously qualifying as a parade and functioning as a means of drawing a crowd to witness the subsequent encounter.

In England, the house-visit form is best represented by those latter-day 'nuptial' forms castigating 'irregular' marriages in connection with the wedding day. In East Anglia, this was designated in terms of a significant feature, the 'rough band' or, specifying a major source of the noise, 'tin kettling', 'tinning' or 'tin panning', and was typically provoked by a discrepancy in the ages of bride and groom.[37] Of one such Suffolk instance, from around 1900, a participant reported that when the wedding feast of an old man and a young girl was well under way, 'us lads', with a view to some impressive rough music, collected metal objects from a nearby blacksmith's, and 'started off round the village hitting blazes out of these tins and things…. The whole village was out in no time to see what was up'. They halted outside the house concerned 'and hit those owd things so you could hear the din for miles'.[38] It may be a local twist that they had beforehand secretly barred the door of the house so those inside could not get out to confront them, but this may also be symptomatic of a more general trend for customary castigations to resemble inversions of engagement customs at the opposite extreme of the spectrum: so while in benevolent house-visits the active group seek acceptance of their entry, here they prevent the exit of the (doubtless enraged) reactive group.

That the demonstrative engagements prompted by irregular nuptials did not exclusively take the form of a customary house-visit on the model of the *charivari* is illustrated by a 1923 instance from Cornwall, where that form was indeed known, but in this case, the 'kiddly band' has a different performance context – a *parade*. On the night of the wedding day of

'Ernie' and 'Eliza' (20 years his senior), a group of locals assembled in a nearby cow-house and broached a barrel of beer, then two fellows impersonated Eliza and Ernie, marching up and down the village to the accompaniment of mouth-organs, comb-and-tissue paper, beating drum, tin-pan, the rattle of bones. Singing went on all through the night, till three or four the next morning.[39]

Here too there may be a hint of inversion, the parade (in the adverse sense) a 'mock' wedding procession; the drinking a wedding feast for those uninvited to the real one.[40] Otherwise, this seems rather like an opportunistic transfer to nuptial auspices of a form of customary castigation more normally directed at marital dysfunction, typically a parade of figures representing the culprits/victims accompanied by rough music and other features.

In relatively recent tradition in northern England, the latter has taken the form of 'stang riding', in which a man is perambulated on a couple of poles borne aloft by others, accompanied by rough music, halting at a number of stations for the rider to explain that he is merely a surrogate for the real offenders, whose identities and faults are proclaimed in doggerel verse.[41] Something very similar, however, was common further south in the early modern period. For example at Wetherden, Suffolk, in 1604, a man rode the stang dressed in women's clothes after his neighbour, returning drunk from the alehouse, had been beaten out and reviled as 'dronken dogg dronken pisspott' by his wife. As elsewhere the parade was accompanied by rough music, and the stang-rider enlivened the occasion by beating spectators and declaiming a warning to wives not to beat their husbands.[42]

Another, perhaps more common, and certainly more spectacular early modern variant involved the parading on horseback of two figures (both men) representing the culprits, the wife in front facing forwards, but turning to belabour the husband sitting behind her and, humiliatingly, facing the rear. To this end, she deploys the large ladle or 'skimmington' which gave this castigatory 'ride' its name, the meanwhile spinning thread on a spindle, a quintessential female occupation.[43] Among much documentation, the most illuminating on performance is the description in the second part of Samuel Butler's mock epic, *Hudibras*, printed in 1664, and William Hogarth's illustration of this passage in an edition from 1726. The central figures are accompanied by others riding and on foot, variously producing a raucous noise (shouting, bagpipes, banging metal vessels) and displaying symbols of female dominance (skirt and shift held aloft) and male subservience (sword reversed), plus horns both blown and (suggesting cuckoldry) displayed. It too might be seen as a grotesque, mocking parody of the offending couple's wedding parade.[44]

Customary castigation could also take the stationary form of an *assembly* in an open venue, where the core active group might stage a performance for the benefit of the community as a whole, in the physical absence, presumably, of the offending party (a rare engagement that was not also an encounter). The form is best documented on the continent,[45] but an extraordinary, presumably not unique, instance was prompted by rumours circulating in the village of Westonbirt, Gloucestershire, in 1736, alleging that George Andrews, the bailiff to an important local landlord, had sodomized a young stranger, Walter Lingsey.[46] The failure of the authorities to intervene prompted some local men to organize what amounted to an ad hoc community festival, deploying the arrangements commonly used for the Whitsun or 'church ales', that is collecting money locally to supply drink and food (in so doing also advertising the event) and to employ a couple of musicians. This too may be an instance of castigation customs perverting celebratory ones.

Performers and audience assembled under a tree close to the church (very likely the customary site for community festivals), and after some feasting and drinking the 'mock groaning' got under way, with Lingsey (motivation uncertain) performing himself. Rather (luckily) than mimicking the 'crime', it offered a grotesque scenario of its imaginary consequences, with Lingsey dressed as a woman, going into labour (hence the title), and giving birth to a straw doll dressed in baby clothes, attended by a midwife (another man dressed as a woman). After further refreshment the entire company repaired to the churchyard, where the 'child' was christened (after its putative father) 'George Buggerer' by a man dressed as a priest (a white apron around his shoulders), and the godfathers were admonished to bring it up to be worthy of its name.

The range of performance contexts surveyed here is usefully summarized by a well-documented 'Hussitting' from Berkshire in 1930, prompted by the failure of the authorities to protect a battered wife from her violent husband.[47] Sustained over several days, it comprised parades through the town of effigies of the husband, his mother and his sister (evidently considered accessories), accompanied by rough music, and at a number of stations the procession halted for the effigies to be whipped. The parade was also punctuated by house-visits as it turned off for a display of the effigies and a burst of rough music at the homes of the three offenders. But the culminating event was the burning of the three effigies on a bonfire, around which the performers danced, and sang insulting ditties about the persons condemned.

Dramatic pastimes and entertainments

Among the many activities associated with the group celebration of seasonal festivals (in post-medieval times typically winter revels and harvest homes) were performances qualifying as 'customary' by virtue of this context, but which were not necessarily restricted to one particular festival.[48] They can be roughly divided into *pastimes*, in which all might participate, given opportunity and inclination, the focus as much upon their mutual enjoyment as on pleasing onlookers, and more outwardly oriented *entertainments*, in which pre-selected and probably rehearsed performers provided a show for others. In their relatively short, simple character, these performances – which could include a range of physical, musical, visual and verbal features – lend themselves to analysis in terms of their varying levels of dramatic sophistication, from activities scarcely differing from the regular games or contests also indulged in under such auspices, to complex forms at the boundary between customary drama and drama in a customary context.

The common, evocative term for recreations at early modern revels was 'gambol', but perhaps most often used for pastimes based on *physical interaction*, including contests of skill and strength. In some, however, there was a modicum of impersonation, even amidst wordless (if not noiseless) fits of rough and tumble between two opposing sides. The latter vary in the permutation of individuals and groups in the confrontation. For example, in what might be termed the 'mobbing' category (most familiar in recent times in the typically cruel party game, 'blind man's buff'), *a group initiates aggression towards an individual*, as in the 'shoeing' or 'riding' of a 'horse' represented by a designated individual. The many references to this among early modern evocations of Christmas revels tend to take the evidently familiar actions for granted, but they can be easily imagined. Variant designations referring to the horse as the 'Mare' and as 'Wild' suggest the selection of a female reveller for subjection, doubtless strenuously resisted, to more or less good natured harassment, shaped to a certain degree in imitation of shoeing and riding (the former implicitly, the latter perhaps implicitly, suggesting a sexual aspect).[49] And this is all there by way of impersonation, with no indication of other dramatic features such as costume or properties.

Such features are present however in instances of the reverse configuration where a *single figure initiates aggressive behaviour towards a group*, typically impersonating a beast of some kind.

The 'speckled stallion' and 'white mare' of Irish wake games are matched in England by the 'crane' reported by John Clare in 1821 from the Soke of Peterborough (a man in a sheet with two jointed sticks as neck and beak), and the 'Old Sow' of Lincolnshire (one or two men under sacking, with a prickly furze-filled sack as a head), both associated with harvest suppers.[50] They are still wordless (protests of the victims aside) and action is improvised within the conceptual framework of the unruly beast.

This is also the case with an example of a gambol with a *one-on-one confrontation* which has an unusually deep historical documentation, 'Skewer' (or 'Shiver') the Goose. It is a mock joust in which the contestants are trussed into a crouching position and grasp a pointed stick emerging between their knees, ostensibly to resemble geese, although the action rather impersonates a cock-fight. In this condition, they hop around lunging and shoving at each other until one is toppled and, unable to rise, is vulnerable to the jabs of his opponent's 'beak'. In the earliest record, where it is performed as a comic feature of the lower-class subplot in the Tudor Interlude, *Fulgens and Lucres* (ca 1495), it is named 'fart-prick-in-cul [arse]' suggesting the beak is mainly aimed at the recumbent opponent's posterior (with farting as the latter's only defence?).[51] A century or so later, it is described in considerable detail as a 'jest or gambol' performed among the pastimes of the servants at the Christmas revels of a transplanted English gentry household in County Down, Ireland, around 1600,[52] and it survived into the nineteenth century as what Lady Alice Bertha Gomme is careful to specify as a 'boy's game'.[53] She does not give a particular context, but (again in an Anglo-Irish context) it was reported as traditional in the nineteenth century not merely at Christmas revels, but at harvest homes and at Hallowe'en.[54] For England, the distinguished folklorist E.C. Cawte (1932–2019) recalled it as a traditional pastime among the pupils when he was attending Salisbury Cathedral School.[55]

Thus far, the semi-dramatic confrontations are unmotivated, except to the extent that beasts are assumed to be naturally aggressive, or subject to various kinds of handling. A predictable elaboration is displayed in forms, now verging on entertainments, where a similar stand-off is *motivated by anterior interaction* between performers who are accordingly closer to dramatic characters (and human as well as beasts). The interaction can nonetheless be largely wordless, or (like the action) improvised.

In an example from Northamptonshire harvest feasts, the violent confrontation is a staff-fight between two male contestants of a kind which would at one time have been among the regular sporting gambols of such revels in its own right. But now the contestants are protected by straw-stuffed blankets, and their fight is the culmination of a routine ('Scotch Peddlars') in which, in the course of droll verbal and physical interaction supposedly at an alehouse, one of them drinks surreptitiously from the other's glass and then drunkenly refuses to pay his full share of the bill.[56]

A further elaboration is illustrated in 'The Dusty Miller', where a hunch-backed, flour-faced Miller (carrying a basket and a broom) and his wife (probably a man in skirts) enter together with their servant ('a kind of Tom fool'). The Miller sits down to eat the food from the basket but it is surreptitiously taken by the wife who sits behind him. After a nonsensical harangue, the Miller beats the servant with the broom, thinking him responsible, but accidentally slays his wife. But this time, there is a sequel in which, after due lamentation, he seeks to revive her, deploying, in turn, the smelling salts and bellows opportunely carried by the servant. The former is doubtlessly applied to her nose; how the latter is deployed Clare leaves us to speculate.[57]

Meanwhile, this revival or 'cure' action can constitute a performance in its own right with only perfunctory motivation. We are again at a harvest home, this time in nineteenth-century

Suffolk, where a male performer costumed as a woman complains of the toothache, prompting the arrival of a doctor (mounted on the back of another, representing a horse by bending forward and supporting his arms on a stool). The ensuing tooth extraction – using tongs which produce an impressive 'tooth' (impersonated by a length of clay pipe) from the mouth of the patient – induces a fainting fit which is also 'cured' by the application of bellows.[58] The introduction of the Doctor figure to accomplish the revival would constitute a further elaboration in the direction of the dramatic if added to a confrontation and slaying sequence like those above, but thus far this conjunction has been encountered only in a couple of quite elaborate Irish wake games.[59]

These latter instances presumably involve some dialogue, but it was dominated by the action, and quite likely improvised. The balance is the reverse in semi-dramatic routines where the confrontation between two characters is in the more amicable form of a *wooing*. Action is largely restricted to a concluding embrace or kiss, with more attention on the antecedent verbal interaction which is accordingly more likely to have scripted dialogue, often in the form of verse, which can be sung. A complex cluster of English folksongs comprising wooing dialogues would make for suitable material, and indeed there are widespread indications, internal and external, that they were rendered in somewhat dramatic fashion.[60]

A good example is the song variously known as the 'Keys of Canterbury (or Heaven or My Heart)' (Roud #573), in which the wooer's various materialistic offers to win the girl's heart are resolutely rejected until he promises the 'keys' specified in the title. Doyen of the folksong collectors, Cecil J. Sharp, remarked:

> I have taken down this ballad many times in Somerset, and in many forms. From what old singers have told me, I gather that the ballad was generally sung by a man and a woman, with much dramatic action.[61]

This would naturally involve distribution of the dialogue stanzas among two – male and female – singers, but as with the violent confrontations, the basic wooing situation can be elaborated – approximating more closely to the mimetic – by a dramatic 'packaging' introducing extra characters and/or motivations. Of this, a relatively straightforward instance is provided by versions of 'The Keys of Canterbury' just discussed, in which the wooer is encouraged by his manservant, the latter and the song both generally known as 'My man Jack'. He does not interfere in the wooing directly, but offers encouragement 'aside' to his master at the beginning or (once or repeatedly) along the way; there can also be a concluding stanza in which the latter expresses his appreciation.

Novelist Thomas Hardy could recall it being performed in his childhood home (a village near Dorchester) around 1844. All the dialogue was sung, and the performers, accompanied by a fiddler, danced part of a 'three-handed reel' after each offer-refusal-encouragement unit, and the whole dance at the end.[62] Hardy does not specify the exact auspices, and this rendition is closer to the children's game forms, but a more conventionally dramatic performance (with some costuming) figured at harvest homes in the nineteenth century, under the title 'Jack an' his maister', as indicated by a Yorkshire source (spelling of the prose here regularized):

Two men used to sing that, one with another. The master began first with

> O Jack, me lad, how can the matter be,
> 'At Ah sud luv a leedy, an' sheea sud not luv me?
> Ner nowder will sheea walk wi' 'mah oonyweer.

Then Jack sang:

> O maister dear! Ah'd hev yah nut to fear,
> 'At sheea will be yer darlin', yer only joy an' dear,
> An' sheea will walk wi' yah onnyweer.

And then the fine lady come in…. She had a fine white muslin gown on, all trimmed round with rows of bright red cat-jugs [rose hips]. And the master sang to her, and she sang back again, and it ended with her taking his arm, and they went off together.[63]

Less constructively, elaboration could take the form of interference by the girl's parents, as in another example from the same Yorkshire source on harvest ('mell') suppers (dramatic enough to deploy a stage property) which opens with a sung dialogue (reported in local dialect) between mother and daughter as the latter sits at her spinning wheel:

> Mudher, Ah'll hev a man,
> If there be yan to be had;
> For there is Andra Carr,
> A boxin', cumly lad.
>
> He sez he likes mah weel,
> An' what can Ah say mair?
> Mudher, if you think fit
> The priest can mak us a pair.
>
> Get out, thou muckle gooad, --
> An' a bonny pair ye'll be!
> How diz tha think he can
> Maintain hiz sel' an' thee?

The mother remains adamant that she marries a man of means, so when subsequently the hapless Andra comes a wooing, it provokes a confrontation which ends with the mother 'braying him out'.[64] Glossed as 'beating or thrashing', this suggests that we are actually dealing with a hybrid in which the wooing functions as the prelude to a violent confrontation.[65]

Another elaboration was the conglomeration of wooing with the hiring of a servant – which itself could be encountered as an independent form.[66] In 'Magherafelt Hiring Fair' collected in Ulster, the prospective employer is a lady and the discussion of terms of employment for her prospective servant an implicit wooing:

> 'Would you hire with me, Tam Bo, Tam Bo?
> Would you hire with me, my heart and my Jo?
> Would you with me? say you and say I,
> And what an'a rantin young widow am I.'
>   (spoken) 'What wages, mistress?'
>
> 'Two pounds five…'
> 'Too little wages, mistress.'
>
> 'Then two pounds ten…'

And so on: his food will be 'potatoes and beef' rather than the 'Sowans [oat-meal puddings] and eels…' first offered, and when for various reasons he refuses to sleep in the loft or with the children, she concedes, 'Well, then we'll get married…'.[67]

A similar combination of motifs, but with the roles reversed between the sexes, occurs in a lengthy harvest-supper entertainment performed in Yorkshire in the early nineteenth century.[68] Here too the scene is set at a hiring fair, and the entertainment opens with 'Polly' fearing that despite her qualifications she will find no one to engage her. There follows a series of sung dialogues in which she is approached, in turn, by three prospective employers: an Old Man and an Old Woman are rejected in single-speech exchanges, but the last, the Squire, is accepted after a lengthier dialogue which develops into an outright wooing, Polly finally acceding to the Squire's offer of marriage. Now an acknowledged entertainment for an audience, it concludes with an explicit epilogue: 'We have no more to sing, now, / We've told you all and done our best'.

One of the most elaborate of the free-standing entertainments recorded also provides an instance of the dramatization of an existing traditional narrative.[69] In the plot of the latter, the 'Golden Ball',[70] two sisters are given golden balls by a mysterious stranger and warned that losing them means death; predictably, the youngest does so, and is taken away to be hanged. This is delayed by the arrival of a series of her relatives and her asking each of them, in turn, if they have brought her ball, which would save her. All respond negatively until it is the turn of her sweetheart, who has indeed done so.[71]

In the version of the tale first published, the editor has inserted a long narrative segment from a different source on exactly how the ball was lost and the adventures of the sweetheart in recovering it (effectively another tale), and this is the form subsequently popularized.[72] The informant who had performed in the dramatic rendition as an 11-year-old girl in South-port, Lancashire, could not remember any of this material, suggesting the interlude may have been based on an independent version. Indeed, the implication of an 'old Mrs. Thompson' supplying the account 'a few years' prior to 1915 may be that the performance antedated or was independent of the publication of the adapted text in 1866.

In Mrs Thompson's recollection, after the girl admitted losing the ball, there was a trial scene, with a judge and jury, then one at the gallows, with the questions and answers (in verse and presumably in song), and when the sweetheart has saved her, in action not specified in the tale (but as if in a successful wooing interlude), '… he prizents 'er with the ball an' hugs 'er and takes 'er away'. There is little detail on staging, other than that performance was both in a local school-room (by adults) and in a cart-house (by children).[73] The ball was a stage property, and whether or not there was a stage, the gallows was an evidently impressive piece of scenery, and the heroine's performance evidently sought, or was considered, to emulate the theatrical – at least in its contemporary melodramatic mode:

> She looks for all the world like the girl in 'The Sign of the Cross', with a bit of a thing round 'er shoulders, to be old-fashioned, and she clasps 'er 'ands and looksup so pitiful, first at the gallus and then at 'er family
>
> —*who look back 'scornful and bitter'.*[74]

House-visit customs

Customary house-visits at the malevolent extreme of the *demonstrative* axis were illustrated above under castigation customs; they are matched at the benevolent extreme by wassailing (where the visitors offer toasts to the good health of the hosts), which has however no significant dramatic features.[75] Towards the positive end of the *interactive* axis, we find a relatively modest house-visit custom, the *mumming*, which has nonetheless played a significant role in folk drama studies.[76] Comprehensively documented in England under this designation from the late medieval period onwards, the mumming was consistently described as a custom in which the visitors intrude into household living-space to engage in a social interaction that, outside these customary auspices (in England typically at Christmas), would be unacceptable from anyone other than a member of the household or an invited guest. This included participation in pastimes, in the early recorded forms notably gaming with dice. Definitive was also the concealment of identity, the minimal disguise of a mask or blackened face often elaborated into a guise impersonating a quite different identity, cross-dressing a characteristic feature.[77]

In larger communities, this anonymity could be and evidently was misused to nefarious purposes (in some instances perhaps modulating into the mischief-visits towards the negative end of the interactive axis),[78] hence the frequent national and local prohibitions. In smaller communities whose members were known to each other, mumming encompassed the extra dimension of wondering who the visitors were, and indeed in some traditions, as recently in Newfoundland, seeking to identify the visitors, even intrusively, became an essential feature of the interaction. Disguise also extended to the vocal dimension, the visitors generally, as the name might suggest, remaining 'mum' throughout.[79]

Such mumming should be distinguished from the cluster of significant house-visit customs whose definitive features are an explicit quest for largesse as reward for an extended entertainment, which includes a dramatic segment qualifying as a 'play' by most criteria, now known as 'mummers' plays'. Following the demise of the ritual origins theory, it has gradually been appreciated by folklorists that the latter emerged, perhaps as late as the eighteenth century, through the intrusion of fully dramatic material into previously non-dramatic or merely sub-dramatic customs.[80]

Given the shared seasonal house-visit context and the overlap in terminology, it is legitimate to anticipate that the host custom concerned was the convivial mumming.[81] But with regard to both purpose and performance realities, the transition would amount to a massive discontinuity – the performers of mummers' plays, in addition to seeking largesse rather than convivial interaction, are rarely disguised and never silent, and the designation 'mummers' play' may indeed owe more to the scholars who studied them than the folk who performed them. Meanwhile in two major regional traditions, the hosts for the inserted dramatic material are demonstrably two quite different (already exactive) house-visit customs, whose performers go by other designations than mummers – the 'trailing' of a decorated plough by ploughboys or plough 'jacks', and the perambulation of sword dancers. Both customs can be traced back to the late medieval period, and furthermore also persisted into the nineteenth century in forms lacking the inserted dramatic interlude.[82]

It may not be a coincidence that their dramatic elaboration occurred subsequent to these two customs ceasing to be 'gatherings' under parish or guild auspices to raise funds for social or devotional purposes, and modulating into something closer to 'cadging' (Peter Harrop's term) for the immediate benefit of the participants (be it spent individually, or collectively on a 'finishing up feast' for the group and its associates).[83] If the same model were to be valid for the most widely distributed, 'Hero Combat' variety of 'mummers' play', the host for the dramatic material would be some other Christmastide gathering under official auspices which went through the same evolution in function and form. There are, for instance, many early modern and some later references to exactive Christmas house-visits by a 'hobby-horse' and his attendants,[84] and the proverbial lament, 'the hobby horse is forgot', may refer not so much to the custom, as to this figure within it, or its subordination in common perception to other features, such as the display by (morris) dancers (or an increasingly dramatic aspect).

But whenever and however they developed, as we have them (in the nineteenth century), the mummers' plays are simply the most elaborate and most dramatic of house-visit customs qualifying as *quêtes* by virtue of their pursuit of largesse, be it in monetary or other forms. Surveying this category as a whole, the show offered by such visitors can range from a simple *quête*-song invoking the largesse associated with a given festive season to that exhibition of a decorated plough, and in between, carol singing; the display of a dead wren tied to a decorated branch, a wax model of Christ wreathed in evergreens, a garland or a beribboned child as 'Valentine'; Molly, Morris, Sword and Horn dances, fools, beasts and men-dressed as women, hobby-horses with diverse supernumeraries – often in various combinations. 'Mummers' plays' are distinguished by encompassing a dramatic interlude alongside a variety of these other features shared with other house-visit *quêtes*,[85] but they are far from the only forms with dramatic features.

Of house-visit customs in which impersonation is a central aspect, the simplest are those in which the visitors consist of a *beast-figure* along with attendants who engage with it, verbally and/or physically, in accordance with the beast's assumed characteristics. Least complex perhaps is the 'Straw Bear' figure, a man completely swathed in straw, who undertook a money-collecting post-Christmas perambulation from house to house in Whittlesey, Cambridgeshire. Nineteenth-century accounts indicate that he or it was led on a string by an attendant, and was made to dance, in imitation of the period's itinerant dancing bears, and equally in expectation of reward. The performance could be either at the doors of houses or, given a large enough kitchen, inside, where the beast is described as becoming unruly ('capering about').[86]

This form is reproduced, but with a horse figure, 'Old Ball' (sometimes 'Baal'), at Eastertide in urban contexts in Lancashire. This beast also differs in terms of construction, being what I would call a 'staff' beast achieved by a man, covered in sacking or the like, bending forward and supporting himself on the staff, to whose top is affixed a horse's skull, enhanced with bottle tops for eyes. With several black-faced attendants, this figure went around aggressively coercing largesse from the households it visited.[87]

Somewhat more complex is the 'Hooden Horse' custom of Kent, a Christmas Eve good-luck visit and *quête* performed by farm labourers on a perambulation to local farmhouses.[88] Performance was in the yard, or in the hall of the larger houses, and the company attending on the beast figure was more variegated, including a Waggoner in a frock coat and top hat, cracking his whip, leading the Horse by a bridle, a Rider (sometimes dressed as a soldier), while a Mollie, a man dressed as a woman, enhanced the impersonation by demonstratively sweeping the ground behind the horse with a broom. There would also be two to three musicians (concertina, tambourine…). The central figure was also staff-beast, the head here made of wood, and with the usual hinged jaw that could be aggressively snapped. As this 'cast' might suggest the performance went on for some time, although there is little consequence: rider and spectators attempted to mount the horse; the horse reared, pranced and snapped its jaws; the Waggoner tried to control it, crying 'whoa!' while Mollie (motivation unspecified) stood on her head. There was no set dialogue, but a brief *quête*-song:

> Three jolly hoodening boys
> Lately come from town,
> Apples or for money
>   We search the country round

which continues with further lines similar to those used in orchard-wassailing (marginally qualifying the visit as benevolent).

Much of this also applies to the Christmas-New Year 'Old Horse' with a distribution in contiguous areas of Nottinghamshire, Derbyshire and Yorkshire in the area around

Sheffield.[89] Attendants can here include a Blacksmith, who at one point attempts to shoe the horse, but dramaturgically more distinctive is the singing of a traditional song, itself of much wider distribution, 'The Poor Old Horse' (Roud 513). This is a lugubrious piece which describes the horse in its prime, its decline and death, and the burial or dismemberment of its corpse, and while it is sung the Horse displays itself before sinking to the ground. It is noticeable even in these simple forms, how the performance context intrudes on the performance content (in contrast to the beast figures touched on earlier which were already 'at home' in a festive context). In the Hooden Horse custom, it was largely restricted to the request for largesse, but here the performance also encompasses the arrival and entry of the visitors:

> We have a poor Old Horse,
> And he's standing at your door,
> And if you wish to let him in,
> He'll please you all I'm sure.
>
> Poor Old Horse, Poor Old Horse

Song, dialogue and action are combined in a different manner in the better-known 'Old Tup' Christmas visit custom of the same region.[90] The beast is of the same construction as the other staff-beasts, only now representing a ram, and the head, when not wooden, could be a sheep's skull. The guise of some attendants reflected their relationship to the Tup in the action that followed; others might have blackened faces. Here too the performance included a song familiar elsewhere as a folksong ('The Derby Ram', Roud 126), and it also told of the animal in its prime and its sorry end (this time slaughter by a butcher), followed by an account of how its monstrous carcass was redistributed. But while the death was also represented, here it was not mimed during the corresponding stanzas, but acted out as a separate dramatic interlude, with scripted or at least standard dialogue, sometimes interrupting the song at the appropriate place, sometimes after the song was completed. One of the attendants, asked by his companion leading the Tup if he knows of a butcher in the neighbourhood, shouts for his brother 'Jack' who comes on in appropriate garb, wielding a large knife, accompanied by his 'wife' (man-woman) and a boy with a bowl, to collect the blood of the beast when it is slaughtered, as duly occurs after some brief comic dialogue. Here too there is packaging facilitating the entry of the performers, usually in the form of extensions to the song ('We brought the tup from Derby and he's standing at your door...').

Within its modest scope, the Old Tup custom offers something of a paradigm for the ambivalent dramaturgical mode characteristic of the larger dramatic forms accorded the accolade of 'mummers' plays' – that is to say an unstable compound of the familiar 'representational' mode of the conventional theatre and a 'presentational' mode more at home in customary contexts.[91] Both modes are options in any sustained performance involving performers who in dress, deportment, action and discourse present themselves as other than they really are ('actors'). In the representational mode of conventional theatre, they engage (sideways) *with each other*, establishing a 'second', dramatic world, so that action is also dramatic interaction and discourse is also dialogue, in a manner conformable with their assumed identities, and potentially elaborated into a plausible sequence qualifying as a 'plot'. In the presentational mode, the performers, although characters, do not engage with each other but (forwards) *with the audience*, remaining in the same 'first', world, through word, comportment and action, typically invoking who and what they are supposed to be: they tend accordingly to be striking, sometimes grotesque, figures. This is the basic mode of the Old Tup custom as the others introduce and describe the beast, which exhibits itself the while, but short though it is, the slaying interlude, deploying costume, properties, purposeful dialogue and 'realistic' action, is thoroughly representational in mode.

The difference between the two modes is particularly striking when there are several characters in close proximity but who, contrary to conventional expectation, engage not with each other but solely with the audience. As *performers*, they can and do interact with each other, but this is in order to achieve the simple mechanics of the performance. For while they can engage with the audience collectively, speaking or singing in unison, just as often each does so individually, in turn. This achieves what (in some variants) is designated by German scholarship as a *Reihenspiel* – literally 'a play with (figures in) a row', or perhaps simply a 'figure-sequence play'.[92] But the procedure can vary. Each performer can simply, unannounced, 'enter' (the performance space), in turn, state or exhibit who they are, and move on to make way for the next. But under customary performance contexts something more emphatic may be suitable, for example, a Presenter who names and heralds ('calls on') each, in turn (the *Hereinrufungskamm* or calling-on stem). Alternatively, the first having been called on and having engaged with the audience, he can herald the entry of the next, and so on in a calling-on-chain (*Hereinrufungskette*).[93] In a final alternative, the verbal and visual aspects can be otherwise distributed, with the group as a whole in chorus heralding and describing the individual figures, as each steps forward, in turn, to strut their stuff.

Such variations of the *Reihenspiel* are historically the default mode for customary drama with more than one guised figure, from the earliest forms of the medieval German *Fastnachtspiele* and the French carnival Fools' plays, the *Sotties* (in the form of the *revue*), through Renaissance pageantry and the maskings parodied by Shakespeare in *Love's Labour's Lost*,[94] to more recent folk tradition.[95] This last may be conveniently represented by the Easter house-visit custom of North West England known as 'Pace-Egging', in that the *quête* is designed, at least ostensibly, to exact largesse in the form of decorated (paschal) eggs (with cash as a thoroughly acceptable alternative). As in the last of the figure-sequence forms just reviewed, the performance encompasses a calling-on song, sung by all performers in unison, whose individual stanzas, between opening greetings and a concluding request for largesse, introduce and describe a series of striking figures, each stepping forward (in front of the others or into the centre of a circle) as their turn comes.[96] This may mean that in so doing they are, paradoxically, the only ones *not* singing, but locally there may have been an alternative mode in which each figure sings his own presentation solo.[97]

With some variation from area to area, the figures most frequently appearing include Lord Nelson, Jack Tar (a sailor), a Lady so Gay, Old Tosspot (a drunkard) and Bessy Brownbags (a female miser). By way of illustration (with built-in indications of costuming and broad hints of expectations):

> The next that comes in is our Lady so gay,
> And from her own country she has run away,
> With her red cap and feather she looks very fine,
> And all her delight is in drinking red wine.
>
>   Fol the diddle ol-I day, Fol the diddle ol-I day

> The next that comes in is our Toss Pot you see,
> He's a valiant old man in every degree,
> He's a hump on his back and wears a pig-tail,
> And all his delight is in drinking mulled ale.
>
>   Fol the diddle ol-, &c[98]

From this perspective, we may return to the mummers' plays,[99] most of which can usefully be perceived as offering an entertainment that includes, often alongside instrumental music, song or dance, both a shorter or longer presentational *Reihenspiel* of displays and statements by or about a sequence of figures, and a dramatic interlude.[100] A pertinent illustration is provided by the Pace-Egging custom just examined, where in some local traditions the figure-sequence is performed alongside a combat and cure interlude familiar from mummers' plays elsewhere.[101]

For the purposes of this survey, it is not an issue whether the compound be construed as a ('Hero Combat') mummers' play with an inserted pace-egging *Reihenspiel* or vice versa. More importantly, here and in other varieties of the mummers' play, the two dramaturgical modes occur in immediate juxtaposition, with the possibility that in the course of iterated performances, they will interact. And while it cannot be ruled out that two 'presentational' characters start to interact with each other, the greater likelihood is that in this dynamic coexistence, the representational mode of the dramatic material will be contaminated by the presentational mode of the entertainment of which it is a part. The latter is established from the outset by the opening address to the household (transforming them into an audience), and whatever happens in the meantime it is re-established in the concluding good wishes and request for largesse.

Symptomatic of such contamination is the procedure in the familiar mummers' plays where characters participating in the dramatic action are 'called on' ('Walk in…!') by a figure already present in the action, and/or present themselves to the audience ('In comes I…!'), before interacting with other characters. It is feasible indeed that representational inter-character action in the interlude (the plot) can be degraded to the extent that some 'characters' are left with only a single speech, and fall into line (the *Reihe*) with other mere 'figures'.[102] To the extent this is the case we might consider applying to the customary figure-sequence the insight offered by folklorist Max Lüthi with regard to another form of folk performance, the folktale – that it readily welcomes material from other forms, but in so doing 'sublimates' them into its own mode.[103]

Notes

1 The field is characterized in conventional folkloristic terms in Thomas A. Green, 'Toward a Definition of Folk Drama', *Journal of American Folklore*, 91 (1978), 843–850, and from a global perspective combining both Folklore and Drama Studies in Steve Tillis, *Rethinking Folk Drama* (Westport, CT: Greenwood Press, 1999), the major English forms examined in ch. 7, 'Rethinking Folk Drama'.

2 See, for example, John Wesley Harris, *Medieval Theatre in Context: An Introduction* (London: Routledge, 1992), ch. 6, 'The Village and the Court'. A very recent instance in an authoritative publication is Jennifer C. Vaught, 'Mummers' Shows and Folk Drama', *The Encyclopedia of Medieval Literature in Britain*, ed. by Sîan Echard and Robert Rouse, vol. 3 (London: Wiley Blackwell, 2017), pp. 1385–1387.

3 For the demise of both theories, see my 'When the Golden Bough Breaks: Folk Drama and the Theatre Historian', *Nordic Journal of English Studies*, 4.2 (2005), 1–40 <https://gupea.ub.gu.se/bitstream/2077/230/1/NJES_4_2_Pettitt.pdf> [accessed 22 February 2020]. There is a survey of Folk Drama scholarship, independent of the theatrical connection, in Lisa Gabbert, 'Folk Drama', *humanities*, 7.1 (2018), 2 <https://www.mdpi.com/2076-0787/7/1/2> [accessed 22 February 2020].

4 The chronological reservation applies to the otherwise most comprehensive explorations in this direction, Robert Weimann, *Shakespeare and the Popular Tradition in the Theatre* (Baltimore, MD: Johns Hopkins University Press, 1978); François Laroque, *Shakespeare's Festive World* (Cambridge: Cambridge University Press, 1991). For a detailed exploration of a specific instance

of such interaction, see my 'Midsummer Metadrama: "Pyramus and Thisbe" and Early English Household Theatre', *Angles*, 5 (2005), 31–43 <https://www.academia.edu/7753285/Midsummer_Metadrama_Pyramus_and_Thisbe_and_Early_English_Household_Theatre>. [accessed 22 February 2020].

5 Scholarly recognition of this development in a major part of the field has culminated in Peter Harrop's, *Mummers' Plays Revisited* (London: Routledge, 2020). See also (within a narrower scope) my 'Beyond the Bad Quarto: Exploring the Vernacular Afterlife of Early Modern Drama', *Journal of Early Modern Studies*, 8 (2019), 133–171 <https://oajournals.fupress.net/index.php/bsfm-jems/article/view/7107/7105> [accessed 22 February 2020].

6 A welcome exception encompassing both aspects is Gordon Kipling's 'Triumphal Drama: Form in English Civic Pageantry', *Renaissaance Drama*, NS. 8 (1977), 37–56.

7 On medieval forms (with some later 'survivals'), see Thomas Pettitt and Leif Søndergaard, 'Traditions of the People: Customs and Folk Drama', in *The Medieval European Stage, 500–1550*, ed. by William Tydeman (Cambridge: Cambridge University Press, 2001), pp. 615–665; still useful is C.R. Baskervill, 'Dramatic Aspects of Medieval Folk Festivals in England', *Studies in Philology*, 17.1 (1920), 19–87. For the early modern period, there is much contemporary documentation in Laroque, *Shakespeare's Festive World*; for a more discursive survey, see my 'Local Drama and Custom', in *A New Companion to English Renaissance Literature and Culture*, ed. by Michael Hattaway (Oxford: Blackwell, 2007), pp. 184–203. For the approach to modern times, see R.W. Malcolmson, *Popular Recreations in English Society 1700–1850* (Cambridge: Cambridge University Press, 1973).

8 For a well-documented and readable survey of recent traditions, see Steve Roud, *The English Year. A Month-by-month Guide to the Nation's Customs and Festivals, from May Day to Mischief Night* (London: Penguin, 2006; repr. 2008). The full period covered by this survey is comprehensively charted (but with less emphasis on performance aspects) by historian Ronald Hutton's *The Rise and Fall of Merry England: The Ritual Year 1400–1700* (Oxford: Oxford University Press, 1994), and *The Stations of the Sun: A History of the Ritual Year in Britain* (Oxford: Oxford University Press, 1996).

9 For earlier periods, a range of sources is invoked in Laroque, *Shakespeare's Festive World*, ch. 5, 'The non-calendary festivals'. Later traditions have attracted sustained attention largely for their relationship to the dire situation of the rural working class: Bob Bushaway, *By Rite. Custom, Ceremony and Community, 1700–1880* (London: Junction Books, 1982), esp. ch. 4, 'Custom and Social Cohesion'; David Hoseason Morgan, *Harvesters and Harvesting 1840–1900: A Study of the Rural Proletariat* (London: Croom Helm, 1982), and more generally E.P. Thompson, *Customs in Common* (London: Merlin Press, 1991).

10 For a study of early modern life-phases and attendant ceremony in general, see David Cressy, *Birth, Marriage and Death: Ritual, Religion and the Life-cycle in Tudor and Stuart England* (Oxford: Oxford University Press, 1997), and more specifically on customs, Laroque, *Shakespeare's Festive World*, pp. 167–175.

11 L.E. Pearson, *Elizabethans at Home* (Stanford, CA: Stanford University Press, 1957), pp. 81–86.

12 There is a comprehensive invocation in George Eliot's *Adam Bede* (1858), ed. by Robert Speaight (London: Dent, 1960; repr. 1972), chs. XXII–XXVI.

13 Ann Jennalie Cook, *Making a Match: Courtship in Shakespeare and His Society* (Princeton, NJ: Princeton University Press, 1991), ch. VII, 'Proposals, Contracts, Weddings'.

14 For an examination of practices at an important transitional period, see Dan Beaver, '"Sown in dishonour, raised in glory": Death, Ritual and Social Organization in Northern Gloucestershire, 1590–1690', *Social History*, 17.3 (1992), 389–419.

15 On Irish tradition, see Sean O'Suilleabhain, *Irish Wake Amusements* (Cork: Mercier Press, 1967), and for medieval English records, C.R. Baskervill, 'Dramatic Aspects', pp. 73–74.

16 For more on early household auspices, see Felicity Heal, *Hospitality in Early Modern England* (Oxford: Clarendon Press, 1990).

17 For the importance of custom in early community life, see Charles Phythian-Adams, 'Ceremony and the Citizen: The Communal Year at Coventry, 1450–1550', in *Crisis and Order in English Towns, 1500–1700*, ed. by P. Clark and P. Slack (London: Routledge, 1972), pp. 57–85.

18 Mervyn James', 'Ritual, Drama and Social Body in the Late Medieval English Town', *Past & Present*, 98 (1983), 3–29 is a highly focused investigation of the relationship between guild custom and social context. I provide a survey of the range of customary performances produced under guild auspices in 'Medieval Performance Culture and the English Guilds: Custom, Pageantry,

Drama', in *Guilds, Towns and Cultural Transmission in the North, 1300–1500*, ed. Lars Bisgaard, Lars Boje Mortensen and Tom Pettitt (Odense: University Press of Southern Denmark, 2013), pp. 131–61 <https://www.academia.edu/9246853/Medieval_Performance_Culture_and_the_English_Guilds_Custom_Pageantry_Drama> [accessed 22 February 2020].

19 Bernard Capp's 'English Youth Groups and *the Pinder of Wakefield*', *Past & Present*, 76 (1977), 127–133 is an initial attempt to transfer to England the ground-breaking insights of Natalie Zemon Davis' 'The Reasons of Misrule', in her, *Society and Culture in Early Modern France* (Stanford, CA: Stanford University Press), 1975, ch. IV.

20 Subjected to sustained and intense scrutiny by Peter and Iona Opie, for example, in *The Lore and Language of Schoolchildren* (Oxford: Oxford University Press, 1959; repr. 1970), ch.12, 'Children's Calendar'. A major resource for semi-dramatic children's games in the nineteenth century and earlier is Lady Alice Bertha Gomme, *The Traditional Games of England, Scotland and Ireland*, 2 vols. (London, 1894–1898; repr. with Introduction by Dorothy Howard, New York: Dover, 1964).

21 A phenomenon explored for the medieval period by Chris Humphrey, *The Politics of Carnival: Festive Misrule in Medieval England* (Manchester: Manchester University Press, 2001), for the early modern by David Underdown, *Revel, Riot and Rebellion. Popular Politics and Culture in England, 1603–1660* (Oxford: Clarendon Press, 1985), and more generally by Bob Pegg, *Rites and Riots. Folk Customs of Britain and Europe* (Poole: Blandford Press, 1981). See also my '"Here Comes I, Jack Straw": English Folk Drama and Social Revolt', *Folklore*, 95.1 (1984), 3–20.

22 A prime instance is Pieter Bruegel the Elder's 'The Fair of St George's Day' [*De Kermis van Sint Joris*]', 1559, in Jacques Lavalleye, *Pieter Bruegel the Elder and Lucas van Leyden: The Complete Engravings, Etchings and Woodcuts* (London: Thames & Hudson, 1967), Pl. 57, where the ambient customary activities include both a sword dance and a St George and Dragon pageant.

23 See my 'Tudor Interludes and the Winter Revels', *Medieval English Theatre*, 6.1 (July 1984), 16–27.

24 See my 'Customary Drama: Social and Spatial Patterning in Traditional Encounters', *Folk Music Journal*, 7.1 (1995), 27–42.

25 For an exemplary study alert to most of these aspects, and juxtaposing performance contexts with literary themes, see Bruce R. Smith, 'Landscape with Figures: The Three Realms of Queen Elizabeth's Country-House Revels', *Renaissance Drama*, NS. 8 (1977), 57–115.

26 Roud, *English Year*, pp. 350–352, 455.

27 Dieter Dünninger, *Wegsperre und Lösung: Formen und Motive eines dörflichen Hochzeitsbrauches* (Berlin: de Gruyter, 1967); Arnold Van Gennep, *Manuel de Folklore Francais Contemporain*, 4 vols., vol. I.i (Paris: Picard, 1937–1958; repr. Paris: Robert Laffont, 1998), pp. 386–396, 'La Barrière'. There is, however, report of an East Anglian custom in which youths and children made a row ('rough music') at the door of the church and would not let the bridal couple emerge until they were given beer or coins: Enid Porter, *The Folklore of East Anglia* (Totowa: Rowman and Littlefield, 1974), p. 27.

28 Major studies, if with main focus on meaning rather than patterns of movement, include Gordon Kipling, *Enter the King: Theatre, Liturgy and Ritual in the Medieval Civic Triumph* (Oxford: Clarendon, 1998); David M. Bergeron, *English Civic Pageantry* (London: Edward Arnold, 1971), and Tracey Hill, *Pageantry and Power: A Cultural History of the Early Modern Lord Mayor's Show, 1585–1639* (Manchester: Manchester University Press, 2011).

29 On the customary parades, interceptions and their interactions, see my 'Moving Encounters: Choreographing Stage and Spectators in Urban Theatre and Pageantry', *Medium Ævum Quotidianum*, 48 (2003), 63–93, reprinted in *European Theatre Performance Practice, 1400–1580*, ed. by Philip Butterworth and Katie Normington (Aldershot: Ashgate, 2014), pp. 239–269.

30 For a systematic analysis, see my 'The Morphology of the Parade', *European Medieval Drama*, 6 (2003), 1–30. Various aspects are examined in *Moving Subjects: Processional Performance in the Middle Ages and the Renaissance*, ed. by Kathleen Ashley and Wim Hüskens (Amsterdam and Atlanta: Rodopi, 2001), non-elite traditions, for example, in James Stokes's 'Processional Entertainments in Villages and Small Towns' (pp. 239–257).

31 There is a useful contemporary survey in Wm. and Hugh Raynbird, *On the Agriculture of Suffolk* (London: Longman, 1849), 'Harvest Customs', pp. 305–310.

32 Karl-S. Kramer, *Grundriss einer RechtlichenVolkskunde* (Göttingen: Otto Schwartz, 1974), 'Rüge', pp. 70–82.

33 The field is reviewed in Thompson, *Customs in Common*, ch. 8, 'Rough Music'. See also my 'Protesting Inversions: Charivary as Folk Pageantry and Folk-Law', *Medieval English Theatre*,

21 (1999), 21–51, and 'Nuptial Pageantry in Medieval Culture and Folk Custom: In Quest of the English *charivari*', *Medium Ævum Quotidianum*, 52 (2005), 89–115 <https://www.academia.edu/4018274/Nuptial_Pageantry_in_Medieval_Culture_and_Folk_Custom_in_Quest_of_the_English_charivari> [accessed 22 February 2020].

34 This aspect of the field, not least the overlap between 'folk' and 'official' laws, has been thoroughly explored in Stephen Banks, *Informal Justice in England and Wales, 1760–1914: The Courts of Public Opinion* (Woodbridge: Boydell & Brewer, 2014).

35 For some instances, see Bob Bushaway, 'The Rituals of Privation and Protest', in *By Rite*, ch. 5, esp. pp. 190–202, 'Protest and the Enemies of the People'; E. J. Jones, '"Scotch Cattle" and Early Trade Unionism in Wales', *Economic History*, 1 (1928), 385–393, repr. in *Industrial South Wales 1750–1914: Essays in Welsh Economic History*, ed. by W.E. Minchinton (London: Routledge, 1969), pp. 209–217.

36 As suggested by the seventeenth-century enclosure riots led by a cross-dressed figure named 'Lady Skimmington' (see below): Christina Bosco Langert, 'Hedgerows and Petticoats: Sartorial Subversion and Anti-enclosure Protest in Seventeenth-century England', *Early Theatre*, 12.1 (2009), 119–135.

37 Porter, *Folklore of East Anglia*, p. 27.

38 George Ewart Evans, *The Pattern under the Plough* (1966; repr. London: Faber & Faber, 1971), ch. 11, 'The Rough Band', pp. 115–118.

39 A.L. Rowse, *A Cornishman at Oxford* (1965; repr. London: Jonathan Cape, 1974), p. 74. For other instances from Cornwall, see M.A. Courtney, 'Cornish Folk-Lore. Part III', *The Folk-Lore Journal*, 5 (1887), 177–220, pp. 216–217.

40 As is sometimes the case with the *charivari*, it is also possible that the ostensible demonstration was concurrently or essentially an exaction, continuing until the unhappy couple paid for the beer.

41 C.R.B. Barrett, 'Riding Skimmington and Riding the Stang', *Journal of the British Archaeological Society*, NS 1 (1895), 58–68; [Eliza] Gutch, *Examples of Printed Folklore Concerning the North Riding of Yorkshire, York, & the Ainsty* (London: Nutt, 1901), pp. 335–337.

42 Cited in Karen Newman, 'Renaissance Family Politics and Shakespeare's *The Taming of the Shrew*', *English Literary Renaissance*, 16 (1986), 86–100, pp. 86–87; see also M. Ingram, 'Ridings, Rough Music, and the "Reform of Popular Culture" in Early Modern England', *Past & Present*, 105 (1984), 79–113, 93.

43 Ingram, 'Ridings, Rough Music'; B.H. Cunnington, 'A Skimmington in 1618', *Folklore*, 41 (1930), 288–290.

44 Samuel Butler, *Hudibras*, ed. by John Wilders (Oxford: Clarendon Press, 1964), Part Two Canto II, ll.585–712. William Hogarth, *Hogarth: The Complete Engravings*, ed. by Joseph Burke and Colin Caldwell (London: Thames & Hudson, 1968), Ill. 103; see also Ill. 88 for a second, contemporary, version. Also valuable is Andrew Marvell's 'The Last Instructions to a Painter' (1667), ll. 376–389, in *The Poems and Letters of Andrew Marvell*, ed. by H.M. Margoliouth, vol. I (Oxford: Clarendon Press, 1971), evidently based on the incident reported in *The Diary of Samuel Pepys* ed. by R. Latham and W. Matthews, vol. VIII (Berkeley: University of California Press, 1974), p. 257, and n. 2 for the connection with Marvell's poem.

45 The most vigorous, or best researched, seem to be the scandal plays of the Basque regions, on which see Joxerra Garcia, 'Basque Oral Ecology', *Oral Tradition*, 22.2 (2007), 47–64, but there is a splendid and fully contextualized Italian instance from 1935 to 1936 in Carlo Levi's autobiographical account, *Christ Stopped at Eboli: The Story of a Year*, trans. Frances Frenaye (New York: Ferrar, Straus & co., 1947), pp. 230–232.

46 The material is presented and discussed in David Rollison, 'Prophecy, Ideology and Popular Culture in a Gloucestershire Village 1660–1740', *Past & Present*, 93 (1981), 70–97, and examined from a broader context in Banks, *Informal Justice*, pp. 41–43. For earlier somewhat analogous instances, see C. J. Sisson, *Lost Plays of Shakespeare's Age* (1936; repr. London: Cass, 1970).

47 Graham Seal, 'A "Hussitting" in Berkshire, 1930', *Folklore*, 98 (1987), 91–94.

48 For early household revels and associated activities, see Laroque, *Shakespeare's Festive World*, pp. 148–153. I have surveyed the field in 'The Folk Interlude: Dramatic Aspects of Traditional Games, Gambols and Songs', *Folk Drama Studies Today: Papers Given at the International Traditional Drama Conference 19–21 July 2002, University of Sheffield, England*, ed. by E. Cass and P. Millington (Sheffield: Traditional Drama Research Group, 2003), pp. 67–88 <https://folkplay.info/sites/default/files/papers/200207/Pettitt2002.pdf> [accessed 22 February 2020].

49 E.g. Robert Herrick, 'A New-Yeares Gift to Sir Simeon Steward', *The Complete Poetry of Robert Herrick*, ed. by J. Max Patrick (New York: Doubleday, 1963; repr. New York: New York University Press, 1963; repr. New York: Norton, 1968), H-319, ll. 15–16: 'the care/That young men have to shooe the Mare'; Francis Beaumont, *The Knight of the Burning Pestle*, ed. by J. Doebler (Lincoln: University of Nebraska Press, 1967), I.i.435ff.: 'I'll have Rafe come and do some of his gambols. – He'll ride the wild mare …'.

50 O'Suilleabhain, *Irish Wake Amusements*, p. 91; E.C. Cawte, *Ritual Animal Disguise* (Cambridge: Brewer, 1978), p. 193; George Deacon, *John Clare and the Folk Tradition* (London: Sinclair Browne, 1983), p. 291.

51 *The Plays of Henry Medwall*, ed. by Alan Nelson (Cambridge: Brewer, 1980), *Fulgens & Lucres*, ll. 1150–1196.

52 Josias Bodley, *Descriptio itineris Capitanei Josiae Bodley in Leculiam apud Ultoniensis. Ann. 1602* [Journey to Lecale], MS. transcribed and translated in Anon, 'Bodley's Visit to Lecale, County of Down, A.D. 1602–3', *Ulster Journal of Archaeology*, 2 (1854), 73–99, and from there, with further commentary establishing the connection to the interlude, in Alan J. Fletcher, '"Farte Prycke in Cule": A Late-Elizabethan Analogue from Ireland', *Medieval English Theatre*, 8.2 (1986), 134–139, 135–136).

53 Gomme, *Traditional Games*, 2, 192.

54 Anon, 'Bodley's Visit to Lecale', p. 94, n.j.

55 Personal communication, 2002.

56 Deacon, *John Clare*, p. 291.

57 Deacon, *John Clare*, p. 291. Somewhat analogous is the routine involving a Miller and his Wife in nineteenth-century Gaelic tradition of the Scottish Highlands and Islands, J.F. and T.M. Flett, 'Dramatic Jigs in Scotland', *Folklore*, 67 (1956), 84–96, 91–94.

58 Raynbird, *On the Agriculture of Suffolk*, p. 307. The same account (with a few discrepancies) had appeared earlier in Hone's *Every-Day Book* (1827), and is quoted in full in Steve Roud, *Folk Song in England* (London: Faber & Faber, 2017), p. 617.

59 Henry Morris, 'Irish Wake Games', *Bealoideas. Journal of the Folklore of Ireland Society*, 8 (1938), 123–141, 124–125; O'Suilleabhain, *Irish Wake Amusements*, pp. 89–90.

60 Surveyed by Roud, *Folk Song in England*, pp. 612–619, including the song-based interludes discussed here.

61 C.J. Sharp and C.E. Marson, eds., *Folk Songs from Somerset*, vol. 3 (London: Simpkin, 1906), p. 74.

62 Roud, *Folk Song in England*, pp. 613–614.

63 Gutch, *Examples of Printed Folk-Lore*, p. 258.

64 The 'out' here balances the explicit reference earlier to Andra coming 'in', suggesting a designated performance space.

65 Gutch, *Examples of Printed Folk-Lore*, pp. 257–258. Further details, on the basis of Gutch's source, are provided by Roud, *Folk Song in England*, p. 618. There is no connection with the two English folksongs known as 'Andrew Carr' (Roud 8166 and 3872).

66 As in the rhymed dialogue called 'The Hiring' reported as a feature of harvest homes in Warwickshire in the nineteenth century: Gomme, *Traditional Games*, I, 319.

67 *Everyman's Book of British Ballads*, ed. by Roy Palmer (London, J. M. Dent, 1980), No. 100, pp. 202–202.

68 Gutch, *Examples of Printed Folklore*, pp. 259–265.

69 Anne C. Gilchrist and Lucy E. Broadwood, 'Notes on Children's Game Songs', *Journal of the English Folk Song Society*, 5 (1915), 228–237, 'The Prickly Bush', pp. 231–234.

70 The tale does not seem to be recognized in the standard *The Types of International Folktales: A Classification and Bibliography Based on the System of Antti Aarne and Stith Thompson*, ed. by Hans-Jörg Uther, 3 vols. (Helsinki: Academia Scientiarum Fennica, 2004); it is not the same as ATU 440: *The Frog Prince or Iron Henry*, which sometimes goes by this title (and can also involve the retrieval of a girl's lost ball).

71 The tale thus supplies an explanation for the questions and answers in the familiar ballad, 'The Maid Freed from the Gallows' (Child 95, Roud 144), but the matter of which came first is not relevant here. The relation between song and tale is discussed in David Shuldiner, 'The Content and Structure of English Ballads and Tales', *Western Folklore*, 37 (1978), 267–280, 270.

72 'The Story of the Golden Ball' is No. 10 in the Appendix of Household Tales contributed by Sabine Baring-Gould to the first edition of William Henderson's *Folklore of the Northern*

Counties of England and the Borders (London: Longman's Green & co., 1866), texts pp. 333–335, Baring-Gould's comments pp. 335–336. The Appendix was dropped from the second edition of 1879. Baring-Gould does not specify the source, other than that the tale is from Yorkshire, and he acknowledges, p. 335, the insertion of narrative material. The tale in this form was subsequently published by Joseph Jacobs in his popular *More English Fairy Tales*, 1894, a sequel to his *English Fairy Tales* of 1890; I have consulted the 1 vol. ed. under the latter title ed. by Donald Haase (Santa Barbara: ABC Clio, 2002), No. 46, pp. 203–205.

73 This may be a glimpse of an arrangement more familiar on the continent (like the German *Stubespiel*) in which, reversing the movement of the house-visit, a group lets it be known that they will offer, at a specified venue and time, a performance which locals are invited to attend.

74 The reference is presumably to the American play by Wilson Barrett, 'The Sign of the Cross', from 1895, whose English performances from 1896 onwards included a production by a travelling company <https://en.wikipedia.org/wiki/The_Sign_of_the_Cross_(play)> [accessed 22 February 2020]. There was also a silent film version from 1914, but this will have been too late for the lady from Southport to have seen it before being interviewed. She could also have seen the postcard, published in London in 1906, with a photograph of what looks like the trial scene, entirely compatible with the description <https://www.ebay.co.uk/itm/Sign-of-the-Cross-Play-Scene-Real-Photo-Postcard-1906-/360983456303> [accessed 22 February 2020].

75 In performance terms, the house-visit wassail should be distinguished from the ceremonial wassailing of apple orchards (where dressing up is a feature of recent revivals). See Roud, *English Year*, pp. 556–559. The spirit of benevolence is well represented in one of the earliest records, poet Robert Herrick's 'The Wassaile', in *The Complete Poetry*, ed. Patrick, *Hesperides*, H.476.

76 For a brief presentation, see my 'Mumming', in *Folklore: An Encyclopedia of Beliefs, Customs, Tales, Music and Art*, ed. by Thomas A. Green, 2 vols. (Santa Barbara: ABC-CLIO, 1997), pp. 2, 566–567.

77 For early records, see Meg Twycross and Sarah Carpenter, *Masks and Masking in Medieval and Early Tudor England* (Aldershot: Ashgate, 2002), ch. 4, 'Mumming'.

78 Although these tended to be at other times of year: Iona and Peter Opie, *The Lore and Language of Schoolchildren* (Oxford: Oxford University Press, 1959; repr. 1970), pp. 255, 276–280.

79 G.M. Sider, 'Mumming in Outport Newfoundland', *Past and Present*, 71 (1976), 102–125; for later traditions in England, see Martin J. Lovelace, 'Christmas Mumming in England: The House-Visit', in *Folklore Studies in Honour of Herbert Halpert*, ed. by Kenneth S. Goldstein and Neil V. Rosenberg (St John's, Newfoundland: Memorial University of Newfoundland, 1980), pp. 271–281.

80 A prescient suggestion along these lines was offered by Michael J. Preston in 'The British Folk Play: An Elaborated Luck-Visit?' *Western Folklore*, 30 (1971), 45–48.

81 Peter Millington, 'The Origins and Development of English Folk Plays', Diss. (University of Sheffield, 2002), pp. 139–144 <http://etheses.whiterose.ac.uk/id/eprint/13> [accessed 22 February 2020].

82 On their historical development, see Hutton, *Stations of the Sun*, pp. 124–133 (plough trailing); 73–76 (sword dancing). In their dramatic forms, they are designated, respectively, 'Plough Plays' (or, because of the dramatic content, 'Wooing Plays') and 'Sword Dance Plays'. The well-established distinctions between these forms and the more widely distributed 'Hero Combat' plays are explicated in studies still invoked as standard (but whose assumptions on ritual origins should be ignored) such as Alan Brody, *The English Mummers and their Plays. Traces of Ancient Mystery* (London: RKP, n.d. [1969]); E.K. Chambers, *The English Folk-Play* (Oxford: Clarendon Press, 1933; repr. 1969); Alex Helm, *The English Mummers' Play* (Woodbridge: D.S. Brewer, 1981). For studies devoted particularly to these forms, see Alun Howkins and Linda Merricks, 'The Ploughboys and the Plough Play', *FMJ*. 6.2 (1991), 187–208; Stephen D. Corrsin, *Sword Dancing in Europe: A History* (Enfield Lock: Hisarlik Press, 1997), ch. 11, 'England, Late Eighteenth to Earlier Twentieth Century'.

83 It may be relevant that in the meantime, one of the most widespread (and possibly most dramatic) of the late medieval gatherings performed by figures representing Robin Hood and some of his associates was falling into desuetude. On this tradition, see John Marshall, 'Robin Hood plays and combat games', in *The Routledge Research Companion to Early Drama and Performance*, ed. by Pamela M. King (London and New York: Routledge, 2017), pp. 177–184; Paul Whitfield White,

Drama and Religion in English Provincial Society 1485–1660 (Cambridge: Cambridge University Press, 2008), ch. 2, 'The parish Robin Hood and religious guilds'.

84 Cawte, *Ritual Animal Disguise*, ch. III, 'The Hobby-Horse in England from 1590 to 1800'.

85 Revealing another awkwardness in the term: 'Mummers' Play' generally refers to the performance as a whole, only part of which is the 'play'–to avoid confusion, the latter is accordingly referred to here as the 'interlude'.

86 Roud, *The English Year*, pp. 24–25, has a succinct account with necessary documentation; for further early accounts, see Pauline Dennis, 'Whittlesey Straw Bear', *English Dance and Song*, 43 (1981), 21–22.

87 Cawte, *Ritual Animal Disguise*, pp. 140–142; Roud, *English Year*, pp. 157–158.

88 The following is based on the still standard work which introduced the custom to folklorists more widely, Percy Maylam, *The Hooden Horse: An East Kent Christmas Custom* (Canterbury: the author, 1909), pp. 2–7 and (for the song), 51–52. A new edition with extra material has been published as *Percy Maylam's the Kent Hooden Horse*, ed. by Richard Maylam, Mick Lynn and Geoff Doel (Stroud: The History Press, 2009). See also Cawte, *Ritual Animal Discguise*, pp. 85–93; Roud, *Englsh Year*, pp. 503–506.

89 S.O. Addy, 'Guising and Mumming in Derbyshire', *Journal of the Derbyshire Archaeological and Natural History Society*, 29 (1907), 31–42, 37–33; Rory Greig, '"We have a poor old horse"', *Lore and Language*, 1.9 (1973), 7–10; Cawte, *Ritual Animal Disguise*, pp. 117–120.

90 Cawte, *Ritual Animal Disguise*, pp. 110–117. Ivor Gatty, 'The Old Tup and his Ritual', *Journal of the English Folk Dance and Song Society*, 5 (1946–1948), 23–30; Ian Russell, 'A Survey of Traditional Drama in North East Derbyshire 1970–1978', *Folk Music Journal*, 3.5 (1979), 399–478.

91 The following can be seen as parallel and supplemental to Tom Brown's interesting meditation on theatrical performance vs. the 'vernacular' style of the mummers' plays in 'Six Actors I've Brought', First Mummers Unconvention (Bath Spa University, 2011) <https://folkplay.info/sites/default/files/papers/201111/Brown2011.pdf> [accessed 22 February 2020].

92 The term is deployed in studies of the late medieval German carnival interlude, or *Fastnachtsspiel*, to distinguish this form from the *Handlungsspiel* (a play with a plot).

93 The German terminology for this distinction is from Karl Meschke, *Schwerttanz und Schwerttanzspiel im germanischen Kulturkreis* (Leipzig and Berlin: Teubner, 1931), p. 131.

94 Eckehard Catholy, *Fastnachtspiel* (Stuttgart: Metzler, 1966), pp. 27–40; Alan E. Knight, 'The Medieval Theatre of the Absurd', *PMLA*, 86.2 (1971), 183–189, 183; *The Riverside Shakespeare*, ed. by G. Blakmore Evans and J.J.M. Tobin (Boston, MA: Houghton Mifflin, 1997), *Love's Labour's Lost*, 5.2.547–715.

95 On the striking similarities in this and other ways between the medieval German and more recent English traditions, see my 'English Folk Drama and the Early German *Fastnachtspiele*', *Renaissance Drama*, NS. 13 (1982), 1–34.

96 The custom and its geographical distribution (including its occurrence as an All Souls' custom in a neighbouring region) are surveyed with characteristic thoroughness in E.C. Cawte's 'The Calling-On Song in the North-West of England', *Folk Music Journal*, 9.4 (2009), 525–580.

97 For example at Thurstaston, Cheshire: see Alaric Hope, 'Pace Egging at Thurstaston', *Cheshire Sheaf*, 3rd ser., 3 (August 1899), 76 (Note 465).

98 Douglas Kennedy, 'Observations on the Sword-Dance and Mummers' Play'. *Journal of the English Folk Dance Society*, 2nd ser., 3 (1930), 13–38, 35–36.

99 For access to the field and its scholarship, see Eddie Cass, Michael J. Preston and Paul Smith, *The English Mumming Plays: An Introductory Bibliography* (London: FLS Books, 2000), and the website of the Traditional Drama Research Group at <http://www.folkplay.info/> [accessed 22 February 2020] (with digital versions of many significant research contributions). There is a full listing of all known local traditions (ca 1,500) at <http://www.mastermummers.org/erd/index.htm> [accessed 22 February 2020], Peter Millington's revised digital edition of the original, E.C. Cawte, Alex Helm and Norman Peacock, *English Ritual Drama* (London: Folklore Society, 1967) incorporating subsequent updates.

100 The historical evolution of the interlude itself is subjected to sustained statistical exploration in Peter Millington's 'The Origins and Development of English Folk Plays'. There are also instances where a local mummers' play has introduced, as well as the main interlude, other dramatic material, typically wooing dialogues similar to those surveyed earlier under pastimes and entertainments.

101 These 'pace-egg plays' are covered in standard works on the mummers' plays; for directly focused studies, see Eddie Cass, 'The Pace-Egg Play – A Traditional Drama in the Lancashire Cotton Towns', *Transactions of the Lancashire and Cheshire Antiquarian Society*, 94 (1998), 111–135; *The Lancashire Pace-egg Play: A Social History* (London: FLS Books, 2001).
102 For a possible instance, see Michael J. Preston, 'The Robin Hood Plays of South Central England', *Comparative Drama*, 10 (1976), 91–100 (a very local phenomenon not to be confused with the late medieval Robin Hood gatherings mentioned in an earlier endnote).
103 Max Lüthi, *The European Folktale: Form and Nature*, trans. John D. Niles (1982; repr. Bloomington: Indiana University Press, 1986), ch. 5, 'Sublimation and All-Inclusiveness'.

2
PERFORMING CALENDRICAL PRESSURES
Shrovetide processions and shroving perambulations in premodern England

Taylor Aucoin

Introduction

When studying folk performance, calendar customs are often treated together as a genus, to illustrate similarities in aesthetic forms and social meanings across calendrical divides. Yet, there is also analytical potential in focusing on one point in the calendar, to discern what separates that point from others, and how such distinctions can lead to the development of unique folk traditions. Training one's eye upon a single spoke in the wheel of the year can show how the calendar, as a stage, structures genres of folk performance. Moreover, it can reveal the historical processes by which the specific pressures and precedents of economic, religious, and social structures, intersecting at one point in calendrical time, have incrementally moulded, altered, and given meaning to those genres over historical time. This chapter adopts the latter approach, taking the pre-Lenten festival of Shrovetide as its spoke of the wheel.

Emerging about a thousand years ago as a distinct festival in the English calendar, Shrovetide is the elastic and moveable pre-Lenten Carnival season. It fluctuates with the date of Easter, can vary in length, and culminates in Shrove Tuesday. Developing in opposition to and preparation for the fasting and penitence of Lent, medieval Shrovetide was a time, on the one hand, for confession (called *shriving*) and charity, and, on the other, for indulgence in pleasures that would be forbidden in the fast to follow. After the Reformation, the English Church retained the Lenten liturgy (though without confession), the English crown retained the ban on meat (though purely on economic grounds), and the English people retained their Shrovetide revels (without any reservations). Centuries of social change, however, have pared Shrovetide down, so that what was formerly a series of festive days is now a singular, yet still much beloved, Pancake Day.[1]

While Carnival elsewhere in Europe and the Americas has long been associated with professional and folk performance, especially parading, masking, and satirical comedies, English Shrovetide has not. Indeed, some scholars have claimed that England lacks a tradition of pre-Lenten public performance, and always has.[2] This claim could be countered in many ways, but perhaps most simply by pointing to the abundance of Shrovetide pageantry that once did (and in some cases still does) fill English streets. As it pertains to folk performance, such street pageantry falls into two main categories: processions (organized marches with pomp and/or ceremony) and perambulations (less structured group performances meandering from place to place). This chapter begins with an overview of premodern Shrovetide processions to illustrate the core seasonal pressures and themes at play during the festival. It then takes a closer look at the impact of those calendrical pressures, and historical change, upon the development and performance of Shrovetide begging perambulations in particular. In the process, the chapter argues that, as structural pressures shaped calendrical folk performance during the premodern period, in turn, these evolving performances and contexts for performance came to provide participants with the thematic means to respond to some of those structural realities.

Survey of Shrovetide processions

Apart from feasting to excess, sports and games were the most common and enduring Shrovetide pastimes in England, with a spirit of competition suffusing even the most mundane activities during Carnival time. This spirit remains visible today in communal pancake-races, but prior to the twentieth century, animal blood sports took top-billing. Most ubiquitous were those targeting poultry, turning pre-Lenten food preparation into cruel games like hen-thrashing, cock-throwing, and cockfighting. Servants, apprentices, and children in general enjoyed the former two as Shrovetide privileges, while the latter was something of an institution in grammar schools. From as early as the twelfth century until the banning of the sport in the 1830s, many English students received a half-holiday on Shrove Tuesday to bring cockerels to their classrooms and set them to fight.[3] The privileges and entertainment extended to schoolchildren did not stop with the tournament, however, for it was in some places followed with a mixture of pomp, pageantry, and procession known as the 'riding about in victory'. Antiquarian John Aubrey described the custom as it was found in his native West Country during the late seventeenth century:

> […] for Cock-fighting, the Schoole-boies continue that Custome still: and have their Victors, that is, he whose Cock conquers or beates the rest […] On Shrove Tuesday shroving when the Victor Boy went thro ye streetes in triumph deckd with ribbons, all his schoole fellowes follow[ed] with drum and a fiddle to a Feast at their Masters schoole house.[4]

Earliest evidence of this custom comes from the marginalia of a fourteenth-century Flemish illuminated manuscript: a triumphant youth holding a cockerel rides upon a rail carried by two companions, while a third marches behind with a banner. This Flemish image, along with fifteenth-century references to Shrovetide 'victors' and 'kings' in the records of Merton College, Oxford, and several abbeys in Normandy, suggests that the tradition was found throughout late medieval north-western Europe. Certainly by the early Tudor period, it was sufficiently popular in English grammar schools for new humanist foundations in London and Manchester to ban the custom; their statutes declaring scholars should have 'no cokfeyghtes nor […] Ryddynge aboute for victorys or other disports had in thyis parties'.[5]

Cockfighting's popularity went beyond the schoolhouse, however, with Shrovetide matches sponsored by royals, nobles, gentry, and civic corporations during the medieval and early modern periods.[6] Evidently, these adult matches could finish with a flourish as well. In his Jacobean treatise on cockfighting, George Wilson wrote how, after his own bird 'Noble Jipsey' emerged victorious in a tournament at Bury St Edmunds, he marched throughout the town with waits, soldiers, and a banner.⁷ While such pageantry was probably found in many cities and towns during the early modern period, schools certainly preserved it the longest. Old grammar schools of the north and southwest maintained the privileges of cockfighting 'victors' and their processions into the eighteenth and early nineteenth centuries, while ridings were still taking place across the border in Scotland as late as the mid-nineteenth century.⁸ There, the victor was made 'king' or 'captain' of the school, and often led a 'grand procession through the town'.⁹ It is in Scotland where we also get some contemporary rationales for Shrovetide cockfighting in schools, and why the tradition was so tenaciously maintained. Edinburgh schoolmaster Robert Blau, writing an oration on the subject in 1696, explained that the privileges conveyed to youths through 'such shows' begat 'in young Students, great Spirits', driving them on 'a vigorous prosecution of Learning, or to military Bravery'.¹⁰

The militaristic spirit implicit in Shrovetide cockfights was made far more tangible in the festival's sports of mass participation. Shrovetide ball games – football and handball – were particularly common and once contested in scores if not hundreds of communities throughout England. Documented from the twelfth century forward, with around a dozen modern survivals, these football matches often pitted communities or subcommunities against one another, with reconciliatory libations shared afterwards. At times involving hordes of participants fighting to advance a ball through streets and across fields, games could come breathtakingly close to an actual battle in their severity and scale.¹¹ But as with cockfighting, a degree of pageantry and ceremony could circumscribe the violence, sometimes in the form of a pregame procession.

One of the oldest and most detailed examples of the latter comes from early Tudor Chester. Every Shrove Tuesday in the early decades of the sixteenth century, a procession snaked its way out of the city to a common field. The Cordwainer Company processed with a football, the Saddler Company with a wooden ball, and every freeman married since the last Shrove Tuesday with a small silk ball. These were all presented to the Merchant Drapers Company, who, under supervision of the mayor, tossed up the balls (which doubled as prizes) for the assembled craftsmen to contest. After 1540, these rough games were reformed into more controllable foot races, horse races, and archery competitions. But the pregame processions remained and were even elaborated, facilitating the Shrovetide sports until the early eighteenth century.¹² These processions ceremonially and practically enabled the sports which followed them, with two distinct groups – craftsmen (i.e. cordwainers and saddlers) and newlyweds – bearing the responsibility of collecting and presenting the necessary balls, prizes, or money to furnish either.

Although precise details varied with locality and time, certain elements of Chester's processions – the enabling function and the central roles played by craftsmen and newlyweds – would recur in other Shrovetide sport processions down through the centuries. From the fifteenth century until the beginning of the seventeenth, for example, the newly married freemen of English-controlled Dublin mounted on horseback every Shrove Tuesday and led their respective craft guilds through the streets. Marching to the sound of trumpets, each newlywed was required to 'bear a ball' to present to the city magistrates.¹³ Centuries later, in nineteenth-century Dorking, Surrey, 'certain grotesquely dressed individuals paraded the streets and suburbs of the town to the sounds of banjo, fife, and drum' prior to the football game on Shrove Tuesday. They collected 'contributions in aid of the expenses and carousal', and bore a 'pole, upon which were placed three large footballs' (Figure 2.1).¹⁴ Similarly in late eighteenth- and early nineteenth-century Alnwick, Northumberland – where a Shrove Tuesday procession and game still survives, albeit much changed – football teams divided

Performing calendrical pressures

Figure 2.1 The band and other processors carrying the footballs aloft before the Shrove Tuesday match in Dorking (1885)

Source: Photograph courtesy of Dorking Museum.

between married and bachelor freemen would march 'from the Townhall, preceded by the band of the Northumberland Militia, and the flags of the Skinners' and Shoemakers' companies'. At the front of the procession was borne aloft a 'circular wreath of laurel, circumscribing a golden ball'.[15]

The drums, fifes, trumpets, and banners of these processions underscore once again the bellicose spirit of Shrovetide. And just as the pageantry of schoolboy cockfights suggests Shrovetide's deep connection to youth, the centrality of craftsmen and newlyweds in football processions implies its close link to work and marriage, respectively. Such themes – work, war, marriage, youth – probably coalesced around Shrovetide during the medieval period due to a mix of material, religious, and social pressures. The relationship between the festival and workers will be explored more thoroughly below, but the warfare connection might be explained as follows. For a warrior society like medieval England, Shrovetide inhabited a transitional period between the winter off-season of training and wargames (i.e. tournaments and football), and the spring recommencement of actual war campaigns. Carnival also represented a last chance for organized violence, since the church technically banned the latter during the fasting season, albeit with limited success.[16]

Likewise, the church's prohibitions on sex and marriage during Advent and Lent may help explain the Shrovetide emphasis on marriage and children. Demographic data from post-Reformation parish registers suggests that such prohibitions were largely adhered to in premodern England, shaping the one- to two-month period between Advent and Lent into an intense social season of coupling, nuptials, and conceptions which climaxed upon Shrove Tuesday. Reinforcing the childhood connection, February and March were also co-incidentally the peak months for births, coming nine months after a different season of love (May/June). As *Poor Robin's Almanac* forecast for the days before Shrovetide in 1674, it was 'roast meat weather where there is marriages and Christenings'.[17] We must thus imagine the performative celebrations which came with such a packed season of life-cycle ceremonies, and how these would have coloured and moulded the traditions of Shrovetide and the more extended Carnival period over time.

One such performance was the wedding procession. A key feature of traditional marriage celebrations in premodern Europe, it was an appropriately jovial method of moving the bridal party from house to church, and back again for the post-nuptial feast and entertainment.[18]

Diarist Henry Machyn describes some especially sumptuous wedding processions in Tudor London, where parties left the church, 'going home to dinner, the trumpets blowing, and after, the flute and drum'.[19] While Machyn focused upon the marriage revelries of the capital's upper classes, humbler folk laid claim to the nuptial procession as well. Indeed, it is among these sorts that the 'big wedding' and its composite parts of public processions and communal participation survived the longest in England, particularly in more rural and remote regions like the north.[20] Here, Shrovetide traditions of marriage and sport met in a folk encounter custom, witnessing the quite literal collision of wedding party processions with communal demands for football and other entertainment. Known as 'ball-money', Victorian MP and antiquarian Egerton Leigh defined the Cheshire version as follows:

> Largesse demanded from a wedding party to obtain which (particularly if the bridegroom is known as a stingy man) a rope is sometimes drawn across the road. It was so called because formerly the money was supposed to go towards the football fund of the parish.[21]

Evidence for this marriage custom spans the British Isles, from the thirteenth century onwards, with vestigial forms surviving today in traditional 'wedding scrambles' for coins in Yorkshire and Scotland (Figure 2.2).[22] While ball-money could be collected at any wedding throughout the year, the custom was strongly associated with winter and Shrove Tuesday, when (as described above) institutions in Chester, Dublin and elsewhere collected a year's worth of marriage dues. According to Georgian antiquarian John Brand, such football dues 'admitted of no refusal', and indeed the repercussions for a 'stingy' bridegroom could be dire.[23] In its exacting nature, and in its pairing of communal entertainment and regulation of the household, ball-money belonged to a larger family of premodern European customs called 'rough music'.

At its simplest, rough music was noise-making – clanging pots and pans, drumming, raucous singing, whooping, and hollering – aimed at publicizing and addressing social transgressions and/or social obligations within a community. Using a typology developed by medievalist and folklorist Tom Pettitt, the custom can be further divided into two broad

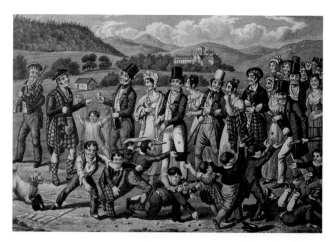

Figure 2.2 Scottish wedding procession with ball-money or ba' siller collection in the fore
Source: Engraving by J. Gleadah, 'Plate 2, Meeting the First Foot', in John Grant, ed., *The Penny Wedding* (London, 1836), Plate 2. National Library of Scotland. CC BY 4.0.

categories, based on target and occasion. *Nuptial rough music* was performed at and because of weddings between mismatched couples (e.g. old-young, widow-bachelor), though in some places all newlyweds were subject to it in a less castigatory manner. Usually, the performers could be bought off with money, fare, or entertainment. *Marital rough music* was not performed at weddings, but in response to specific domestic or sexual transgressions in established households (e.g. adultery, scolding, wife-beating, sodomy). Rarely could these performers be bought off.[24]

As Pettit and other scholars have noted, there is very little evidence of nuptial rough music in medieval or early modern Britain (although ball-money exactions may have been an equivalent or adjacent custom). Marital rough music, however, is well attested across England from the early modern period with particular regional names and forms such as 'riding the stang' in the north and 'riding skimmington' in the southwest.[25] Most 'ridings' involved a procession through town of masked and cross-dressing noisemakers. At its centre was the offender (or some proxy representing them and their social crime) mounted on a pole or backwards on a horse (see front cover). Although usually occasional, arising in direct response to a specific offence, many early modern ridings were performed during festive seasons, Shrovetide being particularly popular. One early and prototypical example comes from an entry in Londoner Henry Machyn's diary, dated to Shrove Monday 1563:

> At Charing Cross there was a man carried by four men, and before him a bagpipe playing, a shawm, and a drum playing. And a twenty links [torches] burning about him because his next neighbor's wife did beat her husband. Therefore it ordered that his next neighbor shall ride about the place.[26]

Scholars have long linked marital rough music like this to Carnival, based on shared performance forms (e.g. masked parades) and similar topsy-turvy symbolism.[27] Yet the connection probably ran deeper than comparable aesthetics and social inversion, or even the free time which all festivals afforded. As we have seen, calendrical pressures shaped Shrovetide and the larger Carnival period into a celebration of household formation, with a focus on marriage and weddings. In the shadow of the penitential Lenten season, it was an ideal time to regulate that household and its normative marital values, using militant performances which mimicked and inverted the classic wedding procession.

Evidence from the nineteenth century suggests that this close relationship between marriage, Shrovetide, and rough music left lasting impressions upon folk performance in some regions, especially the north. In the Lancashire town of Ashton-under-Lyne, for example, inhabitants used Shrove Tuesday as the annual occasion to ritually shame unfaithful spouses.[28] Elsewhere, the act of 'riding the stang' was appropriated into Shrove Tuesday customs which were more light-hearted in their castigation. Villagers in Middleton outside Lancaster, for example, 'stanged' the last person to finish their pancakes on Shrove Tuesday, placing them on a pole to be 'carried by others to middin and there deposited, amid the laughter and jokes of all present'. In Cheshire and Derbyshire, it was the Shrove Tuesday bed-churl (last out of bed) who was stanged to the ash-midden, while in Peak District mining communities, the last one to work was 'balanced upon a pole and tipped down an adjacent hillock'.[29]

During the seventeenth century, aspects of rough music and ridings were also incorporated into a Shrovetide custom far more violent: rioting. Over the course of the century, this developed into an annual tradition, as more than 60 Shrove Tuesday riots occurred or were threatened in cities and towns throughout the kingdom. Most of these took place in early Stuart London, where crowds composed principally of craftsmen, servants, and apprentices attacked a variety of targets, including brothels, playhouses, prisons, and magistrates. The riots often featured the ringing of barber's basins – rough music traditionally employed when carting bawds and prostitutes out of a city – and in one extreme case in Bristol, rioters carried a bawd through the city on a pole after burning her brothel to the ground.[30]

Despite these rough music elements, the riots were more about plebeian appropriations of power and control of the streets than they were about moral policing. Such claims were signalled through quasi-militaristic processions and pitched street-battles against the authorities who came to stop them. Shrove Tuesday crowds marched to the beat of barber's basins, carrying torches, weapons, and makeshift flags of aprons or cleaning rags fixed to broom-handles.[31] While the actors were usually young and male, anyone could harness the militant custom for their purposes. One Shrove Tuesday during the 1640s, for instance, all the women in the town of Preston went 'marching after a drumme, with several weapons against the excize men'.[32]

After the seventeenth century, rioting against buildings and authorities faded as a distinct Shrovetide tradition (i.e. one regularly repeated); yet, militaristic displays continued to be a feature of the festival in many towns and cities. We have already seen this in the sport processions discussed above, but some communities bypassed the pretences of cockfighting and football entirely, holding annual Shrovetide brawls instead. In 1723, for example, the *Gloucester Journal* reported on a Shrove Tuesday tradition in Bristol where 'the blacksmiths of the city assembled in a body in St. Thomas Street, in order to engage their annual combatants, the coopers, carpenters, and sailors there'. Like many football matches, the battle seems to have been preceded with a procession, as a Bristol newspaper would report in 1757:

> Tuesday last, being Shrove Tuesday, the apprentices of coopers and ship-carpenters, with their respective colours and ensigns, made the usual procession through the streets. In the evening, happening to meet on the Quay, and contending for the upper hand, a fight ensued, in which several were wounded [...][33]

The Bristol fights and processions highlight once again certain themes underlying Shrovetide processions, with identities based upon work and youth (e.g. craftsmen and apprentices) expressed through warlike displays.

More general conclusions can be drawn from looking at Shrovetide processions as a whole. Firstly, most could be termed *auxiliary* entertainments rather than focal ones: though they could be spectacular, they were not the main event. Instead, they facilitated the main event (e.g. football processions), celebrated its results (e.g. riding about in victory), or provided a link between more important aspects (e.g. wedding processions). Even Shrovetide rough music ridings and militaristic processions were not performed for the sake of it, but to achieve some other end. This is the overriding difference between English Carnival street pageantry and its counterparts elsewhere in Europe and the Americas, where processions themselves often became the principal attraction (i.e. parades).

Secondly, Shrovetide processions performed the very calendrical pressures which fashioned them, reflected in themes such as childhood/youth, war, work, and marriage. Though diverse and in some ways discordant, these themes fit together coherently when Shrovetide is conceptualized as a festival of the premodern household. More so than at any other festival, Shrovetide performances and their participants emphasized the household's formation (weddings, newlyweds), its biological production (baptisms, children), economic production (servants, apprentices, craftsmen), and even its position as a military and policing unit (warlike displays, communal regulation). Yet the continued social cohesion of the premodern household was in many ways dependent on another fundamental theme of Shrovetide which

Performing calendrical pressures

still needs to be discussed: food and feasting. The next section explores this theme of food and the social relations it underpinned at Shrovetide, examining a perambulatory form of street pageantry, and its development in response to historical change and the distinct calendrical pressures of this 'holiday of the household'.

Shrovetide begging perambulations: a case study

Like many festivals in the traditional English calendar, Shrovetide developed into an occasion for perambulatory begging customs, when groups went house to house asking for food or other gifts, usually in exchange for some kind of performance. Such Shrovetide house-visits have been documented in well over a hundred communities scattered across much of England and Wales (Figure 2.3), dating largely from the nineteenth and early twentieth

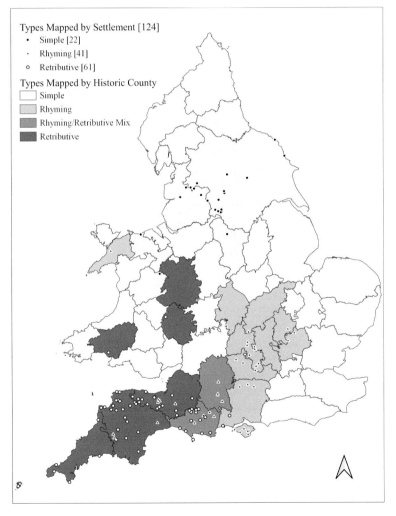

Figure 2.3 Types of Shrovetide Perambulatory House-Visits in England and Wales. Mapped by Settlement and Historic County

Source: Mapping and copyright the author.

centuries. Coming in a dizzying array of regional forms and local names, which also changed over time, these begging perambulations can nonetheless be simplified into three main types, based on the presence and/or absence of certain ritual elements.[34]

Retributive house-visits constitute the first type, where vandalism, housebreaking, or the threat of some other mischief formed a key part of the ritual. This type was most commonly found in southwest England, South Wales, and the Welsh Marches, and although it came in many forms, the central idea was for groups of children or adults to visit houses on Shrove Monday and/or Tuesday, demand pancakes or other fare (usually in verse), and seek destructive retribution if denied. On Shrove Tuesday nights in Victorian Polperro, for example, roving Cornish boys threatened the following:

> Nicky nicky nan,
> Give me some pancake,
> and then I'll be gone.
> But if you give me none
> I'll throw a great stone,
> And down your door shall come.[35]

Spurned visitors made good on their doggerel threat with a broadside of stones or other missiles. Broken pieces of pans or crockery were a less destructive and widely used alternative, resulting in names for the custom and its occasion like Lent-crocking, Lensherding, Pansherd Day, Dappy-door Night, or Sharp Tuesday.[36] This terminology was sometimes incorporated directly into the verses, as in the Devon village of Bridestowe during the 1850s, when children went door-to-door with the following rhyme:

> Lent Crock, give a pancake,
> Or a fritter, for my labour,
> Or a dish of flour, or a piece of bread,
> Or what you please to render.
> I see by the latch,
> There's something to catch;
> I see by the string,
> There's a good dame within.
> Trap, trapping throw,
> Give me my mumps, and I'll be go.[37]

Not all were so longwinded in their poesy, and in fact, concise couplets and singular stanzas characterized most retributive Shrovetide house-visits. In 1865, the lads of Christow, outside Exeter, provided an illustratively blunt example:

> Pancakes and puffins
> a very good store,
> If you don't give me some,
> I'll throw shords at your door.[38]

There were many variations on this basic theme, and in some places the begging element became secondary to the mischief or faded away entirely. In addition to the standard throwing of sherds or stones, perambulating troublemakers might knock upon doors with clubs or sticks, or leave stones tied to them so that they clattered when closed.[39] Cornish boys attempted to take important items from negligent householders, while children in West Somerset and across the Bristol Channel in Carmarthenshire tried to deposit broken crockery or other rubbish inside households without getting caught.[40]

In some villages, gathering pots and pans for ammunition became part of the Shrove Tuesday perambulation, and at the turn of the twentieth century, youths in Kidwelly (Carmarthenshire) and the coastal town of Clovelly (North Devon) made as much noise as possible on the night by 'kicking [...] old tin cans and other utensils along the streets'.[41] In Clovelly, the custom became known as 'tin-canning', and it is the last vestige of Shrovetide retributive house-visits known to survive today.[42] Elsewhere, communal and official tolerance for these abrasive customs steadily declined over the nineteenth and early twentieth centuries so that by the Second World War, they lingered only in the most remote West Country communities.[43]

Rhyming house-visits – the second type – survived far longer, undoubtedly because they were characterized by an *absence* of retribution as well as an invariable presence of rhyming verse. This type brushed shoulders with Lent-crocking in the West Country and predominated in a corridor of small communities from the Isle of Wight up to the southern reaches of Warwickshire and Northampton, and east into Bedfordshire and Hertfordshire. Curiously, customs fitting this description were also found as far afield as Caernarfonshire in North Wales.[44]

In Wales and England, Shrovetide rhyming house-visits often featured lengthier and more complex verses than those found in retributive perambulations. They usually incorporated standard lines, stanzas, and conventions, like lists of desired foods, requests for treats to be homemade, and repetitions of the word 'shroving' – the most common name for the custom. While they could vary greatly in their composition, even within one county, shroving verses largely clustered along regional lines. The following song from late nineteenth-century Freshwater was prototypical of the Isle of Wight:

> Shroven, Shroven, we be come a shroven.
> A piece o' bread and a piece o' cheese,
> And a piece o' your fat bacon;
> White bread and apple pie,
> My mouth is very dry.
> I wish I were so well a-wet,
> To sing en better for a dough-nut.
> Dough-nuts and pancakes,
> All of your own ma-aken.[45]

Verses in northern Hampshire and southern Berkshire were of comparable length and content, but usually started with the line, 'Knick a knock upon the block'. Farther north in Oxfordshire and Buckinghamshire, the standard first line was 'Pit-a-pat! the pan's hot!'.[46]

Those rhyming house-visits found in Somerset and Devon often featured shorter verses and went by different names than their shroving counterparts, like 'tip-toeing', 'dummering', and 'dimmering'. The latter, observed in Cothelstone (Somerset) during the early twentieth century, employed the following:

> Dimmery, dimmery, dinky doe,
> Give me a pancake, then I'll go
> So up with the kettle and down with the pan
> Please put a pancake in my hand.[47]

Shorter still was the doggerel heard in Illmington, Warwickshire:

> Linket lanket,
> Give us a panket.

Unusually, adults collected the pancakes in this village, after tolling the Pancake Bell.[48] Elsewhere, it was invariably children who conducted rhyming house-visits, sometimes in association with the local school. As will be explored more below, such institutional support may explain the comparative longevity this type enjoyed, surviving in some counties into the late twentieth century, and to this day in at least two places, East Hendred (Berkshire) and Durweston (Dorset).[49]

Simple house-visits represent the third and final entry in this typology of Shrovetide begging perambulations, characterized by requests for food, ingredients, or money which were otherwise devoid of elaborate rituals like verses or retribution. Documented mostly in the Victorian and Edwardian periods, customs of this type were found in North Wales and Northern England and can be further categorized according to occasion, region, and desired gift.

Colloping took place on Shrove (or Collop) Monday in small villages clustered around the border between Lancashire and Yorkshire, and in moorland communities around Whitby and Scarborough in the North Riding. Named after the cuts of meat eaten upon the day, children and adults went house to house, asking, 'Pray Dame, a collop, or else a Copper John?'.[50] Collopers used the leftover bacon grease from their collections to make pancakes on the morrow, but further west into Lancashire, in Chipping and the hinterlands of Preston, 'pancaking' customs negated the need for such ingredients. On Shrove Tuesday, children perambulated during the day and older youths at night, with cries of 'Pancake, please!' at each house.[51] In the northeast, near Whitby and in County Durham, the poor spent both Collop Monday and Shrove Tuesday begging, not only for collops, but for flour and milk as well.[52] House-visitors similarly collected pancake ingredients in rural Wales, where the custom was called *blawta a blonega* (lard and flour). Pursued generally by children and the poor on Shrove Tuesday, it was recorded in Anglesey, Denbighshire, and Montgomeryshire.[53]

If simplicity was the distinguishing feature of colloping, pancaking, and *blawta a blonega*, it may also explain why these customs were less well documented than more dynamic forms like Lent-crocking and shroving. Only rarely did collopers employ anything approaching the rhyming couplets or stanzas found in the south. Whitby perambulators might muster a 'Pray you missus, can you give me any aumus? [alms]', while the most sophisticated colloping slogan was recorded in 1896:

> To-day is Collop Monday
> Gie's a collop, an' let's away.[54]

Still, there are tantalizing hints that colloping was not always so simple. According to an 1861 column in the *Preston Chronicle* – the oldest record we have of the custom – adult collopers on the Yorkshire side of the border formerly blackened their faces with soot, dressed in 'ragged unseemly clothes', and otherwise disguised themselves.[55] By the turn of the twentieth century, however, little evidence remained of fancy dress or other intricacies as social changes began to take their toll on the few surviving iterations. Welsh *blawta a blonega* customs were last recorded in Anglesey just prior to the First World War, while colloping lingered until the second in a few Yorkshire settlements in the northern foothills of the Peak District.[56]

Viewed together, the distributions and timelines of these diverse Shrovetide begging perambulations suggest much about their origins, development, and relations to one other, as well as the calendrical pressures underpinning all the above. At first glance, for example, the distance and difference in form between northern colloping and pancaking, and southern shroving and crocking, implies such traditions developed separately. Evidence from Wales and the Welsh Marches, however, complicates this assumption, since all three basic types of begging custom (retributive, rhyming, simple) were in evidence in the region during the nineteenth century. *Blawta a blonega* bears striking resemblance to Shrovetide ingredient gathering in the north, while Lent-crockers in Shropshire shared Shrove Tuesday rhyming couplets with the village of Illmington in Warwickshire, at the north-western fringes of the shroving region.[57] All this may suggest that there was once a much wider contiguous spread of Shrovetide begging customs across England and Wales – perhaps with a common simple form – and that over time they diverged, developed, and died out in different ways. While the scant evidence from North Wales and the Welsh Marches makes this a difficult theory to test, the more robust documentation for the southwest sheds further light. Specifically, a handful of examples from the late seventeenth and early eighteenth centuries offer valuable insight into how these begging customs may have emerged.

The oldest evidence we have pointing to such Shrovetide perambulations is a deposition from the Somerset quarter sessions of 1653, detailing misdemeanours in Bruton. Thomas Gill, a sieve-maker from the latter town, confessed that on 'Tuesday night last beinge Shroue Tuesday', he and four companions 'did throwe many great stones att many doores'. His testimony further implies that there were other, separate groups throwing stones at doors that night as well.[58] Regarded in isolation, this episode does not necessarily suggest a begging custom, but it does suggest a retributive perambulation of the kind so well attested in Somerset at a later date. The next oldest example, however, contains nearly all the familiar elements.

In February 1725, the Oxford antiquarian Thomas Hearne wrote in his diary of a custom in the nearby village of Sunningwell, Berkshire which he supposed 'was formerly in other Places' too. Every Shrove Tuesday at dusk, the boys and girls went about the village saying these verses:

> Beef and Bacon's out of Season
> I want a Pan to parch my Peas on

After repeating the rhymes several times, they then threw 'Stones at all people's doors', prompting the villagers 'generally to shut up their doors that Evening'.[59] While Hearne does not explicitly mention any doles, the verses seem to request essential kitchen implements, perhaps presaging the collection of pots and pans in later retributive examples.

Demands for food were more explicitly described in the final piece of early modern evidence, from mathematician and army officer Robert Health's observations of Cornwall and the Scilly Isles in the 1740s:

> On a Shrove Tuesday each year […] the boys of this island have a custom of throwing stones in the evening against the doors of the dwelling houses […] The terms demanded by the boys are pancakes or money to capitulate.[60]

Together, these accounts from Cornwall, Somerset, and Berkshire provide strong evidence that Shrovetide begging perambulations existed in a recognizable form as early as the late seventeenth century. More specifically, the Bruton incident suggests that adults were once heavily involved, and that it was not solely beggars or young men who participated: Thomas Gill was a craftsman and his group included a father and son duo. Yet the examples from Sunningwell and the Scilly Isles also put paid to any notions that Shrovetide begging unilaterally 'de-evolved' from an adult custom to one for children during the nineteenth century. In these two places at least, children were clearly in full command of the custom from a much earlier period. Most striking, however, is the strong coercive element, backed up by stone-throwing, in all three examples. The uniform presence of this violent act from such an early date, and across almost the entire breadth of both retributive and rhyming territories (Cornwall, Somerset, the Berkshire-Oxfordshire border) is quite significant. It implies that in the south at least, retributive perambulations likely represent the older type of Shrovetide begging custom. Moreover, it suggests that stone-throwing was once the common retribution, and that the regional forms of Lent-crocking or shroving may actually represent later divergent developments from this 'ur-custom', rather than two separate traditions of distinct origins.

Analysis of the history and regional distribution of Lent-crocking and shroving in the nineteenth and twentieth centuries generally supports these hypotheses, showing a gradual shift from retributive stone-throwing, to either (slightly) less offensive crockery throwing and/or benign rhyming. During the eighteenth and early nineteenth centuries, retributive types were found in what would later be the heartland of shroving territory (Berkshire and Hampshire), but were largely gone or replaced with rhyming types by the end of the Victorian Age. For example, in the Berkshire village of Sunningwell, stone-throwing was still present in 1878, but the old verses of 1725 had been changed to standard shroving ones.[61] Likewise, rhyming perambulations appeared in communities deep within Lent-crocking territory (Somerset and Devon), but only from the late nineteenth and early twentieth centuries, as retributive customs began to fade in the region. In Gittisham (Devon), for instance, 'tip-toeing' replaced older forms of 'Lensharding' in the village.[62] All this implies a long-term and widespread retributive-to-rhyming transition across most of the southern distribution.

Although all seasonal begging customs contain an element of social coercion, and some an element of mischief or menace, Shrovetide house-visits seem to have been exceptional in the intensity and persistence of retributive violence displayed over the centuries.[63] They also stood apart from other contemporary seasonal house-visits in additional ways, like the relatively little that perambulators offered in exchange for their gifts. The ritual performances or entertainments which gave house-visits an air of legitimacy, transforming simple begging into (nominally) even exchanges, existed on a spectrum of complexity. This ranged downwards from folk plays, to comedic fancy dress and music, sophisticated songs, and, most ubiquitously, rhymed verses.[64] Shrovetide begging certainly fell at the latter end, implying demand rather than exchange. Northern collopers, for example, offered essentially nothing in return for their gifts, while southern shroving verses were not exactly the height of entertainment. Yet despite their simplicity, Shrovetide verses were generally more varied than the standard rhymes found at other seasonal house-visits. Still more remarkable is that Shrovetide begging perambulations can be traced back with some confidence to the late seventeenth century, while most other seasonal doling customs cannot be reliably dated before the mid-eighteenth. This early modern context, and the medieval one preceding it, may hold clues to the formation of the customs and the distinguishing features of their performance.

While there is no known evidence of such Shrovetide house-visits prior to the 1650s in England, comparable Carnival begging customs involving children and youths were recorded in some German-speaking villages and Low Country towns during the fifteenth and sixteenth centuries.[65] During those same two centuries, similar perambulatory visits also took place in England at other seasons, like hoggling at Christmastide, or plough-light collections on Plough Monday.[66] Shrovetide house-visitors thus would not have been out of place in the medieval period, but their existence remains speculative. Less speculative is the widespread culture of Shrovetide gift-giving, particularly food-giving, which existed in medieval and early modern England.

From the mid-thirteenth century onwards, the accounts of various manors, elite households, monasteries, schools, and civic institutions record gift-giving at Shrovetide, almost invariably to children or stipendiary workers (i.e. those on long-term contracts). The late thirteenth-century Cistercian monks of Beaulieu Abbey in the New Forest of Hampshire, for example, gave all their estate workers pancakes on Shrove Tuesday, with the youngest among them getting a grand feast in the abbey's lay infirmary. In the fourteenth century, the noble lords of Sherbourne manor in Dorset likewise granted their ploughmen dishes of meat on the same day, while the fifteenth-century staff of London Bridgehouse got a Shrove Tuesday 'drinking' each year. To these examples can be added the aforementioned giving of cockerels to children for entertainment and eventual consumption in many medieval grammar schools and individual households.[67] The most common beneficiaries of Shrovetide generosity were thus the lower orders of the economic and familial household, reflecting again the centrality of that institution to the festival.

This pattern of giving also set the season apart from others like Christmastide, Eastertide, or harvest time, when gifts were more universally distributed among the various orders and classes of medieval society. Gervase of Tilbury, writing in the early thirteenth century, explained that during 'so great a feast' as Shrove Tuesday, a good lord should be 'careful to provide well for his household' and guests with 'rich fare'. For with winter stores of meat and grain depleted, 'the circumstances of the season' made Shrovetide a test of good hospitality and household management: it epitomized generosity during a time of privation.[68] With Lent looming, religious pressures also complemented the material ones. As the Augustinian canon John Mirk expounded in a late fourteenth-century homily, Shrovetide was a season for 'full charite wythout feynyng', which he likened to the biblical jubilee, when 'all men and woymen that wern sette wyth seruice and bondage [...] wern made fre in gret joy and murth'.[69] In this way, medieval economic and religious pressures structured Shrovetide into an intense season of social privilege for some, with householders granting food gifts and general liberty to those below them, theoretically in return for continued household cohesion, and perhaps spiritual benefit. This festive social contract was still embraced at the end of the Tudor period, in both rural and urban contexts.[70]

By the seventeenth century, however, rips were beginning to appear in the Shrovetide social contract, as social, economic, and religious changes took their toll on traditions of hospitality, generosity, and charity. The Reformation had already seen a break between salvation and good works, and the dissolution of a medieval welfare system underpinned by monasteries. In the century and a half which followed, there were other erosions: reformers of manners took aim at seasonal customs and privileges now deemed unruly, gentry increasingly spent their winters in London, elite retinues shrank, the great household became less cohesive and more divided between servants and masters, and economic dearth proceeded apace with huge growth in both population and the proportion of labouring, landless poor.[71] In this context, moralists perceived a lost world of good lordship and seasonal generosity, so that in 1683 *Poor Robin's Almanac* ranted how 'harmless mirth, and good housekeeping' at Shrovetide had been 'laid aside | and all to maintain dam'd pride'.[72]

If Shrovetide privileges were indeed under threat, not all gave them up willingly, as we have already seen in the riots of Stuart London. There, new Elizabethan precepts ordering householders to keep servants, apprentices, students, and themselves inside during Shrovetide eventually led to Jacobean pitched battles with constables and billmen, and Caroline bouts with trained bands of militia, as the plebeian crowd effectively defended its age-old claim to the streets during the holiday.[73] It is possible that Shrovetide house-visits either emerged or evolved from a pre-existing form, in a similar manner to the riots: replacing a traditional privilege once freely and happily given with a perceived right violently demanded and defended. Certainly, the core difference between Shrovetide food-giving in medieval and Tudor England, and later Shrovetide begging customs suggests such a shift. The former was embraced and administered on an institutional level, while the latter was not, or at least not in its early retributive form. This follows a broader historical pattern whereby many medieval seasonal collection customs incorporated directly into parish, civic, or manorial institutional practice lost support in the sixteenth and seventeenth centuries, only for begging customs to surface at those same seasons in the eighteenth century.[74]

That Shrovetide house-visits arose out of such a breakdown in medieval and early modern institutionalized practices receives more direct support from the close alignment between their respective regional distributions. More precisely, the medieval schools and manorial estates where Shrovetide food-giving traditions were recorded largely correspond to areas where shroving and Lent-crocking later arose.[75] It is particularly striking, for example, to find nineteenth-century shrovers 'begging for meat and drink at the farm-houses' and throwing 'stones and shards at the door' in the New Forest, where Cistercian monks once rewarded their young farm-hands with Shrovetide pancakes and feasts centuries earlier. Or to find Thomas Gill and his companions perambulating in Bruton, the location of a medieval Augustinian priory that administered Shrovetide gifts to its manors in the fourteenth century.[76]

While these links remain correlative rather than conclusive, the weight of evidence points to a seventeenth-century swing from positive donations, to negative exactions replete with rituals which actively performed and enforced the old Shrovetide social contract. Indeed, those rituals of enforcement may have been directly influenced by other early modern Shrovetide customs like rioting and rough music. Rioters in Stuart London, for example, used stones as their preferred weapons against magistrates and buildings, while rough music was made with the pots and pans that became so central to later Lent-crocking customs.[77] Suggestively, all three customs – retributive perambulations, rough music, and rioting – were found together on that busy Shrove Tuesday night in 1653 Bruton: Thomas Gill, while going door-to-door, witnessed 'ffiue men with visages [masks] and beatinge a brasse pan [go] vp and downe the Streetes' and crowds of 'great multitudes' which 'ouerthrew one another'.[78]

Whatever their impact upon the development of Shrovetide begging customs during the early modern period, the themes and pressures underlying and reflecting in Shrovetide rough music and riots were certainly visible in the retributive house-visits of the nineteenth century. Communal regulation of the household, for example, was on display in places like North Devon, where it was said that Lent-crockers targeted those who 'had rendered themselves obnoxious to the neighbourhood during the past year'. More broadly across all Shrovetide retributive house-visits, it was those stingy households 'not open to hospitality' which faced retaliation.[79] In places or instances where stone-throwing, crocking, or noise-making happened without pre-emptive begging, the privilege of food seems to have been waived for one of general liberty – a right to audibly own the streets and the night which echoed the Shrovetide riots of old.

It was this general sense of social privilege, originally stemming from ideas of charity, hospitality, household cohesion, and real material need, that endured longest for all types of Shrovetide house-visits, be they retributive or otherwise. From as early as the 1740s, Cornish Shrovetide house-visitors claimed that their custom was 'a privilege [...] from time immemorial', and this remained the rallying cry raised in the custom's defence as Lent-crockers were brought to court for damages during the nineteenth century.[80] But as the latter century progressed, the cry increasingly fell on deaf ears, as householders, constables, justices of the peace, and other authorities lost tolerance for a dangerous and destructive pastime. Thus, ironically, it was the violent means of defending and maintaining these privileges that eventually brought them to an end in most West Country communities.

However, as we have seen, Shrovetide performances of privilege survived longer in those communities which eschewed (or perhaps never took up) retributive perambulations in favour of rhyming ones. Schools clearly played a major role in this shift, most visible in the different responses to house-visits adopted in traditional Lent-crocking territory. In the early nineteenth century, a wily schoolmaster in Cerne, Dorset permitted the custom, but only allowed schoolboys to throw pieces of wood at the school door, which he then collected for fuel.[81] As the century progressed, newer schools founded by the National Society were less amiable to the old tradition, and in 1858 two little boys were prosecuted in the magisterial court for 'throwing dirt' and causing 'malicious injury' to the schoolrooms door in Crewkerne, Somerset.[82] By the early twentieth century, most Shrovetide begging customs still maintained in the West Country lacked retributive practices and were closely tied to the local school. In the villages of Langport (Somerset) and Gittisham (Devon), for example, children were released from the school on Shrove Tuesday to collect money. In the latter place, earnings were brought back to the schoolmistress for equal distribution among the pupils.[83]

Increased access to education for the poor during the nineteenth century undoubtedly contributed to the elimination of some retributive house-visits, or the shift to rhyming ones. Yet, as we already know from medieval and early modern traditions of cockfighting and riding about in victory, grammar schools had long distributed food, liberty, and entertainment to students during Shrovetide. And just as early modern rioting and rough music likely influenced the retributive rituals of house-visitors, there is evidence that older school traditions influenced their rhyming rituals. From the fifteenth and sixteenth centuries onwards, Shrovetide was associated in some grammar schools and colleges with the humanist composition of verses. Odes to cockfighting have been found in the records of late medieval grammar schools in Plymouth and St Albans, Tudor students at Eton (Berkshire) spent Shrove Monday composing verses 'in praise of Bacchus', and Georgian scholars of Brasenose College, Oxford wrote elegies to ale.[84] By the nineteenth century, 'setting schoolboys to write verses' was apparently a Shrovetide tradition in many grammar schools.[85]

While we can only speculate the extent to which these institutional verse compositions affected the more formulaic and static rhymes of house-visits, it is a certainty that schools, whether private or public, influenced the development and transmission of the latter to some extent. This was true of both Lent-crocking and shroving. Writing in the 1850s of Lent-crocking verses in Bridestowe (Devon), Philip Hedgeland noted an 'indigenous' version as well as one 'introduced some few years ago by a late schoolmistress, who was a native of another part of the county'.[86] Likewise, children in Berwick St James (Wiltshire) were recorded going door-to-door in 1879 with a standard shroving rhyme, and 'other songs which they have learnt at school'.[87] This central role of schools might explain the relative diversity of Shrovetide begging verses, but it also illustrates a movement of the custom back towards institutional affiliation.

Thus, the pendulum swung from antecedent official gifts freely given (prior to c.1600), to unofficial perambulatory exactions tolerated or condemned (c.1650–1850), and back to semi-official collections accepted or embraced (c.1850-present). Certainly, it is only with the sponsorship of schools and enthusiasm of broader village communities that Shrovetide perambulations have survived in the tin-canning of Clovelly, or the shroving of Durweston and East Hendred.[88] Nonetheless, in the annual calls for money and treats, or the loud racket down the streets, these modern Shrovetide perambulations preserve and perform the much older historical pressures that formed them: the material need for food, the religious imperative for charity, and the social demand for privilege conferred upon the lowest in household and society.

Together with the processions, Shrovetide perambulations show the power of the calendar and historical change in shaping traditions of folk performance. In premodern England, the different seasons and festivals of the calendar represented junctions, where various structural pressures met and exerted force upon individuals and society. Folk performance gave people an outlet to represent, reflect upon, and respond to those forces. Using the thematic elements ingrained into the season, Shrovetide folk performances brought together households, kept them united and productive, regulated their place within society, alleviated material privation, and defended festive social contracts and rights, sometimes with militant force. They were not only products of specific calendrical pressures, but tools used to shape the very same.

Notes

1 On the history of Shrovetide, see Taylor Aucoin, '"When the Pancake Bell Rings": Shrove Tuesday and the Social Efficacy of Carnival Time in Medieval and Early Modern Britain' (unpublished doctoral thesis, University of Bristol, 2019); Ronald Hutton, *The Stations of the Sun* (Oxford: Oxford University Press, 1996), pp. 151–168.
2 For examples see Aucoin, 'When the Pancake Bell Rings', pp. 8–9.
3 Aucoin, 'When the Pancake Bell Rings', ch.1; Hutton, *The Stations of the Sun*, pp. 152–154, 157–159.
4 John Aubrey, *Remaines of Gentilisme and Judaisme*, ed. by J. Britten (London: Folk-Lore Society, 1881), p. 41.
5 Bodleian Library: MS 264, fo. 89r. https://digital.bodleian.ox.ac.uk/inquire/p/784aa20a-1650-4df6-83d2-d0018d169d51; J.M. Fletcher and C.A. Upton, 'The Cost of Undergraduate Study at Oxford in the Fifteenth Century: The Evidence of the Merton College "Founder's Kin"', *History of Education*, 14.1 (1985), 8–9; John Brand, *Observations on the Popular Antiquities of Great Britain*, ed. by Henry Ellis, 2 vols. (London, 1813), I, p. 66; *Records of Early English Drama: Lancashire*, ed. by David George (Toronto, ON: University of Toronto Press), pp. 56, 325.
6 Aucoin, 'When the Pancake Bell Rings', p. 75.
7 George Wilson, *The Commendation of Cockes, and Cock-fighting* (London: Thomas Purfoot for Henrie Tomes, 1607), sig. D3v-D4r.
8 John Symonds Udal, *Dorsetshire Folk-Lore* (Hertford: Austin & Sons, 1922), pp. 139–140; *The Lakes Chronicle*, 8 March 1889, p. 5.
9 Mary Macleod Banks, *British Calendar Customs: Scotland*, 2 vols. (London: Folk-Lore Society, 1937), I, pp. 11–15, 12).
10 Robert Blau, *Praxis oratoria vel suadela victrix Containing Some Select Orations (Both in Latin and English) Introducing One Another* (Edinburgh: George Mosman, 1696), sig. D4v-chi1v.
11 Aucoin, 'When the Pancake Bell Rings', ch. 2; Hutton, *The Stations of the Sun*, pp. 154–155, 159–163.
12 Aucoin, 'When the Pancake Bell Rings', pp. 93–98, 130–138.
13 Aucoin, 'When the Pancake Bell Rings', pp. 114–120.
14 *Sussex Agricultural Express*, 28 February 1857, p. 3; *West Surrey Times*, 12 March 1859, p. 3; *West Surrey Times*, 21 February 1874, p. 6. (For a discussion of face blacking of performers as in Figure 1, refer to Harrop and Roud's 'General Introduction' as well as Harrop's 'Introduction to Part I'.)
15 Gavin Kitching '"From Time Immemorial": The Alnwick Shrovetide Football Match and the Continuous Remaking of Tradition 1828–1890', *International Journal of the History of Sport*, 28.6 (2011), 831–852, 850.
16 Aucoin, 'When the Pancake Bell Rings', pp. 168–169.
17 E.A. Wrigley and R.S. Schofield, *The Population History of England, 1541–1871: A Reconstruction* (London: Edward Arnold for the Cambridge Group for the History of Population and Social Structure, 1981), pp. 288–305; *Poor Robin's Almanac* (London: for the Company of Stationers, 1674), sig. A6r.
18 On the wedding procession and its position within premodern marriage traditions in England, see L.E. Pearson, *Elizabethans at Home* (Stanford, CA: Stanford University Press, 1957), pp. 342–345; John Gillis, *For Better, for Worse: British Marriages 1600 to the Present* (Oxford: Oxford University Press, 1985), pp. 55–83.

19 Henry Machyn, '1560 October 10', in *A London Provisioner's Chronicle, 1550–1563: Manuscript, Transcription, and Modernization*, ed. by Richard Bailey, Marilyn Miller and Colette Moore https://quod.lib.umich.edu/m/machyn/.
20 Gillis, *For Better, for Worse*, pp. 142–145.
21 Egerton Leigh, *A Glossary of Words Used in the Dialect of Cheshire* (London: Hamilton Adama, 1877), p. 12.
22 Aucoin, 'When the Pancake Bell Rings', ch. 2, esp. 138–143; Gillis, *For Better, For Worse*, p. 144.
23 These ranged from fines, levying of property, and imprisonment, to both literal and figurative mudslinging. Brand, 1813, II, p. 79; Aucoin, 'When the Pancake Bell Rings', p. 143.
24 For more on this typology and English rough music, see Thomas Pettitt, 'Towards an Anatomy of English Customary Drama: Theatre, Stage, Play', in Peter Harrop and Steve Roud eds. *The Routledge Companion to English Folk Performance* (Abingdon: Routledge, 2021), 16–43. See also, Tom Pettitt, 'Nuptial Pageantry in Medieval Culture and Folk Custom: In Quest of the English *charivari*', *Medium Ævum Quotidianum*, 52 (2005), 89–115; Martin Ingram, 'Ridings, Rough Music and the "Reform of Popular Culture" in Early Modern England', *Past and Present*, 105 (1984), 79–113; Edward P. Thompson, *Customs in Common* (London: Merlin Press, 1991), see ch. VIII, 'Rough Music'.
25 On these regional forms, see the works in the prior note, as well as entries on 'Stang', and 'Skimmington', in *English Dialect Dictionary Online 3.0*, ed. by Manfred Markus http://eddonline-proj.uibk.ac.at/edd/.
26 Henry Machyn, '1563 February 22', *A London Provisioner's Chronicle*. For additional Shrovetide 'ridings', see *Records of Early English Drama: Somerset Including Bath*, ed. by James Stokes and Robert J. Alexander, 2 vols (Toronto, ON: Toronto University Press, 1996), I, p. 62, II, pp. 637–638; *Records of Early English Drama: Herefordshire/Worcestershire*, ed. by David N. Klausner (Toronto, ON: University of Toronto Press, 1990), pp. 72, 381; Norfolk Record Office: C/S3/44/ Information of Robert Danyell 6 March 1661 (also mentioned in Ingram, 'Ridings', 99–100).
27 See, for example, Peter Burke, *Popular Culture in Early Modern Europe* (1978, rev. repr.; Farnham: Ashgate, 2009), pp. 255–286.
28 Samuel Bamford, *Passages in the Life of a Radical and Early Days*, ed. by Henry Dunckley, 2 vols. (London: Fisher Unwin, 1893), I, p. 122.
29 A.R. Wright, *British Calendar Customs*, ed. by T.E. Lones, 3 vols. (London: Folk-lore Society, 1936–40), I, 30–31.
30 Aucoin, 'When the Pancake Bell Rings', ch. 4, esp. pp. 265 (basin ringing), 273–273 (Bristol riot).
31 For historical, literary, and visual examples of these makeshift ensigns see *REED: Somerset*, I, p. 62; Aucoin, 'When the Pancake Bell Rings', pp. 255, 258.
32 Wigan Archives and Local Studies, D/D An/Bundle 67/19, Letter from Luke Hodgkinson to Hugh Anderton, c.1644.
33 John Latimer, *The Annals of Bristol in the 18th Century* (Bristol, [n.p.] 1893), p. 138.
34 Shrovetide begging perambulations have received relatively less scholarly attention than their counterparts at other seasons, but see Hutton, *The Stations of the Sun*, pp. 163–167; Peter Robson, *Calendar Customs in Nineteenth and Twentieth Century Dorset* (unpublished M.Phil thesis, University of Sheffield, 1988), pp. 182–206; Wright, *British Calendar Customs*, I, pp. 4–6, 16–20.
35 Jonathan Couch, *The History of Polperro: A Fishing Town on the South Coast of Cornwall*, ed. by Thomas Q. Couch (Truro: W. Lake, 1871), p. 152.
36 Philip Hedgeland, 'Lent Crocking', *Notes & Queries*, 1st ser., v. (1852), 77; Edward Vivian and F.W. Mathews, 'The Folk-Lore of Somerset', *Folklore*, 31.3 (1920), 239–249; *Taunton Courier, and Western Advertiser*, 26 March 1949, p. 2; John Mill Chanter, *Wanderings in North Devon*, ed. by Gratiana Chanter (Ilfracombe, 1887), p. 68; J.B.S., 'Custom on Shrove Tuesday', *Notes & Queries*, 2nd ser., v. (1858), 209.
37 Hedgeland, 'Lent Crocking', p. 77.
38 *Western Times*, 14 March 1865, p. 5.
39 Couch, *The History of Polperro*, pp. 151–152; R.L. Tongue, *Somerset Folklore* (London: The Folk-lore Society, 1965), p. 155.
40 Couch, *The History of Polperro*, pp. 151–152; Vivian and Mathews, 'The Folk-Lore of Somerset', pp. 239–240; Trefor M. Owens, *Welsh Folk Customs* (Cardiff: National Museum of Wales, 1957), pp. 76–77.

41 Owens, *Welsh Folk Customs*, pp. 77–78; T. Brown, 'Fifty-fifth Report on Folklore', *Transactions of the Devonshire Association*, 90 (1958), 245–246.
42 Averil Shepherd, 'Clovelly Lentsherd or Tin Can Night', *Calendar Customs: A Guide to British Calendar Customs and Local Traditions*, https://calendarcustoms.com/articles/clovelly-lentsherd-or-tin-can-night/ [accessed 1 May 2020].
43 Hutton, *The Stations of the Sun*, p. 167.
44 For Northampton: *Banbury Guardian*, 24 February 1927, p. 3; Warwickshire: *Warwick and Warwickshire Advertiser*, 8 February 1913, p. 4; Bedfordshire: *Bedfordshire Times and Independent*, 1 March 1940, p. 5; Owens, 1957, p. 74. For the rest of the distribution, see Hutton, *The Stations of the Sun*, pp. 163–164.
45 *Sporting Times*, 7 March 1903, p. 10.
46 Avon Lea, 'Hampshire Folk Lore, Shrove Tuesday', *Notes & Queries*, 1st series, 12 (August 11 1855), 100; Percy Manning, 'Stray Notes on Oxfordshire Folklore', *Folklore*, 14.2 (1903), 167–177.
47 R.P. Chope, 'Devonshire Calendar Customs 1: Moveable Festivals', *Transactions of the Devonshire Association*, 68 (1936), 237; Tongue, *Somerset Folklore*, pp. 156–157.
48 *Warwick and Warwickshire Advertiser*, 1913, p. 4.
49 Averil Shepherd, 'East Hendred Shroving', *Calendar Customs*, https://calendarcustoms.com/articles/east-hendred-shroving/ [accessed 1 May 2020]; Averil Shepherd, 'Durweston Shroving', *Calendar Customs*, https://calendarcustoms.com/articles/durweston-shroving/ [accessed 1 May 2020].
50 *Preston Chronicle*, 23 February 1861, p. 3; *County Folklore Volume 2: North Riding of Yorkshire, York and the Ainsty*, ed. by Mrs. Gutch (London: The Folk-lore Society, 1901), pp. 237–238; *Leeds Mercury*, 18 February 1939, p. 6; *Yorkshire Evening Post*, 13 February 1926, p. 6.
51 *Lancashire Evening Post*, 4 November 1943, p. 2; *Lancashire Evening Post*, 16 February 1926, p. 2.
52 William Brockie, *Legends and Superstitions of the County of Durham* (Sunderland: B. Williams, 1886), pp. 95–96.
53 Owens, *Welsh Folk Customs*, pp. 73–75; *North Wales Times*, 16 February 1907, p. 7.
54 *County Folklore*, 1901, p. 238; *York Herald*, 29 February 1896, p. 12.
55 *Preston Chronicle*, 1861, p. 3.
56 Owens, *Welsh Folk Customs*, pp. 74–75; *Yorkshire Post and Leeds Intelligencer*, 9 February 1932, p. 3.
57 *Warwick and Warwickshire Advertiser*, 1913, p. 4; *Western Morning News*, 8 March 1938, p. 3.
58 *REED: Somerset*, II, pp. 637–638.
59 Thomas Hearne, *Remarks and Collections*, ed. by Oxford Historical Society, 11 vols. (Oxford: Oxford Historical Society, 1907), VIII, p. 330.
60 As quoted in Wright, *British Calendar Customs*, I, p. 18.
61 Hampshire: Christchurch and the New Forest: *Salisbury and Winchester Journal*, 9 November 1818, p. 4; John R. Wise, *The New Forest: Its History and Its Scenery* (London: Smith, Elder, 1867), p. 178. Berkshire (Sunningwell): Hearne, 1907, p. 330; 'A Village Custom', *Notes & Queries*, 5th series, 10 (1878), 447.
62 Somerset: Tongue, *Somerset Folklore*, pp. 156–157. Devon: *The Cornish Telegraph*, 24 February 1910, p. 4; (Gittisham) Chope, Devonshire Calendar Customs, 237; Ralph Whitlock, *The Folklore of Devon* (London: Batsford, 1977), pp. 138–139.
63 Hutton, *The Stations of the Sun*, p. 167.
64 For an overview of these other seasonal begging customs and house-visits, see chapters 6, 7, 11, 14, 19, 23, 36, 39 in Hutton, *The Stations of the Sun*.
65 Aucoin, 'When the Pancake Bell Rings', p. 42 (fn. 36).
66 Hutton, *The Stations of the Sun*, pp. (hogglers) 12–13, 21, (plough-lights) 125–127.
67 For these examples and others see Aucoin, 'When the Pancake Bell Rings', ch. 1.
68 Gervase of Tilbury, *Otia Imperialia: Recreation for an Emperor*, ed. and trans. by S.E. Banks and J.W. Binns (Oxford: Clarendon Press, 2002), pp. 754–757.
69 John Mirk, *Festival: A Collection of Homilies, Part 1*, ed. by Theodor Erbe (London: Early English Text Society, 1905), p. 74.
70 Aucoin, 'When the Pancake Bell Rings', pp. 69–70.
71 On these changes see Felicity Heal, *Hospitality in Early Modern England* (Oxford: Clarendon, 1990), pp. 142–191, 354–365; Hutton, *The Stations of the Sun*, pp. 19–21.
72 *Poor Robin* (London, 1683), sig. A5v.
73 Aucoin, 'When the Pancake Bell Rings', ch. 4.

74 For example, medieval plough-light collections and the eighteenth- and nineteenth-century Plough Monday plays: Hutton, *The Stations of the Sun*, ch. 11.
75 Aucoin, 'When the Pancake Bell Rings', pp. 71–73.
76 Wise, *The New Forest*, p. 178; *REED: Somerset*, II, pp. 637–638.
77 Aucoin, 'When the Pancake Bell Rings', pp. 233, 250.
78 *REED: Somerset*, II, pp. 637–638.
79 Chope, 'Devonshire Calendar Customs', pp. 234, 235.
80 Wright, *British Calendar Customs*, I, p. 18; *North Devon Journal*, 12 March 1857, p. 5; *Western Times*, 14 March 1865, p. 5; *Exeter and Plymouth Gazette*, 6 March 1868, p. 6; *North Devon Journal*, 12 March 1868, p. 5; *Western Times*, 9 April 1875, p. 8.
81 Udal, *Dorsetshire Folk-Lore*, p. 25.
82 Vivian and Mathews, 'The Folk-Lore of Somerset', pp. 241–242.
83 *Western Gazette*, 13 February 1864, p. 6; Chope, 'Devonshire Calendar Customs', p. 237.
84 Nicholas Orme, *Medieval Schools: From Roman Britain to Renaissance England* (New Haven, CT: Yale University Press, 2006), pp. 157–158; Brand, *Popular Antiquities*, I, p. 56; *Brasenose ale: A Collection of Verses Annually Presented on Shrove Tuesday by the Butler of Brasenose College, Oxford* (Boston, MA: Lincolnshire, 1878).
85 *Yorkshire Evening Post*, 16 February 1931, p. 8; *Penrith Observer*, 10 February 1891, p. 6.
86 Hedgeland, 'Lent Crocking', p. 77.
87 *Western Gazette*, 7 March 1879, p. 6.
88 In Clovelly, the council sponsors Lensherd Night. In Durweston, the primary school organizes the shroving, while in East Hendred, the squire of the local manor, Hendred House, maintains the tradition.

3

ROBIN HOOD FOLK-PERFORMANCE IN FIFTEENTH- AND SIXTEENTH-CENTURY ENGLAND

John Marshall

There can be absolutely no doubt that Robin Hood is the most popular and widely known English folklore hero. There are several reasons for this. He has prevailed from the earliest surviving literary reference to him in the late fourteenth century to the present day, appealing to children and adults alike and crossing the boundaries of class and education.[1] The episodic nature of the early tales told about him with their emphasis on hostile challenges leading to physical contests and armed combat makes him ideal material for brief encounters in a wide range of media from orally delivered rhymes to computer-generated images on game platforms and in feature films. The story of Robin Hood also adapts to changing attitudes, anxieties and social and political concerns as much as it does to developments in the media through which it is transmitted. This keeps Robin topical and relevant to each new generation. As the champion of natural justice and freedom from authoritarian control and abuse, he is in constant demand. Notably, he re-emerges anew in periods of social change and political crisis.

In the early material, Robin Hood is a yeoman outlawed in a greenwood for an unspecified and probably fabricated offence. He is loyal to the legitimate king but ruthless in opposing the monarch's greedy and corrupt representatives in the church and state. He robs from the rich but not, initially, to give exclusively to the poor. Rather, he gives to those in desperate need such as the knight who the Abbot of St Mary's in York attempts to defraud.[2]

By the end of the sixteenth century, Robin Hood had largely become gentrified and ennobled as the Earl of Huntington. This may have arisen because of a broadening of the status of the popular audience from the yeomanry and middling sort to include the mercantile class and above. This coincided with the establishment of the London theatres as the most progressive and pre-eminent popular medium of the time. Hardly surprising then that along with kings and queens, Robin Hood was a figure of attraction to playwrights. The ennobling of Robin Hood also provided the opportunity for a generic shift in the telling of the Robin Hood story. Until this moment, the tales of Robin Hood were essentially told as comedies. Even when Robin lost most, if not all, of his contests with adversaries, things generally turned out well for him. The exception being his deception and death at the hands of the Prioress of Kirklees, supposedly, a relative of his.[3]

The newly ennobled Robin Hood and the prominent role given to Maid Marian made possible the placing of him in the alternative context of a tragedy. A transformation registered in the titles of the two 1590s Anthony Munday plays: *The Downfall of Robert, Earle of Huntington* and *The Death of Robert, Earle of Huntington*. The implications of this development were major. Plot, characters, and characterization were elaborated and extended to fit the tragic structure of the wheel of fortune. But much was lost. The immediacy and directness of the scenarios of the earlier material, that acted as a narrative framework for celebrating physical action, were sacrificed in favour of a more classical literary construction.

The beginning of the nineteenth century saw the application of Robin Hood to a specific current concern: English identity. This emerges in a relatively new popular medium, the novel. Following the publication of Walter Scott's *Ivanhoe* in 1820, the dominant national outlook embraced Robin Hood's Saxon heritage and his resistance to the Norman occupation: not unexpected given the very recent Napoleonic Wars.[4] Robin now became a patriotic figure who embodied the qualities of nationhood and bold masculinity. These characteristics created the Robin Hood legend taken for granted in the popular imagination of today. He provided a role model and play figure for generations of children and possibly, a significant inspiration for, amongst others, Baden Powell and the scouting movement.

The next profound media development was the advent of moving pictures. If any medium was destined to become the natural home of Robin Hood, it was film and its offspring television. Silent films relied on swashbuckling derring-do, uncomplicated plots, and the exemplification of good overcoming evil. Robin Hood provided all three. In the twentieth century, not surprisingly perhaps, film and television treatments frequently referenced contemporary political issues. Foremost amongst them were contemporary wars: the coming of the Second World War, its aftermath, the Vietnam War and the plight of veterans, and the questioning of the legitimacy of the Falkland and Iraq wars, all within an imagined medieval setting.

Using the adventures of Robin Hood to refer to and debate the morality and traumatic consequences of wars was not the only political and ethical issue to be explored recently. Matters of feminism and diversity, for example, have featured prominently in film and television versions since the late twentieth century.

This, brief and selective, outline of the changing orientations of the Robin Hood story and the ready adoption of new media shows how adaptable is the form and content of this legendary character. Certain aspects, though, are consistent throughout: his prowess as an archer, his outlawed existence in a homosocial community, his challenge to the maladministration of authority, and the episodic nature of his narrative. Although in spoken and written accounts there is much to enjoy, neither can compete with the excitement and instantaneity of action observed. This is particularly apparent in the twentieth and twenty-first centuries where the prominence of the visual media of film and television quickly assimilated the exploits of Robin Hood.

Almost seven centuries before the invention of film and television, there existed another popular way of celebrating Robin Hood which also recognized the enjoyment value of viewing physical encounters. Unlike the cinematic renderings that have left material evidence, for those of the Middle Ages and early modern period, very little verification has survived. What remains from the early fifteenth century to the early seventeenth century is record evidence from, mainly but not wholly, several towns and villages in Southern and Midland England. The activity that the accounts register involves a costumed Robin Hood actively raising money for local causes. Modern scholars define these events as 'play-games'. This rather imprecise description points to the difficulty of interpreting what took place from the limited documentation. The evidence for them is scanty and primarily financial, accounting for money spent and money received by ale wardens or churchwardens. From these accounts, though, it is possible to assemble a speculative prototypical reconstruction of what is the most folkloric manifestation of Robin Hood. It must be recognized, though, that no one account provides a complete description of the event.

What follows is an extract from the accounts book of the wardens of St John and St George guild of St Brannock's Church, Braunton in Devon. It records the expenses and receipts of a church ale held in 1562.[5]

> Item payd for wood & vorses – iiij s ij d/ Item for Cuppes & quartes – vij d/ Item payd for cloth to make Robyn hoodes Cote xij s/ In primus we payd to Mr Wylliam Bellew Esquyre for vorses – iiij s/ Item for heowyng of þe same – xviij d Item for carydge of þe same vorses – ij s/ Item to Iohn Colemore for wood – viij d/ Item for carrayge of þe same wood – iiij d/ Item to Iohanna Crowne for brewyng our ale – iij s x d/ Item for her gallon of ale – vj d/ Item for our meat & drynke when we brew – ij s iiij d Item for vj li. of hoppes – ij s/ Item for Steanes/Cuppes/quartes – xij d/ Item for ij treing dysshes & a ladle – iij d / Item to Iames Whyte for bakyng our bred & pyes – xvj d/ Item for Robyn hood & hys Company – xij d/ Item for þe poore people þe brotherhed day – vj d/ Item for beryng inof wood of þe churcheyerd – vj d/ Item to Mathew ffosse to be our Cooke – xij d/ Item payd toward þe scolle at heanton – xx d/ Item for making of thys accompt – xij d
>
>   Summa – xlv s x d
>
> Item payd to phylyp walter for þe churche howse & for stones x li. xj s vij d
>
>   Summa Totallis – xij li. xvij s vij d/ So Remeynes of our ales money – xlj s ij d/ So remeynes in our hands þe whole – xvij li. iij s viij d ob. quadrata Item there ys delyvered to Thomas Stote & wylliam Cocke being þe new wardens – xvij li iij s iiij d/&c/
>
>   ffinis
>
> *(In the left-hand margin of this account is the word 'Wytsontyde')*

From the perspective of a cultural historian, the most striking problem with a document like this is that its sole purpose was to balance the books and not to chronicle the activity for posterity. Anything given freely or already in hand does not need recording. Even with these limitations, documents such as the one above give up more information that immediately meets the eye.

The venue, Braunton in North Devon, is known today as the largest village in Great Britain, although no one seems certain whether this refers to size or population. It is one of many places in Devon to have held Robin Hood 'play-games'. In searching local archives for evidence of dramatic performance in England, Wales, and Scotland from the beginnings to 1642, the *Records of Early English Drama* (REED) has done much to bring attention not only to religious plays and minstrelsy but also to the popularity of celebrating Robin Hood. In the Devon volume, 430 parishes were searched of which 43, or 10%, had records surviving. Of these ten, or 23%, recorded Robin Hood's involvement. It is a reasonable assumption that a larger number of extant parish records would have increased the percentage of participation. Even with these figures, it is a remarkable statistic that nearly a quarter of parishes in Devon could have sponsored a Robin Hood ale.

The document transcript above appears much as it does in the manuscript. The layout has been adjusted, though, to save space. The original line breaks are indicated by a forward slash. Some words in the original were written in an abbreviated form rather like an early shorthand. For clarity, they have been silently expanded. Further clarification is needed for those not familiar with pre-decimalization currency, some of the spellings, and words now archaic.

The British currency before the introduction of decimal coinage in 1971 was known as pounds, shillings, and pence (£ s d after the Latin names). The major change was that while there were 240 pence to the pound, there are now 100 new pence. Converting from the earlier currency to decimal is relatively simple: 10 shillings in old money became 50p in the new, 1 shilling was equivalent to 5p, and 2½d to 1p. The first payment in the account is for iiij s ij d or 4s 2d which, as close as possible, converts to 21p.

The following words probably need some explanation:[6]

vorses: furze, a spiny evergreen shrub with yellow flowers. Now more commonly known as gorse.
quartes: quart, a vessel having a capacity of a quarter of a gallon, or two pints.
heowyng: hewing, to cut down or chop-up wood.
steanes: stean, a two handled vessel made of clay for liquids. Used as a pitcher for serving ale and beer.
treining: made from wood as in treen.
scolle: school.
ob. quadrata: ob is an abbreviation for obolus, meaning halfpenny and quadrata, meaning farthing.

The term 'church ale' also needs definition. From the Middle Ages to the early modern period, many parishes, mainly in the south of England, regularly held church ales as holiday gatherings of parishioners and neighbours. This was done to raise funds for local causes. Food and drink were on sale and entertainment of various kinds provided. In the north, bride ales were a popular means of collecting money to bestow upon marrying couples. For those fallen on hard times, help ales were held to financially alleviate some of the hardships. All three types of church ale shared similar motives in seeking to improve the material conditions of individuals, couples, and communities.[7] Some of the general church ales adopted a narrative theme to contextualize the gathering as with Robin Hood in Braunton and elsewhere. At Croscombe in Somerset, Robin Hood church ales, during the early sixteenth century, interchanged with a St George ale. The exchanges do not smoothly alternate but tend to cluster. Never, though, do they appear together in the same year. Robin Hood was much more successful financially than St George, suggesting that in the time of greatest need, the hero rises up.

An insight into the features, practices, and purposes of church ales is provided by what may well be an eyewitness account from the end of the sixteenth century. In 1602 (1603 in the modern rendering of the calendar), Richard Carew, Cornish gentleman and antiquarian, published *The Survey of Cornwall*, the earliest major history and description of the county. He was born in 1555 and had begun the work by 1586 at the latest.

> For the church-ale, two young men of the parish are yearly chosen by their last foregoers to be wardens, who dividing the task, make collection among the parishioners of whatsoever provision it pleaseth them voluntarily to bestow. This they employ in brewing, baking, and other acates [groceries] against Whitsuntide, upon which holidays the neighbours meet at the church house and there merrily feed on their own victuals, contributing some petty portion to the stock, which by many smalls growth to meetly greatness, for there is entertained a kind of emulation between these wardens, who by his graciousness in gathering and good husbandry in expending, can best advance the church's profit. Besides, the neighbour parishes at those times lovingly visit one another, and this way frankly spend their money together. The afternoons are consumed in such exercises as old and young folk (having leisure) do accustomably wear out the time withal.

> When the feast is ended, the wardens yield in their account to the parishioners, and such money as exceedeth the disbursements is laid up in store to defray any extraordinary charges arising in the parish, or imposed on them for the good of the country or the prince's service. Neither of which commonly gripe so much but that somewhat still remaineth to cover the purse's bottom.[8]

These church ales commonly took place in the week of Whitsuntide. The choice of occasion was largely a matter of a combination of time off work and the weather. Before the Reformation, craftsmen and other workers could look forward to several paid and unpaid holidays. Most were single days celebrating the lives of saints. These observances were abolished after the break with Rome. There were also three weeklong unpaid holidays at Christmas, Easter, and Whitsun. The Christmas holiday is fixed in the church calendar and the other two are moveable feasts. Whitsunday falls 50 days after Easter and occurs between 10 May and 13 June. Christmas and Easter are commemorated in very specific scriptural ways and centred in the church. Whitsuntide, or Pentecost, celebrates the gift of the Holy Spirit and the birth of the Christian Church on Whitsunday. The days that follow are available for festive gathering and entertainment. There was also a chance of good weather.

Although the Braunton guild of St John and St George does not specifically refer to their account as a church ale, the list of expenditure makes clear that it was. Most of the money spent goes towards brewing ale and beer and baking bread and pies. The 'vorses' began the process in supplying the kindling necessary to fire up the vessels to boil the water for brewing and the ovens for baking. Furze was also used locally as fuel in limekilns. The vorses had to be bought from the landowners where they grew, then someone was paid for cutting them down followed by transportation to where brewing and baking took place: almost certainly the church house. The process was repeated for the next stage in feeding the fires with wood, some of which came from the extensive churchyard. The payment for vj li (6 lbs) of 'hoppes' signals that beer as well as ale, which was malt based, was being brewed.

It will be noticed in the account that payments are made to procure fuel, drinking and eating vessels, and hops. What is missing are the other ingredients for brewing and baking. This is because the purpose of the church ale was to raise money, within a convivial atmosphere, for the upkeep and enhancement of the parish. To ensure that more money was raised than spent, parishioners, who could, gifted the necessary ingredients. The finished bread, pies, ale, and beer were then sold for a profit.

The brewing of ale was undertaken by 'Iohanna Crowne'. At the time, it was the norm for women, often on an occasional and local basis, to be responsible for the craft. With the capitalization, centralization, and commercialization of brewing in the late sixteenth century, the trade was increasingly dominated by men.[9] 'Matthew ffosse' cooked the food.

By far the largest outlay was for the hire of the church house. The sum of 'x li. xj s vij d' (£10 11s 7d or £10.53) seems colossal when compared with the other payments in the account. The hire was not, though, just for the day of the church ale. As a community facility for the parishioners, the church house would have been where the brewing and baking took place as well as the venue for serving the meat and drink on the day. Many church houses also hired out the necessary equipment for brewing and baking. Some church houses survive from the period including the one adjacent to St Brannock's Church in Braunton, although it no longer serves the original purpose (Figures 3.1 and 3.2).

Another surviving example is the house in the churchyard of St Mary the Virgin in Croscombe, Somerset. Built in about 1481–1482, it was, almost certainly, financed from funds raised by the Robin Hood Revels as they were known there.[10]

Figure 3.1 St Brannock's Church, Braunton, Devon
Source: Photograph © the author.

This reciprocity between Robin Hood and the venue for his celebration brings us back to the most intriguing item of the Braunton account. Along with the ingredients for brewing and baking is the 'ingredient' of Robin Hood. Whatever happened at Whitsuntide in a North Devon village in 1562, the focus of the conviviality and the conduit for charitable giving was Robin Hood. As with Father Christmas, Robin must be instantly recognizable. Like so many other places where he appeared, this was achieved through costume. By far the most common expense in the gatherings was for his coat or tunic. In Wells, Somerset, as well as elsewhere, the colour of the garments worn by his men was 'greene' and where recorded the material was the green cloth of Kendal. This can be assumed to be the case generally as the colour of his attire signified his character more expressively than its shape or fashion. Indeed, at the time, there was no concept of historical costume, Robin and his company would have worn contemporary clothing much like that of a forester. The xij s (12s, equivalent to 60p) spent on Robin Hood's 'Cote' in Braunton appears to be for cloth only: a sum which shows that there was little qualitative difference between the material for making his

Figure 3.2 St Brannock's Church House, Braunton, Devon
Source: Photograph © the author.

costume and that bought by quite wealthy buyers. If the entry is accurate in referring solely to material, the person who turned the cloth into Hood's coat was inadvertently omitted from the account or he/she generously gave their labour free. If the accuracy of the financial calculations is anything to go by, then the former seems the more likely.[11]

The only other related reference in the account is to 'Robyn hood & hys Company – xij d' (12d or 5p). If this is a fee for playing, it is doubtful that the company extended beyond six members with a 2d reward each. It is possible that the payment was for refreshments on the day. Accounts from the Braunton guild in other years provide more information. In one for 1561, there is an item for 'meat & drynke for Robyn hoode & his company ij s' (10p). This is twice as much as that in 1562 but it may not represent a like-for-like expense. This exposes the difficulty in interpreting accounts as the major source of evidence for the play-games. In the event of an apparent contradiction between two or more items, there is a temptation to seek a solution that satisfies congruity rather than acknowledging the limitations of this type of evidence. There also exists a problem with local terminology. The most common term used to describe Robin's band is, as at Braunton, 'his company'. In other places, they are called Hoodsmen, fellows, gentlemen, or simply his men. Were these interchangeable terms or do they indicate a slight variation in essence? Moreover, the numbers involved, where given, vary wildly. Did the size of the company influence the scale and nature of the performance? There is no way of knowing.

Fortunately, the accounts also contain certainties. Where Robin Hood has a named companion, for example, it is nearly always Little John.[12] In the Braunton guild's account for 1564, a payment is made 'for litle Iohns Cote vj s viij d' (6s 8d or 34p). As well as identifying at least one of Robin's company, the item reinforces the importance of costume as a means of recognition and distinction. Further information can be gleaned by comparing the cost of Little John's costume with that of Robin Hood's two years earlier. Robin's cloth only price is almost twice what appears to be Little John's finished coat. His costume was not only cheaper but, presumably, not as striking or elaborate as Robin's. Other accounts from Devon show how ornate and divergent these costumes could be. In 1561, the churchwardens of St Martin's and St Mary's Church in Chudleigh, Devon recorded 'The Count of Robyn Hodde & Litle Iohn'. They begin with a list of the monies raised by the ale: a remarkable total of 'vj li. vj s viij d' (£6 6s 8d or £6.34p). This is followed by a list of expenses:

In primis paid for the clothe of vij Cottes	xl s
Item paid for the Hoodes Cott cloth	xj s iij d
Item paid for the vyces cott	ij s
Item paid for Sylke & bottonse for the same Cottes	vj s iiij d
Item paid for sylke & whyplasse for the Hoodes Cott	iij s
Item paid for making of	ix Cottes x s
Item paid for A pere of showes for the vyce	xvj d

The Chudleigh expenses are for a group of nine players comprising Robin Hood, the 'vyce', or fool, and seven others that included Little John. This suggests an anonymous group of six and a named group of three. Two of the three, Robin and the Vice, are distinguished by their individual coats. The larger group's costumes were probably all identical and trimmed with silk and fastened with buttons. Robin also has a silk adornment but instead of buttons to secure his coat he has 'whyplasse', a thin leather lace. Again, the Robin Hood costume cloth cost twice that allocated for the group of seven. Robin Hood's cloth cost 'xj s iij d' (or 11s 3d equivalent to 56p), whereas each of the seven costumes cost, approximately, 5s 8d (equivalent to 28p). Similarly, Robin's silk and whiplace cost iij s (or 3s equivalent to 15p), while the silk and buttons for the others were priced at about a third of Robin's accessories. Only the Vice had shoes bought for the occasion. This differentiation could indicate that his role in the play-game involved dancing or acrobatics where sure footedness was crucial. His role is further defined by the name given to him. The Vice in medieval morality plays was a personification of evil. His purpose was to distract an everyman figure from his good Christian life to embrace selfish temptation and live a life of sin. To achieve this without thoroughly repulsing his quarry, and to entertain the audience, he adopted the mischievous persona of a fool.

Chudleigh was not the only place to associate Robin Hood with a fool. Some of the fullest records to survive for Robin Hood play-games are from Kingston upon Thames in Surrey. In the account for the year 1509–1510, along with payments to and receipts from Robin Hood, there are costume expenses for Robin, Little John, a friar, morris dancers, and a fool whose coat cost xiiij d (14d or 6p).[13] A fool is a significant figure in early English morris and ring dances where he woos and wins a female figure who is sometimes referred to as the Lady or Maid Marian.[14] The most common number for a morris team is six. This is exactly the number of identical costumes, with Little John removed, that existed in Chudleigh. Is this merely a coincidence? Or is it a likely indication of the dancing role undertaken by the six men?

In addition to the fool making an appearance at Kingston upon Thames, a friar and Maid Marian also appeared. Initially, it seems, as participants in the morris dance that featured as a part of the entertainment with Robin Hood during the Whitsun week festivities. Based on the All Saints churchwardens' accounts between 1504 and 1538, the morris dance only occurred in years when the Robin Hood play-game was performed. In some years, these overlapped with the Kingston King Game, an alternative or tandem fund raiser overseen by a mock king and queen. From the records, there is some evidence that the association of the morris with Robin Hood, especially the characters of a friar and Maid Marian, strengthened over time. So pervasive was this movement that it would be unthinkable today to imagine Robin without a jolly friar as a companion or Marian as female love interest. Strangely, though, there are very few records from Southern and Midland England, other than Kingston, that mention either of them being play-game characters.[15] It is possible that they were silently concealed within Robin Hood's catchall 'company' which ranged from one in most places to 20 in Kingston in 1522–1523.[16] If this was the case, it is surprising that their distinctive appearance was not matched by reference to their costume. More likely, their absence is caused by nothing more sinister than them being surplus to the play-game overall purpose of raising money. This association of the friar and Maid Marian aligned with the morris dance before transferring their attachment to Robin Hood is confirmed by the records of the churchwardens of St Lawrence in Reading, Berkshire for 1529–1530. The church, in some years, had sponsored a May play of Robin Hood. In 1530, there is no mention of it, but in amongst the expenses for morris dancers' clothing, hats, and bells is a payment for 'ffive elles of Canves for a cote for made Maryon'.[17]

Another missing figure, whose absence now would be inconceivable, is the Sheriff. Although he makes a brief appearance in a c.1470 Robin Hood play owned by John Paston II, a Norfolk gentleman, it is not until 1572 in Yeovil, Somerset that he is mentioned in the context of a Robin Hood play-game.[18] The reference records the purchase of a 'grene silke Rebyn for the Sheriffe iiij d'. Whether this was part of his costume or a property is not obvious. It seems unlikely that this was the villainous sheriff of the early poems and ballads as the green silk seems to associate him with Robin rather than oppose him. A later item in the same account might give a clue to its significance: 'paid to Iohn fflacher for fetherynge of Robart Hoodes arrowes iiij d'. A similar payment was made in 1577. The re-feathering of arrows would hardly be necessary if they were only for show. It implies that they were used actively in the play-game. This recalls the highly popular episode where Robin cannot resist an archery contest sponsored by the Sheriff. The green silk may have been a prize given to a disguised Robin rather than a costume embellishment worn by the Sheriff.

This very rare appearance of the Sheriff in a play-game strongly suggests that there was a fundamental difference between the outlawed and anti-authoritarian Robin Hood of the early poems and ballads and the convivial, good-fellow host of the ales. Both aspects are applicable to the character of Robin but are given a different priority according to the occasion and audience expectation.

Unlike the comprehensive recording of main characters and the costumes worn, much less is made of the setting for the festivities. In many instances, the proximity of the church house for dispensing food and drink suggests that the churchyard was the prime location. If a larger area was required, a nearby field might be used. Very few accounts list payments for or disposal of Robin Hood's house or bower.[19] This artificially created outdoor dwelling using natural materials from trees and flowers was where Robin Hood resided to welcome parishioners and visitors and to preside over the ale.

Moving on from the mechanics of a church ale with a Robin Hood flavour, the purpose of the endeavour needs explaining. Like many church fetes in the recent past, the church ale was a celebration of community, fraternity, and charity. The latter is evident in the Braunton account for 1562 where vj d (2½p) is given to e poore people' on the Brotherhood Day: presumably the feast day of either St John, 27 December, or St George, 23 April. The guild also donated xx d (20d or 8p) to 'at heanton'. Heanton Punchardon is a village on the outskirts of Braunton. The giving of alms to the poor from funds raised by Robin Hood was by no means confined to Braunton and could have been the source for the later motif of him taking from the rich and giving to the poor.

Other destinations for the money generated were often quite specific. In most cases, they concerned the maintenance and improvement of the parish church fabric. At Glastonbury and Tintinhull, both in Somerset, the funds were used to replace pews. Although not made explicit in the Braunton records, the Robin Hood ales held there could have served the same purpose as they coincide with an extensive period of pew and bench end replacement. In a similar vein, Stratton in Cornwall had Robin Hood gatherings during the nine years taken to build and install a new rood loft. In 1543–1544, when the final payment for the loft was made, St Andrew churchwardens recorded the sale of the 'wode of Robyn hode is howse' for which they received 'iij s v d' (17p). The wood was bought by a man and a woman who do not seem to be related. The Stratton churchwardens' records show that he was a lime burner. An occupation that required either ownership of, or shared access to, a lime kiln and a regular supply of wood. The woman involved is recorded as having mended church clothing 20 years previously. It is possible that she was a widow by 1543 and supported herself by brewing ale: a craft that also consumed wood. Following the sale, there is no further reference to Robin Hood in Stratton. His work there was done.[20]

In some places, Robin Hood helped build even more substantial structures. In Bodmin, Cornwall, his gathering in 1506 contributed to the Berry Tower building fund: a project that took 13 years to complete. The tower still survives although in a ruinous condition. Similarly, at Kingston upon Thames, the Robin Hood gatherings appear to have supported the reconstruction of the church steeple almost destroyed by lightning in 1445. A cause to which Henry VII gifted iij s iiij d (about 17p), in 1505, to 'the players at kingeston towarde the bilding of the churche stiple'.[21]

The most ambitious church building programme underpinned by Robin Hood was at Croscombe in Somerset. Unlike most places where the occurrence of play-games is relatively sparse, Croscombe had an extensive run of 25 occasions beginning in 1476 and ending in 1526. For the most part, the traditional means of financing everyday church expenses was covered by income from rents, gifts, bequests, annual collections, and guild contributions. What these funds could not cope with was large-scale building work. For the Croscombe churchwardens, the solution lay with Robin Hood. Their accounts of activity show two distinct periods of back-to-back play-games. These were between 1482 and 1485 and for six years out of seven between 1506 and 1512. The first coincides with the construction of the church house and the second with the building of the St George Chapel at the north-east end of the church. Without Robin Hood's aid, these additions could not have been built.

What emerges from all these examples and explains the, generally, intermittent occurrence of them is that Robin Hood play-games were used sparingly to focus attention on the special circumstances that required him. This parallels his interventions in moments of need in the early poems and ballads. It also provides an answer to why the Robin Hood play-games regularly outstripped the sums raised by other church ales.

It is evident that Robin Hood was a highly successful gatherer of funds in the fifteenth and sixteenth centuries. Why was this? First, he was not the mock king that even in a folkloric context might have seemed too aligned with the tax man. Second, he was not a saint with the associated constraints of piety. And third, he was a people's hero; well known, much loved, and widely respected. He invited close affiliation from his audience and, for the most part, they responded by becoming members of his company.

With much going in his favour, he still needed a practical means of gathering in the money. It is possible that he merely collected entrance fees or revenue from the sale of meat and drink. If this was the situation, it not only lacks entertainment, but it ignores the aspects of Robin Hood that made him a folklore legend in the first place. He and his company must have done something more fittingly active to warrant headlining the event.

At Kingston upon Thames, this was partly achieved by the sale of liveries: a means of signifying an allegiance between Robin Hood and his followers. In 1519, 2,000 liveries and 2,000 pins were bought. This huge number was probably more than the entire population of the town and confirms the impression that these ales were open to neighbouring parishes and visitors from further away. In 1507, 1,200 liveries were bought and 40 great liveries. What the difference between them was is unclear. The great ones might have been sold to dignitaries and parish officers or just to those who could afford them. Alternatively, they could have offered greater access to Robin Hood's company or other privileges. The rather precise figure of 24 great liveries was made in 1536. This is close to the 20 members of the company in 1523. Were they worn to identify them when not wearing costume during Whitsun week? This would distinguish them as legitimate collectors. In return, they would recognize the wearers of smaller liveries as having already contributed. Much like a flag-day.

So far what has been said about church ales presided over by Robin Hood is supported by the written evidence of those who organized them. The accounts, between them, provide information on place, time, purpose, characters, and costumes. What was not in their remit was to describe the action that defined the ale. Fortunately, there is circumstantial evidence that points towards an active engagement with the audience.

Where the accounts list the names of those who played Robin Hood and can be identified, the men tend to be young, in their mid to late twenties, and drawn from the more manual trades and crafts. Not only does this suggest that they were in their physical prime but that they embodied the masculine and athletic paradigm that is Robin Hood. Community trust was also important where money was concerned. Many of those chosen to be Robin were, had been, or would become guild and churchwardens with financial responsibility within the parish. This combination of strength in body and selfless service is mirrored in Robin Hood.

Other factors also support a physical dimension to the play-games. Many ales, with or without Robin Hood, featured sporting contests involving archery, wrestling, putting the stone, and casting the axletree: all of which occur in the Paston Robin Hood play mentioned above. In Kingston upon Thames, the churchwardens frequently paid for hats and feathers lost or broken and for repair to costumes, pointing to activity more robust than just collecting donations.

The most convincing evidence for combat being at the centre of the play-games comes from outside the surviving ale accounts. In the telling of the Robin Hood story in the fifteenth and sixteenth centuries, whether in play-games or poems, a central motif is the challenge and physical contest between Robin and an adversary. In the poems, the opponents are mainly outsiders: itinerants, mendicants, and beggars. In contrast, the records of the play-games are overwhelmingly silent on the subject, recording only one or two references to a friar and a late reference to the sheriff. This absence is best explained by the very real possibility that the opposition was drawn from the crowd. It seems reasonable that Robin would have little difficulty in extracting a contribution from parishioners who probably knew where the money was going and stood to benefit from it. But what if a visitor from another parish refused? The answer may lie in the Robin Hood ballads collected by F. J. Child.[22] Of the 38 printed, 16 are of a type known as 'meets his match' where Robin challenges an outsider, often for not paying a fee of passage, and fights him. In these ballads, he wins none of the contests, losing most and drawing the others. Of these opponents, nine decide to join the merry men and receive the livery; the rest leave on good terms. This record of Robin's failure to win is not imposed by the ballad form where any result is possible. But it is essential in the improvised context of a live contest. It is impossible to guarantee a win in these unscripted circumstances, a draw may be controllable, and a loss is easily achieved. The ballad tradition looks to have absorbed the play-game narrative realities rather than constraining performance practice. To a remarkable extent, the play-games of Robin Hood have contributed to the shaping of the legend as much as the more widely acknowledged poems and ballads.

Evidence of this relationship between improvised enactment and written composition, and the centrality of contest to both, survives in an addendum to an edition of *A Mery Geste of Robyn Hoode* printed by William Copland in around 1560. This long poem, written in the late fifteenth century, is followed in Copland's edition by two short plays described by him as 'the Playe of Robyn Hoode, verye proper to be played in Maye games'. The first play is a version of the episode known as 'Robin Hood and the Friar' and the second, 'Robin Hood and the Potter', which resembles, in some respects, the beginning of the second oldest Robin Hood poem to survive. In both plays, Robin confronts a transgressive outsider with whom he has had previous contentious dealings over money. In each case, the conflict provides the justification for a fight that ultimately resolves in reconciliation.[23]

The Robin Hood Ales celebrated communalism and parish autonomy where the individual derived strength from mutual support and good fellowship. They also honoured the rising class of yeomanry and the obligation to assist the poor, bringing the greenwood and the parish into perfect symmetry.

Notes

1. The earliest literary reference to Robin Hood occurs in William Langland, *The Vision of Piers Plowman: A Critical Edition of the B-Text Based on Trinity College Cambridge MS B.15.17*, ed. by A. V. C. Schmidt, 2nd edn (London: Longman, 1995), p. 82, Passus V lines 395–396, where the priest Sloth confesses that he does not know the Lord's Prayer very well, but is familiar with the rhymes of Robin Hood and Randolph Earl of Chester.
2. This episode appears in one of the earliest Robin Hood poems dating from the fifteenth century and known as *A Gest of Robyn Hode*. See, *Robin Hood and Other Outlaw Tales*, ed. by Stephen Knight and Thomas Ohlgren (Kalamazoo: Medieval Institute Publications, 1997), pp. 80–168.
3. This scene concludes *The Gest of Robyn Hode*. See note 2 above.
4. Although the date of publication of Scott's novel is given as 1820 on the title page, it was published in 1819. For the construction of national identity through the legendary figures of Robin Hood and King Arthur, see Stephaniel L. Barczewski, *Myth and National Identity in Nineteenth-Century Britain* (Oxford: Oxford University Press, 2000).
5. Devon Record Office, 1677A/PW1a. The transcription here is based on that from *Devon*, ed. by John M. Wasson, *Records of Early English Drama* (Toronto, ON, Buffalo and London: University of Toronto Press, 1986), pp. 310–311. Unless stated otherwise, references in the text to play-games can be found in the relevant *REED* county volumes by place and date.
6. The definitions given are from the 13-volume *Oxford English Dictionary*.
7. Judith M. Bennett, 'Conviviality and Charity in Medieval and Early Modern England', *Past and Present* 134 (1992), 19–41.
8. Extract from *The Survey of Cornwall by Richard Carew*, ed. by John Chynoweth, Nicholas Orme, and Alexandra Walsham (Exeter: Devon and Cornwall Record Society, 2004), p. 68. I have modernized the spelling and punctuation. Richard Carew appears to have been a moderate Protestant. He criticized the Anglican hierarchy over their objections to holding church ales which they considered to be licentious (*The Survey of Cornwall*, pp. 3–4). Although not mentioned in his description of a church ale, it is possible that he was familiar with the inclusion of Robin Hood. For much of his life, he lived in Antony House in the east Cornwall village of Antony. The St James Collectors and Churchwardens' Accounts record money gathered by Robin Hood in 1554, 1555 (the year Carew was born), 1556, 1558, and 1559. The accounts only survive in an antiquarian copy. Even if these were the only years Robin Hood ales were held, it is quite possible that he was told about them by one of the many older Cornish inhabitants who provided him with local information.
9. For a full account of the trade, see Judith M. Bennett, *Ale, Beer, and Brewsters in England: Women's Work in a Changing World 1300–1600* (Oxford and New York: Oxford University Press, 1996).
10. John Marshall, '"Comyth in Robyn Hode": Paying and Playing the Outlaw in Croscombe', *Porci ante Margaritam: Essays in Honour of Meg Twycross*, ed. by Sarah Carpenter, Pamela King and Peter Meredith, *Leeds Studies in English*, n. s. 32 (2001), 344–368, p. 257. Republished in John Marshall,

Early English Performance: Medieval Plays and Robin Hood Games: Shifting Paradigms in Early English Drama Studies, ed. by Philip Butterworth (London and New York: Routledge, 2020), pp. 248–270.

11   The Braunton account registers 21 items in the first list of expenses and calculates the sum of them as 'xlv s x d' (45s 10d or £2 5s 10d). My reckoning is that the total amounts to £2 2s 1d. Ingeniously, co-editor of this volume, Peter Harrop has posited to me that the discrepancy of 3s 9d (19p) might be accounted for by the tailoring of Robin Hood's costume. Pleasing as this explanation is, it seems unlikely. Two accounts from Kingston upon Thames, Surrey specify the cost of making Robin Hood costumes. In the account for 1507–1508, payment is made 'for makyng of Robyn hodes Cote xvj d' (16d or1s 4d, equivalent to 6½p). In 1518–1519, 14 Kendal coats were made for 'xij s' (12s or 60p). Each coat, if costing the same to make, would amount to 10d or 4p. Even allowing for inflation over half a century, it is doubtful that the cost of tailoring would have increased six-fold. Financial accounts of the time are rarely consistent. We know very little about how they were gathered. Were they, for example, compiled from separate paper bills? Or was there a day when those who owed money for goods and services made their claims verbally before the church or guild wardens? Either way, there is plenty of scope for omissions and slips in recording. In the case of Braunton, the pressure for brevity in expressing the payments might have resulted in unhelpful conflation. It is possible that 'cloth to make Robyn hoodes Cote' condenses the costs of material and manufacture, especially if the provider of the cloth and the tailor were the same person.

12   This is not the case in Cornwall where he does not feature in the extant records.

13   Surrey Record Office KG2/2/1. Extracts from the accounts can be found in Jeffrey L. Singman, *Robin Hood: The Shaping of the Legend* (Westport, CT and London: Greenwood Press, 1998), pp. 181–183. I am extremely grateful to Sally-Beth MacLean, Executive Editor of REED, for her generosity in sharing with me her transcript of the Kingston upon Thames records that she is preparing for publication in the REED volume for Surrey. See also, Sally-Beth MacLean, 'King Games and Robin Hood: Play and Profit at Kingston upon Thames', *Research Opportunities in Renaissance Drama*, 29 (1986–1987), 85–94.

14   John Forrest, *The History of Morris Dancing 1458–1750* (Toronto, ON and Buffalo: University of Toronto Press, 1999).

15   In the household accounts of Prior More of Worcester for the year 1530, there is a payment to the tenants of Cleeve Prior for 'pleying Robyn Whot Mayde Marion & other' (REED volume for Herefordshire and Worcestershire).

16   The number is derived from the payment for the hire of 20 hats for Robin Hood, one of which was lost.

17   The REED volume for Berkshire is online at https://ereed.library.utoronto.ca/.

18   For a history and analysis of the play, see John Marshall, '"goon in-to Bernysdale": The Trail of the Paston Robin Hood Play', *Essays in Honour of Peter Meredith*, ed. by Catherine Batt, *Leeds Studies in English*, n. s. 29 (1998), 183–217. Republished in Marshall, *Early English Performance*, pp. 219–247.

19   Stratton in Cornwall (1544), Abingdon in Berkshire (1567), and Woodbury in Devon (1574) all record either the making or disposing of Robin Hood's house or bower.

20   The REED volume for Dorset and Cornwall records the sale of the wood, but to put this in the wider context of non-dramatic activity in the parish, see *Stratton Churchwardens' Accounts 1512–1578*, ed. by Joanna Mattingly, *Devon and Cornwall Record Society*, n. s. 60 (Woodbridge: The Boydell Press, 2018).

21   Sydney Anglo, 'The Court Festivals of Henry VII: A Study Based Upon the Account Books of John Heron, Treasurer of the Chamber', *Bulletin of the John Rylands Library* 43:1 (1960), 12–45, 39.

22   *The English and Scottish Popular Ballads*, ed. by Frances James Child, 5 vols (Mineola, NY: Dover Publications, 1965), III, pp. 39–233.

23   The two Copland plays are included in Knight and Ohlgren, *Robin Hood and Other Outlaw Tales*, pp. 281–295. For a more detailed exploration of the relationship between these plays and the play-games and the assertion that they involved members of the audience, see John Marshall, 'Robin Hood plays and combat games', in *The Routledge Research Companion to Early Drama and Performance*, ed. by Pamela M. King (London and New York: Routledge, 2017), pp. 170–184.

4

ALONGSIDE THE MUMMERS' PLAYS

Customary elements in amateur and semi-professional theatre 1730–1850

Peter Harrop

Introduction

This chapter addresses points of connection between mummers' plays and other forms of theatre by considering eight performances from the eighteenth into the nineteenth centuries, the period when mummers' plays emerged and took root as a popular form. These examples demonstrate that there were pre-existing household and community contexts for performance into which mummers' plays easily fitted and that those contexts already offered opportunities to amateur and semi-professional performers. As such, they are largely subsumed within the 'temporal customary auspices' discussed elsewhere in this volume, times of year when arrangements were in place for making merry by engaging, for example, in dramatic entertainment of one kind or another.[1]

The selected performances took place in a range of settings across England from the 1730s (the earliest reference for a possible mummers' play) to the 1850s (by which time mummers' plays had spread across much of the country). Some took place on the street; some on trestle or wagon stages in urban or rural settings; some in small homes, others in very grand houses; others took place in and around taverns, inns and public houses; some in fairground booths; at least one in 'a long room over a fish cellar'. Collectively, they illustrate folk, amateur and commercial theatre practices that interwove the customary and traditiony into their local performative fabric. Sometimes this was a matter of content, sometimes a matter of context, sometimes a blend of both. They are of interest because they refute the idea that mummers' plays were ever an entirely singular form subject to occasional corruption by literary influences, or that the performers of mummers' plays operated in theatrical quarantine, unaware of the performing arts of their day. They demonstrate widespread local performance cultures that were semi-professional, popular and often (but not always) reflective of conservative theatrical tastes. This was a theatre that drew on the seasonal and the customary to maximise social and commercial advantages; it suggests a broader 'folk' theatre that is generally discussed.

In 1591, Samuel Cox, secretary to Sir Christopher Hatton (Queen Elizabeth's 'dancing chancellor'), wrote:

> I could wish that players would use themselves nowadays, as in ancient former times they have done, which was only to exercise their interludes in the time of Christmas, beginning to play in the holidays and continuing until twelfth tide, or at the furthest until Ashwednesday, of which players I find three sorts of people: the first, such as were in wages with the king [...] The second sort were such as pertained to noblemen, and were ordinary servants in their house, and only for Christmas times used such plays, without making profession to be players to go abroad for gain [....]The third sort were certain artisans in good towns and great parishes, as shoemakers, tailors, and such like, that used to play either in their town-halls, or some time in churches, to make the people merry...[2]

Cox reminds us that in addition to the rapid emergence of commercial and professional theatres in the sixteenth century, a range of older, local and customary frameworks still persisted. Two well-known examples serve to demonstrate the mix of old and new that arose as modern conceptions of theatre made an entrance into older and by then customary contexts. In the early years of the seventeenth century, the Simpson Company of Egton in North East Yorkshire (comprising artisans of various trades, including shoemakers, and usually numbering around a dozen men and boys) toured the wealthy houses of the Yorkshire moors during an extended Christmas holiday. They performed religious plays (St. Christopher, for example, a now lost Saint's play) and secular plays known to include *The Three Shirleys* (1607), *Pericles* (1609) and *King Lere* (1605 or 1608).[3] They would stay overnight in those homes where they performed, moving on the next day, and it is likely that they broke longer journeys between homes with performances and overnight stays in other lodgings. Such was their commitment to playing that shoemaking and various other trades may have served more as back-up professions and cover for the vagrant activity of acting with which they were eventually charged. (Indeed, so much is known about their itineraries precisely because they fell foul of the authorities, not simply for vagrancy and attached charges, but because the authorities suspected a Catholic recusant dimension to their activities.)

Moving from household to parish theatre, the Stanton Harcourt men from Oxfordshire provide a parallel example.[4] In February 1652, over 300 people had gathered in a first floor room of the White Hart Inn at Witney to watch the company's touring production of the already evergreen *Mucidoros*.[5] As the performance proceeded, the floor gradually gave way and at some point during Act 4 the audience fell into the games room below. Eight people were killed. The performers, all local men, had been rehearsing since late September for a Christmas performance in their own parish, prior to a new year tour of local venues, all within a five-mile radius of their homes. There was, by this time, nothing exceptional about a local semi-professional production at an inn, other than this terrible accident.

The former example provides a contemporary take on older traditions of Christmas entertainment in large and well-to-do households such as participatory revels, maskings, mummings and interludes. The latter example provides a contemporary take on older communal parish entertainments such as Robin Hood games and plays and Ridings at Saints' days – associated with wakes and ales. In short, by the end of the sixteenth and throughout the seventeenth century, whatever the legal and licencing requirements, amateur and semi-professional players were operating in private homes, public houses, town halls, church grounds and other spaces, most commonly under customary seasonal auspices.

Two hundred years after Cox, the antiquarian Joseph Strutt described his understanding of local performers and reiterated Cox's earlier summary:

> In many a place there were local companies formed to visit the houses of the gentlefolk of the immediate district at Christmas and other festive seasons. Such companies could

not properly be termed either amateurs or professionals. They were not amateurs, for they received largesse from their patrons; they were not professionals, for at ordinary seasons they followed their usual town or country occupations.[6]

As Strutt looked back into the eighteenth century to make that remark, and as he considered his contemporary landscape of local performance, the very earliest example of mummers' plays (although it would be a further 50 years before James Halliwell coined that phrase) had appeared.[7] Only a very few – six in the present evidence – can be unequivocally placed as far back as the eighteenth century.[8] One is a chapbook text from Newcastle-upon-Tyne, an early (c1750) example from a 'family tree' of northern chapbook mummers' plays, identified *mise en page* as 'Mock-Plays' and presented as simple acting editions in a mock-heroic style. Another was devised for a specific celebration at the Banks' family estate, Revesby Abbey in Lincolnshire, in 1779 and suggests an early example of the emerging trend for private theatricals (it contains extracts from published plays) while drawing on 'folk' material such as sword and morris dances alongside now familiar mummers' play tropes. We know little of the performative circumstances of the third example, from Truro in Cornwall (1780s), but the performers were linked by family and work ties – it has been termed *The Truro Cordwainers Play* for that reason. Like the Lincolnshire example, Truro intrigues because it contains extracts from earlier published plays and may reflect the fashion for 'spouting' – of performing sections of famous speeches or dialogues, from popular plays of the day, in the style of favoured actors. Pettitt has recently undertaken a detailed analysis of these two latter texts alongside three further nineteenth-century examples, from Keynsham in Somerset (1822), Brant Broughton in Lincolnshire (1824) and Ampleforth in Yorkshire (1860s), that further illustrate a fascinating intertextuality whereby well-known sixteenth-, seventeenth- and eighteenth-century play texts such as *Interlude of Youth*, *Diphilo & Granido*, and *Wily Beguiled* are 'sampled' within eighteenth- and nineteenth-century mummers' plays.[9]

The following provide a selection of theatrical encounters where those who sought enjoyment and income by means of performance capitalised on customary auspices to find their audiences. Brought together in this way, they indicate a theatrical backdrop against which the first folklorists were becoming aware of the first mummers' plays.

Andrew Brice, mayoral election, Devon, 1737

This reference consists of a fragment of text and commentary included in one footnote (among many footnotes) attached to a long satirical poem. The much-abbreviated title of the work is *The Mobiad: Or, Battle of the Voice*.[10] The mayoral election described in the poem took place in 1737 and the poem was written the following year though not published until 1770. Davies, writing in *The Critical Review* for that year, offers the following: 'We fancy we hear our readers say; "the title page is sufficient; we have had enough of this man already"'.[11] Davies also noted the delay between authorship and publication thus:

> It is to be feared that the objects of Mr Brice's poem are too local to promote its extensive circulation. Nay, it will hardly be interesting even to Exeter, for it is written upon an election made in that place thirty years ago.[12]

Brice had sat on the finished material for a long time but he had been fined for libel in 1727 and the risk of repetition may have outweighed any hope of financial gain. When he retired in 1769, despite having sold his business in return for an income, that balance may have shifted.

The reference to mumming occurs in canto IV, page 90, footnote (x) as follows:

> England's Heroe. St. George for England. At Christmas are (or at least very lately were) fellows wont to go about from House to House in Exeter a mumming, one of whom, in a (borrow'd) Holland Shirt most gorgeously be-ribbon'd, over his Waistcoat, &c. Flourishing a Faulchion, very valiantly entertains the admiring spectators thus:
> "Oh! Here comes I Saint George, A Man of Courage bold,
>
> "And with my Spear I winn'd three Crowns of Gold.
> "I slew the Dragon, and brought him to the Slaughter;
> "And by that very means I married Sabra; the beauteous
> "King of Egypt's Daughter – Play Musick.[13]

The member of the public elected to act as the Captain of Constables, a symbolic keeper of the peace for the duration of the mayoral election, is berated in the poem. Brice accuses the 1737 Captain – a local pharmacist – of buying rather than winning the staff of office and rails at his lack of decorum in bearing the silver-tipped truncheon. The only comparable figure Brice can summon up is a lavishly costumed Christmas mummer. The Captain, meanwhile,

> Steers his rigg'd Pageantry of manly Beef [...] Parts in his Frame Paris and Hector crave; / Strong, elegant, brisk, beautiful and brave. / With less Decorum Christmas Mummer struts/Than on He bears his goodly Grace of Guts/Though that same Mummer (x) England's Heroe plays, And Dragon, with his Whineard's Flourish slays. No Hamlet's Ghost can more majestic hold/His Truncheon, nor Stage-Hannibal so bold.[14]

In an essay on the Exeter press, Brushfield noted that 'From the outset of his career, Brice exhibited a great liking for the drama, as well as for the company of actors, to whom he was ever ready to show active kindness, and to entertain at his table'.[15] Tindal, writing in 1781, suggests that this enthusiasm extended to the stage itself: '"Nor did he refrain", it is said, "on any emergency, to appear in any humourous character"'.[16] *Brice's Journal*, which first appeared in 1725, carried advertisements for plays which detailed his authorship of prologues for their local production and offered these for separate sale.[17] His *Journal* also carried long recommendatory notices for productions with which he was involved.

Brice became something of a celebrity to players with his poem *The Play-house Church, or new Actors of Devotion*, written and published in response to two visits to the town by John Wesley in 1739 and 1743. Wesley's local success was regarded as having played a part in the subsequent prosecution of the local players as vagrants and their having to relinquish their theatre which, to add insult to injury, was purchased by the Methodists and converted into a chapel. *The Exeter Flying Post* reported that 'The mob were so spirited up by this poetical invective that the Methodists were soon obliged to abandon the place to its former possessors, whom Mr Brice now protected, by engaging them as his covenant-servants to perform gratis'.[18] Furthermore, 'According to a paragraph in the *London Morning Post* of May 16th, 1745 [...] they created a disgraceful disturbance, and acted with great ferocity to the Methodists, both on entering and leaving their chapel'.[19] He is also reported as 'conniving at the players' illegal performances which masqueraded as concerts of music by selling papers of brick dust under the name of tooth powder at the same price as would have been charged for theatre tickets'.[20]

Brice was reported in *Universal Magazine* to be 'as singular in his speech, as remarkable in his manner and dress; which induced Mr King [the actor] to exhibit him in the character of Lord Ogleby which Mr Garrick introduced in *The Clandestine Marriage*'.[21] Dr Oliver reports that on the completion of the comedy in 1766, 'there was some hesitation what tone would be most suitable to Lord Ogleby – it was decided at last that Mr King should assume

Mr A. Brice's'.[22] Brushfield also tells us that Oliver referred to Brice as facetious and suggests that this was 'a point of character on which Andrew appeared to pride himself, as he sometimes dubbed himself "Merry Andrew," at other times "Andrew surnamed Merry"'.[23]

Given his enthusiasms for satire, confrontation, theatre, and flamboyance it is unsurprising that Brice was alert to the presence of street performers and that he noted or recalled the lines they spoke. The vaunts quoted by him, which are a feature of later mummers' plays, conjure the conceit Brice despises, and serve his satiric purpose well. But to quote lines with an end cue 'Play Musick' is suggestive either of stage direction from a written text or the deliberate and mischievous employ of a stage direction as spoken text. 'Play Musick' (a relatively common stage direction from fifteenth century onwards) may be Brice reaffirming his view that the constable, like the mummer, has taken grandiosity several steps too far. Towards the end of *The Mobiad*, in a telling line, Brice describes the whole election as a 'social play' which confirms both his enjoyment of theatre and a keen sense of *theatrum mundi*.[24]

As far as the mummers' play is concerned Brice tells us little: he suggests that seasonal house performance was taking place in Exeter pre-1770 and indicates an early usage of text that would form part of many later mummers' plays. It is interesting that Brice, a man who loved the theatre and all things theatrical, summons St. George alongside Hamlet's Ghost and a stage-Hannibal, placing mumming alongside the theatre if not quite in it. At the same time, in satirising components of one customary framework – a mayoral election – Brice chooses to introduce another customary framework – Christmas mumming – to affirm his point. The ease with which Brice encompasses customary practice, civic pageantry and commercial theatre is noteworthy. It suggests that he (and perhaps his intended readership) saw a gamut of dramatic activity rather than any immediate distinction between folk drama and theatre.

John Jackson, probably Westmorland, 1740s

The actor, theatre manager and theatre historian John Jackson was born c1730 and spent his early life in the Yorkshire towns of Keighley and Doncaster before being sent to live with relatives near Kirby Lonsdale in Westmorland. His 1793 book *The History Of The Scottish Stage,* [....] *With Memoirs Of His Own Life* recounted a prominent career in the theatre: he had acted with London companies, including Garrick's own, nearly been bankrupted by Mrs Siddons late arrival to an Edinburgh season he was managing, and worked as a strolling player across Britain and Ireland. One of his memories, which he considers 'among the earliest incidents of life', describes a performance he saw 'in a remote part of England'.[25] Although not entirely clear from his memoir, I take the view that the performance took place near Kirby Lonsdale where he resided with his uncle in the early 1740s.[26]

Writing half a century later, he considered the performance to have been part of a range of 'lay compositions and performances [...] which though not expressly theatrical, were notwithstanding of such a kind, as to be analogous with those of the drama'.[27] Such events, he goes on to say, 'were more particularly in practice by the Christmas-gambolers, May-dayers, Maurice-dancers, and maskers'.[28] Jackson thereby marks these performances as customary:

> I recollect seeing, in a remote part of England, one of those sets of irregulars, in that country, called mummers, from which appellation, that outré mode of playing commonly practised by itinerant actors and sometimes even upon the established theatres, we presume stiled mumming: it was composed of young men, farmers' sons and those of decent tradesmen…through the whole of these performances, which had been handed down from father to son, with improvements and alterations for centuries past, appeared the outlines of a Lalouse, a Hippesly and a Lun.[29]

These names are of interest: earlier in his book, Jackson quotes an anonymous contemporary writer who says of Lun (the name under which actor-manager John Rich achieved acclaim performing Harlequin): 'to his instruction we owe a Hippisley, Nivelon, a La Guerre, an Arthur and a Lalouse; all excellent performers in these diverting mummeries'.[30] Jackson particularly appreciates Rich's 'consummate skill in teaching others to express the language of the mind by action'[31] by which, as the prologue for *Harlequin Invasion* puts it, 'every limb had its tongue'.[32] The discussion here is clearly about pantomime: all the listed and reiterated performers were noted for their physicality, for their lightness and speed of movement, for their utter newness and stylistic opposition to the immediate post-Restoration oratorical style. These performers were marked as the antithesis of customary.

Hippisley – variously spelled – was particularly well known for his comic sketch known as 'Hippisley's Drunken Man' (in which a supposedly inebriate actor reads and comments on newspaper articles) as well as his appearances in drolls and harlequinades from 1730 onwards.[33] M. Nivelon is known to have provided a danced afterpiece to a 1741 droll *Darius, King of Persia*.[34] John Laguerre co-owned a Bartholomew Fair Booth from 1734 and produced jointly with Hippisley and others at the George Inn Yard in 1739. Rosenfeld reports that their piece *The Top of the Tree; Or, A Tit Bit for a Nice Palate* incorporated 'the famous dog scene from *Perseus and Andromeda* and the skeleton scene from *The Royal Chace*' in which the actor Arthur, in role as Signor Arthurini, took the part of Pierrot and 'will in this Occasion introduce upwards of 50 Whimsical, Sorrowful, Comical and Diverting faces'.[35] Lalouse is probably the M. Lalauze who opened in London on March 28th 1726 as a member (according to Rosenfeld possibly the master) of the 'Italian Company of Comedians' at the New Theater in Haymarket and engaged in a 'great variety of dancing and tumbling'.[36]

All these performers were well known at the time Jackson witnessed the household performance but, significantly, less so at the time he composed his memoir. This is definitely the voice of Jackson the later historian rather than the youthful spectator; the latter not being in a position to bring the comparison to bear. Holding that in mind, here follows Jackson's description of the household performance (noting that his paragraphs are here re-ordered to reflect the sequence of the performance as he witnessed it):

> 'They had with them, as is customary, a Clown, the ancient *Fool of the Hall*: he had on a patched jacket and trowsers [sic], with a fox's tail to his cap.
>
> The amusements of the evening were prefaced with a song, of perhaps 30 stanzas by way of prologue, the hereditary office, I was given to understand, of the motley fool. The purpose of the composition was to announce the performers, who came on one after another, following the *Clown* in a circle, till the whole, with their characters and abilities, were pointed out to the audience.
>
> > The first verse of this singular production I have endeavoured to recollect,
> > "My name it is Captain Calf-tail, Calf-tail,
> > "And on my back it is plain to be seen;
> > "Although I am simple, and wear a fool's cap,
> > "I am dearly belov'd of a queen."
>
> The first piece, or play, comprised a kind of *Harlequin* plot, with a father, daughter and two lovers. The fool of the hall carried off the lady, to the joy of the rustic audience; the father was reconciled, and the lovers made happy.

> The interlude represented the staggering of a drunkard, with his glass and bottle; and the conclusion, or farce, was a compound of some tricks of the fool, who was supposed to be killed; and after being tumbled about in different positions, frightened his companions from the stage, which closed the scene'.[37]

The earlier description of *The Top of the Tree*, given professionally at the George Inn Yard in 1739, indicates what we might now regard as the sampling, covering or re-performing of extracts from other performances, structured in the popular manner as a juxtaposition of pieces and styles to create an evening's entertainment. Jackson's description of the mummers, probably witnessed by him just three or four years later, suggests something structurally and stylistically similar. At first glance, this seems straightforward – an amateur performance reflecting in some measure the professional theatre of the day.

The prologue will be familiar from later mumming performances and folk dances where it would be termed a 'calling on' song and the fool is dressed in a fashion elsewhere reported by Jackson's contemporary, the antiquarian John Wallis, in his description of a sword dance.[38] Jackson's description of the subsequent play is generically familiar from numerous *Commoedia Del Arte* scenarios as well as indicating those later romantic or wooing plays described by Baskervill and others. The interlude, in this context, is reminiscent of Hippesley's 'drunken man' act. The end-piece farce suggests the tumbling and tricks of the harlequinade and pantomime. Even if Jackson is gently patronising when he sees in the mummers 'the outlines of a Lalouse, a Hippesly, and a Lun', these 'irregulars' do appear to be doing much the same sort of thing – however well or badly – as one would find in the professional drolls of fairground booths during the same period, or as segments of a whole evening at the theatre.

Puzzlingly, Jackson then seems to both reaffirm and deny this. He recalls sufficient glimmer of skill and talent to have put him in mind of gifted professionals; yet, he is adamant that there can be no clear line of influence: 'the exhibitors had never been at a play, nor within the walls of a play-house, the originality of the performances must have been with them'.[39] 'These performances […] had been handed down from father to son, with improvements and alterations for centuries past'.[40]

The contradictions are manifest. Jackson marked the performances as customary yet compared the playing style with that of contemporary performers: he described form and content that was overwhelmingly current, a theatre that simply had not existed for centuries past. That sense of handing down, of face to face transmission of both skills and text, of improvements and alterations over time, was a standard practice in professional theatre as Jackson must have known. Why, then, does he imply that this mode of transmission is worthy of special note in this particular instance, as though it were somehow outwith normal theatrical practice? And why his determination that these particular performers – these sons of farmers and decent tradesmen – had never been at a play? Performances had taken place 12 miles away in Kendal – at least intermittently – from the late 1720s and, in any event, why would this particular insularity of the players' have been brought to his attention at that time? The apparent mirroring of the popular theatre of the day is either a striking coincidence or, in this aspect of Jackson's recollection, he has subjugated his theatre manager to his romantic antiquarian.

William Borlase, Cornwall, 1758

A natural historian with particular interests in geology and antiquities, William Borlase's 1758 description of performance in Cornish homes sought out a sense of historical continuity. Following a brief history and archaeology of medieval performance he describes:

> some faint remains of the same custom I have often seen in the west of Cornwall during the Christmas season, when at the family-feasts of gentlemen, the *Christmas PIays* were admitted, and some of the most learned among the vulgar (after leave obtained) entered in disguise, and before the gentry, who were properly seated, personated characters and carried on miserable dialogues on Scripture subjects; when their memory could go no further, they filled up the rest of the entertainment with more puerile representations, the combats of puppets, the final victory of the hero of the drama, and death of his antagonist.[41]

The distinction between entering in disguise and the 'personation' of characters is not immediately clear. Entering in disguise may mean entering in representational costume, whether masked or otherwise, to play a particular part. Alternatively, disguise may have served two other purposes: firstly, in avoiding the distraction of identifying the player behind the mask; secondly, to provide a neutral base for the playing or 'personation' of multiple roles as required by the content. In the latter case, 'disguise' might suggest the neutral mask of some medieval mummings, which would in this context permit complex playing to allow 'doubling' [whereby actors play more than one role] or 'halving' [whereby actors share roles] as required.[42] In any event, Borlase does not appear to have been a great lover of drama. Not only does he employ the phrases 'miserable dialogues' and 'puerile representations' but also concludes an earlier discussion of the Cornish Ordinaries by lamenting the 'age of ignorance' within which the people 'were to have every truth set before their eyes, by memorials, scenes and symbols, though the most incoherent, unedifying and absurd'.[43]

The scriptural interludes are followed by lighter material. Borlase mentions the combats of puppets but is not specific as to whether any actual puppetry takes place. Pettitt thinks not: 'it is hard to imagine the rustics putting on a regular puppet-show in the houses of the gentry. Borlase may mean the kind of combat which (elsewhere) is performed by puppets'.[44] The broader issue of interaction and interplay between modes of representation such as acting or puppetry is by no means confined to this example. The year 1758, when Borlase published his work, was the same year Samuel Foote had replaced actors with life-sized puppets for a London performance of *Diversions* which itself reprised Henry Fielding's 1730 success in pioneering the idea.[45]

Why does Borlase use the phrase 'when their memory could go no further' to indicate a stylistic break between the scriptural material and the puppet content? It is tempting to think of the (miserable) scriptural material as a necessary penance before the (puerile) fun could begin. This may tell us something about the 'big-house' performer-spectator relationship as well as playing style, suggesting both parties are required to demonstrate propriety in the presentation and reception of dramatic material and social relationships, in order to justify the seasonal exchange of performance for reward? The presentation of scriptural, biblical, religious or otherwise properly moral material would ease the performance of propriety and approval prior to the mutual acknowledgement of levity as seasonally appropriate.

Furthermore, 'when memory could go no further' may indicate that extemporising is acceptable within the playful puppet-like activity but not acceptable in the representation of, for example, biblical characters in serious interactions? But even straightforward puppetry was neither new nor specifically secular. Puppet shows with biblical themes were not uncommon and Rosenfeld mentions that *The Creation of the World and Noah's Flood, with an afterpiece of Dives and Lazarus,* 'held the fair stage for many years and was given by both Matthew Heatley and William Crawley in the early years of the eighteenth century'.[46] Puppet plays had been a fairground mainstay from the seventeenth century and retained a place throughout the eighteenth.

Borlase's phrase, 'I have often seen […] during the Christmas season', places this performance alongside that of Jackson's 'Christmas-gambolers' as seasonal and customary. A decade or so apart, and at opposite ends of the country, these 'most learned among the vulgar', 'farmers' sons and those of decent tradesmen', fulfilled local seasonal expectation while reflecting something of a more contemporary and national engagement with theatre.

John Edwin, Jobson's booth at Bristol Fair, The Siege of Troy, c1770

Elkaneh Settle was a popular Restoration playwright whose early work *The Empress of Morocco* epitomised what Abigail Williams summarises as 'bombastic rhymed drama set in exotic locations', the heroic drama, in short, that had a formative influence on the mummers' play.[47] Settle delivered *The Siege of Troy* for a booth owned by Mrs Mynns, herself a mainstay of large-scale and elaborately staged entertainment. It was enough of a crowd puller to see the name used and re-used as late as 1770 in a much diminished booth performance at Bristol Fair. The actor and singer John Edwin the elder (1749–1790) was among those who saw it there, and his experience is briefly related in a posthumously published biography *The Eccentricities of John Edwin, Comedian*.[48] The production's significance for present purposes is that Edwin records a section of dialogue now associated with the 'cure' component of the mummers' play.

The author of *The Eccentricities* was John Williams (1754–1818) writing under his pseudonym Anthony Pasquin. Williams was usually described as a raffish character, a friend of Garrick and an associate of Hogarth, a journalist, freelancer and theatre critic, who generated strong responses from those around him. He was, for example, reported as famously dirty and described by a contemporary as 'so lost to every sense of decency and shame' that he was 'a fitter object for the beadle than the muse'.[49] At one point, he found himself scouting for pantomime acts in Paris – an opportunity which may suggest a low point for an aspiring man of letters. Nonetheless, he gained access to John Edwin, a young man who had come from a prosperous background but, following his involvement with two London spouting clubs, had abandoned a post at the London Exchequer to pursue acting.[50] While at the fair, according to Williams, Edwin was drawn in by performers 'arranged in a temporary gallery' and an 'old brazen trumpet, which a varlet […] was blowing immediately behind them', to see *Jobson's Comical Family or all the world in a nutshell*.[51] Barely in his twenties at the time of this visit, Edwin was aged about 40 and a successful actor when he provided the reminiscence for *The Eccentricities*. At the time when Williams and Edwin were pulling together those 'original anecdotes', presumably in the late 1780s, they were a double act of bohemian theatre critic and leading actor and singer.

Once in Jobson's booth, the entertainment began with a comic dialogue between Punch and Fiddler for which Williams offers a script (quite possibly a partial script) and a few descriptive notes. This may have been a familiar scene-setting device as Granger, writing in 1769, described a well-known merry-Andrew as 'sometime fiddler to a puppet show; in which capacity he held many a dialogue with Punch, in much the same strain as he did afterwards with the mountebank doctor, his master upon the stage.'[52] This kind of dialogue is described by Strutt as 'mere jumbles of absurdity and nonsense, intermixed with low immoral discourses passing between Punch and the fiddler, for the orchestra admitted of more than one minstrel; and these flashes of merriment were made offensive to decency by the actions of the puppet'.[53] From the Jobson's booth account, it is difficult to tell whether the dialogue is between two puppets (with either one or two operators), or between a puppet and an actor – a ventriloquist act where the human 'Fiddler' talks to the dummy 'Punch'. There is a stage direction preceding the first Punch speech with the advice 'to be spoken nasally'. Williams commentary is interspersed by short sections of script which have Punch both as 'wooden chief' and as 'wooden prey' – the latter usage as Punch is seized and removed by 'a black gentleman' playing a role ascribed as 'Devil', 'Prince of Darkness' and 'satanic majesty' in the space of one sentence. Of course, this could as easily be a second or third puppet as a second actor, although a third puppet would necessitate a second operator.

We are told by Williams that Edwin and his friends were drinking before and during the show (there were 'three Welch girls from Monmouth on the right, and two drunken colliers from Kingswood on the left…Edwin carried some brandy in a pint bottle').[54] He seems to suggest that Edwin mistook Punch for a real person in offering him a drink and engaging him in conversation during the piece.[55] Following on from the initial dialogue, 'Mr Jobson deputed a red haired spinster about fourteen years old, to amuse them with balancing three unsheathed swords upon her comely nose points downward'.[56] We now get to the 'bonne bouche' as Williams has it, the main event which concludes the 'variegated performance' and is described as 'a regular drama' called *The Siege of Troy*. Unfortunately, we have no way of knowing how much of the performance Edwin recalled or Williams' chose to describe, but we do know that their dramatis persona lists four characters and four actors are ascribed those roles. From the given description, a 'large party' of Greeks and Trojans, led by Hector and Achilles, enter from opposing sides of the stage. 'Hector, Achilles and O'Driscol were animated, the rest were very handsomely fashioned out of pieces of pasteboard, and appeared full as majestic as the supernumeraries of the metropolitan theatres'.[57] Whether Williams is praising the designers or damning the London actors remains pleasingly moot (Figure 4.1).

The fight scene is described as though an eighteenth-century boxing match had been transported to the outskirts of classical Troy. Hector and Achilles strip to their shirts, and shake hands and box with 'pugilistic manoeuvres which would not have disgraced [the prize-fighter

Figure 4.1 An imagining of *The Siege of Troy* at Jobson's Booth with live performers. 'Three Welch girls from Monmouth on the right, and two drunken colliers from Kingswood on the left […] Edwin carried some brandy in a pint bottle'

Source: © The author (original artwork Paul Loudon, 2018).

Tom] Johnson'.[58] But these pugilistic manoeuvres are taking place amid a 'large party' of paste board figures. Even in fixed positions, certainly with a capacity to be raised on wires or slid on tracks, then a fight scene could be established which could be played for comedy or dramatic excitement, or both. Edwin's comparison with Tom Johnson (presuming this is not entirely literary licence on the part of Williams) could be comical reference or acknowledge effort at creating tension in a regular drama. In most consideration of the mummers' plays, this image of men boxing on a booth stage, weaving between life-sized paste board figures representing Greek and Trojan soldiers, quite possibly in dramatic earnest, would be a profound dislocation of received wisdom. The outcome of the fight results in a call for the doctor and the arrival of a Quack. This is the point from which Jobson's work has been cited as early evidence for the mummers' play, but it is not helpful to uncouple the material in this way.

Firstly, the dramatis personae reveal an interesting assortment of names. Mr Jobson, presumably the booth owner, plays physician; O'Driscol is played by Mr Murphy which may, of course, simply be an Irishman playing an Irishman but may suggest a comic 'stage Irishman' since Hector is played by Mr *Merryman* (my italics) and Achilles by Mr *Andrew* (again, my italics) as a likely play on Merry Andrew. This was a popular generic for a comedian and Punch, in the preceding sketch, refers to the physic he has ordered from his chemist as 'the balsam of badinage'.[59] There is no way of knowing how complete a record of performance Williams has presented so although no dialogue is reported between Hector and Achilles we cannot be certain that the fight sequence was without speech and there is nothing in the description to confirm whether Hector and Achilles are actors or puppets. Although there are numerous ways in which the material could have been effectively performed, none are reminiscent of later mumming performances.

This is an example of popular professional entertainment in a customary context – an annual fair – drawing content from the repertoire of well-known characters – Punch and the Quack – alongside narrative content from Settle's formerly spectacular telling of the Siege of Troy. Popular entertainment 'in a nutshell' as Jobson's advertising phrased it, with a section of text – and possibly action – that would quickly become central to mummers' plays, but which had already enjoyed a long theatrical life in other plot lines and settings.

Gifford's 'Old Gentleman' c1730; TQM and the Grassington Theatricals, Yorkshire, c1790s–c1800s.

TQM contributed to both volumes of William Hone's antiquarian compilation *The Table Book*.[60] His topic was the Grassington Theatricals in North Yorkshire under the management of Tom Airay which took place in a barn for

> a few weeks in the depth of winter, when the inclemency of the weather [...] rendered the agricultural occupations of himself and his companions impossible to be pursued. They chose rather to earn a scanty pittance by acting, than to trouble their neighbours for eleemosynary support.[61]

TQM is not specific, but I infer a date between the late 1790s and early 1800s, given Airay is clearly still alive and working at the time TQM writes – probably in 1826 or 1827 – though no longer a young man. Furthermore, although the cast may have been younger, their manager surely required some maturity to pull the operation together. TQM informs us that 'The core dramatique…consisted chiefly of young men, (they had no actresses,) who moved in the same line of life as the manager, and whose characters were equally respectable with his'.⁶² He recalls the names Peter W; Isaac G; Waddilove; Frankland of Hetton; Bill Cliff of Skipton; the Hetherington's; Jack Solomon the besom maker; Tommy Summersgill, barber and clock maker; Jack L who migrated to America and Sim Coates, one of the principals, who was club-footed and used to perform *The Fair Penitent*. 'Besides these, there were fifteen or sixteen others from Arncliffe, Litton, Coniston, Kilnsay and other romantic villages'.⁶³

> 'The prices were pit sixpence, and gallery threepence…The stage was lighted by five or six halfpenny candles, and the decorations, considering the poverty of the company, were tolerable. The scenery was respectable; and though sometimes, by sad mishap, the sun or moon would take fire, and expose the tallow candle behind it, was very well managed…The dresses, as far as material went, were good; though not always in character…The audience were always numerous, (no empty benches there) and respectable people often formed a portion'.⁶⁴

TQM undertook additional research and wrote back to Hone with a further inclusion for volume two of the *Table Book*.⁶⁵ He had traced back village theatricals in Linton, a village close by Grassington, to the winter of 1606 and, incidentally, the period when the Simpson Company were operating in the east of the county. On August 1st, 1827, he wrote that 'In the interval of a century from this time, it does not seem that they had much improved their stock of dramas; for within the recollection of old persons with whom I have conversed, one of their favourite performances was "*The Iron Age*" by Heywood'.⁶⁶ Not only is this a recurring usage of the Trojan wars as source material – Heywood then Settle – but TQM also closely echoes an editorial inclusion given some years earlier by Charles Dilke in his 1815 continuation of Dodsley's *Old English Plays*. In an introductory essay to Heywood's *A Challenge to Beauty*, Dilke included a lengthy discussion of Jigs authored by his friend and mentor, the critic William Gifford:

> These jigs, it is certain, continued to be represented in the North of England during the Christmas festivals by young men for the amusement of their friends, long after they had ceased to be so on any regular theatre: and I remember in my early youth to have very frequently been entertained with an account of the dramatic exploits of a very respectable old gentleman, who had been a leading personage on these occasions, had enacted Achilles in Heywood's "*Iron Age*," and figured in several other dramas. He had been a performer in two or three *jigs*, and occasionally repeated and sung portions of the plays and jigs in which he had performed. …. In plays and jigs which he could sing and recite still.'⁶⁷

If we calculate Gifford's (1756–1826) 'early youth' at the commencement of the 1770s and presume an 'old gentleman' to have by then achieved 60 years, these recollections may take us back to the 1730s, some 60 years earlier than those of TQM's informants.

Gifford goes on to say:

> The old gentleman before mentioned, who had by some means acquired the reputation of a poet in his own neighbourhood, used to relate with much humour an application to himself to compose a jig from some scenes of a play which was brought to him; and that a remuneration was offered of somewhat less than a fourth of what is given to Haddit in Taylor's play:⁶⁸ he likewise informed me that the price of admission to see a jig was half that which was given to these rustic performers when they acted a regular play.'⁶⁹

TQM provides a second echo when he implies that the Grassington Company occasionally produced self-authored or self-devised work, sometimes adaptations, perhaps in the manner of earlier drolls. He recalls, though does not name, someone who 'had the reputation of a dramatic manufacturer, though he had, in reality, no talents beyond those of an actor. But his fame drew upon him' and he was able to enhance his earnings.[70]

In Grassington and Linton, TQM continues:

> Sometimes they fabricated a kind of rude drama for themselves; in which case, as it is not very likely that the plot would be very skilfully developed, the performers entered one by one, and each uttered a short metrical prologue, which they very properly chose to call a fore-speech…In these fabrications, I believe, the subjects were frequently taken from printed plays; but the texture was of very inferior workmanship.'[71]

He describes every play, whether tragedy or comedy, as having a 'vice' as 'one of the dramatis personae':

> Armed, as of old, with a sword of lath, and habited in a loose party-coloured dress, with a fur-cap, and fox's brush behind. In some parts of Craven these personages were called clowns, as in Shakespeare's time, and too often and too successfully attempted to excite a laugh by ribaldry and nonsense of their own.[72]

This suggests a well-organised festival of drama, of different types and styles, organised for the Christmas period. It suggests the sustained popularity of Elizabethan plays, available in printed versions, as well as shorter pieces – jigs and possibly droll-like material – locally composed and devised. Lastly, a vice, clown or fool figure seems to have been present both in the full texts and in the shorter pieces, whether occasionally and instinctually liberated from the confines of an existing part (improvising around) or entirely free-floating (we might imagine an anarchic master of ceremonies). In either event, these personages were afforded licence to engage the audience more directly in the action or even to engender additional action by interaction with other actors. These notes are suggestive of customary context and customary content brought together in a comfortable familiarity, pleasing to both performers and audiences.

Frederick Lee and Harry Lupton – Thame Park and the Baronial Hall at Brill c1790–c1840

The Reverend Dr Frederick George Lee (1832–1902) first saw a mummers' play performed in 1839, as a child of seven years, 'in the Hall of the old Vicarage House at Thame'. He later collected the text of the play from 'the lips of one of the performers in 1853'[73] by which time he would have been in his early thirties. As an adult, Lee was in contact with Henry Lupton: 'a local antiquarian and a gentleman of excellent taste and high character'[74] who 'expressed his conviction that my [Lee's] version of the play is most probably the only one that had ever been committed to paper, for the dialogue was purely traditional, and handed down from father to son'.[75] The text that Lee later presented to *Notes and Queries* is clearly a mummers' play but has several features that make it stand out; King Alfred and his Bride, for example, alongside St. George with a talking Dragon as well as a group of morris men.[76] Lee drew on his familiarity with Lupton's works to suggest a varied history for the play he was familiar with:[77]

> I first saw it acted….by those whose custom it had been, from time immemorial, to perform at the houses of the gentle-people of that neighbourhood at Christmas, between St. Thomas's Day and Old Christmas Eve (January 5th). These performers (now long

scattered, and all dead but one, as I am informed) claimed to be the "true and legitimate successors" of the mummers who, in previous centuries, constantly performed at the "Whitsun" and "Christmas Church Ales."[78]

Lupton's 1852 work, however, had drawn on Church Stewards' accounts to describe a clearly separate and different performance associated with sixteenth-century wakes and ales:

> The payments made to the different actors, and the musicians who took part in the celebration of those games, which have been carried out in a manner almost to the present day, by parties travelling in costume from one village to another, with their Lord, Lady, Fool, and other participants, and collecting money on their own account.[79]

The succession Lee referred to can only be that of performance *per se* rather than any specific continuity in content or season. These characters do not accord with the dramatis persona of the mummers' play assigned the same location, and there is no confusing Christmas and Whitsun. In fact, Lupton described two separate successions: first for the mumming (his remark to Lee that it was handed down from father to son), and secondly for the personages of the sixteenth-century Whitsun Ale, still represented into the nineteenth century:

> The last stationary one I recollect was at Brill, when the Baronial Hall, with all its paraphernalia, was carried out to the full extent; and if any wight called anything by its right name, he was fined, or condemned to ride the Lord's high Palfrey, with the Lady.[80]

In addition to the distinctive characters, this suggestion of improvised speech games – the pursuit of non-sequiturs and an insistence on incorrect naming – finds no correlation in the mumming text Lee collected. There may have been a period of overlap when two sets of customary personages made their different seasonal appearances but here, as elsewhere, a local historian does not classify as we might now expect; this is a gathering of customary performance rather than a typology.

Lee goes on to say that the man who provided him with his text had performed at the Baronial Hall of Brill, Buckinghamshire in 1807 and that *his* father had 'done the same' at Thame Park for Lord Wenham c1790. The same source notes that between 1808 and 1814, 'the entertainment was attended by the nobility and gentry for miles round, and is reported to have been produced on a scale of considerable magnificence'.[81] These performances were also given at Brill Hall although the scale of the event is not described. While the mummers' play presents a cast of 11 and a group of morris dancers, it hardly seems 'on a scale of considerable magnificence', a phrase more readily suggestive of grand private theatricals than a humble mummers' play or the characters of a May game.[82] But then, as recently as 1779, the high-profile and influential Banks' family had settled for a similar performance in marking a special occasion at Revesby Abbey in Lincolnshire.[83] Furthermore, as detailed elsewhere in this volume, Lord Stanley and his family appear to have enjoyed a parallel customary entertainment at Alderley Park in Cheshire from the 1820s onwards.

But even as he submitted the text to *Notes and Queries*, Lee inclined to doubt his own aesthetic judgement – not to mention that of the nobility and gentry that constituted at least part of the audience:

> I do not profess to be able to explain the text of the play, nor can I quite admire all its points. Its coarseness, too, is not to my taste. Least of all can I comprehend its purport.

Its anachronisms will be patent to all. But at least its action is vigorous, and, when I was a boy, I confess that I thought the performance most delightful and impressive.[84]

It seems that a mummers' play was performed at Thame Park in the late eighteenth century and formed a centrepiece of lavish Christmas entertainment for some years from the later date of c1810. Something similar, though not on the same scale, took place at the Baronial Hall of Brill during the same period. Lee saw a mummers' play at the Vicarage House in Brill 30 years after that. This is scant evidence but does suggest that the play may have lost an edge of fashionable appeal as we find it recorded at less grand venues. It is possible the mummers' play was originally an assemblage, a characterful dramatic pageant, constructed as a late eighteenth-century Christmas entertainment, with the Church Records providing a *post hoc* historical link to earlier though different parish entertainments, but nevertheless lending cachet through documented continuity. As mummers' plays go, this one presents a fuller catalogue of Merrie England characters than most, including Saint George and the Dragon; Jack and a Giant; King Alfred and his Queen; King William; Old King Cole and Father Christmas.

William Bottrell, Robert Hunt and Thomas Quiller Couch, West Cornwall, c1820s–1860s

Three men born in Cornwall between 1807 and 1826, Robert Hunt, William Bottrell and Thomas Quiller Couch, have all described a range of performance in the west of the county. Their various accounts were published between 1855 and 1871 with both Bottrell and Couch being acknowledged by Hunt in the introduction to his 1865 publication.[85] Couch was a physician and Hunt well-regarded as both geologist and folklorist. Bottrell left Cornwall three times to live and work in France and Spain, then Canada, and then Australia, but retained a life-long interest in learning and telling Cornish folktales. All three writers describe seeing or hearing these performances in their youth or childhood, so it is not always straightforward to determine when the events they describe took place, but all are encompassed by the period 1820 to the 1860s.

The Cornish physician Thomas Quiller Couch was the son of the physician-naturalist Johnathan Couch, and father of the writer and academic Arthur Thomas Quiller Couch. The family lived in Polperro, so his account, which clearly distinguishes between non-play mumming (here goosey dancers or guise dancers) and a Christmas play, is made with reference to a small-town setting.

'On Christmas eve, the mirth begins, when the 'mock' or log is lighted by a portion saved from the last year's fire even the younger children are allowed, as a special favour, to sit up till a late hour to see the fun, and afterwards to "drink to the mock".'[86]

The goosey dancers are house visiting:

> In the course of the evening the merriment is increased by the entry of the 'goosey dancers' (guised dancers), the boys and girls of the village who have rifled their parent's wardrobes of old coats and gowns, and thus disguised dance and sing, and beg money to make merry with. They are allowed, and are not slow to take, a large amount of license in consideration of the season. This mumming is kept up during the week.[87]

In 1865, Hunt expanded his description of geese dancing, first with reference to the Isles of Scilly, but later emphasising the same activity taking place across Cornwall:

> The maidens are dressed up for young men, and the young men for maidens, and, then disguised, they visit their neighbours in companies, where they dance and make jokes […]

in nearly every town and large village in Cornwall, *geese-dancing*, – not goose-dancing formed part of the Christmas entertainments. The term was applied to the old Christmas Plays, and indeed to any kind of sport in which characters were assumed by the performers or disguises worn. These sports were never termed *goose* but always *geese* or *guise* dancing.[88]

In his 1871 *History of Polperro*, Couch again amended his accounts:

[the children] "disguise themselves, their mien, and speech, so cleverly that it is impossible to identify them. They enter without ceremony; dance, sing, and carry on extemporaneous dialogue well spiced with natural wit. After tasting, unasked perhaps, whatever may be on the table, they beg some money to make merry with.[89]

Hunt, meanwhile, had also applied the term to more overtly dramatic material:

In some of the old *geese* dances (*guise* dances from *danse-déguiser*), the giant Blunderbuss and Tom performed a very active part. Blunderbuss was always a big-bellied fellow – his smock-frock being well stuffed with straw. He fought with a tree, and the other giant with the wheel and axle […] The Tinker […] comes in and beats Tom, until Jane comes out with the broom and beats the tinker; and then – as in nearly all these rude plays – St. George and the Turkish Knight come in, but they have no part in the real story of the drama.[90]

Despite carrying the same descriptor, the Christmas play is clearly quite separate in both Hunt's and Couch's minds:

The play is exhibited in the largest room of the inn, or some other public place, and occasionally repeated as one of the entertainments of any feast which may happen in the Christmas week. The players are the young men of the village, and a subscription is made for the purchase of properties, the young damsels contributing their services in the manufacture of the costumes.[91]

This implies that there may be a mobility to play performance and possibly house visiting – the feasts that Couch alludes to. He tells us (1871) that the subject of the play are the achievements of St. George although both Hunt (1865) and Bottrell (1873) describe a different story, involving a serving girl called Duffy, her mother, the squire and the Devil, among other characters.[92] Hunt describes the story as being told by professional Drolls, but also enacted separately by Christmas players:

When I was a boy [Hunt was born in 1807] I well remember being much delighted with the coarse acting of a set of Christmas players, who exhibited in the 'Great Hall' of a farmhouse which I was visiting, and who gave us the principle incidents of Duffy and the Devil Terrytop; one of the company doing the part of the chorus, and filling up by rude description – often in rhyme – the parts which the players could not represent.[93]

Bottrell then describes what seems to be a separate production of the same story, though it is possible that these are the same actors performing in different locations in the same year. My instinct is another group of players, a different version of the story and a different production at a different time. Bottrell says, 'this Droll formed the subject of an old Guise-dance (Christmas Play) which is all but forgotten'.[94] He goes on to offer a dramatis personae and an opening scene which he suggests is recalled from memory but with elements of reconstruction and omission. His prefatory description of remembered performance, however, is vivid:

> Great parts of the dialogue appear to have been improvised, as the actor's fancy dictated. Yet there were some portions in rude verse, which would seem to have been handed down with little variation. Mimical gesticulation expressed much of the story; and when there was unwonted delay in change of scene, or any hitch in acting, in came the hobby-horse and its licenced rider, to keep the mirth from flagging. This saucy jester being privileged to say whatever he pleased kept the audience in good humour by filling up such intervals with burlesque speeches on any matters which had taken place during the past year, that furnished fit subjects for ridicule.
>
> A hall, farmhouse-kitchen, barn or other out-house served for a theatre, and a winnowing-sheet, suspended from key beams or rafters, made a drop-curtain. Father Christmas, as chorus, described the scene, and told the company what characters the actors represented, unless they introduced themselves, as was frequently the case, like St. George, saying 'Here comes I, a champion bold', &c. He also narrated such parts as could not be acted conveniently.
>
> Our simple actors got up their dresses in as old-fashioned and smart a style as they were able to contrive them, by begging or borrowing cast-off finery from the gentry round. [...] their greatest pride was displayed in steeple-crowned or cocked hats, surmounted with plumes and decked with streamers of gay ribbons.
>
> Our rural actresses also wore steeple-crowns fixed high above their heads on pads; stiffen bodies, long-waisted gowns, with bag skirts or long trains; ruffles hanging from their elbows, wide stiff ruffs round their necks; and any other remnants of old finery that they could contrive to get.[95]

Couch, in his *History* of two years earlier, gives further example and detail of the kinds of venues that were converted for purpose, and mentions pre-production fund-raising:

> The theatre was a long room over some fish-cellar, or the largest chamber of the Inn, and the players were the boys and girls of the town. A subscription had been previously made for the purchase of 'properties', and the services of the damsels had been volunteered in arranging the costumes and other adornments.[96]

Bottrell also suggests that these events ended with a dance, to music 'made by Father Christmas'.[97] It is noticeable that the later 1871 and 1873 works both specifically include the girls and women as players. Both versions of Couch's account stress the Christmas plays as an event that had been more popular in the past, and which he believed to be rooted in the *guary mirkl*, the medieval Cornish Mysteries. In a later echo of Borlase (see above), Couch remarks in both 1855 and 1871 that 'the later dramas have not been like the older ones, on Scripture subjects'.[98]

This local interplay between guising, folk tales, dramatised folk tales, mummers' plays and Christmas plays is a striking example of the breadth and fluidity of 'characters assumed' and 'disguises worn'. Overall, it also illustrates the interweaving of the customary and the theatrical at both household and community levels, a central point of this discussion.

Sir Offley Wakeman and the Shropshire Drama – 1830s & 1840s

In 1884, Sir Offley Wakeman published a paper on *Rustic Stage Plays in Shropshire*, which was later reprinted in full by Charlotte Burne in the third volume of her 1886 work on Shropshire Folklore.[99] Here, Burne discussed morris dancing; then morris dancing with associated personages; then the mummers' play; then stage performance, in order to present a tidy evolutionary sequence. For the later stage play section, she drew almost entirely on Wakeman who described performances from the 1830s and 1840s and was able to cite the testimony of elderly former performers in his article. The plays were considered inoffensive (unlike some mummers' plays) though no girls or women acted, and they took place in association with parish wakes which were held around the county between May and October.

> The dresses, ribbons, trinkets &c., as required, were borrowed by the players from the lasses of their acquaintance...the stage was erected on two waggons outside some building, usually in connection with a public house, and was so arranged that the players as they made their exits passed into a sort of Green Room within the building itself... As a rule no more than two players were on the boards at the same time, except in the final scene. On the stage in full view of the audience sat the chairman with his book, who acted as Prompter and Call Boy in one...The actors received no pay but were entertained by the Innkeeper free of expense. The country folk seem to have come from miles round to the representations, as many as 1,000 people being present on some occasions; the performance itself usually lasted about three hours, and was followed by 'fiddling and dancing', in which the spectators joined.[100]

Wakeman goes on to describe the best-known plays as follows:

> *Prince Mucidorus, The Rigs of the Times, St. George and the Fiery Dragon, Valentine and Orson* and *Dr Forster*. In all of them the Fool or Jester seems to have been a very important character; in the local phraseology he is reported to have "played all manner of megrims," and to have been "going on with his manoeuvres all the time."[101] The dress of this important personage included bells at the knee, and a paper mask below a cap of hare skin, with the ears up.[102]

Prince Mucidorous, the popular Elizabethan play, still holds appeal:

> *Prince Mucidorus* seems to have been the favourite piece of all, one old man having played in it no less than 14 times. The plot, as told me by an old blacksmith who as a boy of fourteen took the heroine's part at Chirbury and Priest Weston, was very simple. The heroine (name forgotten) being lost in a wood is attacked by a bear (represented by a man named Whettal dressed in a shaggy skin), and rescued by Prince Mucidorous, who after a terrific contest slays the bear with his sword. At this point of the story the witness came to a stop, and it was only after some pressing that he shyly admitted that the Prince thereupon fell in love with, and eventually married, the heroine.[103]

In the case of St. George and the Fiery Dragon, the Dragon's head was finally struck off to the great amusement of the crowd.[104]

Even in rural communities, in addition to strolling players and nearby theatres, there was a range of seasonal amateur performance, performed and managed by people from the area. Burne suggests that the work represented a '"state of arrested progress" for three hundred years; for nothing in them speaks of a later date than the performances of the "country clowns" in the days of Shakspeare'[sic].[105] The plays themselves have performance histories dating back to c1590 for *Prince Mucidorous* – which Halliwell, in his *Dictionary of Old English Plays*, suggested even then as a kind of droll or farce for the diversion of country people at Christmastime. *St. George and the Fiery Dragon* is also dated as a droll from 1688 but Wakeman and Burne suggest an earlier derivation, citing Chambers, of 1511. Dr Forster was also acted in the 1680s, but Valentine and Orson can be traced back to the 1590s. These unquestionably old plays remained a popular part of the Shropshire repertoire even as they elsewhere entered the scholarly archive; yet, they were of much less interest to the antiquarians than the demonstrably more recent mummers' plays.

Conclusion

The mummers' play took shape in a period when medieval and early modern models of performative house visiting (guising, for example) and household performance (after dinner entertainment, special events for special occasions) continued, especially but not exclusively during the Christmas holidays. Similarly, old fund-raising models, tried and tested through parish wakes, ales, rushbearings, games and performances, began to take on aspects of professional theatre structures, probably through the intermediary examples afforded by the exceptional spread of touring and strolling companies. Both sets of conditions had long since blurred clear distinction between amateurs and semi-professionals or between a social aesthetic (complex local arrangements for having fun while simultaneously meeting a host of obligations) and reward. Although the examples considered here all strike as pretty comfortable, we should not forget that men also went mumming to alleviate poverty and that strolling players, often comprising families as well as individual adults, faced hardship and uncertainty.

Permeating this creative work there are familiar personages, sections of text, event-images and action sequences which conjoin in endless variety. A St. George here, a Quack Doctor there; actors, puppets, animal disguises; fools as agitators, commentators, and mediators; print and manuscript sources; folk tales and Elizabethan plays. These were worked and re-worked, adapted, amended, changed, sampled, re-ordered and juxtaposed. The term *traditional* is problematised by this inconstant yet largely conservative creativity, this battery of bricolage. Notwithstanding, much of this performance took place under customary auspices and might itself – eventually and by default – become traditional. The term *folk* is also problematised by the context of some of this performance, particularly household performance, particularly in big houses where the example of '*Pyramus and Thisbe*' springs uncomfortably to mind. Despite the genuine delight taken in mummers' visits by some of the Stanleys at Alderley Park, for example, one cannot help but wonder what some of the 'nobility and gentry for miles around' made of the mummers' play (if indeed that is what it was) at Thame Park? The line between patronage and patronisation need not be a fine one: neither word sits comfortably with *folk* as 'of the people'; both usages contrast the celebratory, rebellious and resistant associations and undertones of the post-mid-twentieth-century prefix *folk*.

One last point, certainly connecting with those made earlier by Pettitt, is that these theatres can often be distinguished by their mobility. A definitive feature of mummers' plays is that they foreground perambulation, arrival, assemblage, entrance, exit and departure. The variety structure present in these examples of household theatre, and indeed in Jobson's booth, keep prompting the audience to ask who is arriving next and what will they do? In the 'big house' performances, these matters of arrival, assemblage and performance are at least as important for the spectators as for the actors – indeed, all are actors at these social occasions. We do not know enough about the audiences at events like the Grassington theatricals or the Shropshire plays to know whether the same ambitions applied, but it is tempting to imagine that these were special days requiring a special effort on the part of audiences – always happy to meet, converse and impress.

The performers of mummers' plays could only very rarely have worked in a theatrical vacuum. The late nineteenth- and early twentieth-century folkloric determination that mummers' plays should be separate and exceptional to other theatres is itself exceptional. It can only be derived from the intertwining of two Victorian passions – romantic antiquarianism and taxonomy.

Notes

1. Tom Pettitt, 'Towards an Anatomy of English Customary Drama: Theatre, Stage, Play', Chapter 1, this volume.
2. Samuel Cox, 15th January 1591, letter to an unknown correspondent, cited by Edmund K Chambers, *The Elizabethan Stage*, 4 vols. (Oxford: Clarendon Press, 1933), vol. 4, appendix 44, p. 237.
3. See in particular G. W. Boddy, 'Players of Interludes in North Yorkshire in the Early Seventeenth Century', North Yorkshire Record Office Publications, 3 (North Yorkshire County Council, 1976), pp. 95–130; Siobhan Keenan, 'The Simpson Players of Jacobean Yorkshire and the Professional Stage', *Theatre Notebook*, 67.1, (2013), 16–35 and Paul Whitfield White, *Drama and Religion in English Provincial Society, 1485–1660* (Cambridge: Cambridge University Press, 2008), particularly 'The Simpsons: Personnel, Patronage, and Prosecution', pp. 156–167.
4. White, *Drama and Religion*, particularly 'The Stanton-Harcourt Players at Witney', pp. 197–204.
5. *Mucidoros* is an anonymous Elizabethan play from c1590 which keeps cropping up in discussion of provincial theatre. It first appeared in a 1598 first quarto and in 18 subsequent editions by 1668.
6. Joseph Strutt, *Glig-Gamena Angel-Deod, or the Sports and Pastimes of the People of England* (London: Methuen, 1801) Book 3, Chapter 2, p. 141.
7. The OED records the first usage of the collocation 'mummers' play' in James Orchard Halliwell, *Popular Rhymes and Nursery Tales* (London: John Russell Smith, 1849), pp. 231–236, 231.
8. For a full discussion of these six examples, see Peter Harrop, *Mummers' Plays Revisited* (Abingdon: Routledge, 2019), pp. 75–121.
9. Tom Pettitt, 'Beyond the Bad Quarto: Exploring the Vernacular Afterlife of Early Modern Drama', *Journal of Early Modern Studies*, 8 (2019), pp. 133–171.
10. Andrew Brice, *The Mobiad: Or, Battle of the Voice. An Heroic Comic Poem, Sportively Satirical: Being a Briefly Historical, Natural and Lively, Free and Humorous, Description of an Exeter Election. In Six Canto's. Illustrated with Such Notes as for Some Readers May Be Supposed Useful. By Democritus Juvenal, Moral Professor of Ridicule, and Plaguy Pleasant Fellow of Stingtickle College*, vulgarly, Andrew Brice Exon. Exeter (Brice and Thorn, London: T. Davies, 1770). The six cantos run to 178 pages and the first canto, by way of example, contains 37 occasionally cross-referenced footnotes. Many of these relate to the civic and customary year in Exeter.
11. Davies, *The Critical Review: Or, Annals of Literature by a Society of Gentlemen* (30 July 1770) (London: A. Hamilton), entry 16, pp. 312–314, 312.
12. Davies, *The Critical Review*, p. 314.
13. Brice, *The Mobiad*, p. 90.
14. Ibid.
15. T. N. Brushfield, 'Andrew Brice and the Early Exeter Newspaper Press', *Report and Transactions of the Devonshire Association for the Advancement of Science, Literature and Art* (Exeter, July 1888), pp. 163–214, 191.
16. Tindal, 'Memoirs of the Late Mr Andrew Brice of Exeter; with a Striking Likeness of That Singular Character', *Universal Magazine*, 69 (November 1781), pp. 281–283, 283.
17. Brushfield, 'Andrew Brice', pp. 180–181.
18. G. Oliver, 'Biographies of Exonians', *Trewman's Exeter Flying Post*, Thursday, January 4, 1849, 6–7, 7.
19. John Wesley Thomas, *Reminiscences of Methodism in Exeter* (Exeter: The Daily Western Times Office, 1875), pp. 7–8.
20. Ian Maxted, Ian Maxted, Brice, Andrew (1692–1773), printer. Oxford Dictionary of National Biography. Retrieved 17 March 2021, from https://www.oxforddnb.com/view/10.1093/ref:odnb/9780198614128.001.0001/odnb-9780198614128-e-3379.
21. Tindall, 'Memoirs of the Late Mr Andrew Brice', p. 283.
22. Two footnotes (Brushfield, 'Andrew Brice and the Early Exeter Newspaper', p. 193) indicate that Brushfield attempted to check Oliver's sources (see Oliver, *Exeter Flying Post*, Thursday January 4, 1849, pp. 6–7) and appears to have found confirmation in the *Thespian Directory* of 1802.

23 Brushfield, 'Andrew Brice and the Early Exeter Newspaper', p. 214.
24 'Now party battle proves a social play'. Brice, *The Mobiad*, p. 177.
25 John Jackson, *The History of the Scottish Stage, from Its First Establishment to the Present Times; With a Distinct Narrative of Some Recent Theatrical Transactions. The Whole Necessarily Interspersed, with Memoirs of His Own Life* (London: Peter Hill, 1793), p. 409.
26 Alex Helm, *The English Mummers' Play* (Woodbridge: D.S. Brewer for The Folklore Society, 1981), p. 7 cites Jackson's birth date as 1742 in line with earlier editions of the *Dictionary of National Biography* and, in the light of biographical data calculated from that date, reasonably suggests Yorkshire 'approximately circa 1750' as a date and location for the performance described. The current edition of the *Dictionary of National Biography* cites 1729/1730 as Jackson's DOB and I would therefore suggest circa early 1740s as a more likely date for the performance. On pp. 45–47 of his *History*, Jackson describes the complex family situation, political and financial, that led to his removal to his uncle's home in Westmoreland. Although his account is not entirely clear in this respect, it is still suggestive of the 1740s. Finally, the only other usage of 'remote' in Jackson's work refers to Bala in North Wales (pp. 221–222). By way of comparative usage, I would therefore rule out Doncaster on the grounds of population and prefer Kirby Lonsdale to Keighley since the latter was part of an industrialising area. Jackson had been sent to live with his uncle 'on a small paternal estate [...] it was in the neighbourhood of Kirkby Lonsdale in Westmorland' (p. 47).
27 Jackson, *The History of the Scottish Stage*, p. 409.
28 Ibid.
29 Ibid., pp. 409–410.
30 Ibid., p. 369.
31 Ibid.
32 Ibid., p. 367.
33 'The repertoire comic sketch known as "Hippisley's Drunken Man", a monologue in which a supposedly inebriate actor reads and comments on newspaper articles, was quite popular. The original version was performed by the Bristol actor manager, John Hippisley, no later than the 1740s'. See David Worrall, *Celebrity Performance, Reception: British Georgian Drama as Social Assemblage* (Cambridge: Cambridge University Press, 2013), p. 254, note 21. Worrall also provides playbill details of two later revivals. Firstly: 'The much and long desired interlude of the Celebrated Hippesley's drunken man' (1776) and secondly, 'To which is Added Hippisley's Drunken-Man, As altered and spoken by Mr Lee Lewes' (1787).
34 Sybil Rosenfeld, *Theatre of the London Fairs in the Eighteenth Century* (Cambridge: Cambridge University Press. 1960), p. 50.
35 Rosenfeld, *Theatre of the London Fairs*, pp. 45–46.
36 *The Daily Courant*, March 28th, 1726, advertised the Company. See Emmett Avery, 'Foreign Performers in the London Theatres in the Early Eighteenth Century', *Philological Quarterly*, 16.2 (April 1937), pp. 105–123. On p. 113, fn. 30, Avery cites J. Fransen, *Les Comédies Francais en Hollande au XVll et au XlXe siècles* (Paris: Honoré Champion, 1925), p. 267. Fransen suggests this may be Marc-Anthoine Lalauze who performed in Brussels the following season 1726–1727. Rosenfeld, *Foreign Theatrical Companies in Great Britain in the 17th and 18th Centuries* (London: The Society for Theatre Research Pamphlet Series, no. 4. 1954–55, 1955), p. 14, notes The Italian Company as being particularly strong in dancers.
37 Jackson, *The History of the Scottish Stage*, pp. 410–411.
38 John Wallis, *The Natural History and Antiquities of Northumberland*, 2 vols. (London: W and W Strahan, 1769), vol.2, pp. 28–29.
39 Jackson, *The History of the Scottish Stage*, p. 410.
40 Ibid.
41 William Borlase, *The Natural History of Cornwall* (Oxford: W. Jackson, 1758), p. 299.
42 Philip Butterworth, 'Putting On and Removing the Mask: Layers of Performance Pretence', *Early Theatre*, 21.1 (2018), pp. 33–58.
43 Borlase, *The Natural History*, pp. 298–299.
44 Thomas Pettitt, 'English Folk Drama in the Eighteenth Century: A Defense of the "Revesby Sword Play"', *Comparative Drama*, Spring, 15.1 (1981), pp. 3–29, p. 28, note 38.
45 In March 1730, at the Little Haymarket Theatre, Henry Fielding had his first popular success with *The Author's Farce*; its third act, entitled 'The Pleasures of the Town', was played by actors impersonating puppets, in turn, representing well-known personalities of the day. See Martin C.

Battiston, 'Henry Fielding', *ODNB* [accessed 26 April 2020]. Foote's later effort may have been part of a trend or simply a reinvigoration of a popular idea – certainly, by 1758, this was by no means a new idea and was sufficiently successful and controversial (it had angered actors) for Foote to periodically employ the technique into the 1770s. See P.T. Dircks, 'Samuel Foote', *ODNB*, 2000.

46 Rosenfeld, *Theatre of the London Fairs*, p. 14.
47 Abigail Williams, 'Elkanah Settle', *ODNB*, 2004. For a discussion of the ways in which contemporary theatrical style may have shaped the mummers' play, see Harrop, *Mummers' Plays Revisited*, pp. 36–43.
48 See John Williams, *The Eccentricities of John Edwin, Comedian. Collected from His Manuscripts; and Enriched with Several Hundred Original Anecdotes, Arranged and Digested by Anthony Pasquin Esq*, 2 vols. (London: J. Strahan, 1791), vol. 1, pp. 262–264. It was the section of dialogue between O'Driscoll and the physician that first drew the attention of mumming scholars. There is nothing to suggest that either these characters or this dialogue appeared in earlier productions of Settle's work. Indeed, this seems so far removed from Settle's work that it stretches the compass of adaptation.
49 James Sambrook, 'John Williams' [pseudonym Anthony Pasquin] *ODNB*, 2004, cites the allegation of dirtiness. The originator was the famously barbed critic, editor and scholar William Gifford, author of the satiric poem *The Baviad* first published in 1791. In the course of that work, he also described Williams as 'devoid of brains'; then added 'nothing from thy jabbernowl can spring/ but impudence and filth' culminating with 'fit garbage for the hell-hound infamy'. See Gifford, William, *The Baviad and Maeviad* (new and revised edition, London: J. Wright, 1797) pp. 35–36. In 1797, Williams retaliated by suing Gifford for defamation in a famous case involving over 40 booksellers. In any event, as we shall see, both men were possessed of sufficient good qualities that the successful actor John Edwin was content to have his memoirs ghosted by Williams (these were published the same year as *The Baviad*), while the editor Charles Dilke received support from Gifford and was pleased to include a short essay of Gifford's as evidential support (regarding the Jig as a theatre form) within one of his own edited volumes (see note 67 below) published in 1816.
50 The French Horn Tavern in Cheapside and the Falcon in Fetter Lane. See Terry Enright, 'John Edwin the Elder', *ODNB*, 2004.
51 Williams, *The Eccentricities*, vol. 1, p. 255.
52 The description of the performer known as Phillips is from James Granger, *A Biographical History of England etc.*, 4 vols. (2 vols. each in 2 parts) (London: W. Nicholson, 1769), vol. 2, Part 2, p. 561.
53 Strutt, *Sports and Pastimes*, p. 145.
54 Williams, *The Eccentricities*, vol. 1, p. 256.
55 Henryk Jurkowski, *Aspects of Puppet Theatre* (London: Palgrave MacMillan, 2014), p. 105, discusses historical examples of similar confusion but his eighteenth-century example suggests satirical complicity rather than the naivety it alleges. Jurkowski draws on David Erskine Baker, Isaac Reed and Stephen Jones, *Biografia Dramatika or, a Companion to the Playhouse, Containing Historical and Critical Memoirs, and Original Anecdotes, of British and Irish Dramatic Writers*, 3 vols., in 4 pts (London: Longman, 1812), to offer Samuel Foote's example of a country girl who found it difficult to distinguish between puppets and players due to the spirit and truth of the performances. Foote, who owned the Haymarket lease before selling it to Colman in 1776, would have been well known to both Edwin and Williams at their time of writing. He had first employed life-sized puppets in 1758 to mixed reviews and re-engaged with the technique in 1773 when the following text formed part of his live introduction to the opening night:

> Being brought by her friends for the first time to a puppet-show, she was so struck with the spirit and truth of the imitation, that it was scarce possible to convince her, but all the puppets were players; being carried the succeeding night to one of the theatres, it became equally difficult to satisfy her, but that all the players were puppets.
>
> (Baker et al., 1812, vol. 3, 153)

Note 45, above, references Henry Fielding's even earlier – 1730 – engagement with an interplay of life-sized puppets and actors.
56 Williams, *The Eccentricities*, vol. 1, p. 262.
57 Ibid.
58 Ibid., p. 263.
59 Ibid., p. 259.

60 Pseudonyms were commonly adopted by contributors to journals and the anonymous TQM is typical in this respect although he was tentatively identified as the poet Robert Story in *Notes & Queries*, 3rd Series, 10 (1866), p. 209. See TQM, 'Thomas Airay, The Grassington Manager and his Theatrical Company, Craven, Yorkshire', in *The Table Book with Seventy Engravings*, ed. by William Hone (London: Hunt and Clarke, 1827), cols. 69–74. TQM, 'Grassington Theatricals', in *The Table Book, with Forty Six Engravings*, ed. by William Hone (London: Hunt and Clarke, 1828), cols. 247–248.
61 TQM in Hone, *The Table Book with Seventy Engravings*, col. 70.
62 Ibid., col. 71.
63 Ibid.
64 Ibid., col. 72.
65 Ibid., cols. 247–248.
66 Ibid., col. 247. Heywood had been 70 years ahead of Settle in using the Trojan wars as source material for his play, which first appeared in 1632, and this present reiteration demonstrates the sustained popularity of familiar material.
67 The original prologue to Heywood's *Challenge for Beauty* refers to Jigs. In Dilke's edition, the reference is footnoted, with the note taking the form of a disquisition on the form. I had previously supposed this to have been authored by Dilke and am indebted to Tom Pettitt for pointing out Dilke's passing reference to 'the gentlemen alluded to in the preface'. This turns out to be William Gifford the critic, editor and scholar (see note 49 above) who was something of a mentor to Dilke. See Charles Wentworth Dilke, *Old Plays: Being a Continuation of Dodsley's Collection, with Notes Critical and Explanatory* (London: Printed for Rodwell and Martin, 1816), vol. VI, pp. 325–331.
68 The play is *The Hog Hath Lost His Pearl* by Robert Tailor, first performed by the apprentices at Whitefriars in 1613. The character Haddit has been commissioned to write a jig for a player and their interaction concerns a down payment in return for a glimpse of the introduction. Haddit is concerned that the player will visually memorise the introduction and have the piece finished for less by another composer. The player, meanwhile, refuses to pay without hard evidence of progress on the part of Haddit. The player offers two angels; Haddit argues him up to four angels. (The coin changed in value over time but would have been worth somewhere between six and eight shillings. Dilke's 'old man' might therefore have received between three and six shillings.) For a full text, see http://cord.ung.edu/tailhog.html [accessed 26 November 2019].
69 Gifford in Dilke, *Old Plays*, vol. 6, p. 330.
70 TQM in Hone, *The Table Book, With Forty Six Engravings*, vol. 2, col. 248. This seems strikingly coincidental unless TQM and Gifford's 'old gentlemen' were coincidentally known to one another.
71 Ibid., col. 248.
72 Ibid., col. 247.
73 Frederick George Lee, 'Oxfordshire Christmas Miracle Play', *Notes and Queries*, 5th series, vol. 2 (26 December 1874), pp. 503–505, p. 503.
74 Ibid., p. 504.
75 Ibid.
76 All the players are afforded the direction 'Enter' followed by their respective character name. Only the dragon receives the direction 'The Dragon speaks'. This acknowledgement of a 'talking animal' might suggest a mechanical device of some sort rather than (for example) an actor with a hobby, hooden or tourney dragon. The dates suggested by Lee's source, and the date of Lee's correspondence with *Notes and Queries*, coincide with a period of popularity of St. George plays and pantomimes. *Saint George and the Dragon or the Seven Champions of Christendom* in 1822; Beckett and Lemon's *St. George and the Dragon* in the 1830s; Pearson's entire family of talking dragons in his 'entirely new' pantomime at Plymouth Theatre Royal in 1858 and Planch's 1869 *St. George*. In this respect, the text is suggestive of a relatively late interplay between commercial theatre and the mummers' play, both in content and context.
77 These are Harry Lupton, *Extracts from the Accounts of the Proctors and Stewards of the Prebendal Church of the Blessed Virgin of Thame. Commencing …1529 and Ending …1641 etc.* (Thame: Henry Bradford, 1852) and Harry Lupton, *History of Thame and Its Hamlets* (Thame: J. E. & F. Bradford, 1860). Lee suggests that 'some account of these performances are given' in that work. I can find no trace. The earlier work contains a prefatory address to his friends and neighbours wherein Lupton draws our attention (p. iv) to the years 1555 and 1557 where expenditure is detailed in relation to ales and morris dance accoutrements, and further specifies payment to a Vicar who played the part of a Fool. These characters, however, don't match the dramatis personae of the mummers' play that Lee communicates in *Notes and Queries* (note 78 above) and again, some years later, in his own

book on the Church. See Frederick George Lee, *History, Description and Antiquities of the Prebendal Church of the Blessed Virgin Mary of Thame* (London: Mitchell & Hughes, 1883), cols. 53–55 describe both mystery and miracle play performances, whereas appendix IV, cols. 675–678, reprints Lee's 'Oxfordshire Christmas' cited above.

78 Lee, 'Oxfordshire Christmas', p. 503.
79 Lupton, *Extracts from the Accounts*, p. iv.
80 Ibid. My reading of this is that the game (and its personages) remained at the Hall rather than visiting nearby villages – hence 'stationary'. I read 'carried to the full extent' to refer to the extravagance of the event – synonymous with 'going all out' in contemporary usage – at a time when the Hall possessed particular prestige and influence, rather than signifying matters of staging. Whether the palfrey was an actual horse, or stage device, is unclear.
81 Lee, 'Oxfordshire Christmas', p. 503.
82 See Harrop, *Mummers' Plays Revisited*, particularly, pp. 53–74, for a discussion of private theatricals in relation to the hosting of mummers' plays. For a discussion of Georgian private theatricals *per se*, see, for example, Carly Watson, 'Private Theatricals in the Harcourt Family Papers', *Nineteenth Century Theatre & Film*, 38.2 (Winter, 2011), pp. 14–25.
83 See Harrop, *Mummers' Plays Revisited*, pp. 83–92.
84 Lee, 'Oxfordshire Christmas', p. 504.
85 The works referred to are as follows: William Bottrell, *Traditions and Hearthside Stories of West Cornwall*, 2nd Series (Penzance: Beare and Son, 1873); Robert Hunt, *Popular Romances of the West of England; Or, the Drolls, Traditions and Superstitions of Old Cornwall*, First series (London: John Camden Hotten, 1865); Thomas Quiller Couch, 'Thomas Q Couch Continues the Folk Lore of a Cornish Village: Fasts and Festivals', *Notes and Queries,* 1st series, vol. 12 (29 December 1855), p. 507 and *The History of Polperro a Fishing Town on the South Coast of Cornwall by the Late Jonathan Couch, F. L S., with a Short Account of the Life and Labours of the Author, and Many Additions on the Popular Antiquities of the District*, ed. by Thomas Q. Couch (Truro: W. Lake, 1871).
86 Couch, 'The Folk Lore of a Cornish Village', p. 507; 'A Note on the Usage "mock"'. This referred to the root or stump of a tree which was the preferred log to burn at Christmas.
87 Ibid.
88 Hunt, *Popular Romances*, p. 308.
89 Couch, *The History of Polperro*, pp. 161–162.
90 Hunt, *Popular Romances*, p. 37.
91 Couch, 'The Folk Lore of a Cornish Village', p. 507.
92 The source material suggests a version of the existing folk narrative Rumpelstiltskin, also commonly known as Tom Tit Tot (Aarne Thompson Uther Index tale type 500). The dramatisation of existing folk narratives is not uncommon – see, for example, Pettitt's discussion of The Golden Ball, Chapter 1, this volume.
93 Hunt, *Popular Romances*, p. 273.
94 Bottrell, *Traditions and Hearthside Stories*, p. 1.
95 Ibid., pp. 1–2.
96 Couch, *The History of Polperro*, pp. 162–163.
97 Bottrell, *Traditions and Hearthside Stories*, p. 26.
98 Couch, 'The Folk Lore of a Cornish Village', p. 507; Couch, *The History of Polperro*, p. 163.
99 Sir Offley Wakeman, 'Rustic Stage Plays in Shropshire', *Transactions of the Shropshire Archaeological and Natural History Society*, vol. 7 (Shrewsbury: Adnitt & Naunton, 1884), pp. 383–388. This was reprinted in full in Charlotte Sophia Burne, *Shropshire Folk-Lore: A Sheaf of Gleanings from the Collections of Georgina F Jackson*, 3 vols., Part 3 (London: Trubner & Co., 1883–1886 [1886]), pp. 493–499. Because Burne both prefaces and follows her inclusion with useful additional material, I have cited that edition.
100 Burne, *Shropshire Folk-Lore*, p. 494. Burne later adds (p. 499) that Wakeman had informed her of the use of a single manuscript prompt copy from which each individual actor made a record of their own part.
101 Megrim: 'Antics, Tricks, Gesticulations, Grimaces'. *The English Dialect Dictionary*, ed. by Joseph Wright (London, Henry Frowde, 1905), vol. 4, M-Q, p. 80.
102 Burne, *Shropshire Folk-Lore*, p. 495.
103 Ibid., pp. 496–497.
104 Ibid., p. 497.
105 Ibid., p. 493.

5

THE ALDERLEY MUMMERS' PLAY

A story of longevity

Duncan Broomhead

> The play burst unexpectedly into my local pub when I was 18 and I had no idea what was going on, other than a sense that it must be traditional, and that it was great fun. Thereafter, I always wanted to be involved, and a few years of pestering later, I was asked to cover the role of the groom, later graduating to the Doctor in the tragic way that all the main promotions always take place in such plays. Dead men's shoes. Consequently, I'm abundantly aware of the many, many people who've inhabited the role before me, and the responsibility that comes with ensuring many more will after me. The play is joyful. I'm a great believer that tradition shouldn't just be carried out for the sake of it. The Alderley Mummers' play is funny, the costumes flamboyant, the characters daft and likeable. It stands up as good entertainment without the audience needing to understand its history. Traditional performance must be good art in its own right, not performed out of a sense of worthiness or obligation. This play excels on that front. It's a great bunch of people, and I hope to be involved for the rest of my life.
>
> (Tom Kitching, *Doctor*, 31 December 2019)

Introduction

The narrative of the Alderley Mummers' play begins at the start of the nineteenth century and is very much a tale of two families: the Barber family who performed the play and the Stanley family who were its patrons.[1] The Barbers were a large and well-established family centred around Brynlow Farm, tenanted land on the Alderley Park Estate.[2] Other family members lived at nearby Bradford House and Mottram House and though many were farmers, others were employed in various duties on the Alderley Park Estate. Their patrons, the Stanleys, owners of the 4,500-acre estate, moved in the country's highest political and social circles and held the patriarchal outlook of the period towards their tenants and staff. This extended relationship between the two families makes it possible to describe much of the life history of the play, from the original Alderley Mummers (c1804–1937) through to its revival and contemporary performance (1977–2020), a span of over 200 years.

During an interview conducted in 1914, William Barber suggested that the play was started by his Grandfather Samuel, along with Samuel's brother William, 'rather more than a century ago'.[3] Samuel's great grandson Alec, interviewed in 1954, gave a roughly similar date of 150 years.[4] These broad assertions give a range of somewhere between c1804 and c1812.[5] The earlier approximate date has entered the wider record via published works by Alex Helm (1955) and Margaret Dean-Smith (1966).[6] We also know that at least one mummers' play was extant in Cheshire prior to 1788[7] although the 1st Lord Stanley, a keen antiquarian, makes no mention of such dramatic activity or related customs in the record of his pursuit of local customs in the 1790s. This early Cheshire play, forming part of the Douce Manuscripts at the Bodleian Library, has only four characters, Slasher, St. George, Doctor and Prince Saladine, compared to the six who would first feature in the Alderley play. Notwithstanding, textual analysis of this manuscript does show similarities to the Alderley text and it is quite feasible that the Barbers should have learned their play from someone in their neighbourhood, or even from another family member.

From 1803, however, we start to find intriguing mention of seasonal dramatic activity on the Alderley estate.

Pre-1850 (1st Lord Stanley)

> [...] we've found venues where we're appreciated and welcomed.
> (John Portlock, *Beelzebub*, 27/12/2019)

Four references from the first quarter of the nineteenth century mention mumming at the Park. The first two relate to week-long celebrations during the first week of January 1803, marking the birth of twin sons Edward John and William Owen Stanley. The second two references come 21 years later from reports of another week-long celebration, during the second week of January 1824, this time for the boy's coming of age. The first pair of references are from letters written early in 1803 by Maria Josepha, Lady Stanley. On 5th January, she wrote:

> [....] and afterwards on the stage were exhibited performances of various kinds, mummers, snapdragon, a pantomime, including harlequin and columbine and the clown in proper dresses.[8]

In a further letter dated 20th January, she writes about 'Thursday's entertainments':

> [...] a Wild Man, *i.e.* a man in bear's clothing, afforded great amusement to the world in general, and one of the Mummers from Winston sung extremely well.[9]

The next pair of references, those detailing the boy's coming of age, are found in a newspaper cutting bearing the handwritten date of 5 January 1824:

> In the course of the evening, they amused themselves with the usual Christmas gambols of the horse's head and mummers, with various other pastimes.[10]

The Manchester Mercury reported on the same celebrations:

> At intervals, the company received much pleasure from various amusements, such as the hermit, (the character of which admirably supported, the wild man, old hob, &c. &c.[11]

The wild man had also been a feature of the 1803 celebrations; it is unclear what the hermit did, but Old Hob was a recognised horse's head custom in Cheshire.[12] In short, there are elements here of performed customs and various kinds of dramatic enactment, comprising representative examples of seasonal 'big-house' entertainment, but no actual mummers' play as would later be understood. For that, the first definite reference is found in the writing of Louisa Dorothea Stanley, daughter of Maria Josepha and John Thomas Stanley. Her undated papers, categorised by the Cheshire Records Office as '1812–1856', include *The Dialogue or Play of St George as Performed by the Soulers or Mummers at Alderley Park*.[13] The relevant 16 pages of handwritten text include some stage directions and explanatory notes as well as the text of a play for six characters: an unnamed announcer, St. George, Prince Paradine, young Slasher, the Doctor and Beelzebub.

The following marginalia, presumably made by Louisa Stanley herself, are of interest: '*This play I have written from a rough copy I obtained from the man who acts the piece*'[14] and '*In a former copy which I once had & lost many years ago, I think instead this over again it was thus* [sic]

> ST GEORGE *I am St George that valiant Knight*
> *Who shed his blood for England's right*
> *For England's right & England's reason*
> *Therefore I carry this bold weapon.*'[15]

Finally: '*The Doctors speech used to be much longer but the* [two illegible words] *are here omitted*'.[16] So, Louisa Stanley had owned and lost a copy of the play 'many years ago', but fortunately obtained a second rough copy from a performer and was able to produce this fair copy. Her notes are not entirely clear, but she seems to offer an earlier version of a St. George speech – 'I think instead it was thus'? or 'When I think again it was thus'? and she notes that parts of the Doctor's speech appear to have been omitted in the more recent version. Starting on a separate page at the end of the play text is the five-verse song of the '*Soulers or Mummers*' as she titles them. (This flexible usage would be repeated some years later in letters from Katherine Louisa Stanley, daughter of the 2nd Lord Stanley.) Louisa Stanley was sufficiently interested not only to produce a fair copy but to compare her memory of an earlier copy with a new one. Also, she prefaces and concludes her manuscript with acknowledgement of extant published versions of mummers' plays citing George Ormerod's 1819 work *The History of the County Palatine and City of Chester*, which had included an extract from 'The Mock Play, entitled "St. George and Slasher"'.[17] As she puts it, 'Ormerod gives the song very nearly in the same words. I obtained mine from our own actors – Ormerod mentions it as being in Brands' Popular Antiquities'.[18]

1850 to 1869 (2nd Lord Stanley)

> The mummers is a bit of an old family tradition – as performed by my ancestors of the Barber family, in and around Nether Alderley. I do it because it's a buzz and of course for the free beer provided at the pubs in which we perform. It's good entertainment!
> (Nicholas Houseman, *Groom*, 27/12/2019)

The eldest of the twins, Edward John Stanley, a Member of Parliament, a strong Liberal and a member of Palmerston's Cabinet, succeeded as the 2nd Lord Stanley. In 1859, his 15-year-old daughter Katherine Louisa Stanley, known as Kate to her family, wrote two letters about a group of Soulers who had recently visited Alderley Park and performed in the servant's quarters.

On 28th October 1859, she wrote to her mother Henrietta Maria Stanley:

> At 10 o'clock just as we were finishing our Whist we heard a singing outside the windows & we guessed it was the Soulers so we sent Rose to ask & finding they were actors who wished to perform Papa said he was going to his room but we might go & amuse ourselves. We went to see the performance at the bottom of the stone stairs all the maids were there but we were very disappointed when we found they could only sing a one song. They have no play to learn so I wish we could get them one as they are very well got up & and have a very good horse like ours. These are the only idea of the Mummers that the Parish has as the Barbers never perform so they ought to act something. Philip Potts was the one who led the horse & I daresay they would have had some fun if we had not forbidden them to come onto the stairs where the maids all stood. Papa thought it was very slow to have no chase after the maids; it is to be hoped we shall have one this Christmas.[19]

A few days later, on 1st November, Kate wrote a letter about the Soulers to her brother Edward Lyulph Stanley, who would later become the 4th Lord Stanley:

> We had some men here the other day who go about beautifully got up & with a regular Mummers Horse; they go & act at the Farms, that is to say sing, for there is no acting, only a prancing about on the part of the horse. I wish we could get them something short & easy to act; of course they could not invent it themselves & they are the only idea the people have of the Mummers, as the Barbers never act but here. Philip Potts, ex footman was at the head of them.[20]

A number of points can be drawn from these two letters. The terms souling and mumming are still used flexibly, but with some distinctions between them. The Barber family are 'mummers' but only perform at the Hall and, we are told, they have a very good 'horse', an additional character to those referred to by Louisa Dorothy some years earlier. We can infer from Ms Stanley that local people – 'the Parish' – have never seen the Barbers perform but that they are familiar with Soulers, who sang both outside and inside the Hall, and brought their 'very good horse'. Since the leader of the Soulers is an ex-footman, perhaps that explains their visit to the Hall? Might that have provided a special degree of ingress or would any groups of Soulers have been as welcome? The fact that Lord Stanley was disappointed the horse didn't chase the maids (although someone with authority clearly forbade it) suggests a comfortable familiarity with the visitors and the custom, as does Kate's wish that they be given a play to act. Furthermore, these dates for the Soulers' visit coincide with the established Cheshire custom of souling, traditionally performed on 1st and 2nd November. Kate's wish for a 'chase' at Christmas suggests a collating of mumming with Christmas.

Over the next ten years, however, further letters suggest that neither of these customary activities were so fixed. The following year, 1860, Kate mentions mummers in three letters to her brother Edward Lyulph. On 16th November, she wrote to describe events at a house party at Alderley: 'The first evening we had vingt-un & to-night (Thursday) we had the Mummers in the tenants Hall & then competitive Examination & then Billiards'.[21] Two days later, on 18th November 1860, she writes about a house guest, one Mr Ellis, saying: 'I wish I did not make spelling mistakes when I copy anything as Mr Ellis found some in my "Mummers"'.[22] Then, on either 19th or 20th November, Kate tells us that 'Mr Ellis led the horse about last night among the maids & he did it so well & did not frighten them too much'.[23]

These simple references contain tantalising possibilities. If Mr Ellis found spelling mistakes in Kate's 'Mummers', had Kate copied out her grandmother's earlier text, or made a copy of a more recent performance by the Barber's? Had she copied a text from somewhere else or authored her own version? Had such a text formed the basis of a performance by the house guests which featured Mr Ellis as either being 'in' the horse, or playing the horse's groom (since 'he led the horse about')? Is this a case of 'private theatricals' with the guests performing the Barber's Christmas mummers' play in November for the assembled guests? Alternatively, did Kate perhaps refer to a written copy she had made of a souler's song, which might be more easily tied to November? Had a smaller number of guests re-enacted a souler's visit, or had Mr Ellis simply undertaken a one-man costumed chase amongst the maids – presumably sanctioned by all concerned. In any of those events, a 'horse' had to have been readily available, which in itself raises further questions. Whose 'horse' was it? Did it perhaps belong to the Barber family and did they store it at the Hall for the following season?

There is a further relevant letter in Lord Amberley's Journal, written from Alderley Park, dated 8th January 1865.[24] It recounts the visit by the famous traveller and translator of *The Arabian Nights*, Sir Richard Burton. According to the letter, Sir Richard would often mesmerise his wife and whilst she was in the trance, he would consult her about what might happen in the future. Kate's older sister Henrietta Blanche Stanley expressed a desire to be mesmerised and another part of the entry reads: 'After dinner we had the mummers; & then Blanche was actually mesmerized, Maude [another sister] & Airlie [Blanche's husband] being present'. The sequence of mumming and a 'mesmerizing' might, in another context, suggest a theatrical variety show. Being early in January, it may well refer to a late 'Christmas' performance by the Barbers, but the sense of varied 'theatrical' activity remains intriguing.

Further reference**s** from the Amberley Papers reprise Kate's fascination with mumming. Kate had moved away from Alderley Park and a brief entry from her journal dated Friday 17th September 1869 reads: 'The schoolboys came to act the Mummers with Frank [her eldest son], Frank did Slasher & did much the best. Mr Evans the clergyman wrote to object to their learning a play'.[25] Kate must have mentioned this in a letter to her mother who was in Austria at the time for in a letter dated 29th September 1869, she replied: 'What a pity you shd [sic] come across such foolish people as the Clergyman who writes about the Mummers. I wish people would understand that amusement is one of the real lacunas in English peasant life'.[26]

1869 to 1903 (3rd Lord Stanley)

> I do the play because I like the way the old and the new mix; it is an interesting piece of local history that I believe needs to be kept going.
>
> (Tony Lepp, *Prince Paradise*, 26 December 2019)

Henry Edward John Stanley succeeded to the title 3rd Lord of Stanley in 1869. He was a radically different character to his predecessors, a diplomat with a passion for Africa and the East who converted to Islam and became the first Muslim to sit in the House of Lords.

He was also (apparently inadvertently) the husband of a Spanish bigamist, Lady Fabia, who would later be struck from Debrett's. His equally independent siblings included Anglicans, both high and low, an agnostic and a Roman Catholic Bishop.[27] In a generation of Stanleys so little given to tradition, it is unsurprising that visits from soulers and mummers declined, with the latter initially moving from the Hall to farms and large houses in the district.

Alec Barber recalled the time his mother first saw the mummers:

> I remember my mother saying once, they once come, and she lived in Over Alderley, they had that smithy in Over Alderley her father had, and she said they were in the house as kids and me mother. It's a bit since that, because she died in 1964, when she were 90. But anyhow she said she was the only a little child and suddenly there was a lot of banging on the door and it mustn't been locked. They opened the door and they came in, and they had flag floors then and she said they struck floor these great big fellers, she said, they were frightened to death, sparks flew and opened the door and that was in Over Alderley.[28]

His father had spoken to him about the other places the mummers visited during this period.

> But they used to, my dad said they did it more or less, it kept going as they stopped going to the little places and they just did it at the big homes, where the flash people, they reckoned there was more money to handle.[29]

There is also external evidence that this was the period when souling and mumming performances seem to have coalesced around All Souls.[30]

1903 to 1925 (4th Lord Stanley)

> I have played in the horse many times over the years but not so much now, as can be seen from the animal description, and to play it enthusiastically I consider it a young man's part.
>
> Also, I prefer a non-shouty part but still liked to surprise and entertain the audience. I could push and shove the groom about, rising up and pinning the groom to the bar was a favourite as was turning the horses head through 180 degrees or more with the body stationary then trying to escape the grooms grip on the bridle. However, being last on it's a wait and then bent over for several minutes whilst trying to navigate a crowded pub from looking at the floor can be challenging. In addition, working out who is where through a relatively small aperture in the horse's head whilst moving a pole one handed and operating the jaws with the other hand takes a bit of practice.
>
> (Steve Wood, *Young Ball the Horse*, 15/03/2020)

Edward Lyulph Stanley, once recipient of his sister Kate's excited letters about mumming, acceded in 1903 and quickly sought to re-establish the mummers' visits to his seat. By 1907, the *Alderley and Wilmslow Advertiser* was able to report that:

> The "mummers" have again been out in the Alderley district this Christmas. This old custom was not observed in the late Lord's time and when the present Lord Stanley

succeeded, he expressed a desire that it should be revived, and the strange figures are now seen each Christmas. There were great doings in the early times when Lord Stanley [born 1839] was a boy.[31]

At a time when mumming was for the most part in decline across England, the next three decades proved to be a golden age for the Alderley Mummers who flourished and became minor local celebrities. The Christmas festivities at Alderley Park took place over a period of several days. The Hall was decorated, and the houseguests were offered different entertainments on successive nights. One highlight was a large-scale party for the guests, the local schoolchildren and the elderly of the estate. This took place in the Tenants Hall where Christmas gifts were handed out by members of the Stanley family and the mummers performed. The fact that the Alderley Mummers performed at such an important event in the local social calendar assured them considerable press coverage. There were over 100 reports over the next 30 years, ranging from short syndicated reports to lengthy and detailed accounts. 'Local' newspapers from as far afield as Cumbria, Lancashire, Yorkshire, Scotland and Australia carried reports alongside examples in the national press.[32]

The association between the Stanley and Barber families expanded from the mummers' play to embrace larger scale private theatricals. Edward Lyulph's youngest daughter Beatrice Venetia Stanley, better known as Venetia, was 25 years old when she produced the pantomime 'Aladdin' and invited members of the Barber family to take part. Whilst her own family and friends took the leading roles, members of the Barber family took more minor parts. George Barber played the Emperor Ching Chang Chi, and according to the local newspaper[33] 'showed all the dignity that befitted the role'. Other recruits were his nephews Clement Barber, aged 12, who played 'Asbestos – the Spirit of the Lamp.' and Alec Barber aged 8, who played a soldier. (Both Clement and Alec Barber would later become leading members of Alderley Mummers.) Aladdin was produced on a lavish scale with costumes for the leading roles brought in specially from London and Manchester despite there being only two planned performances in what was essentially a domestic setting. In 1913, the Prime Minister, Herbert Henry Asquith, visited Alderley Park for the Christmas celebrations and saw the Mummers perform.[34] On that night, George Barber played Enterer In; William Barber, the leader of the mummers, played St. George. Other Barber family members played the other roles, Ernest was Prince Paradise, Henry was Colonel Slasher, Tom played the Doctor, Ernest took the role of Beelzebub, Albert was the groom and Obadiah the Horse. Alec Barber, who had played a soldier in Aladdin the previous Christmas, specifically recalled meeting Prime Minister Asquith and shaking hands with him.[35]

Asquith saw the Alderley Mummers again in 1914[36] when he made another visit to Alderley Park when, amongst the audience, there were wounded soldiers from the Brookdale Hospital in nearby Alderley Edge.[37] During the First World War, Alderley Park in part became a military hospital and performances of the mummers' play continued under the presumably warm scrutiny of Edward Lyulph. In 1916, Arthur Bowes of Newton-le-Willows, Lancashire, wrote in *Notes and Queries*:

> This family, of the name of Barber, should be a trustworthy authority for the local version, though Lord Sheffield himself is said to act as critic and censor, and has the reputation of being "letter perfect" both in the words and "business."'[38]

Performances continued every year with the date and time of appearance chosen to suit the Stanley's social calendar. On occasion, it could be as early 23rd December and in other years as late as New Year's Day.

William Barber, then the leader of the mummers, died in 1918 and his death was reported in *The Guardian*:

> The death is announced of Mr. W. Barber, leader of the Alderley company of mummers. Alderley has had its mummers for more than a century, and it is a remarkable fact that during all that time only members of one family, the Barbers, have been performers. Lord and Lady Sheffield have always taken a keen interest in the mummers, and their entertainment has been a regular feature of the Christmas gatherings at Alderley Park. Mr. Barber was an old tenant of Lord Sheffield's.[39]

The photographic record of the mummers commenced under the 4th Lord's tenure; unfortunately, there is no earlier information regarding the appearance and costume of the performers. The earliest photograph is circa 1910 and, other than changing one uniform jacket for another, the kit seems to have changed very little until 1937 when (see below) performances ceased (Figure 5.1).

As a member of the 1970s mumming revival side, I was fortunate to have been gifted the remaining items of mummer's kit by Mary Houseman, the daughter of Clement (Clem) Barber. They comprise the complete kit worn by Colonel Slasher alongside a sword and some accessories used by the Enterer In. The latter was played by Clem from 1919 until 1924, at which point he took over the role of St. George. His brother Alec played the part of Colonel Slasher between 1925 and 1937. Although the Alderley Mummers followed the Cheshire tradition of dressing in character, they possessed by far the most ornate and elaborate costume in the county.

The highly decorated bicorn hats worn by both Enterer In and St. George, who were the first two characters to enter the room, were a particular feature. Given present evidence, the shape, style and construction of this ornate headgear were unique in the county. The hats were made from cardboard covered in silver paper, decorated with Christmas decorations with a cow's tail for a plume.[40] The broad design resembles that shown in illustrations from

Figure 5.1 Alderley Mummers 1920. Left to Right: Enterer In – Clement Barber, Doctor – Thomas Barber, Prince Paradise– Alec Barber, St. George – George Barber, Beelzebub – Ernest Barber, Colonel Slasher – Henry Barber, Young Ball (horse) – Obadiah Barber, Groom – Albert Barber
Source: Courtesy of Mary Houseman, Private Collection.

other parts of the country during the mid-nineteenth century, typified for present purposes by a full-page illustration *Christmas Mummers* in a December 1861 edition of *The Illustrated London News*.[41] The family might well have had access to such material. Closer to home, a contemporary photograph believed to show that the Stanley Lodge of the Independent Order of Oddfellows, Manchester Unity Friendly Society, shows men lined up on either side of a Father Christmas character astride a horse. Each man is wearing a bicorn hat of very similar design to those described above and each is holding a ceremonial staff.[42]

Returning to the mummers' costume, the front of St. George's hat bore a large brass Shako plate.[43] The plate is of the 4th Queens Own Light Dragoons, circa 1845 to 1856, the period during which the regiment took part in the Charge of the Light Brigade. Across the front of the hat and in large letters are the initials SG. The jacket is heavily decorated with paper motifs and the performer also wore two crossed sashes and a heart-shaped design on the chest. His sword is that of a British Light Cavalry Trooper of the Napoleonic period. In the photograph taken circa 1910, Colonel Slasher can be seen wearing a modified uniform of an infantry officer from the Napoleonic period. In a photograph from 1920, this has been replaced by the tunic of a Major in the Grenadier Guards from the late Victorian period. On the inside of the tunic, it is possible to make out in part the surname Fox Pitt. The tunic probably belonged to Augustus Henry Lane Fox Pitt-Rivers, who married Alice Margaret Stanley,[44] daughter of the 2nd Lord Stanley. For headgear, Slasher sports a bell crown shako bearing the plate of the Scots Guards Foot Regiment circa 1830. His sword, with a curved blade, was an Ottoman Shamshir, from the period 1801–1840. There are no records of any of the Barber family having served in the Army, so it is most probable that the military clothing and paraphernalia was supplied by the Stanleys. It spans a period of nearly 100 years and incorporates properties and effects of the Napoleonic, Crimean and Boer Wars.

Enterer In's kit was similar but not as ornate as that worn by St. George. His bicorn hat was smaller and not as elaborately decorated. He wore a single sash and cummerbund, both of which were decorated with roundels and surmounted with a cross. His sword was a Victorian Light Cavalry Sword, from the first half of the nineteenth century. It bears a government issue 'proof mark', which shows that it was suitable for military service.[45] The Doctor wore a tall 'Welsh hat' decorated with a large feather. The hat might have come via the Stanleys who owned large estates on Anglesey. (A photograph circa 1914 shows a similar hat being worn by a wizard in one of the Stanley pantomimes.[46]) He also wore a long black clerical cassock with a ruff collar around his neck. Beelzebub wears a grotesque black mask, a hat topped with feathers and a multi-coloured waistcoat and jacket with a hump to his back. His baggy trousers have a playing card motif on the front panel. In short, a colourful and dramatic fusion of different styles that might have come straight from a fancy-dress box. Prince Paradise initially had a blackened face but when Alec Barber took over the role in 1920, he was given black cloth hood to wear, to hide his youthful looks.[47] He wore a long, floor length, red robe and a white shirt. In later years, a broad red sash was added over his shoulder. The groom is dressed representationally with a bowler hat, jacket, jodhpurs and riding boots and he carries a riding crop. The horse consisted of a real horse's skull, painted black with a white blaze and glass eyes, with its lower jaw mounted on a pole. A short handle fastened into the back of the skull allowing the operator to open and shut the jaws. The operator was completely covered by a large blanket decorated with bows at the front. For many years, the horse was played by Obadiah Barber but in 1920, he failed to turn up in time for a performance – a precursor of several such stunts – and the play was performed without either the horse or the groom. The incident was reported by the local paper who politely noted that he had 'missed the bus'.[48]

Part of a report from 1923 is critical of the style and skill of the Mummers performance.

> The acting itself is somewhat crude but after all interest mainely [sic] lies in the fact that it is a typical performance which gives us a definite link with the old days when histrionic performances were in their infancy, and nothing was known of the art of stagecraft, which plays such an important part in present day performance.[49]

Having a cast of members all from the same family can sometimes result in a mismatch and unexpected consequences, as this report from 1924 illustrates:

> There was a heartier roar from those in the know when the "Enterer-In" (Mr Clement Barber, aged 25) lamented over Colonel Slasher (Mr Henry Barber, aged 74) as his "murdered son". The Horse (Mr Obadiah Barber) played his part with true equine sagacity, though at the close he was nearly chased out of the hall by a large dog, who apparently could not "place" his features. Miss Victoria Stanley, Sir Arthur's eight-year-old daughter, was enthusiastic about the play. "I didn't like it the first time I saw it" she said. "I was frightened of Beelzebub and ran away to Mrs Wallace" (the housekeeper).[50]

1925 to 1931 (5th Lord Stanley)

> It's a loud part with a long death with lots of showing off really... I inherited the part from Brian Harker when sadly he didn't 'rise again' after a short illness. When I see the kit, I become Slasher... It's a privilege and I attempt to perform it in the way he and others have done before (whilst adding a gag or too myself) to honour them and respect this simple tradition. The finale at Waters Green Tavern is amazing and is without doubt my favourite night of the year!
>
> (Simon Whomsley, *Colonel Slasher*, 6 November 2019)

During this period, it becomes possible to introduce contextual information regarding the performances and to glean a little more sense of theatrical style and the attributes the actors brought to their characters. Around the time Arthur Lyulph Stanley succeeded as the 5th Lord Stanley, Henry and George Barber died and for the first time the Barbers had to look outside their immediate family to find a replacement. They approached Fred Barber who worked on the Alderley Park Estate; despite the physical proximity, he was actually a distant relative, but he had the right surname and was pressed into action as Enterer In. Alec Barber meanwhile took over as Colonel Slasher – a part he revelled in. He would ham things up and in the death scene he writhed around the floor moaning and groaning, taking an absolute age to die. By this point, a collection was taken up at the end of the play by the horse and groom. Obadiah Barber, as the horse, would reach through his open jaws and collect the cash. On one occasion, Obadiah ran off with the collection. He fled across the fields and was not seen again for days, until he had drunk all the takings. After that, they kept a very close eye on him.[51]

As indicated earlier, there are many colourful stories about Obadiah. A tall man for his time at well over six feet, he was always noted as being of smart appearance and worked as a footman for the Spanish Lady Fabia Stanley, travelling around the country with the family. He was a practical joker and a bit of a rascal. On one occasion, a young man arrived in a horse and trap to court Obadiah's next-door neighbour. Obadiah waited until the couple had gone indoors and took his opportunity to re-arrange the harness, ending up with the horse on one side of a five-bar gate and the trap, re-hitched, on the other.[52] The most repeated story about him is that he used to dress in an old bed sheet and hang from the trees in Alderley Churchyard, pretending to be the ghost of the Grey Lady of the Hall. Sadly, his behaviour became more and more unconventional; he became a kind of a bogey man figure with the local children. By his sixties, he was reduced to living in a makeshift hut in the woods, getting by on handouts. Eventually, there was concern for his well-being and he was taken to a place of safety. In 1927, Obadiah was replaced by Fred Barber Jnr, the son of Fred the Enterer In and a gardener on the estate. This was the final line-up and remained unchanged for the next ten years. During this period, it was reported that Sir James Barrie, author of Peter Pan, had seen the play and had requested a copy of the text.[53]

During the same period, Alec Barber, in the role of Colonel Slasher, was wounded in his fight with St. George. His brother Clement Barber recalled:

> On Saturday night, during one of the duels fought by St. George, his adversary. "Col. Slasher," who is supposed to be slain, actually received a cut close to his rig' eye. Although he was not seriously wounded, the "Colonel's" tunic and gloves were spattered with blood. No break, however, occurred in the play which – to quote the words of Lady Stanley – was "better than ever,"[54]

It would appear to have been quite a cut; the blood stains remain on the tunic to this day. In 1928, there were two critical reports that give further insight into the style of the mummer's performance.

> The play has never been written but is handed down orally from father to son and kept jealously in the family. A fiercely independent play this; it snaps its fingers at the unities and tweaks dramatic convention by the nose; each character hurls forth patches of magnificent rhodomontade in couplets that all but rhyme, and such diverse personages as St. George, the Black Prince, Colonel Slasher, and Beelzebub, meet and mingle in glorious confusion.[55]

The second report summoned the 'good old days':

> We were reminded of those days at Alderley Park on Monday evening, when we had a splendid example of the robust type of melodramatic humour which is reminiscent of those days of Merrie England. This reminder was provided by the Mummers, who gave their annual "command" performance in the magnificently appointed Tenants' Hall at Alderley Park. Neither the text of the play nor the way in which it is usually presented conform to modern ideas with regard to dramatic art – the text is pure doggerel and the histrionic efforts of the artists are crude – but therein lies the charm of the performance: it is a real survival of an ancient custom, and if we view the performance in this light we appreciate its real value.[56]

During the last season of the 5th Lord's tenure, in 1930, the Alderley Mummers performed on New Year's Eve and a local newspaper wrote:

> Some time ago the B.B.C. expressed a desire to broadcast the performance, but the request was declined on the grounds that it would be impossible to convey the atmosphere of the event through the microphone, and the play would thus be unintelligible to listeners.[57]

1931 to 1938 (6th Lord Stanley)

> I've played the same part of 40 years, Enterer In, not everyone enjoys being 1st through the door but I love it. Look forward to it every year and love keeping the tradition going.
> (Dave Houghton, *Enterer In*, 6 November 2019)

In 1931, the 6th Lord Stanley, Edward John Stanley, succeeded to the title and the Christmas celebrations continued for a few more years. Ultimately, financial pressure on the estate as a consequence of death duties meant that radical changes had to be made. In 1933, most of the manor house, but not the Tenants Hall, was demolished. Clem's wife Daisy recalled seeing the Mummers for the first time in 1934, soon after she married. She arrived at the Hall and was greeted by Lord and Lady Stanley. Lord Stanley gave her money from his own pocket to ensure she had enough to give to the horse when it came around at the end of the performance.[58] By 1936, Lord Stanley, now divorced, had moved away from Alderley Park altogether.[59]

At 9.10 pm on 24th December 1937, despite the misgivings of only a few years earlier, the play was included in a radio broadcast which turned out to be the Alderley Mummers final performance. Broadcast for the B.B.C. North Region, the programme was called 'Christian Men Rejoice!' and celebrated 'A Christmas Journey through Four Centuries'. The Mummers, billed as Lord Stanley's Mummers, represented the year 1737.[60]

They broadcast from the Tenants Hall, devoid of all its usual hustle, bustle and Christmas trappings; ironically, they played to their largest audience and to good effect:

> It was a tribute to the Mummers that their first venture on the air gave hundreds of people an exceptionally good interpretation of the play itself. Every word came through with perfect clearness and thus enabled one to visualise the scenes where duels were fought and miracles of healing performed. Never before have the Mummers performed to such good effect. The pace was good, enunciation clear and everything was so perfectly timed that the whole play was through before the Mummers were "faded out" for the next item on the programme.[61]

I was in conversation with Mary Houseman in 2019 when she told me that she was three years old at the time of the broadcast. Whilst she can't remember anything about it, she had been told by her mother that she sat up and looked for her father when she heard his voice on the radio. No recordings of the broadcast are known to exist.

The following year, the entire 4,500-acre estate was put up for auction on 11–14th October 1938. Three months before the auction, Thomas Barber was interviewed by the *News Chronicle*.[62] Described as the leader and director of the famous Alderley Mummers, he rather prophetically said, 'If the Old Hall is sold, we have nowhere to perform'.

The sale, consisting of Alderley Park, 5 smaller halls, 77 farms and 166 cottages, went badly.[63] Only 58 of the 664 lots were sold under the hammer. All the lots were eventually sold incrementally. The Stanley's home for over 500 years was sold for a reputed half a million pounds.

From those initial efforts by Samuel Barber and his brother William, the Alderley Mummers had relied greatly on the patronage of the Stanley family for their continued existence.

It is certain that the Mummers would not have survived into the twentieth century without the intervention of the 4th Lord Stanley. All the members of the Barber family that I have met during 40 years of researching and performing are rightly proud of the Alderley Mummers. The Stanleys, in turn, were proud to have had their 'own' Mummers, a situation that suited generations of both families who in other circumstances could not have enjoyed such a close and unusual relationship – certainly not within the prevailing English class system.

Publication and revival

The legacy of the Alderley Mummers remains to this day, thanks in the main to the work of Alex Helm, who published Alec Barber's version of the text three times.[64] The play text had been jealously guarded by the family for four generations. Alec felt uncomfortable that he had let the text out of the family, thinking that he had betrayed a family trust. Indeed in Helm's manuscripts, there is a clear instruction that the work is 'Not to be reproduced without permission and NOT to be performed by anyone but the Barber family'.[65] Helm reproduced the note in the introduction to his first publication of the play but not in the two subsequent manifestations. The play was now in the public domain: sufficiently so that in 1964 Mike Yates, the folksong collector and researcher, recorded Alec Barber reciting the play and singing the 'Acting Song'. As far as I know, this material was never released commercially but it remains indicative of a considerable shift; this was no longer a matter of written reportage of private performances, but a different mode of entry into a more democratic public sphere.

Publication of the text popularised the formation of 'revival' mummers' sides, including at least five that sprang out of the (relatively) local folk scene during the 1960s and 1970s. Two of these, the Cod End Mummers from Fleetwood who included the play as part of a larger repertoire, and the Monk Coppenhall Mummers, from near Crewe, are now defunct. A third side, the Bollin River Soulers, performed the play for three or four years in the late 1970s. They derived from the Bollin Morris side of Altrincham and subsequently decided to change plays, preferring to concentrate on reviving their local Warburton Souling Play.

Of the two remaining 'revival' sides, one is based in the City of Chester, and the other is the mummers' side that I am associated with. These two sides make an interesting comparison, if only to illustrate what can happen to a play once it has been collected, published and then revived outwith its original context. It demonstrates how two quite different interpretations of the play can be achieved. Both sides are from Cheshire, both have been in existence for over 40 years, both started with links to morris dance sides, both perform seasonally, mainly in Public Houses, and both use their performances to collect for charitable causes. Both sides started off with little more than Helm's published text and a desire to revive a Cheshire mumming play; each side has then taken a very different route to reach their goal and each one is happy with what they have achieved.

The Chester-based side is the oldest of the two, having initially formed in 1971 out of the Jones' Ale Folk Club, but also with a close association to the Chester City Morris Men. Performing the play around the time of All Souls Eve, they call themselves the Jones' Ale Soul Cakers. None of the original members are still performing, having handed the play over to their sons and their sons' friends. As a result, the average age of their cast is the youngest of the Cheshire mumming gangs active today. Their date of performance has since changed to early December. It was customary in Cheshire for the mummers to dress in character and the Jones' Ale costume and kit shows echoes of the style taken by a lot of 'revival' sides from the 1970s. It is a fusion of many periods, ranging from medieval influences up to the modern day. St. George wears a white surcoat with a red cross of St. George. Colonel Slasher has a military-style uniform and Beelzebub is depicted as a devil with horns. Other costumes seem to be fashioned out of old curtains or velvet and some characters wear tights. Even though much of their original kit from the 1970s has been replaced, the overall look remains the same. It is, of course, what the present gang knows as 'the Souling kit', because that was what they saw their fathers wear. The biggest innovation that they have made is in the way they mount their horse's skull. They do not use the usual three-legged mast horse construction whereby a man covered in a blanket crouches behind the skull and operates the horse's jaw. They have chosen to mount their skull on a tall pole whereby the skull is held high and the operator stands beneath it.

Whilst retaining Helm's published text as a basis for the performance, they have embellished it with many asides – always topical yet not too political. Their style of performance has also developed over the years into more all-round entertainment. They have a band who provide a musical introduction for each character along with sound effects and an enhanced dramatic atmosphere. Will Riding, one of the current performers, informed me that 'they don't feel bogged down by tradition'.[66] They are no longer an all-male group and feature men and women as musicians and performers. It may be the Alderley Mummers' text but the Jones Ale Soul Cakers have made it very much their own show.

History of our revival

> I enjoy it, especially when there is a receptive audience. Plus, I can tell non-folkies that we get dressed up, have sword fights in the pub, sing a song and hopefully the landlord gives us a pint for our trouble.
>
> (Roger Jackson, *St. George*, 27 December 2019)

The other side still in existence is the one with which I am associated and remains based within and around Adlington Morris Men and their friends. Through a series of chance meetings and coincidences, the group have taken a quite different approach in interpreting the Alderley Mummers play. In 1977, the Morris Men decided that they wanted to revive a local mummers' play. A chance comment by friends set us on our way: they had bought some old clothes at a farm auction, that they then thought was in Adlington, and as they were leaving, someone said, 'that should not have been sold, that was the old mummers kit'. Thinking we were on the trail of a previously unknown play from Adlington, we set about tracking down the site of the auction. This turned out to be Brynlow Farm, in neighbouring Nether Alderley, the home of the Barber family. In fact, Alec Barber was retiring from farming and selling up. I contacted Mr Barber and later interviewed him on several occasions. He was a charming gentleman and a fount of knowledge regarding the play that had been such a source of pride and enjoyment throughout his life. He still retained that enthusiasm and his face would light up when he spoke of the play. He, in turn, put me in contact with his niece Mary Houseman, daughter of Clem Barber. As a keen family historian, she has proved to be an invaluable contact, filling in many of the gaps in my knowledge, and she remains an enthusiastic supporter of our revival.

The clothes from the auction turned out not to have been part of the old Mummers kit. What items that did remain were already in Mrs Houseman's safe keeping. These have since been gifted to me. Mary was a keen folk dancer, a member of the local W.I. and a founder of the Adlington Folk Dance Club, who had, in turn, spawned the Adlington Morris Men. There seemed too many coincidences: we were by now locked in and keen to revive the Alderley Play. Both Alec Barber and Mary Houseman were supportive of the idea as was Fred Barber Jnr who also agreed to be interviewed. Armed with Alex Helm's book, *Cheshire Folk Drama*, we started rehearsals. Alec Barber attended an early rehearsal and ran us through the action as he remembered it. What we did not realise at the time was that Alec had made a mistake. Perhaps confused by the presence of so many new actors, he attributed some of the Prince Paradise's words to the character of Enterer In. We then incorrectly changed the speakers names in our script to accord with Alec's comments. It was only many years later, in 1988, that we found out about this error and realised that the character names as published by Helm were correct. We had a discussion amongst ourselves but decided to live with the error because, by then, that had become our version of the play. We have also based our costume and properties on those worn and used by the Alderley Mummers because we simply could not see a way to improve on them. Our first public performance took place on 28th December 1978 at a morris dance group Christmas party in Heaton Moor, Stockport. When we perform, each character enters the room, in turn, one at a time, when it is their moment to act. The audience doesn't know who will burst through the door next and each new costume can still draw a gasp.

In 1988, Mary Houseman invited us to perform at the 21st Birthday Party of her son Nicholas.[67] Not unexpectedly, it had a mumming theme, with memorabilia and photographs displayed around the walls. It was there that we were given a copy of the play text that her father, Clement, had written out in 1938. This was just a few months after the final performance by the Barber family, and nearly 20 years before his brother Alec's recitation of the play was recorded. Clem's version contained an extra 12 lines of text which we immediately incorporated into our version of the play. Although we usually act in pubs, we have been lucky enough to perform the play at the Tenants Hall in Alderley Park. It was, by then, a conference centre for the pharmaceuticals company AstraZeneca. The hall had changed little over the years. AstraZeneca have since left the Alderley Park site, which is now being turned into a small luxury housing development. There is a possibility that old Tenants Hall will be converted into a gastro-pub. If so, it would be great to perform there again.

We have also been fortunate to perform the play in front of both the 8th and 9th Lord Stanleys.

On 30th January 1999, we were invited to perform at the Manchester Museum. This was to mark the end of the exhibition. '*Living on the Edge, The Mines, Myths and Merchants of Alderley*' which ran as part of *The Alderley Edge Landscape Project* (AELP).[68] The backdrop for our performance was a life-size enlargement of a photograph of the Mummers from 1920. Thomas Henry Oliver Stanley, 8th Lord Stanley, watched the performance and chatted with us afterwards. On 26th February 2016, we were invited to perform at the Assembly Rooms in Alderley Edge at the book launch of *The Story of Alderley, Living with the Edge* edited by John Prag.[69] The hall was full and Richard Oliver Stanley the 9th Lord Stanley was a guest. After our performance, we had a chance to talk to him and Lady Stanley and have our photographs taken with them both. We have also performed inside St. Mary's Church, Nether Alderley. Brian Hobson, a local historian, gave an illustrated talk and when the topic of mumming was introduced with a photograph of the original Alderley Mummers on screen, there were three loud bangs on the church door. Enterer In burst into the church full of a startled audience. The performance was a great success and particularly atmospheric for the performers, knowing that many of the original mummers lay just a few metres away in the churchyard.

Figure 5.2 Alderley Mummers Play 2016. Left to Right: Enterer In – Dave Houghton, Doctor – Tom Kitchen. Prince Paradise- Tony Lepp, St. George – Roger Jackson, Beelzebub – Geoff Smith, Colonel Slasher – Simon Whomsley, Young Ball (horse) – Peter Jackson, Groom – Nicholas Houseman

Source: Photograph © the author.

We have now been performing the play for over 40 years and there have been many changes of cast although three of the original members are still performing (Figure 5.2). I am one of those, but my role nowadays is perhaps more like that of Thomas Barber, that of leader and Director. During our early performances, it was very rewarding to be approached by members of the audience who as children had seen the original mummers. Their memories of the Christmas celebrations at Alderley Park were always positive and fascinating and informative to listen to. They were a direct link to the play's past.

From the start of our revival of the play, we have all been aware of its history and each new member is given a potted history. Wherever we perform, we seem to get asked questions about the play, the costumes and its history and now take a couple of photos of the original mummers with us (including Figure 5.1).

Why we perform the play

Since first trying to follow leads about those auctioned mummers' costumes, I have met and interviewed members of the Barber family, visited local archives and libraries and trawled through endless old newspapers, books and journals. My research continues and new information is still appearing. After a recent performance, an old acquaintance posted some photos on social media. His Great Grandmother was the sister of Thomas Barber. The story of the mummers had been handed down within his family even though, simply because they were no longer called Barber, their branch had not performed for four generations. I met his father and we exchanged photos and press cuttings about the mummers broadcast, cuttings that the family had treasured for over 80 years.

Finding new information, making new contacts, maintaining old contacts, putting on a good show and continuing an old local tradition is what I enjoy. I have given several illustrated talks about the Mummers to Local History groups; I am not a natural orator and I do not enjoy public speaking, but it is important to me to communicate this aspect of local history and celebrate a continuity. In moments of vanity, I like to think that the old mummers and their audience would recognise what we are doing and appreciate it. Although we try to keep true to the original play, our performances are not intended as re-enactment but rather as a living thing. In common with the Barbers, we may not possess great acting talent; we may declaim our words and disdain over-acting; yet, each performer is encouraged to make their character their own.

I recently asked my fellow mummers why they perform the play and extracts from their replies constitute the text boxes used throughout this chapter.[70] Over the years, a great many of the Barber family have come to see us and I'm pleased they have all been encouraging about our efforts. Nicholas (Nick) Houseman, Clement Barbers grandson, is the fifth generation of his family to perform the play. In January 2020, at the time I was writing this chapter, Mary Houseman came to see our last performance of the season in our 'home pub', the Waters Green Tavern, Macclesfield. The pub was as packed as ever, and the reception was enthusiastic. The entrance of each new character was greeted with loud cheers or boos. After we had finished, I spoke briefly about the history of the play and introduced both Mary and Nick who jointly received a standing ovation. A wonderful and fitting way to end our mumming season.

Notes

1. The relationship of the Barber family to the play, and their sense of ownership of the text in performance, is profound. The fact that no one other than family members had ever performed in the play is stressed – using different words and in multiple formulations – in 38 separate newspaper articles written between 1912 and 1937. In 1932, one account claimed that the Barbers would rather cut a character from the play than allow an outsider to perform. [Anon.], Alderley and Wilmslow Advertiser, Mummers at Alderley Park. Tradition Maintained by Old-Time Performance. Lord and Lady Stanley and Friends Entertained. Childrens Party Postponed 30 December 1932, p. 9, col. c.
2. Ordnance Survey map reference SJ 84 78.
3. [Anon.], 'A Family of Cheshire Mummers – Interesting Performance at Alderley Park', *Alderley & Wilmslow Advertiser*, 2 January 1914, p. 12, col. c–g. The performance date was Tuesday 30th December 1913. Samuel Barber, born 1788, would have been in his late teens when he started mumming.
4. Alec Barber was interviewed by Alex Richardson on the 14th and 21st February 1954 – see London, Special Collections of University College, Alex Helm Collection, vol. 4, p. 103. Furthermore, as will become apparent, the play ceased to be performed in 1937. If it had been performed for 150 years, it would have commenced the year before its claimed originator, Samuel Barber, was born. In 1981, Alec Barber showed the author a newspaper article ([Anon.], *Daily Dispatch*, 17 December 1937, p. 16) citing this date and that may have underpinned the misunderstanding. See immediately below.
5. In fact, there are 59 newspaper accounts dated between 1907 and 1937 that offer a range of start dates from 1787 to 1819. The first claim to an eighteenth-century date didn't appear until 1923 and the date was finally pushed back to 1787 as recently as 1937. No substantiating evidence is provided for any of these dates. They seem to have been premised on casual remarks by performers or audience members.
6. Alex Helm, *The English Folk Play: Part 3* (Manchester: Manchester District of the English Folk Dance & Song Society, 1955), pp. 3–10 and Margaret Dean-Smith, 'An Un-Romantic View of the Mummers' Play', *Theatre Research*, 8, No.2 (1966), pp. 89–99.
7. Oxford, Bodleian Library, MS Douce d.44, pp. 1–7 or see https://folkplay.info/resources/texts-and-contexts/cheshire-play-1788 accessed 10/02/2020.
8. *The Early Married Life of Maria Josepha Lady Stanley with Extracts from Sir John Stanley's 'Praeteritio'*, ed. by Jane H. Adeane (London: Longhams, Green and Co, 1899), pp. 248–251.
9. Ibid. I have been unable to establish a location for Winston or throw any further light on the sung material.
10. Chester, Cheshire Archives and Local Studies Service, Stanley of Alderley collection, Alderley Festivities, Poems & Festivities, DSA 127/3. Account of celebrations at the coming of age of John and William Stanley with additional matter- Festivities 1823/4.

11   [Anon.], Manchester Mercury, Alderley Festivities, 20 January 1824, p. 2, col c.
12   George Ormerod, *The History of the County Palatine and City of Chester* (London: Lackington, 1819), p. LII.
13   Chester, Cheshire Archives and Local Studies Service, Louisa Dorothea Stanley, DSA 127/3 – Poetry, Ballads & Literary, 4 vols., 1812–1856, vol. 3, pp. 107–125. The play is written out on pp. 110–125 of vol. 3, in an undated book.
14   Ibid., p. 110.
15   Ibid., p. 113.
16   Ibid., p. 119.
17   Ormerod, *The History of the County Palatine*, pp. LI–LII.
18   Chester, Cheshire and Chester Archives and Local Studies Service, Louisa Dorothea Stanley, DSA 127/3 – Poetry, Ballads & Literary, 4 vols., 1812–1856, vol. 3, p. 125.
19   *The Amberley Papers, The Letters and Diaries of Bertrand Russell's Parents*, ed. by Bertrand Russell and Patricia Russell (New York: W.W. Norton & Company Inc., 1937), vol. 1, pp. 63–349, 64.
20   Ibid., p. 65.
21   Ibid., p. 100.
22   Ibid., p. 101.
23   Ibid., p. 102.
24   Ibid., p. 349.
25   Ibid., vol. 2, 286–289, 289. Frank is John Francis Stanley Russell born 12 August 1865.
26   The Amberley Papers, vol. 2, pp. 286–287.
27   Peter Edmund Stanley, *The House of Stanley* (Durham, NC: The Pentland Press Ltd, 1998), pp. 396–409, 401.
28   Alec Barber, in recorded interview with Duncan Broomhead, Macclesfield, 29 April 1981.
29   Ibid.
30   Alex Helm Collection, vol. 4, pp. 103–105.
31   [Anon.], *Alderley & Wilmslow Advertiser*, 27 December 1907, p. 5, col. c.
32   The following examples, anonymous in every case, provide a representative sample of these pieces: 'The Mummers', *Nottingham Evening Post*, 27 December 1912, p. 4, col. f.; 'Troupe in Existence for Over a Century', *Daily Citizen* (Manchester), 24 December 1913, p. 5, col. c.; 'Alderley Mummers' Record', *Halifax Evening Courier*, 24 December 1913, p. 4, col. f.; *Mid Sussex Times*, 13 January 1914, p. 2, col. g.; *Hamilton Daily Times*, 23 January 1915, p. 12, col. b.; 'Mumming Party with a History', *Leicester Daily Post*, 29 December 1919, p. 5, col. g.; 'Mumming', *Sheffield Evening Telegraph*, 14 December 1920, p. 4, col. b.; *Hull Daily Mail*, 27 December 1923, p. 1, col. g.; 'Peer's Party for Mummers', Daily Mirror, 2 January 1926, p. 8, col. a.; 'Mummers at Alderley, and Society Farmers at Home', *The Sketch*, 6 January 1926, p. 8, col. half page.; 'Mummers for 130 Years', *Penrith Observer*, 28 December 1926, p. 7, col. a.; 'For Barbers Only', *The Daily News and Westminster Gazette*, 1 January 1929; ''The Alderley Mummers', *Yorkshire Post and Leeds Intelligencer*, 24 December 1929, p. 4, col. a.; 'New Year Revels of Mummers. Century-old Play of St. George. Traditional Jingle', *Daily Dispatch*, Photograph, 1 January 1931, p. 5; 'Play That Is Never Written. Verbal Tradition of the Alderley Park Mummers', *Daily Express*, 1 January 1931; 'Our London Letter, Play about Queen Victoria', *Morning Bulletin, Rockhampton, Queensland*, 14 July 1937, p. 5, col. b.; 'You'll Hear This on the Air. Famous Old Play to be Festival Broadcast', *Daily Sketch*, 17 December 1937.
33   [Anon.], 'Pantomime at Alderley Park: Performance of "Aladdin"', *Alderley & Wilmslow Advertiser*, 3 January 1913, p.6, col. e. The Mummers also got a short report in the same column under the title 'Hereditary Mummers'.
34   [Anon.], 'Prime Minister Returns to London', *Manchester Evening News*, 2 January 1914, p. 3, col. e.
35   Alec Barber in interview with David Watkins, of Nether Alderley, 1983.
36   [Anon.], 'Christmas "Mummers" at Alderley Park', *Manchester Guardian*, 28 December 1914, p. 8.
37   [Anon.], 'The "Mummers" at Alderley Park, St. George and His Thrilling Adventure', *Alderley & Wilmslow Advertiser*, 1 January 1915, p. 6, col. c.
38   Arthur Bowes, untitled, Notes and Queries, Series 12, vol. 1, 13 May 1916, p. 393.
39   [Anon.], *Manchester Guardian*, 12 June 1918, p. 8.
40   Fred Barber, in recorded interview with Duncan Broomhead, Macclesfield, 1982.
41   [Anon.], 'Christmas Mummers', *Illustrated London News*, 21 December 1861, p. 639. The full-page illustration shows a company of mummers performing outside the front door to a large private

residence and with a crowd of onlookers around them. The illustration caption carries the credit 'drawn by A. Hunt' although the illustration itself carries a signature (bottom right) M. Jackson.

42 I am grateful to Brian Hobson, an amateur local historian from Alderley, for drawing this unattributed photograph to my attention.
43 A shako is a nineteenth-century high-sided military headdress; it usually bears a large metal regimental badge at the front, this is known as a Shako plate.
44 Peter Edmund Stanley, *The House of Stanley*, p. 401.
45 I was lucky enough to be able to photograph this sword, which is in the possession of a descendant of Fred Barber Snr. who formerly took the part of Enterer In.
46 Mary Houseman provided me a copy of this photograph from her private collection.
47 Conversations with Alec Barber.
48 [Anon.], 'Christmas at Alderley Park. Lord and Lady Sheffield entertain Young and Old. Mummers Annual Performance', *Alderley & Wilmslow Advertiser*, 31 December 1920, p. 6, col. c.
49 [Anon.], 'Mummers at Alderley Park. Old and Young Entertained by Lord and Lady Stanley', *Alderley & Wilmslow Advertiser*, 28 December 1923, p. 7, col. d.
50 [Anon.], 'The "Mummers." – 120-years-Old Family Tradition', Mary Houseman had in her possession an unidentified newspaper cutting with a handwritten note, *Daily Mail*, 27 December 1924.
51 Alec Barber, In Recorded Interview with Duncan Broomhead, Macclesfield, 29 April 1981.
52 Richard Bourne, *'Mummers', Folk Buzz* (Manchester: Manchester District of the, English Folk Dance & Song Society, Winter 1983), pp. 21–22.
53 Mary Houseman had in her possession an unidentified newspaper cutting with a handwritten date of 'Xmas 1929'.
54 [Anon.], 'Alderley Mummers', *Cheshire Observer*, 7 January 1928, p. 5, col. d.
55 [Anon.], 'Alderley Mummers', *126-year-old Play, The Macclesfield Courier and Herald*, 5 January 1929, p. 3, col. e.
56 [Anon.], 'New Year's Eve Party. Lord and Lady Stanley Entertain Children. Mummers' Annual Performance', *Alderley &Wilmslow Advertiser*, 4 January 1929, p. 9, col. c.
57 [Anon.], 'Revelry at Alderley Park. Quaint Performance by Mummers. St George "sees Red". Lord and Lady Stanley's Annual Party', *Alderley & Wilmslow Advertiser*, 2 January 1931, p. 9.
58 Mrs Daisy Barber in recorded interview with Duncan Broomhead, Adlington, 3 March 1983.
59 Stanley, *The House of Stanley*, pp. 407–408.
60 [Anon.], 'All the Christmas Radio. The King's Message: Big Variety Party: The Festival Abroad: Pantomime. Tonight. 9.10. – Christian Men Rejoice', *Daily Mail*, 24 December 1937, p. 9, col. c. The programme had a different theme to represent each of the four centuries. 1637 was represented by entertainment from Alnwick Castle. 1737 The Alderley Mummers from Alderley Park. 1837 was represented by hymns from Selby Abbey and 1937 by a choir from Lancashire and music by the BBC Northern Orchestra.
61 [Anon.], 'Mummers on the Air. Perfect Broadcast from Alderley Park', *Alderley & Wilmslow Advertiser*, 31 December 1937, p. 9, col. b.
62 [Anon.], 'Estate Tenants' Problem', *News Chronicle*, 8 July 1938. loose press cutting, page unknown.
63 George B. Hill, *Alderley Park Discovered* (Lancaster: Palatine Books/Carnegie Publishing, 2016), p. 81.
64 Collected from Alec Barber by Alex S. Richardson in 1954 and published by Alex Helm in the following works Alex Helm, *The English Folk Play: Part 3*, pp. 3–10; Alex Helm, *Cheshire Folk Drama* (Ibstock: Guizer Press, 1968) Plate 1 opposite, p. 20, Plate 2 opposite, pp. 40, 44–49. https://folkplay.info/sites/default/files/attached/Helm1968.pdf. The play is incorrectly titled as being from Alderley Edge and is also given an incorrect grid reference number; Alex Helm, *Eight Mummers' Plays* (London: Ginn, 1977), pp. 15–24.
65 Alex Helm Collection, vol. 4, p. 103 and *The English Folk Play*, p. 3.
66 Will Riding in telephone interview with Duncan Broomhead, 9 December 2019.
67 In January 2016, Nicholas Houseman went on to join our mummer's gang and took on the role of the Groom.
68 Alderley Edge Landscape Project (AELP), a joint project by Manchester University, Manchester Museum and the National Trust.
69 This is the extensive 1,000-page companion book for the AELP project. *The Story of Alderley, Living with the Edge*, ed. by A.J.N.W. Prag (Manchester: Manchester University Press, 2016).
70 The blocks of quotation used in the text boxes throughout the chapter are taken from e-mails sent to the author on the dates cited and are used here with permission of the individual senders.

6

A PERFORMANCE BESTIARY

Mike Pearson

Monsters

Picture this:[1]

> At Pleugh Jag time there used ter be a gran' percession—men in tall 'ats trimmed wi' belts an' jewellry, an' fine clothes on, used to go first; then there was the 'obby 'orses, made ov a wicker sieve wi' bottom out put round a man an' an 'orse-cloth right over 'im so's just 'is eyes looked out, an' a pair o' ears on. Rear an' kick, they would, these 'ere 'obby 'orses, an' run after folks an' scare 'em nigh ter dead! These 'ud go on afore the Pleugh lads ter the 'ouse where they was wishful ter be. Beesom Bet was the last player an' she reckoned ter sweep up an' leave all tidy after the players.[2]

A grand procession: with men in towering headgear, accompanied by hobby horses (Figure 6.1).

Figure 6.1 West Halton Plough Jags, 1898
Source: Reproduced by permission of North Lincolnshire Museums Service.

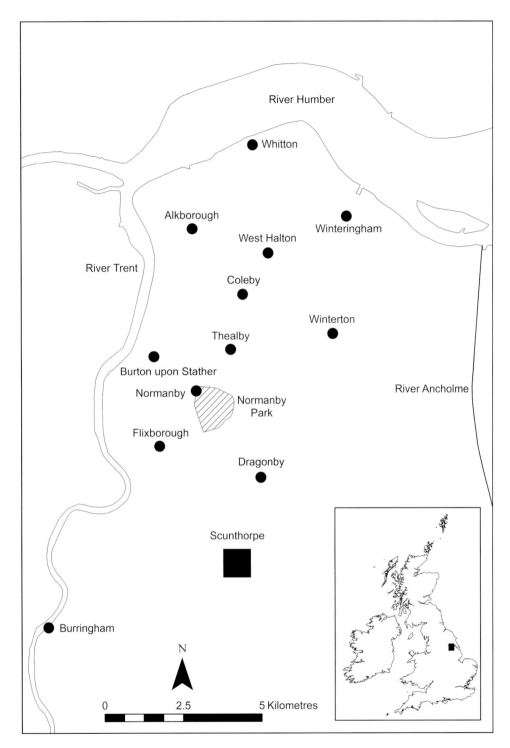

Figure 6.2 Map of North-west Lincolnshire
Source: Map created by Dr Steve Mills, School of History, Archaeology and Religion, Cardiff University.

But in photographs[3] of the teams from Burringham, Burton-upon-Stather and West Halton in north-west Lincolnshire around the turn of the twentieth century, it is strange and disconcerting figures that lurk in the costumed troupes,[4] looking 'more like giant rabbits than horses'[5]; or birds, or polar bears, or ghostly apparitions, or monstrous hybrids (Figure 6.2).

What are they, these 'rather out of the ordinary' creatures,[6] given to causing mayhem and upset?

Pedigree

They are the mutated offspring of sieve horses—a regional type of *tourney horse* in which a covered frame is fitted to the waist of the performer to create the impression of horse and rider. In the Lincolnshire variety, constructed as 'a matter of convenience'[7] from available materials—the detritus of the farmyard—the outer rim of a large corn sieve or potato riddle with the mesh removed was hung at waist level on two straps or ropes from the shoulders of the performer. With his own head protruding, both man and hoop were then draped in a cloak or cloth, hanging below knee level. A small, wooden head with horsehair mane and hinged jaw—that could be operated by pulling a cord—was attached to the front, with a horsehair tail at the rear.

They qualify as horses because of a few essential features of appearance—the head and tail; and because they allow and facilitate performative movement, horse-like and otherwise—the minimum requirement for the enactment of their semblance. But they are a substitute for a horse rather than a portrayal, a creation rather than an imitation.

It's from these beasts that disturbing, fantastical creatures metamorphosed: 'The man's head and body are hidden under the well-fitting white and red horse jacket with earpieces and eyeholes, such as race-horses wear on journeys. So the rider is also the horse—a oneness with the steed'.[8] In place of rider/horse, there is horse/horse. But as a horse's head is long and narrow, the excess material was either left to hang and flap as an amorphous mask; or gathered at the neck and then bound up as a grotesque deformity. With the ears left to droop, or tied up, erect.

Bestiary

They are extinct members of the bestiary of English folk performance: that order of animal figures that occur at times inhabiting the fringes of events, at others as the core around which the activity itself is organised. Those that survive, we encounter in enduring calendar customs. But the dead remain enigmatic: only partially—in fragmentary scripts and faded photographs, eyewitness accounts, oral testimony and antiquarian commentaries—do we catch glimpses of their antics, of their physical horseplay and sexual by-play, of their vivacity and dynamism *in performance*.

From scrutiny of such records, and from observation of existing phenomena in a form of imaginative 'reverse breeding', can we both envisage the Lincolnshire mutants in action, and evoke the world in which they evolved? Can we divine their behaviours, and surmise the likely impacts of the immediate physical and social environment upon their animation and operation? Can we conjure both creature and its habitat, by shifting critical attention from dramatic analysis of the play-text to the apprehension of performance: to those ephemeral episodes in which they appeared fully formed and three-dimensional, albeit hazily from our contemporary standpoint.

Origins

Sieve horses first turn up accompanying plough jags on their annual perambulations. On Plough Monday—the first after Epiphany—groups of farm workers drawing a plough would visit large houses in their parish and beyond, seeking gratuities. To jag is a dialect word meaning 'to tear up': if reward was not forthcoming, the threat was to grub up the boot scraper, or to furrow the front yard or lawn. On this putative day of 'no law', jags regarded their enterprise as inviolable: 'any other night they could be "had up" for exerting their "rights"'.[9] Visits could develop into intimidation and demanding money with menaces, with retribution for non-payment, including setting about the householder with besom shafts 'that they carried for such emergencies'.[10]

The basic form of jagging—going from door to door, sometimes in disguise, to collect a reward 'or rather, a bribe'[11]—was a pattern that could be creatively elaborated to enhance its efficacy: 'We made a tour of the villages and outlying farmsteads, incidentally kicking up a discordant din. Lining up at the doorway of a house we gave a rendering of any old music that we could manage…'[12] Although 'they never performed any play',[13] gangs wore costumes, coloured their faces with soot or burnt cork and included performative figures such as Tom Fool and Besom Bet—a man in female dress—to enliven the effect of the doorstep encounter, and as a function of extra-daily release and mischief.

There were also elements of mock husbandry and of animal impersonation: at Willoughton, jags drew the plough as if they were a harnessed team; one of a Willingham team summoned for their misdemeanours protested, 'I neither pulled nor ploughed, but I was whip'.[14] And until around 1900 at Somerby, 'two or three frisky hobby-horses drew the wooden plough'.[15]

Antiquarian Mabel Peacock recalls a Messingham gang visiting her home at Bottesford Manor in the 1860s: 'Fool […] carried a whip with a bladder at the end of the lash, with which he assaulted the audience, and he also attacked the riotous curvetting Hobby Horse, who my brother says, was always fooling, quarrelling with Betty'.[16] Whilst 'to curvet' means to frolic and leap about, it is a specific term of dressage: a prancing leap in which the hind legs are raised just before the forelegs touch the ground.

Imagine then beasts vigorously active: causing commotion in the confines of a domestic interior, given to extemporised high jinks and squabbling that were likely physical in nature. Existing within the realm of the performative, just beyond our purview.

They emerge in a world of adolescent masculinity: in 'a quite distinct group and part of a quite distinct cultural as well as socio-economic situation', distinctive because of 'the precise material conditions which created and located it'.[17] With the shift of agricultural production following Parliamentary enclosure from villages to newly constructed outlying 'farms in the fields' and as a consequence of the hiring fair system of annual employment, large numbers of young unmarried labourers began to 'live in'—lodging with the farmer, the foreman or the head waggoner—away from parental sanction, in a place of domicile and work combined. In 1851, George Vicars, a bailiff at Roxby, had five unmarried men living in his house, 'their ages ranging from 21 to 16 years'[18]; by 1871, '76% of living-in farm servants in Lincolnshire were aged between 16 and 24'.[19] They were 'employed exclusively on work with horses'[20]—as waggoners and ploughboys—often rising at 4am to have teams ready. Horses were a central part of daily labour, and 'strength, ale and "osses"' were defining features of their milieu.[21] The saddle room and stables were social centres where horsemen from other farms often joined them in the evenings, viewing 'each other's charges with a competitive mixture of admiration and criticism before playing quoits or dominoes to fill in their brief leisure'.[22] From working with horses to playing at horses…

The agricultural depression of the 1870s and 1880s—following the poor harvests and the effect of cheap imports that led to rural depopulation and increased emigration—the 1881 census showing a national decline of 92,250 in agricultural labourers since 1871—and the drift to industrial employment in urban centres such as the nearby burgeoning iron and steel town of Scunthorpe—doubtlessly impacted upon the plough jags.[23] And as the nineteenth century progressed, there was less tolerance of an activity regarded as 'a subsidiary of getting money for drink', leading to 'riot and excess'.[24] 'There is no objection to the amusement as such, but the frequent adjournment to the public houses is a material drawback', protested the *Stamford Mercury* in 1871.[25] By 1888, the *Mercury* noted: 'The "plough jacks" still ply their motley trade, but they are a degenerate race compared with the troupes of former years'.[26]

But the continuing imperative to solicit for the benefit of the participants—and an enduring commitment to local tradition—led to the increasing incorporation of novelty, as 'an addition to' and elaboration of the visit.[27] Gangs adopted and enacted dramatic forms that included costumed characters: as a means to an end, and sufficient to the task, in a 'legitimised wealth transfer transaction'[28] in which recompense is given for evident effort and application rather than simply begging.

Villages in the East Midlands—in north Lincolnshire and in Nottinghamshire—became the setting for 'plough plays', performed annually in the Christmas/New Year season, particularly on Plough Monday. Although the exact chronology is difficult to discern, these rudimentary dramas paralleled and/or were attached to and eventually superseded existing house-visiting customs—plough jagging—that themselves may have been the source of some of the supernumerary characters. Drama transpiring as natural evolution; or as an instance of expeditious genesis…

As local naturalist Adrian Woodruffe-Peacock suggested: 'When times were bad the bands of mummers were larger, the preparations more elaborate, and the play more carefully acted for the younger married men joined with plough-lads in getting up the piece, and wished to please as much as possible, to earn money for their families'.[29] But the casting of the activity as purely mercenary in its objectives is 'extremely reductive', ignoring its role 'in the creation or sustaining of a community identity',[30] and more immediately as a pleasurable pursuit enriching sociability: 'Fun more than anything, entertainment. I don't think for one minute that the money you got was the compelling factor for going round, even though we was all poor'.[31]

As a result of disapproval and censure and the change in the composition and character of jagging, 'ploughs [were] rarely seen in procession'[32] after 1875: 'It seems to have been a logical development to abandon the plough, since it must have been a considerable encumbrance to a team trying to get round their territory'.[33] From plough jagging to plough plays.

Drama

In the late 1880s and 1890s, there was a regional proliferation of the so-called 'Recruiting Sergeant' plays.[34] Largely in verse, Tom Fool introduces the occasion and there is then a three-way operatic scene between the Recruiting Sergeant, the Farmer's Man and the Lady. Encouraged to enlist by the Sergeant, the Man forswears his sweetheart and joins the army. On the rebound, the Lady decides to marry the Fool. Old Dame Jane appears carrying a baby. She claims that the Fool is the father. Beelzebub enters and fights Old Dame Jane, knocking her to the ground. A quack Doctor is called, who raises Jane to life with an intricate, comical cure. The play ends with a song. In a variant, there is an extended sequence of wooing in place of the recruiting scene.

As an eclectic, heterogeneous assemblage or *bricolage* of considerable flexibility—'a fund of speeches, steadily maintained, or even enlarged by borrowing',[35] 'modified and paraphrased during transmission'[36] as 'unmarried labourers took them from one village to another, when they took a fresh "place"'[37]—the drama was open to embellishment or restructuring as the players saw fit, or as memory served during preparation—'slightly altered where memory was not quite accurate'[38]—or as personnel changed, or as happenstance prompted in performance as performing skills varied. Passages altered from year to year and even iteration to iteration, though invariably at the core was the 'dispute with cure'.[39]

Additional figures—usually with a single speech—might be introduced at any point. Whilst not contributing to narrative development, they were important for captivating the audience, and for supplementing their delight and appreciation towards the solicitation and bolstering of reward. They become key figures within local manifestations and acknowledged ways of realising goals.

And so the hobby horses leap in.

'Perhaps the fool and the Hobby-horse belong to both dramas'.[40] Margaret Dean-Smith suggests that the Lincolnshire sieve horses joined the play simply to keep themselves alive, describing them as 'passengers', playing no part in the play, 'nor any recorded dramatic action of their own'[41]: 'The hobby-horse does not contribute to the action of the play, he merely enters and recites a few lines, and he has no connection with the other characters'.[42] Inessential to the main dramatic trajectory maybe—since that has often ended by the time it enters—though always serving as a link to the land.

Ancestors

A horse first appears locally in a recorded script from 'about 1876': 'Here comes a four-year-old colt [cowt], As fine a filly as ever was bought [bowt]'.[43] Around the same time, at Kirton Lindsey, a man 'carried' a hobby horse, with 'a rug on him, with his head stuck up through'[44]; and plough jags at Hibaldstow appeared 'fantastically attired', no longer dragging 'the plough of olden times with them' but accompanied by a 'fiery and curvetting hobby-horse'.[45] Its 'rider' speaks:

> Hoby Horse, No.7.
> In comes a four year old cout,
> As fine as ever was bought:
> He can hotch and he can trot
> 14 miles in 15 hours just like nought[46]

Rider and horse are two distinct entities. Other riders refer to 'my 'oss'—'I bought you last night/But I paid for you this morning/Wo-hop!'[47]—asserting the separate identity of their steed; and boasting of both its physical prowess and its supernatural powers.

At Worlaby: 'The finest filly that ever was bought/Trot fourteen miles in fifteen minutes/And never sweat a dry hair'.[48]

At Barton-upon-Humber: 'He can either bitch-botch, trot or gallop/And carry a butter bowl nine miles high'.[49] The main purpose of the words is a deferred plea on behalf of the team for a handout.

At Elsham: 'If you was as hungry/As my horse is dry/You'd give me a piece of your best pork pie';[50] at Barton, it's 'a pint of beer and a bit of pork pie'.[51]

Sometimes, the presence of a horse is merely alluded to. At North Kelsey, the Farmer's Man struggles to control a mute though energetic beast, not listed in the *dramatis personae*: 'And to my horses I attend/As they go round the end/Gee! Whoa back! Spanker'.[52] On another recorded instance there, it's the Doctor who—from outside—exclaims: 'Whoa! whoa! whoa!/Boy, hold my horse, boy!'.[53] The horse seemingly never makes it in, or maybe exists solely as 'noises off'.

And sometimes, in an instance of transformation, horse and rider become fused as a single equine figure. At Jerusalem, it's the Doctor who describes his beast:

> 'Whoa Whoa Wopsey old boy which of you old boys can 'old my 'orse/'es a donkey 'es a rum un to kick mind he doesn't bite you my lads'.[54]

And at Market Rasen, it's the Doctor too:

> 'Aye, aye, aye hold my hoss/Till I give him a stiff feed o three-penny bits/An' a dose o' thatch pegs'.[55]

Picture then horses in a farm kitchen: first filling the doorway, then circling, demonstrating their prowess. Exhibiting the faculties to which their riders and handlers refer: their bearing and gait springing not only from the mimetic imitation and parody of real horse steps—walking, trotting, galloping—and those invented—hitching, hotching[56] ('whatever pace that word may mean'[57]), bitch-botching, hop-scotching—but also from the manipulation of the sieve contraption—swaying, bending, dipping, crouching. This is in response to particular conditions and context of presentation—the space available, the nature of the audience—and reliant upon the creative resources and energies of the performer: 'the antics, prancing and dramatic action of the horse are dictated by the balletic skills and inventiveness of the rider'.[58]

And in this envisioning, can closer perusal of the performance of existing creatures help illuminate the conduct of their ancestors?

Living relatives (and the recently departed)

A *tourney horse* still accompanies the six Abbots Bromley Horn Dancers who bear an antlered reindeer skull on their daylong peregrination in the surrounding countryside every September. An oval frame is suspended around the waist of the rider, with a skirt draped over it and hanging below the knees. The frame bears a carved, wooden head—with snapping jaws—and a tail. The rider wears a cape that helps cover the frame further, his legs constituting those of the biped animal.

Though 'in skilled hands, the tourney horse can run, jump, skip and dance',[59] The rider at Abbots Bromley keeps it on a tight rein: as it walks in informal procession from traditional station to station, visiting particular farms, large houses and other specific locales; and as it participates with choreographed steps in the formal dances in which it is paired with an attendant bowman.

The latest rider sees its function to be 'in charge of rounding up all the deer and keeping them in order'.[60] His mount is neither particularly horse-like nor given to unbridled misrule, though its wooden under-jaw can snap against the upper.

But it puts in the miles, switching in comportment between informal and formal phases: the 'on' of the dances, the 'off' of the casual promenade.

Mast or *skull-and-pole horses* have a three-legged hobble, with one foreleg and two at rear. A real skull or a wooden replica is mounted on a metre-long staff, which the performer grasps and manipulates whilst bending; he is covered with a cloth attached to the rear of the horse's head. His legs are the horse's back legs; the effect is 'somewhat formless, hardly horse-like'.[61]

In the performance of the Symondsbury Mummers filmed in 1952,[62] Tommy the Pony—a mast horse with hind legs in sacking trousers—appears in a concluding comic interlude with his owner Jan and Jan's wife Bet. He has the propensities of a horse and carries Bet in a trot. But when Jan tries to mount him, he initially shies away; and then when Jan succeeds, bucks, throws and kicks him. In response, Jan strikes him on the head with a knotted stick and knocks him to the ground. Jan and Bet swing their arms as if to keep warm, blow on their hands and then pass them mystically over the inert horse, 'as though to convey warmth to him'.[63] They then try to lift him, falling twice in the effort. Finally, Tommy is righted by four soldiers, after which he turns clairvoyant, responding to prompts to 'Show me the little boy who steals the sugar'. Swivelling his head and looking around, he approaches and identifies a child in the audience by nodding before them, to general delight. But when Bet demands 'Show me the biggest rogue', Tommy paws the ground and chases Jan. 'He must be something of an athlete to perform all that is required of him'.[64] Energetic, comedic, dramatic in its use of timing…

Dick—a 'wild horse' that accompanies the Antrobus Soul Cakers—causes mayhem in his natural habitat, the confined spaces of the crowded pubs that the team visit in early November.[65] His head is made from a blackened and varnished horse's skull, with large artificial eyes, and with its jaws wired so it can 'snap' its teeth. In a noisy entry, Dick drags his Driver who attempts to control his improvised cavortings and misbehaviour as he repeatedly backs into him. Dick clashes his jaws, rears, bangs his front leg on the floor, leaves fake droppings and makes sudden sallies into the audience with his mouth agape, even sitting on their knees. The Driver proceeds in all seriousness, pausing to calm Dick who rears and bangs each time he is spoken to. Or as the performer flexes his spine in response to the extolling of his attributes: of his relative at Tarvin, Dr. Brown declares: 'Come up Dick, whoa! (*Horse winches*)/This Old Horse he's got an eye like a hawk; a neck like a swan/And a foot like a paver's jammack and a tail like a tachinend/Come up Dick, whoa! (*Horse winches*)'[66]; at Alderley, the 'three legged monster' 'could drink a bottle of beer, swallow fire irons and pokers or carry a ladle to collect contributions'.[67]

Violet Alford suggests that the horse act was never part of the play, and that the beast 'seems to have attached himself to the Soul-cakers'.[68] But Dick, though mute, plays an essential and spirited role in the performance, much dependent 'on the inventiveness of the player disguised as the horse'.[69] Irreverent, insistent, engaging…

Notably, when soul cake teams met, they would fight, the victors taking both horses.[70] The Kentish Hooden Horse[71]—also a mast horse —disappeared at the beginning of the twentieth century, though Dobbin—a poor old horse 'exhausted by the hard labour forced on him by the Boss'—reappeared at St Nicholas-at-Wade in 1965, the harbinger of further regional revival. Originally the focus of a house-visiting collecting custom by farm teams, the Horse was led by the bridle door to door by a Groom or Waggoner with a whip, accompanied by a man dressed as woman with a broom (Mollie), and various musicians. Other accompanying figures might include a farm labourer and a boy. On entry, the Horse—decorated with rosettes and ribbons—pranced and clashed its hinged jaw. As the Groom tried to mount, he was often thrown off; on occasion, spectators tried too. The group sang a topical song often mentioning the Horse that may have described its behaviour and/or prompted its mimetic response:

> Our Dobbin's unpredictable, he's calm or can annoy
> We never know what he's about
> He, while we pat him on the snout,
> Gets tough and starts a-kicking out
> Or scrapping with the boy.

In 1828, a pregnant woman died after an encounter with a Hooden Horse. Or was it another member of the party—dressed as a bear—that caused her fright?[72]

There certainly are bears and bear-like creatures in the bestiary. On Plough Monday, at Holton-le-Clay in the Lincolnshire Wolds:

> Many an' manys the time I'se been round wi' the Plough Jags. I can't remember the play as we used ter do, but Straw Man was the first speaker, I remember. Carry this 'ere Straw Man for miles, we did—carried 'im right way into a house, an' set 'im down, tail an' all, an' a soon as 'e was set down 'e made a long speech, after which the play began. Straw Man 'ad ter be a big man, an' 'e was all covered over with straw, an' a great long straw tail that hung down an' trailed be'ind 'im. We never took a plough with us, but we allus took Straw Man.[73]

A creature so large, immobile and imperious that it had to be carried. Spectacular, innovative, makeshift...

The straw bear that dances on the Tuesday following Plough Monday at Whittlesea in Cambridgeshire[74] has no tail but is likely of similar lineage, having 'great lengths of tightly twisted straw bands prepared and wound up the arms, legs and body of the man or boy who was unfortunate enough to have been chosen'. Again this was originally a house-visiting custom: 'He was then taken around the town to entertain by his frantic and clumsy gestures the good folk who had on the previous day subscribed to the rustics, a spread of beer, tobacco and beef'. Banned in 1909 as a form of 'cadging' or begging, the bear—and its junior likenesses—now appears annually.

Constrained by the costume, it dances with lumbering, hopping steps on either leg, and with ungainly twists and spins. It responds to the accompanying music with slow and ponderous steps and finally collapses, legs waving inelegantly in the air. Clumsy, invigorating, poignant...

There are also creatures that have outstripped their horsey origins and become a breed apart. The Padstow Obby Oss is a creature 'black as the devil',[75] 'alarming, even diabolical'.[76] A frame approximately two metres in diameter and extending from the performer's neck is carried on webbing shoulder braces and covered in black sailcloth stretched over the hoop and—skirt-like—reaching the knees. There is a small horse's head with snapping jaw at front, and tail of horsehair at back. A tall pointed mask of 'immense savagery'[77]—with grey whiskers, red lolling tongue and white-circled eyes—completes the creature's mien.

At 11am on May Day, the Old Oss emerges from its 'immemorial home',[78] the Golden Lion public house into an environment made ready, into a town bedecked with sycamore branches, garlands and bunting. It follows an established route, accompanied by an insistent rhythm and cycle of two songs from the attendant drummers, accordionists and Mayers, dressed in contrasting white.

Led by the Teaser who waves his padded club and dances before it—'swaying in hypnotic curves',[79] 'in the fashion of a duel'[80]—it dips, tilts, swings, rolls, spins and prances, gripped inside to aid manipulation: 'It varies from a jaunty walk, with sometimes some swaying of the body to a sinuous twisting of the body in a kind of diving movement'[81]; 'The diabolical, creeping crinoline becomes a completely unrecognizable swirl of shining black magic'.[82] The most extreme manoeuvre is to tip the frame to the vertical, up into a black halo 'that transcends any relation to the shape of horse or man'[83]; and that then descends upon and covers young women. Its progress is punctuated by solemn phases in which it sinks down 'quiet like, dead like',[84] the Teaser stroking the head with his club as the slow verse of the Day

Song is sung: 'O Where is St. George'. 'It is a solemn moment, a dramatic pause before the sudden beat of the drums bring the Oss and everyone back to life'.[85] Urgent, disconcerting, irrepressible...

The Blue Ribbon 'Oss is also on the streets, following a different route as the town is threaded with processional performance. The two creatures finally meet in a joint celebration, though the pressing crowds, who raise their hands to fend off the dangerous gyrations, restrict their fullest freedom of movement. Invasive, unsettling, overwhelming...

The Sailor's Horse at Minehead[86] is also suspended at neck level. Decorated with ribbons and roundels, it is more boat-like in shape, with a plumed mask and long tail. Its movements are buoyant, its swaying advance accentuated by vigorous up and down pumping actions, and by periods of rest with the prow on the ground. It is 'playful and mischievous'.[87] Though its length often moderates its actions in cramped locations, at times it can spin dangerously, lashing its rope tail.

As at Padstow, the sheer exertion involved necessitates the regular swapping of performers. And it too breeds multiples: the unsettling black-ribboned Black Devil; the miniature emulations of children. Exuberant, rhythmical, riotous...

The Derby Tup is a Christmastide custom to collect money in visits to private houses and licenced premises in mining villages south of Sheffield. Now existing in revived, theatricalised form, it was once the preserve of groups of adolescent boys. Centring upon the singing of the eponymous folk song that lauds the attributes of the giant, mythical sheep and lists the extra-ordinary uses to which its prodigious butchered parts might be put, its costumed performers included the Tup, the Butcher, and a variety of ancillary figures. As they all sang, the Butcher sharpened his knife and the Tup made an attempt to escape. At the climax, the Tup was slaughtered, with varying degrees of histrionics. Sometimes there were additional dramatic sequences before, during or after the song, including passages of joke telling to increase the productiveness of the visit.

'From realistic representation through to elaborate and abstract symbolism',[88] the Tup was sometimes a mast animal, sometimes other, but always made from readily available domestic materials: a turnip; a sweeping brush poking out from under a white sheet; a sack with the corners tied to represent horns; a block of wood with marbles for eyes. With a reversed sheepskin coat, rug or curtain to cover the performer, who sometimes grasped a staff, at others entered on hands and knees. At Ridgeway, the snaggle-toothed mast beast, carved from oak, had flashing electric eyes and a patchwork pelt of old fleeces; as the Butcher struck it twice on the snout with his knife, it fell over, baaing pathetically.[89] 'It is the fascination of audiences with the inhuman and the abnormal, the bizarre and the grotesque that ensures its popularity'.[90]

Between 1970 and 1978, Ian Russell observed 41 groups in 14 communities, in a project to relate a transient custom—with few eyewitness accounts—to its social and historical setting.

He notes: the random and arbitrary nature of oral transmission of song, action and costume, and the substantial variations in text from season to season; the importance of inter-generational instruction, as membership varied from year to year; the appreciation of the rewards in both popular and pecuniary responses to artistic elaboration through the application of ingenuity, imagination and attention to detail in the choice of materials, construction and appearance of the Tup; the benefits of rehearsal—with the pitfalls of over-confidence— and of forward planning in selecting routes.

He observes: an empirical understanding of the need for serious application to the task; how groups operate within specific domains, with multiple groups operating in the same area leading potentially to competition, to arguments and violence over trespass on bookings; and how groups move at speed in the unproductive space between one venue and the next. How presentation generally begins with a formal request for entry, followed by the clearing of space at the centre of the room, particularly in the pubs and workingmen's clubs that become the new 'theatre of performance'. How—though performing abilities vary—there is recognition of the need for both adaptability and precision. How there is a conscious introduction of theatricality: the deliberate inclusion of different registers of vocal expression and gesture, of characterisation, comic walks and gruesome sounds such as giving 'a death cry of excessive volume and duration', with humour as an essential ingredient.

He witnesses: a perception of how to create dramatic effect within a particular environment—'Probably pick on a woman and go quietly be'ind 'er and shove it on'er shoulder and tip the face towards her, sort of surprise her'. How delivery is often formal and declamatory and the presentation concise, given pressures of time in which extemporisation would be counter-productive, and as a consequence of the performers' youth, as they 'lack the confidence and experience to match the repartee of their audiences, and so sensibly stick to a uniform style of delivery'. How the response of audiences ranges from indifference to active participation, as spectators heckle, and even grope, prod and grapple with the Tup, attempting to set it on fire. How refusal of entry leads to disappointment and frustration; and how conspicuous welcome might lead to the bestowing of reciprocal gifts, such as drinks for the licensee.

Presaged by a seasonal atmosphere of goodwill, and a sense of occasion and expectation, the groups exist outside parental oversight—whilst intruding into the adult world—as ad-hoc fraternities deriving excitement, collective enjoyment, enhanced status and prestige, and income. Though sometimes exhibiting immoderate elements: with performers on the cusp of adulthood, taking the opportunity to swear, smoke and act belligerently.

What Russell's enquiry offers is a theoretical framework or interpretative methodology for the apprehension of the Derby Tup through close attention to the details of performance. But further, it constitutes a potential optic not only for regarding other contemporary beastly phenomena but also for providing insights that might illuminate the organisation and presentational techniques of equally ephemeral practices in the past.

Imagine then Russell's observations transferred to the nineteenth-century saddle room and village pub, to more or less skilled performers and more or less receptive audiences. To mutant hobby horses: to 'the inhuman and the abnormal, the bizarre and the grotesque'.

Conditions pertaining

In these contemporary examples, there is a crucial relationship between the activity and the particular environment of exposition. Whilst acknowledging likely differences between nineteenth-century physiques fashioned by heavy outdoor labour and twenty-first-century bodies resulting from improved nutrition can contemporary observation inform the tracing of former ecologies, of beasts and their habitats?

To begin, we must need determine and take cognisance of all that is operating at any one time in a set of circumstances: the ramifications of the constituents and conditions of the place of performance, and of the interactions of all components for the conceptualisation, design and implementation of the work. How atmosphere and surroundings might have both benign and adverse repercussions; how performance is always caught between the aspiration and intentionality of its performers and the potential for success, and for misfire and failure in the conditions pertaining.

Can we then summon the past environment of a distinct region: that area of intensive 'high' farming—an intensified capitalist mode of production of massive input of labour, power and fertilisers in arable farming and effort leading to high yields[91]—north of Scunthorpe, close to the confluence of the rivers Trent and Humber. This was no rural backwater but a scene of economically and socially advanced communities: a working rather than a picturesque landscape where in the late nineteenth century there was a resilience and even resurgence in peripatetic dramatic presentation. Surviving as an urge to maintain a custom, as 'what we always do on this day': 'They took it for granted see. Christmas was Christmas, and Christmas was Plough Jags'[92]; as vernacular 'heritage' performance that increasingly included families in both preparation and sequel.

These are the kinds of question we might ask.

How does a performance capitalise upon or is constrained by the set-up and ambience? How is it *mediated* in its nature by its location: by available surface, area, volume; by levels of accommodation in substances, by hardness, texture, give, resistance; by weather, light, acoustic properties? How does it get along: in twilit village street, furrowed field, heated parlour or noisy public bar?

What *affordances* does a place offer performers: 'either for good or ill'; 'benefit or injury, life or death'.[93] How does the terrain affect posture, locomotion and manipulation? How does it is appropriate and take advantage of that which is 'climb-on-able or fall-off-able or get underneath-able…'.[94] In muddy lane, on slippery pavement, amongst jostling drinkers?

And whilst there may be *reciprocity*—congruent 'fit'—between action and location, there may also be *conflict*, the one detrimental to the other. Or *indifference*: to immediate repercussions, one way or the other.[95]

What adjustments might performance need entail to be effective? The costume—and the social context and architecture of place of presentation—might greatly increase or ameliorate *ergonomic* potentialities and challenges for the performer, both assisting and hindering execution: extending, limiting or compromising four vectors of his physical application—his clearance, reach, posture, and ability to apply strength—and requiring adjustment. They may enhance or restrict his expressive gestures, his physical closeness and contact.[96] Increases in hazard and duress may demand excessive energy expenditure, leading to overload, to exhaustion through increased duration.

The performer's methods of coping and techniques of expression as a credible whole in volatile circumstances may include those *planned*, those *improvised*, and those *informed* by previous experience. Through prior advice, worked experience and expedient warning, performers come to know the topography of their performance intimately, as the best place to achieve this or that, as the places where danger lurks. But given changing conditions, performance might be as much tactical as strategic: although the 'what' may be fixed, the 'how', in terms of delivery, timing and quality, may be decided in the moment: applying to varying degrees the resources of voice and gesture; of appearance and the use of accoutrements and properties.

But performance may result essentially from dealing with and confounding such ergonomic problems. Audiences may appreciate the extra-daily degrees of effort and endurance required over extended periods—as at Padstow—and marvel at the extra-ordinary, super-human efforts required to engender the animal.

Through an overlay of contemporary beasts and their environments, imagine bringing into focus—however faintly—and rendering animate extinct creatures and their worlds. Sighting hereditary traits in the youthful manifestation of the Tup; in the arrival of the Hooden Horse, the licence of the 'Obby 'Oss, the antics of Dick…

Imagine wearing the inhibiting framework of the sieve horse where the main potential for action is in the legs: 'to run after folks', to curvet.

Picture the dangers in the un-gritted, icy street…in a state of inebriation.

Consider the combination of necessity and desire, of opportunity and creativity that led to the breeding of unsettling creatures.

Metamorphosis

'Sometimes they come with horse-cloths over their heads and ride hobby-horse'.[97]

> The Soldier, the Lady, and tall hat men, along with the Hobby Horses, attracted considerable attention as they paraded the principal streets and solicited subscriptions. The time for carrying 'The Plough' and pulling up scrapers in order to vent their wrath and fury if refused money has gone by, and the youngsters appear to be on much more familiar terms with the 'Plough Boys' than they used to be. The best gang this year hailed from West Halton.[98]

In the photograph of 1898—by which juncture teams had village affiliation—the West Halton team is large, with 22 performers in all: black-faced 'females', tribal warriors, soldiers in uniform, four men in tall decorated hats, two horn blowers. And two disquieting monsters…

There is here an innate understanding of the nature of performative impact: in the presence of men dressed as women, ornamental hat-men—their headgear 'so heavy that in going from one place to another, where not seen, the wearers would carry them'[99]—and the be-jacketed horses that become ubiquitous in the region. At Winterton in 1901, there are 'two smart and clean Hobby-horses' though the man wearing 'donkey's ears and horns'[100] is surely a misapprehension of the construction.

> The characters in most of the gangs followed much the same pattern […] but the two most dominant were the hobby horses. Dressed in horse rags which were draped over hoops carried by bands over the shoulders, and normally wearing one white and one black stocking (the mark of a thoroughbred) they usually presented a fearsome appearance.[101]

In place of horse/rider, there is now horse/horse, a dangerous abomination with two heads: 'In comes I who's never been before' announces an Alkborough creature,[102] in a familiar formula though now also acknowledging its own transmogrified form. At Burringham, it is the two four-year-old colts who themselves proclaim '*We* can hop-scotch…'.[103] The transition is complete.

These are anomalies, phenomena at the borderline, haunting the fringes of both culture and nature: the result not of evolution, of descent and filiation, but of involution, contagion, infection, between the terms in play and their assignable relations, between man and animal.[104] In donning the horsecloth, the performer becomes other than himself, his everyday identity suspended and dislocated, his behaviour become *extra*-daily and *trans*-gressive, his demeanour *ab*-normal—no longer content to proceed with horsey resemblance that would represent an obstacle or stoppage to new-found liberties.

They cause 'great dread'[105] in children, and chase and frighten girls—'with their horses heads at waist level, which have an obvious sexual significance'.[106]

And yet they are mysteriously beguiling. Young women try to steal luck-bringing hairs from their tails. Unfortunately, these often have 'a piece of leather strap with tintacks in it, their business ends sticking out, so that anyone pulling the tail got scratched'. At Messingham, where there is 'a special array of hobby-horses', any stranger is almost certain to be tempted by offers in pints of beer at the village pub to undertake what is apparently a very easy task: 'He found that, when once he got hold of the tail the difficulty was to let go again; for embedded in the hair were fish-hooks which inevitably found their way deep into fingers, amid roars of unfeeling laughter from those who had been watching'.[107] At Alkborough, one horse—that had a large bell suspended in front and was called 'Bang-up'[108]—is for many years performed by one man, its tail studded too with pins and fish hooks.

Teams range widely: taking different routes as they simultaneously roam the area, following paths—old, pre-enclosure paths—and minor lanes between villages: criss-crossing and threading the landscape with performance. There is general understanding that the plough jags have 'free and unhampered use of the footpaths'[109] on this day of no work, that the land is theirs: to appropriate temporarily, and to inscribe with new escapades.

Just as landscapes are constructed out of the imbricated actions and experiences of people, so people are constructed in and dispersed through their habituated landscape. The plough jags and their horses are living phenomena of a particular *lifeworld*: part of its seasonal rhythms, not separate from other constituents: climate, flora and fauna; settlement, land use and labour; sounds, sights and smells; components of a figuration of landscape as 'nature, culture and imagination within a spatial manifold'.[110] They are active agents within an uneven and differentiated topography in which 'some of the points at which the various affects and bodies cross paths are more heavily trafficked than others'[111]—pubs, farms, track crossings…

Picture the West Halton team setting off for Whitton at 8 on a freezing January morning, then walking on to Winteringham, using 'paths wherever they possibly could'[112]—via Ings Lane by way of Rotten Sykes Path and a short cut via Dole Close Path—calling at the Bay Horse and Ferry Boat pubs, before proceeding to Winterton, Roxby, Sawcliffe or Dragonby, Scunthorpe and Flixborough and then Normanby Hall. Figures in a landscape, of a landscape…

Imagine the palpable excitement generated by the arrival of multiple teams: 'I can remember as many as six gangs, including our own, coming into the village during the day';[113] 'My uncle remembered jagging in its hey-day. He often told me that the village was hardly clear of one gang or another all day'.[114] 'The word would spread "Eh up, plough jags". We would scuttle inside our gate and peer at them from the "safety" of our stackyard. We were frightened of them'.[115]

In 1902 at Whitton, schoolmistress Ada Campbell closes the school as only seven children attend 'it being "Plough Jack Day"'[116]; though at Burringham a correspondent recalls the group 'tapping on the school windows and peering in, they scared the daylights out of me'.[117] Even though these are likely brothers, uncles and cousins, but come in a different, uninhibited guise.

Throughout the day, the West Halton gang are fed pork pies, mince pies, spiced bread and beer at farms, houses and public houses. After Normanby, they visit Burton, Thealby and Coleby before arriving back home for a last pint in The Butcher's Arms—though sometimes it is so late that the pub is shut—and a supper with wives and children in the village school on the day's proceeds.[118]

Imagine too the Burton-upon-Stather team: hearing a drum roll in the village at 7am informing everyone that 'off' is at 8. Marching through the village, playing, singing and dancing but proceeding in 'proper order', accompanied by drums and accordions that play 'any tune that was on the go at that time, real old fashioned tunes' (Figure 6.3).[119]

Figure 6.3 Burton Stather Plough Jags 1907
Source: Reproduced by permission of North Lincolnshire Museums Service.

Their spectacular parade is headed by 'the terrifying horses'[120] and their companion Besom Betty: free to run and prance; and to walk slowly, to smoke, to joke, to catch their breath when no one is watching.

Their arrival at Thealby is announced by the horn blower, going first. Advancing door to door, they begin collecting, wishing the cottager and family:

> A Happy New year
> A pocket full of money
> And a cellar full of beer
> 2 fat pigs and a new bayed cow.
> Mrs and Master would you mind giving us a New Years gift? Thank you![121]

Adjusting the nature and quality of each encounter, the horses modify their demeanour and behaviour according to the familiarity of people and context.

From Thealby, it's on to Coleby, then West Halton where they are given beer at the Butcher's Arms; next across fields to Winteringham, on to Winterton, Roxby and Normanby Hall, concluding with a supper of rabbit pies, Xmas pies, plum pudding and beer at the Ferry House Inn with the money they have collected.

In several villages—Alkborough, Burringham, Burton—there are 'double teams' with duplicate characters, in order to work the sprawling communities more quickly. Indeed, there are sometimes 'triple' and 'quadruple' versions of characters present, enriching the spectacle. At Alkborough, 'all the time a rhythmic dance' is kept up to 'a fiddle or concertina'[122]; though as one correspondent notes 'as they went round they didn't sing, not much chance as they were still going marching on'.[123]

Gangs process along village streets, creating a noisy and colourful display. They visit particular locales—isolated farms and pubs—on their route, where they pause, ask for permission to enter and perform at least part of their play. Their progress is a *punctuated procession*[124]: an articulation of formal and informal passages of movement—'They would go either "steady" or "hurry"'[125]—and of dramatic episodes. A sequence of constituent phases and meetings of differing rhetorical intensities, predicated upon *itinerary*—places to be—and *schedules* to be met: as nodes and journeys in a matrix of movement.

After splitting, they regroup at 'the best and likeliest houses';[126] 'the more "well off" houses to enact the play'.[127] The Fool knocks at the door, announces himself and says that he will be followed by a few of his friends.[128] 'Will you have Plough Jags in please?'.[129] Temporarily shifting into a different register: from procession to exposition. 'They made quite a mess if there was wet or snow but most people took this in good part';[130] 'If the householder did not want the play, they left mince pies and beer in the kitchen and the door left ajar'.[131]

Theirs is an *encounter custom*:[132] a series of deliberate, articulated meetings between two distinct and identifiable groups. Characterised by the *parade* 'in which the active group encounters the reactive by processing through its territory' with the ostensible aim of spreading luck door-to-door; the *house-visit* by costumed figures, leading to senses of anticipation, occasion and expectation; the *encounter* and the *exaction* of recompense. The active group intrudes into more or less welcoming situations. The nature of the *interaction* might be convivial or mischievous; it might reflect 'a relationship—deferential or assertive—with the hosts, or an attitude—benevolent or malevolent—towards them'. Disguise might help to protect identity, to release the inhibitions of participants and to allow a suspension of social constraint: 'disguise licensed freedom of action, especially when combined with alcohol. The élite and the lower orders could mix freely, sexual advances could be made, views could be expressed which would usually be forbidden, and the language "of Billingsgate" swearing and blaspheming, could be used'.[133] The horses are suddenly in the kitchen…

But in small communities, the active group would have been known individuals. The highly localised life of the village was given an intense quality by the restricted, repetitive and personal nature of social relationships: a comparatively small number of people were involved in a wide range of roles—economic, religious, recreational, administrative, ritual. Nearly all the people an individual would ever know, he met frequently—face-to-face—in contexts of work, leisure and worship: 'Everyone in the community is joined to everyone else by a mesh of stories and incidents if not by family relationships'.[134] Such intensity and the demands of work—with the compensatory need for pressure-valves—might give added import to liminal periods of dislocation and misrule: 'processing through the streets was an affirmation of the power of the ordinary person. For one day a year, the common folk asserted their right to take over the world'.[135] It was the continuation of the notion of a temporary, traditionally sanctioned suspension of social order—if not of 'no law'—that engendered transgression.

'Beer flowed freely on "jagging day"' and 'there was often a good deal of high-spirited horseplay among the gangs'.[136] When teams met, it could get violent. The Burringham and Burton gangs often fought, the mutant horses becoming particularly dangerous. Although they carried whips and used them to keep the processional line together, there was no rider left to goad the horse, so instead they lashed out at those they chased, and at innocent bystanders. 'They were usually tall men and were expected to fight the horses from any other team which they met on their travels'.[137] 'If we met any other ploughjags from any other villages when we were out, the hobby-horses would try and knock each other over. Whichever team's hobby-horse won, then that team was 'Cock of the North' or Champions for that particular year'.[138]

As a 'late development',[139] what then precipitated the appearance of monstrous creatures? One key factor was surely the assembling of gangs at Normanby Hall, 'where they had a special invitation to play'.[140] Towards 6pm, they converged in the stable yard where—until 1886—Sir Robert Sheffield and then Sir Berkeley bestowed patronage, perhaps with the aim of 'correcting an evil',[141] in a convention that 'may have kept down horse play'.[142] Unsurprisingly, they were no teams from Normanby itself, an estate village.

There was plum bread and cheese, apple pie and coffee or tea in the servants' hall and dancing with the 'girls from Burton'.[143] But accounts vary widely: gangs from the villages around 'were usually invited by Sir Robert Sheffield to take part in a tug-of-war competition by the light of bonfires'. Or: "ud meet, an' 'ave tugs o'war ower a bonfire; they were given a feed after by Sir Robert Sheffield, but the winnin' team got best supper'. Or: 'Rival gangs of Alkborough, Halton, Burton and Flixborough had a tug of war over a bonfire. The winners called themselves Champions'. Or: 'A huge bonfire was lit and tugs-of-war between the gangs was a feature, in some cases the pull being through the fire'. Or: 'Sir Robert Sheffield staged tug-of war contests over a bonfire followed by a free supper'.[144]

> One year there was a fella a made up 'is mind that 'is team *should* win. Now this 'ere man 'ad an ole 'oss as 'e used fer 'aulin timber, an' 'e fixes 'im on ter the end o' the rope round the corner out o' sight, an' in the dark it was a strange long time afore anyone found out why that team was so almighty strong![145]

'Many a barrel of beer was given by the squire on these occasions, but like many a good thing, got out of hand'.[146]

The first gang to reach the Hall received ten shillings,[147] but at different times all gangs were rewarded with half a sovereign.[148] And prizes were given for the best dressed, hence 'The best gang this year hailed from West Halton'.

And it's the lure of this bonus, this incentive that may have stimulated the development of exaggerated stylistic traits such as the increasingly tall and bedecked hats and the augmentation of the horses, whilst unwittingly encouraging competition and animosity between teams.

The adoption of horse jackets perhaps then originated in a moment of individual innovation—of dressing to impress Sir Berkeley—that spawned copying and cross-fertilisation, as it was taken up by other teams. Resulting in a veritable horse show...

But perhaps too, it sprang from an appreciation of the need for increased visual sophistication[149] in making an impression in a new arena of performance, in Scunthorpe.

'Scunthorpe, its blast furnaces, steel mills and ironstone quarries altered the face and the society of the north-west corner of Lincolnshire'[150]: by 1880, there were 6 works and 20 furnaces; by 1905, there were 173 shops and rows of houses built for miners and furnace workers.

Teams begin appearing on the town's streets. Weird and exotic creatures inhabiting the urban landscape, set against the illuminated shops, and in competition with colourful advertisements. And in its pubs—reflected in the mirrors—where reception is predicated upon meeting and engaging strangers, outside the conventions of village custom.

Scunthorpe is included in the West Halton itinerary: they 'walked all around, called at a very special little pub in Frodingham. The man always used to make a fuss of them there'. They then used the paths to Flixborough 'past behind the works' (Figure 6.4).[151]

On two occasions, the Burringham team are pictured outside Arthur Singleton's photographic studio on High Street. And in the opening passage in this chapter, the 'gran percession' is remembered by a correspondent from Scunthorpe and Crosby.

For some onlookers, a faint recollection of times past, for others a momentary curiosity and for others an object of ridicule or of indifference…

Climate change

The passing of the plough plays and their horses is often attributed to rural depopulation, with the coming of mechanisation, though new machinery actually required substantial

A performance bestiary

Figure 6.4 Burringham Plough Jags, pre-First World War
Source: Reproduced by permission of North Lincolnshire Museums Service.

labour to operate and was for the most part designed to be drawn by horses;[152] to the breaking of large estates; to the dispersal of labourers and the drift to the cities. Few survived the traumatic effects of the First World War and the killing and demoralisation of so many carriers of tradition.

Urban growth certainly contributed. Scunthorpe's ironworks drew large numbers of local young men: 'there was scarcely a labourer's son who stayed upon the land unless he was "half silly"'.[153] Such were the consequences that by the 1890s, there was a shortage of farm workers.

But the waning also proceeded from a change of tone in the nature of rural culture, not only under the influence of educational advancement offered by the 1870 Education Act but wrought by working people themselves: through their embrace of Non-conformism with its anniversaries, charity suppers and tea meetings.

Temperance and Friendly Societies emerged—such as the Oddfellows and Foresters—parading with banners, regalia and bands during which their members momentarily drew attention to themselves; Cow and Pig Clubs with shifting attitudes to prudence and mutual- and self-reliance; and the nascent collectivism of Joseph Arch's National Agricultural Labourers' Union founded in 1872. These movements espoused degrees of independence and offered new varieties of 'rational recreation': pageants, dinners, outings, galas, sporting events. The begging implicit in plough jagging and the attendant consumption of alcohol were viewed as undesirable.

Then there was the increasing availability of new forms of popular entertainment providing alternatives with which the plough play could not compete: Scunthorpe United Football Club was founded in 1899; by 1913, the town had two 'cinematographic halls'.

There were too institutional shifts: the hostility of the police—the rural force established in Lindsey in 1857—and magistrates. In 1898, the whole Barrow team was summoned. Following an incident in which they got their plough stuck in the doorway of the 'Red Lion' in Barton, 'in a violent and drunken mood, they assaulted a local farmer on the street'. 'I think the police really put a stop to a lot of it. It got to be quite rough, quite out of hand. And people began to complain at the rough way that they carried on. And so that's what really finished the plough jags'.[154]

And maybe there is an additional reason for the horses' initial corruption and final extinction: a fundamental change in the nature of the environment itself.

In 1912, John Lysaght opened Normanby Iron Works on land leased from Sir Berkeley Sheffield, joining the established Frodingham and Redbourn works. The development of industrial plant and of huge open cast mines at Crosby Warren, Bagmoor and Sheffield's Hill redrew the map, restricting ease of movement in the landscape.

And perhaps metaphorically, it was the new toxic atmosphere and palls of smoke that darkened the demeanour of the horses, causing them first to be terrifying, and then to succumb to the pollution. Or the thunderous noise and vivid red glow in the night sky as slag was tipped that rendered them now less than wondrous.

Death

But I am repeatedly drawn back to a single symbolic event.

On Friday 7th January 1887, Henry Fowler, an agricultural labourer, aged 25 years, a married man with a wife and three children, died whilst plough jagging.

Shocking Death of a "Plough Jagger" in the Snow
They started [from West Halton] at eight in the morning, about 14 of them.
Snow was on the ground, two or three inches in places, a normal snowfall.
When they got to Winterton some lads gave them some cheek he run them. Well they'd had a drink or two you see and it's thought he fell and hit his head on a stone wall. He wasn't drunk as some people say he was.

Deceased was said to be of intemperate habits.

Deceased had never more than a pint at a time, and 'did' pretty well before they got to Burton Stather, where they called at the Ferry House. They returned towards Alkborough, and when about half way from Burton Stather deceased 'seemed to turn bad', having previously complained of being hungry.

He wanted a rest so he laid down in the snow. The others carried on and left him. When they'd got a little bit further on two of them noticed he wasn't with them. They went back.

He could not walk and they could not carry him, and he seemed very useless and helpless. Deceased's nephew said "Let's leave him; he's acting", and deceased said, "All right, William", these being the first words he had spoken for some time. He said "Well I'll follow up later".

Anyhow he didn't follow up. Well he never got up you see.

Deceased had been left at six in the evening lying on the road, in extremely cold and inclement weather and left there exposed during the whole night, until found by a person casually passing by at eight o'clock the next morning.

A farm lad off a farm in Thealby found him next morning. He got him in his cart and he (took him to) Thealby policeman's house. He was alive then when he got him to the house. They got the doctor to him. The poor chap died on the Saturday morning very early.

After that, the squire, Mr. J. Goulton, Constable of Alkborough, 'set his face against the practice'.[155]

Henry Fowler perished not from exposure but from 'compression of the brain from rupture of a blood vessel', the result of the fall. He died 'having had too much beer and "got down",

A performance bestiary

Figure 6.5 Plough Jags, probably West Halton
Source: Reproduced by permission of North Lincolnshire Museums Service.

as a Lincolnshire farmer would say of a fallen animal that could not get up unaided'.[156] 'I'll tell you what the coroner said, "That old jockey if he didn't give us a lesson. He learned us what things was"'.[157]

Like 'a fallen animal'? An 'old jockey'? Was Henry Fowler then a hobby horse? Were the causeys in Winterton *slape*?[158] Did he kick out: his only option, confined in hoop and cloth, his vision restricted? Was he unable to break his fall, his arms inside the cloth tied tight against the perishing east wind? (Figure 6.5)

Exhibition

Teams did linger until the Second World War, and there is a revival currently at Coleby. The remains of one of last of the original breed—a Burringham horse—hang in a glass case at the North Lincolnshire Museum in Scunthorpe. Like some rare zoological specimen, only its skeleton survives: outer rim; suspension ropes; horsehair tail bound with string; horsehair mane; protruding wooden head, lower jaw hinged with leather—with iron hobnails for nostrils and teeth, to amplify the sound of snapping; and brass studs for eyes. But enough to hint at its power to disturb.

And there on the cross piece are the signs of wear from the hands that once operated the beast.

Picture then the ploughboy—horsecloth pulled tight—grasping that haft: stamping in the January cold, shivering in anticipation, his condensed breath billowing from the orifices…

Notes

1. This formulation echoes the work of US anthropologist Kathleen Stewart (1996) who repeatedly invites her reader in a creative envisioning to 'Imagine this' or 'Picture this'.
2. Ethel H. Rudkin, *Lincolnshire Folklore* (Burgh Le Marsh: Robert Pacey, 1987), p. 42.
3. See 'Plough Jags'. North Lincolnshire Museum Service Image Archive. <http://www.north-lincsmuseumimagearchive.org.uk> [accessed 18 December 2019].
4. The presence of men with blackened faces and in women's dress in the accompanying historical photographs calls for reflection that is beyond the scope of this chapter. For emerging discussions on 'blacking up' in folk performance, see https://www.efdss.org/policies . In this volume, refer to Harrop and Roud's 'General Introduction' as well as Harrop's 'Introduction to Part l'.

5 Peter Millington, 'Burton upon Stather Plough Jags a Photographic Query', *Traditional Drama Forum*, 6 (2003), n.p.
6 Scunthorpe, North Lincolnshire Museum (NLM), Ethel H. Rudkin Collection (EHRC), Box No. 3 (3), 'College' notebook, Ethel H. Rudkin 'The Plough Play' (1958).
7 E.C. Cawte, *Ritual Animal Disguise* (Cambridge: D.S. Brewer Ltd., 1978), p. 9.
8 Violet Alford, 'Some Hobby Horses of Great Britain', *Journal of the English Folk Song and Dance Society*, 3 (4) (1939), 221–240 (p. 224).
9 Rudkin, *Lincolnshire Folklore*, p. 49.
10 Ethel H. Rudkin, 'Plough Jack's Play from Willoughton, Lincolnshire', *Folk-Lore*, 50 (1939), 291–294 (p. 291).
11 Michael J. Preston. 'The British Folk Play: An Elaborated Luck-Visit?', *Western Folklore*, 30 (1) (1971), 45–48 (p. 47).
12 Scunthorpe, NLM, EHRC, Ephemera Box 178, 'Plough Jaggin' Daäy, Gunthorpe', FF.149–150.
13 Rudkin, *Lincolnshire Folklore*, p. 48.
14 Idwal Jones, 'Plough Monday and the Law', *Roomer*, 3 (6) (1983), 41–43 (p. 42).
15 Violet Alford, *The Hobby Horse and Other Animal Masks* (London: The Merlin Press, 1978), p. xxvii.
16 Maurice W. Barley, 'Varia Atque Breviora: Plough Plays in the East Midlands', *Journal of the English Folk Song and Dance Society*, 7 (4) (1955), 249–252 (p. 251).
17 Alun Howkins and Linda Merricks, 'The Ploughboy and the Plough Play', *Folk Music Journal*, 6 (2) (1991), 187–208 (p. 194).
18 T.W. Beastall, *Agricultural Revolution in Lincolnshire*, History of Lincolnshire Vol. VIII (Lincoln: History of Lincolnshire Committee, 1978), p. 119.
19 Howkins and Merricks, 'The Ploughboy and the Plough Play', p. 193.
20 Ibid.
21 Ibid., p. 195.
22 Beastall, *Agricultural Revolution*, p. 121.
23 Ibid., pp. 166–167.
24 See Rex Russell. *From Cock-Fighting to Chapel Building. Changes in Popular Culture in Eighteenth and Nineteenth Century Lincolnshire*. Lincolnshire Archaeology and Heritage Reports Series No 6. (Sleaford: Heritage Trust of Lincolnshire, 2002), pp. 18–20.
25 Russell, *From Cock-Fighting*, p. 19.
26 Ibid.
27 Preston, 'The British Folk Play', p. 47.
28 Eddie Cass, Michael J. Preston, and Paul Smith. *The English Mumming Play: An Introductory Bibliography* (London: FLS Books, 2000), p. 10.
29 Barley, 'Varia Atque Breviora', p. 250.
30 Eddie Cass et al., *The English Mumming Play*, p. 96.
31 Ruairidh Greig, 'The Kirmington Plough-Jags Play', *Folk Music Journal* 3 (3) (1977), 233–241 (p. 240).
32 A.R. Wright and T.E. Lones, *British Calendar Customs: England, II, Fixed Festivals January-May* (London: The Folk-Lore Society, 1938), p. 94.
33 Ruairidh Greig, 'The Plough Play in Lincolnshire', *Tradition Today*, 3 (2013), 20–30 (p. 24).
34 See Peter Millington, 'Mystery History: The Origins of British Mummers' Plays', *American Morris Newsletter*, 13 (3) (1989), 9–16; 'The Ploughboy and the Plough Play', *Folk Music Journal*, 7 (1) (1995), 71–72; 'The Origins and Development of English Folk Plays' (unpublished doctoral thesis, University of Sheffield, 2002); '"Plough bullocks" and other Plough Monday customs in the Nottingham area, 1800–1920', *Transactions of the Thoroton Society of Nottinghamshire*, 109 (2005), 127–137.
35 Maurice W. Barley, 'Plough Plays in the East Midlands', *Journal of the English Folk Song and Dance Society*, 7 (2) (1953), 68–105 (p. 74).
36 Peter Millington, 1989 see <http://petemillington.uk/articles/mysteryhistory.php> [accessed 18 December 2019].
37 Scunthorpe, NLM, EHRC, 3, 'College' notebook, Ethel H. Rudkin 'The Plough Play' (1958).
38 Ethel H. Rudkin, 'A plea for the collection of folklore: shewing that it is of scientific value', *The Lincolnshire Magazine*, 2 (5) (1935), 143–147 (p. 147).
39 Millington, 'The Origins and Development of English Folk Plays', p. 69.

40 London, English Folk Dance and Song Society (EFDSS), Vaughan Williams Library (VWL), Thomas Fairman Ordish Manuscript Collection (TFO), Mabel Peacock, 'Lincolnshire Plough Jags or Plough Jacks 1800–50 or Earlier', TFO/1/16/17. <https://www.vwml.org/search?q=%E2%80%98Perhaps%20the%20fool%20and%20the%20Hobby-horse%20belong%20to%20both%20dramas%E2%80%99&is=1> [accessed 18 December 2019].
41 See Alford, *The Hobby Horse*, pp. xxxiii, xxviii.
42 Cawte, *Ritual Animal Disguise*, p. 134.
43 Mabel Peacock, 'Plough-Jags' Ditties from North Lincolnshire', *Notes & Queries 9th Series*, VII (1901), 323–324 (p. 324).
44 London, English Folk Dance and Song Society (EFDSS), Vaughan Williams Library (VWL), James Madison Carpenter Collection (JMC), 'F. Chafer, Plough Monday', Personalities (JMC.pChaferF), <https://www.vwml.org/search?q=F.%20Chafer&is=1> [accessed 18 December 2019].
45 Eliza Gutch and Mabel Peacock, *Country Folklore Vol 5: Lincolnshire* (London: The Folk-Lore Society, 1908), p. 178.
46 Mabel Peacock, 'Hibaldstow Ploughboys' Play' (1901), *Folk Play Research* <https://folkplay.info/resources/texts-and-contexts/hibaldstow-ploughboys-play-1901> [accessed 18 December 2019].
47 London, EFDSS, VWL, JMC, 'New Barnetby—Hobby Horse', JMC/1/1/3/A, p. 01994 <https://www.vwml.org/search?q=new%20barnetby&is=1> [accessed 18 December 2019].
48 London, EFDSS, VWL, JMC, 'Worlaby – The Plough Jags', JMC/1/1/3/A, pp. 01991-01993. <https://www.vwml.org/search?q=worlaby&is=1> [accessed 18 December 2019].
49 Cawte, *Ritual Animal Disguise*, p. 134.
50 London, EFDSS, VWL, JMC, 'The Plough Jags, Elsham, by Brigg', JMC/1/1/3/A, pp. 01996–02001. <https://www.vwml.org/search?q=elsham&is=1> [accessed 18 December 2019].
51 Cawte, *Ritual Animal Disguise*, p. 134.
52 Rowson Hall, 'A plough jag's play from North Kelsey', *The Village* (The Lincolnshire Local History Society), 20 (1937), 1–4 (p. 3).
53 Russell, *From Cock-Fighting*, p. 91.
54 E.C. Cawte, Alex Helm and N. Peacock, *English Ritual Drama* (London: The Folk-Lore Society, 1967), p. 78.
55 London, EFDSS. VWL, JMC, 'Thomas Sellars, Plough Jags, Morris Dancers', JMC/1/1/3/A, pp. 01970-01975. <https://www.vwml.org/search?view=search&persauthfilter=JMC.pSellarsThos> [accessed 18 December 2019].
56 Eileen Elder, 1977, 135 defines 'hotch' as 'A sort of walking trot'; for Jabez Good, 1973, 45 'to hotch' is' To jog along, to trot'.
57 Peacock, 'Plough-Jags' Ditties', p. 324.
58 Alford, *The Hobby Horse*, p. xxviii.
59 Steve Roud, *The English Year* (London: Penguin Books, 2006), p. 164.
60 See *A Very English Winter: The Unthanks*, BBC Four, 2017. <https://www.bbc.co.uk/programmes/b01pdsvd> [accessed 1 March 2019].
61 Roud, *The English Year*, p. 164.
62 See *'Walk in St George'* (1952) dir. by Alan Simpson, produced by Peter Kennedy on *Here's a Health to the Barley Mow* (bfi/efdss, 2011), [on DVD].
63 Peter Kennedy, 'The Symondsbury Mumming Play', *Journal of the English Folk Dance and Song Society*, 7 (1) (1952), 1–12 (p. 10).
64 Alford, *The Hobby Horse*, p. 49.
65 See 'Antrobus Soul Cakers', online video recording, Vimeo <https://vimeo.com/197543063> [accessed 18 December 2019].
66 Eddie Cass and Steve Roud, *Room, Room, Ladies and Gentlemen* (London: EFDSS, 2002), p. 111.
67 Alex Helm, *Eight Mummers' Plays* (Aylesbury: Ginn, 1978 [1971]), p. 15.
68 Alford, *The Hobby Horse*, p. 56.
69 Helm, *Eight Mummers' Plays*, p. 12.
70 See Helm, *Eight Mummers' Plays*, p. 16.
71 For all quotes, see 'Hoodening' <http://hoodening.org.uk> [accessed 18 December 2019].
72 'Susanna Crow, a heavily pregnant 21-year old woman from Broadstairs, died of "severe contusion from a fall, occasioned by a fit of apoplexy which […] seemed to have been accelerated by fright, occasioned through a party from Margate, who paraded Broadstairs on Christmas Eve with music, and one of whom was habited as a bear in a dress of the most hideous description".

The dress had to be "given up" and the offending "apprentices" were warned that they would be prosecuted if any repetition took place'. See 'Hoodening' <http://hoodening.org.uk> [accessed 18 December 2019].
73 Rudkin, *Lincolnshire Folklore*, p. 42.
74 For all quotes, see 'Whittlesea Straw Bear Festival' <https://www.strawbear.org.uk> [accessed 18 December 2019].
75 Alford, 'Some Hobby Horses', p. 231.
76 See 'Padstow May Day Celebration 2017', online video recording, *YouTube* <https://www.youtube.com/watch?v=i_qcr9xnfWg> [accessed 18 December 2019]. See also *Oss Oss Wee Oss* (1953) dir. by Alan Lomax on *Here's a Health to the Barley Mow* (bfi/efdss: 2011) [on DVD].
77 Donald R. Rawe, *Padstow's Obby Oss* (Padstow: Lodenek Press, 1971), p. 17.
78 Rawe, *Padstow's Obby Oss*, p. 2.
79 Alford, *The Hobby Horse*, p. 40.
80 Rawe, *Padstow's Obby Oss*, p. 2.
81 Cawte, *Ritual Animal Disguise*, p. 160.
82 Richard Southern, *The Seven Ages of Theatre* (London: Faber and Faber, 1979 [1962]), p. 41.
83 Southern, *The Seven Ages*, p. 41.
84 Alford, 'Some Hobby Horses', p. 234.
85 Rawe, *Padstow's Obby Oss*, 3.
86 See '2013 Mayday Minehead Hobby Horse', online video recording, Vimeo. <https://www.youtube.com/watch?v=sDKtRGynhho> [accessed 18 December 2019].
87 Roud, *The English Year*, p. 163.
88 Ian Russell, '"Here Comes Me and Our Old Lass, Short of Money and Short of Brass": A Survey of Traditional Drama in North East Derbyshire 1970–78', *Folk Music Journal*, 3 (5) (1979), 399–478 (p. 462).
89 See *Derby Tup* dir. by Ian Russell on *Here's a Health to the Barley Mow* (bfi/efdss: 2011) [on DVD].
90 Russell, 'Here Comes Me and Our Old Lass', p. 462.
91 Howkins and Merricks, 'The Ploughboy and the Plough Play', p. 192.
92 Greig, 'The Kirmington Plough-Jags', p. 241.
93 James J. Gibson, *The Ecological Approach to Visual Perception* (Boston, MA: Houghton Mifflin, 1979), p. 127.
94 Gibson, *The Ecological Approach*, p. 128.
95 See Bernard Tschumi, *Architectural Concepts: Red Is Not a Colour* (New York: Rizzoli International Publications, 2012), pp. 60–63.
96 In ergonomic terms, the performer's kinesic, proxemic and haptic capacities.
97 Gutch and Peacock, *Country Folklore Vol 5*, p. 175.
98 See *Lindsey and Lincolnshire Star*, 11 January, 1902: 5 in Cass and Roud, 2001, 33.
99 London, EFDSS, VWL, TFO, Mabel Peacock, 'Letter from Mabel Peacock', TFO/1/16/18. <https://www.vwml.org/search?q=mabel%20peacock&is=1> [accessed 18 December 2018].
100 London, EFDSS, VWL, TFO, Mabel Peacock, 'Letter from Mabel Peacock', TFO/1/16/18.
101 Russell, *From Cock-Fighting*, p. 89.
102 Maurice W. Barley, 'The Alkborough Plough Jags Play', *The Local Historian* (Lindsey Local History Society), 8 (1936), 2–4 (p. 2).
103 P.L. Scott, *Burringham: a Pictorial History*. Burringham (Scunthorpe: P.L. Scott, no date), p. 75.
104 See Gilles Deleuze and Félix Guattari, *A Thousand Plateaus: Capitalism and Schizophrenia*, trans. by B. Massumi (London: Athlone, 1988), p. 232ff. In a chapter entitled 'Becoming-Intense, Becoming-Animal, Becoming-Imperceptible…'.
105 London, EFDSS, VWL, TFO, Mabel Peacock, 'Plough-jags at Bottesford in North Lincolnshire A.D. 1862–1872', TFO/1/16/17. <https://www.vwml.org/search?q=Bottesford&is=1> [accessed 18 December 2019].
106 Robert Pacey, *Folk Music in Lincolnshire Volume 1* (Burgh le Marsh: Old Chapel Lane Books, 2015), p. 95.
107 Cass and Roud, *Room, Room*, p. 54.
108 Wright and Lones, *British Calendar Customs*, 11, p. 36.
109 Alan Frost, 'Plough Jags', *Lincolnshire Life*, 7 (6) (1967), 22 (p. 22).

110 Denis Cosgrove, 'Landscape and Landschaft', *German Historical Institute Bulletin*, 35 (2004), 57–71 (p. 69).
111 Jane Bennett, *Vibrant Matter: A Political Ecology of Things* (Durham, NC: Duke University Press, 2010), p. 23.
112 Scunthorpe, NLM, EHRC, 3,'Plough Play Texts'/'Robert Pacey Plough Plays' file, 'West Halton, from Mr. Allan Frost of Winteringham 6 August, 1975'.
113 Russell, *From Cock-Fighting*, p. 89.
114 See Janet Topp Fargion, 'More on Burton upon Stather Plough Plays', *Traditional Drama Forum*, 7 (2003), n.p.
115 Scunthorpe, NLM, EHRC, 3, 'Plough Play Texts'/'Robert Pacey Plough Plays' file, 'Letter from Mrs J. Milson, Horkstow. 12 March 1976'.
116 See *Whitton: Notes on the History of a Parish* <https://spilman.genealogyvillage.com/Whitton/whitton.htm> [accessed 18 December 2019].
117 Scott, *Burringham*, p. 74.
118 See Alan Frost, *'Plough Jags'*, *Winteringham Local History and Geneology* (2019) <http://www.winteringham.info/Memories____/Plough_Jags/plough_jags.html> [accessed 18 December 2019].
119 'West Halton from Mr. Allan Frost of Winteringham 6 August, 1975'.
120 Kevin Leahy and David Williams, *North Lincolnshire: A Pictorial History* (Beverley: North Lincolnshire Council/Hutton Press, 1996), p. 61.
121 Scunthorpe, NLM, EHRC, 3, 'Plough Pay Texts'/'Robert Pacey Plough Plays' file, 'Letter from Mr Osbourne Readhead 1975'.
122 Barley, 'Plough Plays', p. 77.
123 'West Halton, from Mr. Allan Frost of Winteringham 6 August, 1975'.
124 Robert Pacey calls the plough plays 'processional plays'. See Pacey, 2014, 93.
125 'West Halton from Mr. Allan Frost of Winteringham 6 August, 1975'.
126 Barley, 'Plough Plays', p. 75.
127 Scott, *Burringham*, p. 74.
128 See Wright and Lones, *British Calendar Customs*, 11, p. 36.
129 Greig, 'The Kirmington Plough-Jags', p. 235.
130 Scunthorpe, NLM, EHRC, Ephemera Box 178, F.32, 'Letter from N.D.G. Booth', answered 20 June 1964.
131 Scunthorpe, NLM, EHRC, 3, 'College' notebook, Ethel H. Rudkin, 'The Plough Play' (1958).
132 See Thomas Pettitt, 'Customary Drama: Social and spatial patterning in traditional encounters', *Folk Music Journal*, 7 (1) (1995) 27–42 (pp. 31–35).
133 Howkins and Merricks, 'The Ploughboy and the Plough Play', p. 199.
134 Ned Thomas, *The Welsh Extremist* (Talybont: Lolfa, 1978 [1971]), p. 78.
135 Howkins and Merricks, 'The Ploughboy and the Plough Play', p. 199.
136 Russell, *From Cock-Fighting*, p. 89.
137 Pacey, *Folk Music in Lincolnshire*, p. 95.
138 Scunthorpe, NLM, EHRC, 3, 'Plough Play Texts'/'Robert Pacey Plough Plays' file, 'Letter from Mr Osbourne Readhead 1975'.
139 Cawte, *Ritual Animal Disguise*, p. 134.
140 Frost, 'Plough Jags', p. 22.
141 Russell, *From Cock-Fighting*, p. 18.
142 See Scunthorpe History Society [Meeting], Notes no. 21, Lincolnshire Archives: Foster Library, Lincoln, R BOX L. SCUN.367 SCU (1952).
143 'Letter from Mr Osbourne Readhead 1975'.
144 Compiled from Scunthorpe History Society [Meeting] Notes no. 21; Rudkin, *Lincolnshire Folklore*, 1987, p. 42; Wright and Lones, *British Calendar Customs*, 11, p. 97; Fargion, 'More on Burton upon Stather Plough Jags', n.p.; Geoffrey W. Robinson, *The Parish of Burton upon Stather with Normanby and Thealby* (self-published, 1996), p. 60; Greig, 'The Plough Play in Lincolnshire', p. 25.
145 Rudkin, *Lincolnshire Folklore*, p. 43.
146 Robinson, *The Parish of Burton upon Stather*, p. 60.
147 See Barley, 'Plough Plays', p. 75.
148 See Russell, *From Cock-Fighting*, p. 89.

149 In mummer's plays, Peter Harrop notes 'a deliberate embrace of the weird as the nineteenth century moved into the twentieth'. See Peter Harrop, *Mummer's Plays Revisited* (London: Routledge, 2019), p. 158.
150 Beastall, *Agricultural Revolution*, p. 158.
151 'West Halton from Mr. Allan Frost of Winteringham 6 August, 1975'.
152 See Abigail Hunt, 'Scholarly and Public Histories: A Case Study of Lincolnshire, Agriculture, and Museums' (Unpublished doctoral dissertation, University of Lincoln, 2013), pp. 123–134.
153 Nick Lyon, *The Farmworker in North-West Lincolnshire: Commentary and Documents* (Scunthorpe: Scunthorpe Museum, 1984), p. 31.
154 See Peter Kennedy, *'In Comes I, Tom Fool': Lincolnshire Plough Plays* (Folktrax, 1975) [on audio cassette].
155 Compiled from Scunthorpe, NLM, EHRC, 3, 'Plough Play Texts'/'Robert Pacey Plough Plays' file, 'West Halton from Mr. Allan Frost of Winteringham 6 August, 1975' and *The Retford and Gainsborough Times*, 14 January 1887 in Idwal Jones, 1983, p. 8.
156 Barley, 'Plough Plays', p. 76.
157 Scunthorpe, NLM, EHRC, 3, 'Plough Play Texts'/'Robert Pacey Plough Plays' file, 'West Halton from Mr. Allan Frost of Winteringham 6 August, 1975'.
158 'Causey' (causeway) is a local dialect word for pavement, and 'slape' for slippery.

7

PERFORMING COMMUNITY

Village life and the spectacle of worship in the work of Charles Marson

Katie Palmer Heathman

The Christian socialist vicar Charles Marson is known to those interested in the folk revival as the occupier of the vicarage in whose garden Cecil Sharp heard his first folksong, 'The Seeds of Love', sung by Marson's employee, the gardener John England. During his lifetime, however, Marson was better known as an outspoken activist and writer on politics and theology. His folksong collecting was not a sideline or mere hobby, distinct from his Christian socialism, but another expression of this worldview. His notion that community and a common life could be the bond bringing all people together in a better, socialistic society necessitated some form of common culture to anchor those communities. He also envisaged the Church of England and its acts of worship as a similar living community, a bond created and maintained by continuous use of common language, rituals and performance. The idea that Christian worship was a form of performance may sound surprising, even now, and especially in Marson's lifetime, but Marson saw the services of the Church, and especially Holy Communion, as a kind of communal drama:

> The truth is that not only is worship and every other communal act essentially dramatic, but even reason itself is the same. A man who thinks out a problem with closed eyes […] has already erected a stage in his mind, where pro and con, the dramatis personae, argue and fence […]. Particularly in public worship, where God is approached by and through men, there must always be a very marked dramatic element.[1]

Worship as a group was not only a performance of shared cultural heritage, speaking the words, sharing the bread and wine (themselves a symbolic performance of Christ's body and blood), that had been repeated down the centuries, but literally an embodiment of that community, each communicant symbolically taking their part and becoming part of the whole through their participation. Performance of community, and through performance, embodiment, came to be at the centre of Marson's religious, political and social outlook, and his various cultural activities provided material and inspiration for these performances. Many Christian socialists such as Marson took from the incarnation of Christ as a man on earth that the Kingdom of Heaven was also to be realised on earth as an ideal society of individuals in communion with one another. This was itself another embodiment: a living performance of God's goodness. They believed that strong, harmonious communities were the answer, forming the basis of a revitalised society enriched with a shared culture which would itself build and bind these communities together. Folksong represented collective creativity and the concept of useful culture, developed by and according to the needs of those who were to make use of it. This was an idea very important to those wishing to create a socialistic society because it placed at the forefront the needs of a group or community, rather than of any individual.

Marson was a committed activist for the 'social gospel'. For him, the implications of Christian faith were inherently socialistic, and equally, the belief in and practice of socialism not an add-on to faith, but a central aspect of his spiritual life. As he wrote in his clarion-call for Christian socialism, *God's Co-operative Society*, 'it is not necessary for every Churchman to join a Socialist Society, because he has already done this in his baptism'.[2] Many of Marson's clerical appointments were unsuccessful due to his politics: he was refused ordination by six bishops and sacked from five different curacies.[3] Marson finally obtained the living of Hambridge, Somerset in 1895, following a petition by his friends to the Prime Minister, Lord Rosebery, avoiding the need to find an approving bishop.[4] Marson remained there until his death in 1914, and in addition to becoming the site of Cecil Sharp's fateful meeting with John England, Hambridge was the venue, but more significantly the inspiration, for Marson's own most important works.

Marson's diverse activities all shared one aim: the establishment of a socialistic society within which all people could live fulfilling, dignified, but most of all happy lives. This was of course an aim held in common with many of his socialist colleagues, Christian and secular, but Marson's own conception of his role was somewhat unusual. Marson believed that the most important duty of a priest was that of interpretation. The folk revival, along with other movements which interested themselves in the lives and culture of the working classes, has been accused by Marxist scholars of attempting to foist middle-class values and forms of expression onto unwilling working-class recipients in the guise of help.[5] But Marson's conception of this duty was not to translate middle-class ideals to the working classes, but rather to goad his own class into socialist action through a better understanding of working-class lives and culture. Marson admired his contemporaries, the historians J.L. and Barbara Hammond, and recommended that his own readers should read the Hammonds for the full account of what he calls 'that great wrong, the overthrow and downfall of the agricultural labourer, which began with science and ended in grab and brutality, in starvation, despair, ineffective revolt'.[6] The Hammonds, like Marson, raised concerns about the growing social and cultural divisions between classes, particularly in the rural setting: they wrote in *The Village Labourer 1760–1832* that in this period the rich and the poor grew further and further apart, until there remained 'nobody in the English village to interpret these two worlds to each other'.[7] It was this unbridged gulf, still present in the 1890s and 1900s, that Marson sought to cross. He wrote that:

> It is of the first importance that our clergy [...] should study humbly and patiently the lives of the poor, which they do a little; and the views of the poor, which they never do. They must themselves explain those views to the class to which they belong (in the ugly worldly sense of this word class).[8]

This would, Marson hoped, galvanise the comfortable classes into socialist action:

> Then it will follow that all the things which do or can protect the disinherited will be their delight. [...] They will be openly in favour of the existence, strength and health of Unions. They will support all laws [...] which make for the health and are against the helplessness of the governed.[9]

This duty of interpretation was performed by Marson during the majority of his time in Hambridge, and it took three forms which changed over time, sometimes overlapping. These were the collection and dissemination of folk songs, in which he engaged from 1903 to 1906 (terminated by a bitter quarrel with Cecil Sharp, involving disagreements over the presentation of the material but also a feud over Marson's personal life[10]); the production of what he termed 'Shepherd's Plays', contemporary, improvised stagings of the nativity story by Hambridge villagers which took place from 1896 to 1913 and finally, his memoir of and tribute to the people of Hambridge, *Village Silhouettes* (1914).[11]

Marson saw the folksongs sung by the Hambridge parishioners as an expression of rural communal life and values of the kind he wished to interpret to wider society, as well as a demonstration of the bond of common culture and communality he believed would strengthen a socialistic society. But the very act of interpretation was fraught with dangers and deficiencies, particularly in the case of folksong collecting. The fact that songs were intended for publication, and in a respectable format (the *Folk Songs from Somerset* series was dedicated, with her permission, to the Princess of Wales)[12] meant that they had to conform to accompanying standards of decorum and decency, both grammatically and in content. Marson wrote that it was the 'conventions of our less delicate and more dishonest time' which demanded that bowdlerisation, implying that it was not the songs or their original singers in the wrong, but the prudish atmosphere of the drawing room to which the books were destined: 'We plead compulsion and not desire in these alterations', he insisted.[13] In his private letters, Marson exercised his opinions on bowdlerisation, calling the collection of texts he had been reading, including Morley's *Cavalier Ballads and Songs*, 'stupidly bowdlerized for feminine minds', a complaint about the unnecessary and insulting protection of women's sensibilities.[14] Marson's views were already well-developed, long before he considered that these editorial decisions would one day be his to make. When he had become not only an editor but the father of a daughter, Marson continued to defend this premise, namely that directness and simplicity were in themselves nothing offensive. Marson, as the textual editor, has taken most of the blame for the bowdlerisation of the songs in the *from Somerset* series, but his letters demonstrate that he attempted to persuade Sharp to allow some 'improper' lyrics to stand. This was to no avail, despite Marson's assurance that he 'can't imagine how any one could mind it' and that he would teach the song to 'Mary [his daughter, then 12 years old] as soon as I had it'.[15]

Without some measure of bowdlerisation, the collections could not have been published, at least not in a way that could have presented them to the intended middle-class audience for Marson's interpretations. The very role of 'translator' or 'interpreter' between classes which Marson carved out for himself was just that: translating involves the input of the translator, with the material being interpreted inevitably gaining some of the ideas and motives of the interpreter along the way. The presentation of a cultural object in a form other than that in which it was received, in this case a song received aurally and passed on in the form of printed music and text, always involves some degree of interpretation, whether a conscious or unconscious act. Sharp promised that the tunes in the first instalment of their collection were given with 'exact fidelity', but this was impossible, since they were transcribed by a third party.[16] Interpretation was inevitable, even between one 'genuine' folk singer and another, from one performance to the next, because each individual singer altered the tune or words of the songs, either to introduce their own improvements or, if they sang from memory, because they might use slightly different turns of phrase. Of course, Sharp and Marson's interpretations differed from the singers' in that they were deliberately tailored for a specific audience (Sharp noted that most songs were not censored by their original singers, because they 'do not violate the communal sense of what is right and proper')[17] and because their interpretation was preserved in a printed form. But as David Atkinson posits, tradition and revival in fact shared many of the same notions of selectivity. Certain songs or types of song were privileged by their singers using their own 'affective criteria', including continuity with the past, and these criteria often coincided with those of the collectors, allowing for 'a degree of theoretical continuity between traditional and revival activities'.[18] Marson and Sharp's interactions with tradition, though they differed in their printed form, were in line with a larger pattern of interpretation and selective preservation undertaken by the singers themselves.

The interpretative task was important to Marson as a tool in his political arsenal. But the contradiction was that in interpreting this material, damage was inevitably done to the very characteristics which made it so central to his political activities. In preserving one particular interpretation in the printed form, the process of continual alteration and communal improvement in which he and Sharp believed was halted, at least for the new audience. The folksong, wrote Sharp, 'will always be approaching a form which will accurately express the taste and feeling of the community; what is purely personal will be gradually but surely eliminated' through the process of natural selection, with less-popular interpretations falling out of use.[19] This idea was vastly important to Marson politically, as it demonstrated the power of the collective will and the expression of community as a whole, not of powerful individuals: a socialistic art. Sharp wrote that art-music was 'the work of the individual, and expresses his own personal ideals and aspirations only' and 'committed to paper, it is forever fixed in one unalterable form', negatively comparing it to the communal folksong without realising that his publications performed the same function of fixing.[20] Marson made the connection that Sharp missed, having complained that 'The Ballad leaves our head and hearts and gets into our Libraries. So it is much better not to try to date and dissect, but simply to love and enjoy them'.[21] In the programme for a lecture, Marson joked that he would provide ballad 'specimens stuffed and alive', all being 'difficult to obtain, owing to the vice of editing'.[22] Marson clearly believed that the process of printing and publication was damaging to the aesthetic properties of ballads, but seems not to have realised until much later that it was also potentially damaging to the spirit of them as communally made, adaptable and useful 'people's art', one of the reasons which drew him to ballads in the first place. It also echoes Marson's religious outlook: he commented that the Word 'took flesh, not print' to come into our world, prioritising the example of the incarnate Christ on earth as an ideal to live by, rather than the fixed commandments of the Bible.[23] Again, we see his preference for embodied performance, whether of songs or worship.

Marson's final book offers insight into an alternative format of interpretation. *Village Silhouettes*, written in the year of his death, was a celebration of the people of Hambridge, as he had known them over the two decades of his ministry there. The silhouettes are tender portraits of individual parishioners, often tributes to those no longer living. Each piece is illustrated with an artistic silhouette, cut out by Marson himself. The book could be taken as his rejection of the folk revival, or at least the tendency towards fixing immutably in print something that he had enjoyed and valued as a living performance. Marson had withdrawn from the movement in late 1906 following a catastrophic disagreement with Sharp. With *Village Silhouettes*, Marson's focus shifted from the culture of the common people to the people themselves. He had wished through his interpretation of their culture to force his own class to see the working classes as more than economic abstractions. But as he realised, and explained in *Village Silhouettes*, he had himself been guilty of abstraction: in constantly attempting to interpret cultural products of his parishioners, he had cast them as passive carriers of this culture rather than as individuals with rounded lives of their own. He called this failing on his own part 'shameful and blind', and wrote that:

> People were once kind enough to applaud the writer for his discovery of a great gold mine of beautiful song in [...] Now the prospector wishes to proclaim a far greater discovery. The graceful, manly and fine-wrought melodies are not separable accidents, they belong to lives and characters at least as interesting, as full of fine art and exquisite melodiousness, as are the songs [...]. Not only is the expression great, but the life which is so delicately expressed is worthy of our utmost attention and admiration.[24]

This is the task that Marson set for his *Silhouettes*: to express the life, or 'wholeness' of the person hidden behind what would at first seem to be their defining quality. Marson titled each 'Silhouette' with a descriptor designating the interesting quality which marked out this particular person, for example, 'John Moore: The Village Musician' or 'Village Spinsters: I. Ann Warnford'. Yet these simple designations were not what they seemed, for beneath these veneers lay the human qualities, strong personalities and unexpectedness Marson was so ashamed of having discovered too late. Marson's use of the silhouette as a method of illustration implies a tribute, as by this time the silhouette had come to be associated with the frontispieces of biographies.[25] By illustrating his short biographies of the villagers in this way, Marson ascribed dignity and worthiness to their life stories. Black profile art was also used in classical times to depict everyday scenes of working or domestic life in a decorative rather than portrait format on pottery, alongside depictions of mythology and deities. Marson's depiction in silhouette of James Vincent hedging and 'Al-Parn' (Alice Perrin) resting on a gate, along with his frontispiece of agricultural tools and animals, also draw on this heritage of the silhouette as an artistic glorification of everyday life and a visualisation of folklore. The silhouettes function as a sanctification of these tales as modern folklore, a mythology of their time and place. Marson had even declared the ennobling of domestic life as a vital aim in a socialist manifesto written in 1886, and the silhouettes show that these concerns were still in force nearly 30 years later.[26] The use of the word silhouette was also an admission of a fact never addressed in the folksong collections: namely that the depiction was but a *shadow* of the living reality. The lover's silhouette is a keepsake, but the beloved is the true focus. Now it was the people themselves who were important, just as the enjoyment and spirit of the folksongs had become more important than their artistic or political potential. Marson was comfortable enough with the fact that his writing was 'mere' interpretation to acknowledge it directly:

> But all this is hard to say; and when said it is like a silhouette. It is an adumbration rather than an imitation. It has a kind of Platonic abstraction about it, which is the real secret of the silhouette. It is the mere idea of the person, perhaps nearer than we think him. [...] Finally, it always has a sense of fun and laughter in it, which is chiefly why some of us value a form of art which is cheap and quick and very limited. But the poetry, the pen, or even the scissors which laugh, can often say more than even can be got into anything wholly in 'the big bow-wow' vein.[27]

A silhouette is the preservation of a shadow which, for a time, is cast upon the artist. Marson was at pains to point out that his silhouettes were only impressions made upon him, and not imitations of the people he described. His interpretations of the folksongs he edited were the same: they record the impression cast upon Marson and Sharp as they heard the songs, and the editorial work Marson performed was to allow the 'idea' of the song, like the 'idea of the person', to come through within a limited and specific context. There is something paradoxical in the attempt to capture something as fleeting and transient as a shadow, and this is in effect what Marson and Sharp were attempting with their collection. Each version of any song existed only briefly, during the time taken for its performance. So in effect 'fixing' the song through publication was capturing an elusive shadow: the real thing remained at large, flexible and changeable despite the preservation of an impression it once left behind. This very fact leaves Marson's interpretative work in the folksong revival at once profoundly inadequate for the depth of information required to convey everything about folksong *as performed*, but also entirely fitting and suitable as an acknowledgement of the limitations of such work in truly capturing the 'livingness' of communal culture.

We know the 'true' identity of one of the villagers featured in Marson's silhouettes, John Moore, the 'Village Musician', whose name was James Marsh, due to the publication of some of Marsh's poems in *Leisure Hour* and his hymn tunes in *Goodwill*, with Marson having used his publishing connections to support this.[28] Marsh had been a farm labourer all his life but had always maintained a strong interest in music, singing in the choir as a child, and playing violin in the church band and for social dance, and later in life earning a small amount by teaching music to the village children. But according to Marson: 'Folk-songs were abhorrent to John – except, of course, just one or two, but even these he gave up in his later years, and pleaded that he should not even be reminded of them. He was something of a Puritan'.[29]

The folk revival was supposed to rediscover the lost voice of the rural poor, and we know from singer Louie Hooper's letters after Marson's death that she was proud to know that 'her' songs were sung up and down the country.[30] But Marsh was a rural musician whose voice was not heard by that movement. His skills must have formed a significant part of Hambridge's self-image, and he contributed to the village's musical tradition. The folk revival recognised only those songs which they believed had been passed down exclusively through an oral tradition, disregarding music they knew to have been authored by an individual. Marson's emphasis on James Marsh's musical contribution, and especially the award of the title of 'The Village Musician', is therefore significant. The highlighting of Marsh's rejection of folksongs shows that with seven years to reflect on the folk revival, Marson had come to realise that rural musical tradition was much more complex than he and Sharp had believed in 1903.

Marson's insistence on the 'fun and laughter', the vitality of not just the silhouette art form but of the life of Hambridge, is also important. His dissatisfaction with the 'stuffed specimens' of folksong was a part of his larger dissatisfaction with anything made too serious or with the life taken out of it. For Marson, who as a folksong editor and also as an Anglo-Catholic had a strong focus on the past, despaired at the thought that this meant reverence and stuffiness towards tradition:

> Loyalty to the past causes the keys of the kingdom to be so deeply respected that they are hung up in a museum and stared at. We call the museum a Church, and the staring, reverence. Modern wits suggest that the keys might now be put upon the scrap-heap [...] But [...] the keys should be taken down, oiled, and used. [...] The Church [...] was never meant for a museum at all.[31]

To lock away or to preserve untouched was not to respect the past. Irrelevance would soon render even the most important ideas and forms contemptible, if they were allowed to become disconnected from present-day needs and realities. The fact that Marson believed strongly in Christian socialism meant that he saw the Church as holding the potential to become a progressive institution involving itself in contemporary politics. This extended to the belief that churches as buildings had the same potential to become key centres of communal life. Marson saw the Church, in both the organisation and the physical sense of the word, as an element, like folksong, of a shared cultural and national heritage that was not only historically and aesthetically significant, but valuable also because it offered a sense of community and belonging, a cultural possession inherited through the ages:

> The Church service is more and more wonderful as one studies it. […] these cries have fitted the lips of the generations […] Fancy all the folk repeating them in turn, all one's poet friends, Shakespeare listening to them, and Raleigh, Sidney, Colet, Mad Cap Hal, Kings, king-makers, king-haters, rascals, Piers-ploughmen, crusaders. They outlive oaks and empires and democracies and are steeped in the best life of man.[32]

The reason that the Collects were 'steeped in the best life of man' is that they were steeped in communal life, and were part of a chain of continuity linking English culture and common experience through a long history. Both ideas were very important both to the Christian socialists of the time and to the folksong collectors. The words of the church service also appealed to Marson as a performance. The church was not meant for a museum, but as a centre for community, and equally, its services were not mere words on a page, but a human drama, making use of performance to bring souls closer to God and to one another:

> Men must be united into man […] They are united in a living whole, which needs constant feeding and building up […] This work can only be done by the perfect and archetypal man; that is the […] miracle of the Mass, to be set forth with all that is solemn and impressive, with all the appeals to each gate of the soul, the organs of sense, eye-gate, ear-gate, nose-gate, and so on; that is the meaning and use of ritual.[33]

Such performance could be mismanaged, just as the use of the church buildings themselves had been:

> That drama may be (it usually is) mounted with grossly careless stage management, with inattention to dress and deportment […] Yet these very managers, so lacking in manly reason, in theatrical propriety, in the seriousness of the art they have undertaken, […] are the very persons who would […] remodel what they cannot understand, and in the name of development would hugely impoverish the stage upon which they strut so clownishly.[34]

Performance was vital to Marson's entire worldview, and he was highly critical of those who did not understand the importance of ritual as a 'serious' performance used to bring forth a deeper relationship with God and fellow man, and in neglecting the 'stage management', made the performance meaningless. He bemoaned the poor preparation of candidates for ordination in these matters: 'Not a word about reading, voice-production, music, […] the first principles of stage management, without which all public functions, civil or religious, are apt to be ridiculous'.[35] The deep importance of this drama and its management did not mean that it had to be approached without humour, just as the folksongs or the *Village Silhouettes* were meant to be enjoyed. Christ was a human man with human emotions, and laughter and joy were valid as human responses to the experience of worship, and expressive of a living response to that experience. This aspect of Marson's practice was controversial, especially when it came to his Shepherd's Plays.

Marson's wish to make his religious teaching useful to his parishioners by ensuring that it touched their everyday lives, and his belief that the Church should offer opportunities for communal activity found an outlet in performance: he wrote that 'once upon a time almost every village had (or rather was) a dramatic society'.[36] When he moved to Hambridge, Marson began organising a Nativity Play to be performed by the villagers each Christmas. He did not provide a text, but instead encouraged them to improvise their own plays after being told the story as a starting point. The story in question appears, through the similarity of some of the action and characters, such as Mack the sheep rustler, to be the Second Shepherds' Play of the Wakefield/Towneley Mysteries cycle. Dating from the late Middle Ages, the Towneley plays would have been of great interest to Marson with his combined interest in folklore, religious drama and community performance. They would also have been reasonably well-known in educated circles, having been published in two different editions during the course of the nineteenth century: firstly, by the Surtees Society in 1836 under the title *The Towneley Mysteries*, and subsequently in 1897 by the Early English Text Society as *The Wakefield Mystery Plays*. The Second Shepherd's Play, Marson's base story for the Hambridge interpretations, was also published separately from the rest of the cycle in 1835, edited by John Payne Collier as *The Adoration of the Shepherds: A Miracle Play*, and then again the following year as part of a larger volume called *Five Miracle Plays, or Scriptural Dramas*.[37] It is likely that either the Surtees Society or Early English Text Society edition was Marson's source, suggested by his own use of the word 'mysteries' when referring to the play: when he published a transcript of the Hambridge play in *Goodwill* magazine in 1898, he introduced the text by explaining that the cast were 'told the story from the old Mysteries' before improvising their interpretation.[38]

The transcript of the 1898 play in *Goodwill*, along with an extract Marson wrote out in a letter to his friend and subsequent biographer, Francis Etherington, forms the only textual record of the Hambridge interpretations of the play. The extract in the letter is from the play of 1908, the 12th one produced:

I   Some do say there be'ant a God but I say how did thic moon come & they stars? But it do'nt sim like as he do mind w'old shepherds out in the wind.
II May be not! But I have a good hope they zongs of Davud may come to so'thing yet & things be better after a bit.
III Zim so!
I   But d'ee thing folks do live after they be dead?
II They tell so in the Temple & I kind of think so but it's queer to think.
III Ah! T'is so – but there's not much to hope for here, the rich has it all their own way, making motor tracks of poor folk.
    […]
    & after the angels came the shepherds said how glad with the bit of news they were & then went on.
I   The rich wo'nt oppress the poor not any more.
II no! t'is we will begin to oppress they.
III (enthusiastically) – I've often eyed w'old 'Erod & wanted to oppress he, many a time & now I reckon I wull.[39]

The villagers' interpretation of the play gave Marson real insight into the spiritual element of his parishioners' lives. Their improvised script allowed him to catch a glimpse of how they interpreted his teachings, both religious and political, and see how, almost like alterable and orally disseminated folksongs, religious material was shaped by its users. Marson would have been gratified to note that his socialistic interpretations of the gospels were readily grasped by his parishioners, as demonstrated by their discussion of Herod and the oppression of the poor by the rich. The source material, the Second Shepherd's Play, includes the shepherds' complaints of their ill-treatment by the upper classes:

> No wonder as it standys if we be poore,
> For the tylthe of oure lands lyys falow as the
> floore,
> As ye ken.
> We ar so hamyd,
> For-taxed and ramyd,
> We ar mayd hand tamyd,
> Withe thyse gentlery men.
> Thus thay refe us oure rest, Oure Ladye theym
> wary,
> These men that ar lord fest fest thay cause the
> plogh tary.
> That men say is for the best we fynde it contrary,
> Thus ar husbands opprest, in point to myscary,
> On lyfe.[40]

More importantly, Marson was allowed a glimpse of their doubts and scepticism. Marson was conscious of his unusual position in being allowed by his parishioners to hear such subtle musings, indicating more than a superficial liking for or trust in him by his flock. He wrote to Etherington that 'they said wonderful things about God & immortality such as perhaps folk say in cottages, never in our hearing'.[41] The play itself also formed an application of the Christian religion to everyday life in a relevant way, marking a seasonal communal celebration. The villagers in their script moved effortlessly between the setting of first-century Bethlehem and twentieth-century Hambridge, weaving together their own lives and concerns. Linguistically, they moved easily from 'the Temple' used instead of the word church in a nod to their antique setting, to 'motor tracks'.

Marson had published his transcription of the improvised 1898 play in *Goodwill* magazine, demonstrating that he thought the material as worthy of wider dissemination as the folksongs he and Sharp were later to publish. In this earlier version of the play, the actors are children, rather than adults as in the production discussed above. The full transcript shows how much the play is a *Shepherd's* Play, not just a rendering of the nativity story. The majority of the play focuses on them as a rural working community, foregrounding their working lives and concerns:

> 'They do say as they be a goin' to fall our wages again this winter.'
> 'Dunno what us'll do then; we haven't got the price of a pint of cider to spare now.'
> [...]
> 'I'd like old Herod and Pilate to be all night out here, and us have their jobs.'
> Then they slap their chests, and one blows a willow pipe and the others dance.
> 'You take a turn at the piano, and let I do a bit of a gallop now,' they say laughingly to one another.[42]

Joseph is also shown engaged in his own work, in a nod to the Christian socialist notion of Christ the carpenter:

> By the side of the manger sat a little maiden in a blue loose frock, and in the background a bigger boy, in working clothes, was mending a chair.'
> 'What are you doing there?' she asked.
> 'Mending a chair for the landlady; but I haven't got all my tools here, and 'tis a job.'[43]

The story is told almost entirely through from the point of view of the shepherds, except a very few lines from Mary and Joseph. Their reactions to the angel's news and to seeing the infant Christ are central to the production:

> When the song is over the angels withdraw, and shepherds are a little silent.
> 'Beautiful that! I never heard the likes o' that avoor. Where did a' say?'
> "Tis a good job, for certain. Shall us get a bit more to eat now, and not be so cold?'
> 'I don't know what us won't get.'[44]

The importance of Christian teaching to the daily lives of normal people was a major theme in Marson's Christian socialist work, and the focus on the shepherds in the plays was a deliberate expression of both this and Marson's interest in the communal activity of working people, with the Shepherds' Plays becoming almost a contemporary folk play bringing together the Hambridge community in shared artistic purpose.

Of course, as with the folksongs, the published script may not have been an exactly accurate record of the words spoken by the actors of Hambridge, though Marson is at pains to assure the reader that despite the strong relationship to the Towneley source material, the plays were improvised by their performers, referring to himself as 'stage manager' rather than scriptwriter:

> Indeed, they compose the play as well as act it. They were told the story from the old mysteries once or twice, and their characters given them; then a rough platform was erected, and they began to rehearse. They entered into the play with such enthusiasm that all the stage manager had to do was edit a little here and there.[45]

The Hambridge play, delivered in improvised, locally relevant dialogue yet closely tied to the historic source material of the Wakefield Master, functions both as an expression of community and as the voice of a place, as well as situating *fin de siècle* Hambridge and its parishioners within a larger framework of English cultural tradition and performance dating back several centuries. The relationship between the local and specific and the wider whole, itself a macrocosm of the interplay between individuals and their community, was a major feature of Marson and other Christian socialists' work at this time, drawn from Christian socialism's own ties to idealism.

The transcribed words of the Hambridge plays have not been dressed up in pastoral idyll or had their roughest edges smoothed to drawing-room tastes, as the script enraged one reader enough that he wrote to Marson directly to complain:

> I think your 'Drama(?) on the Shepherds' in Dec. No. of 'Goodwill' comes as near rank blasphemy as it is possible to get. It's a very dangerous thing [word illegible] to suggest putting such twaddle in the reach of children.[46]

The complainant, Rev. Arden-Davis, wrote that he was 'not squeamish', but even for him the play was 'beyond endurance'. The 1898 play was not without its irreverent humour, itself a vital part of Marson's worldview which insisted that art, culture and religion all had to be enjoyed to be relevant. Before the shepherds go to offer their simple gifts (a whistle, a ball and a book) to the infant Christ, they must first recover one of their stolen lambs. The lamb has been disguised by the local sheep rustler and his wife as a baby in a cradle, the explanation for baby's ovine appearance being a case of the measles.[47] These are, of course, elements present in the Towneley source material. As Warren Edminster notes, the shepherds comment that Christ laughs and is merry, and the gifts they offer him suggest playfulness and festivity.[48] This interplay of the 'religious and the festive' in the Towneley play displays a Bakhtinian, dialogic 'interactive relationship between the official and unofficial cultures of the Middle Ages', something that Marson with his lifelong interest in folk and community culture and its place in both public life and the church would have deeply appreciated in the plays of the Wakefield Master and strove to develop in his own religious vocation.[49] The Hambridge villagers improvised their own humour beyond the source material: on receiving the sheep-rustling villain, the child playing Mary commented: 'They say he's a bad fellow; but I expect my Son will make something of him'.[50] Even before Arden-Davies' letter, Marson knew that his presentation of the spiritual lives of his parishioners in their own words and with their own imagining of scene, character and meaning would prove controversial, and pre-emptively defended his attempt to allow his parishioners ownership of their communal religious heritage in staging their own localised version:

> surely the story is 'not too bright and good for human nature's daily food'?[51] Is it the worse for the fact that English shepherds found an English Bethlehem, and angels sang in our modern tongue of a modern Saviour? If it did not degrade the Eternal Son of God to take flesh in one age and one place, neither does it degrade Him to appear elsewhere and else-when. There […] is no need to fear the human element in the Eternal Story of the Word made Flesh.[52]

To perform is in effect to make an idea take flesh, to physically embody certain values and ideals. Shared activity, including acting in a play, is an embodiment of community. To perform folksongs, or to dance folk dances, as it was for later folk revivalists, was to physically embody cultural memory.[53] Folksongs had become inadequate for Marson's needs as they were not so easily embodied: it was all too easy to leave them unheard, in books on shelves, and for this reason later Christian socialist activists such as Conrad Noel turned to folk dance in their work to build communities. The Shepherds' Plays fulfilled this need, created by and for the villagers of Hambridge, in a way that Marson had once hoped the folksongs he collected with Sharp would. For Marson as a Christian socialist, the Church was to be a living institution based on a living Christ, useful to Christians because it touched them in their everyday lives, and the new socialist society was to be based on strong communities bound together by shared culture and activity. To perform community, and to give flesh to the Word, went hand in hand as a cultural application and expression of Marson's radical religious and political ideals.

Notes

1 Charles Marson, *God's Co-operative Society: Suggestions on the Strategy of the Church* (London: Longmans, Green and Co., 1914), p. 125.
2 Ibid., pp. 106–107.
3 David Sutcliffe, *The Keys of Heaven: The Life of Revd. Charles Marson, Socialist Priest and Folk Song Collector* (Nottingham: Cockasnook Books, 2010), p. 11.
4 Ibid., p. 196.

5   Dave Harker, *Fakesong: The Manufacture of British 'Folksong' 1700 to the Present Day* (Milton Keynes: Open University Press, 1985), p. 171; Georgina Boyes, *The Imagined Village: Culture, Ideology and the English Folk Revival* (Manchester: Manchester University Press, 1993), pp. 32–33.
6   Marson, *God's Co-operative*, p. 67.
7   J.L. Hammond and Barbara Hammond, *The Village Labourer 1760–1832* (London: Longmans, Green and Co., 1911; repr. Gloucester: Alan Sutton, 1987), pp. 214–215.
8   Marson, *God's Co-operative*, p. 105.
9   Ibid., pp. 106–107.
10 For a summary of this dispute, focused on suspicions of possible infidelity on Marson's part, see Katie Palmer Heathman, *Revival: The Transformative Potential of English Folksong and Dance, 1890–1940*, Appendix I, pp. 210–214. PhD thesis available at https://lra.le.ac.uk/handle/2381/37960
11 Charles Marson, *Village Silhouettes*, 2nd edtn. (London: The Society of SS. Peter & Paul, 1916).
12 Cecil Sharp and Charles L. Marson, *Folk Songs from Somerset: Gathered and Edited with Pianoforte Accompaniment, Second Series*, 2nd edtn. (London: Simpkin, Schott, Taunton: Barnicott and Pearce, 1905; repr. 1911), p. vi.
13 Ibid.
14 Etherington's typescript of Marson's letter of 14 May 1889, A\DFS/2/1, Marson Papers, Somerset Heritage Centre.
15 Typescript of letter from Marson to Sharp, 13 October 1903. A/DFS 1/20, Marson Papers, SHC.
16 Cecil Sharp and Charles L. Marson, *Folk Songs from Somerset: Gathered and Edited with Pianoforte Accompaniment, First Series*, 2nd edtn. (London: Simpkin, Schott, Taunton: Barnicott and Pearce, 1904; repr.1905). p. xvi.
17 Ibid., p. 102.
18 David Atkinson, 'Revival: Genuine or Spurious?', in *Folk Song: Tradition, Revival, and Re-Creation*, ed. by Ian Russell and David Atkinson (Aberdeen: The Elphinstone Institute Occasional Publications 3, 2004), pp. 144–62, 152.
19 Cecil Sharp, *English Folk-Song: Some Conclusions* (London: Simpkin, Novello; Taunton: Barnicott & Pearce, 1907), pp. 11–12.
20 Ibid., p. 15.
21 Text of a lecture. A\DFS/1/20, Marson Papers, SHC.
22 Lectures upon Some Aspects of English Literature, A\DFS/1/20, Marson Papers. SHC.
23 Marson, *God's Co-operative*, p. 34.
24 Marson, *Silhouettes*, pp. v–vi.
25 Emily Jackson, *The History of Silhouettes* (London: The Connoisseur, 1911), p. 18.
26 Manifesto of the Christian Socialist Society, May 1888, repr. in Sutcliffe, *The Keys of Heaven*, pp. 82–83.
27 Marson, *Silhouettes*, p. vi.
28 Sutcliffe, *The Keys of Heaven*, p. 293; Marson, *Silhouettes*, pp. 6–7.
29 Marson, *Silhouettes*, p. 6.
30 'Now Father Marson will never be forgot, when I hear the children sing the tunes to hymns that we gave him years ago. He is always in our minds that make us think of him more. "There is a land of pure delight" in the English hymn book, the tune I gave him. I can't tell you how I feel when I the tune sang to a hymn'. Louie Hooper to Francis Etherington, 11 March 1934. A/DFS 1/20, Marson MSS, SHC. For Christian socialist use of folksongs in the *English Hymnal*, see Katie Palmer Heathman, 'Lift up a Living Nation': Community and Nation, Socialism and Religion in *The English Hymnal*, 1906', *Cultural and Social History*, 14:2, 2017, pp. 183–200.
31 Marson, *God's Co-operative*, p. 123.
32 Letter to Chloe Marson, 9 August 1889. A/DFS1/5, Marson papers, SHC.
33 Marson, *God's Co-operative*, pp. 74–75.
34 Ibid., p. 125.
35 C.L. Marson, 'And Ard', repr. in *God's Co-operative*, pp. 53–65, 58.
36 C.L. Marson, 'The Shepherds (A Drama)', *Goodwill*, 5:12, December 1898, pp. 280–283, 280.
37 'Introduction', in *The Towneley Plays* ed. by Garrett P. J. Epp, (Kalamazoo: Medieval Institute Publications, 2018), n.p. Available at https://d.lib.rochester.edu/teams/text/epp-the-towneley-plays-introduction [accessed 29 July 2020].
38 Marson, 'The Shepherds', p. 280.
39 Letter to Etherington, 4 January 1908. A/DFS1/19, Marson Papers, SHC.

40 Wakefield Master, 'Second Shepherds' Play', in *The Towneley Mysteries*, ed. by James Raine and Joseph Stevenson (London: Surtees Society, 1836), pp. 98–119, 98.
41 Ibid.
42 Marson, 'The Shepherds', p. 280.
43 Ibid., p. 282.
44 Ibid., p. 283.
45 Ibid., p. 280.
46 Letter from Arden-Davies, 4 December 1898. A/DFS1/2, Marson Papers, SHC.
47 Marson, 'The Shepherds', pp. 282, 281.
48 Warren Edminster, *The Preaching Fox: Festive Subversion in the Plays of the Wakefield Master* (London: Routledge, 2005), pp. 144–145.
49 Ibid., pp. 22–23.
50 Marson, 'The Shepherds', p. 283.
51 From William Wordsworth, 'She Was a Phantom of Delight'.
52 Marson, 'The Shepherds', p. 283.
53 Theresa Buckland, 'Dance, Authenticity and Cultural Memory: The Politics of Embodiment', *Yearbook for Traditional Music*, 33, 2001, 1–16, 1.

8

BOXING DAY FANCY DRESS IN WIGAN

Anna FC Smith

Introduction

This former mining town is the principal conurbation of Wigan Metropolitan Borough in north west Greater Manchester. The town's population is 175,405[1] and the wider borough population is 326,088.[2] In 2019, 12% of households were living in fuel poverty, 1% less than north west average, and 1% more than national average.[3] Fifteen per cent of children were living in low-income families in 2018.[4] Historically, it is famed for Rugby League, Northern Soul, its 'pier' (a coal jetty on the canal) and George Orwell's unflattering depiction in *The Road to Wigan Pier*.[5] Wigan has made national waves in recent years through its reorganisation of local government through The Deal and its cultural strategy and exhibition space The Fire Within.

Boxing Day fancy dress, simply referred to locally as 'Boxing Day' or 'Boxing Night', is a custom unique to Wigan.[6] It is a major celebration in the calendar and forms part of the psyche of the town. Its flamboyance seems to be the antithesis of the overly presumed – although in some areas very real – hardships of a former industrial town. This is not an ancient practice but buried within it are echoes of older customary and festive events from within the town and globally. I began my research into 'Boxing Day' in 2017 as part of an Arts Council funded project led by Wigan Library. There had been no previous study done on the custom and I'd noticed the interest shown in the event by the national press over recent years. The press also repeated the claim that no one knew where the custom came from. Having been a regular participant in the event for the last 17 years, I had heard many rumours of its origins. My aim was to find the true origin, knowing that the tradition had likely begun within living memory, but was not something people in their 70s and older recalled from their youth.

Expanding on that work here, and drawing on fieldwork, interviews, social media questionnaires and surveys, local online forums and newspaper articles, I explore how the custom developed, and is enacted. Using the framework of a typical Boxing Night, this chapter will consider the origins and dissemination of the Boxing Day fancy dress custom; the manner in which it 'plays out', how its various elements overlap with other performance customs and how, collectively, the annual costumes function as an ephemeral archive, replaying the internal and external narratives that have marked the people and the year. In an effort to communicate something of my own experience of the event, to explain something more of the prevailing excitement and atmosphere, I have included four short impressionistic accounts. The first of these describes getting ready.

Getting ready

It's Day Two of Christmas, the bigger day. Christmas remnants moved to give space for final preparations. Finishing making masks, papier mâché, lists of things we've forgotten. Nipping into town for a green T-shirt, false eyelashes, a lampshade, a medical gown, string. Texting and calls; who's going out? S's coming now and they need a costume. I'll sort it. *J* is on a walk with her family. She'll get foliage and weeds while she's out. I'd already bought a wig on E-bay last month. Glamour Point, the market, charity shops, pound shops. Calls to ask for face paint. I've got some in my fancy dress box. Don't forget glue. Meet in town then back to mine. Primark, Poundland, B&M's. En-route home, we spot a tree with ideal leaves. *X* has scissors in her bag. Just a few small branches to add to our collection.

In the living room – cutting, trimming and drinking. Make it shorter. Searching for thread and needle. I'm on all fours scratching through leaves and straw. The couch disappears under piles of fabric, discarded outerwear, removed clothes, costume parts and spares. *J* has brought vodka. New tights. Navigating debris. Eyeshadow ground into the rug; mirrors removed from walls and propped against chairs, multiplying the littered landscape. Laptop playing our favourite tunes. I drink some face-paint water. We step across and over each other, vying for mirror spots, pouring more drinks. The atmosphere is anticipatory, excited. We are changing. 'Here, let me get that'. Everyone in charge of their own look. It's a gentle competition as each pushes their look; but we are responsible for each other, assisting and suggesting, physically adjusting, painting and styling. Another layer of makeup. It's a group effort. We don't know when to stop and don't want to. Our joyous cocoon of metamorphosis. Wait till everyone sees how magnificent we look (Figure 8.1).

Figure 8.1 Getting ready at home, 'Labyrinth' theme group, Boxing Day 2017
Source: Image by kind permission of Michael Orrell.

Already, very drunk. The house is strewn with every conceivable thing, including a cabbage. We order taxis. Texts come through to arrange the meeting place. It takes forever to get out. We've lost purses, packed face paint, poured drinks for the bag bar, bumbling. 'Where are the keys?' I've put my purse down again, somewhere. Knock over a drink. No coat fits over this costume. Brave it.

How did this party start?

'Boxing Day' is one of the biggest nights in the Wigan Calendar. It seems to have erupted spontaneously in the twentieth century without conscious direction. Crowds of up to 20,000,[7] ranging in age from 17 to their 50s, descend on Wigan for the event. Partygoers are not all Wiganers, with revellers joining from St Helens, Preston, Bolton and even Newcastle.

> Been up Wigan dropping son & mates off and its already chocka.[8] Fancy dress sights everywhere and on Wigan Lane as well. Wigan town centre's busiest night of the year – mini-buses pulling up from Chorley, Preston and Leigh. Quality Hotel near Sam's Bar booked up tonight with Newcastle fans spending night out in Wigan also in fancy dress.[9]
>
> We've been making the trip over from St Helens for the past ten years or so and always have a great night.[10]

This scale of uptake of the custom belies the fact that Boxing Night is not a promoted event. Though certain clubs or pubs may offer tickets, special DJs and promotional deals to get business, and in more recent years the national press has run photo-stories after the night, it happens because it is tradition. It is sustained and spread by participants; coordination and oversight are at individual or friendship group level.

Many performance customs have a core of organisers, or centralised committees responsible for arranging costumes, routes and activities around which any greater activity revolves. Boxing Night festivity is driven by the micro-coordination of friendship groups, creating clusters of miniature Mas Camps or societies that can begin their organising months in advance.[11] Respondent Andy Curran stated, 'We often start planning early in the new year, especially if the costumes are home-made'.[12] These microcosms merge to create the great mass that is Boxing Night across the extended town. All the people I've interviewed have talked about where they got ready or initially met, emphasising this space as a nucleus to their night out. Though some got ready alone before joining friends, many would congregate in one domestic space to don their costumes. In these miniature Mas Camps, there are frequently named individuals who take the lead on coordinating group looks. Costumes will already have been created by one or more members and accessories bought in advance. Revellers willingly assist as a group in improvising outfits for those who have come unprepared. Andrew Howard and Michael Orrell described their groups as starting preparations in parent's homes and noted the parent's active involvement.[13] Louise Fazackerley[14] and Stephen Kenny[15] told me of their online message groups, running throughout the year, where outfits were debated and planned. George Hale discussed the domestic setting at the start of one of his memorable Boxing Nights:

> Loads of people came to my flat, there was Dick Dastardly, Penelope Pitstop, I think Jimmy was some kind of easy rider thing. Sean Hopkins wore a blue leather coat and the cap, but he didn't have goggles or the nose. It was fun with everyone in the flat, the room was packed, and everyone was dressed ridiculously. Everyone was drinking loads. Andrea came ready because she lived in Leigh, and a lot of people came round and got

ready, used all my things and all my make-up. Some people didn't know what they were doing so they borrowed some of my clothes as well. Music was playing and everyone was drinking, it was really good.[16]

The mycelial spread of Boxing Day fancy dress relies on a word of mouth network. From those I have spoken to, it appears that many participants were initiated by friends or older members of their family, after they had already begun to go out drinking around Wigan, and it is usually first brought up close to Christmas. Though I'd been making the journey over to Wigan from Leigh since the age of 15, it was only in my days at Winstanley College that I was made aware of the custom and invited to take part. This isn't unique; Louise Fazackerly told me she'd been doing Boxing Day since her 17th birthday in 1996.

> I didn't know about it as a child; I found out about it when I was working at KFC. The older staff who were in their early 20s were like 'its Boxing Night and everyone gets dressed up in fancy dress, do you want to come?'[17]

This mirrored Stephen Kenny's initiation:

> The first time I did Boxing Day I was working at The Stag in Orrell and I got dressed up as a schoolgirl in 1997. I heard about it through working in the pub. Even though I'd been going to The Tudor since I was 15, I was always working over Christmas, so I'd never gone out. […] It was only when I started doing it that I encountered other people who were doing it and I don't know if that was because I never really went out round Wigan at Christmas or what really but it just seems like once you've done it once you're invited into the secret club of Boxing Night and all of a sudden everyone is in fancy dress.[18]

This oral transmission of the tradition makes its foundational origins all the more elusive since no authority holds records of its source. Looking through the *Wigan Observer*'s photographic archive I couldn't find early Boxing Day photographs, the majority of their pictures being from the 2000s, though it is well known that the custom goes back further than that. I sought photographs and memories from the public to see how far back I could get historically, to plot out an origin through individual recollections. Most memories clustered around the 1990s and 2000s, but even back through the 1980s people describe taking part in an ongoing tradition as opposed to being in at the start of something. Through a call-out in the *Wigan Observer*, I was contacted by Frank Morgan, the chair of Wigan RUFC. He claimed to have started the Boxing Night fancy dress in 1978, with a fancy dress ball held on 26th December at the Rugby Union club on Wingates Road. This was a ticketed fundraising event to raise money for their Colts [Junior] team forthcoming Easter tours. Attendees would walk to and from the party along Wigan Lane, drinking in the various pubs and subsequently heading to Pemps night club. 'The younger ones would come to our disco until about midnight then they would all fire off round all the clubs, still in their fancy dress'.[19]

Through the 1980s and possibly earlier, The Rugby League football club also held a fancy dress Christmas party at their Riverside nightclub, but this was held in mid-December rather than on Boxing Day. These famous events seem to have been mainly attended by the players, their friends and extended entourage. The Riverside parties are interwoven into some of the theories around Boxing Night's foundation, but the link remains elusive. These parties certainly have a mythical quality to them. Both rugby clubs hold an elite status for many in Wigan: association with them is potentially attainable and definitely aspirational. If Boxing Day did emerge from these parties, it could be argued that the custom was established through emulation; yet, there are many additional and simultaneous genesis theories which have clearer grass roots manifestations.

Fans of both rugby football and soccer would wear fancy dress for Boxing Day matches. These costumes would be the first to populate the pubs during the afternoon of Boxing Days from the 1980s to the 2000s. Again, information is sparse, but it appears that both of these traditional occurrences started after the custom of dressing up was already taking place within the town. Stuart Aspinall's father was a regular at Central Park (Wigan's now demolished rugby ground) since the 1950s. He remembers fancy dress at the Boxing Day matches beginning in the 1980s, concurrent with many images I have been sent of non-match goers in fancy dress, and it ended when the Boxing Day rugby matches ceased in 1995.[20]

According to Wigan Latics football club regular, Dylan Harris,

> The football started in 1999. If I remember correctly it was Martin Tarbuck who runs one of the fanzines who suggested it…it was suggested as it was already a tradition in Wigan at the time. The game was away at Notts County. It was hilarious. Pretty much everyone was dressed up in the Wigan end, the Notts County fans had no idea what was going on. Loads were dressed up as police and were causing chaos. At one point, all the real police waded into the crowd and all you could see was what looked like police fighting with police.[21]

Robin Foxon also recalled the Nottingham County match:

> Football wise it's always a great day, especially if Latics are away as the hosting town will not have a clue. I went to Notts County dressed as a sheepskin jacketed Liam Gallagher. One of our party, who was a chimneysweep, had his broom confiscated as a potential weapon.[22]

The fans seized on the Boxing Day tradition and adopted it as a defining characteristic of being from Wigan, and a means to further assert their identity. Club shirts alone would be enough to distinguish opposing fans, but fancy dress brings a cultural otherness that is both intimidating and irreverent.

During the 1970s, the period of initial popularity for the RUFC fundraising parties, there is simultaneous photographic evidence in the archives of the Wigan Observer for Fancy Dress pub crawl fundraisers. One photograph also appears on the local online forum *Wigan World* captioned 'Mere Oaks Ball and Boot Christmas fancy dress pub crawl 28th Dec 1979'.[23] Work-place or pub-regulars would band together in fancy dress teams and take buckets around pubs to raise money for local causes. This activity was widespread across Wigan neighbourhoods. Tony Topping told me that he believed Boxing Day to have started in Aspull as a consequence of one of these fancy dress pub crawls.[24] I was contacted by Billy Baldwin regarding the same activity in Poolstock:

> I remember well in the early to mid-eighties when we would don fancy dress around the Poolstock area visiting local pubs and clubs collecting for Wigan Hospice which […] was situated there. At that time, the dress code around Wigan was quite strict due to all the trouble which was a regular feature. So, it was a shirt and trousers with shoes (no trainers or T shirts) and an entrance fee of around £10 to £20 on the door of most clubs. We would after collecting for the hospice around Poolstock then go on to Wigan where being in fancy dress the dress code was not enforced and the fact that we had been collecting for charity meant free access to all of the clubs. In the early days as I recall we were the only group in fancy dress, but word quickly spread, and it caught on until there was hardly anyone in

normal clothing around the town centre. Unfortunately, I don't have any photos of those times only the vivid memories and after the Hospice moved to its present location the practice of the annual collections fell off, but the fancy dress tradition continues.[25]

He continued:

> Keith and Norma Holden of the Eckersley Arms sadly no longer with us would organise the collection. The Tippings Arms, The Bold, Honeysuckle Inn, Poolstock Labour Club, Poolstock Cricket Club, Victoria Labour Club were some of those that I can remember. I also recall collecting in Wigan town centre but that was more problematic as we were not known to the landlord and staff and would have to ask permission to collect. Young Keith Holden, Tommy Porter, Baz Marsh, Tony Ratchford and many more regulars would be involved [...] We would split up into groups deciding where each group was going and then meet up back at the Ecks [sic] then later on up to Wigan as described. I remember going to the Cricket Club once and being allowed on stage to announce what we were doing. We got everyone up dancing and the compere said we could do the rest of the night because he hadn't been able to get anyone to take any notice of him never mind dancing. The clubs would help to tot up the cash so they could announce how much had been collected.[26]

There are further claims to a point of origin. Jean Lowe informed me that there used to be fancy dress on New Year's Eve at Turnkey (a club on King Street) but she was 'not sure when or why we changed to Boxing Day'.[27] Pat Jukes told me that 'Ernie Roughley, landlord of Silverwell pub (Scholes) started it' and she 'was told this at his funeral'.[28] Louise Fazackerley remembered that Orrell had its own fancy dress tradition around Christmas and people from Orrell would use the same costume for both nights. Dukki Wiggins contacted me to say that in 1977, people would undertake a pub crawl along Woodhouse Lane to The Bees Knees in the town centre.

All these Boxing Day folk tales and memories coalesce around the late 1970s, coincidentally at the very tail-end of the second folk revival.[29] This would make the Wigan Boxing Day event almost as old as many revived traditional performance customs taking place today, but apart from in its semblance and timing, it is unrelated to past customs. It is difficult to specify what led the larger pub-going populace to adopt Boxing Day fancy dress as a tradition in its own right but cultural phenomena around the time may have primed the town to embrace it. Wigan's summer carnival and district carnivals were revived in the 1970s; there were four or five 'fun pubs' with a camp, kitsch and drag ambience, that were founded in and around Wigan in the early 1980s[30]; Wigan hairdressers engaged in fancy dress at work on Christmas Eve in the early 1980s, and national television programmes such as 'It's A Knockout' achieved popularity through game playing in carnivalesque settings and it influenced carnival games in the town.

The parade

'Taxi's here!' I've trapped one of my branches in the car door. Watch your head. The chatty driver asks what we've come as – the typical joke whenever a driver picks you up. Tonight, it's a genuine question. Some years we've walked, but rain, ice and inappropriate shoes can ruin a night before it's started. 'Drop us at The Tudor'. Others are coming in via Wigan Lane pubs, and some via the pub run from under the railway arches. We'll do the Tudor first, and then get cash out through the churchyard. So many people are back for Christmas! *Y* has come as Harold Shipman. It's a cool suit. Let's go through the churchyard and walk King Street. We might get

Figure 8.2 Putin and friends, Boxing Day 2018
Source: Image by kind permission of Michael Orrell.

on the photos this year. 'April, I've seen four turtles – you must find them'. 'I didn't even recognise you!' In-jokes; esoteric and fabulous. 'Oh, right, I've not seen it'. Bump backs. Gary Glitter? – Boos and shocked laughter. 'No way!' Let's have a toot at the rest of town (Figure 8.2).

We're mobbed in the churchyard by a WW2 soldier and Pamela Anderson with unconvincing sock tits in his red swimming costume. Oompa Loompas arms around each other. They love our look. 'What are you?' Photos taken in a group. On to Wallgate and the crowds begin to amass. To King Street. 'Toreet love'. 'Wahay!' Burly super-heroes with accentuated pecs. Drink deals handed out, every few metres. '118–118!' There's a giant flip-sign finger guarding a bearded cheerleader as he wees behind some bins. I collide with a fellow squid and his shark pal. He thinks he is the better squid, but he is blatantly not. He bought that costume. I made mine. Photos taken anyway, internally seething. A lace-covered, parasol-carrying man pronounces, 'I'm a lady' and he swishes his skirts. So many Jokers, Peaky Blinders, X-men, George Michaels. So many Putins, Kim Jong-uns, Trumps; so many I'm a Celebrity's. 'I love your costume!' Gawping. Checking out the talent, for creativity? I get a wink from Willy Wonka with his hands down his pants. He maintains nonchalance in a top hat. The queues for clubs are an assortment, loomed over by an inflatable T-Rex. 'A-ha!' Alan Partridge. Amply busted wenches with winter tans pout for a selfie. 'You look great!', 'Love that!'. Turning heads and wiggle walks. Waves. Leaning over club barriers with flailing arms. A flailing arm man. A gorilla jumps and squats, beats his chest and grunts in people's faces. Everyone is laughing. Good-humoured jeering. 'She's fit!' Wait. Is that a man? December-defying hot pants. A pack of cards shuffle along. The costumes flow and squeeze in both directions; a sexy Mrs Santa; a sexy pirate; a sexy nurse, squeaky in PVC; five bunny girls. Ambling perambulation. A cowboy riding an ostrich. A series of hunted animal heads on cardboard wall mounts jostle past a knight. People seek the people with the biggest camera lenses. They must be press. Disjointed groups. The Flintstones hug Ali G, monsters flank Jack Sparrow. Should we go in somewhere?

On the dance floor

At the bar, ordering two vodka and Red Bulls. The Mad Hatter is taking their gin in a teacup. Let's dance. Compacted groups nursing drinks undulate with passing revellers. To the dance floor! It's our song!

I dance so hard I get acid reflux flooding my throat. I've brought Rennies – always prepared, a sign of age. Have a Jaegerbomb.

'Let me try your wig?' Items passed overhead; glasses, scalps, caps – swap shop. Costumes come loose. More pins. *F* wears my mask, I keep vigil. Skirts come up, can-can. Neon stockings. Omnipresent cardboard boxes. So versatile. Giant sauce bottles galumph to the beat. There's a bunky dance on Boxing Day – a jolly movement of oversized, unjointed costumes. So many compliments. R's look is well researched – Star Wars fans croon. Shouted conversations about costumes and Boxing Day, analysis of this year's merits, its adherence, the collective effort. Mimicking gestures of character or violating expectations. An old man moonwalks and a rabbit hops. Costumes animate, I swing my tentacles, the robot turns its dials. Someone doffs their cap, showboat with a cane. The Ghostbusters engage their proton packs, 'I ain't afraid of no ghost'.

Groping hands slip around dancing bodies to pinch a bulge. Slip, over. People lift me up in sympathy and disdain. Always me, Bambi. Ginsberg and Dylan. Trump embraces Theresa May. I feel slinky with long silver hair. A body-clinging skeleton leotard jumps into a distended pillow stuffed stomach. The battle of Carnival and Lent. Gripping onto T's bustle, my new mate for the night. 'We're having a gang bang; we're having a ball' Starting a conga. *O* thinks well of themselves, her sinuous gestures jar with the chaos, she likes the attention. Don't we all. Betty Boop looks so good.

H goes over on his ankle and snaps the heel clean off. They were my shoes! *M*'s a toilet-roll cover doll. A labour-intensive hand-crocheted dress. Hand-made.

To the toilets, check the state of our costumes, wee, reconfigure, touch-up. Lipstick re-applied, add more green to the cheek. 'Do you have a brush?' 'I've got a full palette you can borrow' Chats and mirror selfies. 'Have you seen *K*?' 'You look amazing, so funny', 'stunning!' 'Don't worry you look well better than her'. Henry and Henrietta Hoover are in there, their concertina nozzles haven't dried and everything is smeared in paint.

That cello. All you need is love. Arms link shoulders in a circle dance, strangers and friends and new alliances. You can learn how to play the game. In and out, 'all you need is love, da da da da da', kick out, 'love is all you need'.

Lights up and cleared out. Stragglers getting bags; *G* has lost their phone. Heading outside, rolling cigs, with coats tucked under arm. An amorphous congregation forms near the door, planning the next step. Everyone is involved. Home, kebab, taxi, party, 'Indiependance 'till 6?'

The living archive

In its entirety, Boxing Night serves as a dynamic folk performance which expresses ideas, individuals, wider culture and local space. It acts as a news reel, summarising the events of its current year and as a demonstration of the inner lives of Wiganers, consciously through direct costume choice, and unconsciously in how those costumes can be read. It creates a web of connectivity between people. Its patterns repeat and evolve each year, playing out first, amongst the scattered troops of Wigan and its districts, second, amongst the loose mass in the town centre.

Boxing Day in Wigan is what Bastian describes as a 'society-specific, self-contained, and fluid cultural archive'.[31] Its fluidity is due to the continual movement of its 'documents' and in the constantly changing juxtapositions that happen throughout the night. The coming together and clashes of costume, the momentary interactions and the spontaneous performances. Many years of geographical isolation have allowed it to remain self-contained, though media interest and social media, despite their transitory aspect, are beginning to impact on that. No one person would be able to read all its content, its spread is too wide and its annual duration too short. You would need a god's eye view.

Archiving the present – costume and disguise

The costumes people elect to wear are the material documents of the Boxing Day living archive. Diana Taylor suggests that 'What makes an object archival is the process whereby it is selected'[32] and in Wigan those processes of selection are profoundly democratic. As in the late nineteenth-century suburban carnivals described by Dion Georgiou, costume 'provided an escape from everyday dress codes through temporary adoption of an alternative persona'.[33] This could be for personal release, or in order to take oneself less seriously, or to be more provocative; for Billy Baldwin, as noted earlier, it simply allowed access to clubs that might otherwise have remained out of reach.

Just as there are no centralised committees organising the tradition, so there are no set themes. Trends emerging from within the custom suggest seven loose categories, each one manifesting elements of Wigan culture and wider cultures that influence it. In her discussion of carnival more broadly, Bastian claimed that 'to witness and comprehend such a manifestation is central to an understanding of the society itself'[34] which opens up a range of consideration. There are *Christmas* themed costumes, directly referencing the time of year, a large and discordant group of what I would call *generic costumes*, selected for ease, or for comedy value, or because they flatter the wearer: examples might include, a nun, an inflatable t-rex or a sexy nurse. There are *popular media* costumes, taking influences from television, recent films, adverts and current celebrities; *commemorative* costumes relate to something specific that has happened during the year such as the death of a beloved celebrity; *satirical* costumes depict infamous politicians, or comedic or noteworthy events; personal interest or niche costumes could reference anything of importance to the wearer; a favourite singer or food, or an in joke between friends. Lastly, *sick humour* or shock factor which may draw on the year's bad news, occasionally a longer standing story, but will be perverse and controversial, such as representations of paedophile celebrities and other social villains or even victims. All of the above categories of dress might be homemade or hired or bought.[35]

Andrew O'Grady sent me selected images from 1991 to 2012 of Yip Yip puppets from The Muppets, Duff Beer Man, SpongeBob Square Pants, a priest, Gingerbread Man from Shrek, a mouse in cheese and Heath Ledger's Joker.[36] These could be arranged into the categories of *generic*, *popular media* and *commemorative*. In 1988, Angela Garside's friends took their inspiration from a TV advert of the time, *Labatt's Singing Mounties* which is directly in the *popular media* category.[37] Andy Curran described a photograph he appeared in thus:

> That's me wearing way too much blue lycra for a man of my age dressed as 80s cartoon character Ulysses 31. My mates Paul Chorley (as Nien Numb from Return of the Jedi) Tony Quilliam (as Han Solo with a homemade Tauntaun!) and my girlfriend Yvonne Battersby in the Star Trek uniform.[38]

In this instance, these costumes reflect *personal interest* rather than *popular media*; even though they reference the latter, they lack sufficient contemporaneity to 'make the grade' but reflect the wearers personal and longstanding fondness for the characters. The categorisation is evidently loose, and many outfits straddle two or more categories. Kerry Reynolds wrote 'this year [2019] we went as the Handmaid's Tale; we have been going now for about 28 years'.[39] The same year, Louise Fazackerley and her group went as aristocrats from the French revolution, as she explained, 'because of the political context and revolution we thought we'd be aristocracy and some of us would be peasants so they could kill us'.[40] Here are two examples of the *satiric*, underpinning *popular media* referencing on the one hand, and the *generic* on the other.

Boxing Day is without doubt a 'vehicle for social critique'[41] as can be seen in the *satirical*, *commemorative* and *popular media* costumes, but complete social dissent comes within the *sick humour* or shock factor costumes. These may be few and far between, but they stand out against the light-humoured majority. [The extreme bad taste costumes] 'are a little bit niche, a small percentage but you notice them more because you don't notice the third Buzz Lightyear'.[42] Robin Foxon recalls 'the sick costume pushes that year's villain or an unsavoury sentiment in everyone's face. I've seen Madeline McCann, Jimmy Saville and of course the Nazi uniforms from people who definitely had access to other options'.[43]

These looks are purposefully outrageous, breaking with social acceptability and taste. They leap the boundaries of respectability and place Boxing Night within the conceptual tradition of Carnival, described by Natalia Pikli as 'combin[ing] the celebration of exuberant and irrepressible life force, and the questioning, undermining, or twisting [of?] any authority (be it political or linguistic) while joyously degrading the sacred and the powerful'.[44] Like Carnival, Boxing Night collectively permits this. As one interviewee explained, 'there is license for controversial costumes. They normally receive nervous laughter. It's about pushing buttons, being provocative. Some people think its genius in a way'.[45] Those who choose this form of outfit may expect to be viewed with a degree of awe for their audacity. Dave McMahon believes that 'it feeds into quite a common trend among groups of young men in terms of risk-taking and line-stepping as a demonstration of dominance/ bravery'[46] and it may also seek to defeat or accept responsibility for social horror through mockery. The costumes highlight moral lines held by the community, denote stories that have impacted on or disturbed the community, but it also leaves gaps, and what is left out has meaning too. In the past years, Boxing Day has seen the shameful occurrence of blackface and the use of stereotyped cultural dress, from grossly offensive caricatures to the still offensive but erroneously pitched 'ironic' costume as a facet of the shock factor costume. The towns distinctive whiteness created a culture that could be guilty of othering different racial identities, and derogatory characters from past television and comedy have also been used as references. The town has been in a monocultural bubble of unaccountability and ignorance that had allowed this to continue, but societal shifts have brought change and more enlightened attitudes which are continuously reflected in individual costume choices. As McMahon says, 'As awareness grows regarding cultural appropriation and sensitivity this has become less commonplace'.[47]

As with many other customs, cross dressing is prevalent on Boxing Day, and it can be found under any of the previous categorisations. It is a short cut identity change, creating humour through incongruous juxtapositions where burly men genuflect in schoolgirl pigtails or couples and friends switch expected roles. An anonymous interviewee told me, 'my then girlfriend always went out as [men] she fancied'.[48] Louise Fazackerley recalled 'one year me and Sean both went as Freddy Mercury, so he was dressed up as a man dressed up as a woman and I'm a woman dressed as a man, dressed as a woman'.[49]

Cross dressing has played a central role in both British comedy and folk custom but its functions extend beyond frivolity.[50] The licence of Boxing Night has created an accepting space for some to find, or briefly live, a truer self. George Hale, for example, finds an outlet in Boxing Night wherein he part discovered his drag identity. It is a time when he is able to express himself openly in areas of Wigan that are normally threatening for him. He told me: 'I have always felt on Boxing Day I can dress how I want; I feel free because I don't think I will get any hassle […]On Boxing Day no one is going to bat an eyelid, no matter where I go'.[51] In recent years, he has worn drag on general nights out and has felt empowered yet embattled. Though these outfits make him feel 'unstoppable' and he delights in being a self-conscious disrupter, he also gets apprehensive for his own safety: 'but it's different on Boxing Day, I feel safe. It's how it should be really'.[52]

Making vs hiring

Through the 1980s until the late 1990s, fancy dress hire shops would be the first port of call for a revellers costume. There were a number around the districts of Wigan with Louise Fazackerley recollecting at least five. Outfits would be booked out months in advance of Boxing Day so those looking for a last-minute costume would have to take whatever was left. Choice was dictated by what the shops had bought in, limiting the creativity of those who used them. The chances for individual expression would be increased for those who hired early, though still from a set stock. The choices would be of popular figures from the time and generic characters such as an elf or a French maid. Louise Fazackerley recalled

> We all went to the same fancy dress shop in Shevington, and basically picked from what they had[…] My first costume was a French maids outfit, but I was really disappointed with it because it was really long […]not what a 17 year old girl wants to wear when she wants to look sexy.[53]

> I once made the mistake of trying to hire a costume from a shop on Boxing Day morning. I registered the stressed look in the woman's eyes and her facial expression which said 'seriously?' between her over worked gasps for air. I settled for a Spiderman playsuit from the discount box.[54]

The other option was to make your own costume whether it be a technically brilliant kangaroo, or a Christmas present outfit fashioned from left over wrapping and a cardboard box. This allowed for more imagination and creativity with the costume maker-wearer able to create something unique to themselves or their group and more freely reflective of their surroundings and interests. Furthermore, over the last 15 years, the fancy dress shops have declined, to be replaced by the internet, the market, and charity, pound and hardware shops. Costumes are now constructed from online purchases, either bought as a set or made up from an accumulation of items, or they may be homemade as already described, whether in their entirety or in part.

Value is ascribed to costumes on the bases of their originality, of the effort taken in making them and how good someone looks in the outfit. Originality is particularly prised by the alternative culture in Wigan, centred around the Tudor House Hotel, but it is noted elsewhere.

> The costumes in my favourite, the Tudor House Hotel on New Market Street, always reflected obscure films, visual jokes or cult characters like Papa Lazaru. Effort had gone in and also there was a detectable sourcing of materials and use of imagination in putting them together.[55]

This is described by one interviewee as a form of narcissism in being seen as clever and niche[56] which reflects Dion Georgiou's interpretation of fancy dress as 'stressing individuality, impressing upon ones circles of family and friends one's humour, imagination and outgoingness'.[57] Not everybody is concerned with uniqueness or creating their look from scratch (Figure 8.3).

Boxing day fancy dress in Wigan

Figure 8.3   Fancy dress group 'scouser' theme, Boxing Day 2018
Source: Image by kind permission of Micheal Orrell.

> A lot of people want an easy hit, they don't necessarily want to make something, they don't want to stand out, they want to be part of a crowd, they might feel uncomfortable in fancy dress […] there is the opportunity if you're not that way inclined and you want to be anonymous, then you can be an angel or a devil. You've already got the stuff, its cheap, you can assemble it the day before.[58]

Parade as event

Outside space plays an essential part in the Boxing Night narrative. The various pub crawl routes across the town, and King Street, become impromptu sites of interplay, performance and exchange. Movement in these spaces occurs naturally as people commute.

> We got dropped off in the town centre, we were with lots of people then met lots of people there. We started off in the pub on the corner that is now flats, The Queen Vic… then Harry's Bar, We wouldn't normally go there but we'd go to a bigger variety of pubs, it was more of a crawl.[59]

The streets are the veins of the night, ferrying revellers on their way to the pubs and clubs, but they are also the location of the great spontaneous mass of the night. The streets 'happen' before people are syphoned into bars. Boxing Night is spectacle and the streets are the first place to see and be seen. Each group of revellers will have their particular route, some remaining constant over the years, others planning different routes into town each year, hopping from pub to pub from all directions and culminating in the town centre. Travel and geographic location expand with the licence and tolerance of Boxing Night; places normally considered unsafe or unfitting become permitted spaces. This gives the night a flexibility and freedom; the costumes act as a social leveller.

Perambulating is a conscious performative element wherein people seek chance meetings and the opportunity to promenade. As George Hale relates, 'I always want to go to King Street to parade and to shock people'.[60] It is reminiscent of the Monkey Run[61] of the earlier twentieth century where amusement was found in looking and being looked at, in showing off one's costumes and judging those of others. This aspect of the night is notable for the openness of exchange with constant commentary, dialogue and interaction between strangers. There is a conveyor belt of greeting with people drawn to costumes they recognise, ones that are similar to their own and to ones they find striking or attractive. People shout to each other, make remarks, ask questions and proffer compliments. 'Boxing day is a carnival party atmosphere, where everybody is everybody's best friend…I wish it could be like that every single week'.[62]

Spontaneous satire or comedy is enacted through costume contrast and coupling both on the street and in the pubs and clubs. This can be deliberate, where costume relationships are recognised and then performed in public demonstrations like posed photographs, personages temporarily parading together, striking poses and by gathering others to acknowledge the humorous relationship. Or they can be consequent on friendships or romantic encounters made on the night:

> I remember one year one of my friends dressed as a duck, she was very keen on being warm […] she copped off with a Mexican, and it was really funny, aw a ducks copping off with a Mexican […] snogging weird combinations was always fun.[63]

The streets and the club queues are the most concise overview available to an attendee. Repetitions, themes and extreme costumes can be read in aggregate as they store and transmit knowledge. And they function here as 'documents in archival collections' as they 'relate to each other in ways that transcend the information in each document'.[64]

Performance and embodiment

Fancy dress may be altogether too shallow a mechanism to allow the actorly embodying of specific character, but that same dress rests and moves on and with the body to create a compound persona. It is costume rather than disguise: the identity of the wearer is entangled with their costume character to provide a form of self-expression and/or personal enhancement.

> On King Street the costumes are done with broader strokes. Men seem to go for the gigantic torsos of a superhero. The women seem more bothered that their costume must also be flattering- faithfulness to character can't result in looking shit.[65]

The costumes and characters are announced to friends and strangers in uncoordinated sequences, reminiscent of the presentational dramaturgy described by Thomas Pettitt in regard to English mummers plays.[66]

Extempore performances on Boxing Night allow flashes of character creation and the costumes and props drive physical actions and interactions which play out through the night. These are Taylor's 'ephemeral repertoire of embodied practice'.[67] Along with the physical exuberance and spontaneous vocal interaction in the streets, pubs and clubs, revellers will recite catchphrases and replicate walks and body movements of their respective characters as they travel, dance or pose. Performance is enforced by costumes which restrict, facilitate or exaggerate movement, changing the gait of the wearer. These snippets of dramatic allusion are fleeting though continuous flashes everywhere you look, creating a distinctive rhythm to the whole night.

Properties are used by some to stress character:

> When we were Mad Hatter's tea-party we all had tea-cups so we could put our drinks in them and drink out of them. And when we were Clockwork Orange, we spray painted

Figure 8.4 Perambulations, Boxing Day 2018
Source: Image by kind permission of Micheal Orrell.

plastic cups with white so they looked like milk so we looked like we were drinking milk when we had our drinks.[68]

On the dance floor, props and costume elements like masks, tails, hats or long skirts are given life as they are utilised in performances that manipulate and emphasise them. They are combinations of direct physicality and character; a scary costume may be enhanced with threatening actions or a militaristic costume supplemented by salutes and marches. These acts only have an immediate geographical reach, entertaining only the nearest surrounding dancers and onlookers. The bawdy recitals are intimate exhibitions where the impromptu audience also has an interactive and participatory role. There is fluidity in role too, as props and accessories pass amongst the crowds, with a switching of wigs, for example, the revellers become hybrids and act accordingly.

Dramatic allusion also takes place in multiple, random, miniature tableaux off the dance floor, constructed to entertain an immediate audience or for photographs.

In 2009, Brendan O'Leary, Neil Jarvis and I made a last-minute dash for the Boxing Day night! With flour on our faces and boot polish on my head, we entered the night as 3 of the 4 members of Kraftwerk and invited volunteers to man the missing role as we re-created the famous cover of the 1982 album – The Man Machine.[69]

These compact improvisations are more frequent when groups have gone out together in theme. The narratives behind the costumes play out in the group's interaction and are often a part of the photographic records they make. 'We always like doing a photo shoot, like when we were Clockwork Orange, we did a photo shoot in the graveyard, its abandoned then and you can make more of a show of yourselves'.[70] According to Lynn Lunde, 'mumming allows for improvisation of speech and action while allowing the basic structure of the event to carry the action through to a known conclusion'.[71] In the same way, Boxing Night is a continuous set of new improvisations and reactions which conform to an overriding course of action. The novelty is in the characters, speech and interaction, but the general form is repeated year after year (Figure 8.4).

Outside records

For most of its existence, Boxing Night has been barely known to the outside world, exported only through word of mouth or snatched visual experiences at football matches. 'Boxing Night is localised, I see it as its own identity, [its] in a bubble'.[72] This bubble has been slowly expanding over recent years through social media channels and the national papers. This has broadened the night's spatial and temporal reach while also establishing a permanent accessible record.

When the boundaries are opened, the licence permitted on the night is challenged. Positively, this can lead to more socially aware costume choices, but it also threatens the permissive atmosphere of behaviour and idolatry. It is part of the 'epistemic changes brought on through digital technologies'.[73] People perform in accordance to a greater unknown audience which exists and judges beyond the perimeters of the night. The interest that the national press has taken in Boxing Night is regarded in conflicting ways. It has been both welcomed and celebrated as a confirmation of the significance of Boxing Night, and an opportunity to get 15 minutes of fame for those that get photographed. The coverage is also regarded as sneering or titillating; there is a feeling that photographers have entered Wigan with an agenda and there is a distrust of the papers that buy these photographs.

> The day after Boxing Day sees the *Mail* and *Sun*[74] send a freelance voyeur with a wide-angle lens to capture exposed knickers from the pavement, the women lying obscured as faceless torsi. I've had people sending or showing me these 'articles' just because I'm from Wigan [...] [the] paper is here telling its readership how it really sees them, the animalistic working class at play. If you feel one rung above them, you can laugh.[75]

> One thing I don't like about it. I feel the mainstream media cash in a bit on it; the photographers all come on the one night and stay till really late to deliberately take pictures of the girl puking in the corner and then it goes in the Daily Mail, and other press as well. It's nice sometimes looking for your own photo, to see if you got in but actually largely the images they choose to put on are like 'oh look isn't Wigan a mess'. I feel it's unfortunate and not necessarily representative.[76]

No one can deny the debauchery which naturally follows from a carnivalesque and permissive event with alcohol at its heart. The issue that is taken with some of the coverage is the specific focus on the extreme elements by those who have no other knowledge or experience of the night. It is easy for this one-sided external view to feed into the already prevalent disdain towards the town and its people.

Walk of shame

An ensemble has gathered at U's house. We pilfer spirits in mixes we won't remember. We carry on. Lolling. Hours pass. To bed. I am now remnants. Made of bits. Still got the axe. I pass dog walkers. Who gawp at this shadow parade. The low morning sun glints on glitter stuck in my eye. Trip through door and over the living room. The bleak detritus absented of people. It's a frozen snapshot, an archaeological site. Lie amongst the mess, nest, until my head stops banging. Squinting with one eye, I check if we made the papers.

Analysis & conclusion

From these problematic media reports, I was inspired to make the first attempt at discovering the origins of Wigan Boxing Day fancy dress. I wanted to claim back ownership for the town through knowledge of the customs origin. I have been able to identify some substantiated legends and define a time before the custom existed, but the more responses I received, the more varied the origin claims. This half-remembered and complicated genesis actually increases the sense of ownership people have over the custom. Many feel that they have a connection to the founder or can lay some claim in its founding. It genuinely has more than one beginning and this mycelian spawning is sustained by the many who engage in the custom. Ownership manifests through varied understandings of its beginning, its continual spread and repeated observance by the people.

This essay has been an attempt to convey the atmosphere and specific actions of Boxing Night. Taking accounts from many interviewees and from my 17-year experience, I have found unifying factors in both deed and mood, the comradery, the gaiety, the ambivalence and the licence. The actions will have altered across its 40-year span. There are slight changes each year; each attendee will have differing experiences and go to different places through the night; it happens across a wide area. As the outside world alters, so do the costume choices. As the people change, so do their attitudes and actions. Boxing Night is a live tradition, the generic qualities of which have been described by Jose Carlos Mariategui:

> tradition is alive and changing. Those who would forbid it to renew and enrich itself are only fabricating it…tradition is made of heterogeneous and contradictory elements. To try to reduce it to a single concept, to be satisfied with its so-called essence, is to renounce its many crystallizations.[77]

Though a shifting tradition, it still holds as an archival whole which Miller reminds us is 'greater than the sum of its parts [and that] the relationships are as important as the particulars'.[78] The annual costumes function as an ephemeral archive. The manner by which costumes are chosen and how the night is enacted is a cultural expression of the identity of the town, its inhabitants and other attendees. Boxing Night is the archive and repertoire that Diana Taylor says 'preserve[s] a sense of communal identity and memory'.[79] The memory and preservation is in the unsolicited repetition of the night, even if Boxing Night also emphasises novelty. Though it has no formal links to any folk custom or revival, there are thematic overlaps which are reminiscent of other guising customs, but it stands in a unique place due to its location, its isolation, the nature of its formation and its modernity. These factors along with its scale and longevity have earned Boxing Night a place in the folk performance canon.

There are questions as to how long Boxing Night will continue; over recent years, numbers have begun to dwindle, and with coronavirus now threatening communal club and festival life, it is at risk of falling victim. As a festival, it stands as one of Bastian's 'iterative and renewing processes [forming an] essential component of the cultural fabric of all societies'.[80] It may adapt into smaller scale domestic fancy dress parties, maintained in hyper-localised clusters 'perpetuating their collective memory, continuing their traditions, and proclaiming community identity'.[81] No matter what, I will be wearing fancy dress next Boxing Day. As one of my interviewees expressed so perfectly: 'I feel like it gives Wigan a prestige. It is so singular, and the community is unique. It gives me pride to be associated with Wigan'.[82]

Notes

1. https://worldpopulationreview.com/countries/united-kingdom-population/cities/ [accessed 2 April 2020].
2. https://www.google.com/publicdata/explore?ds=jqd8iprpslrch_&met_y=pop&idim=district:E08000010&hl=en&dl=en Data from Data from Office for National Statistics. Last updated: 25 May 2020 [accessed 2 April 2020].
3. https://www.wigantoday.net/lifestyle/thousands-wiganers-living-fuel-poverty-687159 [accessed 2 April 2020].
4. https://www.wigantoday.net/news/quarter-children-borough-living-poverty-709004 [accessed 2 April 2020].
5. George Orwell, *The Road to Wigan Pier* (London: Victor Gallancz, 1937).
6. Boxing Day on 26 December is a holiday observed in the UK and commonwealth countries. It is a bank holiday in the UK. Other fancy dress customs do take place around the UK with Halloween by far the most popular general example. Other localised events take place on New Year's Eve in Looe, Cornwall and Weymouth, Dorset.
7. *Daily Star*. 27 December 2018. https://www.dailystar.co.uk/news/latest-news/boxing-day-fancy-dress-2018-16829127 [accessed 18 March 2020].
8. Colloquial abbreviation of 'chock-a-block' to mean full of people or things, busy.
9. Wigvet, *Wigan World*, Friday, December 26, 2008. https://www.wiganworld.co.uk/ [accessed 25 April 2020].
10. Andy Curran, private e-mail to the author, 25 January 2018, with permission.
11. 'Mas Camps of Caribbean Carnival' A Mas Camp is the headquarters of a Mas Band where the group convene to create their parade costumes, dances and float.
12. Andy Curran, 25 January 2018, Ibid.
13. Andrew Howard and Michael Orrell, audio interview with the author, 24 February 2020.
14. Louise Fazackerley, audio interview with the author, 20 February 2020.
15. Stephen Kenny, audio interview with the author, 24 February 2020.
16. George Hale, audio interview with the author, 26 May 2020.
17. Fazackerley, 2020, Ibid.
18. Kenny, 2020, Ibid.
19. Frank Morgan reported in *The Wigan Observer*, Friday, 26 January 2018. https://www.wigantoday.net/news/rugby-veteran-claims-his-team-inspired-wigans-boxing-day-tradition-712594 [accessed 5 May 2020].
20. Stuart Aspinall, Facebook, Thursday, 14 May 2020.
21. Dylan Harris, Facebook messenger to the author, 14 May 2020, with permission.
22. Robin Foxon, Facebook messenger to the author, 22 May 2020, with permission.
23. Wigan World, 20 October 2009. https://www.wiganworld.co.uk/album/photo.php?opt=8&id=12266&gallery=In+the+Pub&offset=40 [accessed 26 April 2020]. Andy Curran, private e-mail to the author, 25 January 2018, with permission.
24. Tony Topping, Facebook, Tuesday 19 May 2020.
25. Billy Baldwin, private e-mail to the author, 13 January 2018, with permission.
26. Ibid.

27 Jean Lowe, Facebook, Sunday 17 May 2020.
28 Pat Dukes, Facebook, Sunday 17 May 2020.
29 The period from the late 1950s through until the 1970s saw a renewed interest in folk music and folk performances such as morris dancing, with a wide range of revivals of local traditions across the UK. This burgeoning of interest is often loosely termed the second folk revival, following on from the well-known first revival of the early twentieth century.
30 Fun Pubs were eccentrically decorated theme bars that showed variety and cabaret acts. Drag queens served drinks and danced on the bars. Wigan had the Rock Rock café, Henry Afrikas, Clowns Bar, Angels, Sylvester's and others. In conversation with performer, local historian and author Chris D'Bray, he informed me that Preston and Leeds were the only other places to have them.
31 Jeannette A. Bastian, 'Play mas': Carnival in the Archives and the Archives in Carnival: Records and Community Identity in the US Virgin Islands, *Archival Science* 9, no. 1 (2009): 113–125. (Published online: 24 October 2009. Springer Science + Business Media B.V.), p. 115.
32 Diana Taylor, *The Archive and the Repertoire. Performing Cultural Memory in the Americas* (Durham, NC: Duke University Press, 2007), p. 19.
33 Dion Georgiou, *The Meanings of Fancy Dress: Upholding and Inverting Suburban Identities Through Carnival Costumes in Late Victorian and Edwardian London*. Anglo-American Conference of Historians: 'Fashion' (Institute of Historical Research, July 2015). https://www.academia.edu/24443127/The_Meanings_of_Fancy_Dress_Upholding_and_Inverting_Suburban_Identities_through_Carnival_Costumes_in_Late_Victorian_and_Edwardian_London [accessed 16 February 2020] p. 1.
34 Bastian, 2009, p. 115.
35 As unlikely and distasteful as this may sound, Jimmy Saville costumes can be purchased online.
36 Andrew O'Grady, Facebook, 5 February 2018.
37 Angela Garside, Facebook, 12 January 2018.
38 Andy Curran, 2018, Ibid.
39 Kerry Reynolds, Facebook, 7 January 2020.
40 Fazackerley, 2020, Ibid.
41 Lynn Lunde, 'Illegal Acts in Disguise: Mumming as a Component of Collective Social Action in 19th Century Newfoundland', *Mummers Unconvention*, Bath, 2011, pp. 87–97, 88. https://folkplay.info/sites/default/files/papers/201111/Lunde2011.pdf [accessed 18 February 2020].
42 Fazackerley, 2020, Ibid.
43 Foxon, 2020, Ibid.
44 Natalia Pikli, *The Prism of Laughter: Shakespeare's 'Very Tragical Mirth'* (Saarbrücken: VDM Verlag, 2009), p. 91.
45 Anonymous respondent A, 23 March 2020.
46 Dave McMahon, Facebook Messenger to the author, 5 June 2020, with permission.
47 Ibid.
48 Anonymous respondent A, 2020, Ibid.
49 Fazackerley, 2020, Ibid.
50 Terry Gunnel, 'There is Nothing Like a Dame!' Cross-Dressing in Mumming Activities Past and Present. *Cosmos The Ritual Year and Gender*, 25, 2009, pp. 209–217.
51 Hale, 2020, Ibid.
52 Ibid.
53 Fazackerley, 2020, Ibid.
54 Foxon, 2020, Ibid.
55 Ibid.
56 Anonymous respondent A, 2020, Ibid.
57 Georgiou, 2015, p. 2.
58 Fazackerley, 2020, Ibid.
59 Andrew Howard and Michael Orrell, audio interview, 24 February 2020.
60 Hale, 2020, Ibid.
61 This is another barely documented northern custom performed all around the local area from the turn of the last century until the 1950s. Similar to Italy's La Passeggiata where young (and possibly older) people would parade up and down highstreets on a Sunday, dressed in their finest. This was a social performance and 'courting' opportunity.

62 Hale, 2020, Ibid.
63 Fazackerley, 2020, Ibid
64 Taylor, 2007, p. 16.
65 Foxon, 2020, Ibid.
66 Thomas Pettitt, The Man Is Pyramus: A Pre-History of the English Mummers Plays, *Medieval English Theatre*, 22, 2000, pp. 70–99, 74.
67 Taylor, 2007, p. 19.
68 Fazackerley, 2020, Ibid.
69 Phil Rigby, Facebook, 7 January 2018.
70 Fazackerley, 2020, Ibid.
71 Lunde, 2011, p. 88.
72 Anonymous respondent A, 2020, Ibid.
73 Taylor, 2007, p. 18.
74 This is the interviewee's own perception.
75 Foxon, 2020, Ibid.
76 Fazackerley, 2020, Ibid.
77 Jose Carlos Mariátegui, Heterodoxı́a de la tradición, in *Peruani- cemos al Peru* (Lima: Empresa Editora Amauta, 1970 [1927]), p. 117, translated and cited by David M. Guss, *The Festive State: Race, Ethnicity, and Nationalism as Cultural Performance* (Stanford: University of California Press, 2000), p. 17.
78 Fredric Miller, *Arranging and Describing Archives and Manuscripts* (Chicago, IL: Society of American Archivists, 1990), p. 20.
79 Taylor, 2007, p. 18.
80 Bastian, 2009, p. 115.
81 Ibid., p. 115.
82 Anonymous respondent A, 2020, Ibid.

PART II

Folk dance

Peter Harrop

The 1990s was a particularly rich decade in folk dance studies. John Forrest's *The History of Morris Dancing 1458–1750* (1999) provided a solid contextualisation for Keith Chandler's earlier study *Ribbons, Bells and Squeaking Fiddles: The Social History of Morris Dancing in the English South Midlands 1660–1900* (1993). Stephen D. Corrsin's *Sword Dancing in Europe: A History* (1997) provided context for Philip Heaton's later study *Rapper: The Miner's Sword Dance of North-East England* (2012).[1] The latter form of sword dance features complex percussive stepping, which provides a link – not only for purposes of introduction – to a further and broader form, step and clog dancing, reviewed in this volume by the dancer and teacher Alexandra Fisher. Lastly, country dancing – also known by a variety of other descriptors – is considered in both its pre- and post-Edwardian folk revival manifestations. The impact of that first folk revival on English folk dance, in terms of both archival understandings and the experiential repertoire, has been immense. The works mentioned above have been significant in liberating performance history from – in Keith Chandler's excellent phrase – 'the ultimate triumph of "antiquity" over actuality'.[2]

In the present state of the evidence, morris dance is first noted as a courtly and civic form in the fifteenth century; sword dance is a European form, mentioned in England only three times between 1604 and 1712, then developing as a popular form in the North East region from the late eighteenth century. References to what would later be known as country dance largely stem the record of John Playford's choreographic effort in the multiple editions of *The English Dancing Master* (post first edition simply *The Dancing Master*) from 1651 onwards.[3] This was an aspirational teaching manual aimed at dance teachers and their emerging market among the well-to-do. The first records of what would now be recognised as step dance refer to the stage hornpipe of the early eighteenth century; theatrical references then become increasingly common throughout that century prior to the dances spread to dance hall and street in the nineteenth century. None of these four dance forms have ever been just one thing; morris, step and country in particular have found popularity in a wide range of forms and very different social contexts. A 2018 volume of papers on morris dance, for example, highlighted these differences so effectively that one reviewer remarked that 'in the case of morris whilst evolution is undeniable, it is equally plausible that we are dealing with different strands or species of dance development that may have no substantive relationship with each other'.⁴ For these reasons of breadth and duration, morris dance serves as a useful opening.

An example: morris dance

John Forrest's pioneering work brought together the historical records of morris dance, from the earliest in 1458 – the mention in a will of a cup engraved with a morris dance – through to the mid-eighteenth century. That closing date arose from the data pattern which suggested that by then the dances had begun to assume the shapes with which we are familiar today. A predominant form has persisted in the English South Midlands (although there are other forms of morris dance in other parts of the country) and its formations have been addressed by Chandler. First, however, to consider Forrest's findings: the value of his work lies firmly in its entirety but with apologies to him I shall attempt to convey some central points.

Firstly, a strength of the work is its method, seriation. Forrest's data enabled him to determine a range of contexts in which morris dancing had occurred sufficiently often to suggest a trend and to indicate the relative prevalence of morris in those respective contexts over time. Employing the same data to different ends, Forrest is also able to demonstrate a geographical dimension to these trends, and to begin to track the movement of the dances across the country. (Initially, in the late fifteenth and first part of the sixteenth century, westwards from the City of London and the court at Kingston-upon-Thames; then, from the middle of the seventeenth century, demonstrating a contraction away from those places and a subsequent centring upon Chandler's focal area of the South Midlands.) Forrest then utilised his data in two further enquiries: one, to examine patterns of financial support for the dancers and dances and two, official actions pertaining to them. That is to say, support for them, or resistance to them, by official agencies such as royal court, state and civic agencies, church or guild. These trends are not abrupt; they are gradual shifts, occurring differently in different places. Forrest considers a 300-year span during which different forms of dances (all designated 'morris' albeit with multiple spellings) have been danced by people of widely different backgrounds and life experience and have been performed in strikingly different contexts during different periods. A selection of Forrest's chapter headings conveys something of the richness of this array. Royal Court; Urban Streets; Church Property; The Public Stage; Rural Locations; Assemblies and the Country Dance Hall; Private Premises. But despite the accurate dating of specific incidences, and a clearer understanding of trends, this is never a neat or sharp chronology; as Forrest points out, there is never a straightforward succession; individual contexts may have their heydays, but they never entirely supersede one another.

Chandler's two volumes consider morris dancing in the South Midlands from 1660 to 1900 and take a different but equally illuminating approach. His detailed research reminds the reader that dancers are always social individuals with lives and histories, possessed of culture, living in changing and challenging socio-economic circumstances; they should not be traduced as an animated backdrop to *The Wicker Man*. The evidence suggests that

> given the social milieu in which performances typically occurred, the dance forms were jealously guarded for their potential to generate extra income and other tangible benefits (such as alcohol and food), and for the prestige which it conferred on the performers themselves.⁵

The contexts of performance for dancers included Whitsun Ales, benefit society feast days, local tours during which dancers would visit neighbouring feasts and fairs to dance for the crowds – a good income stream – and there is evidence for dancing as an interim income source for men en route to harvest sites as peripatetic workers. Chandler also finds evidence for competitions between teams of dancers. This is semi-professional performance of high order (though occasionally rowdy and inflected by alcohol) by men from the lower rungs of the social ladder, deeply informed by a continuity of local aesthetic (four generations of the same family in one nineteenth-century example), yet regularly reinvigorated by access to the dancing of other teams.

Michael Heaney's more recent and deliberately plural collection *The Histories of the Morris in Britain* reminds us that Cotswold Morris (a twentieth-century generic for the South Midland dancing discussed by Chandler) is one form among several, that morris has taken different forms at different times and that there are marked regional differences between, for example, the South Midlands and North West England.[6] Morris dances of one sort or another have featured at the Jacobean Court; in eighteenth-century election campaigns; in nineteenth-century ales and at Crystal Palace in 1858 accompanied by the band of the Coldstream Guards. Morris dance was a feature of several plays produced from 1589 to the closure of the theatres in 1642 usually as a signifier of a simple, rustic life. They reappeared with some frequency between 1801 and 1910 – the period considered by folklorist Roy Judge – as entr'actes or otherwise self-contained interludes of an evening at the theatre with titles such as *The Ancient Morris Dance*.[7] Though a particular image of morris dance has lodged, post-revival, in the public consciousness, it has in reality been a profoundly multiform activity, presented in theatre, pageantry, dance hall and churchyard as well as on village greens.

Another example: sword dance

Linked hilt and point sword dance stands in contrast; in England, there are multiple local variants but only two forms of the dance, commonly differentiated as longsword and rapper. The major work on the subject has already been mentioned, Corrsin's *Sword Dancing in Europe*. Corrsin makes it abundantly clear that this is a pan-European display dance with the earliest records from the Low Countries in the late fourteenth century, specifically Bruges in 1389. The record persists in that region and from the fifteenth century expands across Central Europe, Scandinavia, Spain and Portugal. From the eighteenth century onwards, there are additional records from the Shetland Islands, the Austria-Hungary region, Italy and Spain. There are scattered sixteenth-century references from mainland Scotland, although nothing from England until the early seventeenth century. All these early records indicate performances by men and boys, at different points of the year, attaching sometimes to widespread festivals such as Shrovetide or Corpus Christi, otherwise to local saints' days, occasionally in honour of distinguished civic guests, or simply as income-raising activity for the performers. They have fallen in and out of favour in different countries at different times. Evidence is variously derived from proclamations, banning orders and account books detailing payment to the dancers, the latter often bearing indication of occasion and location. The sword dance presents as a skilled display, brought forth on special occasions, and Corrsin's evidence suggests that performances attached to larger centres of population.

The English material develops from the later eighteenth century onwards and Corrsin has updated and revised his original research to provide Chapter 10 of the current work. This introduction will therefore focus instead on two evidential outliers, set 74 years apart, even the latter preceding all other examples by 50 years, and both taking place – at least in light of all later evidence – in the 'wrong' part of the country. The following draws on Georgina Boyes closely reasoned explanation from her 2011 lecture to The Early Dance Circle.[8]

The well-known Simpson Company of actors from Westonby, Egton, in what is now North Yorkshire, crop up again in Chapter 4 of this volume. They were particularly active in the first decade of the seventeenth century and the leaders of the company, Robert and Christopher Simpson, were Catholic recusants living in an area described as a 'Bishoppricke of Papists'.[9] The patron of their company was the lord of the manor of Whitby, a port on the North Sea itself described as 'a receptackle to the symenary preists coming from beyond seaes and landing frequently at that port'.[10] In the same period, directly to the west but on the other side of the country, the county of Lancashire held the highest concentration of Catholics in England. Lancashire was home to the Blundell family, with William Blundell (1620–1698) and particularly his grandson Nicholas (1669–1737), separately providing the earliest evidence for sword dancing in England. Both of them, like the rest of the immediate family, were attended and taught by Jesuits. William's own father had been educated in Flanders, and although William was educated by Jesuits in England, he subsequently arranged for his sons and grandson Nicolas to be schooled in Flanders.

William Blundell's mention of a sword dance at Latham, five miles from the Jesuit school at Scarisbrook Hall where Boyes reasons William may have been a student in 1638, refers to an Ash Wednesday performance which would fit with Corrsin's evidence for early performances in the Low Countries. The later description, provided by Nicolas in 1712, tells us he taught a sword dance specially for performance at a party celebrating the 'flowering' of a new marl-pit – a significant agricultural moment befitting a special entertainment. In short, given the regular travel of priests and several generations of pupils between Lancashire and Flanders, and in the absence of any evidence to suggest sword dances elsewhere in England at the time, someone may have brought home from Flanders sufficient 'moves' to teach and reconstruct the dance. Although beyond the scope of this introduction, Boyes may also have thrown light on the later success of the form in Yorkshire and the North East of England where it eventually settled for the duration of the period covered by Corrsin's chapter.

On the one hand, history...

Given the milieux of these earliest references, morris dances at court and in civic processions, sword dances attaching to landed properties, alongside their particularities, what other kinds of dance activity might we know something about?

The terminology of medieval court entertainment is complex and never static but the term that most closely associates with dance is that of 'disguising'. Meg Twycross and Sarah Carpenter trace the usage back to the fourteenth century in the phrase *daunces disgisi* and suggest that 'disguise' in these contexts was closer in meaning to dressing up, but in as opulent a manner as possible to suggest the unfamiliar, strange and exotic. Once people were dressed up for a disguising

> the chief activity at all stages seems to be dance, and richly costumed dance remains the fundamental and most popular form of the disguising right through from the thirteenth until the mid-sixteenth century. The costumes were clearly designed to enhance the spectacle of the dance.[11]

As in other forms of pageantry, matters of entry received greater emphasis, both in terms of arrangements of dressed bodies in procession, and in the use of cars and pageants to wheel people into the performance space. These cars were themselves elaborately scenic; Twycross and Carpenter evidence one dressed as a garden, another set as an elaborate lighting display.

To the modern eye, this suggests a strikingly theatrical entry of costumed dancers, almost always dressed in set groups, engaging in an extended and diverse formation dance display, usually in large halls. The performers and the spectators were often known to each other and the entry was a highlight, a powerful opening image enabling a 'who's who' moment among the participants as the dancers and audience read one another in a mutual spectating. To this modern eye, the descriptions suggest a melding of fashion show and costume ball, formation dance display and voguing, a sustained balance of participatory and spectatorial gaze.

As the early *carole* and *basse danse* were taking shape and elaborating, in the period prior to the earliest morris dancing references, a century before the first English sword dance, here are antecedents if not a precursor of Playford's printed choreographies and, eventually, country dancing.

To reiterate, the earliest reference to a morris dance, at least to an image of a morris dance, is 1458. The first mention of actual morris dances – though with no description – comes as part of a summer parade in London in 1477 sponsored by the Draper's Guild and in 1494 as part of Christmastide celebrations at Court with expenses indicated in Henry VII's account books. 144 years later, in 1638, an Ash Wednesday sword dance takes place at a large house in Lancashire. In 1651, Playford publishes the first of very many editions of *The English Dancing Master*. Onwards a further century and the first mummers' play, a chapbook text, makes an appearance in the city of Newcastle-upon-Tyne. A decade or so later, in 1779, a special performance containing morris dances, sword dances and a mummers' play was given to celebrate the first visit of Dorothea Banks to the family seat of her new husband, Sir Joseph Banks. Sir Joseph and his sister Sarah Sophia were networked in the highest scientific and antiquarian circles – he was the President of the Royal Society – and Sarah Sophia was the leading collector of memorabilia attaching to the then highly fashionable 'private theatricals'. In this very particular evidence grouping, documenting a succession of significant *premières*, there is little that shouts either folk or tradition, but both terms would *eventually* be regarded as applicable, and both would stick fast.

These facts were not at Cecil Sharp's disposal when he first encountered or sought out dances. They are recently accumulated outcomes of many years research. Nevertheless, for the twenty-first-century reader, they serve to exaggerate the oddness of the conclusion Sharp had reached in these matters by 1913:

> In Morris, sword-dance, and [mummers] play we seem to intercept three stages of development, arrested and turned to its own uses by the civilised and social idea of entertainment: in the Oxford Morris-customs the earliest sacramental rite; in the sword-dance the later human sacrifice; in the mumming play the still later half magical presentment on nature's annual death and renewal.[12]

The centrality of that view to the folk revival and its continuation through the first half of the twentieth century cannot be over-emphasised. It unleashed a good deal of creative writing masked as semi-scholarship and it threw multiple grapnels into the public consciousness. There can be no doubt that Sharp's view of the past changed and shaped those dances in his present. The dances we continue to delineate as folk, the dances we are familiar with now, were already an outcome of many different influences when they were repopularised (revived is not the only available word) by a new constituency in the early twentieth century. Of course, this was not the first time an accommodation had been required between known and imagined histories, or in approaches to creativity, authenticity and change. The frames of reference of popular antiquarianism, of Romanticism more broadly, of folklore itself, had already cleared the ground when it came to re-imagining and re-enacting the customary. To restate an important sentiment from the Part I introduction, while history, historicity and historiography should be intellectually separable, if only to understand how they inform one another, they remain resolutely intertwined in performance. Nowhere is that more clearly the case than in the last hundred years of English folk dance.

The interconnection between history, ethnography and intertextuality was also mentioned in passing in the Part I introduction, with reference to Levitt's work on mumming. In the field of English folk dance, the clearest exposition of this complex matter remains Theresa Buckland's 2002 essay, 'Th'Owd Pagan Dance'.[13] In a layered piece, focussing on the example of The Britannia Coco-Nut Dancers and arising from many years of contact with the dancers, she points out that 'the dissemination and repetition of these now discredited academic modes of explanation for dances and dancing thus become part of the ethnographic investigation'.[14] In the case of Sharp's ideas, or a consideration of *The Golden Bough*, for example, a subsequent *scholarly* discrediting on methodological grounds, or on matters of principle relating to comparative evidence, will not have had immediate impact on local origin stories or on extant customary performance that maintained the idea of tradition. Buckland stresses that 'origin narratives cannot be dismissed merely as evidence of ill-informed use of poor and outdated scholarship'.[15] They cannot, because they are unequivocally *part* of the frame of reference, *part* of the idea of the dance, *part* of the performance. And, in a reincorporation of Chandler's effort to understand and appreciate pre-revival dancer's lives, 'they are also a means of claiming and promoting cultural capital' for people and on behalf of places.[16] These *fin de siècle* ideas about the 'very old' have effectively added to the rewards, well-being, status and prestige afforded both to performers and to the places they perform in. They add *value* to the technical mastery of the performers. Origin stories, and the consequent sense of tradition they lend weight to, are intertextual with the facts and with the performers and with the performance. Buckland points out that 'the power of choosing an imprecise or erroneous historical narrative over a more plausible alternative lies precisely in the ambiguity and mystery which such origin texts engender'.[17] This is a persistent feature of the 'metafolklore' as understood by Levitt in the context of mumming; this is the folk belief, the folklore, that accretes to folk performance, and which is such a prominent feature of English folk dance. The researcher Peter Millington has applied the pithy phrase 'mystery history';[18] such stories can be explanatory without having to fully explain and they form an important part of the appeal of folk performance.

While it is straightforward to differentiate between the various forms of dance discussed in the following chapters, and a distinction can easily be made between dances that emphasise theatricality and those that emphasise participation,[19] there are nevertheless no obvious choreographic grounds for a collective separation of all or any of them from 'non-folk' dances. If there are indicators for folk dance as folk dance, for folk dance as a genre, then they lie in those areas outlined in the final section of the Part I introduction. These emphasise the spatial arrangements governing the placing of the dances as much as any internal features; matters of reiteration and duration, temporality and site are perhaps more indicative than any overarching style, technique or form. Even methods of transmission, so often stressed as distinctive in a wider 'folk' discourse, are not entirely separable from those of the academy or the theatre. Although the histories of each of the dances discussed here are different, it is already clear that none of those dance forms could be claimed as consistently 'folk'. In taking the long view, folk dance appears a transitory and contextual determination rather than a choreographic descriptor. But, to tie in with later remarks regarding folk song, these certainly stand as samples of 'what the folk danced'.

Part II: Folk dance

Notes

1. Keith Chandler, *Ribbons, Bells and Squeaking Fiddles: The Social History of Morris Dancing in the English South Midlands 1660–1900* (Middlesex: Hisarlik Press, 1993); Keith Chandler, *Morris Dancing in the English South Midlands, 1660–1900: A Chronological Gazetteer* (Middlesex: Hisarlik Press, 1993); Stephen D. Corrsin, *Sword Dancing in Europe: A History* (Middlesex: Hisarlik Press, 1997); John Forrest, *The History of Morris Dancing 1458–1750* (Cambridge: James Clarke & Co., 1999); Philip Heaton, *Rapper: The Miner's Sword Dance of North-East England* (London: English Folk Dance and Song Society, 2012).
2. Chandler, *Ribbons, Bells and Squeaking Fiddles*, p. 219.
3. John Playford, *The English Dancing Master* [1651] (Binsted: Dance Books, 2013).
4. Vic Gammon, 'The Histories of the Morris in Britain', *Folk Life*, 57.1 (2019), 70–73.
5. Chandler, *Ribbons, Bells and Squeaking Fiddles*, p. 221.
6. Michael Heaney (ed.), *The Histories of the Morris in Britain* (London: English Folk Dance and Song Society & Historical Dance Society, 2018).
7. Roy Judge, 'Merrie England and the Morris 1881–1910', *Folklore*, 104.1/2 (1993), pp. 124–143 and '"The Old English Morris Dance": Theatrical Morris 1801–1880', *Folk Music Journal*, 7.3 (1997), pp. 311–350.
8. Georgina Boyes, '"… our dancers will appear" Popular Culture and Early Records of English Traditional Dance', *The Early Dance Lecture*, 2011. https://www.earlydancecircle.co.uk/events/past-edc-festivals/the-early-dance-lecture-2011/ [accessed 24 November 2020].
9. Jack Binns, *Sir Hugh Cholmley of Whitby 1600–1657: Ancestry, Life & Legacy* (Pickering, Yorks: Blackthorn Press, 2008), p. 10.
10. Ibid., p. 9.
11. Meg Twycross and Sarah Carpenter, *Masks and Masking in Medieval and Early Tudor England* (Aldershot: Ashgate, 2002), p. 133.
12. Cecil J. Sharp, *The Sword Dances of Northern England, Together with the Horn Dance of Abbots Bromley* (London: Novello, 1913), pp. 32–33.
13. Theresa Buckland, 'Th'Owd Pagan Dance': Ritual, Enchantment, and an Enduring Intellectual Paradigm', *Journal for the Anthropological Study of Human Movement*, double issue, 11.4–12.1 (2002), pp. 415–452.
14. Ibid., p. 415.
15. Ibid., p. 442.
16. Ibid. Buckland draws on Pierre Bourdieu's well-known construct, citing his work *Distinction: A Social Critique of the Judgement of Taste* (London: Routledge and Kegan Paul, 1984).
17. Ibid., p. 443.
18. Peter Millington, 'Mystery History: The Origins of British Mummers' Plays', *American Morris Newsletter*, 13.3 (1989), pp. 9–16.
19. As a caveat, I would argue that barn dancing is an extraordinary celebration of the oscillating gaze and that 'losing oneself in the dance' is rarely the whole story. I can't be alone in watching myself, watching my partner, watching my set, watching the whole dance, watching other individuals and couples, watching the band, watching the room, watching who else I might be dancing with and so on. The whole event is persistently spectatorial as well as participatory and therein lies its appeal.

9

MERRY NEETS AND BRIDEWAINS

Contemporary commentaries on folk music, dance and song in the Lake Counties during the Romantic period

Sue Allan

The interest in 'The Picturesque' and the advent of Romanticism from the late eighteenth century brought many visitors to the Lake District, to view not only the dramatic landscapes but also observe the 'manners and customs' of the local people. Their reportage, taken together with the contemporary depictions of local festivities by vernacular/dialect poets, provides valuable insights into the music, dance and song traditions of the Lake Counties of Cumberland and Westmorland.

The modern county of Cumbria comprises the historic 'Lake Counties' of Cumberland, Westmorland, Lancashire north of Morecambe Bay and a corner of the Yorkshire dales, and is perceived in both academic literature and popular imagination as having a strong regional identity.[1] Central to the county is the English Lake District, a mountainous area of some 2,292 square kilometres, designated a National Park in 1951. In 2017, it was inscribed a World Heritage Site as a 'cultural landscape', an acknowledgement of its role in the 'revolution in cultural values' during the second half of the eighteenth century, when mountainous landscapes became attractive and exciting according to the rubrics of, first the Picturesque and then Romanticism.[2] Both movements celebrated the pastoral tradition and helped establish the trope of town versus country, with the Lake District becoming a fashionable destination from the 1760s onwards.[3]

The date commonly attributed to the start of the Romantic period is the publication of Wordsworth and Coleridge's *Lyrical Ballads*, published anonymously in 1798, although this may be better characterised as the beginning of high Romanticism. Wordsworth's preface to the second edition, in 1800, became the movement's de facto manifesto, in which Wordsworth acknowledges his debt to balladry, as presented in Thomas Percy's collection of 1765, as well as to his own experience of the demotic, drawn largely from his childhood.[4] The 'discovery of the people', as part of a quest for authenticity, had begun and along with it the rise of popular antiquarianism, while 'naïve' pastoral scenes and their actors began to be framed as objects of interest to the 'Romantic gaze' of outside observers – musical, visual or literary – and held up as an 'emblem of lost innocence'.[5] 'Artless' and 'wild' became terms of praise, perfectly embodied in the figure of Mary Robinson, the adolescent daughter of a Buttermere innkeeper who attained national celebrity in 1792 through the writings of Joseph Palmer (1756–1815), as the 'Beauty of Buttermere'. Admired as 'the epitome of innocent, unaffected, unspoilt rural upland beauty', her innocence, tragic downfall and redemption made her an inspiration for a number of the Lake Poets.[6] 'The people', as appropriated by the dominant forms of high Romantic culture, went on to be incorporated into poetry, essays on 'customs and manners' and the fashionable descriptive travelogues and guides published by literary travellers.

Observations by visitors to the Lake District

One of the first visiting writers to appreciate the culture as well as the topography of the area was land surveyor James Clarke, whose *Survey of the Lakes of Cumberland, Westmorland and Lancashire* was published in 1789. He discusses the customs of north Cumberland, noting that the women of Carlisle were hardy souls if one judged by what was described in the Border ballads 'Jock-o'-the-Side', 'Hobby Noble' and 'Dick-o'-the-Cow' and also making mention, intriguingly, of a sword dance 'still in vogue in some places contiguous to the Borders', but which he does not elaborate on. He then reports that 'in proportion as you advance into the more lonely and mountainous districts', that is, into the fells and dales of the central Lake District:

> …customs such as the celebration of Christmas seem greater, so much the more is the ancient fashion of that festival perfect; the numbers of pies, and of the rural attendants on conviviality increased; the waits with their fiddles pass from village to village; and the winter merry-nights (as they are called) supply the want of the wakes, which are common (at other seasons indeed) in the more Southern counties.[7]

Clarke makes much of the fact that farming in the fells and dales was a communal culture where neighbours cooperated at peak times like ploughing, sheep shearing, mowing and harvesting on the so-called 'boon days': communal work sessions with an important social aspect. Work and play followed the seasons, with early summer bringing 'boon' clippings (sheep shearing), harvest festivals known as 'kurn suppers' held in the autumn, and then, at the end of the year, came the shepherds' meets and hunt meets.[8]

Sheep 'clipping' was an important event in the fell farming year, usually accompanied by ale, food, sports and dancing late into the night.[9] Cockermouth farmer turned antiquary and writer William Dickinson (1798–1882) describes the feast after a clipping day in a poem chronicling the farming year:

> Than somebody knattles [knocks] on t' teable [table] befoor.
> He says 'lads you mun [must] join in my sang:
> Here's a good health to the man o' this house,
> The man o' this house, the man o' this house,
> Here's a good health to the man o' this house,
> For he is a right honest man.

This old clipping song, he says, frequently degenerated into a raucous drinking game as it progressed and was usually followed by 'O good ale thou art my darlin' and 'The Raven and the Rock Starlin', with 'Tarry woo' traditionally sung by the shepherds.[10] The main social event in the sheep farmer's calendar though was always the shepherds' meet, at the back end of the year, when shepherds from a wide area brought sheep that had strayed into their flocks to return them to their rightful owners at some country inn. After the business of the day, there would be a supper and a chairman appointed to take charge of the evening's entertainment. The shepherd's meet in late November at The Dun Bull at Mardale was one of the oldest and largest, incorporating races, wrestling, hound trails, sheepdog trials and riotous singing at the inn, where 'those that could sing, sang, and those that couldn't, told a story'.[11]

While it is to be expected that music would play an important part in rural celebrations, it is quite surprising to learn that music education was widespread, in at least some parts of Cumberland. Yet in 1820 poet and school teacher Thomas Sanderson of Kirklinton, just north of Carlisle, reported that:

> Church music generally composes a part of the education of a Cumbrian peasant. They are instructed in it by the parish clerk, or by some itinerant professor; and in the course of a few months, by the means of a good ear, and a tuneable voice, acquire as much skill in it as to be able to gratify the taste of a country audience, at least as far as an accurate combination of sounds extends [...] When the school breaks up, they who compose the choir, and he who leads it, have generally a *ball* at the village ale-house, in order to experience jobs of a more *terrestrial* nature than those which spring from psalm-singing.

With a note of disapproval, he adds that, 'Fiddling, dancing, and drinking continue to a late hour: the divine strains, which they lately sung are forgotten; and the heart shut against all the devout feelings which they are calculated to inspire'. It is, however, for dancing and its teaching he appears to be most disdainful:

> Most of the Cumbrian peasantry are instructed in their early years in dancing by some itinerant professor, who commonly carries more merit in his heels than in his head. His pupils are taught country dances, hornpipes, jigs and reels; and if they have any springiness in them, generally attain, after a few months' instruction, sufficient skill and agility in the art, as to be able to amuse the spectators in a rustic assembly room.

Somewhat reluctantly, he admits that dancing

> has so many advocates among the lower, as well as among the higher, classes of the community, that to censure it would probably be to incur the charge of puritanical austerity; but I should think that the time and money expended in acquiring this art might be more usefully applied. Life is too short to waste any portion of it in frivolous amusements…

He also concedes that,

> Amidst all the fatiguing labours which his condition of life subjects him to, the Cumbrian peasant has his festive scenes, which throw a temporary sunshine around him; and by the gratifications which they afford to-day, suspend the thoughts of the hardships and toils of to-morrow.[12]

Some eight years later, under the heading of 'An Evening's Amusement', the local press carried a – mostly quite complimentary – report of both dancing and singing schools in Cumberland:

> On reaching Bromfield, on the 25th ult. on my way from Allonby, a jolly landlord informed me that a grand ball was that evening to be held at his house in consequence of the breaking

up of a Singing School, therefore, resolved to remain awhile, and must confess that I was much gratified with the manner in which the pupils of the worthy Mr McMickin acquitted themselves. On retiring to Mr. Glaister's we were favoured with some choice songs by Mr. McM. And others, and I was also greatly entertained with the attempts of one or two, who succeeded to perfection in imitating the exquisite melody of a pig in a gate.

The mirth of this party getting a little too vociferous, I set off, in company with two friends, for Blencogo. We felt the road rather longer than usual, but on arriving at the place of our destination were delighted to find it all fun and animation, arising from a dancing-school ball: admittance one shilling. We found the room accommodatingly fitted up, and were pleased with the exertions of the youthful votaries of Terpsichore. At length the music ceased, and then ensued a lively scene of rustic gallantry. Happy was the youth who received a smile from his nymph as he assisted her to robe for her journey. 'Pin up your gown', says one: 'bandage your mouth', cries another, 'the mworn's cold, and you have far to go.' In every direction happy couples were taking their departure.[13]

Dancing schools were widespread across the region, which was also notable for its many fiddlers, some of whom were also dancing masters. One such was James Lishman (1777–1849), who is mentioned by Dorothy Wordsworth when visiting a dancing school display on a tour in Scotland in 1822, where she observes that: 'The dancing would not have disgraced the Ambleside *quality* children at Mr Lishman's Ball'.[14] Her brother William's children undoubtedly also have attended dancing lessons, as in a letter dated Christmas 1805 Dorothy describes her niece and nephew in the kitchen at Dove Cottage, Grasmere:

> According to annual custom, our Grasmere Fidler is going his rounds, and all the children of the neighbouring houses are assembled in the kitchen to dance. Johnny has long talked of the time when the Fiddler was to come; but he was too shy to dance with any Body but me, and though he exhibited very boldly when I was down stairs, I find they cannot persuade him to stir again. It is a pleasant sound they make with their little pattering feet upon the stone floor, half a dozen of them, Boys and Girls; Dorothy is in ecstasy, and John looks as grave as an old Man.[15]

An earlier description of a dancing school, in the south Westmorland village of Heversham, appears in Joseph Palmer's *A Fortnight's Ramble in the Lakes*, intended as a light-hearted guide to tourists who wanted to avoid the Grand Tour in Europe because of the instability in France. Palmer and his companion chance upon a dancing school while staying at the Eagle and Child inn, after hearing the sound of a fiddle in the barn next door and seeing about 30 boys and girls assembling for dancing lessons. He remarks that

> The master had more the appearance of a man than of a dancing-master, although he was well qualified for the latter in the opinion of the children's parents. He did not look like one of those Continental beings, who *cabriol* and *pas-grave* themselves into the good opinion of fashion.

The two of them were among a number of spectators in the dancing room where the children performed:

> One of the boys danced a Hornpipe, with hat aside and stick under his arm, tipping most vehemently with head and toe, but in very good time; the master often threw his eyes

> upon the *strangers*, and I took care to give as much satisfaction to my face as I possibly could, though really not more than I felt. After the little hero had sweated over his part, nine girls danced a Cotillon in time and step that would not have disgraced a ball-room; and, what had a singular and rustic effect, whilst they were going the circle in pairs, the odd number stepped into the centre, pulled a red rose from her breast, which she held up as she danced round until she led to another step, and always, when she joined hands with the others, replaced her rose near cheeks that vied with it in healthful beauty. Why should so innocent a dance be called a Cotillon? I think it ought to have an English name, – Where is the harm, then, in my naming it the Rose Dance?
>
> As there was a tall boy, of about seventeen, that had the appearance of a farmer's servant, who wanted to dance, my friend was afraid we should abash him if we remained; so we went away. This lad had the look of a determined candidate for a prize dance. He forced out his toes, until he grinned to it, and looked so eagerly at the dancing girls, I should have thought they were all his sweethearts, but, upon recollection, I am persuaded he was only thinking, 'if I wur dancing, I'd ne'er give out.'[16]

The event was probably the customary end of season 'ball', at which the children performed for their parents the steps they had learned. A similar scene at Grasmere is beautifully described in the poem 'The Children's Dance' by 'Christopher North' – pen-name of Scottish advocate, literary critic and writer John Wilson (1785–1854), who was a friend of Wordsworth when he lived for some years at Windermere, and had a considerable reputation as a dancer himself. Possibly inspired by Robert Burns' 'Cotter's Saturday Night', his opening stanza sets the scene: 'How calm and beautiful the frosty Night | Has stol'n unnotic'd like the hush of sleep | O'er Grassmere-vale!'.

> And lo! the crowded ball-room is alive
> With restless motion, and a humming noise,
> Like on a warm spring-morn a sunny hive,
> When round their Queen the waking bees rejoice.
> Sweet blends with graver tones the silvery voice
> Of children rushing eager to their seats;
> The Master proud of his fair flock employs
> His guiding beck that due attention meets, —
> List! through the silent room each anxious bosom beats!

Although Wilson frames the children in typical Romantic and sentimental fashion as paragons of innocence and purity, his descriptions are lively. The dancing master, he says, is 'No idle, worthless, wandering man', but 'hard-working, patient, and well-liked' – 'a welcome guest, In every cottage-home on hill and vale'. His tunes and skilful playing, are referred to as 'Scottish': a stirring sound that 'speaks of Scotland too – a dear strathspey!' as he makes 'The living bow leaps dancing o'er the strings'. When the ball is finished, the dancing master is encouraged to play again by an old man, who requests:

> [...] a parting tune to play—
> One of those Scottish tunes so sweet and slow!
> And proud is he such wishes to obey.
> Then 'Auld lang syne' the wild and mournful lay
> Ne'er breathed through human hearts unmoved by tears,
> Wails o'er the strings, and wailing dies away!
> While tremblingly his mellow voice he rears,
> Ah me! the aged weep to think of former years![17]

Possibly the best-known description of a Lakeland dancing school is that by poet John Keats (1795–1821), written in 1818. Keats was on a tour of the north of England and Scotland with his friend Charles Brown, which he documented in letters to his brother Tom. At the end of June, Keats and Brown arrived in Ireby in Cumberland, after a walk up Skiddaw, their stay documented in a letter of July 1 sent from Carlisle:

> After Skiddaw, we walked to Ireby the oldest market town in Cumberland – where we were greatly amused by a country dancing school, holden at the Sun, it was indeed 'no new cotillion fresh from France'. No, they kickit & jumpit with mettle extraordinary, & whiskit, & fleckit, & toe'd it, & go'd it, & twirld it, & wheel'd it, & stampt it, & sweated it, tattooing the floor like mad. The difference between our country dances & these scotch figures, is about the same as leisurely stirring a cup o' Tea & beating up a batter pudding. I was extremely gratified to think, that if I had pleasures they knew nothing of, they had also some into which I could not possibly enter, I hope I shall not return without having got the Highland fling, there was as fine a row of boys & girls as you ever saw, some beautiful faces, & one exquisite mouth. I never felt so near the glory of Patriotism, the glory of making by any means a country happier. This is what I like better than scenery. I fear our continued moving from place to place, will prevent our becoming learned in village affairs; we are creatures of Rivers, Lakes, & Mountains.[18]

The quote about 'no new cotillion…' comes from Robert Burns' *Tam o'Shanter*, in the description of the witches dancing in Alloway Kirk: 'Nae cotillion brent new frae France, | But hornpipes, jigs, strathspeys, an' reels, | Pat life an' mettle I' their heels'.[19] The lines are also quoted by Keats' companion Charles Armitage Brown (1787–1842) in his own account of the dancing school:

> Our inn was remarkably clean and neat, and the old host and hostess were very civil and prepossessing – but heyday! What were those obstreperous doings over head? It was a dancing school under the tuition of a travelling master! Folks here were as partial to dancing as their neighbours, the Scotch; and every little farmer sent his young ones to take lessons. We went upstairs to witness the skill of these rustic boys and girls – fine, healthy, clean-dressed and withal, perfectly orderly, as well as serious in their endeavours. We noticed some among them quite handsome, but the attention of none was drawn aside to notice us. The instant the fiddles struck up, the slouch in the gait was lost, the feet moved, and gracefully, with complete conformity to the notes; and they wove the figure, sometimes extremely complicated to my inexperienced eyes, without an error, or the slightest pause. There was no sauntering, half-asleep country dance among them; all were inspired, yet by:
>
>> Nae cotillion brent new frae France;
>> But hornpipes, jigs, strathspeys, and reels
>> Put life and mettle in their heels.[20]

It is, overall, the energy rather than the grace of dancing that visitors to the Lake Counties tend to remark upon, including Joseph Palmer on a return trip to Buttermere, to see once again Mary, the 'Beauty of Buttermere' in the winter of 1797–1798. He is delighted to learn that there is to be a dance, a 'benefit of one Askew, a blind fiddler of Whitehaven' who is described as 'a great favourite with the Cumberland lads and lasses' but also one who has 'much more musical skill than inspires the itinerants of his profession; and much more humour in playing, than many who have the advantage of eyes to lead them by'. At 8pm, bursts of laughter are heard outside and Palmer, who is sitting with the fiddler, asks him to strike up 'Come, haste to this wedding', after which 'a rare parcel of lads and lasses rushed in' and greeted Askew before going upstairs, where 'a reel commenced':

> They were the very rosiest-cheeked mortals I ever saw; – the men kept excellent time and rattled on the floor with a variety of steps; the women danced as easily as the men determinedly. The dance was never long, and the moment the fiddler ceased another set that were ready called a fresh tune and began. I was glad to notice a black-eyed youth hand out Mary and another girl and call for a reel, and I honestly say, I never saw more graceful dancing, or a woman of finer figure to set it off, than in Mary of Buttermere. I was delighted that this exhibition lasted three times longer than any former one. The fidler knew how well she danced; indeed he had told me, and said 'she shall set herself off before you.'

Overhearing a latecomer bemoaning the fact that he cannot dance in his heavy 'iron-bound clogs', Palmer soon observes him among the dancers in his stocking-feet, 'and after they were worn out, barefooted'. Around 11, he is invited to join the women in 'a traditional Christmas posset' downstairs, while the men remained upstairs, where 'all manner of sounding steps, from the shuffle of pumps to the force of iron-clad shoes, were labouring over our heads, with the variety of sound attributed to a Dutch concert'. The party finally broke up and departed for home around two in the morning.[21]

This is not the first time Palmer had remarked upon local fiddlers, or the energy of dancers. On his earlier trip to the Lakes, while trying to retire to bed at an inn in Keswick, he was woken by the sound of a fiddle from the alehouse next door 'and by most violent dancing to it'. Opening his window to listen, he says 'applause and laughter attended every dancer', although he 'could only make out one tune; and, although I never heard any thing like it before, it is still buzzing in my head', but the dancers did not need much 'to induce the heel and toe to beat time to each other; and they were determined to wear leather [...]'. Keswick was evidently a musical place, as he notes a little later that while he is writing 'a blind fiddler is reeling by the inn, and, as well as I can make out, is playing Lady Coventry's minuet, with his own variations'.[22]

In 1800, we find John Housman also remarking on the enthusiasm of the dancers attending fairs, especially the bi-annual hiring fairs where, once the business of the day is done, fiddlers begin 'tuning their fiddles in public houses', most of which seem to having dancing rooms, while the girls 'gently pace the streets, with a view of gaining admirers'. The young men follow after:

> and having eyed the lasses, pick up each a sweetheart, whom they conduct to a dancing room, and treat with punch and cake. Thus they spend their afternoon, and part of their half year's wages, in drinking and dancing [...].

The dancers, he reports:

> [...] attend to exertion and agility, more than ease and grace: minuets and country dances constitute no part of the amusements of these rural assemblies. Indeed these dancing-parties often exhibit scenes very indelicate and unpleasant to the peaceful spectator. No order is observed, and the anxiety for dancing is great; one couple can only dance their jig at the same time, and perhaps half a dozen couple stand on the floor waiting for their turns; the young men, busied in paying addresses to their partners, and probably half

intoxicated, forget who ought to dance next; a dispute arises; the fiddler offers his mediation in vain; nay the interference of an angel would have been spurned at: blood and fur! It must be decided by a fight, which immediately ensues. During these combats the whole assembly is in an uproar; the weaker part of the company, as well as the minstrels, get upon the benches, or stand up in corners, while the rest support the combatants, and deal blows pretty freely among each other; even the ladies will not unfrequently fight like Amazons in support of their brothers, sweethearts, or friends. At length the fight is over, and the bloody-nosed pugilists, and unfeathered nymphs, retire to wash, and readjust their tattered garments; fresh company comes in – all is again quiet, and the dance goes on as before; while the former guests disperse into different public houses, and the reencounter, which generally commences without any previous malice, is rarely again remembered.[23]

In 1827, a contributor to Hone's *Table Book* gives an account of music at another fair, the March Fair at Brough in Westmorland, where two local musicians, fiddler Matthew Horn and John Deighton on clarinet, proclaim the fair first thing in the morning by walking through the town playing 'God save the King', after which the stall holders can start selling their wares. Horn, he says, 'has the best cake booth in the fair', while Deighton is a shoemaker 'and a tolerable good musician'. At the close of the fair, the streets are swept clean, the sweethearts come out and wander around in pairs looking at the entertainment on offer, and at 6pm dancing begins in all the public houses:

> Jack Deighton mostly plays at the greatest dance, namely at the Swan Inn, and his companion, Horn, at one of the others; the dances are merely jigs, three reels, and four reels, and country dances, and no more than three sets can dance at a time. It is a matter of course to give the fiddler a penny or two-pence each dance; sometimes however, another set slips in after the tune's begun, and thus trick the player. By this time nearly all the stalls are cleared away, and the 'merry neet' is the only place to resort to for amusement. The fiddle and clarinet are to be heard everywhere; and it is astonishing what money is taken by the fiddlers.[24]

A night of dancing was the essential finale to most festivals, it seems, including at Grasmere Rushbearing, the best-known of the handful of rushbearing ceremonies, described by Clarke in his 1789 *Survey of the Lakes* as 'an ancient annual custom, formerly pretty universal here, but now generally disused'. At Grasmere Rushbearing, then held in late September but later years moving to July, young women and girls gathered rushes from the fells and processed with them to the church, headed by a 'Queen', who placed a large garland on the pulpit, while the rest strew rushes on the floor. The procession was met at the Church door by a fiddler, who later plays them all to the public house, 'where the evening is spent in all kinds of rustic merriment'.[25] A lively account of the celebrations, dated July 21, is given by T.Q.M., a contributor to Hone's 1827 *Table Book*. He describes the children, mostly girls, parading garlands through the village 'preceded by the *Union* Band':

> In the procession I observed the 'Opium Eater' [Thomas de Quincy], Mr Barber, an opulent gentleman residing in the neighbourhood; Mr & Mrs Wordsworth, Miss Wordsworth and Miss Dora Wordsworth. Wordsworth is the chief supporter of these rustic ceremonies. The procession over, the party adjourned to the ball-room, a hayloft, at my worthy friend, Mr Bell's [The Red Lion)], where the country lads and lasses tripped it merrily and *heavily*. They called the amusement *dancing*, I called it *thumping*, for he who could make the most noise seemed to be esteemed the best dancer; and on the present occasion, I think

Mr. Pooley, the schoolmaster, bore away the palm. Billy Dawson, the fiddler, boasted to me of having been the officiating minstrel at this ceremony for the last six and forty years. He made grievous complaints of the outlandish tunes which 'Union Band chaps' introduce: in the procession of this evening they annoyed Billy by playing the 'Hunters' 'Hunters' Chorus in Friskets.' 'Who,' said Billy, 'can keep time with such a queer thing?'

One of the dancers seizes the writer's collar to introduce himself as 'old Dan Birkett, of Wythburn, 66 years old, not a better jigger in Westmorland' – a resident who, he is told, must be excused his forwardness, having 'been to Lunnon, and so takes liberties'. 'T.Q.M.' is pleased to note that the dancing room was the very one depicted by John Wilson in 'The Children's Dance', and learns that the dancing master 'described so exquisitely' in the poem was one John Carradus. He is less happy to learn from Billy that the custom had undergone change over the years, saying: 'I do not like old customs to change; for, like mortals, they change before they die altogether'. The dancing continues until quarter to 12, when 'a livery servant' comes in to deliver a message to the fiddler:

'Master's respects, and he will thank you to lend him the fiddlestick.' Billy took the hint: the Sabbath morn was at hand, and the pastor of the parish had adopted this gentle mode of apprizing the assembled revellers, that they ought to cease their revelry. The servant departed with the fiddle stick, the chandelier was removed, and when the village clock struck twelve not an individual was to be seen out of doors in the village.[26]

It was, however, Christmas which was the prime season for dancing and music, with Christmas Waits doing their rounds to visit each house on Christmas morning, and dances held in local inns over the holiday period. The Reverend William Hutton of Overthwaite in Westmorland, who wrote in dialect as 'William de Worfat', relates in a prologue dated 'Yule Tide 1784' that his house is very peaceful 'except when the waits gang their raund', and when 'the lads of my family thump the flure [floor] to the tune of Ald Roger' while the children 'merrily carrol the story of the Cherry Tree with other godly Ballads; and lasses dance Jumping Joan and Queen of Hearts.'[27] Even Wordsworth mentions the music of the season, in a poem 'composed at Rydal Mount, Christmas tide 1819':

> The Minstrels played their Christmas tune
> To-night beneath my cottage eaves;
> While smitten by the lofty moon [...]
>
> Through hill and valley every breeze
> Had sunk to rest with folded wings;
> Keen was the air, but could not freeze
> Nor check the music of the strings;
> So stout and hardy were the band
> That scrap'd the chords with strenuous hand.[28]

Christmas was also the season of that archetypal Cumbrian entertainment, the 'Merry Neet' (merry night), defined by Thomas Sanderson in his 1820 'Essay' on manners and customs as 'a night dedicated to mirth and festivity' held at an inn:

> It is generally attended by a numerous company of lads and lasses, the pride and flower of the neighbouring villages, for whose entertainment the landlord takes care to provide pies of different kinds, cards, music and a competent quantity of ale, whisky, gin, and rum. The

dancing commences early in the evening, and continues with unabating spirit, till after midnight. The music, if it be not able to produce the wonderful effects attributed to the strains of Orpheus, has always sufficient powers to move the muscular limbs of an athletic ploughman, and urge him to acts of agility, that often bring his head in contact with the ceiling, or beams of the dancing-room – a feat that never fails to give celebrity to a country performer. At the conclusion of a jig, the fiddler makes his instrument squeak out two notes that say, or are understood to say, 'Kiss her!' – a command which the rustic youth immediately obeys.[29]

Even Wordsworth, not usually given to reporting on local social activities, includes a merry neet in his poem 'The Waggoner'. Benjamin, the waggoner, calls in at a village merry neet at The Cherry Tree inn, Wythburn, Thirlmere, after hearing the welcoming sound of 'a fiddle in all its glee'. The festivities are in full swing, with a feast of food and drink downstairs, and the dancing upstairs:

> What thumping–stumping–-overhead!
> The thunder had not been more busy:
> With such a stir you would have said
> This little place may well be dizzy!
> 'Tis who can dance with greatest vigour–
> 'Tis what can be most prompt and eager;
> As if it heard the fiddle's call,
> The pewter clatters on the wall;
> The very bacon shows its feeling,
> Swinging from the smoky ceiling!

At the end of each dance, 'When every whirling bout is o'er'– | The fiddle's "squeak" – that call to bliss, | Ever followed by a kiss'.[30]

Dialect reportage

The influence of Romanticism undoubtedly focussed literary attention on dialect and the so-called 'peasant poets', especially after Robert Burns' *Poems, Chiefly in the Scottish Dialect*, published in 1786, proved so popular. Burns re-cast the 'pastoral' of that essential precursor to Scottish Romanticism, Allan Ramsay (1684–1758) in vital new linguistic and musical ways.[31] The English Romantic poets, however, while liking the concept of vernacular verse, would not have relished competing in the marketplace for 'scarce book buyers and even scarcer patrons', regarding the 'peasant poets' as 'unjust usurpers' and 'cultural rivals', and certainly within Cumberland Robert Anderson's dialect poetry proved more popular than the poetry of Wordsworth.[32] Meanwhile, despite a stated intention to 'choose incidents and situations from common life' described 'in a selection of language really used by men', Wordsworth almost entirely avoids the use of regional dialect. Nonetheless, the acclaiming, and at times appropriating, virtues of 'low and rustic life' remained a defining element of Romanticism and Romantic antiquarianism.[33]

The publication of works in Cumberland and Westmorland dialects dates back to the middle of the eighteenth century, but had its heyday at the very end of the century and in the early years of the nineteenth century. By 1839, John Russell Smith's bibliography of 'provincial dialects' was able to list 72 works, mainly of poetry from Cumberland and Westmorland.[34] Most of the dialect writers of the period celebrate the lives of Cumbrian 'peasants' and bucolic festivities, populated by a cast of characters, including dancers, fiddlers and singers, and as Michael Baron has noted, 'the cultivation of reportage is itself a regional poetic tradition in the Romantic period'.[35] In this, Robert Anderson (1770–1833) of Carlisle is pre-eminent, or at least most prolific, among the dialect poets in his descriptions of music, song and dance in the early years of the nineteenth century, while his contemporaries Ewan Clark (1734–1811) from Wigton, John Stagg (1770–1823) of Burgh by Sands – who was also a country fiddler – and Mark Lonsdale (1758–1815) also wrote lively and memorable accounts of music and dancing at local festivities.

Reports of singing appear only rarely in dialect literature, perhaps because as many of these poets lean towards comic verse, it is country fiddlers and dance which lend themselves more readily to humorous description. Notable exceptions are the ballad singers and sellers featured in Ewan Clark's 'A Description of Roslay-hill Fair', published in 1779 (not in dialect but in standard English) and Robert Anderson's singers at Carlisle Fair and in his poem 'The Clay Daubin'. In Clark's 'Roslay Fair', a 'motley group' of 'rueful, ragged rogues' appear, whose leader instructs 'pitch-pipe Peg' to exert her 'pithiest strain' to 'make Nancy Dawson ring through all the plain;| Each sense take captive with your syren song, | And turn to statues all the gaping throng'. Peter Placket is then instructed to get 'to reap the fruits, which Peg's soft strains have sown' – that is, to pick the pockets of the crowd, distracted by the singer: a common practice of the time. Not all ballad singers were of course thieves, though: most were simply trying to earn a crust in a practice that was widely regarded as little better than begging. Robert Anderson's 'Jurry Jowlter', for example, with his range of ballads, many of them Anderson's own:

> I chaunt aw maks ov ballets, thro' village or big town,
> An fwok draw geapin roun me, at market an the fair;
> I sing ov British sailors, that ay will rule the deep,
> Ov gallant Nelson's deeth, then aul an young will weep.

> Scairce a dry e'en to be seen! Monie buy the sang, an bliss the neame o' the Hero of the Nile Then I gie them 'Spain in an uprwoar' – 'Success to trade' – 'Irelan in Distress,' and 'The deevil turnt fortune-teller.' Here's luive garlans, fer young fwolk; anacrmontics, fer sots; dwolefu lamentations, fer gloomy aul maids; an 'Crams'– 'Kurn-winnins' – 'Clay-daubins' – 'Murry-neets' – 'Reaces' – 'Weddins' an' 'Fratches', fer 'Canny aul Cummerlan'.[36]

Anderson's 'The Clay Daubin' describes the communal building of a clay-built cottage – for a newly married couple, whereby friends and neighbours work together all day to get the walls up, and then celebrate afterwards with all the helpers. The fiddler Bill Adams is entreated to 'rasp up a lal tune' for the dancing, so he plays 'Chips an Shavings', and later in the evening Deavie offers to 'lilt ye a bit ov a sang':

> He lilted 'The King and the Tinker',
> And Wully struck up 'Robin Hood';
> Dick Mingins tried 'Hooly and Fairly';
> And Martha the 'Babs o' the Wood.[37]

It is dancing, however, which features most in these poems. Dancing was seen as an important preliminary to courtship, so learning to dance was important in rural society, hence the ubiquitous itinerant dancing master. James Lishman and John Carradus of Westmorland have already been mentioned, and in Cumberland we have references to fiddlers Jonathan Brammery, Tom Little, Bill Adams and Ben Wells – some of whom were also dancing masters.

In Ewan Clark's 1805 poem 'The Rustic' (written in Standard English, not dialect), the local dancing master was Tom Little of Thursby, who, 'for upwards of forty years, has figured in his vocation, and exercised the heels of thousands'. After all:

> Who would th' attainment of the dance forego?
> Nor need one buxom lass, or sun-burnt swain,

> To foot the floor by art unskill'd remain;
> T'accomplish this, itin'rant artists will,
> For weekly sixpence, train them into skill;
> Procure some empty barn's commodious site,
> There to instruct each limb to move aright,
> To cross the buckle; thunder one, two, three;
> And bounce a horn-pipe with agility;
> To run a reel, to jump jigs with an air,
> Till all are finish'd for the wake or fair.
> To thee Tom Little, of elastic toe,
> To thee, through friendship, shall one couplet flow;
> Taught by thy skill have thousands ris'n to fame,
> If graceful dancing that distinction claim.[38]

In west Cumberland the fiddler and dancing master of choice for most of the first half of the nineteenth century was Ben Wells, who, according to dialect writer Alexander Craig Gibson (1818–1874) was a fine fiddler. Well-known locally for his rendition of 'The Hunt's Up' on Christmas morning as well as playing for dancing, he was 'remarkably correct, distinct, and strongly marked as to time – in fact, the best possible fiddling to dance to'. He was also a very good teacher:

> The dances as taught by Ben Wells were intricate and required skill and a good memory for the moves and steps. These had to be performed correctly at the dances at which he played because he considered every public dance was a continuation of the last lesson he gave, and the dancers were careful not to put a foot wrong lest he stop the dancing and put it right.

According to Gibson's eponymous poem on the fiddler, his playing 'many a neet, | Gev weel oiled springs to t'heaviest heels' and 'nowt cud match t' sly fiddle squeal, | 'At signall'd kiss i' t' cushion dance'. This dance being the favourite finale, the men dancing around with cushions until the music stopped, when they knelt down in front of the girl they wanted to kiss and take home. After Ben's death, the 'rare top dancers' kept his memory green, but 'T'oald cushion dance went oot o' vogue' as most people became 'owre fine to care, For heamly dance, teun, teal, or sang' ['homely dance, tune, tale, or song'].[39]

Dancing was also an integral part at country weddings in rural Cumberland, which were often 'bidden weddings' (sometimes called 'bridewains' or 'infairs') – uproarious affairs involving the groom and his friends riding around the neighbourhood to invite everyone to the event. The nuptials would be followed by sports, feasting and dancing with a collection made from all the guests for the newly married couple. Such weddings proved a popular subject for vernacular writers, including Cumberland writers Anderson, Stagg and Clark, which describes the feast and sports at Kirkland Common, just outside Wigton, after which 'the aged homewards plod their way; | The young return to dance the night away'.[40] Ann Wheeler (1736–1804) of Arnside wrote about a similar occasion in one of her Westmorland *Dialogues*, where Jennet tells about her experiences there:

> I racken [reckon] we wor twenty on us, lads an lasses, awe dond [all donned] in awr varra best, an blind Tom wor fiddler, an a gud fiddler he is; an we donst [danced] abaut twoa haurs, then they went raund an gidderd [gathered] a penny a-piece fraeth lasses an toopence a-piece fraeth lads.

Figure 9.1 'Arnside Wedding'
Source: Frontispiece to Ann Wheeler's The Westmorland Dialect, with the adjacency of Lancashire & Yorkshire, in Four Familiar Dialogues (1821).

The dancing

> went on a gud bit, en monny a conny jig and reel teya [canny jig and reel too]; then they wor awe for cuntry-donses [all for country dances], an we went dawn yan varra wee [we went down one very well].

The term 'country dance' here refers to a long set dance. However, the next couple to the top call for a different tune (and presumably dance), but when the lad finds he cannot 'lead it off', another offers to show him how but the offer is refused and neither will he 'coo [coo] up anudder [another] tune', so inevitably a fight ensues (Figure 9.1).[41]

Robert Anderson wrote two rollicking poems about weddings, 'The Worton [Orton] Wedding' (written July 10, 1802, published 1805), and 'The Codbeck [Caldbeck] Wedding' (written 1805–1807, published 1808). Sanderson's note to the first says that, 'Among the plebeians of Cumberland the whole day glides away amidst music, dancing, and noisy revelry'.[42] Anderson paints a very lively picture of both events, for example, in Orton:

> Young sour-milk Sawney, on the stuil [stool]
> A whornpeype [hornpipe] danc'd, and keav'd [kicked] and pranc'd;
> He slipp'd, and brak his left-leg shin,
> And hirpl'd [limped] sair about:

> Then cocker Wully lap bawk heet [leapt roof beam height],
> And in his clogs top teyme did beat;
> But Tamer, in her stockin feet,
> She bang'd him out and out,
> And lilted– Whurry whum, &c.

Before long there is a drunken fight, with the fiddler John Stagg in the firing line:

> Blin' Stagg, the fiddler, gat a whack,
> The bacon fleek [flitch] fell on his back,
> And next his fiddle-stick they brack,
> 'Twas weel he was nea waur [It was well he was no worse].[43]

Meanwhile, in Caldbeck, the dancing gets underway to another fiddler, called 'Oggle Willy':

> The breyde wad dance '*Coddle me, Cuddy*';
> A threesome then caper'd Scotch Reels;
> *Peter Weir* cleek'd up [hooked up] auld Auld *Mary Dalton*,
> Leyke a cock round a hen neist [nest] he steals;
>
> *Jwohn Bell* yelp'd out '*Sowerby Lasses*';
> *Young Jwosep*, a lang Country Dance,
> He'd gat his new pumps *Smithson* meade him,
> And fain wad shew how he cud prance.[44]

The food then follows, but it is not long before an all-out drunken fight ensues, a recurring theme in all the dialect wedding poems.

The wedding to cap them all, however, is 'The Bridewain', a carnivalesque dialect masterpiece of 30 stanzas by John Stagg, 'the Blind Bard' and fiddler, about a wedding in north Cumberland.[45] Guests from 10 or 12 parishes attend, and after the nuptials the men race off on horseback to the bride's house, for food and copious quantities of ale, and where we find the fiddlers – Tom Trimmel, Tommy Baxter and Stagg himself – tuning up and 'rozzlin' their bows before striking up 'Cuddy's Wedding', a popular slip jig. After the usual sports – horse racing, wrestling, jumping, gambling, dancing, drinking (and intermittent fighting) continue apace: 'Wi' fiddlin', dancin', cracks, an yell [ale], | The day slipt swiftly owr'. Well into the night 'Lang sair they keyvel'd, danc'd an' sang, [Long sore they kicked, danced and sang]' until it neared the time that 'fwok sud gang to bed'. Some of the company then decide to head off to someone else's house for more dancing:

> Here th'better mak [sort] o' them that com'
>   Wi' country-dances vapour'd [boasted];
> But them that dought [dare] not try sec sprees
>   Wi' jigs an' three-reels caper'd.
> Mull'd yell [ale] an' punch flew roun' leyke mad
>   The fiddlers aw gat fuddled;
> An' monie a lad their sweethearts hed
>   I' nuiks [nooks] an' corners huddled
>   Unseen that neet.

As a new day dawns, some are still drinking, while: 'The fiddlers they i' th' parlour fowte [fought], | An' yen anudder [one another] pelted'. Then, 'just as the sun was peepin', Stagg depicts himself making his way home, 'Hauf wauken an' hauf sleepin'.[46]

A bidden wedding would generally be a summer event, as also would be an 'Upshot' – defined by Mark Lonsdale in his 41-stanza poem of that name as 'a dance or merry meeting projected and conducted by a few of the most spirited young men' in a neighbourhood, which is 'merely for the sake of recreation', whereas 'a common Merry-night' is a commercial event organised by a publican over the Christmas period. He describes his poem as 'a free sketch' of a Cumberland Upshot in Great Orton c.1780.[47] The poem opens with the Orton lads debating where and when to hold the event and which fiddler to book, Jonathan Brammery or John Stagg, and goes on to list all the people attending, Lonsdale himself: 'lytle Markey Lonney'. The accompanying notes say a suitable venue was any farmhouse or barn loft with a boarded floor, with space below for eating, drinking, card players and sweethearts. The fiddler eventually selected was Jonathan Brammery, 'long noted as an itinerant fiddler' according to Lonsdale's notes, but one who was less famed for his 'skill in tormenting cat gut (for he was a sad scraper)' as for his knack of making himself the butt of jokes and pranks, and his party piece 'Hunting the Fox' – 'a kind of duetto between his voice and his instrument' depicting the incidents of the chase 'with a natural snuffle and an affectation of mimicry, vocal and instrumental that made his performance irresistibly laughable'.

When the dancing gets going, it is energetic, the lads spinning girls until they get dizzy. Dancing master Tom Little once more puts in an appearance:

> Tom Leytle, wud a fearfu' bree [bustle],
> Gat hoald o' Dinah Glaister –
> She danc't a famish jig, an' he
> Was Thursby dancin' maister;
> But just as Lytle gev a spang [spring]
> Like a fine squoaerin' Callan ['gesturing youth']
> Loft boards they brack [broke], an' theer he stack [stuck]

A-striddlin' cock'd o'th' hallan [straddling the wooden screen on the floor below].[48] By ten o'clock, the party is in full swing when a pistol shot is heard outside, and a party of maskers enter:

> Oal' Bessey swurl't an' skew't about,
> While fwok to th' skemels brattl't [benches scattered]
> An' lasses whilly-liltit [shouted] out
> As they hed been betrattl't [stupified];
> But th'maister in amang them lap
> Just like a deevil ranty,
> An' browt man Jack, wi' Busy Gapp,
> An' Neddy Tarn an' Lanty.
>
> Reet unkat [uncouth] figures did they cut,
> And ay they skipp'd an' chantit,
> Their spangs an' vapours [springs and swaggers] pass'd for wut [wit],
> An' that was aw they wantit […][49]

The onlookers do their best to try to guess the identity of the maskers, but when the master's mask falls off, they recognise them as weavers from a nearby village. Then the 'Sword Dance com' on' the maskers 'lock't an' meade a bummel [bungle]' because of the clumsiness of one Wulliam Strang. The drama continues when they cut off Hector's head as 'Miss Greace began a' fantin [fainting]', and falls to the floor.[50] After all this excitement, food and drink is called for and a collection taken for expenses – sixpence each, and a penny in the fiddler's hat – and then some of the older folks leave, while 'the young "ans fell to dancin"'. As to the fiddler:

> Oald Brammery sune began to fagg;
> At tymes his mem'ry lwoasin' [losing],

> Yet ne'er a tune was ow'r an dune
> But Jonathan caw't for 'hwozin! [rosin]
>
> Oald clocker Jwonn wad dance a Jigg,
> And Simpson Lass was handy, -
> He arguet sair for 'Shilly-my-gig,'
> An' she for 'Dribbles o' Brandy.'

At this point, however, someone notices that the fiddler has fallen asleep, so the boys burn his wig and dirty his face and waken him with their laughter, and as he'd been dreaming he was 'Huntin' Fox', with 'snuffs an' sneevals' roared out 'yeow! yeow! yeow!' and damns the lads as 'deevals'. The party breaks up in the early hours of the morning, by which time old Brammery is lying asleep, 'drunk as muck'.[51]

> Whilst some of the fiddlers depicted seem of questionable character and ability, one William (Bill) Adams, who appears in Anderson's 'The Clay Daubin' and 'The Kurn-Winnin', was reportedly 'an excellent country musician, particularly noted for playing jigs and strathspeys and a man well known at fairs, merry nights, kurn suppers and 'clay daubins'.'[52] There were many more dances current in the area at the time, as Nichol and Cuddy discuss in Anderson's 'The Cram; Or, Nichol and Cuddy': 'The warl's but a weyl country dance [the world's bit a wild country dance], | Whoar aw caper teane ageane tudder- [where everyone capers one against the other] Nichol observes, while gossiping about the dances at a recent ball held nearby, where:
> [...] They'd jigs, reels, flings, strath-speys, whorn-peypes, cwotilons, minnywhits [minuets], country-dances, dandy walses, an whadreels [quadrilles]. Sec steps, min! yes-twee-three, habbety-nabbety, ledder-te-patch, heel an tae, cross the buckle, gi' me thy daddle, roun-roun-roun, syedlin-seydlin, an kiss an coddle.[...][53] Some of these would undoubtedly be performed at the most famous merry neet in dialect literature, Anderson's 'Bleckell Murry-Neet', written in 1803. The opening verses set the scene:

> Aye lad! sec a murry-neet we've hed at Bleckell,
> The sound o' the fiddle yet rings i' my ear,
>
> Aw reet clipt and heel'd [well-dressed] were the lads and the lasses,
> And monie a clever lish hizzy was there; [many a clever, agile, hussy was there]
> The bettermer swort [better sort] sat snug i' the parlour,
> I' th' pantry the sweethearters cutter'd [whispered] sae soft;
> The dancers they kick'd up a stour [dust] i' the kitchen,
> At lanter [game of Loo] the card-lakers [card-players] sat in the loft.[54]

The clogger of Dalston is declared 'a famish [famous] top hero', stamping with his foot and shouting and roystering until the sweat ran off his chin, and showing off his clog dance steps, which he ended with a flourish:

> He held up ae han leyke the spout of a teapot
> An danc'd 'cross the buckle' an 'ledder te spatch'
> When they cried 'Bonny Bell' he lap up to the ceilin',
> An aye snapt his thoums fer a bit ov a fratch.[55]

The evening continues with much mirth and merriment, food, drink and plenty of ale, before 'Daft Fred' amuses the company with 'smutty stories', a couple of songs are sung – 'Tom Linton' and 'Dick Watters', both Anderson ballads – and the party breaks up at five o'clock on New Year's morning.

Conclusion

The influence of antiquarianism and Romanticism continued throughout the nineteenth century, fostered by the poets of, and visitors to, the Lake District. It spilled out into the writings of the vernacular poets, chronicling the life of the countryside in both Standard English and dialect, their writings taken up, in turn, by 'educated Northern middle-class men, characteristically teachers or booksellers, [who] took to collecting and printing local ballads and songs [...] for a voracious middle-class local reading public, fond of music, who also read poems and even wrote them themselves in local newspapers'.[56]

Dialect poetry is a complex sign: its significance less to do with accurate re-creation of the dialect speech of the past, and more to do with the language's ability to invoke for its audience nostalgia for a mythical 'golden age' when living, loving, working and playing were altogether simpler. It has also, historically, been very important in foregrounding regional identity – promoting a sense of place and belonging. This reached its zenith in the period 1780–1815, when regional poetry flourished as a cultural form in what has been termed the 'emblematic interaction of Romantic aesthetic with pride in regional identity', as shown in the examples given in this chapter.[57]

Although it is tempting to think that the lively narrative poems of Stagg, Anderson and Lonsdale comprise a faithful social history, we need to be wary of making such an assumption. The scenes they depict cannot be regarded in the same light as the more objective reportage of Clarke, Palmer and Housman et al. All were writers skilful at creating atmosphere, theatre and a good story, with a tendency to romanticise their youth and their roots as Cumberland 'peasants', very well aware of their 'intellectual capital' as 'peasant poets', and keen to find ways of 'merchandising' pastoral tropes.[58] Yet neither was the poets' work pure invention, but rather fiction grounded in fact lent an air of authenticity by the names of genuine fiddlers and dancing masters, tunes, dances and songs of the time interwoven into their merry neets, weddings and other festivities. Between them, the reports of the Lake District visitors and the dialect poets offer rare contemporary glimpses – slightly fuzzy snapshots viewed through the prism of both nostalgia and Romanticism – of the music making of working people in the Lake Counties, made possible because of the heightened focus on the area at that time, and the strong sense of place it engendered in people of all classes.

Notes

1. The county of Cumbria came into existence in 1974, following the Local Government Act of 1972. Angus Winchester, 'Regional Identity in the Lake Counties: Land Tenure and the Cumbrian Landscape', *Northern History*, XLII:1 (March 2005), pp. 29–48, 29).
2. *Description of the English Lake District as a World Heritage Site*: https://whc.unesco.org/en/list/422 [accessed 14 July 2020] A 'cultural landscape' is defined as one where the 'combined work of nature and human activity has produced a harmonious landscape in which the mountains are mirrored in the lakes'.
3. Jeremy Burchardt, *Paradise Lost: Rural Idyll and Social Change Since 1800* (London: I. B. Tauris, 2002), pp. 26–29.
4. William Wordsworth, *Lyrical Ballads, with Other Poems. In Two Volumes* (London: T. N. Longman and O. Rees, 1802), Preface. Thomas Percy, *Reliques of Ancient English Poetry* (London: T. N. Longmand and O. Rees, 1765).
5. Philip Connell and Nigel Leask, *Romanticism and Popular Culture in Britain and Ireland* (Cambridge: Cambridge University Press, 2009), p. 31. Matthew Gelbart, *The Invention of 'Folk Music' and 'Art Music'* (Cambridge: Cambridge University Press, 2007), pp. 77, 144.
6. Joseph Palmer (b. Budworth), *A Fortnight's Ramble to the Lakes in Lancashire, Westmorland and Cumberland, by A Rambler* (London: Hookham and Carpenter, 1792), pp. 202–204. 'A Rambler' was the pen-name he used in his regular articles in *The Gentleman's Magazine*. He changed his name from Budworth to his

wife's family name of Palmer in 1812. John K. Walton and Jason Wood, *The Making of a Cultural Landscape: The English Lake District as Tourist Destination, 1750–2010* (Farnham: Ashgate, 2013), p. 75.

7   James Clarke, *A Survey of the Lakes of Cumberland, Westmorland and Lancashire: Together with an Account, Historical, Topographical and Descriptive of the Adjecent Country, to Which Is Added a Sketch of the Border Laws and Customs* (London: printed for the author, 1789), pp. 41, xv, xxxxiv, xxv.

8   A 'churn supper' because 'a quantity of cream, slightly churned, was originally the only dish which constituted it', often called 'kurn' supper in north Cumberland. William Rollinson, *The Cumbrian Dictionary of Dialect, Tradition and Folklore* (Otley: Smith Settle, 1997), p. 91. Ian Whyte, 'The Last English Peasants? Lake District Statemen and Yeoman Farmers in the Late Eighteenth and Early Nineteenth Centuries: The Example of Tom Rumney of Mellfell', *Folk Life*, 46 (2007), pp. 120–130, 126.

9   William Rollinson, *Life & Tradition in the Lake District* (Clapton: Dalesman, 1974), p. 89.

10 William Dickinson, 'Memorandums of Old Times, in Mid-County Dialect', in *Cumbriana, or Fragments of Cumbrian Life* (Whitehaven: Callander and Dixon, 1875), pp. 213–232.

11 Deborah M. Kermode, *The Shepherd's Voice: Song and Upland Shepherds of 19th and Early 20th Century Lakeland* (unpublished MA dissertation, Lancaster University, 2003), p. 35.

12 Thomas Sanderson, 'An Essay on the Character, Manners and Customs of the Peasantry of Cumberland', in *The Poetical Works of Robert Anderson, Author of 'Cumberland Ballads,' & c. to Which Is Prefixed the Life of the Author, Written by himself*, ed. by Thomas Sanderson (Carlisle, B. Scott, 1820), pp. xlvi–xlvii.

13 'A Rambler', 'An Evening's Amusement', *The Citizen*, no. 111, September 1 (Carlisle, 1828), p. 84.

14 Dorothy Wordsworth, 'Journal of My Second Tour to Scotland, 1822', in *Journal of my Second Tour to Scotland, 1822, a Complete Edition of Dove Cottage Manuscripts 98 and 99*, ed. by Jiro Nagasawa (Tokyo: Kenyusha Printing, 1922 [1989]).

15 Dorothy Wordsworth, 'Letter 240: Letter from Grasmere, to Lady Beaumont, December 1805', in *The Early Letters of William and Dorothy Wordsworth 1787–1805*, ed. by Ernest de Selincourt (Oxford: Oxford University Press, 1935), pp. 559–562, 561.

16 Palmer, *A Fortnight's Ramble*, pp. 19–23.

17 John Wilson, *The City of the Plague and Other Poems, 1812* (Edinburgh: Archibald Constable, 1816), pp. 171, 173–174, 185–186.

18 Hyder E. Rollins, *The Letters of John Keats 1814–1821* (Cambridge, MA: Harvard University Press, 1958), p. 307.

19 Carol Kyros Walker, *Walking North with Keats* (New Haven, CT and London: Yale University Press, 1992), p. 159. Robert Burns, *Tam o' Shanter: A Tale (Chapbook)* (Edinburgh: Oliver & Boyd, 1810), p. 6.

20 'Walker', *Walking North with Keats*. Charles Brown published his account as 'Walks in the North' in *The Plymouth and Devonport Weekly Journal* (1, 8, 15 and 22, October 1840).

21 Joseph Palmer, 'A Re-visit to Buttermere 1798', *The Gentleman's Magazine*, LXX (1800), pp. 22–23.

22 Palmer, *A Fortnight's Ramble*, pp. 169–170.

23 John Housman, *A Topographical Description of Cumberland, Westmoreland, Lancashire, and a Part of the West Riding of Yorkshire* (Carlisle: Francis Jollie, 1800), pp. 70, 105.

24 William Hone, *The Table Book of Daily Recreation and Information* (London: Hunt and Clarke, 1827), pp. 159–160.

25 Clarke, *A Survey of the Lakes*, p. 124.

26 T.Q.M., 'Notes on a Tour, Chiefly Pedestrian, from Skipton in Craven, Yorkshire, to Keswick, in Cumberland', in Hone, *The Table Book*, pp. 550–556 (pp. 553–554). T.Q.M. was later identified as Robert Storey in *Notes & Queries*, 3S:10 (September 1866), p. 209.

27 Rev. William Hutton, *A Bran New Wark by William de Worfat, Containing a True Calendar of His Thoughts Concerning Good Nebberhood* (London: Printed and sold by all the Booksellers in Great-Britain, 1785), p. 7.

28 'To the Rev. Dr. W._____ with Sonnets to the River Duddon, &c.', in William Wordsworth, *The River Duddon, A Series of Sonnets: Vaudracour and Julia: And Other Poems. To Which Is Annexed, a Topographical Description of the Country of the Lakes, in the North of England* (London: Longman, Hurst, Rees, Orme and Brown, 1820), pp. 113–114.

29 Sanderson, 'Essay', pp. lii–liii; Francis Jollie, *Jollie's Sketch of Cumberland Manners and Customs*, p. iii.

30 William Wordsworth, 'The Waggoner', in *The Miscellaneous Poems of William Wordsworth: in Four Volumes* (London: Longman, Hurst, Rees, Orme and Brown, 1820), Canto II, pp. 7–47, (pp. 22–23, 25).

31 Gelbart, *The Invention of 'Folk Music'*, pp. 45, 76. Katie Wales, 'Northern English in Writing', in *Varieties of English in Writing: The Written Word as Linguistic Evidence* (Amsterdam, 2010), p. 64.

32 Annette Wheeler Cafarelli, 'The Romantic 'Peasant' Poets and their Patrons', *The Wordsworth Circle*, 26 (1995), pp. 77–87, 84.
33 Michael Baron, *Language and Relationship in Wordsworth's Writing* (London: Longman, 1995), pp. 22–23.
34 John Russell Smith, *A Biographical List of the Works That Have Been Published, towards Illustrating the Provincial Dialects of England* (London: G. Norman, 1839).
35 Michael Baron, 'Dialect, Gender and the Politics of the Local: The Writing of Ann Wheeler', in *Romantic Masculinities: News from Nowhere Vol. 2*, ed. by Tony Pinkney, Keith Hanley, and Fred Botting (Keele: Keele University Press, 1997), pp. 41–56, 51. The term 'peasant' tends to be problematical for us today. For a full discussion of its complex history, see Arthur Knevett and Vic Gammon, English Folk Song Collectors and the Idea of the Peasant', *Folk Music Journal*, 11 (2016), pp. 44–66.
36 *Anderson's Cumberland Ballads, Carefully Compiled from the Author's MS. Containing Over One Hundred Pieces Never Before Published, with a Memoir of His Life, Written by Himself. Notes, Glossary, &c., to Which Is Added Several Other Songs in the Cumberland Dialect by Various Authors* (Wigton: n.d., probably 1843), p. 27.
37 Robert Anderson, *Ballads in the Cumberland Dialect by R. Anderson: With Notes and a Glossary* (Carlisle: W. Hodgson, 1805), 'The Clay Daubin', pp. 113–116, 114, 116; Note LX, p.137. The songs are mostly well-known broadside ballads.
38 Ewan Clark, *The Rustic: A Poem in Four Cantos* (London: Thomas Ostell, 1805), Canto III: 'Manhood', pp. 28–29.
39 Alexander Craig Gibson, *The Folk-Speech of Cumberland and Some Districts Adjacent; Being Short Stories and Rhymes in the Dialects of the West Border Counties* (London: John Russell Smith; Carlisle: Geo. Coward, 1869), pp. 34–36.
40 Clark, *The Rustic: A Poem in Four Cantos*, p. 64.
41 A. Wheeler, *The Westmorland Dialect, with the Adjacency of Lancashire & Yorkshire, in Four Familiar Dialogues: Of Which an Attempt Is Made to Illustrate the Provincial Idiom* (3rd edn.; Kendal, M. and R. Branthwaite, 1821), pp. 58–59. Dialogue III 'Between Sarah and Jennet, or the Humours of a Coquet in Low Life Displayed'. Wheeler's orthography is strikingly different from most of the Cumbrian writers of dialect, and rather more difficult to read.
42 Anderson, *Ballads* (1805), pp. 9–13, Note VI, p. 125. *Ballads in the Cumberland Dialect, with Notes and a Glossary, Chiefly in the Cumberland Dialect, by R. Anderson* (Wigton: R. Hetherton, 1808), pp. 169–175.
43 Anderson, *Ballads* (1805), p. 12.
44 Anderson, *Ballads* (1808), p. 172.
45 John Stagg, *Miscellaneous Poems, Some of Which Are in the Cumberland Dialect* (Workington: W. Borrowdale, 1805), 'The Bridewain', pp. 125–138.
46 Stagg, *Miscellaneous Poems*, pp. 135–138.
47 Mark Lonsdale, 'The Upshot' in Francis Jollie, *Jollie's Sketch of Cumberland Manners and Customs* (Carlisle: Francis Jollie, 1811), pp.1–18, Explanatory notes pp. 19–32, 21–22.
48 Lonsdale, 'The Upshot', stanza 12, pp. 8–9.
49 Lonsdale, 'The Upshot', stanzas 24, 25, pp. 12–13.
50 Lonsdale, 'The Upshot', stanzas 26, 28, pp. 13–14.
51 Lonsdale, 'The Upshot', stanzas 32, 33, 39, pp. 15–16, 17.
52 'The Clay Daubin', Anderson, *Ballads* (1805), pp. 113–116, Note LXI, p. 114. Robert Anderson, 'The Kurn-Winnin; or Shadey an' Jossy', in John Russell Smith, ed., *Dialogues, Poems, Songs and Ballads by Various Writers in the Westmoreland and Cumberland Dialects, Now First Collected, with a Copious Glossary of Words Peculiar to Those Counties* (London: John Russell Smith, 1839), pp. 279–287.
53 Rev. T. Ellwood, ed., *Anderson's Cumberland Ballads and Songs. Centenary Edition* (Ulverston: W. Holmes, 1904), pp. 176–181, 178.
54 Anderson, *Cumberland Ballads* (1893), 'Bleckell Murry-Neet', pp. 68–72, 68. 'Bleckell' is Blackwell, then a village but now a suburb of Carlisle.
55 'Bleckell Murry-Neet', pp. 68–69.
56 Katie Wales, *Northern English: A Cultural and Social History* (Cambridge: Cambridge University Press, 2006), p. 29.
57 Mike Huggins, 'Popular Culture and Sporting Life in the Rural Margins of Late Eighteenth Century England: The World of Robert Anderson, "The Cumberland Bard"', *Eighteenth-Century Studies*, 45.2 (2012), p. 194.
58 Cafarelli, 'The Romantic "Peasant Poets"', p. 81. All three writers wrote with a view to publication, while Anderson also wrote songs performed at London's Vauxhall Gardens and Lonsdale became a manager at Sadler's Wells.

10

SWORD DANCING IN ENGLAND

Texts and sources from the eighteenth and nineteenth centuries

Stephen D. Corrsin

England has made enormous contributions to the modern development of European-linked sword dancing. Documentation is very significant from the late eighteenth century onwards, though very little is known about English dancing before that. In this essay, I will summarize and review the evidence beginning in the late eighteenth century up to the early twentieth century, when Cecil Sharp's compilation, *The Sword Dances of Northern England*, provided the first survey of the two distinct styles of dance which existed, naming them long sword and short sword, or rapper.

The late eighteenth century

The reports which exist for northern England from 1769 to 1789 are of several distinct types. Some are by scholars, describing the history of the region and what they believe to be its ancient customs; one is a well-known transcription of a sword dance play; others include more miscellaneous printed items. The focus stays on northern England. All the reports for the years 1769–1778 place sword dancing in Northumberland, in Tyneside, chiefly in the general area of Newcastle. The reports for 1779–1789 are more scattered, expanding the geographical range south to the city of York and into Lincolnshire, and west to Cumberland – and even as far south as London, when dancers from Cumberland visited.

The first reference is John Wallis's *The Natural History and Antiquities of Northumberland* (1769). Wallis was the curate of Simonburn, on the North Tyne, north of Hexham and some way inland from Newcastle. The reference appears in a discussion of Roman antiquities, specifically those in the area of Hadrian's Wall, west of the town of Hexham, in southern Northumberland, in 'Journey I' of Wallis's book, 'From the *West* to the *East* End of the famous *Roman* wall, and a part of the great military road.'

> The *Saltatio armata* of the *Roman* militia on their festival *Armilustrium*, celebrated 19th October, is still practiced by the country people in the neighbourhood, on the annual festivity of Christmas, the *Yule-Tide* of the *Druids*. Young men march from village to village, and from house to house, with music before them, dressed in an antic attire, and before the *Vestibulum* or entrance of every house entertain the family with a *Motus incompositus*, the antic dance ... or *Chorus armatus*, with swords or spears in their hands, erect,

and shining. This they call, The *sword-dance*. For their pains they are presented with a small gratitude in money, more or less according to each housholder's [sic] ability. Their gratitude is expressed by firing a gun. One of the company is distinguished from the rest by a more antic dress; a fox's skin generally serving him for a covering and ornament to his head, the tail hanging down his back. This droll figure is their chief or leader. He does not mingle in the dance.[1]

Several elements in Wallis's report will appear over and over again. He places the dance at Christmas; refers to costumed young men, carrying swords, travelling and performing with some sort of music; says that they collect money; and notes that there is a distinctively dressed comic character, who is also the leader. Wallis does not describe the actual dance. His view is that this is a Roman relic. But that was a common eighteenth-century explanation for otherwise unusual customs and need not be taken seriously. It does mean, however, that he felt it was an old or at least old-appearing custom.

Another reference is a particularly important one. It has been discussed a number of times and forms the basis for many descriptions of sword dances through the nineteenth century. It comes from the 1777 edition of John Brand's *Observations of the Popular Antiquities of Great Britain*. Brand published it as an expanded edition of Henry Bourne's compilation, *Antiquitates Vulgares, or, The Antiquities of the Common People* (published in 1725). Brand's citation comes from his chapter on Christmas and winter customs. This important passage is worth quoting in its entirety, including his translation of the description by the sixteenth-century Swedish bishop Olaus Magnus, not least because many nineteenth-century descriptions of sword dancing seem to have drawn to a great extent directly from Brand.

> In the North there is another Custom used at or *about this Time,* which if I mistake not, was antiently observed in the Beginning of Lent: The *Fool Plough* goes about, a Pageant that consists of a Number of *Sword Dancers*, dragging a Plough, with Music, and one, sometimes two, in a very antic Dress; the *Bessy,* in the grotesque Habit of an *old Woman*, and the *Fool*, almost covered with Skins, a hairy Cap on, and the Tail of some Animal hanging from his Back: The Office of one of these *Characters* is, to go about rattling a box amongst the Spectators of the Dance, in which he collects their little Donations.
>
> This Pageant or Dance as used at present, seems a Composition made up of the Gleanings of several obsolete Customs followed antiently, here and elsewhere, on this and the like festive Occasions.
>
> I find a very curious and minute Description of the *Sword Dance* in Olaus Magnus' History of the northern Nations. – He tells us, that the northern Goths and Swedes, have a Sport wherein they exercise their Youth, consisting of a Dance with Swords in the following Manner: First with their Swords *sheathed* and erect in their Hands, they dance in a triple Round. Then with their *drawn* Swords held erect as before: Afterwards extending them from Hand to Hand, they lay hold of each other's Hilt and Point, while they are wheeling more moderately round, and changing their Order, throw themselves in the figure of a *Hexagon,* which they call a Rose. – But presently raising and drawing back their Swords, they undo that Figure, to form (with them) a four-square Rose, that may rebound over the Head of each. At last they dance rapidly backwards, and vehemently rattling the Sides of their Swords together, conclude the Sport. Pipes, or songs (sometimes both) direct the measure, which at first is slow, but increasing afterwards, becomes a very quick one, towards the Conclusion.

He calls this a Kind of *Gymnastic Rite*, in which the ignorant were successively instructed by those who were skilled in it: And thus it must have been preserved and handed down to us. – I have been a frequent Spectator of this Dance, which is now performed with few or no Alterations; only they *lay their Swords*, when *formed into* a *Figure*, upon the *Ground* and *dance round* them.

With regard to the *Plough* drawn about on this Occasion; I find the *Monday after Twelfth Day*, called antiently … *Plough Monday*, 'when our northern *Plough Men*, beg *Plough Money* to drink' (it is very probable that they would draw about a *Plough* on the Occasion…)[2]

Brand adds, concerning the characters: 'As to the *Fool* and *Bessy*, they are plainly Fragments of the antient *Festival of Fools*, held on New Year's Day.'[3] He is not specific about places, referring only to 'the North.' Born in 1744 in Washington, south of Newcastle, he was raised in Newcastle, and served as a curate in Cramlington, north of that city, so the report presumably concerns the Newcastle and Tyneside areas. He too regards it as an old dance, and his use of Olaus Magnus (the first time the Swedish bishop appears in English sword dance literature, but far from the last) suggests that he sees it as a Scandinavian dance that had survived in 'the North' of England. One specific exception that Brand makes is that he had seen the swords 'formed into a Figure,' and placed on the ground for the dancers to 'dance round them.' This may be a reference to a common, dramatic, and distinctive characteristic of English sword dances known from later accounts. In this, the swords are interwoven into a 'lock,' 'star,' or 'knot,' and displayed to the audience.

The next major reference is very different, both as a type of source and in the material which it provides. It is the 'Revesby sword dance play,' which was performed on the estate of the naturalist Sir Joseph Banks, Revesby Abbey, in Lincolnshire, on 20 October 1779. The text of the play includes instructions for the sword dance which was part of it. It was first printed by T. Fairman Ordish in 1889, reprinted a number of times since, and analysed from different points of view, including literary history. An intriguing description of the sword dance can be obtained by extracting details from the text.

They foot it once round the Room […]

Then they all foot it round the Room, and follows the Fool out. They all re-enter, and lock their Swords to make the Glass; the Fool running round the Room […]

Then the Fool flings the Glass upon the floor, jumps upon it; then the dancers, every one drawing out his own Sword, and the Fool dancing about the Room […]

Then the Fool, kneeling down, with the swords round his neck […]

Then they draw their Swords, and The Fool falls on the floor, and the dancers walk once round the Fool; and Pickle Herring stamps with his foot, and the Fool rises on his knees again […]

Then the dancers, puting their swords round the Fool's neck again […]

Then the dancers walk round the Fool with their swords in their Hands […]

Then the Fool falls down, and the Dancers with their swords in their Hands […]

The Fool rises from the floor […]

Then the foreman and Cicely dances down, the other Two Couple stand their ground, after a short dance called 'Jack, the brisk young Drummer,' they all go out but the Fool, Fidler, and Cicely […]

Then they dance the Sword Dance, which is called 'Nelly's Gig,' then they run under their Swords, which is called 'Runing Battle,' then Three Dancers dances with 3 Swords, and the foreman jumping over the Swords, then the Fool goes up to Cicely […]

> Then they foot it once round [...]
> Then they foot it round [...]
> [...] and they foot it round[...]
> Then the Dancers takes hold of their Swords, and foots it round the Room, then every Man makes his Obeisance to the Master of the House, and the whole concludes.[4]

It is very likely that the dance has linking elements. The phrase, 'foot it round the room,' probably indicates a circular figure; the dancers 'lock their swords to make the glass,' probably the 'lock' of interwoven swords; they put their swords around the fool's neck, draw them and he falls (twice); and there are figures which seem to consist of passing over and under swords. The cast consists of a fool and five dancers, identified as his sons: a hobby horse, a dragon, and a fiddler. The terms used for the whole group are 'Plow Boys, or Morris Dancers.' There is so much disparate material that one scholar has called it the 'Revesby medley.'[5]

The description is much more detailed than the others from the eighteenth century, but there are some points in common. One issue is the time of year; though the text refers to Christmas, the play was presented in October. But this is simply an example of the fact that sword dances can be held on special occasions or to entertain important people, and not just at set points in the calendar. It is difficult to explain the appearance of sword dancing in Lincolnshire, nowhere near any other known centres. Perhaps a local person or immigrant learned the dance elsewhere and taught it here.

The next important reference is from the city of York. The physician and literary historian Nathan Drake published his *Shakespeare and His Times* in 1817. His comments on sword dancing are chiefly taken from Olaus Magnus and John Brand, but he adds a personal note:

> Of this curious exhibition on Plough-Monday, I have often, during my boyhood, at York, been a delighted spectator, and, as far as I can now recollect, the above description [from Olaus Magnus and Brand] appears to be an actual detail of what took place.[6]

Published references also make it appear that there was sword dancing in Cumberland in this period. In particular, a dance in London by Cumberland dancers on 31 January 1788 was reported. How the northerners got to London is not explained, but perhaps they were brought by a patron or impresario who had seen them dance.

> At the late masquerade-ball in the Pantheon, London, a team of young Cumbrians performed the Cumberland Sword Dance, in stile and character as a company of maskers. The novelty of the spectacle was productive of much entertainment. – Jack and his Master were of the group; nor was Old Bessy forgotten, whose quaint, Northern dialect was the life of the scene.[7]

Another account adds:

> A set of Morrice Dancers from the North, gave an excellent display of the Cumberland Sword Dance. Five of them, dressed in their shirts, trimmed with ribbons, performed their athletick exercise, and the remainder of the nine consisted of Bessey, a Minstrel, Jack, and his Master, who in the characters of Ring Sweeper, Fidler, Songster and Interpreter, added much to the hilarity of the piece.[8]

A brief summary of the eighteenth-century material would be useful. The picture of the circumstances and context of sword dancing in reports from Tyneside (all concerning the years 1769–1778) is clear, albeit when the picture is expanded to include reports from other places, it is less so. The terms used for Tyneside performances are not only sword dance, but also 'morrice dance,' 'fool plough,' 'white plough,' and 'plough stot.' It is a Christmastime custom, occurring in late December to early January. The performers are costumed men or youths with swords, travelling about the area. There is little specific information on the actual dancing, though Olaus Magnus's account, then becoming well known to British scholars, is sometimes mentioned. Otherwise, the reports refer in general terms to the music used, to the custom of plough dragging, and to grotesquely dressed accompanying characters, including fools in animal skins, and a man in old woman's clothes. The collection of money, or 'gifts,' by the performers and their followers is a regular feature. The writers call sword dancing an old custom; but this can simply mean that it appears, in some way, old and unexplained. Some authors suggest the Romans, Saxons, or Scandinavians as the originators of the dancing and related customs.

The reports from 1779 into the 1780s are somewhat different. They expand the geographical range from Tyneside, to the city of York, Lincolnshire, and Cumberland (and London). Some of the references show connections with Christmastime or shortly after (Plough Monday being an agricultural workers' holiday in January, the first Monday after Twelfth Night, 6 January). The dates and venues of the performances shift in these accounts, for instance, to entertain important audiences, such as Sir Joseph Banks, or Londoners. The dancers are, it seems, young men or boys, the same sorts of characters and some of the same customs appearing as in Tyneside.

These reports mostly show how educated observers saw the performances. While some of the references may have material from 'within' the performances as well – the Revesby text, for example – these say nothing about the history or background of the dancing. It is impossible to say for how long sword dancing had been practised in Northumberland, Durham, Yorkshire, Lincolnshire, or Cumberland, before these writers encountered it, or exactly what type of dances these were.

Long sword in nineteenth- and early twentieth-century Yorkshire

Records of sword dances in the nineteenth and early twentieth centuries are distributed across northeastern England, specifically the counties of Yorkshire, Durham, and Northumberland. There are many reports, and in some cases more detail than before. Two separate types of dances come to exist, later known as long sword and rapper, although it is unknown when and how they developed into distinct styles, or what the relationship is between them. We shall begin with the long sword style.

The term 'long sword' seems to date from Cecil Sharp's time, having been coined to distinguish the style from 'short sword,' or rapper, contemporary reports simply referring to 'sword dancing.' Long sword uses rigid swords, or rather sword substitutes, of metal or wood. The evidence for it includes many of the elements seen in the Northumbrian reports of the late eighteenth century: the dancing is noted as taking place during the early winter holidays, though often from Plough Monday rather than Christmas; costumed men or youths dance as they travel around an area; grotesquely dressed characters accompany them; sometimes a short farce or play is presented; and money is collected. While there is some information on the actual dances, detailed descriptions only appear in the early twentieth century. By this time, the dances are usually performed at a steady march or trot, to a variety of popular tunes. There is a common store of figures, always it seems with one or more 'locks' in which the swords are placed in a star shape. But there is a great deal of variety. It is generally assumed that the nineteenth-century dances must have resembled those which were written down later, but there is no way to be certain of this.

Long sword in the nineteenth century is chiefly found in clusters distributed unevenly throughout Yorkshire. Most of the reports come from northern Yorkshire, including the area around Whitby, an important seaport and resort on the coast; from farther west in the North and West Ridings; from the Vale of York and in and around the city of York; and from along the coast, in the area around Flamborough Head. Two distinct dance styles are found around the industrial city of Sheffield, far to the southwest but still in Yorkshire. Definite reports of long sword from outside Yorkshire, from southern County Durham and possibly Derbyshire, are not forthcoming until relatively late.[9]

After the references from 1769 to 1789, there is little information on any style of sword dance until the decade following 1810. This may mean that evidence from these years has not been traced, or that the custom fell into disuse during the difficult years of the French revolutionary and Napoleonic wars. But in May 1811, *The Gentleman's Magazine* published a letter referring to dancing at Christmastime in the North Riding. The account is presented as a contemporary report.

> On the feast of St Stephen also, 6 youths (called sword-dancers, from their dancing with swords), clad in white, and bedecked with ribbands, attended by a fiddler and another youth curiously dressed, who generally has the name of 'Bessy' and also by one who personates a doctor, begin to travel from village to village, performing a rude dance called the sword dance. One of the 6 above-mentioned acts the part of king in a kind of farce which consists of singing and dance, when 'the Bessy' interferes while they are making a hexagon with their swords, and is killed. These frolicks they continue till New Year's Day, when they spend their gains at the ale-house with the greatest innocence and mirth, having invited all their rustic acquaintance.[10]

This corresponds well with the reports from 1769 to 1778. But it should be noted that the swords are made into a 'hexagon' (this term may have been taken from Olaus Magnus and John Brand), a characteristic of later dances as well; and the travelling and performing run from St. Stephen's Day (the next after Christmas) to New Year's Day.

One of the most detailed early descriptions is by George Young, in his *A History of Whitby, and Streoneshalh Abbey* (1817). Young presents Whitby as the local sword dance centre, drawing performers from nearby smaller towns and villages.

> On plough Monday, the first Monday after twelfth day, and for some days following, there is a procession of rustic youths dragging a plough, who, as they officiate for *oxen*, are called *plough-stots*. They are dressed with their shirts on the outside of their jackets, with sashes of ribbons, fixed across their breasts and backs, and knots or roses of ribbons fastened on the shirts and on their hats. Besides the plough draggers, there is a band of six, in the same dress, furnished with swords, who perform the sword-dance, while one or more musicians play on the fiddle or flute. The sword-dance, probably introduced by the Danes, displays considerable ingenuity, not without gracefulness. The dancers arrange themselves in a ring, with their swords elevated, and their motions and evolutions are at first slow and simple, but become gradually more rapid and complicated: towards the close, each one catches the point of his neighbour's sword, and various movements take place in consequence, one of which consists in joining or plaiting the swords into the form of an elegant hexagon or rose, in the centre of the ring; which rose is so firmly

made, that one of them holds it up above their heads without undoing it. The dance closes with taking it to pieces, each man laying hold on his own sword. During the dance, two or three of the company, called *Toms* or *clowns*, dressed up as harlequins in the most fantastic modes having their faces painted or masked, are making antic gestures and movements to amuse the spectators; while another set called *Madgies*, or *Madgy-Pegs*, clumsily dressed in women's clothes, and also masked or painted, go about from door to door, rattling old canisters in which they receive money. When they are well paid, they raise a huzza; when they get nothing, they shout 'Hunger and starvation!' When the party do not exceed 40, they seldom encumber themselves with a plough. They parade from town to town for two or three days, and the money collected is then expended in a feast and dance, to which the girls who furnished the ribbons and other decorations are invited. Sometimes the sword-dance is perfomed differently; a kind of farce, in which songs are introduced, being acted along with the dance. The principal characters in the farce are, the *king*, the *miller*, the *clown*, and the *doctor*. Egton Bridge has long been the chief rendezvous for sword dancers in the vicinity.[11]

Young's account contains many familiar elements. The description of the actual dance is reminiscent of Olaus Magnus and John Brand. Young emphasizes, however, that the dancers lock their swords together so that they can be held up and displayed by one man. This rigid lock of swords is perhaps the single most distinctive feature of modern English sword dances. Young suggests that the dance was originally Scandinavian, so either he thinks it is centuries old, or he is just following Brand.

Reports continue through the nineteenth and into the twentieth century. In general, the picture and context remain consistent, and resemble the late eighteenth- and early nineteenth-century material, including season, venues, performers, and collecting. There is little detail on the dances themselves, though linking elements appear and it is common practice to interweave the swords, and then display them. The writers consistently speak of 'swords,' though substitutes, whether of wood or metal, are known from some reports.

Two of the more interesting accounts from the nineteenth century come from villages south of the city of York. The early one concerns a sword dance and play from Riccall, performed in the 1820s–1830s.

> The sword dancers who usually accompanied or were a part of the Plough Stotts, numbered generally from eight to twelve gaily dressed in breeches and white stocking and white shirts decked with many coloured ribands.
>
> The Swords were thin laths of wood. Having gone through several graceful figures… pointing their swords horizontally to the centre, they interlaced them, and one of the Dancers carried them altogether in his hand.
>
> These dances were seen at Riccall as late as 1836–37…
>
> Each man holds his sword in his left hand and all foot it and rattle their swords. Then each man takes hold of the next man's sword's point with his right hand and threads all through their swords severally, i.e. under any one which two men hold up beginning at the King, until all have gone foremost from the King to the hinderend and then locks their swords.
>
> (Directions for Locking)
>
> Now each man holds his sword in his left hand and the next man's sword point in his right hand, so throws them over their heads and with doing their left hands above each others sword hilt, they will be fast, that is the left hand above and the right below.

They leap over each of their swords and lock and so carry them all first one and then another and so throw them down. Then ride on each of their swords, and after a flourish with them lock them about the neck of a little lad which the clown must call his Kitty.[12]

This account first appeared in print in an article by E.C. Cawte published in 1971, together with the verses of the song, in which the dancers are introduced as various heroes. At the end of the song, 'they cut a figure with swords, all, then they run as the right hand and left, six times around and then another figure.' A 'famous well skilled Doctor' gives a comic speech, and a play follows, with a clown, a king, a lady, and a gentleman. A picture of the sword lock reproduced from the original manuscript shows a lattice shape, with eight swords interlaced, two on a side.

In 1890, William Camidge published a description of Plough Monday in York in the *Yorkshire Gazette* which records quite an elaborate performance by men from the village of Naburn a few miles south of York.

[At one time] Naburn (like other villages) [...] sent a united band of farm servants into the city [of York] on or about Plough Monday, who amused the citizens with their peculiar dress and antics. First in the procession came the band which invariably consisted of from three to six performers, sometimes a clarionet [...]led the musical part of the entertainment – occasionally a brass instrument or two were pressed into the service of the show, whilst at times an accordion or violin was the leading if not the only instrument of the band. A drum was ever considered absolutely necessary [...].

Next to the band came two men-servants dressed as 'King and Queen,' and it was not an uncommon thing for 'his Majesty' to be adorned in an old hussar suit, to carry an old sword and to wear on his head an old helmet; whilst 'her Majesty,' gay with female attire gathered from many homes and sporting many ribbons and laces, hung dependently on his royal highness's arm. It frequently happened that when two or three villages joined to form a company, each village sent a king and queen as a part of their contingent. After the representatives of Royalty followed three or four couple of men who wore outside their waistcoats white shirts profusely adorned with ribbons of every hue whilst their hats bore rosettes, cockades and streamers. They generally carried a wooden sword each, and walked the streets in procession, but at every available spot they danced to the strains of their music, threading their swords in the dance with considerable skill, and going through a series of figures which could only have been perfected by considerable practice and care. Two or three more of their company were dressed up as clowns and begged money from the onlookers. One man was invariably dressed as a tawdrily [sic] woman, and carried a besom which he sometimes used with more freedom than discretion. Another had his face blacked and a third generally had his face coloured and sometimes they wore large spectacles. Before coming into the city they had to secure the consent of the Lord Mayor.[13]

The first attempt at a systematic survey of long sword dancing was made in 1911–1913, when Cecil Sharp published the three parts of his collection, *The Sword Dances of Northern England*. The first two parts had included descriptions from Kirkby Malzeard, in the West Riding of Yorkshire near Ripon; Grenoside, near Sheffield; Sleights, near Whitby; and Flamborough, on the coast south of Whitby, at Flamborough Head. All these four dances were still being performed. Sharp then wrote to many of the parishes in the Anglican Diocese of York, those in the East and large areas of the North Riding, and as a result of this survey was able to print in the third part of his *Sword Dances* accounts from Escrick, Ampleforth, Askham Richard and Haxby, all around York. None was still performed regularly, though there had been dancing a few years before. He also included the dance from Handsworth, a Sheffield suburb, which was still performed by local men. Sharp's letter to the vicars read, in part:

I shall be very much obliged to you if you will kindly inform me –

a   Whether the Sword Dance is still annually performed in your Parish at Christmas or at any other time of the year.
b   And if not, whether it has been so performed within the memory of anyone now living.[14]

In 1955, Norman Peacock studied and summarized the responses, which had come from 157 parishes, about half of those questioned. He prepared both a short article for the EFDSS *Journal* and a longer unpublished summary. He notes:

In 138 parishes no sword dance was, or had been danced […] but in 7 of these, 'Plough Boys' came around and to another 13 dancers came, or had come, from elsewhere.

The Dance had been performed at one time by the inhabitants of 33 parishes, and in 9 more the Dance was still performed; not all of these were in the diocese of York, since some vicars wrote of dances they knew elsewhere.[15]

There were also a few reports from Cumberland and County Durham. Peacock continues:

The replies show that the Sword Dance must have been widely spread in both the East and North Ridings of Yorkshire at one time, but that it died out earlier in the former than in the latter. In the southern and eastern part of the East Riding, Holderness, the Humber plain and the Wolds, it was at best only a vague memory, even in 1912; further north, on the border of the North Riding, it had survived longer, but it flourished only near the North Yorkshire coast and particularly at Skelton-in-Cleveland which was more or less industrial.[16]

Peacock's summary gives a strong sense of a village custom disappearing, presumably under the pressure of intensive social and economic changes. (The 'more or less industrial' comment was not included in the published version, perhaps because it did not fit with the common notion of sword dancing in Yorkshire as a village or rural custom.) It indicates that long sword dances could be found, on the eve of the First World War, chiefly around Flamborough; in North Yorkshire, in East Cleveland and westwards in different locations from Whitby to Kirkby Malzeard, near Ripon; and in Sheffield's suburbs. The style seems to have mostly disappeared from the Vale of York and city of York area, though the dances had been performed relatively recently in the villages of Ampleforth and Bellerby.

But the picture is imprecise. The geography is uncertain, because teams often travelled around to perform, rather than staying in their home villages or towns; the chronology is vague, because of indistinct memories and a dearth of written records. (A study by Michael Heaney of Wychwood Forest morris dance traditions is instructive in this regard. It shows that early dance collectors, and the dancers to whom they spoke, were often wrong about years and even decades. There is no reason to believe that sword dancers were any more accurate.)[17]

Sword dancing has been well known in the general Whitby area at least as far back as George Young's 1817 report. One of the villages studied by Sharp is that of Sleights, inland from Whitby, and we can draw on Sharp's description. He followed the Sleights dancers on Plough Monday

1912, as they toured the area. He writes that the party consisted of six dancers, a fiddler, and seven colourfully dressed 'Toms,' clowns or fools, whose chief role was to collect money. (The money was to be spent on a supper and dance the following Saturday night.) The dancers wore red tunics, with white high collars, and sashes, black trousers, and caps. They carried dull steel 'swords,' with no points, wooden handles without cross bars, and ribbons tied to the tips. These sword substitutes were nearly three-feet long. Sharp was told that the party had once been much larger, and had included a king and queen, the latter a man in women's clothes. Sharp does not say anything about the identities of the dancers; published photographs show young men and older boys. There was also a separate boys' team, which danced in the village itself. The Sleights team performed intermittently for some years after, disbanding finally in the 1930s.

The music consisted of a medley of popular tunes, evidently chosen mostly for pace, rhythm, and phrasing. Among them were 'The Girl I Left Behind Me,' 'Pop Goes the Weasel,' and 'Cock o' the North.' Sharp describes the step as 'a decided march or tramp.' The six dancers began by standing in a ring, and sang:

> Here's fourteen of us all;
> From Sleights town we come,
> And we are going a-ramble-ing
> The country for to see.
> And a holiday we will take,
> Some pastime for to make;
> So freely you will give to us,
> So freely we will take.
> Although we are but young
> And never danced here before,
> Oh we will do the best we can,
> And the best can do no more.
> So now you see us all
> Dressed in our bright array,
> Now we will start our dancing,
> So Music strike up and play.[18]

The dance consists of five 'figures,' figure in this case meaning a complete sequence of movements, ending with a lock of swords, and with a break between each figure. There is, thus, no continuous movement through the whole dance, rather a series of distinct sections. For example, 'Figure 1' consists of 'The Clash,' 'Shoulders-and-Elbows,' 'Your Neighbour's Sword,' 'The Right-and-Left Lock,' and 'The Rose.'[19]

About two dozen long sword dances were described by Sharp and others, in the following decades. There are a number of elements which appear regularly in traditional English long sword, but none appears in every recorded case. Other dances have been composed since, sometimes using and shuffling traditional figures and styles, and sometimes creating new figures.

Both new and old dances are technically complex and share a basic repertory of figures. They normally have a linked circle as the basic figure to which the dance repeatedly returns. Other figures include moving in an unlinked circle, clashing swords held high; stepping one-by-one over swords held low, either 'your own' sword or 'your neighbour's'; moving, singly or in pairs, over or under the opposite swords in the circle, which are held low or high – this serves to invert the circle, and then restore it as dancers return to their places; and rigid locks, displayed to the audience, whether once, or twice, or half a dozen times through the dance. Other figures often appear, such as 'The Hey,' or a poussette figure, with dancers moving in linked pairs. Most reports which refer to the number of dancers mention six or eight. The even number leads to the characteristic symmetry of these dances.

It is not unusual for introductory songs, bits of farce, or short dramas to appear in association with the dances. Sharp and others have felt that the songs, plays, or dramatic or farcical fragments, were surviving parts of an ancient ritual. More specifically, the mock beheadings which were sometimes noted were, in his view, part of a forgotten pagan death-and-resurrection ritual, to ensure fertility or representing the change of the seasons. But it can be pointed out that these elements were far from universal, and that one has to strain mightily to see anything resembling magical rituals in them.

The music for these dances seems to have been whatever was available: fiddle, drum, flute, or accordion, playing medleys or well-known tunes that fit the dances' pace and rhythm. ('The Girl I Left Behind Me' is one such popular tune.) The step generally varies from a steady 'march or tramp' to a fast trot.

The normal performance season is early winter, around Christmas, New Year's Day, or Plough Monday. The dancers wear costumes or at least some kind of distinctive dress; there are accompanying characters (fools, Toms, king and queen, man in women's clothes, doctor), who collect money, and sometimes take part in a piece of the dance, or in a play. The dancers come from villages, smaller towns, and cities – York, Whitby, Sheffield – where larger audiences are easily found, and money more easily collected. The dancers, who are young men or boys, work in various fields, but chiefly in the common working-class trades in their particular communities, whether farming, quarrying, mining, metalworking, or fishing. The dancers carry specially made surrogate swords, usually rigid steel with wooden handles, but without cross hilts. Wooden sword substitutes might also be used.

But exceptions could be found to any common point noted above, in every case that Sharp and others collected. There might be a shuffle-clog step used at times (Grenoside), or a skip (Flamborough); the dance might begin with a lock (Grenoside); a wooden slat might be used as a sword substitute (Flamborough, Haxby); the dancers might hold the hilts in their left hands (Flamborough); there might be no song or drama (Handsworth), or there might be a long one reminiscent of mummers' plays at Christmas or Easter (Ampleforth). In sum, variety – or perhaps local creativity – is and has long been the order of the day.

Rapper dancing in Northumberland and Durham

The other, distinct type of English linked sword dancing is found in northern County Durham and in Northumberland around Newcastle. While nineteenth-century writers usually just referred to 'sword dancing,' at some point the style which became known, after Sharp, as 'rapper' or 'short sword' developed. (The mystery word 'rapper' may have been a mistake caused by Sharp's inability to understand the local dialect. We shall use 'rapper,' which became the standard term.)[20] Rapper dancing features shorter (around two feet, or 60 cm, in length), two-handled, flexible metal 'swords.' This is the defining element of the dance, but the fast shuffle-tap stepping used is also characteristic and distinctive, as is the fact that the style had its home in the coal mining communities of the northeast. While no 'history of long sword' has been written, two comprehensive and capably researched histories of rapper have appeared: E.C. Cawte's 'A History of the Rapper Dance,' published in the *Folk Music Journal* in 1981, and Phil Heaton's *Rapper: The Miners' Sword Dance of North-East England* (2012). Both were published under the auspices of the English Folk Dance and Song Society.[21]

The documentation of the development of rapper is very similar to that of long sword and of eighteenth-century sword dancing. Again, there are a number of brief comments or longer citations by antiquarians, folklore collectors, memoirists, and so forth, throughout the nineteenth century. They come from a well-defined area: Tyneside, around

Newcastle-upon-Tyne on both the Northumberland and Durham sides, and south into Durham past Sunderland. This covers much of the same general area as the reports by Wallis and Brand in 1769–1778.

The nineteenth-century accounts repeat certain important features. They concern Christmastime sword dancing by costumed men and boys, fools and Bessies, money collecting, travelling, and so on. An important new element is that these reports consistently mention pitmen and miners from the coal mining villages in the region. More information appears as the nineteenth century wears on. The nature of the record changes when Sharp's *Sword Dances* appears. As in the case of long sword, this collection presents the first systematic picture of the style. Sharp includes five dances, all of which were still performed.

It was only in the 1950s that researchers revisited the villages where rapper was or had been well known. Bill Cassie, E.C. Cawte, Brian Hayden, and Les Williamson published a series of articles and booklets from the mid-1950s to the 1970s. The culmination of these efforts was Cawte's well-researched essay, 'A History of the Rapper Dance.' A good place to start is his basic description:

> A *rapper* is a strip of spring steel about two feet by 1 ¼ inches [60 × 3 cm], with a handle at each end. Usually the handles are of wood, and one handle has a loose central spindle, so that the blade can rotate while the handle is held firmly. The rapper dance is performed by five men, each holding his own rapper in his right hand, and his neighbour's in his left. Thus linked in a circle, they dance in various patterns so that the rappers are intertwined. Each pattern is called a *knot,* and ends by weaving the rappers into a five-pointed *star,* which is sometimes also called the *knot*.[22]

There are a few points to add to this. The dancing is unquestionably a spectacular style, in which novelty and ingenuity are prized. Older reports typically refer to the Christmas-New Year's season. There are groups of travelling, costumed miners, or pitmen; a couple of characters (a fool, Tommy, or Bessy) collecting money, and sometimes suffering a mock execution; the music consists of standard jig tunes; and often there are introductory songs.

Rapper has been characterized by speed (about 140–160 beats per minute), athleticism (including backward somersaults), and complexity of figures, but it is not known how long these characteristics have been associated with the dance. The stepping has often been remarked upon. At the turn of the twentieth century, shuffle steps were common. But then competitive cloggers became involved, and the standard became a crisp shuffle-tap step.

Perhaps the earliest reference is from ca. 1813, with a verse from the coal mining village of Winlaton, County Durham, which became well known for rapper. It was also the site of the Crowley steelworks, the largest in England at one time. By John Leonard, the poem is 'Winlaton Hopping,' the name of a local fair: 'With Box and Die You'd Sammy Spy / Of Late Sword dancers Bessy-O / All patch'd and torn with tail and horn / Just like a De'el in Dressy-O.'[23] This is intriguing, but it tells nothing about the style of sword dance. The fair took place in May, not the usual sword dancing season, but presumably a good occasion for performers to earn money.

One of the first published references to what is possibly rapper is by a musician, Robert Topliff. His *Selection of the Most Popular Melodies of the Tyne and the Wear* (printed ca. 1815–1820) has the song, 'The Sword Dancers,' with notes on the associated performance:

> The first that I call in, is a squire's son,
> He's like to lose his love, because he is too young,
> Altho he be too young, he has money for to rove,

And he'll freely spend it all, before he'll lose his love.
The next that I call in, he is a sailor bold,
He came to poverty by the lending of his gold.
The next that I call in he is a tailor fine,
What think you of his work, he made this coat of mine.
The next that I call in, he is a keelman grand,
He goes both fore and aft, with his long sett in his hand.

(Note.) After other characters are introduced in a similar manner, the sword-dance takes place, in which one of them is killed, and they again sing.

Alas our actor's dead, and on the ground he's laid,
Some of us must suffer for't young men, I'm sore afraid.
I am sure t'was none of me, that drew his sword so fine,
I'm sure 'twas none of me, I'm clear of the fact,
'Twas him that follows me, that did this bloody act.
Then cheer up my bonny lads and be of courage bold,
We'll take him to the church, and bury him in the mould.

(Note.) The doctor is introduced, and a dialogue of some length takes place, which terminates in his restoring the man to life, the ceremony concludes with the following verses, and a dance to the tune of Kity Bo Bo.

Cox Green's a bonny place, where water washes clean,
And Painshaw's on a hill, where we have merry been,
You've seen them all called in, you've seen them all go round.
Wait but a little while, some past time shall be found,
Then fiddler change the tune, play us a merry jig,
Before I will be beat, I'll pawn both hat and wig.[24]

Topliff, whose song and comments were also used by later writers, continues:

This ceremony, which in its origin is extremely remote, is performed chiefly by pitmen, who at Christmas, emerge from their subterraneous employ, forming themselves into parties, each having a sword by his side, and decorated with all the varied coloured ribbons of his mistress, resort to the more populous towns, whereby their performance, in which they display numberless feats of activity, excite the liberality of the inhabitants. The fool and bessy are two of the most conspicuous characters in this motly group. 'Tis there's [sic] by grimace, gesticulation, and vulgar witticisms to provoke the risible faculties of their audience, and to collect at the end of the entertainment, a reward for their exertions; they have with them a fiddler who accompanies the song in unison with the voice, repeating at the end of each stanza, the latter part of the air, forming an interlude between the verses; during which, the characters are introduced by the singer, make their bow and join the circle, which in deference to their finery, abbreviates the performance.[25]

The type of sword is not described. But the dancers (miners), and the area (the [between the] rivers Tyne and Wear, and the Sunderland area of northeastern County Durham), are the same as for eventual rapper.

The 1902 edition of James Edward Vaux's *Church Folk Lore* provides a report from about 1830 which refers to the swords being of 'flexible iron, with a handle at each end.'[26] It is unfortunate that the dating is imprecise, such recollections being notoriously difficult to trust. But if this report does indeed refer to ca. 1830, it would be the earliest known reference to flexible, two-handled swords used in dancing.

An interesting reference comes from *The Penny Magazine* in 1839.

> There is a curious and ancient game or custom prevalent among the coal-miners of Northumberland and Durham, which, as it is peculiar to these counties, and, perhaps, little known beyond them, it may be interesting to describe. In the places where this Game is practised, it is called 'sword-dancing,' from the circumstance of the performers have each an instrument resembling a sword in appearance, but more elastic, with which they contrive to exhibit many curious feats and figures whilst they are dancing.
>
> With the northern coal-miners, sword-dancing is a Christmas game. It is not, however, practised by them for mere amusement altogether, but partly with the view of making a little money. For this purpose, these sword-dancers, during the Christmas holidays, make excursions among the neighbouring towns and villages in companies of from twenty to thirty in number, where they exhibit their dancing skill. Besides the dancers, there are always two other individuals connected with this, called respectively the *Bessy* and the *Fool*; the former of whom is dressed in petticoats, and in other respects disguised as an old woman; and the latter in the most grotesque costume that can possibly be imagined, -- composed, usually, of the skins of animals. Each of these two personages is provided with an iron or tin box, with which, accompanied with a number of odd gestures, they solicit donations from the by-standers, whilst their brethren are dancing. There is also another person attached to those strolling companies of sword dancers in the capacity of Fiddler. A peculiarity in the dress of the dancers remains to be noticed. Their hats, and the sleeves and breasts of their jackets, are profusely decorated with cockades, made of ribbons of the gayest hues, which give them a picturesque appearance.
>
> Formerly, sword-dancing was a very popular amusement among the coal miners of Northumberland and Durham, during the festive season of Christmas, but it is now but very partially practised by them; and, like many of their pastimes, is gradually giving way to more rational pursuits.[27]

The account printed in William Henderson's *Notes on the Folk Lore of the Northern Counties of England and the Borders* (1866) might be the first recognizable description of rapper.

> But a Christmas in the North would be quite incomplete without a visit from sword-dancers, and this may yet be looked for in most of our towns from the Humber to the Cheviot Hills. There are some trifling local variations both in dance and song: the latter has altered with the times, the former is plainly a relic of the war-dances of our Danish and Saxon ancestors. I had an opportunity last spring of making enquiries into the mysteries of sword-dance from a pitman of Houghton Colliery, Houghton-le-Spring, Joseph Brown by name, and will simply relate what I heard from him on the subject. He was well qualified to speak, having acted as sword-dancer during the past twelve years, in company with eight other men, nine being the number always employed. Five are dancers, one a clothes-carrier, two clowns, and one a fiddler.

The verses are familiar introductory ones, though King George and the King of Sicily now appear with the squire's son, Little Foxey, and a 'pitman bold,' who 'works all underground.' The dancers step forward, in turn:

> The five men then commence dancing round, with their swords all raised to the centre of the ring, till the first clown orders them to tie the points of their swords in 'the knot.'

When this is done, and the five swords are knotted, the knot is held upright by one of the dancers, who they call Alexander, or Alick. Alick then takes his sword from the knot, and retaining it, gives the second dancer his sword; then the second dancer gives the third dancer his sword, the third dancer gives it to the fourth, and the fourth to the fifth.

The first clown, called the Tommy, is dressed in a chintz dress with a belt, a fox's head for a cap, and the skin hanging down below his shoulders.

The second clown, called the Bessey, wears a woman's gown, which of late years has been well crinolined, and a beaver hat.

The five dancers have black breeches, with red stripes at the sides, white shirts decked with gay ribbons, and hats surmounted with streamers.

The dance corresponds most remarkably with the account given by Olaus Magnus of the sword-dance of ancient Goths and Swedes.[28]

Several references appear through the last decades of the century, including mentions of competitions among multiple teams,[29] but the emerging pictorial evidence is particularly interesting. The most important example is a picture by Ralph Hedley, supposed to show the Earsdon dancers, ca. 1880, at Tanfield, south of Newcastle. Five dancers making the 'knot,' with flexible swords, are shown clearly. Joseph Crawhall has a depiction of a two-handled, rapper-style 'sword' in 'The Sword Dancers' section of his mock chapbook, *Olde Ffrendes with Newe Faces* (1883). Another picture is more problematic; versions of it were published by Crawhall in 1883, and in the *Transactions of the Northumbrian Small Pipes Society* in 1894. There are differences between the two versions, but they both appear to show four linked dancers. It is not clear whether the 'swords' are flexible and two-handled. The Society's picture is claimed to be a copy of an old woodcut, depicting a sword dance of the early nineteenth century, though the original has not been identified with certainty. Cawte, however, thinks that 'there is no reason to doubt' the existence of an earlier picture on which both are based.[30]

Further reports are known from around the turn of the century. High points for Earsdon, which became the best known team, came in the years 1906–1908 when they danced for King Edward VII and the future George V, after which they added 'Royal' to their team name. These shows took place at Alnwick Castle, farther north in Northumberland where, according to the local tradition, the team had been performing since earlier in the nineteenth century.

Cawte examines the history of the steel industry in Tyneside in the eighteenth and nineteenth centuries. He shows that suitable steel for the dancing could have been available in the eighteenth century, certainly by the period 1800–1830. He concludes: 'It seems reasonably certain that the origin of the rapper dance lies in the relationship between the steel and coal industries in eighteenth century Tyneside.'[31]

The term 'rapper' has proved untraceable. Accounts in the nineteenth century refer to 'swords' and 'sword dancers,' and Sharp may have been the first to use the word 'rapper' in print in connection with the dance. Probably this represents a misunderstanding deriving from Sharp's inability to understand a local dialect term. In 1890, Richard Oliver Helsop's dialect glossary, *Northumberland Words,* refers to 'rapper' as a 'knocker' or 'a lever at the top of a shaft or inclined plane.' He also states that '*Sword-Dancers*' are 'companies of men, in fantastic dress, who annually perform. They are armed with 'wafters,' which are held aloft and then woven into intricate forms in the dance.' As for 'wafters,' he describes these as 'swords with blunt edges for performances. The swords used by Northumberland sword-dancers are of this character, with handles at each end.'[32] But this is the only reference to 'wafters.'

In fact, the origins of both the 'swords' and of the term 'rapper' remain uncertain. Sharp's descriptions of these implements deserve to be looked at as a group. The rappers seem not to have been standardized. The first account comes from his description of the Swalwell team and dance:

> Each dancer carries a sword, twenty-eight inches [71 cm] in length, called a rapper. The blade, which is without a point, is made of thin, finely tempered steel, and is twenty-two inches long by one and three quarters wide [56 x 4.5 cm]. At one end a round wooden handle, six inches [15 cm] long, is loosely fitted so as to allow the metal haft, attached to the blade, to revolve freely within it; upon each side of the other end two thin blocks of wood, two inches [5 cm] long and of the same width as the blade, are firmly riveted or bound with cord. The rapper is as flexible as a harlequin's wand, to which shape it bears some resemblance.[33]

The 'swords' of other teams visited by Sharp, and from later accounts, have a similar improvised feel to them, in some cases made from discarded saw blades, evidently in mine workshops.[34]

All of Sharp's published descriptions were of dances that were still being performed. The end of the nineteenth century and the first third of the twentieth seem to have represented rapper's heyday in Northumberland and Durham. Four of Sharp's five dances come from the immediate Tyneside area, around Newcastle. These are Earsdon and North Walbottle (the latter actually more associated with Westerhope) on the Northumberland side, and Swalwell and Winlaton from Durham. All were coal mining villages, and the dancers evidently all worked in that industry, or were members of miners' families. Sharp's fifth report comes from the village of Beadnell, 50 miles up the Northumberland coast from Newcastle. Various terms were used for the dancers, including 'guizards' from Swalwell and Earsdon, or 'morris dancers' from Earsdon, but 'sword dancers' still seems a common term, as it was in the nineteenth century.

The typical performance as reported by Sharp is quite consistent. The established period for dancing is from Christmas Eve to New Year's Day, with different teams reporting particular days. The performance often begins with an introductory song, such as the one reported by Topliff. There are five actual dancers (though a sixth or seventh might step in), plus usually a fool and Bessy doing the collecting; the music is a medley of jig tunes, whether on fiddle, accordion, concertina, or whistle; and the costumes are quite elaborate. The dancers move at a fast pace; Sharp reports 140–160 beats per minute.

Information on stepping styles varies. Sharp says that:

> the performers [...] step, or tramp, in time with the music, taking two short, decided steps to each bar. At the end of [...] each section [...] the performers stand still and 'step' as in the Grenoside [long sword] dance.[35]

This would mean a running step in moving figures, and a shuffle in place. But it is also known that in some places around this time, under the influence of competitive clogging, the step was becoming a more difficult and exciting shuffle-tap step. Sharp's comments, and others', show that the step varied quite a bit. However, about this time, thanks to competitive cloggers such as the Earsdon captain, George Osborne (or Osborn), the step became a more important element.

The structure of rapper dances consists of distinct sections ending with a lock of swords, which is often called the 'nut' or 'knot.' An important element is novel ways of tying the 'nut' or 'knot,' which can then be held up and displayed to the audience. Despite the distinct sections or figures, the dance is continuous, and the overall impression is that of tight formations of dancers moving from figure to figure at high speed.

The costumes of the teams described by Sharp are remarkable. They reinforce the idea of rapper dancing as a spectacular display. For Swalwell:

> The dancers wear white shirts, decorated with red, white, and blue rosettes; a red tie, and a sash or belt of the same colour round the waist; dark trousers, or sometimes, white overalls with a red stripe down each leg [...] I am told that about fifty years ago, instead of trousers they wore breeches and white stockings, with ribbons tied round the knees.[36]

Earsdon had new outfits since performing for the King, with 'crimson plush breeches, white linen shirts, a Zouave jacket of crimson plush edged with gold braid, and a broad toreador sash.' But ca. 1880, they wore 'white shirts decorated with bows and rosettes with coloured ribbons, black breeches with alpaca or satinet, knee-ribbons and striped stockings and shoes tied with ribbons.' (This seems to match Hedley's picture.) The Beadnell dancers wore 'blue jerseys and navy blue cloth trousers, and wear, over one shoulder and breast, single baldrics or sashes with pink silk or sateen, four or five inches wide, upon which several large rosettes of different colours are shown.' Winlaton has 'white shirts, sparsely decorated front and back with ribbons, dark trousers and belt.' Finally, North Walbottle wears 'white cambric shirts with a sailor-knotted tie of velvet, violet velveteen breeches, white stockings of rough texture, black shoes, and a broad sash of yellow sateen round the waist, tied in a bow over the left hip.'[37]

Sharp's comments evaluating the significance of rapper are characteristic of his way of thinking.

> [Rapper] must have been the product of extraordinarily ingenious minds, and it is not easy, therefore, to explain its genesis by any theory of evolution. It would be easier to postulate the direct personal influence of some ingenious individual, and that at a comparatively late period.
>
> The Northumberland and Durham dances, though extremely interesting, are, it seems to me, in a sense decadent. There is a kind of perverse ingenuity about them, a striving for effect in detail at the expense of broader features, which is very closely parallel to the rather tortured cleverness of art, or of literature, which has begun to go downhill. Markedly decadent, too, are the rappers, subordinated to the purposes of complex motion until they have lost nearly all the character of the sword [...] [The] Yorkshire dances [i.e., long sword] should, I think, be placed higher in artistic and traditional truth [...][38]

Leaving aside perversity, decadence, and truth, we can see that Sharp makes several good points. He suggests that rapper dancing is a relatively recent invention; that it is a spectacular and complex style; and that the rappers were developed to support 'the purposes of complex motion.' He may well be right, when he refers to an 'ingenious individual.' One can imagine a nineteenth-century Tyneside pitman with some experience in Christmastime sword dancing picking up a saw blade or some other two-feet piece of flexible steel and having a moment of inspiration.

It must be emphasized that the early reports of miners' sword dancing in Northumberland or Durham do not necessarily refer to the rapper dance, as it was known by Sharp's day.

Rigid swords like those of Yorkshire long sword dances may have been used for some time. Like the eighteenth-century dances, the style of the dancing remains uncertain through the early and middle decades of the nineteenth century in Tyneside. Perhaps both rigid and flexible sword surrogates were in use.

But, at some point, flexible, two-handled metal 'swords' began to be used in the dances. The use of such implements, which opened up new possibilities for movements and figures, combined with fast stepping and jig tunes, dancers wearing fancy costumes, and songs and comic characters, caught the imaginations of the miners and their audiences. By the last quarter of the nineteenth century, rapper was well known, and probably had become the sole style of sword dancing in the area. Cawte identifies 13 villages which probably had teams before 1900 (Earsdon and Winlaton, first of all) and 14 in the years 1900–1914.

Conclusion

Reports of sword dances from the late eighteenth to the early twentieth century in England concern three distinct groups: sword dancing in the late eighteenth century, in various places, including Lincolnshire and Cumberland as well as Yorkshire and Tyneside; the style known chiefly from Yorkshire in the nineteenth and early twentieth centuries, which came to be termed long sword; and the style from Northumberland and Durham in the nineteenth and early twentieth centuries, called, at least since Cecil Sharp's day, rapper.

In the last third of the eighteenth century, reports of sword dancing began to appear with some frequency. Some came from Tyneside, from Northumberland and County Durham. The information agrees on a number of points: region, venue, period and occasion, music, costumes, money collecting, and related customs. Little is known of the actual dances; in some accounts linking is suggested, or a lock of swords may be formed. Dances seen in York, Lincolnshire, or Cumberland, may or may not be related to the Tyneside ones. Regardless, we have a cluster of reports which show a northern English custom of Christmas-New Year-Plough Monday sword dancing, focused in Tyneside. In these reports, costumed villagers, men and boys, travel around, and perform, collecting money or 'gifts.' They might perform for distinguished audiences. These early reports were written by educated people, outsiders to the performances by virtue of their education and rank, but also with local ties. They usually regarded the dances as 'old,' though not all say this, and in any case it is not clear what this might mean. Thus, in the late eighteenth century, sword dancing, perhaps of linked varieties, was known in parts of northern England. But it is hard to say anything more definite, with respect to the dancing's development or connections.

There are almost no reports from the late 1780s until the second decade of the nineteenth century. After that a fair amount of information comes from Yorkshire, where there is a consistent pattern of development through the nineteenth and into the twentieth century. Sword dancing is now often connected with the custom of plough dragging, or the 'plough stots.' The dancing is found over large parts of Yorkshire, including the Whitby district in the northeast, and other sections of the East, North, and West Ridings, the suburbs of Sheffield providing late instances. It remains a wintertime custom, young men and boys using the performances to collect money. Details of the dancing itself are limited, but some reports refer to linking during the dancing, and to the swords being locked together as a climax to the show. It is only from the research contained in Sharp's *Sword Dances* that it is possible to survey the existing situation. Many reports also come from farther north, in Northumberland and County Durham, where at some point in the nineteenth century the remarkable style which came to be known as rapper developed. In the early twentieth century, the research of Sharp and others made possible both the codification of these styles and the teaching of them in new regions and to new groups.

What were the key factors in the development of the northern English styles? We can disregard ideas of ancient ritual survivals, Romans, Saxons, Norse, and the like. It is clear that English styles of linked sword dancing were the products of modern ingenuity.

E.C. Cawte's published model of the development of rapper dancing actually concerns English styles of sword dancing in general. He seeks connections between the Tyneside steel industry and the coal miners who became the exclusive performers of rapper in the nineteenth and early twentieth centuries. He is probably right that rapper's immediate origins lie there. More problematic are his views on the chronology of rapper, and on this style's development from Yorkshire long sword styles. He says:

1   The rapper [implement] was in use around 1830, and probably about 1810.
2   There was a sword dance of some type [in Tyneside] about 1769, and probably for 60 years before that.[39]

The first point is derived from sources such as Topliff's and others' written references, and the recollections published by Vaux (which, while referring to perhaps 1830, were not published until 1902). But only Vaux clearly mentions flexible dance implements, and other reports show only that some sort of sword dancing existed. Cawte's second point seems to refer to John Wallis, who was born in 1714. Cawte uses these points to suggest that sword dancing came to Tyneside in the early eighteenth or even in the seventeenth century, perhaps with immigrants from Yorkshire who worked in the steel industry. He believes that they introduced a dance style using rigid swords, which developed into rapper in the eighteenth or early nineteenth century, when flexible sword surrogates became available.[40] The chief problem with this chronology is that it ignores the fact that sword dance was established in Tyneside before it was widely reported in Yorkshire. Further, the only early (1775–1789) Yorkshire reference comes from the city of York.

Models can be proposed for the development of long sword and rapper dancing that fit the available evidence better, and that suggest more probable explanations for relationships between the different styles. Despite the lack of definite documentation, the following is one that I would suggest (with, of course, the proviso that there may be as yet unidentified evidence that would change it significantly).

1   A sword dance style developed in Northumberland, specifically Tyneside, in the eighteenth century. It presumably used rigid swords of some sort, because flexible steel strips (as Cawte shows) would not have been readily available to villagers performing the dance. Its character as a dance style remains unknown, though linking as an important element has been assumed by later writers, and the use of locked swords for display could be found in some cases. It is unknown whether this Tyneside style was related to other dances of the eighteenth century, such as the Revesby, Cumberland, or York reports.
2   This eighteenth-century Tyneside style was the ancestor of the styles that became known, thanks to Cecil Sharp, as long sword and rapper. Sword dancing was well known in northern Yorkshire by the second decade of the nineteenth century; perhaps it spread there directly from Tyneside across a wide area, or else was brought first to York and spread from there. In Yorkshire, it developed into a distinctive style, or clusters of styles, using rigid swords of metal or wood.

3   In Tyneside and Durham, coal miners took over Christmastime sword dancing in the nineteenth century. The first mention of flexible, two-handled sword surrogates may date to around 1830, but by the 1880s they were widely used and had replaced any possible competing styles. These flexible instruments may have been derived from saw blades or some other sort of scrap metal, or from other specific tools.

4   In the early twentieth century, Sharp and others visited the areas where long sword and rapper were known (if not under those names) and wrote down, published, and taught versions of the dances, disseminating them to new regions and new social groups. Folk dance festivals, which were often competitive in nature, also played important roles in the development of these styles in the early decades of the twentieth century. One way or another, the styles became codified.

This model fits the chronology and geography of the documentary evidence relatively well. An assumption on which it is based is that, while long sword and rapper in the twentieth century are very different from one another as styles of dance, they are, in fact, related. This seems probable from their closeness in terms of both the time and locations of their development. There are general stylistic similarities, such as the use of a circle as the base figure, and the small number of dancers. Moreover, the customs which frame both styles – the season, the characters, the songs – are much the same, and connect both long sword and rapper to the late eighteenth-century reports as well.

This model suggests that both styles may have developed as nineteenth-century innovations. Many accounts, from Sharp's day onwards, have seen long sword as the older of the two, and indeed as the ancestor of rapper. But this assumption is not based on documentary evidence. Rather, it seems to rely on the fact that, with its slower movements and use of rigid swords, long sword simply seems 'older' than fast and flashy rapper dancing – the latter, moreover, using flexible sword substitutes that could not have been available before the nineteenth century. In fact, Yorkshire long sword may have been as innovative a style as rapper in the nineteenth century. Presumably the eighteenth-century Tyneside dances used some sort of rigid swords or surrogates, but this does not mean they cannot be the ancestor of both styles.

Other models are possible. Perhaps long sword and rapper arose from separate ancestors: long sword from a Yorkshire style of the eighteenth century (documented only in York), and rapper from the eighteenth-century Tyneside styles. In this case, resemblances would be the result of chance, of the requirements imposed by the use of linked swords of whatever type, and of borrowings both between styles and from the larger stock of English folk culture.

Geography presents difficult problems for any models. For example, if that postulated here is correct, how did the style move from Tyneside to Yorkshire, leaving a sizable gap consisting of most of County Durham? But there appears to be no available evidence to support the idea that Yorkshire long sword could be the ancestor of the eighteenth-century Tyneside dances, or later Northumberland and Durham rapper. The chronology does not fit – that is, sword dancing seems to have been established in Tyneside before Yorkshire; and the same geographical objections arise if movement from Yorkshire to Tyneside is assumed. These models do not refer to other English sword dance styles. The Revesby dance seems isolated; and there is almost no information on the Cumberland dances.

Notes

1. John Wallis, *The Natural History and Antiquities of Northumberland, and So Much of the County of Durham as Lies between the Rivers Tyne and Tweed, Commonly Called, North Bishoprick*, 2 vols. (London: Printed for the author by W. and W. Strahan, 1769), pp. 2, 28–29.
2. John Brand, *Observations on the Popular Antiquities of Great Britain, Including the Whole of Mr. Bourne's Antiquitates Vulgares, with Addenda to Every Chapter of That Work, as Also, an Appendix, Containing Some Articles on the Subject, as Have Been Omitted by That Author* (Newcastle-upon-Tyne: Printed by T. Saint, for J. Johnson, 1777), pp. 175–178.
3. Ibid., p. 179.
4. This is excerpted from T. Fairman Ordish, "Morris Dancers at Revesby," *Folk-Lore Journal*, 7 (1889), pp. 340–353. For the same material, with some variations, see John Ledbury, "An Examination of the Continuing Tradition of Longsword Dancing in Yorkshire by Means of Analysis of Documentary Evidence and Case Studies of Three Recently Formed Dance Teams" (M.A. thesis, University of Sheffield, 1991), p. 37.
5. Thomas Pettitt, "English Folk Drama in the Eighteenth Century: A Defense of the Revesby Sword Play," *Comparative Drama*, 15 (1981), p. 3. Pettitt has recently reconsidered the Revesby material: see "Beyond the Bad Quarto: Exploring the Vernacular Afterlife of Early Modern Drama," *Journal of Early Modern Studies*, 8 (2019), 133–171 as has Peter Harrop in *Mummers' Plays Revisited* (Abingdon: Routledge, 2020), pp. 83–91.
6. Nathan Drake, *Shakespeare and His Times* (Paris: [s.n.], 1838), pp. 66–67.
7. Keith Gregson, "A Cumbrian Sword Dance," *English Dance and Song*, 42.2 (1980), p. 9.
8. Michael Heaney, "Folk Dance and Theatrical Performance in the Eighteenth Century," *Folk Music Journal*, 11.2 (2017), pp. 223–225.
9. For references to Derbyshire, see David Thompson, "By Laying the Swords Cross-bladed on the Ground and Dancing in an Out before Beginning Their Hand Play in the Air," *Morris Dancer*, 4.1 (January 2009), pp. 12–15; and Paul Davenport, "Sword Dance in Derbyshire," *Rattle Up, My Boys: A Quarterly Publication for Those with an Interest in Sword Dancing*, ser. 25.1 (November 2017), pp. 6–8.
10. "Mode of Celebrating Christmas in Yorkshire," *The Gentleman's Magazine*, 81.1 (May 1811), pp. 423–424.
11. George Young, *A History of Whitby, and Streoneshalh Abbey, with a Statistical Survey of the Vicinity to the Distance of Twenty-Five Miles*, 2 vols. (Whitby: Clark and Medd, 1817), vol. 2, pp. 880–881. Egton Bridge is a village on the main road through the valley of the River Esk, running westwards into the North Yorkshire Moors from Whitby and the village of Sleights.
12. E.C. Cawte, "The Riccall Sword Dance," *Folk Music Journal*, 2.2 (1971), pp. 104–106; and Ivor Allsop, *Longsword Dances from Traditional and Manuscript Sources*, edited by Anthony G. Barrand (Brattleboro, Vermont: Northern Harmony, 1996), pp. 234–248.
13. Mrs. Gutch, ed., *Examples of Printed Folk-Lore concerning the East Riding of Yorkshire* (London: Nutt, 1912), pp. 88–89.
14. Norman Peacock, "Report on the Contents of a Parcel Marked 'Sword Dance Information sent to C# [i.e., Cecil Sharp]'," app. 6, p. 3, Vaughan Williams Memorial Library. Peacock published a summary: "Sword Dance Information Sent to Cecil Sharp," *Journal of the English Folk Dance and Song Society*, 8.2 (December 1957), pp. 113–114.
15. Peacock, "Report," app. 1.
16. Ibid., p. 2.
17. Michael Heaney, "Disentangling the Wychwood Morrises," *Traditional Dance*, 3 (1985), pp. 44–81.
18. Cecil J. Sharp, *Sword Dances of Northern England Together with the Horn Dance of Abbots Bromley* (London: English Folk Dance and Song Society, 1985), pt. 2, pp. 12–27 ("decided march") p. 17, song, p. 18.
19. For a fuller and more recent description, see Allsop, *Longsword Dances*, pp. 263–274.
20. See E.C. Cawte, "Watching Cecil Sharp at Work: A Study of his Records of Sword Dances Using His Field Notebooks," *Folk Music Journal*, 8.3 (2003), p. 288; and Phil Heaton, *Rapper: The Miners' Sword Dance of North-east England* (London: EFDSS, 2012), p. 64.
21. See E.C. Cawte, "A History of the Rapper Dance," *Folk Music Journal*, 4.2 (1981), pp. 79–116; and Heaton, *Rapper*.

22 Cawte, "History," p. 81.
23 E.C. Cawte, *Rapper at Winlaton in 1955* (Ibstock, Leics.: Guizer, [1955?]), p. 5.
24 Robert Topliff, *A Selection of the Most Popular Melodies of the Tyne and the Wear: Consisting of 24 Original Airs Peculiar to the Counties of Durham & Northumberland* (London: [R. Topliff], n.d. [ca. 1815–1820]), p. 42.
25 Ibid., p. 42.
26 James Edward Vaux, *Church Folk Lore: A Record of Some Post-Reformation Usages in the English Church, Now Mostly Obsolete* (London: Skeffington, 1902), p. 291.
27 "Sword-Dancing in Northumberland (from a Correspondent)," *The Penny Magazine* (23 March 1839), pp. 111–112.
28 William Henderson, *Notes on the Folk Lore of the Northern Counties of England and the Borders* (London: Longmans, Green, 1866), pp. 51–53.
29 For example, see Gordon Ridgewell, "A Cluster of Nineteenth-century Sword Dance Competitions," *Folk Music Journal*, 1.1 (2016), pp. 67–70.
30 For Hedley's picture, see Sharp, Sword *Dances,* pt. 1, frontispiece. For a detailed discussion, see Eddie Cass, "Ralph Hedley and His Sword-Dance Paintings," *Folk Music Journal*, 8.3 (2003), pp. 335–344. See also Joseph Crawhall, "The Sword Dancers," in his *Olde Ffrendes wyth Newe Faces, Adorn'd with Sutable Sculptures* (London: Field and Tuer, 1883). On the pictures published by Crawhall and the Small Pipes Society, see Cawte, "History," pp. 84–85.
31 Cawte, "History," pp. 106–107.
32 Richard Oliver Heslop, *Northumberland Words: A Glossary of Words Used in the County of Northumberland and on the Tyneside* (Vaduz: Kraus, 1965, repr. of London: Published for the English Dialect Society by Paul, Trench, Trubner, 1892–1894), pp. 516, 714, 762.
33 Sharp, *Sword Dances,* pt.1, p. 73.
34 Ibid., pt. 1, pp. 73, 83, pt. 2 p. 39, pt. 3, pp. 92, 103.
35 Ibid., pt. 1, p. 73.
36 Ibid., pt. 1, p. 72.
37 Ibid., p. 1, pp. 82–83, pt. 2, p. 39, pt. 3, pp. 92, 103. On miners' colourful holiday dress, see "All Dressed Up," *The Nut*, 3 (February 1994).
38 Sharp, *Sword Dances*, pt. 1, pp. 70–71.
39 Cawte, "History," p. 109.
40 Ibid., p. 105.

11

FROM COUNTRY GARDENS TO BRITISH FESTIVALS

The morris dance revival, 1886–1951

Matt Simons

The morris revival of the late nineteenth and early twentieth centuries was a complex and dynamic process of retrieval and invention. What began in the 1880s, deriving impetus from Victorian appetites for expositions of 'Merrie England' by 1914 constituted a national movement with the support of the Board of Education. The early successes of the revival depended on a popular belief that the dances contained 'sacred English truths', crystallised through centuries of transmission.[1] This chapter is concerned exclusively with the variety of morris dancing now commonly described as the 'Cotswold' or 'South Midlands' style, a form based on dances and tunes retrieved from informants in Gloucestershire and Oxfordshire and nearby counties in the early decades of the twentieth century.[2] In the nascent folk revival of the early twentieth century, this form of morris was preeminent. Regrettably, space does not permit for any comparison with the contemporaneous revival and development of morris dancing in the towns of Cheshire and Lancashire, which began in the 1920s and remained quite independent of the revival championed by the English Folk Dance Society (EFDS).[3] This chapter not only provides a chronological overview of the morris revival based on a synthesis of recent scholarship, but also offers an exploration of the highly contested nature of the dances' authenticity.

For convenience, the chapter is divided into a series of phases. After a brief overview of the history of morris from the fifteenth to the late nineteenth century, the first phase encompasses the 1880s–1890s, decades characterised by antiquarianism and 'Merrie England' pageantry. This section focusses on the work of D'Arcy Ferris and Percy Manning in Warwickshire and Oxfordshire, respectively. The second phase is that of 1905–1918, which saw the beginnings of a national revival propagated by the Espérance Club and later the EFDS. It was during this period that the majority of the collecting work took place. Cecil Sharp's view that the morris represented a highly sophisticated dance, akin to an art form, was consciously moulded from his outright rejection of the 'Merrie England' variety willingly embraced by Mary Neal and members of the Espérance Club.[4] The third phase from 1919 to 1929 was one of consolidation and diversification, as the ranks of the EFDS swelled and folk dancing became more firmly entrenched in the national consciousness. The penultimate section concerns the promotion of men's morris during the period 1930–1944, giving rise to the foundation of the Morris Ring in 1934 for the promotion of men's morris clubs.

A final section takes us from the end of the Second World War in Europe in 1945 into the emergence from austerity in the 1950s, with particular attention on the events organised to coincide with the Festival of Britain in 1951.

Precursor to revival

In 1911, an early collector of morris dances, John Graham, wrote 'the worth of morris dances was only appreciated fully when they were dying'.[5] In the decades which preceded Graham's comment, the dances seemed to have all but disappeared, so collectors and revivalists working in the 1900s set about piecing together fragments of an activity which in many places had not been seen for many years. Despite a few brief resurgences of interest in the 1880s, the morris dances of the English south midlands were in a terminal state of decline from the mid-nineteenth century.[6] It was not simply the disappearance of the dances themselves which caused panic among the newly formed communities of collectors and enthusiasts, but the erosion of English village life, to which they were inextricably linked. Perceived as the 'cell from which English society had been built up', the fate of England seemed intertwined with the state of its villages.[7] Thus, the demise of morris dancing was a symptom of a wider decline in rural village life. As Rolf Gardiner described, 'The glory of old England was expressed by this dance, the nostalgia for the England of the Cotswold countryside doomed to die'.[8] Eighteenth- and nineteenth-century enclosures carved up and privatised vast tracts of land, effectively forcing many thousands of people away from agricultural work to throw in their lot and relocate to the industrial towns and cities.[9] Even for those who were not necessarily pushed, in many cases 'rural roots were something to escape, not something to glorify'.[10] At the same time, as fashions of the rural elite and the labouring poor became increasingly polarised, the gentry turned away from the older sports taking with them their patronage.[11] In the latter half of the nineteenth century, morris dancing became both unfashionable and undesirable. Deprived of patronage and willing participants, the dances faded into obsolescence. Without the intervention of outsiders, seeking to capture virtues in old ways of living, morris dancing in the English south midlands may well have faded into total obscurity.

This largely rural phenomenon had not always been the reserve of countrymen: its long and chequered documented history describes a process of translation from the highest echelons of society to a rural plebeian sport. The recorded history of morris dancing in England begins with a payment to a company of morris dancers for their services on the Feast of St. Dunstan, made by the Goldsmiths Company of London in 1448.[12] Despite continuity in terminology, the form and contexts of the dance changed significantly over time. Many of the earliest records describe an entertainment most commonly found in the courts of royalty and nobility.[13] The dancers themselves were usually professional performers, and often received handsome financial rewards for their labours. In this context, the dances probably borrowed from other courtly performances, including those from other parts of Europe, especially pyrrhic entertainments such as the 'Moros y Christianos' and the 'Matachin'.[14] From the early sixteenth century, morris became a common feature in civic processions, grand demonstrations of cities' military force, and legitimacy of governance, which frequently incorporated a Feast of pageantry, pomp, and circumstance.[15] In these processions, the morris took 'martial and exotic' forms, often serving 'a kind of heralding function' attendant to dignitaries.[16] During the mid-sixteenth century, the church provided an important source of sponsorship for morris dancers. Indeed, John Forrest argues that ecclesiastical patronage may have prompted the translation of morris from a largely urban phenomenon to one associated with rural society.[17]

In this context, dancers were usually hired to perform at Church Ales, events designed to raise funds for the upkeep of the parish, principally through the sale of beer.

Puritanical suppression of morris and similar sports commenced in the mid-sixteenth century and gained momentum with the ascension of Elizabeth I to the throne in 1558. It was then further spurred on by zealous clergymen returning from exile in Europe imposed by the counter-reformations of Queen Mary. At this time, morris dancing became 'symbolic of all that was good or ill … depending on where you stood'.[18] Following decades of proscription and prosecutions, by the 1630s, ecclesiastical sponsorship of morris dancing had ceased, resulting in a consequent reduction in the number of recorded dance events. Though the restoration of Charles II in 1660 precipitated a corresponding enthusiasm for revivals of morris, these were in many cases short-lived resurgences. During the eighteenth century, sets of morris dancers became a ubiquitous feature of holiday entertainments throughout the counties of the English south midlands, especially at Whitsun. Dancers usually appeared at Whitsun Ales—secular versions of the earlier Church Ales—which were both 'formal, respectable, dignified, clean and sartorial' as well as 'noisy, animated, busy, [and] competitive'.[19] From the late nineteenth century, morris dancers also participated in events organised by friendly clubs and benefit societies, which adopted a sanitised version of the Whitsun Ales, indicating a widespread cultural trend towards more rational modes of recreation.[20]

Considering the motivations of performers in these contexts, Keith Chandler argues that the dancers were attracted by a combination of tangible benefits—such as the receipt of food, drink, and money—and the status conferred by other members of a community, as well as the bonhomie of a group activity.[21] Thus, Chandler argues that it was not until the folk music revival took sway that abstract appeals to tradition became a significant motivator for dancers. However, it might be countered that the defence of custom, perceived as the 'unwritten beliefs, sociological norms, and usages asserted in practice', was increasingly mobilised by members of the rural working class from the late eighteenth century as a bulwark against state intervention in their lives, especially enclosures.[22] Nevertheless, by the later decades of the nineteenth century, a growing antiquarian interest in old customs and practices emanating from a predominantly urban intelligentsia had set in motion a changing attitude towards morris dancing. The collective result of the work of various antiquarians throughout the nineteenth century was to abnegate the few remaining village sets as a degenerative form, unworthy of consideration.[23] By placing morris securely in the past, they provided a literary basis for theatrical reenactments of 'Merrie England'. Such performances of reconstructed morris dances were therefore both supported by scholarship, albeit of variable quality, and safely distanced from the 'disorderly revels' of more recent times.[24] Moreover, in invoking a timeless 'Merrie England', these performances offered a caricature of history which marked the past apart as a foreign place.

Antiquity and folklore, 1885–1904

The early revival was based on a heady mixing of popular literary myth and anthropological studies, which, according to Chandler, 'in form and content represented the ultimate triumph of "antiquity" over actuality'.[25] Early efforts to inspire a renewed interest in morris traded on popular motifs of 'Merrie England'. With the dances ensconced in a culturally pervasive idyll, early revivalists enjoyed a sense of legitimacy by hitching their efforts to a fashionable idea. Antiquarian studies of the late eighteenth and early nineteenth centuries provided a literary basis to these images. Among the most influential of pioneering antiquaries was Francis Douce who published a lengthy essay on the morris dance as an appendix to his study of 1807 tellingly entitled *Illustrations of Shakespeare and Ancient Manners*.[26] During the late Victorian period, theatrical representations of morris dancers borrowed from historical illustrations and descriptions offered by antiquarians such as Douce and his contemporary Joseph Strutt. As one enthusiast and supporter of the revival later wrote, dances of this kind were 'mummied in literary allusion'.[27] However, in the later decades of the nineteenth century, two men disrupted this precedent for superficial imitation. In 1885, a pageant-master by the name of D'Arcy Ferris instigated a revival of a morris side in Bidford-on-Avon comprising a team of 'rustics'. Forged out of a mixture of antiquarian studies and living informants, D'Arcy Ferris coloured their performances with the imagery of the Elizabethan 'Golden Age': the side was known as the Bidford Shakespearean Morris Dancers. More than a decade later, Percy Manning, a young Oxford-based antiquary of private means, set about collecting information and artefacts relating to the archaeology and folklore of Oxfordshire.[28] Though their methods represented new approaches, which combined fieldwork with performance, they did not directly challenge existing perceptions of 'Merrie England'. Indeed, D'Arcy Ferris positively embraced the idyll, and used it to his own advantage.

Ernest Richard D'Arcy Ferris was born in Bath on 2 April 1855, the son of an official in the Indian Civil Service. In 1885, he embarked upon a career as an organiser of fetes, festivals, and pageants. Embodying a quixotic combination of antiquary and showman, D'Arcy Ferris produced spectacular expositions on 'Merrie England'. Roy Judge described him as a 'full-blooded and thoroughgoing romantic'.[29] Dissatisfied with the vague allusions of antiquarian sources, in the autumn of 1885, Ferris began seeking out living informants with a view to staging a recreation of what he perceived to be the archetypal morris, which he hoped would inspire a national campaign to revive the dances.[30] He soon alighted upon Bidford-on-Avon, a village in southwest Warwickshire, seven miles downstream from Stratford-upon-Avon, where a morris side was known to have existed until the 1850s or 1860s. Resting heavily on Bidford's supposed links to Shakespeare, which centre around a series of infamous drinking competitions in which the Bard is thought to have participated, D'Arcy Ferris styled his new team as 'Shakespearean Morris Dancers'.[31]

The performances were evidently based on syncretic researches, gleaned from books and historical documents as well as the testimonies of old dancers and musicians. Through the course of their inquiries and performances, D'Arcy Ferris and the Bidford Morris succeeded in promoting a revival of interest in morris in several places, including nearby Ilmington. His side comprised a band of young men under the direction of a trainer, William Trotman, who had been a dancer in his youth in Oxfordshire and Gloucestershire.[32] In this role, Trotman received assistance from William Richardson, a veteran of an older Bidford side. During the first six months of 1886, the Shakespearean Bidford Morris Dancers appeared on some 28 occasions at 16 public halls and schoolrooms across the west midlands and occasionally further afield, in each case accompanied by a lecture delivered by D'Arcy Ferris, who also played the part of the 'Lord of Misrule'.[33] The performances were not frivolous, but intended as serious expositions—as one press report from the time described, 'the entertainment was not of the nature of a show or pantomime, but rather of an antiquarian character'.[34] Though the company enjoyed some notoriety with local audiences, outside their 'home' territory, the performances were generally less successful in provoking responses beyond those of faint interest and curiosity.[35]

Following a final concert in Malvern on 1 July 1886—about which one press article reported, 'Their entertainment was not one calculated to make the spectators ecstatic'—D'Arcy Ferris and the Bidford Morris parted company.[36] D'Arcy Ferris was disheartened by his failure to inspire a national revival and the financial disappointment of the enterprise. Nevertheless, the Bidford Morris continued for more than 20 years after his departure, making sporadic appearances in Warwickshire and Gloucestershire until the late 1900s, albeit with a hiatus in activity between the late 1890s and 1904.[37] The remarkable continuity in the core membership was surely testament to their cohesiveness as a group.[38] Scholars have demonstrated how difficult it is to disentangle D'Arcy Ferris' influence in the actual content and style of the dances. Though he sought to present the genuine article, evident in his insistence on the involvement of old dancers as teachers, the final product was perhaps too heavily influenced by his reading of antiquarian literature to be considered a faithful revival of village morris.[39]

Unlike D'Arcy Ferris, Percy Manning largely kept his informants at an arm's length, employing the services of an Oxfordshire labourer to act as his arbiter and collector of information and artefacts. Percy Manning was born on 24 January 1870 into a comfortably middle-class family in Headingley cum Burley, a suburb of Leeds. In 1888, he went up to New College Oxford, where he appears to have spent more time in practical archaeology than on his studies. After several failed exams and interruptions, Manning finally received his degree in 1896, and thereafter committed himself entirely to the independent pursuit of his many interests.[40] Strictly speaking, he was not a scholar but a collector, more concerned with the gathering of information and artefacts than with analysis.[41] He was principally concerned with the archaeology and folklore of the county which had become his home. Beginning in the summer of 1894, Manning conducted a series of enquiries into local morris sides, employing a local labourer, Thomas Carter, as his chief aide and broker. In total, Carter collated information on morris dancers from some 15 communities in Oxfordshire, recording details of their activities, including notes on their costumes, musical instruments, and events attended.[42] Spurred on by the discovery of a photograph of a team of morris dancers from Headington Quarry, a small mining community some three miles to the east of Oxford, Manning sent Carter to interview two members of the side. During two lengthy meetings in November 1897, Carter noted down several tunes from two members of the Trafford family, who had both been members of the team when it last appeared in the 1880s. Following these initial meetings, once again acting on Manning's instruction, Carter convinced the Traffords to arrange a revival of the team.

On 13 March 1899, Manning presented a concert of morris dances and 'old English ballads' at the Corn Exchange in Oxford, featuring the Headington Quarry side. In the lecture which accompanied the performance, Manning explained that he had not interfered with the dancers' rehearsals, stating that it was important to ensure 'there was no *possibility of contaminating the pure tradition*. That is the great danger of today'.[43] The concert proved an enormous success and received praise in the pages of the Oxford press. Undoubtedly buoyed by their experiences at the Corn Exchange, the Headington Quarry Morris made several further performances in 1899, including an appearance in the village at Whitsun and a return to Oxford in December for a fundraising concert at the Constitutional Hall.[44] Perhaps most notably of all, it was the Headington Quarry side, together with concertina player William Kimber, that Cecil Sharp witnessed on Boxing Day 1899, a most fateful encounter which arguably sowed the seeds for the national revival of morris dance from 1905. Notwithstanding the successes of D'Arcy Ferris and Manning in promoting a better appreciation for morris dancing in their respective localities, these efforts ultimately failed to inspire any sustained enthusiasm at a national level. However, their endeavours provided a vital foundation to the national revival which followed in the first decade of the new century. Both the Bidford and Headington Quarry teams played important roles in the nascent revival movement, only they lacked the agency and impetus in themselves to stimulate a national revival.

Towards a national movement

The early decades of the twentieth century marked a rapid growth in commercial entertainment, nurtured especially though not exclusively by the music halls. Commercial forms of music and dance attracted a national following, which reached practically every part of the country, becoming the phenomenon most closely resembling a 'genuinely popular' activity in Edwardian Britain.[45] Social dancing also enjoyed a growth in popularity during this period as a leisure pursuit.[46] Ballrooms and dance halls were spaces in which nearly everybody could perform in accordance with 'authentic, natural emotion', whilst also serving as important sites of sociability.[47] Set against this burgeoning appetite for novel forms of dance and music, the origins of the first national campaign to rescue and revive the ailing morris can be found in a mission based on moral and religious improvement, which looked to the past in search of a panacea for the plight of fracturing urban communities. The national revival of morris dancing began with the Espérance Club in north London in 1905. Instigated by the Club's co-founder, Birmingham-born Mary Neal, with assistance from Cecil Sharp and two members of the Headington Quarry Morris, morris dancing quickly became something of a national phenomenon. The Espérance Club performed the role of vital incubator to the gestative movement, with some of its members travelling across the country to provide tuition. Following a period of fruitful collaboration, from late 1907 the relationship between Neal and Sharp deteriorated into one of antagonistic opposition, manifest in a series of criticisms and reprisals acted out in the pages of the national press. Whilst Neal perceived morris as an idiom, embodying English characteristics and temperament, Sharp believed the dances represented something tantamount to a canon of national folk art. Though the former championed essence and context, the latter argued for the virtues of faithful adherence to technique. Neal's belief in the spiritual importance of morris—as a means of transcendence from stifling modernity—was far removed from Sharp's insistence on good taste. Imbued with the vestigial power of a forgotten ceremonial, Neal's dancers were perceived as agents in social and political change. As she wrote in 1911, 'we may find an inspiration which may help us to make England, the country of our love, a better and fairer land for the generations coming after'.[48]

Founded in November 1895 by Mary Neal and Emmeline Pethick, the Espérance Club aimed to provide a 'spiritual influence' for girls and young women of the working class in St. Pancras, north London.[49] Opening its doors each evening, the Club hosted a programme of activities designed to educate and amuse. Though Neal maintained overall control over their form and contents, the Club's members took a significant degree of personal responsibility for organising and running their own activities. The performance of English folk song was first introduced to the Club's programme in the autumn of 1905 by honorary musical director, Herbert MacIlwaine, who had read a feature on Cecil Sharp's work published in the *Morning Post*. In response to the apparent popularity of these songs, Neal wrote again to Sharp to ask for advice on dances. In return, Sharp informed her of the Headington Quarry Morris and his meeting with William Kimber in December 1899. Following an initial fruitless visit to Headington and a period of strained correspondence, Neal eventually succeeded in persuading Kimber and his cousin, Richard 'Dobbin' Kimber, to provide tuition for the Espérance Club at their Headquarters in Cumberland Market, St. Pancras.[50] After only two visits by the Kimbers during the winter of 1905–1906, the inaugural performance of morris dancing by members of the Espérance Club took place at the Passmore Edwards Settlement, on Tavistock Place, on 15 February 1906. The performance was witnessed by an audience of some 200, comprising Neal's friends and supporters, as well as families of its members.

Among those in attendance was E.V. Lucas, who wrote, 'These morris dances alone would draw me by invisible threads to any hall where they were given—not only for their own unusual alluringness and gaiety, but for their essential merrie Englandism'.[51] Following the success of this concert, Neal quickly organised a public performance, entitled *An English Pastoral*, which took place at the Queen's Hall on 3 April 1906.

Encouraged by Laurence Housman, Neal took a lead in the movement supported by her many allies, who included artists, writers, and politicians.[52] Within a year of the Queen's Hall concert, the Espérance Club introduced morris dancing classes to no fewer than eight counties—including Derbyshire, Devon, Monmouthshire, and Norfolk—as well as several other places in London.[53] From the ranks of young women, Neal appointed a number of instructors, the chief of which was Florence Warren, who was soon employed in this work on a full-time basis. In 1908, Warren was joined by one other full-time instructor, with a further nine engaged in part-time or evening work.[54] For instructors and performers, morris dancing offered young women of the working-class extraordinary opportunities, affording both agency and status. As Neal wrote:

> It is no small thing for a little London dressmaker to stay in the house, as an honoured guest, of a country squire, and ride in his motor car and feel at the same time that she too has something to give.[55]

Neal combined a 'philanthropic zeal and belief in the restorative power of old English culture' as a source of physical as well as mental education.[56]

In the first instance, it seems Sharp's contributions were limited to the provision of musical notation. Though he presented lectures alongside early Espérance performances, it seems these offered little more than elementary details, giving only their titles and a brief description of their form.[57] In the summer of 1906, Sharp began to carry out further investigations into the dances and tunes, and started to collect further material. On 2 June 1906, Neal, MacIlwaine, and Sharp attended a performance of the reformed Bidford Morris, hosted by Lady Isabel Margesson at her home, Foxlydiate House, in Redditch. Here, MacIlwaine and Sharp notated the dances and tunes.[58] The following month, on 5 July, Sharp happened to encounter two men mending the sewers outside his own house in Hampstead, one of whom, William Stagg, was whistling morris tunes. Sharp immediately recognised one of the tunes, 'Bell Isle's March', as a variant of 'Heel and Toe' which he had heard in Redditch.[59] Stagg not only gave Sharp six new versions of tunes recorded elsewhere, but a further nine tunes hitherto unknown to the collector.[60] Perhaps most important of all, Stagg provided him with the address of John Mason, resident of Stow-on-the-Wold Union workhouse, which facilitated four days of collecting in Gloucestershire in March 1907.[61]

In the same month as his serendipitous meeting with Stagg, Sharp and MacIlwaine began work on a handbook of dances and tunes to aid instructors and aspirant dancers. The first part of *The Morris Book* appeared in April 1907. In the introductory remarks, the authors state:

> We have been drawn to the publication of tunes and description of the old English Morris, not primarily for the information of the archaeologist and scholar, but to help those who may be disposed to restore a vigorous and native custom to its lapsed pre-eminence.[62]

This first volume contained notation for 11 dances, taken from the Bidford and Headington Quarry repertories, based on the dancing of Florence Warren. Circumstantial evidence suggests that MacIlwaine was responsible for the notation of dances and the majority of the commentary, whilst Sharp's contribution was limited to arranging the music.[63] A short chapter containing historical notes was followed by a bibliography full of antiquarian texts. Demand for information on morris dances soon required further publications. At around the same time as the appearance of the first part of *The Morris Book*, John Graham published a manual on the Bidford dances, entitled *Shakespearean Bidford Morris Dances*, followed in 1911 by *Lancashire and Cheshire Morris Dances*.[64]

Whilst these publications went some way in assisting many hundreds if not thousands in taking their first steps, both Neal and Sharp agreed that written instructions should only be used in support of demonstration and tuition. By 1907, demand for the services of the Espérance Club in providing instructors was frequently outstripping supply. In November of that year, Neal convened a conference at the Goupil Gallery on Regents Street, London, to discuss how she and her colleagues might collaborate to satisfy the nationwide fervour for morris dancing. This assembly turned out to be a momentous watershed in the relationship between Neal and Sharp, marking the first of a series of skirmishes which led to Sharp's departure from Neal and the Espérance Club. The crux of their disagreement lay in differing attitudes to the transmission of the dances themselves as well as their presentation. Referring to a cartoon and article published in the latest edition of *Punch* magazine, Sharp boldly stated, 'We do not seek to revive the Merrie England of the past, we want to create a Merry England of the present'.[65] Though the *Punch* article was wholly supportive of the revival movement, it emphasised the prevailing pastoral romanticism, choosing for its title 'Merrie England Once More'.[66] Neal later recalled Sharp's immediate response to seeing the article: 'as he looked at it I saw a sort of blind come down over his face'.[67] From this point onwards, Sharp became increasingly wary of allusions to the quaint and picturesque 'Merrie England'. He also began to distance himself from Neal and the Espérance Club.

In early 1908, a provisional committee appointed by the Goupil conference established an Association for the Revival and Practice of Folk Music, an organisation with the expressed support of representatives of the London County Council as well as a number of county education inspectors. In March 1910, the Association was superseded by the Espérance Guild of Morris Dancers, a title which suggested venerability. Through these organisations, which attracted supporters from across the country, Neal emphasised the importance of direct transmission, learning through imitation and intuition. In a letter to *The Observer*, printed soon after the incorporation of folk dance into the recommended curriculum of physical education for schools in 1909, Neal wrote, 'Our teachers were all taught directly by peasant dancers in whose family the traditional dances had been handed down through five generations'.[68] However, as demand for their services grew exponentially, printed instructions became something of a necessary evil, and Neal produced two volumes of *The Espérance Morris Book*.[69]

Sharp too recognised the fundamental inadequacy of written instructions and from March 1909 began to lead classes at the Chelsea College of Physical Education with the assistance of William Kimber. In a leaflet publicising these classes, Sharp wrote, 'No notation can tell the student how to hit the just mean between freedom and reserve, forcefulness and grace, abandonment and dignity'.[70] He also set about making revisions to *The Morris Book*, reflecting developments in his knowledge and attitude towards performance.[71] Though MacIlwaine's name remained on the covers, he had no practical involvement in the preparation of the second edition. Most notably, Sharp omitted the Bidford dances from this revised edition, as he had come to realise the extent of D'Arcy Ferris' influence on their development.[72] It seems that many of his followers uncritically accepted these amendments, believing that the removal of evidences of modern innovation would precipitate a genuine authenticity in their dance: 'revision brought excision'.[73] Just as the contents and description of the dances changed, so too did the interpretation of the dance's history. Resting heavily on E.K. Chambers' *The Medieval Stage*—which adhered to an intellectual framework based on the hypotheses of E.B. Taylor and J.G. Frazer—Sharp described morris as 'one of the seasonal pagan observances prevalent amongst primitive communities and associated in some occult way with the fertilisation of all living things, animal and vegetable'.[74] This analysis is a summary of his notes included in the introduction to *The Sword Dances of Northern England*, published in 1911. Sharp was assisted in the writing of the *Sword Dance* book by one Edward Phillips Barker, a classics scholar based at University College Nottingham, who he credits as a 'joint-author'.[75] From this point onwards, Sharp submitted drafts of all publications on dance to Phillips Barker for scrutiny and comment.[76]

Neal, however, was actually the first to succumb to the enchanting qualities of Frazer's theories. From as early as 1907, she began to suffuse aesthetics of 'Merrie England' with talk of sacrificial rites and priesthood rituals. In October 1907, Neal addressed a meeting of the Southern Cooperative Education Association, and delivered a summary of the dance which married 'Merrie' with a 'Mystic' England: 'the old Morris dancing on the village green, with its accompanying singing and acting, probably formed part of the religious life of the community'.[77] In a serialised account of the revival movement, published in *The Observer* over four instalments in late 1911, Neal claimed that the origins of the dances were 'inspired naturally from the rhythm of earth and sea and the wavering moon'.[78] It was the 'outward and visible sign' of a primitive religion, latterly inherited by rural labourers, 'whose daily toil brings them in touch with the earth and all natural and growing things'.[79] Elsewhere, she referred to her dancers as the transmitters of 'the deep and orderly rhythm of the music which is the inherited tradition of the English race'.[80] Thus, Neal justified her insistence of direct transmission and intuitive learning: interpreted as articles of racial inheritance, morris could not be reduced to inscribed texts.

In a letter of 1911, Sharp wrote, 'Morris dances are not pink pills or any other quack medicine. They are art-products, and as such should be dispensed by artists and trained teachers'.[81] In December of that year, together with a select few allies from the Chelsea School, Sharp called a public meeting to form the EFDS. A press report quoted Sharp's rationale for establishing this new organisation, to 'gather people together into a society which viewed folk-dancing from a purely artistic standpoint'.[82] When he said, 'an artistic movement was very liable to suffer at the hands of philanthropy', it was clear that Sharp's EFDS was in conscious opposition to Neal's Morris Guild. Whilst Neal emphasised the significance of the context in which the dances took place, Sharp was preoccupied with the content of the dances themselves. Though both believed in the importance of subjugating the self to collaborative endeavour, Sharp's insistence on the faithful replication of technical accuracy clashed with Neal's belief that morris was an expression of an inarticulate spirit. Whilst Neal argued that national characteristics were 'racial' and inherited, rediscovered through intuitive dance, Sharp's commitment to discipline revealed a belief that these were ideals which needed to be instilled in people through instruction.

Consolidation and confrontation

During the First World War, both the Espérance Club and its Morris Guild fell into abeyance, out of which they did not emerge. After 1918, Neal withdrew almost entirely from the folk dance movement, redirecting her energies towards social work.[83] Despite the disappearance of his major competitors, Sharp did not necessarily enjoy an unchallenged monopoly on determining the future course of the folk dance movement. Furthermore, the loss of four men from his demonstration side had a hugely detrimental effect on Sharp's confidence. In 1923, he wrote, 'I felt when the dreadful news came that I didn't want to carry on any more, and I still have the same feeling'.[84] Nevertheless, and in spite of a catalogue of health problems, Sharp did not shirk from his role as figurehead of the revival movement, and in 1919 accepted the post of Occasional Inspector for the Board of Education, with special responsibility for reporting on the teaching of folk song and dance in schools.[85] The events of the interwar period provide evidence both for a consolidation of Sharp's attitudes and for a diversification of interpretations. Among the membership of the EFDS, debates over the presentation and dissemination of morris persisted, and new dissidents emerged. Perhaps the most vocal and thorough of these post-war critics was Rolf Gardiner, a charismatic and enthusiastic leader of young people, who styled himself as a self-professed enemy of middle-class respectability.

Though the interwar years brought periods of severe depression, they also witnessed the continued growth of mass commercial leisure, which began in the Edwardian period. For members of the working class, the cinema became an especially important site of entertainment and sociability.[86] Beyond the physical education curricula of British schools, folk dance vied against the cinema and dance halls for participants in a mixed economy of leisure pursuits. Realising the challenges of increased competition, members of the EFDS recognised the need to shake off undesirable associations with misty-eyed pastoral romanticism of the pre-war era. In order to appeal to the post-war generation, they needed to assert the relevance of folk dance to modern audiences. In 1927, long-standing supporter of the EFDS, W.D. Croft reflected on the pre-war caricatures of 'smocks, school children, and flower-show fetes': 'In 1914 folk-dancers were like to be regarded as eccentric, or to be pitied for not having something better to do'.[87] Sharp continued to argue that it was the artistic qualities of the morris dances which provided just reason for their preservation. Indeed, he believed that they deserved to be placed on an equal footing with poetry, music, and the fine arts. As such, he urged his followers to aspire towards excellence in their dancing, stating 'without a fine technique, skilful craftsmanship, [there is] no art'.[88] To this end, Sharp's society eschewed the mop caps and top hats worn by Espérance dancers. Instead, dancers wore costumes more in keeping with physical recreation activities: gym slips for women and white flannels for men.

In addition to Sharp's activities with the Board of Education, the EFDS also organised a programme of classes, competitions, and examinations with a view to promoting technical excellence. In 1921, the editor of the *EFDS News* reminded the readership that competitions both improved the standard of dance and 'preserve[d] the purity of its tradition'.[89] During the 1920s, many places which had hitherto subscribed to the Espérance Club model embraced Sharp's EFDS, a pragmatic response with tangible implications for the style of dancing and their mode of teaching. One such example can be found in the Essex town of Thaxted where morris was first introduced by Blanche Payling of the Espérance Club in December 1910. By the outbreak of the First World War in 1914, morris was firmly established in the town, and local enthusiasm prompted a self-led revival in 1920. By 1925, the Thaxted dancers had aligned themselves with the EFDS. At the local level, however, few enthusiasts took much interest in the pre-war debates between Neal and Sharp. Nevertheless, in the 1920s, the EFDS was not without its dissenting voices.

In the early 1920s, a new figure arrived on the scene, and quickly became a thorn in Sharp's side. Rolf Gardiner was a young rebel intent on dismantling the tenets of urbane respectability. Taking courage from his inspiration, D.H. Lawrence, Gardiner sought to 'smash a few big holes in European suburbanity, [and] let in a little real fresh air'.[90] In 1922, aged only 19, Gardiner entered into an 'open war' with Sharp and the EFDS. He accused Sharp and his followers of betraying morris dances of their true function, lamenting that 'technical skill had triumphed over emotional symbolism'.[91] As a polemicist with a restless pen, Gardiner was frustrated that what he termed 'ruthlessness' was 'often mistaken for bitterness'.[92] In one letter, published in *The Challenge* magazine in 1923, he described the EFDS as 'a platform for the self-display of people who dishonour themselves with shoddy, uncourageous, mediocre work'.[93] Perhaps unsurprisingly, given the frankness of his criticisms, Gardiner became a *persona non grata* in the EFDS and was asked not to attend its meetings.[94] Seldom shying away from controversy, this angry young man was the most vocal and consistent of critics throughout the 1920s.

In the late summer of 1922, Gardiner led 16 dancers and 9 musicians, comprising an 'English Folk Music Company', on a tour of Germany. Based on a self-conscious imitation of travelling English performers of the sixteenth century, Gardiner also hoped that this endeavour would prove a reconciliatory gesture between two embittered nations, 'a political act of the younger generation'.[95] Organised single handedly by Gardiner, the tour took place in defiance of the wishes of Sharp and the EFDS. Though Sharp did not disagree with the tour in principle, he implored Gardiner and his company to confine themselves to villages and small towns, keeping 'away from places of any civic importance'.[96] Fearing Gardiner and his colleagues lacked the requisite expertise to show the dances at their best, Sharp wrote that the dances ought to be introduced to foreign places 'officially, with the full force of our best dancers'—anything else would be 'calamitous'.[97] Chided but not deterred, Gardiner ignored these warnings, and the tour went ahead with performances in some of the largest cities in Germany, including Cologne, Dresden, Frankfurt, and Rothenburg. In addition to morris dances, the programmes included country dances and sword dances as well as folk songs. Gardiner was assiduous in his publicity, writing articles for newspapers, which explained the motivations and rationale for the tour. An article published in the anglophone *Cologne Post* had a distinctively patriotic feel, as he explained:

> It has been forgotten here on the continent and to a shameful degree in our own country itself, that England was once the mistress of music in Europe … In Shakespeare's day, the English were the people for dancing and singing.[98]

Nevertheless, Gardiner's attention was not chiefly aimed at English people in Germany but at the Germans themselves. In fact, at the Cologne performance, English attendees paid more for their tickets than did their German counterparts.

Notwithstanding the acrimony and ill-feeling in England, precipitated by his ignoring Sharp's wishes, Gardiner returned feeling triumphant. Indeed, he considered himself vindicated, arguing that it was 'psychologically and humanly necessary that some form of positive reconciliation should be extended to Germany'.[99] Throughout 1923, Gardiner continued to make public attacks on Sharp and the EFDS, including some especially fraught correspondence in the appropriately titled, *The Challenge*, introduced above, and in a pamphlet entitled *The English Folk Dance Tradition: An Essay*, based on an article originally commissioned by *Die Hellerauer Blätter* in Dresden.[100] Intoxicated by the apparent mystery of the dances, Gardiner accused Sharp of emasculating morris, reducing it to a curious relic for scholars and enthusiasts, and extinguishing the vital spirit of tradition. Gardiner believed that 'he had more the spirit of things in him than anyone', possessing the confidence and foresight to rescue morris dances from the confines of Sharp's classroom.[101]

Together with friend and ally, Arthur Heffer, in the summer of 1924, Gardiner formed the Travelling Morrice, a small band of young morris men who ventured out on 'pilgrimages to holy places', in search of 'a taste of the real thing'.[102] The idea was to embark on a tour of the towns and villages in the Cotswolds, where morris dancing had once been a commonplace activity. Heffer deftly translated Gardiner's lofty aspirations into practical plans. As such, he not only made for an efficient organiser, employing the *Crockford's Clerical Directory* as his chief guide and tool, but he acted as a vital arbiter between Gardiner and the hierarchy of the EFDS, which continued to condemn him.[103] By his collaboration, Heffer provided vital legitimacy to the enterprise, which might otherwise have been wholly tarnished by Gardiner's impetuousness of the previous two years. Only Heffer, a respected dancer and member of the well-known family of booksellers, could reconcile the 'wilder and reckless spirits and cautious constitutionalists' among the Cambridge fraternity.[104] One dancer, Kenworthy Schofield, was especially reluctant to be associated with the rude iconoclast. Even after the tour, Schofield wrote a long and scathing letter, in which he accused Gardiner of 'causing a good deal of unhappiness' to Sharp and members of the EFDS.[105] Though Gardiner had apparently apologised to Sharp in person, Schofield doubted the sincerity of his gesture, writing 'you made no effort to overcome your pride and admit that in the excitement of the moment your pen ran away with you and that you without meaning it had been exceedingly rude'.[106] Not only did Heffer convince Schofield to participate, but he also sought the blessing of Sharp himself, who was at the time in very poor health.

The inaugural tour of the Travelling Morrice took place in June 1924, coinciding with Gardiner's final term at St. John's and his going down from Cambridge. The endeavour promised the fun and adventure of a week's holiday in picturesque countryside. Taking to bicycles, the young men camped under canvas, danced in the streets, and refreshed themselves with 'Rabelaisian quaffing of beer and cider'.[107] Over the course of six days, the eight dancers accompanied by a single musician performed in Burford and Stow-on-the-Wold, as well as several villages, including Adderbury, Bledington, and Leafield, which all once had morris sides of their own. This enterprise constituted 'the first contact of the new generation of morris men with those traditional dancers still surviving'.[108] During the first tour, the Travelling Morrice met with 14 individuals with knowledge of morris dances and tunes, including several old dancers who Sharp had met many years before. Whilst the Cambridge dancers drank in the praise of these veterans, they also delighted in criticism. One especially memorable encounter was that with Henry 'Harry' Taylor of Longborough, a small village some two miles north of Stow. Heffer's Logbook of the tour recorded:

> Mr Taylor was high in his praise in fact all swelled with pride—'Just right quite' was his actual sentence. [sic] [...] Then a wonderful thing happened: old Henry Taylor bless him came up to Arthur and said confidentially 'Pardon me larding in young sir but may an old man what knows what he's talking about suggest that you do Constant Billio a new way to rest you'.[109]

During the 1924 tour, supplemented by a further couple of days' fieldwork carried out by Kenworthy Schofield and Peter Fox, they collected some five new dances and nine tunes, as well as several revisions to existing dances. The comments of Taylor and others suggested to the men of the Travelling Morrice that 'in the anxiety to acquire the necessary control, the vigour of the dances had been rather overlooked'.[110] Schofield produced summaries of their findings in a series of three articles for the EFD(S)S.[111]

The first tour concluded on 23 June, coinciding with the death of Cecil Sharp. Reflecting on this poignant coincidence, Heffer mused:

> Perhaps there is a mystery to be found here in that the magic circle is complete and the dances collected and pieced together by [Sharp] from information supplied by old men have been taken back rejuvenated to the villagers from whom they were originally acquired.[112]

Throughout the 1920s and the decades which followed, the Travelling Morrice made frequent returns to the Cotswolds. Whilst they collected information on morris dances and tunes which contributed towards an expansion of the repertoire at a national level, this band of men also contributed towards the 'encouragement and preservation of local Morris dancing' in the Cotswolds region itself, in many cases giving impetus to local sides and performers, including the Chipping Campden Morris.[113] Despite their success in achieving notoriety among the folk dance fraternity, groups such as the Travelling Morrice remained the exception rather than the rule throughout the 1920s.

Gardiner remained an eccentric outlier, whose influence on the morris revival was circumscribed by his uncompromising idealism. To his frustration, Rolf the 'fresh air fiend' found that many of his colleagues at Cambridge were not so pliant as he might have originally hoped. Indeed, the majority of his compatriots treated Gardiner's schemes with caution and suspicion. As Gardiner himself reflected, 'the majority were indeed profoundly skeptical of mixing up the morris with other things'.[114] Even Arthur Heffer, his closest ally, often willed his friend to exercise restraint and tact in his activities. Gardiner lamented that for his academic colleagues, morris dancing 'was a thrilling pastime' and no more: 'Politics or reformist idealism lay quite outside its scope'.[115]

Men's Morris

In 1923, the EFDS had a membership of more than 650, of which five sixths were women. Though losses in the Great War exacerbated this disparity between genders represented, the Society was from the outset a predominantly female one: in 1913, less than two years after its foundation, women outnumbered men at a rate of four to one.[116] By the mid-1920s, this imbalance was considered an urgent problem by the leadership of the Society. Soon after Douglas Kennedy's appointment as the Director of the EFDS in 1924, the Society's General Council began to hold a series of discussions on the subject of increasing male participation in folk dance, especially in morris and sword. During a conference held as part of the EFDS Cambridge Summer School in August 1925, members discussed practical measures to encourage more men to join. Methods ranged from personal introductions by friends and colleagues, to the provision of classes for men only.[117] At around this time, a number of new men's clubs emerged, including those at Cambridge, Letchworth, and Thaxted. These men's morris sides not only sought to promote the masculine attributes of the dance, but also to pioneer a new approach to teaching and performance, rooted in informal and sociable homosocial groupings, in a kind of imitation of the old village teams of the nineteenth century. From 1926, a series of gatherings took place between these groups of morris men, which aimed to support fledgling sides and encourage new ones to form. These various initiatives culminated in the formation of the Morris Ring in 1934 as an 'informal federation of morris men's clubs', which aimed to provide 'greater solidarity' and encourage public displays.[118]

During the interwar period, fears of 'emasculation' and 'feminisation'—influenced by women's suffrage, unemployment, the emancipating potential of commercial leisure forms, and the physical impact of the Great War—precipitated a reactionary response among some groups of men.[119] Alison Light describes modernist male writers of the 1920s as a group which portrayed 'Britain as the place where it is no longer possible to be properly male—a country gelded ... and emasculated by the aftermath of war'.[120] Together, these fears gave rise to a desire to 'reassert manliness'. Moreover, a national preoccupation with the physical condition of the English people also reinforced 'connections between fitness, manliness and national identity'.[121] Manliness was thus often reconstructed and reproduced through physical training activities. During the 1920s and early 1930s, some men among the EFDS felt that the Society had failed to make any considerable headway in reestablishing morris dancing after the war. Lamenting the depletion of his pre-war demonstration side, Sharp confided to Gardiner that he 'saw no future for the morris now that the women had taken it up'.[122] Whilst Sharp himself did not have any fundamental objection to women dancing morris—explaining that although it 'is not strictly in accordance with ancient usage, no great violence will be done to tradition so long as the dance is performed by members of one sex only'—he did believe that it was of an altogether different character to men's performance. Sharp wrote, 'At its best a woman's Morris must always be of the nature of a free translation rather than an exact reproduction of the traditional dance'.[123]

Beginning in the early 1920s, a growing number of male dancers believed that the encouragement of independent teams meeting together on a regular basis was the 'surest way of "encouraging the practice of morris in its traditional form"'.[124] As Kenworthy Schofield described in 1934:

> It is not denied that men can and do derive much enjoyment in taking part in headquarters or branch demonstrations at which they perform morris dances, but there has grown up a strong feeling among morris men generally that the morris, besides being done in this way, must also be given the chance of a more independent existence, if it is once again to take root.[125]

Among the earliest of the men's clubs was the Cambridge Morris Men, inaugurated at a meeting held on 24 October 1924. The chief objective of the club was to provide a mechanism by 'which former members of Cambridge Morris sides should be kept in touch with men now doing morris at Cambridge'.[126] Though it marked a formalising of existing social networks, it was not necessarily conceived as a formal institution in its own right. At an early meeting in February 1925, the members 'agreed that Christian names should be used', representing a departure from the impersonal university custom of using family names.[127] From 1925, the Cambridge Morris Men developed a group identity, adopting the titles of Squire in place of President and Bagman instead of Secretary, and organising an annual dinner as well as tours of the Travelling Morrice. In many cases, these new groups of morris men were in reality little more than a consolidation of existing teams. This was the case in Letchworth Garden City, where in 1922 the Letchworth Morris Men emerged from the ranks of the established Letchworth Folk Players. Nevertheless, by setting themselves apart with new identities as 'morris men', these entities provided impetus to the promotion of men's dancing. Like the Travelling Morrice, these nascent sides of morris men sought to imitate the old teams, aspiring to present the dance as 'a living thing, not just something which had been taught'.[128]

These men's morris clubs championed teamwork, a conducive agent to instilling a corporate identity. In 1926, a cohort of men in London who had attended EFDS classes together formed the Greensleeves Morris Men, with the hope that 'a really good team can be built up of unpretentious individuals if they practise constantly and regularly together'.[129] In a romantic tone, founder of the Letchworth side Alec Hunter described how the best morris sides comprised a 'communion of spirits' who learned from 'masters of the craft'.[130] The dancers were to be disciplined but not stern. As Hunter explained, 'It is a fine form of team work as there cannot be a really good side until a team has worked together for a long time as friends'.[131] At the instigation of Hunter and Schofield, in May 1926, a gathering of four men's morris clubs took place in Ardeley, a small village in Hertfordshire, hosted by fellow devotee of English folk dance and music, the Reverend Frederic Percy Harton. Though little is known of this meeting, it was evidently successful enough to encourage another such gathering in 1927, which took place on a July weekend in 1927, this time hosted by Conrad and Miriam Noel in Thaxted, near Saffron Walden in Essex. Promoters of morris dancing since 1910, the Noels welcomed the morris men on the condition that dancers attended Mass on Sunday morning.[132] The morris weekend in Thaxted became an annual fixture, advertised in the pages of EFDS publications as opportunities 'to enable men to meet together and learn more about the dance'.[133] Responding to this appetite to take the dance out of the classroom and into rural towns, similar weekend events for morris men were organised elsewhere, and in the summer of 1928, 40 dancers met at Fordingbridge in Hampshire.[134] The following year, men's weekends also took place in Haslemere and at Kelmscott, near Oxford.[135]

During the 1934 Thaxted meeting, the Morris Ring was established as an informal organisation for the support and promotion of men's morris clubs. The Morris Ring was the result of the combined intelligence of Joseph Needham and Arthur Peck of the Cambridge Morris Men. Its origins lay not only in the desire for greater autonomy for morris clubs, but in a wish to incorporate dancers of all social backgrounds without causing embarrassment or unease. As both a Christian and a socialist—who despite his distinctly middle-class upbringing considered himself a member 'by adoption' of the proletariat—Needham was desperate to establish some means of incorporating morris men of all classes into a national federation, which fostered a sense of fellowship and fraternity.[136] The seeds of the idea appear to have been in Needham's encounter with Alfred Cobb during the 11th tour of the Travelling Morrice in 1932. A tiler by trade from Sapperton in Gloucestershire, Cobb was both a dancer and a musician, who Needham deemed 'an outstanding member of the "proletariat"'.[137] The Morris Ring, as conceived by Needham, was to serve as a unifying federation, bringing dancers of the working class and those of the middle class together in one forum. Needham and Peck wished neither to supersede the EFDSS nor to impose a new standard upon men's morris clubs. They believed that prescriptive policies imposed by the Society at a national level were 'contrary to the ethos of Morris teams', which should each have 'a local habitation and a name', that is an identity of their own.[138]

On 20 October 1934, the Morris Ring was inaugurated at a meeting hosted by the EFDSS at Cecil Sharp House. Some 70 men from 13 clubs attended this gathering. Taking the chair as the Director of the Society, Douglas Kennedy announced that Alec Hunter was to be the first Squire and Walter Abson the first Bagman, presenting to the former a silver-mounted staff and to the latter a minute book and money box, gifts of the EFDSS, and symbols of its connection with the Morris Ring.[139] The titles of the officers were influenced by practices established in the Cambridge Morris Men, and these were soon imitated by other clubs in the Morris Ring, representing an informal process of standardisation. By 1935, for instance, Jack Hannah of Letchworth was the 'Bagman of the Morris Men', giving 'a new name for the chap that writes letters'.[140] From 1935, the men's morris weekends were organised under the aegis of the Morris Ring. The format remained largely unchanged, consisting of instruction and public performances, but now also included Feasts, modelled on the formal meals of the Cambridge Morris Men, complete with speeches and toasts. Whilst pubs offered spaces for the morris men to be gregarious and spontaneous, giving opportunities to engage with local people, the Feasts, usually conducted in private, adhered to ritual forms of behaviour which provided a fraternal glue to their association. The Morris Ring took middle-class forms of association and grafted them together with working-class ones, with a view to cultivate an ethos of mateyness, which attempted to transcend the class divide. Set apart from their female counterparts in semi-autonomous groups, under the umbrella of the Morris Ring, the morris men championed informal public performances of dance—which they deemed a more authentic presentation than in formal expositions and competitions—fuelled by homosocial fraternity.

Festival of Britain

Between 1935 and the outbreak of the Second World War in September 1939, the Morris Ring staged 17 gatherings. On Sunday, 10 March 1940, about 70 men convened at Cecil Sharp House for what was to be the final meeting until 1946.[141] By this time, some 37 clubs were members. During an air raid on the night of 27 September 1940, Cecil Sharp House received a direct hit, followed by incendiaries which destroyed many irreplaceable artefacts, including many items recently acquired from the Percy Manning collection.[142] In most places, the war brought about a total halt to activities, as people took on new responsibilities in the war effort. Nevertheless, in Thaxted, morris dancing continued to take place each Easter Monday and Whit Monday, aided by visiting dancers from Cambridge and Letchworth.[143] During the late 1940s, most clubs reformed, supplemented by a modest number of new ones. Between 1946 and 1950, the Morris Ring admitted a further six clubs to membership, including the Headington Quarry Morris. In the aftermath of war, the EFDSS was not simply occupied in the material rebuilding of their headquarters, but also in the rebuilding and revision of their operations. The Committee increasingly focussed on social folk dance, which 'laid themselves open to the charge of neglecting performance in public by specially trained dancers'.[144] Responsibility for the promotion of performance dancing was tacitly conferred upon the Morris Ring and its constituent clubs. The result was the virtual disappearance of opportunity for female participation in morris dancing as the EFDSS turned its attention towards social dancing.

The Festival of Britain remains an important event in modern British history, signifying not only the conclusion of post-war austerity but a resolve to embrace new opportunities, celebrating innovations in architecture, design, and technology. New and old combined in a dynamic conservatism, the Festival used traditional motifs to lend novel exhibits a familiar essence.[145] Furthermore, as David Edgerton argues, it represented a newly formed British nationalism, born of a turning away from empire.[146] Therefore, mottos such as 'The Festival Begins at Home', disseminated through *Picture Post* magazine, carried a double meaning.[147] This event marked the beginning of an end to an era of prolonged austerity, and 'set out to provide a sense of place for a British people in need of location'.[148] Whilst the main exhibition on the South Bank in London was intended to represent 'a great shop window' onto the nation, places like Thaxted were offered up as 'a living stage'. Journalist and broadcaster, James Fyfe Robertson described how 'the audience can walk among the players, and the players will be village people going about their daily work, or combining in their normal recreations'.[149] Elsewhere, communities exploited the opportunity for staging festivals on a smaller scale.

For members of the EFDSS, 1951 was doubly significant, as it also saw the reopening of Cecil Sharp House after many years of rebuilding. However, their attentions were also focussed on promoting a wider awareness of folk dance across the nation. Douglas Kennedy set on the popularising of country dance throughout England as an activity for adults as well as children. He was acutely aware of the types of negative stereotypes which endured, summarising this derision as one which argued that 'folk dancing is "nuts", is sissy, is kid's stuff, is the gymnasium when it's too wet for lacrosse, is sandals and beards or jibbahs, is a hundred girls and a man, etc.'.[150] In addition to a programme of festival concerts at the Royal Albert Hall, the Birmingham Central Hall, and the Nottingham Albert Hall, Kennedy exhorted members of the EFDSS to exploit the opportunity for public gatherings: 'The Festival of Britain is the occasion for "Al Fresco" and informal dancing'.[151] In support of their efforts, the Society published an illustrated brochure entitled *The Dancing English*, in which they set out their stall for the festival year: 'the Society is not just trying to put back something that died long ago, but rather to link up the people of this country with their own traditions and their music and dance inheritance'.[152] Though morris featured heavily in the festival concerts and promotional literature, the EFDSS under Kennedy was principally concerned in popularising country dance as a social activity for mixed gender groupings. With Kennedy's approval, the all-male morris was effectively left in the hands of the Morris Ring, its member clubs providing demonstrations at the EFDSS festival events. Nevertheless, the two organisations remained closely linked, especially through Kennedy himself, who served as the Squire of the Morris Ring from 1938 to 1947.

By the early 1950s, public displays of morris became increasingly commonplace, spurred on to some extent by events organised to mark the Festival of Britain. On 28 July 1951, for instance, the Cambridge Morris Men made their first appearance on the streets of Cambridge, joined by the Winter Morris from Derbyshire, a side with a long history which had only just reformed after a period of abeyance. It had only been during the year before that the Cambridge Morris Men conducted their first dancing tour of Cambridgeshire villages.[153] In London, the newly formed Ravensbourne Morris Men hosted a gathering of morris sides, in the first open air meeting of its type in the city.[154] On a more modest scale, members of the Shoreham Folk Dance Club in Sussex dressed in morris kit for a procession through their town, though it wasn't until 1952 that they decided to learn some morris dances.[155] Nevertheless, their decision to wear morris kit reflected an attitude that morris represented the dancing English.

One of the largest outdoor performances of morris during the Festival year took place in Thaxted on 7 July 1951, one of three events in rural Essex to mark the occasion. The pageant-like event incorporated morris and social country dancing in the streets and yards, already familiar to the people of Thaxted, as well as the Castleton Garland processional and Abbots Bromley Horn Dance, scrupulously devised by Alec Hunter, a man with an eye for theatre and spectacle. A report published in *English Dance and Song* praised his infectious enthusiasm, expressed through his skilful command of the show:

> Mr. Hunter has the supreme gift of being able to persuade an onlooker, in spite of himself, on to the dance floor. On this occasion and on his 'own ground' he was irresistible. Reluctant and bewildered members of the crowd found themselves making up sets and dancing with keen enjoyment.[156]

Framed by the fifteenth-century Guild Hall, with musicians seated on a four-wheeled farmer's wagon, the programme interspersed morris with country dances, mixing the spectacular with the social in an environment in which boundaries of participants and performers were softened, although the morris dancers retained something of an elite status among them. Once more, the Thaxted Morris were joined by their colleagues from Letchworth.[157] By this time, Thaxted was well known for its morris and country dancing—it had been more than 40 years since Blanche Payling of the Espérance Club first arrived to teach dancing to the young people of the town. The fame of the Thaxted Morris was also reflected in their portrayal in a painting by R.T. Cowern, commissioned by British Railways in 1950 for a brochure aimed at promoting increases in passenger traffic on rural Essex lines, including the five-mile branch from Elsenham to Thaxted.[158] By 1951, its status as a crucible of the morris revival seemed secure.

The legacy of the Festival continued for several years, compounded by events marking the Coronation of Queen Elizabeth II in 1953. Throughout the 1950s, the Morris Ring continued to swell as new sides formed across the country. However, just as the Festival of Britain indulged in the nation's cultural heritage, it also represented the beginning of a post-war era which was a thoroughly modern one, manifest in new consumer items and leisure opportunities. Morris dancers continued to be perceived as excitable enthusiasts, and the movement ultimately failed to attract a genuinely popular appeal, though it continued to grow at a modest rate. In spite of the best efforts of reformist dancers to escape from it, popular conceptions of morris dancing continued to be influenced by 'Merrie England'.

Conclusion

Whether or not audiences were always conscious of the illusory qualities, morris nevertheless appeared to provide the public with a sense of reassurance.[159] Throughout the pageantry of D'Arcy Ferris, the socially minded initiatives of Neal and the high-minded aspirations of Sharp, and into the constituent member clubs of the Morris Ring was woven a common thread, which united them all. They believed that the morris dance represented a vestige of a past culture, which had been more authentic and holistic than their own. As such, they perceived the dances to be a bulwark against the supposedly fragmentary and debased forms of popular culture. However, even the most idealistic of advocates for 'Merrie England' recognised that it was impossible and indeed undesirable to turn the clock back. Nevertheless, stuck between past and future, devotees of the morris dance invoked eternal verities, endemic in the amorphous 'spirit' of a social art form. Though morris dancing continued to attract only a tiny proportion of the adult population, this thin layer nevertheless intersected all levels of society. Whilst the clubs in Letchworth and Thaxted continued to attract artisans and labourers, in London, the British Museum, Morley College, and the Royal College of Music each had their own morris side. Meanwhile, Birmingham and Oxford both boasted morris dancing policemen.

Whilst it might appear that dominant tropes of Englishness in the early twentieth century depended on a shared veneration of a stable past—held up as a complete and absolute representation of national culture—hotly contested debates over the very essence of authenticity complicated this process.[160] This reminds us that identities are constantly subject to negotiation and revision, no matter how apparently fixed and stable they may appear on the surface. In the morris revival, authenticity was variously framed by context as well as content. As a vector of a particular strain of Englishness, the morris dance was capable of reflecting various meanings, sometimes simultaneously, depending on an individual's own prejudices and beliefs. Historians of the folk movement can learn from scholars of the social sciences, particularly those who follow a symbolic interactionist approach, after Emile Durkheim. One such recent article cogently articulated how 'The construction and performance of English identity through music is a means by which "the nation" is enacted'.[161] Indeed, as an attempt to revivify enchanted versions of a supposedly ancient form of English culture, the morris revival reveals a number of important truths about national identity in the early twentieth century.

Notes

1. Lee Robert Blackstone, 'The Aural and Moral Idylls of "Englishness" and Folk Music', *Symbolic Interaction*, 40, 4 (2017), pp. 561–580 (p. 565).
2. The first known use of the term 'Cotswold' to describe the various dance traditions of the English south midlands can be found in a short article by Dr. Arthur L. Peck published in 1932: Arthur L. Peck, 'Two Cotswold Morris Men', *Journal of the English Folk Dance and Song Society*, 1, 1 (1932), pp. 71–72 (p. 71).
3. See, for instance, Theresa J. Buckland, 'Institutions and Ideology in the Dissemination of Morris Dances in the Northwest of England', *Yearbook for Traditional Music*, 23 (1991), pp. 53–67.
4. Roy Judge, 'Merrie England and the Morris, 1881–1910', *Folklore*, 104 (1993), pp. 124–143 (pp. 137–138).
5. John Graham, *Lancashire and Cheshire Morris Dances* (London: Curwen and Sons, 1911), cited in Russell Wortley, 'Informal Talk on the Early Morris Revival', *The Morris Dancer*, 1, 3 (1979), pp. 9–14 (p. 9).
6. Keith Chandler, *"Ribbons, Bells and Squeaking Fiddles": The Social History of Morris Dancing in the English South Midlands, 1660–1900* (London: Hisarlik, 1993), pp. 207–224.
7. Martin Wiener, *English Culture and the Decline of the Industrial Spirit, 1850–1980* (Cambridge: Cambridge University Press, 1981), pp. 50–51.
8. Rolf Gardiner, *David's Sling: A Young Man's Prelude* (Cambridge University Library (CUL), MS Gardiner A/2), pp. 51–52 (pp. 172–173).
9. Robert Colls, *Identity of England* (Oxford: Oxford University Press, 2002), pp. 219–220.
10. Emma Griffin, *Liberty's Dawn: A People's History of the Industrial Revolution* (London: Yale University Press, 2013), p. 51.
11. Chandler, *Ribbons, Bells and Squeaking Fiddles*, p. 205 (p. 212).
12. Michael Heaney, 'The Earliest Reference to the Morris Dance?', *Folk Music Journal*, 8, 4 (2004), pp. 513–515.
13. John Forrest, *The History of Morris Dancing, 1458–1750* (Cambridge: James Clark & Co., 1999), pp. 57–91.
14. John Forrest, *Morris and Matachin: A Study in Comparative Choreography* (Sheffield: CECTAL Publications, 1984).
15. Forrest, *History of Morris*, pp. 92–139.
16. Ibid., pp. 101–103.
17. Ibid., p. 140.
18. Ibid., p. 176.
19. Chandler, *Ribbons, Bells and Squeaking Fiddles*, p. 59.
20. Ibid., pp. 81–83.
21. Ibid., pp. 195–204.
22. E.P. Thompson, *Customs in Common* (London: Merlin Press, 1991), p. 100.
23. Judge, 'Merrie England', pp. 124–125.
24. Ibid., p. 125.
25. Chandler, *Ribbons, Bells and Squeaking Fiddles*, p. 219.
26. For a summary of their work, see, for instance, John Cutting, *History and the Morris Dance: A Look at Morris Dancing from Its Earliest Days until 1850* (Alton: Dance Books, 2005), pp. 26–28.
27. E. Phillips Barker, 'Cecil James Sharp', *EFDS News*, 1, 8 (1924), p. 205.
28. Michael Heaney, 'Percy Manning: A Life', in *Percy Manning: The Man Who Collected Oxfordshire*, ed. by Michael Heaney (Oxford: Archaeopress, 2017), pp. 1–47.
29. Roy Judge, 'D'Arcy Ferris and the Bidford Morris', *Folk Music Journal*, 4, 5 (1984), pp. 443–480 (p. 444).

30 Ibid., pp. 447–448.
31 Ibid., pp. 448–449.
32 Roy Judge and Keith Chandler, *Shakespearean Bidford Morris Dancers, 1886: A Source Book* (Eynsham: Chandler Publications, 1985), p. 15.
33 Judge, 'D'Arcy Ferris', pp. 458–459.
34 *Redditch Indicator*, 27 February 1886, p. 5, cited in Judge, 'D'Arcy Ferris', p. 457.
35 Judge, 'D'Arcy Ferris', pp. 466–467.
36 Ibid., p. 469.
37 J. Philip Taylor, *Spotlight on Bidford-on-Avon's Morris Tradition* (Statford-upon-Avon: Shakespeare Morris, 2016), pp. 8–42.
38 Keith Chandler, 'Musicians in 19th Century Southern England: John Robbins of Bidford-on-Avon, Warwickshire (1868–1948)', <https://www.mustrad.org.uk/articles/mus19_16.htm> [accessed 17 July 2020].
39 Michael Heaney, 'Percy Manning, Thomas Carter and the Revival of Morris Dancing', in *Percy Manning: The Man Who Collected Oxfordshire*, ed. by Michael Heaney (Oxford: Archaeopress, 2017), pp. 145–172 (p. 158).
40 Heaney, 'Percy Manning: A Life', p. 8.
41 Judge, 'Merrie England', pp. 125–127.
42 Heaney, 'Percy Manning, Thomas Carter', pp. 151 and 151–156.
43 Ibid., p. 158.
44 Ibid., p. 162.
45 Ross McKibbin, *Classes and Cultures: England, 1918–1951* (Oxford: Oxford University Press, 1998), pp. 390–391.
46 Theresa Buckland, 'From the Artificial to the Natural Body: Social Dancing in Britain, 1900–1914', in *Dancing Naturally: Nature, Neo-Classicism and Modernity in Early Twentieth-Century Dance*, ed. by Alexandra Carter and Rachel Fensham (London: Palgrave Macmillan, 2011), p. 62.
47 Buckland, 'From the Artificial', p. 64.
48 Mary Neal, 'The National Revival of Folk Dancing, II: The Morris Dance', *The Observer*, 5 November 1911, p. 15.
49 Mary Neal, *"My Pretty Maid"* (London: Headley Brothers, n.d.), p. 3.
50 Derek Schofield, *Absolutely Classic: The Music of William Kimber* (London: English Folk Dance and Song Society, 1999), pp. 12–13.
51 Cited in Mary Neal, 'As a Tale That Is Told: The Autobiography of a Victorian Woman', p. 142. Vaughan Williams Memorial Library (VWML) Online, MS Neal, MN/1/1, <https://www.vwml.org/record/MN/1/1> [accessed 12 May 2020].
52 Ibid., p. 146. VWML Online, MS Neal, MN/1/1.
53 Cecil J. Sharp and Herbert MacIlwaine, *The Morris Book*, Part I (London: Novello and Co., 1907), pp. 10–11.
54 Roy Judge, 'Mary Neal and the Espérance Morris', *Folk Music Journal*, 5, 5 (1989), pp. 545–591 (pp. 551–552).
55 Mary Neal, *Set to Music* (n.d. [c.1907]), p. 10. VWML Online, MS Neal, MN/3/3, <https://www.vwml.org/record/MN/3/3> [accessed 12 May 2020].
56 Theresa J. Buckland, 'Pioneering England's Dances Among Late Victorian Youth: On the Early Work of Mary Neal and Grace Kimmins', in *(Re)Searching the Field: Festschrift in Honour of Egil Bakka*, ed. by Anne Margaret Fiskvik and Marit Stranden (Bergen: Fagbokforlaget, 2014), p. 322.
57 Roy Judge, 'Cecil Sharp and the Morris, 1906–1909', *Folk Music Journal*, 8, 2 (2002), pp. 195–228 (p. 195).
58 Paul Burgess, 'The Mystery of the Whistling Sewermen: How Cecil Sharp Discovered Gloucestershire Morris Dancing', *Folk Music Journal*, 8, 2 (2002), pp. 178–194 (pp. 179–180).
59 Burgess, 'The Mystery of the Whistling Sewermen', p. 180.
60 Ibid., p. 182.
61 Ibid., pp. 185–189.
62 Sharp and MacIlwaine, *The Morris Book*, Part I, p. 7.
63 Judge, 'Mary Neal and the Espérance Morris', p. 552.
64 John Graham, *Shakespearean Bidford Morris Dances* (London: Curwen and Sons, 1907).
65 Transcript of the Conference held at the Goupil Gallery, 5 Regent Street, Thursday 14 November 1907, entitled 'English Folk-Music in Dance and Song'. Mary Neal Online Archive, <http://www.maryneal.org/file-uploads/files/file/1907s1b.pdf> [accessed 12 May 2020].

66 'Merrie England Once More', *Punch*, 13 November 1907, pp. 345–347.
67 Neal, 'As a Tale That Is Told', p. 157. VWML Online, MS Neal, MN/1/1.
68 Mary Neal, 'Morris Dances and Education', *The Observer*, 29 August 1909, p. 3.
69 Mary Neal, *The Espérance Morris Book*, 2 vols. (London: Curwen and Sons, 1910–1911).
70 A.H. Fox Strangeways and Maud Karpeles, *Cecil Sharp* (Oxford: Oxford University Press, 1933), p. 78.
71 E.C. Cawte, 'Watching Cecil Sharp at Work: A Study of His Records of Sword Dances Using His Field Notebooks', *Folk Music Journal*, 8, 3 (2003), p. 282.
72 It is probable that Sharp was unaware of D'Arcy Ferris' involvement in morris at Bidford until June 1910. See Judge, 'D'Arcy Ferris', p. 470.
73 Barker, 'Cecil James Sharp', p. 205.
74 Cecil J. Sharp and Herbert MacIlwaine, *The Morris Book, Part I*, 2nd edition (London: Novello and Co., 1912), p. 11.
75 Cecil J. Sharp, *The Sword Dances of Northern England* (London: Novello and Co., 1911), p. 4.
76 Arthur Knevett, 'The Rescue, Reclamation or Plunder of English Folk-Song? A History of the Folk-Song Society, 1898–1932' (Unpublished Ph.D. Thesis, University of Sheffield, 2011), pp. 265–266; Fox Strangeways and Karpeles, *Cecil Sharp*, p. 104.
77 *Co-operative News*, 26 October 1907, p. 67, cited in Judge, 'Cecil Sharp and the Morris', pp. 203–204.
78 Mary Neal, 'The National Revival of the Folk Dance, No. III: Present Day Interpreters of the Folk Dance', *The Observer*, 3 December 1911, p. 20.
79 Neal, 'The National Revival of the Folk Dance', p. 20.
80 Mary Neal, 'To the Thaxted Morris Dancers', *The County Town*, 1, 9 (1911), pp. 8–9 (p. 9).
81 Letter from Cecil Sharp to Hercy Denman, 1911, cited in Fox Strangeways and Karpeles, *Cecil Sharp*, p. 111.
82 'Revival of the Folk Dance: An Artistic Movement', *Morning Post*, 7 December 1911, cited in Derek Schofield, "Revival of the Folk Dance: An Artistic Movement": The Background to the Founding of The English Folk Dance Society in 1911', *Folk Music Journal*, 5, 2 (1986), p. 215.
83 Mary Neal did, however, contribute towards the EFDS fund for a memorial building following Sharp's death in 1924, and attended a meeting of the Morris Ring at Stow-on-the-Wold in September 1938. In 1937, Neal received a CBE for services to folk dance and music.
84 Fox Strangeways and Karpeles, *Cecil Sharp*, p. 114.
85 Ibid., p. 174.
86 McKibbin, *Classes and Cultures*, pp. 186–187.
87 W.D. Croft, 'Fifteen Years' Progress', *Journal of the English Folk Dance Society*, 2, 1 (1927), p. 7.
88 Typescript notes for a lecture on 'Technique and Artistry' by Cecil Sharp, lecture delivered to delegates at the EFDS Aldeburgh Vacation School, August 1923. VWML Online, CJS1/5/54, <https://www.vwml.org/record/CJS1/5/54> [accessed 15 October 2020].
89 Anon., 'On Festivals', *EFDS News*, 1, 2 (1921), p. 20.
90 Letter from D.H. Lawrence to Rolf Gardiner, 9 August 1924, in *The Letters of D.H. Lawrence*, ed. by Aldous Huxley (London: Heinemann, 1956), p. 606.
91 Rolf Gardiner, 'A Brief Account of the Travelling Morrice', *North Sea and Baltic*, 1, 4 (1938), p. 77.
92 Letter from Rolf Gardiner to Maud Karpeles, 8 July 1923. CUL, MS Gardiner, C3/1/12.
93 Rolf Gardiner, 'Correspondence: The English Folk Dance Society', *The Challenge*, 17 August 1923.
94 Letter from Bertram Gavin to Rolf Gardiner, 21 June 1923. CUL, MS Gardiner, C3/1/8.
95 Transcript of a speech by Rolf Gardiner at the 38th Feast of the C.M.M., Christ's College, Cambridge, on 28th October 1961 entitled 'The Travelling Morrice and The Cambridge Morris Men'. Cambridge Morris Men (CMM) Archive.
96 Letter from Cecil Sharp to Rolf Gardiner, 9 July 1922. CUL, MS Gardiner, D2/1.
97 Ibid.
98 Rolf Gardiner, 'English Folk Dance and Song: Performance at the Deutsche Theatre on Sunday', *The Cologne Post*, 31 August 1922. CUL, MS Gardiner, D2/1.
99 Gardiner, 'Correspondence', 1923.
100 Ibid.; Winifred Shuldham Shaw, 'Correspondence: Mr. Rolf Gardiner and the EFDS', *The Challenge*, 10 August 1923; Gardiner, 'Correspondence'; Rolf Gardiner, *The English Folk Dance Tradition: An Essay* (Dresden: Neue Schule, 1923).

101 'David's Sling: A Young Man's Prelude', p. 44. CUL, MS Gardiner, A2/1–6.
102 Transcript of a speech by Rolf Gardiner at the 38th Feast of the C.M.M., Christ's College, Cambridge, on 28th October 1961 entitled 'The Travelling Morrice and The Cambridge Morris Men'. CMM Archives.
103 John Jenner, 'The Travelling Morrice and the Cambridge Morris Men: History and Influences During the Twentieth Century' (2004), p. 8, <http://tradcap.com/archive/histtrav.pdf> [accessed 18 October 2019].
104 Gardiner, 'A Brief Account'.
105 Letter from Kenworthy Schofield to Rolf Gardiner, n.d. [Summer 1924]. CUL, MS Gardiner, C3/1/9.
106 Ibid.
107 Undated summary report of the first tour of the Travelling Morrice by Rolf Gardiner [c.1924]. CUL, MS Gardiner, C/3/4.
108 Arthur Peck, *The Cambridge Morris Men: Twenty-Fifth Anniversary, April 1949* (Cambridge: Cambridge Morris Men, 1949), p. 6.
109 Arthur Heffer, 'A Morris Tour in the Cotswolds Done by the Travelling Morrice'. Log Book of the first tour of the Travelling Morrice (1924). CMM Archive.
110 R. Kenworthy Schofield, 'Morris Dances from Field Town', *Journal of the English Folk Dance Society*, 2, 2 (1928), pp. 22–28 (p. 22).
111 R. Kenworthy Schofield, 'Morris Dances from Longborough', *Journal of the English Folk Dance Society*, 2, 3 (1930), pp. 51–57; R. Kenworthy Schofield, 'Morris Dances from Bledington', *Journal of the English Folk Dance and Song Society*, 1, 3 (1934), pp. 147–151.
112 Heffer, 'A Morris Tour in the Cotswolds'.
113 Katharine M. Briggs, *The Folklore of the Cotswolds* (London: Batsford, 1974), p. 44.
114 Transcript of a speech by Rolf Gardiner at the 38th Feast of the C.M.M., Christ's College, Cambridge, on 28th October 1961 entitled 'The Travelling Morrice and The Cambridge Morris Men'. CMM Archive.
115 Gardiner, "A Brief Account', p. 8. CUL, MS Gardiner, A2/10/3.
116 Christopher J. Bearman, 'The Sorcerer's Apprentice: Rolf Gardiner and Mary Neal', *The Morris Dancer*, 4, 1 (2009), p. 22.
117 'Publicity and Man-Power', *EFDS News*, 1, 10 (1925), p. 297.
118 Letter from Joseph Needham to William Ganiford, 16 April 1934. CMM Archive.
119 Melanie Tebbutt, *Being Boys: Youth, Literature and Identity in the Inter-War Years* (Manchester: Manchester University Press, 2012), p. 24.
120 Alison Light, *Forever England: Femininity, Literature and Conservatism between the Wars* (London: Routledge, 1991), p. 7.
121 Tebbutt, 'Being Boys', pp. 14, 92.
122 Transcript of a speech by Rolf Gardiner at the 38th Feast of the C.M.M., Christ's College, Cambridge, on 28th October 1961 entitled 'The Travelling Morrice and The Cambridge Morris Men'. CMM Archive.
123 Sharp and MacIlwaine, *The Morris Book*, p. 42.
124 R. Kenworthy Schofield, 'The Morris Ring', *E.F.D.S. News*, 4, 3 (1934), pp. 77–79 (p. 79).
125 Ibid., p. 78.
126 Cambridge Morris Men Minute Book, vol. 1, p. 1. CMM Archive.
127 Ibid., p. 3.
128 Maud Karpeles Criticisms on Competition Dances for a forthcoming EFDS Festival, 2 December 1926, cited in in Roy Fenton, 'Destruction not Inscription': How a Pioneering Revival Side Developed', in *The Histories of the Morris in Britain*, ed. by Michael Heaney (London: EFDSS, 2018), p. 156.
129 Excerpt from a letter of 8 June 1926 from N.O.M. Cameron of the Greensleeves Morris Men to a prospective member, Greensleeves MM Log, vol. 1, cited in Fenton (2018), pp. 151–152.
130 Alec Hunter, 'The Spring Meeting of the Morris Ring', *English Dance and Song*, 16, 6 (1952), pp. 199–200.
131 Alec Hunter, 'The English Morris Dance', *The Yaffle*, 1, 1, (1926), [n.p.].
132 Harry de Caux, *Thaxted: " A Desperate Morris Place"* (Thaxted: Thaxted Morris Men, 1983), p. 7.
133 'Men's Morris Week-End', *EFDS News*, 3, 2 (1930), p. 58.
134 'Men's Morris Meetings', *EFDS News*, 2, 18 (1928), pp. 116–117.

135 'Men's Morris Meetings', *EFDS News*, 2, 19 (1928), p. 165.
136 Letter from Arthur Peck to Ewart Russell, 21 April 1966. Essex Record Office (ERO), MS Morris Ring, MR/1704.
137 Arthur L. Peck, 'The Origin of the Morris Ring', summary document in mss. form, 21 July 1934. CUL, MS Needham, A/848/5; Letter from Arthur Peck to Ewart Russell, 21 April 1966. ERO, MS Morris Ring, MR/1704.
138 Joseph Needham, 'Speech at the Golden Jubilee Dinner of the Morris Ring, Birmingham, 12 May 1984', typed manuscript. CUL, MS Needham, A/850.
139 *The First Log Book of the Morris Ring*, ed. by Walter Abson (The Morris Ring, 1991), p. 6.
140 Letter from Morris Sunderland to Ewart Russell, 4 April 1974. ERO, MS Morris Ring, MR/1742.
141 *The First Log Book*, p. 43.
142 Douglas Kennedy and Helen Kennedy, *Folk Dance and Song, 1911–1961* (London: EFDSS, 1961), p. 6.
143 Peck, *The Cambridge Morris Men*, p. 6.
144 Kennedy and Kennedy, *Folk Dance and Song*, p. 8.
145 Sarah Street, 'Cinema, Colour and the Festival of Britain, 1951', *Visual Culture in Britain*, 13, 1 (2012), pp. 97–98.
146 David Edgerton, *The Rise and Fall of the British Nation: A Twentieth Century History* (London: Allen Lane, 2018), p. 29.
147 *Picture Post*, cited in Gillian Darley, 'Essex, 1951', London Review of Books Blog, <https://www.lrb.co.uk/blog/ 2017/07/18/gillian-darley/essex-1951>, [accessed 27 February 2018].
148 Harriet Atkinson, *The Festival of Britain: A Land and its People* (London: I.B. Tauris, 2012), p. 5.
149 Street, 'Cinema, Colour and the Festival of Britain', pp. 97–98.
150 Douglas Kennedy, 'An Open Letter from the Director to the Members of the Society', *English Dance and Song*, 10, 4 (1946), p. 44.
151 Douglas Kennedy, 'Festival of Britain', *English Dance and Song*, 15, 5 (1951), p. 169.
152 EFDSS, *The Dancing English* (London: EFDSS, 1951), p. 11.
153 John Jenner and Arthur Peck, *The Cambridge Morris Men: Fiftieth Anniversary, October 1974* (Letchworth: Hive Printers, 1974), p. 6.
154 Malcolm Ward, 'History of Ravensbourne' <https://www.ravensbourne.org/history> [accessed 14 August 2020].
155 Anon., *Chanctonbury Ring Morris Men: A History* (Sussex: Chanctonbury Ring Morris Men, 1983), p. 6.
156 G.I. Ginn, 'Dancing in Thaxted', *English Dance and Song*, 16, 3 (1951), p. 83.
157 Letter from Alec Hunter to Jack Thompson, 4 February 1952. Letchworth Garden City Collection (GCC) Online, 2012/35/190, <http://www.gardencitycollection.com/object-2012–35–190> [accessed 16 May 2020].
158 'British Railways: Essex' leaflet (1950). ERO, MS Thaxted, T/P 99/1.
159 Judge, 'Merrie England', p. 144.
160 Philip Dodd, 'Englishness and the National Culture', in *Englishness: Politics and Culture, 1880–1920*, ed. by Robert Colls and Philip Dodd (London: Croom Helm, 1986), p. 22.
161 Blackstone, 'The Aural and Moral Idylls', p. 570.

12

THE ENGLISH COUNTRY DANCE, CECIL SHARP AND AUTHENTICITY

Derek Schofield

The rediscovery of John Playford

The first volume of Cecil Sharp's *The Country Dance Book* in 1909 had followed the pattern of his previous and ongoing fieldwork-based approach to the collection and promotion of folk song and morris dances. The second volume in the same series, published barely two years later, was radically different: the dances it contained were culled from John Playford's 1651 work *The English Dancing Master*, and later editions of the same work.[1] In his extensive introduction to that second volume, Sharp wrote of Playford's work: 'For those interested in the revival of folk-dancing, it is the only book in which the English Country Dance, in its earliest, purest, and most characteristic forms, is described'.[2] This represented a major shift in Sharp's working practice, arguably in his broader outlook on tradition, and forms the central focus of this chapter.

Sharp had devoted the previous eight years to collecting, publishing and promoting English folk songs and morris dances. In extending his repertoire of dances for the expanding folk dance revival, the first part of *The Country Dance Book* contained a selection of 18 'traditional' country dances which he had collected from members of the rural working class in Warwickshire, Devon and Surrey. These dances he described as 'the ordinary everyday dance of the country folk'.[3] His informant in Devon, William Ford, was a blacksmith from Upper Pyne, a village north of Exeter. John Lavercombe, a retired bootmaker, lived in Tatsfield, four miles north of Oxted, Surrey, although he had been born in Puddington, Devon, and had also lived in London. In Warwickshire, the dances came from Thomas Hands, a groom and gardener, living in Honington but born in nearby Shipston-on-Stour. All three men were over the age of 60. Sharp met all these informants through his existing network of folk song contacts.[4] It is not clear from Sharp's manuscripts whether any of these three informants actually referred to 'country dances', but the longways formation of the dances he collected was sufficient for Sharp to categorise the dances in that way. Furthermore, for Sharp, these traditional country dances seemed closely related to those outlined by Playford and he believed that the style, if not the actual choreography, had been passed on through the generations for over 250 years.

Playford's *(English) Dancing Master* was published in multiple editions from 1651 until well into the eighteenth century and Sharp's *The Country Dance Book* finally achieved six parts. By the time Part two was published, Sharp had already deciphered 'very nearly all the dances in the first four editions of *The Dancing Master*'.[5] As far as he was concerned, the older the dance, the better, and he was particularly drawn to what he considered the older dances in the 1651 edition of Playford. These dances were in the formations of rounds, squares for eight dancers, a single line of dancers and longways for four, six and eight rather than the 'longways for as many as will' dances which predominated in the later editions of Playford, and which was the style of all the traditional dances Sharp himself collected. These apparently older formations would feature disproportionately in his later publications.[6] Part two of *The Country Dance Book* contained 30 dances from Playford. Part three (1912) had 34, Part four (1916) had 43 and Part six (1922) had 52. (Part five was devoted to the running set that Sharp and Maud Karpeles collected in the USA.) The country dance repertoire of the folk dance revival was therefore predominantly drawn from Playford: his work may originally have been aimed at an elite and literate audience but for Sharp the dances had been drawn from the rural village population, the peasantry.

To Sharp, the value of the dances lay in their age, their 'folk' origin, their 'wholly and demonstrably English' lineage and their purity.[7] These features were all, wrote Sharp, in stark contrast to the practices of ballroom and stage dance repertoires, not just of Edwardian England, but also of the eighteenth and nineteenth centuries.

Sharp was not the first person to have revealed the contents of Playford's collections. Margaret Dean-Smith noted that Jean-Baptiste Malchair (1730–1812), leader of the orchestra at Oxford Music Room, was the first person to examine and study the tunes in the Playford editions, and Malchair's colleague, William Crotch, gave some assistance to William Chappell in the compilation of *Popular Music of the Olden Time*.[8] Chappell's study drew on the various editions of Playford, thereby exposing more of the tunes (but not the dances) to new audiences. Ardern Holt was a regular contributor on fashion and costume for the popular publication *The Queen, The Lady's Newspaper and Court Chronicle*, as well as the author of a book on the subject of costume for fancy balls. In 1888, she wrote that the inclusion of 'old dances' would make fancy balls more attractive and, in addition to promoting the pavane, galliard and minuet, she recommended the Triumph and Cottagers, two dances which are 'often danced now in country places'. Holt included a description of how to dance the former and described the 1686 edition of Playford as 'one of the most interesting and valuable old books on dancing'.[9] Two years later, Frank Kidson, founder member of the Folk-Song Society, published *Old English Country Dances* which included tunes from the Playford editions. His extensive notes and bibliography of published country dance music collections, from Playford's era through to the early nineteenth century, displayed Kidson's detailed knowledge of English tune collections and suggested a more wide-ranging appreciation of English music than that of Sharp.[10]

By 1891, dance teacher Robert M. Crompton, who took full advantage of opportunities to teach historical dances to elite society as well as for the stage, was offering 'Old English Country Dances' amongst the gavottes and minuets.[11] Although more dance teachers started to include country dances in their offer, their sources are uncertain and these country dances, rather like the morris dances of the period, may have owed more to the choreographic imaginations of the teachers than to historical source.[12] However, even after most country dances had disappeared from ballrooms to be replaced by the waltz, quadrille and polka, one particular country dance, 'Sir Roger de Coverley', remained a popular choice for the last dance of the evening. This continued enactment of the longways set may have provided the public with a memory and point of reference for the renewed interest in country dances.

Elsewhere, stemming particularly from the work of Arnold Dolmetsch and an associated interest in early music, there emerged a desire for greater historical choreographic accuracy. Nellie Chaplin (1857–1930) and her two sisters, Kate and Mabel, were all accomplished classical musicians, forming the Chaplin Trio. Having attended a lecture on historical dance in 1903, Nellie was intrigued to find out what the dances looked like.[13] In 1904, she was invited to accompany Dolmetsch on the harpsichord and soon after acquired her own instrument. With the assistance of Carlo Coppi, ballet master and choreographer for Arthur Sullivan's *Victoria and Merrie England* (1897), she gave her first performance of dances, including the pavane, galliard, allemande, courante, sarabande, minuet, gavotte together with national dances: tarantella, jota Aragonese, hornpipe, Irish jig and Scotch reel. This was in July 1904[14] and with Nellie on harpsichord, Kate on *viol d'amore* and violin and Mabel on the *viol da gamba* plus cello, the dances were performed by the pupils, mainly children, of dance teacher Susie Boyle.[15]

Having purchased a copy of the 1665 edition of John Playford's *The Dancing Master*, Chaplin added several of the dances to her concert performances, now billed as 'Ancient Dances and Music'. The first such concert, in St George's Hall, London, on 30 June 1906, featured five 'Old English Dances'.[16] The dances, described in a report as bringing back 'all the simple grace of the countryside', were arranged by Miss Cowper Coles. (Performances sometimes featured spoken passages of explanation and on at least one occasion the orator was Lily Grove, author of a popular work on dance as well as wife to the influential classicist James Frazer.[17]) Alice Cowper Coles (1861–1910) was a dance teacher whose earlier concert, performed in March of the same year, had featured 140 of her pupils. A report described her skill in the 'revival of historic and picturesque national dances of various countries', as well as 'old English country dances executed by some tiny mites in the quaintest of smocks and sun bonnets'.[18] Prior to Cowper-Coles's death, Chaplin was already using the services of an additional dance teacher, Mrs Mary Woolnoth, who added further dances from the Playford publication to the repertoire.[19] Woolnoth was also associated with another promoter of old dances: Grace Kimmins.

Grace Hannam (1870–1954) had married Charles William Kimmins in 1898. He was a psychologist who became chief inspector of education at London County Council. Grace, a social reformer at the West London Mission and then the Bermondsey Settlement, was the founder in 1894 of the Guild of the Brave Poor Things, which assisted poor, physically handicapped children and young people. The same year, she also founded the Guild of Play for children, who performed at the Bermondsey May Day Festival, which had started in 1896.[20] This provided a connection with the work of Mary Neal who also worked alongside Chaplin on several occasions, and shared with Kimmins a deep concern for London's deprived children. Although the work of the Espérance Club was largely focussed on the morris dance, Neal did include traditional country dances from more recent sources in her demonstrations.

By the early years of the new century, musicians and dance teachers started to publish material from their repertoires, no doubt with the intention of further promoting their work and offering encouragement to others.[21] Ardern Holt stood out by virtue of providing a longer publication with commentary and some history, as well as dance notations.[22]

This concentration on the country dance and Playford's publications fitted a wider interest in Tudor and Stuart life and music, with editions of *The Fitzwilliam Virginal Book*, madrigals and Elizabethan love songs all being published at this time. And, as Alun Howkins has written, 'The Tudor World was firmly rural'. Moreover, 'Tudor England and the countryside were to be brought together as a new basis for an English national music'.[23] The later term 'Tudorism', described as the 'post-Tudor mobilization of any and all representations, images, associations, artefacts, spaces, and cultural scripts that have or are supposed to have their roots in the Tudor era',[24] could include – musically – a revival of the music from that period, new compositions in similar style, evoking the Tudor period to establish a political agenda for music, or simply an excuse for 'old English antiquarianism'.[25] In fact, such interest in old music was not confined to the Tudor period, and expanded into the following century and the music of Purcell. Moving away from music, Theresa Buckland has documented the expanding interest in a wide range of old dances in the late Victorian and Edwardian eras. Different forms of this phenomenon extended across the social classes with the common intention, Buckland argues, to portray an image of 'olde England'.[26] Amongst an array of dances from a variety of eras was the country dance.

This interest in the country dance alongside Tudor and Stuart music could be considered part of a broader 'Merrie England' movement, a reference back to an imagined golden age of Queen Elizabeth, Shakespeare and Purcell, a rural myth that 'passed into popular mythology where it was identified as the authentic site of Merrie England'.[27] Roy Judge wrote extensively on this phenomenon, with regard to both May Day and morris dancing before Sharp's revival, describing it as 'A world that has never actually existed, a visionary, mythical landscape, where it is difficult to take normal bearings'.[28] In the midst of the increased interest in old dances and the flurry of publications, Cecil Sharp published *The Country Dance Book*.

Sharp's emerging concept of authenticity

Cecil Sharp (1859–1924) was born in London, the son of a slate merchant. He was educated at Uppingham School and Clare College, Cambridge, where he studied mathematics and reportedly worked harder at his music than his mathematics.[29] Upon graduating, Sharp emigrated to Adelaide, Australia, where he soon followed a music career teaching and conducting and he became a co-director of a college of music. By 1892, Sharp had returned to England, and the following year became a music teacher at a preparatory school, Ludgrove. Later that year, he married Constance Birch and they had four children. He supported the Liberals and later the Labour Party, and in 1900 joined the Fabian Society. Alongside his part-time post at Ludgrove, Sharp became the principal of Hampstead Conservatoire in 1896, resigning in 1905.

In 1899, the Sharp family spent Christmas with his mother-in-law in Headington, Oxford, where, on Boxing Day, he witnessed an out-of-season performance by the Headington Quarry Morris Dancers. He noted some of the tunes from their Anglo-German concertina player, William Kimber, but thought little more about it.

As a music teacher, Sharp was concerned about the quality of music education in schools, including suitable repertoire. Evidence from Ludgrove School archives and former pupils indicates that Sharp was teaching folk and national songs to his pupils in the 1890s, culled from existing song books which drew from Chappell's *Popular Music of the Olden Time*.[30] Not content with existing song books, he published his own collection in 1902.[31] In the introduction to his *Book of British Song*, Sharp explained the criteria for selection: songs that had 'stood the test of time [...] traditional, and, being chiefly of folk origin, are of assured humanity'.[32] Sixty-six of the 78 songs in the book were English, and rather than selecting them from Chappell, he had turned to recent publications by collectors such as Lucy Broadwood and Sabine Baring-Gould to choose songs that had been 'handed down among our peasantry from generation to generation, and are still to be heard in country places'.[33]

Even before he had started his own folk song fieldwork, therefore, Sharp had articulated important elements in his criteria for collection: songs that had lasted, were traditional, of folk origin, passed down through generations of the peasantry, noted directly from the singer, from the countryside and English.

In 1907, by then with the experience of having collected some 1,500 tunes, Sharp published *English Folk-Song: Some Conclusions*. From the introduction alone, it can be seen how similar his 1902 criteria were to those represented by his actual song collecting. The 'English peasant' is the source of songs which are 'genuinely and demonstrably English' and which were being collected in 'rural England'. In order to maintain the authenticity of what he was collecting, Sharp emphasised that the work of collecting was now taking place 'in the right spirit, scientifically, accurately, and above all with a scrupulous honesty and conscientiousness' with 'truthfulness and exactness' in the song transcriptions.[34]

The book also elucidated his criteria and identified other aspects of folk song authenticity. The songs had been created by the 'common people', who were 'unlettered' or 'noneducated', that is, not in close contact with educated people and not influenced by them. They lived in remote areas, having 'escaped the infection of modern ideas'.[35] The genuine folk song was not the product of individual composition, Sharp argued, but rather communal composition, by which he meant that, although a song may have had a single author, it was changed, deliberately or subconsciously, by the process of oral transmission from singer to singer. The folk song was also communal in the way it 'reflects the mind of the community'.[36] Fascinatingly, there is little comment in *Some Conclusions* about singing style, and the sung illustrations included in Sharp's public lectures were delivered by a classically trained singer.

Meanwhile, on noting the interest in morris dance evoked by Mary Neal and the Espérance Club from 1905 onwards, he recognised the potential of promoting the dances he had first seen in 1899 to new audiences. Sharp faced several difficulties when it came to the collection and publication of morris dances. First, unlike song, there were no earlier collections on which to draw and seek inspiration. Second, there was no notation system for dance and he and Herbert MacIlwaine, the Espérance Club's musical director with whom Sharp published the first three volumes of *The Morris Book*, had to devise their own system. Third, in collecting morris dances, Sharp looked to similar sources as his song collecting: the rural working class.[37] In this respect, although Sharp understood many of the dances he collected had been danced by groups of six men, generally he was collecting from single, aged dancers, from variously defunct dance teams. Their memory and physicality must have impacted on the impression Sharp gained.

Additionally, the first volume of *The Morris Book* (1907) contained two significant flaws which Sharp corrected in a second edition (1912).[38] The first was that he and MacIlwaine notated the Headington dances, not from the traditional source, but from one of the Espérance women who had been taught by the Headington dancers: subsequently, all dances in volumes three, four and five were notated from the source dancers. The second flaw was that the other dances came from the Bidford Morris Dancers, a group established in 1886 by a pageant master, Ernest Richard D'Arcy Ferris, with an antiquarian outlook.[39] Sharp wrote in 1912 that the Bidford dances had been omitted from the second edition because 'on further investigation, we found that the traditional authority upon which they rested was less trustworthy then we had believed them to be'.[40] As Judge commented, Sharp was 'rigidly insistent on purity of transmission' and intolerant of the 'variety and changing character of village traditions'.[41]

Further indications of Sharp's criteria for morris dance authenticity were included in the introduction to the third part of *The Morris Book*. The dances from Winster, Derbyshire, were described as 'authentic examples' of an 'ancient and uninterrupted tradition', which were, moreover, 'singularly beautiful and picturesque'.[42]

With the difficulties in dance notation and its interpretation, morris dance transmission within the folk dance revival was highly dependent on personal teaching. For Sharp, it was imperative that teaching should be accurate so that the dances were passed on 'in the purest form possible'.[43] Neal, however, argued that the source dancers did not always demonstrate and teach the dances to the Espérance women in a consistent way, and that variation was part of the transmission process. While accepting variation on the part of the source dancers, Sharp published the steps and movements which 'seemed to be the best and most accurately to represent the type', and thereafter he insisted that this was the prescribed standard.[44] Sharp trained his own teaching staff at Chelsea College of Physical Education, who, in turn, taught at the vacation schools at Stratford-upon-Avon and later in London, all under Sharp's careful eye, with examinations for the dance pupils (many of them school teachers), to ensure that standards were upheld. By comparison, Sharp considered the Espérance-taught dancers to be graceless, undignified and uncouth, and often used the word 'romp' to describe their displays. At first, Sharp had endorsed the performances of the dances by the young women of the Espérance Club, but he and Neal soon fell out over the standards of dancing, teaching methods and the leadership of the emerging song and dance revival.[45]

Sharp, authenticity and the country dance

As described, Sharp's criteria for authenticity were already well established by the time he turned his attention to the country dance. Indeed, the similarity of the longways formation of the dances he had collected to the principal style revealed in Playford's work convinced Sharp that what he had collected was old.

His collecting trip to Warwickshire had taken place in September 1909, and the first *The Country Dance Book* was published before the end of that year, which suggests that Sharp had already determined the method of explaining the dances and had written, or at least drafted, the introduction.[46] The book was divided into four sections: an introduction, a section on the dance formation, steps and figures, and the notation of the dances. Sharp assumed that his audience knew little about the country dance; he gave a diagram of the set indicating the relative positions of men and women and outlined the distance between the two lines of the longways set, and the distance between the couples. This was only the third volume of published dance notations made by Cecil Sharp, and the first that he had published alone. His four sections followed a structure that was similar to that used in the morris dance volumes, that is, figures common to a series of dances were described, then followed by descriptions of individual dances, referencing these 'chorus' figures.

Sharp described 34 separate figures, amounting to 21 pages (a third of the total), compared with 18 pages of individual dance descriptions (one per dance). Although Sharp offered no acknowledgement of Thomas Wilson, the early nineteenth-century dancing master and author, it is clear that Wilson's books inspired Sharp's descriptions. Wilson had published country dance figures, but generally without describing how these figures were used in the make-up of individual dances. Some of the diagrams used by Sharp to describe figures were directly copied from Wilson's books.[47] Wilson's reasoning was that, at that stage, the country dance had a fluid composition, being able to draw on any of a large number of figures. It was the decision of the first or top couple in the set to determine which figures were to be danced.

Even with Wilson's assistance, Sharp's ability to deconstruct dances into series of separate and clearly explained figures, sometimes only a matter of weeks after the dances had been collected, gives an indication of Sharp's developing ability to analyse dance movement.

In his description of the dance formation, Sharp explained that the distinctive longways form of the dance, with lines of men facing lines of women, had several different mechanisms of progression to change the order of the couples so that, for example, the top couple might move down the set to a different position. For Sharp, the progressive feature of the dance 'is the essential and distinctive, as it is the invariable, feature of the Country Dance'.[48] The simplest progression was for the top couple to go to the bottom of the set, then for the second couple to go to the bottom and so on. Less simply, there were also minor set dances in which the figures were 'performed simultaneously by subsidiary sets or groups of two, or sometimes three, adjacent couples'.[49] Sharp explained these minor set formations and progressions using grids of the dance sets, once again taking inspiration from Wilson.[50] Sharp identified duple minor sets and triple minor sets, depending on whether the dancers moved in two or three couple minor sets. The term 'minor set' was used by Wilson, although he did not use the terms duple and triple. It is not clear where Sharp obtained these terms, or whether he invented them himself.

There are no descriptions of the minor sets within the larger longways sets in Sharp's fieldwork manuscripts. This may have been because he only collected from sets of dancers that were too small to split into minor sets: there is no indication how many dancers were available when he collected the dances. Alternatively, he may have been already aware of the way in which the dances he was collecting would be performed, that is to say with longer sets, or perhaps he obtained this information from publications such as Wilson's. Nevertheless, the absence of evidence in his manuscripts must cast some doubt on how accurate the published notations were in terms of the descriptions offered by his informants.

As already noted, a key feature of Sharp's work was his requirement for accuracy, and this is restated in the introduction to the first *The Country Dance Book*. There are, however, several instances which challenge his notion. For example, Christopher Walker reveals that the published version of the dance 'The Triumph' includes the distinctive 'triumph' figure, which is not included in Sharp's manuscripts.[51] There is also ambiguity surrounding the steps to be used in the dances. Sharp failed to note any steps when collecting the dances, but wrote, 'The normal Country Dance step is a springy walking step'.[52] He acknowledged that the galop, polka and waltz steps were sometimes used, and mentions other steps for particular figures, but wrote that the steps should be performed 'very smoothly and quietly; the feet should slide where possible, and, if raised, should not be lifted more than two or three inches from the ground'.[53] Yet when the villagers of Armscote, Warwickshire, gave a display of their dances in Stratford-upon-Avon in 1911, Helen Kennedy recalled: 'The Armscote dancers used the polka step throughout, the men stepping with great vigour, cocking the free leg up behind to get a good send off. The more vigorous the men became the more dainty and demure the women'.[54]

By April 1910, some of the collected and published dances, including 'The Triumph', were already featuring in Sharp's lectures.[55] As we know, Sharp had announced his intention to publish dances from the Playford volumes in his introduction to Part one of *The Country Dance Book*.[56] Even before Part two was published, during the summer of 1911, some of the Playford dances were featuring in his lecture demonstrations, to the detriment of the traditional dances.[57] By this stage, the full range of Sharp's dance collecting was being displayed: morris, long and short sword, alongside traditional and Playford country dances. Sharp was appointed by the governors of the Stratford Memorial Theatre to direct the folk song and dance school in Stratford-upon-Avon for four weeks in July and August 1911, to replace Mary Neal, and in December 1911 the English Folk Dance Society (hereafter EFDS) was founded.[58] Thereafter, Sharp's lecture demonstrations had an additional purpose – to encourage the founding of branches of the EFDS around the country.

Sharp's statements regarding the criteria he used for the collection of authentic folk songs and morris dances would seem to be at odds with his practice regarding those country dances he published and popularised. In spite of his statement that the dances in Playford were the 'earliest, purest, and most characteristic forms', they had not been collected orally, and Playford's intended audience must have been drawn from literate and elite society. There were no further collecting trips specifically to find country dances, and the dances Sharp collected in Goathland in 1914 remained hidden in his manuscripts until the 1950s.[59]

Sharp's defence of the country dance

In trying to distance himself from other promoters of country dance who held a more antiquarian outlook, Sharp felt a need to confirm ideas of authenticity. He pursued this through seeking to establish several criteria: that the dance form should be English, should be of folk origin, should be old but not revived in an antiquarian style and should constitute an art form with a modern outlook.

Sharp believed, though with uncertain evidence and displaying his own aesthetic judgement, that the country dance passed through three phases. The first phase was the 'folk period' when it was a 'genuine' folk dance of 'the village green, the farmhouse and the dancing booths'. The second phase was the fifteenth, sixteenth and seventeenth centuries when it became consciously developed and 'somewhat sophisticated', nevertheless reaching the 'highest pitch of perfection', conveniently coinciding with Playford's initial publication and the golden age of the Tudors and Stuarts. This was when it 'slowly invaded the parlours and drawing-rooms of the wealthy', becoming a refreshing contrast to the more formal dances of polite society. Sharp was keen to emphasise that the dance had never been 'the exclusive possession of any one class'. The third phase was in the eighteenth and nineteenth centuries when it entered 'an age of degeneracy' as a result of the influence of professional dancing masters, who introduced 'the posturings, the elegant steps and posings, the languishing glances'.[60] For Sharp, the period of degeneracy was consequent on the increasingly cosmopolitan nature of English society following the Restoration, when Charles II's introduction of European influences replaced authentic English music and dances.[61] Sharp had already made his views on the neglect of English music well known.

> Since the death of Purcell […] the educated classes have patronized the music of the foreigner, to the exclusion of that of the Englishman. Foreign vocalists, singing in a foreign tongue, have for two centuries monopolized the operatic stage; while English concert platforms have […] been exclusively occupied by alien singers and instrumentalists.[62]

Fortunately, Sharp argued, authentic English song and dance had been carried through the centuries by the peasant singer and dancer.

As already noted, Sharp was clear that the country dance was 'wholly and demonstrably English'. He could quote John Essex (1710) that it was 'originally the product of this nation' and John Weaver (1712) that the country dance was 'the peculiar growth of this nation' and go on to show that the French *contredanse* had itself derived from the English country dance.[63] However, the country dance had continued to be a feature of the ballroom and drawing room from Playford's time into the nineteenth century, so Sharp needed to argue that Playford, especially in the early editions, described the dance in its 'purest' form. But while he stressed the purity of the country dance in the seventeenth century, he was also keen to distance his revival from any hint of antiquarianism.

Sharp resisted performative expressions of Merrie England such as May days, masques and pageants. He had already had his fingers burnt with D'Arcy Ferris's Bidford Morris Dancers and he was little interested in maypole dancing or in the Knutsford May Day.[64] He was not involved in events such as Bermondsey May Day, the May Day English Dance Cycle at the Globe Theatre in May 1912 or Shakespeare's England at Earl's Court in the summer of that year.

Chaplin and the Espérance dancers had performed at the latter two events[65] but, by 1911, Sharp had fallen out with Mary Neal. His opinion of the Espérance dancers and Chaplin can be gauged from a letter he wrote following his visit to a large music festival in Blackpool: 'The rest of the teams were simply execrable – the worst type of Chaplin cum Esperance dancing. I never could have imagined that folk dancing could become so debased and present so gruesome a spectacle'.[66] Press reports indicate that participating school children wore 'old court dress', or were dressed in 'Georgian court dress' as 'fayre ladyes and brave cavaliers'.[67] No doubt for the teachers and audience, these seventeenth-century costumes looked 'authentic' even if not entirely historically accurate. The dress of the dancers performing country dances seemed to be a good indicator, certainly to Sharp, of the Merrie England approach that he deplored. The books referred to in endnote 21 include posed photographs of the children (all girls with some dressed as boys) attired in the 'olde worlde' fashion mentioned above. One of Sharp's supporters and close collaborators, Ralph Vaughan Williams, commented on photographs of Chaplin's dancers: 'those terrible ogling young women who are supposed to be dancing a country dance [...] she [Chaplin] ought to be ashamed of herself!'[68] It is likely that this was also indicative of Sharp's views.

In contrast, Sharp's dancers wore contemporary outfits. He wanted the dances to be relevant in the present day and suited for easy participation, so dressed in a more accessible style. In December 1912, for example, the EFDS dancers gave a concert at the Savoy Theatre, London, where theatre director Harvey Granville Barker was producing Shakespeare's *Twelfth Night*. The women dancers' costumes were designed by Barker's stage designer, Norman Wilkinson: 'blue dresses of almost classical simplicity',[69] and these outfits, or something similar, were used in many subsequent performances. Men were dressed in white shirts and trousers which, with the addition of bells and baldricks, were also used for morris dances. The staging was also simple, a plain white backdrop, drawing press comment: 'absolutely removed [...] from any taint of staginess, it was satisfactory that no attempt was made to give them a background of rural scenery. Such an attempt at realism would at once have made them seem artificial'.[70] Similarly, in contrast to Chaplin's early instruments, Sharp used contemporary accompaniment from the violin and piano.

In 1912, he wrote in the *Daily Mail*,

> There is nothing archaic about this revival. The dances are commended not because they are redolent of a past day and engage the interest of the antiquary, not even because they are English in origin and may be expected to exert a wholesome influence, but solely on their own merits as art forms possessing an attraction for the men and women of today.[71]

Although he was keen to have folk dancing included in schools as part of the new *Syllabus of Physical Exercises*, Sharp regarded its value as an art form to be just as important. This stress on folk dance as an art form was emphasised at the foundation meeting of the EFDS in 1911. The folk dance movement, Sharp was reported as saying, was 'primarily an artistic movement', which was liable to 'suffer at the hands of philanthropy' and be subject to the 'ravages of the Philistines on every side'. The purpose of establishing the EFDS was to view folk dancing 'from a purely artistic standpoint' and to keep it on 'its right lines and prevent it from becoming vulgarised and popularised' although popularisation 'in the best sense of the word' was the aim.[72] The comment on philanthropy was no doubt aimed at Mary Neal and the Espérance dancers, although he may also have had Chaplin and others in his sights with his comments on Philistines and vulgarisation.

Sharp's emphasis on 'art' drew at least two critics. At the conference held in Stratford-upon-Avon during the 1912 summer school as an attempt to reconcile the disagreements between Neal and Sharp, Frank Benson, whose theatre company produced Shakespeare's plays in the town, spoke on the 'danger of over-emphasising the art side at the expense of the unconscious joy side'. He referred to 'the Scylla of academic perfection and the Charybdis of the untutored joy of the savage'. For Sharp, joy and pleasure alone were not enough and art that was not accurate would perish.[73]

Sharp's other 'art' critic was Mary Neal. Writing in *The Observer*, Neal commented on a display by Sharp's dancers:

> the dancing was beautiful, graceful and charming […] it falls into the category of the art and not the folk dance […] beautiful and graceful as their dancing is, it is far removed from what I saw at Bampton at Whitsuntide.[74]

In choosing to distance himself from other promoters of the country dance, Sharp effectively positioned himself as looking forward rather than back. Because nostalgia appeared to be an essential characteristic of folk performance, it was often assumed to be a backward-looking form. However, it was also an idealisation and must therefore have implied hope for a better future. For Sharp and many others, the folk dance revival was both a celebration of artistic authenticity and an alternative to modernity.[75] As such, Sharp's country dance revival practice might be considered part of the broader Arts and Crafts Movement.

Notes

1 John Playford, *The English Dancing Master* (London: John Playford, 1651). For a full bibliographical list of all the subsequent editions of what, from the 1652 second edition onwards, was titled *The Dancing Master*, see Margaret Dean-Smith, *Playford's English Dancing Master 1651: A Facsimile Reprint with an Introduction, Bibliography and Notes* (London: Schott, 1957), pp. xxi–xxxi. Dean-Smith notes that only three known copies of the 1651 edition were in existence.
2 Cecil J. Sharp, *The Country Dance Book, Part II* (London: Novello, 1911), p. 26. Hereafter *CDB* 1911.
3 Cecil J. Sharp, *The Country Dance Book, Part I* (London: Novello, 1909), p. 10. Hereafter *CDB* 1909.
4 Derek Schofield, 'The Everyday Dance of the Country Folk', *English Dance & Song*, 73, 1 (Spring 2011), 12–13.
5 Sharp, *CDB* 1911, pp. 14–15.
6 Ibid., pp. 15–17.
7 Sharp, *CDB* 1909, p. 11.
8 Dean-Smith, *Playford*, p. ix. Alice Little, '"For the Sake of Difference": John Malchair's Categorisations of Tunes, 1760–95', *Folk Music Journal*, 11, 5 (2020), 52–66. William Chappell, *Popular Music of the Olden Time: A Collection of Ancient Songs, Ballads and Dance Tunes, Illustrative of the National Music of England*, 2 vols. (London: Cramer, Beale and Chappell, [1858–59]).

9   Ardern Holt, 'Dances Suitable for Fancy Balls', *The Queen, the Lady's Newspaper and Court Chronicle*, 29 December 1888. Ardern Holt *Fancy Dresses Described; Or What to Wear at Fancy Balls*, 5th edition (London: Debenham & Freebody, 1887) where she wrote that "Country dances are being resuscitated for costume balls" (p. 8).
10 Frank Kidson, ed., *Old English Country Dances, Gathered from Scarce Printed Collections, and from Manuscripts* (London: William Reeves, 1890).
11 Theresa Jill Buckland, 'Dance and Cultural Memory: Interpreting Fin de Siècle Performances of "Olde England"', *Dance Research*, 31, 1 (2013), 29–66, (pp. 37, 46). See also Buckland's 'Crompton's Campaign: The Professionalisation of Dance Pedagogy in Late Victorian England', *Dance Research*, 25, 1 (2007), 1–34.
12 Roy Judge, 'Merrie England and the Morris 1881–1900', *Folklore*, 104 (1991), 124–143 (p. 129).
13 Nellie Chaplin, 'Ancient Dances and Music', *The Sackbut*, 3, 3 (October 1922), 84–87.
14 Ibid., p. 84.
15 'Dances of the Olden Time', *St James's Gazette*, 7 July 1904.
16 Advertisement, *Morning Post*, 12 May 1906.
17 'Ancient Music and Dances', *St. James's Gazette*, 9 January 1905. Lily Grove, *Dancing* (London: Longman, Green, 1895).
18 'Musical Notes', *London Evening Standard*, 24 March 1906.
19 'Gaiety Theatre: Ancient Dances and Music', *Manchester Courier and Lancashire General Advertiser*, 16 February 1910. A list of dances is given in a letter from Nellie Chaplin to Cecil Sharp, 7 November 1910, Cecil Sharp Correspondence Collection, Vaughan Williams Memorial Library, CJS1/12/3/11/2, available online.
20 Ros Black, *Grace Kimmins and Her Chailey Heritage* (Haywards Heath: Arbe, 2017); Theresa Jill Buckland, 'Pioneering England's Dances among Late Victorian Youth: On the Early Work of Mary Neal and Grace Kimmins', in *(Re)Searching the Field: Festschrift in Honour of Egil Bakka*, ed. by Anne Margrete Fiskvik and Marit Stranden (Bergen, Norway: Fagbokforlaget, 2014), pp. 319–330.
21 G.T. Kimmins and M.H. Woolnoth, *The Guild of Play Book of Festival and Dance* (London: Curwen, 1907); Nellie Chaplin, *Ancient Dances and Music: Six Dances from Playford's "Dancing Master"* (London: Curwen, [1909]; Miss Cowper Coles, *Old English Dance Steps: Early Country Dances of the 17th Century* (London: Curwen, 1909); Miss Cowper Coles, *Greensleeves and Other Old Dances Including the Gavotte and Minuet* (London: Curwen, 1910); Nellie Chaplin, *Court Dances and Others* (London: Curwen, 1911); Alfred Moffat and Frank Kidson, *Dances of the Olden Time* (London: Bayley & Ferguson, 1912); Mary H. Woolnoth, *Playford's Country Dances* (London: Curwen, 1913); Frank Kidson, *English Country Dances Arranged for Children's Performance* (London: Curwen, 1914).
22 Ardern Holt, *How to Dance the Revived Ancient Dances* (London: Horace Cox, 1907). The book was dedicated to Nellie Chaplin.
23 Alun Howkins, 'The Discovery of Rural England', in *Englishness, Politics and Culture 1880–1920*, ed. by Robert Colls and Philip Dodd (London, Bloomsbury, 2014 [Croom Helm, 1986]) pp. 85–111 (pp. 94–95).
24 Tatiana C. String and Marcus Bull, 'Introduction', in *Tudorism: Historical Imagination and the Appropriation of the Sixteenth Century*, ed. by Tatiana C. String and Marcus Bull (Oxford: Oxford University Press, 2011), p. 1.
25 Stephen Banfield, 'Tudorism in English Music, 1837–1953', in *Tudorism: Historical Imagination*, pp. 57–77 (p. 60).
26 Buckland, 'Dance and Cultural Memory'.
27 John Burrow, *A Liberal Descent: Victorian Historians and the English Past* (Cambridge: Cambridge University Press, 1981), p. 249, quoted in Howkins 'The Discovery of Rural England', p. 94.
28 Roy Judge, 'May Day and Merrie England', *Folklore*, 102, ii (1991), 131–148 (p. 131); Judge, 'Merrie England and the Morris'.
29 A.H. Fox Strangways, in collaboration with Maud Karpeles, *Cecil Sharp* (London: Oxford University Press, 1933), pp. 1–6.
30 Derek Schofield, 'Sowing the Seeds: Cecil Sharp and Charles Marson in Somerset', *Folk Music Journal*, 8, 4 (2004), 484–512. See also Gordon Cox, *A History of Music Education in England, 1872–1928* (Aldershot: Scolar Press, 1993).
31 Cecil J. Sharp, *A Book of British Song for Home and School* (London: John Murray, 1902).
32 Sharp, *British Song*, p. vi.

33 Sharp, *British Song*, p. vii. See also Schofield, 'Sowing the Seeds', pp. 486–490.
34 Cecil J. Sharp, *English Folk-Song: Some Conclusions* (London: Simpkin, Novello, 1907), pp. vii–viii.
35 Ibid., pp. 3–4.
36 Sharp, *Conclusions*, pp. 10–11, 14.
37 Keith Chandler, *Morris Dancing in the English South Midlands, 1660–1900: A Chronological Gazetteer* (Enfield Lock: Hisarlik for The Folklore Society, 1993), p. 8: "the majority of performers were working-class labourers or, at best, small craftsmen".
38 Cecil J. Sharp and Herbert C. MacIlwaine, *The Morris Book, Part I* (London: Novello, 1907). Second edition 1912.
39 Roy Judge, 'D'Arcy Ferris and the Bidford Morris', *Folk Music Journal*, 4, 5 (1984), 443–480.
40 Sharp and MacIlwaine, *The Morris Book*, 1912, p. 8.
41 Judge, 'D'Arcy Ferris', p. 475.
42 Cecil J. Sharp & Herbert C. MacIlwaine, *The Morris Book, Part III* (London: Novello, 1910), p. 12.
43 Cecil Sharp to Mary Neal, 14 March 1909, Sharp Correspondence, Box 5, Folder A. Quoted in Judge, 'Mary Neal', footnote 69.
44 Sharp and MacIlwaine, *The Morris Book*, 1912, p. 44.
45 Roy Judge, 'Mary Neal and the Espérance Morris', *Folk Music Journal*, 5, 5 (1989), 545–591; Derek Schofield, *Absolutely Classic: The Music of William Kimber* (London: EFDSS, 1999) booklet accompanying CD; Bob Grant, 'When Punch Met Merry', *Folk Music Journal*, 7, 5 (1999), 644–655.
46 The date of publication in the book is 1909; although as the first reviews were not published until March 1910, it is possible that the book was not published until early 1910. Nevertheless, the manuscript must have been with the publisher before the end of 1909.
47 Thomas Wilson, *An Analysis of Country Dancing Wherein Are Displayed All the Figures Ever Used in Country Dances* (London: W. Calvert, 1808); Thomas Wilson, *An Analysis of Country Dancing Wherein All the Figures Used in That Polite Amusement Are Rendered Familiar by Engraved Lines* (London: J.S. Dickson, 1811); Thomas Wilson, *The Complete System of English Country Dancing Containing All the Figures Ever Used in English Country Dancing, with a Variety of New Figures, and New Reels* (London: Sherwood, Neeley and Jones, [1815]).
48 Sharp, *CDB* 1909, p. 18.
49 Ibid., p. 19.
50 Ibid., pp. 17–24.
51 Christopher B. Walker, '"The Triumph" in England, Scotland and the United States', *Folk Music Journal*, 8, 1 (2001), 4–40 (p. 27).
52 Sharp, *CDB* 1909, p. 25.
53 Ibid., p. 26.
54 Helen Kennedy, 'Fifty Years Ago', *English Dance & Song*, XIX, 5 (April–May 1955), 158–159.
55 London Shakespeare League, Mansion House, London. Programme, Vaughan Williams Memorial Library, AS11.
56 Sharp, *CDB* 1909, pp. 12–13.
57 These included a December 1910 performance at Chelsea College: Musicus, 'Sword Dance', *Daily Telegraph*, December 1910. Press Cuttings Book 5, Vaughan Williams Memorial Library; and in January 1911 at the Stationers' Hall for the Worshipful Company of Musicians: 'The Musicians' Company', *Musical Times*, March 1911. Press Cuttings Book 6 and programme, Vaughan Williams Memorial Library, AS11.
58 Derek Schofield, '"Revival of the Folk Dance: An Artistic Movement": The Background to the Founding of The English Folk Dance Society in 1911', *Folk Music Journal*, 5, 2 (1986), 215–219.
59 Derek Schofield, 'Sharp Visits Goathland Again, In Search of Country Dances', *English Dance & Song*, 75, 2 (Summer 2013), 27–28.
60 Sharp, *CDB* 1911, pp. 8–9; 'Mr. Cecil Sharp's Lectures: The Country Dance', *Stratford-upon-Avon Herald*, 15 August 1913. Press Cuttings Book 6, Vaughan Williams Memorial Library.
61 Sharp, *CDB* 1909, p. 7.
62 Sharp, *Some Conclusions*, p. 129. Sharp also refers to English musicians who are trained "to lisp in the tongue of the foreigner" (p. 132).
63 It had been variously argued that the origin of the country dance lay with the *contredanse*. Sharp wrote: "it was the French who adapted one particular form of the English Dance, known as 'A square dance for eight', developed it, called it *contredanse*, and sent it back to England, where in the Quadrille, one of its numerous varieties, it still survives". Sharp, *CDB* 1909, p. 11. For Weaver,

see Richard Ralph, *The Life and Works of John Weaver: An Account of His Life. Writings and Theatrical Productions, with an Annotated Reprint of His Complete Publications* (London: Dance Books, 1985), p. 668. In a 1711 article in *The Spectator*, Weaver described the country dance as the "particular Invention of our own Country"; see Ralph, p. 380.

64 Cecil Sharp to Archibald Flower, 12 February 1911, Sharp Correspondence, Box 5, Folder B, Esperance 2, Vaughan Williams Memorial Library.

65 'English Dance Cycle: May Day Matinee at the Globe Theatre', *The Observer*, 8 May 1912. Press Cuttings Book 10, Vaughan Williams Memorial Library; Marion F. O'Connor, 'Theatre of the Empire: "Shakespeare's England" at Earl's Court, 1912' in *Shakespeare Reproduced: The Text in History and Ideology*, ed. by Jean E. Howard and Marion F. O'Connor (London: Methuen, 1987), 69–98. See also Derek Schofield, 'Visions of English Identity: The Country Dance and Shakespeare-land', in *Folklore and Nation in Britain and Ireland*, ed. by Matthew Cheeseman and Carina Hart (Abingdon: Routledge, forthcoming).

66 Cecil Sharp to Archibald Flower, 14 October 1912, Sharp Correspondence, Box 5, Folder B, Esperance 2, Vaughan Williams Memorial Library.

67 Unidentified Blackpool newspaper, October 1912, Press Cuttings Book 6, Vaughan Williams Memorial Library.

68 Letter from Ralph Vaughan Williams to Lucy Broadwood, 22 January 1913, in Hugh Cobbe, ed., *Letters of Ralph Vaughan Williams 1895–1958* (Oxford: Oxford University Press, 2008), pp. 86–89 (pp. 87–88). Also available online, No. VWL386, http://vaughanwilliams.uk/letter/vwl386 (Accessed 11 September 2020).

69 'Folk Dances and Songs: Display at the Savoy Theatre', *Morning Post*, 3 December 1912. Press Cuttings Book 6, Vaughan Williams Memorial Library.

70 'Display at the Savoy Theatre, London', *Stratford-upon-Avon Herald*, 6 December 1912. Press Cuttings Book 6, Vaughan Williams Memorial Library.

71 Cecil J. Sharp, 'The Newest Dances', *Daily Mail*, 6 December 1912. Press Cuttings Book 6, Vaughan Williams Memorial Library.

72 'Revival of the Folk Dance: An Artistic Movement', *Morning Post*, 7 December 1911, quoted in Schofield 1986.

73 'Stratford-on-Avon Festival: Folk Song and Dance Conference', *Leamington Spa Courier*, 16 August 1912. Press Cuttings Book 2, Vaughan Williams Memorial Library.

74 Mary Neal, 'The National Revival of the Folk Dance. No. III – Present Day Interpreters of the Folk Dance', *The Observer*, 3 December 1911. Bampton refers to the village morris dancing although Neal's comments on style covered all of Sharp's dance genres.

75 See Eric Saylor, *English Pastoral Music: From Arcadia to Utopia, 1900–1955* (Urbana and Chicago: University of Illinois Press, 2017), especially Chapter 1.

13
DOUGLAS KENNEDY AND FOLK DANCE IN ENGLISH SCHOOLS

Chloe Middleton-Metcalfe

Introduction[1]

Douglas Neil Kennedy (1893–1988) was the Director of the English Folk Dance Society (hereafter the EFDS) from 1925 until his retirement in 1961. The EFDS (est. 1911) had been the brainchild of Cecil Sharp, its first director, who passed away in 1924.[2] Kennedy oversaw the EFDS's merger with the Folk Song Society in 1932 creating the amalgamated and extant English Folk Dance and Song Society (hereafter the EFDSS). Most academic attention has so far been directed at the Edwardian folk dance revival; however, Kennedy has been the recipient of growing critical attention.[3] Kennedy was not an acclaimed scholar or folklorist, but he was an excellent publicist, and wrote articles propounding his views with a reach beyond an immediate coterie of enthusiasts.[4] Kennedy also embraced the possibilities opened up by the medium of cinema producing *Wake up and Dance* (1949), a folk dance publicity film which was scripted by his son Peter.[5] His monograph *England's Dances: Folk Dancing To-Day and Yesterday* (1949) provided the introductory text for those interested in the subject for many years.[6] Full public recognition came when he received an OBE (Officer of the Most Excellent Order of the British Empire) for his services to folk dance and song in 1952.[7] In the words of *The Oxford Dictionary of English Folklore*, Douglas Kennedy was 'the official public face of folk dance for decades'.[8]

This chapter explores Douglas Kennedy's folk dance theories, particularly his focus on *vitality* and *naturalness*, the interplay between his ideas and wider approaches to dance, and the gradual decline of officially sanctioned folk dance provision in English schools. Kennedy was primarily concerned with boosting the fortunes of an organisation whose members were mostly interested in social, participatory folk dance, often called *country* dance.[9] After his retirement, Kennedy spent a short time as the president of the Folklore Society from 1964 to 1967 and continued to have active, though somewhat sporadic, engagement with folk dance and folklore until a few years before his death in 1988.[10] This chapter is part of a wider discourse and growing interest in post-Edwardian 'folk' and argues for a reassessment of the place of folk dance in the English education system. This is a story which is often lost in dance histories which have focused on the rise of modern educational dance, in the process losing sight of the comparative popularity of country dance in schools into the 1980s.[11]

By focusing on country dancing and suggesting that its decline was hastened by Douglas Kennedy's adult-centred focus, the second half of this chapter offers an alternative history.

Two key interlinked ideas are explored which are present throughout Kennedy's writings and underpin his approach and orientation to folk dance in education: folk dance as *natural*, and folk dance as *vital*. I go on to compare Kennedy's writings with other approaches published in guidance for physical training (later physical education) teachers between 1933 and 1972. In so doing, I will explore the relationship between folk dance and the educational establishment, charting not only the decline of country dance provision, but also emphasising the continued influence of the EFDSS amongst educationalists into the 1950s. Even after folk dance was completely usurped by modern educational dance as the genre of choice by the various incarnations of the Board of Education, many teachers, both primary and physical education specialists, continued to receive instructions in country dancing. A 1977 survey of 1,336 primary schools in England and Wales found that 77% of schools taught some form of 'folk dance'. This was much higher than the number who taught modern educational or creative dance.[12] Indeed, well into the 1970s, a key source of income for the EFDSS was the fees paid for folk dance provision by Local Education Authorities.[13] Additional research suggests that the genre retained popularity, particularly in primary education, into the 1980s.[14] In any case until the national curriculum was introduced in 1988, official government guidance was often more of an ideal model than a reflection of contemporary practice. As one educational survey printed in 1976 surmised: 'The tendency is for teachers to teach physical education lessons which could not necessarily be described as "modern" or "educational"'.[15] In practice, country dancing left the feet of school children much later than the official physical educational publications, and many subsequent histories of dance education, would indicate.

Douglas Kennedy

Douglas Neil Kennedy was born in the Edinburgh home of his paternal grandmother. Her husband David Kennedy (1825–1886) had been one of the famous 'Singing Kennedys' who toured around the world performing Lowland Scottish songs.[16] David's daughter, Douglas's aunt, Marjory Kennedy-Fraser (1857–1930) was a noted song collector, recognised for her work with Hebridean music.[17] Douglas Kennedy attended a private day school in Scotland before moving to London when he was 14. After living in Strasbourg, Germany, from 1909 to 1910, he returned aged 17 to London and enrolled at the South Western Polytechnic, where he studied Botany, Zoology, and Geology. He also took up military training in the territorial forces, the 14th Battalion of the London Regiment (the London Scottish).[18]

In 1911, his older sister, Helen Dorothy, who was employed at Whitelands College (now part of the University of Roehampton) encouraged him to attend folk dance classes held there.[19] Under the tutelage of Cecil Sharp, Kennedy became part of an elite core of early revivalist dancers who made up the EFDS's first display team.[20] Kennedy's own studies continued at Imperial College, London, until the outbreak of the First World War. He served with the London Regiment, but never saw combat, citing a digestive disorder which prevented him from being sent abroad to fight.[21] When the war finished, Kennedy returned to Imperial College accepting a teaching post on the botany staff.[22] At Cecil Sharp's death in 1924, the future of the EFDS was by no means secure and Kennedy successfully argued the case for continuing the Society without Sharp.[23] Already a committee member and organiser of Sharp's memorial fund, which would eventually raise enough capital to build Cecil Sharp House, a large building in Camden, London, Kennedy was appointed the Organising Director of the EFDS in 1925, and remained in the post until his retirement in 1961.

In 1914, Douglas married Helen Karpeles (1888–1976).[24] Helen was the sister of Maud Karpeles (1885–1976), founder of the International Folk Music Council (est. 1947), and a folk dance and song collector in her own right, although better known as Sharp's secretary and amanuensis.[25] Helen played an active role within the EFDS/S. Sharp had made her the occasional inspector of folk dance in elementary schools in 1920, and during Douglas's time as a director, she continued to work for the Society until retirement. They were even musically active together with Helen playing English concertina and Douglas the side drum in The Square Dance Band which they formed shortly after the end of the Second World War.[26] Helen and Douglas co-authored a number of publications, but Helen also authored articles for the EFDSS's house magazine *English Dance and Song* on her own. They had two sons together, Peter (1922–2006), who is best remembered for his collecting work amongst traditional musicians and singers, and John, who died during naval action in the Second World War.[27] Although this article examines Douglas's work and his words, Helen was an important collaborator whose exact contribution is sadly unquantifiable.[28] I occasionally use the plural form 'the Kennedys' to refer to them both.

Cecil Sharp had successfully lobbied for the introduction of English country dancing into the Board of Education's recommended syllabus for physical training in 1909.[29] Kennedy had witnessed the results of this success, and had found a discrepancy between his own ambitions for the genre and the reality left by Sharp. As Kennedy would argue in an article penned post-retirement, many schoolteachers had:

> only succeeded in killing any impulse to musical or dance expression that might have stirred under other treatment. One of the deterrents to the successful outcome of a crusade through the school children was the typical adult attitude which rejected folk dancing as only kids' stuff. So a determined effort had to be made to ensure that when children left school there were "grown up" occasions where English folk dance and song figured as an acceptable pastime among normal people and not just cranks.[30]

From his contact with EFDS/S members across the country Kennedy felt that the Society attracted only a sub-section of the general population. *Crank* was a pejorative term, associated with fringe lifestyle interests, including sandals, socialism, and fresh air.[31] In one cutting article, Kennedy stereotyped folk dance enthusiasts as being comprised of 'pale-faced intellectuals'.[32] Leisure scholar Robert Snape's work on inter-war folk dancing in Manchester confirms the limited appeal of folk dance during the 1930s. Dance classes appeared to primarily attract single, middle-class women.[33] This dearth of men was a particular area of concern for Kennedy; when he took the directorship, teaching was a female-dominated profession,[34] and dance was also gendered female.[35] Unsurprisingly, a large proportion of the Society's members were female teachers.[36] In addition, the Society offered a tripartite examination scheme which was a recognised qualification by many Local Education Authorities, and therefore attracted interest from the pedagogic profession.[37] One of Kennedy's most overt efforts to re-heterosexualise social folk dance, in an attempt to normalise it as regular adult recreation, was a policy of 'mixed couples only' (that is male-female partners) on the dance floor at the prestigious Saturday night dances held by the Society in London. This policy was instigated in 1945 and the ban only formally lifted in 1974.[38]

Sharp's approach to country dances has been typecast by commentators as being unduly rigid.[39] In the early stages of the revival, Sharp had sought to be recognised as the leading expert in folk dance in opposition to Mary Neal (1860–1944).[40] Neal, first a colleague, but later a competitor of Sharp, had formed the first revival side of folk dancers from a charitable

Methodist mission, the Esperance Club, for young female seamstresses in central London. Their differences in approach are often simplified as being Sharp's 'technique' versus Neal's 'spirit'.[41] Whilst Sharp dictated the exact movements of the morris step, Neal refuted the very concept, teaching that no two traditional dancers perform in the same manner.[42] This binary view has been challenged in research by musicologist Vic Gammon. Gammon's work on Sharp's notebooks provides a rare insight into Sharp's desired aesthetic for social dance, and Gammon's findings test the idea of Sharp the pedant.[43] Rather than technical precision, Gammon argues, it was the concept of 'Gay Simplicity' that appears to have been of greatest importance to Sharp.[44]

A neglected source which supports Gammon's argument can be found in the fourth part of *The Country Dance Book* (1916) which Sharp co-authored with composer and EFDS morris dancer George Butterworth. Sharp and Butterworth make several statements which contradict the idea that Sharp favoured technical precision in country dance above more intangible elements. This supports the view that Kennedy's emphasis on vitality and naturalness could be seen as an extension, rather than a contradiction, of Sharp's view. These statements include:

- 'Technical proficiency, of itself, is of little worth. To the performer who is infected with the true spirit of the dance, technique is merely the vehicle of artistic expression.'[45]
- 'self-consciousness being, of course, the arch-foe of all natural instinctive, artistic expression.'[46]
- 'Although style in the matter of art is intuitive rather than to be acquired by precept, a question of feeling, not of thought, and is altogether too subtle, elusive and intangible a thing to be captured and set down in words.'[47]
- 'The steps prescribed in the Notation are not obligatory. Nor is uniformity necessary […] the arbitrary change of step in the course of a movement is not only permissible, but is in many cases to be commended.'[48]

If we agree with the suggestion that Sharp was less focused on technical precision for country dancing than is often supposed, it could also be argued that Kennedy was less iconoclastic in his approach than might at first be apparent. Although hardly in a position to entirely denounce Sharp's approach, this is certainly the tone which the Kennedys took in print. They referred to an original Sharpian vision which had become lost or distorted over time. Sharp's 'pedantry' was, they felt, 'foreign to his character', and derived from him having to solidify his position against Neal. They argued that given time Sharp would have 'discarded' such notions of technical precision.[49] Whatever Sharp's actual vision, he left behind a legacy of folk dance classes, certification, and vacation schools, all of which contributed to his subsequent reputation as a stickler for technical precision.

Kennedy's plans for change were set into motion after the Second World War and were given a boost by the government's reconstruction fund. This allowed the EFDSS to train staff who could be initiated into Kennedy's new approach.[50] Kennedy established the model for 'folk dance parties', which became the predecessor to the contemporary barn dance or English ceilidh. These parties included a band (rather than a violinist and/or pianist, or small orchestra[51]), a *caller* to teach the dances and give verbal prompts during the dance, and a *walk through* or instruction immediately prior to dancing with music. Kennedy also encouraged the use of a 'dance walk' for country dancing, rather than more complicated footwork or stepping. For Kennedy, proselytisation was an important aspect of folk dance parties; their purpose was to 'infect' dubious attendees with a love of folk dance through instant immersion.[52] Pedagogic methods were reassessed; the folk dance club replaced the folk dance class, as the caller replaced the teacher. Kennedy also changed the repertoire focus of the Society. Seventeenth- and eighteenth-century dances from the publishing house of John Playford, whose content forms the majority of the six volumes of Sharp's *Country Dance Books,* were largely replaced by 'traditional' dances, which were collected at the turn of the twentieth century. These usually used simpler dance figures, and were performed to well-known tunes such as 'Brighton Camp' or 'Soldiers Joy'. Kennedy hoped that these 'traditional' dances, alongside North American square and contra dances, would appeal to a wider demographic. This repertoire could be taught without prior instruction, and the dances contained, he felt, the essential element of rhythmic infection.[53] In 1956, Kennedy abolished the examinations which the EFDS/S had run for country and morris dancing. He argued that examinations had turned out the wrong sort of dancer, for it had been possible to gain one's silver badge (the third and highest examination) and be technically proficient, whilst completely lacking the elusive, vital elements which are key to good dancing.[54] Kennedy surmised: 'in shaping the living traditions to fit the standard moulds we came near to extinguishing the life'.[55] The abolition of examinations was not universally supported within the Society. They were seen by some members as a way to monitor standards, and by others as a way of verifying that folk dance was an activity worthy of study.[56]

During the 1920s, before the firm establishment of modern educational dance, the future of English folk dance in schools might have seemed secure. Kennedy recalled that when he started as the Director, 'the education side of it was pretty satisfactory'; there was a 'constant demand' from teachers for instruction.[57] This complacency perhaps explains the Kennedy's comparatively late contribution to educational literature. *English Folk Dancing in the Primary School* was published only a year before their retirement.[58] A greater concern appears to have been nurturing folk dance as an adult recreation. Many individuals who had been at school when folk dancing was introduced in 1909 were now adults with, on the whole, limited enthusiasm for recreative folk dance. Douglas felt that negative memories of dancing in school turned people away from folk dancing in adulthood.[59] Kennedy's educational writings refer to the right approach in teaching, a key point being the specialism of the teacher. Folk dance should, he felt, be taught by musicians, not physical training instructors.[60] The right approach, by the right teacher, should lead to greater natural, rhythmic, 'infection'[61] which should help to encourage a fondness for folk dance that he hoped might last beyond childhood.

Vitality and naturalness in folk dance

Two related ideas dominate Kennedy's writings about good dancing: *vitality* and *naturalness*.[62] Kennedy was far from a lone voice in advocating the 'naturalness' of his chosen dance form. From the end of the nineteenth century, a number of dance theorists, including American Isadora Duncan (1877–1927) and British Margaret Morris (1891–1980), promoted their various approaches as being a 'natural' alternative to the ballet-derived technique common in theatrical dance performances.[63] Kennedy's concepts of vitality[64] and naturalness intersect, for *vitality* is positioned in opposition to precision, technique, and figurative complexity.[65] Kennedy used the concept of vitality in his argument against formal learning. He argued that the limited revival so far achieved by the EFDS/S was due to the Society's previous focus on technical ability. By changing the emphasis from *technique* to *vitality*, Kennedy hoped to boost recruitment:

> Some of us now regard our past exposition of the English Folk Songs and Dances as having been generally unsuccessful in their effect on the public. […] We were so keen

> that everyone we button-holed should learn everything properly that we built up an elaborate machinery to turn out the "complete folk dancer." The man or girl who just wanted a taste was more of a nuisance than otherwise because he or she didn't fit into the machine and never, by any chance, knew the right dances to be fitted into the right classes.[66]

After becoming better acquainted with English folk dance outside of the EFDS, from those considered to be tradition bearers, such as morris dancers William Kimber (1872–1961) and Sam Bennett (1861–1951), the Kennedys felt able to criticise Sharp's 'dogmatic method of teaching' which they later declared was 'out of step with tradition'.[67] By 1946, they wrote that the 'primary aim' of the EFDSS was not to try and improve those already interested in folk dancing, but to give as many people as possible a 'first taste'.[68]

In a position which would later pit him against the presiding EFDSS patron, the classical composer Ralph Vaughan Williams (1872–1958), Kennedy advocated that good folk dancing does not come from a studied, consciously learnt technique.

> It is far better for dancers to "pick up" the elements of the simplest dances at parties and to acquire a natural unselfconscious approach to rhythmical expression.[69]

Kennedy might have had a very particular reason for his position. As he attempted to move the direction of folk dance away from classes and demonstrations towards parties and participation, this focus on feeling, rather than thought, was part of his campaign to encourage members to change their current practices and to embrace his new style of directorship. He wrote strong criticisms of those that did not (or possibly could not) follow his rhymical approach.

> The over-civilised "heathens" whose ideas of motion are derived from machines and whose idea of a dance-walk is to emphasise each beat, will march about using their limbs as pistons, cogs and levers instead of as living flesh through which the ripples of energy can flow. Such people are the real cranks of this world who will never function properly in a community dance.[70]

In his 1949 monograph *England's Dances*, Kennedy credited the societal changes brought about by industrialisation[71] which resulted in the 'nature of the sophisticated modern man' as the biggest barrier to the popularity of folk dance in contemporary England.[72] Kennedy appeared to hold such views throughout his directorship, for after his retirement he composed two articles with the title 'Folklore and Ecology' wherein he discussed his concept of a 'folk-knack' of mind-body balance, which is found in the 'true countryman' but which can be 'damaged or overlaid by schooling and sophistication'.[73] In these articles, Kennedy advocated folk traditions, including dancing, as a cure to help the 'fragmented individuals' caused by modern society.[74] Tradition, he argued, helps to re-unite individuals with their bodily feelings and thus prevents them from becoming 'social misfits'.[75] Modernist scholar Rishona Zimring has characterised Kennedy's position as 'anti-modern'[76] and it is hard to escape his negative view of technological advance and his unflattering comparisons between folk dancers and machines.[77] However, Kennedy's ideas were far from unique, and were part of a wider European, bourgeoise, intellectual discourse. Anthropologist Sharon MacDonald has discussed how the contrast between modernity and tradition was heightened during the fashion for Darwinian-inspired evolutionary theory in the late nineteenth century. This established, she argues, an 'enduring ambivalence' towards modernity which 'helped fuel quests to salvage traditional culture and restore them to the nation'.[78] Her text refers to museums but the contrast, indeed antagonism, between the concepts of tradition and modernity is equally apparent in other spheres. Even proponents of modern educational dance did not feel that the contemporary world provided an effective path to human happiness. In 1938, modern dance pedagogue Diana Jordan would write of the 'evil effects of town living'. Whilst Kennedy would advocate folk dancing as an antidote, Jordan proposed a new system of movement that she hoped could 'nurture the mind through the body and the body through the mind'.[79]

During the twentieth century, dance was considered to be an especially appropriate method for re-connecting industrial man with his animal self.[80] Curt Sachs's influential *World History of the Dance* (1937) disseminated the simple evolutionist view that dancing comes from the animal world, and that the subsequent complexity of dancing exhibited by cultures corresponds to their supposed level of evolutionary attainment.[81] These ideas were further reinforced by a Descartian-derived dualism and the historical propensity of cultural theorists to privilege textual over bodily communication.[82] Even into the 1990s, popular dance histories would often supply a problematic evolutionarily based framework for the reader, who would pass through chapters on tribal and western folk dance to reach the supposed epitome of developed western theatrical dance culture – ballet.[83] This was a framework which Kennedy seems proud to have helped perpetuate. In a 1973 interview, he was asked to reflect upon the most important developments which he had overseen as a director of the EFDS/S.[84] Kennedy was happy that he had helped to broaden an awareness of folk, that even if people did not like it, they at least had some greater understanding of it. He concluded that the wider acceptance amongst classical music and dance circles of the idea 'that folk is basic to the art' was of the utmost importance. The argument that folk culture should be the basis for new forms of English national art is perhaps best rehearsed in classical music history, most notably amongst biographers of Ralph Vaughan Williams. But such ideas also influenced the approach of Dame Ninette de Valois, founder of the Royal Ballet School, who advocated the learning of English folk forms in order to build a successful and distinct English ballet tradition.[85] The conceptualisation of folk as a foundational form is highly problematic. The idea that artists must explore their indigeneity in order to produce work of great beauty is barely distinguishable from nationalism. Secondly, it reinforces the hierarchical, classed, and raced approaches to art wherein non 'high' forms are perpetually relegated as inferior.

Sharp referred to folk dance as an art form and the revival as an artistic movement; however, Kennedy took an avowedly more populist approach.[86] His claimed greatest achievement, that folk was perceived as 'basic', had important implications for the future allocation of state funding. Kennedy arguably reduced the chances of receiving governmental financial support based on artistic merit. This was tellingly illustrated in 1955 when the EFDSS failed to convince the Inland Revenue that folk music and dance were 'art', and therefore worthy of a tax exemption. The case went to the court of appeal and The Master of the Rolls concluded that:

> the Society's ideas appear to be that the dancer is so taught that he executes with his body, as far as is possible, spontaneous movements said to be expressive of natural or ritualistic physical impulses. The result may be pleasing or picturesque to the beholder but no claim is made to exhibit the beauties of graces of the human form. Artistic performances cannot be said to be the aim, still less the *raison d'être,* of folk dancing.[87]

It was for its role in education, not the arts, that the EFDSS received the majority of its government funding. It was only in 2009, nearly 50 years after Kennedy's retirement, that the EFDSS received a direct grant from Arts Council England. Even here the primary focus was not on folk dance, but on folk music and song, the professional profile of which had been significantly raised by the second folk revival of the 1960s.[88]

Folk dance and education[89]

The decline of country dancing as the dance genre of choice by the educational authorities coincided with a change in pedagogic outlook in the 1920s. In the arts more broadly, modernism was developing as the principle dominant paradigm, and with this emphasis came a stress upon continual invention. Progressivism, an outlook which relegates the role of tradition, was to become increasingly consequential in pedagogic theory and training.[90] As other dance historians have made clear, there was a strong link between progressive educationalists, who stressed the importance of learning directed by the child, and modern dance.[91] Starting in experimental private schools, child-centred experiential approaches to learning advocated by proponents such as John Dewey and Friedrich Froebel were to grow in influence, and would fundamentally alter the approach to dance in physical education. However, this did not happen immediately. In 1931, country dances had received explicit support from influential educationalist William Henry Hadow (1859–1937) who, in 1931, proposed that physical education should contribute towards creating an ephemeral, spiritual movement sensitivity akin to Plato's eurhythmia.

> Dancing is a chief means of cultivating it – provided the dances do not aim at a cheap and superficial 'gracefulness' but are, like many of the old English country dances, full of aesthetic quality as genuine as it is delightful and not only linked with but expressive of simple and beautiful music.[92]

Despite Hadow's support for the genre in the *Syllabus of Physical Training for Schools*, published only two years later, there were concerns over the prescriptive nature of folk dancing. The syllabus advocated free movement and simple made up dances in addition to set 'national' dances.[93] Still, the authors stated that 'folk and national dances are clearly the type of dance best suited to the needs of children'.[94] English country dances, Scottish country dances, the folk dances of different continental nations, and finally morris and sword dances (for both sexes) were given as suitable dance genres. English country dancing was considered to be 'particularly appropriate' because of its 'simple natural steps and attractive music'. The availability of gramophone records lent additional appeal, as country dances were linked to particular melodies and tune substitution was not a common practice. The separate section for infants (3–7 years old) included the advocation of musical folk dance-games such as *Ninepins* and *Pop Goes the Weasel*. The 1933 syllabus also supplied hints on teaching which included theories about rhythm, consciousness, and naturalness. These are similar to ideas found in the writings of contemporary dance pedagogues such as Diana Jordan, as well as folk advocate Douglas Kennedy.[95] For example, the syllabus suggests that: 'The more the attention of the children can be focussed on the music the more rhythmical and unselfconscious do their movements become'.[96]

Kennedy appears to have had some direct influence in the broader dance education world. In 1935, the Ling Association and the National Association of Organisers of Physical Education, two influential physical training bodies, created the Central Council of Recreative

Physical Training (CCRPT). The British government was in the process of establishing National Advisory Councils for improving the fitness of the inhabitants of England, Wales, and Scotland. In 1937, they gave grants to the CCRPT to provide teachers for every type of physical activity from cycling to dancing. A number of dancing groups signed up to the CCRPT, including The Dalcroze Society, The Greek Dance Association, The International Institute of Margaret Morris Movement, and the Scottish Folk Dance Society.[97] Of these, only Douglas Kennedy, representing the EFDSS, had a seat on the CCRPT's executive council. Why the seat was offered to him is unclear, possibly the position reflected the predominance of English folk dance within the education system at that time; however, his influence was not to last.

During the 1920s and 1930s, British physical training advocates were increasingly warming to the movement theories of German modern dance proponents. Starting in the 1920s, a small number of British female educationalists promoted what was then referred to as 'central European' dance.[98] In 1938, Oxford University Press published Diana Jordan's *The Dance as Education*. This presented the case for dance as art, utilising a modern dance framework with key ideas being rhythm, form, and self-expression.[99] Folk, like ballroom, is considered to be a purely 'social' (rather than artistic) form.[100] Jordan argued that teaching children material outside of the 'environment, custom and tradition' in which it had originated resulted in 'sham' dances which 'lack the beauty of spirit and character without which dance is a poor disfigured cripple'.[101] The Kennedy's knew that the tide was turning. In the mid-1930s, they considered emigrating to America when it became clear that 'the educational support which the Society had hitherto enjoyed was now diminishing'.[102]

Ultimately, it was Rudolf Laban (1879–1958), who appears to have had the most influence.[103] Hungarian-born Laban emigrated to Britain from Germany in 1937. Prior to falling out with Joseph Goebbels (the Reich minister for propaganda), he had held two of the most prestigious dance posts in Germany. He choreographed pieces for professional dancers in the new central European style, and pioneered 'movement choirs' which were large group pieces for amateur dancers. Possibly best known today for his movement notation system, he also developed theories of movement utilising key ideas such as space, time, and action.[104] In some instances, he rejected established relationships between dance and music to focus on the dance movement in and of itself.[105] After his arrival in Britain, Laban lived for two years at Dartington Hall, an experimental private school in Devon.[106] There, with assistance from his long-term educational collaborator Lisa Ullmann (1907–1985),[107] Laban grew interest in modern educational dance amongst progressive educationalists. The 1941 Ling Association Conference was a major event in the growth of modern educational dance. The organisers went on to petition the Board of Education to promote the genre and the first of 26 three-week holiday courses was run.[108] In 1946, Laban and Ullman established the Manchester Art of Movement Studio. That same year, they founded an association for teachers, The Laban Guild.

In 1948, two developments occurred. Laban published *Modern Educational Dance*, utilising the movement theories he had developed in his professional dance work, to lay out his schema for dance training in schools. Secondly, the government funded a one-year course for teachers in the Laban method.[109] In 1953, Ullmann moved from her Manchester premises to establish an 'Art of Music Studio' in Surrey with Laban, which focused for many years on providing instruction on modern educational dance in which educational training was an important part.[110] In *Modern Educational Dance*, Laban surmised that traditional/national dances were characterised by the employment of uncreative pattern following. Moreover, as had Jordan, he questioned the propriety and purpose of studying movement supposedly created by societies of the past.¹¹¹ Such negative views of folk dance were taken up by Laban's followers. Joan Russell, author of *Modern Dance in Education* (1958), argued that 'revivals run the risk of becoming self-conscious'. Would it ever be possible, she asked, to have a real revival of folk dances? After all, they had originated in the 'spontaneous communal activities' of past societies now long disconnected from our own.¹¹²

Illustrating the popularity of dance theories which stressed primitivism and animal origins, the 1952 guidance from the Ministry of Education (*Moving and Growing*) describes all types of dance as originating in an 'overflow of feeling, energy or excitement' which perhaps had a ritual or social function 'such as a deliverance from danger'.¹¹³ Country dancing is, however, no longer considered to be the best option for school children. It has been replaced by Laban-derived modern educational dance. Rather than memorising set patterns of dance figures, the Ministry suggested the construction of simple dances as a more appropriate activity. Furthermore, *Moving and Growing* argued that folk dances were originally dances for adults and are, despite previous guidance, unsuitable for children. Kennedy had pushed for folk dance to be recognised as an adult activity; he had even advocated Laban's methods as being more suitable for children.¹¹⁴ He might have been content with the Ministry's new categorisation of folk dance as an 'adult' activity. However, we can see a more child-oriented approach to Kennedy's writings starting in this decade.¹¹⁵ This was perhaps a belated attempt to rejuvenate interest in folk dance amongst educationalists. Using similar language to modern educational dance proponents, Kennedy also started to refer to the care-free approach of children as a model for 'vital' adult participation.¹¹⁶

Although *Moving and Growing* did not support country dancing, its companion publication *Planning the Programme* (1953) did. Moreover, the contents of *Planning the Programme* allow us to infer that Kennedy continued to have some influence amongst physical educationalists. The Ministry explicitly supported Kennedy's change in folk dance repertoire, discouraging teachers from using the dances most favoured by Sharp, seventeenth-century dances such as *Gathering Peascods* and *Rufty Tufty*. They considered these to be too complicated, and they suggested simpler 'traditional' dances collected during the twentieth century named *The Long Eight* and the *Durham Reel*. This mirrored Kennedy's wider approach to the English folk dance repertoire. Thus, his views were still being attended to, but folk dance had already lost its pre-eminent position as the educationalists dance genre of choice. Indeed, Kennedy's view that folk dance should be an adult recreation was now being used to support the complete stoppage of folk dance in schools.¹¹⁷

Movement – Physical Education in the Primary Years (1972) repeated many of the concerns that were established in the 1952/3 guidance. Folk dances of all forms were now considered to be a niche genre within dance education, and they were not specifically recommended by the Department of Education and Science. Indeed, after Laban, there is a noticeable scepticism towards the authenticity of traditional forms:

> Traditional dances express the moods of the people and the setting from which they arise. All dances reflect the attitudes of their time and usually have their origins in a strong emotional surge, but they lose vitality and spontaneity in the process of stylisation and performance far away from the situation that gave them life.¹¹⁸

In this quote, the Department used a Kennedian vocabulary of vitality, naturalness, and spontaneity. The purpose behind the words, however, is to relegate folk dance teaching to the past, rather than encourage a new generation of adult dancers in the present. Kennedy and the Department thus agree that vitality and spontaneity are important characteristics of folk dance. The Department, however, followed the modern educational dance argument, accepting that such characteristics could not be adequately maintained so many years after the dances' initial composition, and that a new approach was therefore required.

Conclusion

Douglas Kennedy pioneered a new approach to folk dancing in England. He removed certification, encouraged the simplification of the dancing repertoire, and replaced teachers and classes with a more informal pedagogy of callers and clubs. His promulgation of figuratively simple 'traditional' dances was part of an attempt to emphasise the more ephemeral aspects of good dancing. Kennedy's ideas of naturalness and vitality in folk dance were one iteration of cultural ideas which had wider resonance. Similar theories can be found in the writings of modern educational dance proponents, as well as in the guidance issued by the various incarnations of the Board of Education. At the start of his directorship, Kennedy appears to have been sceptical of the benefits of teaching children folk dance in compulsory physical education. This raises the question of whether he actually supported the wholesale removal of country dancing from English schools? Arguably, complacency combined with his primary concern to change the way that folk dance was taught blinded him to the benefits of continued promotion and lobbying. In support of Kennedy as an advocate rather than opponent of folk dance in schools, his ideas about vitality, naturalness, and their associated concomitants (unselfconsciousness, spontaneity, etc.) could be seen as a defensive strategy. Foregrounding dance *vitality* countered the chief criticisms placed against folk dance as outdated and meaningless rote-learning. By his retirement in 1961, it would have been clear that the wholesale replacement of folk dance in schools, rather than a modification of approach, was on the horizon.[119] Despite its unpopularity amongst the most influential physical educationalists, in reality, it took many years, and a new generation of teachers, before country dancing finally left the school gymnasium.

Notes

1 This article uses material from my doctoral thesis 'Barn Dances, Ceilidhs, and Country Dancing in England 1945–2020: An Examination of Non-Specialist English Social Folk Dance'. This was instigated at the University of Roehampton under Professor Theresa Buckland and Dr Sara Houston.

2 For more detail, see: Derek Schofield, '"Revival of the Folk Dance: An Artistic Movement": The Background to the Founding of the English Folk Dance Society in 1911', *Folk Music Journal*, 5.2 (1986), 215–219.

3 Academic writing about Kennedy includes Georgina Boyes, *The Imagined Village, Culture, Ideology and the English Folk Revival* (Manchester: Manchester University Press, 1993) and '"Potencies of the Earth": Rolf Gardiner and the English Folk Dance Revival', in *Rolf Gardiner: Folk, Nature and Culture in Interwar Britain*, ed. by Matthew Jefferies and Mike Tyldesley (Farnham: Ashgate, 2010), pp. 65–94; Derek Schofield, 'After the war', and 'Joyful Stratford', *English Dance and Song*, 73.2 (2011), 12–15 and '"Little Ballets": Playford, Sharp and Douglas Kennedy in the 20th century Folk Dance Revival', in *On Common Ground 3*, ed. by David Parsons (London: The Dolmetsch Historical Dance Society, 2001); David Walkowitz, *City Folk: English Country Dance and the Politics of the Folk in Modern America* (New York and London: New York University, 2010); Rishona Zimring, *Social Dance and the Modernist Imagination in Interwar Britain* (Farnham: Ashgate, 2013), pp. 129–168.

4 He was the chosen authority on folk dance for both *Chambers* (1950, 1966) and *Britannica* (1973) encyclopaedias – see Theresa Buckland, 'Definitions of Folk Dance: Some Explorations', *Folk Music Journal*, 4.4 (1983), 315–332. Other examples include Douglas Kennedy, 'Revival of Folk

Dancing in England', *Dancing Times*, 435 (1946a), 128–130; 'Square Dancing in St Pancreas: The Work of Cecil Sharp House', *The St Pancras Journal*, 2.2 (1948), 27–28; 'The Dance as Education', *Dancing Times*, 474 (1950), 345–347; 'Dance Survivals of Pre-History', *The Geographical Magazine*, July (1962), 161–171.

5 This was awarded the documentary Grand Prix at the 1950 Cannes Film Festival.

6 A revised edition *English Folk Dancing: Today and Yesterday* was published in 1964.

7 Derek Froome, 'Douglas Neil Kennedy (1893–1988)', *Folklore*, 99.1 (1988), 127–128. p. 128.

8 Jacqueline Simpson and Steve Roud, *Oxford Dictionary of English Folklore* (Oxford: Oxford University Press, 2003), p. 204.

9 I have utilised the social/performative binary whilst recognising the problems of such a schema. See Chloe Middleton-Metcalfe, *An Introductory Bibliography of Traditional Social Folk Dance* (London: Vaughan Williams Memorial Library, 2019).

10 Roy Judge and Derek Schofield (eds.), 'A Tribute to Douglas Neil Kennedy, O.B.E., 1893–1988', *Folk Music Journal*, 5.4 (1988), 520–536.

11 Such as Janet Adshead, *The Study of Dance* (London: Dance Books, 1981), Catherine Burke, 'Feet, Footwork, Footwear, and "Being Alive" in the Modern School', *Paedagogica Historica*, 54.1–2 (2018), 32–47; Alexandra Carter, 'General Introduction', in *The Routledge Dance Studies Reader*, ed. by Alexandra Carter (Abingdon, Oxfordshire: Routledge), pp. 1–17; Anna Haynes, 'The Dynamic Image: Changing Perspectives in Dance Education', in *Living Powers: The Arts in Education*, ed. by Peter Abbs (London: Falmer, 1987), pp. 141–162; Patricia Vertinsky, 'Schooling the Dance: From Dance under the Swastika to Movement Education in the British School', *Journal of Sport History*, 31.3 (2004), 273–294. More detailed consideration is given to folk dance in Anne Bloomfield 'An Investigation into the Relationship between Philosophical Principle and Artistic Practice with Reference to the Role of Dance in Education' (unpublished doctoral thesis, University of Hull, 1986).

12 Gulbenkian Foundation, *Dance Education and Training in Britain* (London: Calouste Gulbenkian Foundation, 1980), p. 43.

13 In the EFDSS's 1966–1967 Annual Report, government and education authorities made up 33.13% of income. EFDSS, *Annual Report: 1966–1967* (London: English Folk Dance and Song Society, 1967), p. 11.

14 As noted in the Barbara Pagan report (see Janet Dashwood, 'Folk Education in Primary Schools', *English Dance and Song*, 51.3 (1989), 6); and the report by Kate Badrick, *Folk Dancing and the School Curriculum: A Study of the Undervaluation of Part of the English Cultural Heritage in the Education System. Study Report for the Teaching Fellowship Scheme of the Essex Institute of High Education* (Kate Badrick, 1986). Available from The Vaughan Williams Memorial Library, London.

15 N. Whitehead and C.B. Hendry, *Teaching Physical Education in England Description and Analysis* (London: Lepus Books, 1976), p. 19.

16 Douglas Kennedy himself sang such songs for the EFDSS/HMV in 1954: *Hame Cam Oor Guidman at 'Een*; and *The Goulden Vanitee* (HMV B-10836).

17 Per Ahlander, 'Marjory Kennedy-Fraser (1857–1930)', in *Old Songs: New Discoveries Selected Papers from the 2018 Folk Song Conference*, ed. by Steve Roud and David Atkinson (London: Ballad Partners, 2019), pp. 1–18.

18 This account was compiled primarily from three sources. Kennedy's obituary from *The Folk Music Journal*, ed. by Roy Judge and Derek Schofield (1988); Mike Heaney, 'Kennedy, Douglas Neil', *Oxford Dictionary of National Biography* <https://doi.org/10.1093/ref:odnb/54871> [accessed 27 August 2019]; and Kennedy's unpublished autobiography. Known as *The Blue Book*, this is a typescript of oral interview tapes deposited in the VWML (Accession number 228) and is hereafter referenced as Douglas Kennedy, Mss [1973].

19 For more details about the life of Helen Dorothy Kennedy (after marriage Kennedy-North), see Georgina Boyes, 'More About "Madam": Helen Kennedy North and The Abbey School Book', *The Abbey Chronicle: The Journal of the Elsie Jeanette Oxenham Appreciation Society*, 71 (2012), 22–35.

20 Derek Schofield, 'Cecil Sharp and English Folk Song and Dance Before 1915', *Country Dance and Song Online*, 1 (2016) <https://www.cdss.org/programs/cdss-news-publications/cds-online/cecil-sharp-english> [accessed 22 October 2019].

21 Boyes, 'Potencies of the Earth', p. 93. Three of Sharp's six original male demonstration teams died in action during the First World War.

22 Douglas Kennedy, Mss, [1973], p. 165.

23 Ibid., p. 212.
24 Kenneth Loveless, 'Helen Kennedy', *Folk Music Journal*, 3.2 (1976), 188–190.
25 Simona Pakenham, *Singing and Dancing Wherever She Goes: A Life of Maud Karpeles* (London: English Folk Dance and Song Society, 2011).
26 Judge and Schofield, *The Folk Music Journal*, 525.
27 E. David Gregory, 'Roving Out: Peter Kennedy and the BBC Folk Music and Dialect Recording Scheme, 1952–1957', in *Folk Song: Tradition, Revival, and Re-creation*, ed. by Ian Russell and David Atkinson (Elphinstone Institute, 2004), pp. 218–231.
28 In 1959, Kennedy admitted that he had only 'slight' experience in teaching young children folk dance. Douglas Kennedy, 'Inside Out', *English Dance and Song*, 23.3 (1959a), 63–64.
29 Vic Gammon, 'Many Useful Lessons: Cecil Sharp, Education and the Folk Dance Revival 1900–1924', *Cultural and Social History*, 5.1 (2008), 75–97. p. 79.
30 Douglas Kennedy, 'A Jubilee Symposium: Folk Dance Revival', *Folk Music Journal*, 2.2 (1971), 80–90. p. 85.
31 Matthew Simons, 'Morris Men: Dancing Englishness, c.1905–1951' (unpublished doctoral thesis, De Montford University, 2019), p. 24.
32 Douglas Kennedy, 'Revival of Folk Dancing in England', *Dancing Times*, 435 (1946a), 128–130.
33 Robert Snape, 'Continuity, Change and Performativity in Leisure: English Folk Dance and Modernity 1900–1933', *Leisure Studies*, 28.3 (2009), 297–311.
34 At the turn of the century, 73% of teaching staff in English and Welsh schools were female. James Albisetti, 'The Feminization of Teaching in the Nineteenth Century: A Comparative Perspective', *History of Education*, 23.3 (1993), 253–263. p. 255.
35 Athalie Knowles, 'Dance in Schools', in *Dance in Education: Report of the Joint Course Organised by the Arts Council of Great Britain and the Department of Education and Science* (London: Arts Council of Great Britain, 1982), pp. 25–34.
36 Douglas Kennedy, Mss. p. 203.
37 C. Holbrow, 'Letters', *English Dance and Song*, 10.4 (1946), 69.
38 ED&S, 'Saturday Square Dances', *English Dance and Song*, 9.3 (1945), 21.
39 When morris dancer Kenneth Constable recalled Sharp spending 15 minutes correcting his hockle-back (a particular morris dance step) because it was 'too much like Douglas's and his wasn't good' it is assumed by Boyes that Kennedy's dancing lacked the technical precision wished for by Sharp. Boyes, 'Potencies of the Earth', p. 92.
40 Boyes, *The Imagined Village*, pp. 63–86.
41 Roy Judge, 'Mary Neal and the Esperance Morris', *Folk Music Journal*, 5.5 (1989), 545–546.
42 Anon., 'Morris Dancing and Folk Song: The Esperance Clubs at the Kensington Town Hall', *The Practical Teacher*, 30.9 (1910), 547–549. p. 548.
43 Vic Gammon, 'Many Useful Lessons'.
44 A term borrowed by Sharp via Barclay Dun's *Translation of Nine of the Most Fashionable Quadrilles* (Edinburgh: William Wilson, 1818), pp. 13–14. Cecil Sharp, *The Country Dance Book: Part Two*, 3rd ed. (London: Novello and Company, 1927 [1911]) re-print (Wakefield: E.P Publishing, 1972), p. 22.
45 Cecil Sharp, and George Butterworth, *The Country Dance Book: Part Four* (London: Novello and Company, 1916) re-print (Wakefield: E.P Publishing, 1975), p. 30.
46 Ibid.
47 Ibid.
48 Ibid., p. 33.
49 Kennedy and Kennedy, *A Jubilee History*, p. 3.
50 ED&S, 'The E.F.D.S Training Scheme', *English Dance and Song*, 10.4 (1946), 43. Schofield, 'After the War', p. 13.
51 Ibid.
52 Douglas Kennedy, 'Notes on Recruiting', *English Dance and Song*, 10.6 (1946c), 73–74.
53 See Douglas Kennedy, 'What about Playford?', *English Dance and Song*, 4.3 (1940), 32–33; Douglas Kennedy, 'As Easy as A.B.C.', *English Dance and Song*, V.6 (1941), 70 and 75; Douglas Kennedy, 'Where Do We Go from Here?', *English Dance and Song*, 9.2 (1944a), 13–15; Helen Kennedy, 'Traditional and Playford Dances', *English Dance and Song*, 6.2 (1941), 29.
54 Kennedy and Douglas Kennedy, *The English Folk Dance and Song Society: A Jubilee History* (London: The English Folk Dance and Song Society, 1961), pp. 4–5.

55 Kennedy, 'A Jubilee Symposium', p. 83.
56 Betty Ekin, 'Letters', *English Dance and Song*, 10.8 (1946), 108; Holbrow, 'Letters', p. 69.
57 Douglas Kennedy, Interviewed by Jim Lloyd. Radio 3. Produced by Frances Line (11 May 1973). Copy on Casette held at Vaughan Williams Memorial Library, London.
58 Although he did authorise the publication of *English Folk Dancing for Schools* written by EFDSS' employee Sibyl Clark (1956).
59 Kennedy, 'Inside Out', p. 61; Kennedy, 'A Jubilee Symposium', p. 85.
60 Douglas Kennedy and Helen Kennedy, *Do It Yourself: A Guide to Enable Folk Dance Leaders to Tune Up Their Natural Dance Technique* (London: English Folk Dance and Song Society, 1959), p. 35.
61 Kennedy commonly used infection as a metaphor. For example: Douglas Kennedy, 'Community Dancing', *English Dance and Song*, 9.1 (1944b), 3–4. p. 3.
62 Kennedy was not alone in his choice of language to inspire dancers and players. A contemporary, comparable example comes from Ireland in the Gaelic League's book of 30 popular figure dances. Cormac Mac Fionnlaoic would write of the problem of 'Spiritless music' which lacks the '"Rhythmic Vitality" – which is part of the player's own soul'. Cormac Mac Fionnlaoic, *Ár Rinncide Foirne: Thirty Popular Figure Dances. Leabhar 1,2,3* (An Coimisiún le Rincí Gaelacha, 1939) re-print (Kilkenny: Wellbrook Press, Undated), p. 2.
63 Rachel Fensham and Alexandra Carter, *Dancing Naturally: Nature, Neo-classicism and Modernity in Early Twentieth-Century Dance* (Basingstoke: Palgrave Macmillan, 2011).
64 Vitalism was an eighteenth-century scientific philosophy, a reaction to advances in knowledge about human biology. Proponents argued that life cannot be reduced to biological mechanics alone. There must be something else, such as a soul, or vital spark, which animates humanity. Having been a student of the natural sciences, and having studied in Germany prior to the First World War, it is likely that Kennedy would have heard of vitalism, although no direct reference is made in his publications to its key proponents. Vitalism in the early twentieth century was not a wholly unproblematic philosophy; it was linked to theories about evolution which were utilised by the Nazis. Anne Harrington, *Reenchanted Science: Holism in German Culture from Wilhelm II to Hitler* (Princetown, NJ: Princetown University Press, 1996). 'Vitalism', *In Our Time*, BBC Radio Four, 16 October 2008.
65 Kennedy, 'Inside Out'.
66 Douglas Kennedy, 'Open Letter from the Director to the Society', *English Dance and Song*, 10.4 (1946b), 44–45.
67 Kennedys, *A Jubilee History*, p. 3.
68 Douglas Kennedy, 'Open Letter from the Director', p. 44.
69 Douglas Kennedy, 'Awake and Alive', *English Dance and Song*, X.2 (1945), 19–20.
70 Kennedy, 'Community Dancing', p. 4.
71 Boyes (e-mail 29 August 2019) has suggested that Kennedy might have been influenced by Rolf Gardiner's ideas and approaches. Gardiner was a founder member of the Soil Association and a pioneer of organic farming techniques. See also Boyes, 'Potencies of the Earth'.
72 Kennedy, *England's Dances*, p. 135.
73 Douglas Kennedy, 'Folklore and Human Ecology', *Folklore*, 76.2 (1965), 81–89. p. 82.
74 Douglas Kennedy, 'Further Thoughts on Human Ecology', *Folklore*, 77.2 (1966), 81–90. pp. 82–83. Boyes has argued that Kennedy's support for a lost age in part explains his sympathy for the Germanic concept of *Männerbünd* (male-group). German anthropologist Heinrich Schurtz (1863–1903) theorised that *Männerbünde* were an integral, and now lost part of the societies of all primitive peoples. Boyes argued that Kennedy's enthusiasm, or at the very least sympathy for the concept of *Männerbünde*, a concept later associated with Nazism, led to his support for the foundation of the all-male morris dancing organisation The Morris Ring. Boyes, 'Potencies of the Earth', p. 94.
75 Kennedy, 'Further Thoughts', pp. 82–83.
76 Zimring, *Social Dance and the Modernist Imagination*, pp. 140–141.
77 Schofield has cautioned that to apply this label to Kennedy without additional qualification is to ignore Kennedy's explicitly contemporary re-branding of folk dance during the 1940s. Derek Schofield, 'Review of Social Dance and the Modernist Imagination in Interwar Britain by Rishona Zimring' *English Dance and Song*, 76.3 (2014), 42–43.
78 Sharon MacDonald, *Memorylands* (London and New York: Routledge, 2005), p. 142.
79 Diana Jordan, *The Dance as Education* (London: Oxford University Press, 1938), p. 13.

80 Rudolf Laban attended at Delcroze's institute of *Schule für Lebenskunst* (School for the Art of Life) in 1912, where one could 'renounce "civilizational influences"'. Vertinsky, 'Schooling the Dance', p. 277.
81 For criticisms of this idea, see Suzanne Youngerman, 'Curt Sachs and His Heritage: A Critical Review of World History of the Dance with a Survey of Recent Studies That Perpetuate His Ideas', *CORD News*, 6.2 (1974), 6–19; and Drid Williams, *Ten Lectures on Theories of the Dance* (Metuchen, NJ: Scarecrow, 1991).
82 David Michael Levin, 'Philosophers and the Dance', in *What Is Dance?*, ed. by Roger Copeland and Marshall Cohen (Oxford: Oxford University Press, 1982), pp. 85–94.
83 Joann Kealiinohomoku, 'An Anthropologist Looks at Ballet as a Form of Ethnic Dance', in *What Is Dance?*, ed. by Roger Copeland and Marshall Cohen (Oxford: Oxford University Press, 1983), pp. 533–550; Andrée Grau, 'Myths of Origin', *Dance Now* (Winter 1993/4), 38–43; Williams, *Ten Lectures on Theories of the Dance*.
84 Kennedy, Interview, 11 May 1973.
85 Ninette De Valois, *Invitation to the Ballet* (London: John Lane 1937), pp. 188–247; Ninette De Valois, 'Folk Dance and Royal Ballet', *English Dance and Song*, 24.2 (1960), 39–40. Re-printed from *The Dancing Times* May 1960. See also: Roger Savage, *Masques, Mayings and Music-Dramas: Vaughan Williams and the Early Twentieth-Century Stage* (Woodbridge, Suffolk: Boydell, 2014) pp. 165–221.
86 Schofield, 'Revival of the Folk Dance', pp. 215–216.
87 *ED&S*, 'The Rating Appeal', *English Dance and Song*, 20.1 (1955), pp. 8–13. p. 8.
88 Katy Spicer, 'EFDSS Matters', *English Dance and Song*, 71.4 (2009), p. 26.
89 At the beginning of the twentieth century, state infant schools provided education for children under seven, whilst elementary state schools provided education for children up to the age of 14. By the time of *Moving and Growing* (1952), most state schools had been divided into primary (aged 7–11) and secondary (aged 11–16) facilities.
90 Peter Abbs, 'Towards a Coherent Arts Aesthetic', in *Living Powers: The Arts in Education*, ed. by Peter Abbs (London: Falmer, 1987), pp. 9–66. p. 33.
91 Catherine Burke 2018; Anna Haynes 1987; Vertinsky, 'Schooling the Dance'; Patricia Vertinsky, 'Reconsidering the Female Tradition in English Physical Education: The Impact of Transnational Exchanges in Modern Dance', *The International Journal of the History of Sport*, 32.4 (2015), pp. 535–550.
92 The Board of Education, *The Hadow Report: The Primary School* (Board of Education, London: His Majesty's Stationery Office, 1931), p. 95 <http://www.educationengland.org.uk/documents/hadow1931/hadow1931.html> [Accessed 19 December 2019].
93 *Syllabus of Physical Training for Schools* (Board of Education, London: His Majesty's Stationery Office, 1933), p. 59.
94 Ibid., p. 62.
95 Jordan, *The Dance as Education*.
96 Board of Education, *Syllabus of Physical Training*, p. 63.
97 Jeanette Rutherston, 'Dancing and the Physical Fitness Scheme', *Dancing Times*, 328 (1938), 648–650. This source refers to the Scottish Folk Dance Society and not as one might anticipate, the Scottish Country Dance Society.
98 Vertinsky, 'Schooling the Dance', p. 279.
99 Jordan, *Dance as Education*, Passim.
100 Ibid., p. 2.
101 Ibid., p. 3.
102 Kennedys, *A Jubilee History*, p. 6.
103 Valerie Preston-Dunlop, 'Rudolf Laban', in *International Encyclopaedia of Dance*, ed. by Selma Jeanne Cohen (Oxford: Oxford University Press, 1998). <https://www.oxfordreference.com> (Accessed 8 February 2017); Vertinsky, 'Schooling the Dance', p. 279; Vertinsky, 'Reconsidering the Female Tradition', p. 541.
104 For more on Laban, see Karen Bradley, *Rudolf Laban* (London: Routledge, 2018).
105 Preston-Dunlop, 'Rudolf Laban', unpaginated.
106 Vertinsky, 'Schooling the Dance', p. 281.
107 Haynes, 'The Dynamic Image', p. 150; Vertinsky, 'Schooling the Dance', pp. 279, 282.
108 Vertinsky, 'Schooling the Dance', p. 282.

109 Preston-Dunlop, 'Rudolf Laban', unpaginated.
110 Haynes, 'The Dynamic Image', p. 151.
111 Rudolf Laban, *Modern Educational Dance*. 2nd ed. Revised by Lisa Ullmann (London: MacDonald and Evans, 1963 [1948]), pp. 1–12.
112 Joan Russell, *Modern Dance in Education* (London: Macdonald and Evans, 1958), p. 14.
113 Ministry of Education, *Moving and Growing: Physical Education in the Primary School: Part 1* (London: Her Majesty's Stationery Office, 1952), p. 61.
114 Kennedy, 'The Dance as Education', p. 346.
115 Douglas Kennedy, 'Starting Young', *English Dance and Song*, 23.2 (1959b), 35–37; Helen Kennedy and Douglas Kennedy, *English Folk Dancing in the Primary School* (London: Novello, 1960), p. 5.
116 Douglas Kennedy, 'The Director Writes: On the Annual General Meeting', *English Dance and Song*, 23.1 (1959c), 5–6.
117 Ministry of Education, *Physical Education in the Primary School Part 2: Planning the Programme* (London: Her Majesty's Stationery Office, 1953), p. 22.
118 Department of Education and Science, *Movement: Physical Education in the Primary Years* (London: Her Majesty's Stationery Office, 1972), p. 62.
119 Although in the national curriculum active from 1996 to 1999, there was a requirement for children aged 7–11 to be taught 'a number of dance forms from different times and places, including some traditional dances of the British Isles'. Department of Education, *Key Stages One and Two of the National Curriculum* (London: Department for Education, 1995), p. 116.

14
FANCY FOOTWORK
Reviewing the English clog and step dance revival

Alexandra Fisher

Step dance became part of the English Folk Revival just after the Second World War. Although a relatively recent addition to the repertoire of traditional dance forms, step dance has a long and rich social history which has given rise to both clog and hard-shoe stepping traditions. Essentially a solo dance form, step dance has existed for centuries as a social pastime and stage entertainment and, in its heyday, was known to most of the working population: a fact that was noted by Cecil Sharp in 1911.[1] Sharp did not attempt to collect any of this material thinking that it was 'popular' rather than 'traditional', so not in need of revival. It is also the case that, at the time, Sharp lacked the technical knowledge to collect step dance material. After the First World War, the popularity of step dance in England seemed to decline rapidly as communities embraced modernity and were encouraged to move away from the old ways. In the 1950s, when step dance was finally recognised as a traditional dance form, it was the case that some traditions remained active and some were 'just below the surface', but at the time it was not known how and where to locate them. Since then, a gradual process has taken place whereby the revival and its associated research has revealed more about step dance and its history and this, in turn, has shaped and re-shaped the revival.

Clog and step dance material – review and analysis

Seventy years on from the start of the revival, step dance has a considerable presence in the contemporary folk scene. There is an extensive repertoire of clog dance material performed by dance teams in all parts of the country and hard-shoe stepping is attracting an increasing number of solo dancers. Historically, the solo nature of step dance has resulted in much variation of style and technique and, since the revival dancers and researchers have sought ways to distinguish one style from another. This has often led to a belief in the existence of regional styles, where the identity of a step or style of dancing appears to revolve around where it was originally collected, for example, 'Lakeland' steps or 'North-East' steps. This is a common folkloric notion providing useful reference or promotional tools but, in my view, these mask our understanding of the genre as a whole and risk diverting further research.

For a dance form that was virtually unknown at the start of the revival, a well-documented body of knowledge had been amassed, mostly before 1990 through the efforts of a relatively small number of researchers. Fieldwork, although thorough in many cases, has been patchy and spasmodic resulting in an uneven spread of collected material, further reinforcing the perception of regional styles. To counter this assertion, this paper offers an alternative method of viewing step dance material in which we link dance style with social context rather than regional context. To further refine this analysis, I draw upon recent research identifying two basic genres of stepping that have emerged into the twentieth century: the Stage style and the Street style.[2] The two strands had already been noted by clog dance researchers in the 1950s and 1960s when several informants in Lancashire and West Cumberland made a distinction between the 'off-the-toe' dancing of the 'Stage dancer' and the 'heel-and-toe' dancing of the ordinary 'Street dancer' but the evidence had remained largely dormant.[3] As can be seen, the two genres begin to highlight the connection between dance style and context and this can be further refined as follows: the Stage style is characterised by formally structured steps using off-the-toe shuffles and usually performed in a pre-rehearsed routine, whereas Street stepping, being free-form and spontaneous, is characterised by dancing which is 'close-to-the-ground' using heel-and-toe steps and taking place as part of an informal social gathering. Although many dancers would habitually mix these two styles, examples of their default existence still survive.

These two basic genres of step dance, the Stage style and the Street style, offer a framework from which to view the repertoire of steps described in this chapter. The framework offers a structural reference which informs and analyses similarities and differences in terms of both technique and social context. As a clearer picture of step dance as a genre is revealed, the notion of a 'regional' identity for steps increasingly appears as a revival construct.

The stage style

The fact that this genre contains the largest body of collected material and stepping categories is an obvious consequence of its nature as performance repertoire in that it is relatively easy to collect and transmit. Within this genre, I am focusing on three social contexts which have given rise to significant stepping types:

- Dancing masters – the Stage Hornpipe
- Clog dance competitions – the Clog Hornpipe
- Music-hall – Waltz, Schottische and Ragtime steps

Dancing masters – the Stage Hornpipe

The Stage Hornpipe was a solo step dance which became a popular feature on the early eighteenth-century theatre stage as an entr'acte entertainment, appearing on London playbills from the 1720s onwards.[4] Performers displayed increasing amounts of virtuosity reflecting the growing influence of classical ballet and, as dancing in the 'French' style was a prised asset amongst aspiring gentry, the dancing master would become key to acquiring this refinement.[5] Dancing classes and academies for children and adults sprang up in the fashionable towns of Britain from at least 1750 where, as well as the popular social dances of the day, dancing masters taught several stepping dances, including the Hornpipe.[6]

Dancing masters continued to teach into the nineteenth century although stepping dances gradually dropped from their repertoire. However, in more rural areas farthest away from the fashionable centres, itinerant 'old style' dancing masters continued to teach social and stepping dances into the twentieth century. Research has revealed that this was the case in some areas of Scotland and Ireland and also in the Lake District. Hornpipe steps transmitted via 'Lakeland' dancing masters constitute the first of the stepping types included in this review.

Hornpipe steps collected in the Lake District

Hornpipe steps were collected by Tom and Joan Flett in the 1960s in the old counties of Westmorland, Cumberland and North Lancashire and their well-documented research was eventually published in 1979.[7] Their fieldwork revealed that many informants, as children, had regularly attended dancing classes in the early twentieth century. Taught by professional dancing masters, the children learnt the social dances of the day along with Hornpipe steps and other stepping dances. The Flett's main informant was Norman Robinson (1912–1970), the fourth generation of a family who had been operating as dancing masters in the South Lakes area since 1863. The reminiscences of Robinson and other informants created an extensive repertoire of Hornpipe steps as well as a detailed picture of how this family of dancing masters operated. It was typical for a dancing master to run classes in a round of village locations for about ten weeks at a time at the end of which they would organise a Juvenile Ball. This format allowed parents to watch their children perform before an evening's social dancing. It was usual for dancing masters to be good fiddlers, an essential skill that enabled them to accompany their classes and to play for social events.[8]

The Fletts' published research features a number of Juvenile Ball Programmes from 1825 through to 1922 and these indicate that, as well as the Robinson family, there had been several other dancing masters running classes in the area. The Ball Programmes are a wonderful resource, giving information on what dance items were being taught and who was to perform them. Additional Juvenile Ball Programmes collected in recent years, and dating back to 1797, illustrate how dancing masters responded to changing fashions in both the social and stepping dances and it is interesting to note that the popularity of the Hornpipe seemed to increase dramatically in the late nineteenth and early twentieth centuries.[9]

Hornpipe steps remembered by informants demonstrate a distinct style of stepping which, we believe, has its roots on the eighteenth-century theatre stage and several factors seem to confirm this. The steps are performed off-the-toe and are both percussive and visual, beats being made with both toes and heels. The Fletts' research and notation emphasised a 'turn-out' of the legs and feet and also highlighted the aerial quality of the steps along with frequent sideways travel. This and the many 'crossed' steps suggest a link with early ballet technique and indeed, it was discovered that dancing masters would spend time visiting ex-ballet dancers in London and Edinburgh to learn new material.[10] Although performed in clogs today, the Fletts indicate that originally it was probably a hard-shoe dance. The music is an undotted Hornpipe and the steps follow this formal structure, each lasting for eight bars and including an emphasised two-bar finish or 'shuffle-off'. All steps start on the left foot and are not usually repeated off the right.[11]

Because of their distinct nature and well-researched background, these steps have been known to revival dancers since the 1960s as Westmorland or Lakeland steps. This regional label is attractive and useful as a means of identification, but it gives way to the notion that these steps are somehow exclusive to this area of the country and have developed as a distinct 'tradition'. Dancing masters and their steps and methods of transmission were once a national phenomenon and the Fletts' research in the Lake District has revealed valuable details of this piece of dance history through its remarkable persistence into the twentieth century.[12]

Clog dance competitions – the Clog Hornpipe

Tracing the history and development of the competition, Clog Hornpipe is problematic because there is relatively little documented evidence, but the 1880 World Championship clog dance contest acts as a prominent base line. It took place on a Leeds Music-Hall stage and the winner was a young man called Dan Leno.[13] This is believed to be the first World Championship although clog dance contests had been happening in both America and Australia – as well as Britain – since the 1840s.[14] The Clog Hornpipe was a variation of the Stage Hornpipe which, as we have seen, goes back to the eighteenth-century theatre stage. Evidence suggests that the Clog Hornpipe became a frequent act in the early nineteenth century when, according to Bratton (1990), 'an influx of first-generation urban workers swamped the theatre'.[15] Audiences here were thrilled with a menu of impressive physical skills and challenges that were half-familiar but presented in a professional capacity. The dancing of Hornpipes was one such skill and, as well as in clogs, it was performed in many other formats, including on skates, tight-ropes and even horse-back.[16] The Clog Hornpipe, being the most accessible of these stage acts, became 'the people's dance' and seemed to take on a life of its own, appearing as entertainment at circuses, fairs and pub singing rooms. It became one of a number of different physical challenge contests such as boxing and wrestling and was also surrounded by its fair share of betting, bribing and fisticuffs.[17]

In their efforts to comply with the 1843 Theatre Act, many theatres started to cater for a more middle-class audience and were forced to exclude acts which would attract 'rowdy or dangerously lower-class patrons' (Bratton 1990) and by the 1850s many acts, including the Clog Hornpipe, were only to be seen on the newly developing music-hall stage.[18] Aspiring clog dancers, both men and women, would hone their skills in saloon-bars, concert rooms and the illegal free-and-easy establishments where competitions often took place.[19] The Clog Hornpipe had become both a sport and an art and this guaranteed its popularity both in the community and on the music-hall stage, the clog itself becoming the bond between performer and audience.

From about 1860, clog dance competitions were appearing on music-hall stages all over the country but due to further licencing laws, they became increasingly confined to the lower-class halls. They were, however, also held as small local events in pubs, village halls and workplace venues. Competitions were generally advertised by poster, newspaper or by word of mouth and rules concerning dancing and prizes would be stated before-hand. For example, in a small contest, dancers would be required to perform ten steps but at world championship level, it would be 20 steps. The prizes could vary from a leg of mutton, to money, medals, cups and a Championship Belt for high profile contests.[20] A panel of judges, usually ex-champions, were appointed to give marks for timing, beats, originality, execution and carriage. As rivalry was intense, it is said, for beats and timing, that judges would sit under or by the side of the stage so they could not see who was performing.[21]

A considerable number of Clog Hornpipe steps have been collected from informants in many parts of Britain since the 1950s and their similar characteristics identify them as a specific stepping type. With this knowledge, we can view how the Clog Hornpipe has been shaped by the competitions. Clog Hornpipe steps are danced off-the-toe and have a formal structure consisting of six bars of stepping plus a two-bar finish. Competition rules demanded that all steps had to be repeated accurately off both sides of the body and performed on the spot. As dancers were given marks for originality, competition steps employ a large vocabulary of moves, beats being made with all parts of the clog and in fact it could be said that these steps could *only* be performed in clogs. The music required is a dotted Hornpipe but the complexity of the steps demands that it is played in a 12/8 tempo, thus allowing scope for rhythmic variation.[22]

Due to the popularity of clog dance competitions in the late nineteenth and early twentieth centuries, it is interesting to speculate on how working people acquired these complex dance skills. The following examples give a flavour of how this took place:

- John Frith (1874–1957) – a collier from Coppull in Lancashire. Apparently self-taught, he entered many competitions and was once offered professional work in a circus.[23]
- Johnson Ellwood (1899–1977) – a collier and fireman from Stanley in County Durham was taught to clog dance by his father. He entered local competitions and had also danced professionally.[24]
- Sammy Bell (1914–1993) – a collier originally from Linton in Northumberland was taught to clog dance by three different teachers. He entered several competitions and performed as a local amateur.[25]

These brief scenarios are typical of informants from many industrial regions. They illustrate how familiar and accessible clog dancing was at this time particularly, it seems, amongst coal-mining communities, and they highlight the fine line between amateur and professional performances. The information also shows that research has taken place in Lancashire, Durham and Northumberland and that clog dancing clearly persisted here into the twentieth century. Amongst revivalists, this has contributed to the belief that there were distinct differences between competition Hornpipe steps from these three regions but, as we have seen, all competition steps share similar characteristics indicating an accepted uniformity of dance style. As we shall see later, research-based evidence suggests that regional styles (if they existed) were not apparent in competition clog dancing.

Music-hall repertoire – Clog Waltz, Schottische and Ragtime steps

Much of the clog dance material collected from primary source dancers could be said to have come from the music hall and variety theatre stages of the late nineteenth and early twentieth centuries but clog dancing was also a popular 'turn' in local venues. Step dancing was an essential skill for most entertainers at this time, but in a specialist clog dance act, a performer might demonstrate an Exhibition Hornpipe to show off their competition steps and would also include stepping in songs and short sketches, giving scope for different musical tempos and a broader range of steps. Consequently, in addition to Hornpipe steps, material collected from many clog dancers would often include Waltz steps, Schottische steps and Ragtime steps. This repertoire reflects both the importance attached to the Hornpipe and a response to 'new' musical genres.

Clog Waltz

The Clog Waltz was particularly popular in variety theatres all over Britain during the early twentieth century. There are many notated examples of Waltz steps and they seem to consist of quite similar phrases and motifs all danced 'off the toe'.[26] Compared with the serious nature of the Exhibition Hornpipe, it seems that the Clog Waltz was more light-hearted and entertaining, as clog dancer John Surtees (b. 1898) explained: 'you could move about and express yourself'.[27] The Clog Waltz was often known as a 'Dutch Dance' as it was sometimes performed as a comedy courting duet where dancers would wear pseudo Dutch costume, including specially made clogs where the leather uppers were shaped to look like the 'all-wood' Dutch clog.

Schottische steps

Clog dance material collected from several informants included steps known to them as Schottische steps. This type of stepping (or 'Song and Dance' as it was known on the early twentieth-century British variety stage) became hugely popular as an entertainment style. Originating in America as 'Soft Shoe', it is acknowledged as the precursor to Tap dance. Sources indicate that the Soft-Shoe probably developed from a dance called 'The Essence of Old Virginia' which was 'the first popular dance for professionals from the Afro-American vernacular'.[28] For today's Tap dancers, an Essence is a crossed brush-step, and this suggests a connection with the eighteenth-century Stage Hornpipe which would have existed in America at that time.[29]

An important informant here is the step dancer Sam Sherry (1912–2001) who performed at prestigious venues around Britain during the 1920s and 1930s. He referred to the Schottische as a 'a light dance or Soft-Shoe' performed to a 'slow 4-in-a-bar' tempo and he stressed that the most important features were elegance and being able to move smoothly across the stage.[30] Sherry learnt many of his Schottische steps from his father (b.1866) who was a contemporary of Eugene Stratton (1861–1918). Stratton was an American dancer who joined a minstrel troupe in Britain, settling in London and becoming a key figure in the development of the Schottische in Britain. In 1898, he shot to fame with a solo song and dance number entitled *Lily of Laguna*.[31] Schottische steps collected from Sam Sherry and other clog dancers share many of the features described by Sherry; they are light, with subtle taps and involve elegant crossing steps and ingenious travel. There are fancy leg gestures, turns and heel taps and, almost without exception, the favourite tune is *Lily of Laguna*.[32]

Ragtime steps

Sam Sherry's repertoire could be said to incorporate many aspects of the Stage step dance tradition and also to illustrate how it eventually morphed into Tap dance. A particularly good example of this is his Reel or Exhibition routine which he described as a 'fast even-rhythmed 2-in- a-bar style'.[33] Ragtime routines have been collected from several other clog dancers who would perform them in clogs as well as in tap shoes. It is interesting to pick out the characteristics which highlight the transition to a more syncopated result. Although the dancing is off-the-toe and includes fast shuffles, there is considerable use of flat-footed shunts and many steps start on the 'up-beat'.[34]

The Street style

In my analysis, Street stepping styles, in both clogs and hard shoes, can be characterised predominantly by context: usually taking place as part of an informal social gathering. In terms of physical action, this dancing tends to be spontaneous and improvisational and, because it is 'personal', individual style can vary but generally speaking, Street styles of stepping seem to revolve around a heel-and-toe technique rather than an off-the-toe technique. In contrast to the many Stage clog steps that have been collected, notated and transmitted, Street stepping styles have presented far more of a problem to the researcher as they only exist 'in performance' and may appear different each time they are performed. However, many Street step dancers seem to have a small stock of stepping units that are utilised in a random order while nevertheless creating their particular style. Stepping of this nature, it appears, has always been passed on as a gradual process, in a similar way to the oral transmission of a song. Children will witness the joy of seeing older relatives dancing and playing music together on a regular basis and will be encouraged to 'have a go', copy what they see and eventually begin to develop their own performance style.

Hard-shoe stepping styles

In my introduction, I stated that during the early step dance revival of the 1950s some step dance traditions were still 'active'. Consequent research in Devon, East Anglia and the southern counties of England has gradually revealed that this was indeed the case. This is both interesting and fortuitous because the fact that hard-shoe step dance was still being performed in its original social context has enriched both research and analysis. This section will focus on the stepping styles and contexts that have been found in these particular regions.

East Anglia

The research carried out in North Norfolk by Ann-Marie Hulme and Peter Clifton in the late 1970s traced step dancing back to the 1840s and revealed that before the Second World War, 'step dancers and musicians could be found in almost every family', and that step dancing was a common activity at family parties, village events and in the local pub. In describing how dancing might have taken place, they explain that a musician would start playing and one dancer at a time would 'take the floor' and step to the music but that, on occasions, the atmosphere could become competitive with 'each dancer trying to outdo the previous one'.[35]

In terms of style, Hulme and Clifton reject the concept of a common regional style in Norfolk, emphasising that styles generally develop as steps are passed down through families or close communities. However, they do comment on three types of stepping that they observed in the area: first, a heel-and-toe style based around the dancer Dick Hewitt and second, more of a flat-footed style from the West family of the Traveller community. The third influence they noted was an off-the-toe style from the Davies family of Cromer.[36] A common feature, however, was the freestyle nature of the stepping, with dancers using three or four basic motifs put together spontaneously. The preferred music for stepping was usually an undotted Hornpipe but it appeared that dancers only occasionally emphasised a two-bar finish to any eight-bar phrase. A characteristic trait noted in the dancing of the Traveller community involved the practice of using 'a simple limbering up step to set the time' followed by a stamp of the foot to indicate the start of the stepping.[37]

Devon

As in East Anglia, step dancing in Devon has been a popular pastime in pubs, at family gatherings and also as a concert 'turn' but it appears that step dance competitions, particularly on Dartmoor, were also frequent events. Recent newspaper research has revealed that between 1881 and 1939, regular competitions were recorded in at least 16 different village locations (South Zeal and Whiddon Down, for example) and informants have described competitions where prize money would attract as many as 30 contestants from villages far and wide. In a recent review of step dance in Devon, Lisa Sture comments that since the 1950s, with social stepping gradually declining, competitions have kept the tradition alive.[38] In a typical competition, contestants wear hard-soled shoes or hob-nailed boots and must perform on a small raised platform. The music is a continuous undotted Hornpipe and dancers take turns to dance one 'step' each on the platform. One 'step' consists of six bars of a simple 'setting' step with a two-bar finish (repeated off the other foot), followed by six bars of a more complex 'dance' step with a two-bar finish (repeated off the other foot). Each dancer performs three 'steps' and in terms of style, beats are made with toes and heels, flat stamps, shunts and some toe shuffles.[39]

When not in a competition, 'social' stepping would be informal with dancers getting up to perform at any point in the music and displaying a more improvisational style. Many enthusiasts in Devon believe that the stepping of the local Traveller communities could well reflect this social stepping style. Traveller communities in many parts of Britain have retained their interest and involvement in traditional music and step dance and the stepping they perform would fit into my analysis as Street style stepping. In Devon, Sture (2019) refers to the 'heel-and-toe improvisation' of the local Romany dancers and, as mentioned before, it appears that this is also the case in East Anglia. Recent research centred in Hampshire (see below) has found a similar style of stepping within the Traveller community.

Hampshire

Since 2009, Jo and Simon Harmer[40] have focused their research on two dancers, Val Shipley and Janet Keet-Black, both of whom are from Traveller families. Although now settled, previous generations of these families had travelled across many of the southern counties of England. The research identified a heel-and-toe style of stepping and that each dancer 'flowed seamlessly through step combinations which were very obviously led by the music'. The Harmers subsequently visited several Traveller gatherings across Dorset, Hampshire and Sussex where they witnessed similar informal social stepping. They describe the style as 'heel and toe combinations, danced close to the floor' and they also comment that 'what came across most strongly was each dancer's own individuality and personality reflected through the stepping'.[41]

Street clog stepping

If step dancing was a common and much-loved pastime amongst working people right up until the Second World War, it must follow that it was done in all types of footwear, including hard-soled shoes, boots and clogs. Oral history has confirmed that informal stepping in clogs was indeed a common occurrence in clog-wearing communities and many areas of Lancashire still have strong connections with their clog-wearing days. Respondents make mention of informal stepping (in clogs) within the Chorley area and apparently taking place up until the 1950s. Ken Brindle, for example, demonstrated some steps in his working clogs, and described how, as a young boy in the 1940s, he had seen men tapping their clogs outside the pubs and had copied the action in his clogs at home. Brindle called this 'heel and toe' and explained that it was very spontaneous and informal, and the idea was 'to make it sound nice'.[42]

As explained earlier, heel-and-toe stepping had previously been noted in Lancashire and West Cumbria by several researchers who described clog dance steps that were performed close-to-the-ground, using heels and toes only, and were possibly freestyle in nature. People considered this stepping to be 'ordinary', and that it was distinct from 'proper' stage dancing which was performed off-the-toe. They also acknowledged that it was quite normal for a dancer to mix the two styles.

Street stepping styles, by their very nature, are difficult to collect or transmit, so it is not surprising that examples of Street style clog dance are rare occurrences in the post-revival repertoire. However, versions of heel-and-toe clog stepping have been noted from three particular dancers. Pat Tracey (1927–2008) had grown up in East Lancashire and inherited some heel-and-toe steps from her mother and grandfather. From an analytical stance, these steps could be more accurately described as 'toe-and-heel' steps, but they are close-to-the-ground, have no toe shuffles and, as Tracey claims, probably developed as a result of wearing heavy loose-fitting work clogs. While different from Ken Brindle's heel-and-toe technique, they do illustrate a definite connection with clog-wearing. Tracey suggests that this type of stepping originally occurred in East Lancashire as street entertainment and was probably danced freestyle but, since the revival, it has always been taught and performed in dancing clogs as formally structured routines.[43]

There are two other dancers from Lancashire who have routines made up of 'toe-and-heel' steps. Bill Gibbons (b.1898) was born in West Lancashire and worked with his father for many years on the barges, a working community where stepping and music seem to have been widespread. Gibbons' dancing was originally done in working clogs but remains close-to-the-ground even in dance clogs. Analysis has shown it to consist of several randomly arranged motifs that are skilfully phrased with the music.[44] Bert Bowden was born in 1910 in Liverpool and learnt clog steps from his father who had been a keen amateur performer. Bowden also developed an amateur or semi-professional entertainment act as a dancer, comedian and puppeteer. His father taught him a set of Hornpipe steps called 'Old Lancashire steps' and they consist of 'toe-and-heel' steps with the addition of some toe shuffles. Apparently, Bowden's father stressed that the heel drops, or 'chops', should always be emphasised.[45]

The toe-and-heel steps from these three dancers demonstrate certain aspects of the Street style in that they are performed close-to-the-ground and use a different vocabulary from the off-the-toe shuffles of Stage stepping. However, in terms of technique, they seem radically different from the heel-and-toe stepping of Ken Brindle. To find some common ground with his technique, we should look to the clog dance tradition that has developed in Wales. In its solo form, it is essentially freestyle, heel-and-toe (with no toe shuffles) and was originally danced in working clogs. One of the basic skills of this clogging is the 'Pit-a-Pat-a', and this is an exact match for Brindle's heel-and-toe action.[46] Looking further afield, we have already identified this move amongst step dancers in East Anglia, Devon and Southern England and it is also the basis of the 'battering' steps punctuating Irish Set dancing.

In pointing out the difference between heel-and-toe steps and toe-and-heel steps, I am not at this stage attempting an explanation (if there is one), but it is clear that the area needs further research and analysis. An important observation from my experience as a dancer, however, is that the two motifs feel different to perform. Furthermore, toe-and-heel has become integral to many off-the-toe Stage steps, whereas heel-and-toe is never found in Stage style stepping, thereby indicating a distinct technique in its own right.

Concluding remarks

This framework for viewing step dance material offers a helpful and constructive method of analysis for both dancers and researchers. The framework has enabled us to consider several factors, the most important of which is to call into question the linking of dance style with regional orientation. The misleading nature of this was recognised by researcher Chris Metherell in 1981 when reviewing the steps he had collected in the North-East of England. He states that: 'many of the steps in this booklet are however not unique to the North-East, they are found all over the country wherever people clog dance'. As a result of his research, Metherell concluded that there was not a definable North-East style and that any common traits could probably be traced back to certain dominant teachers.[47] Furthermore, in identifying the existence of the Stage style and the Street style, this framework connects step style to social context which enables us to link stepping styles across regions rather than viewing them as distinct traditions. The framework foregrounds aspects of social history, for example, clog dance competitions, and in identifying the Stage style the origin of many steps can be traced back to the eighteenth century. In identifying the Street style, we highlight a lesser known aspect of step dance that warrants further research.

Documenting the revival

Documenting the revival gives an opportunity to reflect upon some of the factors that both initiated it and propelled its momentum. As with other revived folk traditions, the step dance revival has developed through the interplay of fieldwork, research, primary source dancers, transmission and the engagement of revival dancers. Clog and step dance will be reviewed separately but it is useful here to highlight an event which, in 1949, seemed to set the wheels in motion.

A strategic post-war re-organisation of the English Folk Dance and Song Society sought to discover and support folk customs which had not previously been acknowledged as worthy of collection. In order to achieve their post-war mission, EFDSS appointed Area Folk Music Organisers who were sent to take up residence in all parts of the country. Area Organiser Peter Kennedy (appointed to the North-East region in 1947) became aware that there had been a strong clog dance tradition in Durham and Northumberland and he eventually made contact with the clog dancer Johnson Ellwood. At Ellwood's bidding, Kennedy organised a clog dance competition, the Northumberland and Durham Championship, which had last been held in 1938. The competition took place in Hexham and generated interest in clog dance on many levels. Local dancers helped judge the competition and started running classes again, but it was the winner of the Junior contest who opened the door to national recognition for clog dance. Jackie Toaduff, a 14-year-old pitman from Stanley and a pupil of Tiny Allison, was consequently selected by the EFDSS to showcase clog dance within the national folk performance team.[48] These nationwide performances, including several for the EFDSS National Gathering at the Royal Albert Hall, inspired many individuals to become involved in the revival as dancers, teachers and researchers.

Clog dance

Research & primary sources

The early clog dance revival was dependent on locating primary source dancers and enabling their material to be effectively transmitted. In some cases, primary dancers would emerge with the capability to teach their own material but, in the main, primary dancers have been recognised as a consequence of fieldwork and subsequent transmission has taken place via the researcher or group of researchers. Three outstanding examples of dancers as exceptional and committed teachers were Johnson Ellwood, Pat Tracey and Sam Sherry.

Johnson Ellwood, encouraged by the success of the Hexham competition, taught a considerable number of people from 1949 up until his death in 1976. Pat Tracey (1927–2008) had inherited a vast repertoire of steps from her mother's family in East Lancashire. On moving to London in the early 1950s, she had responded to an EFDSS request for information on clog dancing and, by 1959, was teaching her material to a regular class at Cecil Sharp House in London. Sam Sherry (1912–2001), an ex-professional step dancer, had been a member of the Five Sherry Brothers – a 'class act' on the variety circuit involving step dance and acrobatics. Sam, the youngest brother, had retired from the stage in 1956 and when he joined the revival in 1967, at the age of 55, he was regarded as a sensational performer and he was soon teaching and performing regularly at workshop days and festivals.[49] His style and extensive repertoire of steps proved both inspirational and challenging to many dancers and from 1976 he began running a regular class in the Lancaster area.

During the 1950s and 1960s, these three primary source dancers had come forward to fully engage with the revival. They provided the bulk of step dance material for a growing number of enthusiasts, but it was realised that further fieldwork would be necessary to uncover additional sources. Pre-eminent here were Tom and Joan Flett, whose work with Norman Robinson and numerous other informants was particularly significant.[50] This fieldwork also stimulated research in Lancashire by Julian Pilling, who visited several clog dancers and recorded both steps and memories.[51] During the 1970s and 1980s, the Flett's research had inspired a 'research hub' of individuals based in the Reading area. Their activities included research into hard-shoe stepping in Norfolk and Devon as well as the filming of several primary dancers, for example: Dick Hewitt, Sammy Bell, Pat Tracey and Sam Sherry.[52]

A second research hub, based in Newcastle-upon-Tyne, was created in 1980 by the dancer and researcher Chris Metherell, who had carried the torch to Tyneside from Reading.[53] Aware that the North-East was a rich research area, he founded The Instep Research Team who located and interviewed a great many primary clog dancers. The team devised a method of notation to accurately record collected material and sets of steps and informants' biographies were published and made available in the Newcastle Series of booklets. Between 1981 and 1988, Metherell also edited and published INSTEP, a regular journal containing articles, notations, research notes and reviews. The Instep Research Team, now a charity, continue their research activities in all aspects of step dance and their website (www.insteprt.co.uk) contains a wealth of information.

Transmission & participation

The clog dance revival was in full swing by the 1980s with an estimated 60 clog dance teams in existence. These groups occurred in all parts of the country and in many ways their activities echoed those of the longer-established morris-dance teams. Each group was performance orientated: new members being trained by the team to participate in its particular repertoire of dances. Although clog dance is basically a solo activity, teams have generally choreographed their material to perform as groups. Clog dance steps have usually been acquired at specially run workshops, often at folk festivals but, in the early revival, three particular groups started to organise dedicated workshop festivals. Here, participants could learn new material and have opportunities to perform and watch other performances. The first of these, in 1979, was a workshop day organised by the Reading Step and Traditional Dance Group. Formed in 1965, Reading Cloggies had, over the years, developed their research, performance and teaching skills to enable them to run this event on an annual basis.[54] In 1981, the Newcastle Cloggies, a similarly pro-active clog dance group set up by Chris

Metherell, organised the first full weekend workshop festival and the success of this event encouraged a similar weekend to take place in 1984, organised by The Lancashire Wallopers. These three workshop festivals became annual events and, through the years, have contributed greatly to sustaining levels of participation. The Lancashire Wallopers' weekend still takes place today although the Reading and Newcastle festivals have ceased to run. Since 2004, additional annual workshop days have been organised by City Clickers of Bristol and since 2008, by Camden Clog of London.

The clog dance revival has been propelled forward by the enthusiasm of adult groups enjoying both the dancing and the social benefits of the folk movement. Most adults also acknowledge that the skills of clog dancing can be easily acquired by children and young people. Consequently, over the years, children's clog dance groups have come and gone with one in particular, the Fosbrooks of Stockport, still going strong. During the 1990s, funded folk arts projects for young people started to take place and, in the North-East, the Folk Arts agency, Folkworks promoted clog dance in particular. By the end of the decade, Folkworks had also been instrumental in their support for a Folk and Traditional Music Degree course at Newcastle University which later allowed students to pursue stepping as a performance option.

Hard-shoe step dance

Primary sources, research & transmission

East Anglia

Early awareness that traditional step dancing was still taking place in East Anglia came about through BBC audio recordings in 1939 and 1947 from a pub in Eastbridge, Suffolk. Although mainly of singing, the recordings also featured two step dancers and this led folk researchers to make similar recordings in East Anglian pubs during the 1950s and 1960s. Peter Kennedy's recordings in Blaxhall, Suffolk, contributed to the film 'The Barley Mow' (1955) and recordings made by Seamus Ennis in the North Norfolk village of Southrepps resulted in the radio broadcast 'As I Roved Out' (1955) which first featured the step dancer Dick Hewitt. Hewitt's dancing was soon noted by EFDSS and he was consequently invited to perform at the Royal Albert Hall National Gathering in 1959. Marketing himself as 'Dick Hewitt, the Norfolk Step-dancer', he was a prestigious local performer and from 1964, the pub he ran in North Norfolk became a favourite venue for music and stepping. Hewitt was filmed in 1979 and his stepping motifs were notated by step dance researchers Hulme and Clifton in 1981.[55] This is possibly the only attempt to collect and notate stepping in East Anglia but, as we have seen, freestyle stepping is difficult to notate.

As East Anglia became a known location for traditional song, music and dance, individuals associated with the folk revival were attracted to the area. John and Katie Howson moved there in 1978 and set about nurturing and promoting the continuation of these activities in their natural settings. Although not step dancers themselves, they spent the next 20 years creating appropriate contexts and supplying music for the local dancers to carry on stepping in their usual way. Their regular 'Old Hat Music Nights', held in local pubs, gathered together a group of musicians and singers, including step dancers Dick Hewitt, Font Whatling and Cyril Barber. Known as The Old Hat Concert Party, they performed at several folk festivals making step dance more visible to the wider folk scene.[56] In 2000, the Howsons set up the East Anglian Traditional Music Trust with an agenda to encourage greater participation from the local community. From 2002, EATMT inaugurated an annual Traditional Music Day which welcomed performances from any step dancer in attendance. Local enthusiasts decided to hold a Step Dance Day at which there would be informal 'all-comers' stepping competition with no rules or 'style guidance'. In subsequent years, it was decided to run step dance workshops, an unprecedented venture since it had always been acknowledged that the very informality of stepping meant that it could not easily be taught. Interest increased, however, and by 2008 there were two competitions – one for all-comers and one for experienced dancers.[57]

Devon

In a similar way to the start of the clog dance revival, it was a step dance competition that seemed to stimulate the revival in Devon. In 1951, EFDSS Area Organiser Peter Kennedy, fresh from the success of the clog dance competition in Northumberland, took the opportunity to encourage the resumption of the Dartmoor step dance competitions as they had all ceased to run during the Second World War.[58] Kennedy organised a competition in South Zeal, and this event introduced him to two primary source step dancers, Bob Cann (1916–1990) and Les Rice (1912–1996), who were subsequently invited by the EFDSS to perform at the Royal Albert Hall in 1953. Both these individuals were from families who had been involved in music and step dance for generations; Les Rice and his cousin Jack Rice, for example, had several influential uncles, especially Albert Crocker (b.1885), who had won many Dartmoor competitions. Les' daughter, Marlene, was also a step dance champion.[59] A considerable amount of step dance research took place between 1980 and 1991 and information for both Cann and Rice was published by the Instep Research Team.[60] As these dancers were both involved in competitions, it was competition stepping rather than social stepping that entered the record.

Step dancers of Cann and Rice's generation had all learnt their stepping through oral transmission but, in the 1960s and 1970s, when no new dancers were entering the competitions, they began to consider how they could pass on their heritage to younger people. Bob Cann started the Dartmoor Pixie Folk Club at South Tawton where children could learn step dancing and see older dancers perform.[61] In 1977, he began running The Dartmoor Folk Festival at South Zeal, which included step dance competitions, workshops and displays. Les Rice also began to hold some regular step dance classes, gradually involving revival dance enthusiasts, and by 1984 there were enough new dancers to compete, leaving the judging to the older dancers. The step dance competition is now a major feature of the annual Dartmoor Folk Festival and additional competitions have been revived in the Dartmoor villages of Chagford and Okehampton following a 2017 funded community project.[62]

Inside the revival

Competitions & authenticity

We need to acknowledge that step dance can no longer be considered popular culture and that its marginal status is reliant on maintaining and increasing participation. In doing this, individuals and organisations often use the notion of 'heritage' as a promotional tool by attaching a 'regional' label to particular steps or styles of dancing. Although this is an effective way to attract support, there is sometimes conflict between the revival perception of what the dancing represents and the outcome of historical research. This can result in decisions that appear to alter history in order to justify a particular strategic direction, and nowhere is this clearer than the context of the modern step dance competition. The activity connects past and present, is common to both clog dance and hard-shoe stepping and can assert both a positive and a negative influence on the revival dance form. It foregrounds and highlights issues of authenticity and ownership.

Clog dance has been particularly shaped by the competitions that proliferated in the late nineteenth and early twentieth centuries and, as we have seen, in 1949 it was a clog dance competition that launched the clog dance revival. As a result, it was accepted that competitions were an effective way to raise standards and attract new dancers and this stimulated the setting up of new and revived competitions. In 1977, the Durham Folk Festival hosted the Northern Counties Clog Dance Championship, a post-war contest run by Johnson Ellwood between 1953 and 1960. Under his guidance, rules and judging criteria were established and marks would be given for beats, timing, execution and carriage but not for originality, which had always been included in the past. Mike Cherry, a contestant from Berkshire, was particularly concerned about this omission and felt that the rules regarding 'Style' were not easy for an outsider to interpret, thus putting them at a disadvantage.[63] The competition organisers also had difficulty in defining 'Style' but were keen to emphasise that they were trying to preserve the 'purity of the North East Clog Tradition'.[64] Since several styles of clog dancing had been identified in the North-East, it was felt that Style, as defined within the competition, would inevitably be limited to that of the Ellwood family and with no 'originality' criteria included, there was little scope for variation.

A similar dispute occurred over the definition of Style in the setting up of the Lancashire and Cheshire Clog Dance Championship in 1977 which was to take place at the Fylde Folk Festival. The organisers sought advice from Sam Sherry, who lived in Lancashire and was keen for the championship to be established despite having little experience of clog dance competitions. In order to match their perceptions of the North-East's regional style and the success attaching to it, the organisers pondered over how the competition might best reflect a regional style for Lancashire. This was complicated as many different stepping styles had been identified in Lancashire. Notwithstanding, there seemed to be a view that Lancashire clog dancing was done 'off-the-toe', and this was understood to mean that there were no 'heel-beats'. The discovery of several sets of Hornpipe steps which possessed these characteristics *and* were referred to as 'Lancashire' steps was ultimately accepted as proof. It was therefore decided that, for competition purposes, dancers should not use heel-beats and would, indeed, be penalised for doing so.

During the next few years, this created a lot of controversy among both budding contestants and other traditional dancers. Pat Tracey, while recognising the need for rules, argued that from her experience, this would not represent the true picture of clog dancing in Lancashire. Her great-uncle would say 'the one thing you must remember in clog dancing is to use all the wood' and although his competition steps were all performed off-the-toe, they incorporated frequent heel-beats.[65] Alex Boydell (b.1934), reflecting on what he had learned from one of his teachers during the 1940s, stated that he was taught a basic off-the-toe step to establish the 'balance and rhythm' but that once this was mastered, he was 'encouraged to fit in heel drops etc. for they MAKE the step'.[66]

The 'no heel-beats' issue has often been discussed in forums held after the Lancashire competitions take place and, although heel-beats are now allowed in other competitions held during the day, the rule still stands for the prestigious 'Championship Hornpipe'. It has to be acknowledged that this competition has indeed defined a regional style for Lancashire which is now distinct from that of the North-East. In fact, it is said that the 'no-heels' rule had been originally favoured to handicap more experienced dancers from the North-East. A regrettable aspect of the decision, however, is that it diminishes the skill base of the newly defined 'Lancashire style' and this is a sad reflection of the aspirations and capabilities of past Lancashire dancers. In their heyday, clog dance contests involved dancers from all over the country and, in their efforts to perform steps of the utmost complexity, they would certainly have used heel-beats.

In Devon, particularly on Dartmoor, competitions have kept the step dance tradition alive and the characteristics of this style of competition stepping have been handed down from dancers such as Les Rice and Bob Cann. However, with these older dancers now gone, organisers have felt the need to revisit judging criteria and in order to put a local stamp on the dancing, they have sought to reflect, even constitute, a 'Devon Style'. Enthusiasts in Devon are now beginning to consider how the revival has shaped their tradition and are re-evaluating the influence of both competitions and primary source dancers. In this enlightened approach, they have acknowledged that, during the early revival, the teaching of competition steps began to restrict the scope of the dancing. It is now recognised that there is a need to create a better understanding of the tradition: to give it an identity that acknowledges and incorporates the freedom and individualism it had in the past.[67]

Since 2000, a desire to encourage 'new' dancers in East Anglia has embraced competition as a means to an end. Two competitions set up in 2008 provided incentive for both new and experienced dancers while also promoting recognition of an East Anglian style. The rules and judging criteria for 2017 demonstrate an ongoing attempt to negotiate this complex balance. While the aim of the all-comers competition is to 'encourage new dancers to take part', it also stresses the importance of performing in 'the local style' and this is defined as *not* being 'tap, clog, Appalachian or Dartmoor'. The competition for experienced dancers is the Font Whatling Traditional Stepdance Trophy which was set up specifically to highlight traditional East Anglian stepping.[68] The statement that 'You don't have to dance like Font Whatling, but it's really important to dance East Anglian style step dancing' is an interesting piece of guidance that assumes competitors possess, or will develop, an understanding of the East Anglian style however difficult this may be to express in words. The hope is that with many 'traditional' dancers and families still active, the oral nature of the dance form will be enough to sustain it.

There is no doubt that competitions have been and remain a significant factor in the story of English step dance but, as a revival strategy, their impact and effect have been varied. In recent years, competitions have not been a major influence amongst clog dancers who generally prefer to perform their steps in groups rather than as solos. In contrast to this, however, the freestyle nature of hard-shoe step dance is the realm of the solo dancer and so the competition can offer both an incentive and a much-needed performance opportunity. As we have seen, in a revival context, competitions can also create tensions around notions of authenticity as each 'tradition' strives to establish a definitive dance style. Analysis of these tensions from an anthropological perspective can perhaps enrich our understanding of what it means to be involved in a revival dance form.

Why was there a need to establish definitive regional dance styles when it seems that this was not originally considered an important criterion? As already mentioned, across the English Folk Revival as a whole, it was thought that if a cultural form was 'discovered' in a particular region, it formed a traditional part of that region's social history. Running parallel was a post-war awareness of 'the social need to give meaning to our present lives by linking ourselves to a meaningful past'.[69] In their desire to establish an authentic regional dance style, revivalists would habitually consult the 'traditional' dancer with occasional misunderstandings on both sides. Sam Sherry,[70] for example, had no notion of the existence of 'regional styles' prior to his involvement in the revival and in Devon, as we have seen, it is now acknowledged that revivalists, in their efforts to be 'authentic', adhered perhaps too rigidly to Bob Cann's early step dance teaching.

Conclusion

When cultural forms have been separated from what we know of their earlier socio-cultural bases, and are subsequently revived, they can sometimes take on a strangely autonomous existence.[71] This, in turn, opens them to appropriation as items or symbols of cultural significance. Then: 'when different parties develop conflicting notions of authenticity to justify their claims of ownership as regards a dance form, the problematic nature of authenticity as a construct is revealed'.[72] To revive any cultural form can be considered 'strategic and selective'[73] producing intriguing ambiguities that can appear both 'revolutionary and conservative'.[74] So where does that leave us? As the dance ethnologist Anca Giurchescu has pointed out, even when a dance is 'artificially segregated from its social context and considered solely in its physical features', it still 'produces meaning each time it is performed'.[75] The fancy footwork of step dance lures the performer with the appeal of the virtuosic just as it satisfies the spectator with its apparently magical percussive qualities. It has, after all, existed as popular dance for over three centuries. Over the years, it has engaged all sections of society who have danced for joy and self- expression rather than for 'tradition'. Nevertheless, as a revival dance form, step dance has found itself suddenly draped in tradition. Through an appreciation and understanding of this, we can enjoy a tangible sense of history while celebrating the fact that the innate joy of step dance provides its 'endurance in time'.[76]

Notes

1. Georgina Boyes, *The Imagined Village: Culture, Ideology and the English Folk Revival* (Manchester: Manchester University Press, 1993), p. 101.
2. Alexandra Fisher, 'In Search of Street Clog Dance: New Thoughts on Step-Dance Analysis Based on Two Lancashire Clog Dancers', Paper presented at *Stepping On: A Conference on Stepping in Dance*, Cecil Sharp House, London (November 2019).
3. J.F and T.M. Flett, *Traditional Step-Dancing in Lakeland* (London: EFDSS, 1979), pp. 19–20; Julian Pilling, 'The Lancashire Clog Dance', *Folk Music Journal*, 1.3 (1967), 158–162; Patricia Tracey, 'The Lancashire Hornpipe', in *The Hornpipe: Proceedings of the National Early Music Association Conference 1993*, ed. by Janet Adshead-Lonsdale (Cambridge: National Early Music Association, 1993), pp. 15–22 (p. 17).
4. Chris Metherell, 'Some Early Records of Clog Dancing', in C. Metherell (ed.), *INSTEP* No.5 (1982), pp. 3–7.
5. Catherine E. Foley, *Step Dancing in Ireland: Culture and History* (Abingdon and New York: Routledge 2016), pp. 46–49.
6. J.F. and T.M. Flett, *Traditional Step-Dancing in Scotland* (Edinburgh: Scottish Cultural Press, 1996), p. 4. See for example: Mr. Winder, dancing master in Lancaster 1793, advertising the teaching of Minuets, Gavotts, Cotilions, and Hornpipes (copy of dancing master publicity, author's collection).
7. Flett and Flett, *Traditional Step-Dancing* (1979).
8. Flett and Flett, *Traditional Step-Dancing* (1979), pp. 8–10.
9. See for example: Deborah Kermode, *Half-Cut in Clogs: Lakeland's Dancing History* (Ulverston: Old Friends Music & Dance Association, 1998), p. 18.
10. Flett and Flett, *Traditional Step-Dancing* (1996), pp. 5–6.
11. See Ian Dunmur performing Norman Robinson's '17-step routine', https://insteprt.co.uk/lakeland-style-clog-and-step-dancing [accessed on 22 September 2020].

12. See Lakeland Hornpipe steps with Toby Bennett, Chippenham 2013 (YouTube) [accessed 22 September 2020].
13. Caroline Kershaw, '"They've Done Me, They've Robbed Me, But, Thank God, I'm the Champion Still": Clog Dancing in the Victorian Music Hall', in Janet Adshead-Lansdale (ed.), *Border Tensions: Dance and Discourse*, Proceedings of the 5th Study of Dance Conference (Guildford: Dept. of Dance Studies, University of Surrey, 1995), pp. 199–207 (p. 203).
14. Heather Clarke, 'The tradition of step dancing in Australia', *English Dance and Song* (EFDSS, Summer 2018), pp. 14–15 and April F. Maston, 'Challenge Dancing in Antebellum America: Sporting Men, Vulgar Women, and Blacked-Up Boys', *Journal of Social History*, 48.3 (Spring 2015), 605–634.
15. J.S. Bratton, 'Dancing a Hornpipe in Fetters', *Folk Music Journal* 6.1 (1990), 65–82 (p. 68).
16. Kershaw, 'They've Done Me', p. 200.
17. Kershaw, 'They've Done Me', p. 201.
18. Bratton, 'Dancing a Hornpipe', p. 73.
19. Kershaw, 'They've Done Me', pp. 200–201.
20. World Championship Belt won by Dan Leno in 1883 is held in the Victoria and Albert Museum archives.
21. Ernest Frith's memories of his father John Frith in Julie Williams and Alex Fisher, 'A Miner's Tale', *English Dance and Song* (EFDSS Winter 2019), pp. 14–15.
22. See Clog Hornpipe steps from Lynette Eldon https://insteprt.co.uk/reading-clog-and-step-dance-festival-1994 (performers' showcase) [accessed 22 September 2020].
23. Williams and Fisher, 'A Miner's Tale'.
24. Don Watson, 'On Clogs', *Tamlyn* 2.2, (1975) np. See Hornpipe steps from Peter Brown (pupil of Johnson Ellwood), https://insteprt.co.uk/reading-clog-and-step-dance-festival-1996 (performers' showcase) [accessed 22 September 2020].
25. Sammy Bell's Hornpipe Steps, https://insteprt.co.uk/sammy-bells-clog-hornpipes [accessed on 11 September 2020].
26. Waltz steps from Alex Woodcock, https://insteprt.co.uk/alex-woodcock-waltz-1990-2 [accessed 23 September 2020].
27. J. Jarmen and C. Metherell, *The Clog Steps of Mr John Surtees*, Newcastle Series (Newcastle: Instep, 1982).
28. Marshall and Jean Stearns, *Jazz Dance: The Story of American Vernacular Dance* (Boston, MA: Da Capo Press, Inc. 1994), pp. 50–51.
29. See Flett and Flett, *Traditional Step-Dancing* (1979), p. 32.
30. Ann-Marie Hulme and Peter Clifton, '"Actual Stepdancing": Sam Sherry, an autobiography', *English Dance & Song*, 41.2 (1979), p. 3.
31. G. J. Mellor, *The Northern Music Hall* (Newcastle-upon-Tyne: Frank Graham, 1970), p. 73.
32. See, for example, Sam Sherry Schottische steps, https://insteprt.co.uk/sam-sherry-sams-song-1986 [accessed 11 September 2020].
33. Hulme and Clifton, 'Actual Stepdancing', p. 7.
34. See, for example, Alex Woodcock Ragtime steps, https://insteprt.co.uk/alex-woodcock-ragtime-1990 [accessed 11 September 2020].
35. Peter Clifton and Ann-Marie Hulme, 'Solo Step Dancing within Living Memory in North Norfolk', in Teresa Buckland (ed.), *Traditional Dance, Volume 1: Proceedings of the First Traditional Dance Conference* (Crewe and Alsager College of Higher Education, 1981), pp. 29–58.
36. Dancing of Dick Hewitt, https://insteprt.co.uk/dick-hewitt/ [accessed on 11 September 2020]; see also https://eatmt.wordpress.com/step-dancing/ for Percy West (Traditional Music Day 2010) & for Davies family (Cromer lifeboat crew) [accessed on 23 September 2020].
37. Clifton and Hulme, 'Solo Step Dancing', pp. 2–4.
38. Lisa Sture, 'Devonshire Stepdancing: Yesterday, Today and Tomorrow', Paper presented at *Stepping On: A Conference on Stepping in Dance*, Cecil Sharp House, London (November 2019).
39. See dancing of Bob Cann, https://insteprt.co.uk/bob-cann-1987 [accessed on 14 September 2020].
40. See Simon Harmer, https://insteprt.co.uk/simon-harmer/ [accessed on 14 September 2020].
41. Correspondence with Jo Harmer, April 2020.
42. Fisher, 'In Search of Street Clog Dance'; *Chorley Sparks: A Social History of Clog Culture*, DVD (Eccleston Heritage Clog, Eccleston, 2008) Section 3 [accessible in Vaughan Williams Memorial Library, London].

43 Pat Tracey performing Toe-and-Heel steps, https://insteprt.co.uk/pat-tracey-heel-and-toe-1987 [accessed on 11 September 2020].
44 Madeleine Hollis, 'Bill Gibbons, Canal Step Dancer', *INSTEP* 1 (July1981), 1–12 (pp. 7–8) See performance from Melanie Jordan, https://insteprt.co.uk/reading-clog-and-step-dance-festival-1994 (Workshop Showcase) [accessed on 22 September 2020].
45 Madeleine Hollis, 'Bert Bowden, Liverpool Step Dancer & Entertainer', *INSTEP* 10 (October 1983), 10–11.
46 Huw Williams, *Welsh Clog/Step Dancing: A Collection of Traditional Steps and Music* (Brynmawr: H. Williams, 1988), pp. 16, 40.
47 C. Metherell and A. Smith, *An Introduction to Clog Dancing in the North East*, Newcastle Series (Newcastle 1981), p. 1. See also C. Metherell, 'Clog Dancing: An Analysis of Regional Differences', in Theresa Buckland (ed.), *Traditional Dance. Proceedings of the 3rd Traditional Dance Conference* (Crewe and Alsager College of Higher Education 1983), pp. 1–16.
48 Alexandra M. Fisher, 'Clog Dance: Revival, Performance and Authenticity. An Ethnographic Study', unpublished MA Dissertation (University of Surrey 2000), pp. 32–34 [held in Vaughan Williams Memorial Library, London].
49 See Chris Metherell and Barry Callaghan, *Sam Sherry: A Memorial Compilation*, DVD (London: EFDSS, 2007).
50 Flett and Flett, *Traditional Step-Dancing* (1979).
51 See Pilling, 'The Lancashire Clog'.
52 Clifton and Hulme, 'Solo Step Dancing'.
53 See https://insteprt.co.uk/Chris-Metherell/ [accessed 14 September 2020].
54 See programmes and films of Reading Step Dance Festivals, https://insteprt.co.uk/reading-day-of-dance/ [accessed on 16 September 2020].
55 Clifton and Hulme, 'Solo Step Dancing'.
56 See stepping of Cyril Barber, https://eatmt.wordpress.com/profiles/ search 'Old Hat Concert Party' + Swindon 1983 (1) and (2) [accessed on 22 September 2020].
57 Correspondence with Katie Howson: co-director of the East Anglian Traditional Music Trust 2000–2017.
58 Peter Kennedy had become Area Organiser in Devon from 1950.
59 Lisa Sture, 'Devonshire Stepdancing'; see also dancing of Les Rice, https://insteprt.co.uk/leslie-rice-1988 [accessed on 14 September 2020].
60 Ann-Marie Hulme, Peter Clifton, Chris Metherell, Alice Metherell, *Dartmoor Step Dancing*, Newcastle Series (Newcastle 1989), pp. 1–12.
61 Chris Metherell, 'Bob Cann, B.E.M. 1915–1990. Step Dancer', *English Dance and Song*, 53.1 (1991), 13–16.
62 Sture, 'Devonshire Stepdancing'.
63 Mike Cherry, 'A Contestant's View', *INSTEP*, 9 (1983), 4–8.
64 'Interview with Don Watson, organiser of the Northern Counties Championship', *INSTEP* 6 (October 1982), 9.
65 Pat Tracey, 'Off-the-toe Dancing in Lancashire', *INSTEP* 3 (January 1982), pp. 3–4.
66 Alex Boydell, 'Letter Supporting the Views Expressed by Pat Tracey', *INSTEP* 4 (April 1982), np.
67 Sture 'Devonshire Stepdancing'.
68 'Information for Stepdance Competitors' and 'Information for Judges' for the EATMT Stepdance Day 2017 supplied by Katie Howson.
69 R. Bauman (ed.), *Folklore, Cultural Performances and Popular Entertainments* (Oxford and New York: Oxford University Press, 1992), p. 32.
70 Hulme and Clifton, 'Actual Stepdancing', p. 7.
71 Anya Peterson Royce, *Ethnic Identity: Strategies of Diversity* (Bloomington: Indiana University Press 1982), p. 150.
72 Fisher, 'Clog Dance', p. 47.
73 J. Clifford, *The Predicament of Culture. Twentieth-Century Ethnography, Literature and Art* (Cambridge, MA: Harvard University Press 1988), p. 231.
74 Boyes, *The Imagined Village*, p. 3.
75 Anca Giurchescu, 'The Power of Dance Symbol and Its Socio-Political Use', in *Proceedings of the 17th Symposium on Ethnochoreology* (Nafplion Greece: ICTM Study Group, 1992), np.
76 Giurchescu, 'The Power of Dance', np.

15
EXPANDING A REPERTOIRE
Leicester Morrismen and the Border morris

John Swift

Introduction

The term 'Border morris' is now in widespread use and is understood by the morris dancing community to refer to those morris dances which have their origins in the western English counties of Herefordshire, Shropshire and Worcestershire (three of the counties which form the border with Wales).

This chapter aims to provide an overview of the development of Border morris from 1963 onwards, the year of publication of a significant paper on the topic authored by Christopher Cawte in the *Journal of the English Folk Dance and Song Society*.[1] In addition to being a leading researcher of the ceremonial customs of Great Britain, Cawte was a medical doctor with a practice in Leicestershire and, significantly for this chapter, an active member of Leicester Morrismen. The chapter reviews the general progress of Border morris over the following 30 years and describes in some detail the engagement of Leicester Morrismen with the form. The latter element attempts an enduring record of the development whilst the information is still available and provides a case study within the more general story of those 30 years.[2]

The chapter concludes with a brief but broader consideration of Border morris performance alongside a snapshot of the number of teams currently dancing.

How it happened

Background

Cecil Sharp[3] was aware of the morris dances from the counties bordering Wales. His best known encounter was with a team from Brimfield, Herefordshire[4] on Boxing Day 1909, exactly ten years after his first encounter with the Headington Quarry dancers.[5] He did see other performances and had information about dances from at least five other locations[6] but these dances only appear to merit the following fleeting reference in '*The Morris Book*':

> In Worcestershire and Herefordshire, however, where the dance still survives, albeit in a state of decadence, it was performed at Christmas time.[7]

It is suggested that Sharp's view of the Border morris as a decadent or decayed tradition[8] was influential both with subsequent researchers and with dance practitioners. His decision not to include their notation in '*The Morris Book*' would have been a major factor here but subsequent researchers were not very complimentary either. Maud Karpeles[9] records on seeing the Upton-on-Severn dances in 1925 that:

> The dancing was very rough and uncertain as most of the dancers were novice.[10]

Cawte in his 1963 paper records that:

> At Leominster the dance for four men in a square was very poor, and a performance of the four-man version of the Much Wenlock dance, in private, at the Consett meeting of the Morris Ring (1953) was taken to be a joke by some of the audience.[11]

Cawte's paper refers to some 40 locations in the three Welsh Border counties where the dance is recorded as having been performed. In reviewing these records, he alludes to the topic of decadence or decay in the first sentence of his conclusions as follows:

> It is clear that some of these records show the dance in decline, but by drawing conclusions from the better teams, and noting the recurring features throughout, it is possible to suggest the form of the dance at its best.[12]

It is this analysis which, it is assumed, led to the definition of 'Welsh Border Morris' referred to in the next paragraph.

Cawte's 1963 paper was consequent on two significant earlier papers: the first by Joseph Needham[13] published in 1936[14] and the second by Cawte, writing with others, in 1960.[15] Needham's survey of the geographical distribution of ceremonial dance, published in 1936, became a standard work of reference for folk dance studies. His survey defined various categories of dance, including 'Cotswold', 'Derbyshire', 'East Anglian' and 'North-Western'.[16] Dances from the counties of Herefordshire, Shropshire and Worcestershire, including Brimfield, Broseley, Madeley and Upton-on-Severn, were classified by Needham as 'Cotswold' despite several distinctive features. The classification of 'Cotswold' gives the dress as 'usually white with coloured baldrick or other ribbons' and the time of year as 'Whitsun', whereas dances from the counties of Herefordshire, Shropshire and Worcestershire did not use this form of dress and were usually performed in mid-winter. Cawte et al.'s 1960 paper, premised on further geographical and historical evidence, eventually suggested a separate classification for Border morris – actually as 'Welsh Border' – which was then allocated the letter 'B' in their nomenclature and defined as follows:

> Companies of dancers usually eight in number carrying sticks but sometimes handkerchiefs also. In some examples sticks are replaced by percussion instruments of Christy Minstrel type. Costume variable, but basically the ordinary clothes of the performers decorated with ribbons and decorated hats. Some or all of the performers may wear women's clothes or those of circus clown type. Peculiarities: Dancers have blackened faces and sing during the dance. Appears at Christmas.[17]

Cawte's paper on Border morris came three years later but the research undertaken for both papers, essentially the analysis of recurring features of the dance, led to the cumulative conclusion that:

> These features distinguish the morris dance near the Welsh border from other types such as those listed in [Needhams' 1936 paper] and it is proposed that it should be known as the *Welsh Border Morris*.[18]

Next steps after 1963

The publication of Cawte's paper did not lead morris teams to any immediate enthusiasm for Border morris and there is scant evidence for any take up of the dances during the 1960s. Cawte was an active member of Leicester Morrismen during those years and their Squire[19] between 1969 and 1971. He was in a position to take the lead in influencing the team's repertoire but they did not take up Border morris dances at that time. Perhaps they considered the Border dances outside their scope, or perhaps thought the dances too simple, or accepted the lingering influence of Sharp's view that Border morris was 'in a state of decadence'.

That Border morris did subsequently develop into a morris genre owes much to the activities and enthusiasm of Roy Dommett.[20] Dommett began his research into morris dancing in the early 1960s and access to a microfiche reader enabled him to study Cecil Sharp's manuscripts and pursue original research, which added to and on occasions contradicted the information in Sharp's published Morris Books. It should be emphasised at this point that Cecil Sharp and others had been active in the late nineteenth and early twentieth centuries as collectors of folklore material directly from the people who performed, played music for or witnessed the dances. In a few cases, the performances were still current at the time of collection and to explore contradictions between the manuscript and print versions of Sharp's findings, as Dommett did, was regarded by morris enthusiasts as being of significant interest. Dommett's enthusiasm for those original manuscripts culminated in an important contribution to Lionel Bacon's *'A Handbook of Morris Dances'*[21] (hereafter the *'Handbook'*) as well as his own teaching of the Border morris dances.

The material reviewed and augmented by Bacon and Dommett in the *'Handbook'* reaffirmed that each village or town where the dances were collected had particular variants in stepping, hand movements and sequence of figures, and the term 'tradition' was used to identify the dances from each village or town, hence the 'Adderbury tradition', the 'Bampton tradition' and so on. It should be noted however that much of this original collected material was fragmentary in nature. There was a process of interpretation started by Sharp and continued by others which eventually allowed the material to be published in a codified form in the *'Handbook'*. The irony in this chain of events is that what Bacon and Dommett put together in the *'Handbook'* for the Cotswold morris seems like a solid body of material but it is only one method of approach. It is perfectly valid therefore to revisit the original manuscripts, to explore different ways of doing the dances. It should be clear from this that Bacon's *'Handbook'* is not a book of rules although unfortunately, in my view, there are those in the morris dance world who treat it as if it were!

At a time when Dommett was actively promoting Border morris, it is appropriate that Bacon acknowledged his contribution and included the notations (such as they were) for those dances we would now consider Border. However, it is also significant that Bacon formally acknowledged full responsibility for the presentation of the material in the volume since no effort is made to provide a separate category for Border. All the dance traditions in the *Handbook* are simply presented in an alphabetical order by originating town or village. Bacon provided this explanation:

> This book does not set out to include all the known morris dances of England. My initial intention was to restrict it to the Cotswold dances, together with a few others which were included in Sharp's books. However, it became apparent that there is quite a wide range of dances in the West Midlands, up to the Welsh Border, of which there is enough information in the MSS to make them danceable, and I have extended the book to include these. I have also included Lichfield, now a well-established part of the morris man's repertoire, and Winster because the Processional is used at Ring Meetings.[22]

Despite this explanation and the fact that the book was intended as a practical guide, the impression remains that the Border morris dances were still perceived to form a continuum with the Cotswold morris. The absence of the term 'Welsh Border Morris' in the '*Handbook*', ten years after its use was first proposed, tends to support this view.

Border morris comes alive (eventually)

In a paper on Border morris delivered in 1992, Roy Dommett recorded that

> I taught the mss material at the Advanced Morris Weekends at Halsway Manor in the mid to late 1960's, but I am not aware that anyone actually took them away to actually dance out. I was invited to an EFDSS [English Folk Dance and Song Society] staff weekend to pass on the dances which were seen as a possibility for mixed team performance for which a growing need was perceived that could not be met by the Cotswold Morris, at a time when the NW dances were hardly known. Interest picked up enough to ask me to teach the dances at a first workshop for West Midland teams in Ledbury Town Hall in January 1972 and I went on to teach them at Morris Federation workshops.[23]

The workshop held in Ledbury led to the formation of the Original Welsh Border Morris Men. This team first danced out in December 1973 and their tour on the last Saturday before Christmas continues to the time of writing. Their website records the following:

> **Our Foundation**
> The Welsh Border Morris Men were formed in 1973 at the suggestion of John Barker by John, Dave Jones and John Aston, with the objective of running an occasional side, doing just one tour at the traditional time of Christmas, dancing the Welsh Border dances in Worcestershire and Herefordshire.
> **The start (From Scrap Book)**
> A Morris Team was formed with the objective of dancing only dances from the Welsh Border area, principally the counties of Herefordshire and Worcestershire. The procedure that was adopted in 1973 has been followed in subsequent years, namely practices in August and December, culminating with a tour on the Saturday preceding Christmas, this being the traditional time of year for these dances to take place. The side

has members who are also members of other sides, principally Silurian (Ledbury) and Faithful City (Worcester), but membership is open to any man who wishes to further the objectives of the club…[24]

Roy also taught Border morris at the Sidmouth Folk Festival in 1972, as Derek Schofield records:

… on Thursday he [Roy Dommett] taught Border Morris dances from Worcestershire and Herefordshire. At the time there were no Morris teams specialising in these dances and the first ever Border workshop, taught by Roy had only taken place a few months earlier – as ever Roy was pushing at boundaries.[25]

This pushing of boundaries was starting to have some effect and there were essentially two strands of subsequent development.

In 1973, John Kirkpatrick, who danced with Hammersmith Morris Men in London, moved to Shropshire and started the Shropshire Bedlams two years later. He wrote a lively, some might say trenchant, account of the team's formation for *English Dance & Song* in 1979. In this article, Kirkpatrick acknowledges Cawte and Dommett alongside the '*Handbook*' as sources but noted that:

Looking back now at the original material, the way our dances came together seems totally random.[26]

Kirkpatrick's use of 'random' is interesting and perhaps compounded by two further coincidences. The same year Kirkpatrick moved to Shropshire, 1973, the musician Ashley Hutchings recorded the record 'Rattlebone and Ploughjack'.[27] This recording largely consists of recreated music and speech with Border morris on the one side of the vinyl recording and Molly dancing on the other. It created much interest in both traditions, although ultimately was probably more influential in the subsequent development of Molly dancing, the morris dance genre from the eastern counties of England. However, the record was not released until 1976 which coincided, from a Border morris perspective, with the appearance of the group Magic Lantern at the Sidmouth Festival in their street theatre role.[28] Schofield records:

Another Magic Lantern initiative […] was their Border Morris performance. In spite of Roy Dommett's 1972 workshop there was only one revival Morris side specialising exclusively in Border Morris; they were to make their Sidmouth debut in 1977. Taffy had a copy of the 1909 photograph of the Brimfield Morris, and decided to perform the dance round all the venues at the Festival and the pubs in a single evening: it was a one off show but had a lingering impact.[29]

On a personal note, 1976 was the second year I had attended the Sidmouth Festival. As an observer of that performance, my first introduction to Border morris, I can certainly testify to its impact. The following year, however, saw an even greater impact caused by the morris side Schofield alludes to above: Kirkpatrick's Shropshire Bedlams and their companion women's team, Martha Rhoden's Tuppenny Dish. Schofield writes:

They were a sensation at Sidmouth – the appearance, the energy, the flamboyance of the men and the fresh approach of the women. … Over the following few years, the

Bedlams inspired new and existing teams to turn to Border Morris and interpret the dances differently, other teams copied the Bedlams' style rather too slavishly, whilst some teams realised the possibilities of adaption and creation in other styles.[30]

This was one strand of development of Border morris but there was another, running in parallel, which I trace back to the original workshop Roy Dommett ran in Ledbury in 1972. Ledbury was the home of Silurian Morris and their website records the following:

> Established in 1969 by the late Dave Jones, Silurian's original repertoire consisted mainly of Cotswold dances with a few Welsh Border dances for variety. A number of people at this time, especially Dave Jones, were researching the Border tradition, and by 1979 Dave felt that there was sufficient material for the side to perform border dances exclusively. Up until that point Border dances had been performed on Boxing Day tours, dancers wearing their Cotswold Kit with blacked up faces.
>
> However, at the Bromyard festival that year, Silurian emerged in a new costume, based on descriptions of what the Upton Morris Men had worn at the turn of the twentieth century. The first Border Morris revival side, the new kit causing quite a stir amongst traditional Cotswold Morris Ring sides.[31]

It is assumed that Dave Jones introduced the Border morris to Silurian following Dommett's 1972 workshop, that they included these dances in the programme for their Boxing Day tours before Shropshire Bedlams' formation in 1975 and hence their claim to be the first Border morris revival side. Many of the Morris Ring[32] teams dancing Cotswold morris would have been unaware of the development until they saw Silurian dance in 1979 and the performance would indeed have caused 'quite a stir' as Silurian claim.

In the preface to his book, first published in 1988, Dave Jones states that he ran instructionals for the West Midlands Folk Federation and then for the Morris Ring of England 'over ten years ago'.[33] The workshop for the Morris Ring was held in October 1979 and a record of the meeting has been found in the Logbooks of the Morris Ring.[34] It is quoted here in full to enable an understanding of the way in which the instructional was run, which is typical of how the Morris Ring meetings were and indeed continue to be conducted:

> An Instruction Meeting was held at Ledbury, Hereford-shire [sic], from Friday the 19th to Sunday the 21st of October 1979. David Jones, of the Silurian Morris Men, gave instruction in Border Morris. Arrangements for the meeting were by his club; men brought their own bedding and slept in the Youth Centre. Instruction, and all meals except breakfast were in the Royal Oak. Men were given a meal at 8 p.m. on the Friday. From 9.30 until 11.30 p.m. there was instruction in Brimfield. The Saturday went thus: -9.30 a.m., instruction in White Ladies Aston: 10.30 revision of Brimfield and White Ladies Aston: 11.00, coffee: 11.17 instruction in Pershore; 12.45 p.m., lunch: 2.35 p.m., Upton Stick Dance: 4 p.m., tea: 4.20, Upton Handkerchief Dance: 5.30, discussion on "The Value of Instructionals," and on archival work.
>
> There was a Feast at 7.10; with the loyal toast and that of the Immortal Memory [of Cecil Sharp], at 8.30. Five minutes later the Health of the Silurian men was drunk. There was singing until 9.10, when general dancing started and went on until 11 p.m., using the Border dances that had been taught. The men then went to the youth Centre, to dance until Bonny Green Garters at 12.15 a.m.

At 9.35, on Sunday, Bromsberrow Heath and Dilwyn dances were taught; and after coffee at 11 a.m., at 11.20, there was a revision session of all the dances taught during the weekend. At 12.30 there was a discussion on the Border Morris and other topics. Some men stayed to watch, at 2.30 p.m., the filming of the Border Morris as danced by the Silurian club; the rest had left by 2 p.m. Clubs represented at the meeting: – Aber, Chelmsford, Dartington, Datchet, Hereford, Herga, Isca, John o' Gaunt, Kits Coty, Leicester, Mersey, St. Albans, Swindon, Thelwell, Wath-on-Dearne, West Somerset.

The significance of this account is that, for most of those attending, this would have been their first encounter with Border morris and to meet it in the familiar surroundings of a Morris Ring instructional would have made the assimilation of the material much more palatable. It also helped that the dances would have been presented as structured dances with an understandable notation rather than the much more fragmentary material Dommett and Jones had been dealing with a few years earlier.

This, then, is how the second strand to the development and emergence of the Border morris as a separate morris dance genre should be seen.

This emergence in the 1970s may also be part of a wider trend during that decade which recognised the importance of regional identity reflected in dance. Certainly, this trend was apparent in revivals in some of villages where the Cotswold morris had been collected before the First World War and in the North West[35] where as Derek Schofield records:

> the desire to be distinctive, different and focus on something which was locally based became important features once the North-West Morris revival really got going in the late 60s and the 70s.[36]

The first Border morris teams established in the 1970s were similarly based in the region where the Border dances had originally been collected, but there were two emphases at work in the modern dancers' approach. The emerging repertoire and performances of the Shropshire Bedlams, and subsequently the Ironmen and others, were only loosely based on that original collected material. Kirkpatrick, as his 1979 article made clear, having moved to Shropshire and researched the local traditions felt confident that he could create something that could still be regarded as part of that regional tradition. I think it was this confidence stemming from being rooted or grounded in an area with a tradition of dancing that gave those involved the impetus to take that tradition in new directions. Conversely, within the other strand of development identified above, Jones' teaching closely followed the collected repertoire, although, given the limited information in some of the Border morris notations, even in this approach to authenticity, some imaginative interpretation was necessary. As many more Border morris teams formed in subsequent years, these two strands of development became less distinct and more pure invention took place. It seems to me that Sharp had the opportunity to do the same with the Border morris material as he had with the Cotswold material. He had seen a team dance and he had notations in more or less fragmentary form, but he chose not to develop them. One might see Dave Jones as the key person who took this fragmentary material and developed it as best as he could into the dance notations. John Kirkpatrick took the same information and created something rather different, but it would be a brave man who told him that what he had done wasn't based on the regional tradition – and actually the accusation would, in my view, be totally unfair.

The early 1970s was also the time of the formation of the first women's morris dance teams and their numbers expanded significantly through this and subsequent decades. Aside from Martha Rhoden's Tuppenny Dish, the companion team to Shropshire Bedlams, there appeared to be no women's teams exclusively dancing Border morris in those early years. In 1976, the Women's Morris Federation, formed the previous year, issued a list of 41 dances for which they had notation,[37] and this included two Border morris dances, the Pershore Stick dance and White Ladies Aston. Many of the teams at that time performed a mix of dances from the various morris genres and the records of the Women's Morris Federation show that of 14 sides who had joined in 1975, half of them danced at least one Border morris dance but as part of a larger repertoire. The dances listed are Brimfield, Pershore, White Ladies Aston and Upton-on-Severn.

Leicester Morrismen's Border Morris Odyssey

Early years

As recorded above, Leicester Morrismen were represented at the 1979 instructional led by Dave Jones.

Leicester can claim a long involvement with the morris, the earliest references being 1599 and 1603.[38] Dance teams existed in the 1920s and 1930s and the current team formed in 1953. It was not possible in the course of writing this chapter to contact the two men who attended the 1979 workshop, Bill McBean and Colin Seaton, but through the team's scrapbooks,[39] it was established that their first public performance of Border morris was in December 1981 in Great Glen, a village to the south of Leicester (see Figure 15.1). The Squire's notes for November 1981 proposed several weeks practice starting 25th November. There is a record of a further performance in January 1982 at Groby and Mountsorrel, villages to the north of Leicester, and the records show that Border dances continued in the following winter seasons. An item in the minutes of the team's AGM held on 29th September 1983 reads: 'The Border dancing was to be brushed up and was to include more Lichfield dances. The Border Tours were to be continued'.

Figure 15.1 Leicester Morrismen's first border morris performance, December 1981
Source: Photograph copyright the author.

I joined Leicester Morrismen in the summer of 1984[40] and recalled participating in several rather haphazard Border performances in the winter of 1984/85. The performances the following winter, 1985/86, were however given a focus through an invitation to the Whittlesea Straw Bear event at Whittlesey[41] in January 1986. The Squire at the time, Dick Allsop, can take a lot of the credit for this invitation through a chance meeting with one of the main organisers of the event, Brian Kell. Brian was not at all keen to invite yet another Cotswold team but a Border morris team was a different matter and Leicester Morrismen in their winter guise as 'Red Leicester' (see below) have been proud to receive an invitation every year since then. Dick Allsop not only obtained the invitation but succeeded in getting sufficient focus on a consistent kit (the usual morris term for costume and properties) and at least a tolerable standard of dancing in those early years. Both these aspects merit further discussion.

Dressing for Border morris and 'Blacking up'

What Leicester Morrismen wore for Border morris seems to have been taken as a given from the first performances, based on what other teams that had been formed were wearing. It consisted of rag coats, top hats or bowler hats with feathers and a single row of bells. Black face colouring was also initially adopted on this same basis.[42] The only point of consistency I can recall meriting any discussion was the order in which the coloured ribbons were arranged on the hats, although at some point black trousers must have become standard and red sweatshirts under the rag coats (with cooler rugby-style shirts for the summer festivals) became an added refinement. Unlike some teams, I am not aware that the face colouring was seen by Leicester Morrismen as providing a disguise or was invested with any deeper ceremonial significance. It was worn because that was what many Border morris teams had been described as wearing and was what the early border revival teams had adopted.

The practice was however an early concern for some members of the team, given the multicultural nature of the city of Leicester and the city's evident success in promoting this. No written records have been found but there was clearly a discussion over which colour should be used for face colouring. Photographs, which are not definitively dated, were taken during the winter seasons of either 1984/85 or 1985/86 and show the team dancing with a mixture of black and red faces. The recollection is that this mix of different colours was generally agreed to look awful and a decision was taken before the first visit to Whittlesea to use red. Immediately following this decision came the serendipitous discovery that the team for its Border morris performances could be called 'Red Leicester'[43] and this became a readily identifiable defining characteristic for the team. My own recollection is that we were subsequently approached by a local historian who congratulated us on using what would traditionally had been a local material – raddle – used in sheep farming to identify which ewes had been 'served' by the ram. We chose not to disabuse this gentleman of the notion that we had done our research and in fact this became a useful pretext for the practice which became adopted of 'spreading the red' – smudging any apparently willing onlookers with the red face makeup.

The concern in Leicester Morrismen over the use of black face colouring predated what was to become a high profile topic. Nearly two decades later in 2005, Derek Schofield raised the topic in an article in *English Dance and Song* with the title 'a black and white issue?'[44] which included divergent views from several people with an interest in the topic. The discussion continued in the correspondence pages of the next issue which included a strong defence of the practice from John Kirkpatrick of Shropshire Bedlams.[45] The debate continued but in 2013 an article by Chloe Metcalfe (now Middleton-Metcalfe)[46] gave it fresh impetus.

An article in 2016 by Katy Spicer, Chief Executive of the English Folk Dance and Song Society (EFDSS), gave a useful summary of topic and the position of the EFDSS:

> to no longer engage blackface morris sides for EFDSS events …[47]

The article noted that three festivals had also adopted this policy and there have been more since. The debate has resulted in several teams adopting different face colouring or, as, for instance, is the case with Shropshire Bedlams, using masks as an alternative.

There already seemed to be a consensus amongst those who had researched the topic that there is scant evidence for morris dancers in the three Welsh Border counties blacking up before minstrel shows become popular in England from the 1830s. Gordon Ashman, in his detailed consideration of nineteenth-century Shropshire source material, had this to say:

> I can find no genuine reference to blacking up before the popularity of the minstrel show swept the country in a wave after one of the earliest 'Ethiopian Delineators', Thomas Rice, took London by storm with his Jim Crow act in 1836.[48]

Some teams however continue to take the view that blackface is merely a disguise established through traditional use. My own opinion is that the use of blackface is now so clearly established as originating in the United States for the purpose of the racist denigration of the black population that its use is no longer justifiable.

In a recent development, the Joint Morris Organisations, comprising The Morris Federation, The Morris Ring and Open Morris, issued a statement on the matter (July 2020) agreeing that each of them would take action at their respective forthcoming annual general meetings to eliminate the practice from their membership. The first of those meetings, that of The Morris Federation, was held in September 2020 and a resolution passed that no members would wear full face black makeup after the end of the year. The AGM's of Open Morris and The Morris Ring will take place in November 2020 and March 2021, respectively.

Dancing Border morris

During the 1980s, a majority of members of Leicester Morrismen were in their thirties and forties with at least ten years' experience of dancing the 'Cotswold' style of morris. This is a challenging style to dance well, involving multiple coordinated feet and hand movements. Commonly danced in what is termed a 'set' by six or eight dancers in two lines, these movements have to be danced across or up and down the set in sequence. Many of the dances involve additional jumps or 'capers', all of course performed in time with the music. The collected Border morris dances have generally simpler stepping and few of the challenges of the Cotswold morris. Even so, in the first years of dancing Border morris (between 1981 and 1986) Leicester Morrismen only had a very limited number of practices before public performances. Although these performances were low-key in nature, normally outside pubs, it has to be admitted that our performances were rather casual in nature. The invitation to Whittlesea meant that the team would be performing in front of larger crowds, many of whom were either dancers themselves or knowledgeable about the dances. This meant that a new focus on performance was required and here the Squire at the time, Dick Allsop, as already noted was successful in achieving this change. Although practice time was still limited, a more polished performance was delivered and combined with improvements to the consistency of kit and the adoption of red face colouring the team was able to present itself as 'Red Leicester', the winter guise of Leicester Morrismen performing the Border morris.

It needs to be explained that by the mid-1980s, a strong consensus had emerged that the way Border morris should be danced was very different from Cotswold morris. It is hard to find descriptions in the source material of how the dances had traditionally been performed, but an emerging consensus crossed both strands of development described earlier. It has been summed up by Gordon Ashman writing about his team, the Ironmen, in 1987:

> We had been trying to dance "good" Cotswold, which normally seems to be about lightness, about height, about elevation, grace; it is about dancing up, it is about lift. By contrast, we made Border the things we were – weight, heaviness, stomping the earth, dancing down, dramatic movement, sideways movement, clashes, collisions.[49]

Several events became established in the calendar which allowed Leicester's Border repertoire to be performed in public before the annual trip to Whittlesea. Before Christmas, the team was welcomed to dance in both Leicester city centre and in Market Harborough and on the first Sunday after New Year, it became customary to tour through the village of Markfield to the north of Leicester. From 1986 onwards, strenuous efforts were made by the various Squires and those leading the teaching of the Border morris dances to make the styles distinct and 'to stop dancing Border as if it were a different Cotswold tradition'.[50] Ensuring that the musicians also understood their vital role in establishing the distinctive nature of Border morris was a key part of this focus. In a similar way to the style of performance, a consensus emerged that there was a need for a large group of musicians.[51] Leicester was no exception and Roy Thody, dancer, musician and Squire between 1992 and 1995, was a major driver of the efforts to create a distinct style of dancing and a larger band. The team received recognition as a consequence with invitations to dance outside the county, the most notable being to major folk festivals at Sidmouth and Towersey.

Repertoire

There are no formal records of which dances were used in our early years of performing Border. My recollection is that there were only a few, so the well-known Upton-on-Severn stick dance[52] and the Lichfield[53] dances (which we also performed in the summer) were also utilised. In my memory, on at least one occasion, a stick dance from Adderbury[54] was also danced. I was appointed Squire of the team in the autumn of 1987 and took an interest in trying to control the repertoire – an easier task for the limited Border morris repertoire than for the extensive range of Cotswold dances performed. I recorded all the dances performed in public over the three years and condensed the information into a paper titled 'The Role of Repertoire' presented at a conference on morris dancing in 1990.[55] My successor as Squire, Charlie Corcoran, did the same, the results being presented at a subsequent conference in 1992.[56] Charlie's successor, Roy Thody, also collected the data on dances performed, so it is possible to track in some detail the development of the repertoire, although this chapter will only give an outline.

An important comment on the repertoire is that Leicester Morrismen maintain a strong focus on the preservation on the English morris dances as they have been collected and passed down and Bacon's '*Handbook*' serves as a focus in defining and delimiting the repertoire. This approach has its challenges in relation to the Border morris dances but remained a guiding principle during the period covered by this chapter. This emphasis on 'preservation' is quite typical of morris teams like Leicester and is commendable for the desire to perpetuate an essential part of British traditional culture. It is however hard to answer the question of what drove this engagement – or indeed if there is a driver at all beyond this desire for continuation of the tradition – that's the way the team is, that's the culture.

The data show the following:

- Six of the dances taught by Dave Jones at the 1979 workshop were in performance by Leicester Morrismen in the winter of 1988. These were Brimfield, Bromsberrow Heath, Dilwyn and White Ladies Aston together with the Upton-on-Severn Stick and Handkerchief dances, although the stick dance almost certainly differed from that taught at the workshop. The Lichfield dances, The Sheriff's Ride, Milley's Bequest, Ring O'Bells, Vandalls of Hammerwich and The Bower Processional were also danced in Border kit, as was on occasions Brighton Camp from Eynsham.
- The stick dance from Peopleton was introduced that winter, 1988/9. It is not included in the *'Handbook'* and it was taught by Roy Dommett at a workshop for the (then) Women's Morris Federation in 1978 and included in their notation files.[57]
- In 1990, Evesham stick, and Pershore stick and handkerchief dances were introduced.
- In that same year, it was decided that the Lichfield dances would not be danced as order dances. My recollection is that this was the outcome of strenuous lobbying by the then Bagman, Clive Cowx, who, as an ex-Stafford man, was firmly of the view that Lichfield was a Cotswold tradition. Personally, I had always inclined more to Dommett's view that it had many similarities with Border morris but, in any case, the increasing repertoire of dances actually coming from the three Welsh Border counties reduced the need for the Lichfield dances.
- In 1992/3, the Peopleton handkerchief dance was introduced and finally in the winter of 1994/5 Upton Snodsbury came into the repertoire. The notation for Upton Snodsbury in the *'Handbook'* essentially records that there are heys and sticking but Belchamp Morris Men had taught their version of the dance at the Sidmouth Festival in 1994 and subsequently kindly sent me their notation. Leicester took up the nine-man version and found it especially useful for 'show' dances.

I have not been an active member of Leicester Morrismen since 2004 and sight of their list of Border morris dances for winter 2017/8 proved interesting. The team now has another seven dances in its repertoire, only one of which, Much Wenlock, is listed in the *'Handbook'* and hence, as described earlier, would fulfil the criteria for what is regarded as 'traditional'. This is rather in contradiction to what is stated above regarding the team's focus on dances which have been collected and passed down but perhaps also reflects the blurring of the boundaries between the two strands of development of Border morris also described earlier.

Festival experiences

In 1992, Roy Thody and I were invited to the Sidmouth Festival to teach a Border morris workshop and we taught White Ladies Aston to what I recall was an enthusiastic and generally competent body of dancers. We were invited again in 1994, this time to teach two workshops, the first as part of a week-long Border morris series where we taught the Peopleton stick and handkerchief dances and the second as one of a series of 'taster' workshops where we taught Brimfield and Dilwyn. In 1994, we had the support of the Leicester team, in their Red Leicester guise, in the workshops. We also performed informally in the

Expanding a repertoire

town and participated in the torchlight procession, a grand finale of the Sidmouth Festival. This can be presumed to have been well received because the team received an invitation for the following year to participate in a week-long series of workshops intended to allow Border morris dancers to explore all aspects of the tradition, hone their skills and participate in a performance at the end of the week and also in the torchlight procession.

This ambitious programme formulated by the festival's morris advisors, Sue Swift and Sally Wearing, was by their own admission not a great success as these extracts from a letter sent to the team after the festival reveal:

> Leicester MM did a good job in guiding those willing to form a team towards a very creditable performance on the Friday evening. We were pleased that Leicester adapted to cope with the situation that arose and worked hard to make the concept work.

and:

> We realised afterwards that those attending the workshop series were less experienced as dancers and performers than was expected and our overall plans were much too ambitious.[58]

These quotes are instructive in relation to the wider development of the Border morris which is considered further in the concluding section of this chapter. My recollection is that one of the workshop teams (I think there were two) which did perform on that Friday evening named themselves 'Herbaceous Border'. That name was taken up and continues to this day as a 'fringe' Border team which dances on the Esplanade each evening at the Sidmouth Festival and participates in the torchlight procession under the leadership of Kurt Sauter.

Leicester's next, and in the era covered by this chapter last, invitation to a major folk festival as a Border morris team came from Towersey Festival in 1997. As well as performing in all the various venues, we ran a workshop where we taught the Peopleton stick dance and my recollections of this workshop form part of the following section. Figure 15.2 shows the team dancing in the evening ceilidh at Towersey.

As a postscript, invitations to events outside of the county continued, for instance, as an invited team to the Bromyard Folk Festival in 2005. In general, Red Leicester's winter season has continued to follow the pattern established in the late 1980s consisting of

Figure 15.2 Red Leicester at the evening ceilidh in Towersey, August 1997
Source: Photograph copyright the author.

performances in Leicester city centre and other towns (Melton Mowbray in 2018) before Christmas; Boxing Day lunchtime at The Griffin Inn, Swithland, to the north of Leicester; a tour shortly after New Year (on the Great Central Railway in 2018) and finishing with the day at the Whittlesea Straw Bear Festival.

Conclusion

Performance-related aspects

In his entertaining paper on the conversion of the Ironmen from an indifferent Cotswold team to an excellent Border morris team,[59] Gordon Ashman expressed the view that members of Ironmen constituted a 'somatotype', unsuited to Cotswold morris but right for the characteristics of Border morris. Whilst I might take issue with the implied need for a Border morris dancer to be overweight, an important point is made here regarding the different demands of Cotswold and Border morris for the dancer and whether or not teams pursuing a policy of dancing Border only in the winter can ever achieve the excellence required. The year Leicester Morrismen made it as Red Leicester on to the list of invited teams at the Sidmouth Festival, it was as a 'town team'[60] and even then, our principal role was to lead the workshops. The other invited Border morris teams that year were both focussed fully on Border and were Wild Hunt as a 'town team' and Shropshire Bedlams and Martha Rhoden's Tuppenny Dish as the 'arena teams'.

The Border morris is, as collected, a simple dance, consisting predominately of single stepping, mostly simple stick clashing with the hey as possibly the most complex figure. The challenge to give a good public performance of these dances was excellently presented in a paper given at a conference in 1994 by two members of Silurian Morris Men,[61] who pointed out that because of the simplicity of the Border dances, they need to be danced 'spectacularly well' and require '… practice – good hard practice'. It might be seen that the week-long programme organised for the Sidmouth Festival the following year, described above, was an attempt to build on this ethos. Its lack of success indicated that much of the Border morris dancing world was unready for this approach.

At the Towersey Festival in 1997, we taught the Peopleton stick dance, which we thought would interest participants because it, unusually for Border morris, involves both single and double stepping. My recollection is that many of the participants, some of whom had turned up in their Border morris kit, seemed unable to do either of the steps but appeared not to think it important. One can speculate that these people came to our workshop thinking they could already do the dance and since the kit was a large part of what they thought they knew about the performance, of course they wore it. In leading that workshop, it seemed to me that they then couldn't reconcile what they thought they already knew about Border morris with some chap telling them they had to do these steps which didn't come naturally and to coordinate their movements with everyone else. So they rejected what they were being told and carried on with what they thought they already knew.

My reflection afterwards was that there were a lot of people coming to folk festivals at that time who saw teams like Shropshire Bedlams and liked all the excitement, the stick clashing and the shouting but failed to realise that what underpinned the dance, what really made it work was a rigid application of a stepping pattern and a choreography. They probably wanted a short-cut to all the enjoyment of being in a morris team without the pain of having to learn to do difficult things.

Expanding a repertoire

Gordon Ashman mentions[62] an encounter at Whitby in 1986 with:

> a very strange side [...] who had vaguely green splotches on their faces and a few strips of ribbon on their shirts [...] they had weeny little sticks.

On enquiry, they told Ashman (who was not known to them):

> We're Border. We saw a side called the Ironmen, and we thought they were so good we decided to copy them.

Ashman's paper makes no comment on the actual quality of their dancing, but his account immediately led me to recall the attitude of many of the dancers we encountered in our workshop in Towersey some ten years later, described above. Any discussion of the quality of morris dancing is inevitably tricky. It does seem however that many of the teams who have taken up Border morris in recent times have been attracted by the apparent simplicity and immediate visual impact of the dances but have not worked further on the underlying aspects. Thus, sadly, it has to be recorded that many of the teams currently dancing Border morris do not give performances which would be judged by most standards as being of good quality. The mitigating circumstances are aspects such as: in their own towns and villages, these teams might actually be quite well received, the teams might well provide a very nice social milieu for those involved and they are rather carried away with the excitement of it all.

Encouragingly, however, a number of very polished and highly motivated Border morris teams, providing excellent performances, emerged during the 1980s and there have been more since.

Numbers dancing Border morris

The data in Figure 15.3 are a snapshot of immediately available information from three organisations representing morris dancers in the UK for the year 2019.[63]

What is significant in these numbers is the small number of teams in the Morris Ring who dance Border morris to the exclusion of other styles of morris (these six teams are Alvechurch Morris Men, Belchamp Morris, Datchet Border Morris Men, Helier Morris Men, Silurian Border Morris Men and the Original Welsh Border Morris). This might indicate a continuing undercurrent of antipathy to Border morris within the Morris Ring. However, a significant number do perform Border morris dances as part of their repertoire.

	Total Number of Teams	Teams Dancing only Border Morris	Teams Dancing Border Morris with Other Styles of Morris	Total Number of Teams with Border Morris in their Repertoire
Morris Federation	515	75 (15%)	71 (14%)	146 (28%)
Morris Ring	190	6 (3%)	35 (18%)	41 (22%)
Open Morris	137	35 (26%)	21 (15%)	56 (41%)

Figure 15.3 Summary analysis of the number of teams dancing Border morris in 2019
Source: Author's compilation (for further details, see endnote 63).

309

Here, the numbers are not disproportionate to those within the Morris Federation. An assumption might be made that winter would be the usual season for performances by these latter Morris Ring teams, but this would require further investigation beyond the scope of this current chapter. From the perspective of the 1970s, it is remarkable that around 250 teams are dancing Border morris, and more so that those teams should be drawn from a pool of some 850 morris teams overall.

Across these 850 teams, there will be a diversity of reasons for performing the morris dance. Included in these reasons will be the social element of being a member of a club, the physical exercise the dance entails and the challenges of public performance. Another element which is an essential part for me and, I know, many others is continuing a dance tradition which has existed in one form or another for centuries. In the case of Border morris, there are only a handful of dance notations which can be traced back with any degree of certainty even to the nineteenth century. The rest are re-creations but, for instance in the case of Belchamp's Upton Snodsbury dance, made in a way that 'feels right' and are surviving the 'folk process' which discards the indifferent and only preserves the best. Leicester Morrismen's gradual expansion of their repertoire through the inclusion of more recently created dances should be seen as part of this evolutionary process. In this way, we all play our own small part in the preservation and promotion of the wonderful traditional dances of the British Isles.

Acknowledgements

I would like to record my thanks to those listed below for all their valuable help and advice.

Members of Leicester Morrismen, especially Pete Johnson and Charlie Corcoran for the deep dive into the scrapbooks and records as well as Dick Allsop, Martin Barstow, John Bentham and Roy Thody who were all there during the period described in Section 2. All these contributions have made this section as accurate a record as I think is possible; and to Matt Simons, who wasn't there at the time, but has made some useful suggestions, including reminding me of the significance of the *Rattlebone and Ploughjack* record.

Officers of the Morris Ring, particularly Jon Melville and again Charlie Corcoran, in his role as Keeper of the Morris Ring Logbooks, for the extracts which are quoted. John Barker, Annie Jones and Mike Finn for information regarding the early Border morris workshops. Nick Wall at the Vaughan Williams Memorial Library for help with some of the references. Sue Swift and Sally Wearing for permission to quote from their letter, and Sue for help with providing other references. Beth Neill, editor of *Morris Matters* and Mac McCoig, editor of *The Morris Dancer*, for permission to draw on earlier iterations of this material. Derek Schofield for the original motivation, for some useful suggestions and for permission to quote from his 2004 work *The First Week in August*.

Notes

1. E. Christopher Cawte, 'The Morris Dance in Herefordshire, Shropshire and Worcestershire', *Journal of the English Folk Dance and Song Society*, 9.4, (1963), 197–212. Although I have been very selective in what I've written about the history of Border morris prior to 1963, there is in fact a lot of collected information on dances being performed in the three Border counties. In Appendix 1 of his 1963 paper, Cawte gives further details of 25 of the locations mentioned in the paper where the morris dance was known to have been performed and overall, he records around 40 locations.
2. Other iterations of this material have appeared as John Swift, 'The Border Morris – Developments since 1963', *The Morris Dancer*, 6.2, (October 2020), 98–118 and John Swift, 'How Border Morris Developed – a Leicester Perspective', *Morris Matters* 39.2, (2020), 10–14.

3 Cecil Sharp was a pioneering collector of English folk dances and his accounts provide one of the starting points for the history of the morris dance in the twentieth century.
4 See, for instance, Roy L Dommett, 'The Brimfield Morris Dance', *English Dance and Song*, 31.3, (1969), 98. This article includes a reproduction of the photograph taken of the dancers in 1909 and referred to subsequently in this chapter.
5 Headington Quarry is a village to the east of the city of Oxford. The Headington Quarry dancers were the first morris dancers Sharp saw in performance and became something of a benchmark by which subsequent performances were witnessed, described and assessed by Sharp.
6 In addition to Brimfield, which was Sharp's best known and documented encounter with Border morris, he saw a performance at Madley, and at Weobley he saw the dance from Dilwyn performed by a team of children. He also received information about dances in Drake's Broughton, Peopleton, Pershore, Upton-on-Severn and White Ladies Aston. This information is in his field notebooks and manuscripts (as referenced in Cawte's paper) but, as we know, summarised by the single sentence in the 2nd Edition of '*The Morris Book*'.
7 Cecil J. Sharp and Herbert C. MacIlwaine, *The Morris Book, Volumes 1–5 1911–1924* (Letchworth Garden City: Hive Printers for The Morris Ring, 1991), p. 21.
8 Sharp wrote enthusiastically about the qualities and indeed the beauty of the morris dancing which came to be called 'Cotswold' morris. Although he collected quite a lot of information about what we now call 'Border' morris, it seems that he was unimpressed, and the conclusion followed that this was merely a decadent form of 'Cotswold' morris. What exactly Sharp meant by 'decadence' is difficult to know with the passage of more than 100 years but I think all we can do is take the statement at its face value. The Concise Oxford definition entry is 'moral or cultural decline as characterized by excessive indulgence in pleasure or luxury'. I doubt the Brimfield men experienced much luxury, but we could interpret Sharp's view as being that the dance was in 'cultural decline'. My speculation is that he compared the basic nature of the dances unfavourably with the more elaborate Cotswold dances and decided that they were not amongst the dances he wished to promote. I have no doubt that this view, together with the exclusion of the material from the *Morris Books*, was influential.
9 Maud Karpeles was a long-term collaborator with Sharp, a fellow collector and equally influential auditor of dance performance at the time.
10 Maud Karpeles, 'Upton-On-Severn Morris Dances', *Journal of the English Folk Dance and Song Society*, 1.2, (1933), 101–103, (p. 102).
11 Cawte, 'The Morris Dance in Herefordshire etc.', p. 207. The Morris Ring is an organisation established in 1934 for morris dance teams.
12 Cawte, 'The Morris Dance in Herefordshire etc.', p. 206.
13 Joseph Needham was a British biochemist, historian and sinologist best known for his scientific research and writing on the history of Chinese science and technology. He also conducted some significant research into English folk dancing and was a member of Cambridge Morris Men.
14 Joseph Needham, 'The Geographical Distribution of English Ceremonial Dance Traditions', *Journal of the English Folk Dance and Song Society*, 3.1, (1936), 1–45.
15 E. C. Cawte, Alex Helm, R. J. Marriott and N. Peacock, 'A Geographical Index of the Ceremonial Dance in Great Britain: Part One', *Journal of the English Folk Dance and Song Society*, 9.1, (1960), 1–41.
16 Needham's paper gives on pages 3–4 a brief description of each of these morris dance genres but the term 'Cotswold' requires further explanation. Geographically, the Cotswolds describes an area of English uplands from Bath, Somerset in the south running north or north-westwards almost to Stratford-on-Avon, Warwickshire. The term is essentially a misnomer when applied to the body of dances collected from many villages in an area stretching from Oxford in the east to some distance past Stow-on-the-Wold in the west. This area barely overlaps with the Cotswolds yet; because the term is so widely applied as a description of this particular genre of morris dance, it will be used in this chapter. Although each village in this area had its own characteristic way of performing the dances, the body of material collected has sufficient similarities for it to be recognised as a specific genre. The general nature of the dance will be discussed later in this chapter.
17 Cawte et al., 'A Geographical Index of the Ceremonial Dance', p. 7. The reference to 'instruments of Christy Minstrel type' and 'blackened faces' in this definition will strike a jarring note with readers and is discussed later.
18 Cawte, 'The Morris Dance in Herefordshire etc.', p. 207.

19 The titles 'Squire' and 'Bagman' are given in many morris dance teams to the persons who are, respectively, responsible as the leader of the team and for the administrative tasks. In other clubs or societies, the terms 'Chairman' and 'Secretary' would be equivalent.
20 Roy Dommett was an aeronautical engineer who became the UK's chief missile scientist. He was also an enthusiastic morris dancer and researcher.
21 Lionel Bacon, *A Handbook of Morris Dances* (Morris Ring, 1974, 2nd edition, incorporating various corrections (1986).
22 Bacon, *A Handbook of Morris Dances*, p. v.
23 Much of Dommett's archive material is only available on-line. For the Border morris material, it is available on the Morris Federation Notation website and the link to the Index is http://notation.apps.morrisfed.org.uk/document-library/border-morris. The paper from which this quotation is taken was prepared for a conference hosted by the Morris Federation, 'Roots of Border Morris' held in February 1992. The paper is named 'Border Morris as collected v1.0' in the index list and may also be accessed directly through the link: https://drive.google.com/file/d/0B94GzSWSE-eV7aXdVZUczQ0VaSlk/view [accessed 30 October 2019]. An initiative by the English Folk Dance and Song Society to explore the use of Border morris for mixed teams of men and women was clearly short-lived and events moved in another direction. The outcome of Dommett's subsequent workshop at Ledbury was a team only of men but Dommett was also very influential in the subsequent adoption of Border morris more generally.
24 From the home page on http://www.welshbordermorris.co.uk access the page 'History of OWBM' where these quotations can be found or use the direct link https://welshbordermorris.blogspot.com/p/ears-2013-and-still-counting.html. [accessed 30 October 2019].
25 Derek Schofield, *The First Week in August, Fifty Years of the Sidmouth Festival* (Sidmouth: Sidmouth International Festival Ltd, 2004), p. 72.
26 John Kirkpatrick, 'Bordering on the Insane', *English Dance & Song*, 41.3, (1979), 12–14, (p. 13).
27 Ashley Hutchings, *Rattlebone and Ploughjack* (Netherlands: Island Records Limited, 1976), HELP 24.
28 Magic Lantern originally formed as a shadow theatre group performing folk songs and tales. Their leader and key source of inspiration was Taffy Thomas. They turned their hand to street theatre at various festivals but at Sidmouth performed a relatively straight version of the Brimfield dance based very much on the collected notation. Their impact stemmed from the impressive reproduction of the kit from the 1909 photograph, the fact very few of us had seen Border morris before and in my recollection the rather suggestive way the sticking was performed.
29 Schofield, *The First Week in August*, pp. 92–93.
30 Schofield, *The First Week in August*, pp. 99–100.
31 See http://www.silurianmorris.org.uk/history [accessed 30 October 2019].
32 The Morris Ring is an organisation, established in 1934, for morris dance teams. For most of that time, its membership was restricted to men's teams but that rule was relaxed in 2018. For further information, see their website: https://themorrisring.org [accessed 14 April 2020].
33 Dave Jones, *The Roots of Welsh Border Morris* (Putley: Annie Jones, 1995 [September 1988]), p. 2.
34 The Logbooks of the Morris Ring are held by the Keeper of the Logbooks, one of the Morris Ring Archivists, to whom I am grateful for providing me with this transcription.
35 North West Morris is a specific morris dance genre based on traditional dances collected from the counties of Cheshire and Lancashire.
36 Derek Schofield, 'Which Past? The Influences of Tradition and Revival on the North-west Morris in Morris: The Legacy of the Past', *Proceedings of a One-day Conference on Morris Dancing*, Saturday 20 April 1996 (London: The Morris Federation, The Morris Ring & Open Morris, 1996), pp. 94–109 (p. 102).
37 This list and the records referred to in the following sentence are not publicly available at the time of writing and I am grateful to Sally Wearing, Past President of the Morris Federation for the information.
38 William Kelly, *Notices Illustrative of the Drama and other Popular Amusements … Extracted from the Chamberlain's Accounts and Other Manuscripts of the Borough of Leicester* (London: J. R. Smith, 1865), pp. 100–111.
39 The scrapbooks and various other documents referred to in this section are held privately by members of Leicester Morrismen. In addition, I had correspondence with members of the team

who were present at the time and who provided their recollections of various events – see the acknowledgements.

40 I moved to Leicester to take up the position of Quality Manager with a well-known adhesive manufacturer having already had eight years' experience of morris dancing with Kesteven Morris in Lincolnshire. The other members of Leicester Morrismen named in this chapter were at various times Squire of the team and were professional people in a range of employment, including teaching and management consultancy.

41 For general information about Whittlesey, see http://www.strawbear.org.uk/index.html [accessed 30 October 2019].

42 For a broader discussion of this issue, see Harrop and Roud's 'Men in Blackface' in the general volume introduction.

43 The name is a pun since 'Red Leicester' is best known as a cheese which was originally made in Leicestershire. It is actually orange in colour.

44 Derek Schofield, 'A Black and White Issue?', *English Dance and* Song, 67.2, (2005), 12–14.

45 John Kirkpatrick, 'A Black and White Issue?', *English Dance and Song*, 67.3, (2005), 30–31.

46 Chloe Metcalfe, 'To Black Up or Not To Black Up?', *The Morris Federation Newsletter* (Winter 2013), pp. 6–9.

47 Katy Spicer, Facing Up to a Dancing Debate', *English Dance and Song*, 79.4, (2016), 14–15.

48 Gordon Ashman, 'Custom in Conflict: The Morris Dance in the Shrewsbury and Ironbridge Area of Shropshire', *Traditional Dance*, 5/6, (Crewe and Alsager College of Higher Education, 1988), 135–158, (p. 150).

49 Gordon Ashman, 'With One Bound They Were Free: From the Cotswolds to the Welsh Border in One Stride', *Lore and Language*, 6.2, (1987), 105–116, (p. 114).

50 Private communication from Charlie Corcoran.

51 This seems to be at odds with earlier practice. Cawte in his 1963 paper (pp. 206–207) records that 'early nineteenth-century accounts only mention one musician, often pipe and tabor or fiddle, so that the bones, tambourine and so on, seem to be a recent development'.

52 Geoff Hughes, 'The Stick Dance', *The Morris Dancer*, 2.7, (1988), 101–105. In this paper, Geoff Hughes described how he created a new version of this dance which was based on the one collected by Maud Karpeles (see endnote 8). Even though its origin is as a Border morris dance, this version became very popular amongst Cotswold morris teams. Leicester Morrismen had learnt it from Coventry Morris Men in 1978.

53 Lichfield is a relatively small city in the county of Staffordshire where a number of morris dances have been collected. It is neither very close to the Welsh Border counties nor to the 'Cotswold' region; hence, there is a continuing debate over the basis on which the dances are performed as belonging to one or other of these morris genres.

54 Adderbury is a village in Oxfordshire from where a fine set of morris dances was collected, which are firmly within the genre of Cotswold morris. My recollection is that we were short of dances to perform on that particular occasion and a dance which included some vigorous sticking still worked quite well as a Border morris dance.

55 John Swift, 'The Role of Repertoire in The Evolving Morris', in *Proceedings of a One-day Conference on Morris Dancing Held on 20th October 1990* (London: The Morris Federation & The Morris Ring, 1991), pp. 71–89.

56 Charles Corcoran and John Swift, 'Limiting the Repertoire – the Influence of Publications in Influences on the Morris', in *Proceedings of a One-day Conference on Morris Dancing held on 4th April 1992* (London: The Morris Federation, The Morris Ring & Open Morris, 1992), pp. 33–58.

57 An attraction for Leicester Morrismen, who spend much of the year dancing Cotswold morris, was that the dances alternate double stepping in the figures with single stepping in the sticking and hence present a little more of a technical challenge than most of the Border morris repertoire, which is based on single stepping.

The steps in 'single stepping' can be described as 'change, hop, change hop' whilst those in 'double stepping' are 'change, change, change, hop, change, change, change, hop'. This stepping is essentially the first challenge for the novice Cotswold dancer, whilst, as will be noted in a later section, even single stepping appears to be a challenge too far for some Border morris dancers!

58 Letter held privately in Leicester Morrismen's archive.

59 Ashman, 'With One Bound', p. 114.

60 At that time, morris teams invited to dance at the Sidmouth Festival were in two categories. The more elite teams were called 'arena teams' because their programme included performing on the festival's arena stage, whilst 'town teams' principally performed in the town centre.

61 Rob Elliott and Vas Deshmukh, 'Silurian – Greater than the Sum of Its Parts', in *Morris, The Good, The Bad, The Ugly: Proceedings of a One-day Conference on Morris Dancing held on 16th April 1994* (London: The Morris Federation, The Morris Ring & Open Morris, 1994), pp 37–58 (p. 40).

62 Ashman, 'With One Bound', p. 114.

63 The data presented here for the Morris Federation and Open Morris was compiled from the pages on their websites listing the member teams, https://www.morrisfed.org.uk/resources/morrisfed-sidefinder/#!directory/map for the Morris Federation and https://open-morris.org/member-sides-list/ for Open Morris [accessed 30 October 2019]. Open Morris do not aggregate data separately from their website. The Morris Federation membership database does not provide the number of teams dancing only Border morris, so I have used my compiled data in the table above which agrees with the aggregate numbers in the Federation's database to within ±4%.

16
DANCING WITH TRADITION
Clog, step and short sword rapper in the twenty first century

Libby Worth

Introduction

In an interview when nearing his 70th birthday, renowned folk musician and singer Martin Carthy said of folk music that it 'is not an archive. If you see it as that, it becomes like a butterfly in a glass case. Folk music has to live and breathe. I'm not interested in heritage – this stuff is alive, we must claim it, use it'.[1] Folk dance, like folk music, is just such a dynamic tradition, as demonstrated in this chapter through its snapshot of a selection of thriving short sword rapper and step dance communities that do far more than merely cling to the past, or attempt to replicate its traditions. Dancers encountered in pursuing this research, whether through their performances, practice sessions, workshops or interviews, physically demonstrate and discuss the myriad ways that they are engaged in a bodily 'dialogue' with the past. In tune with Carthy's exhortation, they 'use it'. Their relationships with 'tradition' are multiple, complex and ongoing, reflective of contemporary society in which they are embedded. England in the twenty first century is more mobile, fast paced, culturally diverse, urbanised and comparatively newly reliant on digital technology compared to its industrial eighteenth- and nineteenth-century counterparts, during which time many of the dances considered here originated. With the plethora of demands on leisure activity driven by global interconnectivity, relative ease of travel (at least for those with economic means) and a lively and competing range of arts, fitness and sports activities on offer, how is it that dances such as rapper and step have not only survived but could be said to be blossoming?

To set about answering this, the chapter draws on initial research undertaken into short sword (rapper) and clog dancing in Northumberland (2015) that gradually expanded beyond county borders through workshops, spectatorship at festivals, clog dancing classes, rehearsal attendance and interviews.[2] Since my dance background is in site-based improvisation and physical theatres rather than traditional dance, the research methodology moved away from dance ethnography, in which you might expect to be a participant observer for a considerable time within a specified community, and towards a process of listening and spectatorship over a broad field of works that come under the generic and provocative term 'English Traditional Dance'.

I found very quickly that dancers from one form of traditional dance were frequently also participants in a wide range of other forms both within the folk/traditional genre and extending beyond it, to include formal dance training in contemporary or ballet and in a variety of street, national and popular dances styles. Dancers' descriptions of their training, influences and inspirations released spiralling strands of aesthetic and social/cultural roots that, in their interwoven connectivity, prevented appraisal of dances as singular and isolated. This diversity of physical play with, and across, dance forms began to throw light on some of the intriguing features of dances I had seen, such as Toby Bennett's clog dancing with a very particular use of upper body movement and dynamic, the Demon Barber dancers' use of spatial range and Folk Dance Remixed (FDR) hybrid forms combining with hip hop. Subsequent interview material was always planned as a significant contribution to this chapter but, as it turned out, the Covid-19 pandemic struck, resulting in planned attendance at live events being cancelled and Skype interviewing becoming a primary means of developing this research. I am indebted to those dancers who took part in extended interviews in this restricted period during which they have seen performances, tours, competitions, festivals and rehearsals/teaching all decimated. Yet, no matter that dramatic changes have intervened in both stealing livelihoods in some cases and adding extra family responsibilities for others, enthusiasm for, and extensive knowledge about, their dances poured forth. In my selection and framing of this material, I aim to do justice, not just to the information and views offered, but to the timbre and character of the discussions we had.

Why these dances and why these dancers?

The chapter focuses on the idea of living dance traditions and the consequent navigation of aesthetic change as past practices encounter contemporary conditions. I chose dancers, therefore, who were actively engaged in opening up traditional English folk dance forms to new influences, new forms of collaboration across disciplines and genres or to changes in participation and processes of dance development. They are all innovators, who take the generative constraints of traditional dance forms to explore and produce dance material that challenges settled views of what is English, what is folk dance and even, as it turned out, what is dance. They are artists who do not want to abandon traditional forms of rapper and step but rather are caught in the midst of a negotiation of staying true to past choreographies, whilst still pressing their forms beyond what had been received from the physical/oral, notated and written historical archive. All teams and dancers included here are highly respected within their field and beyond for their performances and their knowledge, as shown by their dance awards, audience attraction, reviews, competition successes and written or oral accounts and recommendations. The dancers' accounts of their practices take centre stage. They determined the framing of the chapter as topics of discussion were replicated or emphasised in response to semi-structured interviews. However, as a dancer, I am cognisant of the importance of corporeal transmission of dancing skills, qualities, characteristics, tones and knowledges. Words are not always easy to find to communicate the plenitude and exactness of such processes. With this in mind, our conversations sometimes faltered whilst words and images were sought or, when forms of training, taken for granted within a team, were newly articulated. Therefore, to satisfy ethical concerns on the accuracy and tonal precision of dancers' necessarily spontaneous responses, selected text was returned to respondents for editing. Where I reference live performance/workshops, etc., the descriptions that entail interpretation are mine with no assumption that they reflect the dancers' views.

The primary respondents interviewed for this chapter are all active dancers of at least one of the forms considered: rapper and step/clog dancing. These forms share some components such as use of hard shoe, complex stepping, a sounded percussive performance, ability to be performed in small spaces with a hard floor, close interrelationship with live music and usually quite simple costume or everyday clothes. Yet in other respects, they seem polar opposite with rapper working in teams of five (up to seven) literally bound together by their holding of two handled short 'swords', whilst step dancers are typically solo performers who might work in group formation, but are likely to have their own dances too. Both forms locate important roots for dance creation/developments to specific geographical locations and time periods within the UK. The primary roots for what became known as rapper dancing sprang from the North East mining communities of Durham and Northumberland. Clog and step dancing have more various sources with interviewees referencing dances that emerged from the Lancashire mill workers, Westmorland and Lakeland traditions, Romany and traveller dances, barge dances, Northumberland clog and many more. To talk to dancers working within these traditions is to enter their networks that extend and grow more complex, more nuanced as discussion proceeds. It becomes impossible to talk in generalities as boundaries, whether between nationalities, dance styles, genres and histories, are challenged, exceeded and traversed.

Even a most basic contextualising of the main respondents for this chapter is fraught with difficulty as they each describe their experience of a wide range of traditional dance forms that refuse to sit neatly into a category. The primary focus for each dancer was their experience with step and clog in the case of Toby Bennett (Stepling), Kerry Fletcher (FDR) and Laurel Swift (Gadarene) or rapper dance with Tom Besford (Four Corner Sword and Medlock), Becky Watson (Tower Ravens and Four Corner Sword), Lynne Houston with Linda Sullivan (Whip the Cat Rapper and Clog) and Damien Barber (Demon Barbers).[3] However, this does not mean that their traditional dance experience is restricted in this way, combined they were also familiar with morris, social, ceilidh, Appalachian, Irish and Scottish forms and more. Even a cursory glance at individuals' and teams' respective online presences indicates their far-reaching connectivity across the traditional dance scene in the UK and internationally. Whether professional or amateur, collectively, they are also musicians, composers, choreographers, dancers of different styles (ballet, contemporary, hip hop, etc.), performance producers, academics, festival organisers and teachers, often with day jobs and family caring responsibilities. The chapter consists of journeys through the interviews reflecting on how dancers 'use' traditional forms in current contexts and stimulated by personal aesthetic concerns. Even with this limited sample of respondents, the diversity of approach was extensive, demonstrating motivations that drive fresh approaches to collaboration, opening up to new audiences, integration of internet technology, expression of political attitudes and interest in narrative. The chapter is divided into two primary parts, the first focusing on step and clog dancers' experiences and the second on rapper dance. This fell into place as it became clear that the rapper dancers were working within a more discrete dance framework than others but, illustrative of comments above, teams and dancers exceed any singular definition, so the two sections cross reference.

Tradition

Views on the nature of tradition and traditional dance featured consistently in interviews, whether in response to a direct question, or provoked by the use of the terms in discussion. Toby Bennett voiced a shared concern as to how the relationship of traditional dance to history 'is a really problematic issue because in a way, we do it because it's history and yet that stifles it at the same time'.[4] In much the way that Carthy spoke of the importance of allowing folk music to 'live and breathe', respondents spoke of the balancing act between retaining consistency in steps/figures received by exponents of specific traditional dance forms and introducing changes. Even in the most radical example of traditional English dance fusion considered here, FDR, the responsibility to maintain clarity of traditional steps weighed significantly for Kerry Fletcher, as discussed later. Bennett offers a different twist on the idea of respect for tradition.

> A lot of people find it hard to conceive of themselves as part of the tradition. They see themselves as *recreating* a tradition, rather than that the folk world is a tradition *in itself* and that what they are doing is just as valid as what collectors collected.

In effect, if we try to freeze dances in an effort to be authentic, then what we risk losing is the vitality of the dancers encountering and working with these dances. Bennett agreed with this, 'yes and the vitality of the dances themselves'. He continued, 'it's the real crux of the issue for me and something that's always in my mind. What am I doing? Is it traditional? Does style matter? In some ways it does and in some ways it doesn't and that changes according to what audiences tune into'.

These questions that Bennett raises play out in his dancing. Over the years, he has become associated with a repertoire of Lakeland (also known as Westmorland) stepping which generates a tension for him when he performs, as he wonders if what he is doing is genuinely representing these styles since he has 'increasingly come to question whether what we currently know about tradition is really representative of that tradition in the first place'.

Traditional dancing is not just changing through ongoing practices but understandings of past dances are also unstable, liable to mutation as new information surfaces. Bennett gives an example of this in the way that some contemporary Scottish step dancers he has worked with found fresh links between Lakeland steps and their own 'Scottish' steps. He notes that there are 'clear similarities between the Lakeland steps and the dances from Scotland collected by Tom Flett' and that they share 'very similar features in terms of the steps, step shapes and rhythms they use, with some of them done in clogs'.[5] Bennett has twice won clog dance championships and continues to teach step dance but he does not want to be tied down to a single style.

The complexities of dancing with traditional forms are exhibited in the distinctions Laurel Swift makes between her work in morris and in clog. A musician, choreographer, composer and dancer, Swift was brought up learning morris and, as a young adult, was taught traditional styles of clog dancing by Pat Tracey, herself a descendent of clog dancers from Nelson, an East Lancashire cotton mill town. Swift describes these as the only forms of clog dance she does and, having had Tracey as her teacher at Camden Clog, she feels 'a real duty to try and do them right and to teach them accurately and to be clear about when "here's a thing I got from Pat" and "here's a thing I made up myself"'.[6] With music and morris dancing, Swift experiences greater freedom to innovate through play with compositional components learnt from a variety of sources, rather than coming from 'somewhere that has an intact style'. This is particularly in evidence in Morris Offspring, a company she ran for two years working together with a folk band in which the choreography arose from 'playing' with Morris forms, 'taking it apart and putting it back together again, showing the insides of it'. She sees herself as less innovative in her clogging with the band Gadarene or in duet with Ben Moss (singer, fiddle and melodeon player). She might make a new routine with the steps she knows or elongate a phrase, make small rhythmic change to put 'tension in a tune' and the dance, but this doesn't amount to 'doing anything that Pat wouldn't have done in terms of the steps. She was really innovative in making routines for music hall and for Camden Clog'.

Both Swift and Bennett are caught in the flows and eddies of the confluence between transmission of past dances and making new work. Their responses to questions on traditional dance suggest that this is a dynamic and thought-provoking place that can be creatively stimulating if more rigid views on traditional dance forms are set aside. Swift recollects Martin Carthy's response to the suggestion that if you change tradition, you break it: '"well no, you've just got two". You've got the original one and you've got another one. How important to leave tradition richer than you found it'. Exploring how this enrichment happens in the present, through processes of collaboration, through questioning of basic tenets of what a dance is, where it happens and who participates in it, can additionally offer fresh perspectives on research into historic practices. Does listening to contemporary dance experience described in some depth provide clues as to similar debates and making methods of much earlier times? For instance, as both Damien Barber and Kerry Fletcher talk about their companies, respectively, The Demon Barbers XL and FDR, they make vivid the opportunities afforded them by broadening the pool of cultural dance and music sources drawn upon. This reflects the increasingly multicultural society of an England that is constantly in flux.

Collaboration

Collaboration is so prevalent in traditional dance and music activity that it is easy to take for granted thereby gliding over the tremendous range of processes that contribute to such enmeshed performances. In talking about their divergent experiences of collaboration, some dancers spoke of collision and fusion of styles, others were clearly uncomfortable with and resistant to this. Team-based dancers, as in rapper dancing, where to dance is to literally be linked together by swords, nevertheless revealed difference of method in creating new dances, with some teams preferring a group endeavour, others a single dance writer. Solo step dancers valued the opportunity to develop their own dances with space to improvise, yet were quick to acknowledge the close interweaving with musicians, resulting in bands with dancers such as Stepling and Gadarene. The value of having direct interaction with live musicians, rather than recorded music, arose many times, with Bennett even questioning the rigidity of the boundary between the two art forms. He has chosen to concentrate on solo step dancing often with a single fiddle player in 'duet' form and commented, 'I slightly hesitated because even labelling it as dance is problematic if you are seeing it as a duet with a musician'. Fletcher and Bennett's recurrent use of the term 'foot percussion' confirms this embedded link between dance and music. Fletcher exemplifies this with reference to her time as a guest tutor on Newcastle University's Folk and Traditional Music degree. Laura Connolly, a student at the time, had persuaded the department to allow her to major in foot percussion. She asked Fletcher to work with her, which she did, also teaching musicians playing for dance and the step dancers who had foot percussion as their second instrument.[7]

All the dancers I interviewed for the chapter readily gave examples of how they, or performers with whom they worked, saw themselves as both dancers and musicians. To consider this from the dance perspective in more detail, I look at two pairings of very different forms of dance/music performance making. Toby Bennett with Stepling and Laurel Swift with Gadarene exemplify bands integrated with solo step dancers who perform live, very often in music venues, and produce CDs with the clog as foot percussion. Bennett is primarily a dancer, although he has also learnt to play fiddle, whilst Swift (double bass) with fellow band member Matt Norman (mandolin) move in and out of the band as each performs their distinct step dance style. In both bands, the dancers move with, not to, the music and, in Swift's view

> learning clog dancing is much more like learning an instrument than it is like learning dance. You have to practice on your own and learn all these intricate things. It's a lot of brain space to remember it all and then it becomes muscle memory.

With different tunes, rhythms and time signatures 'if you want to re-jig it and put a step in a different place, then you really have to sort it all out again in your mind'. Swift and Norman dance on a raised box about a metre square with a microphone underneath to amplify their steps. The band's publicity states that they 'take little known dance tunes of the eighteenth and nineteenth centuries and get audiences dancing to them again' whilst 'drawing on Pop, Rock, Funk, Reggae, Electronica and Club Trance'.[8] For the time being, at least, the collaborative element is most evident between the whole band working together, whether as musicians or dancers, rather than between the two dancers who 'rarely dance on the box at the same time, partly because there isn't much room'. This also has to do with the fact that Norman, who has twice been Dartmoor Stepdance Champion, mainly dances to step dance hornpipes which, Swift explains, 'is almost the only rhythm I don't dance to as it's too fast for some steps and too slow for others'. The recurrent word in Swift's discussion of collaborative working was 'play'. Gadarene valued the ability to play with the historic tunes they had unearthed through research and bring them into relationship with many different genres of contemporary music. The process demonstrates the versatility and professional skill of the band, but also a sense of creative curiosity sufficiently flexible to allow in two contrasting forms of traditional dance.

With Stepling, Bennett explores the relationship between dancer and musicians but is quick to note that although step dance included as part of a band is quite new in England, it has a longer history and is more prevalent internationally, especially in Canada. Bennett describes the approach that Stepling has taken as varied, with some arrangements that

> are much more in the traditional mould of 'here's a dance and some music' but with some of them it's much more to do with trying to see the foot percussion as part of the music, and for me, that's been a really interesting and different way of thinking about what I'm doing.

There are similarities with Gadarene in this, but divergence is pronounced in stage configuration with each band's favoured spatial arrangements proving surprisingly significant in indicating the type of relationship between dancer and musician. I was curious as to whether Swift thought that the dancers' movement impacted on the musicians' physicality whilst they played. Swift thought not and instead described how 'I often feel when I'm dancing (or Matt) that the band is focusing in on us and it's channelled through, a bit like you do with a vocalist rather than the whole band putting it out there'. So, although often the audience dance to the band, when the clog dancers take centre stage, they will tend to stop and watch. Spatially, this is evident as the band is spread out behind the dancer who is on the raised box, which further singles her out.

Stepling, conversely, prefers a semi-circular stage arrangement, as Bennett explains:

> we are beginning to experiment more and more with that, with the way we lay ourselves out on stage. I try to resist as much as possible a backing band and me in the front, so I try to avoid being centre stage.

This structure supports Bennett's new focus.

We are beginning to work more on getting radio mics, so we can actually move around. So I've been working very much as a musician rather than as a dancer. We are beginning to get to the position where we can get the musicians to act more choreographically on stage.

Future development is dependent on access to performance space with safe and resonant surfaces to avoid clogging being restricted to a board and the need for the whole band to work with radio microphones to enable mobility. My impression watching the band at Whitby 2019 was that they are well on the way to moving into this new phase. Percussionist Jo May, in particular, was so physically buoyant as she played that she seemed to be having to constrain herself. Deb Chalmers, fiddle player, is also a clog and Morris dancer, so clearly there is much potential for choreographic development within the band.

There were additional elements in Stepling's performance that were arresting. The first was the freedom and softness shown in Bennett's whole upper body that allowed the movement to travel from clog step through to extremities of head and fingers. Movement in the arms and torso were not ostentatious, or even that pronounced, but the whole body was fully mobile with high uplift in the jumps and an easy quality of response. This engendered spread of focus from feet to the whole of the dancer and indeed through to the band. Bennett's professional training in contemporary dance and ballet at Ballet Rambert School and subsequent performance experience with a Belgian opera ballet company must have had much to bring to this, making his contribution to the traditional dance world unusual, even unique. Combined with this softened, fluid upper body, there was joyousness in the dancing with its tremendous variety in rhythmic quality and touching integration with the shifting musical moods. According to Bennett, this response is not unusual, with many audience members experiencing the dances as joyful and affecting. In part, he associates this with the band's intentional stage positioning that allows for eye contact, where 'even just the way we look at each other is choreographic and it just leads into a bodily interaction even when not particularly moving about'. They need to be able to see each other to ensure the intimacy of communication between them that supports the personalities coming through. 'You are expressing something about yourself in this' more fluid, solo form of dancing, as opposed to set team clog dancing. Bennett locates his experience of dancing with Carolyn Francis at a session doing Lakeland songs and jigs as the moment that 'launched all my experimentation and investigations into clog dance'. Her abrupt and assertive response to a second musician attempting to join her fiddle and clog dance duet with Bennett, 'this is just him and me', Bennett found 'completely electric'. She instigated an intensity in the duet relationship through her playing with 'power, drive and rhythm' that 'turned the way I think about performing and the way I was interacting with musicians'. This developed further through working with musician Scott Hartley and in encountering American step dancer Nic Gareiss, whose 'sensitivity and intimacy in performance has been very influential on my performance'.

Bennett spoke of 'dancing not dances' in discussing the improvisatory nature of solo clog dancing, since the 'collecting of set dances were probably in any case just one person's way of dancing'. This is helpful in thinking about two large-scale companies, FDR and Demon Barbers XL, both of which have forged new ways of collaborating with dancers who bring a range of genres as well as English traditional forms. As with Stepling and Gadarene, these are professional companies actively engaged in reinterpretation of English traditional dances and collaborating closely with musicians. However, their additional focus is on engaging with several dance genres practised in England but with markedly varied cultural roots and histories. Both Kerry Fletcher and Damien Barber reveal how this intentional broadening of participation and spectatorship for traditional dance has come with challenges as well as excitement and fulfilment. All four companies are attempting to survive in economic circumstances that shift over the years but are never less than challenging. This is especially evident with these larger companies working with groups of dancers as well as musicians. Even with support from funding bodies, such as Arts Council England, the commercial realities of keeping artists employed consistently make it hard to survive. Despite this, both Fletcher and Barber reflect on how they are driving forward performance productions to open out traditional dance to wider audiences.

Expanding collaboration beyond traditional dance

Barber is a prominent artist in traditional/folk music circles and has worked as a singer/musician (concertina/guitar) for over 30 years. His dance experience took off fully when he and four friends set up Black Swan Rapper in 2000 with one of them, Dan Offord, teaching them the famed Stone Monkey dance that had so impressed the rapper community in 1991. A competitive side rather than purely social, they rapidly developed their own signature dance and over a period of several years from 2002 won most of the major trophies at the yearly competition Dancing England Rapper Tournament (DERT). Phil Heaton, in his comprehensive text on rapper dance history and development, described their dance as 'perfecting a set of evolved figures and movements which reflected the more aggressive and challenging side of the dance'.[9] For Barber, the appeal of the side was the way that they 'were always putting in new figures, making it more acrobatic, raising the standard'.[10] When Offord moved away and the side took on a more social function, Barber eventually left and turned his full attention to the Demon Barbers that were also formed in 2000. This began as a five-piece band launched during Barber's regular spot (Damien Barber and Friends) at the Metropole in Whitby Folk Week but with invited dancers drawn from close contacts and including Black Adder Rapper and Step, Black Swan Rapper and Dog Rose Morris. In a slightly revised configuration, with dancers Fiona and Tiny Taylor rather than the whole of Black Adder, it was named the Demon Barber Roadshow and toured for several years. Barber states that in part this way of working was devised to deal with 'the frustration of not really seeing traditional dance on main stages' at festivals. This discontent was reinforced by increasingly commercialised folk festivals ending free entry for morris and other dance teams; 'the ultimate insult not only were they shoved to the side-lines but charged too!'. Both Demon Barbers and FDR actively work to disrupt the compartmentalising of traditional dance and music that has seen very little dance performance remaining at Cambridge, the largest English Folk Festival of the year, and, as Barber states, pushed to the edges in so many other festival and arts venues.[11]

The Demon Barbers gained a reputation for integrating a wide variety of dance forms but in the early stages these were all English traditional dances with Black Swan Rapper and Dog Rose Morris performing set dances. The Taylor sisters clog dancers, who were also experienced in Irish step dancing, had a somewhat different role, 'coming on as part of the band for maybe half a dozen numbers so that they were quite percussive in the line-up of the band and would provide new material specifically for Demon Barber tracks'. The percussive nature of clog, as experienced by Swift and Bennett, encourages the development of an amalgamated form of sound and visuals but the Demon Barbers differ, in that they are happy to operate more eclectically in devising dances drawn from a variety of traditions. There was opposition to this from some clog dancers external to the band who Barber recalls 'saying, "they are not traditional steps, they are a mishmash of styles"'. But from Barber's perspective,

I wasn't that bothered whether they were North West, South East, Irish steps. I was always more interested in the clogging being exciting and inspirational to an audience. There was no narrative back then, just music and dance for the sake of entertainment.

With this principle at work, Barber was quick to take the opportunity that arose when Black Swan Rapper were invited to take part in the British Dance Edition (2005) at the West Yorkshire Playhouse in Leeds. They were to perform 'what we called our Techno Dance back then, which was a traditional sword dance performed to a techno backing track with fiddle. Often at festivals we'd do it with Ultra Violet lights and with UV paint on the swords'. The dance was received with great enthusiasm by the audience and Bush Hartshorn (then director of Yorkshire Dance) supported Barber's vision to take the company's work into new terrain. Barber explains,

> I'd been thinking for a while about how we could raise the profile of traditional dance even more than we had done with the Roadshow. I wanted to raise it among mainstream audiences, and I knew that it was outside my knowledge then as to how to do that.

With the support of Hartshorn, the company secured two small ACE grants that allowed them studio time to work with choreographer Lucy Suggate, break dancers, a beatboxer and percussionist, alongside the band and clog dancers. Barber recalls the process.

We were interested in looking at similarities between the dance styles because we knew that in theory they came from similar backgrounds. They're performed by everyday people using the facilities and resources they've got around them. So we were interested in how two organic dance forms were similar and this became quite evident very quickly. The footwork of uprock or toprock [in hip hop] is similar to morris and very similar to clog dancing. There's a lot of step hopping, so we focused mainly on the clog dance steps and the break dance steps at that time.

Through learning each other's dances, 'when they put them together it became very difficult to see whether they were hip hop or clog dance steps'. Based on the success of initial short performances within the roadshow, the company 'got funding for a full show, *Time Gentlemen, Please*, which was the forerunner of *The Lock-in*' (Figure 16.1).

Figure 16.1 Demon Barber Roadshow in *Time Gentlemen Please* at Carriageworks Theatre, Leeds, 2010
Source: Photograph with permission, copyright Alan Cole.

These shows both extended the range of dance and music styles and introduced narrative in the form of a light storyline, set in a pub, about mistrust between opposing dance groups eventually resolved through a 'dance off'. As Barber describes it, 'these are two cultures that are very wary of each other – by the end of the show they appreciate where each other is coming from'. In discussing the collaborative process between hip hop and step dancers, Barber found that 'most hip hop dancers that I know really appreciate and love a variety of influences' but dancers from either style could be fixed in their views, 'they don't want it to be diluted and they don't really trust anyone coming in and messing with it'. Some dancers could at times be 'very defensive, unwilling to bend or be flexible with what they are doing' but equally there were positive experiences as, for instance, one company member, Bobak Walker, hip hop dancer who trained at Northern School of Contemporary Dance, describes.

> Once we stripped away the music and costume, to see the two pieces side by side, it was real magic in the studio. I think we were all shocked at how these dances, seemingly worlds apart, were actually variations of the same movements. It was one of those moments where any lingering doubts evaporated and we knew it was going to work.[12]

Having seen the *Demon Barbers XL* show with sections of their new performance *'Rise Up'*, the richness and diversity of the collaborative processes are obvious.[13] The stage is framed by the band members on raised platforms with film projected behind them for the more narrative-based *'Rise Up'*, ensuring that the whole space is alive with lights and action. The unison group clog dance format is disrupted by acrobatic flying movements, high jumping solo morris and forceful floor level break dance moves. It is as if each dance style has been dismantled and reconfigured in kaleidoscopic form, to challenge the viewer to see what might have been familiar moves in innovative configurations. These are not dancers just repeating their routine; rather, they display skills always in relation to other dancers and the musicians whose folk/rock sound is inflected by hip hop, ska and funk. The new show, inspired by 'Kett's Rebellion' of 1549, 'draws striking parallels between this [historic act of] enclosure and the dismantling and privatisation of publicly owned utilities today, emphasised by a short film by Swedish animation artist Mattias Gordon'.[14] The animated film, song lyrics, spoken text and projected photographs take the main load of storytelling, whilst the athletic contemporary, hip hop and clog dancing operate to highlight emotional impact and help drive home the forcefulness, energy and conflict of people's uprising. These are elements that were seen in, for instance, *The Lock In*, but with the edgy playfulness now developed into more potent physical form, befitting a desperate and finally violent rebellion.

Traditional dance and narrative performance

Swift like Barber has opted to produce a show with a centrally placed historic story as content and structuring device. For Swift, this represents a distinct change of direction from her decade-long leadership of Morris Offspring that toured as a dance company with live musicians[15] and where 'everything we did was a morris move one way or another'. It is significant that both artists take the lead in narrative productions, demonstrating confidence in the folk genre as a central component within several contributing dance/music styles. This contrasts with the more typical minor roles assigned to traditional dancers to tutor or choreograph specific elements only within a larger show.[16] Swift's folk musical, *Travelling with Thomas*, interprets stories from the medieval poet/prophet Thomas of Ercildoune, known as Thomas the Rhymer. 'Forced to travel to Fairyland, Thomas is helped and hindered as he tries to find a safe way home. It is a tale of fairness, love, truth and time'.[17] Unlike Barber, Swift opted for the dancers to focus on character development and employed a singer and three dancers, professionally trained but new to traditional dance/music. Swift's and Barber's rehearsal and development processes remain intensely collaborative, including trialling early segments in public contexts to generate audience feedback. Despite Covid-19, Swift persisted with showing a work-in-progress adapted as an online event that was necessarily raw due to isolation rehearsal but that revealed how dancers were responding to Swift's song compositions and the growth of the visual aesthetic. The dances hinted at how morris and clog would be included but Swift was adamant in a Q and A session that this would be developed once they could get together physically.

Due to the pandemic, there is no knowing whether *'Rise Up'* or *Travelling with Thomas* can be completed but, even in these early stages, they illuminate complex questions on the role of traditional dance when integrated with contrasting performance genres. Kerry Fletcher's work with FDR similarly resonates with such questions, as she notes the potential conflict in wanting to open up traditional dance to fresh influences, whilst ensuring that the distinctiveness of each contributing form does not disappear. 'A fusion doesn't need to become a soup, it's more like a salad, you can see the cucumber and tomato… it's not mushed up'. The company formed through Fletcher responding to East London Dance's (ELD) call in 2010 for ideas to contribute to a project called 'Folk Dance Remixed'. Rachel Elliot (Director of Education for English Folk Dance and Song Society, EFDSS) 'was curious as to why more people don't know about folk dance'; Fletcher recalls being put her in touch with Polly Risbridger, Director of ELD who were 'real champions of hip hop and street dance with a set of pathways for young people to get involved'. The idea Fletcher offered was 'Street Dance the Maypole' and, wanting to work with a street dance artist, she began to collaborate with Natasha Khamjani. They, like the Demon Barbers, quickly discovered in the workshops (supported by ELD and EDFSS) that 'toprocking, which is a real kind of battle stepping in hip hop dance, worked really well with step dancing and some morris steps'. Gifted the name from the original ELD project, Fletcher and Khamjani have continued to develop company shows and teaching.

Fletcher has extensive experience of traditional dance ranging from English to Appalachian clogging, morris and more recently Southern English Step Dancing, as learnt with Romany, Gypsy and traveller communities in Kent and Sussex. She continues to dance with Romany dancers such as Janet Keet-Black and Valerie Shipley and folk dancers Rosie Davis, and Jo and Simon Harmer in a group that has built a reputation for reinvigorating southern step dancing through, as Fletcher describes it, 'creating an environment for that to happen more naturally'. As Fletcher explained, 'Cecil Sharp didn't collect step dance because it was so prevalent that he never thought it was in danger. Two world wars later and he was proved wrong', so establishing pub sessions in Falmer, Sussex, for instance, is important in creating a social setting for step dancers to share their steps with live music. This ethos is carried through into FDR's professional performance and workshopping that takes place in large open air venues with traditional dance visibly valued and widely disseminated through embedding free events in everyday social encounter, rather than transporting them to the theatre stage.

Fletcher and Khamjani were adamant that 'we wanted to train our dancers to do it all. This is a fusion, this isn't, now you can see some English Step and clog dance and now hip hop or West African dance' (Figure 16.2).

The difference in a project like FDR is that what might gradually take place over decades is speeded up through the professional company's exploratory workshops, 'music and dance know no boundaries, we get influenced by each other, we are just condensing the time it takes to happen'. Fletcher describes herself as being part of 'a living, thriving tradition' and,

Figure 16.2 'Morris locking' from *Step Hop House* by Folk Dance Remixed performed at Urban Village Fete, Greenwich 2015

Source: Photograph by Natasha Khamjani, courtesy of FDR.

in the context of FDR, she works closely with dancers and musicians who come with the same degree of curiosity and openness bringing dance from their experience of, for instance, African and Caribbean dances, hip hop, Irish stepping, English clog, krump, Bollywood and capoeira. Fletcher and Khamjani are keen to develop a more political show. As a 'culturally very diverse group', Fletcher sees them as already inherently political since they are 'more representative of the population' than many outdoor performance groups, they speak about the cultural histories of the dances and they invite spectator participation. The plan is to make a show based on issues of migration and belonging, reflective of the urgency of current political debate, a subject to which FDR are well placed to contribute.

Playing on the edge: rapper sword dance in 2020

Interviewing rapper sword dancers opened up rather different subjects from those addressed earlier since they are part of a more cohesive community practising with a relatively small set of recorded dance choreographies. Without exception, all dancers referred in the course of discussion to Cecil Sharp's notations of rapper dances in *The Sword Dances of Northern England*[18] and their banter showed great familiarity with each other's sides. All are amateur, practising in leisure time on a designated weekday night or at weekends and the dancers are regular participants in the major competition of the year, DERT. All interviewees were actively engaged in navigating their relationship to rapper traditions, collaboration, maintenance of dance quality and interest in expanding choreographies and participation. However, since the groups shared a common set of dance sources, it was the divergences in motivation, focus, group structure, preferred audience, dancer participation and training that surfaced. Those I interviewed were Tom Besford from the mixed men and women's peripatetic side, Four Corner Sword and the Manchester-based side, Medlock; Becky Watson from London all-female Tower Ravens Rapper and Four Corner Sword, and Lynne Houston and Linda Sullivan from all-female Nottingham-based Whip the Cat Rapper and Clog. Each respondent had a complex history of traditional dance experience that both tracked their geographic work/life journeys together with changing interests or restless curiosity in many forms of dance. The focus in this section is primarily on the teams rather than the individuals and also references Barber's experience with Black Swan Rapper.

Heaton, in his richly detailed and scholarly account of rapper sword dancing history and development through to 2011, is unequivocal in locating its inception.[19] 'The *rapper* sword dance of the Northumberland and Durham coalfield of North-East England is a unique and fascinating tradition developed by the miners of the two counties'.[20] Given that current practitioners of rapper are now more likely to be middle class, highly educated and spread across wide geographical locations, including, for instance, America and Canada, they are far removed from the working conditions and contexts of those village miners whose dance they have inherited. Yet the dispersal of teams through many parts of the UK and beyond has not diminished a strong sense of community that rapper dancers frequently indicate as one of the primary motivations for continuing to participate. Within this overarching network, it was striking how readily and vividly each interviewee characterised their specific group, its distinguishing features and special attraction.

The DERT weekend of competitions takes place in a different part of England (occasionally Scotland) each year, hosted by one or more teams local to that area. Competition was important in the early days of rapper dancing and in Heaton's view the new DERT event that began in Derby 1984 had a dramatic impact.

> After only a few years, the standard of rapper dancing around the country rose dramatically as teams either practised in order to compete, improving their skills and understanding, or stopped dancing rapper in the face of the much better performances of the dancers involved in DERT.[21]

He traces the vicissitudes of the competition as it faded or came back into prominence against a background of concern about the earlier drift in standard of rapper dance caused by too many morris teams adding a poorly executed sword dance to their repertoire. None of the rapper dancers I interviewed reiterated the concerns about the standard of dance currently. Rather, they displayed confidence both in their teams' skill and the vibrancy and standard of dancing within the larger DERT network. Without exception, they were familiar with and had respect for the history and traditions of rapper dancing origins but, as Becky Watson put it, 'I'd say we are part of a new phase of the tradition'.[22] How that 'new phase' is being constructed and sustained is reflected differently in each team.

The Tower Ravens Rapper rehearse in Central London and as a result have a large catchment to draw from. Watson characterises them as being supportive, inclusive, always taking on all sorts of new people.

> We are maybe not the most usual grouping of people but everyone seems to find their space and we feel like a real family and, in this lockdown, we have all been messaging each other. We have weekly meetings and although we wouldn't hang out normally, we all come together to do this thing. Everyone's proud to be a Raven and we want to do well.

Watson suggests that many teams feel this closeness, like being in a 'mini world because it's so intensive and if you do anything wrong in a rapper dance it messes everything up, so you care more maybe, because you are literally connected to people'. Lynne Houston of Whip the Cat responded with not a moment's hesitation to the question of what makes the group special, 'we are like a family'.[23] Like Tower Ravens, they have kept in touch during Covid-19 with the team members that sprawl across East Anglia and into the North East. And, at the end of the interview, Linda Sullivan made a point of reemphasising what she considered the most important aspect of their team compared to other folk dance groups with whom she dances; it 'is the absolute sense of oneness, comradery and closeness we have as a team. We are there for each other, it's a family'. This went beyond pride in dancing well and being 'the only women's team that have that broad age range (19–60s)' to include social fun and playfulness. Sullivan recalls, 'we did a "meet the team" at Sidmouth [Annual Folk Festival] but only Cats would get down and do a flipping plank off!'.[24] Both these female sides with 20–30 memberships experience healthy recruitment, especially after winning DERT major trophies, including Whip the Cat winning the Steve Marris Trophy overall competition (2018).

The significance of the social aspect of teams was also acknowledged by Tom Besford in describing Four Corner Sword. This mixed male and female team is unusual in being peripatetic with weekend meet-ups held in the locale of one of the members. 'There are members dotted all over the country', including London, Newcastle, Littleborough near Rochdale and even one member who lives in Germany. Besford explains, 'you can't be a member of our team unless you actively dance with another team. So everyone is a skilled dancer in their own right'.[25] This enables them to bypass weekly practice, auditioning or having to do anything they do not wish to do. Consequently, they are not to be seen at festivals, apart from Whitby Folk Week and teaching a young people's workshop at Shrewsbury Folk Festival. As Besford spelt out, 'we have no dance commitments whatever. We've got no interest in dancing outside, we've got no interest in dancing with any other team or Morris sides or doing anything like that'. 'We realised that the enjoyment comes from socialising within the group and from cracking a new crawl, one that hasn't been done before, going into pubs and winning round an audience'. It's not a competition side because most of the dancers are competing with their 'home' sides. Likewise, they can engage with reaching competition standard, making new choreographies and teaching newcomers within their home teams. Besford's home team Medlock is based in Manchester and in the weekly practices welcomes newcomers to join and learn to dance. Unlike Tower Ravens and Whip the Cat, teams that love to participate in festivals, competition and crawls, Besford says of Medlock

> we are an extreme version of a crawling team. We only ever do crawls, we only exist to crawl. We do DERT but that's it, we've turned down every other booking we've had and don't dance outside or go to festivals.

Traditional and new dances

All the teams had at least one traditional dance within their repertoire, defined as one of the dances that appears in Cecil Sharp's notated collections from the early twentieth century. In all probability, this is encouraged through DERT, including a traditional dance competition in the weekend event. As Watson said of Tower Ravens, 'We're not a very traditional dance team. We know where the dances came from but also women didn't have a very big place in that tradition'. Their traditional dance is Westerhope, 'we always get quite intense about our Westerhope dance, we're quite proud of that'. This came across clearly in Whitby 2019, when the Tommy introduced it through giving a little of the background of the dance's origin, its village context and the successes of the team that included professional performances in the 1920s. Houston explained how Whip the Cat had three traditional dances with members of the team having done extensive research on two of them, adding to Sharp's notation through using archive footage and 'everything that you could think of people have tried to draw together to imagine how these dances were done'. Houston distinguishes these from their third traditional dance Newbiggin, which is 'a bit snappier and more of a pub dance, a bit more exciting than the traditional dances that can seem repetitive for an audience, whereas a rapper dancer understands the intricacies'.

Four Corner are 'one of the few teams that are saying we do just traditional dances'. Besford quickly qualifies this 'we say the dances are traditional, but they're not. One is Newbiggin-by-the-sea, very similar to how Sallyport Sword Dancers perform it but not quite. The version we do is like one an old team called Triskele used to do, because some of the girls in the team were in Triskele'. Similarly with North Walbottle, Besford put it together a while back with variations on the original. Since they are not doing these to compete, it was more important that they 'deliberately pick two of the easiest dances that you can possible do. We call it rapper by numbers'. In this way, at their bi-monthly gatherings, they could get crawling quickly. Besford offered the following view.

> With the successful teams, everyone on that team has the same ethos. So if you set up a team and say that this team is all about dancing and drinking on pub crawls and doesn't do festivals, then you know where you stand. Or if you say that we are going to do four or five pubs of an evening and we're going to do all the festival slots, another team might say that we are going to build this cult of personality.

Beyond the tweaks and small additions made to the teams' traditional dances, all respondents spoke of new dances they had created. Bearing in mind that dancers remain linked by swords throughout, there are obvious constraints on bodily range of movement, use of space and contrast between dancers, such that innovation must lie elsewhere. The dancers' analyses of their teams' processes of choreographing locate some of these elements and, in the course of doing so, open up questions on, for instance, ownership, who choreographs, what is sought within new choreography and how the making method reflects the ethos and character of the teams. Even within this small sample of rapper sides, considerable diversity became apparent and, interestingly, produced the same degree of success for each team with award-winning dances feted within the rapper community.

For Barber, his interest in Black Swan Rapper was in the challenge of writing new dances and performing to the best standard they could manage. His interest waned when Dan Offord moved away and 'the focus went from being a dynamic, inspirational team to just being more and more a social team, I was always more interested in pushing the boundaries than having a nice weekend away'. In their earliest years, Black Swan went down in rapper history as producing an exceptional dance created, as Barber notes, as a result of their 'always putting in new figures, making it more acrobatic, raising the standards'. With this dance, their performances won a series of DERT trophies and earned inclusion in Heaton's book notations of more recent 'alpha' dances.[26] Typically, no single author is named by Heaton for the Black Swan dance with the assumption therefore that it was created by the whole team. This is by no means always the case and it was clear in talking to Besford that he was a frequent writer of dances for a range of different sides, including the one for which he is credited by Heaton, 'Swearsdell'.[27]

> I'm used to writing dances that are still performed to this day. And I would say that basically everything has been done before. I've a very strong knowledge of the traditional canon and so I've understood what the potential shapes are, so what you are really doing is slightly changing how you are getting into or out of those shapes. And the skill of the choreography is linking figures together, although that said we really pushed the boat out with Medlock. We tried to revert to a more traditional style of movement with the old school pace to it. So Medlock's Gaslamp dance is actually different and looks like no other team's dancing.

Whip the Cat spoke of their new tournament winning dances being created by the teams over a long gestation. Houston describes their 'Mrs Beaton's How to Dance', that won at DERT, as being

> a fast, complicated, exciting dance. It's taken the traditional figures and added a twist to them and changed the way into them, added more to it. People have come up with ideas and added their stamp to it over the course of several years until it's got to the state it's in now, which is finished.

Current workshopping for a new dance is similarly expected to take several years with Sullivan noting that some people have a better idea than others about how to write a dance. Both Houston and Sullivan embraced a process in which 'some things happen completely by accident, it's just that set of five working together and piecing things together'.

Watson describes multiple processes being employed by Tower Ravens dependent on who is leading the group (Figure 16.3). An early version of their competition dance was written by Ffion, who 'was obviously capable of doing that' and subsequently they have worked more as a group relying on each member contributing from their own strengths. She gives the example of how the double team dance came together for the final show at Whitby (2019). Their musician came up with the idea of making use of having two full teams to dance with an imaginary giant sword.

Figure 16.3 Tower Ravens Rapper dancing their Piccadilly dance at Sidmouth Folk Festival, 2018
Source: Photograph with permission of Kyle Baker Photography and Videography.

I thought that sounds like a good idea but my practical side went 'oh no how's that going to work?' We ended up in arches in a long line in display, but how to get out of that? It's not normal. It took several attempts with almost the entire team contributing, headed by the people who actually know how it works. That's an example of how to work a development but to write an entire dance I think it has to be one person, because otherwise it would just take the longest time.

The crawl

For anyone outside the rapper dance world, to enter a pub uninvited, in costume and proceed to dance in a tight knot with loud shoe raps to live music for five minutes or so, have a drink and leave seems audacious, to put it mildly. Yet teams do this repeatedly over an evening, whether it's Whip the Cat's early evening crawl adapted to accommodate the many parents in the group, Tower Ravens' monthly dance outs or Medlock happily clocking up 12 pubs per evening. Besford recounts

> In fact I've got a wonderful crawl diary [collected by one team member] with every single pub we've danced in. It's a fascinating piece of data. So he's got a list showing that we've danced in around 650 pubs since 2014 and how much money we took in each one as well.

As a primary public outlet for rapper dancing, it is surprising that little attention has been paid in research to the skills and often unspoken protocols that underlie this daring and bold means of performance. Rapper dancing is recognised for the extreme contrast between the intense rigour and detailed work entailed in learning many of the dances and their seemingly anarchic, highly energetic, full on delivery. The dancers talked readily about such detail in training, particularly in preparing for competition. Houston, for instance, recalled an interchange '"Oh your hand is at this angle and mine is at this angle. Which should it be?" And you're having a ten minute conversation about a five degree movement in your wrist'. Whether in beginners' workshops with Four Corner or watching Tower Ravens practice, the care taken in such detail is always in evidence and ensures safety and fluidity in sword handling, as well as a sharp precise sound in stepping. But it was Besford who initiated a conversation about the importance too, of preparation to enable dancers to develop both the chutzpah in the dance and behavioural sensitivity necessary for each performance context.

He explained that they often discussed this element with Medlock.

> How you engage with the public. How you hold yourself when you walk into a pub you've never been to before. How you drink, how you stand and nod or smile at the punters who might initially be aggressive or suspicious about what you're doing. Going into pubs that you've never been into before, especially pubs targeted because they are rough, it can go seriously wrong. If you go in there with all nice middle-class pretensions, of course we are all middle class, if you are pretentious, you can very quickly have something turn from a social to not a positive experience. Potentially, it could even be a bit risky or dangerous. But we have perfected in Four Corner and Medlock exactly how you go into a new space and how you engage the public. We chat to people and when sometimes they hint at political ideology that you don't necessarily agree with, you know when to smile and how to give the right amount of stick back. You need to know how to deal with aggression or conflict. All that, I personally love and find fascinating.

Besford recalls one pub they went to that was very run down.

> You could rent rooms by the hour upstairs and inside was real spit and sawdust; there was smashed glass on the floor. But we danced and they loved it. They gave us 30 quid, whereas the more middle class, the more people don't want to engage with us. I love that, that whole social dynamic is one of the things I find most fascinating about where's good to crawl and where's not.

Besford was alert to the irony of the working-class derived dance being represented by primarily middle-class dancers to a working-class audience. And, given Four Corner and Medlock's broad geographic crawl terrain, Besford has become sensitised to the distinctive characteristics displayed across a city's pubs, developing a shrewd sense of likely reception.

Watson, Houston and Sullivan all valued the wild, unpredictable element of pub performing with Watson commenting, 'well there's always that surprise and delight with a little bit of an edge because you're women with swords!'. In a similar vein, Houston noted having to expect the unexpected, 'even when you've been to a pub ten times it's a different atmosphere each time' and Sullivan added, 'it's living on the edge every pub you go in'. They both commented on the importance of having a 'character' (Tommy or Betty) 'to tell the audience what's coming' and, Houston elaborated, to

> intervene too if something is going on and smooth it over. So if someone turns from the bar with two pints in their hands and the dance blocks their way, the Tommy can go 'Oh is one of those for me' and turns it all into a joke as well as explaining that the dance only lasts four minutes.

DERT has a competition for the character dancers in recognition, as Sullivan described, that 'it's about so many things, not just being funny… It's about balance, not getting in the way of a judge [for the DERT competitions judged in pubs], bringing an audience in, it's an art, an absolute art'. But if it becomes impossible like the time they encountered 'two stag parties in a pub with the men coming on to them and hanging onto their costumes. They can call it half way through a dance, "lock, display and off"'.

Watson recollected, after some hesitation, that Tower Ravens do also work to develop pub crawl skills.

> We talk about how you present yourself. Look confident and look like you should be there. When new, learn to do the dance with confidence and a new team member will dance with four experienced dancers. It's useful to come on a crawl before dancing.

They share responsibility for setting up a route and squaring it with pub landlords prior to the crawl. Otherwise, in London, where the landlord is often not present in the evening, the group will not be allowed to dance. Promptness is important and if things do go wrong, as in the Whip the Cat example, they call it a day and leave.

DERT not DERT

There is nothing that quite marks out a twenty-first-century rapper crawl more distinctly than the moment when initially passive drinkers suddenly jump up and start crowding in with their camera phones held high to film the dance and rapidly share it over social media.

Traditional dancers, like everyone, have been impacted by the extraordinary speed of technological developments in communication through internet and phone design with the subsequent ready access that many have to instant dissemination of images. In an essentially bodily art form of live performance with live music that seeks to foster physical trust between participants in close proximity to each other, internet technology might seem to be peripheral. In fact, there was a good deal of divergence in how sides integrated media into their practice and publicity. In general, platforms such as Facebook or Google maps supported organisation of teams, event planning and storage of valuable post event data. Team websites were used by all but with varied degrees of activity ranging from general publicity to extensive visual archives of past performances, links to other sites, articles or interviews. Practices were enabled through being filmed and reviewed, whilst the profile of teams could be actively raised by concerted use of social media platforms. The degree to which these were undertaken very much reflected the character, ethos and interests of the group as described earlier. However, such technology really came into its own and was pushed to its limits through the extraordinary events that forced the cancellation of DERT 2020 planned for 4–5 April.

Whip the Cat were organising DERT in Lincoln and it is easy to imagine the workload this entailed to manage up to 30 teams coming to compete with musicians, families and friends. Venues, catering, merchandise, hospitality, programmes, etc., were all in place by the time Covid-19 began to threaten and after 'two years of work with local businesses to supply the event, they were all let down', although Houston was quick to add that they honoured the contracts that had already completed. In the first weeks of the virus hitting the UK, Houston explained that they were

> planning, planning, planning for it to go ahead but more and more we were having contingency plans. The original idea was to give teams a couple of weeks' notice and ask them at their next practice to film five or six dances, five from a pub crawl and one in a different place (coffee shop, shopping mall etc.).

They emailed a warning but on 16 March, government guidelines warned against congregating in pubs and restaurants and non-essential travel. Houston recalled, 'the first plan went out of the window and we couldn't ask teams to be judged on sub-standard dances from old videos'. 'So it was a team member called Eilidh', Sullivan added, 'she just had some brilliant ideas and we let her run with them'.

The idea was to run a weekend online series of quizzes, games and competitions linked in some way to the usual DERT set-up. Those who had bought tickets for the showcase were invited to the event too and Sullivan said of the experience, 'we were absolutely overwhelmed that so many teams took so much time and made so much effort. It was just phenomenal'. Hosted on Facebook, the technical side was hard to manage especially as all the requested videos for different competitions were still being sent over during the weekend. Houston explained, 'Facebook can be a bit glitchy. So it was best to have just one person running it over the weekend. Something that's improvised and is that big needs just one person in charge'. As an outsider looking in over the weekend, the competitive aspect was still very much visible whether through uploaded videos of excellent solo stepping, or who could come up with the funniest send-up of an event. Some of Sullivan and Houston's favourites were Jonty doing the rapper step named after him. He's filmed in his garden, in costume, ready to do his step and instead he then simply takes one pace onto the step at the edge of the house, end of film, big smile. The Tower Ravens entered the 'buzz competition' with a piece of music made note for note from things that buzz. Houston was impressed with 'the sheer amount of work. Things like the Stone Monkey solo dance, one person did all the five positions in his kitchen and then spliced them together'. But most of all they both agreed 'that it was such a community spirit that weekend, everyone coming together'. The dance that stood out for me was Tower Ravens' compilation of five dancers split across the screen doing their own moves for a dance in time with the musicians and with 'Tommy' Sue shouting in the background. Watson described the layered process of recording the music by two musicians, 'we realised it was hard to know when to go without Number 1 dancer calling, so she recorded herself doing it and calling. Then we used it to listen to and filmed ourselves and put it together, worked with the levels and got Sue [their Tommy] to do her shouting'. In describing this, Watson notes that not only was it good fun but indicative of the character of the team 'that was a prime example of how we wanted it to be really good'.

Conclusion

It is hard to say what the continuing impact of digital media will have on the traditional dances discussed here, as, given the longevity of these forms, the interrelationship is still in its infancy. However, the global pandemic has revealed, with startling clarity, internet technology's potential as a resource that can mitigate the impact of disruption, at least to a degree. The online responses to DERT or Swift's *Travelling with Thomas* Zoom work-in-progress are large-scale examples, reiterated across smaller online team 'practices' that illustrate creative ways of sustaining social contact and dance stimulation to bridge the hiatus in physical connection.

Carthy's defiant call for folk artists to 'claim it, use it' that began this chapter is strikingly illustrated in the subsequent conversations with dancers that revealed their resolute respect for the traditional dance lineages they practise combined with restless curiosity as to how they could press these forms in new directions. This manifests as merging dance and music in the foot percussive work of Stepling or Gadarene, or as the new terrains forged by the Demon Barbers and FDR as they interweave different styles of dance and music in conjunction with film and visual art. Equally, the painstaking work to bring new content to rapper sword dancing, whether through an individual choreographer such as Besford, or through years of collaborative group effort exemplified by Whip the Cat, reveals persistent investment in creative endeavour linked with apparent confidence in the robustness of the dance moving into the future.

Swift, Fletcher and Barber in their moves towards narrative performances 'claim' the central rather than peripheral space for traditional dance and music, inviting collaboration with a range of genres. In so doing, they define their roles as leading, rather than merely contributing, creatives, demonstrating confidence in traditional forms to hold their distinctiveness in the midst of multi-genre productions. This distinctiveness is not simply bound up in specific stepping patterns or team choreographies but is also evident in dancers' explanations of processes, attitudes and ethos operating in each dance group. Such working differences reveal contrasting attitudes to, for instance, ownership, who choreographs, where and to whom dancers perform and the degree to which the individuals or teams are prepared to open to new influences.

This chapter has shown that there are many dancers who, rather than attempting to only replicate past dance forms, consider themselves actively part of tradition and are driven to move that tradition along. The respect and joy they associate with traditional forms of dance are reshaped by their desire to engage with the social and cultural currents of contemporary

England. The valuable insights offered by some of these twenty-first-century dancers in analysing their experiences might simultaneously contribute new perspectives on research into historic traditional dance practices.

Notes

1. Martin Carthy, 'I'm not interested in heritage: this stuff is alive. Interview with Ed Vulliamy', *Guardian*, 17 April 2011, npn. https://www.theguardian.com/music/2011/apr/17/martin-carthy-interview-ed-vulliamy [accessed 10 April 2020].
2. Including, for instance: festivals at Alnwick, Towersey, Cambridge, Sidmouth and Whitby, research with Tower Ravens Rapper, beginners classes with Camden Clog and interviews and co-work with Laurel Swift on a Tate Exchange event.
3. All quotes for these eight dancers refer to the 2020 personal interviews unless otherwise stated.
4. Toby Bennett, personal interview with author, 18 March 2020.
5. See Joan F. & Tom M. Flett, 'What Do We Really Know About Our Dances?', *English Dance and Song*, XXI, 2, (1956), 42–44. For records of dances collected by the Fletts in Scotland and England, see https://insteprt.co.uk/?s=tom+flett.
6. Laurel Swift, personal interview with author, 1 May 2020.
7. Kerry Fletcher, personal interview with author, 25 March 2020.
8. Gadarene, band website, https://www.gadarenemusic.com/Site/Welcome.html [accessed 10 May 2020].
9. Phil Heaton, *Rapper: The Miners' Sword Dance of North East England* (London: English Folk Dance and Song Society, 2012) p. 250.
10. Damien Barber, personal interview with author, 20 April 2020.
11. There are notable exceptions such as Towersey Folk Festival.
12. Damien Barber and Bobak Walker, 'Time Gentlemen Please: Damien Barber, Producer, Performer and Artistic Director of The Demon Barbers and Bobak Walker, Choreographer and performer, reflect on a unique partnership between traditional English Folk dance and Hip Hop'. Foundation for Community Dance. *Animated* magazine, Winter 2011, p. 8 https://www.communitydance.org.uk/DB/animated-library/time-gentlemen-please?ed=14075 [accessed 19 May 2020].
13. The Demon Barbers, *The Demon Barbers XL and 'Rise Up'*, performed at Home, Manchester, 19 October 2019.
14. The Demon Barbers website, Demon Barbers XL 'Rise Up', http://www.thedemonbarbers.co.uk/about/the-demon-barbers-xl-rise-up/ May 2020 [accessed 6 June 2020].
15. Sometimes, they worked with a full band, such as English Acoustic Collective (EAC) or Faustus and at other times with a collection of individual musicians.
16. For example, clog dances in Frederick Ashton's *La Fille Mal Gardée* and David Bintley's *Hobson's Choice* or Pat Tracey invited to tutor the clog dancing sequences in Albert Finney's 1984 Old Vic production of John Arden's play *Sergeant Musgrave's Dance*.
17. Laurel Swift, 'Travelling with Thomas' folk musical work-in-progress. http://www.travellingwiththomas.co.uk/ [accessed 10 May 2020].
18. Cecil Sharp, *The Sword Dances of Northern England*, 3 parts (London: Novello, 1911–1913).
19. For detailed information on early developments of link sword dancing, including rapper, see Stephen D. Corrsin, *Sword Dancing in Europe: A History* (Middlesex: Hisarlik Press, 1997) and 'Sword Dancing in England from the late Eighteenth to the early Twentieth Century', this volume, Chapter 10.
20. Heaton, *Rapper*, p. vii.
21. Heaton, *Rapper*, p. 84.
22. Becky Watson, Personal interview with author, 23 April 2020.
23. Lynn Houston and Linda Sullivan, personal interview with author, 14 April 2020.
24. 'Planking' is an exercise for core muscles in which the body is held in a line (plank) resting on elbows and tucked under toes. A 'plank off' is a competition to see who holds this position for the longest duration.
25. Tom Besford, Personal Interview with author, 17 March 2020.
26. Heaton, *Rapper*, p. 250.
27. Heaton, *Rapper*, p. 257.

17

'SEQUINS, BOWS AND POINTED TOES'

Girls' carnival morris—the 'other' morris dancing community

Lucy Wright

If you should ever find yourself awake and out of the house early on a Sunday morning in the North West of England or North Wales, you might happen upon them: teams of girls and young women in tracksuits and sequinned dresses travelling to weekly competitions in double-deckers festooned with banners and trophies. Pass by a sports hall or leisure centre and you may catch sight of groups of teenagers tracing the moves of a dance routine in a quiet area of the carpark watched over by an attentive trainer. If you're on foot, you will perhaps notice the persuasive thump of pop music emanating from inside the venue, the glint of foil pom-poms overflowing their canvas stuff-sacks, or the allium scent of a food van parked on the verge. You might be surprised for a moment at just how many other people are awake at this time on a weekend, how intergenerational is the crowd and how chaotic and purposeful and electrifying it all is.

The uninitiated could be forgiven for thinking that they were witnessing an event for cheerleaders or Irish dancers: there are some obvious resemblances, although girls' morris is considerably older than cheer and has few direct links with the Irish dancing community.[1] You would probably be less likely to make the connection between these performers and morris dancers, at least in so far as morris dancing is most strongly impressed upon the public imagination. These are not the white-clad men in breeches and flowered hats dancing with handkerchiefs outside of a country pub, or the maelstrom of dancers in tattered coats and grease paint, clashing sticks on the high street. But they are morris dancers nonetheless: in fact, for many of those raised in the girls' morris heartlands of Cheshire, Lancashire and North Wales, they would be the first—perhaps the only—performers the term 'morris dancing' would call to mind (Figure 17.1). A central fixture of community life for some and a fond childhood memory for others, girls' morris is a vital, if largely hidden, aspect of the living heritage of Wales and the North.

It is perhaps counterintuitive that girls' morris became the English folk revival's inconsonant Other. Unlike many of its eponymous cousins, girls' morris dancing can boast a seemingly unbroken history and roots that run at least as deep as almost any other morris style for which there are reliable records in the region. In fact, archival research throws up countless teams of girls performing something called 'morris dancing' in the North West

'Sequins, bows and pointed toes'

Figure 17.1 Members of Orcadia Morris Dancers, 2016
Source: Photograph with permission, copyright the author.

from the 1880s onwards, at least ten years before Cecil Sharp's famous first encounter with Headington Quarry Men on Boxing Day 1899 and almost a century before the women's morris revival of the 1970s and 1980s. Yet girls' morris functions at a fundamental remove from the conventional spaces and contexts of today's folk revival morris dancing community; for decades routinely omitted from its histories and viewed as an object of bemusement or scorn where it was acknowledged at all. Why is this, and what are the implications of its marginalisation for contemporary folk arts practice and scholarship?

In this chapter, I will consider the perceived otherness of girls' morris in the folk revival morris movement, its historical neglect by scholars and continued autonomy as a distinct community of practice. In doing so I hope to persuade that this spectacular and highly skilled dance is not only worthy of attention in its own right, but that it may also play a crucial role in the project of reasserting the significant—but still sorely overlooked—role of women in the folk revival(s). It also points to the need to look outside of the current canon of English folk to identify the other performances which may share comparable and mutually illuminating histories and values, regardless of their genre or type. The many yet-to-be-told stories of the girls' morris dancing community demonstrate that far from being a finite and already-completed project, folk collecting remains rich with potential—if we are open to a more dynamic interpretation of 'the tradition' and we know where to look. This work, which draws on more than eight years of interest and involvement in girls' morris dancing, is my contribution to this ongoing imperative.

What makes girls' morris dancing other?

Girls' morris is a team formation dance, performed by groups of eight or more dancers to a rhythmic musical accompaniment. Participants wear matching costumes (including shoes laced with bells) and carry pom-poms, known as 'shakers', similar to the mollies, tiddlers and garlands used in other forms of North West morris. Routines are activated by a precise and driving triple step strongly reminiscent of the 'ranting' found in clog morris and English country dance and teams often celebrate long histories and place-based identities. So far, so folk…

However, girls' morris performances often bear relatively little resemblance to the better-known morris dances of the English folk revival. Fast-paced, highly synchronised and pristinely executed to an energetic soundtrack of recorded pop music, girls' morris is fiercely competitive and troupes continually update their routines to gain an advantage over their rivals. It is also performed almost exclusively by girls and young women, who often begin dancing at a very early age. If men's morris is sometimes rather uncharitably stereotyped as a dance form characterised by 'beer bellies and beards',[2] then girls' morris dancing might be distinguished by its rather more glamorous 'sequins, bows and pointed toes'.[3] With an estimated 8,000 current participants, it is also extremely popular, almost certainly one of the largest morris dancing communities in existence.[4]

In the sections that follow, I will outline some of the key features of girls' morris dancing—its contexts, communities and choreographies—hopefully dispelling some of the common myths about the performance and demonstrating how this 'other' form of morris dance developed—and flourished—adjacent to the English folk revival.

Performance context

Perhaps the first thing to notice about girls' morris performances, in contrast to those of the folk revival, is the distinct context in which the dancing takes place. While folk revival morris groups typically perform outdoors, often in public locations like pubs and shopping streets, girls' morris events are generally private affairs staged in sports halls and community centres. Instead of an 'incidental' audience of shoppers and members of the public at informal 'dance outs' or the dedicated enthusiasts at outdoor folk festivals and events, girls' morris is primarily performed for an audience of participants and supporters and competitions are generally not widely advertised. For this reason, even for many people living locally, the dance represents a mostly 'hidden' aspect of community cultural life.[5]

It was not always this way. The roots of girls' morris dancing lie in the very public town carnivals and street parades of the mid-nineteenth to late twentieth centuries, and teams would travel widely to perform at dedicated outdoor competitions across the North West and Wales. Indeed, it was while performing at civic events with North West morris teams that the term 'fluffy' morris was coined by the male dancers, in reference to the crepe paper pom-poms carried by members of the girls' teams. However, despite the 'fluffy' moniker having been partially reclaimed by the girls' morris community, it remains somewhat trivialising and many prefer the less contested 'carnival' or 'carnival display' morris in reference to the community's proud historical ties to the town carnival movement.[6]

It is important to say that in this context, 'carnival' is understood quite differently than other, more widespread uses of the term. Although there is photographic evidence to suggest that some girls' morris troupes occasionally performed in the popular West Indian carnivals that have taken place in the UK since the early 1960s, this does not appear to have been commonplace and there are few other overlaps. The 'carnival' in 'carnival morris' is also largely unlike the transgressive historical bacchanals theorised by Bakhtin and Kristeva in their depiction of 'the carnivalesque'.[7] Rather, girls' morris might be more precisely described as a 'Northern British carnival performance', a status it shares with other extant groups such as jazz marching bands (formerly known as 'juvenile jazz bands') in the northeast and South Wales, 'entertaining' or 'entertainer' troupes from Staffordshire and the West Midlands and majorette baton-twirling (found globally), with which the performance shares a history. In common with these close relatives, girls' morris dancers continue to identify strongly with the 'carnival world', the collective term for the community of practice which grew out of the town carnivals movement.

These carnivals had emerged as a form of community self-entertainment in the mid-nineteenth century, in response to changing ideas about leisure time for working people. After 1850, growing middle-class concerns about the poor health and compromised moral character of the newly industrialised poor led to calls for alternative leisure activities that were both respectable and productive, and carnivals were felt to offer a range of ideological as well as physical benefits. Many early carnivals combined nostalgia for a romanticised rural past with what Dan Howison and Theresa Buckland call 'a strand of very up-to-date patriotism' with costumed characters such as John Bull and Britannia processing alongside 'May Queens, Rose Queens, maypole dancers, Jack-in-the-greens, Maid Marians, gleaners, shepherdesses and morris dancers'.[8] The rapid spread of carnivals in the latter part of the nineteenth and early twentieth centuries was also aided by the new railway network which spread across the North of England during the same period, enabling unprecedented numbers to travel across the region to attend events. Teams were often specially created to provide entertainment at the festivities and participation was very popular: Lesley Edwards and Janet Chart reported that at the Great Patriotic Demonstration at Crewe in 1901 there were 200 different sections of participants in the parade, which extended almost three miles in length.[9]

Carnivals continued to play an important role in community social life throughout the middle years of the twentieth century, providing entertainment and opportunities for many working-class people. Inclusive and self-organised, they involved large numbers of people, as both spectators and participants, often with the goal of fundraising for a local cause. Lyn Booth, secretary of the Manchester and North East Cheshire Carnival Organisation (MANECCO) and stalwart of the carnival movement since the 1950s, explained in an interview in 2013:

> [carnivals] were a big array of different things: you'd get your paraders; the pearly king and queen, the Girls' Brigade and Boys Brigade, all the youth clubs who'd be in fancy dress, the pipe bands, all the floats sponsored by different local firms...as well as all your dancing troupes. Some of the bigger carnivals would attract a lot of outside visitors: they had huge acts, like Roy Hudd who was a popular television celebrity and even Diana Dors. The aim was to raise money for local charities while providing social recreation for the communities: it was a wonderful fun day out.[10]

During their popular heyday, almost every town and many villages held their own carnival and many successful troupes had outings every week throughout the summer months. Samantha Hamer, a trainer from Wigan who danced for forty-five years recalled: 'we were out every weekend in the 80s. It was relentless. Saturday, Sunday and Monday if it was a bank holiday... You just put your money in your sock and went out on parade!'.[11]

However, by the mid-2000s, after having been the primary context for girls' morris performance for more than 100 years, troupe attendance at carnivals had declined dramatically. Starting in the 1990s, the community increasingly chose to abandon the town carnival circuit in favour of private competitions in indoor facilities. This shift from public to private is partly explained by the community's growing prioritisation of competition, which had begun to create logistical difficulties for carnival organisers as well as a desire amongst participants to ensure greater predictability of the performance space, including weather conditions. It also reflected a decline in the popularity of town carnivals more generally, as a wider range of leisure opportunities, rising costs and amplified planning regulations rendered the hosting of carnivals a less rewarding process. Today, a handful of carnival organisations, such as Liverpool's Trust, Respect Unity (TRU) and the Mid-Cheshire Independent Adjudicating Panel (MCIAP), continue to host occasional competitions at the remaining town carnivals, for example, in Prestwich and Southport, but these represent an exception within an otherwise indoor season.

Somewhat ironically, although carnival morris troupes are now rarely seen at public carnivals, it is fairly common to find North West morris dancing—as well as other styles of morris, including Cotswold, Border and Molly—performed at civic events, possibly reflecting an increasingly middle-class audience for outdoor festivals or perhaps a symptom of the ossification of divisions between display and competition morris dancing.

Competition

Girls' morris dancing is highly competitive. Routines are judged by up to nine accredited judges (called 'scrutineers') at competitions that are held weekly throughout the performance season from March to October. At the end of the year, a weekend-long championship event is staged at a residential holiday park, at which the prestigious 'Troupe of the Year' award is made. Marks are awarded for costume, appearance, timing, technique, dancing and deportment and troupes hone their routines throughout the season in response to the scrutineers' comments. By contrast, organised competitions no longer play a significant role in the English folk music scene, unlike in Scotland, Wales and Ireland. With the notable exceptions of the annual John Gasson jig competition, held at Sidmouth Folk Festival each August and the popular Dancing England Rapper Tournament (DERT) and Sam Sherry clog dance championship, most forms of folk- and morris dancing do not include a formal competitive element.

Girls' morris competitions are programmed by dedicated carnival organisations who provide adjudication, compering and prizes and hosted by a different troupe each week. Organisations each have their own set of regulations and troupes can select from a range of active groups according to their preferred skill level, preferred atmosphere and location.[12] While it is possible to belong to more than one organisation at a time, most teams choose to remain loyal to one in order to accumulate the necessary number of 'attendances' to be eligible to attend the popular 'End of Season Championships' held in September or October. Historically, large cross-carnival organisations would stage simultaneous competitions for all forms of carnival performance, but today only a few of the longest-running councils continue to provide multi-section events, such as MANECCO which primarily host competitions for entertainer troupes, but also has smaller contests for morris dancers and majorettes.

Weekly events comprise separate competitions for dancers of different age groups, from 'Babies' (dancers from 18 months and upwards), through 'Tinies', 'Dinkies' and 'Juniors' (primary and secondary-school-aged participants) to 'Seniors' (performers aged 18 and over), although not every troupe trains all lines simultaneously. Lines train separately within their home troupe and perform a distinct choreography with its own musical accompaniment and costume design. Since the mid-2000s, some larger organisations have multiple divisions within each age category such as the elite Platinum competition for the most skilful lines and the Diamond division for those newer to the performance. At the end of each event awards are made to the lines that have put in the best performance, with separate awards for the leader (who orchestrates the dancing) and mascot (a younger dancer whose choreography often mirrors that of the leader). Prizes are typically trophies and medals but historically, troupes competed for financial reward, as Samantha Hamer recalls: 'there was always good prize money…probably…£25…well £25 in 1965 was a lot of money!'.[13] In fact, at the 1897 Knutsford Royal May Day, the prizes awarded for morris dancing totalled anywhere between £1,300 and £1,800, when adjusted for contemporary pricing.[14]

For some scholars, such as Howison and Bentley, the long-time emphasis on competition in girls' morris dancing was problematic, representing a departure from purportedly authentic folk processes, as teams chose to 'discard the traditional figures which are considered too simple and to replace them with more grandiose evolutions'.[15] Maud Karpeles too argued that contests functioned to obscure girls' morris dancers' links to 'the traditional dance', opining that '[t]he performers, instead of adhering to the traditional mode of dancing, have been tempted to introduce new features and develop the dance on lines that are calculated to win the approbation of the judge and the audience…this has undoubtedly had an adverse affect [sic] on the dancing'.[16] However, historically competitions were not the exclusive domain of girls' morris troupes: prior to the incorporation of North West morris into the canon of English folk performance, competitions were also commonplace for men's and women's teams—as evidenced in team names like Horwich Prize Medal Morris Men from Bolton. At the same time as Roy Dommett—one of only a few twentieth-century morris historians to conduct fieldwork in the girls' morris dancing community—wrote of the performance in 1986, 'unlike all other traditions it not [sic] had to survive by being artificially encouraged by the 'Revival' or Folk Dancing or the EFDSS'.[17] As such, not only can we regard competition as an integral part of the North West morris tradition, but we might also hold it responsible for the flourishing girls' morris dancing community that continues into the present day. As Samantha Hamer explains, 'they all want to win! They always want to win!'.[18]

Although contests have been a consistent feature of girls' morris dancing for almost the length of its history, competition has also been one of the biggest drivers of change in the girls' morris community. 'The speed, the difficulty, the fitness…everything's got better!', says Samantha Hamer, of the last two decades of indoor competitions.[19] However, what some in the community view as an over-emphasis on penalty- or deficit-based adjudication, where troupes lose marks for any perceived faults in their performance as opposed to gaining them on the basis of their strengths has led some to question whether competition has had a net negative effect on the entertainment value and stylistic variety of performances. For example, many older dancers feel that choreographies have reduced in size, spatially, since the days of outdoor carnival displays, something that Lyn Booth attributes directly to the influence of increasingly strict application of organisation regulations: 'it was a case of what's on them cards. If you were being booked and losing points for spacing, spacing, spacing and lines…it's so much easier to all knit close'.[20] Even costume designs reveal the influence of adjudication: the voluminous bell sleeves now so characteristic of girls' morris dresses were initially introduced to help conceal the detail of dancers' arm movements from the judges' scrutiny. For some, a re-emphasis on entertaining the audience, as opposed to appeasing the judges, would be a welcome development: as Lyn Booth explained, 'I like to see them taking more chances. If they're playing it too safe, I don't tend to like it so much'.[21]

Geography

While the majority of revival morris styles can now be found throughout the UK—and sometimes internationally—girls' morris dancing still remains highly specific to its historical performance territories in the North West.[22] Confined almost entirely to Lancashire, Cheshire and North Wales, with just a handful of satellite troupes in the Peak District and West Midlands (see Figure 17.2), today's teams cluster around the large metropolitan

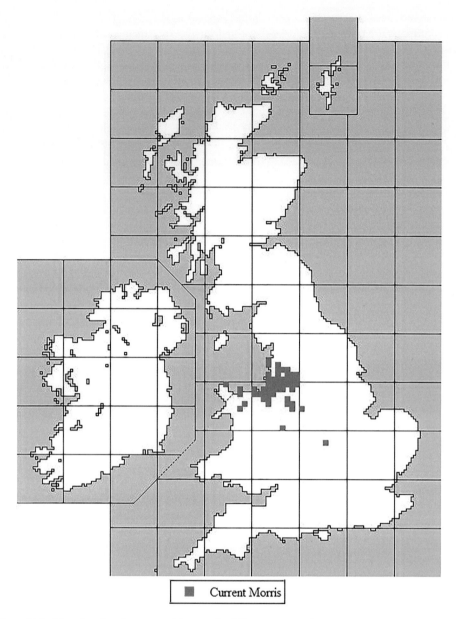

Figure 17.2 Map showing the geographic spread of all current morris troupes

Source: Reproduced with the kind permission of Peter Millington who prepared the maps, and Ian McKinnon, who supplied the data.

settlements in Manchester and Liverpool, with significant pockets of activity in Wigan, Warrington, Salford and Wrexham.

In spite of increased population mobility and a revolution in communications technologies which have enabled the spread of many formerly localised practices, the geography of girls' morris has actually contracted slightly in recent years (see Figure 17.3), probably as a result of the move away from (and overall reduction of) the town carnivals circuit and the decline

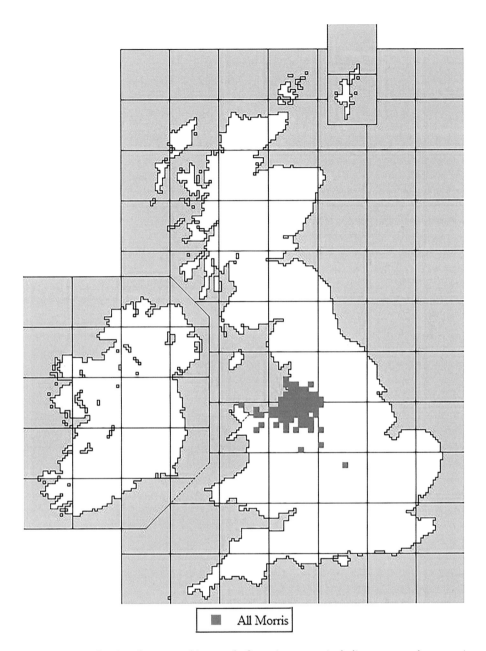

Figure 17.3 Map showing the geographic spread of morris troupes, including teams no longer active

of the large, multi-performance carnival organisations of the past. As the carnival incentive waned, participants' appetite for long-distance travel declined sharply and this, coupled with a steady increase in participant numbers, especially as the younger age divisions were introduced from the 1980s onwards, paved the way for the growth of an increased number of smaller, single-section organisations.[23] Today, the majority of events are highly localised and take place in out-of-town sports facilities and schools, with occasional showcases at popular destinations like Blackpool Tower Ballroom and championship weekends at residential holiday parks such as Pontins in Southport, however in the recent past, troupes travelled long distances for competitions, including attending overseas events held in Spain and the Isle of Man.

Although it is predominantly an urban phenomenon, girls' morris was historically a feature of rural life too, especially in Cheshire and Cumbria where village festivals, galas and rose days were popular annual occurrences. In fact, the acknowledged birthplace of the North West carnival movement is the Cheshire village of Knutsford whose famous Royal May Day celebration was attended by the Prince and Princess of Wales in 1887 (the future King Edward VII and Queen Consort Alexandra), giving the event its regal prefix. Many small parishes, such as Goostrey in Cheshire, gave rise to a succession of carnival teams, who performed locally and sometimes throughout the region, competing against troupes from towns and suburbs. Some teams, such as Lower Withington Morris Dancers in the 1950s–1960s, comprised both a Junior and a Senior division, and—unusual even then—admitted both male and female participants. Such was the appeal of belonging to a carnival troupe that some villages engendered multiple teams all active simultaneously, like Lymm (also in Cheshire) which from 1946 to 1950 had between three and five distinct groups of both morris dancers and entertainers, who often competed against each other at carnivals.[24]

The loss of many rural teams, beginning in the 1960s, is perhaps symptomatic of a wider shift in village demography and class. In addition to the well-documented loss of younger people and net in-migration of older people to an increasingly gentrified countryside, dancers travelling from the inner-cities to perform at rural fetes sometimes clashed with their hosts, in some instances even leading to a morris ban. In 1988, organisers of Goostrey Rose Day announced that girls' morris dancing would no longer be included in the festival programme, having been performed in the village since the 1890s. This decision prompted a petition signed by almost a quarter of the 1,000 local residents demanding its reinstitution within the carnival programme;[25] however, the chairperson of the organising committee was quick to remind people that 'these are not traditional folk dancers and are best compared with majorettes' also pointing to 'the entourage that comes with the dancers [which] has caused problems over the years'.[26] While folk revival morris had come to represent an increasingly middle-class pastime, girls' morris dancers from the towns and inner-cities were felt to represent an unpleasantly proletarian prospect. As Angela Snelson and Sheila Gregory, former members of Lower Withington Juniors recalled: 'somebody objected to the short skirts...it just wasn't the done thing in Goostrey'.[27]

Idealisation of the countryside and an accompanying mistrust of the destabilising influence of the towns has a long history in England, not least amongst many of the leading players of the early folk revival. It is well-recognised that performances associated with industrial areas historically received less attention than those from more rural regions, as Dan Howison and Bernard Bentley noted of North West morris dancing, 'if...[it] is less widely known than the Cotswold tradition, it is not because it died out long ago, but because it was not subjected to the detailed and systematic attention that Sharp devoted to the Cotswold dances'.[28] Indeed, early attempts to document folk performance in the UK virtually excluded industrialised areas, with collectors viewing towns as lacking in the historical depth and demographic stability to host an authentic folk repertoire. For girls' morris dancing this meant not only that its practices were rarely recorded or acknowledged, but also that its very urbanness was viewed as evidence that it had 'los[t] touch with its traditional roots'.[29] Commonly articulated as concern about the evolution of carnival performances in contrast to the perceivedly more consistent morris traditions of the folk revival, girls' morris represents an anomaly to all those whose conception of folk remains rooted in the image of the timeless rural idyll that Georgina Boyes envisaged as 'the imagined village'.[30]

Gender profile

Perhaps the most decisive way in which girls' morris challenges dominant assumptions about morris dancing is in its long history of female leadership. While a small number of boys and men have always been involved in the carnival community, for example holding pastoral roles as trainers, adjudicators and drivers, there are very few male dancers and the performance remains fundamentally female-identified and woman-led.[31] By contrast, the morris dancing associated with the English folk revival is commonly male-identified, in spite of a large influx of female participants since the 1970s. It was not until 2018, for example, that the oldest morris dancing organisation, The Morris Ring, began to admit women as full members for the first time.

However, the enduring perception of folk revival morris as a 'man's dance' is actually at odds with its present-day demographics.[32] The 2017 Morris Census revealed that women now make up 50% of all morris performers (not including girls' morris dancing), representing an increase of 4% since 2014.[33] Almost half of all modern teams are now mixed and 22% are all-female, leaving only 27% as men-only endeavours. In 2019, the BBC 4 documentary, *For Folk's Sake: Morris Dancing and Me* set out to learn 'what can save the male Morris dancer from extinction?', but women's increased participation does not herald the death of men's morris and nor is it a uniquely contemporary phenomenon.[34] In 1600 when Will Kemp morris-danced from London to Norwich, he performed alongside both 'a Mayde not passing 14 yeares of age' with whom he 'was soone wonne to fit her with belles'[35] and 'a lusty country lass' who 'had a good eare' and 'daunced truly', having 'shooke her fat sides, and footed it merrily to Melfoord, being a long myle'.[36] However three hundred years later, Cecil Sharp would denounce these events as part of a 'somewhat ridiculous and very un-Morris-like escapade', and in spite of the many female teachers and collectors involved in the first morris dancing revival in the early 1900s, women were largely discouraged from taking part in folk revival morris until the explosion of the women's morris movement in the 1970s and 1980s.[37]

If the presence of women in morris dancing's more distant past was downplayed by scholars in the first half of the twentieth century, then the role of men was far more fancifully envisaged. In 1928, the rural revivalist Rolf Gardiner posited the view that morris was 'an ancient, magical and priestly dance…employed to gain mastery over the living forces and potencies of the earth',[38] a belief which held traction for some years as part of the popular 'Survivals Theory' of folklore ascribed to Edward Tylor amongst others. Maud Karpeles, for instance, felt that men's North West morris dancing was 'like the Midland morris…of a ritual nature…performed by men only'.[39] Even Mary Neal, better known for her work promoting morris to young working-class women during the early 1900s, was later convinced 'in a devastating moment that these dances were the remains of a purely masculine ceremonial' and that she 'had quite innocently and ignorantly broken a law of cosmic ritual'.[40] Although Survivals Theory was roundly debunked in the years that followed by scholars, including Richard Dorson and Alan Dundes, Georgina Boyes suggests that it may be 'still flourishing in a number of areas of scholarship' as well as in the public imagination.[41]

While few appeared to question the male ownership of morris performances in the Midlands—the site of Cecil Sharp's portentous first encounter—the erasure of women's participation in morris is especially curious in the North West of England where all-female troupes had been commonplace since the 1890s. For many scholars and commentators, the existence of groups of women morris dancing could be explained only as derivation or imitation of an older, all-male form, possibly a result of decreased numbers of men during the two World Wars. Bernard Bentley, for example, viewed girls' morris as a fundamentally post-1950s phenomenon, citing the teaching of the (men's) Mobberley dance to a mixed-sex acrobatic group in Timperley in the mid-1920s, 'thus providing the impetus for 'hundreds of [girls'] troupes all over South Lancashire, Cheshire and North Wales'.[42] However, when Janet Chart and Lesley Edwards conducted their survey of morris dancing in Cheshire they found no evidence to substantiate the claim that women only became involved in morris after the wars, writing 'it is inaccurate to regard females as being used as a last resort where there was a shortage of men as we have evidence of female teams pre-dating male morris teams…this phenomenon is not just a novelty of the 1950s and beyond'.[43]

In fact, women were sometimes the earlier bearers of the morris dancing tradition, as in Robert Chambers description of the 1869 Buxton Well Dressing which states that 'formerly they were little girls dressed in muslin, but as this was considered objectionable, they have been replaced by young men gaily decorated with ribbons, who come dancing down the hill'[44] More than a century later, Pruw Boswell argued that the ultra-masculine revival of North West morris dancing from the 1960s onwards drew heavily on an older tradition associated with children (both boys and girls), writing: 'it is worth noting here that both the dances from Lancaster were originally danced by a team of children…and both had to be re-choreographed and re-named before they became suitable for performance by the men'.[45] And in the 1980s when historian Sue Allan sought information about carnival dances in Cumbria, historically performed by girls and young women (including her grandmother) she discovered that the records lay in the hands of a male morris side whose archivist was unwilling to share them with the 'instigators of women's morris'.[46] The fierce ideological battles provoked by the rise of the women's morris movement in this period must surely go a long way to explaining why girls' morris dancing—already functioning at a remove from the English folk revival—lacked attention and advocacy during the latter stages of the twentieth century.

Conversely, while carnivals historically provided the setting for performances by both men and women, the status of performance as an all-female pastime may have become even more firmly entrenched within the community itself. Appearance, always paramount in girls' morris performance, has become increasingly gender normative with widespread use of pink, glitter and sequins in modern troupe costume designs (although visible make-up is still banned by most carnival organisations).[47] The performance is also yet to experience a comparable surge in the number of male participants, something many involved in the movement would prefer to remain unchallenged. As former dancer and parent, Michelle Grocot explained, 'it's quite frowned upon really in our organisation. It's not a boy thing…I'm not saying that dancing's not for boys, but this kind of dancing's not for boys'.[48] Others suggested that all-male teams would be welcome, but that mixed teams interfered with the uniformity upon which the performances rely. However, there is some precedent for morris troupes comprising both male and female dancers, such as Goostrey- and Lower Withington Morris Dancers in Cheshire, who competed against all-female teams until the early 1960s, and a handful of entertainer and majorette troupes—and many jazz bands—are open to all.[49]

Generational spread

Girls' morris dancing is a markedly intergenerational practice. Dancers typically begin training at a very young age, sometimes performing in their first competitions long before they start school, and many continue to compete throughout their primary and secondary education. There is no upper age limit for belonging to a girls' morris Senior line, but as dancers opt to 'retire' from competitive performance, there are a range of options to stay involved in the performance at a pastoral level, and many former dancers choose to raise their own children, grandchildren and even great-grandchildren—in the community. By contrast, folk revival morris has gained a reputation as an older person's pursuit, in spite of the emergence of new sides with a strong youth involvement, as many of those performers who took up the practice during the revivals of the 1950s and 1970s were not replaced in similar numbers by younger dancers. Although cyclical media outcry that the performance is 'dying out' are almost always unfounded,[50] it is clear that the core demographics of many teams have changed significantly since the 'young men gaily decorated with ribbons who came dancing down the hill' were described in 1869.[51]

There are few such concerns for the girls' morris dancing community: if anything, participants appear to be getting both younger…and older! The introduction of the 'Dinkies' competition in the late 1980s (for dancers aged approximately 6–8 years) followed in the 90s by competitions for 'Tinies' (aged 9–12) and 'Babies' (18 months to 5 years) have opened the performance to large numbers of very young dancers. At the same time, an increasing number of older performers are electing to compete well into their 40s, 50s and beyond. For example, in 2019, Platt Bridge Morris Dancers entered a Senior line popularly nicknamed 'the Chicks' (short for 'Spring Chickens') in reference to the higher than average age of those participating. Their leader, Annmarie Clossett made her first outing as Platt Bridge Senior leader in 1987 aged 20.

Girls' morris is also notable for its primarily matrilineal structure. Not only do many teams comprise one or more family groups, including mothers, sisters, cousins and aunts, but participants also commonly refer to the members of their troupe as a second 'family', reflecting the close ties between participants whether or not they are related. Older members of the troupe sometimes receive honorary terms of address, such as 'Mum' or 'Nana' as markers of affection and respect from the younger dancers. In fact, the concept of the family represents an important metaphor within the girls' morris dancing community, used to express kinship not just between members of a single line or troupe, but with members of other troupes and organisations too. For example, 'the Carnival Family' is often invoked to refer to the close ties felt between participants of different carnival performance styles, such as entertaining and majorettes. This appeal to a sense of family—both as a mode of transmission and set of shared values—is arguably comparable to the use of 'tradition' elsewhere in the folk arts, however where tradition is sometimes mis-equated with conservatism and stasis, the notion of the 'family' offers a generative alternative, based on evolution and adaptation to the needs of new generations of performers.[52]

Choreography

Girls' morris teams perform a single, newly choreographed routine each year. Dances are devised at the start of the performance season and discontinued at its end and troupes rarely, if ever, revisit old routines in their entirety: few complete records are formally kept. This is in marked contrast to the wide repertoires of most folk revival morris groups who usually draw on a number of different local styles predominantly recorded in the early part of the twentieth century by folk dance collectors such as Cecil Sharp, Maud Karpeles and Mary Neal. Although some figures like the 'cross', 'block' and 'reverse semi' have long been in use by carnival performers, modern troupes are equally, if not more likely to invent original formations and features to help distinguish their performance from others on the arena.

Figure 17.4 Platt Bridge Juniors lining up before a performance at Blackpool Winter Gardens, 2019
Source: Photograph with permission, copyright the author.

Girls' morris performances typically follow a similar basic format at competitions, largely prescribed by organisational rules. First the troupe enter the arena and form a single line, usually straight, but sometimes on a right angle, while the leader sets the pace of the musical accompaniment using a variable-speed stereo (Figure 17.4). An adjudicator examines the dancers' costumes, awarding marks for design and deducting them for issues of cleanliness, fit and wear-and-tear. Once the leader is satisfied with the timings, they take their place at the head of the line and the music starts. The leader claps their hands (or bangs a tambourine) and the troupe rise onto their toes and march, with high knees and pointed toes. After 16 steps, the leader signals with raised or outstretched arms and the troupe seamlessly move into the triple step, which will be the only step, other than the march, to be performed throughout the routine. The dancers move through a series of geometric formations for six or seven minutes before converging back into their line, now facing in the opposite direction.[53] The leader signals one last time to indicate that the troupe should perform their final arm movements (known as 'arm-works'). Once completed, the performance ends and the dancers sink back onto their heels and leave the arena, rarely taking their applause. Although troupes align themselves spatially on the arena in relation to the judge's table, there is no fixed front of stage with the audience seated in the round. For this reason, some adjudicators, like Ian McKinnon from the English Town and Country Carnival Organisation (ETACCO) suggests that performances are best viewed aerially.

Highly precise stepping and arm movements are a distinguishing feature of girls' morris performances, not just for the extreme synchronicity of their execution, but also for their unceasing nature within choreographies: stepping is fast and relentless, and once a routine has begun, no member stops moving until it is complete. Perhaps the most important step used in all performances is the march, as this is the first that most dancers learn and is shared by performers across the 'carnival world', although stylistic differences can be observed, particularly in entertainer troupes and jazz bands. Most girls' morris dancing organisations hold separate marching contests at the end of the team competitions for each age group, and choreographies are book-ended with a section of marching, a reminder of the step's significance in carnival processions and street parades.

In addition to the march, two other steps are employed in girls' morris performances, albeit only one per routine. These are the pas-de-bas (also known as the 'pardy') and 'kick-out' steps, both of which are strongly reminiscent of the 'rant'.[54] Today, the pas-de-bas is preferred by most troupes: good technique involves the dancers touching their kneecap (or raising their foot to kneecap height) with the opposite foot at the start of every downward step. The kick-out is less widely used and involves the same triplet rhythm, but with an added lift or kick from the non-supporting foot.[55] Prior to the 2000s, many troupes routinely trained in both pas-de-bas and kick-out steps, with dancers graduating to the kick-out when they entered the Senior line. However, most lines now prefer to focus on a single step for consistency of training: as Samantha Hamer recalled, '[in the 1960s] we were brought up doing both[…]but when our Juniors came up, they couldn't really do it, so we thought it'd be easier for those of us who could do both to just do the pardy'.

The aim of girls' morris performance is to achieve the closest possible uniformity between members of a team. A flawless performance is one in which it is impossible to discern any differences in timing or spacing between dancers and the line moves as a single, cohesive unit. This effect is markedly different from many folk revival morris dances, which usually involve varying degrees of uniformity: for example, rapper teams exhibit fairly high levels of synchronicity between members, while Border and Molly (and to a lesser extent, Cotswold and North West) often permit greater diversity in both choreography and costume. It has been suggested that the close synchronicity that is an essential feature of girls' morris dancing might be traced to a Victorian movement to create conformity and obedience in working-class children,[56] but it is important to note that in spite of their presentational uniformity, modern troupes foster high levels of creative agency in participants who typically play an important role in choreographing their routines in collaboration with their trainers. Although girls' morris dancing does not permit individual interventions in costume or stepping, all members are encouraged to contribute to the devising and execution of a performance, often leading to quite significant innovations in the form.

Musical accompaniment

Girls' morris performances are dynamised by an energetic soundtrack of recorded music, often played at high volume and rapid speed. Pop hits past and present, tunes from the shows and movie themes—in fact almost anything with a strong beat—might be heard over the speakers at competitions. This form of electrified, recorded accompaniment represents quite a difference from the live, acoustic music performed by folk revival morris musicians. However, girls' morris dancing's approach to musical accompaniment closely mirrors developments in music technology and plays an important role in the evolution of the performance across generations.

Recorded music has been a feature of girls' morris dancing for many decades, troupes historically performing to a live musical accompaniment, usually played by a brass band. Regimental marching tunes such as 'The Old Ninety-Five', 'Light of Foot' and '100 Pipers' were popular choices in the 1940s and 1950s, for their stirring quality and regular rhythm which helped to guide foot placement. In street parades, troupes typically marched in time to whichever band was closest to them, but the formal display was usually accompanied by an 'in-house' carnival band provided by the organisers. Some teams, like Goostrey Morris, under trainer, Elsie Maddock, provided musicians with a score to perform, but others such as Lower Withington Senior Morris preferred to use a regular accordionist who travelled with them to competitions, while the Marionnettes from Golborne in Wigan made an arrangement with a local brass band who practised in the same venue.

The switch to recorded music appears to have begun as early as the 1950s, in response to the unpredictable quality and availability of live musicians at carnivals. As John Ryder recalled: 'music was always a bit of a contention [...] At competitions sometimes there was a brass band, but they couldn't always play the music you wanted... I remember we had a vinyl record made [...] performed by a local brass band [...] so we could take it around with us'. However, vinyl records brought their own challenges: 'PA systems developed so you could play vinyls, but they were never at the right speed and you couldn't adjust it!'. Samantha Hamer also remembers using vinyl records as a dancer in the 1960s and 1970s: 'it used to be a record player with adjustable speed. They used to go the end of the track that you'd chosen and then the man used to lift it off and put it back again...' Unfortunately, record players were also no match for the inclement Lancashire weather and records frequently skipped or even blew off the turntable in particularly poor climactic conditions. Later, troupes would switch to other modes of recording technology—cassette tapes, CDs and most recently, MP3s—to ensure their routines could always be reproduced whatever the venue, and variable-speed media players allow dancers to set the pace, depending on their level of fitness and preference.

Musical selection has also loosely followed trends in popular music. Even as early as the 1920s, Margaret Ormrod recalls that bands 'would try to play what was popular then'.[57] Samantha Hamer remembers dancing to Klaus Wunderlich and Lieutenant Pigeon in the 1970s (especially the song 'Mouldy Old Doe'), Rick Astley and John Paul Young in the 1980s and Jean Michel Jarre in the 1990s and early 2000s.[58] Recent selections at competitions have included tracks by Beyoncé, Katy Perry and Nicki Minaj, as well as tunes from musicals, such as 'La Cage Aux Folles' and The Greatest Showman'. However, a number of perennial favourites from the carnivals can still be heard alongside more contemporary records, suggesting that continuity and even nostalgia still have a role in the contemporary world of girls' morris dancing. Patriotic songs like 'Scotland the Brave' and pub classics like 'I'll Tell Me Ma' and 'Campbeltown Loch' remain popular choices for some, especially long-running troupes.

Although not everyone in today's girls' morris community appreciate the use of modern pop music, many view it is an important aspect of safeguarding the performance's popularity into the future. As a number of troupes report struggles to retain older children and teenagers, 'I think the music's helped', Samantha says, 'it helps the girls to dance to something that they know'. In this way, while the specific songs and tunes may not be 'traditional', their popularity and the shared experiences they enable are integral to this tradition's process of 'carrying on'.[59]

Is girls' morris really other?

The contemporary practice of girls' morris dancing undoubtedly presents a challenge to some of the dominant assumptions from and about the English folk revival. On the one hand, the carnival community's emphasis on formal competitions, use of recorded music and glamorous, sequinned costumes seem to render the performance demonstrably 'other' than the morris dances many are more familiar with. On the other hand, it is impossible to deny formal and historical links between girls' morris and other types of North West morris dancing, and by association with the wider morris world to which North West morris is now allied. Put simply, if North West morris is considered to be a 'traditional' dance, then girls' morris dancing should be too.

At the core of girls' morris dancing's 'otherness' are three main conceits which I argue have shaped the canon of English folk performance that we have inherited today. First, as we have seen, the practices of urban dwellers were generally perceived to be less valuable and authentic than those of their rural counterparts, at least during the foundational years of the first folk revival. Cities and towns were felt to lack the population stability and historical depth to support meaningful traditions and as such, contemporary revivalists and scholars have access to fewer materials from and about industrial communities. Second, girls' morris represents one of only a very few examples of female-led folk practices. The paucity of female-identified dance traditions and calendar customs reflects a lack of adequate recognition afforded to women's practices rather than any absence of activity, and one only need look back to the fierce debates that erupted in response to the women's morris movement in the 1970s and 1980s to understand how powerfully an exclusionary patriarchal model informed understandings of tradition and cultural value, the impacts of which we are still coming to terms with. Finally, girls' morris dancing employs a markedly open and generative approach to transmission and continuity, resulting in a performance that looks and feels distinctly modern. That it has been able to adapt to new generations of performers has been key to the survival and continued popularity of the performance in the twenty-first century and it is notable that although the term 'tradition' is rarely used by girls' morris participants, the comparable notion of 'family' is routinely invoked, hinting towards a conception of change and renewal that speaks to the organic, the relational, even the feminine? These three factors do not necessarily make girls' morris fundamentally different from other folk performances—if anything, they perhaps offer a suggestion of how many other traditional practices may have functioned prior to being subsumed by the ideological narratives of the folk revival—but their implications certainly contribute to a distancing effect in the present day.

It would probably be fair to say that the sense of otherness ascribed here to girls' morris dancing in the context of the folk revival may be felt equally on both sides of the divide. I often recall a conversation with members of a girls' morris troupe near Liverpool in which the secondary-school-aged dancers refused to believe that men's morris truly existed, asking, 'do they wear lace socks like ours?!' and laughing uproariously as they imitated men clumsily lifting their knees and pointing their feet. It is not my intention here to suggest that girls' morris dancers need to become better acquainted with the morris performances of the folk revival (unless they want to), but there are some important reasons why I believe that unpicking—and ultimately addressing—the neglect of girls' morris in the folk revival is critical to the future of folk and its scholarship. A big claim? Perhaps, but intentionally or otherwise, the folk movement has long been a gatekeeper and arbiter of the narratives around 'tradition' and 'authenticity' which have served to embrace some and exclude others. While both the folk revival and the carnival movement lack broad mainstream visibility, girls' morris dancing suffers from additional intersectional issues around gender and class, typically lacking the cultural capital of what has become a comfortably middle-class folk scene. If you do not believe me, consider, for example, how men's morris dancing is widely recognised—albeit grudgingly—as a 'symbol of nationhood'[60] while the communities in which girls' morris dancing is practised are more often designated as 'hard-to-reach' or even 'culturally non-participant'.[61]

I believe it is the responsibility of the folk scene to address this imbalance and to consider its wider implications. Firstly, the case of girls' morris dancing underscores the fact that more needs to be done to recover the voices of women and other marginalised groups within the history of the folk movement. The roots of such gender biases can be traced with reference to the pan-European folk revival of the late nineteenth century and they have created a canon which is both arbitrary and disproportionately skewed in favour of white, cis-male practices.⁶² Particularly pertinent to girls' morris dancing, there is an urgency to record the histories of female-identified performances while so much remains in living memory, and to search for the women hidden between the lines of folk performance scholarship. We need to support movements like Fair Plé in the Irish scene and Femfolk in the UK to ensure that the opportunity gap that currently exists for female participants, particularly in folk dance and calendar customs, is closed as soon as possible.

Secondly, if we recognise girls' morris dancing's claim to inclusion in the canon of English folk dance—which I hope to have persuaded that it deserves—such recognition might also prompt us to clarify (again) our working-definition of 'folk'. There is a tendency to perceive folk collection as a limited and already-completed project, no longer relevant or viable in present-day Britain. However, this relies on an outmoded—even colonial—reading of tradition, limited to the practices and customs *of the past*, or elsewhere in the world, discouraging us from looking with an open mind at the activities taking place right outside our doors. Girls' morris dancing reminds us that traditions do not have to *appear* old to *be* old. They do not have to be male-identified, or take place in remote, rural locations, or represent the domain of the 'unlettered peasant'.⁶³ They do not even have to employ the language of tradition to enact it on a daily basis. Girls' morris is not a folk revival performance, but it is traditional nonetheless and it is its otherness—its distance from the rest of the morris dancing world—that makes it so exciting and significant. In paying greater attention to our living traditions, whether or not they identify as 'folk', we are offered a chance to witness at first-hand the evolution of people's performances outside of the ideological frameworks of the folk movement.

Notes

1. Women's participation in cheerleading first started in the 1920s and only became mainstream in the 1940s and 1950s. Prior to this, it had been a men-only activity involving clapping and rhythmic chants. See Natalie Adams and Pamela Bettis, *Cheerleader! An American Icon* (New York: Palgrave, 2003), p. 118.
2. Daisy Bowie-Sell, 'Morris Dancing Isn't Just about Ale, Beer Bellys and Beards', *The Telegraph*, 2011, unpaginated.
3. This motto was coined by Angela Bacon of Orcadia Morris Dancers from Skelmersdale in West Lancashire and adorns the team's branded tracksuits and hoodies.
4. Jack Worth, 'Morris Census: Full Set of Survey Results', *Morris Census: Insights on Morris Dancing in the 21st Century*, 2017 <https://morriscensus.weebly.com> [accessed 2 April 2018].
5. Ruth Finnegan, *The Hidden Musicians: Music-Making in an English Town* (Middletown, CT: Wesleyan University Press, 2007).
6. Town carnival movement is a colloquial term used by some older members of the girls' morris dancing community. Lucy Wright, 'Girls' Carnival Morris Dancing and Contemporary Folk Dance Scholarship', *Folklore*, 128.2 (2017), 157–174 (p. 158).
7. Mikhail Bakhtin, *Rabelais and His World*, trans. by Hélène Iswolsky (Bloomington: Indiana University Press, 1965); Julia Kristeva, *Desire in Language: A Semiotic Approach to Literature and Art* (New York: Columbia University Press, 1969).
8. During this period, 'morris dancing' appears to have been a generic term to describe a range of dances, including by single-sex and mixed groups of men, women and children. Theresa Jill Buckland and Dan Howison, 'Morris Dancers in Crewe before the First World War', *English Dance and Song*, 42.2 (1980), 10–13 (pp. 11, 10).
9. Leslie Edwards and Janet Chart, 'Aspects of Morris Dancing in Cheshire 1880-1914', *English Dance and Song*, 1981, 5–10 (p. 8).
10. Lyn Booth, Interview between Lyn Booth and Lucy Wright, 2012.
11. Samantha Hamer, Interview between Samantha Hamer and Lucy Wright, 2012.

12. To some extent, this mirrors the social role of organisations such as The Morris Ring, The Morris Federation and Open Morris (as well as The North American Morris Dance Organization in the US), albeit without a formal competitive function.
13. Hamer.
14. With thanks to Duncan Broomhead for this information.
15. Dan Howison and Bernard Bentley, 'The North-West Morris—a General Survey', *Journal of the English Folk Dance and Song Society*, 9.1 (1986), 42–55 (p. 46).
16. Maud Karpeles, *The Lancashire Morris Dance: Containing a Description of the Royton Morris Dance* (London: English Folk Dance Society, 1930), p. 5.
17. Roy Dommett, *Roy Dommett's Morris Notes* (Easthampton, MA: CDSS of America, 1986), p. 5.
18. Hamer.
19. Hamer.
20. Booth.
21. Booth.
22. The same can also be said of other carnival performance styles, with the exception of majorette baton-twirling which has long represented a global phenomenon. Jazz marching bands continue to be found primarily in the former coal mining areas of Tyneside, the West Midlands and South Wales and 'entertaining' is almost exclusively practised in Staffordshire with a small number of troupes located in nearby Shropshire and North Wales.
23. This contraction of the performance region might also hint that in spite of currently robust numbers, girls' morris may be struggling to attract new members.
24. In Lymm, four carnival dance troupes, Broomedge Morris Dancing Troupe, The Lymmtonians, The Lymmtoinettes and Pamela Stars, all formed in the years immediately following the end of the Second World War. Geoff Bibby, 'A Brief History of Morris Dancing in the Lymm Area', 2016 <http://www.lymm-morris.org.uk/history/brief/brief-history.html>. Today, although none of these troupes are still running, Lymm is one of only a few rural villages to boast both a girls' morris troupe, Lymm Adivas formed in 2014, and a men's revival side, Lymm Morris Men.
25. Duncan Broomhead, 'Goostrey Morris Dancers – A Journey to the Carnival', *Morris Matters*, 2019, 1–10.
26. Undated newspaper clipping from Sheila Gregory's personal scrapbook.
27. Sheila Gregory and Angela Snelson, Interview: Lower Withington Junior Morris Dancers, 2016.
28. Howison and Bentley, 'The North-West Morris', p. 42.
29. Howison and Bentley, 'The North-West Morris', p. 44.
30. Georgina Boyes, *The Imagined Village: Culture, Ideology and the English Folk Revival* (Leeds: No Masters Co-Operative, 2010).
31. A similar gender profile is found across the carnival world: although many modern jazz marching bands now comprise both male and female participants, they were previously the predominant domain of girls and young women and there are still only a handful of male entertainers and majorettes.
32. Cecil James Sharp, *Folk Dancing in Schools* (Taunton, 1913), p. 12.
33. Worth, 'Morris Census'. The percentage would be much higher if girls' morris were to be included in the calculations.
34. Richard Macer, 'For Folk's Sake: Morris Dancing and Me' (BBC, 2019). <https://www.bbc.co.uk/programmes/m0003vhz>.
35. Will Kemp, *Kemps Nine Daies Wonder. Performed in a Daunce from London to Norwich…Written by Himselfe* (London, 1600), p. 7 <https://www.bl.uk/collection-items/will-kemps-nine-days-wonder-1600>.
36. Ibid. p. 10.
37. John Cutting, *History and the Morris Dance: A Look at Morris Dancing from It's Earliest Days until 1850* (Binsted: Dance Books Ltd., 2005), p. 16.
38. Rolf Gardiner, 'Summer Tour in Germany, 1928', *North Sea and Baltic*, 4 (1938), p. 101.
39. Ibid., p. 6.
40. Mary Neal, 'The Broken Law', *Adelphi*, 16 (1940), 147–150 (pp. 149–150).
41. Boyes, *The Imagined Village*, p. 199.
42. Bernard Bentley, 'Collectors' Corner: The Lancashire and Cheshire Carnival "Morris"', *English Dance and Song*, 23.3 (1959), 65–68 (p. 65).
43. Edwards and Chart, 'Aspects of Morris Dancing', p. 7.

44 Robert Chambers, *The Book of Days: A Miscellany of Popular Antiquities in Connection with the Calendar, Including Anecdote, Biography, & History, Curiosities of Literature and Oddities of Human Life and Character* (Edinburgh and London: W.R Chambers, 1869), p. 819.
45 Pruw Boswell, 'The Lancashire Legacy', in *Morris: The Legacy of the Past, Proceedings of a One-Day Conference on Morris Dancing, Held Saturday April 20th 1996 at Birmingham and Midland Institute, Birmingham Organised by The Morris Federation, The Morris Ring, Open Morris*, 1996, pp. 111–15 (p. 111).
46 In the personal archive of Sue Allan.
47 Lucy Wright, 'Making Traditions: Girls' Carnival Morris Dancing and Material Practice', *Yearbook for Traditional Music*, 49.1 (2017), 26–47.
48 Michelle Grocot, Interview between Michelle Grocot and Lucy Wright, 2016.
49 Howison and Bentley, 'The North-West Morris', p. 44.
50 Richard Savill, 'Morris Dancing "Could Die out If Young Blood Not Recruited Soon"', *The Telegraph*, 2008, unpaginated.
51 Chambers, *The Book of Days*, p. 819.
52 Lucy Wright, '"What a Troupe Family Does": Family as Transmission Narrative in the British Carnival Troupe Dancing Community', *Dance Research*, 37.1 (2019), 35–58 <https://doi.org/10.3366/drs.2019.0252>.
53 Minimum time requirements in place at most organisations, usually approximately six minutes for Junior and Senior lines and five minutes for the younger age brackets.
54 In his handbook on the judging of girls' morris troupes, Ian McKinnon also lists two more steps, the 'down step' and the 'kick forward' or 'donkey step', but these are rarely seen in contemporary girls' morris performances. Ian McKinnon, 'Fluffy Morris, or the Art of Judging Carnival Display Morris Troupes', 2003.
55 A team who notably still use the kick-out step is Platt Bridge Morris Dancers from Wigan.
56 Theresa Jill Buckland, 'Institutions and Ideology in the Dissemination of Morris Dances in the Northwest of England', *Yearbook for Traditional Music*, 23.1 (1991), 53–67 (p. 58) <https://doi.org/10.2307/768396>.
57 Interview between Peter Bearon and Margaret Ormrod, Miss Ditchfields Dancers, 1997.
58 Hamer.
59 *Creativity and Cultural Improvisation*, ed. by Elizabeth Hallam and Tim Ingold (New York: Berg 3PL, 2008), p. 6.
60 Trish Winter and Simon Keegan-Phipps, *Performing Englishness: Identity and Politics in a Contemporary Folk Resurgence* (Manchester: Manchester University Press, 2015), p. 116.
61 Create London, *Panic! What Happened to Social Mobility in the Arts?* (London: Create London, 2015); Chrissie Tiller, *Power Up*, Creative People and Places (London: Arts Council England, 2017).
62 *The Voice of the People: Writing the European Folk Revival, 1760–1914*, ed. by Matthew Campbell and Michael Perraudin (London: Anthem Press, 2013).
63 David Atkinson, *The Anglo-Scottish Ballad and Its Imaginary Contexts* (Cambridge: Open Book, 2014), p. 98.

PART III

Folk song and music

Steve Roud

While 'folk' song and music are undoubtedly part of the wider field of 'folklore', in that they are examples of the home-made unofficial culture of 'the people', there are a number of fundamental aspects which set them apart from other genres. Unlike customs, for example, which are usually restricted both in time of performance and in level of participation, it was the sheer *everydayness* of song (and therefore music) in the past that marks it out, but, paradoxically, makes it so difficult to define and to come to grips with.

As far back as we have records, nearly everybody sang – to themselves and each other, around the home, at work, in the pub, in the playground, at gatherings, after formal dinners, while travelling and so on.

In addition, folk song and music, like social dance, have a much closer relationship to other nominal categories within the wider culture, making it impossible to draw strict lines of demarcation between it and, for example, 'popular' and 'elite' forms. As will be seen, it is often the performer, the style, the social context or even how the performer learnt a song, that marks it as 'folk', rather than the song itself.

Song and music, again like dance, have also been subject to widespread 'revivals', not just of academic interest, but of popular performance. The first great Revival took place in the two decades before the First World War, while the second began in the early 1950s, and is still with us. Folk song and music thus became social *movements* with conflicting agendas, factions, leaders and followers, and even became subject to the vagaries of the music industry, and other 'outside' influences.

In consequence, folk music continues to have an appreciable effect on many people's perceptions of music in society. In the long run, however, folk songs may not have changed the cultural landscape very much, but it can be argued that the cultural landscape has changed folk song beyond recognition.

Revivals are always selective about what gets continued, and what gets changed, invented or forgotten. It is very difficult for newcomers to the field to understand just how different things are today to how they were in, say, 1900 or even 1950, but we still want to call it by the same name.

As will be seen, it is no exaggeration to suggest that modern 'folk' performance, as experienced by most people, is the exact opposite of what would have been recognised by the pioneer collectors of Victorian and Edwardian times. Key features such as folk groups, harmony singing, instrumental accompaniment (especially guitars), musical arrangements, rehearsals, careers, payment, recorded sound, fame outside the immediate community, festivals, concerts and folk clubs have all been introduced in relatively recent years, as 'folk' has become a choice among many musical styles on offer.

Definitions

There is no clear-cut watertight definition of 'folk music', and anyone who needs such a thing, and cannot cope with ambiguity, is warned to avoid the subject of the definition of folk song (or any other kind of music, for that matter).

The problems start with the very name. A significant number of researchers in the field long ago rejected the word 'folk', because of its cultural baggage, and have preferred to talk about 'traditional', 'vernacular' and so on, but these terms have not caught on with the general public, so we have decided to stick with the common word and face its ambiguity as best we can.

But the songs and tunes we are concerned with here have definitely existed, and appear to have had unique characteristics, and to discuss and understand them, and to find out why, we need to talk of categories and agree what is in our remit, and what outside. At all times grounding our perspective on what is or was there, rather than what we want to be there.

The key to unlocking folk song and music is to understand that the discussion needs to take account of much more than just the songs and tunes themselves, and the four main facets, or broad areas of analysis, are *repertoire*, *style*, *personnel* and *context*. These four are reflected in the choice of chapters for this section of this book.

Each of these facets can be sub-divided, of course, and they do not function in isolation. Context, for example, can be seen as pertinent within the community involved, or on a wider social scale. Function, which would be part of context, is clear in certain categories of song, such as a sea shanty or lullaby, but less obvious in a pub sing-song, where community cohesion might be one of the hidden results.

Above all, the essence of 'folk' as a concept is that it is more of a process than a 'thing'. Folk is as folk does.

And, as if all these qualifications were not enough, the timeframe is crucial. Not only do the usual suspects in historical societal change matter a great deal – urbanisation, education, literacy, economic growth – but also developments much closer to our topic, such as the steady rise of commercial popular entertainment. We ignore the timeframe and wider cultural context at our peril.

Before the folk

The basic outline of the development of a consciousness of 'folk' song and music is relatively well documented,[1] and relatively uncontentious, but its *meaning*, value, and whether or not it was a good thing, are hotly debated, now more than ever. Indeed, any folk enthusiast from between the wars would be astonished at how politicised the academic debate has become.

The publication of Bishop Thomas Percy's *Reliques of Ancient English Poetry*, in 1765, is usually cited as the key moment in the development of folklore study. This book was one of the major British contributions to the development of the Europe-wide Romantic movement which changed the face of poetry, art and music for generations to come, and often went hand-in-hand with nationalist movements, in places which needed to assert their national or cultural identity. These people often started by turning to their 'folk' music and culture to find that identity.

In England, as elsewhere, through the nineteenth century, various individuals became interested in aspects of the song and music which could be described as 'popular', in the sense of being 'of the people'. Three main threads are discernible, often distinct but sometimes combined: *literary* (interested mainly in the words, as examples of poetry); *musical* and *local* (concerned with the geographical area and its distinctive culture). And the one constant overarching feature was a growing interest in the twin notions of antiquity and 'heritage'.

For the antiquarians, the past was interesting in its own right; for the 'romantics', the past was better than their current time, and an antidote to corrupt modernism and popular culture.

These threads came together in various ways, but for our purposes the most significant step was the discovery (or some would say invention) of 'the folk', towards the end of the nineteenth century.

The discovery of the folk

The terms 'folk song' and 'folk music' were theoretically available from 1846, with the coining of the word 'folk-lore', but although occasionally used (usually to denote foreign traditions) from the 1850s, they did not catch on straightaway, and most of the key pre-1900 publications avoided the word 'folk' in their titles.[2]

But these books were essential in that they moved the focus from simply 'old' songs to a notion that there existed a definable category of song and music which had been passed on down the generations, relatively free of commercial, foreign and educated influence, and that this material was not only aesthetically pleasing in its simplicity and naivety, but that it represented the musical soul of the nation itself.

Furthermore, the place to find this material was in the mouths of 'the people', or rather one particular segment of 'the people', and not in books of previous eras which only told us about the music of the middle and upper classes. This was the real watershed moment.

The genesis and development of this idea is too complex to investigate fully here, but two major threads can be discerned. In large part, it was a reaction to the dominance of European nations in classical music, particularly Germany, and the regular jibe from continental writers that England was 'the land without music'.[3] But it was also born of a horror of the 'popular' music of the time in the shape of the musical hall of the working classes and the parlour ballads of the piano-playing middle sort, and a distaste for the developing mass popular culture of the period.

It is crucial to understand this latter point. It explains why the collectors felt they were on a mission – real folk music was rapidly being destroyed by the onslaught of mass media pop music as much as by urbanisation and education.

And so 'the folk' were discovered, and they turned out to be, in the main, the ill-educated, elderly rural poor. Elderly because the music was deemed to be dying out, and could only be found on the lips of people born long before compulsory education; rural because geographically and socially protected from modernism and contamination by urban mass culture.

There is no doubt that in their enthusiasm, the collectors exaggerated their singers' lack of education, sophistication and access to the wider culture of their time, and gave the impression that true folk song existed only in the care of 'illiterate peasants'. But on the broad scale they were not completely wrong, nor disingenuous. It is largely a matter of degree. At a time of rapid urbanisation, there certainly was a dichotomy between urban and rural cultures, with the latter being seen as 'backward'. And the old style of home-made singing was indeed dying out in the face of new forms of entertainment, with people increasingly getting their musical pleasure from commercial outlets, where they listened to music rather than made it themselves. Setting, repertoire, style were changing dramatically, unevenly, but inexorably.

The collectors had the lived experience, as well as the blinkers, of their time and place, and sorting one from the other is the ofttimes difficult job of the historian.

Collecting the folk

The development which ushered in the modern idea of 'folk' song and music came with the foundation of the Folk Song Society in 1898. Despite its slow start, and underlying unsureness of its role, the Society created a new era of active collecting, and by 1914 a huge amount of material had been written down and published, and was starting to provide inspiration for fans of the English Musical Renaissance and also to filter into the concert-hall repertoires and home piano-stools.

Folk music was in the air, reported and discussed in the national press, and many people caught the bug and made small collections or sang the songs from the books. After a power struggle over definitions, folk song and dance were introduced to the English school curriculum, and were to stay there until well after the Second World War.

Until the 1970s, the activities of these earlier collectors were taken at face value in terms of their heroic efforts to save the nation's heritage, and pretty much regarded as a closed account, but at that time new researchers started looking more critically at their backgrounds, activities and motives, and they were found wanting.

This new research was timely, and necessary to counter the hagiographic tendencies of previous scholarship, but, in the spirit of the age, and the age-old tendency of those with an axe to grind being more concerned with the axe than a true representation of what was being chopped, the pendulum was made to swing to the opposite extreme.[4]

The collectors were criticised on all fronts, but mainly, at that time, as regards the alleged cultural appropriation of working-class culture by the bourgeoisie, and they were charged not only with this theft but with constructing the whole idea of 'folk song' for their own purposes. Although how they could appropriate what was not really there is never fully explained.

This negative view became the orthodoxy in academic writing for more than a generation and has only recently begun to be exposed as fundamentally flawed. There were welcome signs that its hold was weakening, but at the time of writing it has returned with a vengeance and is now supported by attacks focusing on racism as well as class.

Less controversially, the second Revival also created a wave of new collecting activity, as enthusiasts discovered that there were still many old-style singers to be interviewed and recorded. A wealth of new material was captured for posterity.

Descriptions

In lieu of strict definition, let us attempt a description of what made 'folk song' and music, special up to about 1900, although the main collectors of the time argued that by then 'traditional' music was already heavily infected and dying.

Certain characteristics can be identified and labelled, and they are as much to do with performance as intrinsic structure: everyday, face-to-face, within a community, unaccompanied, mostly solo, non-harmonic, non-commercial, untrained, performed from memory, home-made.

There are always exceptions. Glees and catches were designed to be sung together, as were many cumulative songs, children's rhymes and shanties, and people have always been happy, it seems, to join in the chorus. 'Untrained' signifies lack of formal education, and does not mean that parents did not guide their children, nor that fiddlers did not teach their neighbours' children to play.

In the past, 'unconscious' was high on the list of supposed attributes of folk performance, but we are less comfortable with the concept nowadays, as it seems to deny the singers and musicians any agency or creative input in their art.

Cecil Sharp is the only one of the Edwardian collectors to offer a sustained attempt at definition. He suggested three key elements which define a song as a 'folk song' – Continuity, Selection and Variation.[5]

To become 'folk', a song or tune has to *continue*, to be passed on – horizontally, from person to person, and vertically, down the generations. However, if a song is not *selected* (i.e. by individuals and therefore by the community) for later performance it has no continuity and it dies. Needless to say, this was written before recorded sound took hold. No song really 'dies' while recordings of it survive. Being performed repeatedly, by one performer or many, a song or tune inevitably changes, and some of those *variations* are passed on to the next performer.

Sharp's analysis is overtly based on a notion of social evolution, and particularly natural selection, and one immediate drawback is the assumption that the gradual improvement is firmly aesthetic. It has to be remembered, however, that he was primarily referring to the tunes, rather than the words of songs, and some of our reservations are explained by this fact.

The model can be criticised on a number of relatively mundane points, as well as theoretical ones. It cannot explain, for example, why many good songs have been dropped over the generations, while others, which had not yet reached perfection, continued to be sung. 'Changing fashion' cannot easily be fitted into an evolutionary framework. Nor does it take into account *function* – a bawdy song, or a children's rhyme might succeed precisely because it is 'ugly', or counter-cultural, rather than aesthetically pleasing, or a tune might survive because it has important associations (e.g. the 'National Anthem').

Another reservation concerns his resolutely positive view of the 'oral tradition', as being the process by which a tune is moulded and honed towards perfection, which sits uncomfortably with the commonplace notion that this 'oral tradition' is often degenerative, especially as regards the words. Singers mangle things, forget things, misunderstand things and pass them on.

A closer look also reveals cracks in this idea of an 'oral tradition' (and that term encompasses 'aural', to include instrumental music). Orality is a cornerstone of most descriptions of 'folk', and is essential to the idea of long-term transmission unadulterated by outside influence.

It was abundantly clear to the Edwardian collectors, however, that singers routinely learnt song texts from cheap printed materials such as broadsides and chapbooks, and these mass-produced commercial items, which included brand-new songs as well as old ones, do not fit well with the idea of songs being passed down and moulded by generations of singers. But print and oral traditions are not always in opposition. A person may learn a song from print, but every time they sing it in company, it is back in the 'oral' sphere.

Reviving the folk

Although both Revivals were concerned with folk music, their differences vastly outweigh their similarities. The Folk Song Society remained a small coterie of primarily middle-class musically literate devotees, and counted its success in terms of awakening that middle class to the importance of 'folk' to the national art music culture. There was no attempt to encourage traditional styles or champion traditional singers. Apart from incorporation in classical pieces, their preferred *performance* was by trained artists on the concert platform, accompanied by the piano, or 'folk song in evening dress' as it has been called.

By contrast, the post-war Revival was designed as a grass-roots working-class youth movement, with much of its impetus coming from the left of the political spectrum, although it took on a more middle-class tinge as it developed. It quickly gained a reputation for being a 'protest' movement, with counter-cultural credentials, and various causes were added to its ranks: Campaign for Nuclear Disarmament, anti-capitalism, apartheid, Vietnam War and many others. 'Folk song in denim' might be an appropriate description.

While some fans pursued the idea of 'industrial' songs, others re-discovered the songs collected at the turn of the twentieth century and went in for a new rural nostalgia. Overall, there was a strong belief in the importance of self-made music and artistic expression, and although stars were soon created, they were expected to be as un-star-like as possible.

The Revival soon splintered into factions, termed 'contemporary' and 'traditional' at the time, and each of those groups included sub-divisions. The brief involvement of the music industry in the 1960s clashed with the home-made music philosophy of many followers, upset the counter-cultural credentials of others and bothered the political consciences of the lefties, but brought a mass of new fans, which took 'folk' into the mainstream, and folk groups into the charts. In its heyday, there were thousands of folk clubs around the country, numerous folk festivals and a panoply of shoe-string magazines, record labels and other things necessary to support a national movement.

As already indicated, as regards the song and music itself, the move away from earlier repertoires and styles, although patchy, was swift and was at first manifest in musical accompaniment, although there were always individuals who remained true to the unaccompanied ethos. While followers of the first Revival could barely conceive of a song without a piano, post-war 'folk' took the guitar to its heart.

By the 1980s, the heat and buzz had gone from the Revival, although there were still many fans up and down the land. Time moves on. Musicians and fans often focus on previous revivalists, and in this way the latter become regarded as 'traditional', while a dwindling core of diehards insist on c1900 as the baseline for definitional purposes. But even in 1900 old people were complaining that the young did not understand proper songs and singing.

It is therefore perfectly feasible to take two completely opposing views about the modern 'folk scene'. As already indicated, taking into account the criteria of repertoire, style, personnel and setting, it is possible to argue that a modern folk band bears no relationship at all to the 'folk music' of 1900. However, as the performers have adapted to all the societal and cultural changes of the past century, they have adopted an incremental notion of 'tradition' and can claim for themselves a 'living tradition' – I have my grandad's knife; I have had to replace the blade twice, and I fitted a new handle, but it is still grandad's knife.

They can even argue that this fits perfectly well with Sharp's model of continuity, change and variation, although he did not intend it to. Society gets the folk music it needs. Folk is as folk does.

While our 1900 singers and musicians appear to have been largely content with their role, and did not seek to develop into new realms or styles, this is not true of many modern folk performers. Singers and musicians, even when they start out with notions of authenticity rarely find the older styles satisfying for long, and soon break out of the confines of past practice to develop their own. To survive and prosper, it is said, folk music has to be 'relevant'; it has to communicate with new audiences; it has to be marketed.

Nevertheless, most modern folk musicians, and fans, if asked, still hold to an ideal which can be summed up as 'folk heritage' – folk music as a palpable connection to the ordinary folk of the past, often qualified by class, gender, locality or other factor, but strongly felt. As such, it exists in the emotional sphere, and a provable unbroken and unchanged tradition is not necessary to sustain it. But that is not all, as reported in *The Times* in November 2020; it is their job to move forward:

> It's a living tradition. People think of folk music as just old stories. But old stories can inspire new art. You can revisit old culture and create something new, something that people can feel part of. It's what's missing in a lot of today's music. People are looking for something authentic.[6]

It is interesting to note how easily the notions of 'authenticity', and the perennial claim that 'folk' is in opposition to 'popular' music, are slipped in here to validate 'new art'.

'New' approaches to research

Returning to research, there is evidence of recent changes in the way that insider scholars and commentators look at folk song and music, although, because the field is largely in the hands of amateur enthusiasts outside of the Academy, there is little sense of a 'school of thought' or a cohesive concept of a new orthodoxy.

While valuing the vital contribution of the earlier collectors, and acknowledging the need to scrutinise their methods and conclusions, researchers are nowadays often concerned with getting behind and beyond their towering presence. A new respect for historical evidence has come to the fore, and the use of a much wider pool of resources – singers' manuscripts, newspaper reports, genealogical resources. Of particular note is the growth of an awareness that 'folk' did not exist in a cultural vacuum, and a new interest in the interplay with neighbouring musical genres such as pleasure gardens, music hall, church music and the cheap print trade has been evident.

There are two mantras which sum up key points in the research approaches of many scholars today:

> It is not the origin of a song which makes it 'folk', but what the 'folk' does with it.
> We are not looking for 'folk song' but trying to find out 'what songs the folk sang'.

Notes

1. Steve Roud, *Folk Song in England* (London: Faber, 2017); D.K. Wilgus, *Anglo-American Folksong Scholarship* (New Brunswick: Rutgers University, 1959); E. David Gregory, *Victorian Songhunters* (Lanham: Scarecrow, 2006) and *The Late Victorian Folksong Revival* (Lanham: Scarecrow, 2010).
2. For example, Sabine Baring-Gould, *Songs and Ballads of the West* (London: Methuen, 1889); Frank Kidson, *Traditional Tunes* (Oxford: Taphouse, 1891), and A. Fuller-Maitland and Lucy Broadwood, *English County Songs* (London: The Leadenhall Press, 1893).
3. For example, Carl Engel, *Introduction to the Study of National Music* (London: Longman, 1866), p. 32.
4. See David Harker, *Fakesong: the Manufacture of British Folksong* (Milton Keynes: Open University Press, 1985); and less rabid, but still critical; Georgina Boyes, *The Imagined Village: Culture and Ideology and the English Folk Revival* (Manchester: Manchester University Press, 1991).
5. Cecil Sharp, *English Folk Song: Some Conclusions* (London: Simpkin, 1907).
6. 'A Soundtrack to my watery back garden', interview with Clive Davis, *The Times* (14 November 2020) 'Saturday Review' section, p. 11.

18

RE-CRAFTING LOVE AND MURDER

Print and memory in the mediation of a murdered sweetheart ballad

Thomas Pettitt

Opening remarks: of ballads and broadsides

Whatever its value as a remnant of 'ancient minstrelsy', a source on working-class social conditions or a reflection of popular mentalities, a well-sung folk song is a cultural achievement, and merits appreciation and analysis from that perspective. That its aesthetic characteristics likely deviate from those of the mainstream or 'high' culture of the time and place concerned is not so much a disqualification as a useful indication that they have been achieved by quite different means, and to explore those means is to understand and appreciate song as a form of folk performance.

To this end, it is essential to insist, firstly, that the object of appreciation is the performance, and secondly that the song can and does vary between performances – by different singers, and by a given singer on different occasions. While the stanza form remains fixed, and the melody relatively stable, the words are subject to a 'morphing', which reshapes the song's content and form at various levels. And whatever the talents or tastes of individual singers (or the contexts of individual performances), a major factor in this morphing will be the affordances of the media by which a song is borne between performances, and from which it is generated in performance. This contribution will explore the relationships between verbal morphing, or re-crafting, and mediating systems, with regard particularly to narrative folk songs, or 'ballads', by a close examination of a particular song, which is also of interest from other – generic – perspectives.

The performances to be studied are of those designated by folk song research as 'source' singers. Transcripts or recordings of their performances have been subsequently published in scholarly collections, popular songbooks, or issued on commercial electronic media, but these singers have not learnt their songs from such sources. The media through which the songs have reached *them*, alongside occasional, auxiliary, intervention by writing, have historically been *memory* and *print* (in the form of the broadside or related forms of 'street literature').

From a point of departure in which the English folk songs recorded from performance in the twentieth century were assumed to have been sustained in an 'oral tradition', largely independent of printing, since 'time immemorial' (or the Middle Ages or 'Merrie England'), the last several decades of folk song research have seen a decisive shift towards the realisation, not merely that most of those songs appeared in print at one time or another, but that in most cases those printed songs, or 'broadside ballads', were the original forms from which the performances ultimately derived.[1] This does not necessarily mean, however, that singing is subordinate to print in the mediation of the songs,[2] especially with regard to the re-crafting that produced the forms in which they were sung.

Composed and published with a view to being sung, broadside ballads are significant both for their initiating role and for their contribution to the widespread diffusion of songs. But the print technology enabling the latter is not in itself conducive to verbal morphing. On the contrary, its decisive affordance is the production of multiple copies on which the text of the song is identical for every singer who acquires one. And on each of those copies the text remains fixed, however many times (wherever, whenever, by whomever) it provides the basis for performance. Verbal change can be associated with print only indirectly, when another printer (or the same printer on a subsequent occasion) produces a different 'edition' of a song; but the revision, most likely pen in hand, is external to the printing process.[3]

If and when the printed text is set aside in favour of performance from memory, a song transitions to a different mediating system, deploying exclusively human faculties: retention in and retrieval from memory and delivery by voice (plus any facial expression or gesticulation). It will remain in this system for as long as it is performed from memory and passed on to new singers by their listening to such memory-based performances.

For this medium 'oral tradition' is both inadequate and misleading. 'Oral' (like 'aural') invokes the mouth to ear mediation of the words from one singer to another, but the potential for morphing is much greater, quantitatively and qualitatively, in the passage of the words through the memory of a given singer, from their acquisition (by whatever means), to their reproduction in performance, not least in challenging conditions (domestic, social, festive) where making it work is more important than getting it right. Performance context can also inspire both spontaneous but more conscious change there and then, and premeditated adjustment between performances in the light of anterior experience or the singer's notion of how best the song would work.

Furthermore the implication has generally been that 'oral tradition' encompasses a sustained concatenation of singers over a lengthy period, from a probably unknown origin.[4] Shifting the focus to a 'singing tradition' of memory-based performances does not necessarily encompass a chain of singers. Nonetheless, as soon as there is more than one, their impact on the words in relation to an original will be cumulative, and for any singer after the first, change will not be inhibited by experience of the text in printed form.[5]

From other perspectives the origin of most folk ballads on printed broadsides is a boon to scholarship in identifying the original form of a song and so making it possible to determine, by comparative analysis, exactly what singing tradition has done to it on its way to a given performance with regard to content, form and style. In several exercises of this kind, I have developed the thesis that the resulting performances can in many instances and in several ways be appreciated not merely as the result of haphazard change, but as a re-crafting of the popular, sub-literary, material of the originating broadside, into a verbal product which remains a viable narrative, while displaying a distinct 'vernacular' aesthetic.[6]

Versions of a given song recorded from singing tradition can and do differ from each other in various ways, but they also differ from the original broadsides in the *same* ways – and the same tendency can be noted in applying the same comparative approach to several songs. Purely *casual* changes certainly occur – although adjudication on whether they be classified as 'faults' and their cumulative effect 'garbling' is best left to those for whom the tradition is part of their living culture (in that the aural aspects of singing can establish an independent realm with its own standards of grammar and sense). But the more significant changes in this re-crafting qualify as *systemic* in being in some way related to this memory-and-performance-based media system's distinctive affordances. Steve Roud has remarked, 'The idea that variation is a mark of oral transmission is... too simplistic, although there may be some mileage in looking more closely at the *kinds* of variation to see whether category differences can be identified',[7] and I suggest that this is precisely what these investigations demonstrate – provided we understand 'oral transmission' as a singing tradition comprising reproduction from memory in performance.

That this 'categorical' difference has aesthetic dimensions is because the systemic verbal change involved is not solely quantitative, but qualitative, and not inevitably, as Joseph Ritson once opined, 'a species of alchemy which converts gold to lead'.[8] Nor, as German scholarship once assumed, is the song 'sung to pieces' (*zersungen*), but rather 'sung into shape' (*zurechtsungen*) – subjected to an ameliorative degradation enabling the emergence of narrative and thematic structures which were present in the original, but obscured by sub-literary or journalistic verbiage, and their enhancement by verbal patterning.

The latter point also has generic implications. In the field of folk performance 'ballad' can mean narrative folk songs generally, but historically, for those who composed, sold, bought and sang them, a ballad was any song published on a broadside. In the context of literary studies, 'ballad' has invariably referred to narrative songs from English (and notably Scottish) singing tradition which have aesthetic qualities quite distinct from the broadside ballads, famously dismissed by Francis James Child as 'veritable dunghills'.[9] Having spent decades rooting among them, I agree, but with the important proviso that those much appreciated aesthetic qualities (however else they might be achieved) are precisely what emerges when certain printed ballads are subjected to the systemic affordances of singing tradition (and quite likely the skills of individual singers within these restraints): but only if the core narrative was there in the original. So if 'ballad' is taken in the sense normal in conventional literary histories, this process can also be called the 'balladizing' of a printed song.[10] Generic and aesthetic dimensions come together in the eloquent formulation of Bertrand Harris Bronson, better qualified than most of us to engage with the relationship between ballads in these various senses:

> ... the most brutal and violent, crude and sordid themes, *when passed through the crucible of traditional singing*, sometimes become, not tolerable, merely, but as starkly powerful in their reserve and understatement as all but the very greatest masterpieces of conscious art, and on their own scale of magnitude incomparable.[11]

And as it happens, he goes on to invoke a striking performance (albeit American) of the ballad which is the subject of this enquiry.

'Love and Murder': the ballad

That enquiry will further test and if necessary adjust the assertions just made by applying them to a ballad which is particularly challenging from this perspective, having been subjected to successive re-craftings over two centuries of mediation involving both print and singing tradition. Printed and sung under many titles, it is known to scholarship as Roud 15.[12]

In what qualifies as its pivotal and best known form it was issued in multiple print editions, in broadside (occasionally chapbook) format, from about the 1820s onwards, some under the title redeployed, for its thematic appropriateness, as the title for this chapter, 'Love and Murder',[13] most as 'Polly's Love, or the Cruel Ship's Carpenter', or simply the latter. On occasions when 'the nineteenth-century broadside' may be ambiguous, this form will be referred to as 'Love and Murder' in what follows. While far from all will be cited directly, this study has consulted editions of this nineteenth-century broadside form, issued by some twenty English printers operating in both London and the provinces.[14] With the same proviso on citation, I have juxtaposed it with transcriptions or recordings of derivative performances by 26 English source singers, including a few instances where the collectors, more intent on the music, transcribed only the words of the first stanza sung.[15]

But the results of this comparative analysis will then have to be reconsidered in the light of the complicating factor that the 'Love and Murder' ballad itself derived, by a process as yet undetermined, from a substantially longer broadside version published multiple times in the eighteenth century and a little beyond as 'The Gosport Tragedy'. Under the circumstances, it is a relief to follow the guidelines for this volume and restrict coverage to the song as mediated by English printers and singers.[16]

As a central point of reference, the full text of the nineteenth-century broadside, as issued by the London printer Henry Such, ca 1849–1862 (surviving in more copies than most), is reproduced here, with annotations designed to assist subsequent discussion:[17]

THE COURTSHIP

1. In fair Worcester city and in Worcestershire,
   <u>A handsome young</u> damsel she lived there,
   <u>A handsome young</u> man he courted her to be his dear,
   And he was by his trade a ship carpenter.

THE CRISIS

2. Now the King wanted seamen to <u>go on the sea</u>,
   <u>That caused this young damsel to sigh and to say</u>,
   <u>O William, O William</u> don't you <u>go to sea</u>,
   Remember the vows that you made to me.

THE MURDER

ENTICEMENT TO A LONELY SPOT

3. <u>It was early next morning before it was day</u>,
   He went to his Polly <u>these words he did say</u>,
   <u>O Polly, O Polly</u> you must go with me,
   Before we are married my friends for to see.

4. He led her through groves and valleys so deep,
   <u>And caused this young damsel to sigh and to weep</u>
   <u>O William, O William</u>, you have led me astray,
   On purpose my innocent life to betray.
   INTENT REVEALED

5. It's true, It's true, <u>these words he did say</u>,
   For all the long night I've been digging your grave
   The grave being open, the spade standing by,
   <u>Which caused this young damsel to sigh and to cry</u>.
   PLEA FOR MERCY

6. <u>O William, O William</u>, <u>O pardon</u> my life,
   I never will covet to be your wife,
   I will travel the world over to set you quite free,
   <u>O pardon, O pardon</u>, <u>my baby and me</u>.

KILLING, DISPOSAL OF BODY

7 <u>No pardon</u> I'll give, there's no time for to stand,
So with that he had a knife in his hand,
He stabbed her heart till the blood it did flow,
Then into the grave her fair body did throw.

THE ESCAPE

8 He covered her up so safe and secure,
Thinking no one would find her he was sure,
Then he went on board to sail the world round,
Before that the murder could ever be found.

THE RETRIBUTION

9 <u>It was early one morning before it was day</u>,
The captain came up these words he did say,
There's a murderer on board, and he lately has done,
Our ship is in mourning and cannot sail on.
10 <u>Then up stepped</u> one, indeed it's not me,
<u>Then up stepped</u> another, the same he did say.
<u>Then up</u> starts young William to stamp and to swear,
<u>Indeed it's not me</u> sir, I vow and declare.
11 As he was turning from the captain with speed,
He met his Polly which made his heart bleed,
She stript him and tore him, she tore him in three,
Because he had murdered <u>her baby and she</u>.

Love and murder: the genre

That this song is also a classic Murdered Sweetheart Ballad further recommends it as the object of a case study in representing an unusually well-demarcated, long-lived and numerically significant genre of vernacular narrative song.[18] Fifty or more songs of English origin qualify for inclusion by virtue of their content, all originating in cheap print formats (overwhelmingly broadsides), from the mid seventeenth to the late nineteenth century.

The themes of love and murder, each central to vernacular song in its own right, here collide violently, where the murderer is the accepted lover of the victim. This violent disruption from within of a hitherto conventional couple formation scenario (courtship; acceptance; the inception of a sexual intimacy leading to conception), thwarting the anticipated culmination in marriage, distinguishes the Murdered Sweetheart ballads from those involving femicide in other contexts. The latter include merely 'murdered girl' ballads where the female is the victim of a homicidal maniac (e.g. Roud 2152, 'Fanny Adams'), or killed precisely for *declining* a man's advances (e.g. Roud 561, 'Mary in the Silvery Tide'), or provoking murderous and suicidal jealousy (e.g. Roud 218, 'Oxford City'). Overlapping but nonetheless generically distinct are the many songs in which a (usually pregnant) sweetheart is merely deserted by her lover, even when she subsequently commits suicide.

Uncertainty about inclusion derives less from content than from the way it is handled: there are songs about murdered sweethearts which may qualify as 'ballads' only by virtue of being printed on broadsides. Some, headed 'A Copy of Verses…' and supplementing an extensive prose account, may have been intended for reading rather than singing. They (and others not so labelled) tend more to lachrymose meditation or moralistic exclamation than to the narration of the events (accordingly unsuited to 'balladization' in singing tradition, where they are never encountered).

Among the murdered sweetheart songs also qualifying as ballads by virtue of a strong narrative impulse, two sub-genres can be distinguished in terms of alternative scenarios for the aftermath of the murder, the fatal retribution inexorably visited on the lover. In the majority of cases (increasingly dominant in the nineteenth century), this takes the form of a judicial procedure culminating at the scaffold (the ballads concerned typically presenting themselves as based on real events); in others (as here), a more personal accounting (with supernatural or psychological dimensions) in which the sweetheart can play an active, post-mortem, role.

From the later seventeenth century onwards, authors, singers and audiences are likely to have been aware of the generic paradigm and its characteristic, powerful and evidently popular features. Six of the strongly narrative murdered sweetheart ballads originating in England, plus one on an Irish case (Roud 1412, 'James McDonald'), have been recovered from English singing tradition, some of them frequently printed, and recorded from multiple singers. Among the most successful are 'Maria Marten' (Roud 215), 'The Berkshire Tragedy' (Roud 263, also known as 'The Cruel Miller') and our song of the murderous ship's carpenter.[19] Of the 26 English source singers recorded as knowing at least one stanza of this song, six had another murdered sweetheart ballad in their repertoire.[20] It is quite likely that awareness of the genre and its conventions would influence not merely the composition and reception, but also the mediation and re-crafting, of individual songs.

The genre's resonance with singers and audiences will have been enhanced by its overlap with social realities. While many, perhaps a majority, of the murdered sweetheart ballads are based on actual events, it was of course rare that real-world cases of seduction, pregnancy and desertion also encompassed the murder of the woman. Nonetheless, the scenario without the violent outcome was a common feature of social life, often leading to the woman's social ostracism, and at worst, statistically more significant than femicide, to infanticide by the mother (another favourite ballad theme). In an interesting profile of one of the singers from whom this song was collected in the early twentieth century, Angela Shaw remarks that of the forty-plus songs in her repertoire, thirteen are about seduction, of which nine 'end in a pregnancy that is explicitly ruinous for the girl and/or the child'. Furthermore, the household's composition suggests strongly that both the singer and her aunt had illegitimate children, although the former later married the child's father.[21]

Nineteenth-century broadsides and derivative singing tradition

Against this background, we may turn more concretely to the verbal morphing of our nineteenth-century broadside ballad, both from one broadside edition to another, and from the broadsides to singing tradition. In the case of the broadsides, there being no certainty as to which came first, this will amount to assessing the range of variation between editions. Versions from singing tradition will be compared, for convenience, with the Such broadside given in full above: variations between the broadside editions are occasionally sufficient to permit determination of which was the ultimate source for a given singer's rendition, but this has little relevance for the questions under discussion here. More importantly, the availability of the other editions will avoid attributing to singing tradition variations already established among the broadsides.

At the stanzaic level (and accordingly with regard to higher levels such as episode or theme), the text of the nineteenth-century broadside ballad is extremely stable between editions. All comprise the same eleven stanzas as the Such printing reproduced above, in the same order. Singing tradition displays in contrast a quite complex behavioural profile. Among the 20 singers from whom the collectors recorded more than their first stanza, only four have those same eleven stanzas in the same order (Baldwin, Blake, Hancock, Rowe), and they may plausibly be perceived as having some sense of an original text (possibly having seen a broadside) which they were seeking to reproduce (nonetheless with lesser or greater variation at the sub-stanzaic levels).

At the opposite extreme are what might be termed 'catastrophic' performances that manifestly fail to achieve a viable form of the ballad we can imagine the singer being comfortable with in its traditional performance context. Difficult to determine for outsiders, in some instances nonetheless the evidence is unequivocal. In the sound recordings of Roy Palmer coaxing a few stanzas out of George Dunn, the latter is explicitly aware of their inadequacy. David Marlow opens with a close rendition of the broadside's two opening stanzas, but in an aural equivalent of scribal eye-skip follows the first line of the third, 'Twas early next morning before it was day', which should lead into the murder scene, with 'Our captain stepped up and those words he did say...' (broadside st. 9.2), which should follow this same phrase several stanzas later in connection with the murderer's unsuccessful attempt to escape. Harry Cox sings seven stanzas that provide an adequate rendition of the central narrative thread all the way to the villain's denial of guilt, only to conclude with an apologetic mutter, evidently (and quite exceptionally) unable to recall the climactic final stanza.

Between the complete and the catastrophic lie the performances which evidently seek, and by their own standards probably achieve, a rounded and viable narrative, but with fewer stanzas than the broadside. At its simplest this involves the subtraction of complete stanzas whose absence does not compromise coherence (while enhancing narrative efficiency). For example of the four ten-stanza performances one (Larner) omits the first stanza, whose identification of the location is expendable, and whose information on the relationship of the protagonists is adequately inferred in following stanzas. The ballad's story becomes more generalised as a consequence. The other three (Pike, Tucker, Weenie Brazil) omit the second stanza, which relates the event provoking the crisis (the lover's imminent departure) but which is specific to this story and generically superfluous, as the usual trigger for the murder, evident subsequently, is the sweetheart's insisting on marriage.

Altogether, however many stanzas singers retain, the broadside's first stanza is omitted by six (Larner, Gulliver, Spearing, Danny Brazil, Denny Smith, Wiggie Smith), the second, the most vulnerable of all, by ten (Pike, Tucker, Case, Gulliver, Cox, Spearing, Danny Brazil, 1966, Weenie Brazil, Denny Smith, Wiggie Smith).[22] In sharp contrast, all but one of the non-catastrophic versions retain in its entirety the climactic stanza where the spirit of the sweetheart tears the murderer to pieces, the exception conflating it with the denial of responsibility in the preceding stanza, which is similarly retained in virtually all versions. And most also have at least part of the stanza with the Captain's statement that there is a murderer on board.

The intervening narrative sections encompassing the murder and the escape are subject to various amounts and forms of subtraction, which in versions of less than ten stanzas invariably encompasses sub-stanzaic units. This is rendered significantly more feasible (than with the standard 'ballad stanza') by each stanza comprising readily detachable two-line units, in the form of rhyming couplets (aabb), all lines having four stresses ('long measure'). Here, for example, is how a Mrs. Gulliver handled the climax of the murder scene compared to the Such broadside, reducing two stanzas to one by retaining one line of the first, intruding a new line (5.2, discussed under another heading shortly) and continuing with the second couplet of the next:

Such broadside	Mrs. Gulliver

6 O William, O William, O pardon my life,
   I never will covet to be your wife,
   I will travel the world over to set you quite free,
   O pardon, O pardon, my baby and me.
	5 Oh! pardon for me, poor Polly, she cried
	
	+> For remember, dear William, I'm not fit to die.

7 No pardon I'll give, there's no time for to stand,
   So with that he had a knife in his hand,
   He stabbed her heart
               till the blood it did flow
   Then into the grave her fair body did throw
	So quickaly (sic) he stabbed her,
	               and the blood gan to flew
	And into this cold grave poor Polly he threw

This is a quite viable reduction: the plea for mercy is effective enough without the broadside's elaboration, and the stabbing alone is a clear indication of its rejection.

    Gypsy Wiggy Smith's handling of the murder scene as a whole is more aggressively subtractive, but nonetheless preserves the essential points:

Such Broadside	Wiggy Smith
– narrator's voice	– narrator's voice

4 He led her through groves and valleys so deep,
 	
   And caused this young damsel to sigh and to weep
	2 And he led her through woods and valleys too
	
	   until this poor damsel, her [started] to weep

– her voice:
   O William, O William, you have led me astray,
   On purpose my innocent life to betray.
	– his voice:
	   Lovely Betsy, lovely Betsy, I'm lead you astray

– his voice:
5 It's true, It's true, these words he did say,
   For all the long night
   I've been digging your grave
	– his voice:
	
	   For all of this long night
	             I've been digging your grave.

– narrator's voice:
   The grave being open,
            the spade standing by,
   Which caused this young damsel to sigh and to cry.
	– his voice:
	3 There's your grave lying open
	             and the spade standing near

6 O William, O William, O pardon my life,
   I never will covet to be your wife,
   I will travel the world over to set you quite free,
   O pardon, O pardon, my baby and me.	

7 No pardon I'll give, there's no time for to stand,
   So with that he had a knife in his hand,
   He stabbed her heart till the blood it did flow,
   Then into the grave her fair body did throw.
	– narrator's voice:
	   And into that cold grave her body he threw.

This is not casual forgetting: as my annotations indicate, the subtraction is enabled by astutely transferring to the voice of the murderer (with the necessary adjustment of personal pronouns) statements originally attributed to the girl and the narrator.

Such instances are characteristic of the way the sung versions achieve by subtraction a more efficient narrative: curtailing inessential information, boiling down the broadside's elaborate exchanges between the principals that delay the action sequence, from leading the girl astray to killing and burying her. Altogether in these performances the song is brought closer to what folklorist Max Lüthi, speaking of spoken narrative, called the *Zielform*, which emerges when the affordances of memoral transmission leave only what is most resilient (necessary; memorable),[23] rather as wind and weather reveal an inner structure by wearing down the softer minerals of rocks.

Subtraction is by far the most common change, while among and between both broadsides and sung versions addition occurs only as a feature of substitution, its incidence being greater the smaller the unit substituted (couplet – line – phrase – word), and many instances can be characterised as merely casual – something that happens without seeming to follow a particular pattern or tendency. Their relevance is accordingly somewhat limited, except that incidence is markedly higher in singing tradition than in broadside editing.[24]

In singing tradition however the substitution of verbal material also includes instances that qualify as systemic, that is to say inherent to the cultural system concerned, not least when the material derives from the singing tradition of which this song is a part, be it phrases from particular songs or verbal formulas/commonplaces found in many songs. The process may be perceived as external (verbal) contamination, but it also qualifies as a vernacular equivalent of the *intertextuality* which in literature can colour reception of the host work – Gerald Porter distinguishes it as 'interverbality'.[25]

For example in 1966 Gypsy singer Danny Brazil was recorded performing a version whose eight stanzas are all derived from the broadsides, and in the right order, but which contain several substituted phrases.[26] Most are of indeterminate origin (casual substitutions), but when the murderer is confronted by the spirit of his victim, the new formulation has interesting resonances:

> 11.2 He met his Polly which made his heart bleed (Such broadside)
> 8.2 He met *pretty* Polly, *all dressed up in white* (Danny Brazil).

That 'Polly' should become 'pretty Polly', feels inevitable and is not unique to this singer, but this does not occur in any of the broadside versions. If the contamination is from a specific song, it could have been any of several with a wide diffusion in which, from time to time the female protagonist is named or addressed as 'pretty Polly'.[27] The substituted 'all dressed up in white' is not implausible for a ghost in popular iconography, but the occurrence of the phrase elsewhere in English vernacular song raises the possibility of intertextuality. The most likely source would be another song in the singer's repertoire, a plausible candidate here being Danny Brazil's own 'The False Bride' (Roud 154), in which a young man has been romantically involved with a girl, only to meet her subsequently 'dressed up in white' as someone else's bride (and there too the encounter leads to the lover's death).[28] The powerful intertextual connotation is of course that in Brazil's re-crafting of our ballad the spirit of the murdered sweetheart visits violent retribution on her murderous lover dressed in the bridal gown she would have worn had he fulfilled his promise to marry her.

In the version sung by Harry Cox in the late 1950s, the captain's statement about the murderer on board occurs not '… early one morning before it was day' (Such st. 9.1) but when '… they had not been sailing still days two or three' (st. 6.1). This is certainly a ballad formula heralding fateful (and typically fatal) developments, constructed on the model 'They had not (verb of travel) + (unit of time or distance) + (number + a larger number selected for rhyme).[29] But almost the identical formulation, 'we had not been sailing scarce days two or three' occurs in this singer's version of 'The Bold Princess Royal' (Roud 528),[30] initiating a naval engagement.

When Mrs. Gulliver from Somerset sang this ballad in 1905 (in a stanza quoted above), the broadside's formulation of the sweetheart's plea for mercy, 'I never will covet to be your wife' (Such st. 6.2) is replaced by 'For remember, dear William, *I'm not fit to die*' (st. 5.2). The final phrase is very likely from another murdered sweetheart ballad, 'The Berkshire Tragedy' (Roud 263), not recorded from this singer, but ubiquitous in England in broadside printings and singing tradition. There too the phrase is uttered in vain by the sweetheart immediately before her murder, and those in the singer's audience familiar with this other ballad would be primed to both expect the worst for the victim and anticipate a just retribution.

Alongside this 'external contamination' which can achieve intertextuality with other songs, singing tradition also displays a systemic 'internal contamination', in which verbal material at one point in the song is substituted for that at another point – particularly where something similar is being communicated (by the narrator or the characters). And this, in turn, can achieve (or verbally reinforce) an (intratextual) connection, in the form of a verbal repetition pattern with the line(s) from which the substituted material derived (provided they, too, are retained). An extreme form of the process is illustrated by the version performed by Mrs. Gulliver, which manages to generate a whole new stanza without adding new material:

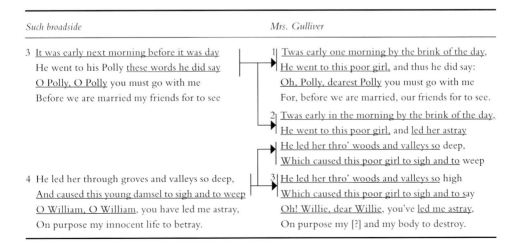

The process also achieves new but very traditional-looking incremental repetitions between the first and second, and the second and third, stanzas.

But impressive as this may be by way of demonstrating the creative systemic change of which singing tradition is capable, it is in this connection that the comparative analysis of broadsides and sung versions raises serious questions about the thesis, otherwise generally supported by the evidence, that memoral tradition re-crafts this ballad in ways not matched by deliberate broadside revisions. While none of the sub-stanzaic variations between the different editions of the nineteenth-century broadside seem to result from external contamination from singing tradition, some do resemble internal contamination (although the direction of change cannot be assumed).

Far more significantly, as indicated (by underlining) on the transcript of the Such broadside provided earlier, many of its lines (I make it 19 out of 44) *already* participate in verbal repetition patterns of one kind or another with other lines. And this, finally, is symptomatic of a more strategic challenge, in that more generally our nineteenth-century broadside form of this ballad exhibits, in relation to the earlier, eighteenth century, form from which it manifestly derives, those same symptoms of systemic re-crafting (strategic subtraction; substitution in the form of external or internal contamination) which subsequently produced its own derivatives in singing tradition: a serious discrepancy meriting closer examination.

The early broadside

The many printings of that earlier broadside version, 'The Gosport Tragedy' (of which fifteen distinct issues have been consulted),[31] differ to the degree of comprising 29, 30, 32, 33, 34 (by far the most frequent), or 35 stanzas (all in the same aabb rhyme scheme and four-stress stanzas as the nineteenth-century form). Which came first, and whether the others were achieved by addition or subtraction, is less interesting here than which of them provided the source for the nineteenth-century abbreviated derivative.[32] The choice effectively lies between the 35- and 30-stanza forms, which alone have the antecedent of the striking line from the murder scene, 'The grave being open, the spade standing by' (Such st. 5.3), forms of which figure in *all* the nineteenth-century broadsides. Verbal discrepancies in other lines reproduced in the later broadside do not decisively favour the one or the other, but in narrative terms the 30-stanza version of the 'Gosport Tragedy' anticipates the later broadside in having the lover fetch the sweetheart at the beginning of the murder sequence, rather than her visiting him, as in the 35-stanza version. The relatively late date of the 30-stanza form's only printing also recommends it as a likely source, appearing as it does in a chapbook published by Shelmerdine of Manchester ca 1820, close to the first appearance of the shorter broadside.

After an opening stanza presenting the protagonists and their relationship, largely reproduced in the later broadside, the Shelmerdine 'Gosport Tragedy' devotes no less than five stanzas to the wooing, before catching up at st. 7 with the short version's second stanza reporting the crisis in the relationship prompted by the lover's imminent departure to sea. The long version's lover reiterates his good faith (sts. 7–9), before again joining the later broadside, now entering only its third stanza, for the murder scene. For a while now they have very similar verbal content, but with the nineteenth-century broadside reducing the sweetheart's plea for mercy from three stanzas to one, and generating those verbal repetitions of the kind normally found in singing tradition (some of them repeating lines elsewhere in the text):

Long broadside (Shelmerdine)	Short broadside (Such)
	2.2 <u>O William, O William</u> don't you go to sea, ...
10 With kindest embraces they parted that night, He went for to meet her <u>next morning e'er light</u>, He says my dear Molly you must go with me, Before we are married a friend for to see.	3 <u>It was early next morning before it was day</u>, He went to his Polly <u>these words he did say</u>, <u>O Polly, O Polly</u> you must go with me, Before we are married my friends for to see.
11 led her thro' groves and valleys so deep, Till <u>this innocent creature</u> <u>began for to weep</u>, She says my dear Will, you have led me astray, On purpose my innocent life to betray.	4 He led her through groves and valleys so deep, And caused <u>this young damsel</u> <u>to sigh and to</u> weep <u>O William, O William</u>, you have led me astray, On purpose my innocent life to betray.
12 True my dear Molly there's none can be save, For I have been all last night a digging your grave: T[h]is innocent damsel she hearing him say so, Her eyes like two fountains began for to flow.	5 It's true, It's true, <u>these words he did say</u>, For all the long night I've been digging your grave The grave being open, the spade standing by, <u>Which caused this young damsel to sigh and to</u> cry.
13 Her hands white as lilies in sorrow she rung, Intreating for mercy cries what have I done; To you my dear Will, that makes you so severe, Unto you own true love that loved you so dear?	
14 She says my dear Will, spare but my life, Let me go destressed if I'm not your wife, Take not my life, lest my soul you betray, Must I in my bloom thus be hurried away.	6 <u>O William, O William</u>, O pardon my life <u>I</u> never <u>will</u> covet to be your wife, <u>I will</u> travel the world over to set you quite free, <u>O pardon, O pardon, my baby and me</u>.
15 A grave and spade she seen, standing by, Must this be the bride's bed for me for to lie: Perjur'd villain she cried thou worst of all men, The heavens will reward you when I'm dead and gone.	
	19 <u>It was early one morning before it was day</u> The captain came up <u>these words he did say</u> 11 4 Because he had murdered <u>her baby and she</u>

In the next stanza in both long and short broadsides, in similar formulations, he kills her, throws her body into the grave and makes his escape, joining a ship that is about to set sail.

Thereafter the later broadside edition continues its process of astute subtraction, wrapping up the narrative in merely three further stanzas (Such sts. 9–11), for which the earlier broadside required no less than 13. In what is retained the generation of repetition patterns also continues, strikingly illustrated by the moment when the villain denies his guilt to the ship's captain. The early version has a simple, almost prosaic, account:

> 26 As William before him stood trembling for fear,
 He began by the powers above for to swear,
 That he of the matter nothing did know,…

which the later broadside develops into a classic instance of balladesque short-form incremental repetition, accompanied by typical modulations into direct speech and parataxis (statements with parallel syntax):

10   <u>Then up stepped</u> one, <u>indeed it's not me</u>,
     <u>Then up stepped</u> another, the same he did say.
     <u>Then up</u> starts young William to stamp and to swear,
     <u>Indeed it's not me</u> sir, I vow and declare.

But otherwise the subtraction is accompanied by substitution. The basic motif is the same – the ghost of the murdered girl haunts the ship – but the earlier broadside (from the generation that produced *The Castle of Otranto*) indulges in a whole sequence of gothick episodes: an unembodied voice uttering curses, modulating into shrieks accompanied by lightening (Shelmerdine sts. 18.3–20.2); the apparition of a beautiful woman with a babe in her arms, who disappears when a crew-member attempts to embrace her (sts. 21–22); a silent appearance which prompts the murderer to confess (st. 27), following which he dies 'in rage and distraction' (st. 29.2). As can be seen in the Such version, 'Love and Murder' replaces all this with a stark, incremental (paratactical), ballad-worthy attack in which three actions divide the body into three parts:

She stript him and tore him, she tore him in three,
Because he had murdered her baby and she' (st. 11.3–4).

The substitution qualifies as the external contamination familiar in singing tradition, and here too the intrusive material may be a common narrative motif (the avenging ghost) or derive from a specific song. A plausible candidate, not least given the propinquity of the settings, is 'The Portsmouth Ghost', a ballad printed in a chapbook format in London in various editions in the late eighteenth and early nineteenth century. It concerns a girl who is courted, impregnated, but merely abandoned, by a soldier who embarks with his regiment for foreign service. She sells her soul to the Devil so her spirit can call up a storm, appear before the sailors to denounce her murderer, and drag him into the sea in a blaze of fire. She also literally 'rips' a body, but it is her own, to destroy his child.[33] Thus, very much in traditional ballad manner, 'Love and Murder' ends, omitting both the longer broadside's wrapping up of the narrative with the conventional discovery of the victim's body and the moralising valediction typical of broadside crime ballads from both periods (Shelmerdine sts. 29.3–30).

Vernacular broadside revision: print as performance?

These considerations suggest that the shorter printed form of this ballad was the result of deliberate revision of the longer antecedent and quite likely under printing house auspices. The motivation would very likely have been to further exploit a demonstrably successful song by adjusting it into conformity with the newly popular, 'slip', format that had room for far fewer stanzas. A prime suspect, the London printer John Pitts, who alone issued both the long and short broadsides,[34] is effectively exonerated when his (34-stanza) version of the 'Gosport Tragedy' lacks that 'grave and spade' line occurring in several other versions, including Shelmerdine's, and in *all* the nineteenth-century editions (including Pitts' own).[35]

In coming to terms with this puzzling material it is necessary to emphasise that the memoral-looking features of the nineteenth-century broadsides were the result of ballad *revision* rather than *composition*: its 'balladesque' character is singularly lacking in the *new* Murdered Sweetheart ballads of this period. And as an exercise more specifically in *abbreviation* it is one of several instances where an earlier, longer broadside ballad was reduced to the shorter form in the nineteenth century. David Atkinson has rightly observed, instancing this ballad among others, that 'These changes are not well documented at the present time and would benefit from detailed research',[36] and an unexpected benefit of this case study may be the revelation that such revision of an earlier ballad with a view to abbreviation *does not necessarily* produce the kind of results we see in the nineteenth-century broadsides – *even when involving the same ballad*.

For a quite different procedure is illustrated by a quite different abbreviated version of the 'Gosport Tragedy' masquerading (if still as Roud 15) under the title 'Nancy's Ghost'.[37] A slip ballad printed by Angus of Newcastle in the decades around 1800,[38] it comprises ten quatrains, all in the same stanza form as the other two broadsides. But while shorter than the nineteenth-century version examined above, it actually retains more of 'The Gosport Tragedy'. Of the 20 couplets making up the ten stanzas of 'Nancy's Ghost', eight are shared with both long and short versions, eight with the long version alone (corresponding to 80% of the whole). The remaining couplets are made up of smaller verbal units similarly corresponding to those in the long broadside or both, or of formulations unique to this version (the latter amounting to four whole lines and three phrases, all doing the same narrative work as the original).

It is not an intermediate between the original 'Gosport Tragedy' and the nineteenth-century 'Love and Murder' broadsides, but a parallel abbreviated version, and it has been achieved by other means. The subtraction is not accompanied by any significant external contamination from elsewhere. As in 'Love and Murder' the retribution is here also reduced to three stanzas, but by simple truncation, omitting the third appearance of the ghost and the murderer's anguished death, so the ballad ends with the girl's curse: '… a ship out of Gosport never shall go, / Till I am revenged for my overthrow' – more like a cheap fiction 'cliff-hanger' than a resolution. Furthermore apart from a reiterated 'spare my life' in the girl's plea there are none of the verbal repetitions achieved by internal contamination in the alternative form.

'Nancy's Ghost' is a relatively straightforward 'literary' (and literate) abbreviation of 'The Gosport Tragedy' with a result whose form and style do not differ significantly from new ballads composed in the same period. Some other, more 'vernacular', process must accordingly be envisioned for the 'Love and Murder' form, and the same will apply to the only other murdered sweetheart ballad first appearing as a lengthy broadside text in the eighteenth century, 'The Berkshire Tragedy' (44 stanzas), subsequently abbreviated to a much shorter (18 stanza) form in the nineteenth, published as 'The Cruel (or 'Bloody') Miller', displaying memoral features similar to those of 'Love and Murder'. And it too, achieved extensive and sustained distribution in singing tradition.

In a discussion of the latter ballad, David Atkinson acknowledges that even the deliberate revision he envisages for the abbreviated broadside 'may have been influenced by the ballad in its orally circulating form'.[39] Something similar might be relevant for 'The Gosport Tragedy', and the existence of such collateral derivatives is suggested by the occurrence, in versions recovered from singing tradition, of faint but thought-provoking echoes of the original, long broadside *not* found in any editions of the abbreviated, nineteenth-century 'Love and Murder' broadside.[40]

For example while the latter merely states that the absconding murderer went 'on board' to sail away (st. 8.3), in Gypsy Denny Smith's performance he enlisted as a 'ship's *carpenter's tale* [sic]' (st. 5.4; emphasis supplied), which may be a garbled rendition of the long version's 'For *carpenters mate* he entered we hear' (Shelmerdine 18.1). And to this end, Denny Smith has it, he went 'to *Bedford* to list straightaway' (st. 5.3; emphasis supplied). Almost 100 miles from the nearest seaport (much further than Worcester, where the action here is set), Bedford is an unlikely place to embark on a naval vessel, and it may not be a coincidence that in an adjacent line in the long broadside, not retained in the short, 'Bedford' was the name of the ship on which the murderer enlisted (Shelmerdine st. 17.3).

George Dunn's fragmentary version, in two of his most sustained attempts, substitutes for the usual opening stanzas the mysterious,

> Two brace of kisses I had late last night
> to rise up in the morning before it was light

before continuing with the murder scene as in the short broadside. This has been recognised as a garbled reminiscence of two lines from 'The Gosport Tragedy' at the same point in the narrative (Shelmerdine st. 10.1–2):

> With kindest em*brace*s they parted that *night*,
> He went for to meet her next *morning* e'er *light*.[41]

More straightforward is the opening of the version sung by Mrs. Emma Hancock (otherwise apparently deriving from the short broadside):

> In Gosport Town a fair damsel did dwell,
> For wit and for beauty none could her excel....

which closely reproduces the first two lines of the 'Gosport Tragedy'.[42]

The balladesque qualities of the nineteenth-century broadside are so ingrained, however, that sporadic influence from versions of the 'Gosport Tragedy' circulating in contemporary singing tradition is hardly a sufficient explanation, and it is tempting to speculate that 'Love and Murder' is effectively a *transcript of* a performance from that tradition, dictated or written down by a singer. This would conveniently accord all its undoubted improvements to singing tradition and its memoral affordances, but the external evidence for this procedure is at best anecdotal, and the same objection would presumably apply to a variant of this scenario in which the reviser was simply writing down his own recollection of the song. At the opposite extreme, however, if the nineteenth-century broadside were a conscious ballad pastiche in the manner of Keats' near contemporaneous 'La Belle Dame sans Merci', we might expect somewhat more structural regularity and stylistic elegance.

The process was plausibly somewhere in between, and in our attempt to look over the shoulder or into the mind of the reviser, some insight may be available in research on medieval texts, where similar memoral symptoms can appear in the process of scribal copying.[43] The connection is more readily appreciated when song transmission is perceived as memoral rather than oral, for while the movement of verbal material for a scribe is not, as for a singer, from ear to voice, but from eye to hand, in both cases a passage through the memory intervenes. It is not feasible to write a legible copy while the eyes are looking at the text being copied, and accordingly, as tireless editor of medieval English texts, George Kane, reminds us, in copying verse, scribes did not copy word by word or even… line by line…. They took up blocks of text, groups of lines such as a stanza or a verse 'paragraph', into the memory by eye… and then, writing from that memory, put their eyes to the page and their hand to the forming of letters.[44]

The less official and authoritative the material, the longer the segments committed to memory were likely to be, potentially increasing the incidence of discrepancy. In the case of very popular, anonymous works, with no sense of obligation to reproduce an authorial original, even longer segments, even more subject to variation, might be encompassed in each transfer, perhaps drifting momentarily into memoral reconstruction if it was material, say a song or a story, with which the scribe was already familiar.

Such circumstances would facilitate both subtraction and substitution, including external contamination with material from other texts. As Kane further notes,

> … everything that the scribe had ever copied or even read was a potential source of disturbance of message from eye to brain to hand because of the possibility of his subconsciously associating it with the copy in hand.[45]

Perhaps for present purposes we can legitimately substitute, 'copied or even *heard*', and in the case of traditional genres like ballads the intrusion of verbal formulas might equally be envisaged.

Kane also observes that the process can likewise induce (internal) contamination from within the text being transcribed (producing verbal repetitions). To all of which can be added the long-standing acknowledgement that scribal copying, not least of secular materials, could be an active, even interventionist process, in which the copyist felt free to achieve 'improvements' by his own lights.[46] He might feasibly also be working to external constraints, say the need to abbreviate or simplify.

Such processes, 'writ large' under the auspices of a nineteenth-century printing house specialising in cheap, popular productions, are quite likely to have been operative in the process by which 'Gosport Tragedy' was re-crafted into something (the nineteenth-century 'Love and Murder' ballad) somewhat resembling what might otherwise have been achieved through unaided singing tradition. On spotting similar but relatively smaller scale variations on the basis of an analogous comparative analysis, Roger de V. Renwick assigns them rather to the compositor in the printing shop, who may have brought an 'oral attitude' to the task, suggesting that as he read the text in front of him *he effectively sang the ballad in his mind*, and set what he heard.[47] The perpetrator here clearly had larger-scale opportunities, and on reflection the process may indeed be related to performance in all directions: to performances recollected from the past; to a mental performance in the present; even to an anticipated pseudo-performance before an 'audience' constituted by those who would acquire a copy of the broadside….

It is in this way, and to this degree, that the material explored in this contribution may be reconciled with, and supply documentation for, David Atkinson's authoritative and intelligently argued suggestion that ballads mediated (from one edition to another) by broadside publication share with those subjected to memoral transmission a 'vernacular' textuality distinct from that of songs in printed books.[48] But it is only *some* broadside ballads, under *some* circumstances, that *can* be re-crafted in a manner similar to, and with results commensurate with, those generated in singing tradition. For those broadside 'ballads' that have not had the benefit of such vernacular re-crafting, abbreviation merely reduces a large lump on the dunghill of cheap print to a smaller one.

★★★

Appendix

Versions of Roud 15 consulted for this contribution

For material available via the following online resources:

> Vaughan Williams Memorial Library (VWML): www.vwml.org.
> Bodleian Library, Oxford: http://ballads.bodleian.ox.ac.uk/
> English Broadside Ballad Archive (EBBA): https://ebba.english.ucsb.edu/

Type into the search box the identification specified below between the angle brackets (which should be omitted). The Madden Collection at the University of Cambridge is not as yet accessible online (all URLs checked 14 February 2020).

The long broadside (eighteenth–early nineteenth century)

- unless otherwise noted, these are all (with slight variations in spelling and capitalization) entitled 'The Gosport Tragedy; or, The Perjured Ship-Carpenter'.
- ordered alphabetically by name of printer or printing house (versions with no imprint at end of list), with specification of copy consulted

Aldermary Churchyard, London (34 stanzas): Yale University. Lewis Walpole Library. online at <https://www.britishtars.com/2014/12/the-gosport-tragedy-or-perjured-ship.html>
Belsey, Exeter (29 stanzas): Madden Collection, 23.48
Cluer, (attrib.), London (34 stanzas): British Library. Roxburghe Collection, III.II.510–511. EBBA <31213>
Evans, London (29 stanzas): Madden Collection, 2.378
Harward, Tewkesbury (33 stanzas): British Library. Document Number CW3311921749
Pitts, Seven Dials, London (34 stanzas): Madden Collection, 2.369
Shelmerdine, Manchester (30 stanzas; chapbook): Bodleian Library 2803.f.4 (not online).
Stonecutter Street, London (34 stanzas): Bodleian <Harding B 3(33)>
Stonecutter Street, London (variant format) (34 stanzas): National Library of Scotland LS. Crawford EB. 655, EBBA <33259>
Storer, Bristol (34 stanzas; chapbook). Bodleian. Firth f.72, no. 33 (not online)
Turner, Coventry (32 stanzas): Bodleian <Harding B.3(34)>
no imprint (34 stanzas): Chetham's Library, <http://www.chethams.org.uk/cat/chethams_library_halliwell_phillipps_0247.jpg>
no imprint (35 stanzas): Houghton Library, Hazlitt EC65. EBBA <35483>
no imprint (35 stanzas): Madden Collection, 2.370
no imprint (34 stanzas): National Library of Scotland, Crawford 656. EBBA <33261>

The short broadside: the 'literary' abbreviation (ca 1775–1825)

'Nancy's Ghost'

> Angus, Newcastle: Bodleian <Harding B 17(207b)>

The short broadside: the 'vernacular' abbreviation (nineteenth century)

> Arranged in accordance with published title

'The cruel ship carpenter'

Cadman, Manchester: Frank Kidson Broadside Collection, VWML </FK/17/239>
Bebbington, Manchester: Bodleian <Harding B 15(74b)>
Forth, Pocklington: Bodleian <Firth c.13(290)>
Jackson and Son, Birmingham: Kenneth Goldstein Collection, University of Mississippi Libraries (goldstein kg04 24 02) <https://egrove.olemiss.edu/kgbsides_uk/341/>
Kiernan/Duckett, Liverpool: Madden Collection, 18.29.
Pratt, Birmingham: Madden Collection, 21.43.
Willey, Cheltenham: Madden Collection, 23.512.
no imprint: Frank Kidson Broadside Collection, VWML <FK/13/146/2>
no imprint: Bodleian <Harding B 11(824)>

'Polly's love, or the cruel ship-carpenter'

Catnach, London: Frank Kidson Broadside Collection, VWML <FK/15/59>
Disley. London: Frank Kidson Broadside Collection, VWML <FK/16/5/2>
Ford, Sheffield: Bodleian <Harding B 11(3058)>
Fortey, London: Bodleian <Harding B 11(3056)>
Harkness, Preston: Bodleian <Harding B 11(3057)>
Hodge, London: Bodleian <Johnson Ballads 458>
Pitts, London: Bodleian <Harding B 11(3053A)>
Pitts, London: Bodleian <Firth c.13(206)>
Such, London: Broadwood Ballad Sheet Collection, VWML <LEB/9/335/1>

'Love and murder'

Armstrong, Liverpool: Bodleian <Harding B 28(24)>
Armstrong, Liverpool: Bodleian <Harding B 28(165)>
Bloomer, Birmingham: Broadwood Ballad Sheet Collection, VWML <LEB/9/337/2>
Pollock, North Shields: Bodleian <Harding B 25(1156)>
Williams, Plymouth: British Library BL HS.74/2008) No.5
no imprint: Bodleian <Harding B 28(285)>

English singing tradition

Alphabetical by singer (with location); followed by collector and date, then the source at or via which the text can be consulted.

Baldwin, George (Tichborne, Hampshire); George Gardiner, June 1907. VWML <GG/1/12/712>

Barnes, Mrs. (unspecified location, Hampshire); George Gardiner, date unspecified. VWML <GG/1/17/1102>

Blake, George (Bitterne, Hampshire); George Gardiner, November 1907. VWML <GG/1/6/343>

Blake, Moses (Lyndhurst, Hampshire); George Gardiner, June 1906. (one stanza only) VWML <GG/1/5/272 >

Bowker, Mrs. (Sunderland Point, Lancashire); Anne Geddes Gilchrist, date not specified. (one stanza only) VWML <LEB/5/163/2 >

Brazil, Danny (Over Bridge, Gloucester); Peter Shepheard, 6 January 1966. *The Brazil Family: Down by the Old Riverside.* Musical Traditions MTCD345–7 (2007). CD 2: track 2.2 (transcript accessible via http://www.mtrecords.co.uk/).

Brazil, Danny (Staverton, Gloucestershire); Mike Yates & Gwilym Davies 19 February 1978. *Gloucestershire Traditions.* The Seamen Song <http://glostrad.com/seamen-song-the/>

Brazil, Weenie (Blairgowrie berryfields, Scotland); Hamish Henderson July/August 1955. *The Brazil Family: Down by the Old Riverside.* Musical Traditions MTCD345–7 (2007). CD 2: track 2.1 (transcript accessible via http://www.mtrecords.co.uk/).

Case, Mrs. (Nicholas, Dorset); H.E.D. Hammond, September 1907. VWML <HAM/5/34/26>

Cox, Harry. (Catfield, Norfolk); Mervyn Plunkett, 1958–1960. VWML <FS/S436285>

Dunn, George (Quarry Bank, Staffordshire); Roy Palmer, 21 June 1971. British Library. Sounds. Roy Palmer English Folk Music Collection. 025M-C1023X0010XX-2600V0>; continued on<025M-C1023X0011XX-0100V0>

Dunn, George (Quarry Bank, Staffordshire); Roy Palmer, 3 December 1971. VWML <FS/S232194>

Gulliver, Mrs. (Combe Florey, Somerset); Henry Hammond, spring 1905. VWML <HAM/2/1/25>

Hancock, Mrs. Emma (Blunsdon, Wiltshire); Alfred Williams, n.d. VWML <AW/4/10>

Larner, Sam (Winterton, Norfolk); Philip Donnellan 13 September 1959. *Good People, Take Warning. Ballads sung by British and Irish Traditional Singers.* The Voice of the People, Topic TSCD 673T 2012, no. 56

Lemming, William (Terwick, Sussex); Clive Carey, February 1911. VWML <CC/1/7>

Marlow, David (Basingstoke, Hampshire); George Gardiner, September 1906. VWML <GG/1/10/565>

Pike, Mrs. (Betsy) (Somerton, Somerset); Mrs. Snow for Cecil Sharp, 18 January, 1906 VWML <CJS2/9/852>

Rowe, John (Duncton, Sussex); Clive Carey, 1912. VWML <CC/1/308>

Smith, Denny (Gloucester, Gloucestershire); Peter Shepheard, 27 April 1966. VWML <FS/S232167>

Smith, James (Westbourne, Sussex); G.B. Gardiner, 19 April 1909 (one stanza only). VWML <GG/1/21/1373>

Smith, Wiggy (Postlip Barn, Gloucestershire); Gwilym Davies 27 June 1998. *Wiggy Smith -- Band of Gold.* Musical Traditions MT CD 307. 2000, track 27 + video of performance at Glostrad Archive Videos <https://www.youtube.com/watch?v=rZarZ8vmSVU>

Smithers, Mrs. Elizabeth (Tewkesbury, Gloucestershire); Cecil Sharp, 9 January 1908 (one stanza only). VWML <CJS2/10/1576>

Spearing, William, aka Spearman (Ile Brewen, Somerset); Cecil Sharp, 6 April 1904 (one stanza only). VWML <CJS2/10/147>

Spearing, William, aka Spearman (Ile Brewen, Somerset); Cecil Sharp, 8 September 1906. VWML <CJS2/9/222> (second page missing)

Stride, Alfred (Dibden, Hampshire); George Gardiner, June 1907 (one stanza only). VWML <GG/1/11/698>

Taylor, Joseph (Brigg, Lincolnshire); Percy Grainger, 28 July 1906 (one stanza only). VWML <PG/5/15>

Thomas, James (Cannington, Somerset); Cecil Sharp, 17 August 1906 (one stanza only). VWML <CJS2/10/1041>

Tucker, William (Ashcott, Somerset); Cecil Sharp, 15 January 1907. VWML <CJS2/9/1171>

Notes

1. In its recent guise, it may have opened with G.M. Laws' essay on 'Ballad Recomposition' in his *American Balladry from British Broadsides* (Philadelphia: American Folklore Society, 1957), pp. 105–122. There is a comprehensive and balanced review in Steve Roud, Introduction, *Street Ballads in Nineteenth-Century Britain, Ireland, and North America: The Interface between Print and Oral Tradition*, ed. by David Atkinson and Steve Roud (Aldershot: Ashgate, 2017), pp. 1–17.
2. An authoritative exponent of this view is David Atkinson's *The Anglo-Scottish Ballad and Its Imaginary Contexts* (Cambridge: Open Book Publishers, 2014).
3. As discussed by Dianne M. Dugaw, 'Anglo-American Folksong Reconsidered: The Interface of Oral and Written Forms', *Western Folklore*, 43 (1984), 83–103.
4. For a disturbing account of the development of this notion, see Paula McDowell, *The Invention of the Oral: Print Commerce and Fugitive Voices in Eighteenth-Century Britain* (Chicago, IL: University of Chicago Press, 2017). There may also be some confusion stemming from the 'oral-formulaic' theory, influential in this and other fields in the second half of the twentieth century, in which 'oral' was effectively synonymous with improvisation-in-performance. Its major manifestation in ballad studies was David Buchan's (in every other way valuable) *The Ballad and the Folk* (London: Routledge, 1972).
5. David Atkinson, in his print-oriented *The Anglo-Scottish Ballad*, p. 34 concedes that in the given conditions, concatenations of up to three singers can have occurred.
6. See, for example, 'From Journalism to Gypsy Folk Song: The Road to Orality of an English Ballad', *Oral Tradition*, 23.1 (2008), 87–117 <https://journal.oraltradition.org/wp-content/uploads/files/articles/23i/07_23.1pettitt.pdf> [accessed 12 February 2020]; 'Written Composition and (Mem)oral Decomposition: The Case of "The Suffolk Tragedy"', *Oral Tradition*, 24.2 (2009), 429–454 <https://journal.oraltradition.org/wp-content/uploads/files/articles/24ii/10_24.2.pdf> [accessed 12 February 2020]; 'The Ballad of Tradition: In Pursuit of a Vernacular Aesthetic', in *Ballads into Books: The Legacies of Francis James Child*, ed. by Tom Cheesman and Sigrid Rieuwerts (Bern: Peter Lang, 1997), pp. 111–123; 'Mediating Maria Marten: Comparative and Contextual Studies of the Red Barn Ballads', in *Street Ballads*, pp. 219–243.
7. Roud, 'Introduction', *Street Ballads*, p. 13 (emphasis supplied).
8. Joseph Ritson, *Scotish* [sic] *Song*, 2 vols. (London: Johnson & Egerton, 1794), I, lxxxi.
9. For the context see Roy Palmer, '"Veritable Dunghills": Professor Child and the Broadside Author(s)', *Folk Music Journal*, 7.2 (1996), 155–166, which provides Child's comment (from 1872) at p. 157.
10. I have explored this aspect of ballad transmission in 'The Late-Medieval Ballad', in *Medieval Oral Literature*, ed. by Karl Reichl (Berlin: Walter de Gruyter, 2011), pp. 429–458.
11. Bertrand Harris Bronson, 'On the Union of Words and Music in "Child" Ballads', *The Ballad as Song* (Berkeley and Santa Barbara: University of California Press, 1969), pp. 112–132 (p. 131) (emphasis supplied).
12. This paper resolutely ignores the nineteenth-century parody version, 'Molly the Betrayed, or the Fog Bound Vessel', Roud V51737.
13. This title also occurs as a sub-title for printed versions of another song, 'The Berkshire Tragedy' (Roud 263).
14. See the Appendix. With regard to identifying and accessing the broadside editions, including versions of the earlier 'Gosport Tragedy', I am happy to acknowledge the assistance of Steve Gardham.
15. See the Appendix. The popularity of the song is also reflected by instances (not considered further here) where only the tune was recorded. In their *New Penguin Book of English Folk Songs* (London: Penguin, 2012), pp. 286–288 (and see Notes p. 81), editors Steve Roud and Julia Bishop assign to singer Henry Burstow (Horsham, Sussex, 1893) a text of this song published by Lucy Broadwood in 'Songs from the Collection of Lucy E. Broadwood (1902)', *Journal of the Folk Song Society*, 1.4 (1902), 139–225 (p. 173). But Broadwood indicates that she collected only the tune from Burstow, and supplies the text from the broadside published by Henry Such.
16. The song occurs only sporadically in Scotland and Ireland, but massively and chaotically, in both print and performance, in North America. For energetic attempts to chart the ballad's international history, see Paul Slade, *Unprepared to Die. America's Greatest Murder Ballads and the True Crime Stories that Inspired Them* (London: Soundcheck Books, 2015), ch. 6, 'Pretty Polly' (pp. 143–177); Richard L. Matteson, 'More English and Scottish Popular Ballads: 1. Gosport Tragedy/ The Cruel Ship's Carpenter/ Pretty Polly', *Bluegrass Messengers* <http://www.bluegrassmessengers.com/1-the-cruel-ships-carpenter-pretty-polly.aspx> [accessed 14 February 2020].

17 Stanza numbers have also been supplied. Broadside texts and published transcripts from performance present the ballad in a variety of formats, but can invariably be resolved, as here, on the basis of syntax and melody, into quatrains (long metre; rhyming aabb) for the purpose of comparison.
18 Earlier studies of the genre include D.K. Wilgus, 'A Tension of Essences in Murdered-Sweetheart Ballads', in *The Ballad Image*, ed. by J. Porter (Los Angeles: Center for the Study of Comparative Folklore & Mythology, University of California, Los Angeles, 1983), pp. 241–256, and the paradigmatic (from a news mediation perspective), Anne B. Cohen, *Poor Pearl, Poor Girl! The Murdered-Girl Stereotype in Ballad and News-paper* (Austin: Univ. of Texas Press, 1981). I have reviewed the genre, its possible origins and its development (on the basis of the 25 songs identified at the time), in 'Journalism vs. Tradition in the Early English Ballads of the Murdered Sweetheart', in *Ballads and Broadsides in Britain, 1500 – 1800*, ed. by Patricia Fumerton, et al. (Aldershot: Ashgate, 2010), pp. 75–90.
19 The others are 'The Cruel Gamekeeper' (Roud 1313), 'Mary Thomson' (Roud 2458) and 'The Suffolk Tragedy' (Roud 18814, another ballad on the Maria Marten case). A further English broadside ballad, 'William Grismond' (Roud V39057) has been recorded only from Scottish singing tradition, as 'Willie Graham' (Roud 953).
20 On the basis of the Roud Folksong Index, these are Harry Cox (Roud 263, 'The Berkshire Tragedy'); Mrs. Emma Hancock (Roud 1313, 'The Cruel Gamekeeper'); Mrs. [Betsy] Pike (Roud 263, 'The Berkshire Tragedy'); Alfred Stride (Roud 263, 'The Berkshire Tragedy'); William Spearing (Roud 263, 'The Berkshire Tragedy'); Joseph Taylor (Roud 215, 'The Murder of Maria Marten').
21 Angela Shaw, 'A Singer in the Quantocks: Jane Gulliver – Her Times and Songs', in *Proceedings of the English Folk Dance and Song Society Folk Song Conference 2013*, ed. by David Atkinson and Steve Roud (Northfield, Minnesota: Loomis House Press, 2015), pp. 48–53 (p. 52).
22 The frequent omission of the stanza (st. 6) in which the sweetheart pleads for her life may be due to its lack of narrative function, but as it contains the only explicit reference to her pregnancy, this may reflect the reticence of singers in the presence of a stranger (from a higher social class) recording the performance.
23 Max Luthi, 'Urform und Zielform in Sage und Marchen', *Fabula*, 9 (1967), 41–54.
24 With the proviso that variation among broadsides is unevenly distributed, with some more prone to small-scale substitution than others.
25 Gerald Porter, 'The English Occupational Song', Diss. (University Of Umeå, Sweden, 1992), p. 75, n.2 <https://www.academia.edu/21018619/The_English_Occupational_Song> [accessed 12 February 2020].
26 *The Brazil Family: Down by the Old Riverside*, Musical Traditions MTCD345-7 (2007), CD 2: track 2.2
27 'Pretty Polly Oliver' (Roud 367); 'Polly Perkins' (Roud 430), not to mention 'The Outlandish Knight' (Roud 21) where it is sometimes used both of the female protagonist (who narrowly avoids becoming a murdered sweetheart) and of her parrot.
28 *The Brazil Family: Down by the Old Riverside*, CD3, track 18.
29 Flemming G. Andersen, *Commonplace and Creativity: The Role of Formulaic Diction in Anglo-Scottish Traditional Balladry* (Odense: Odense University Press, 1985), 12.vi., 'He hadna ridden a mile, a mile /They hadna sailed a league, a league' (pp. 259–265).
30 https://www.vwml.org/record/RoudFS/S400607 (with original MS songbook).
31 See the Appendix.
32 Although not germane to the present enquiry, it would be wrong to not mention David C. Fowler's spirited exploration of its historicity (named people, places and a ship recorded in historical documents) in 'The Gosport Tragedy: Story of a Ballad', *Southern Folklore Quarterly*, 43 (1979), 157–196.
33 Roud V51736. I have consulted the extract (with the full, summarising, title) in *Chap-books of the eighteenth century*, ed. by John Ashton (London: Chatto and Windus, 1882), pp. 70–71. The song is invoked in this connection by Fowler, 'The Gosport Tragedy: Story of a Ballad', p. 191, but while the intrusion is seen as 'the … effect of oral tradition', that effect is characterised as 'adverse'.
34 See the Appendix.
35 Further investigation might do well to shift the focus to Manchester, where Shelmerdine issued his edition, and where 'Polly's Love' was issued at about the same time by three other local printers (Swindells; Bebbington; Cadman).

36 David Atkinson, 'Was There Really a "Mass Extinction of Old Ballads" in the Romantic Period', in *Street Ballads in Nineteenth-Century Britain*, pp. 19–36 (p. 35).
37 Roud Index, https://www.vwml.org/record/RoudFS/S425230.
38 See the Appendix. My attention was drawn to the distinct form of this version of the song by a contribution from Jim Brown to a *Mudcat* thread, 'Origins: Gosport Tragedy / Cruel Ship's Carpenter', on 5 April 2016, <http://awe.mudcat.org/thread.cfm?threadid=159568&page=2&desc=yes> [accessed 14 February 2020].
39 *The Anglo-Scottish Ballad*, p. 51.
40 Although American perspectives will not be pursued in this paper, it can be noted that G. M. Laws, *American Balladry from British Broadsides* (Philadelphia: American Folklore Society, 1957), pp. 268–269, reports distinct derivatives over there from both 'long version' and 'short version' English broadsides (P36A and P36B, respectively).
41 See the exchange between 'Ritchie' (Richard L. Matteson) and Jim Brown, on the thread 'Origins: Gosport Tragedy / Cruel Ship's Carpenter', 3 April 16 – 01:57 AM and 3 April 16 – 10:17 AM. <http://awe.mudcat.org/thread.cfm?threadid=159568> [accessed 14 February 2020].
42 The edition of 'Love and Murder' published by Williams of Plymouth also starts this way, but Mrs. Hancok does not follow its other major idiosyncrasies.
43 Not least romances, on whose mixed transmission, see, for example, Murray McGillivray, *Memorization in the Transmission of the Middle English Romances* (New York and London: Garland, 1990); James R. Hurt, 'The Texts of *King Horn*', *Journal of the Folklore Institute*, 7.1 (1970), 47–59.
44 George Kane, 'The Text', in *A Companion to Piers Plowman*, ed. by John A. Alford (Berkeley: University of California Press, 1988), pp. 175–200 (p. 192).
45 Kane, 'The Text', p. 193.
46 For an early but still valuable contribution along these lines, see Richard A. Dwyer, 'The Appreciation of Handmade Literature', *Chaucer Review*, 8 (1974–1975), 221–240.
47 Roger de V. Renwick, 'The Oral Quality of a Printed Tradition,' *Acta Ethnographica Hungarica*, 47 (2002), 81–89 (pp. 81–82). This may reasonably explain some of the sub-stanzaic verbal morphing discernible between different editions of the nineteenth-century broadside (although the direction of change cannot be determined).
48 David Atkinson, 'Folk Songs in Print: Text and Tradition', *Folk Music Journal*, 8.4 (2004), 456–483 (pp. 471–472).

19

BURLESQUING THE BALLAD

Steve Gardham

The *Oxford English Dictionary* gives the meaning of the noun 'burlesque' most appropriate here as 'that species of literary composition or of dramatic representation which aims at exciting laughter by caricature of the manner or spirit of serious works, or by ludicrous treatment of their subjects; a literary or dramatic work of this kind', and an example of 1667 is given. I would contend that this meaning of the word is that which has prevailed from about 1600 to the present day, albeit other usages have come and gone in that period. As we also use the word as a verb, it seems appropriate to give the same dictionary's verb definition, 'To turn into ridicule by grotesque parody or imitation, to caricature, travesty'.

Prior to 1600, the noun seems to have been used to apply to what we now call 'songs of marvels' or 'impossibilities' such as the well-known 'Martin said to his man/Who's the fool now?'[1]

Whilst many types of literature and dramatic works have been burlesqued over the last four centuries, including the ballad operas of the eighteenth century, this chapter looks at how the traditional ballad, that which has been at some point transmitted orally, has been burlesqued.

An investigation of the topic of burlesques and parodies necessitates close textual comparisons and detailed deconstructions of individual songs, as well as the broad principles which seem to operate in particular genres.

This work is interesting in itself, but it is also valuable as a clear demonstration of how the history of songs, and of singing, needs to take into account the highly complex interplay between commercial and 'folk', which in the past has been seen as a relatively simple relationship. The following case studies lead us through a maze of song milieux, including the oral tradition, printed sources at all levels (broadsides, songsters, sheet music), stage representations (ballad operas, farces, burlettas, pantomimes), commercial pleasure gardens, tavern-singing, semi-professional concert rooms, fully professional music halls and many more.

It is a key definitional element of 'folk song' that songs change over time, both in the individual voice (from performance to performance) and in transmission between singers, down the generations, and so on. Change can be gradual, seemingly organic (and unconscious) or deliberate, but on the whole the 'tradition' appears to be relatively stable and singers relatively conservative rather than innovative and dynamic.

But change can also be abrupt and far-reaching, usually as a result of deliberate individual (and often commercial) intervention. Songs can be re-written, shortened, lengthened, combined, parodied, adapted for a new audience, bawdied or bowdlerised, and generally mucked about, and any of these 'adaptations' can become popular in their own right, and even become 'traditional'.

The complex case of 'Lord Lovel'

Burlesques can act in two quite distinct ways, the obvious one being a burlesque of a single serious work. But the other is when the treatment is of a whole genre, as in the case of the ballad operas of the early eighteenth century, epitomised by Gay's *The Beggar's Opera* which burlesqued the whole genre of Italian opera, dominant in Britain at the time. We therefore commence with a couple of traditional ballads that are very likely not burlesques of individual ballads but of the whole genre of traditional ballads, namely 'Lord Lovel' (Child 75) and 'Giles Collins'/'Lady Alice' (Child 85). Child himself links these two ballads in his headnote to 'Lady Alice' in his seminal *English and Scottish Popular Ballads*: 'This little ballad, which is said to be still of the regular stock of the stalls, is a sort of counterpart to "Lord Lovel"'. Child's comment in his headnote to the latter ballad is even more revealing: 'Lord Lovel is peculiarly such a ballad as Orsino likes and praises; it is silly sooth, like the old age. Therefore a gross taste has taken pleasure in parodying it, and the same with Young Beichan. But there are people in this world who are amused even with a burlesque of Othello'. In a footnote, he refers to the jolly tune and 'cheerful sounding formula, which in the upshot enhances by contrast the gloom of the conclusion'.[2] He does not outright state that in his opinion, 'Lord Lovel' is a burlesque, but the implication is surely there in his 'silly sooth'. In using the word 'parodying', he is more likely referring to the nineteenth-century stage parodies of it, and others.

Bertrand Bronson, who published the traditional tunes associated with the Child ballads, elaborated on the latter's comments, and showed that burlesques could be just as popular as 'straight' songs:

> No light is thrown upon the beginnings of this too insipid ballad by the musical tradition. Its great popularity for at least a hundred years is powerful testimony to the life-giving energy of a memorable tune. For the narrative is of the slightest, and there is no sign in any known version that it has lost much in its passage. The textual tradition is, like the melodic one, unusually compact and consistent. But it is impossible to believe that there is enough nutriment in the story alone to win friends on every hand. Though it dallies with the innocence of love, it could hardly have struck most singers as silly sooth, unless for the reason that it was so strange to common experience. But the tune has been remembered almost note for note by multitudes, we must suppose; and this lack of deviation proves that it was everywhere learned without effort, if not all but involuntarily. There is no obvious bond of sympathy between tripping melody and lachrymose text, but the first effectually removes the curse from the second, so that it can be sung without much loss of self-possession. Whether or not it was born of the eighteenth century, this union of text and tune prettily symbolises a sentimentality too concerned with itself as interesting spectacle ever to be pulled under by the tide of genuine emotion.[3]

Child has very little to say on *Lady Alice*. He gives only two short versions, one a nineteenth-century broadside copy and the other from *Gammer Gurton's Garland* of 1810.[4]

We now know that there were a few earlier versions and many later ones recorded in the twentieth century, both in Britain and in America. The earlier ones, of the second half of the eighteenth century, differ enough between them and between later versions to suggest an even earlier origin. Bronson refers to the possible relationship between this ballad and 'Clerk Colvill' (Child 42), a Scottish rewrite of a very widespread ballad on the continent described in detail by Child in his headnotes. Bronson flags up the very persuasive theory first proposed by Barbara M. Cra'ster,[5] that Child 85 is based on Child 42. These links would not have been available to Child as the versions containing them are largely found in sources recorded after he died. The versions of 'Giles Collins' collected in southern England and some American ones have three extra stanzas at the beginning which are not found in any of the extant earlier versions. The links between the two ballads are that Collins/Colvill meets a maid washing on a stone who he is enamoured with, but the encounter proves fatal to him, and when he gets home he asks his mother to make his bed as he will soon be dead. In *Lady Alice*, he asks his mother to 'bind up my head' which in 'Clerk Colvill' is an action that happens earlier in the story and it is the maid who is asked. Whilst more recently others claim that these links are somewhat tenuous, i.e. the 'mother, make my bed/dead' is a commonplace, I think there is a strong possibility of a connection, and Bronson states 'its plausibility makes a strong appeal'.[6] The earliest extant version of 'Clerk Colvill' was given in Herd's *Ancient and Modern Scottish Songs*[7] of 1769, and even though it is quite likely that it had been written only a few decades earlier, it could easily have been the inspiration for the burlesque 'Giles Collins'.

 The earliest extant versions of 'Lord Lovel' are those sent to Bishop Percy in the 1760s and 1770s.[8] In February 1765, Horace Walpole sent Percy the following version, which he titled 'The Ballad of Lady Hounsibelle and Lord Lovel':

> I fare you well, Lady Hounsibelle,
> For I must needs be gone;
> And this time two year I'll meet you again,
> To end the true love we begun.
>
> That's a long time, Lord Lovel, she said,
> To dwell in fair Scotland:
> And so it is, Lady Hounsibelle,
> And to leave a fair lady alone.
>
> He called unto his stable groom
> To saddle his milk-white steed;
> Hey down, Hey down, Hey, derry down,
> I wish my Lord Lovel good speed.
>
> He had not been in fair Scotland
> Above half a year,
> But a longing mind came over his head,
> Lady Hounsibelle he would go see her.
>
> He had not been in fair London
> Above half a day,
> But he heard the bells of the high chapel ring;
> They rung with a sesora.
>
> He asked of a gentleman,
> That stood there all alone,

What made the bells of the high chapel ring,
And the ladies to make such a moan.

The King's fair daughter is dead, he said,
Whose name's Lady Hounsibelle;
She died for love of a courteous knight,
Whose name it is Lord Lovel.

Lady Hounsibelle died on the Easterday,
Lord Lovel on the morrow;
Lady Hounsibelle died for pure true love,
Lord Lovel he died for sorrow.

Lady Hounsibelle's buried in the chancel,
Lord Lovel in the choir;
Lady Hounsibelle's breast sprung up a rose,
Lord Lovel's a branch of sweet briar.

They grew till they grew to the top of the church,
And when they could grow no higher,
They grew till they grew to a true lover's knot,
And they both were tied together.

There came an old woman by,
Their blessing she did crave;
She cut a branch of this true lover's knot,
And buried 'em both in a grave.[9]

Walpole had written the ballad down from memory having learnt it about 1740. In the accompanying letter, he states, 'I remember to have heard another, which was the exact counterpart to it, called "Giles Colin"', but unfortunately he could not remember any of this. In 1770, Percy received another version from a Reverend P. Parsons of Wye 'from singing'. It is noteworthy that the two versions only differ textually in a few minor points, albeit one is from memory in London and the other from oral transmission only a few miles from London. Walpole's version lacks one stanza of Parsons' version. This stanza comes after stanza 7 in Walpole's version.

He caused the corpse to be set down,
And her winding sheet undone,
And he made a vow before them all
That he'd never kiss woman again.

The closeness of the two versions could suggest that ballad was not very old in the mid-eighteenth century. In the letter, Walpole makes no hint that he considered the ballad comic in any way, but there are numerous features in the ballad that place it into the realms of burlesque. Undoubtedly, whoever composed it was familiar with the characteristics of the ballad of tradition; it is in ballad metre, uses commonplace phrases (somewhat liberally) and a whole stanza sequence, and has the tell-tale leaping and lingering[10] so characteristic of the ballad, but one could say that in this case the leaping and lingering is well overcooked, and there are numerous tell-tale burlesque ingredients in the mix. Just the name Hounsibelle (Ouncebell in Parsons' version) is a hint. Traditional ballads are well-known for using mostly very common first names and whilst the addition of 'belle' onto the end of an existing female given name was common at that time (Nancybelle in later versions), the name here seems to have been unique. The fourth stanza rhymes 'year' with 'go see her' contrived rhymes being typical of burlesques. Both versions have the peculiar use of a well-known refrain as the third line of the third stanza. There are certain situations which suggest that the ballad had not been long in tradition, such as 'He asked of a gentleman that stood there all alone'. The shortening of 'them' in the last line smacks of a comic stage piece. Individually all of these quibbles could easily be dismissed, but collectively to one who has studied burlesque ballads they point to that genre. So the whole has the ring of a burlesque, but a burlesque of what precisely? A suggestion has been made that it was a burlesque of one of the old broadsides 'Fair Margaret and Sweet William' (Child 74), mainly because they have similar plots and both employ the 'rose and briar' commonplace, but my thesis is that both 'Lord Lovel' and 'Lady Alice' are burlesques on the ballad genre as a whole, not on a single ballad, excepting perhaps Lady Alice is a burlesque on 'Clerk Colvill', indeed a possibility.

Another aspect of the burlesque is that in a few cases, on paper, the burlesques looked little different from the serious original and the humour was mostly or all derived from the performance. Both of the ballads so far under scrutiny here appear to have been treated as burlesques in performance in their own urban settings, but in oral tradition when taken directly from the broadside press, became serious ballads in rural areas with little access to stage versions. No doubt 'Giles Collins' existed in many forms in the second half of the eighteenth century, but by 1790 it was certainly a stage burlesque as sung in a 'crying style' by Mr. Needham.[11] But we also know that this version was part of the pleasure garden repertoire in 1763 as its first stanza was included in a medley printed by Thomas Bailey of 110 Leadenhall Street, London,[12] and medleys, by definition, comprise parts of songs already in circulation, and in most cases readily recognisable to their audience.

> Giles Collins he came to his own Father's gate,
> Where he so oft had been a
> And who should come down but his own dear Mother
> For to let Giles Collins in a
> Oh, for to let Giles Collins in a.
>
> Giles Collins he said to his own dear Mother,
> Oh! Mother come bind up my head'en
> And send for the Parson of our Parish,
> For tomorrow I shall be dead en
> Oh for tomorrow I shall be dead en.
>
> Lady Annis was sat in her green Bower,
> And a dressing of her night coif en,
> And there she beheld and as fine an a corpse
> As ever she saw in her life en.
> Oh as ever she saw in her life en.
>
> What bear ye these ye six tall men,
> And a top of your shoulders,
> We bear the body of Giles Collins,
> An old true lover of yours.
> Oh an old true lover of yours.
>
> Settin down, settin down, Lady Annis she said,
> On the grass that grows so green,
> For to morrow morn by ten o' clock,
> Oh my body shall lie by his'n
> Oh my body shall lie by his'n.

> Giles Collins was laid in the East Church yard,
> Lady Annis was laid in the West en
> There sprung a Lilly from Giles Collins,
> Which touch'd Lady Annis's breast en,
> Oh which touch'd Lady Annis's breast en.
>
> Now curse'n the Parson of our Parish,
> For cutting the Lilly in Twain,
> For ne'er was sawn such a pair of true Lovers
> No or e'er will be sawn such again,
> No or e'er will be sawn such again[13]

The addition of the 'a' to the second and fourth lines and the repeat of line 4 are not indicated in those versions sent to Percy, or indeed in later versions, and are characteristic of mainly comic songs of the seventeenth and eighteenth centuries, probably the best-known being 'John Dory' (Child 284) from Ravenscroft's *Deuteromelia*[14] (1609), but mentioned in much earlier literature, which became extremely popular in the seventeenth century. Also in the medley mentioned above printed by Bailey in 1763, a few lines of 'John Dory' immediately follow the fragment of Giles Collins, so it seems reasonable to assume this version used that tune.

As the two ballads progressed into the nineteenth century, 'Giles Collins' appears to have faded as a popular stage piece. The only known sheet music version from this period is a five-stanza version printed in Baltimore c1850,[15] although the song continued to have a lively existence in oral tradition both as a serious ballad and as a comic one. Meanwhile, 'Lord Lovel' took on a new lease of life in the concert halls, taverns, song cellars and supper rooms, having at some point in the early nineteenth century been set to the jolly tune with the comic repeats, and later even having a more obviously burlesque stanza added no doubt by Sam Cowell:

> Then he threw himself down by the side of the corpse
> With a terrible grunt and a guggle,
> Gave two hops, three kicks, heaved a sigh, blew his nose,
> Kicked the bucket, and died in the struggle.

According to the editor of *Notes and Queries* in 1870:

> It first became known in the metropolis by a comic singer of the name of Graham; but it was not received with eclat until poor Sam Cowell brought a copy of it in his pocket from Aberdeen about 1846 when it became a favourite song at Evans's and other Music Halls of the metropolis.[16]

By 1850 a pantomime was being performed at the Theatre Royal, Hull. It was described as *A New Grand Comical, Historical, Legendary, and Lyrical Christmas Pantomime partly founded upon the ancient and affecting Traditionary Ballad of 'The Mistletoe Bough' and partly suggested by another interesting Ditty, both being blended in the wonder-exciting and irresistibly attractive Title of Harlequin Lord Lovel and Nancy Bell and the Fairie of the Silver Oak.* The pantomime combined the Lord Lovel from our ballad with the other one from 'The Mistletoe Bough'. to make one character.

By 1852, the versions being produced by comic singers and song-writers J. W. Sharp and Sam Cowell were all the rage, having been widely published as sheet music and in songsters, and inevitably by the broadside printers. It was one of the first big hits of the embryonic Music Hall era. In comparison with 'Giles Collins', oral versions of 'Lord Lovel' tend to be more consistent in text and tune with little variation from the general stock of stanzas, no doubt due at least partly to its long life and popularity in print and as a commercial piece.

It would be no surprise that successful burlesques often inspire parodies and our two ballads are no exception. Amongst the better-known are 'Giles Scroggins' Ghost', parodying 'Giles Collins', which commences:

> Giles Scroggins courted Molly Brown,
> Fol lol de rol de rol de ra,
> The fairest wench in all the town,
> Fol lol de rol de rol de ra,
> He bought a ring with posy true,
> If you loves me as I love you
> No knife shall cut our loves in two
> Fol lol de riddle lol de ra.

It was written in 1803 by Charles Dibdin Junior to be sung by Mr. Smith in *Two little Gipsies* performed at Sadler's Wells, the music by William Reeve.[17] Actually it has little in common with 'Giles Collins' and perhaps just the name was sufficient to link the two items in people's minds.

'Joe Muggins', the main parody of 'Lord Lovel', follows the wording of its original more closely, and the tune and format are the same:

> Joe Muggins he stood by his old donkey cart,
> Brushing his old black moke,
> When down came his lady love, Sally Bell,
> And thus to her Muggins she spoke, spoke, spoke
> And thus to her Muggins she spoke.[18]

It was written shortly after Sam Cowell and J. W. Sharp made 'Lord Lovel' popular and might well be another of Sam's pieces.

'Oh My Love's Dead'

It would indeed seem that we cannot escape the study of any ballad burlesque without mention of the name Sam Cowell, and the following is no exception. 'Oh, my love's dead' has a long and interesting history worth a brief mention. Those wishing to follow up the early history in great detail should consult *The Roxburghe Ballads*,[19] edited by Joseph Ebsworth (who was Cowell's brother-in-law who also wrote his entry in the *Dictionary of National Biography*). It gives us the original playhouse song 'Captain Digby's Farewell', in three stanzas, first published in 1671 but probably older. This was parodied in 1675 long before it became burlesqued. Here is the fanciful first stanza:

> I'le go to my Love, where he lies in the Deep,
> And in my embraces my Dearest shall sleep;
> When we wake, the kind Dolphins together shall throng,
> And in Chariots of Shells shall draw us along.
> Ah! ah! my love's dead; there was not a Bell,
> But a Triton's shell,
> To ring, to ring out his knell.[20]

The tune became very popular and a favourite with ballad writers and it was not long before the three stanzas were lengthened into a 12-stanza broadside ballad 'The Sorrowful Ladie's Complaint', commencing:

> One morning I walk'd by myself on the shore,
> When the tempest did sing and the Waves they did roar,

> Yet the noise of the winds and the waters was drown'd
> By the pitiful cry and the sorrowful sound
> Of Ah! ah! ah! my love's dead
>   There is not a Bell,
>   But a Triton's shell,
> To ring, to ring, to ring my Love's knell.[21]

The ballad continued to be printed in slightly varying forms during the eighteenth century under such titles as 'Oh My Love is dead' and 'The Drowned Mariner', but by the end of the century and into the nineteenth, much reduced versions were being printed of between four and six stanzas and the chorus had changed somewhat. Here is the first stanza of 'The Lover's Lament for Her Sailor':

> As I was a walking all on the sea-shore,
> Where the wind it blew cool, and the billows did roar,
> Where the wind and the waves and the waters run around,
> I heard a shrill voice make a sorrowful sound,
>   Crying O my Love's gone whom I do adore.
>   He's gone, and I never shall see him more.[22]

The fanciful ideas are retained in the sixth and final stanza, lines 1 and 2:

> The shells of the oysters shall be my love's bed,
> And the shrimps of the sea shall swim over his head.

The pathos of the song ideally suited the fashion of the early nineteenth century and it was widely printed under a variety of titles, but by the middle of the century, it was inevitable that burlesque was its fate. As with 'Giles Collins' having been sung in a 'crying style' by Mr. Needham c1780, Sam Cowell is depicted on the front cover of the original sheet music performing his burlesque version in pathetic character. Even these Music Hall versions were extremely fluid. The three known versions are what is probably the original sheet music written and sung by W. H. C. West and by Sam; one given in *The English Song Book*, with words by Charles Sloman, arranged by T. Westrop[23]; and the third in Ebsworth's *Roxburghe Ballads*.[24] All three are very different. This is the first stanza of West's version:

> As I vos a valking down by the sea shore,
> Vere the vinds and the vaves and the vaters did roar,
> Vith the vinds and the vaves and the vaters all round,
> I heard a young maid, making sorrowful sound,
>   Singing O-o-o-o-oh, my love's dead!
>   Him I adore
>   And I never no never shall see my love more.

There is very little change in text from the broadside as the burlesque was almost all in the exaggerated Coster pronunciation, which is a marked characteristic of the period, and the mock pathetic delivery. Sloman's version is much more altered. Here's his fourth and last stanza:

> She look'd down on the vilds of vide vatery vaste,
> And to pitch in head first she made very great haste,
> Shouting out, now I'll dwell with the lobsters and crabs,
> And live all my days with soles, mussels and dabs,
>   Crying oh! my love's dead, whom I adore,
>   So I never shall see my true Lovier no more.

Sam Cowell made the song famous at the Canterbury Hall in the character of an old salt with pigtail, but the engraving of him on the sheet music portrays the mock pathos of his delivery to perfection.

Villikens and his Dinah

Perhaps the most famous of all the ballad burlesques is that of 'Villikins and his Dinah'. 'The original ballad 'William and Dinah' was written by Henry Horton, a native of Birmingham who used to sing it nightly at an amateur theatrical meeting held at the Red House, New John Street. Horton moved to London where he soon after died. He sang the song at some of the London music rooms. It was very popular and was soon brought upon the stage, but before it was heard at all in London it was popular about the streets of Birmingham'.[25] This reply in *Notes and Queries* by 'Father Frank' was in response to the following request from Henry Mayhew (writer of the seminal *London Labour and the London Poor*):

> Can you or any of your [...] correspondents inform me as the author of *The Wandering Minstrel* in what county or about what year the old song of 'Villikins and his Dinah' was first printed and published? As Mr. Robson sang the song, the words were those originally given by Mr. Mitchell, the first low comedian who appeared in the part, A.D. 1831. He brought the country version to me, and I had to condense and interpolate it, so as to make it 'go' with a London audience.[26]

Although 'Villikins' was written in 1831, it did not become universally popular until Mayhew's one-act burletta *The Wandering Minstrel* was revived in May 1853 at the Olympic in London. Comic actor Frederick Robson had just returned from Dublin and had already appeared in the burlesque of *Macbeth* to great acclaim, in which he introduced several minstrel songs, and he jumped at the chance to play the ballad singer Jem Baggs in the production, and the final song of 'Villikins'. It quickly became the hit of the season and within two years was being sung all over the English-speaking world. Needless to say, Sam Cowell also took it on, and many versions were produced, some with spoken interpolation, and in higher circles it was translated into Greek and Latin amongst other languages.

Davidson's sheet music title runs *The Celebrated Antediluvian and Dolefully Pathetic Lyrical Legend of Willikind and his Dinah with the Melancholy and Uncomfortable fate of ye Dismal Parients, sung by Mr F. Robson at the Royal Olympic Theatre. And by Mr J. L. Toole (Comedian), at the Theatres Royal, Cork, Dublin and Edinburgh, with immense Success; also at the various Literary Institutions in London, in his popular entertainment of 'Sayings and Doings*.[27]

'William and Dinah' and 'Villikins' were widely printed on broadsides and both survived in oral tradition, the former until the English collectors came along and the latter is still sung in folk clubs today, championed by Cockney singers such as John Forman, the latterday Broadside King.

Billy Taylor

Another of Sam Cowell's popular songs was 'Billy Taylor' but in this case the burlesque version was well-known long before the Music Hall era, long before Sam was born in 1820. It was sung by Mr. Emery at the Theatre Royal in Covent Garden in about 1800, and was said to have been a favourite of Sarah Siddons.[28] The earliest extant version of what is very likely the original serious ballad dates back to c1712–20 in *The Female Sailor's Garland*, in three parts, printed by Sarah Bates at the Sun and Bible in Pye Corner, London.[29] It is not divided into stanzas and consists of 200 lines, the equivalent of 25 double stanzas. A later version, 'A New Song call'd the Faithful Lover', printed in *The Faithful Lover's Garland* by John Garnett of Sheffield in 1748[30] is given in double stanzas, but five have been omitted from the earlier version, none of these being those utilised in later versions.

Both of these early versions contribute only five stanzas to the 11-stanza version printed towards the end of the century (NLS LC2856 (2), printed at Kilmarnock c1800,[31] and as Garnett's title suggests, the longer versions have no infidelity or shooting and the ballad ends happily with William and Elizabeth marrying. The other six stanzas, in which William is walking out with another lady, the heroine shoots him and she marries the ship's captain, are new to the short version.

The burlesque, distinguished from all other versions by William being named as Billy, is based on this version and it dates back to at least 1792 when it was printed at Alnwick in a songster simply titled *4 New Songs*.[32] London broadside printer Jemmy Catnach printed a further serious version with four new stanzas,[33] three of them at the beginning distinguished by the first line 'I'll sing you a song about two lovers', and although this was printed much by his successors in the trade and a few others, it was nowhere near as popular as the burlesque.

> Billy Taylor was a brisk young Fellow,
> Full of fun and full of glee,
> And his mind he did discover,
> To a Lady fair and free.
>   Tol de loll, loll loll loll, loll doll doll
>   Fol de loll, loll loll loll, loll loll doll,
>   Loll loll loll, loll doll doll, loll loll, loll loll loll loll loll loll,
>   Doll doll doll, loll loll doll.
>
> Four and twenty brisk young Fellows,
> Drest they were in rich array,
> And they took poor Bill Taylor,
> Whom they press'd and sent to sea.
>
> And his true Love follow'd after,
> Under the name of Richard Car,
> Her lilly white hands were bedaub'd all over,
> With the nasty pitch and tar.
>
> Now behold the first engagement,
> Bold she fought among the rest,
> Till the wind did blow her jacket open,
> And discover'd her lilly white Breast.
>
> When that Captain came for to view it,
> Says he, "What a wind has brought you here?"
> "Sir, I become to seek my true Love
> Whom you press'd, I lov'd so dear."
>
> "If you become to seek your true Love,
> Tell to me his name I pray."
> "Sir, his name is Billy Taylor,
> Whom you press'd and sent to sea."
>
> "If his name is Billy Taylor,
> He is both cruel and severe,
> For rise up early in the morning,
> And you'll see him with his lady fair."

With that she rose up early next morning,
Early by the break of day,
And there she saw bold Billy Taylor,
Dancing with his Lady Gay.

With that she call'd for Sword and Pistol,
Which did come at her command,
And there she shot bold Billy Taylor,
With his true Love in his hand.

When that the Captain came for to know it,
He very much applauded her for what she had done,
And immediately made her the first Lieutenant,
Of the glorious Thunder Bomb.[34]

The *Thunder* was indeed a bomb vessel dismantled in 1800. The burlesque ballad was turned into a burletta by J. B. Buckstone first produced at the Adelphi Theatre, 9th November 1829, and was played upwards of 50 nights during the season. In his introductory remarks to the published script George Daniels attributed the burlesque to Sheridan, 'a whimsy thrown off in one of those joyous moments which gladdened the heart of that eccentric genius'.[35]

As we have seen the burlesque was already extremely popular before Sam Cowell took it to even greater heights in the 1850s. The text of his sheet music version published by B. Williams is almost verbatim the original burlesque with some Coster pronunciations added. The tune is a little more varied in the earlier versions but recognisably the same. As one would expect the serious version tunes are somewhat less jolly. An 1841 version gives the air to the burlesque as 'George Barnwell', which coincidentally is our next ballad.

So in one form or another, this ballad has lasted for more than three centuries, as the burlesque and serious versions based on the broadsides are still sung today in folk clubs, some as hybrids of the two types.

George Barnwell

'An Excellent ballad of George Barnwell an Apprentice of London, who was undone by a strumpet, who having thrice robbed his Master, and murdered his Uncle in Ludlow' was first registered in 1624 at Stationers' Hall and it continued to be printed right through to the middle of the eighteenth century in sets mostly of 98 stanzas (e.g. *Euing Ballads*, p81[36]). Like many of the ballads of the period, it served as warning against vice, in this case to apprentices, who were the main audience for the play based on it by George Lillo first performed at Drury Lane and Covent Garden in 1731. Both Percy and Ritson gave the original broadside version of the ballad the honour of reprinting it. We are told by Joseph Ebsworth again, in the *Roxburghe Ballads*,[37] that the story was burlesqued: '…by James Smith in *The Rejected Address* in 1812; and again by Thackeray in his *George de Barnwell* in 1847'. Smith's burlesque commencing 'George Barnwell stood at the shop door' (perhaps a nod to 'Lord Lovel') was later printed on broadsides, and Thackeray's in *Punch*. It is probable that the popular burlesque *Georgy Barnwell* given below preceded both of these as it was widely printed in the first half of the nineteenth century.

The tune as reported above was the same as that used for Cowell's 'Billy Taylor'.

In Cheapside there liv'd a merchant
A man he vas of wery great fame,

Burlesquing the ballad

And he had a handsome prentice,
Georgy Barnwell vas his name.
Tol hiddy ol tol &c.

This youth he vas both good and pious,
Dutiful beyond all doubt,
And he always staid vithin doors
'Cause his master vouldn't let him out.

And much his master's darter lov'd him,
She slept in next room to him, 'tis said,
And she bored a hole right through the wainscoat,
To look at Georgy going to bed.

A vicked voman of the town, sirs,
Hon him cast a vishful eye;
And she came to the shop one morning,
A flannel petticoat to buy.

When she paid him down the money,
She gave his hand a wery hard squeeze,
Which so frightened Georgy Barnwell,
That together he knocked his knees.

Then she left her card vereon was written,
Mary Millwood does entreat,
That Master Barnwell vould call and see her,
At Cummins's in Dyot Street.

Now as soon as he'd shut the shop up,
He vent to this naughty dicky bird,
And ven he vent home the next morning,
Blow'd if he could speak a vord.

Now soon this voman did persuade him,
Vith her fascinating pipes,
To go down into the country,
And let loose his uncle's tripes.

There he found his uncle in the grove,
Studying hard at his good books,
And Georgy Barnwell vent and struck him,
All among the crows and rooks.

Ven Millwood found he'd got no money,
Not so much as to buy a jewel,
She vent that wery day and peached him,
Now vas not that 'ere werry cruel?

The judge put his three-cornered cap on,
And said –vich Barnwell much surprised,
You must hang until you dead are,
Then you must be a-nat-o-mised.

Now Georgy was hung upon a gibbet,
Molly Millwood died in prison,

At her fate no one lamented,
But every body pitied his'n.

The merchant's darter died soon arter,
Tears she shed, but spoke no vords,
So all young men, I pray take varning,
Don't go vith naughty dicky birds.[38]

The Gosport Tragedy

The following is a burlesque on a very popular ballad 'The Gosport Tragedy, or The Perjured Ship's Carpenter'. Though printed by several provincial printers in the mid- to late nineteenth century, the burlesque had little currency in oral tradition by the time the early collectors came along. In contrast to this, the serious original was extremely popular being widely printed on broadsides since the middle of the eighteenth century. The earlier longer version printed at Bow Church Yard and Aldermary Church Yard in London by the Dicey/Marshall dynasty, had 34 verses and was set in Gosport, whereas some of the later shorter versions were set in Worcester, the burlesque being set in Portsmouth. On this occasion we have a pretty good idea when it was written as the sheet music credits words and music to W. H. C. West. It was published by B. Williams in the late 1850s and also advertises some of Sam Cowell's other burlesques covered in this essay, 'Lord Lovell', 'Billy Barlow' and 'Oh, my love's dead'.

West's first, third, fourth and fifth stanzas seem to be based on an early nineteenth broadside version 'Nancy's Ghost' printed by Angus of Newcastle,[39] and the rest is presumably from West's own pen.

Molly the Betrayed or The Fog-Bound Vessel

In a Kitchen in Portsmouth a fair maid did dwell,
For grammer and graces none could her excel,
Young Villiam he courted her to be his dear,
And he by his trade was a Ship's Carpentier.
    Singing Doddle, doddle, doddle, chip, chum, chow, chooral li ay.

Now it chanc'd that von day ven her vages vas paid,
Young Villiam valk'd vith her, and thus to her said—
"More lovely are you than the ships on the sea."
Then she nudg'd him, and laugh'd, and said "Fiddle de dee!"

Then he led her o'er hills, and down walleys so deep,
At length this fair damsel began for to veep;
Saying, "I fancy, sveet Villiam, you've brought me this vay,
On porpos my hinnercent life to betray!"

He said, "That is true, and we've no time to stand,"
And immediately took a sharp knife in his hand,
He pierc'd her best gown till the blood it did flow
And into the grave her fair body did throw.

That night as asleep in his hammock he lay,
He fancied he heard some sperrit to say,
"Oh vake up young Villiam and listen to hear
The woice of your Molly what lov'd you so dear.

"Your ship bound from Portsmouth it never shall go,
Till I am reweng'd for my sad overthrow,
The anchor is weigh'd, the vinds fair and strong,
But all is in vain for your ship shan't go on.

Then up com'd the Captain vith "Unfurl ev'ry sail."
He guv'd his command but all no avail,
A mist on the hocean arose all around,
And no vay to move this fine ship could be found.

Then he calls up his men vith a shout and a whoop,
And he orders young Villiam to stand on the poop.
"There's summat not right," says he, "mongst this 'ere crew,
And I'm blow'd if I don't think young Villiam it's you."

Then Villiam turned red, and then vite, and then green,
Vile Molly's pale ghost at his side it vos seen;
Her buzzom vos vite, the blood it vos red, --
She spoke not but wanish'd, --and that's all she said!

Now all servant gals who my story does hear,
Just remember poor Molly, and her Ship's Carpentier;
If your sweetheart they axes you vith them to roam,
Just be careful and leave your vages at home[40]

The similarities, particularly with 'Villikins', are remarkable here. The tune changes at various points in the song. The first four stanzas and chorus use a variant of the 'Villikins' tune. In stanzas 5 and 6 as the ghostly part commences the tune changes accordingly, returning to the first tune in the last three stanzas.

Barbara Allen

The most popular of all ballads in the English-speaking world is indisputably that of Child 84 *Barbara Allen*. Part of that popularity has to be down to its constant availability in print and to all levels of society. The first mention, in Samuel Pepys' diary in 1666, is to a 'Scotch' song being sung by an actress/singer friend. The 'Scotch' description was used in the metropolis at that time to describe any song given a northern setting and using pseudo-Scottish dialect, similar to the pseudo-Irish stage songs that held great popularity in the eighteenth and early nineteenth centuries. There were two quite distinct early versions of the ballad and as only one of these contains northern referents it seems reasonable to assume that Pepys was referring to that which commences:

It was in and about the Martinmas time
When the green leaves were a falling
That Sir John Graeme in the West Country
Fell in love with Barbara Allan. (8 more stanzas)[41]

The other, 'Barbara Allen's Cruelty: or the Young-man's Tragedy', was printed by Brooksby, Deacon, Blare and Back of London c1690–96. This starts:

In Scarlet Town where I was bound,
There was a fair maid dwelling,
Whom I had chosen to be my own,
And her name was Barbara Allen. (14 more stanzas)[42]

Which of these is the earlier is a matter for conjecture. William Chappell in his edition of *The Roxburghe Ballads* was of the opinion the Scottish version 'is clearly built upon the English ballad',[43] but as both very likely came from London about the same period it is impossible to declare for certain which is the earliest. Both versions, and others that evolved from the 'Scarlet Town' version, continued to be printed in street literature as long as that medium lasted, and both were greatly anthologised with music for the entertainment of those in higher echelons of society. In 1797, a reduced version of five stanzas was sung in the London theatres by Master Welsh.[44]

Again it appears to have been the pathos that attracted the burlesque treatment. It would be surprising that such a ballad would not be ripe for burlesquing at an early stage, having had such a high profile for so long. However, the earliest so far found was printed by the Glasgow Poet's Box in 1874, no doubt a reissue of an earlier printing as Sam Cowell died in 1864 and he is named on the sheet as one of the singers. It was printed on a two-column sheet along with the standard 'Scotch' version. Indeed under the title 'Barbara Allen the Cruel' it states:

> 'This comic version of 'Barbara Allan', as sung by Messrs Lloyd, Cowell, &c,. is now drawing crowded audiences at all the different theatres and concerts in the kingdom.

> In Reading town a lad was born,
> And a fair maid there was dwelling;
> So he picked her out to be his bride,
> And her name was Barbara Allan,
> And her name was Barbara Allan.
>
> 'Twas in the merry month of May,
> When green leaves they were springing,
> A young man on a sick bed lay,
> For the love of Barbara Allan.
>
> He sent to her his servant man,
> To the place where she was dwelling;
> Now quickly to my master come,
> If thy name be Barbara Allan.
>
> So slowly, so slowly, she walked unto
> The bedside where he was lying;
> And when she looked into his face,
> Says she, Young man, you're dying.
>
> I see death painted in thy face,
> All joy is gone quite from thee;
> I cannot save thee from the grave,
> So farewell, my dearest Johnny.
>
> When she was gone he gave a grunt,
> In expression of his sorrow;
> In his will left Barbara all his blunt,
> And then he died to-morrow.
>
> As she was a-walking thro' the street,
> She met his corpse a-coming;
> Now set'un down, my little brave boys,
> And let I gaze upon him.

The more she look'd, the more she laugh'd,
The further she got from him,
Till all her friends cried out for shame,
Cruel-hearted Barbara Allan.

No wonder that the lady laugh'd,
To see her true love fallen;
Of course she got another spark,
This cruel Barbara Allan.

They buried him in the church porch,
When she died laid her beside 'un,
For she wished to be his bride in death,
Though in life she couldn't abide 'un.

It is worth noting that we do not get a hint of burlesque here until the sixth stanza and even then the comic effect is weakly expressed in a few bits of customary Coster language. As pointed out earlier the main comic effect was produced by the mock pathos assisted by exaggerated body language, grimaces, costume and props, as perfected by the great pantomime clown Joe Grimaldi in the late eighteenth century. The third line of stanza 7 has its equivalent in 'Giles Collins'.

The Twa Sisters

With some ballads, without external evidence and description of audience perception, it can be difficult to assess to what extent they were perceived as burlesques. For instance there are elements of versions of 'The Twa Sisters' (Child 10) that have been at various times described as burlesque. The earliest extant version of the English ballad was printed by Frances Grove of London in 1656.[45] Child's excellent headnotes inform us that the ballad was well-known in Scandinavian countries in close versions to the English, and that equivalent ballads and tales were found all over Europe. Most of these came from relatively recent oral tradition, but at least one, from Iceland, came from the same period as the English ballad.

The early broadside is twice ascribed to a well-known writer of comic verses, Dr. James Smith. Professor Child opined, 'If the ballad were ever in Smith's hands he might possibly have inserted the three burlesque stanzas, 11–13, but similar verses are found in another copy (see later) and might easily be extemporised by any singer of sufficiently bad taste'.[46]

The basic story of the early ballad is that two sisters go down to the sea to watch their father's ships come in, where the elder pushes the younger in. (Most other versions supply a motive in that both sisters are rivals for a suitor and the younger is preferred.) The sister's body (somewhat unlikely) ends up at a miller's dam where her body is recovered and the parts turned into a musical instrument (usually a viol or a harp) which, once constructed, finds its way back to her father's hall where the crime is revealed and punishment meted out.

The broadside cannot be the original as there are obvious gaps in the story provided by other versions. Here are the three 'burlesque' stanzas, part of the body dismantling and use:

What did he doe with her eyes so bright?
With a hie downe downe a downe-a
Upon his violl he played at first sight,
With a hy downe downe a downe-a

What did he doe with her tongue so rough?
Unto the violl it spake enough.

What did he doe with her two shinnes?
Unto the violl they danc'd Moll Syms.

In the Icelandic ballad the sister's body is found by her lover on the sea shore (more realistically) and as in later English, Scottish and Scandinavian versions it is he who strings his harp with strands of her hair. Child was of the very plausible opinion that all of the other uses of the body parts were added later as an easy and natural progression 'till we end with the buffoonery' of the broadside and the following versions.

Two eighteenth-century versions with similar burlesque stanzas to the above were given by Child as his L version and in Additions and Corrections.[47] L was sent in 1852 to *Notes and Queries* by music antiquarian, Edward F Rimbault (1816–1876), having remembered the fragmentary version from his youth as sung by an old maiden lady. The other version was sent to Walter Scott by Anna Seward in 1802 with the following letter:

> The *Binnorie* of endless repetition has nothing truly pathetic, and the ludicrous use made of the drowned sister's body is well burlesqued in a ridiculous ballad, which I first heard sung, with farcical grimace, in my infancy [born 1747] thus:

And O was it a pheasant cock,
Or eke a pheasant hen?
Or was it and a gay lady,
Came swimming down the stream?

O it was not a pheasant cock,
Or eke a pheasant hen,
But it was and a gay lady,
Came swimming down the stream.

And when she came to the mill-dam
The miller he took her body,
And with it he made a fiddling thing,
To make him sweet melody.

And what did he do with her fingers small?
He made of them pegs to his vial.

And what did he do with her nose ridge?
Why to his fiddle he made it a bridge.
Sing, O the damnd mill-dam, O

And what did he do with her veins so blue?
Why he made him strings his fiddle unto.

And what did he do with her two shins?
Why to his vial they danc'd Moll Sims.

And what did he do with her two sides?
Why he made of them sides to his fiddle besides.

And what did he do with her great toes?
Why what he did with them that nobody knows.
Sing, O the damnd mill-dam, O.[48]

These two versions are so close in format and text as to have come from the same source. Rimbault only remembered the first two quatrains in full but described the third in detail. The rest is even sillier than Seward's version and the two quite naturally differ considerably as these couplets easily lend themselves to extemporisation. Both versions show a close affinity to the broadside, the former with 'Moll Sims' and the latter with the 'eyes so bright' stanza. Whilst reading through these two versions, I was struck by the similarity in format to two versions of 'The Herring's Head' I collected locally on the Yorkshire coast. They both have similar introductions before the question and answer sequence and the subject matter is equally silly.

The rest of the many Scottish versions given by Child, mostly from the nineteenth century, are quite different and of the Binnorie/Edinburgh type. They show signs of having stemmed from a single translation from the Scandinavian, albeit with plenty of evidence of oral transmission.

The Three Ravens

Another early ballad that received the burlesque treatment long after its first appearance was 'The Three Ravens' (Child 26), first published in Ravenscroft's *Melismata* in 1611, but very probably of earlier origin. Again the song appears to have had a long popularity and was continually anthologised. Its performance on stage in polite society was what probably led eventually to it being burlesqued, and this time the culprits appear to be the American minstrel stage writers. The following was published in *Christy's New Songster*, in 1863, but in the same year, a slightly different version 'The Four Vultures' was published with music in *Frank Converse's Old Cremona Songster*.

The Three Crows

      As sung by Byron Christy, James Bryant, H. Wilson and G. Weightman.

[Spoken] Three crows they sat upon a tree,
    As black as any crows could be. Sing.
[Repeat the above, sung]

(Same format throughout)

One of these crows said unto his mate,
What shall we do for something to eat?

'Way on that side of yonder plain,
There lies a horse but three days slain.

We'll jump right on his backbone,
And pick out his eyes, one by one.[49]

The style of performance is obviously meant to emulate the repetitions in certain religious ceremonies and is also therefore satirising this as well as the ballad, just as the comic operas were at once satirising Italian opera and contemporary society and politics.

Inevitably the burlesque went quickly into oral tradition producing a wide variety of formats, usually under the title of 'Billy M'Gee Magaw', though the text remained pretty stable; and like the minstrel phenomenon itself soon reached Britain where the song can still be found in oral tradition, usually chanted in mock sermon voice, to a tune such as 'All People that on Earth do Dwell'.

The loyal lover

Another upmarket song that may have contributed to the burlesque canon is that usually found under the title of 'The Loyal Lover'. It is said to have been written by George Syron, an inmate of Bedlam, c1740, and indeed it is sometimes titled 'The Maid of Bedlam'. It immediately became very popular and apart from appearing in many upmarket anthologies with music it was also widely printed on street literature. Today it is still popular with folk singers. This lament has little interest here except that the first half of the second stanza runs thus:

> O cruel were his parents who sent my love to sea,
> And cruel was the ship which bore my love from me!

Whether this was the first usage of this statement is a matter for further research, but the whole song is riddled with clichés and commonplaces, albeit well interwoven. The number of distinct songs in which this couplet subsequently appears in some form has turned it into a commonplace if it was not already that. It reappeared in another lament towards the end of the eighteenth century, usually titled 'The Winter's Evening', or on some slips, 'Oh, Cruel, or The Winter's Evening', taken again from the first half of the second stanza:

> O cruel was my father to shut the doors on me,
> And cruel was my mother the dreadful sight to see.

But this time the format is reiterated in the second half of the stanza:

> And cruel is the winter's night that pierced my heart with cold,
> And cruel was the young man that left his love for gold.

In the early nineteenth century, the burlesque surfaced and this time the format was extended even further. In the following, we have a whole catalogue of ten 'Oh cruels'. It was printed in *Hodgson's New Skylark or Theatrical Budget of Harmony* in 1823:

> Oh, Cruel! Or, The Vagabonding Vagrant And Rantipoling Wife.
> A favourite Comic Duet, as Sung with great Applause at the Royal Coburg, by Messrs. Usher and Stebbing. Tune—Calder Fair.
>
> Oh! cruel vas my parents that forc' my love from me,
> And cruel vas the press-gang that took him out to sea,
> And cruel vas the little boat that row'd him from the strand,
> And cruel vas the great big ship that took him from the land.
>   Too rol, too ral loo rol &c.
>
> Oh! cruel vas the cruel vater that bore my love from Mary,
> And cruel vas the fair vind that wouldn't blow contrary;
> And cruel vas the boatswain, the captain and the men,
> That didn't care a farden if we never met again.
>
> Oh, cruel vas the splinter that broke my poor love's leg,
> Now he's obliged to fiddle for't, and I'm oblig'd to beg;
> A vagabonding vagrant, and a rantipoling wife,
> We fiddles and we limps it, thro' the ups and downs of life.

> Oh, cruel vas the engagement, in which my true love fought,
> And cruel was the cannon-ball that knock'd his right eye out,
> He us'd to leer and ogle me, with peepers full of fun,
> But now he looks askew at me, because he's only one.
>
> My love he plays the fiddle well, and vanders up and down,
> And I follow at his helbow thro', all the streets in town;
> We spends our days in harmony, and wery seldom fights,
> Except when he's his grog aboard, or I gets queer at nights.
>
> Now ladies all take varning, by my true love and me,
> Tho' cruel fate should cross you, remember constancy,
> Like me you'll be revarded, and have all your heart's delight,
> With fiddling in the morning, and a drap of max at night.[50]

It must be earlier, however, as John Pitts printed an answer to it before 1819. Sometime later broadside printer Bloomer of Birmingham printed a close version under the following heading which adds to the comic effect:

> Oh, Cruel!! A very affecting, pathetic sketch of the life of TOMMY STRILL: Sung by Mr. Rayner, on his benefit night, and throughout the Season, at North Shields Theatre, with unqualified Applause. Accompanied by a friend with A wooden leg & one eye. Tune.—"Calder Fair".[51]

The 'rantipoling wife' of the title and stanza 3 of Hodgson had become 'rantpoly wife' in the Bloomer version, and in a still later version, presumably from oral tradition, again printed by Bloomer this had become 'a ranter Polly's wife' giving the name to the title 'Polly and the Fiddler',[52] an early example of a mondegreen.[53] A rantipoling wife was one who was 'on top', originally literally.

The song was immediately popular and provoked answers and parodies. Titles such as 'Another Oh, Cruel' offered a military recruitment version in which a soldier is the maimed victim. This one, not to be outdone, included seventeen 'Oh, cruel' lines. There were also American parodies; a Washington printed version tells of being shanghaied aboard a fishing smack by pirates.[54]

Although already popular, by the rise of the Music Halls a shortened version was published in 1864 *Oh, Cruel were my Parients*, described as 'The Universally Popular Comic Song Sung at the Music Halls and Concerts'. The tune was a variant of 'Sing a Song of Sixpence'.

Lord Bateman

The widespread ballad 'Lord Bateman' (Child 53) did not escape the treatment though the details of how the burlesque relates to the serious ballad are somewhat obscure. Both English and Scottish versions existed on broadsides in the latter half of the eighteenth century. The English version, 'Young Baker',[55] appears to be the immediate predecessor of 'Lord Bateman'. The story of how the burlesque, published in 1839 and illustrated by Cruikshank, came about involves Dickens and Cruikshank, and in some versions, Thackeray. The stories all agree that Cruikshank, who had heard the song being sung in the streets by a ballad singer, sang it in an exaggerated style in the manner of that singer at a dinner of the Antiquarian

Society. Dickens then persuaded Cruikshank to illustrate and publish it and Dickens would provide the humorous notes. The version titled 'Lord Bateman' was widely printed before and after Cruikshank's burlesque version, and although I haven't seen any broadside versions of the burlesque, it no doubt added to the popularity of the serious version.

The burlesque deviates only minimally from the serious ballad; every line is present but it is written in the usual Coster orthography. One stanza of the 21 will suffice here:

> O! avay and avay vent this proud young porter,
> Oh! avay and avay and avay vent he,
> Until he come to Lord Bateman's chamber,
> Ven he vent down on his bended knee.[56]

To give it a happy ending Cruikshank wrote three extra stanzas in which the 'proud young porter' marries Lord Bateman's prospective bride. I have no evidence that this burlesque was ever sung other than by Cruikshank himself although as the music is given in the popular little book, I can imagine it being performed at similar gatherings to that where Cruikshank first performed it. Its popularity no doubt owed more to Cruikshank's humorous cartoons and Dickens' humorous notes.

Sir Eglamore

We have hitherto included ballads that show some evidence of having been part of oral tradition in recent centuries, but there is one example extant in the seventeenth century that did not survive in oral tradition since then. 'The Ballad of Sir Eglamore' is undoubtedly a burlesque based on the third task of slaying a dragon in the French romance *Sir Eglamore of Artois*. In this the first and second tasks, the slaying of a giant and a boar, were also made into a ballad and did survive until recent times in oral tradition. Child titled it 'Sir Lionel' (Child 18). The burlesque, printed on broadsides and published in ballad collections from 1615 to well into the eighteenth century, I give here in full as an early example.

> Courage crowned with Conquest; or, A brief relation, how that Valiant Knight, and Heroick Champion Sir Eglamore, bravely fought with, and manfully slew, a terrible, huge great Monstrous Dragon. To a pleasant new Tune.

> Sir Eglamore that valiant Knight
> With his fa la, lanctre down dilie,
> He fetcht his sword and he went to fight;
> With his fa la lanctre, &c.
> As he went over hill and dale
> All cloathed in his Coat of Male.
> With his fa la lanctre, &c.
>
> A huge great Dragon leapt out of his Den
> Which had killed the Lord knows how many men
> But when he saw Sir Eglamore
> Good lack had you seen how this Dragon did roare.
>
> This Dragon he had a plaguy hide
> Which could both sword and spear abide
> He could not enter with hacks and cuts
> Which vext the Knight to the very hearts blood and guts.

All the Trees in the Wood did shake
Stars did tremble, and men did quake,
But had you seen how the birds lay peeping
'Twould have made a man's heart to fall a weeping.

But it was too late to fear
For now it was come to fight Dog, fight Bare
And as a yawning he did fall
He thrust his Sword in hilt and all.

But now as the Knight in choler did burn
He owed the Dragon a shrewd good turn
In at his mouth his sword he bent,
The hilt appeared at his fundament.

Then the Dragon like a coward began to fly
Unto his Den that was hard by
And there he laid him down and roar'd
The Knight was vexed for his Sword.

The Sword that was a right good Blade,
As ever Turk or Spaniard made
I for my part do forsake it
And he that will fetch it, let him take it.

When all this was done, to the Ale-house he went
And by and by his two pence he spent
For he was so hot with tugging with the Dragon
That nothing would quench him but a whole Flaggon.

Now God preserve our King and Queen,
With his fa la lanctre, &c.
And eke in London may be seen,
With his fa la lanctre, &c.
As many Knights, and as many more,
And all so good as Sir Eglamore.
With his fa la, langtre down dilly.[57]
    London, Printed for F. Coles, T. Vere, and J. Wright, 1672
    (Pepys Ballads, Vol. 2, p134.)

Conclusion

The over-riding feature of the versions of the ballads being burlesqued was pathos, though that was not the only aspect being mocked. Most of them had originated as long ballads and had been deliberately shortened to a fraction of their length to appeal to new audiences at the end of the eighteenth century. But the result was that they had then culminated in an exaggerated leaping and lingering effect, commonly found in ballads that had undergone much oral transmission.

Also in many cases the type of humour intended was that sort of po-faced disaster relation promoted in recent times by the likes of Frankie Howerd, with his 'No, you mustn't laugh!' Another aspect of modern humour that is similar is when we are invited to laugh at pathos in comic animation on our screens. With those old burlesques of ballads the clues lie in the descriptions of performance, relying heavily on presentation, 'in a crying style', the depiction of the pathetic characters portrayed on the sheet music covers. Parted lovers and death predominate, dying for love being heavily mocked. This type of burlesque was already a strong component of urban entertainment by the beginning of the nineteenth century and part of the appeal was that audiences knew what to expect and welcomed it. Though derided at times by polite society, some obviously enjoyed it and even participated, vide, Dickens and Thackeray.

Notes

1. See, for example: Thomas Wright and James Orchard Halliwell, *Reliquiae Antiquae: Scraps from Ancient Manuscripts, Illustrating Chiefly Early English Literature and the English Language* (London: John Russell Smith, 1845), pp. 81–86, 239, 250, 325.
2. Francis J. Child, *The English and Scottish Popular Ballads* Vol 2 (Boston: Houghton Mifflin, 1898), No.85, p. 279.
3. Bertrand H. Bronson, *The Traditional Tunes of the Child Ballads*, Vol 2 (Princeton: Princeton Univ. Press, 1966), p. 189.
4. [Joseph Ritson] *Gammer Gurton's Garland* (London: Triphook, 1810), see Child Vol 2, p. 280.
5. *Journal of the Folk Song Society* 4 (1910), p. 106.
6. Bronson 2 (1966), p. 392.
7. David Herd, *Ancient and Modern Scottish Songs* (Edinburgh: Wotherspoon, 1769), p. 302.
8. Child 2, pp. 207, 212.
9. https://libsvcs-1.its.yale.edu/hwcorrespondence/page.esp?vol=40.
10. 'Leaping and lingering' is the shorthand phrase to describe a common feature of traditional ballad composition. Instead of plodding through the story, blow by blow, the text apparently jumps forward in the plot, and lingers there for a while before leaping forward again.
11. *Collection of English Ballads*, Vol.3. (British Library G308).
12. 'A Medley', in *The Warbling Philomel, A New and Select Collection of the Best Songs Sung this Year in Polite Assemblies, Vauxhall, Ranelagh, etc.* (printed by Bailey of London, 1763), p. 92.
13. https://libsvcs-1.its.yale.edu/hwcorrespondence/page.esp?vol=40.
14. Thomas Ravenscroft, *Deuteromelia* (London, 1609).
15. See Lester S. Levy Sheet Music Collection (https://levysheetmusic.mse.jhu.edu/) 38.155.
16. *Notes & Queries* 4S:5 (1870), p. 521.
17. Writer's own collection.
18. Printed by Glasgow Poet's Box (1865) (Mitchell Library, Glasgow (1287)).
19. *The Roxburghe Ballads*, Vol. 4, pp. 392–400.
20. *The Roxburghe Ballads*, Vol. 4, p. 393.
21. *The Roxburghe Ballads*, Vol. 4, p. 398.
22. Broadside printed by Catnach of London, 1813–1832, Bodleian Broadside Ballads website, Firth c.13 (174).
23. Harold Scott, *The English Song Book* (London: Chapman & Hall, 1926), p. 71.
24. *The Roxburghe Ballads*, Vol. 4, pp. 392–400.
25. *Notes and Queries*, 6S:8 (1883), p. 94.
26. *Notes and Queries*, 6S:8 (1883), p. 67.
27. *Davidson's Musical Treasury* (London) Serial No. 691 (writer's collection).
28. *Notes and Queries* 11S:1 (1910), p. 115.
29. Bodleian Library (Douce PP.183).
30. Sheffield City Libraries, ref MP91S.
31. National Library of Scotland, LC2856 (2).
32. British Library (11606 aa.23.11.1).
33. For an online later issue by Fortey of London, see Bodleian Broadside Ballads website (Harding B11(3010)).
34. *A Collection of Comic Songs* (London: C. Wheatstone, 1811), pp. 74–75 (NLS Glen Collection).
35. *Davidson's Musical Treasury* (London) Serial No. 691 (writer's collection).
36. E.g. *Euing Ballads*, p. 81, online at UCSB EBBA 31764.
37. Joseph W. Ebsworth, *Roxburghe Ballads*, Vol. 8 (London: Ballad Society, 1871–1897), p. 59,

38 John Ashton, *Modern Street Ballads* (London: Chatto & Windus, 1888) p. 116, derived from *The Pickwick Songster* printed by Ford of Chesterfield, but numerous versions on the Bodleian Broadside Ballads website, including one by Batchelar of London dated 1817–1828.
39 Bodleian Broadside Ballads website (Harding B17(207b)).
40 Sheet music printed by B. Williams of London (British Library, H1770).
41 Allan Ramsay, *Tea-Table Miscellany* Vol 4 (1740 edition) p. 343.
42 UCSB EBBA 30145, from British Library, Roxburghe, C.20.f.8.25.
43 Chappell, The Roxburghe Ballads, Vol 3, p. 433.
44 'Well Away, Cruel Barbara Allen', See British Library 993. K28 (3), p. 13.
45 Child 1, p. 126.
46 Child 1, p. 119.
47 Child 4, p. 448.
48 Child 4, p. 448.
49 *Christy's New Songster* (1863), p. 58.
50 *Hodgson's New Skylark or Theatrical Budget of Harmony* (1823) (London: Hodgson & Co., 1823) (British Library 11606.a.29).
51 Cecil Sharp Broadside Collection (VWML online CJS1/10/2/516/1).
52 Madden Collection (Cambridge University Library, Country Printers Vol. 6).
53 'Mondegreen', A verbal interpretation of a misheard word or phrase in a song or recitation that changes the meaning of the original accidentally.
54 Slip titled 'The Pirates and Their Friend', printed at Georgetown, Washington (American Memory website, https://www.loc.gov/item/amss.as111000/).
55 Bodleian Broadside Ballads website, Harding B6 (86).
56 Small upmarket chapbook illustrated by Cruikshank, pub. Bell and Daldy, London in 1871, p. 19.
57 London, Printed for F. Coles, T. Vere, and J. Wright, 1672, online at UCSB EBBA 31635, from Pepys Ballads, Vol. 2, p. 134.

20

THE RISE AND FALL OF THE WEST GALLERY

Popular religious music in the eighteenth and nineteenth centuries

Vic Gammon

What is west gallery music?

What is now described as west gallery music is the repertoire performed in parish churches, rather than cathedrals and abbeys, which emerged and flourished in the period roughly 1750– 1860. It is a distinctive musical style, with characteristic forms of composition and ways of performing. The church provided almost the only institutional basis for music making in many places in this period.

There are exceptions to many generalisations that can and have been made about west gallery music. It is often thought of as a rural form but this was not exclusively the case; examples of this music were performed in towns and industrial villages. Far from being a form with an ancient and rooted history, it was very short-lived. It is often said that west gallery music sits somewhere between folk music and educated art music. There is something in this, but the idea might obscure as much as it illuminates. Those who participated in the music would not have had such ideas; rather, their music was the music they knew and encountered. Some, like the long-celebrated Lancashire weavers of the Rossendale Valley, played some of the compositions of Handel, Croft, Boyce and other leading composers[1]; some certainly participated in what we might now call folk music, instrumental and vocal. West gallery music was a sort of space, a broad continuum of popular practices. The problems of viewing it through our categories of musical perception are exactly that, problems created by our categories and ways of thinking musical differences. This will be a recurring theme of this essay; we cannot necessarily transcend our categories of thinking, but we can at least try to become self-aware of them and their implications.

As Rollo Woods aptly pointed out, 'The phrase "West Gallery Music" would not have been recognised by those who first created it'.[2] At the time, people would write of parochial psalmody, parochial music, rural church music, music in country churches and other terms. There is an association between the music and the place in which it was often, but not exclusively, performed. Galleries were erected at the west end of many churches from the seventeenth to the early nineteenth centuries, in part to extend church capacity in response to a growing population, in part fashion, sometimes in the hope that the creating of a space for singers and instrumentalists would promote an improvement in church music.[3]

At Mayfield in Sussex in 1731, some parties desired to improve singing in the church and the Archbishop of Canterbury granted a permission for west gallery erection to 'be convenient to answer to that end'. The gallery was to be for the sole use of those 'who shall sing psalms skilfully and well' although such people should 'disperse themselves into the body of the said church' in order to help those 'as shall have a pious intention of learning to sing'. Disputes over rights of access over different parts of the building are not uncommon in church history, thus the provisos in the grant.[4] England saw a great deal of gallery construction in the eighteenth and early nineteenth centuries. William Holland took a service at Aisholt (Somerset) in 1812 and commented: 'They have built a new Singing Gallery where the Singers were all arranged in due order. The Gallery improves the church very much'.[5] Some west galleries survive but many were destroyed in the wave of nineteenth-century church restoration and reform, absolutely part of the same movement that ridded the church of the practice of 'west gallery' church music.

At the start of the eighteenth century, after the religious upheavals of the previous two centuries, the Anglican church faced considerable difficulties although it functioned in many ways as an arm of the state. National church it may have been, but it relied on local taxation, the often-resented tithe, and local control and patronage from the landed elite. Becoming a clergyman was often seen as appropriate for younger sons of land-owning families, a respectable occupation of last resort. Some clergymen had little interest in religious matters and in some cases little interest in their parishioners. The fabric of many churches was in a run-down or ruinous state. Some parishes provided very poor livings for clergymen. Richard Brown writes of the parishes being exploited by 'impropriating gentry' giving an example of a local landowner pocketing the bulk of the income that should have gone to the church (a hangover of the Reformation settlement). 'The result of such practice was a direct increase in pluralism, clerical absenteeism and ignorance and decay in the fabric of many churches materially and spiritually'.[6] Some clergymen were well-connected and rich with private incomes; others were extremely poor. Pluralism was the practice of one clergyman holding many 'livings' in different parishes, sometimes putting a low paid curate in post to do the parish work and pocketing the difference between his salary and the income from the living.

Eighteenth-century Anglicanism itself had significant internal divisions and tensions, often reflecting political antagonisms, and sometimes identified as a 'High Church' (Tory supporting) group to which many of the aristocracy and gentry adhered, and a 'Low Church' (Whig supporting) party, generally more sympathetic to non-conformity. In the form of Methodism, Anglicanism suffered a severe shock from within, only after John Wesley's death did Methodism form a church of its own in 1791. Different religious groups held different attitudes to music in church.

By the early nineteenth century, Anglicanism remained unreformed, archaic and very complex in terms of ownership, vested interests and theology. This situation prevailed despite some efforts for renewal. It also faced the challenge of old and new dissent which threatened both congregation size and moral authority. A number of writers criticised 'the un-Christian conduct of the established clergy', denounced the hated and disputed tithes, and generally lambasted the corruption of the Anglican church. The clergy were not popular in many sections of society and the slogan 'More pigs, less parsons' crops up in a considerable number of sources.[7] The 1832 Ecclesiastical Revenues Commission confirmed some of the radical criticisms of Anglican corruption and initiated a process of reform.

Yet pious attitudes and feelings of the rightness of at least some religious observance, even if well-imbued with 'folk Christianity', were widespread. Low attendances and little taking of communion were common.[8] Snape has summed up the general situation well, as his study of Whalley demonstrated that: 'the laity's support for the established church was by no means unconditional, that it was heavily conditioned by customary habits and expectations, and that it was weakening perceptibly by the last quarter of the 18th century'.[9] In addition, Lee has written of the difficulties of the problems of adjustment and integration faced by many of the clergy: 'To many new incumbents, the dislocation from Oxbridge cloister to village green came as a considerable culture shock'.[10]

In the nineteenth century, a movement for reform, backed by the money of some members of the newly affluent middle classes, gathered momentum. The Religious Census of 1851 revealed that almost half of those attending worship were non-conformists and Anglican non-attendance was very high. It so shocked many people that the exercise was never repeated, although it was a spur to church reform. The Anglo-Catholic, Tractarian or Oxford Movement (in origin a reaction to what was seen as too much state intervention in church governance), which flourished from the 1830s, is often 'blamed' for the suppression of the old popular church music. It is true that many Tractarians were keen movers of church music reform, and they believed strongly in individual clergymen working within their parish to effect the changes they felt desirable. These were cultural revolutionaries of their day, who pursued their vision with energy and zeal, but were just one aspect of religious activity and spiritual revival in the middle decades of the nineteenth century. I will show that the pressure to reform church music predates Tractarianism by a number of decades.

The period witnessed attempts to resolve long-standing religious quarrels and conflicts. Such efforts were given new urgency by a fast-changing industrial and intellectual world. It was also a period of rapid development in aspects of music generally, for example, in the emergence of the brass band and choral movements, and new forms of musical entertainment, often with middle-class support and patronage. The popularisation of new and more cheaply produced instruments created conditions for the development of new forms of musical activity.[11]

Thus, the period 1750–1860 was one in which music at the parish level was sometimes deprived of resources, few churches outside prosperous towns had organs and music was a low priority in a church where other demands, parochial interests or self-interests, were seen as more pressing. Clerical governance varied but because of its general weakness, local initiatives could be tried and popular influence over aspects of church life had become a reality, at least until reformers started effectively interesting themselves in such matters. Edward Miller, in the late eighteenth century, wrote: 'It may be alleged that there are many of the clergy who do not think the cultivation of psalmody is a matter of much importance'.[12] The allegation was often true although not universally so; some vestries were supportive to church singers and instrumentalists.[13] The psalms are full of invocations for the people to sing praises, but the question of how that should be done, and who should do it, was a very pressing issue for some, a matter of indifference for others.

Who were the west gallery musicians?

Poverty was widespread in eighteenth- and nineteenth-century England. It is not therefore surprising that the instrumentalists who practised and sustained popular church music in the eighteenth and nineteenth centuries were not, on the whole, drawn from the ranks of the labouring poor. The choice of selling a fiddle or feeding one's family is not really much of a choice. Instrumentalists might need more disposable income than singers in order to maintain their instruments. The overwhelming impression coming from a range of sources is that choir-band members belonged predominantly to the middling sorts of society, artisans, tradesmen. These men had resources above the poorest members of rural society with some disposable income they could spend on instruments. There was, nevertheless, some involvement by people belonging to other strata of society. In a survey I did of 75 nineteenth-century Sussex church musicians using census and other data, the majority (65%) came from trades such as shoemaker, blacksmith, wheelwright, carpenter and bricklayer; 17 were agricultural labourers and servants (23%); there were 7 farmers (9%, though this category could describe anyone from a latter-day peasant to a large-scale capitalist farmer). There was one of each of auctioneer, road surveyor and schoolmaster (4% 'professionals').[14]

There are obviously limitations to these figures, not least of which is geographical (Sussex cannot represent the whole of England) and they represent individuals drawn from many villages. England has always been a country of contrasting communities, even within one county. Being a member of a church choir-band[15] did not necessarily mean that the individual had the purchase, care and maintenance of an instrument, but it often did. The occupations of shoemaker and leather worker (14) are almost as many as agricultural workers (16), whereas in many villages, the latter were a significant majority. Evidence from other studies and sources suggests that this sort of range, with the preponderance of 'middling' or artisan occupations in choir-bands, can be widely observed.

A fairly consistent picture emerges from other documents. At Ardley in the 1840s, Charles Williams, who compiled a manuscript book, was a shoemaker.[16] John Periam recollected that the old church choir at Bampton, Devon around 1847 'consisted of the principle tradesmen and other inhabitants of the little town'; his father was the 'cello player'.[17] At Yetminster c. 1835, the church musicians were aged between 35 and 55 and their occupations were journeyman baker (later a miller), a plasterer, a shoemaker, a thatcher and a schoolmaster and one parish clerk. According to an illustration, a boy and a woman were also involved.[18] At Oldbury-on-Severn in the 1740s, the singers included three fishermen, and the 'rest included a blacksmith, a carpenter, a gentleman, a schoolmaster and two yeomen'.[19] Thomas Clark (1775–1859), the musician and composer of 'Cranbrook' (the tune known today as 'On Ilkley Moor'), was a boot and shoemaker; fellow composer John Barwick (1741–c.1800) was a grocer; both worked in Canterbury, as did the bookseller and composer William Marsh (born c.1780).[20] Thomas Jarman, from Clipston, Northamptonshire, a friend of Clark and one of the most prolific psalmody composers of the early nineteenth century, was a tailor.[21] When Galpin encountered a surviving church band in late nineteenth-century Dorset, a thatcher played the clarinet, a shepherd played the cello and a farm labourer played the flute.[22] In industrial settlements, the situation was inevitably different. The latterly famous 'Larks of Dene' from the industrial Rossendale Valley in Lancashire were mainly weavers, as was Edward Harwood from Darwen who became a professional musician and wrote some celebrated pieces.[23]

An 1839 writer in a Cumberland newspaper looking back saw a cultural difference between those who practised rough sports, such as single stick and wrestling, and what other members of village communities did:

> These were the sports of the ruder part of the peasantry, the artisans, who were more cultivated, had their amusements at home; they were members of the village choir, and on the wake Sunday every one who had a voice, or would lend a hand with hautboy, bassoon, or flute, repaired to the singing-loft church, to swell with heart and voice the psalm or anthem; the clowns below gaping with mute surprise.[24]

A number of fictional accounts reinforce this idea of largely artisan musicians.[25]

We need to generalise to understand, however, the excellent East Midlands researches of Katie Holland remind us that every parish had its own particularities. Using detailed records and studying different types of villages, she sees bands relating to the specific communities in which they practised. In the predominantly industrial and close-knit village of Belgrave, the majority of members of the band were men aged between 20 and 49 and 'framework knitters and stocking or sock makers predominated' but at various times included a miller and a few labourers; a couple of men had multiple occupations and there were even two soldiers. Some of the members fell into poverty at different times. Females took on marginal roles in the choir-band from the 1830s.[26]

In the village of Stubton in the late eighteenth century, almost three quarters of working men were relatively poor agricultural labourers; yet, members of the choir-band came predominantly from people with a relatively high social status and included five substantial farmers or graziers, one carpenter, a parish clerk and only one labourer.[27] In contrast, the village of Lamport in the 1820s was a small closed village with paternalistic, if somewhat eccentric, 'responsible and caring landlords'. The choir-band had a 'mix of labourers and artisans' and included a schoolmaster/artist who left us illustrations of the choir-band.[28]

It is difficult to date precisely when these small ensembles (perhaps two to six instrumentalists, sometimes not so small, reaching into the low teens) began to form part of church music making and how widespread they were. The sources give the impression that they were fairly common from the later eighteenth century through to the second quarter of the nineteenth,[29] although unaccompanied singing also carried on throughout this period. As Weston writes: 'The movement grew, flourished and had virtually died away within a century'.[30] Holland has pointed out that some choir-bands she studied had quite a fluid membership, with members leaving and joining with relative frequency, which contradicts stereotypes of long-lasting and stable institutions, although some stability was provided by the involvement of family groups over considerable periods of time.[31]

The early history of choir-bands is particularly constrained by limited historical sources. There is evidence of a single instrument, usually a bass instrument, being purchased in eighteenth-century church wardens' accounts. Temperley concludes that 'church bands, including treble as well as bass instruments, were uncommon before 1770 but became rather widely popular after that date'.[32] Weston finds the earliest dating for instruments in a choir-band as 1742.[33]

We find the term 'church band' in quite common use by the last quarter of the eighteenth century as when at Colsterworth in Lincolnshire in 1789, 'the church band of music paraded the streets playing "God save the King"' to celebrate George III's recovery from illness.[34] A diarist of 1779 wrote of 'the band of music who perform at church on a Sunday' consisting of an oboe and bassoon, 'the remainder of the band being "composed of eight or nine voices"'.[35] The band performed in a west gallery.

Some church bands had formal society structures with sets of rules; other were less formal in their organisation. Choir-band members got little in the way of recompense for their service, other than funds for a choir dinner in some places, or an outing. Katie Holland stresses the role of sociability in the motivation for joining choir-bands, and their activities sometimes involved visiting and performing in other parish churches.[36] William Holland commented on his Somerset choir-band visiting:

> Very few in church. I never remember so few. The Singers, except a few were gone to Lydiard to Sing and have a dinner given to them and I fear carried many of the congregation with them. Our singers are become famous in the Country, which makes them

vain and fond of exhibiting themselves and I think they think more of their own Praise than(?) the Praise of God.

'We did not buy instruments for the Amusement of other Churches', he added grumpily.[37]

The evidence points to choir-bands flourishing in many parishes during the late eighteenth and early nineteenth centuries, their membership being drawn from a range of the population from labourers to professionals, but with the centre of gravity dominantly among the artisans and craftsmen. This pattern varied in different regions. Women participated in some choir-bands as singers, but I have seen hardly any evidence that they played instruments.[38] The choir-bands left us a considerable body of manuscript and other material that has only really started to be considered in recent decades.

West gallery repertory, instrumentation and performance style

Until the nineteenth century, Anglican congregations mainly sang metrical versions of the psalms. These existed in two dominant forms. The sixteenth-century versifications gathered together by Sternhold and Hopkins, after 1696 usually referred to as the Old Version (OV), and the 'New Version' (NV) of Tate and Brady (1696). Psalms were seen as godly texts derived from the bible, not fallible human productions, and places in the liturgy were designated for their performance. The OV pieces were mainly set in a simple 6868 metre ('common ballad meter' a link with another vitally important popular form). The Tudor versification of the psalms was often lampooned by members of the educated classes for its poor poetry, but there is no doubt that there was both familiarity and fondness among many people for the OV. The Bishop of London in his 1698 preface to the NV found it 'a work done with so much judgement and ingenuity, that I am persuaded, it may take off that unhappy objection, which has hitherto lain against the singing psalms; and dispose that part of divine service to much more devotion'.[39] The NV was not totally triumphant and was sternly objected to by some,[40] but both versions were used well into the nineteenth century. Others tried their hand at making metrical versions of the psalms but within Anglicanism, none had the success of the OV and NV.

Hymns were not generally approved of for use in Anglican churches. Since the time of Sternhold and Hopkins, psalm collections had had an end section of non-psalm material, prayers and liturgy. Some 'occasional' hymns for particular days of the year had been allowed in the Anglican church. Most significantly, 'While Shepherds Watched their Flocks by Night' by Nahum Tate owes its enormous popularity to the fact that it was included in the final section of the NV as 'A Hymn for Christmas Day'. The significant pioneers in hymn creation were different sorts of dissenters, outside the Anglican mainstream, notably Isaac Watts (1674–1748 an ecumenical Congregationalist) and Charles Wesley (1707–1788, Anglican minister and brother of the Methodist leader, John Wesley). These and other writers contributed greatly to the acceptance of non-biblical songs of Christian experience, but Anglicans did not accept this development until well into the nineteenth century, so the OV and NV remained central to Anglican singing long after a court case in 1820 made hymns legal, on an equal status with metrical psalms.[41] That case was by no means the end of controversy; in 1821, we find a critic writing: 'In some cases hymns have been introduced, which are always objectionable, because unauthorised, and often still more so on account of their language or their doctrine'.[42] In a parish history published in 1894, it is reported that at Wollaston in the mid-century '…hymns were not much sung except at Christmas and Easter, they were considered Methodistical'.[43]

Parochial music in the eighteenth century inherited much from the previous two centuries, the old one-note to a syllable strophic psalm tunes (such as 'The Old Hundredth' and 'Winchester Old' – the tune to which 'While Shepherds Watched' is now generally sung[44]) largely derived from Reformation settings. These were sturdy and simple (homophonic) tunes for congregational singing; William Mason wrote that such melodies 'rivalled the words in plainness and simplicity'.[45] Sometimes, psalms were lined out (read, sung or chanted line by line, by an individual [usually the parish clerk], and then sung by the whole congregation). Psalms were sung in unison, sometimes as harmonised melodies (most psalm books prior to 1700 had single line melodies without harmonisation).[46]

From the second quarter of the eighteenth century, there emerged a wholly different musical form, usually referred to as the 'fuging tune'. Temperley defines a fuging tune as one 'designed for strophic repetition with a sacred metrical text, in at least one phrase of which voices enter successively giving rise to overlap of text'. He has gone so far as to say 'the rise of the fuging tune is a phenomenon with few parallels in musical history'.[47] ('Cranbrook' is a popular example of such a tune when sung with all its parts). In addition, in some places, choirs performed through-composed anthems and 'set-pieces' though these were never intended for congregational singing.

To many educated observers, a significant problem with fuging tunes and some anthems was that musical intricacies and overlaps tended to obscure the text. Since the Reformation plainness in church music was upheld as a prime protestant virtue, the religious and educational nature of the words was seen as the great value of psalm singing. Thomas Secker, eighteenth-century Archbishop of Canterbury, preached that '...tunes designed for the multitude to join in, who have never been regularly instructed, must be plain and slow, and such as they have been accustomed to'.[48] A 1768 writer declaimed against fuging tunes: 'in country churches wherever a more artificial kind [of music] has been impudently attempted, confusion and dissonance have been the general consequence'.[49] Edward Miller thought such music 'too complicated and difficult for the congregation to attain by ear, consequently they cannot join in'.[50] Richard Eastcott thought the old simple tunes and some new ones in similar style 'solemn and expressive' but 'The jargon of heterogeneous sounds, introduced of late into our churches, serve to drown devotion in the most clamorous outcries'.[51]

We get a good idea of eighteenth-century developments in religious music in the writings of the enthusiast and reformer, John Arnold. He describes the change from the widespread use of the lining-out system to the formation of choirs fuelled by the publication of harmonised psalms and anthems. He decries the activities of 'country singing masters' who peddle 'very improper' fuging tunes which he considers 'ludicrous compositions'.[52] Arnold's appeal is to a notion of music as a cultivated and educated activity. He favours the use of 'the organ, clerk and charity children with those who understand music'. This would lead congregations 'into a regular method of performing the psalm tunes according to music'.[53]

This outcry against itinerant teachers of psalmody and the music they disseminated is echoed in other sources. Such 'obscure country teachers of psalmody'[54] were not always that obscure. William Tans'ur issued a considerable number of musical publications between the 1730s and 1770s and was a formative influence on the New England school of composers, William Billings et. al. Writing in a book published in 1794, James Merrick railed against such teachers: '...who travel, and style of themselves professors of, and instructors in psalmody, and are furnished with books of their own selections, which are seldom correct, and these are disposed of in every place where they go', adding that the 'harmony is generally very indifferent...'[55] William Riley thought that 'such composers are not acquainted with the first principles of harmony, not even with the species of music which is proper for parochial singing'.[56] A 1779 advertisement for a book of 'capital psalm tunes' hoped that through the use of the book,

> Congregations will be induced to adopt the Tunes in this Book, rather than those vile Productions of itinerant Singing-masters and others, which have prevailed of late, too much, in Country Churches, to the great Disgust of every rational Lover of Church-Music.[57]

Yet such singing masters were responding to popular taste and demand. Other writers saw the possibility of improvement through the use of a 'country singing master' and urged clergy to 'engage some person who knows the notes' to instruct '*by the ear only* such young persons and other parishioners as may wish to learn the plain psalm tunes'.[58]

Our knowledge of singing masters and itinerant teachers of psalmody has been greatly enhanced by recent research. Weston gives some details from church wardens' accounts which show that churches sometimes paid significant amounts of money 'for teaching the singing'.[59] Holland's extensive research has documented some of the ways these teachers operated, although we know more about them from their publications than from church wardens' accounts. Some clearly aimed their publications at particular areas by book tune title. Some were professionals who made a living by combining different musical activities; some had other occupations and operated within a relatively small area.[60] Costs of employing a singing master varied greatly; in certain places, payments appear generous. Holland suggests that teachers could have a good reputation locally but be looked down upon by 'musical elitists'.[61]

The eighteenth century saw a rapid increase in publications of popular psalmody, often aimed explicitly at 'country choirs', some compiled by singing masters.[62] It is clear from the widespread use of the term 'country choirs' after around 1750 that the countryside was perceived as a place of difference, a potential market and often in need of reform or improvement.[63] Abraham Adams, who argued in favour of reform and whose 1765 compilation was 'chiefly intended for the use of country choirs', wanted his collection to 'better improve this excellent and useful part of our service'.[64]

Many of the pieces found in choir-band manuscripts and publications were the creation of itinerant teachers. Temperley has commented:

> The music under discussion was created by unschooled composers. The models were provided by professionals, who distilled and simplified the style of art music of the day. Beyond these they could only build on the established popular traditions of psalm singing and folk music, which preserved within them some features of the art music of much earlier times.

There is significant truth in this passage. The idea that a form of popular music making builds on the musical traditions of those who perform it is self-evidently true, but this is perceived by Temperley as additional and subordinate to the work of educated composers. Such writing puts at the centre the (definitely minority) educated tradition and marginalises the (majority) popular musical culture, always perceived as inadequate, inferior and ignorant. In this, the musicology tends to echo complaints of musical reformers found in the source material. It is possible to think this idea entirely the other way around. The music was created by composers whose learning was built on the established, largely autonomous, vernacular traditions of practical music making, but who also, mainly through their own self-education, incorporated some ideas and techniques of schooled composers.[65] This allows the possibility of a totally different historical perspective which might make more comprehensible some of the cultural antagonisms which feature in the history of church music.

The repertory in church manuscript books was built up over many years. The old 'Reformation' tunes are often present; these date back to Tudor times (and were sometimes imports from continental protestant collections). But later compositions are also present. The tenor part book of Robert Kendal is dated 1791 but contains a number of tunes where the first known date of publication was in the earlier eighteenth century but he included tunes that were quite close to the date the compilation was started.[66] Even at this early date, a few tunes were North American in origin.[67]

If we turn now to musical instruments, the majority of parish churches in the country did not have organs until the second half of the nineteenth century. Prior to that, singing was either unaccompanied or if accompanied then by portable instruments usually brought into the church, at least from about the 1770s. There is plenty of biblical justification for the use of instruments.[68] A number of reformers in the eighteenth century thought that the addition of a bass instrument would help support the singing in a church; thus, some of the earliest financial support from churches are for the cello (sometimes referred to as a 'bass viol' although this name gives rise to ambiguity) and the bassoon. In 1761, we find John Arnold writing:

> The bassoon being now in great Request in many County Churches, [...] makes exceeding good Addition to the Harmony of a Choir of Singers, where there is no Organ, as most of the Bass Notes may be played on it, in the Octave below the Bass Voices.[69]

A few decades later, Richard Eastcott thought that an instrument could improve the quality of church singing: 'almost every village church in the kingdom will give us a grating specimen unless the voices are regulated by an organ or at least a well-tuned, and accurately stopped violincello'.[70] Bass instruments were soon joined, in various combinations, by oboe, flute and clarinet (commonly spelled clarionet) and violin. Less common instruments included the opheclide, the serpent, the keyed bugle and later the concertina. Numbers of instruments varied considerably, very few choir-bands could count their instruments in double figures, three to six instruments seem to have been common, sometimes a solo instrument supported the singing.[71] Weston detects a change over time from a 'double reed period' (roughly 1770–1810) to a string-dominated period (roughly 1800–1840).[72]

We find newspaper advertisements in the 1780s for country town retailers, who dealt in various provisions as well as musical goods. They clearly saw church choir-bands as a potential market. Newcomb of Stamford sold a variety of musical instruments many of which were used in church bands as well as 'ruled paper for copying music in single sheets, quires or books' and added 'Country choirs served on advantageous terms'.[73] An 1830s Boston shop advertised musical instruments 'warranted as to tone and quality' and makes a direct pitch at the choir-band market:

> Country choirs, and military and other bands, supplied with complete sets of instruments, in tune with each other, on the most reasonable terms.[74]

Poor tuning was a regular criticism of church bands by hostile observers. When reformers criticised that church instrumentalists sounded like they were playing dance music, it is in all likelihood because, as many manuscript books attest, they were used to playing dance music. A writer in 1841 complained that 'tunes of the most improper and ludicrous character are too frequently admitted' by choir-bands, complaining that he had heard 'Jenny Jones' (both a song and a dance tune) 'employed in church as a psalm tune'.[75] There is little other than rather unspecific negative observation as to the way instruments were used in the choir-bands; there is more detail when we turn to voices.

Rollo Woods rightly advises caution in the use of hostile and possibly exaggerated accounts of west gallery choirs and urges that 'They can only be used with caution'.[76] He does not stipulate the form that caution should take and caution should not mean avoidance. I argue that if there is consistency within accounts that tells us two things: first, the accounts are referring to something real in the observers' perceptions, there is a shared sense of what this music is like, and second, we need to understand this consistency in terms of different views of music held by the observers and the observed.

In a publication of 1789, T Williams wrote of 'that confusion and dissonance too often heard' in psalm singing and had a section of his collection outlining his concept 'Of Graceful Singing'.[77] An 1825 writer urging music reform wrote of 'the old style of psalmody without an organ, with two or three, or half a score lusty fellows roaring out the strains of Sternhold and Hopkins…'.[78]

There were disparaging comments particularly about the vocal style of both congregations and choirs from an early time.[79] To summarise a great deal of evidence, traditional singing styles used in many churches were not necessarily all the same, but tended to share an emphasis on full chest-voice production and some degree of melodic decoration, such as swoops and turns and end-of-line upward jerks. Where the older styles of British church music have survived, for example in the heterophonic, lining-out traditions of the Isle of Lewis[80] and among some Old Regular Baptist congregations in the US South, these features are clear.[81] Such stylistic features are also clear in the descendants of the eighteenth-century fuging styles such as the carol singing traditions around Sheffield and in parts of the West Country and the shape note traditions of the USA. Eighteenth-century writers observed this full-voiced style of singing: Richard Eastcott admonished loud singers: '…music does not consist in the quantity of tone produced, but in its quality […] it does not consist in noise as too many imagine'. His observation that 'the most vociferous singer is generally considered the most useful' is a glimpse into a popular aesthetic. But it was not just the sound that writers like Eastcote objected to; it was a whole demeanour described as 'the indecent antics and indecorous noise of those celebrated performers, who compose a country choir'.[82]

Relating evidence from early sources to surviving related musical traditions 'will never tell us exactly how an eighteenth-century choir sounded'.[83] I have never encountered a recording of a largely aural or oral-based musical tradition that did not surprise and intrigue me in some way. But Holman's argument that 'the one constant feature of tradition is that it is constantly changing'[84] is a cop-out. Some traditions change faster than others; some sustain consistency for a very long time indeed. The triangulation of evidence between contemporary accounts and descendant musical traditions gets us much closer to an idea of what west gallery music sounded like than many musicologists believe and many revivalists have achieved in their performances. There is overwhelming evidence in numerous sources that 'lusty fellows roaring out' could be a somewhat disparaging but relatively accurate way of describing the singing that went on in many English churches down to the mid-nineteenth century. It is reasonable to assume a consistency between vocal and instrumental styles.

Sometimes theological arguments were introduced to encourage change in singing style. Zabdiel Adams preached that 'God is not the author of confusion but of peace and he expects all things should be done decently and in order'. It was not a matter of indifference to God, 'whether we sing by rule, or irregularly, in a graceful, or in a barbarous manner'. Adams felt that church singers 'are obliged to use their best endeavours to sing in the most regular and agreeable manner possible', 'to sing by rule'.[85] Half a century later, 'W.G.' felt: 'It is really a mockery of the service of the Almighty, to hear the cruel attempts at choral singing in some of our parish churches…'.[86] William Romaine brought stylistic elements into his criticism and complained of the loudness and manner of church singers: 'There are many in our congregations who seem to think they sing best, when they sing loudest. You may see them often strain themselves with shouting, till their faces are as red as scarlet'. He felt that people should 'Sing well, to avoid the tedious drawling manner in use in most of our churches'. He was not optimistic about improvement: 'The abuses here complained of are not to be easily remedied…Some of them are of long standing, not soon to be rooted out' but he earnestly recommended it.[87] Abraham Adams thought music 'ravishing and delightful … when performed with skill in a becoming manner! And how much and unlike itself when made up with harsh and disagreeable sounds'.[88] Yet the psalms, the texts that were constantly sung, repeatedly encouraged the singer to be loud: 'Sing with a loud and cheerful voice' (Psalm 5).

A key notion in much of the writing is decency; Miller thought that God '… expects that *all* things should be done decently and in order'.[89] Zabdiel Adams and other eighteenth-century writers totally opposed the notion of an autonomous tradition: 'it is vain for us to pretend that we need no other instructor than nature in this matter'.[90] More than a century later, the Tractarian clergyman Francis Paget sermonised a similar view: '… the child must learn the rules of music before it can begin to gain the true freedom of the trained musician'.[91] This is still a view one encounters regularly in spite of the fact that the overwhelming quantity of music produced in the world is not made by trained musicians and training itself can create its own limitations as well as enhance techniques.

Some writers have provided evidence that musical reform was possible and high musical standards (judged by educated opinion) could be attained within the choir-band tradition. Drage has reflected on the impressive abilities of some choir-band musicians: '…it would have been useless for composers and compilers to publish pieces that were beyond the capabilities of performers'.[92] Thomas Jarman of Clipston was the 'most prolific and significant Northamptonshire composer of the choir-band period' who led the choir-band at Clipston Baptist Chapel when it 'was held in high repute'.[93] The evangelical clergyman Thomas Haweis, of Aldwincle All Saints, achieved significant musical reform and improvement within the choir-band format and tradition.[94] One hardly feels that the choir-band at Stowey had become 'famous in the country' through incompetence.[95]

During the west gallery period, instrumentalists and singers of very different degrees of competence performed in churches. In societies where largely autonomous musical traditions flourish, it is normal for there to be a wide range of competences displayed. But competence has to be related to style – the collectively held, impermanent, intersubjective notions of what constituted good music. Here different aesthetics come into play, and these ideas were related to music tradition, educational experience and social status. To simplify, there were widely held, popular notions of what constituted good style and there were educated ideas derived from learning and notions of good taste. Add to this, contemporary expectations of the limited capabilities of people from lower social backgrounds, and we begin to appreciate some of the complexities of understanding west gallery music historically.

We also have to deal with changing fashions, the impermanent aspect of the collective ideas of what constitutes good music. In church music, as in anything else, it seems reasonable to think that some of the eighteenth-century music the choir-bands regularly performed began to be perceived as old-fashioned, particularly in a fast-changing world, and largely fell into disuse. An observer of 1839 commented: 'The quavering strains of Arnold, Tansur, Knapp, and Bishop, we hear no more'.[96]

Opposition to and the elimination of the popular church music

Throughout the west gallery period and significantly before it, there was an outcry of opposition to the poor way psalmody in country churches was performed or rather perceived to be performed.[97] Churches were interesting and unique institutions. The intention was that the space be used and occupied by members of all ranks of society. It is not that people met as equals; in most places, social hierarchy was physically present in the allocation and renting of pews and the construction of exclusive spaces and monuments. Patriarchy was physically present in the separation of genders.[98] Some non-conformist groups were less hierarchical than Anglican churches. But it was a space in which people from different social backgrounds, and with different cultural practices, experiences and assumptions, had of necessity to encounter each other. This gave rise to conflicts and tensions, often covert sometimes overt.[99]

It should also be stressed that when dealing with church music reform, there were a number of visions of what form that should take. To evangelicals and many non-conformists, good congregational singing could be the ideal, usually with an organ to deliver its 'grateful violence'.[100] Many non-conformist groups achieved this; to many critics, the success of Methodism could be attributed in good measure to the quality of its singing. To others, those of a high church or Anglo-Catholic persuasion, the ideal of a version of cathedral practice adapted to parish use was much more prevalent. One thing those who favoured reform tended to agree on was that choir-bands were obstacles to musical progress.

Although west galleries and singing pews were often built with the purpose of improving singing in church, the separation of a select group of singers and instrumentalists from the congregation was a recurring complaint among those urging reform, as was their ignorance: '… when a company of illiterate people form themselves into a corner, distinct from the congregation. Here devotion is lost between the impotent vanity of those who sing, and the ignorant wonder of those who listen'.[101] Edward Miller complained about 'the great indulgence given by many of the clergy to *detached sets of singers*' whose music was too complicated and excluded the congregation from participating.[102] A newspaper letter of 1821 argued against such singing exclusivity, reporting that 'an absurd custom frequently consigns it [singing] to a few individuals, whose rude attempts oftener offend than edify'[103] and deplored the lack of congregational singing, which he felt should be encouraged. Many writers complained of select groups of singers monopolising the psalms, William Riley pointed to the title page of the Old Version of the Psalms: 'To be sung of all the people together'.[104]

By the late eighteenth century, William Vincent felt that church music had 'fallen into decay and contempt'. Such a view does not seem to have been held by many of the practitioners of popular church music, but they left little in the way of testimony. Vincent's was one of a number of eighteenth-century schemes advocating church music reform and proposing how this should be done. His *Consideration on Parochial Music* has a chapter entitled 'Means of Restoring Parochial Music'. He stated, 'I imagine there are few clergymen on country benefices, who do not sincerely lament the existence of a select band in the gallery, and wish to remove it, by bringing the whole body of the people to perform their part'.[105] The scheme Vincent proposed is detailed and systematic and involves considerations of the intricacies of the management of parish politics and the organisation of one group of people against another. Vincent was a London rector but obviously had a knowledge of rural church life. If the clergyman is not musical himself, Vincent suggests the employment of a musical instructor for a small price, but he warns against itinerant teachers of singing.

But for this office those persons are not meant, who go about the country as professed teachers of psalmody, as from them and their method the very evil complained of originates.[106]

Vincent anticipates some of the problems that might arise.

> Some ministers will, doubtless, object to disgusting their present band; they will esteem it driving one body of men from the church, before they are sure of securing the attendance of others; they will be desirous of avoiding divisions, and parties in their parish, and envious comparisons between the new and old method.

Vincent felt that such difficulties could be overcome by 'discreet management and gradual means'. If the attempt was made, Vincent argued, 'many difficulties would vanish of themselves in the execution'.[107]

Other members of the clergy were also advocating reform. John Shepherd felt that 'the boisterous and ostentatious clamour of what is called the band of singers may excite disgust but cannot assist devotion'. He defined six objectives for reform: (1) Standing during psalm singing. (2) Singing should not be confined to a select band. (3) 'The Psalms should be sung with modesty and humility: all vociferous roar and squall should be utterly banished'. (4) 'Every attempt at intricacy of execution, all complex air, with whatever is difficult, or carries the appearance of art, should be discouraged [...] The plainer tunes ought therefore to be selected'. The number of tunes used should be limited to 12 or 15. (5) The choice of psalms cannot be left to the parish clerk. (6) The organ is the only instrument that should be allowed in church.[108] Edward Miller produced a similar scheme for reform.[109]

In 1790, Beilby Porteus, Bishop of London, in a much cited sermon, called for the improvement of parochial psalmody and complained of 'a select band of singers who have been taught by some itinerant master to sing in the worst manner, a most wretched set of psalm tunes [...] so complex [...] that it is altogether impossible for any of the congregation to take part...' He wanted this part of worship 'restored to its ancient purity and simplicity, and generally congregational psalmody universally revived'. In country parishes, 'it might be more difficult to restore the psalmody to its primitive state and banish the corruptions of it introduced by the select village choir' but he felt the obstacles 'by no means insuperable'. He proposed training up some of the most promising children and therefore 'a select band will be no longer necessary'.[110] Clearly, by the period of the French Wars, a considerable number of clerics wanted musical reform and had tried to sketch out plans of the form that could take. Most agreed that involved the ejection of choir-bands.

Musical reformers from the 1820s sometimes referred back to authors of the previous century that had pioneered their efforts.[111] Various writers advocated the introduction of organs, ultimately the most common replacement for a choir-band, and proposed practical schemes as to how they might be obtained. Some, though not all, advocated the use of barrel-organs, thus obviating the need for skilled musicians.[112] An advertisement for these instruments stressed their utility for country churches, stating that they could 'entirely supersede the use of other instruments'.[113] A correspondent of 1835 crisply set out the economic constraints of reform:

> Barrel organs are cheaper than finger organs, and do very well for a country church. Finger organs are the best, undoubtedly; but they require an organist, and that organist requires a salary...[114]

In the second quarter of the nineteenth century, the impetus for church music reform, linked to other movements of church renewal, gained significant momentum. Traces of this piecemeal movement can be found scattered in various published and manuscript material of the period. Just two examples of the literature must suffice. In 1831, J A La Trobe published *The Music of the Church*. La Trobe caricatures music events during a service and concludes:

> …I verily believe, that had the taming and bringing into order a country choir been appointed for one of the labours of Hercules, he would have lost his reward. He who undertakes such a task stands in need of every Christian virtue […] He is about to withstand principles, for which obstinate depravity have no rival in the human heart – the principles of ignorant selfishness and petty pride.[115]

Faced with the likely outcome of a withdrawal of support from a choir-band, La Trobe suggests that the clergyman should turn to the Sunday School, where there are 'rich materials for forming a choir'.[116] In some ways, La Trobe built on the critique and detailed plans for church reform that Vincent urged 40 or so years earlier, but his book appeared at the start of a determined and vigorous movement for general church reform and had considerable influence. This book was followed by a magazine *The Parish Choir or Church Music Book*, which ran from 1846 to 1851. This publication contained similar material on reform but actively engaged and supported those attempting reform and provided approved music for new musical arrangements in church. One of the problems writers of the magazine saw working against improving church music were the present musicians: 'Nothing can be more certainly fatal to the good cause, than placing the management of the music in crude and vulgar hands'.[117] The magazine was notable in giving very detailed accounts of attempts to reform what it described in a running heading as 'Refractory Village Choirs'. The personnel, the methods, style and the repertory of the old-style singers and instrumentalists were all under sustained attack. A correspondent of *The Musical World* writing in 1840 believed that the way to affect an improvement in parochial psalmody was by 'creating an interest with the congregation in its performance'. But he issued a caveat: 'How to do this without going too far, and offending the prejudices of these puritanical people, is the rub'.[118] Some clergymen clearly did offend prejudices.

In 1843, in a pamphlet ostensibly about church enlargement and arrangement, John Mason Neale moves from the position of the organ to the subject of galleries (the existence of which he condemned) to the choir-band and the distraction activity in the gallery causes:

> Removed too great distance from the clergyman's eye, having a separate entrance to their seats, possessed of strong *esprit du corps*, and feeling or thinking themselves indispensable to the performance of a certain part of public worship, and too often, alas! privileged to decide what that part shall be, – what wonder if they generally acquire those feelings of independence and pride, which make the singers some of the worst members of the parish. The radicalism both of singers and of bell-ringers is notorious.[119]

Neale is obviously generalising and stereotyping, but this is the sort of thing which the eager young clergymen, imbued with reforming zeal, were absorbing and acting on. We note the insistence on clerical control and oversight, independence and pride make members of the choir-band the worst sort of parishioner.

Many people believe that the old ways of music making simply died out of their own accord, by a sort of natural decay. The late Christopher Turner was a key proposer of such a view. To him, church musicians suffered a 'decline in their morale' and 'unable to sustain themselves [...] bowed to the pressure of change and relinquished their role in the gallery – often without complaint'.[120] This is a sort of 'inevitability of history' argument that does not stand up well to evidence or critical scrutiny. Turner compounds the weakness of his case by claiming that one of the reasons for decline was a fall in population in the countryside in the mid-nineteenth century – no such fall occurred. A decline in the percentage of the rural population as opposed to the urban occurred but in a context of rapidly increasing overall population. The rural population actually increased in the earlier nineteenth century, but not as fast as the urban population. Nor does Turner consider the case of the expulsion of the church bands within the wider context of nineteenth-century changes in popular culture and social relations, 'rational recreation' and 'improvement'.[121]

Conflicts between clergymen and musicians are in some ways a feature of church life and references to unseemly happenings can be found in the writings of a number of ministers. John Skinner, a Somerset Rector in the 1820s, records incidents involving the church singers, including (anticipating Hardy) cases of drunkenness in church.[122] Similarly in Norfolk, the extensive diarist Parson Woodforde had various difficulties with his church singers.[123] The conflicts that became quite widespread in the period 1820–1870 were different in kind, the results of deliberate attempts at parochial church music reform. These reforms sometimes encountered stiff and occasionally violent opposition, occasional defections to other churches and symbolic demonstrations of various kinds.

Weston records the remarkable case at Clipston, probably in 1820, when a reforming curate, the Rev John Bull abolished the choir-band and took a hand in reshaping musical practices. This led to the writing of satirical verses and songs, demonstrations and appearances before the local magistrates. The opposing sides never seemed to reconcile and eventually Bull left the village.[124] Holland gives us extensive details of the case of the argumentative George Atkinson, perpetual curate of Stow-in-Lindsey from 1836, a keen ecclesiologist in a parish where there had not been a resident clergyman for six or seven decades. One of his first acts upon arriving was to remove the singing gallery and ringing platform, dismiss the parish clerk (which he did not have the right to do), stop payments to the choir-band and set about major church restorations without the support of the parish. The village descended into a state of hostility which gave rise to some farcical happenings and lasted in one form or another until the end of his time there. Atkinson wanted to install an organ but did not achieve that; his successor did however.[125] Conflicts over music were never simply just that, but were entangled with other tensions and problems, often theological sometimes social and personal.

John Periam recalled that at Bampton in Devon in the 1840s, 'There were then resident here several people of very good musical taste and knowledge, but the abolition of the old choir put a stop to the whole affair'.[126] Also in Devon, Andrew Jones has documented a number of cases of both attempted musical 'improvement' and the assertion of clerical control over the music and resistance. For example in 1870, Henry Barley, vicar of Branscombe, tried to excommunicate 'those who have been in the habit of singing or playing in the gallery' after their resistance to the use of a newly introduced organ, and for a time there was no music in the church.[127] Robson gives us some very interesting material from Fordington, in Dorset:

> In the early part of the nineteenth century, the vicar, John Palmer, was a vigorous supporter of the church band and is believed to have written some of its music. During his incumbency the west gallery was extended. His successor, Henry Moule, inducted in

1829, quickly fell out with the church band, leading to their striking and to a halving in church attendance. His demolition of the west gallery was greeted by vandalism and the stoning of the vicarage.[128]

Robson provides another very valuable piece of evidence from Whitechurch Canonicorum: 'Great was the heart burning and ill feeling that the dethronement of the old choir occasioned [….] The old hands cut the connection completely and ceased coming to church even'.[129] Similar disruption was caused at Barnham in Kent in the late 1830s when the introduction of a barrel-organ caused the old musicians to go on strike, with just two of them remaining loyal to the church.[130] Such cases were not always clear-cut. Holland gives examples of choir-bands who ceased operation and then recommenced and of their flexibility as when 'eight of the twelve new choristers put in place in 1859 […] were members of the original choir-band',[131] suggesting give and take between the old members and the reforming vicar. Other reports write of the love that existed for the old music, boycotting of tradesmen members of new choirs and even accounts of fights between old and new choirs.[132] There is no simple pattern here, but there is an overall trend.

My work on Sussex uncovered similar happenings and some direct testimony from church musicians involved. James Nye was a labourer, quarry worker, gardener, church fiddle player and composer. When a new clergyman came to his church at East Chiltington, 'the first thing our new parson did was to try to rule the singing'. This caused commotion among the choir and gave Nye 'a good opportunity to leave the church, which I did and this broke up the singing'. This caused more problems as 'the farmers set at the poor parson for interfering with us'.[133] Nye followed his religious inclinations and joined a Calvinistic chapel. Nye's was not a spectacular case but his steadfast withdrawal, his response to a hostile and negative situation may be indicative of the feelings of many choir-band members and relate to the decline in choir-band activity after c.1830.

But some cases were very spectacular. The blowing up of the new church organ at Walsingham in Norfolk in November 1866, while again complex in origin, is a powerful symbolic end to the gallery period.[134] Andrew Jones summed up the transformation with brevity: 'The old music-making clashed head on with the new culture of organs, hymn-books, and surpliced choirs – and lost'.[135]

This 1850 newspaper article gives a succinct account of musical reformation in action, a particular example of a process that was going on all over the country:

> Castle Hedingham Church. – During the last fortnight the singing in connexion with this Church has undergone a great and rapid change, and the effect produced has been highly gratifying to all. The old, but we are happy to say fast-declining, fashion of having most unsacred instruments of various kinds to lead the singing in country churches has unavoidably been the custom here, which, with the accompaniment of a few men's voices, has formed a very poor attempt to "Sing to the praise and glory of God." Through the kind exertions of a visitor of the incumbent of this parish, conjointly with his own and his lady's efforts, the unsolemnizing bassoon and clarionet have been laid aside; a choir of 30 children and a dozen men has been formed, and great credit is due to pupils as well as teachers for the readiness they have shown to promote the needful alteration of this important, but often neglected, part of Divine service. The late singers are entitled to no small praise for the entire absence they have manifested of that foolish pertinacity to adhere to that which custom has made old, and which, in so many instances, has been an insurmountable barrier against improvement.[136]

By 1857, an Anglican publication predicted that 'The days are happily numbered in which a fiddle or bassoon were looked upon as an appropriate accompaniment to a church choir' adding optimistically that few churches were now without organs and the clergy's wives and sisters of the clergy can form 'an excellent staff of organists' where no funds were available to pay professionals.[137] In the 1860s, a once youthful participant in a large choir-band could refer to 'the choir of the olden times', but then realise that the times were 'not so very old'. He wrote of 'the absurdities which were perpetuated with impunity before a perfectly complacent congregation'. There is pleasure in his recollection from old age but he concludes, 'Their's was the error of their day, now in a great deal remedied, and only remembered as a shadow'.[138] This is a more nuanced view than some more triumphalist statements. The same year, a fictionalised account of 'Reforming a Village Choir' stated that, 'The music was in a style fast dying out of rural England; and as well so, for whose risible faculties could stand such an exhibition as we had Sunday after Sunday'.[139] Drage has aptly commented on the way such stories with their 'nostalgic and sometimes patronising accounts of musically incompetent but honest rustics' have 'become a rather comic addition to the national heritage' and 'is all that is remembered of about country church musicians'.[140] In the long term, it is the Hardy's and Eliot's writings that are remembered but, in the short term, the popular writing about choir-bands, often in magazines and newspapers, building on older stereotypes, did much to propagate notions of backward and incompetently comic rustics. For example, in 1865 and 1888, we find a periodical and a newspaper reprinting 'Village Choristers' by M A Scargill which dates from 1835. The story starts with listing difficult to manage animals and carries on '… mules are celebrated for their pertinacity, and donkeys for their stupidity; but all the pigs, rams, mules, and asses in the world, put together, would be more easily managed than a company of singers in a village church'.[141] Clearly, fashion moved against the old music and derided its performers.

During the last three decades of the nineteenth century, two moods dominated writing about the church bands. One is triumphalist and mocking, celebrating the progress made in church music and often ridiculing what had existed before. The other nostalgic and regretful. Sermons and reports of choral festivals or the opening of new church organs became the locus for the new glorification of the present and damning of the past.

At the annual festival of the Nottinghamshire Church Choral Union in 1868, the report comments on improvements in church music 'especially in country parishes'. We are then presented with what became a sort of standard history:

> We are happy to say that a more decent style of service does prevail in country churches than was the case a few years ago. There may be odd villages where the mellifluous clarinet in the hands of the village tailor, or the diaphanous bassoon under the care of the gardener at the hall, still flourish, but we do not think they are near Nottingham.[142]

The account continues with details of 'extraordinary fuges', describing the village choir as a 'motley crew "perched up aloft"' and of enraged musicians (listeners not performers, referencing Hogarth) after hearing performances. A writer syndicated in not less the 15 newspapers declared in 1874: 'The ancient village choir, with its flutes and its fiddles, has been swept away. Its pretensions were no doubt greater than its powers'.[143]

The progress of musical reformation was piecemeal. Church choral associations and choral unions were formed in the 1840s and 1850s in various places with the express aim of improving singing in church.[144] Like brass bands and secular choral societies, they are characteristic cultural organisations of mid-nineteenth-century English society: rational, improving and respectable. They practised regularly in formal singing classes with a competent choir-master, with a view to improve congregational singing. They charged a small subscription and raised money in other ways. No doubt, less formal but equally effective arrangements were carried on throughout the country.

Preaching at a choral festival in Leamington in 1894, the Dean of Hereford looked back on the 'wonderful improvement in church music throughout the country during the last quarter of a century'. Then came the inevitable sketch of a dark age: when the hymn was given out, then from the 'vest-end [sic] gallery proceeded discordant sounds from instruments out of tune, and quivering voices of veteran minstrels, who declined to retire from the choir in which they had taken part for half a century. Irreverence then predominated, and the church services and the building were much neglected'. Now was an age of renovated churches, greater reverence and better music arising from the influence of cathedrals. Had the old ways continued, 'the churches would have been devoid of worshippers'.[145]

In contrast to this triumphalism, interesting statements of regret come from a number of writers. Curwen's 1897 statement is perhaps surprising coming from a champion of mass choralism: '…the disestablishment of these rural instrumentalists was a mistake. It would have been better […] to have reformed them than to have suppressed them'.[146] Galpin expressed similar sentiments feeling that 'the suppression of these bands as a relic of a barbarous age and the introduction of organs […] has not been an unmixed good'. He felt 'Reformation was, no doubt, needed but not extinction'.[147]

Alfred Williams, whose folk song collecting was motivated by a wish to leave 'a permanent record of the language and activities of the district', rather than just preserve and publish songs, deplored the effect of the abolition of the choir-bands which 'dealt a smashing blow at music in the villages':

> They laboured to make themselves proficient and the training they took both educated them and exerted an unmistakable influence upon the everyday life of their fellows. But when the organ came, the village band was dismissed from the church; they were not wanted any more. Their music was despised. There was no further need of them, and the bands broke up. For a while the fiddle sounded at the inns and at the farm feast but was soon heard no more.[148]

Williams, notwithstanding his romanticism, reminds us that the church had had a vital role in providing an institutional base for a great deal of diverse music making. So, what really caused the demise of west gallery choir-bands? Holland, the best writer that has considered the subject in recent years and put her work on a firm empirical basis, would put the emphasis on social change as a more powerful explanation than the conflict between elite and popular musical values (which pre-existed the demise) and the coming of organs, church restoration and the activities of reforming clergy. The disappearance of many choir-bands predated these developments; they were often ephemeral, locally organised groups.[149] She points to the lessening of institutional support for choir-bands by church vestries (which usually consisted of 'substantial' householders in a parish, farmers, gentry and sometimes aristocrats) in the East Midlands in the 1840s; vestries were the very bodies that had bought instruments and provided supplies and choir suppers previously.[150]

I have a lot of sympathy for this view. Social historians are drawn to the dramatic events and conflicts that illustrate deeply held attitude and values, but interesting as they are, these are only part of the story. Some choir-bands clearly died of 'natural' causes. But perhaps it is wrong to see musical reform and social/cultural change as not intrinsically connected.

The 1820s and 1830s was a time of massive historical realignment and change. Holland has done a great service in showing that a simple scheme of development from choir-bands to church organs and surpliced choirs does not fit all cases. There are gaps, and some cases of reinstatements of choir-bands, also cases where choir-bands and organs co-existed for a period.[151] Real life is messy and the actual development depended much on local conditions and local personalities. In the early years of the nineteenth century, choir-bands were relatively numerous; by 1870, they were rare survivals.

Ideas and cultural values are important but these operate within social, economic and institutional constraints and in the case of church music reform, within a village community framework. Ideas have to be there in order to have their day and the idea that choir-bands should be abolished was there soon after they had come into being. Significant change occurred in the second quarter of the nineteenth century. This was a result of important shifts in attitude among some of the laity and increasing professionalisation and control exercised by members of the clergy. What had been previously encouraged and supported was now discouraged and resources were put in other directions: to organs, reformed choirs and church choral associations. In some places, where the old tradition and culture were strong, change was resisted; in other places, it was not, although we have relatively little evidence of any feelings of resentment that might have been experienced.[152]

West gallery literature and scholarship

Significant writing about what we now call west gallery music can be thought of as existing in three chronological and in some ways overlapping phases which we could call literary, antiquarian and scholarly.

Popular church music making was used as literary material by a number of nineteenth-century fiction and poetry writers who wanted to tell stories, often retrospective, with a setting in village life. Hardy was the most significant writer to deal with the subject of west gallery music, but by no means the only one. A useful overview of nineteenth-century writers is contained in Gillian Warson's work. As well as Hardy, George Eliot, Samuel Butler, Thomas Hughes and Arnold Bennett all include significant mentions of aspects of popular church music. Sometimes the subject adds local colour, sometimes it adds to the drama of the work, sometimes it is used for comic effect. The US author, Washington Irving, was an early writer on the subject although he set the comic, whimsical and gently derisory tone that would be taken up by many writers, including obscure contributors to periodical publications who explored the dramatic, humorous and sentimental possibilities of the subject. Most often, old-style church music is seen to represent a lost world which larger social changes within rural society had cast away, generally for the better but sometimes with a sense of loss and regret. A significant number of nineteenth-century clergymen deal with the subject in their memoirs and diaries; these are not always tinged with romanticism or regret.[153]

Thomas Hardy is the most significant writer to have taken popular church music as a subject. In *Under the Greenwood Tree* (1872) and some short stories and poetry, Hardy depicts a church band (the Mellstock choir) its activities and in the novel its demise. Hardy was able to set down 'a fairly true picture' of a church band as his father had been a member of one and some of his manuscripts were owned by his son, who also played the fiddle. But years after the novel's publication, Hardy had some regrets. His 1896 preface gave more detail about the historical background of the church bands and puts them in a positive light. His 1912 preface is a fascinating document as Hardy laments the limitations of his earlier writing:

> In rereading the narrative after a long interval there occurs the inevitable reflection that the realities out of which it was spun were material for another kind of study of this little group of church musicians than is found in the chapters here penned so lightly, even so farcically and flippantly at times.[154]

Hardy was not the most farcical writer on the subject by a long way but it is interesting that he wrote this about his own work. His influence on later writers and researchers has been significant.

Towards the end of the nineteenth century, we find the first stirrings of what we could describe as factual antiquarian writing on church music. The tone was set by Rev Francis W Galpin, famous for his work on the history of musical instruments, who produced a short article entitled 'The village church band, an interesting survival' in 1883 and followed this with a 1906 piece called 'Notes on the old church bands and village choirs of the past century'. In the 1883 piece, Galpin describes his encounter with a three-piece instrumental band at Winterbourne Abbas in Dorset consisting of clarinet, flute and cello. He found the effect 'most picturesque' and commented on 'the quaintness of the surroundings' but did mention how 'the little building resounded with the lusty voices of the villagers'. Galpin's 1906 piece is more expansive though still based on material from his native Dorset; it has some interesting detail and is much influenced by Thomas Hardy. Galpin thought that the 'rivalry which existed between these church bands greatly conduced to their efficiency and maintenance'.[155]

The most significant of these antiquarian writers was Canon K H MacDermott. His first book, *Sussex Church Music in the Past*, was published in 1922 and this was followed by *The Old Church Gallery Minstrels*, in 1948, which took a wider geographical perspective. These books are rambling and thoroughly antiquarian in approach but are based on interest in the subject that dated back into the nineteenth century. They contain some interesting detail but rather revel in quaint and what are portrayed as ludicrous episodes in church life – his work is undermined by his delight in recounting the odd and the sensational. MacDermott's saving grace is that he acquired a lot of information and a considerable number of church music manuscripts and books he bequeathed to the Sussex Archaeological Society. In that he interviewed people that had experienced the older style church music; his work is valuable, in that his method was to write down a few remembered impressions; his work represents a great lost opportunity.[156]

Mention should be made of Charles Pearce's 1921 paper 'English Sacred Folksong of the West Gallery Period'.[157] The paper is conceptually problematic (I do not think the pieces discussed are 'folk song' by any definition of his day or ours), but it is a serious attempt to explore the musicality of once widely used pieces. Pearce, a pillar of the London musical establishment, spoke up for the musical qualities of some west gallery music and decried the W H Monk sausage-machine tune editing for *Hymns Ancient and Modern* (1861) though I do not think he would have wanted a return to the west gallery style of performance.

In the inter-war period, Percy Scholes, editor of the *Oxford Companion to Music*, demonstrated a wonderfully wide-ranging interest in all things musical, including popular church music. Other interest was mainly from local historians and those (usually members of the Galpin Society) concerned with organology and musical archaeology. Conventional histories of church music generally ignored, discounted or denigrated the music of the choir-band period. Bernarr Rainbow, in writing on the tonic sol-fa movement and the reform of church music, assumes much of the contemporary criticism of choir-bands was justified and criticises the romanticism of prior writing about the west gallery period.[158]

The modern wave of interest in the subject did not emerge until the 1970s when it came in a sense from two directions, scholarly musicology and folk music studies. The pioneer of the scholarly study of popular church music was Nicolas Temperley, an English scholar resident and working in the USA. His magisterial *The Music of the English Parish Church* was first published in 1979.[159] This is linked to a series of important journal essays. The subject had never been covered before with such ambition and comprehensiveness and he devotes a substantial chapter to 'Country psalmody, 1685–1830'. Crucially, Temperley was influenced by colleagues he encountered in the USA who had taken the US vernacular religious music as a serious subject of study. Writing about the fuging tunes, he draws attention to the interest the US scholars had paid to a subject ignored by English writers:

> Naturally, country church music of the 18th century occupies a much more important place in American musical history than in European; America boasts little in the way of opera, art song, or instrumental music, and almost no professional church music, from that period. Many who have studied this music during the last 50 years have been attracted by the freshness of fuging tunes, and by their boldness. Some, grown accustomed to their strange idiom, have come to like them.[160]

In this passage, we can detect both the freshness of Temperley's approach and some of its limitations. One has to ask to whom fuging tunes are a 'strange idiom' and why? It was a strange idiom to the US music historians at first, but not once they had assimilated its characteristics and conventions. Clearly, it was not a 'strange idiom' to the west gallery musicians who relished their performance, or to the singers who perpetuated the shape note tradition in the USA, nor to west gallery revivalists in this country. The very fact that people have taken to this material must put into question central assumptions and practices of much conventional musicology. Strangeness does not cancel out validity; rather, it points to the cultural limitations of the observer, though clearly such a view is hard for anyone with solid cultural preconceptions to accept or even to understand.

In recent years, there have been a number of publications and academic works that have sought to throw light on this music. Much of this has been linked to the west gallery revival. Rollo Woods' *Good Singing Still: A Handbook on West Gallery Music* remains the best popular introduction to the subject, demonstrating the writer's knowledgeable and considered approach. In contrast, Harry Woodhouse's *Face the Music: Church and Chapel Bands in Cornwall*, a latter-day emulation of K H MacDermott's work, contains some interesting material but is a throw-back to an earlier age of antiquarianism. A significant amount of music from period sources has been published for west gallery revivalists in recent decades, some of which includes informative introductory material.[161]

A number of research degrees which relate to west gallery music have been completed in recent decades, and some of these are available online. Some have been mentioned above where elements of the work have been addressed, for example, Sally Drage, Peter Robson and Gillian Warson but some other work should be cited. Fanella Bazin has documented popular church music in the Isle of Man.[162] Stephen Weston's empirical work has provided us with much detail about the choir-band movement, particularly the musical instruments.[163] Holland's careful work on churchwarden's accounts and vestry minutes has given us fascinating insights into the history and workings of choir-bands at a village level.[164] More recently, Rebecca Dellow has explored a similar area but in a very focussed way, considering manuscripts dating from c. 1860 to 1880. She has very interesting things to say about the interaction between aural and literate practices, and the role of popular publications in the acquisition of skills and repertoire.[165]

Stephen Campbell has conducted a study of contrasting manuscript books, including church music manuscripts. He has some critical and interesting things to say and is good on the way that forms of mediation have skewed our perception of vernacular music practice in the eighteenth century. He provides a useful critique of the 'mismatch between the current perception of vernacular music and the actuality of that music in its original context'. He argues for the existence of a 'multifaceted mainstream culture' writing 'It is all too easy to compartmentalise music into defined genres associated with particular social classes, but in fact the social distribution of music is complex'. He makes a good case for the 'permeability of class barriers' and 'the ability of some music to gain acceptability across social divides'. Well said, but I think his work underplays the role of conflict within musical discourses and lacks insight to be gained from a wider attention to the history of popular culture.[166]

I will turn to some more general considerations relating to west gallery music. In the writing of any sort of history, differences in approach related to cultural experience and scholarly tradition are bound to emerge. In terms of evaluation, a folk song studies or cultural history approach has much in common with Dell Hymes' characterisation of folklore studies:

> Succinctly put, folklorists believe that the capacity for aesthetic experience, for shaping of deeply felt values into meaningful, apposite form, is present in all communities and will find some means of expression among all […] our work is rooted in recognition that beauty, form, and meaningful expression may arise wherever people have a chance, even half a chance, to share what they enjoy or must endure. We prize that recognition above fashions or prestige.[167]

Those who have found west gallery music from the background of musicology and the Western classical tradition (albeit often from the somewhat marginalised sub-field of 'early music') have made a significant step in questioning some basic assumptions, and that should be recognised and celebrated. They nevertheless bring with them significant assumptions about the nature of music itself. Equally, people from a folk song background have attitudes and values (sometimes equally unexamined) that are at odds with those schooled in the 'classical' tradition. The tensions between these approaches are manifested in the revival as well as the scholarship of west gallery music.

Nowhere does this show more significantly than in the too easy acceptance of the evaluation of the poor quality of west gallery music and performance so common in the historical sources. We might accept this as almost inevitable from those brought up within the confines of Western music and musicology but this is true of some of those who accept such a view but are otherwise engaged in the active revival of west gallery music. Take Harry Woodhouse's sweeping statement 'Reading books on church history makes it clear that the musical standards of the minstrels often left something to be desired'.[168] The author does not take account of who these authors were, their attitudes and values nor the particular ideas they wished to promote. Nor does he take account of the gaps in the historical record, particularly the sparse evidence of the attitudes and values of people who performed the music some of whom, where we have such evidence, were hugely enthusiastic about what they did.

I have pointed out in another place how similar the accounts of observers, usually critics, of popular church music are to the observers of overseas travellers to the music of 'natives' that they came across.[169] The musical standards in west gallery music were no doubt very variable (as they are in many fields of musical performance today), encompassing a range from the outstanding and exceptional to the awful and abysmal.

There is, for want of a better term, a colonialist attitude, that is evident when Nicholas Temperley expresses a degree of surprise that some of his colleagues might actually enjoy fuging tunes or when he writes of 'unschooled composers' as if this were sufficient explanation. It is there in Holman's 'need to devise new methods of evaluating psalmody'[170] and Drage's rapid leaps to value judgements. For example, she states that unaccompanied metrical psalm tunes were sung 'slowly and unrhythmically by an apathetic congregation', as if this were a universal characteristic: 'slowly' is attested in many sources, 'unrhythmically' is true in a narrow way, in that there is no discernible regular beat, but the term rhythmic can be used to describe regular patterns of change and lined-out psalm singing certainly has these in its alternation of solo and group voices and the fact one senses surges and falling back. Perhaps using the terms 'flowing rhythm' or 'free rhythm' is helpful here.[171] Finally, do we know that congregations were apathetic just because some observers said they were? Some descriptions of lined-out psalm singing underline the enthusiasm of the congregation as do some modern recordings.

Drage has the courage and honesty to admit that her primary intention when she set out on her research was not fulfilled:

> The main focus of my research was to be the [way?] didactic prefaces of tune books informed the performance of the music, but these subsequently proved to be less enlightening than expected. There was little originality and considerable repetition between books with most of the material taken from earlier treatises.[172]

Sometimes the prefaces were intended to try to correct intrenched elements of popular style. Take, for example, the 'Rudiments of Music' prefacing various US shape note song books; the extent to which the actual practice of shape note singing varies from the prescriptions is clear for anyone who bothers to read these writings and listens to shape note performances – going back as far as we have recorded examples. In any case, it would be hard to measure the way that such introductions informed performance. Drage's work is held back by her too ready acceptance of the opinions of some of her sources and her inability to question critically the cultural assumptions she has absorbed. This is a shame because her scholarship can be impressive.

The antagonism between what Holman described as 'a philosophical or even ideological gulf between two groups' (those with a folk music background and those from the early music revival) became very clear at the 1995 conference held in Clacton, which nevertheless produced a useful set of papers.[173] One general point I would make about what I will call the 'musicological' school is their shocking lack of familiarity with largely oral/aural musical traditions. Though exhibiting a wide variety of forms, these often have many recognisable characteristics in common. These become particularly apparent when people from this background try to recreate dominantly oral forms of music. Holman totally misrecognises the situation when he hopes that he is not misrepresenting the situation by suggesting that the west gallery movement 'is effectively a branch of ethnomusicology' – I doubt that many modern west gallery performers have read much ethnomusicology, even if they know what it is.

In his introduction, Holman observes that the approaches of both Drage and myself have weaknesses. Of course, this is the case; the past is, in many ways, radically unknowable. He puts forward the defensive argument that as a tradition is constantly changing, we can never be sure 'how much 20th century recordings can tell us about the practice of the 18th and 19th century'.[174] The response to Holman's 'how much' could well be: much more than you think. Many musicians attempt 'historically informed' performances, but choice is exercised as to what is chosen to inform. What Holman fails to recognise is the attempt in my writings to triangulate different types of evidence, looking for the links, consistencies and consonances between historical evidence and what can be observed of modern survivals. I think this is so far out of the comfort zone of some historical musicologists that it cannot even be considered.

Holman wishes to devise 'new methods of evaluating psalmody' and adds insightfully 'it is no good judging it by the standards of art music'. Absolutely true, but the perceived need to evaluate may itself be the central problem; evaluation by whom for whom? Drage obviously feels no embarrassment at writing the sentence: 'When examining music written mostly by amateurs it is not surprising to find some fairly incompetent compositions'.[175]

One key problem inherent in the 'musicological' approach lies in habitual and often unconscious ways of responding to music and in the judgement of one kind of music in terms of another. This lack of reflectivity cannot take on board a broadly relativist stance that, in the first instance, asks why do these people like this? Older anthropologists tended to call this 'cultural relativism' but it is better described by what Tilley has termed 'methodological contextualisation' and 'methodological neutralism'.[176] All of us come to a fairly settled aesthetic view related to our education, experience, social factors and personal inclinations, but not to see a non-evaluative approach as important in musical research is a significant failure, a failure of empathy.

This judging of a form of music by standards of another comes through clearly in some of the sources. Edward Miller wrote: 'Perhaps the excellent musicians we hear at the opera, have in some measure contributed to render the present performance of parochial psalmody so intolerable to our ears'.[177] In the eighteenth century, Burney cautioned against writing off historical music which did not accord with the educated tastes of his day 'however uncouth the compositions of these times may appear'. We need to apply the implications of Burney's insight. Different musical systems can exist within a society at any given time. Burney argued that 'those productions, which […] universally afforded delight to the best judges of their merit, were well entitled to examination and respect…'. The key question becomes who, in terms of popular church music, were the best judges? I suggest that it was not the clerics and musical reformers but the people who put time and effort into singing, playing, performing and lovingly compiling manuscript books of the church music they enjoyed, should be the judges. Though they left little in terms of direct testimony, that is our problem not theirs. They deserve better than to be largely remembered by the enormous condescension of musical posterity. Frederick Jones, a veteran of the Falmer church band, recollected his performances before 1864: 'Alas they were indeed happy meetings, notwithstanding the disdain, shall I say contempt with which a more educated public regarded our old compositions with their repeat and twiddle'.[178]

Survival and revival

It is notable that examples of west gallery music survived in active use into the twentieth and twenty-first centuries. To survive in popular practice is to have enduring appeal. That west gallery music has been actively revived in recent years is a testimony to the fact that a significant number of people have found the material worthwhile, enjoyable and interesting.

The most notable survivals are the traditions of carol singing around Sheffield extensively recorded, studied and in part revived by Professor Ian Russell.[179] There are also significant survivals in the West Country, in the carol singing tradition of Padstow in Cornwall by Doc Rowe[180] and carol traditions recorded by Bob and Jacqui Pattern.[181] There are also some distinctively west gallery pieces in the repertory of the Copper family of Sussex.[182] The survival and further development of west gallery music is strongly there in the tradition of shape note singing in the USA.[183] These survivals are significant but, using Raymond William's useful term, they are residual. West gallery music passes though all three of William's stages: it is an *emergent* form in the eighteenth century, it is *dominant,* at least in rural areas, in the late eighteenth and early nineteenth centuries, thereafter it is a *residual* form, albeit one available for revival when the time was right.[184]

Academic interest in and the revival of west gallery music are closely related. In 2010, Temperley looked back to his 1970s research on 'Country Psalmody' and reflected:

> … I found that the subject had not only been neglected, but had actually been suppressed by some earlier writers who didn't think it was worthy of serious attention. My curiosity was aroused, and I felt that there was an entirely new story to be told […] about a whole musical culture that had been almost entirely forgotten. But although I found it fascinating and moving myself, I never really expected that it would interest anyone except a few musicologists and historians. I did end the chapter by saying that 'judgement must be reserved until the music of the English country parish churches has been […] thoroughly explored and revived.' But this was a forlorn hope.[185]

Temperley then expressed his surprise on learning of the formation of groups to perform this music. The West Gallery Music Association was formed in 1990 based on the enthusiastic groundwork done, by particularly Gordon Ashman, a former RAF officer and great musical enthusiast,[186] Dave Townsend, a professional musician and concertina player, Rollo Woods, a former librarian and instrumentalist and others. It was set up 'to study, preserve, perform, teach and enjoy the sacred and secular music and song of west gallery and allied traditions, together with their settings within a social and historical context'.[187]

I have tried to keep myself largely out of this account but need to say something about my involvement with the early west gallery revival movement. Prompted by my friend Anne Loughran, I had discovered the MacDermott collection in the Sussex Archaeological Society Library. I did my MA thesis on popular church music in Sussex in 1978 and around that time formed a group called 'Hope in the Valley' to try out some of the Christmas material I found in manuscripts. I led this group for a few years but handed it over to other people who wanted to sustain it, and through various name changes, permutations and revivals, it exists to the present day.

I was in touch with and aware of Gordon Ashman's and Dave Townsend's interests because of folk music networks and I took part in some of the early events which led to the formation of the WGMA. What is particularly interesting is that it was not one person who kicked off the revival in west gallery music; rather, it was the result of a few people in different parts of the country – and in Temperley's case in the USA – thinking and acting along similar lines.

At the time of writing, over 30 groups are associated with the WGMA in various parts of England and the Isle of Man and there is an associated group in Boston, USA. There are other groups performing west gallery music not associated with the organisation. A considerable body of music, from printed and manuscript sources, has been located and performed, some of it published and a number of recordings made and some issued commercially. The work of the WGMA and the recording and documentation of surviving music of this type have had an influence on the general repertory of hymn and carol singing, for example, in the content of *The New Oxford Book of Carols*.[188]

There is no doubt that the west gallery movement has brought to light, as Temperley remarked, 'a whole musical culture that had been almost entirely forgotten'. But it has done this within the pressures and confines of musical revivalism. Musical revivals have been explored by various writers, notably by Tamara Livingstone, and the revival of west gallery music certainly contains the 'basic ingredients' she has outlined: a 'small group of core revivalists' in the form of scholars and enthusiasts of the 1970s and 1980s who drew attention to west gallery materials; 'original sources' in abundance in the form of manuscript and printed books of music, a 'revivalist ideology and discourse' linked to discovering a hidden aspect of our musical past, not always without disagreement but vigorous in its day; a 'revivalist community' and 'revivalist activities' created by the formation of west gallery choirs and the WGMA; and creation of a 'revivalist market' mainly in the form of publications and recordings.[189] Hill and Bithell write of a revival as 'the project of reclaiming, reimagining, and transforming the past' and consider it 'a recurring universal phenomenon'.[190] Revivals are often written off as being prompted by nostalgia for a lost past or a golden age. There is something in this, but the motivation can also be prompted by a dissatisfaction with the past as known and presented, by the discovery of something which contradicts the accepted story or orthodox view. That a lot of the interest in west gallery music is antiquarian in nature is undeniable (it has this in common with a great deal of popular interest in the past) but that does not invalidate attempts at historical understanding, partial and inadequate as it is, if for no other reason than if we do not investigate the past, we simply imagine or invent it.

The west gallery music revival has given rise to a number of major areas of difficulty and contention. The question as to whether west gallery performers should consciously try to adopt an appropriate performance style, and what that style should be, has been influenced by the living traditions, for example, carolling around Sheffield and US shape note music. Some groups however are unaware or give scant attention to such ideas and a style close to the present-day singing in many Anglican churches is sometimes adopted.

Whether or not to dress in period costumes has been another area of contention. It is notable that on the 'Quire Information' page of the WGMA website, one of the first pieces of information given is whether the group is costumed or non-costumed.[191] Some people feel that such theatricalism takes attention away from the music and will have none of it, others, as with other re-enactment groups, get a great deal out of the carnivalesque inhabiting of a pretended role, although this can lead to yokel-type buffoonery. This links to the tradition of comic and patronising writing about west gallery music and can give a trivial impression of the genre.

In any act of revivalism, there is a process of decontextualisation (taking material from a different time and place) and recontextualisation (presenting that material in a new setting and situation). In that process the material itself is altered, modified and selected no matter what efforts are made to perform it in what may be considered to be an authentic way. Most significantly here is the tension between participative performance and performance for an audience (although as noted above some choir-bands certainly were performers for an audience).

Finally, there is the question of localism. Many within the movement promote the connection between place and music – sometimes even fictionalised places – providing a sense of identification and belonging, but imbuing the music with a sprung-from-the-earth aura that does not bear the weight of critical scrutiny. This inclination goes back to the sources of the music: as Holland points out in respect of eighteenth- and nineteenth-century psalm collections, 'Some compilers, with local markets in mind, cleverly renamed tunes to reflect parishes in the area'[192] and some even gave their collections county names.[193]

There is no 'solution' to the problems created by revivalism. The past will always be mediated and misinterpreted when we revive elements of it and it is easy to make fun of revivalist efforts. Yet the act of revival can be enriching and the revival of west gallery music has revealed an aspect of our musical past more stimulating and interesting than anyone previously anticipated.

Notes

1. Nicholas Temperley, *The Music of the English Parish Church*, Vol. 1 (Cambridge: Cambridge University Press, 1979), 199–200. Sally Drage, 'Larks of Dean: Amateur Musicians in Northern England', in: R. Cowgill and P. Holman (eds.), *Music in the British Provinces, 1690–1914* (Aldershot: Ashgate, 2008) 195–221.
2. Rollo G Woods, *Good Singing Still: A Handbook on West Gallery Music* (England: West Gallery Music Association, 2017) 15. Hardy referred to 'the old west-gallery period of church-music', Thomas Hardy, *A Laodicean* (London: Sampson Low, 1881) 9, and the term gained a boost from Charles W. Pearce, 'English Sacred Folk Song of the West Gallery Period (Circa 1695–1820)', *Proceedings of the Musical Association*, 48th Sess. (1921) 1–27.
3. See the listing at West Gallery Churches, 'Galleries', <http://www.westgallerychurches.com/index.html> 14 June 20.
4. Vic Gammon, 'Popular Music in Rural Society: Sussex 1815–1914', (Sussex, 1985) 41–42.
5. W. Holland and J. Ayres, *Paupers & Pig-Killers: The Diary of William Holland, a Somerset Parson, 1799–1818* (Stroud: Sutton, 2003) 233.
6. Richard Brown, *Church and State in Modern Britain 1700–1850* (London: Routledge, 1991) 98.
7. John Wade, *Black Book* (London Walker's Pond Press, 1832).
8. Barry Reay, *Popular Cultures in England 1550–1750* (London: Longman 1998) 87. Holland and Ayres, *Paupers & Pig-Killers*, 126, 151, 228, 270.
9. Michael Francis Snape, *The Church of England in Industrialising Society: The Lancashire Parish of Whalley in the 18th Century* (Woodbridge: Boydell, 2003) 41.
10. Robert Lee, *Rural Society and the Anglican Clergy, 1815–1914* (Woodbridge: Boydell & Brewer, 2006) 30.
11. Dave Russell, *Popular Music in England, 1840–1914: A Social History* (2nd edn.; Manchester: Manchester University Press, 1997).
12. Edward Miller, *Thoughts on the Present Performance of Psalmody in the Established Church of England* (London, 1791) 8–13.
13. Katie Holland, 'Anglican Choir-Bands in the East Midlands: A History C.1700–1860' (University of Nottingham, 2010) particularly 125–164.
14. Vic Gammon, '"Babylonian Performances": The Rise and Suppression of Popular Church Music, 1660–1870', in: Eileen Yeo and Stephen Yeo (ed.), *Popular Culture and Class Conflict 1590–1914: Explorations in the History of Labour and Leisure* (Brighton: Harvester, 1981) 62–88.
15. I am adopting Weston's sensible usage 'choir-band', except when quoting source material; it is the best term to convey the idea of a combination of singers and instrumentalist to readers. Stephen J Weston, 'The Instrumentation and Music of the Church Choir-Band in Eastern England' (Dissertation; Leicester, 1995) 5.
16. Gillian Warson, *From Psalmody to Hymnody: The Establishment of Printed Hymnbooks within Hymn Singing Communities* (Dissertation; Sheffield, 2001) 108.

17 Anonymous, 'Music Sixty Years Ago', *The Musical Herald*, 592 (1 July 1897) 210.
18 Frederick David Lang, 'The Anglican Organist in Victorian and Edwardian England (c. 1800– c. 1910)' (Dissertation; University of Hull, 2004) 21.
19 Sally Drage, 'The Performance of English Provincial Psalmody c. 1640– c. 1860' (Dissertation; Leeds, 2009) 82.
20 A Kent Psalmody Manuscript. Facsimile CD Rom (Retford: Nick Parkes, 2003).
21 Weston, 'Instrumentation and Music' 55.
22 F. W. Galpin, 'Notes on the Old Church Bands and Village Choirs of the Past Century', *The Antiquary* (1906) 101–106.
23 Drage, 'Performance…', 66.
24 *Kendal Mercury* (Saturday 16 March 1839) 1.
25 Gillian Warson, 'The English Choir-Band in Literature', in: Christopher Turner (ed.), *The Gallery Tradition: Aspects of Georgian Psalmody* (Ketton: SG Publishing, 1997) 9–16. Warson, *From Psalmody to Hymnody*, 54, 55, 66, 108, 114.
26 Holland, 'Anglican Choir-Bands…', 202–204, 206.
27 Ibid., 212–216.
28 Ibid., 176–183.
29 Temperley, *English Parish Church*, 197 concurs with this view.
30 Weston, 'Instrumentation and Music', 1.
31 Holland, 'Anglican Choir-Bands…', 224, 335 and passim.
32 Temperley, *English Parish Church*, 196. Weston, 'Instrumentation and Music' 68–73 (Weston has added greatly to our understanding of the chronology of choir-bands. particularly in the East Midlands).
33 Weston, 'Instrumentation and Music', 73.
34 *Stamford Mercury* (13 March 1789) 3. For a similar account, see *Staffordshire Advertiser* (24 October 1801) 4. The term 'band' in the eighteenth century was widely held to mean a group or collection of people and is not exclusively connected with instrumentalists; Perry defined a choir as 'a band of singers'. William Perry, *The Royal Standard English Dictionary* (Boston, 1800) 143.
35 Peregrine Phillips, *A Diary Kept in and Excursion to Little Hampton, near Arundel and Brighthelm-stone, in Sussex in 1779* Vol. 1 (London 1780) 13–14.
36 Katie Holland, 'The Nottinghamshire History Lecture 2010: Harmony and Good Company: The Choir-Band as a Vehicle of Sociability in Nottinghamshire, c. 1750–1830', *Transactions of the Thoroton Society of Nottinghamshire* (2010) 114.
37 Holland and Ayres, *Paupers & Pig-Killers*, entry for Sunday July 12 1807, p. 151.
38 Weston found one lone woman cellist, Phoebe Brown, who performed at Matlock (d. 1854). Weston, 'Instrumentation and Music' 109. Women singers are depicted in some representations but J.M. Neale remarked disapprovingly of women in west galleries 'where women-singers are allowed' suggesting that they were not allowed in some churches. He thought 'the notice which they attract from their station in front of the gallery might well enough befit a theatre, but is highly indecorous in the House of God'. [J M Neale], 'Church Enlargement and Church Arrangement', in: *Cambridge Camden Society* (ed.) (Cambridge: Cambridge University Press, 1843) 17.
39 Nicholas Brady and Nahum Tate, *A New Version of the Psalms of David : Fitted to the Tunes Used in Churches* (London, 1704).
40 William Beveridge, *A Defence of the Book of Psalms, Collected into Metre by Thomas Sternhold, John Hopkins, and Others: With Critical Observations on the Late New Version, Compar'd with the Old* (London, 1710).
41 Temperley, *English Parish Church*, 208.
42 Anon, 'Thoughts on the Music and Words of Psalmody 1793–1826; Oct 1821; 16, British Periodicals Pg. 337', *The British Critic* 16 (October 1821) 337–356.
43 Weston, 'Instrumentation and Music' 169, quoting A. Whigello, *The Annals of Wollaston* (2nd ed.; Wellingborough, 1894) 13.
44 First published in *The Whole Book of Psalmes*, T. Este, 1592.
45 William Mason, *Essays, Historical and Critical, on English Church Music* (York, 1795) 167.
46 Nicholas Temperley, 'John Playford and the Metrical Psalms', *Journal of the American Musicological Society*, 25:3 (1972) 331–378.

47 Nicholas Temperley, 'The Origins of the Fuging Tune', *Royal Musical Association Research Chronicle*, 17 (1981) 1–32.
48 Thomas Secker, *The Works of Thomas Secker, Ll. D.: Late Lord Archbishop of Canterbury* (3; London, 1811) 465.
49 Anon, *The Lyric Muse Revived* (London, 1768) 79.
50 Miller, *Thoughts on the Present Performance*, 7.
51 Richard Eastcott, *Sketches of the Origin, Progress and Effects of Music*, … (Bath: printed and sold by S. Hazard; sold likewise by Messrs. G. G. J. and J. Robinson; Cadell, Dilly, and Vernor and Hood, London, 1793) 173, 172.
52 John Arnold, *Church Music Reformed* (London, 1765) v–vi.
53 Ibid., v.
54 Ibid., contents page.
55 James Merrick, *Improved Psalmody*, Vol.1 (London, 1794) 15.
56 William Riley, *Parochial Music Corrected* (London: Printed for the Author, 1762) 1.
57 *Derby Mercury* (15 January 1779) 4.
58 Miller, *Thoughts on the Present Performance*, 8, 56.
59 Weston, 'Instrumentation and Music', 29–30, 37, 215.
60 Holland, 'Anglican Choir-Bands…', 143, 145–155.
61 Ibid., 155.
62 See, for example, *Bath Chronicle and Weekly Gazette* (27 October 1763), 2 for advertisement for A. Williams' *The Universal Psalmodist*.
63 *Ipswich Journal* (26 Mar 1768) 4. *Derby Mercury* (15 October 1779) 4.
64 Abraham Adams, *The Psalmist's New Companion* (10th edn.; London, c.1765). Title page and preface.
65 The argument here is similar to that between proponents of 'proper English' and linguistics scholars who look for the coherence and structure within any language variant (dialect). As Harry Ritchie has argued in a popular article 'Almost all judgments about someone's language … have no linguistic justification and reflect only the prejudice of the judger'. Harry Ritchie, 'It's time to challenge the notion that there is only one way to speak English' *The Guardian* (13 December 2013).
66 Robert Kendal's Book, 1791 (Manuscript Music Book) Facsimile CD Rom (Nick Parkes, Retford, 2003).
67 Ibid. Robert Kendal's Book, 1791 – Psalm Tunes, etc. – A Table of Reference. Chris Brown, 'American Tunes in West Gallery Sources', <http://originalsacredharp.com/2014/11/12/american-tunes-in-west-gallery-sources/> Consulted 1 May 2020.
68 See, for example, Gilbert Boyce, *A Candid and Friendly Reply to Mr Dan Taylor's Dissertation on Singing in the Worship of God* (Wishbech, 1787) 10.
69 John Arnold, *The Compleat Psalmodist* (5th edn.; London: Robert Brown, 1761) iv.
70 Eastcott, *Sketches of the Origin, Progress and Effects of Music*, …, 209.
71 Temperley, *English Parish Church*, 197 for a useful table. Weston, 'Instrumentation and Music', gives a great deal of information on instrumentation.
72 Weston, 'Instrumentation and Music', 80.
73 *Stamford Mercury* (19 June 1789) 3. Holland has cast considerable light on ways choir-bands obtained things they needed and the role of bookshops as intermediary suppliers. Holland, 'Anglican Choir-Bands…', 125–131.
74 *The Lincoln Rutland and Stamford Mercury* (30 November 1821) 1.
75 *The Church of England Quarterly Review*, IX (1841) 468.
76 Woods, *Good Singing Still*, 61.
77 T Williams, *Psalmodia Evangelica: A Complete Set of Psalm and Hymn Tunes for Public Worship* (London: S.A and P. Thompson, 1789) i, 19–23.
78 'On the Present State of Church Music in England': *Bristol Mercury* (28 February 1825) 4.
79 This is an area where there has been much controversy and I have written extensively on it in the past. See particularly Vic Gammon, 'The Performance Style of West Gallery Music', in: Christopher Turner (ed.), *The Gallery Tradtion: Aspects of Georgian Psalmody* (Corby Glen: SG Publishing, 1997) 43–51, and Vic Gammon, 'Problems in the Performance and Historiography of English Popular Church Music', *Radical Musicology*, 1 (17 May 2006).

80 It is incorrect to claim Hebridean heterophonic psalm singing as 'one of the most distinctively Scottish musical traditions'; the style was once widespread throughout Britain, although certainly with local variations. See Simon Mckerrell, *Focus: Scottish Traditional Music* (Kindle Edition edn., Focus on World Music Series; New York and Abingdon: Routledge (Taylor and Francis), 2016). The fact that the same sound world survives on both sides of the Atlantic with no obvious common root is testimony to the longevity and diffusion of some traditional styles.
81 Jeff Todd Titon, *Powerhouse for God: Speech, Chant, and Song in an Appalachian Baptist Church* (Austin: University of Texas Press, 1988).
82 Eastcott, *Sketches of the Origin, Progress and Effects of Music*, … 176.
83 Peter Holman, 'Introduction', in: Christopher Turner (ed.), *The Gallery Tradition: Aspects of Georgian Psalmody* (Ketton: SG Publishing, 1997) X.
84 Ibid., x.
85 Zabdiel Adams, *The Nature, Pleasure and Advantages of Church-Musick* (Boston, 1771) 20.
86 W.G. *The Musical World*, London Vol. 20, Iss. 11. (13 March 1845) 125.
87 William Romaine, *An Essay on Psalmody* (London, 1775) 89, 95, 99–101, 129, 134.
88 Abraham Adams, *The Psalmist's New Companion*. Title page and preface.
89 See also Miller, *Thoughts on the Present Performance*, 8.
90 Zabdiel Adams, *The Nature, Pleasures and Advantages of Church-Musick* (Boston, 1771) 24–25.
91 Frances Paget, *The Spirit of Discipline* (London: Longmans Green, 1891) xxx.
92 Drage, 'Performance', 280.
93 Weston, 'Instrumentation and Music' 54, 56 quoting from T.S.H. Elwin, *The Northamptonshire Baptist Association* (London 1964) 101–102.
94 Ibid., 172–173.
95 Holland and Ayres, *Paupers & Pig-Killers*, 151.
96 *Kendal Mercury* (16 March 1839) 1.
97 It is interesting to note that a parallel reform movement to that in England was active in the American Colonies from the early eighteenth century. See Charles Hamm, *Music in the New World* (New York: Norton, 1983) 39–41. Richard Crawford, *America's Musical Life* (New York: Norton, 2001) 125–136. It is possible to argue that much 'west gallery' music is the product of attempts to regulate singing that took on its own popular dynamic.
98 Amanda Flather, *Gender and Space in Early Modern England* (Woodbridge: Boydell, 2011) 135–172.
99 John Charles Bennett, 'The English Anglican Practice of Pew-Renting, 1800–1960', (Dissertation; University of Birmingham, 2011). Richard Gough, *Antiquities & Memoirs of the Parish of Myddle, County of Salop* (Shrewsbury: Adnitt & Nauton, 1875); Snape, *The Church of England in Industrialising Society*, 38–40 and passim.
100 This telling phrase is from a sermon by Gabriel Towerson, *A Sermon Concerning Vocal and Instrumetal Musick in the Church.* (London 1696) 26. See Temperley, *English Parish Church*. 101.
101 Anon, *The Lyric Muse Revived*. 80. Holland, 'Anglican Choir- Bands…', gives evidence that literacy among choir-bands was high, 38, 139, 141, 188, 216, 223, 226, 333, 335.
102 Miller, *Thoughts on the Present Performance*, 7.
103 *Bristol Mirror* (20 January 1821) 4
104 Riley, *Parochial Music Corrected*, 1.
105 William Vincent, *Considerations on Parochial Music* (2nd edn.; London, 1787) 16.
106 Ibid., 18.
107 Ibid.
108 John Shepherd, *A Critical and Practical Elucidation of the Book of Common Prayer* Vol.1 (London: Rivington, 1817) 301–304.
109 Miller, *Thoughts on the Present Performance*, 8–10.
110 Beilby Porteus, *Works of the Right Reverend Beilby Porteus, Late Bishop of London: With His Life, Volume 6* (London: T Cadell, 1823) 241, 242.
111 'On the Present State of Church Music in England', *Bristol Mercury* (28 February 1825) 4.
112 'Parochial Psalmody' *The British Magazine* (8 December 1835) 679–680.
113 Canon Noel Boston and Lyndesay G. Langwill, *Church and Chamber Barrel-Organs: Their Origin, Makers, Music and Location – a Chapter in English Church Music* (Edinburgh: Lyndesay G. Langwill, 1967) 3. This dates from the 1840s.
114 'Correspondence – Parochial Psalmody', *The British Magazine* (December 1835) 679.

115 John Antes La Trobe, *The Music of the Church Considered in Its Various Branches, Congregational and Choral: An Historical and Practical Treatise* (London: Seeley & Burnside, 1831) 89.
116 Ibid. 92. For a contemporary review, see 'The Music of the Church considered in its various Branches, …' *The British critic, quarterly theological review and ecclesiastical record* (July 1831) 120–136.
117 *The Parish Choir* 1, no. 7 (August 1846) 55–56.
118 Correspondence. LAICUS *The Musical World* (24 September 1840) 14, 245.
119 [Neale], 'Church Enlargement and Church Arrangement', 15–16.
120 Christopher Turner, 'The Decline of the Gallery Tradition', in: Turner, *The Gallery Tradition*, 71–80, 77.
121 These arguments are more fully developed in Vic Gammon, Problems in the Performance and Historiography of English Popular Church Music. *Radical Musicology* 1 (2006): 73 pars. (17 May 2007) <http://www.radical-musicology.org.uk>.
122 J. Skinner et al., *Journal of a Somerset Rector: John Skinner, A.M., Antiquary, 1772–1839. Parochial Affairs of the Parish of Camerton, 1822–1832*. British Museum Mms. Nos. 33673–33728 (J. Murray, 1930) 8, 22, 96.
123 J. Woodforde and J. Beresford, *The Diary of a Country Parson, 1758–1802* (Canterbury Press, 2011) 24, 41, 43, 45.
124 Weston, 'Instrumentation and Music', 58.
125 Holland, 'Anglican Choir- Bands…', 290–298. James Obelkevich, *Religion and Rural Society: South Lindsey 1825–1875* (Oxford: Clarendon Press, 1976) 111–112.
126 Anon, 'Music Sixty Years Ago', 210.
127 Andrew Jones, *Victorian North Devon: A Social History* (Bridport: A. Jones, 2010) 216.
128 Peter Robson, 'Thomas Hardy as a Source for the Study of Traditional Culture in Dorset' (Dissertation; University of Sheffield, 2004) 116, referenced to Richard Grosvenor Bartelot, *The History of Fordington*, (Dorchester: Henry Ling, 1915). For other evidence on expulsions, see Gammon, '"Babylonian Performances"', 79–80, and Gammon, 'Popular Music in Rural Society', 56–63.
129 Quoted from Robson, 'Thomas Hardy as a Source for the Study of Traditional Culture in Dorset', 116, referenced to Dorset County Library Collection, Broom.
130 British Library, Add. MS, 47775A, 10 (MacDermott MS).
131 Holland, 'Anglican Choir- Bands…', 202, 314.
132 *The Parish Choir*, I, 17 (1847) 137 and I, 18, (1847) 145.
133 James Nye, *A Small Account of My Travels through the Wilderness* (Brighton: QueenSpark, 1982) 16.
134 *Norfolk News* (10 November 1866) 5; *Norfolk News* (8 December 1866) 6; *Norfolk Chronicle* (8 December 1866) 7.
135 Jones, *Victorian North Devon: A Social History*, 214. See also Warson, *From Psalmody to Hymnody*, 67.
136 *Essex Standard* (27 September 1850) 2.
137 E.D. Mackerness, *A Social History of English Music* (London: Routledge and K. Paul, 1964) 195.
138 'The Country Choir'. *Musical Standard* (15 August 1862) 1, 2, 14.
139 *Gloucestershire Chronicle* (1 February 1862) 3, abridged from 'London Society'.
140 Sally Drage, 'A Reappraisal of Provincial Church Music' in David Wyn Jones (ed.), *Music in Eighteenth-Century Britain* (Abingdon: Routledge, 2016) 175.
141 M A Scargill, *Provincial Sketches* (London: Edward Churton, 1835) 211–239. *Newbury Weekly News and General Advertiser* (22 November 1888) 2.
142 *Nottinghamshire Guardian* (29 May 1868) 8.
143 *Daily Gazette for Middlesbrough* (30 May 1874) 3.
144 See for example *Manchester Courier and Lancashire General Advertiser* (26 November 1853) 9. *West Middlesex Herald* (6 October 1855) 2; *Bucks Herald* (31 October 1857) 5; *Nottinghamshire Guardian* (16 September 1858, 5; *Norfolk Chronicle* (21 July 1860) 5.
145 *Birmingham Daily Post* (25 October 1894) 5.
146 Quotes in Weston, 'Instrumentation and Music', 8. The vocabulary is very interesting, particularly in view of the criticism that my use of the term 'suppression' has received.
147 Galpin, 'Notes on the Old Church Bands…' 106.
148 Alfred Williams, *Folk Songs of the Upper Thames* (London: Duckworth, 1923) 9, 23.
149 Holland, 'Anglican Choir- Bands…', 337.
150 Ibid., 307–308. It is worth pointing out that these were basically the same people who would administer the new and harsh poor law after 1834.
151 Weston, 'Instrumentation and Music' 108. Holland, 'Anglican Choir- Bands…', 304.

152 Some examples of resistance are given in my thesis: Gammon, 'Popular Music in Rural Society', 57–63.
153 Warson, *From Psalmody to Hymnody*, 16, 31,32, 34, 39, 40, 65.
154 Thomas Hardy, *Under the Greenwood Tree* (London: Macmillan, 1872).
155 Francis W.Galpin, 'The Village Church Band; an Interesting Survival', *Musical News* (8 July 1883, and 15 July 1883) pp. 31–32 and 56–58. Galpin, 'Notes on the Old Church Bands…', 106.
156 MacDermott's material formed the basis of my initial research in this field and my MA thesis. It is interesting that both MacDermott and Galpin were clergymen, as were many antiquarians of their time. Lee, noticing late nineteenth-century antiquarian interest of many members of the clergy, has aptly remarked, 'Strikingly … after half a century during which so many interest groups seemed to be working to secure its demise, the decline of popular culture suddenly became a cause for anxiety and regret'. Lee, *Rural Society and the Anglican Clergy, 1815–1914*. 31.
157 Pearce, 'English Sacred Folk Song'.
158 Bernarr Rainbow, *The Choral Revival in the Anglican Church 1839–1872* (London: Boydell, 1970). B. Rainbow, *The Land without Music: Musical Education in England, 1800–1860 and Its Continental Antecedents* (London: Novello, 1967).
159 Temperley, *English Parish Church*.
160 Temperley, 'The Origins of the Fuging Tune', 2.
161 See http://www.wgma.org.uk/publications.htm.
162 http://www.wgma.org.uk/Articles/manx.htm accessed 30 May 2020; see also Fanella Crowe Bazin, 'Music in the Isle of Man up to 1896' (University of Liverpool, 1995).
163 Weston, 'Instrumentation and Music'.
164 Holland, 'Anglican Choir- Bands…'.
165 Rebecca Dellow, ''Fiddlers' Tunebooks' - Vernacular Instrumental Manuscript Sources 1860–C1880: Paradigmatic of Folk Music Tradition?', (Disseration: Sheffield, 2018).
166 Stephen William John Campbell, 'Reconsidering and Contextualising the Vernacular Tradition: Popular Music and British Manuscript Compilations (1650–2000)' (Dissertation; York 2012) 2–3, 46, 81, 131.
167 Dell Hymes, 'Folklore's Nature and the Sun's Myth', *Journal of American Folklore* (1975) 345–369, 346.
168 Harry Woodhouse, *Face the Music: Church and Chapel Bands in Cornwall* (St Austell: Cornish Hillside Publications, 1997) 5.
169 Gammon, 'Problems in the Performance and Historiography of English Popular Church Music', Observations largely based on Frank Harrison, *Time, Place and Music: An Anthology of Ethnomusicological Observation C.1550 to C.1800* (Amsterdam: Frits Knuf, 1973).
170 Turner, *The Gallery Tradition*, xi.
171 Martin R. L. Clayton, 'Free Rhythm: Ethnomusicology and the Study of Music without Metre', *Bulletin of the School of Oriental and African Studies, University of London* 59:2 (1996) 323–332.
172 Drage, 'Performance', 278.
173 Turner, *The Gallery Tradition*.
174 Holman, 'Introduction'.
175 Sally Drage, 'A Reappraisal', 175.
176 John J. Tilley, 'Cultural Relativism', *Human Rights Quarterly* 22 (May 2000) 501–547, 508.
177 Miller, *Thoughts on the Present Performance*, 172.
178 Sussex Archaeological Society, MacDermott Manuscript, I pp. 53–54 (letter from Frederick Jones to K H MacDermott 1 June 1917. MacDermott softens this in his published version leaving out the words 'shall I say contempt'. K. H. Macdermott, *Sussex Church Music in the Past* (Chichester: Moore & Wingham, 1922) 11. I make no excuse for using this fascinating quote again.
179 See http://www.villagecarols.org.uk for a way into Russell's extensive work, and his thesis, Ian Russell, 'Traditional Singing in West Sheffield, 1970–1972', (Dissertation; University of Leeds, 1977). This is available online at http://www.villagecarols.org.uk/articles/traditional-singing-in-west-sheffield.html.
180 'Harkey, Harkey' [Padstow Carols recorded by Doc Rowe] Rezound Records, 2000.
181 Various recordings in Bob and Jacqueline Patten Collection https://sounds.bl.uk/World-and-traditional-music/Bob-and-Jacqueline-Patten-Collection.
182 The Copper Family, *Coppers at Christmas: The Carol Collection of the Copper Family of Rottingdean Sussex* (Coppersongs CD, 2007).

183 There are many recordings of and publications on shape note singing; one of the best ways into this subject is the Sacred Harp website https://fasola.org.
184 Raymond Williams, *Marxism and Literature* (Oxford: Oxford University Press, 1977) 121–127.
185 Anonymous, *Let Our Joys Be Known: Twenty Years of the West Gallery Music Association* (Oxford: West Gallery Music Association, 2010). Foreword.
186 https://www.theguardian.com/news/2003/oct/06/guardianobituaries.artsobituaries (Consulted 10 February 2020).
187 http://www.wgma.org.uk/aboutus.htm (Consulted 10 February 2020).
188 Hugh Keyte and Andrew Parrott (eds.), *The New Oxford Book of Carols* (Oxford: Oxford University Press, 1992) particularly xix.
189 Tamara E. Livingston, 'Music Revivals: Towards a General Theory', *Ethnomusicology*, 43:1 (1999) 66–85.
190 Juniper Hill and Caroline Bithell, 'An Introduction to Music Revival as Concept, Cultural Process, and Medium of Change', in: Juniper Hill and Caroline Bithell (eds.), *The Oxford Handbook of Music Revival* (New York: Oxford University Press, 2014) 1.
191 http://www.wgma.org.uk/choirs.htm, consulted 7 May 2020.
192 Holland, 'Anglican Choir- Bands…', 136.
193 John Barwick, *Harmonia Cantica Divina, or the Kentish Divine Harmonist* (London: Printed for the Author, 1783). John Arnold, *The Leicestershire Harmony* (London 1759).

21

THE DRIVE FOR AN ENGLISH IDENTITY IN MUSIC AND THE FOUNDATION OF THE FOLK-SONG SOCIETY

Arthur Knevett

The main activists who were engaged in collecting folk-songs outlined the criteria they set for the songs they were seeking and identified the older members of rural communities as the people that would know such songs. The migration of people from the countryside to the towns to seek employment in the new factories and workshops that needed labour; the introduction of compulsory education; the growth of popular commercial music, and its perceived degenerative effects all militated against the conditions necessary for the continuation of a vibrant folk-song tradition as defined by the early field collectors. This gave a sense of urgency to the task and the 'Irish' impetus behind the founding of a society to draw folk-song collectors together would eventually bring about the founding of a society dedicated to folk-song. The leading musicians of the day recognised that English folk-song could contribute to the establishment of an English identity in music to challenge the domination of German music and this, in turn, could be used to counter the degenerative effects of commercial music and urban living and re-kindle patriotism in the working-class.

One can point to a number of factors in the nineteenth century that gave rise to a mindset that was favourable to the development of the folk-song movement, and I will limit myself here to some that seem particularly germane.

Industrialisation

The First Industrial Revolution began in Britain in the eighteenth century. By the mid-nineteenth century, the continuing development of the factory system required an ever increasing workforce and the resulting exodus of people from the countryside to the towns fulfilled that need. The continuing developments in manufacture required an educated workforce. Improved literacy resulting from the Education Act of 1870, which built on the work of the Church schools and other voluntary agencies, helped to provide this. It was the younger, more able that left the country for the towns; John Saville states that: 'In the nineteenth century, the majority of those who left the rural areas of England and Wales, whether they were going abroad or to urban areas within Britain, were under 35 years of age'.[1] W. E.

Forster speaking to the House of Commons for the 1870 education bill said:

> We must not delay. Upon the speedy provision of elementary education depends our industrial prosperity. It is of no use trying to give technical education to our artizans [sic] without elementary education; uneducated labourers – and many of our labourers are utterly uneducated – are, for the most part unskilled labourers and if we leave our work-folk any longer unskilled [...] they will become overmatched in the competition of the world.[2]

Machine tools used in factories and workshops had brought about major advances in manufacturing techniques resulting in faster production and such techniques required workers with a new set of skills. The development of systems of mass production in Britain ahead of the rest of the world allowed British-manufactured goods to dominate world trade. Peter Mathias wrote that 'Britain's was the first industrialization of any national economy in the world'.[3]

The new manufacturing processes pioneered in Great Britain inevitably spread to other countries; J. L. and Barbara Hammond wrote that: 'It was from England that the new processes, the new machinery and the new disciplines passed to the continent of Europe'.[4] They went on to say that the inventions of Watt, Arkwright, Crompton, and Stephenson '[...] were decisive events in history: decisive because mass production depends on those inventions and mass production is an integral part of the new system'.[5] As the factory system continued to develop, it was generally agreed that a more literate and numerate workforce would be a necessity if the United Kingdom was to maintain its place as the leading industrial nation.

The period from c.1870 to 1900 witnessed rapid industrial development in Western European countries, the USA and Japan and competition from these countries caused a significant drop in Great Britain's share of the world market. As H. L. Beales put it: 'The determining factors which govern the character of the period from the British standpoint, were first the improving mechanism and industrialism, and second the advance of other countries to competitive power'.[6] This period of industrialisation in these countries is commonly referred to as the Second Industrial Revolution. Germany in particular made huge advances and became a major competitor in all areas of manufacture and trade. Furthermore, the development of shipboard refrigeration enabled the import of cheap foreign meat and butter, as well as wheat, and New Zealand, Australia, the USA, and Argentina became important suppliers of food for the British market.[7] These developments resulted in what was termed a 'Great Depression' giving rise to the 1886 Royal Commission on the Depression in Trade and Industry.

In 1892, a very influential book by Ernest Edwin Williams entitled *Made in Germany* was first published, subsequently running into five editions. Commenting on the fourth edition, the 5th Earl of Rosebery, formerly the Liberal prime minister, wrote:

> Year after year our consuls and our various officials of the Board of Trade have called the attention of the community to the fact that we are no longer, as we once were, undisputed mistress of the world of commerce, but that we are threatened by one very formidable rival, at any rate, who is encroaching on us, as the sea encroaches on the weak parts of the coast, – I mean Germany.[8]

England: the un-musical nation

In the cultural field, Germany's long-standing dominance in music was also keenly felt during this period and England was regarded as an un-musical nation, but the focus here is upon art or classical music, as distinct from popular or vernacular music. As early as 1840, the German poet Heinrich Heine wrote in an article published in the *Pariser Berichte* that:

> These people have no ear, neither for the beat nor indeed for music in any form, and their unnatural passion for piano playing and singing is all the more disgusting. There is verily nothing on earth so terrible as English music composition, except English painting.[9]

This reputation persisted and in 1881 the music critic Frederick Crowest wrote that we have '[...] the continental reputation of being the Great Un-musical Power of Europe – strong enough in commerce and steam, but devoid of musical talent, invention and discrimination, [...]'.[10] In the same year, the Duke of Edinburgh, the Duke of Albany, and Prince Christian each gave an address at the Free Trade Hall in Manchester to raise funds for the creation of a Royal College of Music (RCM). The Duke of Edinburgh drew attention to the need to promote the advancement of music in England and called for support to raise funds for '[...] the establishment of a central public institution ranking in importance with the national Conservatoires on the Continent'.[11] The Duke of Albany observed that:

> [...] there is already more music in England than in any other country. The most eminent artists of the Continent are to be heard here. [...] How is it, then, that while such an abundance of music is brought to us and made for us, we often hear it said from the other side of the Channel that England is not a musical nation?' He went on to draw attention to the lack of public interest in music and said; I am convinced that the subject only wants to be brought before the country, [...] by a properly organised system of instruction, such as that for which we are now pleading for this discreditable state of things to be changed.[12]

The campaign was successful and the RCM was established by royal charter in 1882. In the same year, the music critic Joseph Bennett wrote a review of the premier performance at the Birmingham Festival of Hubert Parry's First Symphony and said that it gave '[...] capital proof that English music had arrived at a renaissance period'.[13] He would later write, after the foundation of the RCM, that:

> [...] English music was never so fortunate as now. We have among us four composers whose good repute has recently conquered German prejudice [...]. Mr. Cowen's 'Scandinavian' Symphony, Mr. Goring Thomas's 'Esmeralda', Mr. Villiers Stanford's 'Savonarola' and Mr. A. C. Mackenzie's 'Colomba' [...]. The victory of these English composers is 'as the letting out of water'. They have made a hole in the dyke [...]. To a large extent they have the immediate future of English music in their hands [...].[14]

According to Michael Kennedy, the 'so-called renaissance of English music and musical life' started around 1880 and he goes on to say that:

> The choice of any specific year is bound to be arbitrary, [...]. The Corporation of the City of London founded the Guildhall School of Music in that year, George Grove's *Dictionary of Music and Musicians* was published in 1879–80 and a twenty-eight year old composer, Charles Villiers Stanford (1852–1924) wrote his Evening Service for the Festival of the Sons of the Clergy in St Paul's Cathedral. In their different ways, these

unconnected events represented the coming to fruition of the gradual change in attitudes to music in Britain [...]'[15]

However, the negative musical reputation was slow to change and as late as 1896, Ernest Williams, noting a consistency across the economic and cultural fields, wrote: 'At midnight your wife comes home from an opera that was made in Germany, has been here enacted by singers and conductor and players made in Germany, with the aid of instruments and sheets of music made in Germany'.[16] Nonetheless, the quest for an English identity in music was underway. Commenting on this period, the composer and musicologist Cecil Forsyth wrote that musicians began to ask themselves what it was that German musicians depended upon for their inspiration. The answer, he concluded, was 'their nationality' and this realisation led to the 're-discovery of folk-song'.[17] But it was not until the later years of the nineteenth century and the early years of the twentieth century that composers started to take notice of the fruits of the labours of the folk-song collectors and endeavour to establish an English style of music. They started to take inspiration from English folk-song melodies rather than imitating composers from 'the other side of the Channel'. Michael Kennedy asserts that: 'As significant a feature as any in the musical renaissance, [...], was the bridging of the gap between the meretricious ballad and the art-song'. He argues that the song compositions of Maude Valerie White and the operatic soprano Liza Lehmann played a significant part in raising the standards and he goes on to say that: 'Nor should the growing interest in folk-song be underestimated in this respect. [...] In its influence on a new generation of composers, the folk-song revival was nothing but beneficial in its impact on the composition of English songs'.[18]

The folk-song collectors

Alongside the developments that were taking place in art music circles, the enthusiasts involved in collecting folk-songs had been operating largely independently of each other and there had been little co-ordination between them. They had discovered that folk-songs were being sung to modal tunes and were worried that this neglected store of native music and song was under threat of erosion. This, they felt, was due to the increasing availability in the rural areas of alternative commercial forms of musical entertainment which had been made more accessible to the rural population by an improving communication network. This gave rise to a sense of urgency for the recovery of folk-songs. Eventually, events would bring the players together and there would be sufficient agreement among them to bring about the establishment of a society which would have as one of its expressed aims the co-ordination of such collecting activity for the preservation and perpetuation of the folk-song tradition.

The Hammonds, commenting on the changes in nineteenth-century Britain, said that '[...] when the factory was taking the place of the craft, the newspaper the place of the pageant, illiteracy was the worst disenfranchisement a man could suffer'.[19] It was the older members of rural communities that were most likely to be unlettered and these were the people that the folk-song collectors would seek out. The theory being that these people would be more likely to know 'genuine' folk-songs because they would be more reliant on an oral tradition for news and entertainment and not be directly influenced by the printed word. Indeed, Cecil Sharp, writing in 1907, thought that it was a waste of time to collect songs from singers under the age of 60 and concluded that: 'Their songs are nearly all modern; if by chance they happen to sing an old one, it is so infected with the modern spirit that it is hardly worth gathering'.[20]

The foundation of the Irish Literary Society of London and the 'Irish' impetus for a Folk-Song Society

In parallel with these developments in the field of English music, there was a clearly discernible mood among Irish writers, poets, and musicians which manifested itself as an Irish literary revival. Pioneering work in the collecting of Irish folk music had been undertaken in earlier years by the likes of Edward Bunting and George Petrie. The late nineteenth-century revival grew out of a desire to reassert an Irish cultural identity. The movement was inextricably linked in some minds to the campaign for Irish Home Rule. The 1885 general election had resulted in the Liberals winning more parliamentary seats than the other parties, but not an overall majority. William Ewart Gladstone, the Liberal prime minister, supported Home Rule for Ireland and, with the support of the Irish Nationalist Party, tried to push through a Home Rule Bill. However, a breakaway group of 93 Liberal MPs, known as the Liberal Unionists, who saw themselves as defenders of the Union of Britain and Ireland and could not tolerate the prospect of Irish independence, voted against their own government. In consequence, Gladstone and his Cabinet recommended that the queen dissolve Parliament, and she reluctantly agreed.

A new election took place in 1886 and, as Herbert Woodfield Paul, barrister and Liberal MP at the time, wrote in his biography of Gladstone:

> The results of the General Election were disastrous to Home Rule. There were returned 316 Conservatives, 78 Liberal Unionists, as those Liberals who left Mr. Gladstone called themselves, 191 Liberals who adhered to him and 85 Parnellites as before. This gave the Conservatives and Liberal Unionists combined a working majority of 113.[21]

By the 1890s, the campaign for Irish Home Rule had suffered a near-fatal blow. The scandal surrounding the Irish Nationalist Party leader, Charles Stewart Parnell, and his adulterous affair with Katharine ('Kitty') O'Shea, the wife of one of his MPs, during the 1880s had severely damaged his reputation. Parnell was named as a co-respondent when Captain O'Shea filed for divorce in 1889–1890, a case that received widespread publicity.[22] This was then followed by Parnell's premature death in 1891, just four months after his marriage to Kitty O'Shea, leaving the Irish Nationalist Party in a state of disarray. At the next general election, in 1892, Gladstone was once again returned to power, but he was only able to form a government with Irish Nationalist support. Herbert Paul wrote:

> Never was a Government formed under greater difficulties. The Prime Minister was eighty-two, and though his strength was unabated, the infirmities of age were creeping upon him. His majority was entirely dependent upon the Irish vote, and the Irish party itself had not been reunited by the death of Mr. Parnell in October 1891.[23]

These cultural and political developments added to a general air of apprehension and gloom that pervaded certain groups and factions at the fin de siècle. The historian Richard Shannon argues that a general air of pessimism overshadowed the whole decade of the 1890s and that 'fin-de-siècle was invoked by many writers as a literal and emotional fact'.[24] This feeling had produced a reaction within the musical establishment that encouraged the quest for an English musical identity, in part to address the lack of identity to which Carl Engel and others had drawn attention earlier in the century.[25] This English quest coincided with the Irish renaissance to consolidate a revival of English folk-song and music – but it was the product of historical chance rather than something either planned or inevitable.

The Irish Literary Society of London

Significant figures among the Irish nationalists increasingly turned from politics to cultural enterprises in order to re-establish an Irish identity. In 1891, the Celtic scholar and poet Douglas Hyde (a future president of the Irish Republic) and the celebrated poet and writer William Butler Yeats (he was appointed as a Senator of the Irish Free State in 1922) founded the Irish Literary Society of London (ILSL).

Alfred Perceval Graves was a founder member of the ILSL (he was also the father of Robert Graves, the celebrated poet and writer) and in his autobiography, he wrote, 'Plans for the formation of the society had been hatched in Mr. W. B. Yeats' rooms in Fitzroy Square', and he went on to identify 'the young active spirits in the movement' as Yeats, Lionel Johnson, Frank Fahy, and Graves's cousin, Thomas Rolleston.[26] Nevertheless, it was W. B. Yeats who was the acknowledged leader of the Irish literary renaissance. In 1889, he had written a long poem, 'The Wanderings of Oisin', which expresses strong nationalistic sentiments.[27] He was also fascinated with Irish legends and the occult, and in 1890 he had joined the Hermetic Order of the Golden Dawn, which the literary critic John Carey has described as 'part of a widespread revival of occultism' during the 1890s.[28] In 1892, Lionel Johnson wrote a review of 'The Countess Kathleen and Various Legends and Lyrics' by W. B. Yeats and said that: '[...] Mr Yeats makes his profession of faith and loyalty towards Ireland, and justifies the tone of his poems, [...] because in singing of these he is singing of Ireland and for Ireland'.[29]

The first president of the ILSL, Sir Charles Gavan Duffy, was an ardent Irish nationalist, who at this time had retired from public life and was living in France but retained his interest in and involvement with Irish political and literary matters.[30] He evidently helped with the preliminary arrangements to establish the ILSL. Graves wrote:

> Late in the spring of 1891, at the invitation of the council of the newly formed Irish Literary Society of London, which had been organised by Sir Charles Gavan Duffy and a set of his literary friends, I presided over an inaugural meeting in Hart Street, Bloomsbury.[31]

Duffy's involvement with the society and his appointment as the president are a strong indicator of the nationalist sentiments and aims of the society, albeit to be pursued through cultural enterprises rather than political action. The initiative for the founding of the ILSL had grown out of the frustration felt by Irish nationalists at the continuing failure to achieve Home Rule. The general election of 1895 dealt a crushing blow to both the 'Home Rulers', who wanted Home Rule for Ireland while remaining a part of the Union with Britain, and the 'Separatists', who wanted complete independence. The Unionists, comprising the Conservatives and Liberal Unionists, were returned with a majority of 152. As for the Separatists, *The Times* commented that the election of 1895 'will be remembered for the most crushing defeat that has been inflicted on any political party since 1832'.[32] It was against this political backdrop that Irish nationalists started to look towards a cultural revival of all things Irish in order to assert their independence as a nation. As the historian Seamus Deane has written, 'it meant that the young generation in Ireland turned in disgust from politics and gave their energies to cultural revival'.[33]

The foundation of the ILSL was a pioneering part of this revival. The ILSL attracted to its ranks both Separatists and those who desired Home Rule while remaining part of the union. Their common ground lay in the desire to re-establish an Irish cultural identity. It was from this perhaps unexpected quarter that the real impetus for the founding of the

Folk-Song Society (FSS) then came. Christopher Bearman states: 'The initiative for the Folk-Song Society's foundation came from the Irish Literary Society, in particular from two people [Alfred Perceval Graves and Kate Lee], both Anglo-Irish',[34] but we need to ask, why should a group of exiled Irish and Anglo-Irish people have been the prime movers behind the formation of a folk-song society in London?

Alfred Perceval Graves, Kate Lee, and the idea for a folk-song society

Alfred Perceval Graves was the son of Charles Graves, Bishop of Limerick (Church of Ireland), Charles Graves was also one of the 23 vice-presidents of the Society for the Preservation and Publication of the Melodies of Ireland, founded in 1851.[35] Alfred Perceval Graves took over as the secretary of the ILSL from his cousin Thomas Rolleston in 1895. At this time, he was one of Her Majesty's Inspectors of Schools, a post he held from 1875 to 1910. He was progressive in his views on education, wanting the best education for all children, and he took a particular interest in physical education.[36] Graves was a supporter of Home Rule; he wanted Ireland to have its own parliament but to remain in the Union. This is made apparent in his autobiography when he said of the Isle of Man that 'Here was an island blessed with Home Rule [...]'.[37] However, he was far from being a radical and remained conservative in his outlook.

Graves had collaborated with the Irish composer Charles Villiers Stanford (they had been friends since childhood) in the publication of song collections entitled *Songs of Old Ireland* (1882) and *Songs of Erin* (1892). Graves wrote and compiled the songs, which were then set to music and arranged by Stanford. Stanford had long taken an interest in Irish music, and he went on to edit the collection made by George Petrie.[38] Stanford was a professor of music at Cambridge, a post he held for 40 years, and a key figure at the RCM, where he taught composition.[39] He was one of 'the principal architects of the English Musical Renaissance', and firmly believed in the potential of music in education to bring about 'the refinement of the masses' and to produce model citizens of Victorian society[40]; he was a staunch Conservative and Unionist.

Graves, in keeping with others in the Irish literary revival, followed the practice established by Thomas Moore in the early nineteenth century of setting many of his songs to music using the traditional Irish airs to be found in the collections of Edward Bunting (1773–1843), George Petrie (1789–1866), and F. W. Joyce (1827–1914). These earlier musicians and collectors had been primarily interested in the tunes and tended to ascribe much less value to the words of songs. The Irish musician and folk-song collector Seán O'Boyle has summarised their practice very well:

> Petrie collaborated with Bunting and Joyce worked with Petrie and so formed throughout the nineteenth century a continuous chain of collectors imbued with the antiquarian spirit. Petrie may speak for all of them. He conceived it as a duty, he said [. . .] to preserve the native melodies, because of a deep sense of their beauty, a strong sense of their archaeological interest and a desire to aid in the preservation of remains so honourable to the national character of the country.[41]

O'Boyle goes on to say, 'But collectors never took down Gaelic words and music together in the field and English language texts, when used at all, were censored or bowdlerised or completely changed'.[42] He describes how this practice led to the production of artificial Irish folk-songs as the habit of writing new words to be set to the traditional tunes took hold.

O'Boyle calls Thomas Moore (1779–1852) the chief practitioner in this respect. In his collection of *Irish Melodies* (1808–1834), Moore wrote verses to be set to tunes, many of which 'were sought out in the collections of Bunting and elsewhere',[43] and he even changed some of the melodies to fit his words. O'Boyle then writes:

> Later on, other poets, like Samuel Lover, Samuel Ferguson and Alfred Percival [sic] Graves used tunes in the printed collections to produce what I may call ersatz Irish songs – songs for an elite coterie and never assimilated into the repertory of the folk-singers [. . .] These were songs written in English by sophisticated poets for sophisticated audiences.[44]

Prior to his appointment as the secretary of the ILSL, Graves had a number of books to his credit, one of which was *The Irish Song Book*, published in 1894.[45] His editorial practice of changing or removing words or even whole stanzas is clearly explained in the introduction:

> For this treatment of Irish song I shall no doubt be roundly attacked by those to whom every syllable of the 'Battle of the Boyne' and 'Shule Agra', or every single verse of our more recent national lyric is sacred [. . .] Modern taste will not tolerate the chanting of a dozen verses or more to the same tune. Few songs should exceed four or five, and a ballad, if it runs to greater length, can generally be compressed within a reasonable vocal compass.[46]

The songs mentioned above are two of the seven traditional items in the collection. With respect to the practice of setting poems or songs to traditional tunes, Graves writes, 'It will be recognised that I have found fresh partners for a few favourite airs and lyrics'.[47]

He concludes with what sounds almost like a pre-echo of Cecil Sharp:

> It is indeed high time for us to restart a school of national Irish music. If not, we shall assuredly forfeit our national birthright of song; for, Antæus-like, our musicians have lost their power since they have been lifted from the touch of their native earth. If this collection of songs and airs, which from its size cannot pretend to give more than a fair sample of Irish lyrics, sets them thinking in this direction it will have served the main purpose for which it was compiled.[48]

In his introduction, Graves uses the term 'folk songs' to describe the contents. The matter of definition was, however, to be a contentious issue when the FSS was founded. Although Graves was not a Separatist, the inclusion in *The Irish Song Book* of two strongly nationalistic songs dating from the United Irishmen rebellion of 1798 – 'The Wearing of the Green' and 'The Wind that Shakes the Barley' – suggests that he had at least some sympathy with the cause, although the songs were sufficiently historical not to cause him any serious political embarrassment. The inclusion of Jacobite songs in Stanford's *National Song Book* would later mirror this practice.[49] In these publications, the celebration of a more turbulent past is presented as a stage in the development towards a stable present.

Mrs Kate Lee (née Spooner) was the daughter of an English father and an Irish mother. She was a folk-song collector and had, in the 1890s, developed a short-lived career as a concert singer. She was also an active member of the Folklore Society (FLS). In 1895, she joined the ILSL. Graves said of her, 'A striking personality joined the I. L. S. at this time in Mrs Kate Lee, the wife of an English M. P. with West Indian estates, who presented us with a piano and helped us at all our concerts'.[50] In fact, her husband, Arthur Morier Lee, had been unsuccessful in his bid to become an MP, having stood as a Liberal Unionist candidate in the 1895 general election for the constituency of Newcastle-under-Lyme, which he narrowly lost to William Sheppard Allen, a Gladstonian Liberal. Kate Lee's interest in the ILSL was, presumably, fuelled by her Irish ancestry. In his autobiography, Graves recalls the meeting at which the idea for a folk-song society was first mooted:

> After a conversation which took place between Mrs. Kate Lee, Mr. Plunket Greene, my brother Charles and myself it was decided that an attempt should be made to draw all collectors of folk-song together into one society for the promotion of its best interests.[51]

The founding of the Folk-Song Society: 'fakers' and preservationists

Plans were made to explore the viability of establishing a folk-song society and a meeting was arranged for 27 January 1898. A circular letter was prepared by Kate Lee and distributed to all interested parties, including Alfred Nutt, the president of the FLS. The circular was printed on one side of a single sheet which was folded to make two pages, each measuring 193 mm (7⅝") × 120 mm (4¾"). The title 'Proposed Folk Song Society' was printed in red. Figure 21.1 shows the only known copy of this document.[52]

The circular was among the papers of J. F. Gill deposited in the Manx National Heritage Library in 2000, but the circular itself only came to light in 2009.[53] It was found together

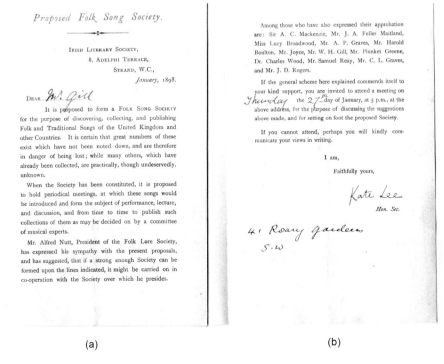

(a)   (b)

Figure 21.1 The circular letter that announced the Folk-Song Society in 1898
Source: Courtesy of Manx National Heritage (MS 09702).

449

with a letter dated 10 February 1898 to J. F. Gill from his brother, W. H. Gill, in which he writes, 'You will be interested to hear of a project to form a Folk Song Society (see circular letter enclosed, which please return)'.[54] Gill also makes specific reference to Kate Lee, saying of her that she is 'a strong friend & supporter of Manx music'. There is also a mention of the circular in a letter from Frank Kidson to Lucy Broadwood; he writes:

> I have received today (probably at your suggestion) a circular. Such a society worked on proper lines, would be a capital idea but its success and its usefulness would fully depend on its managing committee and their earnestness. I trust that you would be on the committee.[55]

The call for a meeting to discuss the founding of a folk-song society was added to the agenda and discussed at a meeting of the council of the FLS that took place on 11 January, where it was decided that a deputation should attend the proposed meeting.[56] That meeting went ahead as planned, on 27 January, at the premises of the ILSL, just off The Strand. A report of the meeting was printed in the *Musical Times* which stated that:

> The preliminary meeting was held at 8, Adelphi Terrace, when amongst those who took an active part in the proceedings were Messrs. Alfred Nutt, J. A. Fuller Maitland, E. F. Jacques, F. Kidson, A. P. Graves, Mrs Gomme and Miss Lucy Broadwood [. . .] The Folk-Lore Society has since stretched out a very sympathetic hand, and its president, Mr. Nutt, has made the committee a generous offer which it is hoped it will be able to accept.[57]

On the face of it, the meeting provided an opportunity for folk-song collectors, musicians, the musically interested, FLS members, Irish Unionists, and Celticists to come together, to pool resources, and to promote a common interest in folk-song.

At the meeting, four of those present addressed the assembly: Lucy Broadwood, J. A. Fuller Maitland, Kate Lee, and A. P. Graves. Broadwood notes in her diary that 'Graves talked of "restoring" traditional songs, which I objected was the last thing that such a Society should do. Mr. J. A. F. M. and Mr. Gill supported me'.[58] The meeting was also reported in the *Daily News*, which recorded that 'Some difference of opinion seemed to exist on the question whether any "adaption" or "restoration" should be countenanced, or whether everyone should rigidly set down what is heard'.[59] The differences between the two camps can be clearly observed by comparing the ideas expressed by Graves in his introduction to *The Irish Song Book* and the preface to Broadwood and Fuller Maitland's *English County Songs*. In a letter that Fuller Maitland sent to Lucy Broadwood on 21 January, shortly before the meeting of 27 January, he writes:

> After I had read and pondered yours and Mrs Lee's letter of last night, there came another letter from her. It seems that she offended Mr. A. P. Graves by putting herself down as Hon. Sec.; that he wrote to her so rude a letter that she can only withdraw from the concern altogether; and that (according to her) H. Boulton is to act as Secretary! Of course we must take all that for what it is worth, and I do not think it very materially alters our position with regard to the ostensible objects of the Society. But I think it does indicate that the 'faking' party is stronger than we thought. This being so, I think our action should be (meaning by 'our' you, Kidson and I) to show that we are willing to co-operate if things are to be carefully and 'cleanly' done. It would not do to hold aloof from it because there are fakers on the committee.[60]

Harold Boulton was a musician and song-writer. The exclamation mark after his name in Fuller Maitland's letter suggests that he regarded him as one of the 'fakers' – that is, those who would compose song lyrics, set them to traditional tunes, and then describe them as folk-songs. One of Boulton's most famous compositions was 'The Skye Boat Song', which was included in a collection of songs entitled *Songs of the North*.[61] This collection was extremely popular and ran to 20 editions. It includes some folk-songs and some new songs, by Boulton and others, set to traditional tunes. In this respect, Boulton's approach to Scottish tunes and songs was the same as Graves's treatment of Irish material.

Graves's idea that Boulton should act as honorary secretary suggests that he had already formulated plans as to how the society should be run and the policies it should adopt. Kate Lee had signed the circular as 'Hon. Sec.'. It is clear from Fuller Maitland's letter of 21 January that she had taken it upon herself to act in this capacity and had not discussed it with Graves, who evidently had other plans. Graves's objection to Kate Lee is notable and strongly suggests that he felt that control of the foundation of the society was being taken from him – which supports the case that the idea for a society was his. Nevertheless, it was Kate Lee who was the activist, and it was her efforts that turned the idea into reality. Her actions in getting things moving have been widely recognised, not least by Graves. Bearman writes that 'it has to be admitted that it was Kate Lee who did most of the work and who has the greater right to be honoured as our founder'.[62]

That may be so – but if Graves had never put forward the idea for such a society it may never have happened. Kate Lee did, however, become honorary secretary when it was founded, so presumably some sort of compromise had been reached and she was persuaded to continue her involvement. Graves served as a committee member until 1921,[63] but never took a particularly active role.

Lucy Broadwood was also supported in her opposition to Graves's idea of 'restoring' songs by W. H. Gill, the Manx musician and folk-song collector, who worked for the General Post Office in London. W. H. Gill, in collaboration with his brother, J. F. Gill, and Dr John Clague, had published a collection called *Manx National Songs* in 1896. This was made up of Manx traditional tunes to which new words – some of them composed by Graves – had been set, because the original songs had been sung in the Manx language. On the face of it, Gill should have been included among the 'fakers'. However, in the preface to the collection, he makes it very clear that the purpose was to get the melodies back into circulation and that the work was popular rather than antiquarian. He explains that the Manx language is practically dead, that 'In many cases the original words possess little literary merit, or historic interest, and in many others they are unfit for publication', and goes on to say, 'The English words here given, whilst in some cases referring to the subject of the originals, are in no sense translations, and in the majority of instances [. . .] have no connection with the original themes'.[64] He also refers the reader to other, earlier collections where they could access the original Manx song texts. One can only assume that it was this openness that, in the view of Broadwood et al., set Gill apart from the other 'fakers'.

The defeat of what Fuller Maitland described as the '"faking" party' was crucial to the future success and achievement of the FSS. With hindsight, it is clear that the value of what the society achieved lay in the accurate record that its collector members tried to make of what they were able to glean from traditional singers. The collectors had their limitations and failures – the representation of a song performance in a manuscript or in the pages of the *Journal of the Folk-Song Society* (*JFSS*) can only capture a part of the richness that the collector experienced. When collecting and classifying folk material, it is inevitably taken out of its natural environment and its quotidian meaning is lost, or at the very least misunderstood. Nevertheless, the society produced a body of material that is unique in its provenance and is of continuing interest. This would not have been the case had the 'fakers' prevailed. Indeed, Bearman makes the point that if Graves and Boulton 'had been the official voices it is likely that the Folk-Song Society's efforts would have been steered away from field collection [. . .] and directed more towards printed material and National Songs'.[65]

The foundation of the Folk-Song Society

Frank Kidson's entry for the Folk-Song Society in *Grove's Dictionary of Music and Musicians* states: 'FOLK–SONG SOCIETY. This society was definitely established in London on June 16, 1898, for the preservation and publication of folk-songs and melodies'.[66] However, there are no minutes or record of the proceedings at that meeting but in an article celebrating the society's 50th anniversary, the composer and former committee member Frederick Keel states that at the first general meeting, which took place on 2 February 1899, 'The Hon. Secretary's Report given at this meeting is the one clear statement that the Society was publicly constituted on June 16th 1898'.[67]

When the FSS was founded, Charles Villiers Stanford, along with C. Hubert H. Parry, Sir John Stainer and Sir Alexander Mackenzie were appointed as the four Vice-Presidents of the Society and as Donald Wilgus put it 'The Society had the support of the principal academic musicians; [...]'.[68] Here we see the beginnings of a network of educationalists and professional musicians that had an interest in, to use a generic term, vernacular song, and music. However, Dibble has pointed out that in spite of his support for the FSS, Stainer held reservations about the use of folk-songs in schools and 'did not consider the folk song an ideal educational agency, owing principally to the wide range of the melodies for children's voices'.[69] Dibble went on to point out that the composer Charles Villiers Stanford took a very different view which he had expressed in a paper delivered to the London School Boards in 1889, an 'unbridled desire to see the teaching of folk songs' as part of the school curriculum.[70]

At the Inaugural Meeting of the FSS held on 16 May 1898, at which the Society was formally constituted, Fuller Maitland reported that negotiations with the FLS '[...] came to nothing because, from the beginning they were carried out under misunderstanding, and the society now to be formed would be quite independent'.[71] A committee was elected and the minutes record that:

> The following names were submitted for the proposed Committee, and unanimously elected: – - Mr. Kidson, Mr. E. F. Jacques, Mr. J. A. Fuller Maitland, Mrs Gomme, Miss Broadwood, Sir Ernest Clarke, Mr. W. H. Gill, Mr. A. P. Graves, Mr. Kalisch, Mr. Corder, Mr. J. D. Rogers, Mrs Lee.
> Mrs Lee was elected secretary. The Committee to appoint its own Treasurer.[72]

Following the public formal constitution of the society (16 June 1898), the elected committee of management met again on 6 July 1898, and at this meeting Fuller Maitland took the chair and read a letter from Lord Herschell accepting the presidency. Lord Herschell had been Gladstone's solicitor-general in the 1880s and in the 1890s served as the Lord Chancellor. The foundation of the FSS was reported in a number of newspapers both national and regional.

Lucy Broadwood, Fuller Maitland, and Frank Kidson: a preservationist alliance

At this point, it is useful to give a little biographical information on Lucy Broadwood (1858–1929) since she was later to become a key figure in the FSS. Lucy's father, Henry Fowler Broadwood, took over the famous piano-making firm, John Broadwood and Sons in 1851 following the death of his father. Lucy was born at Melrose, Scotland and was the youngest of nine surviving children. As a child, she moved from Scotland to the family estate in Lyne near the Surrey-Sussex border. Lucy remained at the family home in Lyne until her father's death in 1893; she then moved to London taking up residence with her mother at the Broadwood's town house in Pimlico. Following her mother's death in 1898, she gave up the lease on the town house and moved into a mansion flat in Westminster which she shared with her niece Barbara Cra'ster. She remained single all her life but she was able to support herself through private means and thus maintain her independence. E. David Gregory writes of Lucy Broadwood that: '[…] she evidently had plenty of time to devote to her chosen pursuits. The main ones were religion, art, reading and music'.[73] When she was 26 years old (in 1884), her brother James became engaged to her friend Evelyn Fuller Maitland. This resulted in closer contact between the two families and as a result Lucy became much better acquainted with Evelyn's brother J. A. Fuller Maitland, or Alec Fuller Maitland as he was known. She was later to collaborate with him in the publication of a collection of folk-songs, *English County Songs* (1893), that would come to be regarded as a seminal piece of work. Alec Fuller Maitland was a composer, author, and, from 1889 to 1911, the chief music critic of the *Times*.[74] In 1904, he edited a new edition of *Grove's Dictionary of Music and Musicians*.

Lucy's interest in folk-song was inspired by the discovery of her uncle's collection when she was still an adolescent; the collection had been privately published in 1847 before she was born. Her uncle John had noted the songs having himself learnt them orally by 'hearing them sung every Christmas'.

Lucy was familiar with folk-songs because her father, who had also collected songs at the same time as his brother, occasionally sang them at home to entertain the family. Lucy decided to re-publish her uncle's collection to which she added a further ten songs. As she worked on preparing this new edition for publication to be called *Sussex Songs: Popular Songs of Sussex* (1890), she was unhappy with the arrangements that G. A. Dussart had produced for the original edition and she enlisted the help of her cousin, Herbert Frederick Birch-Reynardson. He agreed that Dussart's 'hymn-like'[75] pianoforte arrangements needed to be replaced. Broadwood admired her cousin's musical compositions and in particular the music he had composed for *A Masque of Flowers*, a production at the Prince of Wales Theatre in London, her diary records that she was 'enchanted with it'.[76] She was confident that he was the right person for the job and he agreed to do it. This joint project became public knowledge within London music circles and consequently Broadwood was approached by William Alexander Barrett who asked her for examples of Sussex songs that he could include in the collection of folk-songs he was compiling for publication at that time. Alfred James Hipkins, who was one of the chief advisors on pianos for the family firm, had become an 'avuncular figure to young Lucy with whom he shared an interest in folksong'[77] and he was also a friend of Barrett. Hipkins had written to her and asked her for permission to give Barrett her address so that he could write to her.[78] Hipkins was an influential character in the London music circle; Fuller Maitland wrote of him that

> A. J. Hipkins was a benefactor to all the young pianists who were trained in England or who flocked over from abroad; he himself had been the tuner preferred above all others by Chopin on his visits to England, [...].[79]

Presumably she gave permission very promptly because Barrett wrote to her a few days later. In a letter dated 11 April 1889, he asked if he could use examples of songs from her uncle's collection to add to the one-hundred he already had for his forthcoming collection to be published under the title of *Quaint Songs*.[80] The 1 March 1889 edition of *The Musical Times* carried a short news item which, in effect, advertised Barrett's forthcoming work. It stated:

> The suggestion made by Mr. Andrew Lang that an effort should be made to collect the popular songs has, to some extent, been already carried into effect by Mr. W. A. Barrett and a series of quaint songs, words and music derived chiefly from traditional sources and from the presses of the "Broadside" ballad printers, will shortly be published.[81]

Barrett, who in 1876 was promoted from Assistant Vicar Choral to Vicar Choral at St Paul's Cathedral,[82] was also the music critic for the *Morning Post* from 1866 until his death. He was also one of the 150 Assistant Inspectors for schools and worked closely with John Hullah, the government inspector (HMI) of music in schools and training colleges. Hullah had subscribed to Chappell's work *Popular Music of the Olden Time*.[83] The music historian Gordon Cox wrote that 'Chappell's influence was profound. He personally encouraged John Hullah's work, *The Song Book* (1866), which was comprised of national songs and was based largely on Chappell's collection'.[84] It may be that Barrett was influenced by Hullah and his own interests were fired by Hullah's interest in national song which then led him to extend the study of national song and investigate the oral song tradition.

In addition to his work as an Assistant Inspector and music critic, Barrett was also the editor of *The Musical Times* and he was the co-author of a musical dictionary with another HMI, and colleague at St Paul's, John Stainer, later to become Sir John Stainer and a vice-president of the FSS. Stainer had been a Professor of Music at Oxford University and in 1872 accepted the post of organist at St Paul's Cathedral with a salary of £400 per year. The composer C. Hubert H. Parry had been a pupil of Stainer's at Oxford and was quick to congratulate him on his new appointment. In his biography of Stainer, Dibble quoted from a letter from Parry in which he said:

> My dear old Professor
>
> I really can't express to you how delighted I was at seeing by accident in the papers your translation to the see of St Paul's. Of course one must feel sorry for poor Oxford, but from every other point of view one must congratulate oneself and the country as well as you. [...] I feel almost inclined to fancy you and Barrett cooperating in the work of regeneration in which direction his pen and influence are always straight.[85]

However, with regard to Barrett's request to Lucy Broadwood for help, her response was that she felt unable to assist him in this matter. No doubt she wanted to avoid any possibility of duplication between the two collections. Nonetheless, in 1891 William Barrett published his collection under the title *English Folk Songs* and not *Quaint Songs* as originally planned. Tragically, later in the same year, he very suddenly and unexpectedly died aged only 57.[86] Given Barrett's own interest in folk-song and his collaboration and friendship with both Hullah and Stainer, it is quite probable that he too would have been a member of the FSS had he survived.

Also in 1891 Frank Kidson had privately published his collection of songs entitled *Traditional Tunes* and Hipkins sent Lucy a copy,[87] and she wrote in her diary that it was 'very interesting'.[88] A few months later, Broadwood wrote to Kidson about his collection and this was the start of a lifelong friendship and fruitful musical collaboration. Presumably her interest lay in the fact that Kidson, like her uncle, had adopted a strict antiquarian approach. He recorded tunes exactly as they were sung, though he did, as her uncle had done, edit some song texts, but unlike her uncle he presented the texts and tunes without piano accompaniment. At this time, Broadwood and Maitland were preparing their collection *English County Songs* (1893) for publication. They had decided to present the collection with accompaniment and they justified this decision when they stated:

> While to give the tunes without accompaniment is doubtless the most scientific method of preserving the songs, it has the disadvantage of rendering them practically useless to educated singers. The accompaniments have been kept as simple as possible, and in all cases the editors have endeavoured to preserve the character of the period to which they suppose the tune to belong.[89]

The reference to 'educated singers' is a clear indicator that the volume was aimed at as wide a market as possible. The practice of presenting only the air as the singer gave it would appeal, at this time, only to a limited market and this is probably why Kidson's collection was restricted to a run of 200 copies and published privately. The Rev. Sabine Baring-Gould and Rev. H. Fleetwood Sheppard published *Songs of the West* in four parts, parts one and two in 1889, part three in 1890, and part four in 1891. Later in 1891, the collection was published as a single volume. Baring-Gould had also heard of Broadwood's work and he wrote to her about songs that he had collected in the West Country. Broadwood acknowledged the work of Barrett, Kidson, and Baring-Gould in a letter she wrote to the FLS, published in the December 1892 edition of the society's journal. The letter requested that readers contribute to her any songs that they may have noted. Presumably this was part of the strategy she used in order to gather songs from each of the English counties for the forthcoming collection that she and Fuller Maitland were working on. She wrote:

> Sir, – May I draw the attention of the members of the Folk-Lore Society to the branch of work in which I am especially interested, namely, the collecting of all kinds of *traditional tunes and songs*, chiefly of Great Britain?
>
> There have from to time been published a few small books giving rustic ballads with their tunes: the Rev. S. Baring-Gould in his *Songs of the West,* has rescued a great deal of old music lingering in Cornwall and Devonshire; Mr. Heywood Sumner's *Besom-Maker* is a small contribution; *Sussex Songs* embodying the collection made by the Rev. John Broadwood [...] with additions from myself; and Dr. Barrett's *English Folk-Songs* are others; besides the admirable volume of *Traditional Tunes* published by Mr. F. Kidson of Leeds, which deserves to be far better known than it is. [...]. If any members of the Folk-Lore Society should wish to help in this work, any contributions will be most welcome if sent to Miss Lucy Broadwood, Lyne, Rusper, Horsham.[90]

At the time of writing this letter, the FLS was the only forum for folk-song collectors to either publicise or discuss their work. The fact that Broadwood was a member of the FLS and that her declared interest was in folk-song is a clear indication that she felt a need for such a forum. It is not surprising, therefore, that she embraced the suggestion, when it was first mooted, for a society dedicated to folk-song and had strong views on the policies such a society should adopt.

Political allegiances of the Folk-Song Society's founders – 'a new level of struggle'?

The first annual general meeting of the FSS took place at the home of Rachel and Frederick Beer, in Mayfair on Thursday, 2 February 1899, just seven months after the foundation of the society. At this meeting of the FSS, the committee comprised 12 members, and in accordance with Rule VI, 6 members stood down. Rule VI states that: 'At each General Meeting half of the Members of the Committee shall retire from office, but shall be eligible for re-election'.[91] Five of them put themselves forward for re-election, and were all unanimously re-elected. Mrs [Rachel] Frederick Beer was newly elected to replace Mr Frederick Corder, who was unable to continue as a committee member. Rachel Beer's biographers, Eilat Negav and Yehuda Koren, wrote that:

> To her growing list of memberships Rachel added the Folk Song Society [...]. Mrs Beer was offered a seat on the committee; it gave her an opportunity to display her patriotism and to continue her campaign for quality entertainment, and she promoted the society with lengthy articles and interviews in the *Sunday Times*.[92]

The committee membership now comprised the following people:

> Mrs Frederick Beer; Miss Lucy Broadwood; Sir Ernest Clarke; W. H. Gill, Esq.; Mrs Laurence Gomme; A. P. Graves, Esq.; E. F. Jacques, Esq.; Frank Kidson, Esq.; J. A. Fuller Maitland, Esq.; J. D. Rogers, Esq.; W. Barclay Squire, Esq.; Dr. Todhunter. Hon. Secretary; Mrs Kate Lee; Hon. Treasurer; A. Kalisch, Esq.[93]

Rachel Beer is not listed as being present at the general meeting, even though it took place in her home. It may be that she was busy making preparations for the conversazione that was to follow the meeting.

Rachel Beer (née Sassoon) was the aunt of the poet Siegfried Sassoon and she was famous in her own right as the first female editor of a national newspaper. She was the editor of the *Observer*, which was owned by her husband, and she was also owner-editor of the *Sunday Times*. The former Liberal prime minister William Gladstone, his wife Catherine, and their family had been 'guests of honour' at the marriage of Frederick and Rachel and they had hosted the Beers' wedding breakfast at their home on 4 August 1887.[94] The Gladstones '[...] had watched Rachel grow up, and now that she was an adult and had married into more money, Catherine Gladstone was ready to link her with one of her many charities'.[95]

Following the sudden death of Lord Herschell in March 1899, Viscount Cobham succeeded him as the president of the FSS, serving from 1899 to 1904. Viscount Cobham was Gladstone's nephew and had served as a Liberal MP from 1868 to 1872. It is probable that Rachel Beer invoked her friendship with Gladstone, who had died the previous year, to secure Cobham's agreement to become the president of the FSS. At the time, he was serving as a commissioner reporting to the Board of Trade in connection with the Railway and Canal Traffic Act.

I have already mentioned some of the political associations of the group that was responsible for the foundation of the FSS. Irish Nationalists and Unionists, some of them profoundly conservative like Stanford and to a lesser extent Graves, played important roles. Lucy

Broadwood and Fuller Maitland were also conservatives, while other members favoured the Liberal Party. It was only later, in the early years of the twentieth century, that some folk revivalists would display what looked like more radical colours – for example, Cecil Sharp's membership of the Fabian Society, and Mary Neal's support for the Woman's Social and Political Union and the Independent Labour Party.

It is worth asking why some Liberals should have been attracted to the idea of folk-song collecting. A new social emphasis developed in Liberalism in the late nineteenth century, including an interest in the social conditions of the poor (for example, the work of Charles Masterman, Liberal M.P., and Rachel Beer) and in what would later be termed 'labour history' (for example, the work of J. L. and Barbara Hammond). The thrust of this 'New Liberalism' was to address some of the social and political developments outlined in the first section of this chapter. We could suggest that Liberals in the late nineteenth century wanted to move towards a more harmonious society, and that in folk-song, a cultural artefact from the past, they found something that, however vaguely, might help them do so.

Of the collectors who were active in the period before the FSS, we know that Sabine Baring-Gould was a strong Liberal and supporter of Gladstone. He wrote: 'My father was a very pronounced Liberal and I had contracted similar principles'.[96] Lucy Broadwood, however, was a Conservative and supporter of the Primrose League, an organisation dedicated to spreading Conservative principles, but also a supporter of women's suffrage.[97] Their different political leanings did not stop them becoming friends and collaborators.

After the first general meeting, Sir Hubert Parry, one of the vice-presidents, gave a short inaugural address. Parry was very well connected; he was a friend of Arthur Balfour, leader of the Conservative Party and prime minister from 1902 to 1905. He was the father-in-law and a friend of Arthur Ponsonby who was married to Parry's eldest daughter, Dorothea. Ponsonby was a one-time member of the Liberal Party who later opposed Britain's involvement in the First World War and, in the 1920s, became a Labour MP and peace campaigner. Parry was also a friend of Spencer Lyttelton, who was Gladstone's private secretary at various times. Jeremy Dibble in his biography of Parry concludes that Gladstone was his 'political mentor'.[98] In collaboration with Robert Bridges, Parry composed a cantata called The Spirit of Darkness and Light, which was 'written as an apotheosis to Gladstone'.[99] Nevertheless, the composer and poet Sir Arnold Bax depicted Parry as a 'Victorian man of convention, the conservative squire',[100] which became the generally accepted view of Parry. His daughter Dorothea, however, strongly repudiated that opinion, writing in a letter to the *Musical Times*, 'He was a Radical, with a very strong bias against Conservatism – he writes somewhere that he found himself continually in a minority of one, and reduced to silence by the champions of Conservatism'.[101]

Parry's inaugural address provides us with a clear view of what he saw as the vulgarising effects of 'the common popular songs of the day', and of urban life in general, and admirably illustrates the 'air of gloom' of the fin de siècle:

> If one thinks of the outer circumference of our terribly overgrown towns where the jerry-builder holds sway; where one sees all around the tawdriness of sham jewellery and shoddy clothes, pawnshops and flaming gin-palaces; where stale fish and the Covent Garden refuse which pass for vegetables are offered for food – all such things suggest to one's mind the boundless regions of sham. It is for the people who live in these unhealthy regions – people who, for the most part have the most false ideals, or none at all [. . .] It is for them that the modern popular music is made, and it is made with a commercial intention out of snippets of musical slang.[102]

He went on to say that the purity of folk music must be cherished and the music and songs preserved, and that this would go some way towards re-establishing the finer qualities of life for the people in general. Parry concluded his address by expressing the hope that:

> [...] our puzzling friend Democracy, has permanent qualities hidden away somewhere, which may yet bring it out of the slough which the scramble for false ideals, the strife between the heads that organise and the workmen who execute, and the sordid vulgarity of our great city-populations, seem in our pessimistic moments to indicate as its inevitable destiny.[103]

Georgina Boyes in her analysis of Parry's address contends that he '[...] proposed a solution which went beyond exclusively musical concerns'. She draws attention to the fact that Parry believed that it was not only the musical form of folk music and song that was uncontaminated by the trappings of modern life, but the content of the songs themselves. She points out that he believed that the values embodied 'In "true" folksong', in which there was '[...] no sham, no got up glitter, and no vulgarity, nothing common or unclean' provided contemporaries with a summary of the 'qualities of the race'. Folk music and song had been collectively created by ordinary people and embodied 'their deepest feelings, characteristics and aspirations'. She goes on to argue that Parry believed that this would provide a 'cultural standard which could be drawn upon to reverse the process of degeneration, and restore the old social balance', and that 'from recognition of this national core, a new socio-cultural consensus could develop to restore the status quo'.[104]

Dave Harker makes much the same point, but rather more forcefully, when he states:

> Yet it is perfectly clear that what Parry and the Folk Song Society feared was bound for "extinction" was not only that idealised "golden age" of pre-industrial rural bliss, but their very own material security which was being thoroughly tested by a "Democracy" which they suspected was not their "close friend" at all.[105]

Harker goes on to argue that, even though they might not fully have realised it, the founders of the FSS were involved in what he terms 'a new level of struggle', whereby a musical culture, reshaped through their own mediation, would displace the commercial popular music and songs of the music halls.[106] In fact, according to Harker, Parry was expressing a view that accepted 'crucial eugenic factual beliefs' – and which, according to the political philosopher Allen Buchanan, had become generally accepted by the 'bourgeoisie'. Buchanan writes:

> The belief that the major social problems of capitalist society were not due to its defective institutions, but rather to unseen biochemical entities within the bodies of "the dangerous class", was comforting to those who benefited from those institutions and diverted attention from the possibility that they needed to be reformed or replaced by better institutions.[107]

It is true that the members of the FSS and the musical establishment in general were members of the middle and upper-middle classes of Victorian and Edwardian societies. No doubt they held views in keeping with their social status and class interests, without necessarily being aware that in so doing they were acting politically. Boyes's and Harker's analyses, however, ascribe to the founders of the society a political awareness and level of political activity that is simply not corroborated by the available evidence.

The members of the FSS were preoccupied with the recovery of what they saw as a fast-disappearing musical cultural heritage. To them, this recovery would have practical and beneficial qualities in terms of what it could contribute to national cultural life. As far as their political allegiances are concerned, the evidence suggests that in general, but with some notable exceptions, they supported the Liberal cause and what might be termed progressive Conservatism.

However, their main concern was the recovery and rescue of folk-songs. If, in the process of recovering and repackaging this cultural heritage, they had the effect of inculcating feelings of nationalism and patriotism, then, as far as they were concerned, so much the better. Furthermore, if such a process helped produce model citizens who would be content with their lot, then this would be a welcome side effect, but there is nothing to suggest that these were the unwritten aims of the society or that there was a unified view among FSS members. Indeed, the minutes of committee meetings provide no evidence of political allegiances, let alone activities, at all – and if the members had been politically motivated, that is the one place where one would expect to find some evidence of it. Instead, the minutes simply log the decisions made and the actions required for the day-to-day running of the society – although no doubt there was also some 'off the record' discussion. Furthermore, if their aim was to displace the commercial popular music and songs of the music halls with 'a musical culture, reshaped through their own mediation', it achieved very limited success.

Conclusion

The decline and collapse of the Irish Home Rule movement prompted a renaissance in Irish poetry, literature, and music, and the founding of the ILSL was a part of this. The initiative for the foundation of the FSS in 1898 came from the ILSL, at a time that witnessed a general air of fin de siècle apprehension and gloom and also coincided with a perceived need to establish an English identity in music. The founding of the FSS was a reaction to these socio-political and cultural developments, and to the perceived need to save a dying cultural heritage. With this aim in mind, it attracted a range of people – principally folk-song collectors, but also musicians, the musically interested, FLS members, Celticists, and Irish Unionists. Politically, a number of the early movers of the FSS had strong links with the Liberal Party, but members articulated a range of political views.

The available evidence points to Alfred Perceval Graves, and not Kate Lee, as the originator of the idea for a folk-song society, but without Kate Lee's enthusiasm and commitment to the enterprise it might have remained simply an idea. There is complexity in trying to understand cultural movements. In any historical context, people are subject to pressures and constraints and are influenced by ideas circulating at the time. Men and women do make their own histories, but within the cultural, economic, and intellectual contexts of their period, though some may be forward-thinking, and we describe such people as being 'ahead of their time'. Some kinds of historical evidence, particularly those related to the connectedness of things and the relationships between them, are not possible to prove as 'facts'. We observe the known facts and from them make judgements and interpretations, which are inevitably coloured by our own ideas and preconceptions. The formation of the FSS happened within a particular historical, social, and intellectual context – it was in part a product of a certain historical conjuncture, but it was also, crucially, the result of the actions of key individuals, who were themselves the product of particular social contexts. We should welcome attempts to understand such things in a wider historical context, but, on balance, it seems that it is easy to overstate the place of the FSS in the class and cultural politics of its day. It was the institutional expression of a desire to preserve traditional songs on the part of a small group of activists – who, in the process and with all their limitations, did something rather unique and valuable and we owe those pioneers a huge debt of gratitude.

Notes

1 John Saville, *Rural Depopulation in England and Wales 1851–1951* (London: Routledge & Kegan Paul, 1957), p. 89.
2 W.E. Forster House of Commons Debate on Elementary Education, 17 February 1870, *Hansard* Vol. 199, cc 438–498 (c 465).
3 Peter Mathias, *First Industrial Nation: The Economic History of Britain, 1700–1914* (2nd edn; London: Routledge, 1983), p. 4.
4 J.L. Hammond and Barbara Hammond, *The Rise of Modern Industry* (4th edn; London: Methuen, 1930), p. 1.
5 Ibid., p. 3.
6 H.L. Beales, 'Revisions in Economic History 1: The Great Depression in Industry and Trade', *Economic History Review* 5.1 (1934), 65–75 (p. 74).
7 G.D.H. Cole and Raymond Postgate, *The Common People, 1746–1946* (2nd edn; London: Methuen, 1946), p. 445.
8 Archibald Philip Primrose (Earl of Rosebury), *The Decline and Fall of British Industrial Supremacy* (London: United Empire Trade League Publications No. 12, 1895), p. 1.
9 Heinrich Heine, *Pariser Berichte*, 29 July, 1840, trans by Bryan Townsend, cited in *The Music Salon Blogshot*, 9 September, 2012. Available at <https://www.themusicsalon.blogshot.com2012/09> accessed 17 October 2019.
10 Frederick J. Crowest, *Phases of Musical England* (London: Remington, 1881), p. vii.
11 *Music in England: The Proposed Royal College of Music. Three Addresses Delivered by HRH The Duke of Edinburgh, HRH The Duke of Albany, HRH Prince Christian, at the Free Trade Hall, Manchester Dec. 12 1881* (London: John Murray, 1882), p. 3.
12 Ibid., pp. 9–10.
13 Joseph Bennett, 'Hubert Parry's First Symphony', *The Daily Telegraph* (4 September 1882).
14 Joseph Bennett, 'English Music in 1884', *The Musical Times and Singing Class Circular*, 25.496 (1 June 1884), pp. 324–326 (p. 326).
15 Michael Kennedy, 'Music', Chapter 10 in: Boris Ford (ed.) *The Cambridge Cultural History of Britain: Volume 7 Victorian Britain* (London: Folio Society, 1995), p. 283.
16 Ernest Edwin Williams, *Made in Germany* (4th edn; London: Heinemann, 1896), p. 11.
17 Cecil Forsyth, 'Song and Folk-Song', Chapter 10 in: Charles Villiers Stanford and Cecil Forsyth (eds.), *A History of Music* (New York: Macmillan, 1918), pp. 200–13 (pp. 208–209).
18 Kennedy, 'Music', pp. 281–282.
19 Hammond, *The Rise of Modern Industry*, p. 231.
20 Cecil J. Sharp, *English Folk-Song Some Conclusions* (London: Simpkin Novello, 1907), p. 119.
21 Herbert Woodfield Paul, *The Life of William Ewart Gladstone* (London: Thomas Nelson, 1901), p. 271. (Note, using the figures given by Herbert Woodfield Paul the 'working majority was 118).
22 See, for example, 'The Connemara Divorce Suit', *The Times* (17 November 1890), p. 3.
23 Paul, *William Ewart Gladstone*, pp. 319–320.
24 Richard Shannon, *The Crisis of Imperialism, 1815–1915* (St Albans: Paladin, 1976), p. 273.
25 Carl Engel, *An Introduction to the Study of National Music* (London: Longmans, Crew, Reader and Dyer, 1866), p. viii.
26 Alfred Perceval Graves, *To Return to All That: An Autobiography* (London: Jonathan Cape, 1930), p. 262.
27 See Michael J. Sidnell, 'The Allegory of *The Wanderings of Oisin*', *Colby Library Quarterly*, 15.2 (1979), 137–151.
28 John Carey, *The Intellectuals and the Masses: Pride and Prejudice among the Intelligentsia, 1880–1939* (London: Faber, 1992), p. 71.
29 Lionel Johnson, A review of 'The Countess Kathleen and Various Legends and Lyrics' *The Academy*, July – December 1892 [1 October 1892] in: A. Norman Jeffares (ed.), *W. B. Yeats: The Critical Heritage* (London: Routledge and Kegan Paul, 1977), pp. 78–82 (p. 80).

30 Duffy was initially a member of the Repeal Association, an organisation set up to campaign for the repeal of Act of Union between Britain and Ireland, but he and others subsequently broke away to form the more militant grouping known as Young Ireland, which had a lasting influence as a political, cultural, and social movement.
31 Graves, *Return to All That*, p. 261.
32 *The Times* (31 July 1895), p. 6.
33 Seamus Deane, *A Short History of Irish Literature* (London: Hutchinson, 1986), p. 176.
34 Christopher James Bearman, 'The English Folk Music Movement 1898–1914' (unpublished doctoral thesis, University of Hull, 2001), pp. 40, 82.
35 *The Complete Collection of Ancient Irish Music, as Noted by George Petrie*. Edited from the Original Manuscripts by Charles Villiers Stanford, 3 vols. (London and New York: Boosey & Co. 1902–1905), pp. i, iii.
36 For a summary of Graves views on education in Ireland, see Joseph Lee, *The Modernisation of Irish Society: 1848–1918* (3rd edn; Dublin: Gill and Macmillan, 2008), p. 31. For his views on physical education, see Alfred Perceval Graves, 'Physical Education in Primary Schools', *Contemporary Review*, 85 (1904), 888–898.
37 Graves, *Return To All That*, p. 182.
38 C.V. Stanford (ed.), *The Complete Collection of Irish Music as Noted by G. Petrie*, 3 parts (London: Boosey, for the Irish Literary Society, 1902–1905).
39 'In Memoriam, Charles Villiers Stanford 1852–1924', *Musical Times*, 65.975 (1 May 1924), 402–403.
40 Gordon Cox, *A History of Music Education in England* (Aldershot: Scolar Press, 1993), p. 69.
41 Seán O'Boyle, *The Irish Song Tradition* (Dublin: Gilbert Dalton, 1976), p. 12.
42 Ibid., p. 13.
43 John Francis Waller, 'A Prefatory Memoir', in *Moore's Irish Melodies: Lalla Rookh, National Airs, Legendary Ballads, Songs Etc.* (London: William Mackenzie, [1897]), p. xvi.
44 O'Boyle, *Irish Song Tradition*, p. 14.
45 This was an edited collection of 112 songs from 54 authors and an additional 7 traditional songs. The book was one of a series of titles in publisher T. Fisher Unwin's New Irish Library. The series editor was Sir Charles Gavan Duffy and the assistant editors were Douglas Hyde and Thomas Rollerston.
46 Alfred Perceval Graves, ed., *The Irish Song Book* (4th edn; London: T. Fisher Unwin, 1897), pp. v–vi.
47 Ibid., p. vii.
48 Ibid., p. xv.
49 See, for example, 'Charlie Is My Darling', and 'Wha Wadna Fecht for Charlie?' in Charles Villiers Stanford, *National Song Book*, vol. 1 (London: Boosey, 1906), pp. 82, 91, respectively; and compare Christopher A. Whately, 'Scotland: A Truer Picture', *History Today*, 62.7 (2012), 57–58 (p. 57): 'Tartan and the kilt once feared to the extent that they were outlawed, were by the end of the Napoleonic Wars in 1815 the dress of heroes: the loyal, brave Highland regiments'.
50 Graves, *Return to All That*, p. 266.
51 Ibid., p. 266.
52 Douglas, Isle of Man, Manx National Heritage Library, MS 09702, Deemster J.F. Gill Papers.
53 Stephen Miller, '"You will be interested to hear of a project to form a Folk Song Society": W. H. Gill and the Founding of the Folk-Song Society', *Folk Music Journal*, 10.1 (2011), 73–88.
54 Douglas, Isle of Man, Manx National Heritage Library, MS 09702, Deemster J.F. Gill Papers, Box 2, letter from W.H. Gill to Deemster J.F. Gill, 10 February 1898.
55 London, Vaughan Williams Memorial Library, Lucy Broadwood manuscript Collection, LEB/4/95, letter from Frank Kidson to Lucy Broadwood (9 January 1898).
56 London, Folklore Society Archives, Minutes of Meeting of Council (11 January 1898).
57 'Occasional Notes', *Musical Times and Singing Class Circular*, 39.661 (1 March 1898), 165.
58 Woking, Surrey History Centre, Broadwood Papers, 6782/12, Lucy Broadwood Diaries (27 January 1898).
59 'This Morning's News', *Daily News* (28 January 1898).
60 Broadwood Papers, 2185/LEB/67, SHC, Letter from J.A. Fuller Maitland to Lucy Broadwood (21 January 1898).
61 A.C. Macleod and Harold Boulton, eds, *Songs of the North, Gathered Together from the Highlands and Lowlands of Scotland*, 3 vols (London: Field & Tuer, [1885]).

62 C.J. Bearman, 'Kate Lee and the Foundation of the Folk-Song Society', *Folk Music Journal*, 7.5 (1999), 627–643 (p. 635).
63 Vaughan Williams Memorial Library, Minutes of the Folk-Song Society (12 March 1921).
64 W.H. Gill, *Manx National Songs with English Words, Selected from the MS. Collection of the Deemster Gill, J. Clague and W. H. Gill* (London: Boosey, 1896), p. ii.
65 Bearman, 'Kate Lee', p. 635.
66 J.A. Fuller Maitland, ed. *Grove's Dictionary of Music and Musicians*, 5 vols (London: Macmillan, 1904–1910), II, 70.
67 Frederick Keel, 'The Folk-Song Society 1898–1948', *Journal of the English Folk Dance and Song Society*, 5.3 (1948), 111–126 (p. 113 n).
68 D.K. Wilgus, *Anglo-American Folksong Scholarship Since 1898* (New Brunswick: Rutgers University Press), p. 128.
69 Jeremy Dibble, *John Stainer: A Life in Music* (Woodbridge: Boydell Press, 2007), p. 276.
70 Ibid., p. 276.
71 Vaughan Williams Memorial Library, Minutes of the Folk-Song Society, 'Inaugural Meeting' (16 May 1898), p. 2.
72 Ibid., p. 8.
73 E. David Gregory, 'Before the Folk-Song Society: Lucy Broadwood and English Folk Song, 1884–97', *Folk Music Journal*, 9.3 (2008), 372–414 (p. 374).
74 Frank Howes, 'Obituary: J. A. Fuller Maitland, April 7th 1856–March 30th 1936', *Journal of the English Folk Dance and Song Society*, 3.1 (1936), 78.
75 Dorothy de Val, *In Search of Song: The Life and Times of Lucy Broadwood* (Farnham: Ashgate, 2011), p. 46.
76 Gregory, 'Before the Folk-Song Society', p. 375.
77 Dorothy de Val, *In Search of Song*, p. 36.
78 Broadwood Papers, Ref.2185/LEB/1/4, SHC. Letter from A.J. Hipkins to Lucy Broadwood, 5 April 1889.
79 J.A. Fuller-Maitland, *A Door-Keeper of Music* (London: John Murraay, 1929), p. 110.
80 Broadwood Papers, Ref.2185/LEB/1/5, SHC. Letter from W.A. Barrett to Lucy Broadwood, 11 April 1889.
81 'Miscellaneous Concerts, Intelligence, &c.', *Musical Times and Singing Class Circular*, 30.533 (1 March, 1889), 168.
82 Dibble, *John Stainer*, fn. p. 177.
83 W. Chappell, 'List of Subscribers' in *Popular Music of the Olden Time* (London: Chappell, 1858–1859), p. xviii.
84 Gordon Cox, *History of Music Education in England*, p. 67.
85 Dibble, *John Stainer*, p. 144.
86 'Obituary: "William Alexander Barrett"', *Musical Times and Singing Class Circular*, 32.585 (1 November 1891), 659–660.
87 This copy is no. 75 of a limited edition of 200. It has the inscription 'To Miss Lucy Broadwood from A J Hipkins, 1891'. It is among the Lucy Etheldred Broadwood Holdings, item ref. 6192/2/80, SHC.
88 Lucy Broadwood diaries, 30 June, 1891, Lucy Ethelred Broadwood Holdings, Ref.6782/9, SHC.
89 Broadwood and Fuller Maitland *English County Songs*, p.v.
90 Lucy Broadwood, 'Correspondence: Folk-Songs and Music, To the Editor of Folk-Lore', *Folk-lore*, 3.4 (1892), 551–553 (pp. 551–552).
91 'Rules', *Journal of the Folk-Song Society*, 1.1 (1899), iv.
92 Eilat Negev and Yehuda Koren, *The First Lady of Fleet Street: The Life, Fortune and Tragedy of Rachel Beer* (London: Robson Press, 2012), p. 242.
93 'Committee', *Journal of the Folk-Song Society*, 1.1 (1899), i.
94 Negev and Koren, *First Lady of Fleet Street*, p. 137.
95 Ibid., p. 142.
96 S. Baring-Gould, *Early Reminiscences, 1834–1864* (London: John Lane, 1922), p. ix.
97 De Val, *In Search of Song*, p. 3.
98 Jeremy Dibble, *C. Hubert Parry: His Life and Music* (Oxford: Clarendon Press, 1992), p. 356.
99 Ibid., p. 358.
100 Ibid., p. 499.

101 Dorothea Ponsonby, 'Hubert Parry' [Letter to the Editor], *Musical Times*, 97.1359 (May 1956), 263.
102 Sir Hubert Parry, Mus. Doc., Vice-President 'Inaugural Address', *Journal of the Folk-Song Society*, 1.1 (1899), 1–3 (pp. 1–2).
103 Parry, 'Inaugural Address', p. 3.
104 Georgina Boyes, *The Imagined Village: Culture Ideology and the English Folk Revival* (Manchester: Manchester University Press, 1994), pp. 26–27.
105 Dave Harker, *Fakesong: The Manufacture of British 'Folksong' 1700 to the Present Day* (Milton Keynes: Open University Press, 1985), p. 171.
106 Ibid., p. 171.
107 Allen Buchanan, 'Institutions, Beliefs and Ethics: Eugenics as a Case Study', *Journal of Political Philosophy*, 15 (2007), 25–45 (p. 30).

22

'NO ART MORE DANGEROUS' – EVE MAXWELL-LYTE AND FOLK SONG

Martin Graebe

Before the second folk song revival of the 1950s, there were very few professional singers who specialised in folk song. In the 1930s and 1940s, Clive Carey, Harry Plunket-Greene, Steuart Wilson, and others sang arrangements of traditional songs as part of a repertoire of mostly classical music. A few others, like Albert Richardson, sang predominantly humorous songs, from or based on the tradition, to audiences who preferred rather lighter fare.

From 1930 until her untimely death in 1955, Eve Maxwell-Lyte made a successful career performing folk songs on the concert platform, on the radio, and in early television broadcasts, though the style of her performances was very different from those of today, lying between the classical and the popular.

Verona Eve Maxwell-Lyte was born in Kensington on 1 April 1908. Her parents were Walter and Verona (Finch) Maxwell-Lyte and she was their first child. Her great-great-grandfather was Rev. Henry Lyte, the composer of the hymn, 'Abide with me'. It was reported that:

> ... she sang even before she talked, her first solo at the age of eighteen months being the popular ragtime 'Yip-i-addy-i-ay'! By the time she was three years old she could sing all the English nursery rhymes perfectly in tune. Her talent for acting also developed early, and while she was still in the nursery she started writing plays which were performed by her brother and sister and herself. [...] Throughout her school career she was invariably chosen for the chief part in the end-of-term plays, and to sing the solos at concerts, and she carried off numerous prizes for singing and elocution.[1]

She came from a privileged background and her name appeared frequently on the lists of those attending society weddings. Like other young women of her time and class, she was presented at court. In the changed society after the First World War, there was no barrier to women of her class entering the musical profession, so she became a professional soprano in her late teens, performing a range of classical material.

Her performances can be tracked through advertisements in national and local newspapers and an idea of the content of her concert programme can be formed from reviews. While learning her craft, she appeared several times on London stages such as that of the Wigmore Hall, but many of her performances were in small towns and village halls. She

Figure 22.1 Eve Maxwell-Lyte in her stage costume
Source: From a publicity brochure (courtesy of the Dartington Trust).

also performed frequently in schools and took part in many charity concerts, some of which she organised.

In the early 1930s, her repertoire shifted in favour of older songs and she frequently appeared in costume, often with her friend, Iris Gibb. There is a short film of the two women performing *The Street Cries of Old London*, made by Pathé in 1931.[2] In the first song, there is a young girl with them, who does not sing. She is identified as 'Meg' and is, in fact, Maxwell-Lyte's sister Margaret Eglington Maxwell-Lyte, then aged 10, but who went on to become an actress. In the same year, Eve Maxwell-Lyte added a number of the songs collected by Cecil Sharp in Somerset to her repertoire. She also joined the English Folk Dance Society, the predecessor of EFDSS, at this time and she was to appear several times in concerts at Cecil Sharp House (Figure 22.1).

The 'Diseuse'

In 1932, she gave a recital of songs at the Aeolian Hall entitled 'Traditional Songs of Many Lands'. The programme included French Folk-Songs, English and French Ballads, English, Scottish, Irish, and Welsh Folk-Songs as well as traditional songs of Germany and Italy. In this recital, she adopted a style of performance that was to become her trademark, that of what was described at the time as a *diseuse* – that is, someone who acted the songs she presented. She no longer wore period costume as she had in the past but adopted a dress for her performances which incorporated a very full skirt with a contrasting lining which enabled her to take on an appearance appropriate to the song she was singing. The Nova Scotian folk song collector, Helen Creighton, reported that:

> There were set ideas about how folk songs should be sung and I was told that, in England, purists objected to the beautiful costume she wore. We loved it and were fascinated by the way she used her voluminous skirts for a shawl at one time when she impersonated an old woman, and to cradle a baby when she sang a lullaby.[3]

The recital was considered a success, though the reviewer in *The Times* had some reservations:

> There is no art more dangerous than that of tricking out folk-songs into a sophisticated entertainment. Miss Maxwell-Lyte, who embarked upon this risky enterprise in a recital at Aeolian Hall on Tuesday night, has certain prophylactics which enable her to keep clear of many difficulties of the bastard art; she is musical, sings in time and in tune, she has that kind of personal charm which evades some of its falsities, and she has a sound taste. Indeed the sincerity of her own attitude emphasised rather than concealed these difficulties of which she did not appear to be wholly aware. […] Miss Maxwell-Lyte has an excellent repertory and she has the makings of a voice. If she would apply herself to the singing rather than the decoration of folk-songs she would quickly put herself among the small number of those who can present folk songs with the concealed art that they require in modern conditions.[4]

In the 1930s, as now, the folk song 'Establishment' had reservations about this style of performance, as expressed in a lecture on 'The Singing of English Folk-Songs' given to the EFDS School at Bridport, Easter 1930 by William Kettlewell, in which he included the use of gesture and costume among his list of 'don'ts', saying that they were 'un-English and unnecessary'.[5]

Her approach appears, however, to have been a winning formula with the audiences for her later concerts and the majority of reviews were favourable. A *Times* reviewer, for example, wrote:

> There is a good deal to be said in theory against the art of the diseuse. In practice it justifies itself if the diseuse invests it with a charm and ingenuity of her own contribution, and it is so with Miss Eve Maxwell Lyte. Her voice is fresh and true, and in this perilous art she knows when to be resourceful and when restrained.[6]

Nova Scotian songs

In July 1938, Helen Creighton was at her home in Halifax, listening to a shortwave radio broadcast from England of Canadian Folk Songs. She was surprised and delighted to hear 'When I Was in My Prime' and other songs that she had collected. She said, 'The voice would fade and static interfered but we heard enough to realise this was a lovely voice and the choice of songs was to my liking'.[7] The singer was Eve Maxwell-Lyte and Creighton wrote to her immediately, saying how much she had enjoyed the performance and giving her the contact details for her English co-collector, Doreen Senior. Maxwell-Lyte arranged to meet

Senior and a note from her was enclosed with a letter from Senior to Creighton, reporting their meeting:

> Dear Miss Creighton
>
> I was simply delighted to get your letter written to me at Broadcasting House, and I was so glad that you had heard the broadcast of Canadian Songs on July 4th and were pleased with 'When I Was In My Prime' which I love and think is one of the most lovely folk songs. I at once got in touch with Miss Senior and was waiting to write until I had seen her – but she is posting a letter to you and suggested I should write a note now to go with hers. […] We have a great plan in hand to do a group of Nova Scotian Songs at my London recital in the Autumn arranged by her.[8]

There is no indication of how Maxwell-Lyte acquired the songs from Creighton's collection, but those she was singing at that time were all from the book *Songs and Ballads from Nova Scotia*.[9] Doreen Senior had brought two copies of this home with her from a collecting trip in Nova Scotia in 1933, one of which was presented to the Library at Cecil Sharp House.[10] It was probably here that, taking advantage of her membership of the Society, the singer discovered the book and a new source of songs. In her autobiography, Creighton says that Maxwell-Lyte told her that 'she had wondered if she should have asked permission to sing our songs but thought "it's the middle of the night; nobody will be listening in Canada"'.[11]

Doreen Senior was a teacher and a trained musician. She had been sent out by EFDS in 1932 to teach English folk dancing at a summer school for teachers in Halifax, Nova Scotia. There she met Helen Creighton and agreed, after the summer school was finished, to go out with her to note the tunes from the singers while Creighton focused on the words of their songs. Their partnership was a success and was repeated in the following years until the Second World War intervened. Their work together was published after the war as *Traditional Songs from Nova Scotia*.[12]

Following the meeting with Maxwell-Lyte, Senior made a number of arrangements of songs from Creighton's book, as well as some that they had collected together during their joint collecting trips in Nova Scotia. Some of these were performed by Maxwell-Lyte at the Aeolian Hall, London on 25 November 1938. The publicity for the concert claimed 'Entirely new programme, including first performance in England of English Folk Songs from Nova Scotia'.[13] One of the attendees at the concert was Helen Creighton's brother, Mac, who sent her a telegram the following day saying, 'Lyte says your songs greatest success of all. Prime [i.e. "When I Was in My Prime"] one of loveliest songs ever collected. Hall Full. Am very proud'.[14] In a letter to Helen Creighton, Eve Maxwell-Lyte said:

> Your brother was so sweet. I think he was *really* pleased about the concert and my singing of the songs. Miss Senior less so – she is a purist and doesn't approve of me acting the songs. – it is a point of view – I do not feel somehow that *you* would mind. I do not do anything much but do not just stand in the orthodox concert fashion and sing. I feel myself and so do many others that I give the songs life and humanity and more beauty than the average concert singer. I wish you *could* see and hear me and pass your own verdict.[15]

Maxwell-Lyte had arranged a long tour of Canada for the early part of 1939. She arrived in Halifax on 7th January of that year and visited Helen Creighton before starting her tour. She gave her a copy of a recording of her singing two songs: 'When I Was in my Prime' and 'The Broken Ring'.[16] Senior was asked to provide arrangements for further Nova Scotian songs for the tour but, because of her teaching workload, she was still working on these while the tour was in progress.

Maxwell-Lyte's tour took her all over Canada, but she returned to Halifax to give a 'Recital of Traditional Songs of All Nations' on 16th March for the 'large and critical audience' of the Halifax Ladies Music Club which had been arranged by Helen Creighton. The concert of 28 songs included 5 from Creighton's collection. Once she was back in England, Maxwell-Lyte sent Creighton her thanks and the gift of two books of Appalachian Nursery Rhymes.[17]

The war years

As 1939 wore on the likelihood of war with Germany increased and, at the end of August, Doreen Senior cut short her collecting trip with Helen Creighton to race across the Atlantic in a ship with no lights showing in case of U-boats. The day after she arrived, she was evacuated, with all the children from her London school, to spend the next three years in Ely. In the early years of the war, Maxwell-Lyte worked as a volunteer, helping to fit gasmasks. But she then became involved in a full-time capacity for CEMA (Council for the Encouragement of Music and the Arts) giving concerts all over the country, accompanied by Joan Davies.[18]

> She sang to audiences in air-raid shelters, while the bombs fell overhead; in rest centres for the homeless in the devastated cities; at midnight and in the small hours to night shifts of factory workers; and lonely communities of evacuees in remote villages. She journeyed, ate, and slept as best she could, and worked hard. It is said that in one year she gave 360 concerts – not, perhaps, a matter for boasting by a professional singer in peacetime, but in those strange years a record to be proud of.[19]

On the afternoon of 25 February 1940, Maxwell-Lyte gave a recital entitled 'Folk Songs of Nova Scotia' at Cecil Sharp House, a few weeks before the building was seriously damaged by a bomb. She sang 12 songs, accompanied on the piano by Doreen Senior. The recital was prefaced with an introductory talk by Senior about her experiences as a song collector with Helen Creighton. The Danish-Icelandic singer, Engel Lund, another great exponent of folk song at the time, was in the audience with her accompanist Ferdinand Rauter and in a letter to Senior after the event, Maxwell-Lyte said:

> Sunday was lovely wasn't it? I don't know when I have enjoyed a concert more, the audience was so absolutely marvellous and praise from those people like Jean Sterling Macaulay, Engel Lund & Ferdinand Rauter is worth having because they really do know what they are talking about and would not say what they didn't mean.[20]

One of the songs that was performed in the recital was 'The Cruel Mother' and Maxwell-Lyte gives us an idea of how she feels about the song in this passage from the same letter:

> ... you know I don't think I make a bad job of it at all. I give *myself* the shudders – perhaps that's why it doesn't come off to you and others, I maybe feel it *too* much myself. It is always an exposure and an exhausting one to sing it well in practice – and I know that if you feel a thing too much it never gets over – That must be it, it only gets across to people who are closely attuned to *me*.

After the war

Maxwell-Lyte appeared on television for the first time in 1934, before she had made a radio broadcast. On 10 July 1939, she gave a recital on BBC National Radio in which she included songs from Nova Scotia and Newfoundland as well as some from European countries, including a Portuguese song collected and arranged by Rodney Gallop. This was the start of a lasting friendship and working relationship. Gallop's arrangements of songs from Portugal and the Basque Country were regularly featured in Maxwell-Lyte's concerts.

As well as her CEMA concerts, Maxwell-Lyte had continued to appear on the radio throughout the war. Television was suspended immediately after the war broke out and was not resumed until 1946. Maxwell-Lyte made her first post-war appearance in the medium in February 1947 with Ernest Lush at the piano for another recital of English folk songs. Her appearances on radio in the post-war period included a regular slot singing folk songs during Children's Hour. She was also involved in one episode of the series, 'English Folk Songs and Ballads', devised by Steuart Wilson.

In 1948, she married Sidney Saunders. They had met before the war, but he was a Lieutenant in The Kings Royal Rifle Corps and was taken prisoner and spent several years in a German prison camp. He was, by profession, an accountant but he now became Maxwell-Lyte's regular accompanist. The birth of a son was announced in April 1949, but there is not now any trace of him, and it seems likely that he died in childhood.

Maxwell-Lyte suffered periods of illness but continued to tour. In 1955, she and her husband made a very successful tour of South Africa. After returning to England, they then went on a motoring tour in the French Alps, taking with them Eve's sister, Margaret (Meg), who had taken part in the 1931 film of street cries, and had gone on to become a successful actress. On 31 August, their car left the road and struck a tree. The two women were fatally injured and died at the hospital in Grenoble shortly afterwards. Sidney Saunders, who was driving, was injured but survived. Eve Maxwell-Lyte was then 47 years old.

The accident was reported widely and there were a number of obituaries published. *The Times*, a newspaper that had not always been kind about her performances in earlier days, carried three separate items about her, which were much more appreciative of her art. It is worth quoting extracts from them because of the light they throw on her personality and on the reaction of other people to her. The first, published the day after she died, focused on her work with Rodney Gallop, who had been strongly associated with the EFDSS.

> Her interpretations of the many lovely songs collected by the late Rodney Gallop in the Basque country, Portugal, Spain, and Greece were notable. She took the care to achieve authentic renderings, using dialect and at times the peasant singer's uncultivated quality of tone. The results were often almost as dramatic as an operatic scena and her recitals at Cecil Sharp House, the last of which took place in March last year, were always memorable.[21]

A week later, in another short obituary, a *Times* reviewer said a little about his personal experience of her:

> The radiance that Eve Maxwell-Lyte brought to the concert platform was not just a stage technique: it was a reflection of her own gay and loving personality, and whether she was before an audience or among friends one always felt a spontaneous give-and-take of warmth and sympathy. She approached her art with sincere humility, and everyone

> who worked with her knew that her nature had no trace of the touchiness and petulance which sometimes beset professional artists. The courage and steadfastness which underlay her charm made her friendship something to be treasured. It was a unique pleasure to spend an evening in her home and hear her running through a pile of folk songs at random, her lovely, clear voice accompanied on the piano by her husband, to whom the deepest sympathy must go out in this double tragedy.[22]

On the following day, a longer item was published, from which I have already quoted. This was a much more considered assessment of her artistic contribution and of the personality that lay behind it.

> London audiences and musicians mourn the death of Eve Maxwell-Lyte. There was no one quite like her in her particular art, dramatic folk song. But it should be remembered that she was personally known and loved by audiences all over the British Isles. She had, perhaps, as large a following as anyone who was not a radio star. During the war years she was one of those devoted musicians who worked "full-time" for the Council for the Encouragement of Music and the Arts (now the Arts Council of Great Britain), and as such she travelled the length and breadth of the country.
>
> [...] What counted, of course, was her personality. She had extraordinary sweetness of nature, and a kind of calm (at least to the outside world) unusual in such a sensitive artist. When other people showed their tiredness in frayed tempers, she was always gay, with a caustic wit that made her an enchanting companion in good times and bad. She looked lovely, and her looks were part of the radiance of her character. All over the country, among people of every degree, she made friends, and they were lasting ones, whom she never deserted in the later years of professional success. It was surely in part this vigorous personality which gave her work as a dramatic singer its special quality. She married, not so long ago. and found great happiness. It is good to know that one of her recent triumphs was a concert tour of South Africa, during which her husband acted as her accompanist on the piano.[23]

The writer in *The Times* was identified as 'M.G.' for two of these and for some of the past reviews in the same newspaper. M.G. was also responsible for the obituary that appeared in the *Journal of the English Folk Dance and Song Society*. For an audience that was more likely to hold strong views about ways of singing folk songs, he wrote:

> There are widely differing schools of thought about the interpretation of folk songs, ranging from the purists who would refrain from any attempt to reproduce a song outside its authentic setting, to the singer who merely uses it as a variation of a repertoire, without any attempt at understanding or feeling for the circumstances which gave it birth. For Eve, a folk song was something organic, not to be imitated so much as relived, and even developed to give enjoyment to those for whom the original form would have been no more than a museum piece. Her own warm humanity enabled her to enter into the emotions and experiences of people of many and varied lands, and to transmit the songs without entirely robbing them of their original character. Many singers have met disaster through using mannerisms which are at their best meaningless, and at their worst embarrassing. Eve's own sincerity was the bond between the original folk singer and the cultivated audience.[24]

Finale

Sixty-five years after her death, Eve Maxwell-Lyte is nearly forgotten. The film clips referred to above are, at present, the only performances by her that are readily available to the public. There are some recordings of her singing in the British Library Sound Archive and there is the tantalising possibility that the recording she gave to Helen Creighton will turn up in the Nova Scotia Archive.

But this style of performance, in a liminal space between Art Music and 'Folk', is long gone and, like Maxwell-Lyte, performers such as Steuart Wilson and Harry Plunket-Greene are as dead to us as the Victorian and Edwardian singers who trod the boards before them. In the years after the Second World War, a new generation of singers created their own folk revival with its own values, repertoire, and styles of performance, taking traditional song and making it their own.

Maxwell-Lyte and others of those years are a link between the two revivals, drawing inspiration from the first and then keeping the songs alive until the singers of the second revival took them up, and re-interpreted them. Many of that generation, my generation, might, as children, have heard Maxwell-Lyte singing songs like 'When I was in my Prime', or 'Sprig of Thyme' on the radio – part of their experience of 'Children's Hour' – and a seed was sown. In our later years, the performance seems rather old-fashioned, but the beauty of the song endures.

Notes

1. Michel Maskiewitz, 'Eve Maxwell-Lyte, an Appreciation', *Eve Maxwell-Lyte, Traditional Songs of Many Lands* (London: The Athenaeum Press, n.d.), pp. 3–4. Publicity Brochure in Doreen Senior Files, Devon Heritage Centre, DS 1 D, Letters, 1940–1941.
2. This film can be viewed on YouTube – https://www.youtube.com/watch?v=6CLpxmPA05g (accessed 4 November 2019). In the film, Maxwell-Lyte is the shorter and more animated of the two women. It is interesting to compare the songs and performances with the sequence accompanying the song 'Who will Buy?' in Carol Reed's 1968 film version of *Oliver*.
3. Helen Creighton, *A Life in Folklore* (Toronto: McGraw-Hill Ryerson, 1975), p. 121.
4. 'Recitals of the Week, Miss Eve Maxwell-Lyte', *The Times*, 24 June 1932, p. 10.
5. W.R.W. Kettlewell, 'The Singing of English Folk-Songs', *E.F.D.S. News*, Volume 2, No. 23 (May 1930), pp. 267–272.
6. This paragraph is quoted in the publicity brochure *Eve Maxwell-Lyte, Traditional Songs of Many Lands*. It is attributed to *The Times*, but I have not been able to locate the article in the on-line archive of the newspaper, in which there are several review articles over the years which discuss Maxwell-Lyte's singing style and that of the diseuse generally. Some of these articles were much more critical of the 'pernicious' art of the diseuse though others such as this place Maxwell-Lyte above others of her kind.
7. Creighton, *A Life in Folklore*, p. 120.
8. Undated note from Eve Maxwell-Lyte to Helen Creighton in Nova Scotia Archive, Halifax MG 2815 no 109.
9. Helen Creighton, *Songs and Ballads from Nova Scotia* (Toronto, ON: J.M. Dent & Sons, 1932).
10. Then known as the Cecil Sharp Library and opened in April 1931.
11. Creighton, *A Life in Folklore*, p. 120.
12. Helen Creighton and Doreen Senior, *Traditional Songs from Nova Scotia* (Toronto, ON: The Ryerson Press, 1950).
13. The four Nova Scotian songs performed at the Aeolian Hall were 'When I was in my Prime' (Roud 3), 'The Kangaroo' (a version of 'The Carrion Crow', Roud 891), 'The Broken Ring' (Roud 264), and 'The Farmer's Curst Wife'. The first was arranged by Elsie Spooner and the last three by Doreen Senior. This was not, in fact, the first performance of Nova Scotian songs in

England by Maxwell-Lyte. The London concert had been delayed and she had given a recital in Petersfield a week earlier in which she had included five Nova Scotian songs.
14 Entry in Creighton's Diary for 31 October 1938, Nova Scotia Archive, MG1 2830 No 2 – Diary 1938–1944.
15 Letter of Eve Maxwell-Lyte to Helen Creighton, 8 December 1938, Nova Scotia Archive, MG 2815 No 109.
16 It is believed that this recording is in the Nova Scotia Archive, but it has not, yet, been located.
17 It is likely that these were the two books edited by Cecil Sharp, *Nursery Songs from the Appalachian Mountains*, London: Novello, 1921 [First Series], 1923 [Second Series].
18 After the war, the CEMA became the Arts Council.
19 'Miss E. Maxwell-Lyte', *The Times*, 9 September 1955, p. 13.
20 Letter of Eve Maxwell-Lyte to Doreen Senior, 27 February 1940, Doreen Senior Files, Devon Heritage Centre, DS 1 D, Letters, 1940–1941.
21 'Miss E. Maxwell-Lyte', *The Times*, 2 September 1955, p. 11.
22 'Miss E. Maxwell-Lyte', *The Times*, 8 September 1955, p. 14.
23 'Miss E. Maxwell-Lyte', *The Times*, 9 September 1955, p. 13.
24 'Eve Maxwell-Lyte, Died August 31st, 1955', *JEFDSS*, Vol. 7, No 4, p. 263.

23

CREATIVITY VERSUS AUTHENTICITY IN THE ENGLISH FOLK SONG REVIVAL

Brian Peters

Introduction

The folk revival in England has always been factional. Those who enjoy old songs, performed in a relatively unadorned manner – let's call them 'traditionalists' – are regularly mocked by modernists who prefer newly written songs or musically daring arrangements. Traditionalists are 'purists' and 'butterfly collectors' who wish to 'preserve songs in aspic' or 'put folk music in a museum', while a shadowy constabulary, 'the folk police', lurks ready to pounce at the first twang of an electric guitar string. The remarkable truth, however, is not how closely traditionalists have followed the model of the vernacular singers they venerate, but how many liberties they have taken. Perhaps we should not be surprised, for as Bert Feintuch has written regarding the revivals in Northumbrian bagpiping and American old-time music:

> The term *revival* implies resuscitation, reactivation and rekindling, and many revivalist musicians assert that they're bolstering a declining musical tradition. But rather than encourage continuity, musical revivals recast the music – and culture – they refer to. They are actually musical transformations, a kind of reinvention. And in reality, each revival achieves its own momentum with its own standard repertoire and styles and its own selective view of the past.[1]

It is difficult to pinpoint exactly the moment when the second English folk revival began.[2] In a fascinating biography of one of its chief progenitors, A. L. 'Bert' Lloyd, Dave Arthur remarks that its history is 'a tangled web of misinformation, disinformation, supposition, contemporary myth, vested interest, hyperbole, ignorance and romanticism'.[3] The American song collector Alan Lomax was undoubtedly an important catalyst, but perhaps the key event was the meeting, probably in 1951, between Lloyd, a well-travelled journalist whose interest in folk song had been kindled by his experiences on an Australian sheep station and in an East Anglian 'singing pub', and Jimmy Miller (later known as Ewan MacColl), actor, scriptwriter, songwriter and political activist.[4] Their working relationship, cemented by a shared Marxist outlook as well as their musical enthusiasm, was the driver throughout the 1950s and 1960s of a new and significant cultural movement that survives to this day, albeit attenuated in its following and crusading spirit. The young performers who led the revival's creative explosion during the 1970s, whether slogging around England's many hundreds of acoustic folk clubs or applying electrodes to the music in the field of folk-rock, were deeply influenced by the practices these two towering characters had established. As the revival blossomed once more in the twenty-first century, their shadow still hung heavy across the new generation.

Lloyd and MacColl created a new sound for English folk song. Both led by example, performing and recording copiously, and were influential in two further ways: Lloyd by passing the material he had researched – and in many cases substantially reworked – to the most accomplished and creative emerging artists, and MacColl through the 'Critics Group', a singers' collective he led with Peggy Seeger, that explored techniques for presenting the songs effectively. Although Lloyd's followers have been the more significant in their hold over revival repertoire, MacColl and Seeger's ideas have continued to resonate through the teaching of their disciples.

Ellen Stekert remarks from a North American perspective that: 'A folksong is a blend of text, tune, style of presentation and function'.[5] I shall deal in detail with the first three, but it is worth remarking in passing on the fourth. Folk song in England had existed over the previous hundred years in the context of mostly rural, working-class life: at home, at work or in the pub.[6] The revival, by contrast, appealed mostly to urban or suburban youth, broadly speaking well-educated and upwardly mobile.[7] Although the folk club concept that was developed in the 1950s shared with rural communal singing a preference for licenced premises, and was certainly less formal than most art music venues, it nonetheless demanded a more conscious performance style than the 'one singer, one song' practice of country pubs.[8] Moreover, the revival's function – at least in the minds of its pioneers – was as much political as social and musical.

Presentation style, text and tune were all considered malleable. The 'correct' way to sing a folk song was endlessly discussed, taught and revised, with multiple styles emerging as the movement developed. Meanwhile, the evolution of a canon of songs that would appeal to a post-war audience in the midst of technological and cultural change was achieved through careful selection and refurbishment. The revival paid lip service to what had gone before, but few of its protagonists even pretended that authenticity was their prime object.

Decisions and divisions

As with any movement driven by a crusading spirit and fanatical enthusiasm, splits in the emerging folk revival were inevitable. The first significant division resulted from a far-reaching decision in the late 1950s concerning repertoire. Many of the dynamic young musicians flocking to the cause came fresh from the skiffle craze; Martin Carthy, Shirley Collins, Ashley Hutchings, Roy Bailey and Sandra Kerr were all former skifflers.[9] Although Lloyd and MacColl performed mostly traditional songs, the 'Ballads and Blues' club they founded in London in 1953 with Alan Lomax and Seamus Ennis, Peggy Seeger arriving in 1956, initially reflected skiffle's American influences and a sense of internationalism, fostering an easy-going attitude in which French, Yiddish or Spanish songs were acceptable and MacColl could sing 'Sixteen Tons' alongside his Scots ballads. This eclecticism, however, did not survive the watershed moment when Seeger, the daughter of folklorists and familiar with black American music, burst out laughing at a young skiffler's performance of Leadbelly's 'Rock Island Line' in a London accent. The heated discussion that ensued resulted in a major change of direction (and of name, to the Singers Club), with the adoption of 'the Policy' which demanded that performers at the club should restrict themselves to songs from their own culture, in their own language.[10] Controversial from the outset, it has been derided as dictatorial, a kill-joy limitation upon the choices of British musicians who might wish to dabble in blues or bluegrass. Nevertheless, the Policy, although formulated originally for one specific folk club, shaped and arguably enabled the entire folk revival.

One effect was to erect a divide between 'traditional' and 'contemporary' repertoires and their enthusiasts. Many 1960s folk club singers were more interested in Bob Dylan or Tom Paxton than in 'Searching For Lambs' and, finding their repertoires frowned upon in 'policy clubs' promoting English song, left for clubs that reflected their own tastes.[11] The traditionalists, meanwhile, had to seek material from their own culture – once they had decided what their own culture was. Sandra Kerr, a Singers Club regular, remains a staunch defender of the Policy:

> It's been misinterpreted as dictatorial bullying, but all it said to people was: why are you singing songs from another culture, why not look at the glories of your own culture and how you identify with it? I was an urban folk singer who was singing American blues, for heaven's sake; why should a 17-year-old white girl from the East End of London be singing 'House of the Rising Sun'? If it hadn't been for Ewan I would never have come to understand that there was a tradition that really related to me. It was crucial; we went looking for London songs, and turned up some absolutely gorgeous material. And the same was happening in Birmingham, Manchester and Glasgow.[12]

The search for regional material was particularly important to the folk clubs of Northern England, and dovetailed perfectly with Bert Lloyd's promotion of industrial songs, as we shall see. Many singers, however, identified simply as English, and mined the rural songs published by Cecil Sharp, Baring-Gould and their colleagues in the *Journal of the Folk Song Society*, thereby embracing the first revival's selective concept of what constituted 'folk song'.[13] Whether the repertoire chosen was national or regional, however, the exploration of traditional English songs was a direct consequence of the Policy.

The rules established, MacColl and Seeger in 1964 set up the Critics Group, a discussion and teaching forum in which aspiring singers like Sandra Kerr could hone their skills through vocal exercises, tuition on technique, and theatrical approaches such as the Stanislavski method, and bring their musical efforts to the assembled company for appraisal.[14] Lloyd kept his distance, and a section of the movement rejected it altogether, feeling that everything was becoming too academic. The singing workshops, the erudite LP sleeve notes, the comparison of variants and the lengthy onstage introductions mentioning Child ballad numbers or describing how Cecil Sharp had collected the song in Muchelney Ham were anathema to those who believed that such self-consciousness was the opposite to the attitude of traditional singers who just 'got up and did it'. This faction, including the grassroots musician Reg Hall, and the Newcastle singer Bob Davenport, refused to accept the belief implicit in the very notion of a 'revival' – that the tradition was essentially dead.[15] For Davenport, context, rather than 'folk' repertoire, was everything, and he would as a matter of principle include popular songs in his repertoire. His relationship with MacColl in particular became incendiary. A meeting at the John Snow pub in London, intended as an opportunity for reconciliation between the belligerents, ended in noisy acrimony, with the influential journalist Karl Dallas reporting that:

> The basic divergence of opinion is not between the Dylanites and the traddies, nor between the purists and the commercialists, nor yet again between the serious students

and the entertainers. The only argument of any significance is between the intellectual discussion wing of the revival, headed by MacColl, and anti-intellectual primitivism, represented by Davenport.[16]

The charge was essentially one of snobbery, as a letter to *English Dance and Song* magazine made clear:

> People in the revival still seem to me to be far too much with Percy in his study, rather than with Bob Davenport and (far too few) other singers in the public bar… This seems to me lacking in humility, as is the notion that the folk are 'wrong' if they sing 'Nellie Dean'.[17]

While reigning in its excesses, the 'intellectual discussion wing' eventually gained the ascendancy, and reverential audiences, fact-filled song introductions and copious sleeve notes became the norm. Nonetheless, Davenport's faction opened a successful club at The Fox in Islington conceived as the antithesis of the Singers Club, in which traditional singers and musicians were welcomed regardless of the purity of their repertoire, and allowed to perform naturally in an informal atmosphere. Peta Webb, one of the revival's most accomplished singers in traditional style, remembers:

> I sang regularly at the Fox. The policy was to book traditional singers and musicians to be part of an enjoyable, inclusive, sociable event. Bob would sing comic and music hall songs as well as serious ballads, and Irish monologuist Freddy McKay was a regular. I found the Singers Club atmosphere rather worthy and stifling; I felt that MacColl and Seeger dominated the sessions too much, and I resented being 'auditioned' by MacColl in the corridor before being allowed to sing one song from the floor. But I flourished in the all-embracing atmosphere of The Fox – it remains the model for the Musical Traditions Club founded in 1990 by Keith Summers, Ken Hall and myself.[18]

The Musical Traditions Club, and similar gatherings which invite traditional singers from England, Ireland and Scotland to perform in an informal setting, may be fringe events when compared with successful mainstream concerts and festivals, but for their adherents they represent the beating heart of the folk revival.

Finding a voice

Divorced from the singing practices of the English countryside, the revival had to find a style in which to sing folk songs convincingly. MacColl, a least, had a strong connection to Scottish tradition, since his father, mother and aunt had all been ballad singers.[19] Lloyd had no familial connections to folk singing, but he had heard it in the wild, having collected songs (controversially) in Australia as a young man, and made field recordings at the Eel's Foot pub at Eastbridge, Suffolk, in 1939.[20] As the prime movers in the nascent revival, it fell to these two to set the direction.

In an article entitled 'The English Folk Voice', Simon Featherstone discusses how MacColl and Lloyd addressed the issue.[21] He contends that, in divorcing themselves both from the drawing-room arrangements of Cecil Sharp and from the American folk revival, they were forced to develop a synthetic style, based on a nasal tone, elongated vowels, tremelo and an undefined quality called 'wah', and proposes that this 'folk voice' inspired Kenneth

Williams' parodic 1960s character, 'Rambling Syd Rumpo'. Unfortunately, the two songs by MacColl and Lloyd cited in evidence sound nothing like Rambling Sid, and MacColl's 'Sixteen Tons' is neither English, traditional, nor typical of his output. Rumpo was no wickedly accurate parody of folk revival singing, but simply a comedian putting on a yokel accent and singing nonsensical but archly suggestive words to well-known folk tunes. Although some folk club singers *have* strayed close to the precipice of self-parody, none sounded like this.

From the outset, pastiching old singers was rejected. Lloyd recommended that 'people find their own forms of competent expression, without having to imitate "old Bob" or "young Sam"' since such attempts would only 'produce a kind of museum atmosphere, which is distasteful'.[22] MacColl concurred, according to Critics Group stalwart Jim Carroll:

> MacColl never pretended to be someone who faithfully and accurately produced what he heard from traditional singers… He didn't attempt to imitate […] and had little time for those who did. Having said that, the first thing he said to anybody who asked his advice was, 'Go and listen to the old men and women singers, take what they have to offer and use it to make the songs your own, and if you feel the inclination, lift the corner and find out what's underneath, that's all part of the making of a singer.[23]

The *raison d'etre* of the Critics Group was to guide inexperienced singers towards an appropriate style. As Peggy Seeger recalled:

> It was an attempt to keep the folksongs *folksongs*, not turn them into classical pieces or pop songs or anything-goes songs. We analysed vocal styles and accompaniment, and, tried to expand our abilities […] so that we could tackle different kinds of songs […] and still keep the songs true to themselves. If we became evangelical and sounded dictatorial, well – that's the way things go. The intentions were honourable.[24]

Recordings of the group's workshops, often led by Seeger with interjections by MacColl, reveal a well-informed and thorough approach.[25] To develop both vocal technique and style, voice exercises were prescribed alongside tuition in breathing, phrasing and the various types of ornamentation. For all the objections raised in some quarters to this micro-management, much of the advice was sound, and the approach remains influential through the work of former group members like Sandra Kerr, a key tutor on the folk music degree course at Newcastle University, and Frankie Armstrong, whose voice workshops have benefited a host of singers.

The Critics did not forbid instrumental accompaniment, Seeger having mastered English system concertina, guitar, banjo and lap dulcimer to accompany herself and MacColl, although 'inappropriate' arrangements like the folk/jazz/world music collaboration of Shirley Collins with guitarist Davey Graham were frowned upon. Outside the group, Lloyd employed as accompanists Alf Edwards, a master of the concertina schooled in variety shows, or the fiddle virtuosity of a young Dave Swarbrick; others, like Shirley Collins and Cyril Tawney, used guitar or banjo. Although no-one could blame these folk pioneers in the midst of a pop music explosion for deciding that unaccompanied singing was unlikely to win a mass following, it is worth noting how profoundly this distanced their performances from a singing tradition in which accompaniment was all but unknown. Apart from the provision of harmonic texture, instruments tended to impose a regular beat upon songs traditionally performed by untutored singers whose rhythm was so irregular that collectors had often been obliged to utilise multiple time signatures to transcribe them. Some revival musicians were able eventually to adapt their playing to something freer, but any idea of strict authenticity was inevitably compromised.

An understanding of MacColl and Lloyd's early approach can be gained from their monumental 8-LP set devoted to the Child ballads, released in the USA in 1956.[26] The material is treated with reverence and deliberation, the delivery is generally stentorian and declamatory, and the pace is unhurried, several of MacColl's offerings lasting over ten minutes. How much of MacColl's style derived from his family is difficult to judge, but his use of hard head tones and the rasp of an exaggerated Scots accent lend his voice a quality unlike that of most traditional singers. Lloyd's contribution reveals his talent as a dramatic and expressive interpreter, but also a tendency to drift markedly sharp in pitch, so that the high notes he relished would become progressively strained. His singing remained perennially wayward, but he was able to adapt it to his advantage in adopting a more conversational style; Peggy Seeger describes his 'lovely voice that could barely hold on to a pitch… like listening to a breeze sing'.[27] MacColl too became less declamatory with time. Possessing an actor's instinct, he would choose his approach according to context, attacking the dramatic and brutal 'Baron of Brackley' with ferocity and gimlet-sharp accuracy, while reserving a softer, more intimate tone for a sly tale of seduction like 'The Beggar Man'.[28] In his autobiography he laid out an exhaustive blueprint for performing 'Lamkin', detailing every momentary 'increase in tempo' and 'infinitesimal pause', while dismissing all charges of self-consciousness and claiming that 'the genuine folk singer' was perfectly capable of self-analysis in matters of style.[29]

Vocal decoration was a topic that exercised the minds of many revival singers. MacColl and Seeger were of the opinion that the singers to be heard in English field recordings were mostly elderly and a bit past it:

> There were much better singers in Scotland and Ireland than there were here – they were mostly old men who had no style left, even if they knew the songs, so we were trying to rehabilitate what might have been the singing style. I taught decoration to get some vocal agility into people, and to make the songs a little bit more interesting.[30]

To provide role models, Paddy Tunney and Joe Heaney, singers from Ireland capable of elaborate vocal ornamentation, were invited to the Singers Club. However, any assumption that traditional singers in England conformed to a straightforward, unadorned style needs to be questioned. Joseph Taylor of Brigg, Lincolnshire, gives the lie to it spectacularly; Percy Grainger who recorded him in 1908, remarked on his 'effortless high notes, sturdy rhythms, clean unmistakable intervals, and his twiddles and "bleating" ornaments'.[31] Taylor was much studied by revival singers, as was Phil Tanner of the Gower, who on his 1930s recordings displays a flair for decoration as well as wonderful exuberance. Other well-known traditional singers like Harry Cox, Sam Larner and Bob Copper were well capable of adding grace notes, mordants or slides to their melody lines, and Lloyd was quick to absorb such devices. Despite opting to sing an alternative variant of 'Henry Martin' instead of Phil Tanner's spectacular version, the ornamentation he added was almost a homage to Tanner.

No revival singer mastered vocal decoration better than Anne Briggs. She became hugely influential, partly because of the platform afforded to her by Lloyd's support and inclusion in his projects, but also because she possessed a remarkable ability to pluck from the air the most elaborate vocal curlicues without apparent effort. Briggs developed her skill independently of the Critics Group, by emulating Isla Cameron, an accomplished singer from MacColl's circle.

> I really went a bit wild on the decoration because that was what I enjoyed doing. It wasn't decoration to me, it was part of the way to sing the song […] it could convey so much more in terms of emotive feeling and atmosphere […] It was an instinctive feeling for the association with […] those old traditional songs that, subconsciously and without knowing a thing about it, I felt was *right*.[32]

Two outstanding female vocalists who emerged during the 1970s and remained at the pinnacle of the revival long thereafter, June Tabor and Maddy Prior, were greatly influenced by Briggs. Tabor bought one of her recordings and 'copied it exactly […] twiddle for twiddle', citing it as the principal source of her technique.[33] Not every women singer favoured such elaboration, though. Shirley Collins, who came from a working-class rural family, including several singers, was immediately impressed when she heard Harry Cox and George 'Pop' Maynard at Cecil Sharp House in the 1950s.

> I had grown up listening to my beloved Granddad singing old songs […] and with Harry I felt that same sense of affection and admiration […] I listened to all of Peter Kennedy's recordings of Harry, and the more I heard, the more convinced I was of his absolute greatness, how melodious and graceful was his singing and how perfectly paced.[34]

Wanting nothing to do with the 'pompous and pretentious' Critics Group, Collins sang in much the same way that her mother and grandfather had, using her own accent, a soft, natural tone, and only occasional decorations, believing that the English style was essentially 'restrained and unadorned'.[35] Despite a long absence from performing, her recordings enjoyed a fresh burst of popularity in the twenty-first century, becoming a significant influence on young singers.

The outstanding male performers of the revival during the 1960s and 1970s, such as Martin Carthy, Louis Killen and Nic Jones, tended towards head tones, decoration and pitching towards the upper end of their ranges. Cyril Tawney, however, a significant interpreter of traditional song as well as a songwriter, stood apart in his use of a largely unembellished and mellow baritone owing more to Burl Ives than MacColl. Peter Bellamy was the opposite, pitching his songs coruscatingly high and showering his listeners with ornaments, 'bleats' and other vocal tricks learned variously from MacColl, traditional singers from his native Norfolk, and foreign styles such as Appalachian and Blues. He recalled that Joe Heaney had instructed him 'how to decorate, in the bar of the Pinder of Wakefield',[36] and claimed Harry Cox as an influence, though with a caveat:

> I suppose really I was trying to sound like Harry Cox. But I was aware that even if one could do a really good job of trying to sound like Harry Cox, that one was going to get nowhere in terms of communicating with the majority of the people out here now… there has got to be a line which you can walk that embodies the traditional elements but that is still relevant to today. It's no good trying to be an imitator of a style which is archaic.[37]

Compare, for example, Bellamy's 'Betsy the Servingmaid' with the recording by Cox, which Bellamy admitted to having 'altered a lot, not always unintentionally'.[38] The pitch is raised significantly, the pace is increased by 50%, the 'bleat' decoration is used in preference to Cox's occasional mordant and, most notably, the melody is wrested from the major to the Aeolian mode. For all of his study and absorption of traditional style, Bellamy sounded like no English country singer.

Although now revered as a great individualist, during the 1970s Bellamy was one of the chief offenders, according to the folk music press, in the cardinal sin of 'mannerism'. Amongst others brought before the court of journalistic opinion to answer for this crime were June Tabor, Mike Waterson, Nic Jones and Maddy Prior, while Tony Rose was accused of a vocal idiosyncrasy dubbed 'the strangles'.[39] No singer had his mannerisms dissected more thoroughly than Martin Carthy. Reviewing his 'Shearwater' LP in 1972, Karl Dallas acknowledged that Carthy was 'one of our principal stylists', but complained that:

> Unfortunately, a rather sterile sort of formalism has entered into Carthy's work in this period, which has tended to focus attention upon the tricks played by the voice rather than upon the content of what the voice is singing… it would be a very good thing for all concerned if some of our leading singers were able to distinguish between style and mannerism.[40]

What concerned Dallas particularly were the 'upward portamento slides' that Carthy had apparently borrowed from 'Irish tinkers', and which other reviewers felt had infected the style of Maddy Prior too, during their collaboration in Steeleye Span. Eventually, Carthy subjected himself to a wholesale reappraisal:

> At first I did follow Ewan's way quite slavishly, just standing up and delivering the song deadpan – I was almost puritan. I learned to do decoration and all that nonsense, and at one point I adopted an all-purpose West Country accent because I wasn't happy singing like a Londoner, which was nonsense – you need to sing like what you are. It took time to get the mannerisms out of the way. I went into the studio and I delivered what I thought was a great performance of a particular song, but when I went back and listened to it, I was horrified. I woke up to what I was doing, leaving the whole spirit of the thing behind. I realised I'd gone up a blind alley and I had to start again as far as my singing was concerned. On *Because It's There* it was different from anything that had gone before.[41]

It is interesting to compare Carthy's earlier and later styles. The vocal tone becomes less adenoidal, the slides and scoops disappear along with any surviving hint of a West Country accent, the decoration is pared back and one other notable mannerism has been expunged: the pronunciation of the word 'my' as 'me', which became almost *de rigeur* amongst revival singers in the wake of Lloyd and MacColl.[42] Carthy initially embraced the affectation, but it is notably absent in his later work, so a phrase he once rendered as '*Me* hat is frozen to *me* head, and *me* feet they are like two lumps of lead' came to sound less piratical.[43] His earlier style probably did contribute to the generic 'folk voice' that developed amongst some club singers and a few professionals, who adopted exaggerated nasal tones and yokel-esque vowels. Most leading performers, however, avoided it, and were quite different stylistically from one another.

'All folk songs are forgeries'

The history of the publication of folk song and balladry is shot through with high-minded editorial interventions ranging from mere tampering to outright fakery. Thomas Percy's 1765 *Reliques of Ancient English Poetry*, a key text for the English Romantic movement, set the course by subjecting ballads to 'additions, subtractions, alterations, amalgamations and inventions' in order to suit the tastes of the time.[44] Collectors like Sir Walter Scott also collated and edited ballads for publication so that, in assembling his *English and Scottish Popular Ballads* Francis James Child, made it his business to obtain the original, unadulterated manuscripts from which Percy, Scott and others had worked.[45] England's first folk song revival saw further interventionism, Sabine-Baring Gould notoriously bowdlerising or completely rewriting lyrics that offended him,[46] while Cecil Sharp excised bawdy lyrics from his books of songs.[47] Bearing in mind that texts obtained from rural singers were often incomplete or incoherent, the temptation to mix and match versions to produce a coherent lyric was understandable, although there is undoubted irony in collectors professing reverence for their source material while deploying their skills to make it better. The second revival persisted in the practice, presenting an idealised version of each song, as 'the folk' *should* have sung it. As Peggy Seeger explains:

> A lot of the English texts were handed down with imperfections, through the memories of older people: the song had travelled, but not all of it had travelled, bits and pieces of it had fallen off along the way. But you could get books that printed this version and that version, and they showed what that song had been before the bits dropped off, so what Ewan, Bert and I did was to put those pieces back on. It's only what Robert Burns did! Ewan made up tunes when he couldn't find one that he liked.[48]

MacColl admitted that both he and Lloyd had made 'adaptations and borrowings'. Lloyd was entirely comfortable creating in the traditional idiom: when the Singers Club 'Policy' sent its members scuttling to find fresh material, he teased them by making up ersatz 'traditional songs' on the spot.[49] MacColl believed that Lloyd 'lacked the special talent' to become a songwriter, but 'to the task of cobbling […] patches on to an English song, or strengthening a run-down text by rewriting a line or even a whole stanza, Bert brought skill and taste'.[50] Lloyd's interventions, however, went beyond mere patching. An interview in 1974, unpublished until recently, confirms what song detectives who had taken their magnifying glasses to Lloyd's repertoire had long suspected:

> I sing very few songs as I receive them… Old Vaughan Williams once said to me, the practice of altering folksong is an obnoxious one and I trust nobody to do it, except myself… But I do like to alter and remake songs… If a song's going to be nicer if you splice three or four variants of it together and make the story more or less complete, so much the better. It's better than having it hang around as a ruin… I don't feel that, in popular performance, the existing traditional model is sacrosanct. For study purposes, that's quite another matter, of course. If one's dealing with a thing on any plane of scholarship, then it's necessary to be as precise as one can.[51]

Few revival singers would quarrel with this practice – although whether Lloyd lived up to his expressed ideals regarding scholarship is another matter. Modern interpreters of folk songs, and Child ballads in particular, often find the published texts in need of editing or collation. Martin Carthy's epic arrangement of 'The Famous Flower of Serving Men' (Child 106), one of the most dramatic songs the revival has ever produced, is an outstanding example; Carthy set out with a four-stanza fragment:[52]

> The most important thing in a ballad is momentum, and those first four and a half verses are momentum personified; it seems like the ultimate wrong for a mother to actually

seek to destroy her daughter by killing her child. But there was this huge gap in the story, so I hunted through Child, ballad by ballad, to find something to fill it. I lit upon 'The Lord of Lorne and the False Steward', where the lord is betrayed by his steward but he's bound to silence and can tell no human being what the problem is, not even the woman he loves. So she persuades him to tell the horse he's grooming the whole story, and conceals herself so she hears everything. I thought, I'll try and get that idea in. I was writing down odd lines on bits of paper and tossing them on to the floor, then after some months I picked up all the bits, put them on the bed and rearranged them. And there was the song, like it was handed to me as a gift. There is a bit I made up myself, about the milk-white hind – and I'm really happy with that.[53]

Few performers, however, possessed Carthy's imagination. 'Standard' versions of many titles have attracted successive singers like wasps to a jam jar, and often they turn out to have been planted in the canon in an 'improved' form scarcely resembling the original. The revival favourite, 'To the Begging I Will Go' is a good example. MacColl recorded it in 1966, with erudite sleeve notes mentioning its origins in seventeenth-century drama and subsequent popularity in Scotland, before citing 'a version from 19th century Lancashire' as his source.[54] In fact, he had collected it himself in 1947, from Becket Whitehead, an expert in local history and dialect who lived up on the moors to the East of Oldham not far from MacColl's home. MacColl passed it to Carthy, whose 1965 recording inspired a plethora of cover versions by performers celebrated and humble, culminating in an explosive instrumental and vocal extravaganza by big-band festival headliners Bellowhead in 2010. Only two verses in MacColl's version, however, corresponded to what Becket Whitehead actually sang; stanzas mentioning the local towns of Dukinfield and Shaw, and 'noisy looms', appeared mysteriously, as if to cement its Lancashire credentials. Meanwhile, Mr Whitehead's major-key tune, which he performed with brimming *joie de vivre*, was supplanted by a lugubrious melody in a minor key, lending a world-weary and ironic slant to verses extolling the attractions of begging as a lifestyle.[55] What became the revival 'standard' for 50 years bore scant resemblance to anything collected from the man credited as its source, and was surely the artfully judged work of Ewan MacColl himself.

Does this matter, if the result was so obviously successful? MacColl was unrepentant, claiming continuity with traditional practice: 'In a sense, all folk songs are forgeries… All that we possess is a body of texts and tunes in a state of constant change, of evolution and devolution'. Traditional singers, he reminded his readers, had always modified their material; even Harry Cox had learned 'Van Diemen's Land' from a broadside and made up his own tune.[56] The problem was that MacColl and Lloyd were not always frank about their interventions, and many went by without attracting attention:

> Bert didn't acknowledge it, and Ewan didn't acknowledge it. Bert never said where he got them from, and he put his own versions in [his book] as 'folk songs.'[57]

The revival repertoire was riddled with songs like 'To the Begging' that had been altered almost out of recognition from the source material. Even that perennial folk club favourite 'The Wild Rover' was assembled from English and Australian sources by revival musicians, before being transplanted to Ireland.[58] The alterations, carried out with such flair by Lloyd, MacColl and others, did not merely render the songs more attractive and 'singable'; they were part of a wholesale re-imagining of the traditional canon.

Meddling with the modes

The sound of the second folk song revival is coloured by the scales in which many of the melodies are set – scales which do not conform to the conventions of classical or much popular music. According to Cecil Sharp, such modal scales were a throwback to the church music of medieval times and an indication of the antiquity of the songs.[59] The three commonest in English folk song after the major are the Mixolydian – in which the seventh note is flattened, as in The Beatles' 'Norwegian Wood' – the Dorian, and the Aeolian, which share a minor third. In the Dorian, a whole-tone gap between the fifth and sixth notes lends a slightly exotic feel, but in some folk tunes, the sixth is missing altogether, giving a minor tonality without the Dorian/Aeolian differentiation.

Edwardian collectors nursed a passion for the modal scales, favouring them in publications despite a majority of the tunes they noted in the field (about two thirds, according to Sharp) being major. Two-thirds of the songs Vaughan Williams placed in the *JFSS* were modal, while Lucy Broadwood displayed a similar bias.[60] Of Sharp's *One Hundred English Folk Songs* only 43% were major, the author admitting in one case that 'I have taken down fifteen different versions of this song, but the tune given in the text is the only one that is modal'.[61] This favouritism might have reflected the influence of survivalist doctrines (assuming 'modal' equalled 'ancient'), a preference for the unusual, or mere aesthetics. As a composer, Vaughan Williams certainly valued the modes: his *Folk Song Suite* contains twice as many Dorian and Aeolian tunes as major ones, while the *Norfolk Rhapsody* is built on three modal airs. Delius' Brigg Fair borrows a tune from Joseph Taylor rendered strikingly Dorian as a result of a mistranscription by Grainger.

The second revival was no less infatuated. Although Lloyd sniffed in his seminal book *Folk Song in England* that, 'A kind of fetishism attaches to the manner of folk song modes, especially among younger students', he nonetheless carefully explained modal theory in Sharpian style.[62] In *The Penguin Book of English Folk Songs*, a hugely important source of material for revival singers, co-editors Lloyd and Vaughan Williams made selections that favoured the modes no less than Sharp's had.[63] As a performer, Lloyd was very conscious of melodic characteristics, adding a modal analysis of each song to the sleeve notes of one album,[64] and he also allowed his preferences to influence his theorising. Vic Gammon, scrutinising Lloyd's claim that a profound change had occurred in English vernacular song around 1750, from 'square, robust, common-chord-based' airs, to tunes which tended to 'wander along with no clear idea of which direction to take', concluded that such wayward tunes, while quite rare in oral tradition, actually characterised Lloyd's own repertoire.[65] But Lloyd was not merely winnowing the collections for the tunes in minor modes, with wide pitch ranges, unusual contours and the 'hovering, meandering qualities' he enjoyed so much. He was actively *creating* them.

The LP 'Leviathan', one of Lloyd's most successful recordings, is an atmospheric collection of whaling songs.[66] His sleeve notes recall nostalgically his experiences on the whaler *Southern Empress* 30 years earlier, describing vividly a concert given by singers and musicians amongst the crew. 'I like to think', he mused, 'the sound was a bit similar to what you hear on this record'. One might assume that most of the songs had actually been sung aboard, but only a couple were (supposedly) collected from crew members, while the majority hailed from Scottish or American printed sources and some were scarcely known in oral tradition.[67] Lloyd's reworking of 'Farewell to Tarwathie' and 'The Weary Whaling Grounds' is well-established.[68] He based 'The Bonny Ship the Diamond' on a version from Gavin Greig's collection, changing ship and place names and substituting the original major tune with one in the Dorian mode, creating a revival hit.[69] Another key track was 'The Coast of Peru' a grim and gory account of the slaughter of a sperm whale, collated from American sources and embellished with a few racy touches: the description of Tumbez harbour, famed for its carnal delights, as a place where a man could 'buy a whorehouse for a barrel of flour' is classic Lloyd. But the song's power owes much to the dark and jagged melody – surely original – that batters repeatedly the Dorian sixth and seventh. Stirring into *Leviathan* authentically traditional songs with modal tunes – 'The Cruel Ship's Captain' and 'The Twenty-third of March' – and creating new melodies for 'Rolling Down to Old Maui' and probably 'Off To Sea Once More',[70] Lloyd gave 9 out of the 15 tracks a minor tonality, creating moods of excitement, horror or melancholy, as appropriate. It was a triumph for modal recasting.

Ewan MacColl was no less capable of crafting tunes in these scales, as witness 'To the Begging I Will Go'. Martin Carthy is in no doubt there were others:

> Of course Ewan made up tunes, or refashioned tunes that were already there, and you can often tell they're his He made up the tune for 'Scarborough Fair' and one for 'The Sheffield Apprentice', which is a fabulous song, but it's a Ewan tune… and why not?

'Scarborough Fair' is one of the best-known English folk songs, thanks to its performance by Simon and Garfunkel in the film *The Graduate*, Paul Simon having appropriated it from Carthy's repertoire. Carthy himself learned it from MacColl, who claimed to have collected it from Mark Anderson, a retired lead miner in Teesdale he had encountered in 1947. But although Anderson (actually a quarryman) committed several songs to Alan Lomax's tape recorder in 1951, 'Scarborough Fair' was not amongst them, and suspicion attaches to its provenance.[71] 'The Sheffield Apprentice', as sung by MacColl, has a soaring Dorian/Aeolian tune spanning 13 notes, traditional in style but somehow grander than anything that the archives ever seem to produce.

Carthy himself was equally enchanted by the modes. His 1965 debut LP included not one song in the major, and all of his solo albums over the next seven years showed a marked preponderance of modal (usually minor) tunes, although he sourced mostly authentic versions from *The Penguin Book* and the *JFSS*. The same modal preference applied to the early recordings by electric folk band Steeleye Span, of which Carthy was a member, although Anne Briggs, Shirley Collins and Nic Jones were more even-handed in their melodic selections. Singers establishing a Northern identity had different priorities. Harry Boardman, seeking out industrial and dialect material from his native Lancashire, was content to set his broadside texts and poems to the likes of 'The Girl I Left Behind Me' or jaunty major tunes of his own. MacColl, a former friend, was not impressed, remarking scathingly in a radio programme:

> …his musical judgement tends to be rather less developed than his sense of local pride, with the result that his repertoire is overloaded with items chosen because of their dialect rather than because of their musical value.[72]

Boardman had chosen not to use the kind of grand melodies that MacColl enjoyed, so his 'musical judgement' had to be faulty, for all his undoubted success in reviving Lancastrian folk song. In general, though, the traditional camp in the folk revival was thoroughly seduced by the kind of modal tunes so attractive and exotic that Vaughan Williams once suggested they barely sounded English.[73] Lloyd, MacColl, Carthy, Steeleye Span and other leading lights had set a course that held steady for decades; the 'sound of folk' had been established, and it did not sound much like the public bar of the Eel's Foot.[74]

Colliers and cotton weavers

Lloyd decided that, in order to attract a wide audience, the revival would have to choose its repertoire wisely, commenting to MacColl, 'There's no use beginning with all those old country songs that I sing. We've got to start with something which is much closer to them in time, with the industrial songs'.[75] This was not just window-dressing: both men, as committed Marxists, were dedicated to the idea that folk song did not begin and end with ploughboys and milkmaids, but had been created also by industrial workers, particularly in the coal fields and cotton mills of the North. 'Industrial Song' became Lloyd's 'Big Idea', and the publication of *Come All Ye Bold Miners* in 1952 marked its unveiling.[76] In *Folk Song in England* he insisted that the songs he was interested in were 'quite distinct from the non-folkloric labour anthems' but were made by 'singing miners, mill-hands and foundry-workers' in true folk song style: 'the benevolent ghosts of the fine oral culture of the past are still strongly present in some corners, ready to surprise us with their "melodious twang"'.[77] The majority of the industrial songs he published came from nineteenth-century broadsides, such as 'The Bury New Loom' and 'The Haswell Cages' which were reproduced faithfully. A second tranche came from the pen of 'Pitman Poet' Tommy Armstrong, acclaimed by Lloyd as the personification of a major developmental shift in vernacular song making, 'seen on tiptoe in the half light crowing like a cock to herald the dawn'.[78] A third segment consisted of mining songs submitted in response to Lloyd's appeal in the newsreel *Mining Review* in 1951;[79] Lloyd's *Folk Song in England* also introduced the important pieces 'Rap 'Er to Bank' and 'Jowl, Jowl and Listen', collected by Birtley headmaster Walter Toyn, who also passed them to Jack Elliott, miner and patriarch of the famous singing family. Lloyd displayed scarcely less selectivity than Cecil Sharp with this material, declaring only a minority of the submissions true 'industrial folk songs', while shutting parlour ballads and stage songs outside the coalhouse door.[80] Another problem arose through his determination to prove the continuing vitality of industrial song by blurring the line between vernacular tradition and revivalists actually inspired by his own book. *Folk Song in England* included contemporary songs by folk club artists, and disingenuously presented as the designated tune for 'Trimdon Grange Explosion' a Mixolydian air with which Louis Killen had replaced Tommy Armstrong's original choice.[81]

Further doubts about Lloyd's industrial songs concern their authenticity, most seriously in the case of 'The Recruited Collier'. Supposedly submitted in response to the 1951 appeal by a miner named J. T. Huxtable, Roy Palmer has exposed it as a concoction based on an early nineteenth-century, rurally set poem, its central ploughboy character replaced by a collier and a smattering of mining references inserted to bolster the deception.[82] Garnished with a suitable tune, it was handed to Anne Briggs, who delivered it affectingly on *The Iron Muse*, an important LP of industrial songs for which Lloyd deployed a variety of the day's leading artists.[83] 'The Recruited Collier' ran like wildfire through the folk song world, and was recorded by countless performers well into the twenty-first century, knowledge of its dubious provenance notwithstanding.[84] Even the traditional singer Fred Jordan had a go at it.

The revelation that 'The Recruited Collier' was a fabrication provoked a re-examination of some of Lloyd's other significant contributions to the industrial song canon. *The Iron Muse* also hosted 'The Weaver and the Factory Maid', allegedly supplied to Lloyd by an otherwise obscure denizen of Widnes, William Oliver, who had a 'recollection' of seeing it on a broadside which subsequent research failed to trace. There is in fact plenty of broadside evidence of a composition about a weaver falling for a *servant* maid of lower status, while Lloyd's striking Mixolydian melody in 5:4 time belonged to a related song about the unrequited love of a weaver for a rich girl; the 'factory maid', however, was unknown outside Mr Oliver's memory – or possibly Lloyd's imagination.[85] This did not prevent her from striding in clogs and shawl through the next 50 years of revival covers, from Steeleye Span to Brass Monkey, The Imagined Village and Bellowhead.

The doubts surrounding tracks on *The Iron Muse* do not stop there. 'With Me (sic) Pit Boots On' was credited by Lloyd as 'a Durham miners' version' of a widespread song about work clothes being worn to bed during an amatory encounter. The lyric of 'Pit Boots', however, is so similar – but for a few carbonaceous substitutions – to the comic ditty Cecil Sharp had collected about a rural labourer's apron as to stretch the limits of coincidence.[86] 'The Blackleg Miners', sung by Louis Killen and again highly popular in the revival, relied for its provenance on Lloyd's claim to have heard it from a Mr Sampey of Bishop Auckland in 1949, another source otherwise unknown to folklorists. Only one other variant of the song has ever been unearthed: 'The Yahie Miners', in George Korson's American collection *Coal Dust on the Fiddle*.[87] Although Lloyd suggested that Korson's Nova Scotia version might be a parody of a Durham original, some would judge the reverse more likely.

Ewan MacColl was hardly a bystander in the matter of industrial song. He conferred the title *The Shuttle and Cage* on both a book and an LP containing compositions of his own alongside older pieces from Scotland and Northern England.[88] From his collecting trip to Teesdale came 'Fourpence A Day', which he performed in an uncharacteristic and somewhat approximate Yorkshire accent. 'The Four Loom Weaver', probably the most celebrated song of industrial protest in the revival repertoire, was credited to Becket Whitehead of Delph, although curiously it is not amongst his BBC recordings. The song's history is entangled with a family of dialect broadsides printed around the Manchester area in the early 1800s describing the adventures of 'Jone O' Grinfield', and often highlighting working-class poverty. In *Ballads and Songs of Lancashire* John Harland reproduced several such ballads, noting the popularity of one he called 'Jone O' Grinfield Junior', which began 'Aw'm a poor cotton-wayver, as mony a one knaws'.[89] This piece was printed on several nineteenth-century broadsides, and Lloyd included in *Folk Song in England* a similar text set to the tune of 'The Chapter of Kings', which served generically for all the 'Jone' broadsides.[90] MacColl's 'Four Loom Weaver' is clearly the same beast, but the text is edited radically and emerges leaner and punchier, while the old tune is replaced by a dramatically soaring Dorian air resembling uncannily that of 'Scarborough Fair'. Bearing in mind MacColl's documented practice of recycling existing tunes through judicious tweaks, and his preference for the Dorian mode,[91] one wonders whether Becket Whitehead ever sang 'The Four Loom Weaver' in this form, or whether it owes more to the creative powers of its 'collector'.

Although Dave Arthur believes that Lloyd overstated the importance of industrial song to the revival's success,[92] the notion was correct as far as the North of England was concerned. In Newcastle Johnny Handle, newly converted from skiffle to folk, took to describing rural songs from 'doon sooth' derisively as 'pooks of hay' referencing a phrase from a rural broadside which epitomised a world far removed from the colliery where he had worked.[93] In 1958 he met Louis Killen, newly returned to Newcastle after spending time in London, with MacColl's advice to 'sing the songs from where you come from' ringing in his ears and a copy of *Come All Ye Bold Miners* in his pocket.[94] Having grown up hearing the likes of 'Cushie Butterfield' and 'The Blaydon Races' from C. E. Catcheside-Warrington's *Tyneside Songs* sung at family soirees, Handle was in no doubt what his 'own culture' meant, and built his repertoire on a combination of local vernacular favourites, Lloyd's industrial ballads and songs from his own pen.

In Manchester, Harry Boardman, founder of the first folk club in the city in 1954, was similarly inspired. Like Johnny Handle, he had in boyhood experienced performances of local repertoire as a part of everyday working-class life, with dialect verses by the likes of Edwin Waugh or Sam Laycock featuring prominently.

> They were very well known. At any sort of 'do' – in a church hall or in somebody's house – somebody would inevitably get up and recite 'Bonny Brid' or 'Bowton's Yard', or sing a setting of a poem.[95]

Boardman, like several revivalists a member of the Young Communist League, had heard Lloyd lecture at a Workers' Music Association Summer School in 1951, and been inspired by Lloyd and MacColl's *Ballads and Blues* series on the radio. Encouraged to develop a regional repertoire by Tyneside singers, he was fortunate in making the acquaintance of the colourful local collector Paul Graney, who directed many a Lancastrian broadside his way. Having done some collecting himself in Pennine villages, Boardman, like Handle, developed a repertoire, including dialect, comic, nostalgic and industrial material, and effectively invented 'Lancashire folk song' as a genre. With groups like the Oldham Tinkers showing a flair for new compositions in the style, Boardman curated two LPs, *Deep Lancashire* and *Owdham Edge*, which enjoyed great commercial success. He credited the concept of industrial folk song as his inspiration:

> 'As Bert Lloyd has suggested, there has been very little research done into industrial songs and ballads [...] the Folk Song Revival with its industrial 'wing' has provided an opportunity for a revival in regional dialect songs [...] Lancashire will not be left behind in this revival.'[96]

'Industrial folk song' has, however, been bedevilled by a scarcity of evidence that the soot-stained Victorian broadsides seized upon by Lloyd, MacColl and Boardman ever had the kind of traction in oral culture that Sharpian folk song had in the countryside, or popular dialect material came to exert in the North.[97] It is worth remembering that the rurally focussed song collectors of the Edwardian boom (Frank Kidson being an exception) would have been unlikely to encounter such songs, though we know at least that 'Jone O' Grinfield Junior' was sung by an old weaver in Droylsden, and that the Luddite 'Croppers' Song' was chorused in a pub near Huddersfield.[98] Whatever its traditional footprint, the importance of industrial song to the revival in the North and Midlands was considerable, as the demand for a book like Roy Palmer's broadside collection *A Touch on the Times*, and the popularity in Northern folk clubs of 'Poverty Knock' (collected from an elderly Yorkshire weaver who probably wrote most of it himself) attests.[99] For the historian Raphael Samuel the coalfield ballads in particular represented 'the very basis of the Folk Club movement',[100] but whether Lloyd's claim that *The Iron Muse* truly represented 'songs made by working people out of their own tradition for their own use' is questionable.[101]

Mowers and maidenheads

For the seeker after folk songs that would appeal to young people in the liberated 1960s, sex was an obvious topic. Lloyd was very interested in erotic songs, proclaiming their ancient roots and relishing earthy sexual metaphors he claimed had 'survived more or less unaltered over the last [...] three thousand years'.[102] Following *The Iron Muse*, another concept album was assembled, *The Bird in the Bush* proving at least as influential as its begrimed predecessor.[103] Enlisting Anne Briggs and Frankie Armstrong, Lloyd produced a work that again demonstrated his remarkable affinity for the *zeitgeist*. His sleeve notes were careful to distance the songs from crude bawdiness, and to relate them to the ancient beliefs of a pre-Christian culture:

> The songs were made by men and women in close touch with nature, in tune with the run of the seasons, the growth of the crops, the increase of stock, the fruitfulness of their own kind [...] modern city writers have remarked on the 'disconcerting ease' with which young women in the folk songs become pregnant, forgetting that for societies in healthy condition the arrival of children is vital and joyous because, among other things, it means more hands to help with the work. So it's not surprising that the idea of trying out a girl to be sure of her fertility lies within many an amatory folk song where pregnancy is only unwelcome if the girl is deserted, and not always then.[104]

There is a basic flaw in this argument.[105] The traditional repertoire is replete with songs describing precisely the situation Lloyd brushes aside: the young woman left pregnant by a feckless man and facing a desperate situation alone. In many cases the end is tragic: suicide in 'The Butcher Boy', death in childbirth in versions of 'The Foggy Dew', or abandonment by a ruthless philanderer, as befalls a 13-year-old in 'Abroad as I Was Walking'. No such negativity was allowed across the threshold of *The Bird in the Bush*. The sex was invariably consensual and mutually satisfying, with the women often making the running. Where pregnancy ensued, it was greeted with equanimity; in 'Pretty Polly', a young mother's rueful thoughts about her conception were replaced by Lloyd with a line stating that she 'never regretted' it. As for the sex act, symbols like the cobblers awl, the hunter's gun or the meadow desperately in need of mowing took the place of the copulatory detail Lloyd loathed in the songs 'passed round in rugger dressing-rooms, and bawled by the mock-hearty company who wear their male supremacy like a jockstrap'.[106]

To fill an LP with themed songs that were titillating yet subtle, Lloyd researched widely. The *JFSS* would yield nothing earthy, but unexpurgated texts could be found in the collectors' field notebooks, while the Child ballads and other Scottish and American collections were plundered, and Harry Cox supplied 'The Long Pegging Awl'. Some songs were ingeniously sexed up. 'The Stonecutter Boy' (reset to the Dorian tune of Cox's 'Pretty Ploughboy') was amended to introduce a 'little scream' of female pleasure, the shape-shifting sexual pursuit of 'The Two Magicians' gained a suggestive 'cock pigeon' in place of a dove, and to 'The Old Man from Over the Sea' (from Lloyd's own *Penguin Book*) were added new couplets like: 'My mother told me to show him what to do / But the silly old cod couldn't learn how to screw'. In another invention, the exhausted hero of 'The Mower' was begged by his partner, 'I'll strive to sharpen your scythe, if you set it in my hand'. 'The Bonny Black Hare', one of the most explicit songs on the record, with its 'sporting gun' metaphor, insatiable maid and hunter's limp ramrod, represented a radical rewrite, although Lloyd conjured from the ether an 'immigrant Irish potato-lifter' in Suffolk, from whom he claimed to have heard the song. His lyric was quite unlike the broadside texts, but instead followed almost word-for-word two versions from the Ozark mountain collection of Vance Randolph,[107] while the Dorian melody in a beguilingly irregular rhythm had no precedent in either England or the Ozarks, and was surely Lloyd's own work.[108] Randolph was clearly his main source for 'Pretty Polly' as well.

Only 4 out of the 14 tracks on the record had melodies in major keys, with the majority either straight Dorian or Dorian/Aeolian hybrids. Filtered through the skilled interpretations of the three singers, the effect was to bestow a cutting edge on 'The Old Man From Over the Sea' and 'The Two Magicians', but a shimmering, dreamlike quality on songs like 'Stonecutter Boy' or 'Gathering Rushes'. A similar quality suffused the title track; Lloyd's sleeve notes, after waxing lyrical about the phallic peregrinations of Boccaccio's nightingale and the dove of the Annunciation, remarked that the song's 'symbolic language and mysterious tune create a scene that is sensual in the extreme'.[109] Ignoring a score of light-hearted major versions collected in England, Lloyd had happened serendipitously upon a modal tune from Scotland published in JFSS by Anne Gilchrist for comparative purposes,[110] which provided the perfect atmosphere of bewitchment via Frankie Armstrong's almost mystical rendition. Anne Briggs and Shirley Collins both took up 'The Bird in the Bush', and it became another revival favourite, even reaching the popular historical TV drama 'Sharpe'.

In the final analysis, only three songs on *The Bird in the Bush* are presented without significant emendations to the original text or melody, and Lloyd appears to have made up almost half of the predominantly modal tunes. Martin Carthy & Dave Swarbrick, The Young Tradition, Andy Irvine & Paul Brady, Fairport Convention and Steeleye Span were amongst many leading acts to record songs from the album, while twenty-first-century artists such as Bellowhead and the Dublin band Lankum have also raided it. Other risqué songs subjected to Lloyd's refurbishments, like 'My Husband's Got No Courage in Him' and 'Three Drunken Maidens', were fed into the revival and proved especially popular with women singers.[111] Although not all of his erotic pieces have survived the scrutiny of modern feminism,[112] the spirited and sexually adventurous women who populated them chimed perfectly with the mores of the age.

Faeries and foul fiends

A third key element in the appeal of revival folk was a steer towards dark and mysterious themes more alluring for many than the pastoral adventures of ploughboys and shepherdesses. Popular culture was in the embrace of sword-and-sorcery, the gothic and the macabre, from Tolkein's *Lord of the Rings* to Dennis Wheatley's novels and Hammer Films' horror classics. The revival was not slow to clamber aboard the tumbril as it lurched away from 'The Farmer's Boy' and 'Buttercup Joe' towards a repertoire flirting constantly with the ancient, the other-worldly and the disturbing. Essential to the process was the eager pillaging of F. J. Child's ballad collection. These lengthy narratives are regarded by many performers as the most gripping pieces in the repertoire, none more than the epic ballad of 'Tam Lin' (Child 39), a tale of sorcery, shape-shifting and a triumphant romantic conclusion that can take ten minutes to perform. For the impatient, it epitomises the 'long, boring ballad'; many a drinks-carrier, waiting outside the folk club door for the current song to end, has groaned, 'I hope they're not doing bloody "Tam Lin" in there!' In the right hands, however, it tells its tale so thrillingly that Lloyd's admission to having 'cobbled it together' seems unduly modest.[113] His rendition was inspirational and, according to Carthy, encouraged the younger generation of performers not only to cover 'Tam Lin' itself (Briggs, Armstrong and Mike Waterson took up Lloyd's version, while Fairport Convention and others recorded alternative reconstructions), but to embrace lengthy ballads as a genre.[114]

David Atkinson has written that the Child canon constitutes 'a cornerstone of the postwar English revival repertoire', suggesting that it was precisely the ballads' remoteness from everyday life that cemented their appeal.[115] Their universal themes of love, jealousy, betrayal, heroism and murder are set in a timeless quasi-Arthurian world populated by lords, ladies and page-boys, where every horse is a 'milk-white steed', bloody murders are carried out with a 'good broadsword' or a 'little pen-knife', and the supernatural prowls the shadows. Such tales were catnip to a generation gripped by Tolkein's stories of brave warriors, gilded elves and anthropomorphic trees, and the arrival of Bertrand Bronson's mammoth opus *The Traditional Tunes of the Child Ballads* during the 1960s provided a wealth of British and American material to those willing to undertake the research.[116] Any idea that ancient ballads were the staple fare of English traditional singers needs, however, to be corrected. Although 'Barbara Allen', 'The Gipsy Laddie', 'The Outlandish Knight' and 'Lord Bateman' were certainly popular,[117] much of Child's material was rare in oral tradition, and a large proportion was Scottish. This did not deter traditionalists in the revival. MacColl and Seeger regarded ballads as an anchor for every performance – 'without them, the evening is like a ship drifting in the tide' – and remarked approvingly that young singers were exploring them zealously.[118] MacColl claimed that Lloyd had dismissed ballads as 'boring old songs' and did not rate him as a ballad interpreter,[119] but Lloyd's book declared them 'some of the oldest as well as greatest folk songs we have', and he was scarcely less prolific in their performance than MacColl.[120] The subsequent prominence of Child in the revival was reliant on the next generation of performers, whose reworked versions provided emotional highlights in their repertoires and became trademark pieces. Fans of Martin Carthy would await eagerly his latest blockbuster ballad, be it 'Prince Heathen', 'The Famous Flower', or 'Willie's Lady', while Frankie Armstrong became known for bravura performances of Lloyd's 'Tam Lin' and her own 'Lady Diamond', and Nic Jones put together excellent versions of 'Little Musgrave' and 'Annachie Gordon'. The folk-rock bands of the 1960s and 1970s (whose efforts Lloyd encouraged) regarded the ballads as ripe for dramatic arrangement, while often playing the game of 'one song to the tune of another'. Apart from 'Tam Lin', Fairport Convention set their Appalachian 'Matty Groves' to 'Shady Grove', and 'Sir Patrick Spens' to 'Hugh the Graeme', while Steeleye Span used the melody of 'When I Was a Little Boy' for 'King Henry', and 'The Bells of Paradise' for 'Alison Gross', splattering both with electrified Gothic mayhem.

Although violence and death – the bread and butter of the Child canon – always held a macabre fascination, one aspect was especially favoured. There are many tales of the supernatural between Child's covers, and revivalists homed in with delight on the elfin sorcery of 'Tam Lin', the ghostly revenants of 'The Grey Cock' and 'The Unquiet Grave' and the infernal manifestations of 'The False Knight on the Road' and 'The Demon Lover'. Many of the most spectacular supernatural ballads came from Anna Brown, a native of eighteenth-century Aberdeen venerated by Child as his most important single contributor, the sole source for the witching ballads 'Willie's Lady', 'Alison Gross' and 'King Henry', and the best for 'Thomas the Rhymer'.[121] Many scholars believe, however, that this well-read daughter of a university professor had a hand in the composition of these rare and elaborate texts.[122] Once again the revival had chosen to fish in the remotest backwaters in order to hook the most exotic specimens, which were then assumed to be typical of the tradition. The press release for a high-profile folk fusion project in 2007 declared:

> Every age re-invents the past to its own fancy. When Edwardian song collector Cecil Sharp roamed England, he imagined the country's history as a rural idyll, filled with flower meadows and genial shepherds, even though the songs he found were frequently about poverty, death and fornication with faeries.[123]

Cecil Sharp would never have found a song about fornication with faeries in rural England had he deployed an army of cyclists with notebooks. One wonders who was actually 're-inventing the past' here.

Early enthusiasts for occult subject matter were the influential duo Dave and Toni Arthur, whose 1970 LP *Hearken to the Witches Rune* presented their own versions of supernatural ballads of witchcraft, faeries and ghosts, before the folk-rock bands had cottoned on to the idea.[124] Researching links between Wiccan magic and folklore, they joined a coven organised by 'King of the Witches' Alex Sanders, and wove their ballads together in performance with traditional dance and magical rituals. Bert Lloyd, inevitably, had set the ball rolling. A friend of notorious occultist Aleister Crowley, and an enthusiast for James George Frazer's *Golden Bough*, with its fanciful ideas about fertility rites and human sacrifice, he devoted much space in *The Singing Englishman* to 'witchcults in the Middle Ages' which as a good Marxist he was eager to portray as an oppositional political movement as well as a primitive magical religion. Songs like 'The Derby Ram' and 'The Herring's Head' were survivals of 'dark and sinister hymns' celebrating animal transformations.[125] Perhaps such notions informed his notorious addition to 'Reynardine' of the line 'his teeth did brightly shine', at a stroke transforming an outlaw romance to a vulpine version of the werewolf legend, and persuading a generation of traditionalists that such other-worldly phenomena were the very essence of English folk song.[126]

Lloyd was fascinated by 'John Barleycorn', the 'supremely beautiful [...] song of the death and resurrection of the Corn King, who features in magical cults all over the world'.[127] He returned to the theme when contributing sleeve notes to the Watersons' 1965 LP of seasonal and ritual songs, *Frost and Fire*, for which he had supplied much of the material, including a version of 'John Barleycorn' from Sharp's collection with another fine Dorian tune. His writings contributed significantly to a perceived connection between folk music and paganism; 'John Barleycorn' plays a 'totemic' role in modern pagan rituals, despite the song post-dating the end of paganism by 800 years.[128] The same spirit informs the twenty-first-century musical sub-genre known as 'dark folk' or 'wyrdfolk', in which relatively young bands perform atmospheric and ethereal pieces, old and new, again regarding 'John Barleycorn' as a key text.[129] The knot was sealed in the public mind by the 1973 horror film *The Wicker Man*, in which traditional customs hailing from diverse parts of the British Isles, from sword dancing to a Padstow-style hobby horse, were thrown together on a remote Scottish island to a soundtrack of risible folk song pastiches, before a climactic human sacrifice. As one critic noted, 'the effect is one of a folkloric amusement park'.[130]

This sense of strangeness permeated the revival, Karl Dallas writing that 'Anne Briggs takes us into [an] unreal world, where madness chatters round the corner'.[131] It was facilitated too by the sound of the music. Minor tonalities can provoke various emotional responses, but they fit particularly well with tales of violent death and strange manifestations in the darkness. Where traditional singer Sam Larner saw no incongruity in singing the grisly ghost ballad 'Pretty Polly' to an anodyne air from the 'Villikins' family, revivalists preferred to select variants with suitably sinister modal tunes, or make up new ones to suit the mood. Bert Lloyd's setting of 'Lucy Wan' in the uncommon and alien-sounding Lydian mode rendered the ballad's disturbing account of incest, murder and dismemberment even more horrifying, especially as performed by Martin Carthy and Dave Swarbrick with a queasily droning fiddle. Carthy himself has questioned the tune's authenticity, but declared, 'I don't give a toss, because the feel it generates is, for me, unforgettable'.[132] In the 1970s, Carthy who, like many folk revival guitarists, was using alternative tunings that better fitted modal tunes began experimenting with 'moving the tonal centre' – essentially, accompanying the song in a different key from that suggested by its starting and end notes.

> I heard Ewan singing 'The Broomfield Hill' with Peggy playing dulcimer – the tune was in D but the tonal centre was G, and I was completely thrilled by it. I've done it with a few songs over the years, and it really changes the character of a tune; it darkens the whole thing. Changing the tonal centre can inject a bit of mystery even into a simple song.[133]

The extent to which lyrical and musical strangeness had seduced the revival became clear when Steve Roud and Julia Bishop brought out *The New Penguin Book of English Folk Songs* in 2013 having, unlike previous compilers, selected songs according to their statistical popularity in oral tradition. Child ballads were markedly less prominent than in Sharp's or the original *Penguin Book* collections, and optimistic major scales accounted for 80% of the tunes. One astute reviewer, admiring the scholarship but missing the 'eerie, ambiguous moods' of the usual revival repertoire, commented wryly: 'the corbie croak of the Old Weird England has been lost amongst the larks in the morning'.[134]

Conclusion

It is abundantly clear that the mainstream folk revival in England never regarded as a priority the kind of 'authenticity' pursued by the urban musicians Stekert dubbed 'imitators', who attempt to reproduce accurately specific traditional styles, risking incongruity or even parody.[135] While admiring traditional singers and adopting elements of their techniques, English revivalists from the first began to recast the songs textually and melodically, and to develop their own singing styles, fit for the new context the movement had created. As Canadian performer and scholar Sheldon Posen concluded, 'middle class urban people like myself "had" folklore too, which we performed in our appropriate surrounds involving interaction with peers and reflecting the values of our group'.[136] Although the revival, with its small and shabby venues, ungenerous artist fees and anti-elitist 'floor singer' system, earnestly rejected commercialism, even the most high-minded professional artist was always aware of the pressure to sell records and 'put bums on seats'. Thus, only a tiny minority of traditionalists attempted to build a career on unaccompanied singing, and few practised absolute faithfulness to traditional material. There was instead a commitment to the spirit of the songs, as Peggy Seeger makes clear:

> I didn't come from the mountains – I came from Washington DC. I sing as truly as I can to *who* I am, and that's my function in the world, because I love the songs, and I want to sing them to tell the story. If the text doesn't suit me I find another text – which is a folklorist's nightmare – and I mix them so that the genius of the people who made the songs comes through. Authenticity really comes from where the songs came from.[137]

Martin Carthy believes that the practices of the revival are analogous to what went on amongst traditional singers:

> I've often said that the only thing you can do to hurt a song is not to sing it. Traditional song, music and dance has never been a sort of musical Grade Two Listed Building, it's a fluid thing with a basic truth running through it. There was a whopping reappraisal of traditional song going on when people like George Maynard, or Harry Cox, or Sam Larner interpreted the broadsides – it's been happening for a hundred years, it's what happened in the 1970s, and it's still happening now. I don't believe there's anything

wrong with treating the material as yours and mauling it about, getting it to work, finding a way of marshalling it so that it thrills everybody else the way it thrilled you. It's not about authenticity, it's about truth.[138]

It is true that traditional song in England has always been subject to evolution and change, though perhaps not to the purposeful and wholesale interventions perpetrated by the revival.

And, where Carthy and his contemporaries have generally been transparent about their sources and revisions, he accepts that this was not the case with his mentors:

Neither Ewan nor Bert were ever candid about where their stuff came from, and so much of it was down to their imagination. That could be maddening. If you asked Bert a question about something like 'Reynardine', you'd get a fabulous reply that danced all around it, and at the end you'd ask yourself, 'did he answer the question…?'

MacColl and Lloyd, through their performances, recordings, publications and sleeve notes, established themselves as oracles, so their concealment matters, especially since folk songs were viewed by many followers as a window into the past. Lloyd's *Folk Song in England* remains wonderfully readable, and was considered both an inspiration and the last word in scholarship in the early stages of the revival, but its historical contextualisation is often far-fetched. It retreated from some of the fantasies of *The Singing Englishman* and drew a discreet veil across 'The Recruited Collier' and 'Reynardine', presumably to retrieve some semblance of accuracy, but it included in full 'The Mower' and 'Gathering Rushes' (both credited mysteriously to Lloyd as collector), quoted stanzas from 'The Bonny Black Hare', and remarked without a blush on the sensuality of 'The Bird in the Bush'. The 1978 revision of *Come All Ye Bold Miners*, moreover, retained both 'The Recruited Collier' and 'The Blackleg Miners'. To pass off heavily edited texts and tunes as 'traditional', even to the point of inventing bogus sources, is unforgivable amongst scholars; Winick states baldly that Lloyd 'probably lied' about 'Reynardine', while Steve Roud gives short shrift to defenders who plead, 'He may have told us lies, but he gave us good songs'.[139] Lloyd's high-minded comments regarding the separation of performance and scholarship ring rather hollow today.

However, the flowering of creativity, musical excellence and historical curiosity that the revival encouraged was initiated principally by these two extraordinarily talented if flawed characters, and perpetuated by a generation of musicians whose artistic achievements rested firmly on an openness to innovation and a determination not to be trammelled by strict adherence to some arbitrary notion of authenticity. Although it never conquered the mainstream, the folk revival was a significant cultural movement that enriched many lives. Even as its fabrications are gradually unpicked, its artistic success should be celebrated wholeheartedly.[140]

Notes

1 Burt Feintuch, 'Musical Revival as Musical Transformation', in: Neil V. Rosenberg, ed. *Transforming Tradition: Folk Music Revivals Examined* (Urbana: University of Illinois Press, 1993), pp. 183–193.
2 The 'second revival' was separated by five decades from the first, which was executed by genteel Edwardian enthusiasts like Cecil Sharp.
3 Dave Arthur, *Bert: The Life and Times of A. L. Lloyd* (London: Pluto Press, 2012), p. 205.
4 Arthur, *Bert*, pp. 206–208.
5 Ellen Stekert, 'Cents and Nonsense in the Urban Folksong Movement: 1930–66', in: Rosenberg, *Transforming Tradition*, p. 94.

6 Steve Roud, *Folk Song in England* (London, Faber, 2017), pp. 29, 321–345.
7 Niall MacKinnon, *The British Folk Scene* (Buckingham: Open University Press, 1993), pp. 42–50.
8 Roud, *Folk Song in England*, pp. 594–596.
9 MacKinnon, *British Folk Scene*, pp. 23–24; Arthur, *Bert*, pp. 193–197, Fred Woods, *Folk Revival: The Rediscovery of a National Music* (Poole: Blandford Press, 1979), pp. 53–54.
10 Peggy Seeger, *First Time Ever* (London: Faber, 2017), pp. 186–192.
11 MacKinnon, *British Folk Scene*, p. 28.
12 Sandra Kerr, interviewed by the author, December 2019.
13 Roud, *Folk Song in England*, pp. 119–160.
14 Ewan MacColl, *Journeyman: An Autobiography* (Manchester: University Press, 2009), pp. 305–308.
15 Arthur, *Bert*, p. 269.
16 Karl Dallas, 'Time for a Truce', *Folk Music Ballads and Songs* 2 (1966), p. 2.
17 Letter from Pete Nalder, *English Dance and Song*, 32:1 (1970), p. 32.
18 Peta Webb, personal communication.
19 MacColl, *Journeyman*, p. 341; MacColl's mother can be heard on the LP by Betsy Miller and Ewan MacColl, *A Garland Of Scots Folksong* (Folk-Lyric FL 116, 1960).
20 Arthur, *Bert*, pp. 11–36, 103–105.
21 Simon Featherstone 'The English Folk Voice: Singing and Cultural Identity in the English Folk Revival, 1955–65', in: Susan C. Cook and Sherril Dodds, eds., *Bodies of Sound: Studies Across Popular Music and Dance* (London: Routledge, 2016), pp. 73–84.
22 Barry Taylor, 'Some Reflections': An Interview with Bert Lloyd on 2 February 1974, with an introduction by the author. <https://www.mustrad.org.uk/articles/lloyd2.htm> accessed 4 September 2020.
23 Jim Carroll on the Mudcat Cafe forum, 14 February 2014, www.mudcat.org.
24 Peggy Seeger, 'Ewan MacColl Controversy', *The Living Tradition* <https://www.folkmusic.net/htmfiles/edtxt39.htm> accessed 27 September 2020.
25 Critics Group recorded archive, kindly provided by Jim Carroll.
26 Ewan MacColl and A.L. Lloyd *The English and Scottish Popular Ballads, Vols. 1–4*, Riverside RLP 12, 621–628 (USA, 1956).
27 Peggy Seeger, interviewed by the author, December 2019. His later singing style is well represented on *An Evening with A.L. Lloyd*, Fellside FECD220 (CD, UK, 2010).
28 A.L. Lloyd and Ewan MacColl, *English and Scottish Folk Ballads*, Topic LP, 12T103 (1964).
29 MacColl, *Journeyman*, pp. 341–349.
30 Peggy Seeger, interview.
31 Notes to *English Folk-Songs Sung by Genuine Peasant Performers*, The Gramophone Company, 31st July 1908.
32 'June Tabor Feature', *Swing 51* 13 (1989), p. 12.
33 'June Tabor Feature', p. 11.
34 East Anglian Traditional Music Trust website.
35 *fROOTS* 349 (2012) 25–29.
36 *Folk Music Ballads and Songs* 2 (1966), p. 5.
37 Peter Bellamy feature, *Swing 51* 5 (1982), pp. 8–18.
38 Sleeve notes, *The Young Tradition* Transatlantic LP TRA 142 (1966).
39 *Folk Review* 7:2 (1977), p. 34; *Folk Review* 2:8 (1973), p. 29; *English Dance and Song* 33:1 (1971), p. 36.
40 *Folk Review* 1:6 (1972), p. 20.
41 Martin Carthy, *Because It's There*, Topic LP 12TS389 (1979).
42 For example, MacColl's 'The Sheepstealer' on *The Manchester Angel* Topic LP 12T147 (1966), or Lloyd's 'The Bonny Black Hare'.
43 Compare 'Cold Haily Windy Night' on *Shearwater* (1972) and the 1999 performance with Steeleye Span on *The Carthy Chronicles*, Free Reed FRQCD 60.
44 Roud, *Folk Song*, pp. 53–55.
45 Francis James Child (ed.), *The English and Scottish Popular Ballads* (Boston, MA: Houghton, Mifflin, 1882–1898), 5 vols; the editorial practices of ballad collectors is discussed in David Atkinson, *The Anglo-Scottish Ballad and its Imaginary Contents* (Cambridge: Open Book, 2014), pp. 119–147.
46 Martin Graebe, *As I Walked Out: Sabine Baring-Gould and the Search for the Folk Songs of Devon and Cornwall* (Oxford: Signal Books, 2017), pp. 212–229; see also Roud, *Folk Song in England*, pp. 97–98.

47 Harker, *Fakesong* (Milton Keynes: Open University Press, 1985), pp. 195–197 claims that Sharp's amendments were substantial and unacknowledged; his analysis is contradicted by Christopher Bearman in *The English Folk Music Movement, 1898–1914* (Ph.D. thesis, University of Hull, 2001), pp. 169–177, and by the present author's unpublished research.
48 Peggy Seeger interview.
49 Seeger, *First Time Ever*, p. 191.
50 MacColl, *Journeyman*, p. 291.
51 Barry Taylor, 'Some Reflections'.
52 Child, *ESPB*, p. 429.
53 Martin Carthy, interviewed by the author, February 2020.
54 Ewan MacColl, *The Manchester Angel*, Topic Records LP 12T147 (1966).
55 This and a few other songs were recorded from Whitehead by Seamus Ennis for the BBC in 1952, BBC 18136; see also Peter Kennedy, *Folksongs of Britain and Ireland* (London: Oak, 1975), p. 497.
56 Ewan MacColl, *Journeyman*, p. 291.
57 Peggy Seeger, interview.
58 Brian Peters, 'The Well-Travelled Wild Rover', *Folk Music Journal* 10:5 (2015), pp. 609–636.
59 Cecil Sharp, *English Folk-Song: Some Conclusions* (London: Simpkin, Novello, 1907), pp. 36–45.
60 Julian Onderdonk, 'Vaughan Williams and the Modes', *Folk Music Journal* 7 (1999), pp. 609–626; Vic Gammon, 'Folk Song Collecting in Sussex and Surrey' 1843–1914', *History Workshop Journal* 10 (1980), pp. 61–89.
61 Note to 'The Cuckoo', Cecil Sharp, *One Hundred English Folk Songs* (Boston, MA: Oliver Ditson, 1916), p. xxix.
62 A. L. Lloyd, *Folk Song in England* (London: Lawrence & Wishart, 1967), p. 49.
63 Ralph Vaughan Williams and A.L. Lloyd, *The Penguin Book of English Folk Songs* (Harmondsworth, Penguin Books, 1959).
64 Lloyd and MacColl, *English and Scottish Folk Ballads*.
65 Lloyd, *Folk Song in England*, pp. 229–234; Vic Gammon, 'A. L. Lloyd and History: A Reconsideration of *Folk Song in England* and Some of His Other Writings', in: Ian Russell, ed., *Singer, Song and Scholar* (Sheffield Academic Press, 1986), pp. 146–164.
66 A.L. Lloyd, *Leviathan*, Topic LP 12T174 (1967).
67 Gavin Greig, *Folk Song of the North East* (Folklore Associates: Hatboro, 1963); Gale Huntingon, *Songs the Whalemen Sang* (Barre: Barre Publishing, 1964).
68 Arthur, *Bert*, pp. 192–193.
69 Gavin Greig, *Folk-Song of the North-East* art. LXXXV; for an accurate record, see Basil Lubbock, *The Arctic Whalers* (Glasgow: Brown, Son & Ferguson, 1937), p. 210.
70 Lloyd claimed to have heard it from a crew-mate, Ted Howard of Barry, but other variants collected in the Welsh port are all major.
71 Mike Bettison, 'Tracking Down Scarborough Fair', *English Dance & Song* 75:2 (2013), pp. 16–19.
72 Quoted in Barry Taylor, 'Some Reflections'.
73 Elizabeth James, 'The Captain's Apprentice and the Death of Young Robert Eastick of King's Lynn: A Study in the Development of a Folk Song', *Folk Music Journal* 7:5 (1999), p. 579.
74 Lloyd's field recordings are available on *Good Order! Traditional Singing & Music from The Eel's Foot*, Veteran CD VT140CD (2000).
75 Arthur, *Bert*, p. 208.
76 A.L. Lloyd, *Come All Ye Bold Miners: Ballads & Songs of the Coalfields* (London: Lawrence & Wishart, 1952).
77 Lloyd, *Folk Song in England*, pp. 316–318.
78 Lloyd's sleevenotes to *Tommy Armstrong of Tyneside* Topic LP 12T122 (1965).
79 Arthur, *Bert*, pp. 209–210.
80 Harker, *Fakesong*, pp. 243–245.
81 Jude Murphy, *Heritage and Harmony* (MA Dissertation, University of Sunderland, 2003), p. 85.
82 Roy Palmer, 'A. L. Lloyd and Industrial Song', in: Russell, *Singer, Song and Scholar*, pp. 133–147.
83 A.L. Lloyd (arranger), *The Iron Muse: A Panorama of Industrial Folk Music*, Topic Records LP 12T86 (March 1963).
84 Jon Boden wrote on his blog 'A Folk Song a Day': 'There's something very convincing about this song, regardless of how far Lloyd re-wrote it'.
85 Roy Palmer, 'The Weaver in Love' *Folk Music Journal* 3:3 (1977), pp. 261–274.

86 'The Kettle Smock', Cecil Sharp MSS, Folk Words pp. 1166–1167/Folk Tunes, p. 1176.
87 George Korson, *Coal Dust on the Fiddle* (Philadelphia: University of Pennsylvania Press, 1943), pp. 334–335.
88 Ewan MacColl, *The Shuttle and Cage: Industrial Folk-Ballads* (Workers' Music Association, 1954), p. 29; Ewan MacColl with Peggy Seeger *Shuttle and Cage: Industrial Folk Ballads*, Topic Records 10" LP 10T13 (1957).
89 John Harland, *Ballads and Songs of Lancashire* (2nd edition; London: Routledge, 1875), pp. 169–172.
90 Examples from the Bodleian Library include 2806 c.17(197), Firth c.26(2), Harding B 20(80). Lloyd, *Folk Song in England*, pp. 325–327.
91 Peggy Seeger, ed., *The Essential Ewan MacColl Songbook* (New York: Oak, 2001), pp. 15–16.
92 Arthur, *Bert*, p. 208.
93 Pete Wood, *Johnny Handle: Life and Soul* (self-published, 2017), pp. 17–18.
94 Peggy Seeger recalls Killen staying with her and MacColl, and being so advised.
95 Derek Schofield, 'A Lancashire Mon', *Folk Review*, April, (1975), pp. 4–7.
96 Harry Boardman, 'Now't to do in't Mill', *Folk Music Ballads and Songs* 4, (1966), p. 5.
97 Roud, *Folk Song in England*, pp. 569–584.
98 Palmer, *Working Songs*, p. 131.
99 Roy Palmer, *A Touch on the Times: Songs of Social Change 1770–1914* (Harmondsworth: Penguin, 1974); A.E. Green, the collector of 'Poverty Knock', believed his source Tom Daniel to have composed it, according to his acquaintance Pete Coe.
100 Murphy, *Heritage and Harmony*, p. 79.
101 Sleeve notes, *The Iron Muse*.
102 Arthur, *Bert*, pp. 114–115.
103 A.L. Lloyd, Anne Briggs and Frankie Armstrong, *The Bird in the Bush*, Topic LP 12T135 (1966).
104 *The Bird in the Bush*, sleevenotes.
105 See also Vic Gammon, 'Song, Sex, and Society in England, 1600–1850', *Folk Music Journal*, 4:3 (1982), pp. 208–245.
106 *The Bird in the Bush*, note to 'Pretty Polly'.
107 Vance Randolph, *Unprintable Ozark Folksongs and Folklore: Roll Me in Your Arms, Vol. 1* (Fayetteville: University of Arkansas Press, 1992), pp. 42–43. This source was not available to Lloyd, but Dave Arthur (personal communication) suggests that he accessed Randolph's MS through its editor Gershon Legman.
108 Lemmy Brazil sings 'The Bonny Black Hare' on *The Brazil Family: Down by the Old Riverside* (Musical Traditions, MTCD345-7) to a major tune resembling examples collected by Sharp and Gardiner; the Ozark tune is in triple time and major.
109 *The Bird in the Bush*, note to 'The Bird in the Bush'.
110 *Journal of the Folk-Song Society* 4 (1910), p. 94.
111 Kathy Henderson, Frankie Armstrong and Sandra Kerr, *My Song Is My Own* (London: Pluto Press, 1979), an influential feminist songbook, includes both titles. 'My Husband' was collected by Sharp, but the modal tune is probably Lloyd's; his sexing up of 'Three Drunken Maidens' is described in Graebe, *As I Walked Out*, pp 217–219.
112 The group Lady Maisery rewrote 'Two Magicians' for their CD *Mayday* (RootBeat RBRCD19, 2013), rejecting the revival version's 'predatory feel and connotations of sexual harassment'.
113 Anne Briggs, *Anne Briggs* (Topic 12T207, 1971); Lloyd's tune is from Scots traveller Willie Whyte, on *The Muckle Sangs, Classic Scots Ballads*, School of Scottish Studies: University of Edinburgh.
114 Arthur, *Bert*, pp. 339–340; a live performance can be heard on *An Evening with A.L. Lloyd*.
115 David Atkinson, 'The English Revival Canon: Child Ballads and the Invention of Tradition', *Journal of American Folklore* 114 (2001), pp. 370–380.
116 Bertrand H. Bronson, *The Traditional Tunes of the Child Ballads Vols. 1–4* (Princeton, NJ: Princeton University Press, 1959–1972); Revivalists often used Appalachian variants, e.g. Nic Jones' 'Edward' and 'The Outlandish Knight'.
117 Steve Roud and Julia Bishop, *The New Penguin Book of English Folk Songs* (London: Penguin, 2012), p. 490.
118 MaColl, *Journeyman*, p. 302; sleeve note to Ewan MacColl and Peggy Seeger, *The Long Harvest: Traditional Ballads in their English, Scots & North American variants*, Argo (Z)DA 66–75 (1967–1968).
119 MacColl, *Journeyman*, p. 290.

120 Lloyd, *Folksong in England*, pp. 135–168.
121 Sigrid Rieuwerts, ed., *The Ballad Repertoire of Anna Gordon, Mrs Brown of Falkland* (Woodbridge: Boydell and Brewer, 2011).
122 David C. Fowler, *A Literary History of the Popular Ballad* (Durham, NC: Duke University Press, 1968), pp. 294–331.
123 Press release for *The Imagined Village* <https://realworldrecords.com/releases/the-imagined-village/> accessed 15 September 2020].
124 Dave and Toni Arthur, *Hearken to the Witches Rune,* Trailer LP LER 2017 (1970).
125 Lloyd, *The Singing Englishman*, p. 28.
126 Stephen D. Winick, 'A. L. Lloyd and Reynardine: Authenticity and Authorship in the Afterlife of a British Broadside Ballad', *Folklore* 115 (2004), pp. 286–308.
127 Lloyd, *The Singing Englishman*, p. 28.
128 Andy Letcher, 'Paganism and the British Folk Revival, in: Donna Weston, ed., *Pop Pagans: Paganism and Popular Music* (Acumen Publishing, 2013), pp. 91–109; Peter Wood, 'John Barleycorn: The Evolution of a Folk-Song Family', *Folk Music Journal* 8 (2004), pp. 438–455.
129 Various Artists, *John Barleycorn Reborn*, Cold Spring CD CSR84CD (2007).
130 Mikel J. Koven, 'The Folklore Fallacy. A Folkloristic/Filmic Perspective on The Wicker Man', *Fabula*, 48 (2007), pp. 1–11.
131 Karl Dallas, 'Review of Shirley Collins', *Folk Music Ballads and Songs* 4 (1966), p 18.
132 Sleeve notes, Martin Carthy and Dave Swarbrick, *Skin and Bone*, Special Delivery (Topic Records) CD SPDCD 1046 (1992).
133 Martin Carthy, interviewed by the author, February 2020.
134 Raymond Greenoaken, *Stirrings* 152 (2012), p. 51.
135 Stekert, 'Cents and Nonsense', p. 97.
136 Sheldon Posen, 'On Folk Festivals and Kitchens', in Rosenberg, ed., *Transforming Traditions*, p. 135.
137 Peggy Seeger, interview.
138 Martin Carthy, interview.
139 Winick, 'A. L. Lloyd and Reynardine', p. 301; Roud, *Folk Song in England*, p. 55.
140 My thanks are due to Peggy Seeger, Martin Carthy, Sandra Kerr, Peta Webb, Dave Arthur, Derek Schofield, Jim Carroll, Nick Dow and Raymond Greenoaken. The online resources The Mudcat Discussion Forum and Mainly Norfolk have also been invaluable.

24

FOLK CHOIRS

Their origins and contribution to the living tradition

Paul Wilson and Marilyn Tucker

Introduction

Folk choirs in England have evolved over the past 30 years, a modern adaptation of the solo, unaccompanied English folk song tradition. They have built on the oral tradition by encouraging learning by ear and embraced contemporary modes of learning which themselves hark back to the self-taught traditional singer. Folk choirs embody principles of 'open access', widespread through the folk world, allowing that anybody can, and has the right to, sing.

To understand what a folk choir is, we need to define the terms 'folk' and 'choir', and to understand where choral or ensemble singing fits within the English folk tradition. The folk choir forms a bond: the individual solo singer and the desire to preserve the essence of English traditional folk songs become intertwined with creative artistry and collective celebration:

> … [the way] you sing a song on your own is different from when you sing in the choir […] I don't want [the choir] to sound like a bunch of people belting out folk songs in the pub at a session as well, yes it is fun but who wants to listen to that.[1]

For many, there is little distinction between a folk choir and a community choir, and indeed many folk choirs operate as community choirs. These two forms share many characteristics (e.g. vocal tone and voice pitching), are located within the same pedagogical framework and emerged from similar social and cultural contexts. Both community and folk choirs are typically non-auditioned, open access, non-judgemental entities where every type of voice can find an expression and a place to sing. There is also some shared repertoire, with folk choirs existing on a spectrum with regard to how much emphasis is placed on traditional English folk song. For those calling themselves folk choirs, the defining difference when compared to a generalised community choir is the respect for, and development of, the entity that we have come to recognise as an 'English traditional folk song'.

Through this chapter, we will examine the origins of the concept of folk music, including our journeys as singers and folk choir leaders; how the folk have sung in ensemble, in both formal and informal settings; the skill of the folk choir arranger in preserving the melodic, narrative form of English folk songs, making them suitable for singing by large groups in harmony, and briefly where this inspiration can be found; the cultural and social contexts that gave rise to the folk choir movement.

In this chapter, we present a practitioner's perspective and a personal memoire, incorporating reflection and analysis from ourselves and from colleagues who were with us through the birth and growth of English folk choirs.

Folk music revivals: music of the people

The concepts presented here are discussed in more detail in other parts of this volume, but certain aspects are particularly relevant, in particular the way in which the collectors and scholars presented 'folk' music and the impact this has had on the way we view the genre. The difference between the study of music for its own sake and for its use as raw material (e.g. using traditional tunes in 'classical' composition) is generally understood in folklore writing, but what is often ignored are the practical ramifications in terms of creation, revival and development of repertoires, styles and contexts. This has affected both the evolution of folk choirs and the way they can be interpreted by both the participants and the outside commentator.

Folk is a relatively recently invented genre. The term 'volk' was first used by a German Romantic Philosopher with humble beginnings and a great intellect, Johann Gottfried von Herder (1744–1803), and ever since it has been something of a struggle to define it.

> In Herder's usage, Volk meant low- and middle-class people who […] were […] 'creatures that are closer to nature than scholars.' […] He saw these values most clearly articulated in Volkslieder, [folksongs] a product of the *Volk*.[2]

Throughout the nineteenth century, the search for a 'national' folk music spread across Europe and was taken up in England by Victorian and Edwardian English folk song collectors such as Devon squarson Sabine Baring-Gould (1834–1924) and London music teacher Cecil Sharp (1859–1924) and these collections have set the standard for what we regard as folk song.

The main defining features of the genre for Sharp were continuity, variation and selection. Put these together with the idea of origins, song families and the oral/aural transmission of the repertoire and what emerges is a romantic idea of the folk and their song.

> Folk-song is in verity the product of the people […] English peasantry clung to their ancient melodies, and modified them imperceptibly as time went on, but the current of folk-song never mingled with the stream of classic music in England.[3]

The prevalence of lyrical songs and ballads within these collections, and the individual singers they were collected from have led to a conventional wisdom that English folk song is a solo unaccompanied tradition.

From the early 1950s onwards, there was another folk revival in England, quite often dubbed the 'second' or 'post war' revival. The Topic Folk Club in Bradford in 1956 and the Singers Club in London in 1953 were among the earliest to establish a weekly audience.

Ewan MacColl, Peggy Seeger, Bert Lloyd (A.L. Lloyd) and others formed a loose team of energetic performers, writers, anthologists and commentators who brought a class perspective to the repertoire. They maintained that because it was ordinary working people who provided the overwhelming proportion of the songs, performers and scholars needed to be aware of this to understand and best represent this repertoire.

> I think the best way to understand these songs is to relate them to the times and circumstances they were made up in. These are songs of the common people. How those common people lived and thought, how they went about their work and what return they got for it, and what happened to them in history, is all reflected in the folksongs.[4]

This perspective is a reframing of the earlier definitions of folk song, on the lines of 'Folk-song is in verity the product of the people', and both are included in this overview of what is folk song, to provide an understanding of the historical context of the music itself as being 'of the people', thus lending itself to being sung in greater numbers by the people.

This second revival then also reinforced the notion that folk song is about solo singing and choral or ensemble singing is incidental. Since the English tradition is largely monophonic and unaccompanied, some would assert that a 'folk choir' is an oxymoron.

This concept is not without merit, because it is the nature of folk choirs to take the songs from this solo tradition and form them into choral pieces, while still retaining the melodic nature of English folk song.[5]

Although the term 'folk choir' has not been in common usage, we can find examples of both formal and informal examples of folk songs being sung in traditional choral or ensemble settings over the centuries.

Sharp's folk song collecting in Somerset led him to Captain John Short of Watchet. Sharp not only found him a powerful and captivating singer with an impressive musical ear, but records that he had the ability as a leader to shape and motivate a group of sailors to get tasks finished with a good will on board the old 'yankee' sailing ships; a lesson for any community choir leader:

> This was another skill of the shantyman – to pick the right song for the task in hand: with the correct rhythm and speed for the job, not too long lest the story is not completed and not too short so that an excess of unrelated additional verses has to be used.[6]

One of Sharp and Baring-Gould's major collaborations was to publish *English Folk Songs for Schools* in 1906, which was prepared for singing by groups of children.[7] They identified that folk songs as they received them from the singers could not simply be transferred into this new context, but needed some curation and adaptation to be suitable for groups to sing.

Ralph Vaughan Williams (1872–1958) was both a composer and a folk song collector. He made a huge contribution to the choral singing culture of this country by marrying folk melodies to the words of popular hymns, lowering the musical pitches to be comfortable for the majority of natural voices in the congregations and publishing the results as *The English Hymnal*[8] in 1906. This one volume produced a rise in engagement in singing in England.

At roughly the same time as the post war folk revival was getting under way, the BBC instigated an unparalleled attempt to collect the folk songs of the British Isles employing folk song collectors and this helped a whole generation of listeners not only to become aware of the folk songs of England, but many to aspire to sing them. The radio programme *As I Roved Out* ran for six series between 1953 and 1958.[9]

The folk clubs of the post war folk revival had their peak in the 1970s and early 1980s, giving thousands upon thousands of people a weekly contact with a standard folk repertoire.

Martin Carthy said, 'In the very early sixties there weren't that many clubs, but in 1970 somebody did a count up of clubs in London and there were 400.' Peggy Seeger conducted a wider survey which suggested 'there were about three thousand clubs in the country, just an unbelievable number.'[10]

Through the folk revival, then, we have a generation of people knowing and identifying with this material together with an underlying belief that anyone can do it. This is sometimes to the detriment of an entertaining night out, when the fourth murder ballad in a row gets sung at a singaround evening, but the truth remains that anyone can get up and sing, get applause and occasionally feed back on their performance.

This sense of 'can do' has fed into and now permeates the folk choir movement. The advent of the 'folk choir' as a recognisable entity in the later 1980s might be seen as being built on a generation of audience members and performers alike who had grown up with a strong sense of what our traditional music sounded like through the clubs. Many of the vanguard of folk choir leaders are drawn from this stable of folk singers, and some have been interviewed for this chapter.

The choir as folk and the folk as choir

THE CHOIR: An organised group of singers […] for singing in […] performances.[11]

Further back in history, it becomes more difficult to distinguish between genres of music in general. This is also true of choral and ensemble singing. This section presents some examples of different forms of organised group singing and how they related to an oral tradition, and how informal groups of people have sung folk songs in ensemble either for social satisfaction or as work related to help the task along.

The pictures that we have in books in the fourteenth and fifteenth centuries show us that a small number of musicians often gathered very close to one another singing to God often but also singing to one another.[12]

From the sixteenth into the seventeenth centuries, madrigals notated for group singing in harmony have come down to us intact. However, this seems a far cry from the enthusiastic rumpus we can hear sounding out through the descriptions of psalmody and more informal musical groupings. We have a few fascinating details about group singing, made all the more precious for being really quite rare. 'Already in 1602 Carew had found Cornwall notable for its "Three men songs, cunningly contrived for the ditty and pleasantly for the note"'.[13]

It's not clear whether a folk song repertoire was part of what Madrigal Society members sang for their own pleasure, but sing other things they did. One rule from The Madrigal Society in 1748 enacted that

> All musical performances shall cease at half an hour after ten o'clock, unless some of the members shall be cheerfully incited to sing catches, in which case they shall be indulged half an hour, and no longer.[14]

Among the members of that society were mechanics, Spitalfields weavers and some 'well-versed in psalmody' which was seen as an advantage.

The psalmody movement started to grow from the final decade of the seventeenth century. Psalmody mixed amateur and professional skillsets and attempted to systematise the teaching and engaging of ordinary people in singing, offering harmony singing for mass participation. Many psalmody features and practices resonate with modern folk choirs: itinerant singing leaders, regular choir rehearsals, published books of music and writings on pitching and voice production. Most interesting for modern folk choir leaders is the way the vocal harmony parts were offered and arranged. In the psalmody movement, two- and three-part arrangements were common with the tenor voice in the middle often taking the tune and the whole arrangement transposed up or down or simplified to suit the voices available.[15]

Local Christmas carol traditions present a crossroads where harmony singing which had been started for religious purposes then found a life outside the church.

> The mid 18th century saw a beginning of the spirit of independence that later so vexed the clergy, many of them suspicious from the start of singing societies propensity to exercise their hobby in gatherings separate from worship and beyond the confines of the parish, for, like bell-ringers, neighbouring groups visited each other's turf.[16]

There are some pieces which are still sung by choirs as part of their 'folk carols' repertoire – for example, 'Hark The Glad Sound', and the tune for 'While Shepherds Watched' known as 'Cranbrook', also used for the secular Yorkshire folk song 'On Ilkley Moor Baht 'At'. Local carol groups may still identify a tune to each other by calling out the place name associated with the tune. It is of further interest that these tunes have occasionally picked up local alternative nicknames, for example around Dunster in Somerset the tune 'Lyngham' for 'While Shepherds Watched' is referred to as 'The Roller'.

Singing at work

There are strong examples through history of groups of people singing at work, or attendant on work. The earliest of these is generally taken to be the ox-driving songs from the thirteenth-century *Fleta*.

There are the songs recorded from many occupations: for example, group singing while quarrying stone, deep sea sailing, shearing sheep, waulking tweed or weaving cloth.

> Handloom weavers formed their own musical societies. They would re-arrange their working hours to rehearse and would practise musical pieces whilst working, propping up musical scores where they could be seen from the looms.[17]

Harvesting the hops in Kent in August and September every year, was like a holiday for some and they made it into a social and musical one. We have much oral history and many commercially published folk song collections from Gipsies and Travellers, showing how they and the East End Londoners sang as they harvested this crop.

> In the late 1950s, hop picking was industrialised with the introduction of hop-picking machines and the last widespread singing at work culture [...] fell silent.[18]

Speaking of the old-style Exmoor sheepshearing, Fred Winzer, a retired shearer, remembered teams of 20 or 30 shearers all dressed in white with a couple of pairs of shears each travelling around farms on Exmoor. They would shear all day for about a fortnight to get all the farms done within a certain area. They sang during the day's work but the main singing was in the evenings when the host family on each farm would put up a supper for the workers.

Fred recalls that after the tables were cleared 'Some chaps would start the fun and you'd sing for half the night' at the shearing parties at the end of each days work.[19]

Working and singing have gone together for centuries and sometimes a repertoire born of the occupation finds a life outside that community and particular work-space. This comes into sharp focus with the Port Isaac shanty crew Fisherman's Friends.

> A male shanty group of ten or eleven singers, they have achieved runaway musical success on the basis of what seems like a very traditional multitrade portfolio centred on the little village and its harbour and amounting to two occupations per person on average. The Fisherman's Friends harmonic tuning is superb, and at the sustained peak of committed performance on these local fronts, the distinction between amateur and professional has ceased to have any meaning in terms of standard here.[20]

Fisherman's Friends now enjoy large-scale performances, sometimes of national significance. The group do not wear a choir uniform and do not aspire to wear one. They have deep local connections through families and employment and display a loyalty, unity, mutuality and trust which goes way beyond and sits alongside the musical commitment. Fisherman's Friends both rode the rising tide of popularity of shanties and, in turn, spawned a whole wave of shanty crews.

For singing at work, there were often no musical scores, but still there is recurrent evidence that to get through a day's work, singing together helps either with the morale of the workers, overcoming fatigue, co-ordinating heavy tasks or possibly easing the effects of the revelry of the previous night.

Community singing

The First World War fractured many things, including the folk revival movement as it was then developing. Group singing was a huge part of the national psyche during the war either engendered for propaganda purposes from 'central musical command' or used to comment on the situations people found themselves in – songs about the awful food, taking the rise out of the enemy and so on. It is striking that quite a few songs from this period have not only survived but flourished on people's lips with and without the helping hand of any external media.

After the war, there was a perceived need to re-build people's morale and so the National Community Singing Movement came into being, appropriating many of the songs from the earlier revival and providing group and choir singing experiences for huge numbers of people. The *Daily Express*, along with other newspapers of the time, published its *Community Song Book* because it wanted to sell more papers, but the spin off has completely outstripped that initial commercial impetus in terms of both public group singing and longevity.

> The National Community Singing Movement was a distinctive feature of English popular musical life in the mid 1920s. Seen as essentially educational by the individuals who initiated it, it was rapidly appropriated by sections of the press and especially the *Daily Express* as an instrument in the circulation wars of the period.[21]

The *Express* songbook, published in 1927, contains a number of songs now considered mainstream folk repertoire from 'Barbara Allen' and 'The Wraggle Taggle Gipsies' through to regional songs such as 'Ilkley Moor Baht' At' and 'Widdicombe Fair'. The heady mix of some 240 songs is completed with shanties, hymns, children's songs and national songs along with the English folk songs.

Over the next decades, we see a number of song anthologies appearing from various societal groups; Scouts, Guides, The Youth Hostel Association, Clarion Cycling and Walking Clubs for example. The contents of these books were a matter for the editor in each case, but we can feel a resurgence of the earlier pre WW1 revival coming through in the choice of songs. The contents of *The Holiday Fellowship Book of Holiday Songs* June 1935 is remarkable for the high number of folk songs which can be classed as traditional English; 'Widdecombe Fair', 'Barbara Allen', 'Early One Morning' and 'Seventeen Come Sunday' alongside the more predictable 'Cockles And Mussels', 'Rio Grande', and 'A-Roving'.[22]

All these initiatives served to reinforce folk song within a community singing movement. But if we examine these anthologies, the vocal arrangements or accompaniments do not conform to a folkloric musicality. They are often presented for unison singing or as conventional Soprano, Alto, Tenor, Bass (S.A.T.B.) vocal arrangements.

Football terraces

The Community Singing movement energised another oral tradition. The *Express* launched Community Singing as a feature of the FA Cup in 1926 and this continued until 1971, when it was discontinued through lack of support among fans. It should be noted here that football terraces are still a place where the folk can be heard singing:

> (Manchester) City fans concocted a song commemorating that great 1956 Cup Final victory that's still sung [...] 'Bless 'Em All' has remained in common currency in football grounds ever since, albeit adapted in rather cruder fashion along the way.[23]

Such parodies were created from the 'bottom up' and taken up and sung by large groups on the terraces and sat alongside the 'top down' initiatives of the original deriving from a published song book.

Folk song in school

For many, the introduction to group singing and folk song came at school, along with playground lore and songs among children as its own oral tradition. These songs were passed around groups of youngsters seemingly unaided by any external media. Alongside this 'bottom up' culture were folk songs presented as a classroom activity. *Singing Together* was started in 1939 as a temporary schools project by the BBC. It ran for 65 years and at its height it was estimated that eight out of ten schools in England were tuning in every week to listen and sing along with the broadcast songs. Songbooks were produced containing lyrics, basic melodies and accompanying graphics. These were mailed out to schools each term and the selection of songs contained a good number of folk and 'folk style' pieces. Many young people learned some folk songs as a result and there is a connection with current folk choirs through certain songs. When the song 'Turpin Hero' was presented to a Devon choir in 2019, it elicited the response from some singers that it was familiar to them through *Singing Together*.

Street choirs

In England, from the 1930s onwards, Communist Party members returning from the Spanish Civil War had heard revolutionary anthems and experienced the power of group singing in Europe. They returned and wanted to create similar choirs over here. Clarion Camping,

Walking and Cycling Clubs sang as they camped, walked and cycled. Socialist holiday associations had been around since the turn of the century at least. It was thus a relatively small cultural and musical step to link these two and this was how the Clarion Choir was formed in 1939.

> My parents would go (during WWll) in the night to the night shifts in the factories and give performances to the workers and then go back home to bed […] and then do their own day's work [..] and I think, particularly at that time, even just singing good honest sort of music (as opposed to singing for a profit) was a political act in itself: to do that for working people.[24]

From that day to this, a movement of street choirs has been singing for peace, freedom, justice and socialism in England, taking in folk songs, protest songs and occasionally pop and classical pieces which chimed with a specific campaigning purpose. Meeting in pubs, as free and open spaces, was undeniably a help to the street choir movement who would typically hold a meeting as part of any rehearsal to focus and fuse thoughts, lyrics, songs and practical action into a musical campaign.

Street choirs often refashioned and reworked lyrics to fit pre-existing tunes for a particular situation or support a certain perspective or campaign. This reworking of lyrics connects directly with the folk singer's predisposition to refashion songs and performances and 'make it their own' reflecting the 'can do' spirit of the post-war folk revival. Community choirs, world choirs, folk choirs and street choirs have all borrowed the technique of re-shaping songs and passing them around, revisiting for themselves Sharp's earlier definitional features of continuity, variation and selection.

> The various workers' rambling and holiday associations […] were less preoccupied with political programmes than with enlarging the individual personality through creative activities, the development of 'fellowship' and a group life which foreshadowed the collectivity of the socialist society for which they were striving.[25]

As part of the same era and a similar socialist impetus, the Workers Music Association was founded in 1936 when five London Choirs met to perform together.

Cultural and social contexts

If we look at the wider context of the late 1980s and early 1990s, several factors provided the right conditions for folk choirs to emerge. The growth of the community arts movement and the eventual emergence of Community Music in its own right with the founding of Sound Sense, the professional organisation for community music in 1989; the popularity of world music; women achieving a more visible presence in the folk revival; a general dwindling of folk club audiences and the dedication of public funds to promote Folk Music Development.

As the 1980s progressed, the community arts movement gathered strength, the magazine *Mailout* was started in 1987 'as a newsletter supporting community arts companies in England's East Midlands. Over the years it evolved into a national magazine'.[26]

Community Arts at this time was mostly dominated by print shops and street theatre, with music not being very prevalent in its own right. Companies like Welfare State International or Charivari did use music but this was usually within a multi-arts context, the leading idea being performance art/theatre. During the early/mid-1980s, Wren Music's co-founders

Paul Wilson and Marilyn Tucker were invited to national community arts conferences to give workshops and talks on how music, and particularly folk music, could be used as a community art. At this time, Wren Music's starting point focussed on finding out what was extant or within living memory in the oral tradition, and stimulating revivals at a neighbourhood or village level.

Later in the decade, there was concern at a national level at the under-representation of folk music within the Arts Council funded organisations, and the Folk Development movement was stimulated: Folkworks in Gateshead was started in 1988 by Alistair Anderson and Ros Rigby and it was quickly followed by others; Traditional Arts Projects (TAPS) by Roger Watson in Southern England in 1989 and Folk South West in 1992 by Eddie Upton. It was Eddie who, as far as we can ascertain, started the first overtly named 'folk' choir in 1987, The Caedmon Choir. Folk choirs quickly became an integral part of these Folk Development programmes, opening up access to singing folk songs to more people, outside the established folk scene.

Alongside the development of the folk choir, interest was developing in other types of folk related initiatives and revivals. The first WOMAD festival was held in Shepton Mallet in 1982. The West Gallery Music Association was formed in 1990 to study, revive and enjoy the sacred music of the Georgian era. People's carrolling traditions, in Cornwall, Sheffield, Derbyshire and Exmoor also gained the attention of folk music activists. Foremost among these endeavours was Ian Russell's establishment of a biennial festival of carols in and around Sheffield from 1994.

The folk scene in the 1980s was changing its attitude to women, and leading folk singers were making strides to redress the balance. The now iconic book *My Song Is My Own* (Kathy Henderson, Frankie Armstrong and Sandra Kerr) was published in 1979 'on the back of a huge wave of optimism and activism which women had spearheaded'.[27]

The voice workshop emerged as a participatory event, led by some of these same female folk singers, where singers were able to explore and find both their physical and metaphorical voices. Voice workshops started to appear at folk festivals but also, significantly, in more community-development type of settings, often linked with the feminist movement. The choir leaders interviewed for this chapter all speak of starting out by running 'voice workshops', where the emphasis was on releasing and finding the voice rather than singing folk songs.

> I came to do a lot more voice production, improvising, body work and therefore shorter songs that I could teach in the shorter time which I didn't feel I could do with songs in English. Most of the Bulgarian songs were relatively short and then I learned a few of the Georgian and then some Italian and some African. The whole voice workshop world moved into embracing harmony songs from cultures that grew up in recent years or decades or centuries with harmonies at the core of what they did.[28]

The relationship between the voice workshop and the folk choir is very close. Much of the vocal technique used within folk choir work is based on the notion of the 'natural voice' as pioneered by Frankie Armstrong, and it is worth noting here the strengths of this approach as it fits with the ethos of inclusivity, and most folk choirs would expect to start a rehearsal with a vocal warm-up linked to 'Body, Breath, Voice' and the use of the natural voice.

Natural Voice is about celebrating the voice you were born with, rather than trying to train it to an ideal of perfection. It's about building accepting, non-judgemental communities that sing together. It's about welcoming all voices into a group without audition and

> ## Case study 1
>
> ### *Wren Music: Folk Choirs: Voices in Common*
>
> In 1987, members of Dartmoor Folk Club run by Wren Music suggested that they undertake a 'Mini-bus Wassail', a glorified pub crawl, singing wassail songs from the west country tradition. This marked Wren Music's first project arranging a traditional song in harmony for a community ensemble, with rehearsals. The Dartmoor Wassail song, a collation of two other wassail songs, was created and arranged in two parts, with male and female voices on each part creating the impression of four-part harmony.
>
> From this, Wren graduated to running a 'Performers Workshop', where folk enthusiasts came together once a week to share their progress in playing and singing, and it was a natural progression to arrange some community concerts for these performers. It soon became obvious that what these performers wanted most was to form a choir, and in response to funding being offered from Exeter City Council, Voices in Common, Wren Music's first ever community folk choir was established in 1989.
>
> The Voices in Common model has grown into other areas of Devon and there are currently five such community folk choirs. These choirs pre-date the twenty-first-century explosion in community choirs brought about by TV programmes led by Gareth Malone, and they presented one of the few non-formal choral singing opportunities, and so acted as much as a community choir as a folk choir. The repertoire reflected this: a blend of traditional English songs, songs from folk choral traditions from around the world, songs in folk style about contemporary issues and some old pop songs.
>
> Some members of the Voices in Common choirs have made the transition into folk club floor singers or professional artists after being introduced to folk songs through the choir, taking us back to the solo tradition.

working from there to make a group sound. It's about making learning by ear accessible to the whole group so that nobody needs to be able to read music.[29]

> It comes from […] Frankie Armstrong all comes from her she's the goddess of community choir singing and this idea that you are not kind of creating an artificial sound but you're working with your voice. And I definitely follow that principle.[30]

Pedagogical frameworks

Contemporary with the growth of democratisation in the arts through the community arts movement, there were different approaches developing in education: formal, informal and non-formal. Informal and non-formal pedagogical models were emerging and gaining currency. The 1990s saw the Organisation for Economic Co-operation and Development (OECD) and the European Union (EU) adopting policies for lifelong learning, and this increased recognition of the informal and non-formal, in turn, gave credence to community-based learning, which included non-formal models of music education, preparing the ground for folk choirs to flourish.

Folk music in general could be described as an autodidactic informal model, where learning is more about the individual or small group of people learning through the oral/aural tradition, often on their own and picking up things as they go along, allowing for great enjoyment but perhaps a lack of knowledge of what real skills and techniques are required. In informal ensemble singing this is where we find football chants, folk club choruses, shanty crews and perhaps Woodcraft Folk camp songs, where a book of core repertoire may be shared. A strong feature of the English folk club scene is chorus singing by the audience. This is classic informal participation. People are free to make up their own harmonies on the spot, and these will sometimes be genuinely innovative. More usually, since innovation is not a required feature of this singing, the harmonies may be taken from a raft of harmony options developed over many repetitions by the same crowd meeting in the same place.

> I think the tradition is probably linear rather than chordal that we've got, based on beautiful melodies that people can sing and we can sing them together in unison easily and we do because that's what folk clubs are all about …[31]

Formal music education is focussed on the individual progressing on specific instruments or voice. Formal pedagogy is defined by being structured and has learning objectives. This approach is represented in amateur choirs by male voice choirs and choral societies, for example, where there is an adherence to the score as written, and the voices within the choir, Soprano, Alto, Tenor, Baritone, Bass are allocated according to standard vocal ranges.

> So I'm still I'm challenging Soprano Alto Tenor Bass, that's an invention from [..] two centuries ago now but you know that makes people pigeon hole themselves. I say 'why don't you go and sing lower than you usually do or higher than usual, you might be surprised.' My interest is in the whole voice and its possibilities, and folk cultures are much more likely to give you the possibility of experimenting and exploring that than things that are for me a bit too sanitised.[32]

The non-formal model allows for the freedom of the individual within the framework of group learning with guidance from professional music leaders. In folk and community choirs, this is illustrated by singers being invited to choose which part to sing (high, middle or low) suggesting repertoire, and arrangements created especially for that particular choir. The role of the professional choir leader/conductor is always respected and the leader is free within this framework to arrange to their own set of rules:

> The other thing is obviously that wider sense of the term folk which was its inclusivity, in that it was for people first of all, not singers first of all. One of the great joys for me, and it still is I have to say, one of the great joys of working in that movement is to see people who do not think of themselves as singers [..] in Werca's Folk and in Sidmouth folk choir (that's another major element of my work) I still have people in those choirs who say 'well I'm not really a singer' but there they are, they've developed, they have confidence they make lovely sounds or they make characterful sounds you know I think that in that sense that's another aspect of the term folk.[33]

There is no conservatoire, no nationally validated qualification and no formal structure which the aspiring folk choir leader can join. This obviously has weaknesses in that there is no standard quality check on what is being delivered. Folk choir leaders can themselves be eclectic in their choice of training. By and large it seems they have to take whatever they find useful from a number of disciplines, methods and organisations. However, there are also benefits in that anyone can set up as a song leader. Some would say this is preferable to the highly didactic and openly dismissive tone of earlier singing manuals and handbooks.

> Singing teachers and authors of these singing manuals would have no compunction about using excessively negative and censorial language. Examples of bad habits or poor practice are cheerfully lambasted as 'terrible', 'painful', 'repellent', 'an ugly habit', 'a serious offence', or 'a sin.'[34]

This reminds us forcibly of the violence done to our national singing culture by such theories and explains the received culture that folk choir leaders often hear from new members. Remarks such as 'I was told to mime at school choir concerts' or 'I was told I was tone deaf' and a host of perceptions which do not become less agonising to listen to the more they appear.

The distance travelled towards 'allowing, empowering, accepting' attitudes is certainly huge and this has helped fuel the explosion of choirs, many of which are partly or entirely based on folk song.

Folk groups in harmony

Combined with these external cultural and social contexts there were musical influences within the folk scene which played a further part in the emergence of folk choirs.

As well as the proliferation of informal group singing with folk club choruses and shanty singing already described, there was more considered harmony singing going on within the folk scene, and groups such as The Watersons, The Young Tradition and Staverton Bridge took inspiration from traditional singers like the Copper Family of Sussex.

The Coppers represented a continuous harmony singing tradition spanning several generations and were inspirational for many folk revival harmony groups.

The singing of the Coppers focussed around two main vocal lines being typically the tune and a lower harmony. These two lines were passed on orally, often from grandparent to grandchild, 'leapfrogging' the generations and guaranteeing the harmony singing continued. The songs were collected in a family song book and provided a valuable connection with a much earlier age.

The Watersons were also a family, Mike Waterson and his two sisters, Norma and Elaine (known as Lal), originally formed the group together with a cousin, John Harrison. The group disbanded in 1966 but re-formed in 1972 and played an enormous part in bringing traditional songs sung in unaccompanied harmony to a huge audience. Individual members especially in the shape of Norma Waterson and husband Martin Carthy are a reminder of their far-reaching influence through albums and performances. Musically, the arrangements seemed quite organic and instinctive, unison singing of the tune expanding into harmony at the ends of lines or where the audience was encouraged to join in.

The three voices of the Young Tradition had a natural division of voices where the lead voice was placed in the middle (Peter Bellamy) a male bass line below (Royston Wood) and female higher line (Heather Wood – no relation). Their sound was ear-catching and self-consciously stylish.

Other harmony groups were to follow. For example, Staverton Bridge were a professional trio who met at music college, and took inspiration from both The Watersons and The Young Tradition. They were performing unaccompanied folk songs in harmony on a national basis between 1972 and 1977. They took a conscious approach borrowing different musical conventions as each song seemed to require. They did also add instruments selectively, but took care to allow the vocal lines to flourish as the main focus. Through professional performances by such groups, many audience members discovered a joy in singing in harmony pretty spontaneously.

All these musical influences combined in the 1970s, to provide an energetic and varied culture built on the central idea of singing English folk songs in harmony, although this was not the norm for people singing together. As Frankie Armstrong has said:

> Even though I made albums with Peggy [Seeger] and Sandra [Kerr] for example we didn't do arrangements as such we might throw in the odd harmony but mostly you know we sang things in unison or solo.[35]

Arranging for folk choirs

For this chapter, the defining feature of the folk choir is the interaction between the repertoire and the vocal arrangement. This marks their unique contribution to a living tradition, in the way in which songs gleaned from the standard folk song collections, and identified as coming from the melodic, solo often narrative tradition, are then arranged for choral singing, to preserve the integrity of both the melodic tradition and the meaning and the story of the lyrics. This is what differentiates the folk choir proper from the classical choir singing folk songs arranged according to conventional four-part harmony rules, the shanty crew singing in unison with improvised harmonies, or the community singing movement of the early twentieth century where folk songs were often sung in unison, with more attention paid to the act of singing than the meaning of the lyrics.

> One of the things about our music if you like is its melody structure, one of the things that differentiate anyways that is its melody structures, the fact that it's modal, the fact it has different time signatures and [...] whole kind of style that is other to classical music and I certainly felt that whatever arrangements of this music I made I wanted melody at its core.[36]

The quality of melodies which abound in folk song collections is just wonderful. Folk song collectors from late nineteenth century were attracted by this. While it is true that many English folk songs are in the common major scale (the Ionian mode), the more 'exotic' minor musical modes were prioritised by the early collectors and have been an enduring fascination for anthologists and composers for well over a hundred years. There are also the open five-note (pentatonic) or six-note (hexatonic) tunes and those ending on a note or cadence which might not sound 'finished' as defined by western classical or pop music soundscapes. As a result of all this, modern folk choir leaders have a sumptuous box of musical variety to choose from.

The rhythmic function of any folk song tune is to carry meaning and allow the lyrics space to breathe and become intelligible and credible. Sometimes, this calls for a steady regular rhythm for a drinking song or easy participation in singing a chorus. Sometimes, this brings forward a wonderful rhythmic complexity, especially with the more lyrical story songs or love songs. Some folk songs move effortlessly into uneven rhythms like 5 beats in a bar because it's the most comfortable fit for the lyrics. There are worksongs, tricky tongue twister songs, seasonal celebration songs and call-and-response songs where the leader may be required to skip or extend a beat. All these and more can give folk choirs access to a rich variety of rhythmic modes without once leaving the very middle of English traditional song.

Some of the lyrics are compelling and provide us with all kinds of insights into other social groups and worlds through a succinctly told tragic or comic story, a riddle song, a lullaby, a wish for good fortune, an annual custom or an expression of exuberance at the end of a job of work. The economy and brevity of many of the songs also recommend them as choir pieces. This echoes the economy and power of ordinary people's speech and is a permanent reminder that the songs grew up often out of a necessity for someone to tell a story, grieve over a loss or give a musical focus to a celebration.

Central to the repertoire of many folk choirs, reflecting the regional nature of folk song itself, are songs with stirring local connections. There exist very localised songs referring to places, incidents, particular trades or regional variations of well-known traditional songs. This gives the folk choir a natural connectedness which is not seen as strongly with other genres of music.

This same regionality sometimes presents a challenge of pronunciation, as dialects and accents have receded in our society, and the majority of choir singers are most likely to speak in Received Pronunciation (RP) English. It is important that we respect the locally correct pronunciation while not turning to parody and mimicking the local accent.

Here is an examination of three traditional songs in folk choir arrangements from three different choir leaders/arrangers.

> 'Whittingham Fair'[37]
> Are you going to Whittingham Fair?
> Parsley, sage, rosemary and thyme
> Remember me to one who lives there
> For once she was a true lover of mine

'Whittingham Fair' is one of the classic ballads of the English folk tradition. It is a close relation to Scarboro Fair famously sung by Martin Carthy and Paul Simon while Whittingham Fair itself has been recorded by Sandra Kerr and others. The theme of the song is a familiar one in folklore. Two lovers set each other impossible tasks and the woman wins, or at least has the last word, and Sandra Kerr created a version with vocal harmonies in 2005 for her women's choir Werca's Folk.

The vocal arrangement Sandra made allows the beautiful melody to be heard. The melody itself is in the Aoelian mode, the 'natural' minor, with flattened third, sixth and seventh degrees of the scale. The tune itself spans nine notes, containing some lovely leaps so characteristic of Northumbrian melodies. There is a close harmony part which weaves around using the notes of the tune, apart from the two highest. The harmonies are built mostly from the notes of the tune, but a third lower part brings in a new note – a sharpened sixth – to great effect. This spins us into the Dorian mode for a note or two and is further used twice to point up crucial moments in the dialogue.

There are nine verses in all and the arrangement takes the listener through a range of musical textures, with the first verse totally in unison, and four of the remaining verses in the three-part harmony described above. Where the story changes and the challenges are thrown down in verses five and nine, the music changes and the arrangement uses the 'canon' technique; voices coming in at different times similar to a 'round'. On a further couple of verses the tune is taken by a different group with the other two harmony groups singing moving drones; long single notes. The whole arrangement gives the tune plenty of space to work and also employs folk techniques – drones, canons and close harmony writing – to enhance the story. The piece is brought to rest on an unexpected final chord possibly implying that the story is 'unfinished'.

Finally, there is a local twist in the pronunciation of Whittingham, where the 'g' is sounded as a soft 'g' like a 'j' This just appears once in the first line, as part of the scene-setting (Figure 24.1).

Figure 24.1 'Whittingham Fair'
Source: Arranged by Sandra Kerr.

Whittingham Fair

2

(music notation, measure 25)

Voice 1: hope he will an-swer as man-y for me and then he'll be a true lov-er of mine

Voice 2: mar-y and thyme He'll ans-wer and then he'll be a true lov-er of mine

Voice 3: ans-wer as ma-ny for me and then he'll be a true lov-er of mine

1
Are you going to Whittingham Fair?
Parsley, sage, rosemary and thyme
Remember me to one who lives there
For once she was a true lover of mine
2
Tell her to make me a cambric shirt
Parsley, sage, rosemary and thyme
Without any seam or needlework
Then she'll be a true lover of mine
3
Tell her to wash it in yonder dry well
When never sprung water nor rain ever fell
4
Tell her to dry it on yonder thorn
Which never bore blossom since Adam was born
5
Now he has asked me questions three
Parsley, sage, rosemary and thyme
I hope he will answer as many for me
Then he'll be a true lover of mine
6
Tell him to find me an acre of land
Between the salt water and the sea sand
7
Tell him to plough it with a ram's horn
And sow it all over with one peppercorn
8
Tell him to reap it with a sickle of leather
And bind it up with a peacock's feather
9
When he has done and finished his work
Parsley, sage, rosemary and thyme
Tell him to come and he'll have his shirt
Then he'll be a true lover of mine

Sequence of singing

Verse 1 - All voices unison tune

Verses 2 and 3 - 3part harmony (Letter A)

Verse 4
Group 1 takes tune
Group 2 drone (ooo) on note D,
    rising to F on the word 'mine'
Group 3 - drone on note A,
    rising to B natural on the word 'mine'

Verse 5
3-part canon (Letter B)

Verse 6 - 3-part harmony (Letter A)

Verse 7 as verse 4 viz:
Group 1 takes tune
Group 2 drone (ooo) on note D,
    rising to F on the word 'mine'
Group 3 - drone on note A,
    rising to B natural on the word 'mine'

Verse 8 - 3-part harmony (Letter A)

Verse 9
3 part canon (Letter B)

Figure 24.1 (Continued)

'The Lark In The Morning'[38]
The lark in the morning awakes from her nest
She mounts in the air with the dew on her breast
Oh the lark and the ploughboy together can sing
And return to her nest in the evening
Return to her nest in the evening

'The Lark In The Morning' is one of those English songs which have a beautifully shaped tune and a pretty constant tonal centre. This opens a number of musical possibilities. Playing the tune against a one-note drone or singing the tune in canon, creates momentary clashes adding richness for the listener. The tune is in a minor mode which is mainly Aeolian, but with a variable 7th and with the harmony lines treating the mode as flexible with variable 5ths and 6ths.

The song itself is typically English and bucolic and talks of courtship and celebration when the day's work is done.

Arranger and choir leader Sarah Owen has used the canon technique to great effect in the choir arrangement of this song and also allowed the tune to flourish and breathe. The arrangement starts with the first verse with all singers in unison. The second verse has the singers in two groups, one group singing the main melody and another group singing the same lyrics and tune but at half speed, joining up on line four to finish together. Verses three and four then spin into full three-part harmony with the tune in the middle, the high part providing a rhythmic drone effect and the low part a moving harmony line which complements the tune. Finally, the first verse is repeated in three-part canon, with sustained drone notes used to finish the canon section and with the whole choir joining in quiet unison at the end of the piece.

The final line of each verse repeats and Sarah has used this as an opportunity to provide optional solo lines – a soloist being asked to sing the first iteration of the line and the choir joining in with the repeat, reminiscent of many a traditional song session in more informal settings. Bar lengths at the ends of some lines are extended to allow the chords to fully sound and the choir to tell the story. This is a perfectly natural technique recorded from many solo traditional singers but here some of these extensions are written out to allow the choir to enjoy this flexibility – a good mix of being responsive and prescriptive at the same time.

This arrangement was created for a massed youth choirs event for Exeter Cathedral, where four youth choirs would meet and after just one rehearsal would perform the song as part of a showcase of Excellence In Singing. It therefore became expedient to add precise performance instructions, including dynamics, speed markings and phrasing and also circulate audio guides, sheet music and lyric sheets to the choirs beforehand (Figure 24.2).

'The Sweet Nightingale'[39]
My sweetheart come along, don't you hear the fond song?
The sweet notes of the nightingale flow
You shall hear the fond tale of the sweet nightingale
As she sings in the valley belo-o-ow
As she sings in the valley below

'The Sweet Nightingale' is arranged to be deliberately closer to what might be heard in a tuneful and harmonious folk club or song session by simply borrowing what is often improvised by a group of singers. The parts have then been reworked and tidied slightly for a choir arrangement. The song tells of courtship, rejection, reconciliation and marriage all in five short verses written as a dialogue between the protagonists. The chorus consists of an extended melisma on the word 'below' and a repeated last line, making it very easy to join in.

The melody is in triple time and a really familiar and accessible major scale (Ionian mode). The arrangement has parts labelled Soprano, Alto, Tenor, Bass. For the short two-line verses, the sopranos sing with the tenors and the altos with the basses, doubling at the

Figure 24.2 'The Lark in the Morning'
Source: Collected by S. Baring-Gould, arranged by Sarah Owen.

The Lark In The Morning

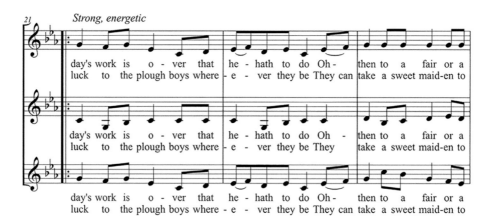

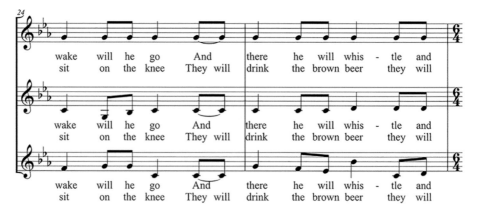

(b)

Figure 24.2 (Continued)

The Lark In The Morning

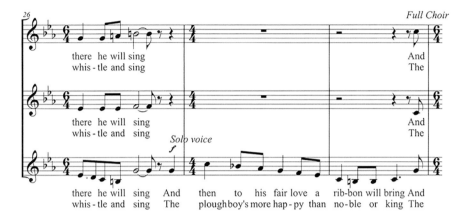

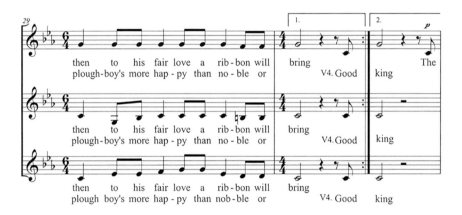

(c)

Figure 24.2 (Continued)

The Lark In The Morning

(d)

Figure 24.2 (Continued)

Folk choirs

The Sweet Nightingale

Traditional Cornish
Arranged Paul Wilson 2005

Only the last verse is scored here, to show how the harmonies come together. If desired in the preceding verses, the voices can be apportioned to underpin the dialogue. The tenors and sopranos hold the tune for the lyrics of the verses.

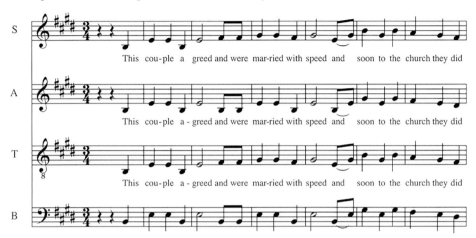

www.wrenmusic.co.uk

(a)

Figure 24.3 'The Sweet Nightingale'
Source: Arranged by Paul Wilson.

Verse 1
"My sweet heart come along, don't you hear the fond song?
The sweet notes of the nightingale flow"
Chorus - "You shall hear the fond tale of the sweet nightingale
  As she sings in the valley below
  As she sings in the valley below"

Verse 2
"Pretty Betty don't fail, for I'll carry your pail
Safe home to your cot as we go"
Chorus - "You shall hear the fond tale . . . . "

Verse 3
"Pray let me alone I have hands of my own
And along with you, sir, I'll not go"
Chorus - "For to hear the fond tale . . . . "

Verse 4
"Come sit yourself down with me on the ground
On the banks where the primroses grow"
Chorus - "You shall hear the fond tale . . . . "

Verse 5
This couple agreed and were married with speed
And soon to the church they did go
Chorus - No more she's afraid for to walk in the shade
  Or to sit in the valley below
  Or to sit in the valley below

www.wrenmusic.co.uk

(b)

Figure 24.3 (Continued)

Folk choirs

octave a two-part arrangement. This also allows the voices to be split in different ways to underpin the dialogue.

The simple chorus then fans out to four parts, the sopranos taking the tune, with the altos often running in thirds below. The tenors have been given a high held tonic note, before coming down to a classic 5–4–3 suspension for the last chord. The basses have an easy and satisfying I, IV, V type line with short ascending and descending scale passages.

The parts are labelled for the four voices but the actual harmony parts are closer than is often the case in classical repertoire. The lowest, the bass, is not very low and the highest, the soprano, not very high. The harmonies are not complex and can be quickly taught and sung successfully. This gives any newcomers to folk song a safe place to stand and the thrill of experiencing the closeness of the harmonies in a folk choir (Figure 24.3).

World harmonies

In writing harmonies for English folk choirs, arrangers have been able to draw on examples from the world cultures where harmony singing exists within a folkloric tradition. The discovery of harmony singing of folk choirs from other countries has excited folk choirs in England, with some learning the pieces to incorporate into their programmes and others taking some of the musical ideas into their arrangements. Here are examples from four cultures which have given us new sounds and ideas to incorporate or exchange with our own developing folk harmony practice.

From Bulgaria, we have the sustained discords and 'open throat' tone used to great effect by English folk singer Frankie Armstrong back in the 1970s, and further popularised by the arrival of choir leader Dessislava Stefanova around 20 years later.

Folk harmony singing from The Republic of Georgia brings thrilling unison endings, many songs in three voice parts and clashing 1–4–5 chords. Georgia took a leap into people's consciousness through the visit to this country in the 1990s by Georgian singing leader and ethnomusicologist Edisher Garakanidze and his choir Mtiebi.

An awareness of Corsican and Sardinian parallel fifths, tonal shifts and the polyphonic songs sung by shepherds and fishermen was helped by the BBC radio programmes made by Andy Kershaw in 2005.[40] Sardinia also boasts 'folk masses' with harmony parts passed on orally down the generations echoing the transmission style of The Copper Family of Sussex.

The folklorisation of church harmonies and call-and-response structures of South Africa have been a popular feature for English choirs for many years. Songs from African traditions are sometimes featured in concert programmes which are otherwise of completely English material.

In addition to these exciting musical features, there are strong parallels in the functions of songs. Folk choirs elsewhere seem to have songs for every occasion – harvest, birth, death, songs about work and for weddings. It can inform, enliven and energise a folk choir in England to know that these parallels exist and the wish to exchange repertoire and establish international social links between choirs is strong and increasingly acted on.

Examples of other traditions of folk-based harmony around the world can provide a wonderful selection of sounds and ideas to create arrangements for folk choirs in England. Arrangers might use clashing adjacent notes, parallel triads, discordant 'sus 4' chords, polyphonic accompanying lines, super-close harmonies and a host of other features. All these indicate the existence of a musical spectrum which is distinct, different and grounded in folk practice, as opposed to the rather predictable four-part harmony styles of hymn writers and the world of western classical music.

> **Case study 2**
>
> 'My Coffin Shall Be Black'[41]
> My coffin shall be black
> Four little angels at my back
> Two to watch and two to pray
> And two to carry my soul away
>
> This is an extraordinary piece, the lyrics spoken by a boy in Cornwall in 1893 and contained in the Baring Gould MS, while the tune was communicated to Ralph Vaughan Williams by a Northumberland Schoolteacher in 1906.
>
> The song is epic in theme – death, resurrection, last wishes and attendant angels – but small both in tune compass and amount of words. Both chorus and the verses are sung to the same simple, repetitive tune. There are no other variants of this song recorded in England, but the piece is striking enough and well referenced enough to warrant inclusion in a folk choir repertoire.
>
> In his collection, Baring-Gould notes versions from the rest of Europe, including Sardinia and so this arrangement borrows features from that harmony singing tradition.
>
> The simple repetitive tune is preserved totally intact in the centre of the arrangement. The harmony changes around this to produce a fuller sound for the verses adding one lower and two higher harmony lines. The chorus is delivered in stark parallel fifths, outlawed by conventional harmony writing. It is therefore very easy for singers opting for the tune to learn their line, while the harmony parts provide an acoustic change for the audience and a shift in tonal centre. With these features and the first line statement from a solo voice which gives pitch, speed and a lead into the lyrics, the arrangement borrows both from Sardinian practice and medieval music.
>
> Within the Wren Music groups, it is sung by Wren's male chorus and has also been featured at a festival in Sardinia by a specially formed 11-strong choir. The arrangement is designed to produce a 'shiver' in the listener and Wren's male chorus have sung it in a local cave and also in Exeter Cathedral, the long echoes adding to the sense of 'other worldliness'.

Folk song and other repertoire

Although the practice of what material a folk choir tackles can sometimes be vague and fluid, the genre is becoming increasingly well defined. There has been an explosion of participatory singing in recent years. Big Choral Census in 2017 co-ordinated by Voices Now found that there were at least 40,000 choirs and 2.14 million people singing regularly in the UK – this they also said was likely to be an underestimate. Although this includes all types of choirs singing a range of genres of music, 'folk' came high in the list of genres.

> [The survey found that] although classical music is still popular, contemporary songs are sung by 62 percent of choirs, with classical appealing to 60 percent. Folk songs are next in demand, on 48 percent.[42]

There are two designations of community choir which bear close comparison with folk music. The first are those choirs calling themselves 'global' or 'world' choirs and another are the gospel choirs drawing mainly on black music from Africa or North America. The genre boundaries between these choirs and folk choirs can sometimes seem quite fluid, since they often tend to encompass folk music of other countries.

Singing in other dialects or languages calls for another set of essentials; lyric sheets, audio guides, pronunciation guides, a literal translation and some basic information about the cultural context of the song. For songs with dialect words, foreign languages or from another class, occupational or societal background this kind of attention to detail can also bring a strong sense of authenticity and connectedness.

There are some areas of repertoire that overlap with or are on the fringes of folk choir:

> …that's using the term 'folk' [in] a wider sense rather than just traditional song. I think The Beatles songs will be… you know, in years to come people will classify them as folk songs and I mean, I think it's the ongoing tradition.[43]

There could be an argument that old pop songs should make it into the repertoire of a folk choir, if they had undergone what Latvian folklorist Ilmars Pumpurs (of the Latvijas Nacionālais kultūras centrs) identifies as the process of 'folkorisation'.[44] This occurs when the song is initiated as a pop song and then taken up by the folk and emerging through the oral tradition with a number of variations.

We can find songs within the established folk canon that can chart a similar route. For example, an early version of 'The Sweet Nightingale' which is so prevalent and popular in oral tradition, can be traced back to a ballad opera from 1761, *Thomas and Sally* by Isaac Bickerstaff and Thomas Arne.

There is an interesting dilemma produced by songs like Leonard Cohen's 'Hallelujah'. It fulfils Cecil Sharp's criteria of continuity, variation and selection and would seem to be becoming a folk song, with dozens of variants, people making their own harmonies, adding lyrics and differing versions of the tune. A recent arrangement of 'Hallelujah' for a 30-voice Exeter choir conducted as an experiment, divided the choir with three singers reluctant to sing it – 'that's not a folk song' – around ten singers delighted to learn it – 'it's part of my own oral tradition' – and the rest of the choir, the majority, happy to go along with it as a different flavour to add to their existing repertoire of folk songs.

There are an increasing number of newly written songs in the 'folk style' which are well on the way to becoming folk songs themselves, being so widely sung that the original composer is overlooked and the piece gets described as 'traditional'. The title of the piece or some words have sometimes been changed and people clearly have taken 'ownership' of the song. However, this is not always the case and some 'new' folk songs have their writer's names firmly attached to them. These 'new' pieces may have been written at any time over the last 50 years or so, some have a consistent popularity and longevity. Taken together, this means that many fulfil some or all three of the criteria; continuity, selection and variation. Some folk choirs feel these pieces complement the traditional songs they sing and have arranged them and taken them into repertoire. Here are two examples to illustrate the point.

'The Grey Funnel Line', written in 1959 by Cyril Tawney, was the last song he wrote before leaving the Royal Navy. Recorded by many artists, including June Tabor, Emmylou Harris, Dolores Keane and Mary Black and making appearances on BBC Radio 3, in the repertoire of folk choirs, in folk clubs, concerts and on the lips of many soloists and duos, it has proven wide appeal. The wistful, melancholic lyrics strike an authentic emotional note. The slow-moving tune is built around just five notes: the pentatonic scale. Its musical features include the first two notes being a rising tonic and fifth of the scale, followed by the third clearly establishing the tonal centre. This means that harmony lines almost suggest themselves. The tune has sometimes had new words put to it, for example appearing as 'The NAPE Picket Line' for a Trade Union inspired song project on songs of work in Newfoundland, Canada, sung in harmony by Gerry Strong and Jim Payne. Although there are few variations to the tune, harmonic structure and lyrics of the original, choir leaders and arrangers clearly feel that this song belongs alongside its more traditional counterparts, although the criterion of variation is weak.

'Keep You In Peace' is another such recent song, although in this case it was written specifically for choirs to sing in harmony. It has become so widespread in the folk and community choirs movement that it is well on its way to fulfilling the holy trinity of continuity, variation and selection. 'Keep You In Peace' was written in 1992 by the choir leader, composer and writer Sarah Morgan.

Sarah Morgan's reworking of the lyrics (elsewhere similar lyrics are known as 'The Celtic Blessing') and the marrying of her new lyrics with a beautiful traditional tune (elsewhere a similar tune is known as 'Mrs. Jamieson's Favourite') has created a heart-warming piece now known and sung by thousands of people around the world, and often selected for use at funerals.

Although 'Keep You In Peace' has strong Celtic connections, the creation by this Dorset choir leader has become deservedly popular throughout the UK and around the world, being sung and recorded by community choirs in Gloucester, The Lake District, Edinburgh, Devon and Sarah's own Dorset. Around the world, we can find versions being sung by the Tokushima Ensemble in Japan and The Caspian Choir in Azerbaijan. The lyrics are also quoted in *Singing For Our Lives*,[45] a book on street choirs and is clearly sung, known and loved by many street choirs throughout England.

> Unlike many arrangers, my aim is not to use a folk song as the basis for a choral work, but to create an arrangement that will give a choir the pleasure of singing a folk- song in harmony.[46]

Conclusion

Ordinarily through our work, we strive to share practice, and we take a step-by-step approach to demystify the practicalities of being a community folk practitioner. With this chapter, we have resisted the urge to create a 'handbook' for folk choir leaders, and rather we have sought to share our perspectives on the birth and growth of the English folk choir.

We noted that for many, the term 'folk choir' is synonymous with 'community choir', and while these two forms have some similarities, we have sought to describe features that we believe to be specific to the folk choir. Since the TV series *The Choir* was broadcast in 2007, there has been a significant increase in community choral singing in England, but we have not seen an equivalent increase in the number of folk choirs.

We provided information about the invention of 'folk' as a genre with examples of group singing through history and in various social and occupational contexts. We then described how the folk choir emerged from social and cultural initiatives in the 1980s and built on the long-established folk club traditions of England: a melodic, modal song tradition, blended with elements from historic and folkloric group singing from England and around the world.

To illustrate this, we provided song examples with an analysis of the musical arrangements. It should be noted that folk choirs have not replaced folk clubs, but rather folk choirs represent a more recent addition to the complex web of activities that constitute the folk music traditions of England.

Folk choirs have made the singing of folk songs accessible to singers who value the collective activity of learning. They have created a particular kind of choir experience with the rehearsal and performance of repertoire that has historical significance, sometimes hyper-local historical significance. This has given a folk music opportunity to members of the general public, the folk, for whom rehearsing on their own and delivering a solo performance may be unthinkable. Some folk choir leaders noted that their membership is drawn from people already enthusiastic about folk music, as well as people who are generally interested in singing in a choir. This would suggest the folk choir has the potential to be an effective vector for transition between these sectors. However, folk choir leaders further noted that while those interested in choir singing often transition into folk enthusiasts (performing at local folk clubs) the inverse transition (where folk enthusiasts join other non-folk choirs) is very rare. Folk choirs provide a strong base from which to introduce new audiences to folk songs, and are likely to continue to feed the solo singing tradition.

We believe this combination of factors shows that folk choirs embody the concept of a living tradition, through the demonstration of simultaneous continuity and change. Continuity through the re-presentation of old songs, with respect for the traditions of both the melodic form and the collective expression of singing together, and change through the intentional structuring of harmonies, the formalisation of rehearsals and the professionalisation of the role of folk choir leader. The future of the folk choir will be secure for as long as folk choir leaders have the vision and tenacity to embrace this duality.

Notes

Unless otherwise indicated, all 'interviews' are lodged in the Marilyn Tucker and Paul Wilson Personal Collection

1. Matt Norman, Interview with Marilyn Tucker (June 2020).
2. Alyson Sue Vaaler, 'Modern Antiquity: Modern Interpretations of Folk Sources in Gustav Mahler's Songs from Des Knaben Wunderhorn' (Master's thesis, University of Wisconsin-Milwaukee May 2013) p. 10.
3. Cecil J. Sharp, and Sabine Baring-Gould, *English Folk Songs for Schools* (London: Curwen, 1906), Introduction.
4. A.L. Lloyd, *The Singing Englishman – An Introduction to Folksong* (London: Workers Music Association, 1944) p. 2.
5. For a summary of these perspectives, see Steve Roud, *Folk Song in England* (London: Faber, 2017) and for contrasted reading A.L. Lloyd, *Folk Song in England* (London: Lawrence and Wishart, 1967).
6. Tom Brown, *A Sailor's Life – The Life and Times of John Short of Watchet* (S&A Projects, 2014) p. 62.
7. Sharp and Baring-Gould, *English Folk Songs for Schools*.
8. Ralph Vaughan Williams, *The English Hymnal* (Oxford: Oxford University Press, 1906).
9. *Radio Times* description of the first programme September 27 1953: 'In this programme you are invited to listen to some of the folk songs and music still sung and played in the British Isles'.
10. J.P. Bean, *Singing From The Floor – A History of British Folk Clubs* (London: Faber, 2014) p. 122.
11. Collins online Dictionary.
12. Dr Lisa Colton, University Of Huddersfield, contributor to: *A Choral History of Britain – Presenter Roderick Williams* (BBC Radio 4 27th September 2017 – Producer Chris Taylor).
13. Stephen Banfield, *Music In The Westcountry* (Woodbridge: Boydell Press, 2018) p. 110.

14 Charles Mackeson, *The Madrigal Society* (Grove's Dictionary of Music and Musicians, 1900).
15 Sally Drage, 'The Performance of English Provincial Psalmody c.1690–c.1840', (Doctoral Thesis; University of Leeds School of Music, 2009) chapters 3 and 9.
16 Banfield, *Westcountry*, 2018, p. 85.
17 Marek Korcynski, Michael Pickering and Emma Robertson, *Rhythms of Labour* (Cambridge: Cambridge University Press, 2013) p. 47.
18 Korcynski, Pickering and Robertson, *Rhythms*, p. 50.
19 Testimony from Fred Winzer, Exford, Exmoor 1979 (Marilyn Tucker and Paul Wilson personal collection).
20 Banfield, *Westcountry*, pp. 111–112.
21 Dave Russell, 'Abiding Memories: The Community Singing Movement and English Social Life in the 1920s', *Popular Music* 27:1 (2008) pp. 117–133.
22 *The Holiday Fellowship Book of Holiday Songs* (London: Holiday Fellowship, 1935).
23 Colin Irwin, *Sing When You're Winning* (London: Andre Deutsch, 2006) p. 137:

>Bless 'em all, bless 'em all
>Bert Trautmann, Dave Ewing and Pau
>Bless Roy Little who blocks out the wing
>Bless Jack Dyson the penalty king
>And with Leivers and Spurdle so tall
>And Johnstone the prince of them all
>Come on the light blues, It's always the right blue
>So cheer up me lads, Bless 'em all

24 Campaign Choirs Writing Collective, *Singing for Our Lives – Stories from the Street Choirs* (Bristol: Hammer On Press, 2018); Quote from Jane Scott the 'conductor' of the Birmingham Clarion Choir p. 135.
25 David Prynn, 'The Clarion Clubs, Rambling and the Holiday Associations in Britain since the 1890s', *Journal of Contemporary History* 11:2–3 (1976) pp. 65–77.
26 Description from Mailout website – https://mailout.co/magazine/.
27 Sandra Kerr quoted in *The Guardian* (10 March 2014); Kathy Henderson, Frankie Armstrong and Sandra Kerr *My Song Is My Own* (London: Pluto Press, 1979).
28 Frankie Armstrong, Interview with Marilyn Tucker (June 2020).
29 Natural Voice Network website: https://naturalvoice.net/.
30 Matt Norman, Interview with Marilyn Tucker (June 2020).
31 Janet Russell, Interview with Marilyn Tucker (June 2020).
32 Frankie Armstrong, Interview with Marilyn Tucker (June 2020).
33 Sandra Kerr, Interview with Marilyn Tucker (June 2020).
34 Caroline Bithell, *A Different Voice, a Different Song – Reclaiming Community through Natural Voice and World Song* (Oxford: Oxford University Press, 2014) p. 45.
35 Frankie Armstrong, Interview with Marilyn Tucker (June 2020).
36 Sandra Kerr, Interview with Marilyn Tucker (June 2020).
37 'Whittingham Fair' (Child 2, Roud 12) in by John Stokoe and John Collingwood Bruce, *Northumbrian Minstrelsy* (Newcastle: Soc. of Antiquaries of Newcastle-upon-Tyne, 1882) Alternative titles – The Elfin Knight : Scarboro Fair.
38 'The Lark In The Morning' Baring Gould collection, tune from Robert Hard of South Brent, Devon and words from Samuel Gilbert of Mawgan-in-Pyder, Cornwall.
39 'The Sweet Nightingale' (Roud 371). R. Bell, *Ballads and Songs of the Peasantry of England*, (London: John W Parker and Son, 1857) p. 247. Ralph Dunstan, *Cornish Song Book*, (London: Ascherberg Hopwood and Crew, 1929) p. 41. Baring-Gould collection; H. Westaway, Belstone, Devon and J. Parsons Lewdown, Devon. Also cited by Baring-Gould: *Thomas and Sally*, Ballad Opera, Lyrics, Isaac Bickerstaff, Music, Dr. Arne, 1761.
40 Andy Kershaw, *Corsica and Sardinia*. BBC Radio 3 (14 August 2005).
41 Origins: From the Baring-Gould MS collection: SBG Personal Copy Volume 2. Lyrics spoken by a boy at Altarnun, Cornwall 5 February 1893. Tune communicated to Ralph Vaughan Williams by Mr Kinnaid a schoolmaster at Dunstan, Northumberland 7th August 1906. Published – Imogen Holst and Ursula Vaughan Williams, *Yacre of Land* (Oxford: Oxford University Press, 1961) p. 19.

42 Abigail Le Marquand-Brown, and Elanor Caunt, *Big Choral Census – Voices Now* (Oxford: Oxford University Press Choral, 2017).
43 Janet Russell, Interview with Marilyn Tucker (June 2020).
44 Ilmars Pumpurs, 'Folk Music as Community Music', Talk given as part of MusInc seminar and training event, Riga, 23 September 2017.
45 Campaign Choirs Writing Collective, *Singing For Our Lives*.
46 Sarah Morgan, 'Community Choirs – A Musical Transformation', (doctoral dissertation, University of Winchester, September 2013).

25

'PAST PERFORMANCES ON PAPER'

A case study of the manuscript tunebook of Thomas Hampton

Rebecca Dellow

Introduction

Thomas Hardy, writing in his 1896 preface to *Under the Greenwood Tree*, describes vernacular musicians and their manuscripts from approximately 50 years before:

> Their music in those days was all in their own manuscript, copied in the evenings after work, and their music-books were home-bound. It was customary to inscribe a few jigs, reels, horn-pipes, and ballads in the same book, by beginning it at the other end, the insertions being continued from front and back till sacred and secular met together in the middle, often with bizarre effect.[1]

Tunebooks like these preserve remnants of a chiefly amateur, monophonic, instrumental practice, participated in by 'ordinary' people in nineteenth-century England. They provide a largely unexplored insight into the repertoire and life of vernacular nineteenth-century musicians. There are about 300 surviving manuscripts known to date, comprising chiefly pre-existing melodies, which are scattered across the country, held in libraries, museums, record offices and private ownership. They represent the repertoire of amateur musicians who played for personal pleasure, dances and informal gatherings throughout the last 300 years. They do not necessarily represent the musicians' entire repertoire. Likewise, it is not clear whether the transcribed tunes are those which were commonly played, those that were more unusual or tunes that the musicians wanted to learn.

Nearly 100 years after Hardy's writing, my fiddle-playing grandfather gave me a manuscript like those Hardy describes. It had belonged to my great-great-grandfather, Thomas Hampton, who had been a fiddle player in Hereford during the mid-late nineteenth century. At first, I found that the tunes in Hampton's manuscript did not conform to my notion of 'proper' folk tunes and it was not until 20 years later, when working on Medieval manuscripts, evaluating them as contextual and musicological artefacts, that I began to reassess the manuscript's importance. Around this time, I also became aware of the warped historiography and problematic definitions surrounding folk music. Reviewing my 'Fiddlers' Tunebook',[2] I could see how my preconceived notions played into the dialectic between popular music and folk music which has persisted in the scholarly discourse of vernacular song and instrumental music since the terms first appeared, and is still around today.

When I cast aside my ancestor's manuscript, I was perhaps guilty of the same prejudice said by some to be applied by the early folk song collectors,[3] deriding the more ephemeral tunes, and making assumptions regarding definitions based on its literate manuscript form. Intrigued, I set out to unravel what these manuscripts tell us about mid-late nineteenth-century vernacular musical practice. It became abundantly clear that not only is the musical practice represented by these manuscripts a much-neglected area of English music history, but the manuscripts constitute a rare and important synchronic capture of the process of folk tradition at work.

Current definitions of folk music still cite orality as a key factor, as a cursory glance at Wikipedia will show,[4] and it is apparent in more reliable sources too.[5] The field of folk song and the wider discipline of history have now accepted that textual influence was inescapable,[6] but the degree of oral/aural reliance is only now beginning to be examined within the field of instrumental tunes. Although the manuscripts are inherently textual by their medium, and the research also reveals a strong reliance on direct textual sources, this does not mean that the manuscripts were not subjected to oral/aural influences.

The manuscripts' heterogeneous repertoire (in both content and source materials) can also add to controversy regarding their inclusion in English folk music tradition. As will be shown, the manuscripts mainly contain contemporary tunes and songs, often newly composed by a known composer and widely available from commercial print. As such, it could be argued that the manuscripts are more simply part of nineteenth-century popular music making, in a vernacular milieu. Developing the idea of tradition as a 'process', rather than defining by 'origins', Steve Roud describes a folk song as 'the process through which the songs pass, in the brains and voices of ordinary people, which stamps them as folk'.[7] Therefore, the origin of the song (be it 'art', minstrel, music hall or an older historic song) does not define the song. Essentially, any song can become a folk song, '*it is not the origin of a song which makes it "folk", but what the "folk" do with it*'.[8] Likewise, in this study, I refer to a folk tradition taking the form of a process,[9] and it becomes clear that these manuscripts are an integral part of a folk tradition.

Who compiled instrumental manuscript tunebooks?

My grandfather, Charles Hampton (1913–1999), gave me the manuscript in 1990 along with a collection of contemporaneous printed music, both of which had been owned by my great-great-grandfather, Thomas Hampton (1844–1896).[10] The neatly inscribed ink title on the front cover reads: *Dances For violin* and contains 57 tunes, spanning contemporary popular songs and dance tunes, older tunes and some Nonconformist hymns, dating from c1870s to 1880s and is the work of two main scribes.

Thomas Hampton was baptised in the rural Gloucestershire village of Blaisdon, in March 1844.[11] He was the fifth child of Elizabeth and John Hampton,[12] a charcoal runner.[13] Thomas' mother died in 1849, and he then lodged with William Blewett in Blaisdon along with his older sister Ann and younger brother, William.[14] In 1861, his father and brothers were living on a charcoal barge, the '*Mary*', which plied the Hereford and Gloucester Canal.[15]

The Hereford and Gloucester Canal was prosperous in the early to mid-nineteenth century, 1860 being the most successful year financially.[16] Ironically, this was due in part to extra traffic resulting from the building of the railways. There followed a long decline,

Figure 25.1 Walter Soobroy's name written on printed music and matching handwriting in the manuscript

starting in 1862, when the canal company agreed to the Great Western and West Midland Railways taking over the canal for conversion, leading eventually to its closure in 1881.[17] It is likely that this played a part in the Hampton family's relocation to Hereford city centre to seek alternative employment. Thomas, now a general labourer, married Ann Wyatt, from Droitwich, at the Hereford Register Office in March 1870,[18] and he lived most of his married life close to the canal wharf, directly next to the prison and workhouse. This location, coupled with Thomas' future occupation as a skinner, suggests a modest existence. Thomas and Ann remained there, until Thomas' death from chronic pneumonia, asthma and phthisis, aged 52 in 1896.[19] The publication dates of some of the tunes suggest that the manuscript was compiled when Thomas lived in Hereford, although some of the melodies may have been known to him as a boy in rural Blaisdon.

The majority of the tunes and titles are written quite scruffily, and are thought to be written by Thomas; yet, the opening nine pieces are in a neat, well-educated hand. The printed music passed down alongside the manuscript held the key to identifying this scribe. Figure 25.1 shows the name 'Walter Soobroy' written in smart handwriting,[20] in a copy of *Hopwood & Crew's Selection [...] Book 4*. The first four letters ('Walt') are directly comparable with those found in the word 'Waltz' in Hampton's manuscript. Other stylistic letter formations leave no doubt that the first manuscript scribe was Walter Soobroy.

Walter Soobroy (1851–1931)[21] was the son of Mary Soobroy, a laundress, and grandson of Mary Gough and step-grandson of Richard Gough, with whom he lived since birth.[22] In 1871, around the date of the manuscript, Walter was living a minute's walk away from Thomas Hampton, and was working as a brush-maker's assistant.[23]

The circumstances surrounding the relationship between the two men, and how and why the manuscript book transferred from Soobroy to Hampton, are unknown. However, it is relatively safe to assume that 26-year-old Thomas and 20-year-old Walter knew each other. Soobroy's superior hand and the inclusion of some pedagogic items conceivably place him in the role of teacher, although a simpler explanation such as Soobroy offering the remaining empty pages of his manuscript to Hampton remains feasible.

Received history of archetypal folk musicians depicts an image of rural, elderly, poor men who lack education. This view is likely prompted by the early folk song collectors' descriptions, summed up in Cecil Sharp's conclusion that folk song is part of the culture of 'the non-educated, or "the common people" [...] the unlettered [...] the remnants of the peasantry [...] who resided in the country and subsisted on the land',[24] causing much contention throughout twentieth-century folk song discourse.[25] In the most recent scholarly writings on the subject, characteristics of the folk can be seen to encompass a much broader scope. The image of nineteenth-century vernacular musicians includes people of any age, gender, habitat (urban or rural) and, to some degree, level of education, the key over-riding factor being that they are 'ordinary'.[26] This fits quite well with the majority of manuscript compilers from this period who were young, skilled or semi-skilled working-class men from rural backgrounds. Hampton conforms relatively well to this profile, apart from his city location and his unskilled labouring job, putting him at the lower end of the demographic scale.

What did the manuscripts contain?

The manuscript contains a thorough mix of repertoire made up predominantly of post-1830 tunes and song melodies. About a third of the tunes are older, and these more historic tunes are possibly evidence of having passed through the selection and survival process of tradition, with some dating from before 1750. The most common genre is dance tunes made up of hornpipes and waltzes.[27] The manuscript is representative of other manuscripts, notwithstanding a distinct lack of quadrilles and marches, probably due to the slightly later date.

Historic tunes (pre-1750)

Although it becomes clear that many of Hampton's historic tunes were sourced from contemporary print,[28] the history of some of these tunes is striking, a handful of which I have highlighted below. For example, the unidentifiable tune title 'Runn's Hornpipe' (Figure 25.2) is a close variant of both Winter,[29] and Rose's,[30] 'Harlequin Gambols' and Davoll's, 'Harlequin's Hornpipe'.[31] It was published with this title in 1816 in Wilson's *Companion to the Ball Room*,[32] and also in 1810–1822 in Blackman's *A Selection of the most favorite Hornpipes for the Violin*,[33] indicating early nineteenth-century popularity. Philip Heath-Coleman identified the tune as a version of 'Master Byrons Hornpipe', dating from circa 1697 from 'a publication attributed to Purcell',[34] perhaps an aural mis-interpretation from 'Byron' to 'Runns'.

The song, 'Last Rose of Summer', was published in Thomas Moore's extremely popular early nineteenth-century collection *Irish Melodies*, a series described as a 'veritable corner-stone of bourgeois "popular song"',[35] which would account for its popularity in Victorian repertoires. However, reputedly Moore took the melody from Alfred Milliken's

Figure 25.2 'Runns Hornpipe'

eighteenth-century song, 'The Groves of Blarney', who is said to have borrowed the tune from a seventeenth-century harp melody.[36]

A version of 'Cawder Fair' appears in Hampton's manuscript in shorthand, under the guise of the mid-nineteenth-century popular dance form of a Highland Schottische (see Figure 25.4).[37] Known by several names ('Calder Fair', 'Cawdor Fair', 'Hawthorn Tree of Cawdor' and 'Go on Boys and Give a Tune'),[38] the 'Very Old' tune was published in 1817.[39] The tune is reminiscent of the melody of the nursery rhyme 'Sing a Song of Sixpence', which may date to the early seventeenth century.[40]

1750–1830

Just over 10% of Hampton's tunes have origins dating back to the mid-late eighteenth and early nineteenth centuries. Christopher Walker indicates that 'The Triumph' was introduced into ballrooms in the late eighteenth century, although it is possible that older tunes were 'recycled' and the tune existed before this time.[41] The earliest reference I can find to 'The Ratcatcher' is as a broadside ballad dated 1813–1833.[42] As a song, it became immensely popular throughout the century, perhaps fuelled by the celebrity of singer Sam Cowell (1820–1864) in the 1840s,[43] and remained popular in printed music during Hampton's time.[44] Clearly a pervasive song, a 1855 *Musical World* correspondent complains: 'Everywhere I go in London…I cannot escape the infliction of having my ears stunned with some hideous words relating to the daughter of a ratcatcher and a seller of sand, set to the most vile tune'.[45] The melody of 'Tight Little Island' is related to the song of the same name by Thomas Dibdin (1771–1841), Charles Dibdin's illegitimate son,[46] 'at the time of the threatened Napoleonic invasion'.[47] The tune found its way into the morris dance repertoire, collected by the early twentieth-century folk song collectors.[48]

Post-1830

In line with other tunebooks over half of Hampton's tunes are relatively contemporary, with hornpipes, minstrel songs and waltzes especially popular. These are often attributed to composers about whom little is now known, but who were evidently very prevalent at the time. Alongside fashionable Victorian dances of waltzes, polkas, schottisches and a galop, Hampton also includes a varsoviana, a popular mid-century dance form which by 1888 was 'seldom danced now, though it formerly had a sort of ephemeral popularity. We always considered it as rather a boisterous sort of performance, and more suitable for the casino than the private ballroom'.[49] Two of the dance tunes ('Wedding Galop' and 'Mina Waltz') were written by Charles Coote (Junior). In the nineteenth century, both Charles Coote (Senior (1809–1880))[50] and Charles Coote Junior (1831–1916)[51] were prolific composers and arrangers but are little known now. Similarly, another prolific composer/arranger whose legacy did not survive is W. H. Montgomery. He appears to be the source of several arrangements found in Hampton's repertoire, not least, 'Silver Lake', 'The Rigoletto Waltz', 'The Last Rose of Summer' and the minstrel song 'The Gipsy's Warning'.

Hampton includes the melodies for five 'blackface-minstrel' songs in his tunebook, reflecting their wider popularity in the later nineteenth century. 'The Gipsy's Warning' was written (or arranged)[52] by Henry A. Goard,[53] which became popular from 1864, remaining so throughout the early 1870s. 'Mollie Darling', written in 1871 by William S Hays,[54] remained popular well into the twentieth century. Similarly, ''Tis but a Faded Flower' was popular amongst instrumentalists, existing in American sheet music from at least 1860,[55] and was part of The Christy Minstrels' repertoire,[56] circa 1870.

'Art' music, carols, religious tunes

Hampton transcribed popular arrangements of classical music (such as excerpts from opera) as well as hymns. His religious music is all Nonconformist, probably sourced from Dwight Lyman Moody and Ira David Sankey's popular nineteenth-century hymn book, *Sacred Songs and Solos*. 'Safe In the Arms of Jesus', subtitled 'No. 25', in the manuscript can be found in *Sacred Songs and Solos*, where it is also numbered '25' in the 1890, 1880 and 1870 editions of the book.

Hampton's inclusion of the popular carol, 'O Come all ye faithful', is noteworthy (see Figure 25.3). His transcription would suggest that he either copied this hurriedly from nineteenth-century print or perhaps wrote it out aurally, 'by ear' as there is an absence of barlines and key and the rhythmic notation appears to be in shorthand. As an English carol, it is thought to date from 1789,[57] but the origins of the original Latin version, 'Adeste Fideles', are explored by Bennett Zon in his 1996 article in *Early Music*.[58] Zon interpreted the absence of barlines and peculiar rhythmic notation in Hampton's transcription as an indication that Hampton had sourced and copied the tune from a much older free-rhythmic source.

Hampton's tune choice did not then exclusively comprised historic, older 'traditional' dance tunes and looking beyond the evidence in Hampton, it is abundantly clear that an eclectic mix of age and style of melody was the norm. It is fascinating to see that some tunes written down (and presumably played) by Thomas Hampton are instantly recognisable today and are still played amongst today's folk musicians, and indeed make up part of the repertoire of my children – his great-great-great granddaughters – 150 years on. Similarly, that some of his tunes can be found in printed or manuscript collections over 100 years before appearing in the manuscript demonstrates a remarkable longevity for certain tunes.

Inward transmission and sources

Inward transmission refers to the way the tunes were transferred directly into the manuscripts. In its broadest sense it distinguishes aural/oral transmission from copying although the terms are not mutually exclusive. The findings contrast acutely with inherited views regarding the role of orality/aurality in folk music, dispelling this as a direct means of transmission into the manuscripts and indicating copying instead. It is quite clear that the majority

Figure 25.3 'O Come all ye faithful'

of tunes were sourced from the contemporary, mass-published tune collections, indicating a much-understudied area of musical printed resources. However, it is crucial to acknowledge the possibility that the men had a vast unwritten repertoire, committed to memory which could have been acquired by aural/oral or textual means of which we have no knowledge.

Inward transmission

Initially, it is important to consider what is meant by the term oral/aural transmission. 'Aural' is more relevant to the instrumental tune field, and my preferred term, as items are passed on by ear rather than by mouth; yet, 'oral' is the term more generally associated with folk music because of its specific relevance to song. There are several different permutations of the form. For example, a tune can be written down 'by ear', at the same time as it is being played or sung by another musician, thus removing any memorising element from the exercise. It can be written 'by ear' from memory, in which case the tune may have entered the mind of the transcriber via either a prior textual route or a prior aural route, or the tune may have existed purely orally and been passed down through an oral to aural source and subsequently transcribed. It is difficult to state categorically that a tune has not had influence of printed text at any time, so despite the compiler transcribing a tune from either a direct oral source or aurally from memory, 'oral transmission' as a term meaning passed down aurally through generations of course cannot be proven, and is highly improbable.[59]

The influence of text on transmission suggests that the rare occasions in the tunebooks, where a tune does appear to have been written from memory or 'by ear' it is likely to represent either of the first two possibilities outlined above rather than a long line of exclusive aural transmission. As such, the tunes written from memory are not necessarily representative of an inherited view of an aurally transmitted tune. This can be seen in the manuscripts. For example, Figure 25.4 shows a shorthand transcription which might indicate having been written from memory, or by ear. However, the title indicates that the source of the tune is contemporaneous as the schottische was a popular Victorian dance; thus, a long aural line is unlikely.

A further possibility exists whereby the tune appears to be written by ear or from memory but is a tune well known to the compiler and has in fact been hurriedly copied, perhaps to save time and space, only the 'bare bones' required in order to bring the tune back to the musician's fingers.

It is clear that Hampton and other compilers were copying the majority of their tunes from printed, published music (or possibly other manuscript copies), rather than writing down aurally transmitted tunes or tunes from memory.[60] In some cases, a potential 'parent' or direct source was discovered. This revealed not only that the tunes were copied, but that the compilers were copying from contemporary printed sources. Four tunebooks were

Figure 25.4 'Highland Schottische'

identified which it is quite clear were consulted and copied by Hampton namely *Hopwood & Crew's Selection of Quadrilles Bk 4*,[61] *Hopwood & Crew 100 Country Dances for the Violin*,[62] *Westrop's 120 Country Dances*[63] and *Kerr's Merry Melodies Bk 1*,[64] along with several other potential direct sources. It is clear that well over 90% of the tunes were copied, with approximately 98% of these copied from contemporary sources.

Sources

The types of sources used by the compilers were budget publications specific to amateur monophonic instrumentalists and were frequently referred to as 'cheap' works. They were published chiefly in London and varied in price between one shilling and eighteen pence, although were often sold at half or a third of the cover price. They covered all popular genres, including extracts and arrangements from opera, minstrel songs, popular song, modern dances, jigs, reels and hornpipes, reflected in the heterogeneous assortment found in the manuscripts. Interestingly, this shows that despite containing a wide mix of tunes from across a broad spectrum of genres and provenance, the manuscript compilers were drawing on a body of contemporary source material which was actually narrow in chronological and geographical range.

It is interesting to consider why, when this source material was advertised as 'cheap', the compilers chose to copy rather than purchase the printed music. Although possibly comparatively cheap, and sold below the marked price, in reality, printed music remained a luxury item for the lower end of the demographic, and unaffordable in many cases. Further, the selection process afforded by a self-made compilation fulfils personal taste across all genre boundaries and creates adaptability in function, resulting in a unique, individual collection which is compact and easily transportable. It is likely that this format was favoured by amateur musicians for its adaptability and economic advantages, despite the labour involved.

Acquiring general and musical literacy skills

The fact that these men were copying tunes raises another question – that of literacy. As with other compilers, although Hampton wrote a manuscript book he did not sign his marriage certificate. Both he and his wife marked the certificate with a cross,[65] implying illiteracy. Hampton's marriage and manuscript date from the same time, removing the likelihood that one reflects skills learnt later in life. This provides fascinating evidence of a cultural or social effect which occurred within the nineteenth-century working-class psyche, proving that it is impossible to fully understand the past. Furthermore, this dramatically reduces the validity of twentieth-century research into nineteenth-century literacy levels based on marriage certificate signage,[66] research which is still relied upon in current scholarship.[67] Perhaps this represents a general practice, possibly due to modesty,[68] inclusivity,[69] to avoid embarrassing a partner, or fear of poor handwriting,[70] rather than suggesting that despite compiling a musical manuscript book, none of the compilers could write their own names.

Using statistics of nineteenth-century marriage certificate signatures has likely resulted in historians assuming a lower level of nineteenth-century literacy than existed. In the same way, it is important not to make assumptions regarding lack of aurality based on the textual and literate nature of the manuscripts. Despite proving that the compilers' method of inward transmission was by copying from print, implying they could read and write music, it does not mean that was their sole source of the tunes – they could have learnt the tunes aurally (either years ago or contemporaneously) and subsequently sought them in accessible 'cheap' print for speedier copying. As such, it remains possible that the inward textual transmission method into the manuscripts is potentially skewing the actual reliance on aurality.

It is quite clear that general literacy was not out of reach of the mid to lower levels of society and in reality was likely to be more widespread than is perceived. Likewise, musical literacy was not inaccessible to lower classes. However, what is not clear is from where these skills were emanating, especially as education was not compulsory during Hampton's childhood.

General literacy, musical literacy and musical skill are different skills and not all are required in order to achieve proficiency in one. Musical skill can be acquired independently as the illiterate 'ear-players' demonstrate.[71] They can play tunes without being able to read music and also do not necessarily need (or have) a skill in general literacy in order to do so. Similarly, being able to read music does not inevitably imply instrumental musicianship, and so too does not prove an ability to read or write in general terms. With guidance, young children are capable of rudimentarily reading music and playing that music on an instrument before learning to read words. Basic musical notation relies on identifying the position of symbols, rather than complex ordering of letters.

However, a general skill in literacy can enable a subsequent skill in musical literacy. In Medieval music, Reinhard Strohm argues that musical literacy could have expanded dramatically from as early as the late Middle Ages, in line with an increase in general literacy, 'which with little educational effort, could be turned into musical literacy'.[72] This is interesting, not least because it opens up the possibility of a nineteenth-century musician reading pedagogic material to acquire those skills. Vic Gammon observes this in church band musicians who were able to self-teach musical literacy (and skill) using psalm collections 'and other sorts of self-tutor'.[73] It is also possible to see a connection between this method and the self-improvement movement.

Just because some young children can read simple music notation, they are not necessarily capable of transcribing it. This may suggest that, in line with general literacy, the ability to read music is acquired prior to the skill of writing it. The concept of copying music could be seen as an intermediate stage between reading and writing music, as copying does not require an ability to understand and therefore be wholly musically literate. In Medieval music, scholars debate the role and ability of the copyists, questioning whether the scribes were mindlessly copying the repertoire from exemplars into chansonniers or if they actually did possess some level of musical literacy and compositional skill.[74]

It is clear that being capable of copying a tune title suggests they had the capacity to copy and then learn at the very least, their own name and thus illiteracy is unlikely. Added to this, copying was a time-consuming, laborious task. It is fair to assume that they would only commit to this effort if it offered advantages of speed, ease and reliability and they could actually read the tunes and translate them into a sound on their instruments compared to learning the tune 'by ear'. Given the potential interactions and independence of the different skills it is important that assumptions are not made based on the evidence of one skill. Evidently Hampton's ability to read music is established. Furthermore, his shorthand transcription of some tunes (showing a tune hastily copied or written by ear to act as an aide-memoire rather than a note for note imitation) suggests a fair level of musical literacy and subsequently a good level of musical skill to interpret the rough transcriptions into music.

We do not know from where Hampton gained his general and musical literacies. He was listed as a scholar in 1851, although this does not necessarily mean he attended school.[75] Blaisdon's National School was established in 1847, 'in the old poorhouse by the church',[76] but no extant records exist for this period so it is not clear if he was enrolled there. Even if he had attended school, the evidence suggests that he would not have been guaranteed a comprehensive and systematic education. Further, evidence of notational musical provision in schools is rare.

It is possible he learnt his musical and literacy skills at home – perhaps from a family member, but such informal passing on leaves a distinct lack of evidence. Some evidence can be found in oral narratives of other musicians of the time such as Stephen Baldwin who learnt to play the violin from his father[77] and brothers, Walter and John Chamberlain Bulwer, who were taught to both play violin and read music by their father in the late nineteenth century.[78] Membership in the church bands could be the root of the skills in these circumstances, discussed in detail by Vic Gammon,[79] and touched on below.

It is well known that Anglican churches contributed much to musical ability and literacy in the early mid part of the century but more from 'inside' involvement rather than deliberate education. 'A Village Choir', a mid-nineteenth-century painting by Webster, even shows members of a West Gallery church band reading from music, corroborating levels of both general and musical literacies.[80] The skills of a band member could be 'assimilated through upbringing and exposure',[81] thus acquiring musical literacy through self-teaching using psalm collections and self-tutors (relying too on general literacy), and 'the encouragement of others'.[82] Whilst churches clearly had a role in the early part of the century, the disbandment of the bands mid-century would have seriously affected their place in the transmission of musical skill as the century progressed. Gravestones and baptism records show that the Hampton family had connections with Blaisdon parish church. According to the Churchwarden's accounts, payments appear for organ blowing and tuning from 1869, so it is possible that a church band existed there before organ installation during Thomas' childhood,[83] but no records show names of specific musicians.

Nonconformist chapels would also have provided a place to hear music and possibly participate and acquire musical skill.[84] Vic Gammon noted 'large scale defections to the Methodists',[85] which he attributes in part to a backlash to the introduction of the organ and subsequent disbandment of the church bands. As such, existing musical literacy and skill would be shared across denominations. Furthermore, a strong current of education, literacy and self-improvement existed in Nonconformist denominations.[86]

It is also likely that an influential source of skills for Hampton was from the self-improvement or autodidactic movement, strongly supported by the Nonconformist church. The autodidactic movement was a massive part of the cultural and social make-up of Victorian England. Not only did the autodidactic 'revolution' amongst the lower classes teach literacy skills but opportunities were also available to learn new musical skills in the form of both playing an instrument, reading and writing musical notation, alongside lectures and concerts and providing a stage on which to perform. At a more informal end of the scale, Jonathan Rose quotes the Chartist, Robert Lowery, detailing an informal culture in the pubs of nineteenth-century Newcastle,[87] conjuring up images of like-minded musicians sharing and learning both instrumental skill and notational skill, perhaps poring over a borrowed printed tunebook and learning the skills to make their own copy.

Many Subscription Reading Rooms and The Working Men's Club and Institute Union had libraries and held classes.[88] By the mid-century, the Mechanics' Institute had become 'a recognised part of the educational scene, not only in the industrial cities but in rural market towns and even in quite small hamlets'.[89] They had libraries, and the subject of music, 'both vocal and instrumental',[90] often appeared on their curriculum, quite possibly a source for the compilers. Vic Gammon and Dave Russell cite such institutions as providing actual instrumental classes,[91] in 'the form of cheap class lessons'.[92] Russell lists 'part-time teachers, usually musically inclined clerks and skilled manual workers who swelled their income by giving

Figure 25.5 'Waltz' by S. Musgrave, showing octave doubling

lessons for as little as 3d an hour to the aspiring amateurs of the neighbourhood'.[93] An educational relationship between a skilled manual worker and an aspiring amateur puts forward a plausible explanation for the association between Soobroy and Hampton, suggesting some informal or formal self-improvement through the initial nine pedagogic and popular tunes. These are written in Soobroy's neater and possibly more educated hand and strengthen the argument that Hampton acquired at least some of his skill via the autodidactic route.

Soobroy was a capable musician. The newspaper extract given below shows him leading a string band,[94] and although an apprenticed brush maker in his youth, by 1891 he was a bugler for the Shropshire Light Infantry,[95] and following his discharge in 1897[96] worked as a 'violinist/music' in 1901.[97] His musical career did not last though, as by 1911 he was working as a carter.[98] Not only are Soobroy's writing and notation skills neater, appearing far more educated, controlled and advanced than Hampton's but perhaps this first section is indicative of Soobroy using the manuscript to teach Hampton. Examples of pedagogy can be found in the initial section of the manuscript, including a D major scale detailing third position fingering in the higher register, a bowing and intonation scalic exercise and this later addition (the ink is darker in comparison) of octave doubling below the melody, offering an easier option to avoid moving into third position (Figure 25.5).

It is impossible to say whether Soobroy's instruction was limited to musical literacy, if indeed it were at all, or if Hampton was also receiving instrumental lessons (and/or general literacy) in this way. Hampton's subsequent notation and transcriptions are perhaps too accurate and fluid to suggest that Soobroy alone was Hampton's only access to musical literacy and technical skill. Whilst Hampton's technical skill and some tune melodies may have been acquired as a boy in Gloucestershire, the opportunity of self-improvement in his urban setting and the pedagogic associations with Soobroy suggest that this was a viable route for him to acquire or improve his musical literacy skills and either improve or learn to play the violin.

Acquiring sources

Having put forward some ideas as to where men like Hampton acquired their skills, I now return to examine where the men may have acquired their sources. As an urban compiler, Hampton had plenty of access to music sellers; yet as discussed above, purchasing printed music, especially on a regular basis, given the popular trends in evidence in the manuscripts, could be unaffordable to a lower-working-class musician. Instead, it is probable that compilers were borrowing a printed copy, selecting specific tunes, copying them into their manuscripts (thus creating their bespoke repertoire) and returning the printed source. In the manuscript, evidence of this is seen in the 'cluster copying' (where a selection of tunes from one source is copied down, followed by a cluster of tunes from a different source), the haphazard tune ordering (Hampton's manuscript is not laid out in dance sets ready for continuous performance or in genre type or alphabetically for easy retrieval) and the untidy handwriting suggesting rushed transcription.[99] It appears that the compilers copied out groups of tunes or a single tune they liked or wanted to learn, when they came across them in a printed book.

It is possible that the musicians were borrowing printed copies (or indeed manuscripts) from friends,[100] or from libraries belonging to the self-improvement institutions, some of whom had specific music libraries,[101] although maintaining an up-to-date musical library to match trends in popular fashion could have put constraints on these charitable institutions. Instead, it is possible that a much larger social and cultural influence was involved. When searching through contemporary newspaper advertisements for music sellers, a much-understudied yet seemingly widespread nineteenth-century social and cultural phenomenon became apparent: Musical Circulating Libraries. These libraries could account for the hurried, cluster copying and ad hoc layouts in the manuscripts and offer a feasible place from which the compilers accessed their tunes.

The number of newspaper advertisements mentioning these circulating libraries implies that they were commonplace; yet, I have found only four academic papers written about them,[102] and the most recent dates from 1982. In it, Hans Lenneberg proposes that the 'matter-of-fact tone' given in references to these libraries implies 'that by the middle of the nineteenth century musical lending libraries were common'.[103] He suggests that they were disapproved of due to 'the musical world [having] misgivings about the practice of lending […] [they] seem to have been held in contempt by publishers and booksellers',[104] and that general lending libraries had a bad reputation due to their role in the dissemination of 'erotic literature'.[105]

Nineteenth-century musician and poet, John Clare, 'usd [sic] to seize the leisure that every wet day brought me to go to Drurys shop to read books & to get new tunes for my fiddle'.[106] Trade directories are scant for Clare's locale and period; yet, Mina Gorji names the 'New Public Library' owned by Edmund Drury 'an early supporter of Clare's and a source of much of his early reading',[107] who operated as a bookshop and lending library, and presumably also acted as a music seller. Although no mention is made of whether he also ran a Musical Circulating Library, it is quite likely; otherwise, Drury might have given Clare short shrift! The possibility of a musical library as an everyday part of John Clare's contextual background not only explains Clare's actions but indicates no direct mention of a library, perhaps as it was unnecessary due to widespread public knowledge, thus their subsequent absence in the historical record.

The range of music offered by these libraries was extensive and catered not only for ensembles or the Drawing-room genre but directly reflected the popular instrumental repertoire included in the manuscripts as well. From what can be determined, terms of borrowing vary not only between different libraries, but between the different services a borrower required.[108] An advertisement for Duck's 'Cheap Music Repository' shows an annual subscription of 21 shillings,[109] which would equate to a weekly subscription of just under five pence, excessive for the compilers' demographic but affordable if shared between a group of musical friends. This fee would offer access to vast quantities of tune collections for a whole year costing much less than a one-off purchase of one copy of Chappell's 'Cheap Works' outright. However, it is possible that the compilers' sources were more along the lines of a smaller Musical Circulating Library detailed by Trevor Fawcett which offered a copy on a nightly rate of one penny.[110] This time-limit would corroborate the sense of urgency inferred in the copying.

As the century progressed, these libraries and the need to compile manuscripts became redundant as, combined with mass production lowering prices, and the real-time pay increases from the 1870s taking effect, the lower classes had more disposable income to purchase their own copies of music. Consequently, the once commonplace Musical Circulating Libraries were a short-lived phenomenon whose existence has been largely forgotten. The significance of manuscripts such as Hampton's is raised by their ability to show a synchronic period, demonstrating popular taste at that time and moreover personal selection of this taste, which cannot be perceived by examining the content of the printed sources alone.

Outward transmission

Tune titles indicate that the majority of the secular tunes are dances, but the often-informal occasions and environments for performance by amateur musicians are not well documented and information is incredibly scant. Thus, establishing the outward transmission, i.e. when, where and for what function the compilers played their tunes, is difficult. The outward transmission, or function, fulfilled by the musicians would undoubtedly have had a large impact on the selection and thus diversity of repertoire. For example, selecting hornpipes could result from accompanying step-dancers in the local pub and waltzes to accompany informal and formal dances. It is also feasible that the function was more simply for personal enjoyment and entertainment, the inclusion of a song or waltz having no purpose other than it was popular and the compiler liked it or wanted to learn it.

It is sometimes through incidental means, such as court reports in newspapers, that we learn of the activities of amateur musicians. However, searching local newspaper articles for the mention of Hampton in both musical and non-musical environments proved fruitless. On face-value, this might suggest that he was not involved in the secular musical activities of his community. However, toiling for hours copying out tunes, collating a repertoire possibly in candlelight, after a long day at work and presumably putting in time to learn the tunes and improve technical skill, without a rewarding outlet for such a repertoire is unlikely.

Nevertheless, Soobroy's musical activity did make the newspapers. In 1891 a report in the *Ross Gazette* mentions Soobroy and his 'string band' playing for a gymnastics display (see Figure 25.6).[111] The article suggests that the music was incidental music, presumably on a non-commercial, voluntary basis accompanying the sporting event. Although a tune programme is not given, the string band performed an overture of tunes to open each half of the evening, the National Anthem at the close and possibly some background music during the display, suggested by the 'Musical Maze'. It is fascinating to find Soobroy mentioned in a newspaper article and raises the possibility of 47-year-old Hampton being an unnamed member of the band, 5 years before his death.

It is possible that Hampton played the fiddle to accompany dancing, as suggested by the title of his tunebook – 'Dances for Violin' – and some of the tune titles. This does not necessarily mean that Hampton was a member of an organised dance band, and the participatory element, if there was one at all, could have been for smaller community events or for own entertainment. His involvement could have leant towards more informal activities, gathering to play for dances on a smaller scale, such as at club day feasts, Whitsun ales, village feast days, revels, harvest homes, ringers' suppers, shearing feasts[112]; servant's balls,[113] weddings, wakes and hiring fairs, at various locations ranging from gentry country houses and assembly rooms to barns, village halls and pubs.[114]

Several of Hampton's tunes are popular for Morris dancing, indicating that he could have played for a Morris team. It is possible that Hampton knew the Baldwin family of

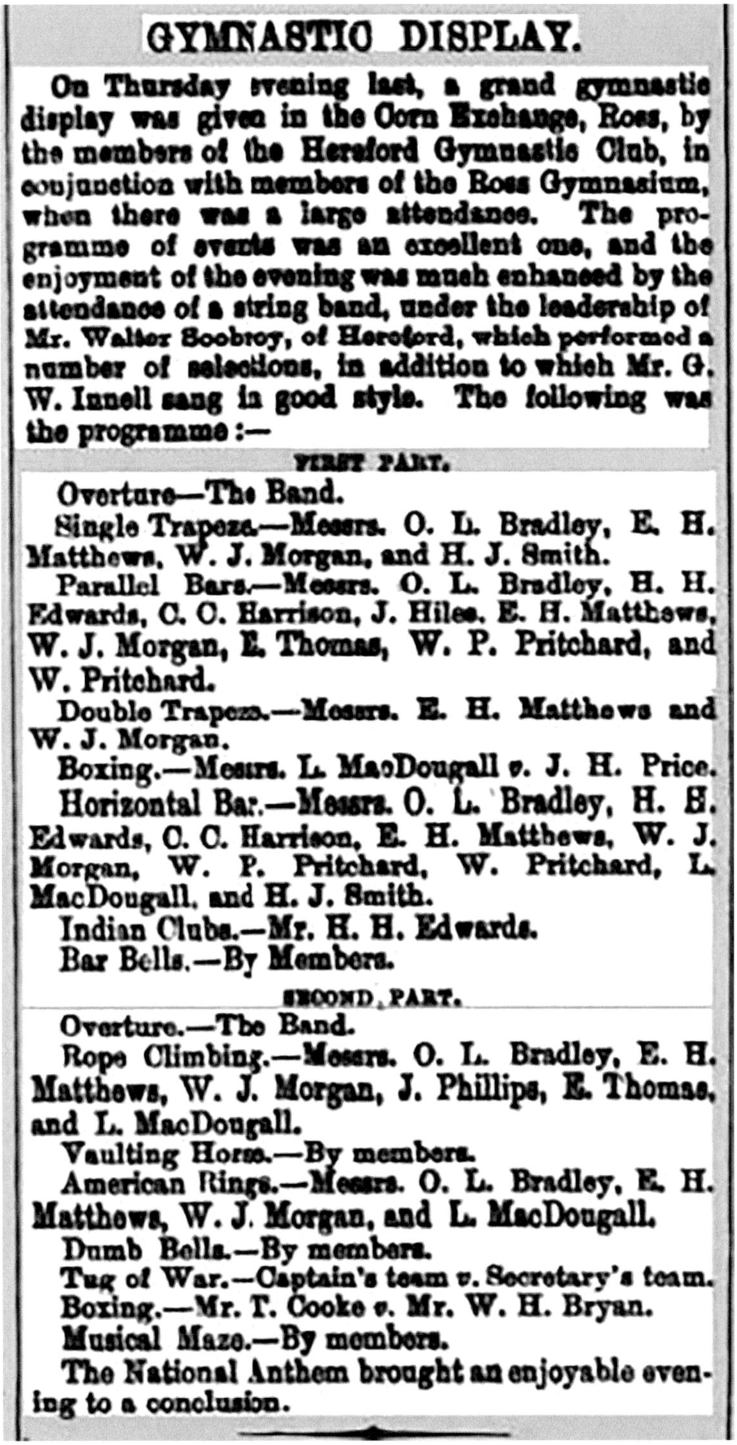

GYMNASTIC DISPLAY.

On Thursday evening last, a grand gymnastic display was given in the Corn Exchange, Ross, by the members of the Hereford Gymnastic Club, in conjunction with members of the Ross Gymnasium, when there was a large attendance. The programme of events was an excellent one, and the enjoyment of the evening was much enhanced by the attendance of a string band, under the leadership of Mr. Walter Soobroy, of Hereford, which performed a number of selections, in addition to which Mr. G. W. Innell sang in good style. The following was the programme:—

FIRST PART.

Overture—The Band.
Single Trapeze.—Messrs. O. L. Bradley, E. H. Matthews, W. J. Morgan, and H. J. Smith.
Parallel Bars.—Messrs. O. L. Bradley, H. H. Edwards, C. C. Harrison, J. Hiles, E. H. Matthews, W. J. Morgan, E. Thomas, W. P. Pritchard, and W. Pritchard.
Double Trapeze.—Messrs. E. H. Matthews and W. J. Morgan.
Boxing.—Messrs. L. MacDougall v. J. H. Price.
Horizontal Bar.—Messrs. O. L. Bradley, H. H. Edwards, C. C. Harrison, E. H. Matthews, W. J. Morgan, W. P. Pritchard, W. Pritchard, L. MacDougall, and H. J. Smith.
Indian Clubs.—Mr. H. H. Edwards.
Bar Bells.—By Members.

SECOND PART.

Overture.—The Band.
Rope Climbing.—Messrs. O. L. Bradley, E. H. Matthews, W. J. Morgan, J. Phillips, E. Thomas, and L. MacDougall.
Vaulting Horse.—By members.
American Rings.—Messrs. O. L. Bradley, E. H. Matthews, W. J. Morgan, and L. MacDougall.
Dumb Bells.—By members.
Tug of War.—Captain's team v. Secretary's team.
Boxing.—Mr. T. Cooke v. Mr. W. H. Bryan.
Musical Maze.—By members.
The National Anthem brought an enjoyable evening to a conclusion.

Figure 25.6 Soobroy's string band
Source: From Ross Gazette, 1891.

fiddlers, known to Cecil Sharp and researched by Philip Heath-Coleman.[115] Stephen, born in Hereford in 1873, played for morris, country dances and gypsy weddings.[116] Like Hampton, Stephen had connections to Hereford and the Forest of Dean, but it is more probable that Stephen's father, and fiddle teacher Charles Baldwin was a connection.[117] Born in Newent (only seven miles from Blaisdon) in 1827, Charles also moved in geographically similar locations to Hampton. Remarkably, Charles was living in Hereford, a mile away from Thomas in 1871 and it is feasible that the two fiddlers knew each other during this time. Not only do they share a mutual musical interest, but in 1861, when Thomas' father and brothers were transporting charcoal on the Hereford and Gloucester Canal, Charles was working as a charcoal burner in Newent,[118] through which the canal passed.[119]

Alongside the potential social or work-related connection between the Hampton and Baldwin families comes a similarity of repertoire. The recording of Stephen and the collection of Charles' and Stephen's tunes show six tunes in common with Hampton's repertoire.[120] The function of the recordings and Sharp's collecting was to find traditional tunes. If a more popular repertoire were included, there could be even more tunes in common. Furthermore, Hampton and Baldwin share an unusual tune name in both their repertoires suggesting similar sources. Philip Heath-Coleman's research shows that Charles played for the Clifford's Mesne morris, which is directly between Blaisdon and Newent.[121] Hampton's potential connection with Baldwin, his location and the inclusion of Morris tunes in the manuscript indicate that Hampton may also have played for the morris side.

Hornpipes are one of the most represented dance or tune genres in Hampton's manuscript. The hornpipes are all of the 4/4 'new' style and not the 3/2 hornpipes of earlier centuries. It is highly likely that the hornpipes' presence in the manuscripts is due to their role in accompanying the thriving nineteenth-century solo exhibition dance practice of step-dancing and clogging; see Figure 25.7.[122]

Step-dancing is documented in oral narratives recorded by Keith Chandler and Reg Hall, with Chris Holderness recording an oral narrative stating that 'most men done a little bit of stepping years ago'.[123] Step-dancing occurred at informal locations such as the pub, and during functions such as feasts and wakes. However, there is very little written about this practice in the wider nineteenth-century musical or social history and it is interesting that the manuscripts might document or support these oral narratives.

Figure 25.7 'Step Dancing in the Tap Room'
Source: *The Graphic*, 22 October 1887.

Hornpipes also appear in the programmes of penny concerts and amateur concerts,[124] and the possibility exists that the music in the manuscripts was beginning to represent music for music's sake and that the hornpipes were played purely for aural enjoyment rather than needing to fulfil a function such as accompanying a dance. As such, an aesthetic function of the manuscripts, or the musical practice they represent, is possible, the tunes existing simply for personal recreation. This is further corroborated by the inclusion of song melodies as well as dance tunes within many manuscripts. The revelation of the stand-alone aesthetic value of the manuscripts' contents adds another dimension to their functionality and to the activities of the musicians.

Thus, a potential role opens up for the musicians as informal entertainers for their own and an audiences' auditory pleasure. This can occur on several levels: personal and private in a domestic situation; informal in a social, perhaps in a 'tune-up',[125] in a pub setting; or on more formal level. It is hard to ascertain whether a truly autotelic instrumental musical practice took place in these environments, in a similar way that an exclusively tune session might occur today, or rather the instrumentalists were always in an accompaniment role be it for singers or dancers.

Steve Roud quotes a colourful narrative from Edwin Waugh's *Lancashire Sketches*, dated 1855, in which instrumental musicians are playing in a pub, albeit in an accompaniment role:

> In another corner you might hear the fiddler playing the animated strains of the 'Liverpool Hornpipe' or 'Th' Devil Ript his Shirt', while a lot of hearty youngsters, in wooden clogs, battered the hearthstone to the tune. In the room above, the lights flared in the wind, as the lads and lasses flitted to and fro in 'The Haymaker', 'Sir Roger De Coverley', or 'The Triumph', or threaded through a reel and set till the whole house shook.[126]

Dave Russell also provides evidence of a tune-up tradition in Suffolk: 'local singers and instrumentalists gathered in the taproom of a set hostelry and entertained each other, anyone refusing or unable to contribute being forced to buy drinks'.[127] He describes the class of those participating as similar to Hampton whilst 'the 'respectable' classes kept at safe distance in the parlour or saloon bar'.[128]

Julian Taylor's collection of newspaper extracts provides evidence of numerous informal fiddle and dance events. These give an insight into informal pub culture, via incidental reports; for example, the suicide of Robert Clough, a fiddler who played at 'The Boat' public-house two nights a week.[129] Chandler's study of nineteenth-century musicians also indicates a vibrant informal rural pub music culture,[130] as does Hall's research.[131] Researching newspapers local to Hampton, uncovered an article depicting informal music and dancing events at pubs, once again in an unrelated section, in which the report focusses on the crime of selling beer after time and theft, but paints a wonderful picture of informal step-dancing and fiddle-playing at a pub.

The report suggests the local pub environment had spontaneous and informal music, corroborated by personal oral narrative. According to family narrative, Thomas was in a Hereford pub, participating in a pub activity whereby if you could play or sing without making a piglet squeal, you won the piglet. Thomas duly won the piglet, but during the process had evidently consumed a fair bit of ale and on his way home, with pig and fiddle under his arm, he stumbled over and broke the fiddle. Whether he managed to hang on to the pig is not known![132]

Conclusion

Manuscripts such as Thomas' have value as historical artefacts, informing on both musicological and non-musicological levels, and thus validate their role beyond a personal tune repository to a primary and important historical resource. Musicologically, they are able to act as a primary source on a topic which has had little academic attention and which, because of the status of its informants, audience and participants and the informal nature of its content, is not often preserved in the historical record. The manuscripts are able to give an insight into Victorian popular musical tastes, technical ability, and social and cultural activities previously reliant on oral narrative and non-musical archival research. As more general historical sources, the manuscripts hold vital information regarding non-musical aspects of nineteenth-century culture, making them significant in wider social and cultural history disciplines. They enable us to observe unwritten cultural and social rules (consequently potentially destabilising research on nineteenth-century literacy levels) and provide evidence of wider social and cultural movements, such as religious and autodidactic practices.

Perhaps their most significant role as musical artefacts is their survival when compared to the printed sources which they replicate. If it were not for these manuscripts, our knowledge of the extent of these musicians' repertoires would be skewed. The repertoire of 'ear-playing' nineteenth-century amateur musicians was open to mediation by collectors hunting out and selecting historic tunes from their repertoire and as such may not be wholly representative.[133] Similarly, many of the contemporary tunes and songs do not exist in modern collections such as the Traditional Tune Archive, nor are they easily accessible in the original, printed publications and it is only through the manuscripts that we are re-acquainted with this repertoire. Without these manuscripts, our knowledge of a mid-late nineteenth-century amateur, vernacular, instrumental musical practice, its participants, repertoire and sources, would be lacking. Without these manuscripts, there is a danger that an entire chapter in the historiography of nineteenth-century English music would be omitted.

Whether the tunes in the manuscripts fall under the definitions of folk music or historic popular music may depend on your own interpretation of those difficult terms. Regardless, it is clear that in the context of a traditional 'process' the manuscripts have a very important part to play. Steve Roud compares this traditional process which 'turns' a song into a folk song to a 'sausage machine: put a pleasure-garden song into the tradition, and if it is not spat out as unsuitable, it emerges at the other end as a clearly different kind of song'.[134] The textual medium of the manuscripts provides a synchronic capture of the 'process of tradition', at work, and gives a valuable insight into the progression from a contemporary popular tune into a folk or traditional tune when viewed retrospectively in the context of subsequent (and current) instrumental players' repertoire. The manuscripts enable the inner working of Roud's 'sausage machine' to be viewed.[135] As such the manuscripts have a vital role in the 'process' of folk music tradition.

Notes

1 Thomas Hardy, *Under the Greenwood Tree* (Ware, Hertfordshire: Wordsworth Editions Limited, 2004) p. xxiv.

2 This is a term used to describe the books although they were not exclusively compiled by fiddle players but also include the repertoires of other monophonic instrumentalists such as flautists and cornet players.

3 For example, David Harker, *Fakesong : The Manufacture of British 'Folksong' 1700 to the Present Day* (Milton Keynes: Open University Press, 1985) p. xiii.

4 Wikipedia, 'Folk Music', *Wikipedia* (2017) <https://en.wikipedia.org/wiki/Folk_music> [accessed 14 October 2017].

5 For example, Maud Karpeles, *An Introduction to English Folk Song* (London: Oxford University Press, 1973, 1987) p. 2; Ralph Vaughan Williams, *National Music and Other Essays*, 2nd edn (Oxford: Oxford University Press, 1986) pp. 28–33.

6   See for example: David Atkinson, 'Folk Songs in Print: Text and Tradition', *Folk Music Journal*, 8.4 (2004), 456–483; Adam Fox, *Oral and Literate Culture in England 1500–1700* (Oxford: Oxford University Press, 2000).
7   Steve Roud, *Folk Song in England* (London: Faber, 2017) p. 22.
8   Roud, *Folk Song in England*, p. 23.
9   Roud, *Folk Song in England* p. 22.
10 'Thomas Hampton', *Baptism Record for Thomas Hampton, 30 March 1844* (Gloucestershire Archives; Gloucester, England; Gdr/V1/410) <www.ancestry.co.uk> [accessed 20 April 2017].
11 The village was small with a population of 280 in 1851: 'Blaisdon', *Post Office Directory of Gloucestershire, Bath & Bristol* (1856) (p. 242) <http://specialcollections.le.ac.uk> [accessed 4 December 2016]. In 1861, it had risen to 282: 'Blaisdon', *Slater's Directory of Glos, Herefs, Mon, Shrops & Wales* (1868) (p. 252) <http://specialcollections.le.ac.uk/cdm/> [accessed 2 April 2017]. Baptism Record for Thomas Hampton.
12 'John Hampton', *1841 England Census Return (Class: HO107; Piece: 369; Book: 1; Civil Parish: Blaisdon; County: Gloucestershire; Enumeration District: 1; Folio: 7; Page: 8; Line: 2; GSU roll: 288780)*, <https://www.ancestry.co.uk> [accessed 3 October 2015]; 'Elizabeth Hampton', *Baptism Record for Elizabeth Hampton, 22 January 1843* (Fhl Film Number: 91516) <www.ancestry.co.uk> [accessed 21 April 2017].
13 'John Hampton', *Certified Copy of Death Certificate for John Hampton, 29 February 1884* (Application Number 3114128–2: Hereford Register Office, 2011).
14 'Thomas Hampton', *1851 England Census Return (Class: HO107; Piece: 1959; Folio: 420; Page: 2; GSU roll: 87359)*, <www.ancestry.co.uk> [accessed 4 October 2015].
15 'John Hampton', *1861 England Census Return (Class: RG 9; Piece: 1821; Folio: 107; GSU roll: 542873)*, <www.ancestry.co.uk> [accessed 17 October 2015].
16 David E. Bick, *The Hereford & Gloucester Canal* (Newent, Glos: The Pound House, 1979) p. 34.
17 Bick *Ibid.*, (1979) pp. 37–41.
18 'Thomas Hampton', *Certified Copy of Marriage Certificate for Thomas Hampton and Ann Wyatt*, 7 March 1870 (Application Number 8111747/1: Hereford Register Office, 2017).
19 Certified Copy of Death Certificate for Thomas Hampton.
20 *Coote, Hopwood & Crew's Selection of Quadrilles, Waltzes, Polkas &C. Edited and Expressly Arranged for the Violin Book 4*. Copy in the author's possession.
21 'Walter Soobroy', *Marriage Record for Walter Soobroy, 2 July 1874* (Fhl Film Number: 992807) <www.ancestry.co.uk> [accessed 6 October 2015]; 'Walter Soobroy', *Death Record for Walter Soobroy, 1931* (Herefordshire Volume: 6a Page: 571) <www.ancestry.co.uk> [accessed 7 October 2015].
22 'Walter Soobroy', *1861 England Census Return (Class: RG 9; Piece: 1821; Folio: 84; Page: 8; GSU roll: 542873)*, <www.ancestry.co.uk> [accessed 16 September 2015]; 'Walter Soobroy', *1871 England Census Return (Class: RG10; Piece: 2700; Folio: 36; Page: 22; GSU roll: 835344)*, <www.ancestry.co.uk> [accessed 16 September 2015].
23 'Walter Soobroy', *1871 England Census Return*.
24 Cecil Sharp, *English Folk Song, Some Conclusions* (London: Simpkin, 1907) p. 3.
25 See for example: A.L. Lloyd, *Folk Song in England* (London: Lawrence & Wishart, 1967); David Harker, *Fakesong : The Manufacture of British 'Folksong' 1700 to the Present Day* (Milton Keynes: Open University Press, 1985); C.J. Bearman, *English Folk Music Movement 1898–1914* (PhD thesis, Hull University, 2001).
26 Roud, *Folk Song in England*, p. 27.
27 A complete list and analysis on the content can be found in my PhD thesis available online at https://etheses.whiterose.ac.uk/. Rebecca Dellow, *'Fiddlers' Tunebooks' – Vernacular Instrumental Manuscript Sources 1860–c1880: Paradigmatic of Folk Music Tradition?* (PhD thesis, University of Sheffield, 2018).
28 This is discussed in Part 4.
29 Geoff Woolfe, *William Winter's Quantocks Tune Book* (Crowcombe: Halsway Manor, 2007) p. 74.
30 Colin Thompson and Tim Laycock, *Benjamin's Book : The Complete Country Dance Manuscript of Benjamin Rose* (Colin Thompson and Tim Laycock, No date) p. 39.
31 Charles Menteith and Paul Burgess, *The Coleford Jig Traditional Tunes from Gloucestershire* (Cheltenham: Charles Menteith and Paul Burgess, 2014) p. 62.
32 Andrew Kuntz and Valerio Pellicconi, 'Harlequin Hornpipe 4', *Traditional Tune Archive* (2017) <http://tunearch.org> [accessed 13 March 2018].

33 Chris Walshaw, 'Harlequin's Hornpipe. Bhp.09', *abcnotation* (2017) <http://abcnotation.com> [accessed 13 March 2018].
34 David Kettlewell, 'Master Byrons Hornpipe', *English Dance & Song*, 43.3 (1981), p.19; Philip Heath-Coleman, *Email Correspondence* (24 June 2015).
35 Derek Scott, *The Singing Bourgeois : Songs of the Victorian Drawing Room and Parlour* (Milton Keynes: Open University Press, 1989) p. 25.
36 Scott, *The Singing Bourgeois*, (1989) p. 27.
37 The tune can be found in Kerr's (although not Hampton's direct source) titled '"Cawdor Fair" Highland Schottische'. Kerr, *Kerr's First Collection of Merry Melodies for the Violin* (Glasgow: James S Kerr, No date) p. 20.
38 Andrew Kuntz and Valerio Pelliccioni, 'Cawdor Fair', *Traditional Tune Archive* (2017) <http://tunearch.org> [accessed 16 March 2018].
39 The annotation 'Very Old' is given in Gow. Neil Gow, *Gow's Repository of the Dance Music of Scotland* (Edinburgh: Robert Purdie, 1817).
40 Iona Opie and Peter Opie, *The Oxford Dictionary of Nursery Rhymes* (London: Oxford University Press, 1951) pp. 394–395.
41 Christopher Walker, '"The Triumph" in England, Scotland and the United States', *Folk Music Journal*, 8.1 (2001), 4–40 (p. 4).
42 Broadside Ballads Online from the Bodleian Libraries, 'Results: Roud Number:13883', *Bodleian Libraries University of Oxford* (No date) [accessed 3 March 2018].
43 Derek Scott, *Sounds of the Metropolis : The Nineteenth-Century Popular Music Revolution in London, New York, Paris, and Vienna* (Oxford: Oxford University Press, 2008) p. 174.
44 A direct source was found for Hampton: Thomas Westrop, *120 Country Dances* (London: Charles Sheard & Co., No date) p. 9. The tune also appears in Boosey, *Boosey's Hundred Reels, Country & Other Dances. For the Violin*, p. 10.
45 Scott, *Sounds of the Metropolis*, (2008) p. 174.
46 Scott, *The Singing Bourgeois*, (1989) p. 35.
47 Scott, *The Singing Bourgeois*, (1989) p. 35.
48 Frank Kidson and Mary Neal, *English Folk-Song and Dance* (Cambridge: Cambridge University Press, 1915) p. 129.
49 Frederick Warne, *The Ballroom Guide* (London: Frederick Warne, 1888 [2012]) p. 61.
50 Frank Greene, 'People Coote Charles', *TheMusicSack* (2017) <http://musicsack.com/PersonFMTDetail.cfm?PersonPK=100067546> [accessed 26 September 2017].
51 Musopen, 'Charles Coote' (No date) <https://musopen.org/composer/charles-coote/> [accessed 26 September 2017].
52 British Library Catalogue, 'Three Rondos, No 1, the Carnival, No 2, the Tarantella, No 3, the Pulcinella, for the Piano Forte, From … The Gipsy's Warning … No. 3.', *British Library* (No date) <http://explore.bl.uk> [accessed 3 March 2018].
53 Michael R. Turner, *The Parlour Song Book* (London: Michael Joseph, 1972) p. 241.
54 Ray B. Browne, *The Alabama Folk Lyric: A Study in Origins and Media of Dissemination* (Ohio: Bowling Green University Popular Press) p. 97.
55 The Lester S. Levy Sheet Music Collection, ''Tis but a Little Faded Flower. Ballad', *John Hopkins Sheridan Libraries & University Museums* (2017) <http://levysheetmusic.mse.jhu.edu> [accessed 3 May 2017].
56 The Sheetmusic Warehouse, ''Tis but a Little Faded Flower – Ballad Sung by the Christys Minstrels', *The Sheetmusic Warehouse* (No date) <https://www.sheetmusicwarehouse.co.uk> [accessed 7 June 2017].
57 Hymns and Carols of Christmas, 'Adeste, Fideles – Notes on the Hymn', *Hymns and Carols of Christmas* (No date) <http://www.hymnsandcarolsofchristmas.com> [accessed 5 October 2016].
58 Bennett Zon, 'The Origin of "Adeste Fideles"', *Early Music*, 24.2 (1996), 279–288.
59 For a discussion on this in the folk song field, see Atkinson, 'Folk Songs in Print: Text and Tradition'.
60 For more details of the methods I used, please consult my PhD thesis: Dellow (2018).
61 Coote, *Hopwood & Crew's Selection of Quadrilles, Waltzes, Polkas &C. Edited and Expressly Arranged for the Violin Book 4*.
62 Jones, *Hopwood & Crew's 100 Country Dances for the Violin, Arranged by S. Jones.London, [1875] Music Collections E.269.(3.)*.
63 Westrop, *120 Country Dances*.

64 Kerr, *Kerr's First Collection of Merry Melodies for the Violin*.
65 Certified Copy of Marriage Certificate for Thomas Hampton and Ann Wyatt.
66 For example, see David Vincent, *Literacy and Popular Culture : England 1750–1914* (Cambridge: Cambridge University Press, 1989) pp. 16–18.
67 'Literacy statistics are difficult to calculate but the commonly accepted measure is "signature literacy"; the most comprehensive survey of this in the Victorian period is on marriage certificates'. Paul Rodmell, 'Introduction', in *Music and Institutions in Nineteenth-Century Britain*, ed. by Paul Rodmell (London and New York: Routledge, 2016) (p. 3).
68 Flora Thompson, *Lark Rise to Candleford* (London: Oxford University Press, 1939) p. 80.
69 Thompson *Ibid.*, (1939) p. 192.
70 Richard Sykes, 'The Evolution of Englishness in the English Folksong Revival, 1890–1914', *Folk Music Journal*, 6.4 (1993), 446–490 (p. 453).
71 Keith Chandler, 'Musicians in 19th Century Southern England', *Musical Traditions Internet Magazine* (2000), <http://www.mustrad.org.uk> [accessed 14 October 2015].
72 Reinhard Strohm, 'Unwritten and Written Music', in *Companion to Medieval & Renaissance Music*, ed. by Tess Knighton and David Fallows (Oxford: Oxford University Press, 1992) pp. 228–33 (p. 231).
73 Vic Gammon, *Popular Music in Rural Society: Sussex 1815 – 1914* (PhD thesis, University of Sussex, 1985) p. 35.
74 Elizabeth Aubrey, 'Literacy, Orality and the Preservation of French and Occitan Medieval Courtly Songs', *Revista de Musicologia,* 16 (1993), 2355–2366 (p. 2357).
75 'Thomas Hampton', *1851 England Census Return*.
76 British History Online from Victoria County History, 'Blaisdon: Education', *Institute of Historical Research, University of London* (2017) <http://www.british-history.ac.uk/vch/glos/vol10/pp10-11> [accessed 27 April 2017].
77 Philip Heath-Coleman, *Stephen Baldwin 'Here's One You'll Like, I Think'* (Musical Traditions, 2005) MTCD334 p. 3.
78 Chris Holderness, 'Walter and Daisy Bulwer. Recollections of the Shipdham Musicians by Members of Their Community. Mt185', *Musical Traditions Internet Magazine* (2009), <http://www.mustrad.org.uk/articles/bulwer.htm> [accessed 27 April 2017].
79 Gammon, *Popular Music in Rural Society*, p. 34.
80 Victoria & Albert Museum, 'A Village Choir (Oil Painting) (1847 Webster)'.
81 Gammon, *Popular Music in Rural Society*, p. 34.
82 Gammon, *Popular Music in Rural Society*, p. 34.
83 Gloucestershire Archives, *Churchwardens' Accounts and Vestry Minutes*, P49/CW/2/1 (1820–1874).
84 Alan Ainsworth, 'Religion in the Working Class Community, and the Evolution of Socialism in Late Nineteenth Century Lancashire: A Case of Working Class Consciousness ',*Histoire Sociale Social History,* 10. 20 (1977) 369.
85 Gammon, *Popular Music in Rural Society*, p. 63.
86 Dave Russell, *Popular Music in England 1840–1914: a Social History.* (Manchester: Manchester University Press, 1987), p. 189.
87 'Every branch of knowledge had its public-house where its disciples met…There was a house were the singers and musicians met – a house where the speculative and free thinking met…' Jonathan Rose, *The Intellectual Life of the British Working Classes*, 2nd edn (London and New Haven, CT: Yale University Press, 2010) p. 38.
88 Rose *Ibid.*, p. 79.
89 E.D. Mackerness, *A Social History of English Music* (London: Routledge, 1964) p. 148.
90 Mackerness *Ibid.*, p. 148.
91 Gammon, *Popular Music in Rural Society*, p. 288.
92 Russell, *Popular Music in England*, p. 172.
93 Russell, *Popular Music in England*, p. 172.
94 'Gymnastic Display', *Ross Gazette*, 16 April 1891, <https://www.britishnewspaperarchive.co.uk> p. 4.
95 'Walter Soohry', *1891 England Census Return England Census Return (The National Archives of the UK (TNA); Kew, Surrey, England; Class: RG12; Piece: 2062; Folio: 79; Page: 5)*, <https://search.ancestry.co.uk> [accessed 4 June 2018].
96 'Walter Soobroy', *Royal Hospital Chelsea Pensioner Admissions and Discharges, 1715–1925 England Census Return (Royal Hospital Chelsea: Length of Service Pensions, Admission Books; Class: WO 117; Piece Number: 51)*, <https://search.ancestry.co.uk> [accessed 4 June 2018].

97 'Walter Svobrory', *1901 England Census Return England Census Return (Class: RG13; Piece: 2481; Folio: 86; Page: 26)*, <https://search.ancestry.co.uk> [accessed 4 June 2018].
98 'Walter Soobroy', *1911 England Census Return England Census Return (Class: RG14; Piece: 15710; Schedule Number: 168)*, <https://search.ancestry.co.uk> [accessed 4 June 2018].
99 For detailed evidence of this, please see my PhD thesis.
100 Perhaps Soobroy's printed music was borrowed by Hampton and not returned.
101 In 1821, The Bradford Musical Friendly Society was founded 'as a music library for local musicians'. Russell (1987) p. 196. And just as music was sold by non-specific shops such as booksellers, so it is possible that the general libraries also held music.
102 Trevor Fawcett, 'Music Circulating Libraries in Norwich', *The Musical Times*, 119. 1625 (1978), 594–595; Hans Lenneberg, 'Early Circulating Libraries and the Dissemination of Music', *The Library Quarterly: Information, Community, Policy*, 52. 2 (1982), 122–130; Alec Hyatt King, 'Music Circulating Libraries in Britain', *The Musical Times*, 119.1620 (1978), 134–138; Victor A. Perch, 'Music Circulating Libraries', *The Musical Times*, 122.1663 (1981), 601–601.
103 Lenneberg, *'Early Circulating Libraries'*, p. 123.
104 Lenneberg, *'Early Circulating Libraries'*, pp. 125–126.
105 Lenneberg, *'Early Circulating Libraries'*, p. 126.
106 George Deacon, *John Clare and the Folk Tradition* (London: Frances Boutle Publishers, 2002) p. 305.
107 Mina Gorji, *John Clare and the Place of Poetry* (Liverpool: Liverpool University Press, 2008) <https://books.google.co.uk> [Accessed 27 April 2017].
108 For example, Novello, Ewer & Co's Musical Circulating Library offered six different classes (appropriate for town or country borrowers). They ranged from 5 Guineas per annum for a town dwelling band leader to borrow instrumental parts, up to 18 pieces daily, down to 3 shillings on a weekly basis to borrow 12 pieces per week (for a town dweller), or 20 pieces (for a country dweller). *Catalogue of Novello, Ewer & Co.'S Circulating Music Library*.c1890?
109 'Duck's Cheap Musical Repository', *Bath Chronicle and Weekly Gazette*, 11 January 1866, <http://www.britishnewspaperarchive.co.uk> [accessed 28 April 2017] p. 8.
110 Fawcett, 'Music Circulating Libraries in Norwich', p. 594.
111 'Gymnastic Display', *Ross Gazette*, 16 April 1891, <https://www.britishnewspaperarchive.co.uk> p. 4. A transcription of the first section is provided in Appendix F.
112 Sabine Baring-Gould, *Old Country Life*, 2nd edn (West Yorkshire: EP Publishing, 1975) p. 243.
113 Vic Gammon, 'Manuscript Sources of Traditional Dance Music in Southern England', *Traditional Dance*, 4 (1986) pp. 53–72 (p. 70).
114 Andy Hornby, *The Winders of Wyresdale* (Andy Hornby, 2013) p. 3.
115 Heath-Coleman, *Stephen Baldwin 'Here's One You'll Like, I Think'*.
116 Menteith and Burgess, *The Coleford Jig*, p. ii.
117 Heath-Coleman, *Stephen Baldwin 'Here's One You'll Like, I Think'*, p. 2.
118 Heath-Coleman, *Stephen Baldwin 'Here's One You'll Like, I Think'*, p. 3.
119 Herefordshire & Gloucestershire Canal Trust, 'Maps', *Herefordshire & Gloucestershire Canal Trust* (No date) <http://www.h-g-canal.org.uk> [accessed 26 April 2017].
120 Menteith and Burgess, *The Coleford Jig Traditional Tunes from Gloucestershire*.
121 Heath-Coleman, *Stephen Baldwin 'Here's One You'll Like, I Think'*, p. 4.
122 Image courtesy of Reg Hall; from *The Graphic*, 22 October 1887, p. 457; an engraving by Charles J. Staniland, the venue is 'The King's Head', Hoverton, Wroxham, Norfolk and the fiddler is the landlord, Mr Jimpson. Reg Hall, 'I Never Played to Many Posh Dances… Scan Tester, Sussex Musician, 1887–1972', Keith Summers (ed.) *Musical Traditions* (1990) <https://www.mustrad.org.uk/pdf/scan05.pdf> [accessed 12 April 2018]; Reg Hall, *Email Correspondence* (13 April 2018).
123 Chris Holderness, 'Hindringham. Traditional Music and Dancing in This North Norfolk Village. Mt285', *Musical Traditions* (2013) <http://www.mustrad.org.uk/articles/hindring.htm> [accessed 23 April 2017].Paragraph 10.
124 See, for example, advertisements for concerts which include hornpipes: 'Harp Recitals Chesterfield and Brampton Mechanics' Institute', *Derbyshire Courier*, 21 October 1871, <http://www.britishnewspaperarchive.co.uk> [accessed 27 April 2017] p. 2.
125 A tune-up is an English equivalent to the Irish music 'session', whereby musicians will sit in a pub and take turns starting a tune generally to which others can join in.

126 Roud, *Folk Song in England*, p. 324; Edwin Waugh, *Sketches of Lancashire Life and Localities* (London: Whittaker, 1855 and 1857).
127 Russell, *Popular Music in England*, p. 183.
128 Russell, *Popular Music in England*, p. 183.
129 Julian Taylor, 'Music of North West England', Julian Taylor (No date), <http://www.fiddlemusic.co.uk/north-west-music.htm> [Accessed 11 November 2014].
130 Chandler, 'Musicians in 19th Century Southern England'.
131 Hall, 'I Never Played to Many Posh Dances'.
132 In trying to ascertain some foundation to this story, I searched for mention of a similar practice (presumably most occurrences were not worthy of mention as the activities occurred as a lower-class pursuit in a public-house). However, I found a late nineteenth-century newspaper report of a similar event whereby the game was to sing and prevent the pig squirming or moving rather than squealing: 'A 'Pig-Carrying' Competition', *Edinburgh Evening News*, 18 July 1896, <http://www.britishnewspaperarchive.co.uk> [accessed 27 April 2017] p. 6.
133 See David Atkinson, 'Revival: Genuine or Spurious?' in *Folk Song Tradition, Revival, and Re-Creation*, ed. by Ian Russell (Aberdeen: The Elphinstone Institute University of Aberdeen, 2004) pp. 144–162 (p. 145).
134 Roud, *Folk Song in England*, p. 671.
135 Roud, *Folk Song in England*, p. 671.

26

THE PERFORMERS IN THE PLAYGROUND

Children's musical practices in play

Julia Bishop

Children may not be the first group of people who come to mind when we think about folk performance. Widespread and persistent ideas of 'tradition' as age-old, unchanging and the preserve of older people mean that we tend to overlook children's status as 'folk'. This is coupled with adults' tendency to overlook or dismiss children's everyday culture. Yet, theirs is a dynamic tradition, embracing conservative and innovative practices, right under our noses, as Iona and Peter Opie, two of the leading researchers into children's folklore in the mid-twentieth century, observe:

> The tradition is truly a living one, and while some parts of it are declining others are burgeoning. The songs and actions may change, but the important thing is that childhood continues to sing in the freedom of its own tatterdemalion world.[1]

The aim of this chapter is to explore some of these informal vocal performances of young people, from the age of roughly six years upwards, in the street and school playground, during their leisure time when they are relatively free of the control of adults. For reasons of space, the emphasis is on performances that take place as part of play and games. This excludes those arising in non-game situations, such as children's calendar customs (house visiting at Shrovetide, May Day and Christmas, for example), dramatic performance (such as the 'Old Tup' play) and humorous exchange (topical songs and parodies), which have received less attention in research but are no less important.

There has been increased recognition of contemporary children's musical play in recent years resulting in a number of in-depth studies.[2] As well as highlighting the findings of this work, we will review the evidence for musical play in the past in light of those findings. In what ways have practices and repertoire been passed on between different generations of children, in different places and times, and how have they been adapted and changed in response to social change more widely? Secondly, we hope to extend the focus on musical performance in the more obviously musical games, such as hand-clapping, to other forms of play, such as ball-bouncing, skipping and counting out, which might not immediately be thought of as musical or performative.

One of the most obvious of the broader developments is in media and technology which have significantly influenced the ways in which music is experienced by everyone, including young people. Adults perennially express the fear that these developments are responsible for a perceived decline in children's abilities to play, interact with each other and be creative. In particular, certain forms of musical play, such as singing games and skipping, are among those regularly cited as evidence of this supposedly dire state of affairs. It is timely then to review both continuity and change in children's musical play.

A consideration of the musical and performative elements of play in the past, however, is dependent on the nature of the evidence available to us today. Among the earliest sources of children's games, songs and rhymes in England is the work of James Orchard Halliwell, especially his two publications, *Nursery Rhymes of England* (1842) and the sequel *Popular Rhymes and Nursery Tales* (1849).[3] Clearly, before sound recording, photography and moving image, the documentation of children's songs and singing play had to be through the written transcription of the words and, where relevant, description of the movements, and musical notation of the tune.[4] This limits the extent to which we can understand this early evidence in terms of performance. Sound recordings of children's singing and play only begin to emerge in the 1930s, followed by a number of recordings made by folk song collectors from mid-century as part of the second 'folk revival'.[5] It was not until around 1970, however, with the advent of portable magnetic tape recorders for domestic use, that audio recording of children's play came within easy reach of researchers and the general public.

Remarkable by its rarity in the nineteenth century is the use of drawings or diagrams to convey the formations of games, written descriptions being preferred. The drawings and diagrams by J. P. Emslie, touched on below, are a notable exception. In the twentieth century, there are several collections of photographs and film of children's performances but, again, such visual sources are not numerous and it is not until comparatively recently that audio-visual documentation of children's play has become the norm. With the recent development of the wearable camera, allowing documentation of the child's point of view in play and performance, it will be interesting to see what further insights this may afford.

Meanwhile, the discussion below draws particularly on historical sources that have been made publicly accessible as part of established online resources and readers may wish to consult these sources in conjunction with the text.[6]

Another important consideration with existing sources is the extent to which we can glimpse the multimodal nature of children's performances. By multimodal, we mean the ways in which verbal and musical aspects are entwined with other modes of expression and communication, such as gesture, movement, touch and spatial arrangement.[7] Another central concern is whether the evidence we have, past and present, derives directly from children. Adults' memories of childhood play are certainly valuable and often vivid but, as the Opies pointed out, may be selective, omit mundane but important details, and be tinged with nostalgia.[8] The Opies therefore opted to collect from young people, for whom these practices were part of their everyday life and in general we draw on sources that do likewise here.

A final point is that we are also interested in gleaning any evidence of children's experiences of musical play. What is the appeal or otherwise of a game with musical elements, and what is it like to play it?

Rhyme, rhythm and song

The Opies proposed that children had two distinct kinds of oral rhymes, those which regulate their games and relationships with each other, such as ball-bouncing, skipping and counting out rhymes, and 'those, seemingly almost as necessary to them, which are mere expressions of exuberance: a discordant symphony of jingles, slogans, nonsense verses, tongue-twisters, macabre rhymes, popular songs, parodies, joke rhymes, and improper verses'.[9] In this chapter, we count these verses, rhymes and chants as forms of musical play alongside songs. This is because the line between speech and song is neither clear-cut nor consistent in this area of folk performance. Children use a whole range of vocal styles, including heightened speech, sing-song delivery and rhythmic intonation, without fixed pitches.[10] At the same time, an emphasis on the beat or pulse and the rhythm is a key feature in their performance. An inclusive approach thus seems to be called for which considers 'rhymes' (rhymed and rhythmic verse) and 'chants' (unrhymed phrases with a pronounced rhythm) as musical performance, together with 'songs' (rhymed or unrhymed, rhythmic verses sung to a series of fixed pitches). We will refer to them collectively as 'vocalisations'.

Ball-bouncing, skipping and counting out as musical performance

Musical play can be divided into games in which musical performance is the central goal and those in which it is an accessory to the central goal. Ball-bouncing, longrope skipping and counting out are all examples of this latter category. In these games, children's vocal performance is subordinate to bouncing the ball, jumping over the rope or choosing a person to be 'It', respectively, but is nonetheless integral, helping to regulate the game in specific ways.[11]

In the past, the vocalisations accompanying ball-bouncing, skipping and counting out have typically been documented as text. Even when they have been audio-recorded, the sound made by the rope or the ball is often absent as in-context recordings, made while the game was in progress, are rare. Clearly, the nature of the games, especially ball-bouncing and skipping, and the accompanying game movements, suggest that a regular beat is a feature of the vocal performance, but what can we learn about the specifics of their delivery by looking at individual examples?

In ball-bouncing, the player generally plays alone using one or two balls which are repeatedly bounced against a hard surface. While the ball is in flight between throws, she also undertakes additional hand and leg movements. All of this is coordinated with the chosen vocalisation which may take the form of a song, rhyme or chant. The repertoire of vocalisations, as documented by the Opies and others in the third quarter of the twentieth century, is very diverse.[12] As well as dedicated ball-bouncing ones, there are examples taken from the counting out and skipping repertoire. Others were adapted from advertising slogans, such as 'Drinka pinta milka day, M-I-L-K' (Roud 32905).[13] Many have a humorous or curious twist to them.[14]

Most ball-bouncing vocalisations contain four stressed beats, as in

> Mrs Brown went to town
> With her knickers hanging down;
> Mrs Green saw the scene
> And put it in a magazine.
>
> (Roud 12982)[15]

A few comprise three stressed beats plus (one infers) a one beat rest, as in

> Big Ben strikes ten
> T-E-N.
>
> (Roud 19549)[16]

Any intervening unstressed syllables may be performed in a swung rhythm, as in the 'One Two Three A-Leary' and 'Plainsie Clapsie' (Roud 19541) examples discussed below, or a march-like rhythm, as suggested by the 'Drinka Pinta Milka Day' slogan. It is not possible to judge from a written text whether the delivery was swung or straight, however, and it may be that this varied between children even in connection with the same item.

Though there are earlier examples, ball-bouncing really took off in popularity from the 1920s when balls made of India rubber became cheaply and widely available.[17] From this time it has been documented pretty much exclusively as being a girl's activity.[18] There were several different ways of playing. One was simply to pat the ball against the ground creating a constant beat. In this case, the sound of the ball striking the ground coincided with each of the stressed beats of the text. This can be seen in the 1957 film *One Potato, Two Potato*, by the Irish writer and educator, Leslie Daiken, which features a game of 'One Two Three A-Leary' (Roud 18310), one of the best-known ball-bouncing vocalisations, as transcribed below (Figure 26.1).[19]

The ball is bounced approximately twice per second, and on the stressed syllables of the words 'a-leary' and 'over', the player swings her leg over the ball while it is bouncing. The Opies acknowledge the musicality of the performance in their comment that, 'when the player is skilful, it is a dainty performance, almost a dance'.[20] There are many variants of 'One Two Three A-Leary',[21] which was performed as a chant, as in the Daiken film, or as a song, as in the following example, recorded by Iona Opie at St Clements School in Ordsall, Manchester, in 1970 (Figure 26.2).[22]

The melody resembles that of the singing games 'Mrs Macaroni' (Roud 13203) and 'Dusty Bluebells' (Roud 13206), which is, in turn, related to 'Bobby Shaftoe' (Roud 1359).[23]

The vocalisation sometimes names or enumerates the actions that have to be accomplished by the player and the sequence in which they must occur. These make up the entirety of 'Plainsie Clapsie', as documented on the *One Potato Two Potato* film,[24] illustrating the local terminology that develops for the various movements (Figure 26.3).

Plainsie *(no movement)*
Clapsie *(clap)*
Twirl the wheel to *(roll hands)*

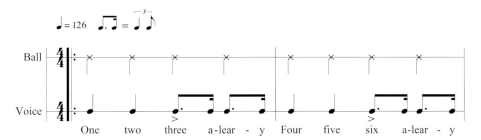

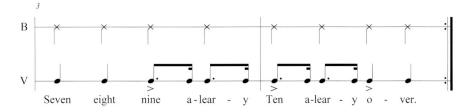

Figure 26.1 'One Two Three A-Leary'
Source: From One Potato, Two Potato (1957) Transcribed by Julia Bishop.

Figure 26.2 'One Two Three A-Lairy'
Source: Ordsall children (1970) Transcribed by Julia Bishop

> Backsie (*clap behind*)
> First your heel (*touch heel*)
> And then your knee (*touch knee*)
> Then your toe (*touch toe*)
> And under you go (*under-knee throw*).

This time the ball is bounced against the wall and coincides with every other beat of the pulse, half the rate of the ball-bouncing in 'One Two Three A-Leary' (see Figure 26.1 above):

Other games involved juggling two balls against the wall, the players likewise energetically repeating the short patterns and set moves as many times as possible without a break. Sometimes several players lined up, each one seamlessly taking over the game with the same ball and chant before passing on to the next.

The game is thus a veritable multimodal challenge for the player, as the filmed games show. Most obviously, she must avoid dropping the ball or stopping partway through, but also be able to recite the rhyme fluently, without stumbling on the words and while maintaining a consistent tempo and rhythm. This calls for judgement as to the physics of bouncing of the ball against the available surface, as well as excellent hand-eye coordination, a cool head and acute skills of anticipation and in-the-moment adjustments, while maintaining a fluent musical performance. The player could slightly stretch the pulse of the vocalisation to take account of the speed at which the ball returns to her so as to be able to maintain the game and successfully repeat the sequence without stopping. The challenge was clearly an important part of the game's appeal and the Opies highlight the extent to which girls would practise to perfect the skill.[25]

The vocalisations not only indicate when a 'fancy throw' is to be made, or when the balls should be passed to the next player. They also form the oral 'yardstick' by which each player's achievement is measured.[26] The vocalisations make throwing and catching a ball a bit more 'extreme', introducing risk and self-challenge to the undertaking.

Ball-bouncing has declined to near non-existence among children in England since the 1970s. Conversely, hand-clapping games have grown in popularity in the latter part of the twentieth century and into the twenty-first. From a musical point of view, clapping games can be seen as the heirs of ball-bouncing. Players use their own and their partner's hands to produce a regular percussive beat (the equivalent of the bouncing ball), interspersed with gestures and moves, and accompanied by the performance of a chant, rhyme or song. These are discussed more fully below.

Another recent parallel, involving a sound-producing object (but one which is definitely not to be bounced), and whose movements have to be controlled as part of the game, is

Figure 26.3 'Plainsie Clapsie'
Source: From One Potato, Two Potato (1957) Transcribed by Julia Bishop.

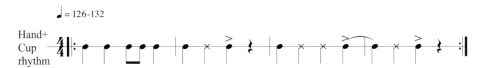

Figure 26.4 Rhythmic ostinato of 'The Cup Song' ('When I'm Gone') (Roud 32904)
Source: Lulu and the Lampshades (2009). Transcribed by Julia Bishop.

'The Cup Song'. In this, the player produces an ostinato rhythm by performing a series of moves. These involve tapping on a table with the hands and manipulating a glass or beaker to produce percussive beats, while singing a song. The range of moves involved in the sequence results in beats of varying strength, creating a syncopated effect in bars 3 and 4 (Figure 26.4).

The song's rhythm is distinct from, but coordinating with, that of the ostinato accompaniment and the whole routine requires a high level of skill. Spread via the internet and given an additional boost when featured in the 2012 film *Pitch Perfect*, it seems that 'The Cup Song' originated in a light-hearted recording made by members of a London band, Lulu and the Lampshades, in 2009.[27] It is still going strong among children in primary and secondary schools, and there are many performances and arrangements, including some by professional music groups, to be found on YouTube.

Returning to ball games, songs, chants and rhymes also feature in football and other ball games commonly played by boys, but in these cases the vocalisation has a different role, encouraging the players or celebrating the scoring of a goal. In a rather different example, 'My Man John' (Roud 13192), from the early twentieth century, the vocalisation regulates the pounding of players who are 'out', in a game resembling 'Ball He' or Dodgeball.[28] It was documented by Alice Gillington, a literary figure and important collector of folk songs and singing games during this period,[29] and published in her book *Old Isle of Wight Singing Games* (1909), as follows (Figure 26.5).

No. 12.
MY MAN JOHN.

BALL GAME.

This is a boy's game, though girls sometimes join in it. A ball is thrown up against the wall of a house and caught again, whilst the others are running round, then thrown at the runners (much in the manner of Rounders) and whoever the ball hits has to be "My Man John," and is beaten first with one fist, singing:—

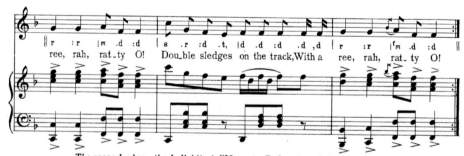

The second whom the ball hits is "My man Redcap," and the song goes on:—

Beating my man Redcap
With a ree, rah, ratty O!

The third is:—

My man Bluecap, etc.

The fourth is:—

My man Greencap, etc.

And so on to the end of the game, choosing a different coloured cap each time a boy is hit and taken.

5685

Figure 26.5 'My Man John'
Source: Gillington (1909).

The performers in the playground

Figure 26.6 Photograph of 'My Man John'
Source: Gillington (1909) Image by courtesy of The University of Liverpool Library SPEC Scott Macfie A.7.50(5).

The game has similarities with 'Daddy Whacker', in which the child who is caught is whacked with a stick, but the vocalisation of 'My Man John' regulates the 'whacking' into a rhythmic and potentially more stylised form of hitting.[30]

Gillington's books appear to have been aimed at teachers and parents wishing to teach the games, given the piano accompaniments and stage by stage instructions as to how to play. Her style of presentation is interesting in that she places the instructions for play at the relevant points within the music notation, whereas it was more usual at the time to describe the game separately or in relation to the verbal text alone.

Another notable feature of Gillington's books is the inclusion of photographs showing children in the midst of playing some of the games, among them 'My Man John' (Figure 26.6).

Posed as some of these photographs may strike us today, due to limitations of contemporary photography with regard to capturing figures in motion, they still convey additional information about the identity of the performers, such as their relative ages, and the proximity and spatial arrangement of the players, as well as evoking a more vivid sense of the game than comes from contemporary written descriptions alone.

Like ball-bouncing, skipping in a longrope is an activity overwhelmingly reported as undertaken by girls. No longer as popular as it was in the mid-twentieth century, it is now found almost exclusively as an adult-led activity. Group skipping is thus regularly cited as evidence that children have 'lost the ability to play' and that the 'old traditional games' are dying out.[31] Yet, group skipping to an accompanying vocalisation is not extensively documented prior to the nineteenth century, so this 'classic' game is perhaps not as old as some would believe.[32]

As the Opies shrewdly observe, longrope skipping 'is a game that has seldom been carefully observed by adults',[33] and for a general picture, alert to its multimodal challenge and the participants' point of view, the Opies' eloquent description is hard to beat:

Here is no leisurely gambolling in the rope, no airy-fairyness. The expert skipper reminds one not of a fluttering butterfly but a machine gun. The two 'enders' turning the rope stand surprisingly close to each other. The rope screams as it is turned and cracks as it hits the ground. The skipper seems to be suspended in the air; she rises barely an inch from the ground as the rope whips under feet. She seems to rebound from the ground rather than jump from it. She may seem unconcerned (perhaps she has hands in the pockets of her overcoat), but her feet are working like pistons.[34]

Again, in-context sound recordings and films of skipping are rare. The following transcription of the skipping game 'Rosy Apple' (Roud 6492) has been made from a sequence in the 1959 BBC documentary, *Morning in the Streets*.[35] It attempts to capture the aural backdrop of the rope striking the ground in a regular incessant beat and the counterpoint between the rope's beat, the skipper's jumping and the song. The cross-head notes indicate the noise of the rope against the ground (Figure 26.7).

Figure 26.7 '[Rosy Apple]', Skipping
Source From Morning in the Streets (1959) Transcribed by Julia Bishop.

As can be seen, the skipper jumps in the rope on every beat, the rope creating an upbeat to the jumps on the first and third beats of the bar. Between these are smaller, lighter jumps. Together, they produce the characteristic skipping rhythm – a-*one* two, a-*three* four.

The girls in this example skip to 'Rosy Apple',[36] sung to the tune of the 'King Pippin Polka' (discussed below). Nevertheless, skipping vocalisations can be chanted (as in 'Salt, mustard, vinegar, pepper'), rhymed or sung, the variability in their mode of performance perhaps relating to the amount of breath needed for skipping and the number of other players available to sing while the skipper is in the rope. The Opies highlight that these are work songs,[37] performing a crucial role by providing a common point of reference for the 'enders' and the skipper to coordinate their respective roles in the game. In particular, they indicate to each party the tempo of their rope-turning and the jumping, and enable them to vary that tempo and remain synchronised.

The repertoire of skipping chants, rhymes and songs documented over the course of the twentieth century is voluminous and varied in subject matter, including action chants, advertising jingles and divination rhymes. As Roud has pointed out, 'although some of it is mundane and closely tied to the physical needs of the activity, there are also many flashes of humour, surrealism and sheer poetry'.[38] Variants created by children themselves have also been documented.[39] These may often be relatively ephemeral but suggestive of the same kind of improvisatory and experimental approaches identified by Marsh in her study of children's clapping and singing games and discussed in more detail below.[40]

Counting out is a widespread preparatory game which allows the selection of an individual to be 'It', that is, the chaser or other key role in the ensuing game. Counting out seems to have been a common practice even in the nineteenth century and it is still going strong. Halliwell included the words of many counting out rhymes in his *Popular Rhymes and Nursery Tales* (1849) and provided a description of the method of counting out which pretty much describes the basic game as it is played today:

> The operation of counting-out is a very important mystery in many puerile games. The boys or girls stand in a row, and the operator begins with the counting-out rhyme, appropriating a word to each, till he comes to the person who receives the last word, and who is accordingly 'out.' This operation is continued till there is only one left, who is the individual chosen for the hero of the game, whatever it may be.[41]

Counting out as a process of elimination is very common. The vocalisation is performed solo by the counter, regulating their movements as they count off each player, in turn. Counting off players is done in a number of ways, such as pointing at each person, or touching their outspread fingers or shoe (placed in a circle with the others) or their clenched fist or clasped hands (such as is used with the chant 'Coconut Crack'). The counter has a dual role in that they must include themselves in the counting out, necessitating pointing at themselves, their own shoe, their other fist or an imaginary fist respectively. While the chanting is done by the counter alone, there may be intervening actions (often cued by the vocalisation in lines such as 'change your black shoe' or 'coconut crack') which are done by the others or by the counter themselves.

The speed at which the counting out is accomplished can vary according to how much time is available, how many players there are to be eliminated and how impatient the players are to get on with the subsequent game. Nevertheless, the vocalisations take the form of chants and rhymes (sung vocalisations to fixed pitches appear to be rare or non-existent in the English language), whose rhythmicised delivery necessarily articulates the words more slowly and deliberately than normal speech and emphasises the ritual quality of the performance.

As Arleo highlights, a feature of the counting out chants and rhymes is their 'rich texturing of sound', especially in the way that they commonly employ nonsense words.[42] Many are rhymes, sometimes employing internal rhyme as well, while alliteration and assonance are also prevalent in both rhymes and chants, as in the following examples:

> Ickle ockle chocolate bockle
> Ickle ockle out.
>
> (Roud 20650)[43]

> Ip dip, sky blue
> Who's it? Not you.
> God's words are true,
> It must not be *you*.
>
> (Roud 32897)[44]

> Coconut coconut coconut crack.[45]

The counter not only performs the vocalisation but also chooses it, and thereby the associated method of counting. One of the few studies as to how this role is negotiated among the players was undertaken by Roemer who refers to this process as 'bidding'. In a study of children in the US in the 1970s, she draws attention to several different approaches. The first of these is appropriation, as in the following example:

JACK: Wait a minute. I got it. I got it. [bid]
PUT OUT THESE [PUTS OUT FISTS]
ENGINE, ENGINE . . .

Another is through soliciting and receiving permission:

SAUNA: I have a good 'un.
CANI: O.K.
SAUNA: Put your hands in, 'K?
KATIA: 'K.
SAUNA: Monkey, monkey…[46]

In an example on the British Library's Playtimes website, a group of Anglo-Punjabi and Anglo-Bengali children from West Yorkshire were filmed playing 'Akkar Bakkar' (Roud 32903) (the Punjabi version of the counting out game 'Eeny Meeny Miny Mo', Roud 13610) in 2002. The players negotiate who will lead and take turns to perform the rhyme and count the others' fingers.[47] These instances show the interest of the lead up to the performance of counting out as well as the vocalised elements and actions themselves.

The way in which the role of counter is negotiated is of particular interest given the degree of power they have in the game. More experienced counters, for example, can calculate how to influence who is ultimately selected by their choice of vocalisation and with whom they choose to begin counting.[48] Another strategy is for the counter to append a 'coda' to the vocalisation, such as 'If you do want to play / You can "sling your hook" away',[49] which can likewise affect the outcome of the game. What appears at first sight to be a game of chance, accepted as 'fair' and random, can in fact involve the strategic use of mathematical and performance skills to favour or single out other players.

The rhythm of counting out vocalisations has fascinated researchers over many years.[50] Early studies focused on cross-cultural comparison, seeking universal patterns of prosody. There can, however, be a marked difference between the implied or ideal meter and rhythm as written down on the page and the ways it is performed by players themselves. As filmed examples from 2009 to 2010 on the British Library *Playtimes* website show, there is more variety than one might expect and these may be linked to factors such as how experienced a child is at counting out and the ways in which the counter performs the associated movements. In 'Ip Dip Do' (Roud 32898), for example, the counter points to a player on every syllable of the vocalisation ('Ip dip do / Cat's got the flu / Chicken's got the chicken pox and out goes you'), including the unstressed ones, leading to a slower and more deliberate performance. In 'Onica Bonica' (Roud 32899), counting takes place on the stressed beats only and the counter is careful to re-start each repetition of the vocalisation on the next player, in turn. In the final rendition, when the outcome has become predictable to all, the counter no longer bends down to count the feet but counts from standing up, in preparation for the immediate start of the ensuing chase game.[51] The 1957 *One Potato Two Potato* film demonstrates still another approach to counting out in which the rhyme referred to in the title of the film (Roud 19230) is delivered in a markedly declamatory style with a decisive blow on the fists of each player to match.[52]

Children's evolving performance practices in singing games

Singing games are performances in which two or more players sing a song while undertaking a sequence of movements in the manner of a dance, or in particular formations. Associated gestures, mimed actions and movements suggested by the content of the song are often involved as well. They are thus examples of play in which musical performance is the central aim of the game.

The performers of singing games are often reported to be girls, from the age of roughly 6–12 years. From the work of the Opies and subsequent researchers, we know that children often learn them from each other at school, and also from children in their neighbourhood, cousins and adult relatives and midday supervisors at school, or at out-of-school activities. Film and television have also proved an important source and more recently the Worldwide Web, particularly video-sharing platforms such as YouTube.

Singing games are the children's games that, above all others, have been recognised by collectors as musical and, as it would be termed today, multimodal. This applies even to Halliwell, for example, in his two books of children's folklore of 1842 and 1849. Halliwell provides the words of the songs and a description of how the associated games are played. He mentions that some of the texts are sung, and occasionally references melodies published elsewhere. So, for example, 'The Bramble Bush' (Roud 7882) is described as 'a ring dance imitation-play, the metrical portion of which is not without a little melody'. Particularly striking is that, in comparing the actions undertaken in a variant game, 'The Mulberry Bush', Halliwell coins the term 'motion-cries' to mean the lines of text with accompanying movements, such as 'This is the way we mend our shoes'. He shows how these differ from those of 'The Bramble Bush' and implies that the 'motion-cries' of 'The Mulberry Bush' are semi-improvised by the performers, in that 'the dance may be continued by the addition of cries and motions, which may be rendered pretty and characteristic in the hands of judicious actors'.[53] This, in turn, suggests that he or his correspondent has observed the game actually being played on one or more occasions.

The person who laid the foundation for the collection and study of singing games, and established the term itself, was the folklorist Alice Bertha Gomme, in her monumental study, *The Traditional Games of England, Scotland and Ireland* (published in two volumes, 1894 and 1898). This contains nearly 800 games and their variants, including numerous singing games, gathered from published sources, from personal recollection and from observation of children, by Gomme herself and a network of correspondents. It covers 112 locations, of which 89 were in England.[54] Gomme brought together the available evidence for each, including the singing game tunes which were notated 'as sung by the children, either by myself or by correspondents…and are unaltered'.[55] Her book was also ground-breaking in its inclusion of visual evidence. These were drawings of children, intended to convey their actions in the game, and diagrams illustrating the more complicated figures and changes in their form created by John Philipps Emslie, a topographical artist and fellow folklorist.

Gomme's work helped inspire much subsequent research into children's games and musical play,[56] including many turn-of-the-century English folk song collectors, such as Anne Gilchrist, Lucy Broadwood, Cecil Sharp, Frank Kidson, Janet Blunt and Percy Grainger.[57] Anne Gilchrist in particular applied her extensive knowledge of song and tune histories to the singing games with fascinating results. In one study, she traces the origin of the singing game song 'Sweet (or Queen) Mary' (Roud 6281) song to an eighteenth-century Scottish song, 'Nae Bonnie Laddie Will Tak' Me Awa' (Figure 26.8).[58]

Comparing the texts of the collected versions, she also shows how children, unfamiliar with Scots, have varied the words 'tak' me awa'' to 'take me a walk', and 'give me a waltz'. We can see how such changes have a knock-on effect on the song's imagery and frame of reference for the performers, and it is probable that this, in turn, occasions further variation, although it is difficult to document the unfolding sequence of these changes.[59]

The melody of the 'Queen Mary' singing game is very consistent among the collected versions we have from the late nineteenth and twentieth centuries. Gilchrist identifies it as a variant of the dance tune 'Bonnie Dundee'. She had herself transcribed 'Bonnie Dundee' from a tunebook of 1838 compiled by the Lake District fiddler, William Irwin, although the tune was known in many other spheres of music-making during the nineteenth century.[60] Compared to that of Irwin, the singing game melody as collected by Gilchrist from the 'Liverpool girls' shows a strong melodic resemblance to the first part, especially in bars 2, 4 and 6. Both have the same phrase structure as well (ABAB). The distinctive upward leap of an octave at the end of 'Queen Mary' shows parallels with the descending octave leaps in bars 3 and 7 of Irwin's tune (Figure 26.9).

Figure 26.8 '[Queen Mary]', Liverpool girls (c.1915)
Source: *Journal of the Folk Song Society* 5 (1915)

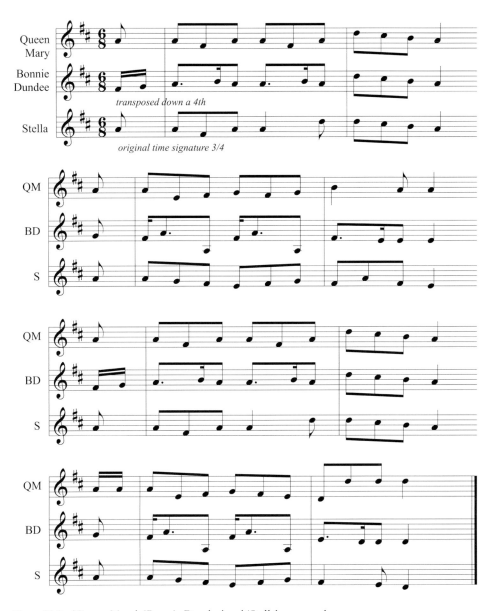

Figure 26.9 'Queen Mary', 'Bonnie Dundee' and 'Stella' compared

The singing game differs slightly from the fiddle tune in its alternation between two notes a third apart (bars 1 and 5), which the Opies identify as a musical trait of singing games.[61] The range of the singing game is also confined to an octave, in contrast with the fiddle tune. Furthermore, the children's melody tends to cluster around the fifth degree of the scale which is midway between these octave extremes. A limited range is another common feature of singing games,[62] making them less effort to sing in the context of a physically exerting game, and requiring a lesser degree of vocal skill, increasing their accessibility.

Gilchrist's study not only illustrates children's appropriation of words and tunes from adult culture, but also that the direction of influence is not purely one-way. She gives a detailed account of the 'Queen Mary' tune's adoption as a hymn tune, known as 'Stella' (see Figure 26.9).

> Henri Hemy, of 'Pianoforte Tutor' fame, noted the tune about sixty years ago from the singing of little girls in the mining village of Stella, four miles from Newcastle-on-Tyne – in which town he was the organist of a Catholic church–and set it to a hymn 'Hail, Queen of Heaven, the ocean star' for which he had previously been unable to find a suitable tune. It first appeared in his collection of *Easy Music for Church Choirs*, 1851, and afterwards in the *Crown of Jesus Music*, 1864, from which it passed into other collections. The idea of adapting the game-tune to an English translation of the hymn to the Virgin, *Ave, maris stella*, may first have entered Hemy's mind through the chance association of 'Queen Mary' and Stella – an odd case of suggestion, if so.[63]

Hemy's actions also provide evidence of the singing game itself as played by children over 40 years earlier than the next reports of its existence. We will see further examples of this interchange between children's and adult culture below.

The first sound recordings made in England of children's singing games were gathered in the early 1930s by an American folk song collector, James Madison Carpenter.[64] He used a Dictaphone cylinder machine to record the songs, usually only the initial stanza or two, as his aim was to capture the tune rather than document the performance as such. His collection contains both recordings of adults singing children's songs of their youth and a handful of singing games performed by children themselves.[65] As far as we can tell from his documentation, the child performers are Edith Wagstaff, Lily Crowther and several other unnamed children in Thorpe Audlin, West Riding of Yorkshire. Official records give Edith Wagstaff as being born in 1916 so she would have been in her mid-to-late teens when the recordings were made.

Among the Thorpe Audlin children's singing games is 'The Big Ship Sails' (Roud 4827), a singing game that has been regularly reported throughout the twentieth century and yet was unknown to Alice Gomme at the end of the nineteenth (Figure 26.10)[66].

'The Big Ship Sails' is based on the movement pattern of a much older game, 'Thread the Needle', in which players hold hands in a line and dance under an arch made by the raised arms of the end-most players.[67] In 'The Big Ship Sails', and also in a number of country dances and parallel children's games elsewhere in Europe, the players 'thread the needle' in a slightly different manner, which anchors the game to a particular spot, as Carpenter describes:

> Children form line by clasping hands, first holding one hand against object. As song begins, line, led by last man, begins skipping dance as it circles toward[s] first child, who makes arch with right hand held against tree or building, for the line to pass under. As they circle and re-approach, second child makes arch and receives them under her right arm. So on to the last. Then first child circles and clasps hand of last, completing circle.

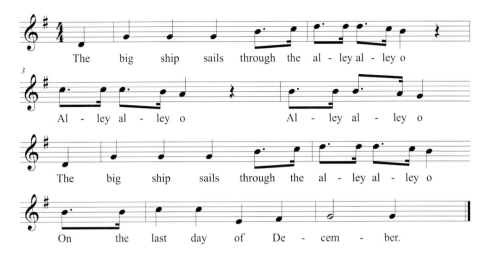

Figure 26.10 'The Big Ship Sails'
Source: Edith Wagstaff and children of Thorpe Audlin [1929–35] Transcribed by Julia Bishop.

>Then again resumes first position, and the line begins to 'unwind', going back under the 'arches' in reverse order.[68]

These movements are accomplished to a single stanza of song, repeated over and over. In some versions, though, the players remain in circle formation, performing appropriate actions to one or more subsequent stanzas, such as:

>The captain said, 'That will never never do'…[etc.] (*wagging finger*)
>The big ship sank to the bottom of the sea…[etc.] (*crouching down*)
>We all dip our head in the deep blue sea…[etc.] (*heads bowed*)[69]

Some have claimed that the song's core stanza refers to the opening of the Manchester ship canal in 1894, but the earliest recorded version comes from New Zealand in 1870 which makes this unlikely. The association of the singing game with northwest England was nevertheless boosted by its use in the 1961 film, *A Taste of Honey*, which was set in the region and features the Manchester Ship Canal. It is more productive to consider the words of the song in relation to those who sang it. For the players of any singing game, the words of the song evoke a narrative or scenario which they interpret or imagine in line with their experiences and knowledge. In the case of 'The Big Ship Sails', for example, the Opies report that some children referred to the arch made by the players' arms as the 'alley', suggesting these particular children saw themselves as the ship sailing through the 'alley' as they go under the arch, their own version of the 'threading the needle' metaphor.[70] For others, the song may have recalled images of actual ships they had seen, particularly if they lived near docklands or, indeed, the Manchester ship canal. We can only infer these as possibilities but there is evidence that the song resonated in children's minds with current affairs involving ships. The sinking of the Lusitania in 1914 prompted additional stanzas which, according to the Opies, were still circulating among children ten years later:

>The big ship's name was the Lusitania…[etc.]
>The Germans sank the Lusitania…[etc.]
>My father was the captain of the Lusitania…[etc.][71]

'The Big Ship Sails' is also featured in Daiken's 1957 *One Potato, Two Potato* documentary. Filmed in London, this segment shows seven girls flocking to a bombsite where they play the game with gusto.[72] The game concludes with a cry of 'Shoot, bang, fire!' as the girls simultaneously launch their hands above their heads in a final flourish. The Opies note a variety of such vigorous multimodal codas to 'The Big Ship Sails' and a number of others (both singing and clapping games), a detail of performance that might repay closer study in the future.[73]

The tune tradition of 'The Big Ship Sails' as reported in England is very consistent, revealing only a small degree of melodic variation. Like 'Queen Mary' it typically has the range of an octave but is for the most part concentrated on just five consecutive pitches and has a clear-cut major tonality. Its march-like feel is underlined by the use of a repeated pitch on the first two or three beats of every bar (the three G's in bar 1, the two D's in bar 2, etc.). The use of the half-line at the end of line 1 repeated twice over to make the second line of each stanza is a technique also found in other children's songs, such as 'Here We Go Round the Mulberry Bush', and the tunes echo each other in parts.[74] The tune of 'The Big Ship Sails' is, however, closest in melodic outline to that of another singing game, 'Poor Mary Sits a-Weeping', of which it is a four-time transformation (Figure 26.11).[75]

Figure 26.11 'The Big Ship Sails' and 'Poor Mary'
Source: 'Poor Jenny', collected by Iona and Peter Opie, 1975.

Despite this, most of the documentation of children's singing games in the second and third quarters of the twentieth century is in the form of transcriptions or sound recordings, rather than film. Worthy of note are actuality recordings of four singing games dating from the late 1930s and made by the BBC.[76] 'The Muffin Man' (Roud 7922), 'Dusty Bluebells' (Roud 13206) and 'Lucy Locket' (Roud 19536) were recorded in Millwall, and 'Sally Go Round the Moon' (Roud 11591) at a school in Wandsworth. Several of these feature descriptions of the game given by individual children in response to the questions of a female reporter ('How do you play ['Sally Go Round the Moon']?' 'Make a ring. And dance round and sing. And cocks your legs up and then say "Oops"'. 'Oh, that sounds a very jolly one!'). Importantly, from the point of view of gaining insights into performance, the ensuing part of the recording clearly captures children actually playing the game, making these the first audio recordings to do so.

Although not numerous, the Carpenter and the BBC recordings feature a mixture of older and newer games. The extensive research of the Opies in the post-war period went on to confirm this decline and renewal. With it, they noted a shift in emphasis away from those which involved the choosing of one of the children and which had their roots in courtship dances of young people of marriageable age in earlier times.[77] Of the 113 singing games the Opies included in *The Singing Game* (1985), they regarded only 82 as 'true' singing games, in the sense that they were formerly used in courtship and customs. Others, like 'The Big Ship Sails', were offshoots of older games which had come to have their own identity. They regarded the others as songs and fragments 'commandeered to make singing games on the old pattern – for once a pattern exists, it will be copied'.[78] Despite their interest in and emphasis on continuity elsewhere in their writing, then, they recognised the validity of these newer items of repertoire and young people's associated performance practices. In particular, they included 'impersonations' and dance routines, many inspired by popular culture, and focusing particularly on those which were widespread at the time or had stood the test of several decades. Brian Sutton-Smith, a contemporary play researcher, summed up the changes thus:

> Despite their interest in origins, what the Opies actually give us is a picture of historical change as much as a picture of historical continuity […] Most striking in their work, and not commented on by the Opies, is the remarkable upsurge in post-television years of games of buffoonery, impersonation, dance routines, and clapping […] While there are historical forerunners to many of these games, what most strikes our attention is their fadlike character and their ephemerality. Children's folklore appears in many games to have taken on the character of modern mass-media culture, with its cycles of fashion and popularity. Dance routines, in particular, come and go as quickly as the topical songs that stimulate them. There is, in addition, a more explicit vulgarity and sexuality in many of these than was the case in the singing games of the prior century.[79]

This is evident in the collection of sound recordings made by the Opies. Following their national written surveys of young people in the 1950s and 1960s, from the late 1960s and up to 1983, Iona Opie traversed the country with a tape recorder to record singing games from school-aged children from a wide range of locations in England, and a number in Scotland. The resulting collection consists of 85 open-reel and cassette tapes and is now deposited at the British Library where it has been digitised and made available as the 'Opie Collection of Children's Games and Songs'.[80]

There are many performances of interest in the collection which are not included in *The Singing Game*.[81] In response to her enquiries among the children for singing games, Iona received a great deal of information from the children about their performances in the playground more generally, including the latest hit songs. These illustrate the scope of the repertoire current among these children, their knowledge of older and newer items, and their facility with a variety of musical styles and performance practices. Iona also recorded some of these performances, one example being a rendition of 'Mama, He's Making Eyes at Me' by a group of girls in Coram Fields, London, in July 1974.[82] The girls give a highly accomplished performance, one as soloist and the others as backing group. The details clearly indicate that their immediate source was 10-year-old Lena Zavaroni, whose performance of the song earlier that year had won her the television talent show *Opportunity Knocks*, and whose recording had reached the top 10 in the UK album charts. In their analysis of this and other examples among the Opie recordings, Jopson, Burn and Robinson argue that such performances can involve 'complex forms of musical mastery [...] and the production of a powerful vocal style [suggesting] a musical sophistication considerably greater than the orthodox systems of music education allow for'.[83] While 'traditional singing games and the "new" pop songs [...] appear to co-exist contentedly alongside one another' among children, it is also clear that the associations and status of individual songs give them a certain cachet which children, in turn, can lay claim to through their own performances.[84]

The Opies were aware that, 'a printed page cannot convey the exuberance of children singing these games on their own. We have tried to give [our] book life by assembling as much evidence as we could of a still rich tradition, and by using the children's own words to describe it'.[85] They were true to their word. Just one example is their description of 'In and Out the Dusty Bluebells'[86] which they note with characteristically dry humour is 'one of the most popular of song-games in the present day, and with good reason: it is humorous, cumulative, has a good tune plenty of action, is seldom found in recreation manuals, and is little known to the older generation'. The game appears fairly demure on paper, but a different picture emerges from the children's comments: '"I like this game," confessed a nine-year-old, "because in the end you get muddled up"'. Likewise, in the second half of the game in which one player taps on the shoulders of another, the Opies observe:

> their actions belie their words. The shoulders are not patted but thumped; and when a girl links up she tends to hold on to her forerunner's skirt ('It's awful, they nearly pull your skirt off'); and if they join up by putting their hands on the shoulders of the girl in front of them, they will feel it necessary each time they come to 'Tippity tappitty on your shoulder', to thump the shoulders of the girl in front them. The game, therefore, is not lacking in action.[87]

This recalls the 'My Man John' ball game example collected by Alice Gillington, exemplified above, and counters essentialised views of gender in children's games. The other big shift that the Opies' work documents so well at this time is the rise of clapping games in the second half of the twentieth century, discussed in the following section.

The Opies' research made a big impact on subsequent generations of researchers, particularly school teachers, inspiring them to make their own studies of children's games, including musical play.[88] These studies are more delimited in geographical scope than those of the Opies but are more in-depth. They are also able to take advantage of contemporary technological developments, especially improved portability and sound quality, but growing public concern about photographing and filming children due to concerns about safeguarding and privacy have militated against visual documentation of children at play. Exceptions to this are two recent studies undertaken by researchers at University College London and the University of Sheffield. Concerned with continuity and change between the past and the present, the multimodal nature of children's practices in the school playground and the impact of media and commerce on children's play, they have involved extensive video-recording, including by the children themselves, most recently using wearable cameras.[89]

A noticeable gap in the Opies' research as published,[90] and that which came after it, is attention to the repertoires and practices of those who came to Britain to settle from the mid-1950s, and in earlier times. (Head)teacher researcher, Nigel Kelsey, for example, recorded several versions of 'Brown Girl in the Ring' (Roud 13195), a singing game from the West Indies, in London schools in the early 1980s. He also had evidence of the game circulating in London 60 years previously,[91] prompting him to wonder if the game had persisted or had been reintroduced more recently by members of the Caribbean community. Either way, it seems likely that the game had been boosted by the popularity of the song which became a hit for the Caribbean and European group Boney M in 1978.

While this example might be interpreted as a evidence of a singing game repertoire enriched by new games from other parts of the world, the way 'Brown Girl in Ring' was played and children's experiences of playing it show negative as well as positive experiences of playing. As one woman of colour recalled of her school days during this period,[92] being the 'brown girl in the ring' was to be marked out as different and disempowered in the context of the playground.

There is a passing mention in the Opies' work that 'immigrant children play English singing games before they can speak English, reproducing the words as pure sound', and more recent studies elsewhere have confirmed the ease with which children assimilate each other's songs and rhymes in multilingual playgrounds.[93] However, Curtis and Marsh distinguish between playgrounds in which children from a Black, Asian and minority ethnic background are in the minority and those where there is more of a critical mass from the same background.[94] In the former situation, those in the minority preferred not to introduce items they played at home that departed from the established repertoire at that particular school.

In the schools with a large population of children from an Asian background studied by Curtis in the 1990s in West Yorkshire, though, she found examples of singing games brought from the families' home country. One of these was a Bangla game which roughly translated as 'Why are you crying? Wake up and wash your face. Choose your partner'. The game bears a striking resemblance to an older English-language game, 'Here sits poor Sally on the ground / Sighing and sobbing for her young man' (Roud 4509).[95] Curtis also uncovered examples of English-language singing games translated into other languages and some bi-lingual examples as well.[96] Bollywood songs and dance routines also formed part of the mix. Another important international and multi-cultural collection is that of Dan Jones, available at the British Library.[97] Clearly, though, much more research needs to be done on questions of race in children's vernacular song performance and musical play in this country.

Clapping games and the playground beat

Writing in the early 1980s, the Opies described clapping games as 'the most zestful, speedy, and energetic of the singing games, and . . . one of the chief growth areas'.[98] From the vantage point of the early 2020s, we can see that their observations were spot on. The popularity of clapping games, and similar kinds of musical play such as cheerleading routines and handshakes, has increased in the second half of the twentieth century and continues into the twenty-first. The old-style singing games, skipping and ball-bouncing games, however, have pretty much completely dropped out of fashion among young people in the same period, unless fostered by adults. Some bewail this shift, but what has occasioned it and what can it tell us about young people, their changing worlds and their informal everyday performances during this period?

In clapping games, the players undertake a repeated sequence of clapping patterns and prescribed gestures, with one or more partners, to the accompaniment of their own singing. Like skipping and ball-bouncing, it requires agility, timing and a host of perceptual skills to get it right, and that is largely what makes the game both compelling and fun. There is also sociability and a mix of teamwork and friendly rivalry in performing the routine with others.

In contrast to ball-bouncing, skipping and singing games, clapping can easily be undertaken indoors and out, and requires no plaything, no vertical surface and little space. Players may clap in pairs or, less commonly, in a circle of up to six people. They stand on the spot to clap, their movements primarily confined to the upper body.

In Britain, clapping games go back to at least the mid-nineteenth century.[99] Reports of them are sporadic, though, and there is no mention in Halliwell's books of popular rhymes, nor Gomme's *Traditional Games*, nor among the collectanea of the folk song collectors.[100] They were played on occasion, it seems, but were unremarkable to adults. Then, in the early 1960s, an influx of new repertoire revitalised their appeal and they spread like wildfire.

Up to this point, the repertoire was rather limited. A commonly mentioned example was 'My Mother Said I Never Should'. It was sung to the tune of 'The King Pippin Polka', written by Charles D'Albert, a dancing master and composer, in c.1860, one of many dance tunes produced in the wake of 'polkamania' which had swept Europe in the mid-nineteenth century.[101] 'My Mother Said' to the 'King Pippin Polka' tune was noted by Anne Gilchrist who calls it an 'early polka "Doodle"' (Figure 26.12).

The song must have captured children's imagination as it has variously been reported as a singing game, dance and drama, as well as a clapping song.[102]

In the clapping game, according to an earlier account by the Reverend Addison Crofton (c.1875), children would 'clap their hands together, alternately their own and their partner's hands':

> My mother *said* (clap)
> That I never *should* (clap)
> Play with the gipsies (clap)
> In the wood (clap)
> Because she said (clap)
> That if I did (clap)
> She'd smack my bottom (clap)
> With a saucepan lid! (clap)[103]

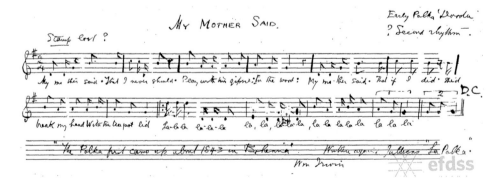

Figure 26.12 'My Mother Said' (n.d.)

This pat-a-cake pattern, sometimes combined with crossing hands over the chest and slapping thighs, is still practised by children today in 'A Sailor Went to Sea Sea Sea' (Roud 18338), which is often one of the first games to be learnt. A new clapping sequence became widely adopted in the 1960s, though, in which children held their palms horizontally, one facing up and the other down, to clap their partner's hands in an Up/Down movement. This was followed by clapping their partner's hands in the pat-a-cake or 'high 10' manner, then clapping their own hands. We can describe this using the following abbreviations:

U   Up/Down clap with horizontal hands
P   Clap Partner's hands with pat-a-cake or 'High 10' hands
O   Clap Own hands

The sequence produced a 3-beat pattern. Since clapping songs are almost always in 2- or 4-time, players often introduced a rest before repeating the pattern, according to the Opies, which aligned the stressed notes and words of the song with the same clapping move each time and allowed for a gesture or action to be performed.[104] Many of their sound recordings evidence a continual clapping beat, though,[105] and those more skilled in clapping games nowadays employ this and more extended patterns which create a cross-rhythm between the song and the clapping. An example of this is the performance of 'My Mummy Sent Me Shopping' (Roud 20093), performed by a group of 10–11-year-old girls, and partway through a boy of the same age, at a primary school in Sheffield in 2010.[106] The group form a circle and adapt the 3-way clapping pattern above to clap with the person on either side of them simultaneously. Figure 26.13 shows the way in which the clapping actions are fitted to the four-time melody being sung in this performance,[107] making it apparent at once that the verbal and musical stresses coincide with a different clapping action within and between the phrases.

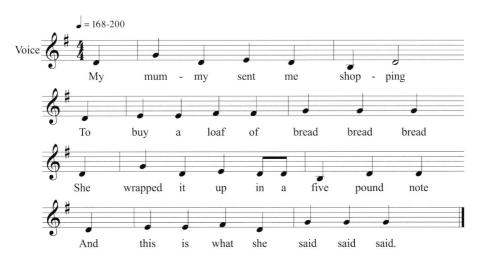

Figure 26.13 'My Mummy Sent Me Shopping'
Source: Sheffield schoolchildren (2010). Transcribed by Julia Bishop.

Line 1	U My	P mum -	O my	U Sent	P me	O shop -	U ping	P —
Line 2	O To	U buy	P a	O Loaf	U of	P bread	P bread	P bread
Line 3	O She	U wrapped	P it	O Up	U in a	P five	O pound	U note
Line 4	P And	0 this	U is	P What	O she	U said	P said	P said

The performers manage these cross-rhythms fluently on the whole which, considering that they sing these parts of the game at tempos of 168–200 beats per minute, is no mean feat!

As seen in singing games and in this example, the final word/note of phrases 2 and 4 is often repeated three times, and matched by the repetition of the 'clap partner' (P) clapping action which the players use to re-establish synchronisation before continuing.

Whatever the clapping pattern used, it is interspersed with gestures and actions. These can be embedded in the clapping section or form a whole section of the game in their own right. In the above example, the transition is made by singing the first line of the new section, 'My name is Tracy Beaker' (Roud 20422), and then changing to rhythmicised speech for the rhythm of the new verse, which now includes syncopation and is performed at a different tempo. The vocal style and the body language is forthright and uncompromising:

My name is Tracy Beaker, I'm a movie star (*miming holding a microphone*)
I've got the curly wurly knickers (*circling hands at hip level*)
And the see-through bra (*drawing in-turned palms outwards across chest*)
I've got the hips, the lips and the sexy legs (*touching hips, lips and sliding palms down side of each leg*)
If you want to marry(?) me, just count to three (*standing still*)
1–2–3! (*3 jumps extending legs further apart in manner of the splits*)

The actions stress the parts of the content that might be considered risqué from the adult point of view, especially in a school setting, and involve the performers highlighting their own bodies. At the same time, the movements are exaggerated, as if the sexual glamour of film stars is simultaneously being emulated and parodied.[108] It is notable that this same section was performed as a separate routine 60 years ago, the film stars referred to then being Diana Dors and Marilyn Monroe.[109] Nowadays, it is often a female pop singer, such as Katy Perry or Britney Spears. References to gender are a feature of a number of clapping games and offer rich possibilities for interpretation by those playing the clapping games, as researchers have shown.[110]

It is important to note that the 'My Mummy Sent Me Shopping' section of this game goes back 60 years as well when it was often sung with the opening line 'I went to a Chinese restaurant'. It was combined with a second section in which what was 'said, said, said' comprised a series of humorous nonsense words and phrases, such as

Alli alli
Chickerlye chickerlye
Om pom poodle
Walla walla whiskers
Chinese chopsticks
Indian chief says 'How!'

The Opies point out that the rhyme and the rigmarole had previously been current for counting out in the 1920s, and was certainly known in the 1880s.[111] Many other games likewise employ racial tropes. These reflect not only cultural forms and the social structures that supported them at the time they were adopted by children but also the cultural forms and social structures of ensuing periods during which they were perpetuated. At the same time, what was appropriated by children was for their own distinctive purposes and was re-created by each generation. Few studies have addressed this paradox and, in current times, it seems all the more important to do so.

Not only did a new clapping pattern become established in the 1960s, but also a new tune. Of the 28 clapping games documented by the Opies in *The Singing Game*, nine were sung by children all over the country to the same tune. Not only this, but the same tune has persisted to the present day and is still associated with six of the same sets of words as found by the Opies – 'A Sailor Went to Sea Sea Sea', 'My Mummy Sent Me Shopping', 'When Susie Was a Baby' (Roud 20199), 'My Mother Is a Baker' (Roud 32900), 'My Mother Gave Me Necklace' (now known as 'My Boyfriend Gave Me an Apple', Roud 12986), as well as several others.[112] The re-use of the same basic tune with different sets of words is a characteristic of adult traditional singing in England.[113] Like adults, the players regard these as separate clapping games and do not notice the recurrence of the tune. The consistency with which children sing a clapping song to the same tune all over the country and over many years is much greater than in adult tradition, though, and is quite remarkable given the number of times these songs must have been passed on from one generation of children to another over the last 70 years.

The origin of this particular melody is something of a mystery. The Opies attribute the new wave of interest in clapping in the 1960s to an influx of 'sparkling and spirited chants' from America in the second half of the twentieth century.[114] One of the earliest examples of these was 'I Am a Pretty Little Dutch Girl' (Roud 12986) which was first documented in the UK in 1959 and spread quickly among the child population, as, for example, reported to the Opies in this headteacher's letter (Figure 26.14).[115]

The song 'I Am a Pretty Little Dutch Girl', albeit with slightly variant words, had already been circulating for skipping and clapping in the US from the 1940s, being reported from New York and West Virginia.[116] The melody goes back even further though. Its origin appears to be the first part of a fiddle tune called 'Chinese Breakdown', which was recorded by the Stripling Brothers, an old-time country music duo from Alabama, in 1934.[117] The tune re-appeared a few years later in adapted form as the chorus of 'The Merry-Go-Round Broke Down', written by Tin Pan Alley songwriters Cliff Friend and Dave Franklin (1937).[118] Friend and Franklin's song was rapidly taken up as the theme tune for Warner Brothers' *Looney Tunes* animation series which introduced such well-known characters as Bugs Bunny and Daffy Duck to children across the world.[119]

Figure 26.15 compares 'Chinese Breakdown' and 'The Merry-Go-Round Broke Down' with the clapping song. They are not exactly alike, the clapping song being a simpler form of the tune, but the resemblance in the opening motif and in other melodic elements, coupled with the tune's wide circulation via on children's film, makes a connection plausible.

The interplay between commercial popular culture and clapping games, and their skipping and ball-bouncing predecessors, does not end here. A number of clapping songs have their roots in popular music, such as 'Under the Bram Bush' (Roud 18988) and 'See, See, My Playmate' (Roud 16805). Further investigation often uncovers that the popular songs may themselves draw on children's oral culture. Both 'My Mother Told Me (if I was goody)' (Roud 17597) and '3, 6, 9, The Goose Drank Wine' (Roud 18987) were in circulation

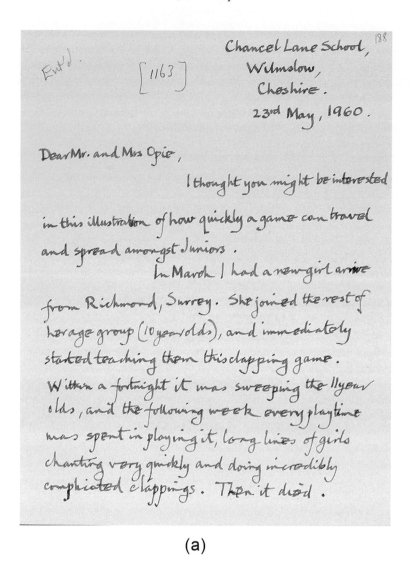

(a)

Figure 26.14 Letter from headteacher to Iona and Peter Opie, 23 May 1960

long before Shirley Ellis recorded them in combination with 'The Clapping Song' in 1965. Likewise, the clapping game 'Eeny Meeny Dessameeny' (32901), popular in the twenty-first century and often featuring a 12-beat clapping pattern, grew from a whole family of counting out rhymes popular in the US from at least the late nineteenth century, and was later recorded by the Philadelphia doo-wop group Lee Andrews and the Hearts as part of 'Glad to Be Here' in 1957, and featured in 'Eenie Meenie' in 1963 by Vito and the Salutations, from Brooklyn, New York.[120] This exchange may happen multiple times. As Kathryn Marsh observes, 'children's dialectical relationship with the media results in cycles of appropriation and reappropriation whereby material derived from the media is appropriated for play purposes by children, reappropriated in this play form by the media, then reappropriated and regenerated in modified form by children'.[121] This process has a long history and is not

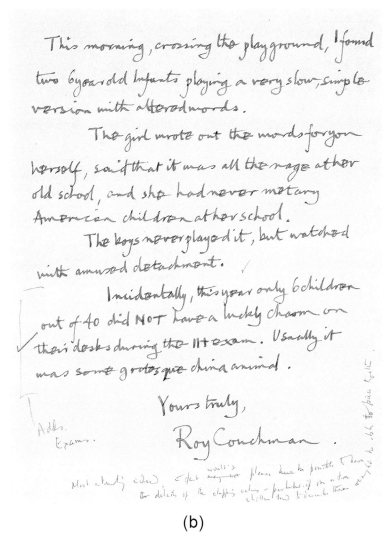

(b)

Figure 26.14 (Continued)

confined to the age of electronic media. Appearances in commercially produced versions may give a boost to the game among children for a while, and can have the effect of standardising words, tunes and movements or act as a prompt for experimentation and re-creation.

In the twenty-first century, however, young people have access to many more sources of information than ever before for clapping games. They increasingly watch television programmes and films online, some of which feature or suggest ideas for clapping games and movement routines which are developed in children's offline play. These sources supplement existing face-to-face learning and transmission in the school playground, home and neighbourhood, rather than replacing them, as some adults fear. More than this, the development of mobile technology and ease of film production, coupled with the growth of the participatory web, especially video-sharing platforms, has created a powerful new means by which clapping

Figure 26.15 'Chinese Breakdown' (1934), 'Merry-go-round Broke Down' (1937) and 'Pretty Little Dutch Girl' (1977) compared

games can be circulated. YouTube (launched in 2005) hosts numerous films in which children and young people perform, demonstrate, teach and talk about the games. An increasing proportion of these are peer-to-peer productions, created by and for young people. They showcase their skills, pass on tips and capture the fun and the challenge of hand-clapping. The plethora of versions available works to prompt variety rather than standardisation.[122]

The Opies' research in the 1950–1980 period also observed that young people experimented with producing their own clapping games, drawing on existing models and fitting clapping patterns and gestures to other songs with which they were familiar.[123] These creations were usually transient, however, and so have not been documented as much as the more enduring songs. Children continue to compose their own clapping games right up to the present time. The following game, 'iPhone', was being played by two girls, aged 6–7, in the playground of a London primary school in 2018, and was filmed as part of a research project.[124] One of the girls had learnt it from her sister and taught it to the other girl.

> OMG (*clap-clap clap*)
> Chat, chat, chat (*clap-clap clap*)
> On my phone (*clap-clap clap*)
> Snapchat (*clap-clap clap*)
> OMG, chat, chat, chat
> On my phone, Snapchat
> Turn around – Oh no, my battery's dead (*turn, palm upturned as if holding mobile phone*)
> Freeze.[125] (*strike a pose*)

The new composition is modelled on the clapping game, 'Lemonade', with its punchy rhythm and rhyme, which was regularly played at the school at the time (Figure 26.16).

> Lemonade (*clap-clap clap*)
> Ice Tea (*clap-clap clap*)
> Coca Cola (*clap-clap clap*)
> Pepsi (*clap-clap clap*)
> Lemonade, Ice Tea
> Coca Cola, Pepsi
> Turn around, touch the ground (*turn, touch ground*)
> Flick your hair, I don't care (*hair flick, finger wag*)
> Freeze! (*forearm cross over chest*)
> Star, star, star, star
> Icky icky yah yah (*forearm cross over chest, tap hips*)
> Boom! (*shoulder bump*)
>
> (Roud 32902)[126]

The researchers who documented this example suggest that young people draw on their lifeworlds, experience of traditional models and immediate environment to create meaning in such compositions and to make their interests evident. In this case, these include their response to contemporary technologies and social networking, as well as the 'Lemonade' clapping game. Another researcher, Kathryn Marsh has made an international study of children's musical play in the late 1990s and early 2000s. She highlights the way that children compose at the same time as they perform and so composition is a collaborative effort by the players.[127] Marsh observed that children compose by going through cycles of experimentation followed by regularisation and control and so does not result in 'a clearly identifiable, unchanging product to be preserved'.[128]

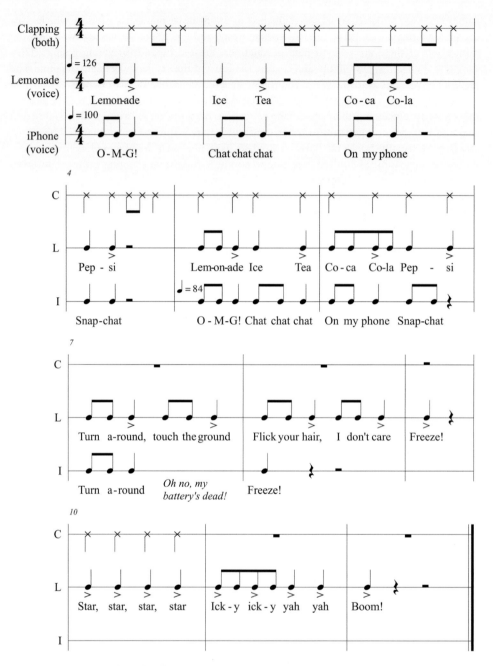

Figure 26.16 'Lemonade' and 'iPhone' compared
Source: Collected by John Potter and Kate Cowan, London, 2018. Transcribed by Julia Bishop.

A recording of 'A Sailor Went to Sea Sea Sea' as played by two 5–6 year old girls at a school in Sheffield in 2010 illustrates this same composition in performance and collaborative approach.[129] The girls extend the familiar game by improvising additional stanzas and associated gestures. The additions likewise draw on their lifeworlds and vernacular knowledge (such as in 'A sailor went to bed, bed, bed' and the mime for 'sleeping') and their immediate surroundings ('A sailor went to tree, tree, tree'). A process of friendly competition emerges as they vie to become the first to make a suggestion and introduce their favoured associated gesture. That they are able to keep the game going at the same time, with few hesitations, and instantly adjust to the new suggestion, involves expert timing and anticipation, as well as close observation of their partner.[130]

Clapping games have flourished rather than been diminished by the fads and fashions in commercial popular music and changing technologies which also provide even more sources for children to draw on. Practices continue to develop and go in and out of fashion.

Children continue to find them a viable form of performance and a means of expression as well as a sphere for experimentation. Meanwhile, YouTube in particular has created a completely new source for researchers into musical play and children's performances, providing a rich source of information on musical and multimodal performance which has yet to be fully tapped and offering exciting possibilities for future research.

Conclusion

Children's musical play, when an accessory to, or a goal of, the game, can be productively viewed as folk performance. They constitute everyday forms of vocal music among communities of children, learnt and performed in informal, non-professionalised and non-commercial settings. There is no slavish imitation of 'originals' or aspiration to 'correctness', and a diversity of styles is accepted. In this, they conform to the definition of folk song, articulated by Roud.[131] His criterion of face-to-face learning and performance is also applicable, but is extended by transmission through the participatory web which, despite being asynchronous and digitally mediated, has much in common with face-to-face learning and transmission and intertwines with it.[132] Even more than in adult folk performance, however, children's performances within play exemplify Turino's concept of 'participatory performance' in which social interaction with each other is as at least as important as the music being produced, and the performance is for the players themselves, rather than an outside audience.[133]

It is also clear that children's performance traditions are dynamic, adapting to wider changes and influences at the same time as drawing on existing resources within their peer culture. In particular, contemporary children have been quick to adapt to and draw on the far wider range of cultural resources available to them than in the past and employing them for their own aesthetic and expressive ends. A focus on the history of tunes found in musical play has also provided clues to instances of the dynamic interchange between children's peer cultures and adult popular culture in the past.

As the Opies and others have highlighted, the twentieth century witnessed a number of shifts in the popularity of musical games and games with musical elements. Ball-bouncing has died out but, as we have suggested here, it has been superseded by clapping play which has burgeoned, and the importance of rhythm and a driving beat has continued. Longrope skipping is rarely played, except when led by adults, its decline possibly due to the higher concentration of children playing in available play spaces. Counting out, however, has continued in much the same way as before, with new repertoire coming in since the collecting work of the Opies. Finally, children still play singing games but in a form very different from their forebears a hundred years ago, again attributable to the changing nature of available play spaces and greater access to media culture, among other factors.

Earlier evidence goes some way towards indicating multimodal aspects of musical play. In order to further the historical study of performance practices within play, however, there is a need to identify and review the body of audio and audio-visual evidence from the twentieth century to identify in-context recordings. Consideration of all the sonic elements of a performance and how children execute them sheds new light on the nature of their practices as players and musicians. Likewise, contemporary technology allows for the documentation of ephemeral and transient moments within play, shedding light on creative practices and the importance of experimentation and improvisation within children's performance traditions.

The question of gender still requires much more detailed investigation. The evidence suggests that musical play has never been exclusively undertaken by girls, and that we need to broaden our purview to notice and understand the roles boys take in relation to musical play, as well as the influence of social structures and constructions of gender.

We have also noted an almost complete lack of attention to ethnic diversity in children's play in this country, in the past and present, and the urgency of addressing this issue. We have also seen how children's actual experiences of playing specific games, and consideration of actual performance practices rather than idealised or generalised ones, are crucial to understanding the role of social structures such as gender and race within musical play.

Clearly, there is much else still to be explored in terms of children's performance, within play and also beyond. We have, it is hoped, reviewed sufficient evidence to conclude that, children do indeed continue to sing and vocalise, as the Opie quotation with which we began proposed, but nowadays within the freedoms and constraints of their contemporary social worlds, as active performers, and co-creators and re-creators of the things that they perform.

Notes

1 Iona and Peter Opie, *The Singing Game* (Oxford: Oxford University Press, 1985), p. vii.
2 See, for example, Eve Harwood, 'Memorized Song Repertoire of Children in Grades Four and Five in Champaign, Illinois'(unpublished doctoral dissertation, University of Illinois, Urbana-Champaign, 1987); Patricia Shehan Campbell, *Songs in Their Heads: Music and Its Meaning in Children's Lives* (New York: Oxford University Press, 1998); Kathryn Marsh, *The Musical Playground: Global Tradition and Change in Children's Songs and Games* (New York: Oxford University Press, 2008), Kyra D. Gaunt, *The Games Black Girls Play: Learning the Ropes from Double-Dutch to Hip-Hop* (New York: New York University Press, 2006); *Children's Games in the New Media Age: Childlore, Media and the Playground*, ed. by Andrew Burn and Chris Richards (Farnham: Ashgate, 2014); Tyler Bickford, *Schooling New Media: Music, Language, and Technology in Children's Culture* (New York: Oxford University Press, 2017).
3 James Orchard Halliwell, *Nursery Rhymes of England* (1842) and *Popular Rhymes and Nursery Tales* (1849).
4 For more on the musical transcription of folk song by ear in the field, see Julia Bishop 'Our History 3: Tuning a Song: Collecting the Music', in *Folk Song in England*, ed. by Steve Roud (London: Faber, 2017), pp. 185–216.
5 See, for example, Peter Kennedy, *One Two Three a-Loopa* (Folktrax cassette FTX-201, 1975), and *Somebody Under the Bed* (Folktrax cassette FTX-202, 1975).
6 The Iona and Peter Opie Archive (www.opiearchive.org), the Vaughan Williams Memorial Library digital archive (www.vwml.org), the British Library Sounds collection (https://sounds.bl.uk/) and the British Library educational resource, *Playtimes: A Century of Children's Games and Rhymes* (www.bl.uk/playtimes).

7 For more on multimodality, see Carey Jewitt, Jeff Bezemer, and Kay O'Halloran, *Introducing Multimodality* (London: Routledge, 2016).
8 For a fuller examination of the Opies' research methods, see Julia C. Bishop, 'From "Breathless Catalogue" to Beyond Text: A Hundred Years of Children's Folklore Collecting', *Folklore*, 127 (2016), 123–149.
9 Iona and Peter Opie, *The Lore and Language of Schoolchildren* (1959), p. 17.
10 See Hazel Hall, 'Musical and Poetic Characteristics of Children's Folklore', in *The Oxford Companion to Australian Folklore*, ed. by Gwenda Beed Davey and Graham Seal (Oxford: Oxford University Press, 1993), pp. 257–271. Compare with the work of Susan Young on musical play among children in the early years, e.g. 'Seen But Not Heard: Young Children, Improvised Singing and Educational Practice', *Contemporary Issues in Early Childhood*, 7 (2006), 270–280.
11 In my own research, I have also seen primary school children holding handstand competitions in which the players were coordinated via a call-and-response performance with the leader/judge. See Jackie Marsh and Julia C. Bishop, Changing Play: Play, Media and Commercial Culture from the 1950s to the Present Day (Maidenhead: Open University Press, 2013), pp. 41–43.
12 See, for example, Opie, *Children's Games with Things*, pp. 138–146, and Steve Roud, *The Lore of the Playground* (London: Random House, 2010), pp. 197–203.
13 From an advertising campaign run by the Milk Marketing Board from the late 1950s.
14 Opie, *Children's Games with Things*, p. 138.
15 Opie, *Children's Games with Things*, p. 143.
16 Roud, *Lore of the Playground*, p. 194.
17 Roud, *Lore of the Playground*, p. 196.
18 Opie, *Children's Games with Things*, p. 128.
19 Leslie Daiken, *One Potato, Two Potato* (British Film Institute, 1957). This clip is available to view on the British Library *Playtimes* website.
20 Opie, *Children's Games with Things*, p. 136.
21 Opie, *Children's Games with Things*, pp. 137–138.
22 *Opie Collection of Children's Games and Songs*, British Library Sounds, C898/39 (00:08:12–00:08:30), available at https://sounds.bl.uk/Accents-and-dialects/Opie-collection-of-children-s-games-and-songs. Transcribed a semitone lower than sung.
23 Opie, *Singing Game*, pp. 336–339, 366–367.
24 The game follows on from 'One Two Three A-Leary' and is also available to view on the British Library *Playtimes* website.
25 Opie, *Children's Games with Things*, p. 128.
26 Opie, *Children's Games with Things*, p. 151.
27 Robert Samuel, '"Cups," the newfangled patty-cake game that's gone viral among young girls', *Washington Post*, 26 February 2013.
28 Cf. Iona and Peter Opie, *Children's Games in Street and Playground* (Oxford: Oxford University Press, 1969), pp. 73–74.
29 Michael Yates, and Steve Roud, 'Alice E. Gillington: Dweller on the Roughs', *Folk Music Journal* 9.1 (2006), 72–94.
30 Opie, *Children's Games in Street*, pp. 72–73. Douglas (1916: 153) also mentions a game called 'Daddy Red-Cap' with an associated song which may be the same as 'My Man John'.
31 For a more detailed discussion, see the introduction to *Play Today in the Primary School Playground*, ed. by Julia C. Bishop and Mavis Curtis (Buckingham: Open University Press, 2001), pp. 1–19 (especially pp. 8–10).
32 Roud, *Lore of the Playground*, pp. 171–174.
33 Opie, *Children's Games with Things*, p. 167.
34 Opie, *Children's Games with Things*, pp. 167–168.
35 Dennis Mitchell and Roy Harris, *Morning in the Streets* (BBC, 1959). The skipping game is featured at 13:39–13:58 of the full-length (35-minute) film, copies of which can be found on YouTube.
36 Also played as a singing game, Opie, *Singing Game*, pp. 164–166.
37 Opie, *Children's Games with Things*, p. 207.
38 Roud, *Lore of the Playground*, p. 182.
39 Opie, *Children's Games with Things*, pp. 211–212.

40 Opie, *Children's Games with Things*, pp. 207–306; N. G. N. Kelsey, *Games, Rhymes, and Wordplay of London Children*, ed. by Janet E. Alton and J. D. A. Widdowson (London: Palgrave Macmillan, 2019), 271–337.
41 Halliwell, *Popular Rhymes and Nursery Tales*, p. 134.
42 Andy Arleo, 'Counting-Out and the Search for Universals', *Journal of American Folklore*, 110 (1997), 391–407.
43 Roud, *Lore of the Playground*, p. 350, noted as collected in Northamptonshire, 1950s.
44 Opie, *Children's Games in Street*, p. 31.
45 Roud, *Lore of the Playground*, p. 348.
46 Danielle Roemer, unpublished paper (n.d.), quoted in Roger D. Abrahams and Lois Rankin, *Counting-Out Rhymes: A Dictionary*, American Folklore Society Bibliographical and Special Series, vol. 31 (Austin: University of Texas Press, 1980), p. xiv.
47 British Library, *Playtimes* website.
48 Kenneth S. Goldstein, 'Strategy in Counting Out: An Ethnographic Folklore Field Study', in *The Study of Games*, ed. by Elliott Avedon and Brian Sutton-Smith (New York: Wiley, 1971), pp. 167–178.
49 Norman Douglas, *London Street Games* (London: St Catherine Press, 1916), p. 63.
50 Constantin Brăiloiu, 'La rythmique enfantine', in *Problèmes d'ethnomusicologie, ed. by* Constantin Brăiloiu (Geneva: Minkoff Reprint, 1973 [1956]), pp. 4–37; Robbins Burling, 'The Metrics of Children's Verse: A Cross-Linguistic Study', *American Anthropologist*, 68(1966), 1418–1441, and Andy Arleo, 'Counting-out and the Search for Universals', *Journal of American Folklore*, 110 (1997), 391–407.
51 The clip of 'One Potato, Two Potato' is available on the British Library *Playtimes* website.
52 Clip available on the British Library *Playtimes* website.
53 Halliwell, Popular *Rhymes*, pp. 127–128.
54 For further information about her methods, see Alice B. Gomme, Preface, *The Traditional Games of England, Scotland and Ireland*, 2 vols (London, Nutt, 1894, 1898), I, pp. vii–x, and critical appreciations of her work, Georgina Boyes, 'Alice Bertha Gomme (1852–1938): A Reassessment of the Work of a Folklorist', *Folklore*, 101 (1990),198–208, and Steve Roud, 'Books Worth (Re)-Reading', *International Journal of Play*, 3 (2014), 349–351.
55 Gomme, *Traditional Games*, p. ix. Charlotte Burne had been the first to include tune notations of singing games some ten years before, from the children in a gipsy family. See her *Shropshire Folk-Lore* (London: Trübner, 1883, 1885, 1886).
56 Although her interpretations of the games as remnants of ancient rituals reflect a now discredited theoretical approach, the excellence of her documentation makes her books a standard reference work in children's play.
57 They collected at firsthand, from children and adults, and also via correspondents.
58 Anne G. Gilchrist and Lucy E. Broadwood, 'Notes on Children's Game-Songs', *Journal of the Folk-Song Society* 5.19 (1915), 221–239 (p. 221).
59 Julia C. Bishop, '"That's how the whole hand-clap thing passes on": Online/Offline Transmission and Multimodal Variation in a Children's Clapping Game', in Burn and Richards, *Children's Games*, pp. 53–84, attempts to do this with a clapping game in the context of one school playground over a period of several years.
60 William Irwin, 'Bonnie Dundee', Traditional Tune Archive, https://tunearch.org/wiki/Bonnie_Dundee_(2).
61 Opie, *Singing Game*, p. vii.
62 Opie, *Singing Game*, p. vii.
63 Gilchrist and Broadwood, 'Notes', p. 223.
64 Julia C. Bishop, '"Dr Carpenter from the Harvard College in America": An Introduction to James Madison Carpenter and his Collection', *Folk Music Journal*, 7.4 (1998), 402–420.
65 Apart from 'The Big Ship Sails', discussed below, the other children's games are 'Steal a Horse and Buy a Gig' (Roud 12981), 'Wallflowers' (Roud 6307), 'The Wind Blows High' (Roud 2649), 'Margaret Made a Pudding' (Roud 13324), 'Oranges and Lemons' (Roud 13190) and 'Poor Mary Sits a-Weeping' (Roud 2118). All are audible in succession on James Madison Carpenter Collection, JMC/1/10/96, Cylinder 095 which can be found online as part of the Vaughan Williams Memorial Library digital archive, www.vwml.org/record/VWMLSongIndex/SN19209.

66 https://www.vwml.org/record/VWMLSongIndex/SN25903 and https://www.vwml.org/record/VWMLSongIndex/SN19209. Carpenter's transcription gives the following alternatives for the final line, 'On Christmas day in the morning' and 'On [a] cold and frosty morning'.
67 Opie, *Singing Game*, pp. 29, 33–40.
68 Carpenter Collection, JMC/1/1/1/J, p. 00997, www.vwml.org/record/VWMLSongIndex/SN25903
69 British Library *Playtimes* website and Opie, *Singing Game*, pp. 50–51.
70 Opie, *Singing Game*, p. 50.
71 Opie, *Singing Game*, p. 52
72 Available at the British Library *Playtimes* website.
73 Opie, *Singing Game*, pp. 50–52; cf. pp. 398–400 ('Sally Go Round the Sun'), and pp. 453–455 ('Under the Bram Bush').
74 See Richard Chase, *Singing Games and Playparty Games* (1949; reprinted New York: Dover, 1967), p. 46, for a 1948 Massachusetts version of 'The Big Ship Sails' sung to a simple time transformation of the 'Here We Go Round' melody.
75 There are also similarities with the French Canadian fiddle tune, 'Reel du Tadoussac', also known as 'Glise à Sherbrooke', recorded by Joseph Allard in 1928, itself potentially based on the melody of Henry Bishop's 'Home Sweet Home'. See Traditional Tune Archive entries for each at https://tunearch.org/wiki/TTA.
76 See London Sound Survey at www.soundsurvey.org.uk.
77 Opie, *Singing Game*, pp. 1–31.
78 Opie, *Singing Game*, p. 29.
79 Felicia R. McMahon and Brian Sutton-Smith, 'The Past in the Present: Theoretical Directions for Children's Folklore', in *Children's Folklore: A Source Book*, ed. by Brian Sutton-Smith, Jay Mechling, Thomas W. Johnson, and Felicia R. McMahon (New York: Routledge, 1995), p. 294.
80 See note 7 above.
81 See Laura Jopson, Andrew Burn and Jonathan Robinson, 'The Opie Recordings: What's Left to be Heard?' in Burn and Richards, *Children's Games*, pp. 31–51.
82 British Library Sounds, C898/26.
83 Jopson et al., 'The Opie Recordings', p. 38.
84 Jopson et al., 'The Opie Recordings', pp. 38–39.
85 Opie, *Singing Game*, p. vii.
86 Opie, *Singing Game*, pp. 366–367.
87 Opie, *Singing Game*, p. 367.
88 See, for example, the articles in 'The Lifework and Legacy of Iona and Peter Opie', a special issue of the *International Journal of Play* 3.3 (2014).
89 See Burn and Richards, *Children's Games*, and Rebekah Willett et al., *Children, Media and Playground Cultures: Ethnographic Studies of School Playtimes* (Basingstoke: Palgrave Macmillan, 2013).
90 It is possible that the research files kept by the Opies contain documentation on this that was not written up and published.
91 Kelsey, *Games, Rhymes, and Wordplay*, pp. 194–195.
92 Yinka Olusoga, conversation with author, 17 June 2020.
93 Opie, *Singing Game*, p. 29; Kathryn Marsh, 'It's Not All Black or White: The Influence of the Media, the Classroom and Immigrant Groups on Children's Playground Singing Games', in Bishop and Curtis, *Play Today*, pp. 80–97.
94 Mavis Curtis, 'The Multicultural Playground' in Roud, *Lore of the Playground*, pp. 393–394.
95 Curtis, 'The Multicultural Playground', pp. 403–404.
96 Mavis Curtis, 'Zig Zag Zoo and Other Games: The Oral Tradition of Children of Asian Origin in Keighley, West Yorkshire', *Folk Life*, 38 (2000), 71–82, and 'The Multicultural Playground', pp. 393–410.
97 See 'Dan Jones Collection of Children's Games and Songs', British Library Sounds, C1664.
98 Opie, *Singing Game*, p. 446.
99 Opie, *Singing Game*, pp. 442–443, and Douglas, mentioned above.
100 Carpenter's interwar collection contains only one example of a clapping game, collected from Jeannie Campbell in Aberdeenshire, Scotland, and noted as 'learned at school – used as a clapping game' (https://www.vwml.org/record/VWMLSongIndex/SN25924).

101 *The King Pippin Polka* (London: Chappell, [c.1860?]), British Library Music Collections h.721.k.(17.). See also 'Albert, Charles Louis Napoléon d'', by A. J. Hipkins, revised by David Charlton (2001), in *Grove Dictionary Online*, 2001. 'My Mother Said', noted by Anne Gilchrist, Gilchrist collection AGG/7/196e, https://www.vwml.org/record/AGG/7/196e.

102 Alice Gillington noted it in the Isle of Wight, for example, as 'formerly played by boys and girls standing either in a ring or on opposite sides, taking up alternate verses in answer to each other. Nowadays it is played either by two children clapping hands together, as they sing, or in the following way [sung and acted out].' See *Old Isle of Wight Singing Games*, pp. 12–13. Cf. Opie, *Singing Game*, pp. 441, 442.

103 'Folklore Notes of Rev. Addison Crofton', Bodleian Libraries, Oxford, MSS. Eng. misc. e. 39–42. Quoted in Opie, *Singing Game*, p. 441.

104 Opie, *Singing Game*, p. 444.

105 See, for example, 'Under the Bram Bush' on the British Library *Playtimes* website.

106 British Library *Playtimes* website.

107 The transcription relates to the second rendition of this section of the game, beginning at 00.36. There are slight variations among some of the players each time.

108 Cf. Marsh, 'It's Not All Black'.

109 Opie, *Singing Game*, pp. 415–417.

110 See, for example, Marjorie Harness Goodwin, *The Hidden Life of Girls: Games of Stance, Status, and Exclusion* (New York: Wiley, 2008).

111 Opie, *Singing Game*, pp. 465–467.

112 Mavis Curtis, 'A Sailor Went to Sea: Theme and Variations', *Folk Music Journal*, 8.4 (2004), 421–437.

113 Bishop, 'Our History'.

114 Opie, *Singing Game*, p. 441.

115 Oxford, Bodleian Libraries, MS. Opie 32 fol. 188r and MS. Opie 32 fol. 188v.

116 Opie, *Singing Game*, p. 452, and Roger D. Abrahams, *Jump-Rope Rhymes: A Dictionary* (Austin: University of Texas Press, 2014), p. 69.

117 'Chinese Breakdown I' entry, Traditional Tune Archive, https://tunearch.org/wiki/Chinese_Breakdown_(1), and 'Stripling Brothers' entry, Wikipedia.

118 'The Merry-Go-Round Broke Down' entry, Wikipedia.

119 'Miss Susie Had a Steamboat' (Roud 15421) entry, Wikipedia.

120 Julia Bishop, "Eeny Meeny Dessameeny': Continuity and Change in the 'Backstory' of a Children's Playground Rhyme', unpublished paper, 2011.

121 Marsh, *Musical Playground*, p. 181.

122 Bishop, 'That's how the handclap thing'.

123 Opie, *Singing Game*, p. 445.

124 John Potter and Kate Cowan, 'Playground as Meaning-Making Space: Multimodal Making and Re-making of Meaning in the (Virtual) Playground,' *Global Studies of Childhood*, 10 (2020), pp. 248–263.

125 In a further development observed by the researchers, the second girl who was playing 'iPhone' then went on to compose her own version of the game, 'Bluetooth'. See Potter and Cowan, 'Playground as Meaning-Making Space'.

126 A similar performance of 'Lemonade' from a different school, recorded in 2010, is available on the British Library *Playtimes* website.

127 Marsh, *Musical Playground*, pp. 199–202.

128 Marsh, *Musical Playground*, p. 202.

129 See British Library *Playtimes* website.

130 More detailed discussion is in Julia C. Bishop and Andrew Burn, 'Reasons for Rhythm: Multimodal Perspectives on Musical Play', in Burn and Richards, *Children's Games*, pp. 89–119.

131 Roud, *Folk Song in England*, pp. 23–25.

132 Bishop, 'That's how the whole hand-clap thing passes on'.

133 Thomas Turino, *Music as Social Life: The Politics of Participation* (Chicago, IL: University of Chicago Press, 2008).

INDEX

Note: **Bold** page numbers refer to tables, *italic* page numbers refer to figures and page numbers followed by "n" refer to end notes.

Abson, W. 239
actor 34, 81, 84–87, 95
Adams, A. 418
Adams, B. 194
The Adoration of the Shepherds: A Miracle Play (Collier) 152
African and Caribbean dances 326
The Alderley Edge Landscape Project (AELP) 115, 119n68
Alderley Mummers' play *108, 116*; Barber family 101, 105, 117n1; 1850 to 1869 (2nd Lord Stanley) 103–105; 1869 to 1903 (3rd Lord Stanley) 105–106; history of revival 114–116; 1903 to 1925 (4th Lord Stanley) 106–110; 1925 to 1931 (5th Lord Stanley) 110–111; 1931 to 1938 (6th Lord Stanley) 112–113; play performance 116–117; Pre-1850 (1st Lord Stanley) 102–103; publication and revival 113–114; Stanley family 101
Ales, W. 178, 227
Alford, V. 10, 12, 127
Alfred Nutt, J. A. 450
Allan, S. 2, 4
All Saints 71, 418
All Souls 42n96, 106, 113
amusement dancing 191
Anderson, Alistair 506
Anderson, Pamela 164
Anderson, Robert 193, 194, 195
anti-capitalism 360
apartheid 360
The Arabian Nights 105
Armstrong, Frankie 507, 521
'arm-works' 348

Arnold, John 416
Arthur, Dave 473, 486, 491
Arthur, Toni 491
Ash Wednesday sword dance 181
Asquith, Herbert Henry (Prime Minister) 107
assemblies 20–21
Astley, Rick 350
Aston, John 298
Atkinson, George 422

Bailey, Roy 474
Baldwin, Billy 166
ball-bouncing, skipping and counting out: 'My Man John' 555, *556*, 557, *557*; 'Plainsie Clapsie' 553, *555*; Rhythmic ostinato of 'The Cup Song' 555, *555*; '[Rosy Apple]' Skipping *558*, 558–559
'ball-money' 48
Banks, Joseph 181, 205, 207
'Barbara Allen' 397–399
Barber, Damien 317, 319, 321
Barber, George 110
Barker, Harvey Granville 256
Barker, John 298, 310
Baron, Michael 193
Barrett, W. A. 454
Barrie, J. 111
Barwick, John 411
The Beggar's Opera (Gay) 385
Bell, Sammy 281, 287
Bennett, J. 443
Bennett, Sam 266
Bennett, Toby 317
Bentley, Bernard 344, 346

Index

Bidford Shakespearean Morris Dancers 228
'Billy Taylor' 392–394
Black Adder Rapper and Step 322
Blackface 5–6; camouflage 5; disguise 5; representational 5, 6; symbolic 5
Black, Mary 523
Black Swan Rapper 322, 327
blawta a blonega 54–55
Blundell, Nicholas 180
Blundell, William 180
Blunt, Janet 562
Boardman, Harry 487
Bollywood 326
'boon days' 185
Border morris: background 295–297; development of 300; Leicester Morrismen and (*see* Leicester Morrismen's Border Morris Odyssey); next steps after 1963 297–298; numbers dancing Border morris 309, 309–310; Original Welsh Border Morris Men 298; performance-related aspects 308–309; 'Rattlebone and Ploughjack' 299; at Sidmouth Folk Festival 299; teams, establishment 301–302
Borlase, W. 84
Bottrell, William 91, 92, 93
Boulton, Harold 451
Bourne, H. 10
Bowden, Bert 285
The Bower Processional 306
Boxing Day fancy dress, Wigan: activity in Poolstock 162–163; analysis 173–174; Boxing Night festivity 160–161; costume and disguise 166–168; cross dressing 167; on the dance floor 164–165; fancy dress group 'scouser' theme, Boxing Day 2018 *169*; folk tales and memories 163; getting ready *159*, 159–160; 'Labyrinth' theme group, Boxing Day 2017 *159*; living archive 165; making vs hiring 168–169; Nottingham County match 162; outside records 172–173; parade 163–164, 169–170; perambulations, Boxing Day 2018 *171*; performance and embodiment 170–172; Putin and friends, Boxing Day 2018 *164*; RUFC fundraising parties 162; Rugby League football club 161–162; walk of shame 173; Wigan Latics football club 162; *Wigan Observer* 161; *Wigan World* 162
Boydell, Alex 290
Brady, Nicholas 413
Brammery, Jonathan 194
Brand, J. 209
Brice, Andrew: *Brice's Journal* 80; Christmas mumming 81; *The Critical Review* 79; *The Exeter Flying Post* 80; mayoral election, Devon, 1737 79–81; *The Mobiad: Or, Battle of the Voice* 79; *The Play-house Church, or new Actors of Devotion* 80; reference to mumming 80; *Universal Magazine* 80
Briggs, Anne 489
British Dance Edition 323
Broadwood, Lucy 562
Bronson, Bertrand Harris 364, 385
Brown, Charles Armitage 189
Brown, Richard 409
Buchanan, A. 458
Buckstone, J. B. 394
Bunting, Edward 447
Burlesquing The Ballad: Barbara Allen 397–399; Billy Taylor 392–394; complex case of 'Lord Lovel' 385–390; George Barnwell 394–396; Gosport Tragedy 396–397; Lord Bateman 403–404; loyal lover 402–403; 'Oh My Love's Dead' 390–392; Sir Eglamore 404–405; Three Ravens 401; Twa Sisters 399–401; Villikens and his Dinah 392
Burne, C. 14, 93
Burns, Robert 193
Burton, Richard 105

calendrical pressures: shriving 44; Shrovetide perambulations (case study) 44, 51–60; Shrovetide processions survey 44, 45–51
Camidge, W. 210
Campaign for Nuclear Disarmament 360
Campbell, Stephen 429
Cann, Bob 289, 291
capoeira 326
Carlson, M. 15
Carradus, John 192
Carter, Thomas 229
Carthy, Martin 315, 474, 484, 491, 511
Cassie, Bill 214
castigating malfeasance (folk law) 23; conjugal irregularity 24; customary castigation 26; form and content 24; house-visit castigation 25; material context 24; model of the *charivari* 25; nuptial irregularity 24; *parade* 25; range of offences triggering 24–25; rough music 27; sexual irregularity 24
Catcheside-Warrington, C. E. 486
Cavalier Ballads and Songs (Morley) 147
Cawte, Christopher 12
Cawte, E.C. 28, 210, 213, 214, 221, 296
Central Council of Recreative Physical Training (CCRPT) 268–269
'central European' dance 269
Chambers, E.K. 233
Chandler, Keith 177, 227
Chaplin, Nellie 250
Chappell, William 398
character: 'balladesque' 375; dancers 332; Father Christmas 5, 109; of Lord Ogleby 80; of Robin 72
charivari see rough music

Cheshire Folk Drama (Helm) 115
Child, F.J. 74
'Chinese Breakdown' 573
Christmas 4, 5, 11, 22, 27, 28, 33, 34, 68, 69, 78, 80, 81, 84, 85, 88–93, 95, 102, 104–108, 112, 115, 116, 124, 131, 152, 159, 161–163, 166, 168, 185, 187, 190, 192, 195, 198, 203, 204, 206, 207, 211, 213, 215, 216, 251, 295, 296, 298, 305, 413, 432, 502, 550
Clague, J. 451
clapping games and playground beat: Chinese Breakdown, Merry-go-round Broke Down and Pretty Little Dutch Girl compared 573–574, *576*; 'Lemonade' and 'iPhone' compared 577, *578*; Letter from headteacher to Iona and Peter Opie, 23 May 1960 573, *574–575*; 'My Mother Said' 570, *570*; 'My Mummy Sent Me Shopping' 571, *571*
Clare, J. 28, 539
Clark, E. 194
Clark, Ewan 194
Clark, Thomas 411
Clarke, J. 185
Clifton, Peter 283
clog dance: competitions, the Clog Hornpipe 280–281; material 277–278; in Northumberland 315; research & primary sources 286–287; transmission & participation 287–288
Clog Hornpipe 280–281
Clog Waltz 281–282
Collier, J.P. 152
Collins, Giles 386
Collins, Shirley 474, 479, 489
community, performance of: Christian socialism 151, 154; folksong collection 147; *God's Co-operative Society* 146; God's goodness 145–146; *Goodwill* 152, 153; Holy Communion 145; notion of Christ 153–154; notions of selectivity 148; process of printing and publication 148; role of 'translator' or 'interpreter' 147; 'Shepherd's Plays' 147, 152–153, 155; socialistic society, establishment of 146; *Village Silhouettes*, Marson's 148–150, 151
community singing: folk song in school 504; football terraces 504; street choirs 504–505
Community Singing movement 504
Community Song Book 503
Copper, Bob 478
Corcoran, Charlie 310
Corrsin, S.D. 4
costumes, *Christmas*: commemorative costumes 166, 167; generic costumes 166–167; popular media costumes 166–167; satirical costumes 166, 167; sick humour or shock factor 166, 167
Cotswold Morris 179, 225, 226, 236, 237, 243n2, 296–298, 300, 301, 303–306, 308, 311n8, 311n16, 313n53, 313n54, 313n57, 340, 344
Council for the Encouragement of Music and the Arts (CEMA) 468
country dances 4, 177–178, 186, 189–191, 196, 235, 241, 248, 261–265, 268, 337, 535, 542, 564; *see also* English country dance
Covid-19 pandemic 316, 325, 328, 333
Cowell, Sam 389, 390, 391, 392, 394, 532
Cowern, R.T. 242
Cox, Harry 371, 478, 492
'Cranbrook' 502
Crawhall, Joseph 217
Crawley, W. 84
creativity *vs.* authenticity in English folk song revival: 'All folk songs are forgeries' 480–482; Colliers and cotton weavers 485–487; decisions and divisions 474–476; Faeries and foul fiends 489–492; finding a voice 476–480; Meddling with the modes 483–485; Mowers and maidenheads 487–489
Creighton, Helen 466, 468, 471
Crocker, Albert 289
Crowest, Frederick 442
Crowley, Aleister 491
'The Cruel Miller' 367
'The Cruel Ship's Carpenter' 365, 379, 484
custom: annual 17; biographical incidence 17–18; *blawta a blonega* 54; 'Boxing Day' or 'Boxing Night' 158; castigation 24; Cheshire custom of souling 104; Christmastide 129; Christmastime 11, 207; Easter housevisit 35; European 22; Halloween 11; 'Hooden Horse' 33–34; Lent-crocking, Lensherding, Panshered Day, Dappy-door Night, or Sharp Tuesday 52; Old Tup 34; Pace-Egging 36; of plough dragging 220; Shrovetide 49; 'tin-canning' 53
customary plays (performances) 23–36; castigating malfeasance (folk law) 23, 24–27; dramatic pastimes and entertainments 23, 27–31; house-visit customs 23, 31–36
customary stages (material contexts) 20–23; assemblies 20–21; encounters 21–23
customary theatres (auspices) 17–18; biographical incidence 17; temporal auspices (incidence) 17–18

Daily Express 503
D'Albert, Charles 570
The Dalcroze Society 269
Dallas, Karl 491
The Dance as Education (Jordan) 269
dancer: Border morris 308; clog 281, 286, 321; "complete folk dancer" 266; folk 115; hip hop 324; morris 264, 321, 345; rapper 329; solo 291; stage 278; step 282, 287–289, 321; street 278; sword 216; traditional (*see* traditional dancing)

Index

Dancing England Rapper Tournament (DERT) 322, 327, 329, 340
Daniels, George 394
'dark folk' or 'wyrdfolk' 491
David Gregory, E. 453
Davies, Joan 468
Davis, Rosie 325
Deane, S. 446
Dean-Smith, Margaret 125, 249
The Death of Robert, Earle of Huntington (Munday) 65
Deighton, John 191
Demon Barber Roadshow 322, *323*
Demon Barbers XL show 324
Derrida, J. 13
Deuteromelia (Ravenscroft) 389
Devon 283–284; Street style 283–284
Dibdin, Charles 390
Dickinson, W. 185
Dog Rose Morris 322
Dolmetsch, Arnold 250
Dommett, Roy 299, 300, 341
Dors, Diana 339
Dorson, Richard 345
The Downfall of Robert, Earle of Huntington (Munday) 65
drama 124–125; communal 145; English customary drama 16–36; folk 1–4, 9–15, 81; heroic 85; regular 86–87; religious 5, 152; rude 89; seventeenth-century 482; TV 489
dramatic pastimes and entertainments 23, 27–31; gambol with one-on-one confrontation 28; 'Keys of Canterbury (or Heaven or My Heart)' 29; 'mobbing' category 27; physical interaction 27; revival or 'cure' action 28–29; Yorkshire source 29–31
Drury, Edmund 539
Duffy, Charles Gavan 446
Duncan, Isadora 265
Dundes, Alan 345
Dunn, George 368, 376
Durham Reel 270
Dussart, G.A. 453
'Dutch Dance' 282
Dylan, Bob 475

East Anglia: Street style 283
Easter 11, 17, 33, 35, 44, 68, 161, 213, 240, 413, 466
Eastcott, Richard 414, 416, 417
Ebsworth, Joseph 390
Edgerton, D. 240
Edminster, W. 155
Education Act of 1870 441
Edward, James 215
Edwin, John: *The Eccentricities of John Edwin, Comedian* 85; Jobson's booth at Bristol Fair 85–86, *86*; *The Siege of Troy* 86–87, *87*

Ellwood, Johnson 281, 286, 287
Emslie, J. P. 551, 562
encounters: contextual encounter 21; customary encounter 22; house-visit performance 21–22; parade 23; reception 22; socio-cultural engagement 21; spatial encounter 21
Engel, Carl 445
English clog 326
English country dance: authenticity, Sharp's emerging concept of 251–253; rediscovery of John Playford 248–251; Sharp and authenticity 253–255; Sharp's defence 255–257
English County Songs 455
English customary drama: customary plays (performances) 23–36; customary stages (material contexts) 20–23; customary theatres (auspices) 17–18; history of 16–17; socio-cultural auspices (function) 18–20; 'traces of ancient mystery' 16
English Dance and Song 476
The English Dancing Master (Playford) 177, 248
English Folk Dance and Song Society (EFDSS) 261
English Folk Dance Society (EFDS) 13, 225, 235–237
English identity in music: Alfred Perceval Graves and Kate Lee 447–449; England, un-musical nation 442–444; folk-song collectors 444; Folk-Song Society 447–452, 456–459; industrialisation 441–442; 'Irish' impetus 445; Irish Literary Society of London 445, 446–447; Lucy Broadwood, Fuller Maitland, and Frank Kidson 453–455
English Romantic movement 480
English Town and Country Carnival Organisation (ETACCO) 348
Essex, John 255
European Union (EU) 507
Evelyn, J. 453
Evesham stick dance 306

Face the Music: Church and Chapel Bands in Cornwall (Woodhouse) 428
fairground theatre: John Edwin, Jobson's booth at Bristol Fair, The Siege of Troy. c1770 85–87
fancy footwork: clog dance 277–278, 286–288; competitions & authenticity 289–291; documenting the revival 286; hard-shoe step dance 288–289; Lancashire and Cheshire Clog Dance Championship i 290; music-hall repertoire 281–282; 'no-heels' rule 290–291; Northern Counties Clog Dance Championship 290; notion of 'heritage' 289; stage style 278–281; step dance material 277–278; Street style 282–285
Fazackerly, Louise 161, 166, 167
Ferguson, S. 448

Finn, Mike 310
First Industrial Revolution 441
Five Miracle Plays, or Scriptural Dramas (Collier) 152
Fletcher, Kerry 317, 318, 321, 325, 326
folk choirs: arranging for 510–511, 514, 521; choir as folk and the folk as choir 501–502; community singing 503–505; cultural and social contexts 505–507; folk groups in harmony 509–510; folk music revivals 499–501; folk song and other repertoire 522–524; 'The Lark in the Morning' *515–518*; music of people 499–501; pedagogical frameworks 507–509; singing at work 502–503; 'The Sweet Nightingale' *519–520*; 'Whittingham Fair' *512–513*; World harmonies 521; Wren music (case study) 507, 522
Folk Club movement 487
folk dance 4–5, 267; Ash Wednesday sword dance 181; *carole* and *basse danse* 181; disguising dance 180–181; and Douglas Kennedy (*see* Kennedy, Douglas); eighteenth- and post-eighteenth-century dance 4; ethnography and intertextuality 182; history 180–182; morris dance 177–178; sword dance 4, 179–180; twentieth-century 4
folk dance-games: *Ninepins* and *Pop Goes the Weasel* 268
Folk Dance Remixed (FDR) hybrid forms 316
folk drama: mummers' play 3–4; performativity 1; reiteration and duration, time and place 14–15; Romanticism, context and technique 15; spatial arrangements 14; 'stages' 3; theatre and performance 1, 3–4, 9–15
'folk heritage' 360–361
folklore 1–2, 13
Folklore Society 13
folk music *see* folk song and music
folk performance: 'English folk performance' 2; performance skills 13; role in formation of cultural memory 1
'folk scene' 360
folk song and music 6–7; collecting folk 358; definitions 356; descriptions 358–359; discovery of folk 357–358; before folk 356–357; 'new' approaches to research 361; reviving folk 359–361; 'sweetheart murder' ballads 6
folk-song society 13; Alfred Perceval Graves and Kate Lee 447–449; circular letter *449*; committee membership 456, 459; Conservatism 457; 'fakers' and preservationists, founding of 449–452; foundation of 452; founders, political allegiances of 456–459; Irish impetus for 445; musical establishment 458; political associations 456–457; purity of folk music 458
'folk' theatre 11–12

'folk tunes' 7
fool plough 208
Forrest, John 177
A Fortnight's Ramble in the Lakes (Palmer) 187
Franklin, Dave 573
Frazer, J.G. 233, 491
Friend, Cliff 573
Frith, John 281
'fuging tune' 414
Fuller Maitland, E. F. 450
Fuller Maitland, J.A. 453

Gammon, Vic 537
Gardiner, Rolf 226, 234
Gareiss, Nic 321
Garnett, John 393
Gathering Peascods 270
George Barnwell 394–396
Georgiou, Dion 166
Gibbons, Bill 285
Gifford, W.: Grassington Theatricals, Yorkshire, c790s - c1800s 87–88; 'Old Gentleman' c1730 88; TQM 87–89
Gilchrist, A. 489
Gilchrist, Anne 562, 570
'Giles Collins'/'Lady Alice' 385, 387–389
'Giles Scroggins' Ghost' 390
Gillington, A. 555, 568
Gill, W. H. 450, 451
Girls' carnival morris: cheerleaders or Irish dancers 336; cheerleading 352n1; choreography 347–349, *348*; community self-entertainment 339; competition 340–341; English folk revival 338, 352; 'fluffy' morris 338; gender profile 345–346; generational spread 346–347; geography 341–344, *342*, *343*; jazz marching bands 338; Members of Orcadia Morris Dancers, 2016 *337*; musical accompaniment 349–350; otherness 350–351; performance context 338–340; recording technology 349; regimental marching tunes 349; rhythmic musical accompaniment 337
Gladstone, William Ewart (Prime Minister) 445, 456
Goard, Henry A. 532
Good Singing Still: A Handbook on West Gallery Music (Woods) 428
Gordon, Mattias 324
'The Gosport Tragedy' 396–397
Graham, J. 226, 232
Grainger, Percy 562
Greek Dance Association 269
Gregory, Sheila 344
The Guardian (Barber) 108

Hadow, William Henry 268
Hale, George 160, 167
Halloween 11, 12, 174n6

Hamer, Samantha 340, 341, 349
Hammond, B. 146, 442
Hammond, J.L. 146, 442
Hampshire: Street style 284
Hampton, Thomas 529
Hancock, Emma 376
handkerchief dance 306
Hannah, Jack 239
Hannam, Grace 250
hard-shoe step dance: Devon 289; East Anglia 288–289; primary sources, research & transmission 288–289
hard-shoe stepping styles 283
Hardy, T. 29, 528
Harker, Dave 458
Harmer, Simon 284, 325
Harris, Emmylou 523
Harry Plunket-Greene 471
Harton, F. 239
Hatton, C. 77
Haweis, T. 418
Hayden, B. 214
Heaney, Joe 478
Heaney, M. 4
Heaton, Philip 177
Helsop, Richard Oliver 217
Henderson, William 216
Hero-Combat plays 32, 36, 41n82
Hewitt, Dick 287, 288
hilt and point 4, 179, 204
hip hop 326
Hipkins, A. J. 453
Hippisley, J. 82
'Hippisley's Drunken Man' 82, 97n33
The Histories of the Morris in Britain (Heaney) 179
The History of Morris Dancing 1458–1750 (Forrest) 177
The History of the County Palatine and City of Chester (Ormerod) 103
A History of Whitby, and Streoneshalh Abbey (Young) 208
Holden, Keith 163
The Holiday Fellowship Book of Holiday Songs 504
Holland, William 412
Holt, A. 249
Hone, W. 87, 88
Horn, Matthew 191
hornpipe steps: collected in Lake District 279
Horton, Henry 392
household performance: Frederick Lee and Harry Lupton – Thame Park and the Baronial Hall at Brill c1790–c1840 89–91; John Jackson, probably Westmorland, 1740s 81–83; William Borlase, Cornwall, 1758 83–85; William Bottrell, Robert Hunt and Thomas Quiller Couch, West Cornwall, c1820s–1860s 91–93

house-visit customs 23; Christmas-New Year 'Old Horse' 33–34; customary drama 35; in England and Wales *51*, 51–52; 'figure-sequence play' 35; 'Hero Combat' mummers' play 36; 'Hooden Horse' custom of Kent 33; 'mummers' plays' 32–33; mumming 31–32; 'Old Ball' 33; 'Old Tup' Christmas visit custom 34; Pace-Egging custom 36; 'The Poor Old Horse' 34; retributive house-visits 52–53; rhyming house-visits 53–54; simple house-visits 54–56
Housman, John 190
Housman, Laurence 231
Howard, A. 160
Howison, Dan 344
Howkins, A. 250
Hudd, Roy 339
Hulme, Ann-Marie 283
Hunt, Robert 91, 92
Hutchings, Ashley 474
Hyde, Douglas (President) 446

Illustrations of Shakespeare and Ancient Manners 228
Interlude of Youth, Diphilo & Granido 79
International Institute of Margaret Morris Movement 269
Irish Home Rule movement 459
Irish Home Rule movement, collapse of 459
Irish Literary Society of London (ILSL) 446–447
The Irish Song Book 448
Irish stepping 326

Jackson, J.: 'Hippisley's Drunken Man' 82; *The History Of The Scottish Stage, […]With Memoirs Of His Own Life* 81; household performance 82; *The Top of the Tree* 83
Jacques, F. 450
James, Francis 364
Jarman, Thomas 411
Jarre, Jean Michel 350
Johnson, L. 446
Johnson, Pete 310
Johnson, Tom 87
Jones, Andrew 423
Jones, Annie 310
Jones, Dave 298, 300, 306
Journal of the English Folk Dance and Song Society (Cawte) 295, 470
Journal of the Folk-Song Society (*JFSS*) 451
Joyce, F. W. 447
'juvenile jazz bands' 338

Karpeles, Maud 263, 341, 347
Keane, Dolores 523
Keats, J. 189
Keet-Black, J. 325, 284
Kell, Brian 303

Kendal, Robert 416
Kennedy, Douglas: country dance 261; Darwinian-inspired evolutionary theory 266–267; Director of English Folk Dance Society 261; EFDS/S members 263, 265; *England's Dances: Folk Dancing To-Day and Yesterday* 261, 266; *English Folk Dancing in the Primary School* 265; folk dance and education 262, 268–271; history of 262–263; leading expert in folk dance 263–264; *The Oxford Dictionary of English Folklore* 261; plans for change 264; 'spirit' 264; vitality and naturalness in folk dance 261–262, 265–268; *Wake up and Dance* 261
Kennedy, Michael 443, 444
Kennedy, Peter 289
Kerr, Sandra 474, 475, 477
Kettlewell, William 466
'Keys of Canterbury (or Heaven or My Heart)' 29
Khamjani, Natasha 325, 326
'kick-out' steps 349
Kidson, Frank 562
Kimber, William 229, 232, 251, 266
Kimmins, C.W. 250
King Lere 78
Kirkpatrick, John 299, 301, 303
krump 326
'kurn suppers' 185

Laban, Rudolf 269
Lady or Maid Marian 71
'Lake Counties,' Romantic period: 'An Evening's Amusement' 186–187; 'boon days' 185; Cumbrian entertainment, the 'Merry Neet' (merry night) 192–193; Cumbrian peasantry 186; dancing room, spectators 186–187; energy of dancers 190; enthusiasm of dancers 190–191; night of dancing 191; observations by visitors 185–193; Romantic and sentimental fashion 188–189; sheep 'clipping' 185; T.Q.M. 191–192; visitors to 189–190; witches dancing 189; World Heritage Site 184
'Lancashire' steps 290
'Lancashire style' 291
'The Lark In The Morning' 514, 515, 526n38
Larner, Sam 478, 492
Lawrence, D.H. 234
Laycock, Sam 487
Lehmann, Liza 444
Leicester Morrismen's Border Morris Odyssey: dancing Border morris 304–305; dressing for Border morris and 'blacking up' 303–304; early years 302–303; festival experiences 306–308; first border morris performance December 1981 *302*; 'Herbaceous Border' 307; *'The Morris Book'* 295–296; Morris Ring 296; next steps after 1963 297–298; Red Leicester, in Towersey, August 1997 307–308, *307*; repertoire 305–306; *see also* Border morris
Leonard, John 214
The Lichfield dances 306
Lillo, George 394
Ling Association 268
Lishman, J. 187
Little, Tom 194
Liverpool's Trust, Respect Unity (TRU) 340
Lloyd, A. L. 473, 487, 489, 493, 499
Lomax, Alan 473, 484
The Long Eight 270
'Lord Bateman' 'Love and Murder' 364–366, 374–377, 379, 383n42
long sword: in 1911–1913 210–211; dances 212–213; description 207–208; description of Plough Monday 210; in early twentieth-century Yorkshire 208–209; EFDSS *Journal* 211; music, medley of tunes 212; in nineteenth century 208, 209; Sleights dancers on Plough Monday 211–212; songs 213; 1820s–1830s 209–210
Longways (dance set) 248, 249, 253, 254
Lonsdale, Mark 194
'Lord Lovel,' case of 385–390; 'The Ballad of Lady Hounsibelle and Lord Lovel' 386–387; extant version of 386; traditional tunes 385
Lover, S. 448
loyal lover 402–403
Lucas, E.V. 231
Lupton, Henry 89
Luthi, M. 36, 370
Lyrical Ballads (Wordsworth and Coleridge) 184

MacColl, Ewan 486, 499
MacColl, Kirsty 481, 482, 483, 484, 487, 493
MacDonald, Sharon 266
MacIlwaine, Herbert 230, 252
Mackenzie, Alexander 452
Madgies, or *Madgy-Pegs* 209
Magnus, O. 209
MANECCO 340
Manx National Heritage Library 449
Mariategui, Jose Carlos 173
marital rough music 49
Marsh, Baz 163
Marsh, James 150
Marsh, Kathryn 577
Marsh, William 411
Mason, John 231
Mason, William 414
Mathias, P. 442
Maynard, George 492

McKay, Freddy 476
Men's Morris: clubs championed teamwork 238–239; consolidation of existing teams 238; encouragement of independent teams 238; fears of emasculation and feminisation 238; Morris Ring 239–240; teaching and performance 237
Merrick, James 414
'Merrie England' movement 251
merry neets and Bridewains: 'Arnside Wedding' 196; ballad singers and sellers 194; 'Bleckell Murry-Neet' 199; country dance 196; country weddings 195; dancing masters 194–195, 198; dialect poetry 200; dialect reportage 193–199; English Romantic poets 193; observations by visitors to lake district (see 'Lake Counties,' Romantic period); 'Oggle Willy' 197; rollicking poems 196–197; 'Sword Dance com' 198–199
Mid-Cheshire Independent Adjudicating Panel (MCIAP) 340
Miller, Edward 414, 419, 420
Miller, Jimmy 473
Milley's Bequest 306
Ministry of Education *(Moving and Growing)* 270
Mirk, J. 57
Modern Dance in Education (Russell) 270
Modern Educational Dance (Laban) 269–270
modes (musical): Aeolian mode 479, 483, 484, 489, 514; Dorian mode 483, 483, 486, 488, 511; Major mode 32, 479, 483, 510, 514, 538; Mixolydian mode 483, 485, 486
Molly dancing 299
Monk, W.H. 427
Montgomery, W. H. 532
Moody, Dwight L. 533
Moore, T. 448, 531
The Morphology of the Parade (Pettitt) 14
morrice dance 208
Morris, Border 298, 301
morris dance 177–178; antiquity and folklore, 1885–1904 227–229; consolidation and confrontation 233–237; 'Cotswold' or 'South Midlands' style 225; Elizabethan 'Golden Age' 228; Festival of Britain 240–242; Men's Morris 237–240; 'Moros y Christianos' and 'Matachin' 226; precursor to revival 226–227; seriation 178; towards a national movement 230–233
Morris, Hammersmith 299
Morris, Margaret 265
Morris, Neal 233
Morris Ring 239–240, 296, 300–301, 312n32
'movement choirs' 269
Movement – Physical Education in the Primary Years 270

Moving Encounters; Choreographing Stage and Spectators (Pettitt) 14
mummers' plays 32, 81; Andrew Brice, mayoral election, Devon, 1737 79–81; Christmastime custom 11; Cox's earlier summary 77–79; 1377 'mumming' 11; 'pace-egg plays' 43n101; *The Truro Cordwainers Play* 79
music *see individual entries*
music-hall repertoire: Clog Waltz 281–282; Ragtime steps 282; Schottische steps 282
musician: country 199; folk 315; lower-working-class 538; Manx 451; nineteenth-century 536, 539; professional 418, 432; rural 150; Village 149–150
'My man Jack' 29

National Association of Organisers of Physical Education 268
National Community Singing Movement 503–504
The Natural History and Antiquities of Northumberland (Wallis) 203
Neal, M. 4, 230, 231, 232, 233, 234, 252, 255, 257, 263, 345, 347, 457
Needham, J. 239, 296
'New Version' (NV) 413
New Year's Day 107, 205, 208, 213, 218
New Year's Eve 111, 163, 174n6
'No Art More Dangerous,' Eve Maxwell-lyte and folk song: after war 469–470; Carthy's epic arrangement 481–482; Critics Group 477, 479; The 'Diseuse' 465–466; Eve Maxwell-Lyte *465*; finale 471; Nova Scotian songs 466–468; vocal decoration 478; war years 468
Norman, Matt 319
North-West Morris 301, 312n35, 337, 338, 340, 341, 344–346, 350
Notes and Queries (Lancashire) 107, 389
Notes on the Folk Lore of the Northern Counties of England and the Borders (Henderson) 216
nuptial rough music 49
Nursery Rhymes of England 551

Observations of the Popular Antiquities of Great Britain (Brand) 204
'Oh My Love's Dead' 390–392
The Old Church Gallery Minstrels (MacDermott) 427
Old English Country Dances (Kidson) 249
'Old Hat Music Nights' 288
Old Version (OV) 413
O'Leary, Brendan 172
Oliver, William 485
Organisation for Economic Co-operation and Development (OECD) 507
Orrell, Michael 160
Owen, Sarah 514

'Pace-Egging' 35
Palmer, J. 185, 189
Palmer, Roy 368
Pancake Day 44
'pardy' 349
Parry, Hubert 457
pas-de-bas steps 349
'Past Performances on Paper': acquiring general and musical literacy skills 535–538; acquiring sources 538–540; 'art' music, carols, religious tunes 533; 'Highland Schottische' *534*; historic tunes (pre-1750) 531–532; instrumental manuscript tunebooks 529–531, *530*; inward transmission and sources 533–534, 533–535; manuscripts 531; 'O Come all ye faithful' *533*; outward transmission 540–543; Post-1830 532; 'Runns Hornpipe' *531*; 1750–1830 532; Soobroy's string band *541*; sources 535; 'Step Dancing in the Tap Room' *542*; 'Waltz' by S. Musgrave, showing octave doubling *538*
Paul, Herbert 445
Paul, John 350
Paxton, Tom 475
'peasant poets' 193
Peck, A. 239
Percival, A. 448
performance *see individual entries*
Performance Bestiary: adoption of horse jackets 136; ancestors 125–126; bestiary 121; Blue Ribbon 'Oss 129; Burringham Plough Jags 136, *137*; climate change 136–138; conditions pertaining 130–132; death 138–139; Derby Tup 129–130; Dick, 'wild horse' 127; drama 124–125; encounter custom 135; exhibition 139; Hobby Horses 132–133; Kentish Hooden Horse 127–128; living relatives 126–130; mast or skull-and-pole horses 126; metamorphosis 132–136; monsters 120–121; North-west Lincolnshire *122*; origins 123–124; Padstow Obby Oss 128–129; pedigree 121; "Plough Jack Day" 133–134, *134*, *139*; punctuated procession 134; Sailor's Horse at Minehead 129; Tommy the Pony 127; tourney horse 126; West Halton Plough Jags, 1898 *120*
performative 'folk law' 10
performers in playground: ball-bouncing, skipping and counting out 552–561; children's evolving performance practices in singing games 561–569; children's musical play 550; clapping games and playground beat 569–579; rhyme, rhythm and song 551–552
performing community *see* community, performance of
Periam, John 422
Pericles 78
Pershore stick dance 306

personage 2, 9, 88, 94
Pethick, Emmeline 230
Petrie, George 447
Pettitt, Thomas 11, 14
Phillips, Edward . 233
Pilling, Julian 287
place of performance (county and town/village) 130
Planning the Programme 270
Playford, J. 177; *The English Dancing Master* 248, 250; rediscovery of 248–251
The Play-house Church, or new Actors of Devotion 80
Plough Monday 17, 56, 123, 124, 128, 140n34, 206–208, 210, 211, 213, 220
Plough plays 41n82, 124, 136, 137
plough stot 208
Plunket-Greene, Harry 471
Poems, Chiefly in the Scottish Dialect (Burns) 193
popular and courtly mumming, mummers' plays 10–11
popular antiquities to performance studies 12–14
Popular Music of the Olden Time (Chappell) 249, 251
Popular Rhymes and Nursery Tales 551
Porter, Tommy 163

Queen Elizabeth II 242, 251
The Queen, The Lady's Newspaper and Court Chronicle (Holt) 249
Quiller Couch, T. 91

Ragtime steps 282
Ramsay, A. 193
Randolph, Vance 488
rapper dancing 4; characterization 214; *Church Folk Lore* 215; costumes of the teams 219; description of 216–217; development of 213–214, 221; history of 213; nineteenth-century 213–214, 217; in Northumberland and Durham 213–220; origins of 218; *The Penny Magazine* 216; Sharp's day 219–220; significance of 219; sprang 317; structure of 218–219; sword dance in 2020 326–328; 'The Sword Dancers' 214–215, 217; Tyneside style 221
Rapper: The Miner's Sword Dance of North-East England (Heaton) 177
re-crafting love and murder 379; ballads 362–366; broadsides 362–364; 'catastrophic' performances 368; 'the cruel ship carpenter' 379; early broadside 372–374; the genre 366–367; 'literary' abbreviation (ca 1775–1825) 378; long broadside (eighteenth–early nineteenth century) 378; nineteenth-century broadsides and derivative singing tradition 367–372; 'Polly's love or cruel ship-carpenter' 379; short broadside 378–379; at stanzaic level

367–368; sub-stanzaic units 368; 'vernacular' abbreviation (nineteenth century) 378; vernacular broadside revision 374–377; Versions of Roud 15 378; *Zielform* 370
'Recruiting Sergeant' plays 124
Reeve, William 390
Reliques of Ancient English Poetry (Percy) 356, 480
Renwick, Roger de V. 377
retributive house-visits 52–53
Reynolds, K. 166
rhyming house-visits 53–54
Ribbons, Bells and Squeaking Fiddles (Chandler) 177
Rice, Les 289, 291
Richardson, Albert 464
Rigby, Ros 506
Riley, William 414, 419
Rimbault, Edward F. 400
Ritson, Joseph 364
Robert M. Crompton 249
Robertson, Fyfe 240
Robin Hood folk-performance: 'Cote' in Braunton 69–70; decimal coinage, introduction of 67; English identity 65; expenses and receipts of church ale, 1562 66–68; Father Christmas 69; in fifteenth and sixteenth-century England 64–75; 'for litleIohns Cote vj s viij d' 70–71; gatherings 73; house or bower 72; *A Mery Geste of Robyn Hoode* 75; 'play-games' 65, 71–72, 74; *Records of Early English Drama* (REED) 66; 'Robin Hood and the Friar' 75; 'Robyn hood &hys Company – xij d' 70; Saxon heritage 65; St Brannock's Church in Braunton 68, 69, 70
Rolleston, T. 447
Romaine, W. 418
Rose, Jonathan 537
rough music 9–10, 48; descriptions 10; marital rough music 49; nuptial rough music 49
Roxburghe Ballads (Ebsworth) 391
Royal College of Music (RCM) 443
Rufty Tufty 270
Russell, Dave 537, 543
Russell, Ian 432

Sanderson, T. 186
Sankey, Ira D. 533
Saville, J. 441
Saville, Jimmy 167
Schofield, Derek 4, 299
Schottische as 'a light dance or Soft-Shoe' 282
Schottische steps 282
Scottish Folk Dance Society 269
Scott, W. 65, 400, 481
Second Industrial Revolution 442
Seeger, Peggy 481, 499, 510
shakers 337

Shakespeare and His Times (Drake) 206
Shakespeare, W. 16, 35, 151, 228, 251, 256
Shannon, Richard 445
Sharp, C. J. 29, 231, 232, 234, 235, 240, 248, 249, 251, 253, 262, 277, 287, 295, 297, 326, 329, 345, 347, 444, 469, 475, 479, 483, 499, 542: 'art' critic 257; and authenticity 251–255; collection of authentic folk songs 255; concept of 'Gay Simplicity' 264; and country dance 253–255; *The Country Dance Book* 248–249, 253, 254, 264; criteria for collection 251–253; defence of country dance 255–257; *English Folk-Song: Some Conclusions* 252; expressions of Merrie England 256; fieldwork manuscripts 254; history 251; 'minor set' 254; *The Morris Book* 252–253; of morris dances 252; *The Sword Dances of Northern England* 326; *Syllabus of Physical Exercises* 256–257; technique 264; 'The Triumph' 254
Sharp, J.W. 389, 390
Shepherd, John 420
The Sheriff's Ride 306
Sherry, Sam 282, 286, 287, 292
Shipley, Val 284, 325
short sword *see* rapper dancing
shriving 44
Shrovetide perambulations (case study) 44, 51–60; house-visits in England and Wales 51, 51–52; Lent-crocking and shroving 54–56; nineteenth century 59–60; retributive house-visits 52–53; rhyming house-visits 53–54; by seventeenth century 57–58; simple house-visits 54–56
Shrovetide processions survey 44, 45–51; auxiliary entertainments 50; Bristol fights and processions 50; Chester's processions 46–47; food and feasting 51; football game, Shrove Tuesday 46–47, 47; marriage and children 47; rough music and ridings 48–50; sports and games 45–47, 47; wedding procession 47–48, 48
The Siege of Troy ('a regular drama') 86
Silurian dance 300
Simon, Paul 511
simple house-visits 54–56
Simpson, Christopher 180
Simpson, Robert 180
singer: ballad 392, 403; comic 392; concert 448, 467; dramatic 470; English folk 521; 'floor singer' system 492; 'genuine' folk 147, 478; peasant 255; pop 572; self-taught traditional 498; solo 498; traditional 485, 491; urban folk 475
singing games, children's evolving performance practices in: 'The Big Ship Sails' 565, 566; 'Poor Mary' 566, 566; 'Queen Mary,' 'Bonnie Dundee' and 'Stella' compared 563, 564; '[Queen Mary]', Liverpool girls 562, 562

'Sir Eglamore' 404–405
Sloman, Charles 391
Smith, James 394, 399
Snelson, Angela 344
Social and Spatial Patterning in Customary Encounters (Pettitt) 14
socio-cultural auspices (function) 18–20; association 18–19; community 18; distribution, communication, interaction 19–20, *20*; engagements 19; household 18; participants 18
Solomon, Jack 88
song: 'Acting Song' 113; bawdy 359; calling-on 35, 83; clapping 570, 573–574; English folk 230, 263, 475, 481; folk (*see* folk song and music); game 562; 'Industrial Song' 485–487; Manx 451; *quête* 33; riddle 511; 'Scotch' 397; solo 282; traditional 34, 288, 479, 492–493, 514
The Song Book (Hullah) 454
Spicer, Katy 304
'Stage dancer' 278
Stage Hornpipe 278–279
stage style: clog dance competitions – the Clog Hornpipe 280–281; dancing masters – the Stage Hornpipe 278–279; hornpipe steps collected in Lake District 279
Stagg, J. 194, 197
Stainer, John 452, 454
Stanford, Charles Villiers 443
step dance 282, 287–289, 321; material 277–278
stick dance 306
stingy man 48
Stone Monkey dance 322
The Story of Alderley, Living with the Edge (Prag) 115
strange familiars 12
Stratton, Eugene 282
street clog stepping 284–285
'Street dancer' 278
Street style 282–285; Devon 283–284; East Anglia 283; Hampshire 284; hard-shoe stepping styles 283; street clog stepping 284–285
Strutt, J. 78, 228
Sullivan, Arthur 250
Summersgill, Tommy 88
Surtees, John 281
The Survey of Cornwall (Carew) 67
Survey of the Lakes of Cumberland, Westmorland and Lancashire (Clarke) 185
Sussex Church Music in the Past (MacDermott) 427
Swarbrick, Dave 491
'The Sweet Nightingale' 514, 519, 523
sword dance: style 221
sword dance plays 14, 181, 203, 205, 209

Sword Dances (Sharp) 220
The Sword Dances of Northern England (Sharp) 210
sword dancing 4, 179–180, 213; Ash Wednesday sword dance 181; Christmastime sword dancing 222; in Cumberland 206; descriptions of 205–206; in England 4; *Festival of Fools* 205; late eighteenth century 203–207; long sword in nineteenth- and early twentieth-century Yorkshire 207–213; nineteenth-century descriptions of 204–205; rapper dancing in Northumberland and Durham 213–220; Tyneside performances 207
Sword Dancing in Europe (Corrsin) 177, 179
Syron, George 402

Table Book (Hone) 191
Tabor, June 523
Tate, Nahum 413
Tawney, Cyril 523
Taylor, Diana 173
Taylor, E.B. 233
Taylor, Joseph 483
Temperley, N. 428
'Three Ravens' 401
The Three Shirleys 78
thumping 191
time of performance (in relation to calendar) *see* calendrical pressures
'tin-canning' 53
Tracey, Pat 285, 286, 287, 318
tradition *see individual entries*
traditional dancing: 'alpha' dances 329; Black Swan Rapper 329; collaboration 319–322; complexities of 318; crawl 331–332; dance/music performance making 319–321; dances and dancers 291, 316–317; Dancing England Rapper Tournament (DERT). 322; 'dancing not dances' 321–322; DERT not DERT 332–334; East London Dance's (ELD) 325; expanding collaboration 322–324; hip hop or West African dance 325, *326*; history of dance 317; and narrative performance 324–326; Newbiggin 329; rapper sword dance in 2020 326–328; relationship between dancer and musicians 320; 'Rise Up' 324–325; 'Scottish' steps 318; song 34, 288, 479, 485, 491, 492–493, 514; Southern English Step Dancing 325; team-based dancers 319; Tower Ravens 330, *330*; transmission of past dances 319; *Travelling with Thomas* 324–325; Westerhope dance 329
Tucker, Marilyn 506
Tunney, Paddy 478
'Twa Sisters' 399–401
Twelfth Night (Shakespeare) 256
Tylor, Edward 345

Ullmann, Lisa 269
Under the Greenwood Tree (Hardy) 528
Upton, Eddie 506

Vandalls of Hammerwich 306
Victoria and Merrie England (Sullivan) 250
Victorian movement 349
Vietnam War 360
village theatre Gifford's 'Old Gentleman' c1730; TQM and the Grassington Theatricals, Yorkshire, c1790s – c1800s. 87–89; Sir Offley Wakeman and the Shropshire Drama – 1830s & 1840s 93–95
'Villikens and his Dinah' 392
Vincent, James 149
Vincent, William 419
Vitalism 261–262, 265–268, 274n64
Von Herder, Johann Gottfried 499

Walker, Christopher 532
Wallis, John 83, 85, 221
Walpole, H. 386, 387
Warren, Florence 231, 232
Watts, Isaac 413
Waugh, Edwin 487
Weaver, John 255
Wells, Ben 194
'Welsh Border Morris' 296
Wesley, Charles 413
Wesley, J. 80, 409
West Gallery music 6, 408; abolition of choir-bands 425–426; 'capital psalm tunes' 415; Castle Hedingham Church 423–424; champion of mass choralism 425; choir-band and distraction activity 421; choir-band manuscripts and publications 415; Church choral associations and unions 424–425; church singing 416; critic writing 413; dramatic events 425; eighteenth-century Anglicanism 409; existence of 'multifaceted mainstream culture' writing 429; 'fallen into decay and contempt' 419; 'flowing rhythm' or 'free rhythm' 430; 'folk Christianity' 409–410; 'fuging tune' 414; 'historically informed' performances 431; 'inevitability of history' argument 422; literature and scholarship 426–431; musical reformers 420;
musical taste and knowledge 422–423; musicians 410–413; *The Music of the Church* 421; in nineteenth century 410; objectives for reform 420; old 'Reformation' tunes 416; opposition to and elimination of popular church music 419–426; *Oxford Companion to Music* 427–428; parochial music 414; period 1750–1860 410; poor tuning 416–417; popular music making 415; process of decontextualisation 433; religious music 414; repertory, instrumentation and performance style 413–418; scholarly musicology and folk music studies 428; Singing Gallery 409; and singing pews 419; survival and revival 431–434; Temperley's approach 428; West Gallery Music Association 432–433; Whitechurch Canonicorum 423
Weston, Stephen 428
West, W. H. C. 391
White, Maude Valerie 444
white plough 208
Whitsun 3, 17, 26, 68, 71, 90, 178, 227, 229, 296, 540
Whitsuntide 67, 68, 69, 257
'Whittingham Fair' 511, 512, 526n37
Wilgus, Donald 452
William Borlase: 'big-house' performer-spectator relationship 84; combats of puppets 84; 1758 description of performance 83–84; disguise and personation of characters 84
William, R. 432
Williams, Alfred 425
Williams, B. 394, 414
Williams, Ernest Edwin 442
Williams, J. 85, 86
Williamson, Les 214
Williams, Ralph Vaughan 256, 266, 267, 500
Williams, T. 417
Williams, Vaughan 481, 483, 484
Wilson, J. 188, 192
Wilson, Paul 506
Wilson, Steuart 469, 471
Wilson, Thomas 253
Wily Beguiled 79
World History of the Dance (Sachs) 267

Yeats, W. B. 446